ENGLISH-GREEK
DICTIONARY

ΛΕΞΙΚΟ
ΕΛΛΗΝΙΚΑ · ΑΓΓΛΙΚΑ
ΑΓΓΛΙΚΑ · ΕΛΛΗΝΙΚΑ

COLLINS
GEM
DICTIONARY

GREEK · ENGLISH
ENGLISH · GREEK

ΕΛΛΗΝΙΚΑ · ΑΓΓΛΙΚΑ
ΑΓΓΛΙΚΑ · ΕΛΛΗΝΙΚΑ

Harry T. Hionides

New Edition by / Νέα Έκδοση
Niki Watts, Helen George-Papageorgiou

HarperCollins*Publishers*

first published in this edition 1987

© William Collins Sons & Co. Ltd. 1987

latest reprint 1998

ISBN 0 00 472222 1 Paperback

Collins Gem® is a registered trademark
of HarperCollins Publishers Limited

Harry T. Hionides

new edition by / νέα έκδοση
Niki Watts, Helen George-Papageorgiou

consultant / σύμβουλος
Roger Green

editorial staff / εκδοτικό προσωπικό
Val McNulty, Susan Dunsmore

Printed and bound in Great Britain by
Caledonian International Book Manufacturing Ltd,
Glasgow, G64

ΕΙΣΑΓΩΓΗ

INTRODUCTION

Ο χρήστης που επιθυμεί να διαβάσει και να καταλάβει Αγγλικά θα βρει σ' αυτό το λεξικό έναν περιεκτικό και σύγχρονο κατάλογο λέξεων, καθώς και σημαντικό αριθμό φράσεων που χρησιμοποιούνται σήμερα. Επίσης θα βρει σε αλφαβητική σειρά τους κύριους ανώμαλους τύπους με παραπομπή στο βασικό τους τύπο, καθώς και μερικές από τις συνηθέστερες συντομογραφίες, αρκτικόλεξα και γεωγραφικές ονομασίες.

Ο χρήστης που επιθυμεί να εκφραστεί και να επικοινωνήσει στα Αγγλικά θα βρει όλους τους τρόπους χρήσης των βασικών λέξεων. Όπου μια λέξη έχει πολλές σημασίες, οι αντίστοιχες μεταφράσεις δίνονται κατά σειρά προτεραιότητας ανάλογα με τη συχνότητα των Ελληνικών εννοιών,

The user whose aim is to read and understand Greek will find a comprehensive and up-to-date wordlist which includes the most common scientific and technical terms. The official ("monotonic") accent system has been used throughout, and a high proportion of Demotic words and Demotic versions of words which also have Katharevousa forms have been included.

The user who wants to communicate and express himself in Greek will find clear and detailed treatment of all the basic words, with numerous indicators pointing to the appropriate translation and helping him to use it correctly.

ABBREVIATIONS

a	adjective	επίθετο
abbr	abbreviation	σιντομογραφία
ad	adverb	επίρρημα
AGR	agriculture	γεωργία
ANAT	anatomy	ανατομία
ARCH	archaeology	αρχαιολογία
ARCHIT	architecture	αρχιτεκτονική
ASTR	astronomy	αστρονομία
attr	attributive	επίθετο
AUT	automobile	αυτοκίνητο
AVIAT	aviation	αεροπορία
BIBL	biblical	βιβλικός
BIOL	biology	βιολογία
BOT	botany	βοτανική
Brit	British usage	αγγλισμός
CARP	carpentry	ξυλουργική
CHEM	chemistry	χημεία
CINE	cinema	κινηματογράφος
cj	conjunction	σύνδεσμος
col	colloquial	κοινός
collect	collective	περιληπτικός
COMM	commercial	εμπορικός
comp	comparative	συγκριτικός
compd	compound	σύνθετος
COMPUT	computers	ηλεκτρονικοί υπολογιστές
dim	diminutive	υποκοριστικό
DIP	diplomacy	διπλωματία
ECCL	ecclesiastical	εκκλησιαστικός
ECON	economics	οικονομία
ELEC	electricity	ηλεκτρισμός
esp	especially	ειδικά
excl	exclamation	επιφώνημα
f	feminine noun	θηλυκό
fig	figuratively	μεταφορικά
FIN	finance	οικονομία
GEOG	geography	γεωγραφία
GEOL	geology	γεωλογία
GRAM	grammar	γραμματική
HUNT	hunting	κυνήγι
impers	impersonal	απρόσωπο
infin	infinitive	απαρέμφατο
interj	interjection	επιφώνημα
inv	invariable	αμετάβλητος
irreg	irregular	ανώμαλο
LING	linguistics	γλωσσολογία
lit	literal	κυριολεκτικός
LITER	literature	λογοτεχνία
m	masculine noun	αρσενικό
MATH	mathematics	μαθηματικό
MECH	mechanical	μηχανισμός
MED	medical	ιατρική

MIL	military	στρατιωτικός
MUS	music	μουσική
n	noun	ουσιαστικό
NAUT	nautical, naval	ναυτικός
nt	neuter	ουδέτερο
num	numeral	αριθμός
old	old-fashioned	απαρχαιωμένος
o.s.	oneself	εαυτός
PARL	Parliament	κοινοβούλιο
part	participle	μετοχή
pej	pejorative	υποτιμητικός
pers	personal	προσωπικός
PHIL	philosophy	φιλοσοφία
PHON	phonetics	φωνητική, φωνολογία
PHOT	photography	φωτογραφία
PHYS	physics	φυσική
pl	plural	πληθυντικός
POET	poetry	ποίηση
POL	politics	πολιτική
poss	possessive	κτητικός
pp	past participle	μετοχή αορίστου
pred	predicative	κατηγορούμενο
prep	preposition	πρόθεση
PRINT	printing, typography	τυπογραφία
pron	pronoun	αντωνυμία
pt	past tense	αόριστος, παρατατικός
(R)	registered trademark	σήμα κατατεθέν
RAD	radio	ραδιοφωνία
RAIL	railways	σιδηρόδρομος
REL	religion	θρησκεία
SCH	school	σχολείο
sing	singular	ενικός
sl	slang	λαϊκός
s.o.	someone, somebody	κάποιος
sth	something	κάτι
sup	superlative	υπερθετικός
TECH	technical	τεχνικός
TEL	telecommunications	τηλεπικοινωνίες
TEX	textiles	υφαντά
THEAT	theatre	θέατρο
TV	television	τηλεόραση
UNIV	university	πανεπιστήμιο
US	American usage	αμερικανισμός
v	verb	ρήμα
vi	intransitive verb	ρήμα αμετάβατο
vt	transitive verb	ρήμα μεταβατικό
vti	transitive and intransitive verb	ρήμα μεταβατικό και αμετάβατς
ZOOL	zoology	ζωολογία

ΣΛΝΤΟΜΟΓΡΑΦΙΕΣ

αθλητ	αθλητικά	athletics, sport
αερο	αεροπορία	aviation
αιτ	αιτιατική	accusative
αμ, αμετ	ρήμα αμετάβατο	intransitive verb
ανατ	ανατομία	anatomy
αρνητ	αρνητικός	negative
αρχιτεκ	αρχιτεκτονική	architecture
αστρον	αστρονομία	astronomy
βλ	βλέπε	see (cross-reference)
βοτ	βοτανική	botany
γεωγρ	γεωγραφία	geography
γεωμ	γεωμετρία	geometry
γραμμ	γραμματική	grammar
εκκλ	εκκλησιαστικός	religion
εμπόρ	εμπόριο	commerce
επίθ	επίθετο	adjective
επίρ	επίρρημα	adverb
επιφ	επιφώνημα	exclamation
ζωολ	ζωολογία	zoology
ηλεκ, ηλεκτ	ηλεκτρισμός	electricity
ιατρ	ιατρική	medicine
κτλ	και τα λοιπά	et cetera
μαθημ	μαθηματικά	mathematics
μηχαν	μηχανισμός	mechanical
μεταφ	μεταφορικά	figuratively
μουσ	μουσική	music
ναυτ	ναυτικός	nautical, naval
νομ	νομική	law
οικ, οικον,	οικονομικά	economics
όνομ, ουσ	όνομα, ουσιαστικό	noun
πλ	πληθυντικός	plural
πολιτ	πολιτική	politics
πρόθ	πρόθεση	preposition
π.χ.	παραδείγματος χάρη	e.g. (for example)
στρατ	στρατιωτικός	military
σύνδ	σύνδεσμος	conjunction
τεχν	τεχνολογία	technical
τηλεπ	τηλεπικοινωνίες	telecommunications
τυπογρ	τυπογραφία	printing, typography
φιλοσ	φιλοσοφία	philosophy
φωτογρ	φωτογραφική	photography
χημ	χημεία	chemistry

PRONUNCIATION OF MODERN GREEK

Each letter in Greek nearly always represents the same sound. The few exceptions are listed below and on page viii. The pronunciation system used in the text (given in brackets after each Greek main entry) transcribes the letters of Greek into the English alphabet, with one special character used to represent a less obvious sound. A list of the sounds which the English alphabet is used to represent is given below. When you read out the pronunciation you should sound the letters as if you were reading an English word.

GREEK LETTER		CLOSEST ENGLISH SOUND	SHOWN BY	EXAMPLE		PRONOUNCED
Α	α	hand	a	άνθρωπος		anthropos
Β	β	vine	v	βούτυρο		vooteero
Γ	γ	see page viii	g	γάλα		gala
		yes	y	για, γέρος		ya, yeros
Δ	δ	this	ð	δάχτυλο		ðakteelo
Ε	ε	met	e	έτοιμος		eteemos
Ζ	ζ	zone	z	ζώνη		zonee
Η	η	meet	ee*	ήλιος		eeleeos
Θ	θ	thin	th	θέατρο		theatro
Ι	ι	meet	ee*	ιππότης		eepotees
Κ	κ	key	k	και		ke
Λ	λ	log	l	λάδι		laðee
Μ	μ	mat	m	μάτι		matee
Ν	ν	not	n	νύχτα		neehta
Ξ	ξ	rocks	ks	ξένος		ksenos
Ο	ο	cot	o	όχι		ohee
Π	π	pat	p	πόλη		polee
Ρ	ρ	carrot see page viii	r	ρόδα		roða
Σ	σ, ς	sat	s	σήμα		seema
Τ	τ	top	t	τράπεζα		trapeza
Υ	υ	meet	ee*	ύπνος		eepnos
Φ	φ	fat	f	φούστα		foosta
Χ	χ	see page viii	h	χάνω		hano
				χέρι		heree
Ψ	ψ	lapse	ps	ψάρι		psaree
Ω	ω	cot	o	ώρα		ora

* The letter i is used to represent the "ee" sound a) when two such sounds occur together; b) when "ee" is followed by "e"; c) before a stressed vowel; e.g.

ικανοποίηση	eekanopieesee
βίαιος	vieos
κριός	krios

COMBINATIONS OF LETTERS

The combinations of letters shown below are pronounced as listed.

GREEK LETTERS	CLOSEST ENGLISH SOUND	SHOWN BY	EXAMPLE	PRONOUNCED
ει	meet	ee	είδος	eeδos
οι	meet	ee	οικογένεια	eekoyeneea
αι	met	e	αίμα	ema
ου	food	oo	που	pou
μπ	beer	b	μπύρα	beera
	or amber	mb	κάμπος	kambos
ντ	door	d	ντομάτα	domata
	or bend	nd	πέντε	pende
γκ	good	g	γκάζι	gazee
γγ	angle	ng	Αγγλία	angleea
τζ	adze	dz	τζάμι	dzamee

The pairs of vowels shown above are pronounced separately if the first has an acute accent (΄) or the second a dieresis (¨); e.g.

παιδάκι	peδakee	παϊδάκι	paieeδakee
καιρός	keros	Κάιρο	kaeero

Some Greek consonant sounds have no English equivalent.

GREEK LETTER	REMARKS	EXAMPLE	PRONOUNCED
Ρ,ρ	slightly trilled r	ρόδα	roda
Χ,χ	like ch in loch	χάνω	hano
	or like a rough h	χέρι	heree
Γ,γ	like a rough g	γάλα	gala
	or like y	για	ya
		γέρος	yeros

STRESS

All Greek words of two or more syllables have an acute accent which indicates where the stress falls. For instance, άγαλμα is pronounced agalma and αγάπη is pronounced agapee.

ΑΓΓΛΙΚΗ ΠΡΟΦΟΡΑ

Φωνήεντα και δίφθογγοι	Σύμφωνα
Αγγλικό παράδειγμα	Αγγλικό παράδειγμα

	Αγγλικό παράδειγμα		Αγγλικό παράδειγμα
ɑ:	father	b	bat, baby
ʌ	but, come	d	mended
æ	man, cat	f	fine, raffle
ə	father, ago	g	get, big
ɜ:	bird, heard	dʒ	gin, judge
ɛ	get, bed	ŋ	sing
ɪ	it, big	h	house, he
iː	tea, see	j	young, yes
ɒ	hot, wash	k	come, mock
ɔ:	saw, all	l	little, place
ʊ	put, book	m	ram, mummy
uː	too, you	n	ran, nut
aɪ	fly, high	p	pat, pope
aʊ	how, house	r	red, tread
ɛə	there, bear	s	sand, yes
eɪ	day, obey	t	tab, strut
ɪə	here, hear	v	vine, river
əʊ	go, note	z	rose, zebra
ɔɪ	boy, oil	ʃ	she, machine
ʊə	poor, sure˙	tʃ	chin, rich
		w	water, which
		ʒ	vision
		θ	think, myth
		ð	this, the

Το σημείο * σημαίνει ότι το τελικό 'r' δεν προφέρεται στα Αγγλικά εκτός αν η λέξη που ακολουθεί αρχίζει με φωνήεντο. Το σημείο ['] καθορίζει την τονιζόμενη συλλαβή.

GREEK-ENGLISH
ΕΛΛΗΝΙΚΑ-ΑΓΓΛΙΚΑ

Α, α

α-, αν- (negative particle) in-, un-, il-, ir-, -less.

αβαθής [avathees] shallow.

αβάπτιστος [avapteestos] unbaptised.

αβάσιμος [avaseemos] groundless || (υποψία) unfounded.

αβάστακτος [avastaktos] unbearable || (δύναμη) uncontrollable.

άβατος [avatos] inaccessible || untrodden.

άβγαλτος [avgaltos] inexperienced.

αβγό, το [avgo] egg.

αβγολέμονο, το [avgolemono] sauce or soup with eggs and lemon.

αβέβαιος [aveveos] doubtful || uncertain.

αβίαστος [aveeastos] unforced, natural.

αβίωτος [aveeotos] unbearable, intolerable.

αβλαβής [avlavees] (έντομο κτλ) harmless.

αβοήθητος [avoeetheetos] without help.

άβολος [avolos] inconvenient || (κάθισμα κτλ) uncomfortable.

άβυσσος, η [aveesos] abyss.

αγαθός [agathos] good, kind || (αφελής) naive || (τίμιος) honest.

άγαλμα, το [agalma] statue.

άγαμος [agamos] unmarried, single.

αγανακτώ [aganakto] be irritated.

αγανάκτηση, η [aganakteesee] indignation, anger.

αγάπη, η [agapee] love, affection.

αγαπημένος [agapeemenos] dear, beloved || (πράγμα) favourite.

αγαπητός [agapeetos] βλ **αγαπημένος**.

αγαπώ [agapo] love || (μου αρέσει) like.

αγγαρεία, η [angareea] chore || drudgery.

αγγείο, το [angeeo] vase || (πήλινο) pot || (ανατ) blood vessel.

αγγειοπλαστική, η [angeeoplasteekee] pottery.

αγγελία, η [angeleea] announcement || (εμπορ) advertisement.

αγγελιαφόρος, ο, η [angeleeaforos] messenger || (στρατ) orderly.

αγγελικός [angeleekos] angelic(al).

αγγέλλω [angelo] announce, declare.

άγγελμα, το [angelma] message, notice.

άγγελος, ο [angelos] angel.

αγγίζω [angeezo] touch.

Αγγλία, η [angleea] England.

αγγλικά, τα [angleeka] English (language).

αγγλικός [angleekos] English.

Αγγλίδα, η [angleeδa] Englishwoman.

Άγγλος, ο [anglos] Englishman.

αγγούρι, το [angouree] cucumber

αγελάδα, η [ayelaδa] cow.

αγέλαστος [ayelastos] morose, sullen.

αγέλη, η [ayelee] herd || (προβάτων) flock || (λύκων) pack.

αγένεια, η [ayeneea] rudeness.

αγενής [ayenees] rude, impolite.

αγέραστος [ayerastos] ever young.

αγέρωχος [ayerohos] haughty, arrogant.

αγιάζι [ayazee] hoarfrost, cold || (αύρα) breeze.

αγιάζω [ayazo] (γίνομαι άγιος) become a saint.

αγιασμός, ο [ayasmos] blessing with holy water.

αγιάτρευτος [ayatreftos] incurable.

αγίνωτος [ayeenotos] (φρούτο) unripe, raw.

άγιος [ayos] holy || (πρόσωπο) saint.

αγκαζάρω [angazaro] reserve, book || hire.

αγκαζέ [angaze] arm in arm || (πιασμένο) engaged, taken, occupied.

αγκάθι, το [angathee] thorn, prickle.

αγκαλιά, η [angalia] embrace || (επιρ) armful.

αγκαλιάζω [angaliazo] embrace, hug.

αγκίδα, η [angeeða] splinter, thorn.

αγκινάρα, η [angeenara] artichoke.

αγκίστρι, το [angeestree] hook.

αγκομαχώ [angomaho] gasp, pant.

αγκύλες, οι [angeeles] brackets.

άγκυρα, η [angeera] anchor || σπκώνω ~ weigh anchor.

αγκυροβολία, η [angeerovoleea] mooring.

αγκυροβολώ [angeerovolo] anchor, drop anchor.

αγκώνας, ο [angonas] elbow.

αγναντεύω [agnantevo] see from a distance.

άγνοια, η [agnea] ignorance.

αγνός [agnos] chaste, modest.

αγνοώ [agnoo] be ignorant of || (περιφρονώ) ignore.

αγνωμοσύνη, η [agnomoseenee] ingratitude.

αγνώμων [agnomon] ungrateful.

αγνώριστος [agnoreestos] unrecognizable.

άγνωστος [agnostos] unknown || (ουσ) stranger.

άγονος [agonos] infertile, barren || ~ γραμμή unprofitable shipping line.

αγορά, η [agora] (το μέρος) market || (η πράξη) purchase.

αγοράζω [agorazo] purchase, buy.

αγοραίος [agoreos] for hire || (μεταφ) vulgar, common.

αγορανομία, η [agoranomeea] market inspection police.

αγορεύω [agorevo] make a speech || (με στόμφο) harangue.

αγόρι, το [agoree] boy, lad.

άγουρος [agouros] unripe, green, sour.

αγράμματος [agrammatos] illiterate, uneducated.

άγραφος [agrafos] unwritten.

αγριάδα, η [agriaða] fierceness, savageness.

αγριεύω [agrievo] be infuriated, become angry.

αγρίμι, το [agreemee] wild animal || (μεταφ) rude fellow.

άγριος [agreeos] wild || savage.

αγροίκος [agreekos] coarse, unrefined.

αγρόκτημα, το [agrokteema] farmland.

αγρός, ο [agros] field || country.

αγρότης, ο [agrotees] farmer || peasant.

αγροφυλακή, η [agrofeelakee] agrarian police.

αγρυπνώ [agreepno] stay awake, lie awake || (επαγρυπνώ) be watchful.

αγύμναστος [ageemnastos] untrained, unexercised.

αγχιστεία, η [anghisteea] relationship by marriage.

αγχόνη, η [anghonee] gallows, hanging.

άγχος, το [anghos] anxiety.

άγω [ago] lead, conduct, guide.

αγωγή, η [agoyee] breeding, conduct || (νομ) lawsuit.

αγώγι, το [agoyee] fare.

αγωγός, ο [agogos] conductor || (σωλήνας) pipe, conduit.

αγώνας, ο [agonas] struggle, fight || (αθλητ) game, contest || **αγώνες** πλ games, sporting events.

αγωνία, η [agoneea] agony || anxiety.

αγωνίζομαι [agoneezome] struggle, fight, strive.

αγωνιστής, ο [agoneestees] contestant, fighter || (πολιτ) militant.

αγωνιώ [agoneeo] be in agony || be anxious.

αγωνιώδης [agoneeodees] anxious, troubled.

αδαής [adaees] inexperienced, unfamiliar (with).

αδάμαστος [adamastos] untamed || (λαός) unconquered || (θάρρος) unbroken.

άδεια, η [adeea] leave, permission || (γάμου κτλ) licence, permit.

αδειάζω [adeeazo] empty || (ευκαιρώ) have time.

άδειος [adeeos] empty, unoccupied.

αδέκαστος [adekastos] incorruptible || (αμερόληπτος) impartial, unbiased.

αδελφή, η [adelfee] sister.

αδέλφια, τα [adelfeea] πλ brothers, brother and sister.

αδελφικός [adelfeekos] (αγάπη) brotherly || (φίλος) dear.

αδελφός, ο [adelfos] brother.

αδένας, ο [adenas] gland.

αδέξιος [adekseeos] awkward, clumsy.

αδέσμευτος [adesmeftos] (μεταφ) under no obligation || (χώρα) non-aligned.

αδέσποτος [adespotos] stray, without an owner.

άδηλος [adeelos] uncertain, doubtful || **άδηλοι πόροι** invisible income.

αδήλωτος [adeelotos] undeclared.

Άδης, ο [adees] Hell || Hades.

αδηφάγος [adeefagos] voracious || (μεταφ) greedy.

αδιάβαστος [adiavastos] (βιβλίο) unread || (μαθητής) unprepared.

αδιάβατος [adiavatos] impassable.

αδιάβροχο, το [adiavroho] raincoat.

αδιάθετος [adiathetos] (υγεία) unwell || (κεφάλαιο) unspent.

αδιαίρετος [adieretos] indivisible || undivided.

αδιάκοπος [adiakopos] uninterrupted, continuous.

αδιάκριτος [adiakreetos] imperceptible || (χαρακτήρας) indiscreet.

αδιάλλακτος [adialaktos] implacable, uncompromising.

αδιάλυτος [adialeetos] indissoluble, undissolved.

αδιάντροπος [adiantropos] brazen || (ενέργεια) impudent.

αδιαπέραστος [adieaperastos] impenetrable.

αδιάρρηκτος [adieareektos] unbreakable || (μεταφ) indissoluble.

αδιάσπαστος [adiaspastos] unbroken || inseparable.

αδιάφορος [adiaforos] indifferent.

αδιαχώριστος [adieahoreestos] inseparable.

αδίδακτος [adeedaktos] untaught.

αδιέξοδος, η [adieksodos] impasse || (δρόμος) cul de sac, dead end.

αδικία, η [adeekeea] injustice, wrongdoing, offence.

άδικος [aδeekos] unjust, unfair || έχω άδικο I'm in the wrong.

αδικώ [aδeeko] do wrong || (κάποιον) be unjust to.

αδιόρθωτος [aδeeorthotos] irreparable || (χαρακτήρας) incorrigible.

αδίστακτος [aδeestahtos] unhesitating, resolute.

άδολος [aδolos] guileless, innocent.

άδοξος [aδoksos] inglorious.

αδούλευτος [aδouleftos] unwrought, raw || (αγρός) uncultivated.

αδράνεια, η [aδraneea] inertia || (μεταφ) indolence.

αδράχτι, το [aδrahtee] spindle.

αδύνατος [aδeenatos] thin || (δεν γίνεται) impossible.

αδυναμία, η [aδeenameea] (πνεύματος) deficiency || (σώματος) weakness.

αδυνατώ [aδeenato] be unable to.

αδυσώπητος [aδeesopeetos] relentless, implacable.

άδυτο, το [aδeeto] (εκκλ) sanctuary.

αειθαλής [aeethalees] evergreen.

αεικίνητος [aeekeeneetos] in perpetual motion.

αείμνηστος [aeemneestos] late, fondly remembered.

αεράμυνα, η [aerameena] air defence.

αεραγωγός, η [aeragogos] air duct.

αερίζω [aereezo] ventilate, air.

αερισμός, ο [aereesmos] ventilation, airing.

αέριο, το [aereeo] gas.

αεριούχος [aereeouhos] aerated, gaseous.

αεριστήρας, ο [aereesteeras] ventilator.

αεροδρόμιο, το [aeroδromeeo] airport.

αερόλιθος, ο [aeroleethos] meteorite.

αερολιμένας, ο [aeroleemeenas] airport.

αεροπλάνο, το [aeroplano] aeroplane.

αεροπορία, η [aeroporeea] air force.

αεροπορικώς [aeroporeekos] by air.

αερόστατο, το [aerostato] balloon.

αετός, ο [aetos] eagle || (μεταφ) clever person || (χαρταετός) kite.

αζήτητος [azeeteetos] unclaimed || (εμπορ) not in demand.

άζυμος [azeemos] unleavened.

άζωτο, το [azoto] nitrogen.

αηδής [aeeδees] loathsome, sickening.

αηδία, η [aeeδeea] disgust, loathing.

αηδιάζω [aeeδeeazo] feel disgust for, loathe.

αηδόνι, το [aeeδonee] nightingale.

αήττητος [aeeteetos] undefeated, unbeatable.

αθανασία, η [athanaseea] immortality, eternity.

αθάνατος [athanatos] immortal, deathless.

αθέατος [atheatos] invisible, unseen.

άθελα [athela] unintentionally.

αθέμιτος [athemeetos] illegal, unlawful.

άθεος [atheos] godless || (ουσ) atheist.

αθεόφοβος [atheofovos] impious || (ουσ) rogue.

αθεράπευτος [atherapevtos] incurable || (μεταφ) incorrigible.

αθετώ [atheto] break one's word, violate.

άθικτος [atheektos] untouched, unharmed.

αθλητής, ο [athleetees] athlete.

αθλητικός [athleeteekos] athletic || (σώμα) robust.

αθλητισμός, ο [athleeteesmos] athletics.

άθλιος [athleeos] wretched, miserable.

άθλος, ο [athlos] feat, exploit.

αθόρυβος [athoreevos] quiet, silent.

άθραυστος [athravstos] unbroken || (αντικείμενο) unbreakable.

άθρησκος [athreeskos] irreligious.

αθροίζω [athreezo] add up, count || (στρατ) gather, assemble.

άθροισμα, το [athreesma] sum, total.

αθυμία, η [atheemeea] dejection, depression.

αθυρόστομος [atheerostomos] indiscreet, impertinent.

αθώος [athoos] innocent.

αθωώνω [athoono] acquit, exonerate.

αίγλη, η [eeglee] splendour || (ονόματος κτλ) grandeur, glory.

αιγόκλημα, το [egokleema] honeysuckle.

Αίγυπτος, η [eyeeptos] Egypt.

Αιγύπτιος, ο [eyeepteeos] Egyptian.

αιγυπτιακός [eyeepteeakos] Egyptian.

αιθέριος [ethereeos] ethereal, essential.

αιθήρας, ο [etheeras] (χημ) ether || air.

αίθουσα, η [ethousa] large room, hall || (σχολικ) schoolroom.

αίθριος [ethreeos] clear, bright || (καιρός) fair.

αίμα, το [ema] blood.

αιματηρός [emateeros] bloody, bloodstained.

αιματοχυσία, η [ematoheeseea] bloodshed.

αιμοβόρος [emovoros] bloodthirsty || (μεταφ) ferocious, cruel.

αιμοδοσία, η [emodoseea] blood donation.

αιμομιξία, η [emomeekseea] incest.

αιμορραγία, η [emorayeea] haemorrhage.

αιμοσφαίριο, το [emosfereeo] blood corpuscle.

αίνιγμα, το [eneegma] enigma, riddle.

άιντε [aeede] (επιφ) come now!, come on!

αίρεση, η [eresee] heresy.

αιρετικός [ereteekos] heretical.

αισθάνομαι [esthanome] feel.

αίσθημα, το [estheema] sensation, feeling || **αισθήματα** πλ feelings.

αισθηματικός [estheemateekos] sentimental.

αίσθηση, η [estheesee] sense, sensation.

αισθητικός [estheeteekos] aesthetic || **ο** ~ beautician.

αισθητός [estheetos] perceptible, noticeable.

αισιόδοξος [eseeodoksos] optimistic.

αίσχος, το [eshos] shame, disgrace.

αισχροκέρδεια, η [eshrokerdeea] profiteering.

αισχρολογία, η [eshroloyeea] obscenity, filthy talk.

αισχρός [eshros] shameful, infamous.

αίτηση, η [eteesee] application, petition, request.

αιτία, η [eteea] cause, reason, motive.

αιτιατική, η [eteeateekee] (γραμμ) accusative (case).

αίτιο, το [eteeo] cause || (εγκλήματος) motive.

αιτιολογία, η [eteeoloyeea] explanation || (οίκον) particulars.

αίτιος [eteeos] responsible.

αιτώ [eto] request (κάτι) **αιτούμαι** beg (κάτι).

αιφνιδιασμός, ο [efneedeeasmos] surprise.

αιχμαλωτίζω [ehmaloteezo] capture || (μεταφ) captivate.

αιχμάλωτος, ο [ehmalotos] captive, prisoner.

αιχμή, η [ehmee] (βελόνας) point || (βέλους) head.

αιώνας, ο [eonas] age, century.

αιώνιος [eoneeos] eternal || perpetual.

ακαδημία, η [akadeemeea] academy.

ακαθαρσία, η [akatharseea] filth, dirt.

ακάθαρτος [akathartos] dirty, filthy.

ακάθεκτος [akathektos] unrestrained, unchecked.

ακαθόριστος [akathoreestos] undefined.

ακακία, η [akakeea] (δένδρο) acacia.

άκακος [akakos] harmless, innocent.

ακαλαισθησία, η [akalestheeseea] lack of taste.

ακάλεστος [akalestos] uninvited.

ακαλλιέργητος [akalyergeetos] uncultivated || (άνθρωπος) uncultured.

ακαμάτης, ο [akamatees] loafer.

άκαμπτος [akamptos] unbending.

ακανθώδης [akanthodees] thorny, prickly.

ακανόνιστος [akanoneestos] unregulated || (σχήμα) irregular || (σφυγμός) uneven.

ακαριαίος [akareeayos] instantaneous.

άκαρπος [akarpos] unfruitful || (μεταφ) fruitless.

ακατάβλητος [akatavleetos] indomitable || (χρέη) unpaid.

ακατάδεκτος [akatadektos] disdainful, haughty.

ακατάληπτος [akataleeptos] incomprehensible.

ακατάλληλος [akataleelos] unsuitable, unfit.

ακαταλόγιστος [akatalogeestos] not responsible (for) || irrational.

ακατανόητος [akatanoeetos] inconceivable, unintelligible.

ακατάπαυστος [akatapavstos] unceasing, endless.

ακατάστατος [akatastatos] untidy || (καιρός) changeable.

ακατοίκητος [akateekeetos] uninhabited.

ακατόρθωτος [akatorthotos] unfeasible, impossible.

ακέραιος [akereos] integral, whole || (τίμιος) upright || — **αριθμός** integer.

ακεφιά, η [akefia] dejection, gloom.

ακίνδυνος [akeendeenos] safe, harmless.

ακίνητος [akeeneetos] immovable || (περιουσία) estate, property.

άκλιτος [akleetos] indeclinable.

ακμάζω [akmazo] flourish, thrive.

ακμαίος [akmeos] vigorous, sturdy || (γερός) robust.

ακμή, η [akmee] height, peak || (ιατρ) acne.

ακοή, η [akoee] hearing || **εξ ακοής** by hearsay.

ακοινώνητος [akeenoneetos] unsociable || (εκκλ) not having taken first communion.

ακολασία, η [akolaseea] debauchery, excess.

ακολουθία, η [akoloutheea] retinue, suite || (εκκλ) church service || **κατ** ~ **ν** in consequence.

ακόλουθος [akoloutos] (ουσ) attendant || (στρατ) attaché || (επίθ) following, next.

ακολουθώ [akoloutho] follow.

ακολούθως [akolouthos] consequently, afterwards || **ως** ~ as follows.

ακόμα [akoma] yet, more || ~ **και** even if.

ακονίζω [akoneezo] sharpen, whet.

ακόντιο, το [akonteeo] javelin, dart.

άκοπος [akopos] not cut || (εύκολος) easy || (ξεκούραστα) untiring.

ακόρεστος [akorestos] insatiable.

ακούμπι [akoumbo] lean.

ακούραστος [akourastos] indefatigable, unwearied.

ακούρδιστος [akourðeestos] not tuned || (ρολόι) not wound up.

ακούσιος [akouseeos] unintentional || involuntary.

ακουστικό, το [akousteeko] (τηλεφ) receiver.

ακουστικός [akousteekos] acoustic.

ακουστός [akoustos] famous, celebrated.

ακούω [akouo] hear, listen to || (εισακούω) obey.

άκρα, η [akra] end, tip, extremity.

ακραίος [akreos] extreme, utmost.

ακρατής [akratees] intemperate, incontinent.

ακράτητος [akrateetos] impetuous, rash, unrestrained.

άκρη, η [akree] βλ άκρα.

ακριβά [akreeva] dearly.

ακρίβεια, η [akreeveea] accuracy, precision || (μεταφράσεως κτλ) exactness || (τιμής) costliness.

ακριβής [akreevees] exact || (ωρολόγιο κτλ) accurate || (υπολογισμός) correct || (σε ραντεβού) punctual.

ακριβός [akreevos] dear, expensive.

ακριβώς [akreevos] precisely, accurately.

ακρίδα, η [akreeða] locust, grasshopper.

ακρόαση, η [akroasee] hearing, listening || (συνάντηση) audience, interview.

ακροατήριο, το [akroateereeo] audience.

ακροατής, ο [akroatees] listener || (πανεπιστημίου) auditor.

ακροβάτης, ο [akrovatees] acrobat.

ακρογιάλι, το [akroyalee] seashore.

ακρόπολη, η [akropolee] acropolis || citadel.

ακρωτηριάζω [akroteereeazo] maim, mutilate.

ακρωτήριο, το [akroteereeo] cape, promontory.

ακτή, η [aktee] shore, beach, coast.

ακτίνα, η [akteena] ray, beam || (ελπίδος) gleam || (ενεργείας) range || (τροχού) spoke || (κύκλου) radius.

ακτινοβολία, η [akteenovoleea] radiation.

ακτινογραφία, η [akteenografeea] X-ray.

ακτινοθεραπεία, η [akteenotherapeea] radiotherapy.

ακτοπλοΐα, η [aktoploeea] coastal shipping.

άκυρος [akeeros] invalid, void.

ακυρώνω [akeerono] nullify, invalidate || cancel.

αλάβαστρο, το [alavastro] alabaster.

αλάδοτος [alaðotos] (φαγητό) without oil.

αλαζονεία, η [alazoneea] arrogance, boastfulness.

αλάθητος [alatheetos] infallible.

άλαλος [alalos] speechless, dumb.

αλάνθαστος [alanthastos] infallible, certain.

αλάργα [alarga] far off.

αλάτι, το [alatee] salt || αλατιέρα saltcellar.

αλατίζω [alateezo] salt.

Αλβανία, η [alvaneea] Albania.

αλβανικός [alvaneekos] Albanian.

Αλβανός, ο [alvanos] Albanian.

άλγεβρα, η [alyevra] algebra.

Αλγερία, η [alyereea] Algeria.

Αλγερινός, ο [alyereenos] Algerian man || **α~** (επθ) Algerian.

αλγερίνικος [alyereeneekos] Algerian.

αλέθω [aletho] grind.

αλείβω [aleevo] coat, smear, rub.

αλείφω [aleefo] βλ **αλείβω.**

αλεξικέραυνο, το [alekseekeravno] lightning conductor.

αλεξιπτωτιστής, ο [alekseeptoteestees] parachutist.

αλεξίπτωτο, το [alekseeptoto] parachute.

αλεπού, η [alepou] fox || (μεταφ) sly person.

άλεσμα, το [alesma] grinding.

αλέτρι, το [aletree] plough.

αλεύρι, το [alevri] flour.

αλήθεια, η [aleetheea] truth || (επιρ) really, indeed.

αληθεύω [aleethevo] be true.

αληθινός [aleetheenos] real, genuine, true.

αλησμόνητος [aleesmoneetos] unforgettable.

αλήτης, ο [aleetees] vagabond, vagrant.

αλιεία, η [alieea] fishing || fishery.

αλιεύς, ο [alievs] fisherman.

αλιεύω [alievo] fish (for).

αλκοολικός [alkooleekos] alcoholic.

αλκυόνα, η [alkeeona] kingfisher, halcyon.

αλλά [ala] but, however, yet.

αλλαγή, η [alayee] change || variation.

αλλάζω [alazo] change, alter.

αλλαντικά, τα [alanteeka] πλ sausages.

αλλεπάλληλος [alepaleelos] repeated, successive.

αλλεργία, η [aleryeea] allergy.

αλληλεγγύη, η [aleelenyiee] mutual help, solidarity.

αλληλένδετος [aleelenδetos] interdependent, bound together.

αλληλογραφία, η [aleelografeea] correspondence.

αλλοδαπός, ο [aloδapos] foreigner, alien.

αλλοίθωρος [aleethoros] cross-eyed.

αλλοίμονο [aleemono] (επιρ) oh dear!

αλλοιώνω [aleeono] alter, change.

αλλοιώς [alios] otherwise, in a different way.

αλλοίωση, η [aliosee] change, alteration || (τροφίμων) adulteration.

αλλοιώτικος [alioteekos] different, unlike || (πρόσωπο) odd, strange.

αλλόκοτος [alokotos] queer, strange, odd.

άλλος [alos] (an)other, else || (επόμενος) next || (διαφορετικός) different || (επί πλέον) more || **κάθε άλλο!** anything but!

άλλοτε [alote] formerly || sometime.

αλλού [alou] elsewhere.

άλλωστε [aloste] besides, on the other hand.

άλμα, το [alma] jump, leap || **~ τώδης** by leaps and bounds.

άλμη, η [almee] brine, pickle.

αλμυρός [almeeros] salty || (μεταφ) costly.

άλογο, το [alogo] horse || **αλογόμυγα** horsefly.

αλοιφή, η [aleefee] ointment.

αλουμίνιο, το [aloumeeneeo] aluminium.

άλσος, το [alsos] grove, thicket.

αλύγιστος [aleeyeestos] inflexible.

αλύπητος [aleepeetos] pitiless, cruel.

αλυσίδα, η [aleeseeδa] chain.

άλυτος [aleetos] (που δεν ελύθη) unsolved || (δεν μπορεί να λυθεί) unsolvable.

άλφα, το [alfa] the letter A.

αλφάβητο, το [alfaveeto] alphabet.

αλώνι, το [alonee] threshing floor || αλωνίζω thresh || (σκορπώ) scatter.

άλωση, η [alosee] fall, capture, conquest.

άμα [ama] as soon as || (εάν) if.

αμαζόνα, η [amazona] amazon.

αμάθεια, η [amatheea] ignorance, illiteracy.

αμαθής [amathees] ignorant, illiterate.

αμάν [aman] (επιφ) for heaven's sake!

αμαξάς ο [amaksas] coachman, cab driver.

αμάξι, το [amaksee] carriage || (αυτοκίνητο) car.

αμαξοστοιχία, η [amaksosteeheea] train.

αμαρτάνω [amartano] sin.

αμαρτία, η [amarteea] sin || είναι ~ απ' το Θεό it's a pity!

άμαχος [amahos] non-combatant.

άμβωνας, ο [amvonas] pulpit.

αμέ [amme] (επιφ) why not? || of course!

αμείβω [ameevo] reward, compensate.

αμείλικτος [ameeleektos] implacable, inexorable.

αμείωτος [ameeotos] undiminished.

αμέλεια, η [ameleea] negligence, carelessness.

αμελής [amelees] negligent || (μαθητής) lazy.

αμελώ [amelo] neglect.

άμεμπτος [amemptos] irreproachable, blameless.

αμερικάνικος [amereekaneekos] American.

Αμερικανός, ο [amereekanos] American.

Αμερική, η [amereekee] America.

αμέριμνος [amereemnos] carefree, heedless.

αμερόληπτος [ameroleeptos] impartial.

άμεσος [amesos] direct, immediate.

αμέσως [amesos] at once, immediately.

αμετάβλητος [ametavleetos] unchanged || immutable.

αμετάκλητος [ametakleetos] irrevocable.

αμεταχείριστος [ametaheereestos] unused, new.

αμέτοχος [ametohos] exempt, not participating in.

αμέτρητος [ametreetos] countless, immeasurable.

αμήχανος [ameehanos] perplexed, embarrassed.

αμηχανία, η [ameehaneea] perplexity, confusion.

αμίαντος, ο [ameeantos] asbestos.

αμίλητος [ameeleetos] silent, quiet.

άμιλλα, η [ameela] emulation, rivalry.

αμίμητος [ameemeetos] inimitable.

άμισθος [ameesthos] unsalaried, without pay.

άμμος, η [ammos] sand.

αμμουδιά, η [amoudia] sandy beach.

αμμώδης [amodees] sandy.

αμμωνία, η [amoneea] ammonia.

αμνησία, η [amneeseea] amnesia.

αμνηστία, η [amneesteea] amnesty.

αμνός, ο [amnos] lamb.

αμοιβαίος [ameeveyos] mutual, reciprocal.

αμοιβή, η [ameevee] reward, recompense.

άμοιρος [ameeros] unfortunate, destitute.

αμόνι, το [amonee] anvil.

άμορφος [amorfos] shapeless.

αμόρφωτος [amorfotos] uneducated, unrefined.

αμπαζούρ, το [ambazour] lampshade.

αμπάρι, το [ambaree] storeroom || (ναυτ) hold.

αμπέλι, το [ambelee] vine ||
vineyard.

αμπραγιάζ, το [ambrageeaz]
clutch.

άμπωτη, η [ambotee] ebb tide.

αμυγδαλές, οι [ameegðales] πλ
tonsils.

αμύγδαλο, το [ameegðalo] almond.

αμυδρός [ameeðros] dim, faint.

άμυλο, το [ameelo] starch.

άμυνα, η [ameena] defence.

αμφιβάλλω [amfeevalo] doubt.

αμφίβιος [amfeeveeos] amphibious.

αμφίβολος [amfeevolos] doubtful,
dubious.

αμφίεση, η [amfiesee] dress, attire,
clothing.

αμφιθέατρο, το [amfeetheatro]
amphitheatre.

αμφίρροπος [amfeeropos]
undecided, in the balance,
wavering.

αμφισβητώ [amfeesveeto] dispute.

αμφορέας, ο [amforeas] amphora,
pitcher.

αμφότεροι [amfoteree] πλ both.

αν [an] if, whether || ~ **και** although,
though.

ανά [ana] along, over || ~ **εις** one by
one || ~ **την πόλη** through the
city.

αναβαίνω [anaveno] βλ **ανεβαίνω**.

αναβάλλω [anavalo] put off,
postpone, delay.

ανάβαση, η [anavasee] ascent.

αναβολή, η [anavolee]
postponement, adjournment.

αναβρασμός, ο [anavrasmos]
agitation, excitement ||
fermentation.

ανάβω [anavo] light || (φως κτλ) turn
on, switch on || (θυμώνω) get
provoked.

αναγγέλλω [anangelo] announce,
make known.

αναγγελία, η [anangeleea]
announcement, notice.

αναγέννηση, η [anageneesee]
revival, renaissance.

αναγκάζω [anangazo] force,
compel.

αναγκαίος [anangeyos] necessary,
essential, needed.

αναγκαστικός [anangasteekos]
compulsory || (προσγείωση κτλ)
forced.

ανάγκη, η [anangee] need,
necessity, want.

ανάγλυφο, το [anagleefo] bas-
relief.

αναγνωρίζω [anagnoreezo]
recognize || (παραδέχομαι) admit.

αναγνώριση, η [anagnoreesee]
recognition, acknowledgement.

ανάγνωση, η [anagnosee] reading.

αναγνώστης, ο [anagnostees]
reader.

αναγούλα, η [anagoula] nausea,
disgust.

ανάγω [anago] raise || (μετατρέπω)
reduce, convert.

ανάγωγος [anagogos] ill-bred, ill-
mannered.

αναδάσωση, η [anaðasose]
reafforestation.

αναδιοργανώνω [anaðeeorganono]
reorganize.

αναδιπλασιασμός, ο
[anaðeeplaseeasmos] (γραμμ)
reduplication.

ανάδοχος, ο [anaðohos] godparent,
sponsor.

αναδρομικός [anaðromeekos]
retroactive, retrospective.

αναζητώ [anazeeto] search for,
seek.

αναζωογονώ [anazoogono] revive,
invigorate.

αναζωπυρώ [anazopeero] relight,
rekindle || (μεταφ) revive.

ανάθεμα, το [anathema] curse ||
(εκκλ) excommunication.

αναθέτω [anatheto] commission,
entrust || (αφιερώνω) dedicate.

αναθεώρηση, η [anatheoreesee] revision, review.

αναθυμίαση, η [anatheemeeasee] stench, exhalation, fumes.

αναίδεια, η [anedeea] impudence.

αναιδής [anedees] impudent, shameless.

αναίμακτος [anemaktos] bloodless.

αναιμία, η [anemeea] anaemia.

αναίρεση, η [aneresee] refutation.

αναισθησία, η [anestheeseea] unconsciousness || (μεταφ) insensibility.

αναισθητικό, το [anestheeteeko] anaesthetic.

αναίσθητος [anestheetos] insensitive || (στους πόνους) unconscious, insensible || (ασυγκίνητος) unmoved.

ανακαινίζω [anakeeneezo] renovate, renew.

ανακαλύπτω [anakaleepto] discover, detect.

ανακαλώ [anakalo] recall || (άδεια, διάταγμα) repeal, abrogate || (διαταγή κτλ) cancel, withdraw || (υπόσχεση) retract.

ανακατώνω [anakatono] mix, stir || (συγχέω) confuse.

ανακάτωμα, το [anakatoma] mixing || (φασαρία) confusion || (στομάχου) nausea.

ανακεφαλαίωση, η [anakefaleosee] recapitulation.

ανακηρύσσω [anakeereeso] proclaim, declare.

ανακινώ [anakeeno] stir up || (μεταφ) bring up, raise.

ανάκληση, η [anakleesee] revocation, recalling.

ανακοινώνω [anakeenono] announce.

ανακοπή, η [anakopee] checking || (νομ) reprieve || (ιατρ) heart failure.

ανακουφίζω [anakoufeezo] relieve, alleviate, lighten.

ανακριβής [anakreevees] inaccurate.

ανάκριση, η [anakreesee] interrogation, inquiry.

ανακριτής, ο [anakreetees] examining magistrate.

ανάκτορο, το [anaktoro] palace.

ανακωχή, η [anakohee] armistice, truce.

αναλαμβάνω [analamvano] undertake || recover.

ανάλατος [analatos] (μεταφ) dull.

ανάληψη, η [analeepsee] (εργασίας) resumption, undertaking || (του Χριστού) ascension.

αναλλοίωτος [analeeotos] unchanging, constant, unaltered.

αναλογία, η [analoyeea] relation, proportion, ratio || portion.

αναλογικός [analoyeekos] proportionate.

ανάλογος [analogos] proportionate || (μαθημ) proportional.

αναλόγως [analogos] proportionately, according to.

ανάλυση, η [analeesee] analysis.

αναλυτικός [analeeteekos] analytical || detailed.

αναλφάβητος [analfaveetos] illiterate, ignorant.

αναμένω [anameno] wait for, expect.

ανάμεσα [anamesa] in between, among.

αναμεταξύ [anametaksee] between, among || στο ~ in the meantime, meanwhile.

αναμιγνύω [anameegneeo] mix, blend || implicate.

ανάμικτος [anameektos] mixed.

ανάμιξη, η [anameeksee] mixing, interfering.

άναμμα, το [anama] lighting || (προσώπου) inflammation || (έξαψη) excitement || (μοτέρ κτλ) ignition.

αναμμένος [anamenos] alight, burning.

ανάμνηση, n [anamneesee] recollection, memory.

αναμονή, n [anamonee] expectation, waiting.

αναμφισβήτητος [anamfeesveeteetos] indisputable, unquestionable.

ανανάς, ο [ananas] pineapple.

ανανεώνω [ananeono] renew, renovate.

ανανέωση, n [ananeosee] renewal, renovation.

ανάξιος [anakseeos] unworthy, unfit, inefficient.

αναπαράσταση, n [anaparastasee] representation || (εγκλήματος) reconstruction.

ανάπαυλα, n [anapavla] respite, rest.

ανάπαυση, n [anapavsee] rest, repose || (στρατ) stand easy!

αναπαυτικός [anapavteekos] comfortable, restful.

αναπαύομαι [anapavome] rest, relax.

αναπηδώ [anapeedo] jump up, leap up, start.

ανάπηρος [anapeeros] disabled || (διανοητικώς) deficient.

ανάπλαση, n [anaplasee] reforming, remodelling.

αναπληρώνω [anapleerono] replace || substitute || refill.

αναπνέω [anapneo] breathe.

αναπνοή, n [anapnoee] breath, breathing, respiration.

ανάποδα [anapoda] backwards || (μέσα έξω) inside out, topsy-turvy.

αναποδιά, r [anapodia] reverse, bad luck || contrariness.

αναποδογυρίζω [anapodogeereezo] turn upside down.

ανάποδος, r [anapodos] reversed || (άνθρωπος) difficult, cantankerous.

αναπόφευκτος [anapofevktos] inevitable, unavoidable.

αναπτήρας, ο [anapteeras] cigarette lighter.

ανάπτυξη, n [anapteeksee] development || (εξήγηση) explanation.

αναπτύσσω [anapteeso] unfold, develop || (λόγο) expound, explain.

αναρίθμητος [anareethmeetos] countless, innumerable.

ανάρπαστος [anarpastos] quickly bought up.

ανάρρωση, n [anarrosee] convalescence, recovery.

αναρχία, n [anarheea] anarchy.

αναρχικός [anarheekos] anarchical || (ουσ) anarchist.

αναρωτιέμαι [anarotieme] ask o.s., wonder.

ανάσα, n [anasa] breath, breathing || rest, respite.

ανασηκώνω [anaseekono] lift up, raise.

ανασκαφή, n [anaskafee] excavation.

ανάσκελα [anaskela] on one's back.

ανασκόπηση, n [anaskopeesee] review, weighing up.

ανασταίνω [anasteno] revive, restore to life.

ανασταλτικός [anastalteekos] restraining, holding back.

ανάσταση, n [anastasee] resurrection.

ανάστατος [anastatos] in disorder, agitated, excited.

αναστατώνω [anastatono] disturb, upset.

αναστέλλω [anastelo] stop, stay, suspend.

αναστενάζω [anastenazo] sigh, groan.

αναστηλώνω [anasteelono] restore, erect.

αναστήλωση, n [anasteelosee] restoration, erection.

ανάστημα, το [anasteema] height, stature.

αναστολή, n [anastolee] reprieve || suspension || restraint.

ανασυγκρότηση, n [anaseengrot_eesee] reconstruction.

ανασύρω [anaseero] raise, pull out, pull up, draw up.

ανατаράσσω [anataraso] stir up, upset.

ανατέλλω [anatelo] (ήλιος) rise || appear.

ανατίμηση, n [anateemeesee] price rise || revaluation.

ανατινάζω [anateenazo] blow up || spring up.

ανατίναξη, n [anateenaksee] explosion.

ανατοκισμός, ο [anatokeesmos] compound interest.

ανατολή, n [anatolee] east || (ήλιου) sunrise || **'Απω 'Α~** Far East || **Μέση 'Α~** Middle East.

ανατολικός [anatoleekos] eastern || oriental.

ανατομία, n [anatomeea] anatomy.

ανατρέπω [anatrepo] upset || (βάρκα κτλ) overturn, capsize.

ανατρέφω, [anatrefo] rear, bring up, raise.

ανατρέχω [anatreho] refer back to, go back to.

ανατριχιάζω [anatreeheeazo] shiver, shudder.

ανατροπή, n [anatropee] upset, overthrow || (νομ) refutation, reversal.

ανατροφή, n [anatrofee] upbringing, breeding.

ανάτυπο, το [anateepo] offprint, reprint.

άναυδος [anavdos] speechless, dumbfounded.

αναφέρω [anafero] mention, cite || report || relate.

αναφλέγω [anaflego] inflame, ignite.

ανάφλεξη, n [anafleksee] combustion, ignition.

αναφορά, n [anafora] report || (αίτηση) petition.

αναχαιτίζω [anaheeteezo] check, restrain || (επίθεση) repel.

αναχρονισμός, ο [anahroneesmos] anachronism.

ανάχωμα, το [anahoma] mound, bank, dyke.

αναχώρηση, n [anahoreesee] departure.

αναχωρώ [anahoro] leave, depart, go.

αναψυκτικά, τα [anapseekteeka] πλ refreshments.

αναψυχή, n [anapseehee] recreation.

ανδρεία, n [anδreea] bravery, valour.

ανδρείος [anδreeos] brave, courageous.

ανδρικός [anδreekos] manly, virile, male.

ανεβάζω [anevazo] raise, lift up || (θέατρο) put on.

ανεβαίνω [aneveno] ascend, climb, go up.

ανέβασμα, το [anevasma] going up || lifting || (έργου) production.

ανεβοκατεβαίνω [anevokateveno] go up and down || (τιμές) fluctuate.

ανέγγιχτος [anengeehtos] untouched, new.

ανέγερση, n [aneyersee] erection || (οπλώμα) getting up.

ανειλικρινής [aneeleekreenees] insincere || false.

ανέκαθεν [anekathen] always, ever, from the beginning.

ανέκδοτο, το [anekδoton] anecdote, funny story.

ανεκμετάλλευτος [anekmetalevtos] unexploited.

ανεκτικός [anekteekos] tolerant, patient, indulgent.

ανεκτίμητος [anekteemeetos] priceless, inestimable.

ανεκτός [anektos] bearable, tolerable.

ανέκφραστος [anekfrastos] inexpressible, indescribable || (ηθοποιός) expressionless || (βλέμμα) vacant.

ανελλιπής [aneleepees] flawless || (οργάνωση) complete || (φοίτηση) continuous.

ανέλπιστος [anelpeestos] unexpected || (γεγονός) unforeseen.

ανεμίζω [anemeezo] ventilate, air || (σίτο) winnow.

ανεμιστήρας, ο [anemeesteeas] fan, ventilator.

ανεμοβλογιά, η [anemovloya] chickenpox.

ανεμόμυλος, ο [anemomeelos] windmill.

άνεμος, ο [anemos] wind.

ανεμοστρόβιλος, ο [anemostroveelos] whirlwind.

ανεμπόδιστος [anembodeestos] unhindered, unimpeded.

ανεμώνα, η [anemona] anemone.

ανένδοτος [anendotos] unyielding, inflexible.

ανενόχλητος [anenohleetos] undisturbed.

ανεξάντλητος [aneksantleetos] inexhaustible.

ανεξαρτησία, η [aneksarteeseea] independence.

ανεξάρτητος [aneksarteetos] independent.

ανεξέλεγκτος [anekselengtos] unconfirmed || (δαπάνη κτλ) unexamined.

ανεξήγητος [anekseeyeetos] inexplicable.

ανεξίτηλος [anekseeteelos] indelible.

ανεπαίσθητος [anepestheetos] imperceptible, slight.

ανεπαρκής [aneparkees] insufficient, inadequate.

ανέπαφος [anepafos] untouched, intact.

ανεππρέαστος [anepeereastos] unaffected, uninfluenced.

ανεπιθύμητος [anepeetheemeetos] undesirable.

ανεπίσημος [anepeeseemos] unofficial.

ανεπιτυχής [anepeeteehees] unsuccessful.

ανεπιφύλακτος [anepeefeelaktos] unreserved.

ανεπτυγμένος [anepteegmenos] (άνθρωπος) cultured || (σωματικώς) developed.

άνεργος [anergos] unemployed, idle.

ανέρχομαι [anerhome] ascend, climb || (λογαριασμός) amount to.

άνεση, η [annesee] ease, comfort.

ανεστραμμένος [anestramenos] reversed, inverted.

άνετος [anetos] comfortable, easy.

άνευ [anev] without.

ανεύθυνος [anevtheenos] irresponsible.

ανεφάρμοστος [anefarmostos] inapplicable || (μη εφαρμοσθείς) unapplied.

ανέφικτος [anefeektos] unattainable, impossible.

ανεφοδιάζω [anefodeeazo] provision, restock.

ανέχομαι [anehome] tolerate.

ανεψιά, η [anepsia] niece.

ανεψιός, ο [anepsios] nephew.

ανήθικος [aneetheekos] immoral, corrupt.

άνηθο, το [aneetho] dill, anise.

ανήκουστος [aneekoustos] unheard of, incredible.

ανήκω [aneeko] belong (to).

ανήλικος [aneeleekos] under age || minor.

ανήμερα [aneemera] on the same day.

ανήμπορος [aneemboros] indisposed.

ανησυχία, η [aneeseeheea] uneasiness, concern.

ανήσυχος [aneeseehos] uneasy, anxious.

ανησυχώ [aneeseeho] be anxious, be worried.

ανήφορος, ο [aneeforos] uphill road || ascent.

ανθεκτικός [anthekteekos] endurable, resistant.

ανθίζω [antheezo] blossom, flourish.

ανθίσταμαι [antheestame] resist, oppose.

ανθοδέσμη, η [anthodesmee] bouquet, nosegay.

ανθοδοχείο, το [anthodoheeo] flowerpot, vase.

ανθολογία, η [antholoyeea] anthology.

ανθοπώλης, ο [anthopolees] florist.

άνθος, το [anthos] flower.

άνθρακας, ο [anthrakas] coal || (ιατρ) anthrax.

ανθρακικός [anthrakeekos] carbonic.

ανθρακωρυχείο, το [anthrakoreeheeo] coalmine.

ανθρωπιά, η [anthropia] civility || good breeding.

ανθρώπινος [anthropeenos] human.

ανθρωπιστής, ο [anthropeestees] humanist.

ανθρωποκτονία, η [anthropoktoneea] homicide.

ανθρωπολόγος, ο [anthropologos] anthropologist.

άνθρωπος, ο [anthropos] man, person.

ανθρωπότης, η [anthropotees] mankind, humanity.

ανθυγιεινός [antheeyeeinos] unhealthy, unwholesome.

ανία, η [aneea] boredom, weariness, ennui.

ανίατος [aneeatos] incurable.

ανίδεος [aneedeos] unsuspecting || ignorant.

ανικανοποίητος [aneekanopieetos] unsatisfied.

ανίκανος [aneekanos] incapable, unable, unfit || impotent.

ανισόρροπος [aneesoropos] unbalanced.

άνισος [aneesos] unequal, uneven.

ανίσχυρος [aneesheeros] powerless, weak, feeble.

ανίχνευση, η [aneehnevsee] tracking, searching.

άνοδος, η [anodos] ascent, accession.

ανοησία, η [anoeeseea] folly, foolishness, nonsense.

ανόητος [anoeetos] foolish, silly, absurd.

ανόθευτος [anothevtos] unadulterated, pure.

άνοιγμα, το [aneegma] opening, aperture.

ανοίγω [aneego] open || (βρύση) turn on || (ούρτη) draw || (ομπρέλλα) put up || (φώτα κτλ) turn on, switch on || (ουζήτηση) open, broach || (χάρτη) unfold || (χορό) lead, open || (πηγάδι) dig || (κουρτίνες) draw || (για χρώμα) fade.

ανοίκιαστος [aneekeeastos] unlet, unrented.

ανοικοδομώ [aneekodomo] rebuild.

ανοικτός [aneektos] open || (επί χρωμάτων) light.

άνοιξη, η [aneeksee] spring, springtime.

ανοιχτόκαρδος [aneehtokardos] open-hearted, cheerful.

ανοιχτοχέρης [aneehtoheerees] open-handed, magnanimous.

ανομβρία, η [anomvreea] drought.

ανόμοιος [anomeeos] dissimilar, unlike.

ανοξείδωτος [anokseedotos] stainless, rustproof.

ανοργάνωτος [anorganotos] unorganized.

ανορεξία, η [anorekseea] loss of appetite || (μεταφ) half-heartedness.

ανορθογραφία, η [anorthografeea] misspelling.

ανοσία, η [anoseea] immunity.

άνοστος [anostos] insipid, unsavoury || (μεταφ) ugly, disagreeable.

ανοχή, η [anohee] forbearance, tolerance || **οίκος ανοχής** brothel.

ανταγωνίζομαι [antagoneezome] compete, vie (with).

ανταγωνισμός, ο [antagoneesmos] competition, contest, rivalry.

ανταλλαγή, η [antalayee] exchange.

αντάλλαγμα, το [antalagma] thing exchanged, recompense.

ανταλλακτικό, το [antalakteeko] spare part, refill.

ανταλλάσσω [antalaso] exchange.

ανταμείβω [antameevo] reward, recompense.

ανταμώνω [antamono] meet, join.

αντάμωση [antamosee]: **καλή ~** goodbye, farewell.

αντανάκλαση, η [antanaklasee] reflection.

αντανακλώ [antanaklo] reflect.

αντάξιος [antakseeos] worthy, deserving.

ανταποδίδω [antapodeedo] return, repay.

ανταποκρίνομαι [antapokreenome] be like, correspond to, respond, suit.

ανταπόκριση, η [antapokreesee] correspondence || (εφημερίδας) dispatch.

ανταποκριτής, ο [antapokreetees] correspondent, reporter.

ανταρσία, η [antarseea] rebellion, revolt, mutiny.

αντάρτης, ο [antartees] rebel, insurgent, guerrilla.

άντε [ante] (επιφ) come on!, get a move on!

αντένα, η [antena] aerial, antenna.

αντεπίθεση, η [antepeethesee] counterattack.

αντεπιτίθεμαι [antepeeteetheme] counterattack.

άντερο, το [antero] intestine.

αντέχω [anteho] endure, hold firm, last.

αντζούγια, η [andzouyeea] anchovy.

αντηλιά, η [anteelia] glare.

αντηχώ [anteeho] resound, echo.

αντί [antee] instead of, in exchange for || (τιμή) for || **~ για** instead of || **~ να** instead of.

αντιαεροπορικός [anteeaeroporeekos] anti-aircraft.

αντιγραφή, η [anteegrafee] copy, copying.

αντίγραφο, το [anteegrafo] copy, transcript.

αντιγράφω [anteegrafo] copy, imitate || (στο σχολείο) crib.

αντίδι, το [anteedee] endive.

αντίδικος, ο [anteedeekos] opponent.

αντίδοτο, το [anteedoto] antidote.

αντίδραση, η [anteedrasee] reaction, opposition.

αντιδραστικός [anteedrasteekos] reactionary, reactive.

αντιδρώ [anteedro] react, counteract, oppose.

αντίδωρο, το [anteedoro] (εκκλ) holy bread.

αντίζηλος [anteezeelos] rival.

αντίθεση, η [anteethesee] contrast || opposition.

αντίθετος [anteethetos] contrary, opposite.

αντίκα, η [anteeka] antique.

αντικαθιστώ [anteekatheesto] replace, substitute || relieve.

αντικανονικός [anteekanoneekos] irregular, against the rules.

αντικατάσταση [anteekatastasee] replacement || substitution.

αντικαταστάτης, ο [anteekatastatees] substitute || successor.

αντίκειμαι [anteekeeme] be opposed to.

αντικειμενικός [anteekeemeneekos] objective.

αντικείμενο, το [anteekeemeno] object, thing || topic.

αντικλείδι, το [anteekleeðee] passkey.

αντικοινωνικός [anteekeenoneekos] unsocial.

αντικρούω [anteekrouo] oppose, refute.

αντίκρυ [anteekree] opposite, face to face.

αντικρύζω [anteekreezo] face, front || meet.

αντίκτυπος, ο [anteekteepos] repercussion, effect, result.

αντίλαλος, ο [anteelalos] echo.

αντιλαμβάνομαι [anteelamvanome] understand || perceive, notice.

αντιλέγω [anteelego] object, contradict.

αντιληπτός [anteeleeptos] perceptible || understandable.

αντίληψη, η [anteeleepsee] understanding, opinion || quickness of mind.

αντιλυσσικός [anteeleeseekos] anti-rabies.

αντιμετωπίζω [anteemetopeezo] confront, face.

αντιμέτωπος [anteemetopos] face to face, facing.

αντιναύαρχος, ο [anteenavarhos] vice-admiral.

αντίο [anteeo] (επιφ) goodbye!

αντιπάθεια, η [anteepatheea] antipathy, aversion.

αντιπαθητικός [anteepatheeteekos] repulsive, repugnant.

αντιπαθώ [anteepatho] dislike.

αντίπαλος, ο [anteepalos] adversary, opponent || (στρατ) enemy.

αντιπερισπασμός, ο [anteepereespasmos] distraction || (στρατ) diversion.

αντίποινα, τα [anteepeena] πλ reprisals.

αντιπολίτευση, η [anteepoleetevsee] opposition.

αντίπραξη, η [anteepraksee] opposition, thwarting.

αντιπρόεδρος, ο [anteeproeðros] vice-president, deputy chairman.

αντιπροσωπεία, η [anteeprosopeea] representation || delegation.

αντιπροσωπεύω [anteeprosopevo] represent, stand for.

αντιπρόσωπος, ο [anteeprosopos] representative || (εμπορικός) agent.

αντίρρηση, η [anteereesee] objection, contradiction.

αντισηπτικός [anteeseepteekos] antiseptic.

αντισταθμίζω [anteestathmeezo] balance || (μηχανική) compensate.

αντίσταση, η [anteestasee] resistance, opposition.

αντιστέκομαι [anteestekome] resist, oppose.

αντίστοιχος [anteesteehos] corresponding, equivalent.

αντιστράτηγος, ο [anteestrateegos] lieutenant-general.

αντιστρέφω [anteestrefo] invert, reverse.

αντίστροφος [anteestrofos] reverse, inverse.

αντισυνταγματικός [anteeseentagmateekos] unconstitutional.

αντιτίθεμαι [anteeteetheme] be opposed.

αντίτιμο, το [anteeteemo] value, price.

αντιτορπιλλικό, το [anteetorpeeleeko] destroyer.

αντίτυπο, το [anteeteepo] copy.

αντίφαση, η [anteefasee] contradiction, discrepancy.

αντιφάσκω [anteefasko] contradict o.s.

αντίχειρας, ο [anteeheeras] thumb.

αντλία, η [antleea] pump.

αντλώ [antlo] pump, draw (off) || derive.

αντοχή, η [antohee] endurance, strength, resistance.

άντρας, ο [antras] man || husband.

αντρίκιος [antreekeeos] βλ **ανδρικός**.

αντρόγυνο, το [antroyeeno] married couple.

αντωνυμία, η [antoneemeea] pronoun.

ανύπανδρος [aneepanðros] unmarried, single.

ανύπαρκτος [aneeparktos] non-existent.

ανυπαρξία, η [aneeparkseea] non-existence, lack.

ανυπολόγιστος [aneepoloyeestos] incalculable.

ανυπόμονος [aneepomonos] impatient, anxious.

ανυπόπτος [aneepoptos] unsuspecting || not suspect.

ανυπόστατος [aneepostatos] groundless, unfounded || unsubstantial.

ανυπότακτος [aneepotaktos] insubordinate || (λαός) unsubdued.

ανυπόφορος [aneepoforos] intolerable.

ανυψώνω [aneepsono] raise || (μεταφ) praise, elevate, extol.

άνω [ano] up, above || ~ **κάτω** in confusion, upset || (μέρος) above, over.

ανώδυνος [anoðeenos] painless.

ανωμαλία, η [anomaleea] irregularity, unevenness || anomaly.

ανώμαλος [anomalos] (επιφάνεια) irregular, uneven || (άνθρωπος) erratic, eccentric.

ανώνυμος [anoneemos] anonymous || ~ **εταιρεία** limited company.

ανώτατος [anotatos] supreme, uppermost.

ανώτερος [anoteros] superior, higher, upper || ~ **χρημάτων** above money.

άξεστος [aksestos] uncouth, rough, unpolished.

αξέχαστος [aksehastos] unforgotten || unforgettable.

αξία, η [akseea] worth, value, price.

αξιαγάπητος [akseeagapeetos] amiable, lovable.

αξιέπαινος [akseiepenos] praiseworthy, laudable.

αξίζω [akseezo] be worth, cost || merit || **αξίζει να τιμωρηθεί** he deserves to be punished.

αξίνα, η [akseena] pickaxe.

αξιοθαύμαστος [akseeothavmastos] wonderful, admirable.

αξιοθέατος [akseeotheatos] worth seeing || **τα αξιοθέατα** the sights.

αξιοθρήνητος [akseeothreeneetos] lamentable, deplorable.

αξιόλογος [akseeologos] remarkable || distinguished.

αξιόπιστος [akseeopeestos] trustworthy, reliable.

αξιοπρεπής [akseeoprepees] dignified, decent.

άξιος [akseeos] capable || deserving || worthy, worth.

αξιοσημείωτος [akseeoseemeeotos] noteworthy, notable, remarkable.

αξιότιμος [akseeoteemos] estimable, honourable.

αξιωματικός, ο [akseeomateekos] officer.

άξονας, ο [aksonas] axis || axle, pivot, shaft.

αξύριστος [akseereestos] unshaven.

άοπλος [aoplos] unarmed.

αόριστος [aoreestos] invisible, indefinite || (γραμμ) aorist.

άοσμος [aosmos] odourless, scentless.

απαγγελία, η [apangeleea] recitation, declamation || diction.

απαγόρευση, η [apagorevsee] prohibition.

απαγορεύω [apagorevo] prohibit, forbid.

απαγωγή, η [apagoyee] abduction || (παιδιού) kidnapping.

απάθεια, η [apatheea] indifference, apathy.

απαισιόδοξος [apeseeoδoksos] pessimist.

απαίσιος [apeseeos] frightful, sinister, horrible.

απαίτηση, η [apeteesee] claim || demand.

απαιτητικός [apeteeteekos] demanding, exacting, importunate.

απαιτώ [apeto] claim, demand, require.

απαλλαγή, η [apalayee] deliverance || release || dismissal.

απαλλάσσω [apalasso] deliver, free || (κάθαρση) relieve.

απαλλοτριώ [apalotreeo] expropriate, alienate.

απαλός [apalos] soft || gentle.

απάνθρωπος [apanthropos] inhuman, cruel.

άπαντα, τα [apanta] πλ complete works.

απάντηση, η [apanteesee] reply, answer, response.

απαντώ [apanto] answer, reply || meet.

απάνω [apano] up, above || upstairs || ~ **κάτω** approximately || **από πάνω** on top, from above || **έως** ~ to the top || ~ **που** at the moment when || ~ **από** above, more than || ~ **σε** at the moment of.

απαράδεκτος [aparaδektos] unacceptable, inadmissible.

απαραίτητος [apareteetos] indispensable.

απαράλλακτος [aparalaktos] identical || unchanged.

απαράμιλλος [aparameelos] unrivalled, incomparable, peerless.

απαρατήρητος [aparateereetos] unnoticed, unobserved.

απαρέμφατο, το [aparemfato] (γραμμ) infinitive.

απαρηγόρητος [apareegoreetos] inconsolable.

απαριθμώ [apareethmo] enumerate, count.

απαρνούμαι [aparnoume] renounce, deny, disavow, disown.

απαρτίζω [aparteezo] form, constitute.

απασχόληση, η [apasholeesee] occupation.

απασχολώ [apasholo] occupy, busy.

απατεώνας, ο [apateonas] cheat, deceiver, swindler.

απάτη, η [apatee] deceit, fraud || illusion.

απατηλός [apateelos] deceptive, false, fraudulent.

απατώ [apato] deceive, cheat, defraud.

απεγνωσμένος [apegnosmenos] desperate.

απειθαρχία, η [apeetharheea] insubordination, lack of discipline.

απεικονίζω [apeekoneezo] represent, portray, depict.

απειλή, η [apeelee] threat, menace.

απειλητικός [apeeleeteekos] threatening.

απειρία, n [apeereea] inexperience || (μέτρο) infinity, immensity.

άπειρος [apeeros] inexperienced || (αριθμός) infinite, boundless.

απέλαση, n [apelasee] deportation, expulsion.

απελευθερώνω [apeleftherono] set free, emancipate.

απελευθέρωση, n [apeleftherosee] liberation, emancipation.

απελπίζομαι [apelpeezome] despair.

απελπισία, n [apelpeeseea] despair || είναι ~ it's hopeless!

απέναντι [apenantee] opposite.

απεναντίας [apenanteeas] on the contrary.

απένταρος [apentaros] penniless, broke.

απέραντος [aperantos] immense, boundless, endless.

απεργία, n [aperyeea] strike.

απερίγραπτος [apereegraptos] indescribable.

απεριόριστος [apereeoreestos] unlimited.

απεριποίητος [apereepeeetos] neglected, untidy.

απερίσκεπτος [apereeskeptos] thoughtless, foolish, heedless.

απερίσπαστος [apereespastos] undistracted.

απέριττος [apereetos] simple, plain, concise.

απεσταλμένος, ο [apestalmenos] envoy, minister, delegate.

απευθύνομαι [apeftheenome] apply, appeal, address.

απεχθάνομαι [apehthanome] detest, abhor.

απεχθής [apehthees] odious, repulsive, detestable.

απέχω [apeho] abstain || be distant, be far from.

απήχηση, n [apeeheesee] effect || echo.

άπιαστος [apeeastos] not caught || intact, intangible.

απίθανος [apeethanos] unlikely, improbable.

απίστευτος [apeestevtos] unbelievable, incredible.

**απιστία, [apeesteea] infidelity || incredulity.

άπιστος [apeestos] unbelieving || faithless, infidel.

απιστώ [apeesto] be unfaithful.

άπλα, n [apla] spaciousness.

απλά [apla] simply.

άπλετος [apletos] abundant.

απλήρωτος [apleerotos] unfilled || unpaid.

απλησίαστος [apleeseeastos] unapproachable.

άπληστος [apleestos] insatiable, greedy, avid.

απλοϊκός [aploeekos] naïve, simple.

απλός [aplos] simple || (εισιτήριο) single || (ντόσιμο) plain.

απλότητα, n [aploteeta] simplicity, naivety, plainness.

απλούστατα [aploustata] simply.

άπλυτος [apleetos] unwashed || τα άπλυτα dirty linen.

άπλωμα, το [aploma] spreading, unfolding || (χεριών) stretching || (ρούχων) hanging out.

απλώνω [aplono] spread, stretch || (ρούχα) hang out.

απλώς [aplos] simply, merely, plainly.

άπνοια, n [apneea] lack of wind.

από [apo] from, of || by || through || than || ~ καιρού σε καιρόν from time to time || ~ φόβο out of fear || ~ μνήμης by heart || ~ τον ίδιο δρόμο by the same road || ~ το παράθυρο through the window || ξέρω περισσότερα ~ σένα I know more than you || (προθ) μέσα ~ out of || πριν ~ before.

αποβάθρα, n [apovathra] pier, wharf.

αποβάλλω [apovalo] reject, expel, dismiss || (μωρό) miscarry.

απόβαση, n [apovasee] disembarkation, landing.

αποβιβάζω [apoveevazo] disembark, unload.

αποβλέπω [apovlepo] consider || aim at, look forward to || regard.

αποβολή, n [apovolee] dismissal || (μωρού) miscarriage, abortion.

αποβραδίς [apovraðees] yesterday evening, since last night.

απογειώνομαι [apoyeeonome] take off.

απογείωση, n [apoyeeosee] takeoff.

απόγεμα, το [apoyema] afternoon.

απόγνωση, n [apognosee] despair, desperation.

απογοήτευση [apogoeetevsee] disappointment, disillusionment.

απογοητεύω [apogoeetevo] disappoint, disillusion.

απόγονος, ο [apogonos] offspring, descendant.

απογραφή, n [apografee] (πληθυσμού) census || (εμπορ) inventory.

αποδεικνύω [apoðeekneeo] prove, demonstrate.

αποδεικτικό, το [apoðeekteeko] certificate.

απόδειξη, n [apoðeeksee] proof || receipt.

αποδεκατίζω [apoðekateezo] decimate.

αποδεκτός [apoðektos] acceptable || accepted.

αποδέχομαι [apoðehome] accept || admit.

απόδημος [apoðeemos] living abroad, migrant.

αποδίδω [apoðeeðo] give back, return || (τιμές) grant, award || (κάτι σε κάτι) attribute || (ελευθερία)

restore || (μετάφραση) express || (έργο) produce.

αποδοκιμάζω [apoðokeemazo] disapprove of || demonstrate against.

αποδοκιμασία, n [apoðokeemaseea] disapproval, rejection || booing.

απόδοση, n [apoðosee] (επιστροφή) return, repayment || (μηχανής κτλ) efficiency, capacity || (εργοστασίου) output || (της γης) yield, produce || (έργου) rendering.

αποδοχή, n [apoðohee] acceptance || acceptation || **αποδοχές** πλ salary, fees.

απόδραση, n [apoðrasee] escape.

αποδυτήριο, το [apoðeeteereeo] changing room.

αποζημιώνω [apozeemeeono] compensate, indemnify.

αποζημίωση, n [apozeemeeosee] compensation, indemnity.

αποθαρρύνω [apothareeno] discourage.

απόθεμα, το [apothema] deposit || stock, reserve.

αποθέωση, n [apotheosee] apotheosis || (μεταφ) rousing reception.

αποθηκεύω [apotheekevo] store up.

αποθήκη, n [apotheekee] storage room, storehouse, warehouse.

αποθρασύνομαι [apothraseenome] become arrogant.

αποικία, n [apeekeea] colony, settlement.

αποκαθιστώ [apokatheesto] rehabilitate, restore || (κόρη) marry.

αποκαλύπτω [apokaleepto] disclose, unveil, reveal.

αποκάλυψη, n [apokaleepsee] revelation || (θρησκεία) Apocalypse.

αποκαρδιωτικός [apokarðeeoteekos] disheartening.

αποκατάσταση, η [apokatastasee] restoration, resettlement || (κόρης) marriage.

απόκεντρος [apokentros] outlying, remote, out-of-the-way.

αποκέντρωση, η [apokentrosee] decentralization.

αποκεφαλίζω [apokefaleezo] decapitate, behead.

αποκήρυξη, η [apokeereeksee] denunciation, proscription.

αποκηρύσσω [apokeereeso] renounce, disavow || proscribe, outlaw.

αποκλεισμός, ο [apokleesmos] exclusion, blockade, boycott.

αποκλειστικός [apokleesteekos] exclusive.

αποκλείω [apokleeo] exclude || debar || boycott || **αποκλείεται** it's out of the question.

αποκληρώνω [apokleerono] disinherit.

αποκλίνω [apokleeno] lean, diverge, incline.

αποκοιμίζω [apokeemeezo] lull to sleep.

αποκοιμούμαι [apokeemoume] fall asleep.

αποκομίζω [apokomeezo] carry away || derive.

απόκομμα, το [apokoma] press-cutting || (κομματι) bit.

αποκοπή, η [apokopee] cutting off || amputation.

απόκρημνος [apokreemnos] precipitous, steep, abrupt.

αποκριές, οι [apokries] πλ carnival.

αποκρίνομαι [apokreenome] answer, reply.

απόκρουση, η [apokrousee] repulsion || (κατηγορίας) refutation.

αποκρούω [apokrouo] repulse || reject.

αποκρύπτω [apokreepto] conceal, hide, cover.

απόκρυφος [apokreefos] secret || (εκκλ) apocryphal.

απόκτηση, η [apokteesee] acquisition.

αποκτώ [apokto] obtain, get || (παιδί) have.

απολαβή, η [apolavee] gain, profit, income.

απολαμβάνω [apolamvano] gain, earn || (διασκεδάζω) enjoy.

απόλαυση, η [apolavsee] enjoyment.

απολίθωμα, το [apoleethoma] fossil.

απολογία, η [apoloyeea] defence, plea, excuse.

απολογισμός, ο [apoloyeesmos] financial statement, account, report.

απολογούμαι [apoloyoume] justify o.s., apologize.

απολύμανση, η [apoleemansee] disinfection.

απόλυση, η [apoleesee] release || dismissal.

απολυτήριο, το [apoleeteereeo] discharge certificate || (σχολείου) school leaving certificate, diploma.

απόλυτος [apoleetos] absolute || (αριθμός) cardinal.

απολύτως [apoleetos] absolutely || entirely.

απολύω [apoleeo] release || (διώκνω) dismiss || (από το στρατό) discharge.

απομακραίνω [apomakreno] remove, send away, keep off.

απόμαχος, ο [apomahos] veteran, pensioner.

απομεινάρια [apomeenaria] πλ remains, left-overs, remnants.

απομένω [apomeno] remain, be left || (κατάπληκτος) be left speechless.

απομίμηση, η [apomeemeesee] imitation, copy.

απομνημονεύματα, τα [apomneemonevmata] πλ memoirs.

απομονώνω [apomonono] isolate || (ηλεκτ) insulate.

απονέμω [aponemo] bestow, allot || confer, award.

απονομή, n [aponomee] award.

αποξενώνω [apoksenono] alienate, estrange.

αποξήρανση, n [apokseeransee] draining, drying.

απόπειρα, n [apopeera] attempt, trial.

αποπεράτωση, n [apoperatosee] completion.

αποπλάνηση, n [apoplaneesee] seduction || (φωτός) aberration.

αποπλέω [apopleo] set sail, sail away.

απορία, n [aporeea] doubt || uncertainty, perplexity.

άπορος [aporos] needy, poor.

απορρέω [aporeo] flow, stem (from), emanate.

απόρρητος [aporeetos] secret.

απορρίματα, τα [aporeemata] πλ rubbish, refuse.

απορρίπτω [aporeepto] cast off || (προσφορά κτλ) reject, refuse || (στις εξετάσεις) fail.

απορροφώ [aporofo] absorb.

απορρυπαντικό, το [aporeepanteeko] detergent.

απορώ [aporo] be at a loss, wonder, be surprised.

απόσβεση, n [aposvese] extinguishing || (χρέους) liquidation (of debt).

αποσιωπητικά, τα [aposeeopeeteeka] πλ points of omission.

αποσιωπώ [aposeeopo] hush up, pass in silence.

αποσκοπώ [aposkopo] aim, have in view.

απόσπασμα, το [apospasma] extract, excerpt || (στρατ) detachment || εκτελεστικό ~ firing squad.

αποσπώ [apospo] detach, tear || (στρατ) detach.

απόσταξη, n [apostaksee] distillation.

αποστασία, n [apostaseea] revolt, defection || apostasy.

απόσταση, n [apostasee] distance || remoteness.

αποστειρώνω [aposteerono] sterilize.

αποστέλλω [apostelo] dispatch, send, transmit.

αποστερώ [apostero] deprive.

αποστηθίζω [aposteetheezo] learn by heart.

απόστημα, το [aposteema] abscess.

αποστολέας, ο [apostoleas] sender, shipper.

αποστολή, n [apostolee] sending, consignment || (εμπορική κτλ) mission.

αποστομώνω [apostomono] silence.

αποστράτευση, n [apostratevsee] demobilization.

απόστρατος, ο [apostratos] retired officer, ex-serviceman, veteran.

αποστρέφω [apostrefo] avert, turn away.

αποστροφή, n [apostrofee] repugnance, aversion, abhorrence.

απόστροφος, n [apostrofos] apostrophe.

αποσύνθεση, n [aposeenthesee] decay, decomposition || disorganization.

αποσύρω [aposeero] withdraw || retract.

αποταμιεύω [apotamievo] save, put aside || (τρόφιμα) lay up.

αποτελειώνω [apoteleeono] complete || finish off.

αποτέλεσμα, το [apotelesma] result, effect || αποτελεσματικός effective.

αποτελούμαι [apoteloume] consist of, be composed of.

αποτεφρώνω [apotefrono] reduce to ashes, burn down.

απότομος [apotomos] sudden, abrupt || (στροφή) steep, sheer || (τρόπος) curt, gruff.

αποτραβιέμαι [apotravieme] withdraw, give up.

αποτρέπω [apotrepo] avert, turn aside, ward off.

αποτρόπαιος [apotropeos] abominable, hideous, horrible.

αποτροπή, η [apotropee] averting, warding off, dissuasion.

αποτσίγαρο, το [apotseegaro] cigarette end, stub, fag end.

αποτυγχάνω [apoteenghano] fail, fall through, miss.

αποτυπώνω [apoteepono] impress, imprint.

αποτυχία, η [apoteeheea] failure, reverse.

απουσία, η [apouseea] absence || απουσιάζω be absent.

αποφασίζω [apofaseezo] decide, resolve, determine.

απόφαση, η [apofasee] decision, resolution || (νομ) verdict || το παίρνω ~α make up one's mind.

αποφασιστικός [apofaseesteekos] decisive, determined.

αποφέρω [apofero] yield, bring in || produce.

αποφεύγω [apofevgo] avoid, keep clear of || (κάπνισμα κτλ) abstain from.

απόφοιτος [apofeetos] school leaver || university graduate.

αποφυγή, η [apofeeyee] avoidance, evasion.

αποφυλακίζω [apofeelakeezo] release from prison.

απόφυση, η [apofeesee] excrescence || protuberance.

αποχαιρετίζω [apohereteezo] wish goodbye, bid farewell.

αποχαιρετισμός, ο [apohereteesmos] farewell, goodbye.

αποχέτευση, η [apohetevsee] draining, drainage.

απόχρωση, η [apohrosee] shade, tone || (χρώματος) fading.

αποχώρηση, η [apohoreesee] withdrawal, retirement, departure.

αποχωρητήριο, το [apohoreeteerio] W.C., lavatory || (στρατ) latrine.

αποχωρίζομαι [apohoreezome] part with, be separated from.

αποχωρισμός, ο [apohoreesmo] separation, parting.

αποχωρώ [apohoro] withdraw, retire, leave.

απόψε [apopse] tonight, this evening.

αποψινός [apopseenos] tonight's.

άποψη, η [apopsee] view, sight || (μεταφ) view, idea.

άπρακτος [apraktos] unsuccessful || unachieved.

απραξία, η [prakseea] inactivity || (οικ) stagnation, standstill.

απρέπεια, η [aprepeea] indecency, bad manners.

απρεπής [aprepees] indecent, improper, unbecoming.

Απρίλης, ο [apreelees] April.

απρόβλεπτος [aprovleptos] unforeseen, unexpected.

απροετοίμαστος [aproeteemastos] unprepared, unready.

απροθυμία, η [aprotheemeea] reluctance, hesitancy.

απρόθυμος [aprotheemos] unwilling, reluctant, hesitant.

απρόοπτος [aprooptos] unforeseen, unexpected.

απρόβλητος [aprosvleetos] unassailable || invulnerable.

απροσδόκητος [aprosdokeetos] unexpected, unforeseen, sudden.

απρόσεκτος [aprosektos] inattentive, careless, remiss.

απροσεξία, η [aprosekseea] inattention, inadvertence.

απρόσιτος [aproseetos] inaccessible, unapproachable.

απροστάτευτος [aprostatevtos] unprotected || forlorn.

απρόσωπος [aprosopos] impersonal.

αποχώρητο, το [aprohoreeto] limit, dead end.

άπτερος [apteros] wingless.

απτόητος [aptoeetos] undaunted, intrepid.

απύθμενος [apeethmenos] bottomless.

απωθώ [apotho] repel, repulse, thrust back || (μεταφ) reject.

απώλεια, η [apoleea] loss || (θάνατος) bereavement.

απώλητος [apoleetos] unsold.

απών [apon] absent, missing.

απώτατος [apotatos] furthest, remotest, most distant.

απώτερος [apoteros] farther, further || ~ σκοπός ulterior motive.

άρα [ara] so, thus, therefore, consequently.

άρα [ara] I wonder if, can it be that?

αραβικός [araveekos] Arabian, Arabic.

αραβόσιτο, ο [aravoseeto] maize, corn.

άραγε [araye] is it?, can it be?, I wonder if.

άραγμα, το [aragma] anchoring, mooring.

αραδιάζω [aradeeazo] put in a row, line up || (ονόματα κτλ) enumerate.

αράζω [arazo] moor, anchor, drop anchor.

αραιός [areos] sparse, scattered || (επισκέψεις) infrequent, rare.

αραιώνω [areono] (σάλτσα κτλ) thin

down || (γραμμές κτλ) spread out || (επισκέψεις) lessen, cut down.

αρακάς, ο [arakas] (common) pea.

αράπης, ο [arapees] negro, dark person || (φόβητρο) bogey.

αραπίνα, η [arapeena] negress, dark woman.

αράχνη, η [arahnee] spider || cobweb.

'Αραβας, ο [aravas] Arab.

αργά [arga] slowly || late.

αργαλειός, ο [argalios] loom.

αργία, η [aryeea] holiday, closing day || idleness.

άργιλλος, η [aryeelos] clay.

αργοκίνητος [argokeeneetos] slow-moving, sluggish.

αργομισθία, η [argomeestheea] sinecure.

αργοπορία, η [argoporeea] slowness, delay.

αργός [argos] slow || idle, inactive.

αργόσχολος [argosholos] idle, unoccupied.

αργότερα [argotera] later, then.

άργυρος, ο [aryeeros] silver.

αργώ [argo] be late || (μαγαζί) be closed.

άρδευση, η [ardevsee] irrigation.

'Αρειος [areeos]: ~ Πάγος Supreme Court.

αρεστός [arestos] agreeable, pleasing, gratifying.

αρέσω [areso] please, delight, like || μου αρέσει I like it.

αρετή, η [aretee] virtue.

αρετσίνωτος [aretsenotos] unresinated.

αρθρίτιδα, η [arthreeteeδa] arthritis.

αρθρογράφος, ο [arthrografos] journalist.

άρθρο, το [arthro] article, clause, term.

άρθρωση, η [arthrosee] articulation, joint || good articulation.

αρίθμηση, n [areethmeesee] numbering, counting, pagination.

αριθμητική, n [areethmeeteekee] arithmetic.

αριθμός, ο [areethmos] number.

αριθμώ [areethmo] count, enumerate.

άριστα [areesta] very well || (βαθμολογία) excellent.

αριστερά [areestera] left hand || (επιρ) on the left, to the left.

αριστερός [areesteros] left, left-handed || left-wing.

αριστοκρατία, n [areestokrateea] aristocracy.

αριστούργημα, το [areestouryeema] masterpiece.

αρκετά [arketa] enough, sufficiently.

αρκετός [arketos] enough, sufficient, adequate.

αρκούδα, n [arkouda] bear.

αρκτικός [arkteekos] Arctic, northern.

αρκώ [arko] be enough, suffice || **αρκεί να** as long as.

αρλούμπα, n [arloumba] foolish talk, nonsense.

άρμα, το [arma] chariot || (στρατ) ~ **μάχης** tank.

αρματώνω [armatono] arm || equip.

αρμέγω [armego] milk || (μεταφ) fleece.

Αρμένης, ο [armenees] Armenian.

αρμενίζω [armeneezo] set sail, sail.

άρμη, n [armee] brine.

αρμόδιος [armodeeos] qualified, competent || propitious.

αρμοδιότης, n [armodeeotees] province, jurisdiction.

αρμόζω [armozo] fit || befit, be becoming, be proper.

αρμονία, n [armoneea] harmony, concord.

αρμός, ο [armos] joint.

αρμοστής, ο [armostees] high commissioner, governor.

αρμύρα, n [armeera] saltiness.

αρμυρός [armeeros] salty.

άρνηση, n [arneesee] refusal || denial || negation.

αρνί, το [arnee] lamb || (μεταφ) docile person.

αρνούμαι [arnoume] refuse, deny, decline || disown.

άροτρο, το [arotro] plough.

αρουραίος, ο [aroureos] field mouse, rat.

άρπα, n [arpa] harp.

αρπαγή, n [arpayee] rapine || rape || stealing.

αρπάζομαι [arpazome] take hold of || come to blows.

αρπάζω [arpazo] grab, snatch || steal, pinch || (ευκαιρία) seize || (λέξεις) catch, pick up.

αρπακτικός [arpakteekos] greedy || (ζώο) rapacious, predatory.

αρραβώνες, οι [aravones] engagement.

αρραβωνιάζω [aravoneeazo] betroth (old), engage.

αρραβωνιαστικιά, n [aravoneeasteekia] fiancée.

αρραβωνιαστικός, ο [aravoneeasteekos] fiancé.

αρρενωπός [arenopos] manly, masculine.

άρρην [areen] male.

αρρωσταίνω [arosteno] make sick || fall ill.

αρρώστια, n [arosteea] illness, sickness.

άρρωστος [arostos] ill, sick, unwell.

αρσενικός [arseneekos] male || (γραμμ) masculine.

άρση, n [arsee] removal, lifting || (μεταφ) raising, abrogation.

αρτηρία, n [arteereea] artery || (οδός) thoroughfare.

άρτιος [arteeos] whole, entire || (αριθμός) even.

αρτοποιείο, το [artopieeo] bakery, baker's shop.

αρτοπωλείο, το [artopoleeo] baker's shop.

άρτος, ο [artos] bread.

άρτυμα, το [arteema] seasoning, sauce.

αρχαιοκαπηλία, η [arheokapeeleea] illicit trade in antiquities.

αρχαιολόγος, ο [arheologos] archeologist.

αρχαιολογία, η [arheoloyeea] archeology.

αρχαίος [arheos] ancient || antiquated.

αρχαιότης, η [arheotees] antiquity || (στα γραφεία) seniority.

αρχάριος [arhareeos] beginner, novice, apprentice.

αρχείο, το [arheeo] archives, records.

αρχέτυπο, το [arheteepo] archetype, original.

αρχή, η [arhee] beginning, start || (φιλοσ) principle || (διοίκ) authority || κατ' αρχήν in principle.

αρχηγείο, το [arheeyeeo] headquarters.

αρχηγία, η [arheeyeea] command, leadership.

αρχηγός, ο [arheegos] commander, leader, chief || (οικογενείας) head.

αρχιεπίσκοπος, ο [arhiepeeskopos] archbishop.

αρχιερέας, ο [arhiereas] prelate, high priest.

αρχίζω [arheezo] begin, start, commence.

αρχικός [arheekos] initial, first, original.

αρχιστράτηγος, ο [arheestrateegos] commander-in-chief, generalissimo.

αρχιουντάκτης, ο [arheeseentaktees] editor-in-chief.

αρχιτέκτων, ο [arheetekton] architect.

άρχοντας, ο [arhontas] lord, master, elder.

αρχοντιά, η [arhontia] distinction, nobility || wealth.

αρχοντικός [arhonteekos] fine, of distinction, lordly.

αρωγή, η [aroyee] help, assistance, aid.

άρωμα, το [aroma] aroma, perfume, odour || αρωματικός scented.

ας [as] let, may || ~ είναι so be it, let it be.

ασανσέρ, το [asanser] lift, elevator.

ασαφής [asafees] obscure, vague.

ασβέστης, ο [asvestees] lime.

ασβεστώνω [asvestono] whitewash.

ασέβεια, η [aseveea] disrespect || impiety.

ασεβής [asevees] disrespectful || impious.

ασέλγεια, η [aselya] lewdness, debauchery.

άσεμνος [asemnos] indecent, obscene, immodest.

ασήκωτος [aseekotos] unraised || (βαρύς) impossible to lift.

ασήμαντος [aseemantos] insignificant, unimportant.

ασημένιος [aseemeneeos] silver(y).

ασήμι, το [aseemee] silver || ασημικά ηλ silverware.

άσημος [aseemos] obscure, insignificant, unimportant.

ασθένεια, η [astheneea] sickness, illness.

ασθενής [asthenees] ill, weak || (ο άρρωστος) patient.

ασθενικός [astheneekos] sickly.

ασθενώ [astheno] be ill, fall sick, get sick.

άσθμα, το [asthma] asthma.

ασιτία, η [aseeteea] undernourishment.

άσκηση, η [askeesee] exercise, practice || drill.

ασκητής, ο [askeetees] hermit.

άσκοπος [askopos] pointless, aimless, purposeless.

ασκός, ο [askos] (skin) bag || wineskin.

ασκούμαι [askoume] exercise, practise.

ασκώ [asko] exercise, practise.

ασπάζομαι [aspazome] kiss, embrace || (μεταφ) adopt, espouse.

ασπασμός, ο [aspasmos] embrace, kiss || greeting.

άσπαστος [aspastos] unbroken || unbreakable.

άσπιλος [aspeelos] immaculate, spotless.

ασπιρίνη, η [aspeereenee] aspirin.

ασπίδα, η [aspeeδa] shield.

άσπλαχνος [asplanghnos] hard-hearted, pitiless, unmerciful.

άσπονδος [asponδos] irreconcilable, relentless.

ασπούδαστος [aspouδastos] uneducated, ignorant.

ασπράδι, το [aspraδee] white spot || (ματιού, αυγού) white.

ασπρειδερός [aspreeδeros] whitish.

ασπρίζω [aspreezo] whiten, bleach || (γίνομαι άσπρος) turn white.

ασπρομάλλης [aspromalees] white-haired.

ασπροπρόσωπος [asproprosopos] uncorrupted || successful.

ασπρόρουχα, τα [asprorouha] πλ underclothes, linen.

άσπρος [aspros] white.

άσσος, ο [asos] ace.

αστάθεια, η [astatheea] instability, inconstancy, fickleness.

άσταθής [astathees] unsteady, fickle, unstable.

αστακός, ο [astakos] lobster.

άστατος [astatos] fickle, unstable.

άστεγος [astegos] homeless || roofless.

αστειεύομαι [astievome] joke, jest.

αστείο, το [asteeo] joke, pleasantry.

αστείος [asteeos] humorous, funny.

αστείρευτος [asteerevtos] inexhaustible, limitless.

αστέρι, το [asteree] star.

αστερισμός, ο [astereesmos] constellation.

αστεροσκοπείο, το [asteroskopeeo] observatory.

αστήρικτος [asteereektos] unsupported || (μεταφ) untenable.

αστιγματισμός, ο [asteegmateesmos] astigmatism.

αστικός [asteekos] urban || civic || ~ κώδικας civil code.

αστοιχείωτος [asteeheeotos] unlearned, ignorant.

αστόχαστος [astohastos] thoughtless, imprudent.

αστοχία, η [astoheea] failure || carelessness.

αστοχώ [astoho] miss the mark, fail || (λησμονώ) forget.

αστράγαλος, ο [astragalos] anklebone.

αστραπή, η [astrapee] lightning.

αστραπιαίος [astrapieos] lightning, quick.

αστράπτω [astrapto] lighten || flash, glitter.

αστρικός [astreekos] stellar, astral.

άστριφτος [astreeftos] not twisted.

άστρο, το [astro] star.

αστρολογία, η [astroloyeea] astrology.

αστρολόγος, ο [astrologos] astrologer.

αστροναύτης, ο [astronaftees] astronaut.

αστρονομία, η [astronomeea] astronomy.

αστρονόμος, ο [astronomos] astronomer.

αστροπελέκι, το [astropelekee] thunderbolt.

αστροφεγγιά, η [astrofengia] starlight.

άστρωτος [astrotos] (κρεββάτι) unmade || (τραπέζι) unlaid || (πάτωμα) bare || (δρόμος) unpaved.

άστυ, το [astee] city.

αστυνομία, η [asteenomeea] police.

αστυνομικός [asteenomeekos] policeman, of the police.

αστυνόμος, ο [asteenomos] police officer.

αστυφύλακας, ο [asteefeelakas] police constable.

ασυγκίνητος [aseengkeeneetos] unmoved, unfeeling.

ασυγκράτητος [aseengkrateetos] unsuppressible.

ασύγκριτος [aseengkreetos] incomparable.

ασυγύριστος [aseeyeereestos] untidy, disarranged.

ασυγχώρητος [aseenghoreetos] inexcusable, unforgivable.

ασυζήτητος [aseezeeteetos] unquestionable, incontrovertible.

ασυλία, η [aseeleea] asylum, immunity, inviolability.

ασύλληπτος [aseeleeptos] elusive, not caught || (μεταφ) inconceivable.

ασυλλόγιστος [aseeloyeestos] rash, thoughtless.

άσυλο, το [aseelo] shelter, refuge, asylum.

ασυμβίβαστος [aseemveevastos] irreconcilable, incompatible.

ασύμμετρος [aseemetros] disproportionate.

ασυμπλήρωτος [aseembleerotos] uncompleted, incomplete.

ασύμφορος [aseemforos] disadvantageous, not profitable.

ασυναγώνιστος [aseenagoneestos] unbeatable, unrivalled.

ασυναίσθητος [aseenestheetos] unconscious, inconsiderate.

ασυναρτησία, η [aseenarteeseea] incoherence || inconsistency.

ασυνάρτητος [aseenarteetos] incoherent || inconsistent.

ασυνείδητος [aseeneedeetos] unscrupulous, unconscionable.

ασυνέπεια, η [aseenepeea] inconsequence, inconsistency.

ασυνεπής [aseenepees] inconsistent.

ασυνήθιστος [aseeneetheestos] unusual, uncommon.

ασυρματιστής, ο [aseermateestees] wireless operator.

ασύρματος, ο [aseermatos] wireless || **σταθμός ασυρμάτου** wireless station.

ασύστολος [aseestolos] impudent, brazen.

άσφαιρος [asferos] blank.

ασφάλεια, η [asfaleea] security, safety || (ζωής κτλ) insurance || (αστυνομία) police || (ηλεκτ) fuse || (όπλου) safety catch.

ασφαλής [asfalees] safe, secure, sure.

ασφαλίζω [asfaleezo] secure, assure || (ζωή κτλ) insure.

ασφαλιστήριο, το [asfaleesteereeo] insurance policy.

ασφάλιστρο, το [asfaleestro] insurance premium.

άσφαλτος, η [asfaltos] asphalt || (δρόμος) tarred road.

ασφαλώς [asfalos] surely, certainly || safely.

ασφυκτικός [asfeekteekos] suffocating.

ασφυξία, η [asfeekseea] suffocation, asphyxia.

άσχετος [ashetos] irrelevant, unrelated, unconnected.

ασχήμια, η [asheemeea] ugliness, deformity.

άσχημος [asheemos] ugly || unsightly || bad.

ασχολία, η [asholeea] occupation, business, job.

ασχολούμαι [asholoume] be occupied with, keep busy.

άσωτος [asotos] dissolute || prodigal, wasteful.

αταίριαστος [atereeastos] incompatible || dissimilar.

άτακτος [ataktos] irregular || disorderly || (παιδί) naughty, unruly.

αταξία, η [atakseea] confusion, disorder || unruliness.

ατάραχος [atarahos] calm, composed, quiet.

αταραξία, η [atarakseea] composure, calmness, serenity.

άταφος [atafos] unburied.

άτεκνος [ateknos] childless.

ατέλεια, η [ateleea] defect || (δασμού) exemption || (χαρακτήρος) imperfection.

ατελείωτος [ateleeotos] endless || unfinished, incomplete.

ατελής [atelees] incomplete || defective || (φόρου) tax-free.

ατελώνιστος [ateloneestos] duty-free || not cleared through customs.

ατενίζω [ateneezo] gaze, stare at, look fixedly at.

ατζαμής [adzamees] unskilled || awkward, clumsy.

ατίθασος [ateethasos] stubborn || (άλογο) difficult to tame.

ατιμάζω [ateemazo] dishonour, disgrace || (βιόζω) rape, ravish.

ατιμία, η [ateemeea] dishonour, disgrace, infamy.

άτιμος [ateemos] dishonest, infamous, disreputable || (συμπεριφορά) disgraceful.

ατιμώρητος [ateemoreetos] unpunished.

ατμάκατος, η [atmakatos] small steamboat.

ατμάμαξα, η [atmamaksa] locomotive.

ατμοκίνητος [atmokeeneetos] steam-driven.

ατμομηχανή, η [atmomeehanee] steam engine, locomotive.

ατμοπλοΐα, η [atmoploeea] steam navigation.

ατμόπλοιο, το [atmopleeo] steamship.

ατμός, ο [atmos] steam, vapour || (κρασιού) fume.

ατμόσφαιρα, η [atmosfera] atmosphere.

άτοκος [atokos] without interest.

άτολμος [atolmos] timid, faint-hearted.

ατομικιστής [atomeekeestees] egoist.

ατομικός [atomeekos] personal || (ενέργεια κτλ) atomic.

ατομικότητα, η [atomeekoteeta] individuality.

άτομο, το [atomo] (θυσική) atom || (άνθρωπος) individual, person.

ατονία, η [atoneea] langour, weakness, dejection.

άτονος [atonos] languid, dull || (γραμμ) unaccented.

ατού ο [atou] trump.

ατόφυος [atofeeos] solid, massive.

άτριφτος [atreeftos] not rubbed, not grated.

ατρόμητος [atromeetos] bold, dauntless, daring.

ατροφία, η [atrofeea] atrophy.

ατροφικός [atrofeekos] atrophied, emaciated.

ατρύγητος [atreeyeetos] ungathered, unharvested.

άτρωτος [atrotos] unwounded, unhurt || invulnerable.

ατσαλένιος [atsaleneeos] of steel, steely.

ατσάλι, το [atsalee] steel.

άτσαλος [atsalos] untidy, disorderly, unkempt || (ζωή) riotous, lawless.

ατσίδα, n [atseeda] alert person, wide-awake person.

ατύχημα, το [ateeheema] mishap, accident, misfortune, injury.

ατυχής [ateehees], **άτυχος** [ateehos] unfortunate, unlucky, wretched.

ατυχία, n [ateeheea] misfortune, bad luck.

ατυχώ [ateeho] fail, have bad luck, meet with misfortune.

αυγερινός, ο [avgereenos] morning star.

αυγή, n [avyee] dawn, daybreak.

αυγό, το [avgo] egg.

αυγολέμονο, το [avgolemono] lemon and egg sauce or soup.

αυγοτάραχο, το [avgotaraho] botargo.

αυγουλιέρα, n [avgouliera] eggcup.

Αύγουστος, ο [avgoustos] August.

αυθάδεια, n [avthadeea] audacity, insolence.

αυθάδης [avthadees] impertinent, saucy.

αυθαιρεσία, n [avthereseea] high-handed act.

αυθαίρετος [avtheretos] arbitrary, high-handed.

αυθεντία, n [avthenteea] authority, authenticity.

αυθεντικός [avthenteekos] authentic, authoritative.

αυθημερόν [avtheemeron] on the very same day.

αυθόρμητος [avthormeetos] spontaneous.

αυθυποβολή, n [avtheepovolee] auto-suggestion.

αυλαία, n [avlea] curtain.

αυλάκι, το [avlakee] channel, ditch, trench || (ξύλου κτλ) groove.

αυλακωτός [avlakotos] grooved, furrowed, scored.

αυλή, n [avlee] yard, courtyard || (βασιλέως) court.

αυλόγυρος, ο [avloyeeros] enclosure, surrounding wall.

αυλός, ο [avlos] pipe, flute, reed.

άυλος [aeelos] immaterial, incorporeal.

αυξάνω [avksano] increase, augment || (ταχύτητα) accelerate.

αύξηση, n [avkseesee] increase || (γραμμ) augment.

αυξομείωση, n [avksomeeosee] fluctuation, variation.

αύξων [avkson] increasing || ~ αριθμός serial number.

αϋπνία, n [aeepneea] sleeplessness, insomnia.

άυπνος [aeepnos] sleepless, wakeful.

αύρα, n [avra] breeze.

αυριανός [avreeanos] of tomorrow.

αύριο [avreeo] tomorrow.

αυστηρός [avsteeros] severe, rigorous, austere.

αυστηρότητα, n [avsteeroteeta] severity, strictness, austerity.

Αυστραλία, n [avstraleea] Australia.

αυστραλιακός [avstraleeakos] Australian.

Αυστραλός, ο [avstralos] Australian.

Αυστρία, n [avstreea] Austria.

Αυστριακός, ο [avstreeakos] Austrian.

αυταπάρνηση, n [avtaparneesee] self-abnegation.

αυταπάτη, n [avtapatee] self-delusion, self-deception.

αυτάρεσκεια, n [avtareskeea] complacency.

αυτάρκεια, n [avtarkeea] contentment.

αυτάρκης [avtarkees] self-sufficient, satisfied.

αυταρχικός [avtarheekos] authoritative, dictatorial.

αυτί, το [avtee] ear.

αυτοβιογραφία, η
[avtoveeografeea] autobiography.

αυτόγραφο, το [avtografo]
autograph.

αυτοδημιούργητος
[avtoðeemeeouryeetos] self-made.

αυτοδιάθεση, η [avtoðeeathesee]
self-determination.

αυτοδικαίως [avtoðeekeos] of
right, de jure.

αυτοδιοίκηση, η [avtoðieekeesee]
self-government.

αυτοθυσία, η [avtotheeseea] self-
sacrifice.

αυτοκέφαλος [avtokefalos]
independent || (εκκλ) autocephalous.

αυτοκινητιστής, ο
[avtokeeneeteestees] motorist.

αυτοκίνητο, το [avtokeeneeto]
car, automobile (US).

αυτοκινητόδρομος, ο
[avtokeeneetoðromos] motorway,
highway.

αυτοκρατορία, η [avtokratoreea]
empire.

αυτοκράτωρας, ο [avtokratoras]
emperor.

αυτοκτονία, η [avtoktoneea]
suicide.

αυτοκτονώ [avtoktono] commit
suicide.

αυτόματος [avtomatos] automatic.

αυτονόητος [avtonoeetos] self-
explanatory, obvious.

αυτοπεποίθηση, η
[avtopepeetheesee] self-confidence,
self-reliance.

αυτοπροσώπως [avtoprosopos]
personally.

αυτόπτης, ο [avtoptees]
eyewitness.

αυτός [avtos] he || ο ~ the same.

αυτοσυντήρηση
[avtoseenteereesee] self-
preservation.

αυτοσυντήρητος
[avtoseenteereetos] self-supporting.

αυτοσχεδιάζω [avtosheðeeazo]
improvise, extemporize.

αυτοσχέδιος [avtosheðeeos]
improvised, impromptu, makeshift.

αυτοτελής [avtotelees] self-
sufficient || independent.

αυτού [avtou] there.

αυτουργός, ο [avtourgos]
perpetrator.

αυτοφυής [avtofiees] indigenous,
natural.

αυτόφωρος [avtoforos] in the very
act, red-handed.

αυτόχειρας, ο [avtoheeras]
suicide.

αυτόχθων, ο [avtothhon]
indigenous, aboriginal, native.

αυτοψία, η [avtopseea] (ιατρ)
autopsy || (νομ) local inspection.

αυχένας, ο [avhenas] nape of the
neck || cervix || (μεταφ) neck.

αφάγωτος [afagotos] uneaten || not
having eaten || untouched.

αφαίμαξη, η [afemaksee]
bloodletting.

αφαίρεση, η [aferesee] deduction,
subtraction || (φιλοσ) abstraction.

αφαιρούμαι [aferoume] be absent-
minded.

αφαιρώ [afero] deduct, subtract ||
(κλέβω) steal, rob.

αφαλός, ο [afalos] navel.

αφάνεια, η [afaneea] obscurity,
oblivion.

αφανής [afanees] obscure,
unknown || invisible.

αφανίζω [afaneezo] ruin, destroy.

αφάνταστος [afantastos]
unimaginable.

άφαντος [afantos] invisible, unseen.

αφασία, η [afaseea] muteness,
aphasia.

αφειδής [afeeðees] lavish,
extravagant.

αφελής [afelees] simple, ingenuous,
guileless.

αφέντης, ο [afentees] master, boss || owner.

αφεντικό, το [afenteeko] governor, boss, employer.

αφερέγγυος [aferengeeos] insolvent.

άφεση, η [afesee] remission || discharge.

αφετηρία, η [afeteereea] starting point || beginning.

αφή, η [afee] sense of touch || (αίσθηση) feeling.

αφήγηση, η [afeeyeesee] narration, account.

αφηγούμαι [afeegoume] narrate, relate, tell.

αφηνιάζω [afeeneeazo] bolt || (για ανθρώπους) run amok.

αφήνω [afeeno] let, permit || (μόνος) let alone || (ελευθερώνω) let go of || (εγκαταλείπω) abandon.

αφηρημάδα, η [afeereemaδa] absentmindedness.

αφηρημένος [afeereemenos] absentminded || (φίλος) abstract.

αφθαρσία, η [aftharseea] indestructibility, incorruptibility.

άφθαρτος [afthartos] incorruptible, indestructible.

άφθαστος [afthastos] unsurpassed, incomparable, unexcelled.

αφθονία, η [afthoneea] abundance, profusion.

άφθονος [afthonos] abundant, plentiful, profuse.

αφθονώ [afthono] abound with, teem with, be plentiful in.

αφιέρωμα, το [afieroma] offering, dedication.

αφιερώνω [afierono] dedicate, devote || (βιβλίο κτλ) inscribe.

αφιέρωση, η [afierosee] dedication, devotion.

αφιλοκερδής [afeelokerδees] disinterested, selfless.

αφιλότιμος [afeeloteemos] wanting in self-respect, mean.

αφίνω [afeeno] βλ **αφήνω**.

άφιξη, η [afeeksee] arrival, coming.

αφιόνι, το [afionee] poppy || opium.

άφλεκτος [aflektos] nonflammable.

άφοβος [afovos] intrepid, fearless, bold.

αφομοιώνω [afomeeono] assimilate.

αφομοίωση, η [afomeeosee] assimilation.

αφοπλίζω [afopleezo] disarm || (φρούριο κτλ) dismantle.

αφοπλισμός, ο [afopleesmos] disarmament.

αφόρετος [aforetos] unworn, new.

αφόρητος [aforeetos] intolerable, insufferable.

αφορίζω [aforeezo] excommunicate.

αφορισμός, ο [aforeesmos] excommunication.

αφορμή, η [aformee] motive, pretext, cause.

αφορολόγητος [aforoloyeetos] untaxed, free from taxation.

αφορώ [aforo] concern || regard || **όσον αφορά** as regards.

αφοσιώνομαι [afoseeonome] devote o.s., be attached to.

αφοσίωση, η [afoseeosee] devotion, attachment, affection.

αφότου [afotou] since, as long as.

αφού [afou] since, after.

άφρακτος [afraktos] unfenced, unwalled.

αφράτος [afratos] light and crisp || frothy, foamy || (δέρμα) soft.

αφρίζω [afreezo] foam || (μεταφ) be furious.

αφρικανικός [afreekaneekos] African.

Αφρικανός, ο [afreekanos] African.

Αφρική, η [afreekee] Africa.

αφροδισιολόγος, ο [afroδeeseeologos] venereal disease specialist.

αφροδίσιος [afrodeeseeos] venereal.

αφρόντιστος [afronteestos] neglected, uncared for.

αφρός, ο [afros] foam || (κοινωνίας) cream || (σαπουνιού) lather.

αφρώδης [afrodees] frothy, foamy.

άφρων [afron] foolish, thoughtless, rash.

αφυδάτωση, η [afeedatosee] dehydration.

αφύπνιση, η [afeepneesee] awakening || (μεταφ) dawning.

αφύσικος [afeeseekos] unnatural || (προσποιητός) affected.

άφωνος [afonos] mute, speechless, silent.

αφώτιστος [afoteestos] dark || (άνθρωπος) unenlightened.

αχ [ah] (επιφ) ah!, oh!, alas!

αχαΐρευτος [ahaeerevtos] scoundrel.

αχανής [ahanees] immense, enormous, vast.

αχαρακτήριστος [aharakteereestos] unprincipled, indescribable.

αχαριστία, η [ahareesteea] ingratitude.

αχάριστος [ahareestos] ungrateful.

άχαρος [aharos] ungraceful, awkward, unsightly || unpleasant.

αχηβάδα, η [aheevada] cockle, sea shell, shellfish.

αχθοφόρος, ο [ahthoforos] porter.

αχινός, ο [aheenos] sea urchin.

αχλάδι, το [ahladee] pear.

άχνα, η [ahna] βλ **αχνός**.

αχνάρι, το [ahnaree] footprint || (μεταφ) pattern.

άχνη, η [ahnee] mist, evaporation || (χημ) corrosive sublimate.

αχνίζω [ahneezo] evaporate || steam.

αχνός, ο [ahnos] vapour, steam || (χρώμα) pale, colourless.

αχόρταγος [ahortagos] insatiable, greedy || (ζώο) voracious.

αχούρι, το [ahouree] stable, stall || (μεταφ) untidy place, pigsty.

αχρείαστος [ahreeastos] unnecessary, needless.

αχρείος [ahreeos] wicked, vile.

αχρησιμοποίητος [ahreeseemopieetos] unused.

αχρηστεύω [ahreestevo] make useless.

αχρηστία, η [ahreesteea] obsoleteness, uselessness.

άχρηστος [ahreestos] useless, worthless.

αχρονολόγητος [ahronoloyeetos] undated.

αχρωμάτιστος [ahromateestos] unpainted, uncoloured, plain.

άχρωμος [ahromos] colourless, uncoloured.

άχτι, το [ahtee] yearning, longing.

αχτίδα, η [ahteeda] ray, beam.

αχτένιστος [ahteneestos] uncombed, unkempt || (λόγος κτλ) unpolished.

άχυρο, το [aheero] straw, hay.

αχυρώνας, ο [aheeronas] barn, hayloft.

αχώνευτος [ahonevtos] undigested || indigestible.

αχώριστος [ahoreestos] inseparable.

άψητος [apseetos] not cooked, underdone.

αψηφώ [apseefo] disregard, disdain, scorn.

αψιμαχία, η [apseemaheea] skirmish.

αψίδα, η [apseeda] arch, vault || apse.

άψογος [apsogos] faultless, irreproachable.

αψυχολόγητος [apseeholoyeetos] ill-considered, impolitic.

άψυχος [apseehos] lifeless || (δειλός) cowardly, timid.

άωτον, το [aoton]: άκρον ~ acme, height of.

B, β

βαγόνι, το [vagonee] carriage || (εμπορικό) wagon, truck || (βαγκόν-λι) sleeping car.

βάδην [vaðeen] at a walking pace.

βαδίζω [vaðeezo] walk || (στρατ) march || (πηγαίνω) go.

βάδισμα, το [vaðeesma] step, walk, gait.

βαζελίνη, η [vazeleenee] vaseline.

βάζο, το [vazo] vase.

βάζω [vazo] put, set, place || (φορώ) put on || (φόρους κτλ) impose, lay || ~ εμπρός start, begin || ~ χέρι lay hands on || ~ τα δυνατά μου do my best.

βαθαίνω [vatheno] deepen || βλ και βαθύνω.

βαθειά [vatheea] deep(ly), profoundly.

βαθμηδόν [vathmeeðon] by degrees, gradually.

βαθμιαίος [vathmieos] gradual, progressive.

βαθμίδα, η [vathmeeða] step, stair || (μεταφ) rank.

βαθμολογία, η [vathmologeea] (οργάνου) graduation || (μαθήματος) grades, marks.

βαθμός, ο [vathmos] degree || (στρατ) grade, rank || (μαθήματος) mark.

βάθος, το [vathos] depth, bottom || (φόντο) back, background.

βαθούλωμα, το [vathouloma] hollow, depression.

βαθουλώνω [vathoulono] hollow out || become hollow.

βάθρο, το [vathro] (βάση) basis, foundation || (αγάλματος κτλ) pedestal || (γεφύρας) pillar.

βαθύνω [vatheeno] deepen, hollow out, become deeper.

βαθύπλουτος [vatheeploutos] opulent.

βαθύς [vathees] deep || (σκότος κτλ) heavy, deep || (ύπνος) sound || (αίσθημα) profound || (πνεύμα) penetrating, sagacious.

βαθύτητα, η [vatheeteeta] depth, profundity, deepness.

βαθύφωνος [vatheefonos] bass, deep-voiced.

βάιο, το [vaeeo] palm branch.

βακαλάος, ο [vakalaos] cod.

βάκιλλος, ο [vakeelos] bacillus.

βακτηρίδιο, το [vakteereeðeeo] bacillus.

βαλανίδι, το [valaneeðee] acorn || βαλανιδιά oak tree.

βάλανος [valanos] acorn.

βαλβίδα, η [valveeða] valve.

βαλές, ο [vales] knave (in cards).

βαλίτσα, η [valeetsa] suitcase, (hand)bag.

Βαλκάνια, τα [valkaneea] πλ the Balkans.

βάλς [vals] waltz.

βάλσαμο, το [valsamo] balsam, balm || (μεταφ) consolation.

βαλσαμώνω [valsamono] embalm || (μεταφ) console, comfort.

βάλσιμο, το [valseemo] placing, setting, laying.

βάλτος, ο [valtos] marsh, fen, bog.

βαλτός [valtos] instigated, planted.

βαμβακερός [vamvakeros] of cotton.

βαμβάκι, το [vamvakee] cotton.

βάμμα, το [vamma] tincture, dye.

βαμμένος [vamenos] dyed, painted.

βάναυσος [vanavsos] rough, coarse, rude.

βάνδαλος, ο [vandalos] vandal.

βανί(λ)ια, η [vaneeleea] vanilla.

βαπόρι, το [vaporee] steamship.

βαπτίζω [vapteezo] baptize, christen || dip, plunge.

βάπτιση, η [vapteesee] βλ **βάπτισμα**.

βάπτισμα, το [vapteesma] baptism, christening.

βαπτιστικός [vapteesteekos] baptismal || (ουσ) godchild.

βάπτω [vapto] (χάλυψ) temper || (μπογιά) paint || (παπούτσια) polish.

βάραθρο, το [varathro] abyss, gulf, chasm.

βαραίνω [vareno] weigh down, make heavier || (κουράζω) weary || (αισθάνομαι βάρος) feel heavy || (μεταφ) carry weight.

βαράω [varao] βλ **βαρώ**.

βαρβαρικός [varvareekos] barbaric.

βάρβαρος [varvaros] barbarous, brutal, savage.

βάρδια, η [vardeea] watch, duty, shift.

βαρέλι, το [varelee] barrel, cask.

βαρετός [varetos] annoying, boring, tedious.

βαρήκοος [vareekoos] hard of hearing.

βαριά, η [varia] (σφυρί) hammer || (επιρ) seriously.

βαρίδι, το [vareedee] (counter)weight.

βαριέμαι [varieme] be bored, be tired (of) || (δε θέλω) not want (to) || **δε βαριέσαι** never mind!, don't bother!

βάρκα, η [varka] small boat, rowing boat, dinghy.

βαρκάρης, ο [varkarees] boatman.

βαρόμετρο, το [varometro] barometer.

βάρος, το [varos] weight, load, burden || **σε ~ του** at his expense.

βαρύθυμος [vareetheemos] sad, depressed.

βαρύνω [vareeno] weigh down, lie heavy || βλ και **βαραίνω**.

βαρύς [varees] heavy || (ποινή) severe, harsh || (σφάλμα) serious ||

(ύπνος) deep, heavy || (ζυγός) oppressive || (ευθύνη) grave || (άνθρωπος) slow, dull-witted.

βαρυσήμαντος [vareeseemantos] significant, grave, momentous.

βαρύτιμος [vareeteemos] precious, costly, valuable.

βαρύτονος [vareetonos] baritone || (γραμμ) with a grave accent.

βαρύφωνος [vareefonos] deep-voiced, bass.

βαρώ [varo] beat, hit, shoot || (σάλπιγγα) sound || (καμπάνα) toll.

βασανίζω [vasaneezo] torture, torment || (ένα θέμα κτλ) examine thoroughly, go into || (το μυαλό) rack.

βασανιστήριο, το [vasaneesteereeo] rack, torture chamber.

βάσανο, το [vasano] pain, trial, ordeal || (μεταφ) nuisance.

βασίζω [vaseezo] base.

βασικός [vaseekos] primary, basic, fundamental.

βασιλεία, η [vaseeleea] kingdom || reign.

βασίλειο, το [vaseeleeo] kingdom.

βασιλέας, ο [vaseeleas] king.

βασιλεύω [vaseelevo] reign, rule.

βασιλιάς, ο [vaseelias] βλ **βασιλέας**.

βασιλική, η [vaseeleekee] basilica.

βασιλικός [vaseeleekos] royal, royalist || (ουσ) basil.

βασίλισσα, η [vaseeleesa] queen.

βασιλομήτωρ, η [vaseelomeetor] queen mother.

βασιλόπιττα, η [vaseelopeeta] New Year's cake.

βασιλόφρων [vaseelofron] royalist.

βάσιμος [vaseemos] sound, trustworthy.

βάση, η [vasee] base, foundation || (βαθμών) pass mark.

βασκανία, η [vaskaneea] evil eye.

βαστώ [vasto] (φέρω) bear, hold,

support || (συγκρατώ) hold, control || (ύφασμα κτλ) keep, wear || (κρατώ) carry, hold.

βατ(τ), το [vat] watt.

βατόμουρο, το [vatomouro] blackberry.

βατός [vatos] (δρόμος) passable || (ποτάμι) fordable || (ύφωμα) accessible.

βάτραχος, ο [vatrahos] frog, toad.

βαυκαλίζω βαφή, n [vafee] dyeing || shoe polish || dye.

βάφομαι [vafome] make-up.

βαφτίσια, τα [vafteeseea] πλ christening.

βαφτισιμός, ο [vafteeseemios] godson.

βάφω [vafo] βλ **βάπτω**.

βάψιμο, το [vapseemo] painting, make-up.

βγάζω [vgazo] take off, raise, draw out || (εξαλείφω) get out, wash out || (λάδι, χυμό κτλ) press, squeeze || (νόδι, χέρι) dislocate || (καπνό κτλ) give off || (παράγω) produce || (χρήματα) make, earn || (βουλευτή κτλ) elect || (διακρίνω) make out, read || (δίδω όνομα) name, call || (αποδεικνύω) prove || (αφαιρώ) take from || (εφημερίδα κτλ) publish || (περίπατο) take for a walk.

βγαίνω [vgeno] go out, come out, get out || (ανατέλλω) rise || (κυκλοφορώ) be out || (εκλέγομαι) be elected || (εξαλείφομαι) fade, come out.

βγαλμένος [vgalmenos] taken off, removed.

βγάλσιμο, το [vgalseemo] extraction, removal || (κοκκάλου) dislocation.

βδέλλα, n [vðella] leech.

βέβαιος, o [veveos] certain, sure, convinced.

βεβαιώνω [veveono] confirm, affirm, assure || certify.

βεβαίως [veveos] certainly, surely.

βεβαίωση, n [veveosee] confirmation || (χαρτί) certificate.

βεβαρημένος [vevareemenos] marked || (συνείδηση) heavy.

βέβηλος [veveelos] profane, sacrilegious, impious.

βεβιασμένος [veveeasmenos] forced.

βελάζω [velazo] bleat.

βελανίδι, το [velaneeðee] acorn.

βελγικός [velyeekos] Belgian.

Βέλγιο, το [velyo] Belgium.

βέλο, το [velo] veil.

βελόνα, n [velona] needle.

βελονιά, n [velonia] stitch.

βέλος, το [velos] arrow, dart.

βελούδο, το [velouðo] velvet.

βελτιώνω [velteeono] improve, better.

βελτίωση, n [velteeosee] improvement.

βενζινάκατος, n [venzeenakatos] small motorboat.

βενζίνη, n [venzeenee] petrol.

βεντάλια, n [ventaleea] fan.

βεντέττα, n [venteta] vendetta || (ηθοποιός) star.

βέρα, n [vera] wedding ring.

βεράντα, n [veranta] veranda, porch.

βέργα, n [verga] stick, rod, switch, twig.

βερεσέ [verese] on credit, on trust.

βερίκοκκο, το [vereekoko] apricot.

βερνίκι, το [verneekee] varnish, polish || (μεταφ) veneer.

βέρος, o [veros] genuine, true, real.

βέτο, το [veto] veto.

βήμα, n [veema] step, pace || (βίδος) pitch, thread || (έλικος) twist || (έδρα) rostrum.

βηματίζω [veemateezo] step, pace, walk.

βήτα, το [veeta] the letter B.

βήχας, o [veehas] cough.

βήχω [veeho] cough.

βία, n [veea] force, violence || hurry || (μετά βίας) with difficulty.

βιάζομαι [veeazome] be in a hurry, be rushed.

βιάζω [veeazo] force, compel || (παραβιάζω) break open || (παραβαίνω) violate || (ασελγώ) rape, ravish.

βίαιος [vieos] violent, forcible || fiery, passionate.

βιαιότητες, οι [vieoteetes] πλ acts of violence.

βιαίως [vieos] violently, forcibly.

βιασμός, ο [veeasmos] rape, violation.

βιαστής, ο [veeastees] ravisher, rapist.

βιαστικός [veeasteekos] urgent, pressing, hurried.

βιασύνη, n [veeaseenee] haste, urgency.

βιβλιάριο, το [veevleeareeo] booklet, card, bank book.

βιβλικός [veevleekos] biblical.

βιβλιογραφία, n [veevleeografeea] bibliography.

βιβλιοθηκάριος, ο [veevleeotheekareeos] librarian.

βιβλιοθήκη, n [veevleeotheékee] bookcase || library.

βιβλίο, το [veevleeo] book.

βιβλιοπώλης, ο [veevleeopolees] bookseller.

βίβλος, n [veevlos] Bible.

βίδα, n [veeδa] screw || (μεταφ) whim, caprice.

βιδώνω [veeδono] screw.

βίζα, n [veeza] visa.

βίζιτα, n [veezeeta] visit, call || visitor.

βίλλα, n [veela] villa.

βιογραφία, n [veeografeea] biography.

βιολέττα, n [veeoleta] violet.

βιολί, το [veeolee] violin, fiddle || αλλάζω ~ change one's tune.

βιολόγος, ο [veeologos] biologist.

βιομηχανία, n [veeomeehaneea] industry || manufacture.

βιομηχανικός [veeomeehaneekos] industrial.

βιοπαλαιστής, ο [veeopalestees] breadwinner.

βιοπάλη, n [veeopalee] working hard to make a living.

βίος, ο [veeos] life.

βιός, το [veeos] wealth, property.

βιοτεχνία, n [veeotehneea] handicraft.

βιοχημεία, n [veeoheemeea] biochemistry.

βιταμίνη, n [veetameenee] vitamin.

βιτρίνα, n [veetreena] shop window, showcase.

βίτσιο, το [veetseeo] bad habit.

βιώσιμος [veeoseemos] viable, feasible.

βλαβερός [vlavero] harmful || (έντομο) noxious.

βλάβη, n [vlavee] harm, damage || (μηχανής) motor trouble, breakdown.

βλάκας, ο [vlakas] blockhead, fool, idiot.

βλακεία, n [vlakeea] nonsense, silliness.

βλακώδης [vlakoδees] stupid, silly.

βλάπτω [vlapto] harm, injure, damage.

βλαστάρι, το [vlastaree] sprout, bud || (οικογενείας) scion.

βλάστηση, n [vlasteesee] sprouting || (φυτεία) vegetation.

βλαστός, ο [vlastos] shoot, sprout || (μεταφ) scion, offspring.

βλασφημία, n [vlasfeemeea] blasphemy, curse.

βλασφημώ [vlasfeemo] curse, revile.

βλάχος, ο [vlahos] (μεταφ) bumpkin, boor.

βλέμμα, το [vlemma] look, glance, eye.

βλεννόρροια, η [vlenoreea] gonorrhoea.

βλέπω [vlepo] see, look at.

βλεφαρίδα, η [vlefareeda] eyelash.

βλέφαρο, το [vlefaro] eyelid.

βλήμα, το [vleema] projectile.

βλογιά, η [vloya] smallpox.

βλοσυρός [vloseeros] fierce, stern, grim.

βόας, ο [voas] boa.

βογγητό, το [vongeeto] groan, moan.

βογγώ [vongo] moan, groan || roar.

βόδι, το [vodee] ox.

βοδινό, το [vodeeno] beef.

βοή, η [voee] shout, cry, humming, roaring || (όχλου) clamour.

βοήθεια, η [voeetheea] help, aid, assistance.

βοήθημα, το [voeetheema] help, assistance, relief.

βοηθητικός [voeetheeteekos] auxiliary || (άνεμος) favourable, fair.

βοηθός, ο [voeethos] assistant, helper, collaborator.

βοηθώ [voeetho] help, aid, give a hand, relieve.

βόθρος, ο [vothros] cesspool, ditch.

βολάν [volan] steering wheel, driving wheel.

βολβός, ο [volvos] bulb, kind of onion || (ματιού) eyeball.

βολεύομαι [volevome] get comfortable || get fixed up.

βολεύω [volevo] accommodate, fit in, suit || **τα ~** get along, do well.

βολή, η [volee] throw, blow, stroke, shot || (απόσταση) range.

βόλι, το [volee] ball, bullet.

βολιδοσκοπώ [voleedoskopo] sound.

βολικός [voleekos] convenient, handy, easy.

βολίδα, η [voleeda] sounding lead ||

(αστρο) meteor || (σφαίρα) bullet, ball.

βόλτα, η [volta] walk || (στροφή) revolution || (κοχλίου) thread || **κόβω βόλτες** I stroll about.

βόμβα, η [vomva] bomb.

βομβαρδίζω [vomvardeezo] bomb, bombard || (μεταφ) assail.

βομβαρδισμός, ο [vomvardeesmos] bombing.

βομβαρδιστικό, το [vomvardeesteeko] (αερο) bomber.

βόμβος, ο [vomvos] hum, buzz, buzzing.

βορειοανατολικός [voreeoanatoleekos] north-east(ern).

βορειοδυτικός [voreeodeeteekos] northwest(ern).

βόρειος [voreeos] north(ern).

βορείως [voreeos] northwards, to the north, north.

βοριάς, ο [vorias] north wind.

βορράς, ο [vorras] north.

βοσκή, η [voskee] pasture.

βοσκός, ο [voskos] shepherd.

βοσκοτόπι, το [voskotopee] pasture land.

βόσκω [vosko] graze || (μεταφ) drift.

βοτάνι, το [votanee] plant, herb.

βοτανικός [votaneekos] botanic(al).

βότανο, το [votano] herb, plant.

βοτανολόγος, ο [votanologos] botanist.

βότρυς, ο [votrees] bunch of grapes.

βότσαλο, το [votsalo] pebble.

βουβάλι, το [vouvalee] buffalo.

βουβός [vouvos] dumb, mute.

βουδδιστής, ο [voudeestees] Buddhist.

βουή [vouee] βλ **βοή.**

βουίζω [voueezo] buzz, hum.

Βουλγαρία, η [voulgareea] Bulgaria.

Βουλγαρικός [voulgareekos] Bulgarian.

Βουλγαρός, ο [voulgaros] Bulgarian.

βούλευμα, το [voulevma] decision, ordinance, decree.

βουλευτής, ο [voulevtees] member of parliament, deputy.

βουλή, η [voulee] parliament, chamber || (θέληση) will, volition.

βούληση, η [vouleesee] desire, will || κατά ~ at will.

βούλιαγμα, το [vouleeagma] sinking, submergence || collapse.

βουλιάζω [vouleeazo] sink || (μεταφ) ruin, be ruined.

βουλιμία, η [vouleemeea] insatiable appetite.

βουλλοκέρι, το [voulokeree] sealing wax.

βούλλωμα, το [vouloma] sealing, stamping || (το αντικείμενο) cork, stopper.

βουλλώνω [voulono] seal || (πωματίζω) stop, choke up, fill.

βουνήσιος [vouneeseeos] mountainous || (ουσ) highlander.

βουνό, το [vouno] mountain.

βούρδουλας, ο [vourdoulas] whip, lash.

βούρκος, ο [vourkos] mud, mire || (μεταφ) mire, gutter.

βουρκώνω [vourkono] fill with tears.

βούρλο, το [vourlo] (bul)rush.

βούρτσα, η [vourtsa] (hair)brush || (ρούχων) clothes brush || (δοντιών) toothbrush.

βουρτσίζω [vourtseezo] brush, brush down.

βουστάσιο, το [voustaseeo] ox stall, cowshed.

βούτηγμα, το [vouteegma] plunging, dipping || (μεταφ) plundering, stealing.

βούτημα, το [vouteema] hard biscuit.

βουτηχτής, ο [vouteehtees] diver || (μεταφ) thief.

βουτιά, η [voutia] dive || (μεταφ) snatching, stealing.

βούτυρο, το [vouteero] butter.

βουτώ [vouto] plunge, dip || (κλέβω) steal, snatch.

βραβείο, το [vraveeo] prize.

βραβεύω [vravevo] award, reward.

βράγχια, τα [vrangheea] πλ gills || (ιατρ) branchiae.

βραδιά, η [vradia] evening.

βραδιάζω [vradeeazo]: **βραδιάζει** it's getting dark.

βραδινός [vradeenos] evening.

βράδυ, το [vradee] evening.

βραδύνω [vradeeno] be late, be slow.

βραδύς [vradees] slow, sluggish, tardy.

βραδύτης, η [vradeetees] slowness, tardiness.

βράζω [vrazo] boil, ferment, seethe.

βρακί, το [vrakee] trousers || underpants.

βράσιμο, το [vraseemo] boiling, fermentation.

βράση, η [vrasee] boiling || (μούστου κτλ) fermentation.

βρασμός, ο [vrasmos] boiling || (μεταφ) agitation, excitement.

βραστός [vrastos] boiled || boiling, hot.

βραχιόλι, το [vraheeolee] bracelet.

βραχίονας, ο [vraheeonas] arm, forearm || branch.

βραχνιάζω [vrahneeazo] become hoarse.

βραχνός [vrahnos] hoarse.

βράχος, ο [vrahos] rock.

βραχυκύκλωμα, το [vraheekeekloma] short circuit.

βραχυπρόθεσμος [vraheeprothesmos] short-dated || short-term.

βραχύτητα, η [vraheeteeta] shortness, brevity, conciseness.

βραχώδης [vrahoðes] rocky.

βρε [vre] (επιφ) you there!, hey, you!

βρεγμένος [vregmenos] wet, moist.

βρέξιμο, το [vrekseemo] wetting, watering, moistening.

βρεφοκομείο, το [vrefokomeeo] foundling hospital, public nursery.

βρέφος, το [vrefos] baby, infant.

βρέχω [vreho] water, wet, dampen, rain.

βρίζω [vreezo] abuse, swear at, insult || outrage.

βρισιά, η [vreesia] abuse, insult, outrage.

βρισίδι, το [vreeseeðee] stream of abuse.

βρίσκομαι [vreeskome] be, find o.s.

βρίσκω [vreesko] find || (τυχαίως) come across, discover || (σκέπτομαι) think, deem || (παίρνω) get, procure || (μαντεύω) guess.

βρογχίτιδα, η [vrongheeteeða] bronchitis.

βροντερός [vronteros] thundering, noisy.

βροντή, η [vrontee] thunder.

βρόντος, ο [vrontos] noise, roar || heavy fall || **στο βρόντο** in vain.

βροντώ [vronto] (μεταφ) knock, make a noise.

βροχερός [vroheros] wet, rainy.

βροχή, η [vrohee] rain || ~ **ψιλή** drizzle.

βρυκόλακας, ο [vreekolakas] vampire, ghost.

βρύο, το [vreeo] moss || seaweed.

βρύση, η [vreesee] fountain, spring || (μεταλλική) tap.

βρυχώμαι [vreehome] roar, bellow.

βρώμα, η [vroma] filth, stink || (για πρόσωπο) hussy, bitch, slut.

βρωμερός [vromeros] stinking, smelly || (υπόθεση) nasty, odious, vile || (άτομο) stinking, dirty, slovenly.

βρώμη, η [vromee] oats.

βρωμιά, η [vromia] filth, dirt || (μεταφ) nasty business, corruption.

βρωμίζω [vromeezo] stink, dirty, sully.

βρώμικος [vromeekos] dirty, grubby || (μεταφ) nasty, odious, vile.

βρωμώ [vromo] give off a stench, smell badly, stink.

βυζαίνω [veezeno] suckle || (μεταφ) suck.

βυζαντινός [veezanteenos] Byzantine.

βυζί, το [veezee] breast.

βυθίζω [veetheezo] sink, plunge, dip.

βύθιση, η [veetheesee] sinking, submersion.

βύθισμα, το [veetheesma] (ναυτ) draught || sinking.

βυθοκόρος, η [veethokoros] dredger, dredge.

βυθός, ο [veethos] bottom of the sea.

βυρσοδεψείο, το [veersoðepseeo] tannery.

βύσσινο, το [veeseeno] sour cherry.

βυτίο, το [veeteeo] cask, barrel.

βωβός [vovos] dumb, mute, silent.

βώλος, ο [volos] clod || **βώλοι** πλ marbles.

βωμολοχία, η [vomoloheea] obscenity, scurrility.

βωμός, ο [vomos] altar.

Γ, γ

γαβάθα, η [gavatha] earthenware vessel || wooden bowl.

γάγγλιο, το [gangleeo] ganglion.

γάγγραινα, η [gangrena] gangrene || (μεταφ) canker.

γάδος, ό [gaðos] cod(fish).

γάζα, η [gaza] gauze.

γαζί, το [gazee] stitch || (της χειρός)

handstitch || (της μηχανής) machine-stitch.

γάζωμα, το [gazoma] stitching.

γάιδαρος, ο [gaeedaros] ass, donkey || (μεταφ) boor, ass.

γαϊδουράγκαθο, το [gaeedourangatho] thistle.

γαϊδουριά, η [gaeedouria] rudeness.

γαιοκτήμονας, η [geokteemonas] landowner.

γάλα, το [gala] milk.

γαλάζιος [galazeeos] azure, blue.

γαλαζοαίματος [galazoematos] blue-blooded.

γαλαζόπετρα, η [galazopetra] turquoise.

γαλακτερός [galakteros] milky, of milk.

γαλακτικός [galakteekos] lactic.

γαλακτοκομείο, το [galaktokomeeo] dairy farm.

γαλακτοπωλείο, το [galaktopoleeo] dairy.

γαλακτώδης [galaktoðees] milky, milk-white.

γαλάκτωμα, το [galaktoma] emulsion.

γαλανόλευκος, η [galanolevkos] the Greek flag.

γαλανομάτης [galanomatees] blue-eyed.

γαλανός [galanos] blue.

Γαλαξίας, ο [galakseeas] Milky Way.

γαλαρία, η [galareea] gallery.

γαλατάς, ο [galateas] milkman.

γαλβανίζω [galvaneezo] galvanize || (μεταφ) electrify, rouse, stimulate.

γαλέρα, η [galera] galley.

γαλέτα, η [galeta] hard tack.

γαληνεύω [galeenevo] calm, quieten down.

γαλήνη, η [galeenee] calm, peace, serenity.

γαλήνιος [galeeneeos] calm, composed, serene.

Γαλλία, η [galeea] France.

γαλλικός [galeekos] French.

Γάλλος, ο [galos] Frenchman.

γαλόνι, το [galonee] (μέτρο) gallon || (στρατ) stripe, pip.

γαλοπούλα, η [galopoula] turkey hen.

γάμα, το [gama] the letter G.

γαμήλιος [gameeleeos] nuptial, bridal || γαμήλιο ταξίδι honeymoon.

γάμπα, η [gamba] calf, leg.

γαμπρός, ο [gambros] bridegroom || son-in-law || brother-in-law.

γαμψός [gampsos] hooked, crooked.

γάντζος, ο [ganðzos] hook, grapple.

γαντζώνω [ganðzono] hook.

γάντι, το [gantee] glove.

γαργαλίζω [gargaleezo] tickle || (μεταφ) tempt, allure.

γαργάρα, η [gargara] gargle.

γαρδένια, η [garðeneea] gardenia.

γαρίδα, η [gareeða] shrimp, prawn.

γαρνίρισμα, το [garneereesma] adornment, garnishing, decoration.

γαρνίρω [garneero] garnish, trim.

γαρνιτούρα, η [garneetoura] garniture, trimming.

γαρυφαλιά, η [gareefalia] carnation || (μπαχαρικό) clove tree.

γαρύφαλλο, το [gareefalo] carnation || (μπαχαρικό) clove.

γαστραλγία, η [gastralyeea] stomachache.

γαστρικός [gastreekos] gastric.

γαστρίτιδα, η [gastreeteeða] gastritis.

γαστρονομία, η [gastronomeea] gastronomy.

γάτα, η [gata] cat.

γαυγίζω [gavyeezo] bark.

γαύγισμα, το [gavyeesma] barking, baying.

γδάρσιμο, το [gðarseemo] (πράξη) flaying || (αποτέλεσμα) scratch.

γδέρνω [gderno] flay, skin || (μεταφ) fleece.

γδύνομαι [gdeenome] get undressed, strip.

γδύνω [gdeeno] undress || (μεταφ) rob.

γεγονός, το [yegonos] event, fact.

γειά, η [ya] health || ~ σας hello || so long, goodbye.

γείσο, το [yeeso] (αρχιτεκ) eaves || cornice || (κασκέτου) peak.

γειτονεύω [yeetonevo] be close to, be adjoining.

γειτονιά, η [yeetonia] neighbourhood, vicinity.

γελαστός [yelastos] smiling, pleasant, cheerful.

γελάω [yelao] βλ **γελώ.**

γελιέμαι [yelieme] be deceived, be mistaken.

γέλιο, το [yeleeo] laugh, laughter.

γελοιογραφία, η [yeleeografeea] caricature, cartoon.

γελοιοποίηση, η [yeleeopieesee] ridicule, derision.

γελοιοποιούμαι [yeleeopeeoume] make o.s. ridiculous.

γελοιοποιώ [yeleeopeeo] make ridiculous, ridicule.

γελοίος [yeleeos] ludicrous, ridiculous.

γελώ [yelo] laugh || (μάτια κτλ) smile, twinkle || (εξαπατώ) deceive, take in.

γεμάτος [yematos] full || (δρόμος κτλ) crowded, swarming || (όπλο, δέντρο κτλ) loaded || (δωμάτιο κτλ) packed, crammed || (παχύς) stout, plump.

γεμίζω [yemeezo] fill up || (πλοίο) load || (μαξιλάρι κτλ) stuff || (συμπληρώνω) fill out.

γέμισμα, το [yemeesma] filling || (στρώματος) stuffing || (φεγγαριού) waxing || (όπλου) charging, loading.

γεμιστός [yemeestos] stuffed.

Γενάρης [yenarees] January.

γενεά, η [yenea] race, generation, breed.

γενεαλογία, η [yenealoyeea] genealogy, lineage, pedigree.

γενέθλια, τα [yenethleea] πλ birthday, anniversary.

γενειάς, η [yenias] beard.

γενειοφόρος, ο [yeneeoforos] bearded.

γένεση, η [yenesee] origin, birth || (εκκλ) Genesis.

γενέτειρα, η [yeneteera] native country, birthplace.

γενετή, η [yenetee]: **εκ γενετής** from birth.

γενετήσιος [yeneteeseeos] productive, generative, sexual.

γενίκευση, η [yeneekevsee] generalization.

γενικεύω [yeneekevo] generalize.

γενική [yeneekee] general, universal, wide || (γραμμ) genitive (case) || βλ και **γενικός.**

γενικός [yeneekos] general || βλ και **γενική.**

γενικότητα, η [yeneekoteeta] generality.

γέννα, η [yena] birth, childbirth || (μεταφ) breed.

γενναιοδωρία, η [yeneodoreea] generosity.

γενναιόδωρος [yeneodoros] generous, magnanimous.

γενναίος [yeneos] courageous, brave.

γενναιότητα, η [yeneoteeta] courage, bravery.

γενναιοφροσύνη, η [yeneofroseenee] generosity, liberality.

γενναιόφρων, ο [yeneofron] magnanimous, liberal.

γενναιόψυχος [yeneopseehos] generous, brave.

γέννημα, το [yeneema] offspring, product || (μωρό) progeny.

γέννηση, η [yeneesee] birth.

γεννητικός [yeneeteekos] genital, sexual.

γεννήτρια, η [yeneetreea] generator.

γεννώ [yeno] (για γυναίκα) give birth to, bring forth || (για άλογα) drop a foal || (για κουνέλια, γουρούνια) litter || (για πτηνά) lay || (μεταφ) create, breed, cause.

γεννώμαι [yenome] be born.

γένος, το [yenos] race, family, line || το ανθρώπινο ~ mankind || (ζώων, φυτών) kind, species || (γραμμ) gender.

γερά [yera] strongly, hard, vigorously.

γεράκι, το [yerakee] hawk.

γεράματα, τα [yeramata] πλ old age.

γεράνι, το [yeranee] geranium.

γερανός, ο [yeranos] (πτηνό) crane || (μηχάνημα) crane, winch.

γερατειά [yeratia] βλ γεράματα.

Γερμανία, η [yermaneea] Germany.

γερμανικός [yermaneekos] German.

Γερμανός, ο [yermanos] German.

γέρνω [yerno] lean, bend || (για βάρκα κτλ) lean, tilt || (για ήλιο κτλ) go down, sink.

γερνώ [yerno] age, grow old.

γεροντικός [yeronteekos] senile.

γεροντοκόρη, η [yerontokoree] old maid, spinster.

γεροντοπαλήκαρο, το [yerontopaleekaro] old bachelor.

γέρος, ο [yeros] old man.

γερός [yeros] (άνθρωπος) vigorous, sturdy || (κράση) sound, healthy || (τροφή) solid, substantial, hearty || (ξύλο) sound || (πάτωμα) solid, firm || (τοίχος) strong || (επιχείρημα) strong, valid.

γερουσία, η [yerouseea] senate.

γερουσιαστής, ο [yerouseeastees] senator.

γεύμα, το [yevma] meal, dinner.

γεύομαι [yevome] taste, try.

γεύση, η [yevsee] taste, flavour.

γέφυρα, η [yefeera] bridge.

γεφυρώνω [yefeerono] bridge || build a bridge.

γεωγραφία, η [yeografeea] geography.

γεωγράφος, ο [yeografos] geographer.

γεώδης [yeodees] earthy.

γεωλογία, η [yeoloyeea] geology.

γεωλόγος, ο [yeologos] geologist.

γεωμετρία, η [yeometreea] geometry.

γεωμετρικός [yeometreekos] geometric(al).

γεωπονία, η [yeoponeea] agriculture.

γεωργία, η [yeoryeea] agriculture, farming.

γεωργικός [yeoryeekos] agricultural.

γεωργός, ο [yeorgos] farmer.

γεώτρηση, η [yeotreesee] drilling.

γεωτρύπανο, το [yeotreepano] drill.

γη, η [yee] earth, land, ground.

γηγενής [yeegenees] native, indigenous.

γήινος [yeeinos] earthly, terrestrial.

γήπεδο, το [yeepedo] ground, sportsground.

γήρας, το [yeeras] old age.

για [ya] for, because of, on behalf of || γι' αυτό therefore || ~ καλά for certain, for good || ~ την ώρα for the time being || ~ πού whither? || ~ το Θεο for God's sake || (επίρ) as, for || (συνδ) ~ να in order to || ~ φαντάσου! fancy that! || ~ πες μου tell me.

γιαγιά, η [yayia] grandmother.

γιακάς, ο [yakas] collar.

γιαλός, ο [yalos] seashore.

γιαούρτι, το [yaourtee] yoghurt.

γιασεμί, το [yasemee] jasmine.

γιατί [yatee] why? || (συνδ) because.

γιατρεύω [yatrevo] cure, heal, treat.

γιατρός, ο [yatros] doctor.

γιγάντιος [yeeganteeos] gigantic.

γιγαντόσωμος [yeegandosomos] huge (in size).

γίγας, ο [yeegas] giant.

γίδα, η [yeeda] goat.

γιδοβοσκός, ο [yeedovoskos] goatherd.

γιλέκο, το [yeeleko] waistcoat.

γίνομαι [yeenome] be done, become || (μεγαλώνω) grow || (στρέφω) turn || (γεγονός κτλ) happen, occur || (ωριμάζω) ripen || ~ **καλά** recover || **τι γίνεσαι;** how are you?

γινόμενο, το [yeenomenon] product.

Γιουγκοσλαβία, η [yougoslaveea] Yugoslavia.

γιουγκοσλαβικός [yougoslaveekos] Yugoslavian.

Γιουγκοσλάβος, ο [yougoslavos] Yugoslav.

γιουχαΐζω [youhaeezo] hoot, jeer.

γιρλάντα, η [yeerlanta] garland, wreath.

γιώτ, το [yot] yacht.

γκαβός [gavos] cross-eyed || (κατ επέκτασιν) blind.

γκάζι, το [gazee] gas || πατώ ~ step on the gas.

γκαζιέρα, η [gaziera] cooking stove, primus stove.

γκαζόζα, η [gazoza] lemonade.

γκαρίζω [gareezo] bray.

γκαρσόνι, το [garsonee] waiter.

γκαρσονιέρα, η [garsoniera] bachelor flat.

γκάφα, η [gafa] blunder.

γκέμι, το [gemee] bridle, reins.

γκίνια, η [geeneea] bad luck.

γκιώνης, ο [geeonees] (scops) owl.

γκουβερνάντα, η [gouvernanta] governess.

γκρεμίζω [gremeezo] demolish, pull down, wreck.

γκρεμίζομαι [gremeezvome] fall, crumble, collapse.

γκρεμνός, ο [gremnos] sheer drop, crag.

γκρίζος, ο [greezos] grey.

γκρίνια, η [greeneea] grumble, nag, murmur.

γκρινιάζω [greeneeazo] complain, nag, grumble.

γλάρος, ο [glaros] seagull.

γλάστρα, η [glastra] flowerpot.

γλαύκωμα, το [glavkoma] glaucoma.

γλαφυρός [glafeeros] elegant, graceful.

γλείφω [gleefo] lick.

γλεντζές, ο [glenðzes] fun-loving person, reveller.

γλέντι, το [glenðee] party, feast.

γλεντώ [glenðo] amuse || (απολαμβάνω) enjoy || (επί χρημάτων) squander.

γλεύκος, το [glevkos] must.

γλιστερός, ο [gleesteros] slippery.

γλίστρημα, το [gleestreema] slide, slip || (μεταφ) blunder, mistake.

γλιστρώ [gleestro] slide, slip || (μεταφ) slip away.

γλοιώδης [gleeoðes] slimy, sticky || (πρόσωπο) slippery.

γλόμπος, ο [glombos] globe.

γλουτός, ο [gloutos] buttock, rump.

γλύκα, η [gleeka] sweetness.

γλυκά, τα [gleeka] πλ pastries, confectionery.

γλυκαίνω [gleekeno] sweeten, make mild, soften.

γλυκάνισο, το [gleekaneeso] anise.

γλύκισμα, το [gleekeesma] cake, pastry.

γλυκομίλητος [gleekomeeleetos] soft-spoken, affable.

γλυκομιλώ [gleekomeelo] speak tenderly, speak kindly.

γλυκό, το [gleeko] jam, sweetmeat.

γλυκόξινος [gleekokseenos] bittersweet.

γλυκοχάραγμα, το [gleekoharagma] daybreak, twilight.

γλυκός [gleeko] affable, sweet || (καιρός) mild || (φως) subdued, mellow || (χρώμα) delicate || (ήχος) soft, sweet || (κρασί) sweet || (όνειρα) pleasant.

γλύπτης, ο [gleeptees] sculptor.

γλυπτική, η [gleepteekee] sculpture.

γλυπτός [gleeptos] sculptured, carved.

γλυτώνω [gleetono] save, deliver || (αμεταβ) escape.

γλύφω [gleefo] βλ **γλείφω**.

γλώσσα, η [glossa] tongue, language || (ψάρι) sole.

γλωσσάς, ο [glossas] chatterbox, gossip.

γλωσσικός [glosseekos] linguistic.

γλωσσολογία, η [glossologeea] linguistics.

γλωσσολόγος, ο [glossologos] linguist.

γλωσσομαθής [glossomathees] polyglot, linguist.

γνάθος, ο [gnathos] jaw.

γνέθω [gnetho] spin.

γνήσιος [gneeseeos] genuine, real || (παιδί) legitimate.

γνησίως [gneeseeos] genuinely, authentically.

γνωμάτευση, η [gnomatevsee] opinion, adjudication.

γνώμη, η [gnomee] opinion, view.

γνωμικό, το [gnomeeko] maxim, saying, adage.

γνωμοδότης, ο [gnomodotees] adviser, councillor.

γνωμοδοτώ [gnomodoto] give one's opinion, judge.

γνώμων, ο [gnomon] set square, level || (μεταφ) criterion, model.

γνωρίζω [gnoreezo] let it be known,

inform || (έχω γνώση) know, be aware of || (αναγνωρίζω) discern, distinguish || (έχω σχέσεις) know, be acquainted with || (παρουσιάζω κάποιο) introduce.

γνωριμία, η [gnoreemeea] acquaintance, familiarity.

γνώριμος [gnoreemos] known, intimate.

γνώρισμα, το [gnoreesma] sign, mark, indication.

γνώση, η [gnosee] knowledge, notion || **γνώσεις** πλ knowledge, learning.

γνώστης, ο [gnostees] expert, connoisseur, specialist.

γνωστικός [gnosteekos] prudent.

γνωστοποίηση, η [gnostopieesee] notification, announcement.

γνωστοποιώ [gnostopeeo] notify, inform, advise.

γνωστός [gnostos] known || (φίλος) acquaintance.

γογγύλη, η [gongeelee] turnip.

γοερός [goeros] plaintive, woeful.

γόης, ο [goees] charmer.

γοητεία, η [goeeteea] charm || attractiveness.

γοητευτικός [goeetevteekos] charming, captivating.

γοητεύω [goeetevo] charm, attract.

γόητρο, το [goeetro] prestige, reputation.

γομάρι, το [gomaree] load || (μεταφ) simpleton, beast.

γόμμα, η [gomma] gum || (σβυσίματος) india rubber, eraser.

γόμωση, η [gomosee] stuffing || (όπλο) charge.

γονατίζω [gonateezo] (make to) kneel || (μεταφ) humble || (αμεταβ) kneel down || (μεταφ) give way, yield.

γονατιστά [gonateesta] on one's knees, kneeling.

γόνατο, το [gonato] knee.

γονεάς, ο [goneas] father || **γονείς**
πλ parents.

γονιμοποίηση, η
[goneemopieesee] fertilization,
impregnation.

γονιμοποιώ [goneemopeeo]
fecundate, fertilize.

γόνιμος [goneemos] fertile, prolific
|| (μεταφ) inventive.

γονιμότητα, η [goneemoteeta]
fecundity, fertility.

γόνος, ο [gonos] child, offspring ||
(απέρμα) sperm, seed.

γόπα, η [gopa] bogue (fish) ||
(τσιγαρου) cigarette butt.

γοργός [gorgos] rapid, quick.

γορίλλας, ο [goreelas] gorilla.

γούβα, η [gouva] cavity, hole.

γουδί, το [goudee] mortar.

γουδοχέρι, το [goudoheree] pestle.

γουλί, το [goulee] stalk, stump ||
(μεταφ) bald.

γουλιά, η [goulia] sip.

γούνα, η [gouna] fur.

γουργουρητό, το [gourgoureeto]
rumbling, rumble.

γούρι, το [gouree] good luck.

γουρλώνω [gourlono] open (eyes)
wide, goggle.

γουρούνι, το [gourounee] pig, hog.

γουρσούζης, ο [goursouzees]
luckless person, unlucky person.

γουρσουζιά, η [goursoozia] bad
luck.

γουστάρω [goustaro] desire, feel
like || (ευχαριστούμαι) delight in,
enjoy.

γούστο, το [gousto] taste ||
(φιλοκαλία) good taste || **για ~** for
the hell of it.

γοφός, ο [gofos] haunch, hip.

Γραικός, ο [grekos] Greek.

γράμμα, το [gramma] letter,
character.

γραμμάριο, το [grammareeo]
gram(me).

γραμματεία, η [grammateea]
secretariat, secretary's office.

γραμματέας, ο [grammateas]
secretary.

γραμματική, η [grammateekee]
grammar.

γραμμάτιο, το [grammateeo] bill
of exchange || (χρεωστικό)
promissory note.

γραμματοκιβώτιο, το
[grammatokeevoteeo] letterbox,
postbox.

γραμματόσημο, το
[grammatoseemo] (postage) stamp.

γραμμένος [grammenos] written ||
(μεταφ) destined.

γραμμή, η [grammee] line, row ||
(επιρ) straight, in a row || **πρώτης
~ς** first-class.

γραμμικός [grameekos] linear.

γραμμόφωνο, το [grammofono]
gramophone.

γρανίτης, ο [graneetees] granite.

γραπτός [graptos] written.

γραπτώς [graptos] in writing.

γραπώνω [grapono] seize, snatch.

γρασίδι, το [graseedee] grass.

γρατσουνίζω [gratsouneezo]
scratch.

γρατσούνισμα, το
[gratsouneesma] scratch.

γραφειοκράτης, ο
[grafeeokratees] bureaucrat.

γραφειοκρατία, η
[grafeeokrateea] bureaucracy.

γραφείο, το [grafeeo] desk, bureau
|| (δωμάτιο) study || (ίδρυμα) office,
bureau.

γραφικός [grafeekos] of writing,
clerical || (μεταφ) picturesque,
colourful.

γραφικότης, η [grafeekotees]
picturesqueness, vividness.

γραφίτης, ο [grafeetees] graphite.

γραφομηχανή, η [grafomeehanee]
typewriter.

γράφω [grafo] write, record, compose || enrol.

γράψιμο, το [grapseemo] writing.

γρήγορα [greegora] quickly, promptly.

γρηγορώ [greegoro] watch, be alert || be awake.

γριά, η [greea] old woman.

γρίλλια, η [greeleea] grille.

γρίππη, η [greepee] influenza.

γρίφος, ο [greefos] riddle, puzzle, enigma.

γριφώδης [greefodees] enigmatic(al), obscure.

γροθιά [grothia] fist || punch.

γρονθοκόπημα, το [gronthokopeema] boxing, punch.

γρονθοκοπώ [gronthokopo] punch, pound.

γρουσούζης [groosoozees] βλ γουρσούζης.

γρυλισμός, ο [greeleesmos] grunting, snorting.

γρυλλίζω [greeleezo] grunt, squeal.

γρύλλος, ο [greelos] piglet || (έντομο) cricket || (μηχάνημα) jack.

γυάλα, η [yeala] glass, jar || (ψαριών) bowl.

γυαλάδα, η [yealada] brilliance, shine, gloss.

γυαλάδικο, το [yealadeeko] glassware || glass works.

γυαλένιος [yealeneeos] glass.

γυαλί, το [yealee] glass || πλ spectacles, glasses.

γυαλίζω [yealeezo] polish, shine.

γυάλισμα, το [yealeesma] polishing, glazing.

γυαλιστερός [yealeesteros] polished, glossy.

γυαλόχαρτο, το [yealoharto] glasspaper, sandpaper.

γυιός, ο [yos] son.

γυμνάζομαι [yeemnazome] train o.s., exercise, practise.

γυμνάζω [yeemnazo] exercise, train, drill.

γυμνασιάρχης, ο [yeemnaseearhees] secondary school headmaster.

γυμνάσια, τα [yeemnaseea] πλ manoeuvres.

γυμνάσιο, το [yeemnaseeo] secondary school, high school.

γυμναστήριο, το [yeemnasteereeo] gymnasium.

γυμναστής, ο [yeemnastees] P.T. instructor.

γυμναστική, η [yeemnasteekee] πλ gymnastics || exercise.

γύμνια, η [yeemneea] nudity, nakedness || poverty.

γυμνιστής, ο [yeemneestees] nudist.

γυμνός [yeemnos] naked, bare, nude.

γυμνώνω [yeemnono] bare, expose || (μεταφ) strip.

γύμνωση, η [yeemnosee] disrobing || denudation || fleecing.

γυναίκα, η [yeeneka] woman || (σύζυγος) wife.

γυναικάς, ο [yeenekas] womanchaser, rake.

γυναικείος [yeenekeeos] womanly, feminine.

γυναικολογία, η [yeenekologeea] gynaecology.

γυναικολόγος, ο [yeenekologos] gynaecologist.

γυναικόπαιδα, τα [yeenekopeða] πλ women and children.

γυναικοπρεπής [yeenekoprepees] womanly, effeminate, womanish.

γυναικωνίτης, ο [yeenekoneetees] harem.

γυνή [yeenee] βλ γυναίκα.

γύπας, ο [yeepas] vulture.

γυρεύω [yeerevo] ask for, call for || (ελεημοσύνη) beg for || (να βρω κάτι) look for, seek || (αποζημίωση κτλ) claim || (διαζύγιο) apply for || (βοήθεια) request.

γυρίζω [yeereezo] turn, rotate,

revolve || (σβούρα) spin || (στρέφω)
turn || (αναστρέφω) turn ||
(επιστρέφω) return || (αμεταβ) turn,
rotate || (ταινία) shoot.

γύρισμα, το [yeereesma] turn,
revolution || (δρόμου, ποταμού) turn,
twist, winding.

γυρισμός, ο [yeeresmos] return,
coming back.

γυριστός [yeereestos] curved,
turned up, crooked.

γυρνάω [yeernao] βλ γυρίζω.

γυρολόγος, ο [yeerologos] hawker,
pedlar.

γύρος, ο [yeeros] circle,
circumference || (φορέματος) hem ||
(περιστροφή) turn, revolution ||
(περπάτημα) walk || (βαρελιού) hoop.

γυρτός [yeertos] bent, inclined,
curved.

γύρω [yeero] round, around, about,
round about.

γυφτιά, η [yeeftia] stinginess,
avarice, shabbiness.

γύφτος, ο [yeeftos] gipsy.

γύψινος [yeepseenos] plaster.

γύψος, ο [yeepsos] plaster of Paris.

γυψώνω [yeepsono] plaster.

γωνία, η [goneea] angle, corner ||
(εργαλείο) square, set square ||
(απόμερος τόπος) nook, den ||
(ψωμιού) crust of bread.

γωνιακός [goneeakos] angular ||
(της γωνίας) corner.

γωνιόλιθος, ο [goneeoleethos]
cornerstone.

γωνιώδης [goneeodees] angular.

Δ, δ

δα [δa] (indeclinable particle) όχι
~ certainly not! || τόσος ~ only
so tall, so small.

δάγκωμα, το [δangoma] bite.

δαγκώνω [δangono] bite.

δαδί, το [δaδee] pinewood,
firewood.

δαίδαλος [δeδalos] labyrinthine,
intricate, complicated.

δαιμονίζω [δemoneezo] enrage,
infuriate.

δαιμονισμένος [δemoneesmenos]
(μεταφ) mischievous || possessed.

δαιμόνιο, το [δemoneeo] genius ||
(διάβολος) demon, fiend.

δαιμόνιος [δemoneeos] very clever,
marvellous, divine.

δαίμων, ο [δemon] demon, devil,
fiend.

δάκρυ, το [δakree] tear.

δακρύζω [δakreezo] shed tears,
weep || (επί φυτών) sweat.

δακτυλήθρα, η [δakteeleethra]
thimble.

δακτυλίδι, το [δakteeleeδee] ring.

δακτυλικός [δakteeleekos] digital,
dactylic.

δάκτυλο, το [δakteelo] βλ
δάκτυλος.

δακτυλογράφος, ο, η
[δakteelografos] typist.

δάκτυλος, ο [δakteelos] finger ||
(ποδιού) toe || (μονάς μήκους) inch.

δαμάζω [δamazo] tame, subdue.

δαμαλισμός, ο [δamaleesmos]
vaccination.

δαμάσκηνο, το [δamaskeeno]
plum || (ξηρό) prune.

δανείζομαι [δaneezome] borrow.

δανείζω [δaneezo] lend, loan.

δάνειο [δaneeo] loan.

δανειστής, ο [δaneestees] lender,
creditor.

Δανία, η [δaneea] Denmark.

δανικός [δaneekos] Danish.

Δανός, ο [δanos] Dane.

δαντέλλα, η [δantella] lace.

δαπάνη, η [δapanee] expenditure,
expense, cost.

δαπανηρός [δapaneeros] costly,
expensive.

δαπανώ [δapano] spend, consume.

δάπεδο, το [δapeδo] floor || ground.

δαρμός, ο [δarmos] βλ δάρσιμο.

δάρσιμο, το [darseemo] beating || (γάλακτος) churning.

δασκάλα, η [δaskala] teacher, schoolmistress.

δασκαλεύω [δaskalevo] coach, teach.

δάσκαλος, ο [δaskalos] teacher, schoolmaster.

δασμολόγιο, το [δasmoloyeeo] tariff.

δασμός, ο [δasmos] tax, (customs) duty.

δάσος, το [δasos] forest, woodland.

δασύς, ο [δasees] thick, bushy, hairy.

δασώδης [δasoδees] wooded, woody.

δαυλί, το [δavlee] torch, firebrand.

δάφνη, η [δafnee] laurel, bay tree, bay.

δε [δe] and || but || on the other hand || ο μεν... ο ~ the one... the other.

δεδομένα, τα [δeδomena] πλ data, facts.

δεδουλευμένος [δeδoulemenos]: ~ τόκος accrued interest.

δέηση, η [δeesee] prayer, supplication.

δείγμα, το [δeegma] sample, specimen || (ένδειξη) token, sign.

δειγματολόγιο, το [δeegmatoloyeeo] sample, collection.

δεικνύω [δeekneeo] show, point out || (επί οργάνων) mark, indicate.

δείκτης, ο [δeektees] indicator || (χειρός) forefinger || (ωρολογίου) hand || (ζυγού) index, cock || (πυξίδος) needle.

δεικτικός [δeekteekos] indicative || (γραμμ) demonstrative.

δειλά [δeela] timidly, faintheartedly.

δείλι, το [δeelee] (late) afternoon.

δειλία, η [δeeleea] timidity, cowardice.

δειλιάζω [δeeleeazo] lose courage, be afraid.

δειλινό, το [δeeleeno] (late) afternoon.

δειλός [δeelos] timid || cowardly, fainthearted.

δεινός [δeenos] horrid || (ικανός) able, clever, expert.

δεισιδαιμονία, η [δeeseeδemoneea] superstition.

δεισιδαίμων [δeeseeδemon] superstitious.

δείχνω [δeehno] βλ δεικνύω.

δέκα [δeka] ten.

δεκάδα, η [δekaδa] set of ten.

δεκαδικός [δekaδeekos] decimal.

δεκαετηρίδα, η [δekaeteereeδa] decade || (εορτή) tenth anniversary.

δεκαετής, ο, η [δekaetees] ten-year-old.

δεκαετία, η [δekaeteea] ten years, decade.

δεκάζω [δekazo] corrupt, bribe.

δεκάλογος, ο [δekalogos] Decalogue, Ten Commandments.

δεκανέας, ο [δekaneas] corporal.

δεκανίκι, το [δekaneekee] crutch.

δεκαπενθήμερο, το [δekapentheemero] fortnight.'

δεκαπλάσιος [δekaplaseeos] tenfold.

δεκάρα [δekara] one tenth of a drachma.

δεκάρι, το [δekaree] ten-drachma piece || (στα χαρτιά) ten.

δεκασμός, ο [δekasmos] bribery, corruption.

δέκατος [δekatos] tenth.

Δεκέμβριος, ο [δekemvreeos] December.

δέκτης, ο [δektees] receiver.

δεκτικός [δekteekos] capable of, susceptible to, receptive to.

δεκτός [δektos] accepted || (γνώμη) admissible.

δελεάζω [δeleazo] tempt, entice, bait.

δελεαστικός [deleasteekos] tempting, attractive.

δέλτα, το [delta] (γράμμα) delta || (ποταμού) delta.

δελτίο, το [delteeo] bulletin || (υγείας) report || (ψηφοδέλτιο) ballot.

δελφίνι, το [delfeenee] dolphin.

δέμα, το [dema] (πάκο) bale, bundle || (ταχυδρομικό) parcel.

δεμάτι, το [dematee] bundle || (καρότων κτλ) bunch || (φρυγάνων) faggot.

δε(ν) [de(n)] (negative particle) no, not.

δενδρολίβανο, το [dendroleevano] rosemary.

δένδρο, το [dendro] tree.

δενδρόφυτος [dendrofeetos] full of trees, wooded.

δένω [deno] bind, tie || (με αλυσίδα) chain, link || (γραβάτα κτλ) tie || (βιβλίο) bind || (προσδένω) fasten, fix || (καράβι) moor, berth || (γλυκό κτλ) thicken || (μεταφ) bind.

δεξαμενή, η [deksamenee] tank, reservoir || (ναυτ) dock, basin.

δεξιά, η [deksia] right hand || (πολιτ) right wing || (επιρ) to the right.

δεξιός [dekseeos] right || right-handed || (πολιτ) right-wing || (επιτήδειος) clever.

δεξιότητα, η [dekseeoteeta] skilfulness, cleverness.

δεξιόχειρας, ο [dekseeoheeras] right-handed (person).

δεξιώνομαι [dekseeonome] receive, welcome.

δεξίωση, η [dekseeosee] reception.

δέον, το [deon] what is necessary.

δεόντως [deondos] suitably, fitly, properly.

δέος, το [deos] awe, fear, fright.

δέρας, το [deras] fleece || **χρυσόμαλλον ~** the golden fleece.

δέρμα, το [derma] skin, pelt || leather.

δερμάτινος [dermateenos] of leather.

δερματίτιδα, η [dermateeða] dermatitis.

δέρνω [derno] beat, flog || (γάλα) churn.

δέσιμο, το [deseemo] tying, binding || bandage.

δεσμά, τα [desma] πλ chains, fetters, bonds.

δέσμευση, η [desmevsee] tying, binding.

δεσμεύω [desmevo] bind by a promise, pledge.

δέσμη, η [desmee] bunch || (φύλλων) bundle.

δέσμιος, ο [desmeeos] prisoner, captive.

δεσμός, ο [desmos] tie, bond.

δεσμοφύλακας, ο [desmofeelakas] prison warder.

δεσπόζω [despozo] dominate, rule || (υπέρκειμαι) tower above, overlook || (μεταφ) rise above.

δεσποινίς, η [despeenees] young lady || Miss.

δεσπότης, ο [despotees] ruler, master || (εκκλ) (arch)bishop.

δεσποτικός [despoteekos] despotic.

δετός [detos] tied, bound.

Δευτέρα, η [ðevtera] Monday.

δευτερεύων [ðevterevon] secondary || subordinate.

δευτεροβάθμιος [ðevterovathmeeos] secona-degree.

δευτερόλεπτο, το [ðevterolepto] second.

δεύτερος [ðevteros] second || (σε ποιότητα) inferior.

δευτερότοκος [ðevterotokos] second-born.

δέχομαι [ðehome] accept, receive || (παραδέχομαι) approve || (δεξιούομαι) welcome, greet ||

(υφίσταμαι) receive || (ανέχομαι) tolerate.

δήθεν [deethen] apparently, as if, so-called.

δηκτικός [deekteekos] biting, scathing.

δηλαδή [deeladee] that is to say, namely, viz.

δηλητηριάζω [deeleeteereeazo] poison || (μεταφ) corrupt, taint.

δηλητηρίαση [deeleeteereeasee] poisoning || (μεταφ) corruption.

δηλητήριο, το [deeleeteereeo] poison, venom.

δηλώνω [deelono] declare, state || (γέννηση κτλ) register, give notice || (εμπόρευμα) enter (goods).

δήλωση, η [deelosee] declaration, statement || (γέννηση κτλ) register.

δημαγωγία, η [deemagoyeea] demagogy.

δημαρχείο, το [deemarheeo] town hall || city hall (US).

δήμαρχος, ο [deemarhos] mayor.

δήμευση, η [deemefsee] confiscation.

δημεύω [deemevo] confiscate, seize.

δημητριακός [deemeetreeakos]: τα δημητριακά cereals, crops.

δήμιος, ο [deemeeos] executioner, hangman.

δημιουργία, η [deemeeouryeea] creation.

δημιουργικός [deemeeouryeekos] creative.

δημιουργός, ο [deemeeourgos] creator.

δημιουργώ [deemeeourgo] create || establish.

δημοδιδάσκαλος, ο [deemodeedaskalos] primary schoolteacher.

δημοκράτης, ο [deemokratees] democrat.

δημοκρατία, η [deemokrateea] democracy || republic.

δημοκρατικός [deemokrateekos] democratic, republican.

δημοπρασία, η [deemopraseea] auction.

δήμος, ο [deemos] municipality.

δημοσία [deemoseea] (επιρ) publicly.

δημοσίευμα, το [deemosievma] newspaper article, publication.

δημοσίευση, η [deemosievsee] publication.

δημοσιεύω [deemosievo] publish, make known.

δημοσιογράφος, ο [deemoseeografos] journalist, reporter.

δημόσιο, το [deemoseeo] the state, the public.

δημόσιος [deemoseeos] public || (κρατικός) national.

δημοσιότητα, η [deemoseeoteeta] publicity.

δημότης, ο [deemotees] citizen.

δημοτική, η [deemoteekee] demotic (Greek).

δημοτικός [deemoteekos] municipal || (δημοφιλής) popular.

δημοτικότητα, η [deemoteekoteeta] popularity.

δημοφιλής [deemofeelees] popular, well-liked.

δημοψήφισμα, το [deemopseefeesma] plebiscite.

δημώδης [deemodees] popular, folk.

διά [δia] for, by, with, about || (μετά γενικής) through, across, by means of || ~ παντός forever || ~ μιας at one go || ~ θαλάσσης by sea.

διαβάζω [deeavazo] read, study || (μετά προσοχής) peruse.

διαβάθμιση, η [deeavathmeesee] grading, graduation.

διαβάλλω [deeavalo] slander, defame, calumniate.

διάβαση, η [deeavasee] crossing, passage || (στενό) pass, ford.

διάβασμα, το [δeeavasma] reading, lecture || studying.

διαβασμένος [δeevasmenos] learned, prepared (for examination).

διαβατήριο, το [δeevateereeo] passport.

διαβάτης, ο [δeeavatees] passer-by.

διαβατός [δeeavatos] passable || (ποταμός) fordable.

διαβεβαιώνω [δeeaveveono] assure, assert, affirm.

διαβεβαίωση, η [δeeaveveosee] assurance, affirmation.

διάβημα, το [δeeaveema] step, measure, move.

διαβήτης, ο [δeeaveetees] pair of compasses || (ιατρ) diabetes.

διαβιβάζω [δeeaveevazo] transmit, forward, convey.

διαβίβαση, η [δeeaveevasee] transmission, forwarding.

διαβιβρώσκω [δeeaveevrosko] corrode || (οκουλίκι) eat into || (θάλασσα κτλ) erode.

διαβίωση, η [δeeaveeosee] living.

διαβλέπω [δeeavlepo] discern, penetrate, foresee.

διαβόητος [δeeavoeetos] notorious.

διαβολεμένος [δeeavolemenos] shrewd, cunning || (μεταφ) devilish.

διαβολή, η [δeeavolee] slander, calumny.

διαβολικός [δeeavoleekos] satanic, diabolical.

διάβολος, ο [δeeavolos] devil, satan || (φασαρίας) noisy, boisterous.

διαβουλεύομαι [δeeavoulevome] deliberate, confer || (μηχανορραφώ) plot.

διαβρέχω [δeeavreho] wet, soak, steep.

διάβρωση, η [δeeavrosee] corrosion.

διαγγέλλω [δeeangelo] announce, notify.

διάγνωση, η [δeeagnosee] diagnosis.

διάγραμμα, το [δeeagrama] diagram, drawing, plan.

διαγραφή, η [δeeagrafee] cancellation.

διαγράφω [δeeagrafo] trace out || (σβήνω) efface, cancel.

διάγω [δeeago] live, pass one's time.

διαγωγή, η [δeeagoyee] behaviour, conduct, deportment.

διαγωνίζομαι [δeeagoneezome] compete, contend.

διαγώνιος [δeeagoneeos] diagonal.

διαγωνισμός, ο [δeeagoneesmos] competition || (εξετάσεις) examination.

διαδέχομαι [δeeadehome] succeed, follow.

διάδηλος [δeeaδeelos] manifest, evident.

διαδήλωση, η [δeeaδeelosee] demonstration, manifestation.

διάδημα, το [δeeaδeema] crown, diadem.

διαδίδω [δeeaδeeδo] spread, circulate, propagate.

διαδικασία, η [δeeaδeekaseea] procedure, legal inquiry.

διάδικος, ο, η [δeeaδeekos] litigant.

διάδοση, η [δeeaδosee] spreading || rumour.

διαδοχή, η [δeeaδohee] succession.

διάδοχος, ο, η [δeeaδohos] successor, crown prince.

διαδραματίζω [δeeaδramateezo] play (a role), act.

διαδρομή, η [δeeaδromee] course, distance || (εμβόλου) stroke.

διάδρομος, ο [δeeaδromos] passage, corridor, hall.

διαζευκτικός [δeeazevkteekos] (γραμμ) disjunctive.

διάζευξη, η [δeeazevksee] separation, severance.

διαζύγιο, το [deeazeegeeo] divorce.

διάζωμα, το [deeazoma] frieze.

διαθέσιμος [deeatheseemos] available, free.

διάθεση, η [deeathesee] arrangement, disposal || (κέφι) mood, humour.

διαθέτω [deeatheto] dispose, arrange || (χρησιμοποιώ) employ, use, make available || (διανέμω) allot.

διαθήκη, η [deeatheekee] will, testament.

διάθλαση, η [deeathlasee] refraction.

διαίρεση, η [dieresee] division, separation || (μεταφ) discord, difference.

διαιρέτης, ο [dieretees] divisor, divider.

διαιρώ [diero] divide, separate.

διαισθάνομαι [diesthanome] feel, have a presentiment.

διαίσθηση, η [diesthesee] presentiment.

δίαιτα, η [dieta] diet.

διαιτησία, η [dieteeseea] arbitration.

διαιτητής, ο [dieteetees] arbiter || (ποδοσφαίρου) referee || umpire.

διαιωνίζω [dieoneezo] perpetuate || protract.

διαιώνιση, η [dieoneesee] perpetuation.

διακαής [deeakaees] ardent, fervent, eager.

διακανονίζω [deeakanoneezo] regulate, adjust, settle.

διακατέχω [deeakateho] possess.

διάκειμαι [deeakeeme] be disposed, be inclined.

διακεκριμένος [deeakekreemenos] distinguished, eminent.

διάκενος [deeakenos] empty, hollow, vacant || **το διάκενο** void, vacuum.

διακήρυξη, η [deeakeereeksee] declaration, proclamation.

διακηρύττω [deeakeereeto] declare, proclaim, announce.

διακινδυνεύω [deeakeendeenevo] risk, endanger, hazard.

διακλάδωση, η [deeaklaðosee] fork || (δρόμου κτλ) branch.

διακομίζω [deeakomeezo] transport, carry.

διάκονος, ο [deeakonos] deacon.

διακοπή, η [deeakopee] suspension, interruption, recess || (ρεύματος) cut.

διακόπτης, ο [deeakoptees] switch, stopcock.

διακόπτω [deeakopto] suspend, cut off, interrupt, discontinue.

διάκος, ο [deeakos] deacon.

διακόσμηση, η [deeakosmeesee] decoration, embellishment.

διακοσμητής, ο [deeakosmeetees] decorator.

διάκοσμος, ο [deeakosmos] ornamentation, decoration.

διακοσμώ [deeakosmo] decorate, adorn.

διακρίνω [deeakreeno] discern, discriminate.

διάκριση, η [deeakreesee] distinction || (κρίση) discretion.

διακύμανση, η [deeakeemansee] fluctuation, undulation.

διακωμωδώ [deeakomoðo] ridicule, satirize.

διαλαλώ [ðeealalo] proclaim, cry out, broadcast.

διαλεγμένος [ðeealegmenos] selected, chosen.

διαλέγω [ðeealego] choose, select, pick out.

διάλειμμα, το [ðeealeema] interval, recess || intermission.

διάλειψη, η [ðeealeepsee] irregularity.

διαλεκτική, η [ðeealekteekee] dialectics.

διαλεκτός [δeealektos] chosen, select.

διάλεκτος, η [δeealektos] dialect, idiom.

διάλεξη [δeealeksee] lecture || conversation.

διαλεύκανση, η [δeealevkansee] elucidation.

διαλλακτικός [δeeallakteekos] conciliatory.

διαλογή, η [δeealoyee] sorting.

διαλογίζομαι [δeealoyeezome] meditate, consider.

διαλογισμός, ο [δeealoyeesmos] reflection, thought.

διάλογος, ο [δeealogos] dialogue, conversation.

διάλυμα, το [δeealeema] solution.

διάλυση, η [δeealeesee] dissolution, decomposition || (εντός υγρού) solution || (εταιρείας κτλ) liquidation || (στρατ) disbanding.

διαλυτός [δeealeetos] soluble, dissolvable.

διαλύω [δeealeeo] dissolve || (εταιρεία) liquidate || (συμβόλαιο κτλ) annul, cancel || (εχθρό) disband, defeat, scatter || (αμφιβολία κτλ) dispel.

διαμάντι, το [δeeamantee] diamond || διαμαντικά πλ jewellery, gems.

διαμαρτυρόμενος, ο [δeeamarteeromenos] Protestant.

διαμαρτυρία, η [δeeamarteero] protest.

διαμάχη, η [δeeamahee] dispute, fight.

διαμελίζω [δeeameleezo] dismember.

διαμένω [δeeameno] reside, live, stay.

διαμέρισμα, το [δeeamereesma] region, constituency, district || (οικία) apartment, flat.

διάμεσος, ο [δeeamesos] intermediary, intermediate.

διαμέτρημα, το [δeeametreema] bore, calibre.

διάμετρος, η [δeeametros] diameter || gauge.

διαμοιράζω [δeeameerazo] distribute, share.

διαμονή, η [δeeamonee] stay, residence, sojourn.

διαμορφώνω [δeeamorfono] model, shape, form.

διανέμω [δeeanemo] distribute || divide.

διανόηση, η [δeeanoeesee] thought || intelligence.

διανοητικώς [δeeanoeeteekos] intellectually.

διάνοια, η [δeeaneea] intellect, mind.

διανοίγω [δeeaneego] open (up).

διανομέας, ο [δeeanomeas] distributor || (ταχυδρομικός) postman.

διανομή, η [δeeanomee] distribution.

διανοούμενοι, οι [δeeanooumenee] πλ intellectuals.

διανυκτερεύω [δeeaneekterevo] spend the night || stay open all night.

διανύω [δeeaneeo] go through, cover, terminate.

διαξιφισμός, ο [δeeakseefeesmos] sword-thrust || fencing.

διαπασών, η [δeeapason] tuning fork || (μουσ) octave.

διαπεραστικός [δeeaperasteekos] piercing, sharp || (βροχή) drenching.

διαπερνώ [δeeaperno] pierce, penetrate, pass through.

διαπιστευτήρια, τα [δeeapeestevteereea] credentials.

διαπιστώνω [δeeapeestono] ascertain, find out, confirm.

διαπίστωση, η [δeeapeestosee] ascertainment.

διάπλαση, n [δeeaplasee] (con)formation || moulding.

διαπλάσσω [δeeaplaso] form, shape || (μεταφ) educate, train.

διάπλατα [δeeaplata] wide-open.

διαπλάτυνση, n [δeeaplateensee] widening.

διαπλέω [δeeapleo] cross over, sail through.

διαπληκτισμός, ο [δeeapleekteesmos] dispute, quarrel.

διαπνοή, n [δeeapnoee] respiration.

διαποτίζω [δeeapoteezo] soak, saturate.

διαπραγματεύομαι [δeeapragmatevome] negotiate || discuss.

διαπραγμάτευση, n [δeeapragmatevsee] negotiation.

διαπράττω [δeeaprato] perpetrate, commit.

διαπρεπής [δeeaprepees] eminent, distinguished.

διαπρέπω [δeeaprepo] excel.

διάπυρος [δeeapeeros] red-hot || (μεταφ) fervent, eager.

διάρθρωση, n [δeearthrosee] articulation, joint, structure.

διάρκεια, n [δeearkeea] duration.

διαρκώ [δeearko] last, endure || continue.

διαρκώς [δeearkos] continually, constantly, always.

διαρρέω [δeeareo] traverse || (δοχείο) leak || (υγρού, νέα κτλ) leak out || (χρόνος) elapse, pass.

διαρρηγνύω [δeeareegneeo] tear, burst open, break.

διάρρηξη, n [δeeareeksee] breaking, rupture || (κλοπή) burglary.

διαρροή, n [δeearoee] flow || (σωλήνος) leakage.

διάρροια, n [δeeareea] diarrhoea.

διαρρυθμίζω [δeeareethmeezo] arrange, regulate.

διαρρύθμιση, n [δeeareethmeesee] arrangement, regulation.

διασαφηνίζω [δeeasafeeneezo] clarify, elucidate.

διασαφήνιση, n [δeeasafeeneesee] clarification, elucidation.

διασάφηση, n [δeeasafeesee] βλ **διασαφήνιση**.

διάσειση, n [δeeaseesee] concussion, shock.

διάσελο, το [δeeaselo] pass.

διάσημος [δeeaseemos] famous, celebrated, renowned.

διασκεδάζω [δeeaskeδazo] scatter, dispel || (ψυχαγωγώ) divert, amuse || (αμεταβ) amuse o.s.

διασκέδαση, n [δeeaskeδasee] dispersion || (ψυχαγωγία) entertainment.

διασκεδαστικός [δeeaskeδasteekos] diverting, entertaining.

διασκευάζω [δeeaskevazo] arrange, modify, alter.

διασκευή, n [δeeaskevee] arrangement, adaptation, modification.

διάσκεψη, n [δeeaskepsee] deliberation || conference.

διασκορπίζω [δeeaskorpeezo] scatter, disperse || (χρήμα) waste.

διάσπαση, n [δeeaspasee] distraction || (ατόμου) splitting.

διασπείρω [δeeaspeero] disseminate, disperse, scatter || (μεταφ) circulate.

διασπορά, n [δeeaspora] dispersion, scattering.

διασπώ [δeeaspo] sever, rupture.

διασταλτικός [δeeastalteekos] dilating, dilative.

διάσταση, n [δeeastasee] separation, disagreement || (μέτρο) dimension.

διασταυρώνω [deeastavrono] cross || meet.

διασταύρωση, η [deeastavrosee] crossing || (δρόμων) intersection.

διαστέλλω [deeastelo] distinguish || (διανοίγω) distend, expand.

διάστημα, το [deeasteema] space, interval, period || **κατά διαστήματα** from time to time || at intervals.

διαστολή, η [deeastolee] distinction || (καρδιάς) diastole || (γραμμ) comma.

διαστρεβλώνω [deeastrevlono] twist, bend || (μεταφ) alter, distort.

διαστρέφω [deeastrefo] twist, bend || (μεταφ) pervert, corrupt.

διαστροφή, η [deeastrofee] perversion, distortion.

διασύρω [deeaseero] (μεταφ) defame, slander, backbite.

διασχίζω [deeasheezo] tear || (μεταφ) cross, travel through.

διασώζω [deeasozo] preserve, rescue, deliver.

διάσωση, η [deeasosee] deliverance, rescue, preservation.

διαταγή, η [deeatayee] order, command, instruction.

διάταγμα, το [deeatagma] order, decree, edict.

διάταξη, η [deeataksee] arrangement || (νόμου κτλ) provision.

διατάραξη, η [deeataraksee] disturbance, upheaval.

διαταράσσω [deeataraso] disturb, agitate.

διατάσσω [deeataso] arrange || order, command.

διατείνομαι [deeateenome] maintain, declare.

διατελώ [deeatelo] be, stand.

διατέμνω [deeatemno] intersect, split.

διατήρηση, η [deeateereesee] maintenance, preservation, conservation.

διατηρώ [deeateero] hold, maintain || preserve, conserve || (ψυχραιμία) keep.

διατίμηση, η [deeateemeesee] tariff, rate, price list.

διατιμώ [deeateemo] fix the price of, regulate the sale of.

διατομή [deeatomee] cross-cut, cut.

διατρέφω [deeatrefo] keep, feed, support.

διατρέχω [deeatreho] run through || (απόσταση) cover, traverse.

διάτρηση, η [deeatreesee] perforation, drilling, cutting.

διάτρητος [deeatreetos] perforated, drilled.

διατριβή, η [deeatreevee] stay || (μελέτη) study, thesis || (ασχολία) pastime.

διατροφή, η [deeatrofee] food, board || (εн διαζυγίου) alimony.

διατρυπώ [deeatreepo] pierce, bore through.

διάττων, ο [deeaton] shooting star.

διατυμπανίζω [deeateembaneezo] divulge, let out, give away.

διατυπώνω [deeateepono] formulate, state.

διαύγεια, η [deeavyeea] clearness, transparency.

διαφαίνομαι [deeafenome] show through, appear, come in sight.

διαφανής [deeafanees] clear, transparent.

διαφέρω [deeafero] be different from, differ.

διαφεύγω [deeafevgo] escape, get away, evade.

διαφημίζω [deeafeemeezo] advertise.

διαφήμιση, η [deeafeemeesee] advertisement, advertising.

διαφθείρω [deeaftheero] spoil, damage || (μεταφ) corrupt.

διαφθορά, η [ðeeafthora] corruption, depravity.

διαφορά, η [ðeeafora] difference || dissension, contention.

διαφορετικός [ðeeaforeteekos] different, dissimilar.

διαφορικό, το [ðeeaforeeko] differential.

διαφορικός [ðeeaforeekos] differential.

διάφορο, το [ðeeaforo] profit, interest, gain.

διαφοροποίηση, η [ðeeaforopieesee] differentiation.

διάφορος [ðeeaforos] different, various, mixed || **τα διάφορα** miscellaneous.

διάφραγμα, το [ðeeafragma] partition || (ανατ) diaphragm.

διαφυγή, η [ðeeafeeyee] escape, evasion || (υγρού κτλ) leak, leakage.

διαφύλαξη, η [ðeeafeelaksee] preservation, protection.

διαφυλάσσω [ðeeafeelaso] preserve, protect, keep.

διαφωνία, η [ðeeafoneea] discord, disagreement.

διαφωνώ [ðeeafono] disagree, differ.

διαφωτίζω [ðeeafoteezo] clear up || enlighten.

διαφώτιση, η [ðeeafoteesee] enlightenment.

διαχειρίζομαι [ðeeaheereezome] administer, manage, handle.

διαχείριση, η [ðeeaheereesee] management, handling, administration.

διαχειριστής, ο [ðeeaheereestees] administrator || (στρατ) pay corps officer.

διαχέω [ðeeaheo] diffuse, give out.

διάχυση, η [ðeeaheesee] diffusion || (μεταφ) effusiveness, gaiety.

διαχυτικός [ðeeaheeteekos] effusive, gushing, demonstrative.

διάχυτος [ðeeaheetos] diffuse.

διαχωρίζω [ðeeahoreezo] separate, divide.

διαχώριση, η [ðeeahoreesee] separation.

διαψεύδομαι [ðeeapsevðome] contradict o.s., fail.

διαψεύδω [ðeeapsevðo] deny, give the lie to || disappoint.

διάψευση, η [ðeeapsevsee] denial, contradiction || disappointment.

διγαμία, η [ðeegameea] bigamy.

δίγαμος, ο [ðeegamos] bigamist.

δίγλωσσος [ðeeglosos] bilingual.

δίδαγμα, το [ðeeðagma] teaching, moral || (εκκλ) lesson.

διδακτικός [ðeeðakteekos] instructive, didactic.

διδακτορική, η [ðeeðaktoreekee] (διατριβή) doctorate.

δίδακτρα, τα [ðeeðaktor] πλ tuition fees.

διδάκτωρ, ο [ðeeðaktor] doctor.

διδασκαλία, η [ðeeðaskeleea] teaching, instruction.

διδάσκω [ðeeðasko] teach, instruct.

δίδυμος [ðeeðeemos] twin.

διεγείρω [ðieyeero] excite, rouse, incite.

διέγερση, η [ðieyersees] excitation, stimulation.

διεζυγμένος [ðiezevgmenos] divorced.

διεθνής [ðiethnees] international.

διείσδυση, η [ðieesðeesee] penetration, piercing.

διεισδύω [ðieesðeeo] penetrate, enter, advance.

διεκδίκηση, η [ðiekðeekeesee] claim, vindication.

διεκδικώ [ðiekðeeko] claim, contest.

διεκπεραιώνω [ðiekpereono] bring to a conclusion || (στέλλω) forward.

διεκπεραίωση, η [ðiekpereosee] forwarding, consignment.

διεκφεύγω [ðiekfevgo] slip away, escape.

διέλευση, η [ðielevsee] crossing, passing.

διένεξη, η [ðieneksee] dispute, quarrel.

διενεργώ [ðienergo] operate, effect, hold.

διεξάγω [ðieksago] conduct, accomplish, carry out.

διεξέρχομαι [ðiekserhome] traverse, travel through || (μεταφ) look into.

διεξοδικός [ðieksoðeekos] lengthy, extensive, detailed.

διέξοδος, η [ðieksoðos] issue, outlet || (μεταφ) way out, alternative.

διέπω [ðiepo] govern, rule.

διερεύνηση, η [ðierevneesee] investigation, research.

διερευνητικός [ðierevneeteekos] searching, exploratory.

διερευνώ [ðierevno] search, explore, examine.

διερμηνέας, ο [ðiermeeneas] interpreter, translator.

διερμηνεύω [ðiermeenevo] interpret, translate.

διέρχομαι [ðierhome] pass by, cross.

διερωτώμαι [ðierotome] ask o.s., wonder.

διεσπαρμένος [ðiesparmenos] dispersed.

διεστραμμένος [ðiestramenos] perverse, wicked.

διετής [ðietees] lasting two years || (επί φυτών) biennial.

διετία, η [ðieteea] (space of) two years.

διευθέτηση, η [ðievtheteesee] arrangement, settlement.

διευθετώ [ðievtheto] arrange, settle || adjust.

διεύθυνση, η [ðievtheensee] address || direction || (εταιρείας) management.

διευθυντής, ο [ðievtheentees] director || (σχολής) principal ||

(μουσ) conductor || (θεάτρου) manager || (εφημερίδος) editor || (φυλακών) governor, warden || (σωματείου) president || (προσωπικού) personnel manager.

διευθύνω [ðievtheeno] direct, guide || (επιχείρηση) manage || (εφημερίδα) edit || (βιομηχανία) handle, manage, direct || (έργα) superintend, oversee || (ορχήστρα) lead, conduct.

διευκόλυνση, η [ðievkoleensee] easing, help.

διευκολύνω [ðievkoleeno] facilitate, help forward.

διευκρινίζω [ðievkreeneezo] clear up, explain.

διευκρίνιση, η [ðievkreeneesee] elucidation, explanation.

διεύρυνση, η [ðievreensee] widening, broadening, enlargement.

διεφθαρμένος [ðieftharmenos] corrupt, immoral, dissolute.

δίζυγο, το [ðeezeego] parallel bars.

διήγημα, το [ðieegeema] story, tale.

διήγηση, η [ðieegeesee] narration.

διηγούμαι [ðieegoume] narrate, relate, tell.

διήθηση, η [ðieetheesee] filtration, percolation.

διηρημένος [ðieereemenos] divided, separated.

διίσταμαι [ðieestame] (μεταφ) stand apart || (μεταφ) disagree.

διισχυρίζομαι [ðieesheereezome] maintain.

δικάζω [ðeekazo] try, judge.

δικαιόγραφο, το [ðeekeeografo] title deed.

δικαιοδοσία, η [ðeekeeoðoseea] jurisdiction, province.

δικαιολόγηση, η [ðeekeeoloyeesee] justification, excuse.

δικαιολογητικά, τα [ðeekeeoloyeeteeka] πλ documentary proof.

δικαιολογία, η [δeekeologeea] justification, excuse.

δικαιολογώ [δeekeologo] justify, excuse, vindicate.

δίκαιο, το [δeekeo] justice, right || law.

δίκαιος ο [δeekeos] fair, just, righteous.

δικαιοσύνη, η [δeekeoseenee] justice, fairness.

δικαιούχος, ο [δeekeouhos] beneficiary.

δικαιώνω [δeekeono] side with || justify, vindicate.

δικαίωμα, το [δeekeoma] right, claim.

δικαίωση, η [δeekeosee] justification, vindication.

δίκανο, το [δeekano] double-barrelled shotgun.

δικάσιμος, η [δeekaseemos] day of trial.

δικαστήριο, το [δeekasteereeo] law court, court of justice, tribunal.

δικαστής, ο [δeekastees] judge, justice, magistrate.

δικαστικός [δeekasteekos] judicial, judiciary.

δικέφαλος [δeekefalos] two-headed.

δίκη, η [δeekee] trial, suit, lawsuit, case.

δικηγόρος, ο, [δeekeegoros] lawyer, barrister, attorney.

δικηγορώ [δeekeegoro] practise as a lawyer, plead.

δικογραφία, η [δeekografeea] file of proceedings || (δικηγόρου) brief.

δικονομία, η [δeekonomeea] procedure.

δίκταμο, το [δeektamo] dittany.

δικτατορία, η [δeektatoreea] dictatorship.

δικτατορικός [δeektatoreekos] dictatorial.

δίκτυο, το [δeekteeo] net, network || (μεταφ) snare, trap.

δικτυωτό, το [δeekteeoto] wire netting, lattice, grille, trellis.

δίλημμα, το [δeeleema] dilemma.

διμερής [δeemerees] bipartite.

διμοιρία, η [δeemeereea] platoon, section.

δίνη, η [δeenee] whirlpool, whirlwind.

δίνω [δeeno] give, grant || (τιμή) offer || (παράγω) produce, yield || (μάχη) give battle || (γροθιά) deal a blow to.

διογκώνω [δeeongono] swell, inflate.

διόγκωση, η [δeeongosee] swelling, inflation.

διόδια, τα [δeeoδeea] πλ toll || (ναυτ) port toll.

δίοδος, η [δeeoδos] passage, pass, defile.

διοίκηση, η [δeeekeesee] administration, command.

διοικητήριο, το [δeeekeeteereeo] prefecture, commissioner's office.

διοικητής, ο [δeeekeetees] governor, commissioner, commandant.

διοικητικός [δieekeeteekos] administrative.

διοικώ [δieeko] administer, govern, rule, command.

διόλου [δeeolou] (επιρ) not at all || όλως ~ entirely, quite.

διοξείδιο, το [δeeokseeδeeo] dioxide.

διοπτεύω [δeeoptevo] observe with binoculars || (ναυτ) take bearings of.

διόπτρα, η [δeeoptra] binoculars.

διόραση, η [δeeorasee] perspicuity.

διορατικός [δeeorateekos] clear-sighted || (πνεύμα) shrewd, keen.

διορατικότητα, η [δeeorateekoteeta] perspicacity.

διοργανώνω [δeeorganono] organize, form, arrange.

διοργάνωση, η [δeeorganosee] organization, arrangement.

διορθώνω [đeeorthono] correct, put straight || (παντελόνι) patch, mend || (μεταφ) remedy, make good.

διόρθωση, η [đeeorthosee] correction, putting right.

διορθωτής, ο [đeeorthotees] (τυπογρ) proofreader.

διορία, η [đeeoreea] time limit, term, delay.

διορίζω [đeeoreezo] appoint || order, fix.

διορισμένος [đeeoreesmenos] appointed.

διορισμός, ο [đeeoreesmos] appointment.

διόροφος, ο [đeeorofos] two-storeyed.

διόρυξη, η [đeeoreeksee] digging, excavation.

διότι [đeeotee] because.

διουρητικός [đeeoureeteekos] diuretic.

διοχέτευση, η [đeeohetevsee] (ηλεκ) conduct || (ύδατος) conveyance.

διοχετεύω [đeeohetevo] conduct, convey || (μεταφ) transmit, divert.

δίπατος [đeepatos] two-storeyed.

δίπλα, η [đeepla] fold, pleat, wrinkle.

δίπλα [đeepla] (επιρ) by, near, next door, close.

διπλά [đeepla] twice as much.

διπλανός [đeeplanos] nearby, next-door, adjacent.

διπλαρώνω [đeeplarono] accost || (ναυτ) come alongside.

διπλασιάζω [đeeplaseeazo] double.

διπλασιασμός, ο [đeeplaseeasmos] reduplication.

διπλάσιος [đeeplaseeos] double, twice as much.

διπλός [đeeplos] double.

δίπλωμα, το [đeeploma] diploma, degree || (τύλιγμα) folding, wrapping.

διπλωμάτης, ο [đeeplomatees] diplomat.

διπλωματία, η [đeeplomateea] diplomacy.

διπλωματικός [đeeplomateekos] diplomatic.

διπλωματούχος [đeeplomatouhos] having a diploma, holding a degree.

διπλώνω [đeeplono] fold.

δίπλωση [đeeplosee] folding, wrapping.

δίποδος [đeepodos] two-legged, two-footed.

διπρόσωπος [đeeprosopos] two-faced, deceitful.

δίς [đees] twice.

δισάκκι, το [đeesakee] saddlebag, travelling bag.

δισέγγονο, το [đeesengono] great-grandchild.

δισεκατομμύριο, το [đeesekatomeereeo] billion.

δίσεκτο, το [đeesekto]: ~ έτος leap year.

δισκίο, το [đeeskeeo] (ιατρ) tablet.

δισκοβόλος, ο [đeeskovolos] discus thrower.

δίσκος, ο [đeeskos] tray || (ζυγού) pan, scale || (αθλητ) discus || (πλίου κτλ) disk || (εκκλ) collection plate || (γραμμοφώνου) record.

δισταγμός, ο [đeestagmos] hesitation, doubt.

διστάζω [đeestazo] hesitate, doubt.

διστακτικός [đeestakteekos] hesitant, irresolute.

δίστιχο, το [đeesteeho] distich, couplet.

δισύλλαβος [đeeseelavos] of two syllables.

δίτροχος [đeetrohos] two-wheeled.

διϋλίζω [đieeleezo] filter, distil, strain.

διύλιση [đieeleesee] filtering, straining.

διϋλιστήριο, το [dieeleesteereeo] filter, strainer || (πετρελαίου) refinery.

διφθερίτιδα, η [deefthereeteeða] diphtheria.

δίφθογγος, η [deefthongos] diphthong.

διφορούμενος [deeforoumenos] ambiguous.

δίφραγκο, το [deefrango] two-drachma piece.

δίφυλλος [deefeelos] two-leaved.

διχάζομαι [ðeehazome] (μεταφ) become disunited, disagree.

διχάζω [ðeehazo] divide, split || (μεταφ) estrange, disunite.

διχάλη, η [ðeehalee] pitchfork.

διχαλωτός [ðeehalotos] forked, cloven.

διχασμός, ο [ðeehasmos] division || disagreement.

διχόνοια, η [ðeehoneea] dissension, discord.

διχοτόμος [ðeehotomos] bisector.

διχοτομώ [ðeehotomo] bisect.

δίχρονος [ðeehronos] (μηχανή) two-stroke (engine).

δίχως [ðeehos] without || ~ άλλο without fail.

δίψα, η [ðeepsa] thirst.

διψασμένος [ðeepsasmenos] thirsty, eager (for).

διψώ [ðeepso] feel thirsty || thirst for, be eager for.

διωγμός [ðeeogmos] persecution.

διώκω [ðeeoko] pursue, chase, expel, persecute || (μεταφ) banish, dispel.

δίωξη, η [ðeeoksee] persecution, hunting.

διώρυγα, η [ðeeoreega] canal.

διώχνω [ðeeohno] βλ διώκω.

δόγμα, το [ðogma] dogma, creed, doctrine.

δογματικός [ðogmateekos] dogmatic(al).

δόκανο, το [ðokano] trap || (μεταφ) lure, snare.

δοκάρι, το [ðokaree] beam, rafter, girder.

δοκιμάζω [ðokeemazo] taste, try out || (αυτοκίνητο) test, try || (ρούχα) fit || (υποφέρω) undergo, suffer.

δοκιμασία, η [ðokeemaseea] suffering.

δοκιμαστικός [ðokeemasteekos] trial, test || ~ σωλήνας test tube.

δοκιμή, η [ðokeemee] trial, test, testing || (θέατρο) rehearsal || (ρούχα) fitting.

δοκίμιο, το [ðokeemeeo] treatise || (τυπογρ) printer's proof.

δόκιμος [ðokeemos] esteemed, first-rate || ~ cadet.

δοκός, η [ðokos] girder, beam.

δόλιος [ðoleeos] fraudulent, crafty.

δόλιος [ðoleeos] wretched, unlucky, poor.

δολιότης, η [ðoleeotees] deceit, fraudulence, fraud.

δολοπλόκος [ðoloplokos] treacherous, artful.

δόλος, ο [ðolos] fraud, deceit, guile.

δολοφονία, η [ðolofoneea] murder.

δολοφονικός [ðolofoneekos] murderous.

δολοφόνος, ο, η [ðolofonos] assassin, murderer.

δολοφονώ [ðolofono] murder, assassinate.

δόλωμα, το [ðoloma] bait, decoy.

δόνηση, η [ðoneesee] vibration || (σεισμός) tremor, shock.

δόντι, το [ðontee] tooth || (ελέφαντος) tusk || (μηχαν) cog.

δονώ [ðono] vibrate, shake.

δόξα, η [ðoksa] glory.

δοξάζω [ðoksazo] glorify, celebrate, extol.

δοξάρι, το [ðoksaree] (μουσ) bow.

δοξολογία, η [ðoksoloyeea] doxology, Te Deum.

δόρυ, το [ðoree] spear.

δορυφόρος, ο [ðoreeforos] satellite.

δοσίλογος [ðoseelogos] quisling.

δόση, η [ðosee] portion || dose || (πληρωμή) instalment.

δοσοληψία, η [ðosoleepseea] transaction.

δοτική, η [ðoteekee] (γραμμ) dative (case).

δούκας, ο [ðoukas] duke.

δούκισσα, η [ðoukeesa] duchess.

δουλεία, η [ðouleea] slavery, servitude.

δουλειά, η [ðoulia] work, affair, business.

δούλεμα, το [ðoulema] teasing.

δουλευτής, ο [ðoulevtees] hard worker, industrious worker.

δουλεύω [ðoulevo] work, operate || (έχω δουλειά) have a job || (ρολόι κτλ) work, operate || (περιπαίζω) tease.

δούλη, η [ðoulee] slave.

δουλικός, η [ðouleekos] servile, slavish.

δουλοπρεπής [ðouloprepees] servile, mean.

δούλος, ο [ðoulos] slave || servant.

δουλώνω [ðoulono] enslave, subjugate.

δούπος, ο [ðoupos] thump, bump.

δοχείο, το [ðoheeo] receptacle, vessel, pot.

δρακόντειος [ðrakonteeos] (μεταφ) severe, harsh.

δράκος, ο [ðrakos] ogre, dragon.

δράμα, το [ðrama] drama || (μεταφ) trouble.

δραματική, η [ðramateekee] πλ dramatics.

δραματικός [ðramateekos] dramatic, tragic.

δράμι, το [ðrameeo] dram || (μεταφ) tiny amount.

δραπετεύω [ðrapetevo] escape.

δραπέτης [ðrapetees] fugitive.

δράση, η [ðrasee] activity, action || άμεσος ~ flying squad.

δραστήριος [ðrasteereeos] active, energetic, vigorous.

δραστηριότητα, η [ðrasteereeoteeta] activity, energy, effectiveness.

δράστης, ο, η [ðrastees] perpetrator, culprit.

δραστικός [ðrasteekos] efficacious, drastic, effective.

δραχμή, η [ðrahmee] drachma.

δρεπάνι, το [ðrepanee] sickle.

δριμύς [ðreemees] sharp, bitter, severe, keen.

δρομάς, η [ðromas] dromedary.

δρομέας, ο [ðromeas] runner.

δρομολόγιο, το [ðromoloyeeo] itinerary || timetable.

δρόμος, ο [ðromos] road, street || (αθλητ) race || (απόσταση) distance.

δροσερός [ðroseros] cool, fresh.

δροσιά, η [ðrosia] freshness || dew.

δροσίζομαι [ðroseezome] refresh o.s., cool down.

δροσίζω [ðroseezo] cool, refresh || get cool.

δροσιστικός [ðroseesteekos] refreshing.

δρυμός, ο [ðreemos] forest, wood.

δρυοκολάπτης, ο [ðreeokolaptees] woodpecker.

δρύς, η [ðrees] oak.

δρω [ðro] act, do, take effect.

δυάδα, η [ðeeaða] couple, pair.

δυαδικός [ðeeaðeekos] binary || dual.

δυϊκός [ðieekos] (γραμμ) dual (number).

δύναμαι [ðeename] can, may || be able to.

δυναμική, η [ðeenameekee] dynamics.

δυναμικός [ðeenameekos] energetic, dynamic.

δύναμη, η [ðeenamee] strength, might, power, force.

δυναμίτιδα, η [δeenameeteeδa] dynamite.

δυναμό, το [δeenamo] dynamo.

δυνάμωμα, το [δeenamoma] intensification, strengthening.

δυναμώνω [δeenamono] strengthen, make stronger || (υγεία) become stronger.

δυναμωτικός [δeenamoteekos] fortifying, strengthening || (ιατρ) tonic.

δυναστεία, η [δeenasteea] dynasty, regime, rule.

δυνάστης, ο [δeenastees] ruler, potentate || (μεταφ) oppressor, despot.

δυνατά [δeenata] strongly, hard || loudly.

δυνατός [δeenatos] strong, powerful || (κυβέρνηση) powerful || (φωνή) loud || (άνοδος) possible || δυνατό! possibly!, maybe!

δυνατότητα, η [δeenatoteeta] possibility.

δύο [δeeo] two.

δύοσμος, ο [δeeosmos] mint, spearmint.

δυσανάγνωστος [δeesanagnostos] illegible.

δυσανάλογος [δeesanalogos] disproportionate.

δυσανασχετώ [δeesanasheto] be anxious, be indignant, get angry.

δυσαρέσκεια, η [δeesareskeea] displeasure, discontent.

δυσάρεστος [δeesarestos] unpleasant, disagreeable.

δυσαρεστημένος [δeeasaresteemenos] displeased, dissatisfied.

δυσαρεστώ [δeesaresto] displease, dissatisfy.

δυσβάστακτος [δeesvastaktos] unbearable, heavy, overwhelming.

δύσβατος [δeesvatos] inaccessible, rough.

δυσειδής [δeeseeδees] ugly, unsightly.

δυσεντερία, η [δeesentereea] dysentery.

δυσεπίλυτος [δeesepeeleetos] difficult to solve.

δυσεύρετος [δeesevretos] difficult to find.

δυσθυμία, η [δeestheemeea] sadness, depression.

δύσθυμος [δeestheemos] depressed, sad.

δύση, η [δeesee] west || (ηλίου) setting || (μεταφ) decline.

δύσκαμπτος [δeeskambtos] rigid, stiff, inflexible.

δυσκινησία, η [δeeskeeneeseea] sluggishness.

δυσκοιλιότητα, η [δeeskeeleeoteeta] constipation.

δυσκολεύομαι [δeeskolevome] find difficult, find hard, be hard put to.

δυσκολεύω [δeeskolevo] make difficult, make hard.

δυσκολία, η [δeeskoleea] difficulty.

δυσκολο- [δeeskolo] (first component) difficult, hard.

δύσκολος [δeeskolos] difficult || (άνθρωπος) hard to please.

δυσμένεια, η [δeesmeneea] disfavour, disgrace.

δυσμενής [δeesmenees] adverse, unfavourable.

δύσμορφος [δeesmorfos] deformed, ugly.

δυσνόητος [δeesnoeetos] difficult to understand.

δυσοίωνος [δeeseeonos] inauspicious, ill-omened.

δυσοσμία, η [δeesosmeea] bad smell, stench, offensive odour.

δυσπεπτός [δeespeptos] indigestible.

δυσπιστία, η [δeespeesteea] mistrust, incredulity.

δύσπιστος [δeespeestos]

incredulous, distrustful, unbelieving.

δυσπιστώ [deespeesto] distrust, mistrust.

δύσπνοια, η [deespneea] difficult breathing.

δυσπρόσιτος [deesproseetos] inaccessible.

δυστοκία, η [deestokeea] difficult birth || (μεταφ) indecision.

δύστροπος [deestropos] perverse, peevish.

δυστροπώ [deestropo] behave peevishly.

δυστύχημα, το [deesteeheema] accident, stroke of bad luck.

δυστυχής [deesteehees] unhappy, unfortunate.

δυστυχία, η [deesteeheea] unhappiness, adversity, poverty.

δυστυχισμένος [deesteeheesmenos] βλ **δυστυχής**.

δυστυχώ [deesteeho] be unhappy, be unfortunate, be poor.

δυσφημίζω [deesfeemeezo] defame, slander.

δυσφήμιση, η [deesfeemeesee] calumny, slander.

δυσφόρητος [deesforeetos] hard to endure.

δυσφορώ [deesforo] be displeased || (με κάτι) be discontented.

δυσχεραίνω [deeshereno] impede, make difficult.

δυσχέρεια, η [deeshereea] difficulty || hardship.

δυσχερής [deesherees] difficult.

δύσχρηστος [deeshreestos] unwieldy, inconvenient, awkward.

δυσωδία, η [deesodeea] stench, stink.

δύτης, ο [deetees] diver.

δυτικός [deeteekos] west(ern).

δύω [deeo] set || (μεταφ) decline, wane.

δώδεκα [dodeka] twelve.

δωδεκάγωνο, το [dodekagono] dodecagon.

δωδεκαδάκτυλο, το [dodekadakteelo] duodenum.

δωδεκάδα, η [dodekada] dozen.

δωδεκαετής [dodekaetees] twelve years old.

δωδεκαπλάσιος [dodekaplaseeos] twelve-fold.

δωδέκατος [dodekatos] twelfth.

δώμα, το [doma] flat roof, terrace || apartment.

δωμάτιο, το [domateeo] room || (ύπνου) bedroom.

δωρεά, η [dorea] bequest, present, gift || ~ν (επιρ) gratis, free, for nothing.

δωροδοκία, η [dorodokeea] bribery, corruption.

δωροδοκώ [dorodoko] bribe, corrupt.

δώρο, το [doro] gift, present.

δωσίλογος [doseealogos] responsible, answerable.

Ε, ε

έ [e] (επιφ) well!, hey!, hallo!

εάν [ean] βλ **αν**.

έαρ, το [ear] spring.

εαυτός [eaftos] oneself || **καθ'εαυτού** really, exactly, precisely.

εβδομάδα, η [evdomada] week.

εβδομαδιαίος [evdomadieos] weekly.

έβδομος [evdomos] seventh.

εβραϊκός [evraeekos] Jewish.

Εβραίος, ο [evreos] Hebrew, Jew.

έγγαμος [engamos] married.

εγγίζω [engeezo] draw near || (μεταφ) touch.

εγγλέζικος [engleezeekos] English.

Εγγλέζος, ο [englezos] Englishman.

εγγόνι, το [engonee] grandchild.

εγγονός, ο [engonos] grandson.

εγγραφή, η [engrafee] registration, record, entry.

έγγραφο, το [engrafo] document.

εγγράφω [engrafo] register, enrol || (μάθημ) inscribe.

εγγύηση, η [engieesee] security, guarantee, bail.

εγγύς [engees] near, at hand.

εγγυώμαι [engeeome] guarantee, vouch for.

εγείρω [eyeero] raise, build.

έγερση, η [eyersee] raising, building || (από ύπνο) awakening.

εγκαθίσταμαι [engkatheestame] settle, put up, settle o.s.

εγκαθιστώ [engatheesto] set up, settle, establish.

εγκαίνια, τα [engkeneea] πλ inauguration, opening.

έγκαιρος [engkeros] timely, opportune.

εγκάρδιος [engkarðeeos] cordial, affectionate.

εγκάρσιος [engkarseeos] transverse, slanting, oblique.

εγκαταλείπω [engkataleepo] abandon, desert.

εγκατάσταση, η [engkatastasee] installation, establishing.

έγκαυμα, το [engkavma] burn.

έγκειται [engkeete] **σε σας ~** it rests with you.

εγκέφαλος, ο [engkefalos] brain.

εγκλείω [engkleeo] enclose || confine || lock up.

έγκλημα, το [engkleema] crime | sin || **~ τίας, ο** criminal || **~ τικός** criminal || **~ τικότης, η** delinquency, wrongdoing, crime.

εγκοπή, η [engkopee] incision, notch, groove.

εγκόσμιος [engkosmeeos] mundane, worldly || social.

εγκράτεια, η [engkrateea] sobriety, moderation, temperance.

εγκρίνω [engkreeno] approve, ratify.

έγκριση, η [engkreesee] approval, sanction.

εγκύκλιος, η [engkeekleeos] circular letter.

εγκυκλοπαίδεια, η [engkeeklopeðeea] encyclopaedia.

έγκυος [engkeeos] pregnant.

έγκυρος [engkeeros] valid, sound, well-grounded.

εγκώμιο, το [engkomeeo] praise.

έννοια, η [egneea] care, anxiety, concern.

εγχείρηση, η [engheereesee] operation.

εγχειρίδιο, το [engheereeðeeo] manual.

έγχρωμος [enghromos] coloured.

εγχώριος [enghoreeos] local, native, domestic.

εγώ [ego] I || (ουσ) **το ~** ego || **εγωϊσμός, ο** pride, conceit, selfishness.

έδαφος, το [eðafos] ground, earth, soil.

έδρα, η [eðra] seat, chair || (ανατ) bottom || (εκκλ) see.

εδραιώνω [eðreono] establish, strengthen, make firm.

εδρεύω [eðrevo] reside, have one's seat.

εδώ [eðo] here || **~ και τρία χρόνια** three years ago.

εδώλιο, το [eðoleeo] bench, seat.

εθελοντής, ο [ethelontees] volunteer.

εθελουσίως [ethelouseeos] voluntarily.

έθιμο, το [etheemo] custom, tradition || habit.

εθιμοτυπία, η [etheemoteepeea] formality, etiquette.

εθνάρχης, ο [ethnarhees] national leader.

εθνικός [ethneekos] national.

εθνικότητα, η [ethneekoteeta] nationality.

εθνικόφρων [ethneekofron] patriotic, nationalistic.

έθνος, το [ethnos] nation.

ειδάλλως [eedalos] if not, otherwise.

ειδεμή [eedemee] otherwise.

ειδήμων [eedeemon] expert, skilled, well-informed.

ειδήσεις, οι [eedeesees] πλ news.

ειδικός [eedeekos] special, particular || (άνθρωπος) specialist.

ειδοποίηση, η [eedopieesee] notification, notice.

ειδοποιώ [eedopieo] notify, inform, advise.

είδος, το [eedos] sort, kind, type || (βοτ) species || **τα είδη** goods, wares || kinds.

ειδύλλιο, το [eedeeleeo] love affair || idyll.

ειδωλολάτρης, ο [eedololatrees] pagan, heathen.

είδωλο, το [eedolo] idol || image.

είθισται [eetheeste] it is the custom.

εικασία, η [eekaseea] conjecture, guess.

εικαστικός [eekasteekos] conjectural || **εικαστικαί τέχναι** fine arts.

εικόνα, η [eekona] image, picture || (εκκλ) icon.

εικονίζω [eekoneezo] portray, depict, represent.

εικονικός [eekoneekos] figurative || (επίθεση) sham || (πράξη) bogus || (τιμή) conventional.

εικόνισμα, το [eekoneesma] portrait || (αγιογραφία) icon.

εικονογραφία, η [eekonografeea] illustration || (εκκλ) iconography.

εικονοστάσι(ο), το [eekonostasee(o)] (εκκλ) shrine, screen.

είκοσι [eekosee] twenty.

εικοστός [eekostos] twentieth.

ειλικρίνεια, η [eeleekreeneea] sincerity, frankness.

ειλικρινής [eeleekreenees] sincere, candid.

είμαι [eeme] I am, I'm.

είναι [eene] be, is, it is || **το ~** being.

ειρήνη, η [eereenee] peace.

ειρηνικός [eereeneekos] peaceful.

ειρηνοδικείο, το [eereenodeekeeo] magistrate's court.

ειρμός, ο [eermos] train of thought, continuity.

ειρωνεύομαι [eeronevome] speak derisively, speak ironically.

ειρωνεία, η [eeroneea] irony, mockery.

εις [ees] in, among, at || (χρόνο) within || to, into, on.

εισαγγελέας, ο [eesangeleas] public prosecutor || district attorney (US).

εισάγω [eesago] import || (νομοσχέδιο) introduce || (φέρω πρώτα) introduce for the first time || (παρουσιάζω) present ||

εισαγωγέας, ο importer ||

εισαγωγή, η importation || (παρανόιαση) introduction ||

εισαγωγικά, τα inverted commas.

εισβάλλω [eesvalo] invade || (ποταμός) flow into.

εισβολή, η [eesvolee] invasion.

εισέρχομαι [eeserhome] come in, enter, go in.

εισήγηση, η [eeseeyeesee] report || suggestion.

εισηγούμαι [eeseegoume] propose, move || introduce.

εισιτήριο, το [eeseeteereeo] ticket.

εισόδημα, το [eesodeema] income, revenue.

είσοδος, ο [eesodos] entry, entrance || admission.

εισπνέω [eespneo] inhale, breathe in.

εισπράκτορας, ο [eespraktoras] conductor || collector.

είσπραξη, η [eespraksee] collection || receipt.

εισπράττω [eesprato] collect.

εισφορά, η [eesfora] contribution.

εισχωρώ [eeshoro] penetrate, intrude, get in.

είτε [eete]: ~ ... ~ either ... or, whether ... or.

εκ [ek] from, out of, by, of || **εξ ανάγκης** of necessity || ~ **νέου** again || **εξ ίσου** equally.

εκ-, εξ- [ek, eks] out, off || completely, wholly.

έκαστος [ekastos] each, every one || **καθ' εκάστην** every day || **τα καθ' έκαστα** the details.

εκάστοτε [ekastote] each time.

εκατέρωθεν [ekaterothen] on both sides, mutually.

εκατό [ekato] hundred || **τά ~ per cent.

εκατομμύριο, το [ekatomeereeo] million.

εκατομμυριούχος, ο [ekatomeereeouhos] millionaire.

εκατονταετηρίδα, η [ekatontaeteereeδa] century || centenary.

εκατονταπλάσιος [ekatontaplaseeos] hundredfold.

εκατοστάρι, το [ekatostaree] hundred-drachma note.

εκατοστόμετρο, το [ekatostometro] centimetre.

εκατοστός [ekatostos] hundredth.

εκβάλλω [ekvalo] take out, extract || (απομακρύνω) repudiate || (εχθρό) drive out || (επί ποταμών) flow into.

έκβαση, η [ekvasee] issue, outcome, result.

εκβιάζω [ekveeazo] (κάποιο) force, compel || blackmail || (διάβαση κτλ) force.

εκβολή η [ekvolee] ejection || (ποταμού) mouth, estuary.

έκδηλος [ekδeelos] manifest, evident, obvious.

εκδηλώνω [ekδeelono] show, reveal.

εκδίδω [ekδeeδo] issue, publish || (απόφαση) pronounce || (συναλλαγματική) draw || (εγκληματία κτλ) extradite.

εκδίκηση, η [ekδeekeesee] vengeance, revenge.

εκδικητικός [ekδeekeeteekos] revengeful, vindictive.

εκδικούμαι [ekδeekoume] take revenge on, get even with.

εκδιώκω [ekδeeoko] expel, oust || (στρατ) dislodge, drive out.

εκδορά, η [ekδora] abrasion || skinning.

έκδοση, η [ekδosee] publication, edition || (χαρτονομίσματος) issue || (παραλλαγή) version, story || (εγκληματία κτλ) extradition.

εκδότης, ο [ekδotees] publisher, editor.

εκδοτικός [ekδoteekos] publishing || ~ **οίκος** publishing house.

εκδοχή, η [ekδohee] interpretation, version.

εκδρομή η [ekδromee] excursion, outing, trip.

εκεί [ekee] there || ~ **που** instead of, while, whereas.

εκείνος [ekeenos] he, that one there.

εκεχειρία, η [ekeheereea] truce, armistice.

έκθαμβος [ekthamvos] dazzled, astounded.

έκθεμα, το [ekthema] exhibit.

έκθεση, η [ekthesee] (στο ύπαιθρο) exposure || (ανθέων κτλ) exhibition || (εμπορευμάτων) display, exposition || (γραπτή) composition.

εκθέτης, ο [ekthetees] exhibitor || (μαθημ) exponent.

έκθετος [ekthetos] exposed.

εκθέτω [ektheto] expose, display,

exhibit || (την ζωή) expose, imperil || (τέκνο) abandon || (σχέδια) state, disclose || (μεταφ) lay bare, expose.

εκθρονίζω [ekthroneezo] dethrone.

εκκαθαρίζω [ekathareezo] clear out, clean || (λογαριασμό) liquidate, settle.

εκκεντρικός [ekentreekos] eccentric.

εκκενώ [ekeno] empty (out), vacate || (ποτήρι κτλ) drain || (όπλο) fire || (οικία) leave.

εκκένωση, η [ekenosee] evacuation, emptying || (ηλεκ) discharge.

εκκίνηση, η [ekeeneesee] departure, starting off.

εκκλησία, η [ekleeseea] church || **εκκλησιαστικός** ecclesiastic(al).

έκκληση, η [ekleesee] appeal.

εκκρεμής [ekremees] unsettled, pending.

εκκωφαντικός [ekofanteekos] deafening.

εκλέγω [eklego] choose, pick out || elect.

έκλειψη, η [ekleepsee] eclipse || (μεταφ) disappearance.

εκλεκτικός [eklekteekos] choosy, selective.

εκλεκτός [eklektos] choice, select, picked || **οι εκλεκτοί** élite.

εκλιπαρώ [ekleeparo] entreat, implore.

εκλογέας, ο [eklogeas] elector, voter.

εκλογή, η [eklogee] choice, selection || election.

εκλογές, οι [ekloges] πλ elections.

εκλογικός [eklogeekos] electoral.

εκμαγείο, το [ekmayeeo] (plaster) cast.

εκμαιεύω [ekmeyevo] extract, elicit.

εκμεταλλεύομαι [ekmetalevome] exploit.

εκμηδενίζω [ekmeedeneezo] annihilate.

εκμίσθωση, η [ekmeesthosee] leasing, lease.

εκμισθωτής, ο [ekmeesthotees] lessor, hirer.

εκμυστηρεύομαι [ekmeesteerevome] confide a secret, confess.

εκνευρίζω [eknevreezo] annoy, exasperate.

εκούσιος [ekouseeos] voluntary || willing.

εκπαίδευση, η [ekpedevsee] education, training.

εκπαιδευτήριο, το [ekpedevteereeo] school, institute.

εκπαιδευτικός [ekpedevteekos] educational || (δάσκαλος) schoolteacher.

εκπαιδεύω [ekpedevo] educate, train, instruct.

εκπατρίζω [ekpatreezo] expatriate.

εκπέμπω [ekpembo] send forth, emit || (από ραδιοφώνου) broadcast.

εκπίπτω [ekpeepto] decline, fall || (μεταφ) deduct, reduce, lower.

εκπληκτικός [ekpleekteekos] astonishing, surprising.

έκπληξη, η [ekpleeksee] surprise, astonishment.

εκπληρώ [ekpleero] fulfil, perform.

εκπλήσσω [ekpleeso] surprise, astonish.

εκπνέω [ekpneo] exhale || (πεθαίνω) die || (μεταφ) expire, terminate.

εκποιώ [ekpeeo] sell, dispose of.

εκπομπή, η [ekpombee] emission || (ραδιοφώνου) broadcast.

εκπρόθεσμος [ekprothesmos] overdue.

εκπρόσωπος, ο [ekprosopos] representative.

εκπροσωπώ [ekprosopo] represent.

έκπτωση, η [ekptosee] decline, fall || (δικαιωμάτων) loss || (τιμής κτλ)

reduction, rebate, discount, deduction.

εκρήγνυμαι [ekreegneeme] explode, erupt, burst.

εκρηκτικός [ekreekteekos] explosive.

έκρηξη, η [ekreeksee] explosion, eruption, outburst.

εκσκαφή, η [ekskafee] excavation, cutting.

έκσταση, η [ekstasee] ecstasy, rapture.

εκστρατεία, η [ekstrateea] expedition, campaign.

εκσφενδονίζω [eksfendoneezo] fling, throw, hurl.

έκτακτος [ektaktos] temporary, emergency || (ειδικός) special, exceptional, excellent.

εκτάκτως [ektaktos] temporarily || extraordinarily, unusually.

έκταση, η [ektasee] extent, stretch.

εκτεθειμένος [ektetheemenos] exposed || compromised.

εκτείνω [ekteeno] stretch, extend, prolong.

εκτέλεση, η [ektelesee] execution || performance, fulfilment.

εκτελεστικός [ektelesteekos] executive.

εκτελώ [ektelo] execute || perform, carry out.

εκτενής [ektenees] extensive, lengthy.

εκτεταμένος [ektetamenos] extensive, long.

εκτίθεμαι [ekteetheme] be embarrassed || display.

εκτίμηση, η [ekteemeesee] esteem, estimation, appreciation.

εκτιμώ [ekteemo] esteem, value, appreciate, estimate.

εκτοξεύω [ektoksevo] shoot, cast, hurl.

εκτοπίζω [ektopeezo] displace, dislodge || (εξορίζω) exile.

εκτόπισμα, το [ektopeesma] displacement.

έκτος [ektos] sixth.

εκτός [ektos] outside, save (for) || ~ **της πόλεως** outside the city || ~ **από** apart from, besides, except for || ~ **αν** unless || ~ **κινδύνου** out of danger.

έκτοτε [ektote] ever since, since then.

εκτρέπομαι [ektrepome] deviate from || (μεταφ) go astray.

εκτρέπω [ektrepo] deflect, turn aside, divert.

εκτροχιάζομαι [ektroheeazome] become derailed || (μεταφ) go astray.

έκτρωμα, το [ektroma] monster, freak.

έκτρωση, η [ektrosee] abortion, miscarriage.

εκτυλίσσομαι [ekteeleesome] develop, evolve.

εκτυπώνω [ekteepono] print || emboss.

εκτυφλωτικός [ekteefloteekos] blinding.

εκφέρω [ekfero] express.

εκφοβίζω [ekfoveezo] intimidate, frighten.

εκφορά, η [ekfora] funeral, burial.

εκφορτωτής, ο [ekfortotees] unloader, docker.

εκφράζω [ekfrazo] express, reveal.

έκφραση, η [ekfrasee] expression.

εκφραστικός [ekfrasteekos] expressive.

εκφυλισμός, ο [ekfeeleesmos] degeneration.

εκφωνώ [ekfono] deliver a speech || read aloud.

εκχύλισμα, το [ekheeleesma] extract.

εκχωρώ [ekhoro] transfer, assign, cede || (θέση) make way.

έλα [ela] (επιφ) come, come now.

ελαιογραφία, η [eleografeea] oil painting.

ελαιόλαδο, το [eleolaðo] olive oil.

έλαιο, το [eleo] olive oil, oil.

ελαιοτριβείο, το [eleotreeveeo] olive press.

ελαιόχρωμα, το [eleohroma] oil paint.

ελαιώνας, ο [eleonas] olive grove.

έλασμα, το [elasma] metal plate, sheet iron.

ελαστικό, το [elasteeko] tyre || rubber, elastic.

ελαστικός [elasteekos] flexible, elastic.

ελατήριο, το [elateereeo] spring || (μεταφ) incentive, motive.

έλατο, το [elato] fir, fir tree.

ελάττωμα, το [elatoma] defect, fault.

ελαττώνω [elatono] diminish, lessen, decrease.

ελάττωση, η [elatosee] decrease, curtailment.

ελάφι, το [elafee] deer.

ελαφρόπετρα, η [elafropetra] pumice stone.

ελαφρός [elafros] light, slight || (καφές κτλ) mild, thin, weak.

ελαφρώνω [elafrono] reduce, lighten || feel relieved.

ελάχιστα [elaheesta] very little.

ελάχιστος [elaheestos] least, very little || του λάχιστο(ν) at least.

Ελβετία, η [elveteea] Switzerland.

Ελβετίδα, η [elveteeða] Swiss woman.

ελβετικός [elveteekos] Swiss.

Ελβετός, ο [elvetos] Swiss man.

ελεγκτής, ο [elengtees] inspector, auditor.

έλεγχος, ο [elenghos] inspection, examination || (λογαριασμού) verification, control, auditing || (μηχανής) testing, overhauling || (μεταφ) censure, check, reproach.

ελέγχω [elengho] check, control, test.

ελεεινός [eleyeenos] pitiful, wretched, vile.

ελεημοσύνη, η [eleyeemoseenee] alms, charity.

έλεος, το [eleos] mercy, pity.

ελευθερία, η [elefthereea] liberty, freedom.

ελεύθερος [eleftheros] free || (εργένης) unmarried.

ελευθερώνω [eleftherono] redeem, set free, release, rid.

ελεφαντόδοντο, το [elefantoðonto] tusk || ivory.

έλεφας, ο [elefas] elephant.

ελεώ [eleo] give alms to, commiserate with || ελέησον (επιφ) Lord have mercy!, for Heaven's sake!

ελιά, η [elia] olive, olive tree || (προσώπου κτλ) mole.

ελιγμός, ο [eleegmos] twisting, winding || (στρατ) manoeuvre, movement.

έλικα(ς),η, ο [eleeka(s)] coil, spiral || (προπέλλα) screw, propeller || (βοτ) tendril.

ελικόπτερο, το [eleekoptero] helicopter.

ελίσσομαι [eleesome] wind, coil, twist || (στρατ) manoeuvre.

έλκηθρο, το [elkeethro] sledge, sled.

ελκυστικός [elkeesteekos] attractive, winsome.

ελκύω [elkeeo] charm, attract || draw, pull.

έλκω [elko] draw, pull, haul.

Ελλάδα, η [elaða] Greece.

Ελλάς, η [elas] Greece.

έλλειμμα, το [eleema] deficit, shortage.

έλλειψη, η [eleepsee] lack, want, deficiency || (μαθημ) ellipse.

Έλλην(ας), ο [eleen(as)] Greek (person).

Ελληνίδα, n [eleeneeða] Greek woman.

ελληνικά, τα [eleeneeka] πλ Greek (language).

ελληνικός [eleeneekos] Greek.

ελληνισμός, ο [eleeneesmos] the Greek people.

ελληνιστί [eleeneestee] in Greek.

ελλιπής [eleepees] defective, wanting.

έλξη, n [elksee] pulling, traction, drawing, attraction.

ελονοσία, n [elonoseea] malaria.

έλος, το [elos] marsh, swamp, morass.

ελπίδα, n [elpeeða] hope, expectation || **παρ' ~** contrary to expectation.

ελώδης [eloðees] marshy, swampy.

εμβαδό, το [emvaðo] area.

εμβαθύνω [emvatheeno] (μεταφ) examine thoroughly, probe deeply.

έμβασμα, το [emvasma] remittance (of money).

εμβατήριο, το [emvateereeo] march.

έμβλημα, το [emvleema] emblem, crest, symbol.

εμβολιάζω [emvoleeazo] (φυτό) graft || (άνθρωπο) vaccinate, inoculate.

εμβόλιο, το [emvoleeo] vaccine || (φυτό) graft.

έμβολο, το [emvolo] piston, rod || (πλοίου) ram.

εμβρόντητος [emvronteetos] thunderstruck, stupefied.

έμβρυο, το [emvreeo] embryo, foetus.

εμένα [emena] me.

εμείς [emees] we.

εμετικός [emeteekos] emetic.

εμετός, ο [emetos] vomiting.

εμμένω [emeno] adhere to || persist, insist.

έμμεσος [emesos] indirect.

έμμηνα, τα [emeena] πλ menstruation.

έμμισθος [emeesthos] salaried, paid.

έμμονος [emonos] persistent, obstinate, persevering.

εμπάθεια, n [empatheea] animosity, ill feeling.

εμπαίζω [empezo] tease, mock, deceive.

εμπειρία, n [embeereea] experience, skill.

εμπειρογνώμων, ο, n [embeerognomon] expert, specialist.

έμπειρος [embeeros] experienced, skilled (in), able.

εμπιστεύομαι [embeestevome] (εν)trust, confide.

εμπιστευτικός [embeestevteekos] confidential.

έμπιστος [embeestos] trustworthy, reliable, faithful || **εμπιστοσύνη, n** trust, confidence.

εμπλοκή, n [emblokee] (στρατ) engagement || (μηχανής) jamming || gear of car.

εμπλουτίζω [emblouteezo] enrich.

εμπνέομαι [embneome] feel inspired.

έμπνευση, n [embnevsee] inspiration.

εμπνέω [embneo] inspire.

εμποδίζω [emboðeezo] hinder, obstruct, prevent || hold back, impede.

εμπόδιο, το [emboðeeo] obstacle, impediment, obstruction.

εμπόρευμα, το [emborevma] merchandise.

εμπορεύομαι [emborevome] engage in commerce || deal in, trade in.

εμπορικός [emboreekos] commercial, mercantile.

εμπόριο, το [emboreeo] trade, commerce.

έμπορος, ο [emboros] merchant, trader, vendor.

εμποροϋπάλληλος, ο, η [emboroeepaleelos] shop assistant || clerk (*US*).

εμπρησμός, ο [embreesmos] arson.

εμπρηστικός [embreesteekos] incendiary || (μεταφ) fiery.

εμπρόθεσμος [embrothesmos] within the time limit.

εμπρός [embros] forward(s), before, in front of || ~ **σε** compared with || **πηγαίνω** ~ to succeed || ~ **από** in front of || **το ρολόι πάει** ~ the clock is fast || ~ **μου** in front of me || ~! hallo, come in || **βάζω** ~ to start.

εμφανής [emfanees] apparent, obvious, clear.

εμφανίζομαι [emfaneezome] appear, present o.s., make an appearance.

εμφανίζω [emfaneezo] exhibit, reveal || (φωτογρ) develop.

εμφάνιση, η [emfaneese] appearance, presentation || (φωτογρ) development.

έμφαση, η [emfasee] stress, emphasis.

εμφύλιος [emfeeleeos]: ~ **πόλεμος** civil war.

έμφυτος [emfeetos] innate, inherent, intuitive.

εμψυχώνω [empseehono] encourage, stimulate.

εν [en] in, at, within || ~ **τούτοις** however, nevertheless || ~ **τάξει** all right.

εν(α), το [en(a)] one || a, an.

εναγόμενος [enagomenos] defendant.

ενάγω [enago] sue, bring action against.

εναγωνίως [enagoneeos] anxiously, with anguish.

εναέριος [enaereeos] aerial, overhead || airy.

εναλλαγή, η [enalayee] permutation, exchange, interchange.

εναλλάξ [enalaks] alternately, in turn.

εναλλάσσω [enalaso] alternate, exchange.

έναντι [enantee] towards, against || **βλ και απέναντι.**

ενάντια [enanteea] adversely, contrarily || ~ **σε** against.

εναντίο(ν) [enanteeo(n)] against || contrary to.

εναντίο(ν), το [enanteeo(n)] the contrary.

ενάντιος [enanteeos] adverse, contrary, opposite || **απ' εναντίας** on the contrary.

εναπόκειται [enapokeete]: **σε σένα** ~ it's up to you.

ενάρετος [enaretos] virtuous, upright.

έναρθρος [enarthros] articulate, jointed.

εναρκτήριος [enarkteereeos] inaugural.

εναρμονίζω [enarmoneezo] harmonize.

έναρξη, η [enarksee] opening, beginning, inauguration.

ένας, ο [enas] one || a, an || ~ **one by one** || ~ **κι** ~ especially good, very bad || **ο** ~ **τον άλλο** one another.

ενασχόληση, η [enasholeesee] occupation, employment.

ένατος [enatos] ninth.

ένδεια, η [endeea] deficiency || poverty.

ενδεικνύομαι [endeekneeome] be called for, be necessary.

ενδεικνύω [endeekneeo] indicate.

ενδεικτικό, το [endeekteeko] certificate.

ενδεικτικός [endeekteekos] indicative.

ένδειξη, η [endeeksee] indication, sign.

ένδεκα [endeka] eleven.

ενδέχεται [endehete] it is possible, it is likely.

ενδεχόμενο, το [endehomeno] eventuality, possibility.

ενδιάμεσος [endeeamesos] intermediate, in-between.

ενδιαφέρομαι [endeeaferome] be interested in.

ενδιαφέρον, το [endeeaferon] interest, concern.

ενδιαφέρω [endeeafero] concern, interest || ~ν interesting.

ενδίδω [endeedho] give way to || give way, bend.

ένδικος [endeekos] legal, judicial.

ενδοιάζω [endeeazo] hesitate, waver.

ενδο- [endo] (combining form) within, in.

ένδοξος [endoksos] celebrated, glorious, illustrious.

ενδότερος [endoteros] inner, interior.

ενδοχώρα, η [endohora] hinterland.

ένδυμα, το [endeema] dress, garment, clothes || ~σία, η suit, dress, garb.

ενέδρα, η [enedra] ambush.

ένεκα [eneka] on account of, because of.

ενενήντα [eneneenta] ninety.

ενέργεια, η [enerya] energy, action || (φαρμάκου) efficacy.

ενεργητικός [eneryeeteekos] energetic, active || (φάρμακο) effective.

ενεργός [energos] active || effective.

ενεργούμαι [energoume] move the bowels || take place.

ενεργώ [energo] act, take steps ||

(φάρμακο κτλ) take effect, work || (καθαρτικό) purge.

ένεση, η [enesee] injection.

ενεστώς, ο [enestos] (γραμμ) present tense.

ενετικός [eneteekos] Venetian.

ενεχυροδανειστής, ο [eneheerodhaneestees] pawnbroker.

ενήλικας [eneeleekas] of age, adult.

ενηλικιούμαι [eneeleekeeoume] come of age, reach majority.

ενήμερος [eneemeros] aware, informed.

ενημερώνω [eneemerono] inform, bring up to date.

ενθάρρυνση, η [enthareensee] encouragement, cheering up.

ενθαρρύνω [enthareeno] encourage, cheer up, hearten.

ένθερμος [enthermos] ardent, warm, hearty.

ενθουσιάζομαι [enthouseeazome] be enthusiastic about.

ενθουσιασμός, ο [enthouseeasmos] enthusiasm.

ενθύμιο, το [entheemeeo] keepsake, souvenir, memento.

ενθυμούμαι [entheemoume] recall, remember, recollect.

ενιαίος [enieos] single, uniform.

ενικός [eneekos] (γραμμ) singular (number).

ενίσχυση, η [eneesheesee] reinforcement, strengthening || (πλεκ) amplification.

ενισχύω [eneesheeo] support, reinforce, assist.

εννέα [ennea] nine || ~ κόσιοι nine hundred.

εννιά [ennia] nine.

έννοια, η [ennea] sense, concept, meaning, interpretation.

έννοια, η [enyea] concern, worry || (σκοτούρα) anxiety || ~ σου (επιρ) take care!, don't worry!

έννομος [ennomos] lawful, legal, legitimate.

εννοείται [ennoeete] it is understood, certainly.

εννοώ [ennoo] understand, mean, intend.

'ενοικιάζεται [eneekeeazete] 'to let', 'for rent'.

ενοικιάζω [eneekeeazo] rent, let, hire.

ενοικιαστής, ο [eneekeeastees] tenant || (νομ) lessee.

ενοίκιο, το [eneekeeo] rent.

ένοικος, ο [eneekos] tenant, lodger.

ένοπλος [enoplos] armed, in arms.

ενορία, η [enorea] parish.

ενόρκως [enorkos] under oath, on oath.

ενόσω [enoso] as long as.

ενότητα, η [enoteeta] unity, concord.

ενοχή, η [enohee] guilt, culpability.

ενόχληση, η [enohleesee] trouble, annoyance, inconvenience.

ενοχλητικός [enohleeteekos] troublesome, inconvenient, annoying.

ενοχλώ [enohlo] trouble, annoy, pester, inconvenience.

ενσάρκωση, η [ensarkosee] incarnation, embodiment.

ένσημο, το [enseemo] stamp.

ενσκήπτω [enskeepto] happen suddenly, break out || break into.

ένσταση, η [enstasee] objection.

ένστικτο, το [ensteekto] instinct.

ένταλμα, το [entalma] warrant, writ.

ένταση, η [entasee] strain, tension || intensity, intensification.

εντατικός [entateekos] intensive.

ενταύθα [entavtha] here || (ένδειξη επιστολής) in town, local.

εντείνω [enteeno] stretch || (τις προσπάθειες) intensify || (τις σχέσεις) overstrain.

έντεκα [enteka] eleven.

εντέλεια, η [enteleea] perfection.

εντελώς [entelos] completely, entirely, totally.

εντερικός [entereekos] intestinal.

έντερο, το [entero] intestine.

εντεταλμένος [entetalmenos] responsible for, charged with || (ουσ) delegate.

έντεχνος [entehnos] skilful, artistic, ingenious.

έντιμος [enteemos] honest || (οικογένεια κτλ) respectable, honourable.

έντοκος [entokos] with interest.

εντολή, η [entolee] order, mandate || authorization, commission.

εντομοκτόνο, το [entomoktono] insecticide.

έντομο, το [entomo] insect.

έντονος [entonos] (προσπάθεια) strenuous, intense || (φως) strong || (χρώμα) bright, deep.

εντοπίζω [entopeezo] localize || (πυρκαϊά) restrict, confine.

εντόπιος [entopeeos] local, native, indigenous.

εντός [entos] within, inside, in, into || ~ ολίγου soon.

εντόσθια, τα [entostheea] πλ entrails, intestines.

εντριβή, η [entreevee] massage || (μηχανική) friction.

έντυπο, το [enteepo] printed matter.

έντυπος [enteepos] printed.

εντυπωσιακός [enteeposeeakos] impressive, striking.

εντύπωση, η [enteeposee] impression, sensation, feeling.

ενώ [eno] while, whereas, since.

ενώνω [enono] unite, join, connect.

ενώπιον [enopeeon] in the presence of, in front of.

ένωση, η [enosee] union || (ηλεκτ) short circuit.

εξ [eks] βλ εκ.

εξαγοράζω [eksagorazo] buy off, redeem, ransom, obtain by bribery.

εξαγριώνω [eksagreeono] infuriate, enrage.

εξάγω [eksago] take out, extract || (εμπόριο) export || (φίλοο) deduce.

εξαγωγή, η [eksagoyee] export || (οδόντος) extraction.

εξάδελφος, ο [eksaðelfos] cousin.

εξαερίζω [eksaereezo] ventilate, air.

εξαεριστήρας, ο [eksaereesteeras] ventilator.

εξαίρεση, η [ekserese] exception, exemption (from), immunity (from).

εξαιρετικός [eksereteekos] exceptional, unusual, excellent, remarkable.

εξαίρετος [ekseretos] excellent, remarkable.

εξαιρώ [eksero] except, exempt.

εξαίσιος [ekseseeos] excellent, splendid.

εξακολουθώ [eksakoloutho] continue.

εξακόσιοι [eksakosiee] six hundred.

εξακριβώνω [eksakreevono] verify, ascertain, establish, clear up.

εξαλείφω [eksaleefo] efface, rub out, remove, obliterate.

έξαλλος [eksalos] beside o.s., frenzied.

εξάμβλωμα, το [eksamvloma] monstrosity.

εξαναγκάζω [eksanangazo] compel, force, coerce.

εξάνθημα, το [eksantheema] rash, pimples.

εξανίσταμαι [eksaneestame] rebel, protest.

εξαντλώ [eksantlo] exhaust.

εξαπατώ [eksapato] cheat, deceive, delude || be unfaithful to.

εξάπλωση, η [eksaplosee] spreading out, extension.

εξαπολύω [eksapoleeo] let loose, hurl.

εξάπτω [eksapto] excite, provoke || (περίεργεια κτλ) rouse, stir.

εξαργυρώνω [eksargeerono] cash, turn into money.

εξάρθρωση, η [eksarthrosee] dislocation.

έξαρση, η [eksarsee] (μεταφ) elevation, exaltation.

εξαρτήματα, τα [eksarteemata] πλ gear, tackle, rigging, accessories.

εξάρτηση, η [eksarteesee] dependence.

εξαρτώμαι [eksartome] depend on, turn on.

εξασθένηση, η [eksastheneesee] weakening, enfeeblement.

εξάσκηση, η [eksaskeesee] exercise, practice, training.

εξασκώ [eksasko] exercise, practise || (πίεση) exert.

εξασφαλίζω [eksasfaleezo] assure || (θέση) book, reserve.

εξατμίζω [eksatmeezo] evaporate || (μεταφ) vanish, melt away.

εξάτμιση, η [eksatmeesee] evaporation || (αυτοκινήτου) exhaust.

εξαφανίζομαι [eksafaneezome] disappear, vanish.

εξαφανίζω [eksafaneezo] eliminate, wipe out, destroy.

έξαφνα [eksafna] all of a sudden.

έξαψη, η [eksapsee] fit of anger || excitement, elation.

εξεγείρομαι [ekseyeerome] rise, rebel.

εξέδρα, η [ekseðra] platform, stand || (λιμανιού) pier.

εξελιγμένος [ekseleegmenos] developed, evolved.

εξέλιξη, η [ekseleeksee] evolution, development.

εξελίσσομαι [ekseleesome] unfold, evolve, develop.

εξερευνητής, ο [ekserevneetees] explorer.

εξερευνώ [ekserevno] investigate, explore.

εξέρχομαι [ekserhome] go out, leave || βλ και **βγαίνω**.

εξετάζω [eksetazo] examine, interrogate, investigate.

εξέταση, η [eksetasee] examination, inspection.

εξεύρεση, η [eksevresee] discovery, finding out, invention.

εξευτελίζω [eksevteleezo] cheapen, lower, humiliate.

εξέχω [ekseho] stand out, project || excel.

έξη, η [eksee] habit, custom, use.

εξήγηση, η [ekseeyeesee] explanation, interpretation.

εξηγούμαι [ekseegoume] explain, make clear, give an explanation.

εξηγώ [ekseego] explain || interpret.

εξή(κο)ντα [eksee(ko)nta] sixty.

εξημερώνω [ekseemerono] tame.

εξηντλημένος [ekseentleemenos] exhausted, used up.

εξής [eksees]: **ως ~** as follows || **τα ~** the following || **στο ~** henceforth || **και ούτω καθ' ~** and so on.

εξιλεώνω [ekseeleono] appease, pacify || atone for.

εξίσταμαι [ekseestame] be astonished, wonder at.

εξίσωση, η [ekseesosee] balancing, equalizing || (μαθημ) equation.

εξόγκωμα, το [eksongoma] swelling, tumour, bulge.

εξογκώνω [eksongono] swell || (μεταφ) exaggerate.

έξοδο, το [eksodo] expense.

έξοδος, η [eksodos] opening, emergence || (πόρτα) exit || (στρατ) sortie || (εκκλ) exodus.

εξοικειώνω [ekseekeeono] familiarize, accustom.

εξολοθρεύω [eksolothrevo] exterminate, destroy.

εξομαλύνω [eksomaleeno] smooth down || level.

εξομοιώνω [eksomeeono] assimilate to, liken to, rank together.

εξομολόγηση, η [eksomoloyeesee] confession, acknowledgement.

εξομολογώ [eksomologo] confess.

εξοντώνω [eksontono] annihilate, exterminate.

εξοπλίζω [eksopleezo] arm, equip.

εξοργίζω [eksoryeezo] enrage, make angry.

εξορία, η [eksoreea] banishment, exile.

εξορίζω [eksoreezo] exile, banish.

εξορκίζω [eksorkeezo] conjure, exorcise.

εξουδετερώνω [eksoudeterono] neutralize.

εξουσία, η [eksousea] power, authority, government.

εξουσιοδοτώ [eksouseeodoto] give authority to, authorise, empower.

εξοφλώ [eksoflo] (λογαριασμό) pay off, liquidate || (μεταφ) fulfil.

εξοχή, η [eksohee] countryside || (εδαφική) eminence, protrusion || **κατ' ~** preeminently, par excellence.

εξοχικός [eksoheekos] country, rural, rustic.

έξοχος [eksohos] excellent, eminent, notable.

εξοχότης, η [eksohotees] excellence || **η αυτού ~** His Excellency.

εξύβριση, η [ekseevreesee] abuse, insult, offence.

εξυμνώ [ekseemno] praise, celebrate.

εξυπακούεται [ekseepakouete] it is understood, it follows.

εξυπηρέτηση, η [ekseepeereeteesee] assistance, service, attendance.

εξυπηρετικός [ekseepeereteekos] helpful, useful.

εξυπηρετώ [ekseepeereto] serve, assist, attend upon.

εξυπνάδα, η [ekseepnaδa] cleverness, shrewdness.

έξυπνος [ekseepnos] clever, intelligent, smart, witty.

εξυψώνω [ekseepsono] elevate, raise || (μεταφ) exalt, extol, glorify.

έξω [ekso] out, outside, without, abroad || απ' ~ from outside || (μάθημα) by heart || ~ από outside, except for || μια και ~ at one go.

εξώγαμος [eksogamos] illegitimate, bastard.

εξώθυρα, η [eksotheera] outside door, gateway.

εξωθώ [eksotho] drive, push, force.

εξωκκλήσι, το [eksokleesee] chapel, (country) church.

εξώπορτα, η [eksoporta] βλ **εξώθυρα.**

εξωραΐζω [eksoraeezo] beautify, decorate, embellish.

έξωση, η [eksosee] eviction, expulsion.

εξώστης, ο [eksostees] balcony.

εξωτερικό, το [eksotereeko] exterior || foreign country, abroad.

εξωτερικός [eksotereekos] external || foreign.

εξωτικό, το [eksoteeko] spook, spectre, wraith.

εξωτικός [eksoteekos] exotic || outlandish.

εξωφρενικός [eksofreneekos] crazy || maddening || unreasonable, absurd.

εξώφυλλο, το [eksofeelo] cover, flyleaf || (παραθύρου) shutter.

εορτάζω [eortazo] celebrate.

εορτή, η [eortee] holiday || name day || festival.

επάγγελμα, το [epangelma] profession, vocation ||

επαγγελματίας, ο craftsman, businessman.

έπαθλο, το [epathlo] prize, trophy.

έπαινος, ο [epenos] praise.

επαινώ [epeno] praise, speak highly of.

επακόλουθα, τα [epakoloutha] nλ consequences.

επακολουθώ [epakoloutho] follow, come after.

επάκρο, το [epakro]: **στο ~** extremely, to the extreme.

επαλείφω [epaleefo] smear (with), anoint (with).

επαληθεύω [epaleethevo] establish, verify.

επάλληλος [epaleelos] successive, one after another.

επανάγω [epanago] bring back (again).

επανακτώ [epanakto] recover.

επαναλαμβάνω [epanalamvano] repeat, resume.

επανάληψη, η [epanaleepsee] resumption, repetition.

επανάσταση, η [epanastasee] revolution.

επαναστάτης, ο [epanastatees] revolutionary, rebel.

επαναστατικός [epanastateekos] revolutionary.

επαναστατώ [epanastato] revolt, rebel.

επαναφέρω [epanafero] restore, bring back.

επανειλημμένος [epaneeleemenos] repeatedly.

επανέρχομαι [epanerhome] return.

επάνοδος, η [epanoδos] return.

επανόρθωση, η [epanorthosee] reparation, restoration.

επαξίως [epakseeos] deservedly, worthily.

επάρατος [eparatos] (μεταφ) hateful, abominable.

επάρκεια, η [eparkeea] sufficiency, adequacy.

έπαρση, η [eparsee] conceit, haughtiness.

επαρχία, η [eparheea] province, district.

επαρχιώτης, ο [eparheeotees] provincial.

έπαυλη, η [epavlee] villa || country house.

επαφή, η [epafee] contact, touch.

επείγομαι [epeegome] be in a hurry, make haste.

επειγόντως [epeegontos] urgently.

επείγων [epeegon] urgent, pressing.

επειδή [epeedee] because, as, for, since.

επεισόδιο, το [epeesodeeo] episode, incident || (καυγάς) quarrel, dispute.

έπειτα [epeeta] next, then, afterwards || moreover || ~ από after.

επέκταση, η [epektasee] extension.

επεκτείνω [epekteeno] extend, prolong.

επεμβαίνω [epemveno] interfere, intervene.

επέμβαση, η [epemvasee] intervention, interference || (ιατρ) operation.

επένδυση, η [ependeesee] lining, covering || (οικον) investment.

επεξεργασία, η [epeksergaseea] processing, elaboration.

επεξήγηση, η [epekseeyeesee] explanation, elucidation.

επέρχομαι [eperhome] come suddenly, occur, happen.

επέτειος, η [epeteeos] anniversary.

επευφημώ [epefeemo] cheer, applaud.

επί [epee] on, upon, over, above || (διάρκεια) for || ~ πλέον furthermore || ~ τέλους at last.

επιβάλλομαι [epeevalome] assert o.s. || be indispensable.

επιβάλλω [epeevalo] impose, inflict.

επιβαρύνω [epeevareeno] burden.

επιβατηγό, το [epeevateego] passenger ship.

επιβάτης, ο [epeevatees] passenger.

επιβατικό, το [epeevateeko] passenger vehicle, passenger ship.

επιβεβαιώνω [epeeveveono] confirm, corroborate.

επιβιβάζομαι [epeeveevazome] embark, go on board.

επιβιβάζω [epeeveevazo] put aboard.

επιβλαβής [epeevlavees] harmful.

επιβλέπω [epeevlepo] supervise.

επιβλητικός [epeevleeteekos] imposing.

επιβολή, η [epeevolee] imposition, infliction.

επιβουλεύομαι [epeevoulevome] plot against.

επιβραδύνω [epeevradeeno] retard, delay.

επίγειος [epeeyeeos] earthly, worldly.

επίγνωση, η [epeegnosee] knowledge, understanding.

επίγραμμα, το [epeegrama] epigram.

επιγραφή, η [epeegrafee] inscription || (βιβλίου) title.

επιδεικνύομαι [epeedeekneeome] show off, be pompous.

επιδεικνύω [epeedeekneeo] display || show off.

επιδεικτικός [epeedeekteekos] showy.

επιδείνωση, η [epeedeenosee] aggravation.

επίδειξη, η [epeedeeksee] display || showing off.

επιδέξιος [epeedekseeos] skilful.

επιδερμίδα, η [epeeðermeeða] complexion || epidermis.

επίδεσμος, ο [epeeðesmos] bandage.

επιδέχομαι [epeedehome] allow, be susceptible to, tolerate.

επιδημία, η [epeedeemeea] epidemic.

επιδιόρθωση, η [epeedeeorthosee] repair, mending.

επιδιώκω [epeedeeoko] aim at, pursue, seek.

επιδοκιμάζω [epeedokeemazo] approve.

επίδομα, το [epeedoma] allowance, extra pay.

επίδοση, η [epeedosee] presentation, delivery || (νομ) deposit || (μεταφ) progress, development || (αθλητ) record.

επίδραση, η [epeedrasee] effect, influence.

επιδρομή, η [epeedromee] invasion, raid.

επιδρώ [epeedro] influence, act upon.

επιεικής [epieekees] lenient, indulgent.

επιζήμιος [epeezeemeeos] harmful, injurious.

επιζώ [epeezo] survive, outlive.

επίθεση, η [epeethesee] attack || application.

επιθετικός [epeetheteekos] aggressive.

επίθετο, το [epeetheto] adjective || surname.

επιθεώρηση, η [epeetheoreesee] inspection || (περιοδικό) review || (θέατρο) revue.

επιθυμία, η [epeetheemeea] desire, wish.

επιθυμώ [epeetheemo] wish for, desire.

επίκαιρος [epeekeros] timely, opportune || topical.

επικαλούμαι [epeekaloume] invoke.

επίκειμαι [epeekeeme] be imminent || impend.

επικερδής [epeekerðees] profitable.

επικεφαλίδα, η [epeekefaleeða] headline || title.

επικίνδυνος [epeekeenðeenos] dangerous, hazardous.

επικοινωνία, η [epeekeenoneea] contact, communication.

επικοινωνώ [epeekeenono] communicate.

επικός [epeekos] epic.

επικράτεια, η [epeekrateea] state, dominion.

επικρατώ [epeekrato] prevail, predominate.

επικρίνω [epeekreeno] criticize, censure.

επικροτώ [epeekroto] approve.

επικυρώνω [epeekeerono] ratify, confirm, sanction.

επιλαχών, ο [epeelahon] runner-up.

επιληψία, η [epeeleepseea] epilepsy.

επιλογή, η [epeeloyee] selection, choice.

επίλογος, ο [epeelogos] epilogue || conclusion.

επιλοχίας, ο [epeeloheeas] sergeant-major.

επίμαχος [epeemahos] disputed || controversial.

επιμελής [epeemelees] diligent, industrious, careful.

επιμελητήριο, το [epeemeleeteereeon] (εμπορικό) chamber of commerce.

επιμελητής, ο [epeemeleetees] superintendent || (university) tutor.

επιμελούμαι [epeemeloume] take care of.

επιμένω [epeemeno] insist, persist.

επιμήκης [epeemeekees] oblong, elongated.

επιμονή, η [epeemonee] insistence, perseverance.

επίμονος [epeemonos] persistent, stubborn, obstinate.

επινοώ [epeenoo] invent, contrive, devise.

επίπεδο, το [epeepedo] level || (βιοτικό) standard of living.

επίπεδος [epeepedos] plane, level, flat || even.

επιπίπτω [epeepeepto] fall upon.

έπιπλα, τα [epeepla] πλ furniture.

επιπλέω [epeepleo] float || (μεταφ) keep afloat.

επίπληξη, η [epeepleeksee] reproach, rebuke.

επιπλήττω [epeepleeto] reproach, chide.

επιπλοκή, η [epeeplokee] complication.

επιπλώνω [epeeplono] furnish.

επίπλωση, η [epeeplosee] furnishing.

επιπόλαιος [epeepoleos] superficial || frivolous.

επίπονος [epeeponos] laborious, toilsome.

επίρρημα, το [epeereema] adverb.

επιρροή, η [epeeroee] influence.

επίσημος [epeeseemos] official, formal.

επίσης [epeesees] likewise, also, too.

επισιτισμός, ο [epeeseeteesmos] provisioning, provisions.

επισκεπτήριο, το [epeeskepteereeo] visiting card || visiting hour.

επισκέπτης, ο [epeeskeptees] visitor.

επισκέπτομαι [epeeskeptome] visit, call upon.

επισκευάζω [epeeskevazo] repair, mend.

επισκευή, η [epeeskevee] repairing, mending.

επίσκεψη, η [epeeskepsee] visit, call.

επίσκοπος, ο [epeeskopos] bishop.

επισπεύδω [epeespevdo] hasten, rush.

επιστάτης, ο [epeestatees] supervisor || overseer || attendant.

επιστήθιος [epeesteetheeos]: ~ φίλος bosom friend.

επιστήμη, η [epeesteemee] science.

επιστημονικός [epeesteemoneekos] scientific.

επιστήμων, ο, η [epeesteemon] scientist, professional (person) || expert.

επιστολή, η [epeestolee] letter.

επιστράτευση, η [epeestratevsee] mobilization, call-up.

επιστρέφω [epeestrefo] return.

επιστροφή, η [epeestrofee] return.

επίστρωμα, το [epeestroma] covering.

επισυνάπτω [epeeseenapto] annex, attach.

επισύρω [epeeseero] attract, draw, catch one's eye.

επισφαλής [epeesfalees] precarious, risky || unstable.

επιταγή, η [epeetayee] order || cheque.

επιτακτικός [epeetakteekos] imperative.

επίταξη, η [epeetaksee] requisition.

επιτάφιος, ο [epeetafeeos] Good Friday procession.

επιταχύνω [epeetaheeno] accelerate, speed up.

επιτελείο, το [epeeteleeo] (general) staff.

επιτετραμμένος, ο [epeetetramenos] chargé d'affaires.

επίτευγμα, το [epeetevgma] achievement.

επίτευξη, η [epeetevksee] attainment || obtaining.

επιτήδειος [epeeteedeeos] suitable for || clever, skilful.

επίτηδες [epeeteedes] on purpose, purposely.

επιτηδευμένος [epeeteedevmenos] affected.

επιτηρώ [epeeteero] supervise, oversee, watch.

επιτίθεμαι [epeeteetheme] attack, assail, assault.

επίτιμος [epeeteemos] honorary.

επιτόκιο, το [epeetokeeo] compound interest.

επίτομος [epeetomos] abridged, shortened, condensed.

επί τόπου [epeetopou] on the spot.

επιτρέπω [epeetrepo] allow, permit.

επιτροπή, η [epeetropee] committee, commission.

επίτροπος, ο [epeetropos] guardian, trustee || commissioner.

επιτυγχάνω [epeeteenghano] attain, get || get right || (κατά τύχην) meet, find || (στη δουλειά) succeed.

επιτυχής [epeeteehees] successful.

επιτυχία, η [epeeteeheea] success.

επιφάνεια [epeefaneea] surface.

επιφανής [epeefanees] eminent, prominent.

Επιφάνια, τα [epeefaneea] πλ Epiphany.

επιφέρω [epeefero] bring about, cause.

επιφυλακή, η [epeefeelakee]: σε ~ at the ready, on the alert.

επιφύλαξη, η [epeefeelaksee] circumspection || reservation.

επιφυλάσσομαι [epeefeelasome] reserve, intend.

επιφώνημα, το [epeefoneema] (γραμμ) interjection.

επιχείρημα, το [epeeheereema] argument || attempt.

επιχειρηματίας, ο [epeeheereemateeas] businessman.

επιχείρηση, η [epeeheereesee] undertaking || (οικον) enterprise, business || (στρατ) operation.

επιχρυσώνω [epeehreesono] gild.

εποικοδομητικός [epeekodomeeteekos] constructive, edifying.

επόμενος [epomenos] next, following.

επομένως [epomenos] consequently, therefore.

επονομάζω [eponomazo] surname, name.

εποπτεύω [epoptevo] supervise, oversee, inspect.

επουλώνω [epoulono] heal.

εποχή, η [epohee] epoch, era || (του έτους) season.

επτά [epta] seven.

επτακόσιοι [eptakosiee] seven hundred.

επώδυνος [epodeenos] painful.

επωμίδα, η [epomeeda] epaulette.

επωμίζομαι [epomeezome] shoulder (a burden).

επωνυμία, η [eponeemeea] (nick)name || surname || (εταιρείας) title.

επώνυμο, το [eponeemo] surname, family name.

επωφελής [epofelees] profitable, beneficial, useful.

επωφελούμαι [epofeloume] take advantage, avail o.s., profit.

έρανος, ο [eranos] fund, collection.

εραστέχνης, ο [eraseetehnees] amateur.

εραστής, ο [erastees] lover.

εργάζομαι [ergazome] work || function.

εργαλείο, το [ergaleeo] tool, implement.

εργασία, η [ergaseea] work, job, business || (επιδεξιότητα) workmanship.

εργαστήριο, το [ergasteereeo] laboratory || studio || workshop.

εργάτης, ο [ergatees] labourer, worker || (ναυτ) windlass.

εργατιά, η [ergateea] working class.

εργατικός [ergateekos] industrious, of the working class.

εργένης, ο [ergenees] bachelor.

εργοδηγός, ο [ergodeegos] foreman.

εργοδότης, ο [ergodotees] employer.

εργολάβος, ο [ergolavos] contractor.

έργο, το [ergo] work || act, deed || (βιβλίο) book || (σινεμά) film.

εργοστάσιο, το [ergostaseeo] factory || works.

εργόχειρο, το [ergoheero] handiwork || (κέντημα) embroidery.

ερεθίζω [eretheezo] irritate, excite.

ερεθισμός, ο [eretheesmos] irritation.

ερείπιο, το [ereepeeo] ruin, wreck.

έρευνα, η [erevna] (re)search, investigation.

ερευνητής, ο [erevneetees] researcher || explorer.

ερευνώ [erevno] search, investigate.

ερημιά, η [ereemeea] solitude || wilderness.

έρημος, η [ereemos] desert || (επιθ) desolate, deserted.

ερημώνω [ereemono] lay waste, devastate.

έριδα, η [ereeda] dispute, quarrel.

ερίφι, το [ereefee] kid.

έρμαιο, το [ermeo] prey || victim.

ερμηνεία, η [ermeeneea] interpretation.

ερμηνεύω [ermeenevo] interpret.

ερμητικός [ermeeteekos] hermetic.

ερπετό, το [erpeto] reptile.

έρπω [erpo] crawl, creep.

ερυθρόδερμος, ο [ereethrodermos] redskin.

ερυθρός [ereethros] red.

έρχομαι [erhome] come.

ερχόμενος [erhomenos] coming, next.

ερχομός, ο [erhomos] coming, arrival.

ερωμένη, η [eromenee] mistress.

ερωμένος, ο [eromenos] lover.

έρωτας, ο [erotas] love, passion.

ερωτευμένος [erotevmenos] in love.

ερωτεύομαι [erotevome] fall in love.

ερώτημα, το [eroteema] question, problem.

ερωτηματικό, το [eroteemateeko] question mark.

ερωτηματολόγιο, το [eroteematoloyeeo] questionnaire.

ερώτηση, η [eroteese] question, query.

ερωτικός [eroteekos] erotic || amatory.

ερωτύλος [eroteelos] amorous.

ερωτώ [eroto] ask, inquire || question.

εσκεμμένος [eskemenos] premeditated || deliberately.

εσοδεία, η [esodeea] crop, harvest.

έσοδο, το [esodo] income, revenue, receipt.

εσοχή, η [esohee] recess, indentation.

εσπεριδοειδή, τα [espereedoeedee] πλ citrus fruits.

εσπερινός, ο [espereenos] vespers.

εσπευσμένος [espevsmenos] hasty, hurried.

εστία, η [esteea] hearth, fireplace || (σπίτι) home || (ηλίκνου) cradle || (σόμπας) burner.

εστιατόριο, το [esteeatoreeo] restaurant.

έστω [esto] so be it || ~ και even, if.

εσύ [esee] you.

εσχάρα, η [eshara] grill, gridiron, grid.

έσχατος [eshatos] extreme, utmost, last.

έσω [eso] within, inside.

εσωκλείω [esokleeo] enclose.

εσώρρουχα, τα [esorouha] πλ underclothes, underwear.

εσωτερικός [esotereekos] interior, inner, internal || domestic.

εταιρεία, n [etereea] company, society, firm, partnership.

ετερογενής [eterogenees] heterogeneous.

έτερος [eteros] (an)other || **αφ' ετέρου** on the other hand.

ετήσιος [eteeseeos] annual, yearly.

ετικέττα, n [eteeketa] label, price tag.

ετοιμάζομαι [eteemazome] get ready, prepare.

ετοιμάζω [eteemazo] prepare, make ready.

ετοιμασία, n [eteemaseea] preparation.

έτοιμος [eteemos] ready.

έτος, το [etos] year.

έτσι [etsee] thus, so, like this, like that, in this way || ~ **κι** ~ middling || in any case, || ~ **κι αλλοιώς** in any case, either way.

ετυμηγορία, n [eteemeegoreea] verdict.

ετυμολογία, n [eteemologeea] etymology.

ευ- [ev] well, easily.

ευαγγέλιο, το [evangeleeo] gospel.

Ευαγγελισμός, ο [evangeleesmos] Annunciation.

ευάερος, ο [evaeros] well-ventilated, airy.

ευαισθησία, n [evestheeseea] sensitivity.

ευαίσθητος [evestheetos] sensitive.

ευανάγνωστος [evanagnostos] legible.

εύγε [evye] (επιφ) bravo!, good show!

ευγένεια, n [evgeneea] courtesy, politeness.

ευγενικός [evyeneekos], **ευγενής** [evyenees] polite, courteous.

εύγευστος [evyevstos] palatable, tasty.

ευγλωττία, n [evgloteea] eloquence.

ευγνωμοσύνη, n [evgnomoseenee] gratitude.

ευγνώμων [evgnomon] grateful, thankful.

ευδαιμονία, n [evðemoneea] prosperity || happiness.

ευδιάθετος [evðeeathetos] in good humour.

ευδιάκριτος [evðeeakreetos] discernible, distinct.

ευδοκιμώ [evðokeemo] succeed || thrive || prosper.

ευδοκώ [evðoko] be pleased to, deign, consent.

ευέξαπτος [eveksaptos] irritable, excitable.

ευεργέτης, ο [everyetees] benefactor.

ευεργετικός [everyeteekos] beneficial, beneficent, charitable.

εύζωνας, ο [evzonas] evzone.

εύηλιος [eveeleeos] sunny.

ευημερώ [eveemero] prosper.

ευθεία, n [evtheea] straight line || **κατ'** ~ direct, straight.

εύθετος [evthetos] suitable, proper, convenient.

εύθικτος [evtheektos] touchy, sensitive.

εύθραυστος [evthravstos] fragile, brittle.

ευθύγραμμος [evtheegramos] straight, rectilinear.

ευθυμία, n [evtheemeea] gaiety, cheerfulness.

εύθυμος [evtheemos] merry, gay, cheerful.

ευθύνη, n [evtheenee] responsibility.

ευθύνομαι [evtheenome] be responsible, be accountable.

ευθύς [evthees] (επιρ) immediately, at once.

ευθύς [evthees] straight, upright || (τίμιος) honest, straightforward.

ευκαιρία, η [evkeereea] opportunity, chance || (εμπόριο) bargain.

εύκαιρος [evkeros] opportune || (ελεύθερος) available, free.

ευκάλυπτος [evkaleeptos] eucalyptus.

εύκαμπτος, ο [evkambtos] flexible, pliable.

ευκατάστατος [evkatastatos] well-to-do, well-off.

ευκίνητος [evkeeneetos] agile, nimble.

ευκοιλιότητα, η [evkeeleeoteeta] diarrhoea.

ευκολία, η [evkoleea] ease, convenience || (χάρη) favour.

εύκολος [evkolos] easy || convenient.

ευκολύνω [evkoleeno] facilitate.

ευκρατής [evkratees] temperate, mild.

ευλαβής [evlavees] devout, pious.

ευλογία, η [evloyeea] blessing, benediction.

ευλογιά, η [evloya] smallpox.

ευλογώ [evlogo] bless.

ευλύγιστος [evleeyeestos] flexible, supple, pliant.

ευμενής [evmenees] benevolent, kind, well-disposed.

ευμετάβλητος [evmetavleetos] changeable, inconstant.

ευνόητος [evnoeetos] easily understood || intelligible.

εύνοια, η [evneea] favour, goodwill.

ευνοϊκός [evnoeekos] propitious, favourable.

ευνοούμενος [evnooumenos] favourite.

ευνοώ [evnoo] favour.

ευπαθής [evpathees] sensitive, delicate.

ευπαρουσίαστος [evparouseeastos] presentable, imposing.

εύπιστος [evpeestos] credulous, gullible.

εύπορος [evporos] well-off, prosperous.

ευπρέπεια, η [evprepeea] propriety || decency.

ευπρεπίζω [evprepeezo] put in order || adorn, embellish.

ευπρόσδεκτος [evprosðektos] welcome, acceptable.

ευπρόσιτος [evproseetos] accessible, approachable.

ευρετήριο, το [evreteereeo] index, catalogue.

ευρέως [evreos] widely, largely.

εύρημα, το [evreema] find, discovery.

ευρίσκω [evreesko] βλ **βρίσκω**.

ευρύς [evrees] wide, extended, broad.

ευρύχωρος [evreehoros] spacious, roomy.

ευρωπαϊκός [evropaeekos] European.

Ευρώπη, η [evropee] Europe.

ευσέβεια, η [evseveea] piety, devoutness.

ευσεβής [evsevees] pious, devout.

ευσπλαγχνία, η [evsplanghneea] compassion, pity.

ευστάθεια, η [evstatheea] stability, firmness.

εύστοχος [evstohos] well-aimed, proper.

εύστροφος [evstrofos] agile, nimble, versatile.

ευσυνείδητος [evseeneeðeetos] conscientious || scrupulous.

εύσωμος [evsomos] well-built, stout, sturdy.

ευτέλεια, η [evteleea] meanness, baseness, cheapness.

ευτελής [evtelees] cheap, mean, worthless.

ευτύχημα, το [evteeheema] good luck, lucky thing.

ευτυχής [evteehees] lucky, fortunate, happy.

ευτυχία, η [evteeheea] happiness, good fortune.

ευτυχισμένος [evteeheesmenos] βλ **ευτυχής.**

ευτυχώς [evteehos] luckily, happily, fortunately.

ευυπόληπτος [eveepoleeptos] reputable, esteemed.

εύφλεκτος [evflektos] inflammable.

ευφορία, η [evforeea] fruitfulness, fertility.

ευφράδεια, η [evfraðeea] eloquence.

ευφυής [evfiees] intelligent, witty, clever.

ευφυΐα, η [evfieea] intelligence, wit, ingenuity.

ευχαρίστηση, η [evhareesteese] satisfaction, pleasure.

ευχαριστίες, οι [evhareesties] πλ thanks.

ευχάριστος [evhareestos] pleasant, agreeable.

ευχαρίστως [evhareestos] gladly, with pleasure.

ευχαριστώ [evhareesto] thank || please, gratify || thank you.

ευχέρεια, η [evhereea] ease, facility.

ευχή, η [evhee] prayer || wish || blessing.

εύχομαι [evhome] wish, hope.

εύχρηστος [evhreestos] useful, handy || in general use.

εφ [ef] βλ **επί.**

εφάμιλλος [efameelos] equal to, on a par with, a match for.

εφάπαξ [efapaks] in a lump sum, once only.

εφαπτόμενη, η [efaptomenee] tangent.

εφαρμογή, η [efarmoyee] application, fitting.

εφαρμόζω [efarmozo] fit || apply || enforce.

έφεδρος, ο [efeðros] reservist.

εφεξής [efeksees] henceforth, hereafter.

έφεση, η [efesee] (νομ) appeal.

εφετείο, το [efeteeo] court of appeal.

εφέτος [efetos] this year.

εφεύρεση, η [efevresee] invention.

εφευρετικός [efevreteekos] inventive, ingenious.

έφηβος, ο [efeevos] youth, adolescent.

εφηβικός [efeeveekos] of youth, of puberty || **εφηβική ηλικία** adolescence.

εφημερεύω [efeemerevo] be on duty.

εφημερίδα, η [efeemereeða] newspaper, journal, gazette.

εφιάλτης, ο [efeealtees] nightmare.

εφικτός [efeektos] possible, attainable, feasible.

εφιστώ [efeesto]: ~ **την προσοχή** draw attention to.

εφόδια, τα [efoðeea] πλ supplies, equipment || **εφοδιάζω** supply, equip, furnish.

έφοδος, η [efoðos] charge, assault, attack.

εφοπλιστής, ο [efopleestees] shipowner.

εφορεία, η [eforeea] tax office, revenue department.

έφορος, ο [eforos] inspector, director, keeper, curator.

εφτά [efta] βλ **επτά.**

εφτακόσιοι [eftakosiee] βλ **επτακόσιοι.**

εχεμύθεια, η [ehemeetheea] secrecy, discretion || **υπό** ~ **ν** under pledge of secrecy.

εχθές [ehthes] yesterday.

έχθρα, η [ehthra] enmity, hostility.

εχθρεύομαι [ehthrevome] hate, dislike.

εχθρικός [ehthreekos] hostile, (of the) enemy, inimical.

εχθρικότητα, η [ehthreekoteeta] hostility.
εχθροπραξίες, οι [ehthropraksies] πλ hostilities.
εχθρός, ο [ehthros] enemy, foe.
έχιδνα, η [eheeðna] viper, adder.
έχω [eho] have, keep || consider || cost, be worth || ~ **δίκιο** I am right || **τι έχεις;** what's wrong?, what's the matter?
έψιλο, το [epseelo] the letter E.
έως [eos] till, until, to || as far as.

Ζ, ζ

ζαβολιά, η [zavolia] cheating, trickery.
ζαβός [zavos] crooked, perverse || clumsy.
ζακέτα, η [zaketa] jacket.
ζαλάδα, η [zalaða] giddiness, dizziness || headache.
ζάλη, η [zalee] dizziness.
ζαλίζομαι [zaleezome] become dizzy, become confused.
ζαλίζω [zaleezo] make dizzy, confuse, daze, stun.
ζαμπό, το [zapo] ham.
ζάπλουτος [zaploutos] very rich, opulent.
ζάρα, η [zara] crease, wrinkle.
ζάρια, τα [zareea] πλ dice.
ζαρκάδι, το [zarkaðee] roe(buck).
ζάρωμα, το [zaroma] creasing, wrinkling || crease, wrinkle.
ζαρώνω [zarono] crease, wrinkle || shrink.
ζαφείρι, το [zafeeree] sapphire.
ζαχαρένιος [zahareneeos] sugary || (μεταφ) honeyed.
ζάχαρη, η [zaharee] sugar.
ζαχαροκάλαμο, το [zaharokalamo] sugar cane.
ζαχαροπλαστείο, το [zaharoplasteeo] confectioner's (shop), cake shop.

ζαχαρωτά, τα [zaharota] πλ sweets.
ζεματίζω [zemateezo] scald || be very hot.
ζεματιστός [zemateestos] scalding, boiling.
ζενίθ, το [zeneeth] zenith.
ζερβός [zervos] left-handed || left.
ζέση, η [zesee] boiling || (μεταφ) warmth, fervour.
ζεσταίνομαι [zestenome] get warm, feel hot.
ζεσταίνω [zesteno] heat up, warm.
ζεστασιά, η [zestasia] warmth, heat.
ζέστη, η [zestee] heat, warmth || **κάνει ~** it's hot, it's warm.
ζεστός [zestos] hot, warm.
ζευγαράκι, το [zevgarakee] pair (of lovers).
ζευγάρι, το [zevgaree] pair, couple || (βοδιών) yoke.
ζευγνύω [zevgneeo] yoke, harness, link.
ζεύγος, το [zevgos] pair, couple.
ζεύξη, η [zevksee] yoking || bridging, junction.
ζέφυρος, ο [zefeeros] light breeze.
ζήλεια, η [zeeleea] envy, jealousy.
ζηλευτός [zeelevtos] enviable, desirable || much desired.
ζηλεύω [zeelevo] envy, be jealous of.
ζηλιάρης [zeeleearees] envious, jealous.
ζήλος, ο [zeelos] zeal, ardour, eagerness.
ζηλότυπος [zeeloteepos] βλ **ζηλιάρης.**
ζημιά, η [zeemeea] damage, loss, injury || harm.
ζημιώνω [zeemeeono] damage, cause a loss, injure.
ζήτα, το [zeeta] the letter Z.
ζήτημα, το [zeeteema] question, subject, matter || **είναι ~** it's doubtful (whether).

ζήτηση, η [zeeteesee] demand || search, pursuit.

ζητιανεύω [zeeteeanevo] beg, ask for alms.

ζητιάνος, ο [zeeteeanos] beggar.

ζήτω [zeeto] (επιφ) long live!, up with!

ζητώ [zeeto] seek, ask for, look for, demand || beg.

ζητωκραυγή, η [zeetokravgee] cheer.

ζιζάνιο, το [zeezaneeo] (μεταφ) naughty person || (βοτ) weed.

ζόρι, το [zoree] force, violence || difficulty || **με το ~** against one's will.

ζορίζω [zoreezo] force, exert pressure on.

ζόρικος [zoreekos] hard, difficult || (επι ανθρώπου) hard to please, irksome.

ζούγκλα η [zoungla] jungle.

ζουζούνι, το [zouzounee] insect.

ζούλισμα, το [zouleesma] squeezing, crushing.

ζουμερός [zoumeros] juicy, succulent.

ζουμί, το [zoumee] juice || broth || (ψητού) gravy.

ζουμπούλι, το [zoumboulee] hyacinth.

ζούρλα, η [zourla] lunacy, folly.

ζουρλομανδύας, ο [zourlomandeeas] strait jacket.

ζοφερός [zoferos] dark, gloomy.

ζοχάδα, η [zohaða] peevishness, sourness, sullenness.

ζυγαριά, η [zeegaria] pair of scales, balance.

ζυγίζομαι [zeeyeezome] hover over.

ζυγίζω [zeeyeezo] weigh.

ζυγός, ο [zeegos] yoke || (παλαντζας) scale, beam.

ζυγός [zeegos] even (number) || **μονά ζυγά** odd or even.

ζυγώνω [zeegono] draw near.

ζύθος, ο [zeethos] beer, ale.

ζυμάρι, το [zeemaree] dough || ζυμαρικά pastry, pies, cakes.

ζύμη, η [zeemee] leaven, dough.

ζύμωμα, το [zeemoma] kneading.

ζυμώνομαι [zeemonome] ferment.

ζυμώνω [zeemono] knead || ferment.

ζύμωση, η [zeemosee] fermentation.

ζω [zo] live, experience || lead a life.

ζωγραφιά, η [zografia] painting, drawing.

ζωγραφική, η [zografeekee] painting.

ζωγραφιστός [zografeestos] painted.

ζωγράφος, ο [zografos] painter, artist.

ζώδιο, το [zoðeeo] sign of the zodiac.

ζωέμπορος, ο [zoemboros] cattle dealer.

ζωή, η [zoee] life, living || lifetime.

ζωηρεύω [zoeerevo] become lively || brighten up.

ζωηρός [zoeeros] lively, vivid || (θερμός) warm, animated || (χρώματος) bright || (εύθυμος) gay, full of life.

ζωηρότητα, η [zoeeroteeta] heat, warmth || (κινήσεως) quickness, promptness || (βλέμματος) vivacity, brightness.

ζωικός [zoeekos] animal || vital, necessary.

ζωμός, ο [zomos] broth, soup.

ζωνάρι, το [zonaree] belt, sash, girdle, waistband.

ζώνη, η [zonee] zone || βλ και **ζωνάρι.**

ζωντανεύω [zontanevo] revive, return to life.

ζωντάνια, η [zontaneea] liveliness, alertness.

ζωντανός [zontanos] living, live, vivid || lively.

ζωντοχήρα 89 ημερολόγιο

ζωντοχήρα, n [zontoheera] divorced woman, divorcée.

ζωντοχήρος, ο [zontoheeros] divorced man, divorcé.

ζωογονώ [zoogono] animate || (μεταφ) stimulate, excite.

ζωοκλοπή, η [zooklopee] cattle rustling, sheep stealing.

ζωολογία, η [zooloyeea] zoology.

ζώο, το [zoo] animal || (μεταφ) fool, ass.

ζωοτροφές, οι [zootrofes] πλ animal fodder, food stuffs.

ζωόφιλος [zoofeelos] fond of animals.

ζωπυρώ [zopeero] rekindle, revive.

ζωτικός [zoteekos] vital.

ζωτικότητα, η [zoteekoteeta] vitality || (μεταφ) vital importance.

ζωύφιο, το [zoeefeeo] insect, louse || πλ vermin.

Η, η

η [ee] the.

ή [ee] or || ~ ... ~ either ... or || (συγκριτικός) than.

ήβη, η [eevee] puberty.

ηγεμόνας, ο [eeyemonas] prince, sovereign || governor.

ηγεσία, η [eeyeseea] leadership.

ηγέτης, ο [eeyetees] leader, chief.

ηγούμαι [eegoume] lead, command.

ηγούμενος, ο [eegoumenos] abbot.

ήδη [eedee] already, even now.

ηδονή, η [eedonee] delight, sensual pleasure, lust.

ηδονικός [eedoneekos] delightful || sensual.

ηθική, η [eetheekee] ethics || morality.

ηθικό, το [eetheeko] morale || morality, morals.

ηθικός [eetheekos] ethical, moral || virtuous, modest.

ηθογραφία, η [eethografeea] folk customs, folklore.

ηθοποιία, η [eethopieea] acting.

ηθοποιός, ο, η [eethopeeos] actor, actress.

ήθη, τα [eethee] πλ manners, habits, customs.

ήθος, το [eethos] character, nature, manner.

ηλεκτρίζω [eelektreezo] electrify.

ηλεκτρικό, το [eelektreeko] electricity.

ηλεκτρικός [eelektreekos] electric.

ηλεκτρισμός, ο [eelektreesmos] electricity.

ηλεκτρολόγος, ο [eelektrologos] electrician.

ηλεκτρονική, η [eelektroneekee] πλ electronics.

ηλεκτρόνιο, το [eelektroneeo] electron.

ηλεκτροπληξία, η [eelektropleekseea] electric shock.

ηλιακός [eeleeakos] of the sun, solar.

ηλίαση, η [eeleeasee] sunstroke.

ηλίθιος [eeleetheeos] idiotic, stupid, silly.

ηλικία, η [eeleekeea] age.

ηλικιωμένος [eeleekeeomenos] aged, advanced in years.

ηλιοβασίλεμα, το [eeleeovaseelema] sunset.

ηλιοθεραπεία, η [eeleeotherapeea] sunbathing.

ηλιοκαμένος [eeleeokamenos] sunburnt, tanned.

ήλιος, ο [eeleeos] sun || (φυτό) sunflower.

ημέρα, η [eemera] day || της ~ς fresh, today's.

ημερεύω [eemerevo] tame, domesticate || calm down, appease.

ημερήσιος [eemereeseeos] daily, everyday.

ημερολόγιο, το [eemeroloyo]

calendar, almanac || (πλοίου) logbook || (ατόμου) diary.

ημερομηνία, η [eemeromeeneea] date.

ημερομίσθιο, το [eemeromeestheeo] daily wage.

ήμερος [eemeros] domesticated || tame, gentle.

ημερώνω [eemerono] tame || calm down, pacify.

ημιαργία, η [eemeearyeea] half-day (holiday).

ημιεπίσημος [eemiepeeseemos] semi-official.

ημιθανής [eemeethanees] half-dead.

ημίθεος, ο [eemeetheos] demigod.

ημικύκλιο, το [eemeekeekleeo] semicircle.

ημιμαθής [eemeemathees] half-learned (person), having a smattering of learning.

ημίμετρα, τα [eemeemetra] πλ half-measures.

ημιπληγία, η [eemeepleeyeea] stroke, paralysis.

ημισέληνος, η [eemeeseleenos] crescent.

ήμισυ, το [eemeesee] half.

ημισφαίριο, το [eemeesfereeo] hemisphere.

ημιτελής [eemeetelees] half-finished.

ημίφως, το [eemeefos] twilight || dim light.

ημίχρονο, το [eemeehrono] (αθλητ) half-time.

ημίωρο, το [eemeeoro] half-hour.

ηνίο, το [eeneeo] rein, bridle.

ηνωμένος [eenomenos] united, joint || **Ηνωμένο Βασίλειο** United Kingdom || **Ηνωμένες Πολιτείες (Αμερικής)** United States (of America).

ήπαρ, το [eepar] liver.

ήπειρος, η [eepeeros] continent || mainland, land.

ηπειρωτικός [eepeeroteekos] continental.

ήπιος [eepeeos] mild, indulgent || (ασθένεια) benign.

ηρεμία, η [eeremeea] quietness, tranquility, serenity.

ήρεμος [eeremos] calm, tranquil, peaceful, still.

ηρεμώ [eeremo] be calm || keep quiet, keep still.

ηρωικός [eeroeekos] heroic.

ηρωίνη, η [eeroeenee] heroin.

ήρωας, ο [eeroas] hero.

ηρωίδα, η [eeroeeda] heroine.

ηρωισμός, ο [eeroeesmos] heroism.

ησυχάζω [eeseehazo] grow quiet, rest, calm down.

ησυχία, η [eeseeheea] quietness, peace, serenity.

ήσυχος [eeseehos] quiet, peaceful, composed.

ήτα, το [eeta] the letter H.

ήττα, η [eeta] defeat, beating.

ηττοπάθεια, η [eetopatheea] defeatism.

ήττον, το [eeton] less.

ηττώμαι [eetome] be defeated, succumb.

ηφαίστειο, το [eefesteeo] volcano.

ηχηρός [eeheeros] loud, ringing, resonant.

ηχητικός [eeheeteekos] producing sound, resounding.

ήχος, ο [eehos] sound.

ηχώ, η [eeho] echo, sound || (μεταφ) repercussion.

ηχώ [eeho] ring, sound, strike, reverberate.

Θ, θ

θα [tha] shall, will, should, would.

θάβω [thavo] bury, inter || (μεταφ) hide.

θαλαμηγός, η [thalameegos] yacht.

θάλαμος, ο [thalamos] room || (νοσοκομείου) ward || (ποπλότου κτλ) inner tube || (όπλου) chamber.

θάλασσα η [thalassa] sea || **τα κάνω ~** mess up, fail.

θαλασσινά, τα [thalaseena] πλ shellfish.

θαλασσοδέρνω [thalassoðerno] buffet || (μεταφ) struggle against (adversity).

θαλασσολύκος, ο [thalasoleekos] sea dog, mariner.

θαλασσοπόρος, ο [thalasoporos] navigator, seafarer.

θαλασσώνω [thalasono]: **τα ~** turn things topsy-turvy, mess it up.

θαλερός [thaleros] green, in bloom || (μεταφ) fresh, vigorous.

θάμβος, το [thamvos] astonishment, wonder.

θάμνος, ο [thamnos] bush, shrub, scrub.

θαμπός [thambos] (χρώμα) lifeless, without lustre || dim, cloudy.

θάμπωμα, το [thamboma] dazzle || astonishment || (ματιού) dimness || (μυαλού) confusion.

θαμπώνω [thambono] dazzle || tarnish, blur, dim || grow dim.

θαμώνας, ο [thamonas] habitué, regular customer, frequent visitor.

θανάσιμος [thanaseemos] deadly, fatal.

θανατηφόρος [thanateeforos] deadly, murderous.

θανατικός [thanateekos] capital, of death.

θάνατος, ο [thanatos] death.

θανατώνω [thanatono] execute.

θανή, η [thanee] death || funeral.

θαρραλέος [tharaleos] plucky, daring, bold.

θαρρετός [tharetos] βλ **θαρραλέος.**

θαρρεύω [tharevo] venture, dare, hazard.

θάρρος, το [tharos] daring, courage, spunk, mettle.

θαρρώ [tharo] believe, think.

θαύμα, το [thavma] miracle, wonder.

θαυμάζω [thavmazo] wonder at, admire, be amazed at.

θαυμάσιος [thavmaseeos] admirable, marvellous, superb.

θαυμασμός, ο [thavmasmos] wonder, admiration, astonishment.

θαυμαστής, ο [thavmastees] admirer, fan.

θαυμαστικό, το [thavmasteeko] exclamation mark.

θαυμαστικός [thavmasteekos] admiring.

θαυμαστός [thavmastos] admirable, astonishing.

θαυματουργός [thavmatourgos] wondrous, miracle-making, miraculous.

θάψιμο, το [thapseemo] burial.

θεά, η [thea] goddess.

θέα, η [thea] view, sight, aspect.

θέαμα, το [theama] spectacle, show || **θεαματικός** spectacular, wonderful.

θεατής, ο [theatees] spectator, onlooker.

θεατός [theatos] visible, perceptible.

θεατρικός [theatreekos] theatrical || (μεταφ) pompous, showy.

θεατρίνος, ο [theatreenos] actor.

θέατρο, το [theatro] theatre, stage.

θεία, η [theea] aunt.

θειάφι, το [theeafee] sulphur.

θεϊκός [theyeekos] divine.

θείος, ο [theeos] uncle.

θείος [theeos] divine, holy, sacred.

θέλγητρο, το [thelyeetro] charm, enchantment, attraction.

θέλγω [thelgo] charm, enchant, fascinate.

θέλημα, το [theleema] will, wish, desire || θελημτικός voluntary || willing.

θέληση, η [theleesee] will, volition, will power.

θελκτικός [thelkteekos] seductive, attractive, captivating.

θέλω [thelo] wish, want, require, need || be willing || ~ να πω I mean to say || θέλει δεν θέλει whether he likes it or not.

θέμα, το [thema] subject, point, topic || (γραμμ) stem, theme.

θεμέλιο, το [themeleeo] foundation || (μεταφ) basis, groundwork.

θεμιτός [themeetos] lawful, legal || permissible.

θεόγυμνος [theoyeemnos] stark naked.

θεοκρατία, η [theokrateea] theocracy.

θεολογία, η [theoloyeea] theology.

θεολογικός [theoloyeekos] theological.

θεολόγος, ο [theologos] theologian.

θεομηνία, η [theomeeneea] natural disaster, calamity.

θεοποιώ [theopeeo] (μεταφ) idolize, praise, laud.

θεόρατος [theoratos] enormous, colossal.

θεός, ο [theos] god.

θεοσεβής [theosevees] pious, devout.

θεότητα, η [theoteeta] deity.

Θεοτόκος, η [theotokos] the Virgin Mary.

θεοφάνεια, τα [theofaneea] πλ the Epiphany.

θεοφοβούμενος [theofovoumenos] godly, pious.

θεραπεία, η [therapeea] cure, treatment || recovery.

θεραπευτήριο, το [therapevteereeo] hospital, clinic || (σχολής) infirmary.

θεραπευτικός [therapevteekos] curative.

θεραπεύω [therapevo] cure, treat || (μεταφ) satisfy.

θεράπων, ο [therapon] servant || attendant.

θέρετρο, το [theretro] resort || country house.

θερίζω [thereezo] mow, cut || reap || (μεταφ) annihilate.

θερινός [thereenos] summer, summery.

θερίο, το [therio] beast.

θερισμός, ο [thereesmos] reaping, mowing, cutting.

θεριστής, ο [thereestees] reaper, mower.

θεριστικός [thereesteekos] of reaping, for mowing || sweeping.

θερμαίνομαι, η [thermenome] be feverish.

θερμαίνω [thermeno] heat up, warm up || (μεταφ) revive.

θέρμανση, η [thermansee] heating, warming.

θερμαστής, ο [thermastees] stoker.

θερμάστρα, η [thermastra] (heating) stove, furnace.

θέρμες, οι [therme] πλ hot springs.

θέρμη, η [thermee] fever || (μεταφ) ardour, zeal.

θερμίδα, η [thermeeda] calorie.

θερμόαιμος [thermoemos] hot-blooded, irritable, touchy.

θερμοκήπιο, το [thermokeepeeo] hot house, greenhouse.

θερμοκρασία, η [thermokraseea] temperature.

θερμόμετρο, το [thermometro] thermometer.

θερμός [thermos] warm || (μεταφ) passionate, fervent, heated.

θερμοσίφωνας, ο [thermoseefonas] water heater.

θερμοστάτης, ο [thermostatees] thermostat.

θερμότητα, η [thermoteeta] heat, warmth || (μεταφ) zeal, earnestness.

θερμοφόρος, η [thermoforos] hot-water bottle.

θέρος, ο [theros] harvest.

θέρος, το [theros] summer.

θέση, η [thesee] place, seat || position || (στρατ) emplacement, location || (εργασίας) employment, job, office || (χώρος) room, space || (κατηγορία) class.

θεσμός, ο [thesmos] institution, law, decree.

θεσπίζω [thespeezo] decree, legislate, enact (laws).

θετικός [theteekos] positive, real, actual || (πληροφορία) definite.

θετός [thetos] adopted || foster.

θέτω [theto] put, set || impose.

θεωρείο, το [theoreeo] (θεάτρου) box || (τύπου κτλ) gallery.

θεώρημα, το [theoreema] theorem.

θεώρηση, η [theoreesee] visa || (εγγράφου) certification.

θεωρητικός [theoreeteekos] theoretical || imposing.

θεωρία, η [theoreea] theory.

θεωρώ [theoro] consider, regard, look at || certify, visa.

θήκη, η [theekee] box, case || (εργαλείων) toolbag.

θηλάζω [theelazo] suckle, nurse.

θηλαστικό, το [theelasteeko] mammal.

θηλειά, η [theelia] noose, loop, slipknot || buttonhole.

θηλή, η [theelee] nipple, teat.

θηλυκό, το [theeleeko] female.

θηλυκός [theeleekos] female || (γραμμ) feminine.

θηλυκότητα, η [theeleekoteeta] femininity.

θηλυπρεπής [theeleeprepees] effeminate, womanish.

θημωνιά, η [theemonia] stack, pile || (σανού) haystack.

θήρα, η [theera] chase, hunt || (κυνήγι) game, quarry.

θήραμα, το [theerama] game, prey.

θηρίο, το [theereeo] wild beast, brute || (μεταφ) monster, fiend.

θηριώδης [theereeodees] fierce, savage, brutal, bestial.

θησαυρίζω [theesavreezo] hoard up, accumulate || become wealthy.

θησαυρός, ο [theesavros] treasure || (μεταφ) storehouse, thesaurus.

θησαυροφυλάκιο, το [theesavrofeelakeeo] treasury.

θήτα, το [theeta] the letter Θ.

θητεία, η [theeteea] military service || term of office.

θιασάρχης, ο [theeasarhees] manager, impresario.

θίασος, ο [theeasos] cast, troupe.

θίγω [theego] touch (upon) || (μεταφ) offend, insult.

θλάση, η [thlasee] breaking || (ιατρ) fracture, bruise.

θλιβερός [thleeveros] sad || (γεγονότα) deplorable, painful.

θλίβω [thleevo] press, crush || (μεταφ) afflict, distress.

θλιμμένος [thleemenos] distressed, afflicted || in mourning.

θλίψη, η [thleepsee] crushing || (μεταφ) grief, sorrow.

θνησιμότητα, η [thneeseemoteeta] death rate, mortality.

θνητός [thneetos] mortal.

θόλος, ο [tholos] (αρχιτεκ) vault, dome || (ουρανίσκου) roof.

θολός [tholos] dull, blurred || (κρασί) turbid || (κατάσταση) confused.

θολώνω [tholono] make dull || (το μυαλό) confuse, disturb || (νερό κτλ) muddy || (ουρανός) get overcast.

θολωτός [tholotos] vaulted.

θόρυβος, ο [thoreevos] noise, turmoil, clamour.

θορυβούμαι [thoreevoume] worry, be uneasy.

θορυβώ [thoreevo] create a disturbance || disturb.

θορυβώδης [thoreevoδees] noisy, boisterous.

θρανίο, το [thraneeo] (school) desk, bench, seat.

θράσος, το [thrasos] impudence, insolence.

θρασύς [thrasees] impudent, brazen, saucy, bold.

θραύση, η [thravsee] fracture || destruction, ruin.

θραύσμα, το [thravsma] fragment || (λίθου) splinter.

θραύω [thravo] break, smash, crack.

θρεμμένος [thremenos] well-fed.

θρεπτικός [threpteekos] nourishing, nutritious.

θρέφω [threfo] βλ τρέφω.

θρέψη, η [threpsee] feeding, nourishing.

θρήνος, ο [threenos] lamentation, wailing.

θρηνώ [threeno] lament, mourn || complain.

θρησκεία, η [threeskeea] religion.

θρησκευτικός [threeskevteekos] religious || (ακρίβεια) scrupulous.

θρησκόληπτος [threeskoleeptos] fanatically religious.

θρήσκος [threeskos] religious.

θριαμβευτικός [threeamvefteekos] triumphant, triumphal.

θριαμβεύω [threeamvevo] triumph || (μεταφ) excel, prevail.

θρίαμβος, ο [threeamvos] triumph, victory.

θρόισμα, το [throeesma] rustle.

θρόμβωση, η [thromvosee] thrombosis.

θρόνος, ο [thronos] throne.

θρούμπα, η [throumba] ripe olive.

θρυλικός [threeleekos] legendary.

θρύλος, ο [threelos] legend || rumour.

θρύμμα, το [threema] fragment, scrap || θρυμματίζω break to pieces, shatter.

θυγατέρα, η [theegatera] daughter.

θυγατρικός [theegatreekos]: ~ ή εταιρεία subsidiary.

θύελλα, η [thiela] storm.

θυελλώδης [thieloδees] stormy.

θύλακας, ο [theelakas] satchel, pouch.

θύμα, το [theema] victim.

θυμάμαι [theemame] βλ θυμούμαι.

θυμάρι, το [theemaree] thyme.

θύμηση, η [theemeesee] memory, remembrance.

θυμητικό, το [theemeeteeko] memory.

θυμίαμα, το [theemeeama] incense.

θυμιατό, το [theemeeato] censer.

θυμίζω [theemeezo] remind, recall.

θυμός, ο [theemos] anger, rage.

θυμούμαι [theemoume] remember, recall.

θυμώνω [theemono] make angry, infuriate || get angry, flare up.

θύρα, η [theera] door, gate, doorway.

θυρίδα, η [theereδa] small window || (θεάτρου) box office || (τραπέζης) counter.

θυρωρός, ο [theeroros] hall porter, concierge.

θύσανος, ο [theesanos] crest, tuft || tassel.

θυσία, η [theeseea] sacrifice || θυσιάζω sacrifice.

θωπεία, η [thopeea] petting, patting, stroking, caress(ing).

θωρακίζω [thorakeezo] plate with steel.

θώρακας, ο [thorakas] cuirass, breastplate || thorax.

θωρηκτό, το [thoreekto] battleship.

θωριά, η [thoria] air, appearance || colour, complexion.

θωρώ [thoro] see, look.

Ι, ι

ιαματικός [yamateekos] curative, medicinal.

ίαμβος, ο [eeamvos] iambus.

Ιανουάριος, ο [yanouareeos] January.

Ιάπωνας, ο [yaponas] Japanese (man).

ιαπωνέζικος [yaponezeekos] Japanese.

Ιαπωνία, η [yaponeea] Japan.

ιάσιμος [yaseemos] curable.

ίαση, η [eeasee] cure, healing, recovery.

ιατρείο, το [yatreeo] doctor's surgery, clinic || infirmary.

ιατρική, η [yatreekee] medicine.

ιατρικός [yatreekos] medical.

ιατρός, ο, η [yatros] doctor, physician.

ιβίκος, ό [eeveeskos] hibiscus.

ιδανικό, το [eedaneeko] ideal.

ιδανικός [eedaneekos] ideal.

ιδέα, η [eedea] idea || notion, thought.

ιδεαλιστής, ο [eedealeestees] idealist.

ιδεολογία, η [eedeoloyeea] ideology.

ιδεολόγος, ο, η [eedeologos] idealist.

ιδεώδης [eedeodees] ideal.

ιδιάζων [eedeeazon] typical, singular.

ιδιαίτερος [eedieeteros] special, characteristic || ο ~ private secretary || **τα ιδιαίτερα** private affairs.

ιδιαιτέρως [eedieeteros] in particular || privately.

ιδιοκτησία, η [eedeeokteeseea] ownership || property, estate.

ιδιοκτήτης, ο [eedeeokteetees] owner, proprietor || landlord.

ιδιόκτητος [eedeeokteetos] privately owned.

ιδιοποιούμαι [eedeeopeeoume] appropriate, usurp.

ιδιόρρυθμος [eedeeoreethmos] peculiar, original, eccentric.

ίδιος [eedeeos] same || own, oneself || particular || ~ **με** same as || **εγώ ο ~** I myself.

ιδιοσυγκρασία, η [eedeeoseengkraseea] temperament, idiosyncrasy.

ιδιοτελής [eedeeotelees] selfish, self-centred.

ιδιότητα, η [eedeeoteeta] property, quality, characteristic.

ιδιότροπος [eedeeotropos] peculiar, eccentric || singular.

ιδιοφυής [eedeeofiees] talented, gifted.

ιδίωμα, το [eedeeoma] idiom, dialect || property, characteristic || **ιδιωματικός** idiomatic.

ιδιωματισμός, ο [eedeeomateesmos] idiom.

ιδίως [eedeeos] specially, particularly.

ιδιωτικός [eedeeoteekos] private, particular.

ιδιώτης, ο [eedeeotees] individual, layman.

ιδού [eedou] (επιφ) look!, behold!, here it is!

ίδρυμα, το [eedreema] institution, foundation || establishment.

ίδρυση, η [eedreesee] establishment, founding.

ιδρυτής, ο [eedreetees] founder.

ιδρύω [eedreeo] found, establish.

ιδρώνω [eedrono] perspire, sweat.

ιδρώτας, ο [eedrotas] sweat.

ιεραπόστολος, ο [ierapostolos] missionary.

ιερέας, ο [iereas] priest.

ιεροκήρυκας, ο [ierokeereekas] preacher, missionary.

ιερό, το [iero] sanctuary, holy of holies.

ιερός [ieros] holy, sacred.

ιεροσυλία, η [ieroseeleea] sacrilege.

ίζημα, το [eezeema] sediment.

ιθαγένεια, η [eethageneea] nationality, citizenship.

ιθαγενής [eethagenees] native, indigenous.

ικανοποίηση, η [eekanopieesee] satisfaction, contentment.

ικανοποιητικός [eekanopieeteekos] satisfactory, sastisfying.

ικανοποιώ [eekanopeeo] satisfy, please || (τα πάθη) satiate || (πείνα) appease.

ικανός [eekanos] capable, able || sufficient || (εργάτης) skilful.

ικανότητα, η [eekanoteeta] capacity, competence, skill.

ικετεύω [eeketevo] implore, beg.

ίκτερος, ο [eekteros] jaundice.

ιλαρά, η [eelara] measles.

ιλιγγιώδης [eeleengeeoδees] giddy, dizzy.

ίλιγγος, ο [eeleengos] giddiness, dizziness.

ιμάντας, ο [eemandas] strap || (μηχανής) belt, band.

ιματιοθήκη, η [eemateeotheekee] wardrobe || cloakroom.

ίνα, η [eena] fibre, filament.

ίνδαλμα, το [eenδalma] ideal || illusion, fancy.

Ινδία, η [eenδeea] India.

Ινδιάνος, ο [eenδeeanos] (Red) Indian || ~ turkey.

ινδικός [eenδeekos] Indian.

Ινδονησία, η [eenδoneeseea] Indonesia.

ινδονησιακός [eenδoneeseeakos] Indonesian.

Ινδονήσιος, ο [eenδoneeseeos] Indonesian.

Ινδός, ο [eenδos] Indian.

ινστιτούτο, το [eensteetouto] institute || ~ **καλλονής** beauty salon.

ίντσα, η [eentsa] inch.

ινώδης [eenoδees] fibrous || (κρέας) stringy.

ιξώδης [eeksoδees] glutinous, sticky, gummy.

ιός, ο [yos] venom || (ιατρ) virus || (μεταφ) malice, spite.

Ιούλιος, ο [youleeos] July.

Ιούνιος, ο [youneeos] June.

ιππασία, η [eepaseea] horsemanship || riding.

ιππέας, ο [eepeas] rider, horseman || (σκακιού) knight.

ιππικό, το [eepeeko] cavalry.

ιπποδρομίες, οι [eepoδromies] πλ races.

ιππόδρομος, ο [eepoδromos] racecourse || hippodrome.

ιπποδύναμη, η [eepoδeenamee] horsepower.

ιπποπόταμος, ο [eepopotamos] hippopotamus.

ίππος, ο [eepos] horse.

ιππότης, ο [eepotees] knight, chevalier.

ίπταμαι [eeptame] fly, soar.

ιπταμένη, η [eeptamenee] air hostess.

ιπτάμενος, ο [eeptamenos] flyer.

Ιράν, το [eeran] Iran.

ίριδα, η [eereeδa] rainbow || (ματιού) iris.

ιριδισμός, ο [eereeδeesmos] iridescence.

Ιρλανδία, η [eerlanδeea] Ireland.

ιρλανδικός [eerlanδeekos] Irish.

Ιρλανδός, ο [eerlanδos] Irishman.

ίσα [eesa] equally, as far as ||

straight, directly || ~ ~ exactly, precisely || ~ **με** up to, until.
ίσαμε [eesame] βλ **ίσα με.**
ισάξιος [eesakseeos] equivalent (to).
ισάριθμος [eesareethmos] equal in number.
ισημερία, n [eeseemereea] equinox.
ισημερινός, ο [eeseemereenos] equinoctial || (ουσ) equator.
ισθμός, ο [eesthmos] isthmus.
ίσια [eeseea] βλ **ίσα.**
ίσιος [eeseeos] straight, erect || honest || equal to.
ισι(ι)ώνω [ees(ee)ono] straighten || make even, smooth.
ίσκιος, ο [eeskeeos] shade, shadow.
ισόβιος [eesoveeos] for life, lifelong.
ισόγειο, το [eesoyeeo] ground floor.
ισοδύναμος [eesodeenamos] equivalent || equal in force.
ισοδυναμώ [eesodeenamo] be equivalent to.
ισοζύγιο, το [eesozeeyeeo] balancing, balance || ~ **πληρωμών** balance of payments.
ισολογισμός, ο [eesoloyeesmos] balance sheet.
ισόπαλος [eesopalos] evenly matched, of equal strength.
ισοπεδώνω [eesopedono] level up, level down, smooth.
ισόπλευρος [eesoplevros] equilateral.
ισορροπημένος [eesoropeemenos] well-balanced.
ισορροπία, n [eesoropeea] balance, equilibrium.
ισορροπώ [eesoropo] balance.
ίσος [eesos] equal to, the same as || **εξ ίσου** likewise.
ισότητα, n [eesoteeta] equality.
ισότιμος [eesoteemos] equal in rank || equal in value.
ισοφαρίζω [eesofareezo] equal, make equal || be equal to.

Ισπανία, n [eespaneea] Spain.
ισπανικός [eespaneekos] Spanish.
Ισπανός, ο [eespanos] Spaniard.
Ισραήλ, το [eesraeel] Israel.
ισραηλινός [eesraeeleenos] Israeli.
Ισραηλίτη, ο [eesraeeleetee] Israeli.
ιστιοπλοΐα, n [eesteeoploeea] sailing.
ιστιοφόρο, το [eesteeoforo] sailing ship.
ιστορία, n [eestoreea] history || story, tale.
ιστορίες, οι [eestories] πλ trouble, scene, quarrel.
ιστορικός [eestoreekos] historic(al) || (ουσ) historian.
ιστός, ο [eestos] mast, pole || (βιολ) tissue.
ισχιαλγία, n [eesheealyeea] sciatica.
ισχίο, το [eesheeo] hip.
ισχνός [eeshnos] lean, thin || (βλάστηση) scanty, sparse.
ισχυρίζομαι [eesheereezome] assert, maintain, declare.
ισχυρισμός, ο [eesheereesmos] assertion, contention, allegation.
ισχυρογνώμων [eesheerognomon] stubborn, headstrong, obstinate.
ισχυρός [eesheeros] strong, sturdy || (φωνή) loud || (άνεμος) stiff, strong.
ισχύς, n [eesheess] strength, power, force || (νόμου κτλ) validity.
ισχύω [eesheeo] have validity || be in force.
ισώνω [eesono] βλ **ισι(ι)ώνω.**
ίσως [eesos] perhaps, probably, maybe.
Ιταλία, n [eetaleea] Italy.
ιταλικός [eetaleekos] Italian.
Ιταλός, ο [eetalos] Italian (person).
ιτιά, n [eetia] willow tree.
ιχθυοπωλείο, το [eehtheeopoleeo] fishmonger's shop.
ιχθύς, ο [eehthees] fish.

ιχνογραφία, η [eehnografeea] sketching, drawing.

ίχνος, το [eehnos] footprint, track || trace, vestige || (μεταφ) mark, sign.

ιώδιο, το [yodeeo] iodine.

ιωνικός [yoneekos] Ionic, Ionian.

ιώτα, το [yota] the letter I.

Κ, κ

κάβα, η [kava] wine cellar.

καβαλιέρος, ο [kavalieros] escort, partner.

καβάλλα, η [kavala] riding || (επιρ) on horseback || (σε τοίχο κτλ) astride.

καβαλλάρης, ο [kavalarees] rider, horseman || (εγχόρδου) bridge.

καβαλλέτο, το [kavaleto] easel.

καβαλλικεύω [kavalekevo] mount a horse || (μεταφ) dominate.

καβαλλώ [kavalo] βλ **καβαλλικεύω.**

καβγαδίζω [kavgadeezo] quarrel, wrangle, squabble.

καβγάς, ο [kavgas] row, quarrel.

καβγατζής, ο [kavgatzees] grouch, wrangler.

κάβος, ο [kavos] cape, headland || (ναυτ) cable.

καβούκι, το [kavookee] shell.

κάβουρας, ο [kavooras] crab || crawfish.

καβουρδίζω [kavourdeezo] roast, brown || scorch.

καβούρι, το [kavouree] βλ **κάβουρας.**

καγκελάριος, ο [kangelareeos] chancellor.

κάγκελο, το [kangelo] (παραθύρου κτλ) bar || (σκάλας) balustrade || (κήπου) railings || (δικτυωτό) grille.

καγκάζω [kanghazo] guffaw.

κάδος, ο [kados] bucket, vat, tub, small barrel.

κάδρο, το [kadro] (πλαίσιο) frame ||

(πίνακα) frame || (χάρτου) border || (φωτογραφία) framed picture.

καπμένος [kaemenos] (μεταφ) miserable, wretched.

καπμός, ο [kaemos] longing, yearning.

καθαίρεση, η [katheresee] dismissal, degradation.

καθαιρώ [kathero] dismiss, discharge || (ιερέα) unfrock.

καθαρεύουσα, η [katharevousa] formal Greek (language).

καθαρίζω [kathareezo] clean, clear || (κουκιά, φρούτα) peel, pare, shell || (μεταλλικά είδη) burnish || (ποτήρια) polish || (εξηγώ) explain, clarify || (λογαριασμούς) settle, clear up.

καθαριότητα, η [kathareeoteeta] cleanness, cleanliness || brightness.

κάθαρμα, το [kathareesma] cleaning || peeling || polishing.

καθαριστήριο, το [kathareesteereeo] dry cleaner's.

καθαρίστρια, η [kathareestria] charwoman, cleaning lady.

κάθαρμα, το [katharma] (μεταφ) rogue, rascal, scamp.

καθαρόαιμος [katharoemos] thoroughbred.

καθαρός [katharos] (πρόσωπο κτλ) neat, tidy || (φωνή) clear, distinct || (χρυσός) pure || (ουρανός) clear || (απάντηση) plain, straightforward || (ιδέα) clear, distinct || (κέρδος) clear, net || (έννοια) obvious, manifest, evident.

καθαρότητα, η [katharoteeta] cleanness, purity || clearness.

κάθαρση, η [katharsee] cleansing, refining || catharsis || quarantine.

καθαυτό [kathavto] exactly, precisely || really.

κάθε [kathe] each, every || ~ άλλο far from it || ~ τι everything.

κάθειρξη, η [katheerksee] βλ **φυλάκιση.**

καθέκαστα, τα [kathekasta] πλ details, particulars.

καθελκύω [kathelkeeo] (ναυτ) launch.

καθένας [kathenas] everyone, each one, everybody.

καθεξής [katheksees] so forth, so on.

καθεστώς, το [kathestos]: **το ~** regime, status quo.

κάθετος [kathetos] vertical, perpendicular, upright.

καθηγητής, ο [katheeyeetees] professor, teacher.

καθήκι, το [katheekee] chamberpot || (μεταφ) rogue, vicious person.

καθήκον, το [katheekon] duty, task || **καθήκοντα** πλ functions, duties.

καθηλώνω [katheelono] pin down, fix || immobilize.

καθημερινός [katheemereenos] daily, everyday.

καθημερινώς [katheemereenos] daily.

καθησυχάζω [katheeseehazo] (ένα φόβο) calm, reassure, pacify || become calm.

καθιερώνω [kathierono] consecrate, dedicate || establish, validate.

καθίζηση, η [katheezeesee] subsidence, landslide.

καθίζω [katheezo] seat, place || (πλοίο) run aground.

καθισιό, το [katheesio] idleness, unemployment, inactivity.

κάθισμα, το [katheesma] chair, seat || (πλοίο) stranding.

καθίσταμαι [katheestame] become, get, grow.

καθιστός [katheestos] sitting (down).

καθιστώ [katheesto] (εγκαθιστώ) establish, install || (κάποιον) make, render || (διορίζω) appoint.

καθοδηγώ [kathoδeego] instruct, guide, lead.

κάθοδος, η [kathoδos] descent || alighting.

καθολικός [katholeekos] catholic || (γνώμη) unanimous || universal.

καθόλου [katholou] generally || (διόλου) not at all, no way.

κάθομαι [kathome] be seated, sit down, sit.

καθομιλουμένη, η [kathomeeloumenee] the spoken language.

καθορίζω [kathoreezo] determine, define, fix, decide.

καθορισμός, ο [kathoreesmos] defining, fixing, determination.

καθόσο [kathoso] as || according to what || being.

καθρέφτης, ο [kathreftees] mirror, looking-glass.

καθρεφτίζω [kathrefteezo] reflect, mirror.

καθυστερημένος [katheestereemenos] backward || late.

καθυστέρηση, η [katheestereesee] delay, lateness.

καθυστερούμενα, τα [katheesteroumena] πλ arrears.

καθώς [kathos] as well as, like, as || **~ πρέπει** proper.

και [ke] and, also, too || **~ ... ~** both ... and || **~ να** even if.

καΐκι, το [kaeekee] caique, sailing boat.

καϊμάκι, το [kaeemakee] cream || (του κοφέ) froth.

καινοτομία, η [kenotomeea] innovation.

καινούργιος [kenouryos] new, fresh.

καιρικός [kereekos] of the weather.

καίριος [kereeos] timely || (πλήγμα) deadly, mortal || (σημείο) vital, important.

καιρός, ο [keros] time, period ||

καιροσκοπώ 100 καλάμι

weather || **με τον καιρό** in course of time.

καιροσκοπώ [keroskopo] wait for an opportunity, be an opportunist.

καισαρικός [kesareekos] Caesarean.

καίτοι [ketee] though, although.

καίομαι [keome] be on fire.

καίω [keo] burn.

κακά [kaka] badly, ill || bad things.

κακάο, το [kakao] cocoa.

κακαρίζω [kakareezo] cluck, gobble.

κακεντρέχεια, η [kakentreheea] malevolence, spite.

κακία, η [kakeea] wickedness, malice.

κακίζω [kakeezo] reproach, blame, reprimand.

κακοβαλμένος [kakovalmenos] untidy || badly placed.

κακόβουλος [kakovoulos] malicious.

κακογλωσσιά, η [kakogloseea] slander, calumny || gossip.

κακοήθης [kakoeethees] dishonest, vile || (ιατρ) malignant, serious.

κακόηχος [kakoeehos] dissonant, unpleasant to hear.

κακοκαιρία, η [kakokereea] bad weather.

κακοκεφιά, η [kakokefia] depression, bad mood.

κακομαθαίνω [kakomatheno] (μωρό κτλ) spoil || acquire bad habits.

κακομαθημένος [kakomatheemenos] ill-bred, spoilt, rude.

κακομεταχειρίζομαι [kakometaheereezome] maltreat, abuse.

κακομοίρης [kakomeerees] hapless, wretched.

κακό, το [kako] evil, harm, wrong, bad, mischief.

κακοπέραση, η [kakoperasee] privation, hardship.

κακοπιστία, η [kakopeesteea] perfidy, faithlessness.

κακοποιός [kakopeeos] criminal, ill-doer.

κακοποιώ [kakopeeo] maltreat || rape.

κακός [kakos] bad, wicked || (παιδί) mischievous || nasty, serious.

κακοσμία, η [kakosmeea] stench, stink.

κακοσυνηθίζω [kakoseeneetheezo] πλ **κακομαθαίνω**.

κακοτυχία, η [kakoteeheea] misfortune, bad luck.

κακούργημα, το [kakouryeema] crime, villainy, felony.

κακουργιοδικείο, το [kakouryodeekeeo] criminal court.

κακούργος, ο [kakourgos] criminal || (μεταφ) villain, rogue.

κακουχία, η [kakouheea] hardship, privation.

κακοφαίνεται [kakofenete]: **μου** ~ it displeases me, it offends me.

κακοφτιαγμένος [kakofteeagmenos] badly made, badly wrought.

κακόφωνος [kakofonos] discordant, dissonant.

κάκτος, ο [kaktos] cactus.

κακώς [kakos] badly, wrongly.

κάκωση, η [kakosee] ill treatment || (αποτέλεσμα) suffering, hardship.

καλά [kala] well, all right || properly, thoroughly.

καλάθι, το [kalathee] basket || ~ **αχρήστων** wastepaper bin.

καλαισθησία, η [kalestheeseea] good taste, elegance.

καλαμάρι, το [kalamaree] inkstand, inkpot || (ψάρι) cuttlefish, squid.

καλαματιανός [kalamateeanos] (dance) of Kalamata.

καλάμι, το [kalamee] reed, cane || (ψαρέματος) fishing rod || (άνατ) shinbone.

καλαμοζάχαρο, το
[kalamozakharo] cane sugar.

καλαμπόκι, το [kalambokee]
maize, corn.

καλαμπούρι, το [kalambouree]
joke, pun.

κάλαντα, τα [kalanta] πλ carols.

καλαπόδι, το [kalapoðee]
(shoemaker's) last, shoe last.

καλαφατίζω [kalafateezo] caulk.

κάλεσμα, το [kalesma] invitation.

καλεσμένος [kalesmenos] invited ||
(ουσ) guest.

καλημαύκι, το [kaleemavkee]
priest's high hat.

καλημέρα [kaleemera] (επιφ) good
morning.

καληνύχτα [kaleeneehta] (επιφ)
good night.

καληνυχτίζω [kaleeneehteezo] bid
good night.

καλησπέρα [kaleespera] (επιφ)
good afternoon || good evening.

κάλι, το [kalee] potash.

καλιακούδα, η [kaleeakouða]
crow.

καλλιέργεια, η [kalierya]
cultivation, tilling || (μεταφ)
cultivation.

καλλιεργώ [kaliergo] cultivate, till,
grow.

καλλικάντζαρος, ο
[kaleekandzaros] sprite, spook,
goblin.

καλλιστεία, τα [kaleesteea] πλ
beauty competition.

καλλιτέχνης, ο [kaleetehnees]
artist.

καλλιτεχνικός [kaleetehneekos] of
art, of artists, artistic.

καλλονή, η [kalonee] beauty.

κάλλος, το [kalos] beauty, charm.

καλλυντικά, τα [kaleenteeka] πλ
cosmetics, make-up.

καλλωπίζω [kalopeezo] beautify,
decorate, adorn.

καλμάρω [kalmaro] become calm,
relax.

καλντερίμι, το [kalntereemee]
cobbled street, paving stone.

καλό, το [kalo] good, benefit ||
favour || blessing || στο ~ ! so long!

καλοαναθρεμμένος
[kaloanathremenos] well brought
up.

καλοβαλμένος [kalovalmenos]
well turned out, well-groomed, tidy.

καλόβολος [kalovolos]
accommodating, easy-going,
complaisant.

καλόγερος, ο [kaloyeros] monk ||
(σπυρί) boil, carbuncle || (παιχνίδι)
hopscotch.

καλόγρια, η [kalogreea] nun.

καλοζώ [kalozo] live well || support
comfortably.

καλοήθης [kaloeethees] moral,
virtuous || (ιατρ) benign.

καλοθρεμμένος [kalothremenos]
well-nourished || well-bred.

καλοκάγαθος [kalokagathos] kind-
natured, good.

καλοκαίρι, το [kalokeree] summer
|| καλοκαιρία fine weather ||
καλοκαιρινός summer, summery.

καλοκαμωμένος [kalokamomenos]
well-made || handsome.

καλοκάρδος [kalokarðos] good-
hearted, cheerful.

καλοκοιτάζω [kalokeetazo] look
closely at || look after well || ogle.

καλομαθαίνω [kalomatheno] spoil,
pamper, pet || develop good habits.

καλομαθημένος
[kalomatheemenos] pampered.

καλοντυμένος [kalonteemenos]
well-dressed.

καλοπέραση, η [kaloperasee]
comfort, happy life, good life.

καλοπερνώ [kaloperno] lead a
pleasant life || be well treated.

καλοπιάνω [kalopeeano] coax,
treat gently.

καλοπροαίρετος [kaloproeretos] well-disposed, obliging.

καλοριφέρ, το [kaloreefer] central heating || radiator, heater.

καλορρίζικος [kaloreezeekos] lucky.

κάλος, ο [kalos] corn.

καλός [kalos] (άνθρωπος) kind, good || (εργάτης) skilful || (υπάλληλος) able, efficient || (νέα) good, favourable || (τροφή) wholesome || (καρδιά) kind.

καλοσυνηθίζω [kaloseeneetheezo] βλ **καλομαθαίνω.**

καλούπι, το [kaloupee] form, mould.

καλούτσικος [kaloutseekos] not bad, passable, adequate.

καλπάζω [kalpazo] gallop || walk fast, run.

κάλπη, η [kalpee] ballot box.

κάλπικος [kalpeekos] counterfeit, false || (μεταφ) worthless.

κάλτσα, η [kaltsa] sock, stocking.

καλύβι, το [kaleevee] hut, cabin, hovel.

κάλυμμα, το [kaleema] wrapper, cover || (κρεββατιού) blanket, coverlet || (κεφαλής) cap, headdress || (τραπεζικού) margin, cover.

κάλυκας, ο [kaleekas] (βοτ) calyx || (στρατ) cartridge || (ανατ) calix.

καλύπτω [kaleepto] cover, veil, hide || (προθέσεις) cloak, mask, conceal.

καλύτερα [kaleetera] better.

καλυτερεύω [kaleeterevo] improve || get better.

καλύτερος [kaleeteros] better.

κάλυψη, η [kaleepsee] covering.

καλώ [kalo] call, beckon, name || (σε δείπνο) invite || (νομ) summon.

καλώδιο, το [kalodeeo] rope || cable.

καλώς [kalos] well || rightly, properly || έχει ~ good, agreed || ~ ωρίσατε (επιφ) welcome!

καλωσορίζω [kalosoreezo] welcome.

καλωσύνη, η [kaloseenee] goodness, kindness || (καιρός) fine weather.

καμάκι, το [kamakee] harpoon, fish spear.

κάμαρα, η [kamara] room.

καμάρα, η [kamara] arch, archway, arcade || (θόλου) vault.

καμάρι, το [kamaree] pride, boast.

καμαριέρα, η [kamariera] chambermaid, parlourmaid.

καμαρότος, ο [kamarotos] steward, cabin boy.

καμαρώνω [kamarono] take pride in, glory in.

καμαρωτός [kamarotos] (αρχιτεκ) arched, vaulted || (υπερηφάνεια) proud, haughty.

καμέλια, η [kameleea] camellia.

καμήλα, η [kameela] camel.

καμηλοπάρδαλη, η [kameeloparðalee] giraffe.

καμινάδα, η [kameenaða] chimney, smokestack || funnel.

καμινέτο, το [kameeneto] spirit lamp.

καμίνι, το [kameenee] furnace, kiln.

καμιόνι, το [kameeonee] lorry, truck.

καμιά [kamia] βλ **κανένας.**

καμουτσίκι, το [kamoutseekee] whip.

καμουφλάζ, το [kamouflaz] camouflage, disguise.

καμουφλάρω [kamouflaro] camouflage, disguise.

καμπάνα, η [kambana] bell.

καμπαναριό, το [kambanario] belfry, steeple.

καμπαρντίνα, η [kambarndeena] gabardine.

καμπή, η [kambee] bend, turn || (σωλήνα κτλ) elbow, knee.

κάμπια, η [kambeea] caterpillar.

καμπίνα, n [kambeena] cabin.

καμπινές, ο [kambeenes] toilet, rest room, W.C.

κάμπος, ο [kambos] plain, flat country.

κάμποσος [kambosos] considerable, some.

καμπούρα, n [kamboura] hump, hunch.

καμπούρης, ό [kambourees] hunchback.

καμπουριάζω [kamboureeazo] hunch || stoop.

κάμπτομαι [kambtome] bow || yield, sag || (τιμές) go down.

κάμπτω [kambto] bend, turn, curve.

καμπύλη, n [kambeelee] curve, bend.

καμπύλος [kambeelos] curved, rounded || crooked.

καμφορά, n [kamfora] camphor.

κάμψη, n [kampsee] bending, flexion || (τιμών) fall, drop.

καμώματα, τα [kamomata] πλ affected manners, antics.

καμώνομαι [kamonome] pretend, feign.

καν [kan] at least, even || **ούτε ~** not even || **~ ... ~** either ... or.

Καναδάς, ο [kanadas] Canada.

καναδικός [kanadeekos] Canadian.

Καναδός, ο [kanados] Canadian.

κανακάρης [kanakarees] petted, spoilt || (ουσ) only child.

κανάλι, το [kanalee] channel, canal.

καναπές, ο [kanapes] sofa.

καναρίνι, το [kanareenee] canary.

κανάτα, n [kanata] jug, pitcher.

κανείς [kanees] someone, anyone || no one, nobody.

κανέλλα, n [kanela] cinnamon.

κανένας [kanenas] anyone, one, some || no, no one.

κανναβάτσο, το [kanvatso] canvas, pack cloth.

κάνναβι, το [kanavee] hemp.

κάννη, n [kanee] barrel of a gun.

καννίβαλος, ο [kaneevalos] cannibal.

κανόνας, ο [kanonas] rule || (εκκλ) canon.

κανόνι, το [kanonee] cannon.

κανονίζω [kanoneezo] regulate || (υποθέσεις) settle, arrange || (λογαριασμός) settle, close, pay off.

κανονικός [kanoneekos] regular, usual, ordinary || (εκκλ) canonical.

κανονισμός, ο [kanoneesmos] regulation, rule(s), by-laws.

κάνουλα, n [kanoula] tap || faucet (US).

καντάδα, n [kantada] serenade.

καντήλι, το [kanteelee] small olive-oil light, nightlight.

καντίνα, n [kanteena] canteen.

κάνω [kano] do, make, create, build || (υποκρίνομαι) play, sham || **τα ~ θάλασσα (n σαλάτα)** to make a mess of it || **~ παιδί** to have a child || **~ νερά** to leak || (μεταφ) to hedge || **~ πως** to pretend that || **τι κάνετε;** how are you?

κάπα, n [kapa] peasant's cloak.

καπάκι, το [kapakee] lid, cover.

καπάρο, το [kaparo] deposit.

καπαρώνω [kaparono] give a deposit || book, engage.

καπέλλο, το [kapelo] hat.

καπετάνιος, ο [kapetaneeos] captain, skipper, chief.

καπηλεία, n [kapeeleea] (μεταφ) huckstering, exploiting.

καπηλειό, το [kapeeleeo] wine shop, taverna.

καπίστρι, το [kapeestree] bridle, halter.

καπλαμάς, ο [kaplamas] veneer.

καπνέμπορος, ο [kapnemboros] tobacco dealer, tobacconist.

καπνιά, n [kapnia] soot, lampblack.

καπνίζω [kapneezo] smoke || cure.

κάπνισμα, το [kapneesma] smoking.

καπνιστής, ο [kapneestees] smoker || (κρέατος) curer.

καπνιστός [kapneestos] smoked, smoke-cured.

καπνοδόχος, η [kapnodohos] chimney || (πλοίου) funnel.

καπνοπώλης, ο [kapnopolees] tobacconist.

καπνός, ο [kapnos] smoke || tobacco || (μεταφ) έγινε ~ he vanished (into thin air).

κάποιος [kapeeos] someone || a certain.

καπότα, η [kapota] shepherd's cloak.

κάποτε [kapote] from time to time, now and again, sometimes || once.

κάπου [kapou] somewhere || ~ once in a while || ~ δέκα about ten.

κάππα, το [kappa] the letter K.

κάππαρη, η [kapparee] caper.

καπρίτσιο, το [kapreetseeo] caprice, whim, fancy.

κάπως [kapos] somehow, somewhat.

καραβάνα, η [karavana] mess tin || platter.

καραβάνι, το [karavanee] caravan.

καράβι, το [karavee] ship, boat, vessel.

καραβίδα, η [karaveeda] crawfish.

καραβοκύρης, ο [karavokeerees] owner of a vessel || captain.

καραγκιόζης, ο [karangeeozees] (μεταφ) comical person, comedian.

καραδοκώ [karodoko] watch for, look out for || waylay.

καρακάξα, η [karakaksa] magpie.

καραμέλα, η [karamela] sweet || caramel.

καραμούζα, η [karamouza] toy flute || (αυτοκινήτου) horn.

καραμπίνα, η [karambeena] carbine.

καραντίνα, η [karanteena] quarantine.

καράτι, το [karatee] carat.

καρατομώ [karatomo] behead, decapitate.

καράφα, η [karafa] carafe || (κρασιού) decanter.

καράφλα, η [karafla] baldness.

καρβέλι, το [karvelee] (round) loaf.

καρβουνιάρης, ο [karvouneearees] coal merchant || coalman.

κάρβουνο, το [karvouno] coal, charcoal.

κόργα [karga] quite full || tightly, closely.

κάρδαμο, το [karðamo] cress.

καρδιά, η [karðia] heart || (φρούτου) core, centre.

καρδιακός [karðiakos] affected with heart disease.

καρδιολόγος, ο [karðiologos] heart specialist.

καρδιοχτύπι, το [karðiohteepee] heartbeat || (μεταφ) anxiety.

καρέκλα, η [karekla] chair, seat.

καρίνα, η [kareena] keel.

καρκίνος, ο [karkeenos] cancer || crab.

καρκίνωμα, το [karkeenoma] carcinoma.

καρμανιόλα, η [karmaneeola] guillotine || (στα χαρτιά) dishonest card game.

καρμπόν, το [karbo] carbon paper.

καρναβάλι, το [karnavalee] carnival.

καρότο, το [karoto] carrot.

καρούλι, το [karoulee] reel, spool || pulley.

καρούμπαλο, το [karoumbalo] bump (on the head).

καρπαζιά, η [karpazia] clout on the head.

καρπός, ο [karpos] fruit || (ανατ) wrist.

καρπούζι, το [karpouzee] watermelon.

καρπούμαι [karpoume] reap the fruits of || (μεταφ) benefit by.

καρποφόρος [karpoforos] fruitful || effective || lucrative.

καρποφορῶ [karpoforo] produce fruit || (μεταφ) succeed.

καρρέ, το [karre] (στα χαρτιά) foursome || (φουστανιού) open neck of dress.

καρρό, το [karo] (στα χαρτιά) diamond || (σχεδίου) check.

κάρρο, το [karo] cart, wagon.

καρροτσάκι, το [karotsakee] handcart, barrow || (μωρού) pram.

κάρτα, η [karta] postcard || visiting card.

καρτέρι, το [karteree] βλ **ενέδρα**.

καρτερῶ [kartero] persevere, persist || wait for, expect.

καρύδι, το [kareedee] walnut || Adam's apple || **καρυδιά, η** walnut tree, walnut (wood).

καρύκευμα, το [kareekevma] seasoning || (το μπαχαρικό) condiment, spice.

καρυοθραύστης, ο [kareeothravstees] nutcracker.

καρυοφύλλι, το [kareeofeelee] clove || (όπλου) flintlock.

καρφί, το [karfee] nail.

καρφίτσα, η [karfeetsa] pin || (κόσμημα) brooch.

καρφώνω [karfono] nail, pin || (μεταφ) fix.

καρχαρίας, ο [karhareeas] shark.

κασετίνα, η [kaseteena] (σχολική) pencil box || (κοσμημάτων) jewellery box.

κάσ(σ)α, η [kasa] case, box || (χρηματοκιβώτιο) safe || (μεταφ) coffin, bier.

κασέλα, η [kasela] wooden chest, trunk.

κασκέτο, το [kasketo] cap.

κασμίρι, το [kasmeeree] cashmere.

κασόνι, το [kasonee] packing case.

κασσίτερος, ο [kaseeteros] tin.

κασταvιά, η [kastania] chestnut tree.

κάστανο, το [kastano] chestnut.

κασταvός [kastanos] chestnut-coloured, maroon.

καστόρι, το [kastoree] beaver || felt.

κάστρο, το [kastro] castle, fortress.

κατά [kata] against, upon, during, according to, by, about || ~ **τύχη** by chance || ~ **βάθος** at bottom || **καθ' εκάστην** every day || ~ **διαβόλου** to the devil, to hell.

καταβαίνω [kataveno] βλ **κατεβαίνω**.

καταβάλλω [katavalo] overthrow, overcome, exhaust || (προσπάθειες) strive, endeavour || (χρήματα) pay, put down.

κατάβαση, η [katavasee] descent, alighting, getting off.

καταβιβάζω [kataveevazo] let down, take down || (ύψος) lower, reduce.

καταβολή, η [katavolee] (χρημάτων) paying in, deposit.

καταβρέχω [katavreho] sprinkle, soak, water.

καταβροχθίζω [katavrohtheezo] devour, eat ravenously, gulp down.

καταγγελία, η [katangeleea] denunciation || annulment, revocation.

καταγής [katayees] on the ground, on the floor.

καταγίνομαι [katayeenome] busy o.s. with, see to.

κάταγμα, το [katagma] fracture.

κατάγομαι [katagome] be descended from, come from.

καταγωγή, η [katagoyee] descent, origin, lineage.

καταγώγιο, το [katagoyo] hovel, hideout, den of vice.

καταδέχομαι [katadehome] deign, condescend.

κατάδηλος [kataðeelos] evident, clear.

καταδίδω [kataðeeðo] denounce, betray.

καταδικάζω [kataðeekazo] condemn, sentence || (μεταφ) doom, proscribe.

καταδίκη, η [kataðeekee] sentence, conviction || censure, blame.

κατάδικος, ο, η [kataðeekos] prisoner, condemned person.

καταδιωκτικό, το [kataðeeokteeko] fighter (plane).

καταδιώκω [kataðeeoko] pursue, chase || (πολιτικώς) persecute, oppress.

κατάδοση, η [kataðosee] betrayal, denunciation.

καταδρομή, η [kataðromee] pursuit.

καταδρομικό, το [kataðromeeko] cruiser.

καταδυναστεύω [kataðeenastevo] oppress.

καταδύομαι [kataðeeome] dive, plunge.

καταζητώ [katazeeto] pursue, chase.

καταθέτω [katatheto] deposit, lay down || (σαν μάρτυρας) give evidence || (οπλα) lay down || (σχέδιο) introduce.

καταθλιπτικός [katathleepteekos] crushing, overwhelming.

καταιγίδα, η [kateyeeða] tempest, storm, hurricane.

κατάϊφι, το [kataeefee] kind of oriental cake.

κατακάθι, το [katakathee] residue, sediment, dregs.

κατάκειμαι [katakeeme] lie flat, lie down.

κατάκαρδα [katakarða] deeply, seriously, profoundly, to heart.

κατακέφαλα [katakefala] headlong, on the head.

κατακλύζω [katakleezo] flood, inundate || (μεταφ) invade, overrun.

κατακλυσμός, ο [katakleesmos] flood.

κατάκοιτος [katakeetos] bedridden.

κατάκοπος [katakopos] exhausted, deadbeat, dog-tired.

κατακόβω [katakovo] cut to pieces, cut up, lacerate.

κατακόρυφο, το [katakoreefo] zenith || (μεταφ) acme.

κατακόρυφος [katakoreefos] vertical, perpendicular.

κατακρατώ [katakrato] withhold, keep illegally.

κατακραυγή, η [katakravyee] outcry || protestation.

κατακρεουργώ [katakreourgo] butcher, massacre.

κατακρημνίζω [katakreemneezo] demolish, pull down.

κατακρίνω [katakreeno] blame, criticize, condemn.

κατάκτηση, η [katakteesee] conquest, subjugation.

κατακτώ [katakto] conquer, subjugate.

καταλαβαίνω [katalaveno] understand.

καταλαμβάνω [katalamvano] take, lay hold of, seize || (χώρο) take up.

καταλήγω [kataleego] end in, come to, result in, come to an end.

κατάληξη, η [kataleeksee] termination, ending.

καταληπτός [kataleeptos] comprehensible, intelligible, clear.

κατάληψη, η [kataleepsee] occupation, capture || (ιδέας) understanding, comprehension.

κατάλληλος [kataleelos] suitable, appropriate, fit, proper.

καταλογίζω [kataloyeezo] attribute, impute, ascribe.

κατάλογος, ο [katalogos]

κατάλοιπα catalogue, list || (φαγητών) menu || (τιμών) inventory, register, roll.

κατάλοιπα, τα [kataleepa] waste || **ραδιενεργά ~** radioactive waste.

κατάλυμα, το [kataleema] lodging, housing || (στρατ) barracks, billeting.

κατάλυση, n [kataleese] abolition || (χημ) catalysis.

καταλύω [kataleeo] abolish, do away with || take up lodging.

καταμερίζω [katamereezo] share out, distribute, apportion.

καταμεσής [katamesees] in the very middle.

κατάμεστος [katamestos] quite full, crowded.

καταμετρώ [katametro] measure, survey, gauge.

κατάμουτρα [katamoutra] point-blank.

καταναλίσκω [katanaleesko] consume, spend, use up || (ποτά) drink.

κατανάλωση, n [katanalosee] consumption.

καταναλωτής, ο [katanalotees] consumer, customer.

κατανέμω [katanemo] distribute || (ευθύνες) allot, assign, share.

κατανόηση, n [katanoeesee] understanding, comprehension.

κατανοώ [katanoo] understand, comprehend.

κατάντημα, το [katanteema] wretched state.

καταντώ [katanto] be reduced to, bring to, end up as.

κατάνυξη, n [kataneeksee] compunction, piety.

καταπακτή, n [katapaktee] trap, pitfall.

καταπατώ [katapato] violate, encroach upon.

κατάπαυση, n [katapavsee] cessation, stopping, halting.

καταπέλτης, ο [katapeltees] catapult.

καταπέτασμα, το [katapetasma]: **τρώω το ~** to eat to bursting point.

καταπιάνομαι [katapeeanome] undertake, enter upon, engage upon.

καταπιέζω [katapiezo] oppress, crush, harass.

καταπίνω [katapeeno] swallow, gobble up || (για κύματα) engulf.

καταπίπτω [katapeepto] fall down, come down || collapse || (λιγοστεύω) diminish.

καταπλακώνω [kataplakono] flatten, crush.

κατάπλασμα, το [kataplasma] poultice.

καταπλέω [katapleo] sail in, sail down.

καταπληκτικός [katapleekteekos] amazing, wonderful, marvellous, astonishing.

κατάπληκτος [katapleektos] stupefied, amazed.

κατάπληξη, n [katapleeksee] surprise, astonishment.

καταπλήσσω [katapleeso] astonish, surprise, amaze, stupefy.

καταπνίγω [katapneego] strangle, throttle, suffocate || (εξέγερση) suppress, put down.

καταποντίζομαι [kataponteezome] go down, sink.

καταπραΰνω [katapraeeno] pacify, mollify, appease, calm, assuage.

κατάπτυστος [katapteestos] despicable, abject, low, villainous.

καταπτώση, n [kataptosee] downfall || (εδάφους) landslide || (μεταφ) prostration, exhaustion || dejection, depression.

κατάρα, n [katara] curse, imprecation || (μεταφ) hell, woe, damnation.

καταραμένος [kataramenos] cursed, damned.

καταργώ [katargo] abolish, annul, cancel.

καταριέμαι [katarieme] curse, damn, call down curses on.

καταρράκτης, ο [kataraktees] cascade, waterfall || (τεχν) sluice.

καταρρέω [katareo] collapse, fall down || (μεταφ) give out.

καταρρίπτω [katareepto] (κάποιο) knock down || (τοίχο) pull down, demolish || (επιχείρημα) prove to be wrong || (ρεκόρ) beat, break || (αερο) shoot down.

καταρροή, n [kataroee] catarrh, head cold.

κατάρτι, το [katartee] mast.

καταρτίζω [katarteezo] organize, establish, form, prepare, construct.

καταρώμαι [katarome] βλ **καταριέμαι**.

κατάσβεση, n [katasvese] extinction, blowing out || (μεταφ) suppression || (δίψας) slaking, quenching.

κατασκευάζω [kataskevazo] construct, make, erect, build || (ιστορία κτλ) invent, concoct, fabricate || (έργο τέχνης) fashion, model.

κατασκεύασμα, το [kataskevasma] fabrication, concoction || construction, creation.

κατασκευή, n [kataskevee] making, construction || (έργο) structure, edifice, building || (εφεύρεση) invention, fabrication.

κατασκήνωση, n [kataskeenosee] camp, encampment || camping.

κατάσκοπος, ο [kataskopos] spy, secret agent.

κάτασπρος [kataspros] pure white, white as a sheet.

κατασταλάζω [katastalazo] (μεταφ) end in, conclude, settle out.

κατάσταση, n [katastase] situation, condition, state || (περιουσία) wealth, property || (ονομαστική) register, list.

καταστατικό, το [katastateeko] (εταιρείας) statute.

καταστέλλω [katastelo] suppress, overcome || curb, control, contain.

κατάστημα, το [katasteema] establishment, institution || shop, store || **καταστηματάρχης** shopkeeper.

κατάστιχο, το [katasteeho] accounts book || register.

καταστολή, n [katastolee] suppression || checking, bridling, controlling.

καταστρεπτικός [katastrepteekos] destructive, devastating, ruinous.

καταστρέφω [katastrefo] destroy, ruin, devastate || spoil, damage.

καταστροφή, n [katastrofee] destruction, ruin, disaster, catastrophe.

κατάστρωμα, το [katastroma] deck.

καταστρώνω [katastrono] draw up, make up, frame || lay down.

κατάσχεση, n [katashesee] seizure, confiscation || (λόγω χρέους) attachment.

κατάταξη, n [katataksee] classification, sorting, grading || (στρατ) induction.

κατατάσσομαι [katatasome] enlist.

κατατομή, n [katatomee] profile || vertical section, cutoff.

κατατόπια, τα [katatopeea] πλ locality, every nook and cranny.

κατατοπίζομαι [katatopeezome] find one's bearings.

κατατοπίζω [katatopeezo] direct, explain, inform.

κατατρέχω [katatreho] persecute, harass.

καταφανής [katafanees] obvious, evident, manifest.

καταφατικός [katafateekos] affirmative, positive.

καταφέρνω [kataferno] persuade, convince, accomplish, succeed || τα ~ succeed, manage.

καταφέρω [katafero] deal, strike || βλ και **καταφέρνω**.

καταφθάνω [katafthano] arrive || overtake, catch up, overhaul.

κατάφορτος [katafortos] overloaded.

καταφρονώ [katafrono] scorn, despise.

καταφύγιο, το [katafeeyo] refuge, hiding place.

κατάφυτος [katafeetos] covered with vegetation.

κατάφωτος [katafotos] profusely illuminated.

κατάχαμα [katahama] on the ground, on the floor.

καταχθόνιος [katahthoneeos] infernal, fiendish, devilish.

καταχραστής, ο [katahrastees] embezzler, defaulter.

καταχρεωμένος [katahreomenos] deep in debt.

κατάχρηση, η [katahreese] abuse, misuse, breach of trust.

καταχρώμαι [katahrome] abuse, take advantage of, presume upon.

καταχωρώ [katahoro] enter in a register, insert, register, record.

καταψηφίζω [katapseefeezo] vote against, oppose.

κατάψυξη, η [katapseeksee] refrigeration.

κατεβάζω [katevazo] let down || (αποσκευές) take or bring down || (θερμοκρασία κτλ) lower, reduce || (κόστος) lessen, decrease || (αυλαία) drop.

κατεβαίνω [kateveno] come down, go down, descend.

κατέβασμα, το [katevasma] descent, lowering, taking down.

κατεβασμένος [katevasmenos]

(τιμή) reduced || (κατηφής) depressed.

κατεδαφίζω [katedafeezo] demolish, pull down, raze.

κατειλημμένος [kateeleemenos] occupied, reserved.

κατεργάζομαι [katergazome] elaborate, work out, shape, fashion.

κατεργάρης, ο [katergarees] rascal, rogue || (επιθ) cunning, tricky.

κατέρχομαι [katerhome] βλ **κατεβαίνω**.

κατεύθυνση, η [kateftheensee] direction, line, course.

κατευθύνομαι [kateftheenome] turn, head (for).

κατευθύνω [kateftheeno] direct, guide, aim, turn.

κατευνάζω [katevnazo] calm, pacify, appease, mollify.

κατέχω [kateho] possess, own, have, hold || (θέση) occupy || (γνωρίζω) know.

κατεψυγμένος [katepseegmenos] frozen, icy, frigid, polar.

κατηγορηματικός [kateegoreemateekos] categorical, explicit.

κατηγορητήριο, το [kateegoreeteereeo] indictment.

κατηγορία, η [kateegoreea] accusation, charge || category, class, division.

κατήγορος, ο [kateegoros] plaintiff, accuser || δημόσιος ~ public prosecutor.

κατηγορούμενο, το [kateegoroumeno] (γραμμ) complement || attribute.

κατηγορούμενος [kateegoroumenos] the accused || defendant.

κατηγορώ [kateegoro] accuse, charge || blame, criticize.

κατηφής [kateefees] gloomy, depressed.

κατήφορος, ο [kateeforos] descent, slope.

κατηχώ [kateeho] (εκκλ) catechize || (σε οργάνωση) initiate.

κάτι [katee] something || some.

κατοικία, η [kateekeea] dwelling, residence, home.

κατοικίδιος [kateekeedeeos] domesticated.

κατοικώ [kateeko] live in, dwell in, inhabit, reside.

κατολίσθηση, η [katoleestheesee] landslide.

κατόπι(ν) [katop(i)ee] after, close after || then || behind || ~ν από after.

κατοπτρίζω [katoptreezo] reflect, mirror || (μεταφ) represent.

κατόρθωμα, το [katorthoma] achievement, feat.

κατορθώνω [katorthono] succeed in, perform well.

κατορθωτός [katorthotos] feasible, possible, practicable.

κατουρλιό, το [katourlio] urine, piss (col).

κατουρώ [katouro] piss (col), urinate.

κατοχή, η [katohee] possession || (στρατ) occupation || (νομ) detention.

κάτοχος, ο [katohos] possessor, occupier || experienced person.

κατοχυρώνω [katoheerono] fortify || (μεταφ) secure, safeguard.

κατρακυλώ [katrakeelo] bring down, tumble down, come down.

κατράμι, το [katramee] tar, asphalt.

κατσαβίδι, το [katsaveedee] screwdriver.

κατσάδα, η [katsaδa] scolding, dressing-down, reprimand.

κατσαρίδα, η [katsareeδa] cockroach.

κατσαρόλα, η [katsarola] saucepan.

κατσαρός [katsaros] curly, curled, fuzzy.

κατσίκα, η [katseeka] goat.

κατσικήσιος [katseekeeseeos] of a goat.

κατσίκι, το [katseekee] kid.

κατσουφιάζω [katsoufeeazo] look sour, look sullen, frown.

κάτω [kato] down, under, underneath, below || on the ground || στο ~ ~ after all || απάνω ~ approximately, about || άνω ~ upset, in a turmoil.

κατώτατος [katotatos] lowest, least, undermost.

κατώτερος [katoteros] lower || poorer (quality), inferior.

κατώφλι, το [katoflee] threshold, doorstep || (μεταφ) eve.

καυγάς, ο [kavgas] quarrel, wrangle, squabble, argument.

καύκαλο, το [kavkalo] skull || shell, carapace.

καύσιμα, τα [kavseema] πλ fuel.

καύσιμος [kavseemos] combustible, inflammable.

καύση, η [kavsee] burning || (χημ) combustion.

καυστικός [kavsteekos] caustic.

καύσωνας, ο [kavsonas] heatwave.

καυτερός [kavteros] hot || (υγρό) scalding || (μεταφ) caustic, biting.

καυτηριάζω [kavteereeazo] cauterize || (ζώα) brand || (μεταφ) stigmatize.

καυτός [kavtos] scalding, boiling, hot.

καύχημα, το [kavheema] boast, pride, glory.

καυχιέμαι [kavhieme] boast of, be proud of.

καφάσι, το [kafasee] trellis, lattice || (σε φρούτα) crate.

καφενείο, το [kafeneeo] coffee house.

καφές, ο [kafes] coffee.

καφετζής, ο [kafetsees] coffee-house keeper.

καφετιέρα, η [kafetiera] coffee pot.

καχεκτικός [kahekteekos] sickly (person), weakly (person).

καχύποπτος [kaheepoptos] suspicious, distrustful.

κάψα, η [kapsa] excessive heat.

καψαλίζω [kapsaleezo] singe, broil || toast.

κάψιμο, το [kapseemo] burning || scald.

καψούλι, το [kapsoulee] (ιατρ) capsule.

κέδρος, ο [keðros] cedar tree, cedar (wood).

κείμενο, το [keemeno] text.

κειμήλιο, το [keemeeleeo] heirloom, treasure.

κελαϊδώ [kelaeeðo] sing, warble, chirp.

κελεπούρι, το [kelepouree] bargain || windfall, godsend.

κελευστής, ο [kelevstees] petty officer.

κελλάρι, το [kelaree] cellar || larder.

κελλί, το [kelee] cell || honeycomb.

κέλυφος, το [keleefos] shell, husk, bark.

κενό, το [keno] void, empty space, vacuum || (μεταφ) gap.

κενός [kenos] empty || (οικία) unoccupied, vacant.

κέντημα, το [kenteema] sting, bite || embroidery || (μεταφ) exhortation.

κεντρί, το [kentree] sting || thorn.

κεντρίζω [kentreezo] (βόδι) prick, goad || (άλογο) spur || (δένδρο) graft || (μεταφ) rouse, stir up.

κεντρικός [kentreekos] central, middle || principal.

κεντρομόλος [kentromolos] centripetal.

κέντρο, το [kentro] (πόλης) centre || (γεωμ) centre || (διασκέδασης) (night) club, taverna ||

τηλεφωνικό ~ telephone exchange.

κεντρόφυγος [kentrofeegos] centrifugal.

κεντώ [kento] embroider || (μεταφ) incite, rouse, awaken, stir up.

κενώνω [kenono] empty || (δρόμο) drain || (συρτάρι) clean out || (σπίτι) evacuate.

κένωση, η [kenose] emptying, clearing out || bowel movement.

κεραία, η [kerea] antenna, feeler || (ασυρμάτου) aerial.

κεραμίδι, το [kerameeðee] tile, slate || **κεραμίδα η** roof.

κεραμική, η [kerameekee] ceramics.

κεράσι, το [kerasee] cherry || **κερασιά, η** cherry tree.

κέρασμα, το [kerasma] treat.

κερατάς, ο [keratas] cuckold.

κέρατο, το [kerato] horn || (για άνθρωπο) obstinate, perverse.

κεραυνοβόλος [keravnovolos] like lightning.

κεραυνός, ο [keravnos] thunderbolt.

κερδίζω [kerðeezo] win, earn || get, gain || profit by.

κέρδος, το [kerðos] earnings, winnings || advantage.

κερδοσκοπώ [kerðoskopo] speculate.

κερένιος [kereneeos] wax, waxen.

κερί, το [keree] wax || taper, wax candle.

κερκίδα, η [kerkeeða] tier of seats.

κέρμα, το [kerma] fragment || coin || (για μηχάνημα) token.

κερνώ [kerno] treat || stand or buy a drink.

κετσές, ο [ketses] felt.

κεφαλαιοκρατία, η [kefaleokrateea] capitalism.

κεφάλαια, τα [kefalea] πλ funds, capital.

κεφάλαιο, το [kefaleo] capital, funds || (βιβλίου) chapter.

κεφαλαίο, το [kefaleo] capital (letter).

κεφαλαιώδης [kefaleoðees] essential, fundamental.

κεφαλή, η [kefalee] head || leader, chief.

κεφάλι, το [kefalee] head || (μεταφ) brains.

κεφάτος [kefatos] well-disposed, merry, jovial.

κέφι, το [kefee] good humour, gaiety || **στο ~** merry, mellow.

κεφτές, ο [keftes] meatball, rissole.

κεχρί, το [kehree] millet.

κεχριμπάρι, το [kehreembaree] amber.

κηδεία, η [keeðeea] funeral (procession).

κηδεμόνας, ο [keeðemonas] guardian || curator.

κήλη, η [keelee] hernia, rupture.

κηλιδώνω [keeleeðono] stain, dirty || (μεταφ) sully, tarnish.

κηλίδα, η [keeleeða] spot, stain || (μεταφ) slur, blemish.

κήπος, ο [keepos] garden.

κηπουρική, η [keepoureekee] gardening, horticulture.

κηπουρός, ο [keepouros] gardener.

κηρήθρα, η [keereethra] honeycomb.

κηροπήγιο, το [keeropeeyo] candlestick, taper-stand.

κήρυγμα, το [keereegma] proclamation || (εκκλ) sermon, preaching.

κήρυκας, ο [keereekas] herald || (εκκλ) preacher.

κηρύσσω [keereeso] proclaim, announce || (εκκλ) preach.

κήτος, το [keetos] cetacean, whale.

κηφήνας, ο [keefeenas] drone || (μεταφ) idler, loafer.

κιάλια, τα [kialeea] πλ binoculars, opera glasses.

κίβδηλος [keevðeelos] adulterated, counterfeit || (μεταφ) fraudulent.

κιβώτιο, το [keevoteeo] chest, box || **~ ταχύτητων** gearbox.

κιγκλίδωμα, το [keengleeðoma] (φράκτης) barrier, fence || (σιδερένιο) grating || (ξύλινο) lattice work || (παραθύρου) bar.

κιθάρα, η [keethara] guitar.

κιλό, το [keelo] kilogram.

κιμάς, ο [keemas] minced meat.

κιμωλία, η [keemoleea] chalk.

Κίνα, η [keena] China.

κινδυνεύω [keenðeenevo] endanger || be in danger, risk, venture.

κίνδυνος, ο [keenðeenos] danger, peril, hazard, jeopardy.

κινέζικα, τα [keenezeeka] πλ Chinese language.

Κινέζικος [keenezeekos] Chinese.

Κινέζος, ο [keenezos] Chinese, Chinaman || **οι Κινέζοι** the Chinese.

κίνημα, το [keeneema] movement || (μεταφ) rebellion, revolt.

κινηματογράφος, ο [keeneematografos] cinema.

κίνηση, η [keeneesee] movement || (κυκλοφορίας) flow of traffic || (αξιών) transactions.

κινητήρας, ο [keeneeteeras] motor.

κινητός [keeneetos] movable.

κίνητρο, το [keeneetro] motive.

κινίνη, η [keeneene] quinine.

κινούμαι [keenoume] move.

κινώ [keeno] set in motion, move, rouse, make go, set going.

κιόλα(ς) [keeola(s)] already, also, even.

κιονοστοιχία, η [keeonosteeheea] colonnade.

κιόσκι, το [keeoskee] kiosk.

κίσσα, η [keesa] magpie.

κισσός, ο [keesos] ivy.

κιτρινίζω [keetreeneezo] go yellow, make yellow, pale.

κίτρινος [keetreenos] yellow || sallow, pale.

κίτρο, το [keetro] citron.

κλαδευτήρι, το [kladevteeree] pruning hook, pruning scissors.

κλαδεύω [kladevo] prune, trim.

κλάδος, ο [klados] branch, sector.

κλαίγομαι [klegome] complain, gripe.

κλαίω [kleo] cry, weep || feel sorry for, weep for.

κλάμα, το [klama] crying, wailing, weeping.

κλάνω [klano] break wind, fart (col).

κλαρί, το [klaree] small branch.

κλάση, η [klasee] class, age group, category.

κλάσμα, το [klasma] fraction || fragment.

κλασσικός [klaseekos] classic(al) || (μεταφ) standard, standing.

κλαψιάρης [klapseearees] given to complaining || tearful, plaintive.

κλάψιμο, το [klapseemo] crying, grumbling.

κλέβω [klevo] βλ **κλέπτω**.

κλειδαριά, η [kleedaria] lock || (ασφαλείας) safety lock || (κρεμαστή) padlock.

κλειδαρότρυπα, η [kleedarotreepa] keyhole.

κλειδί, το [kleedee] key.

κλειδώνω [kleedono] lock up || (περιορίζω) confine, coop up.

κλείδωση, η [kleedosee] joint.

κλείνω [kleeno] close, shut, shut up, seal || (με σύρτη) bolt || (βρύσση) turn off || ~ το **μάτι** wink || ~ τα **εξήντα** I'm nearing sixty.

κλείσιμο, το [kleeseemo] closing, locking up || (μεταφ) conclusion.

κλεισούρα, η [kleesoura] pass || mustiness.

κλειστός [kleestos] shut, closed.

κλέπτης, ο [kleptees] thief, burglar || (πορτοφολιών) pickpocket.

κλέπτω [klepto] (κάτι) steal || (κάποιο) rob || (με απάτη) cheat, swindle.

κλεφτά [klefta] furtively, stealthily || hurriedly.

κλέπτης, ο [kleftees] thief || klepht.

κλεφτοπόλεμος, ο [kleftopolemos] guerrilla warfare.

κλεφτός [kleftos] stolen || furtive, stealthy.

κλεψιά, η [klepseea] βλ **κλοπή**.

κλέψιμο, το [klepseemo] theft, robbery, burglary.

κλεψύδρα, η [klepseedra] water clock, sandglass.

κλήμα, το [kleema] vine || **κληματαριά**, η vine arbour, climbing vine || bower || **κληματόφυλλο**, το vine leaf.

κληρικός [kleereekos] clerical, of the clergy.

κληροδότημα, το [kleeroδoteema] legacy, bequest.

κληρονομιά, η [kleeronomeea] inheritance || heritage, legacy.

κληρονομικός [kleeronomeekos] hereditary.

κληρονόμος, ο, η [kleeronomos] heir, heiress.

κληρονομώ [kleeronomo] inherit, come into an estate.

κλήρος, ο [kleeros] lot, fate || (εκκλ) clergy || (μεταφ) lot, fortune.

κλήρωση, η [kleerosee] drawing of lottery, prize drawing.

κλήση, η [kleesee] call, calling || writ of summons.

κλητήρας, ο [kleeteeras] clerk || (δικαστικός) bailiff.

κλίβανος, ο [kleevanos] oven, kiln, furnace.

κλίμα, το [kleema] climate || (μεταφ) atmosphere.

κλίμακα, η [kleemaka] staircase,

stairs, ladder || scale || (μουσ) gamut, scale.

κλιμακωτός [kleemakotos] graduated.

κλιματισμός, ο [kleemateesmos] air conditioning.

κλινήρης [kleeneerees] bedridden.

κλινική, η [kleeneekee] clinic, (private) hospital.

κλίνω [kleeno] lean, bend || (έχω τάση προς) tend || (γραμμ) decline, conjugate.

κλίση, η [kleesee] inclination, slope || proneness, tendency || (γραμμής) slope || (γραμμ) declension, conjugation || (γραμμ) slant.

κλονίζομαι [kloneezome] stagger || (μεταφ) hesitate, falter, waver.

κλονίζω [kloneezo] shake, unsettle || (υγεία) damage, ruin.

κλονισμός, ο [kloneesmos] shaking, concussion || (μεταφ) hesitation, wavering.

κλοπή, η [klopee] theft, robbery, burglary.

κλοπιμαίος [klopeemeos] stolen || furtive, stealthy.

κλουβί, το [klouvee] cage.

κλούβιος [klouveeos] bad, rotten || (μεταφ) empty-headed, stupid.

κλύσμα, το [kleesma] enema.

κλώθω [klotho] spin.

κλωνάρι, το [klonaree] branch (of tree) || shoot.

κλώσιμο, το [kloseemo] spinning.

κλώσσα, η [klosa] (brooding) hen.

κλωστή, η [klostee] thread, string.

κλωτσιά, η [klotsia] kick.

κλωτσώ [klotso] kick.

κνήμη, η [kneemee] shin || leg.

κόβομαι [kovome] cut o.s.

κόβω [kovo] (ψωμί) cut, slice || (μαλλιά) cut, trim || (νύχια) pare || (κρέας) carve || (νομίσματα) coin, mint || (νερό) turn off || (καφέ, σιτάρι) grind, mill || (κεφάλι) behead || (εφόδια) cut off || ~ μονέδα

make money || ~ εισιτήριο buy a ticket || ~ δεξιά turn right.

κόγχη, η [konghee] marine shell || (ματιού) eye socket || (αρχιτεκ) niche.

κοιλάδα, η [keelaδa] valley, vale.

κοιλιά, η [keelia] belly, abdomen || (τοίχου) bulge.

κοίλος [keelos] hollow, sunken.

κοιλότητα, η [keeloteeta] hollowness || concavity.

κοιμάμαι [keemame] sleep, be asleep.

κοίμηση, η [keemeesee] (εκκλ) Assumption || sleeping.

κοιμητήριο, το [keemeeteereeo] cemetery, graveyard.

κοιμίζω [keemeezo] put to sleep || quiet, lull, beguile.

κοιμισμένος [keemeesmenos] (μεταφ) sluggish, stupid, dull.

κοιμούμαι [keemoume] βλ κοιμάμαι.

κοινοβουλευτικός [keenovoulevteekos] parliamentary, parliamentarian.

κοινοβούλιο, το [keenovouleeo] parliament || (στην Αγγλία) Houses of Parliament.

κοινό, το [keeno] the public.

κοινοποιώ [keenopeeo] notify, inform, announce || serve (a notice).

κοινοπολιτεία, η [keenopoleeteea] commonwealth.

κοινός [keenos] common || ordinary, vulgar || (εργασία κτλ) collective || (γραμμ) common (noun) || κοινή γνώμη public opinion || από κοινού in common, together.

κοινότητα, η [keenoteeta] community || parish || Βουλή των Κοινοτήτων House of Commons.

κοινοτοπία, η [keenotopeea] commonplace || banality.

κοινωνία, η [keenonea] society,

community, association || (εκκλ) Holy Communion.

κοινωνικός [keenoneekos] social, sociable || **κοινωνικός λειτουργός** social worker.

κοινωνώ [keenono] receive Holy Communion || administer Holy Communion.

κοιτάζω [keetazo] look at, pay attention to || consider, see || attend.

κοίτασμα, το [keetasma] layer, deposit, stratum.

κοιτίδα, η [keeteeda] cradle || (μεταφ) origin, birthplace.

κοιτώνας, ο [keetonas] bedroom || dormitory.

κοκεταρία, η [koketareea] smartness, coquetry, stylishness.

κόκκαλο, το [kokalo] bone || (ναπουτσιού) shoehorn || **έμεινε ~** he was astounded.

κοκκινέλι, το [kokeenelee] red wine.

κοκκινίζω [kokeeneezo] redden, blush, turn red.

κοκκινογούλι, το [kokeenogoulee] beetroot, beet.

κοκκινομάλλης [kokeenomalees] red-haired.

κόκκινος [kokeenos] red, scarlet || (μάγουλα) ruddy, rosy.

κόκκος, ο [kokos] grain || (καφέ) bean || (σκόνης) speck.

κοκκύτης, ο [kokeetees] whooping cough.

κόρκορας, ο [kokoras] cock, rooster.

κοκορέτσι, το [kokoretsee] sheep's entrails.

κολάζω [kolazo] punish, chastise.

κολακεία, η [kolakeea] flattery, softsoaping.

κολακευτικός [kolakevteekos] complimentary.

κολακεύω [kolakevo] flatter, fawn upon.

κόλακας, ο [kolakas] flatterer, wheedler.

κόλαση, η [kolasee] hell.

κολατσιό, το [kolatsio] snack.

κολικός, ο [koleekos] colic.

κολιός, ο [kolios] kind of mackerel.

κόλλα, η [kola] glue, gum, paste || (κολλαρίσματος) starch || (χαρτιού) sheet of paper.

κολλάρο, το [kolaro] collar.

κολλέγιο, το [koleyo] college.

κόλλημα, το [koleema] glueing, sticking || soldering.

κολλητικός [koleeteekos] contagious, infectious.

κολλητός [koleetos] soldered || close-fitting || (εφαπτόμενος) contiguous.

κολλιέ, το [kolie] necklace.

κόλλυβα, τα [koleeva] πλ boiled wheat (given after funerals).

κολλώ [kolo] glue, stick, paste || solder, fuse || (αρρώστεια) get, catch || (σε κάποιο) stick to, attach to.

κολοκύθι, το [kolokeethee] vegetable marrow, pumpkin.

κολόνα, η [kolona] βλ **κολώνα**.

κολόνια, η [koloneea] eau de Cologne.

κολοσσιαίος, ο [kolosieos] colossal, enormous.

κολοσσός, ο [kolosos] colossus, giant.

κόλπο, το [kolpo] trick, artifice, deceit.

κόλπος, ο [kolpos] breast, bosom || (γεωγραφικός) gulf, bay.

κολυμβήθρα, η [koleemveethra] font.

κολυμβητής, ο [koleemveetees] swimmer.

κολύμπι, το [koleembee] swimming.

κολυμπώ [koleembo] swim.

κολώνα, η [kolona] pillar, column.

κόμβος, ο [komvos] knot || junction.

κόμης, ο [komees] count, earl.

κομητεία, η [komeeteea] county, shire.

κομήτης, ο [komeetees] comet.

κομιστής, ο [komeestees] carrier, bearer.

κόμιστρα, τα [komeestra] πλ carriage fees.

κόμμα, το [koma] (πολιτικό) party || (γραμμ) comma || (μαθημ) decimal point.

κομματάρχης, ο [komatarhees] party leader.

κομμάτι, το [komatee] piece || (ψωμί) slice || (ζάχαρη) lump || fragment, chip || (επιρ) a bit.

κομματιάζω [komateeazo] cut up, parcel out, tear, break.

κομμένος [komenos] sliced, cut || (κουρασμένος) exhausted.

κομ(μ)οδίνο, το [komodeeno] bedside table.

κομμουνιστής, ο [komouneestees] communist.

κόμμωση, η [komosee] hairdressing, hair style.

κομμωτήριο, το [komoteereeo] hairdressing salon.

κομπιάζω [kombeeazo] (μεταφ) hesitate.

κομπίνα, η [kombeena] racket (col).

κομπιναιζόν, το [kombeenezon] slip, petticoat.

κομπόδεμα, το [komboðema] hoard of money, savings.

κομπολό(γι)ι, το [kombolo(y)ee] string of beads, worry beads.

κόμπος, ο [kombos] βλ **κόμβος**.

κομπόστα, η [kombosta] compote.

κομπρέσσα, η [kombresa] compress.

κομφόρ, τα [komfor] πλ home comforts, necessities.

κομψός [kompsos] fashionable, stylish, smart.

κονδύλιο, το [konðeeleeo] item, entry.

κονιάκ, το [koneeak] cognac, brandy.

κονίαμα, το [koneeama] mortar || plaster.

κονσέρβα, η [konserva] tinned food, canned food, preserve(s).

κονσέρτο, το [konserto] concert.

κοντά [konta] close to, close by, near || almost, nearly || ~ **σε** near, next to || ~ **στα άλλα** moreover.

κονταίνω [konteno] shorten, curtail || get shorter.

κοντάρι, το [kontaree] pole || (σημαίας) staff || (ναυτ) mast.

κοντεύω [kontevo] be about to, be nearly finished, be on the verge (of) || (πλησιάζω) approach, come near, draw near.

κόντημα, το [konteema] shortening, shrinking.

κοντινός [konteenos] neighbouring, near(by) || (δρόμος) short, quick.

κοντός [kontos] short || (ουσ) pole, post, stake.

κοντοστέκω [kontosteko] pause || hesitate, waver.

κόντρα [kontra] against, opposite.

κοπάδι, το [koraðee] flock || herd, drove || (λύκων) pack || (ανθρώπων) crowd, throng.

κοπάζω [kopazo] calm down, grow quiet, subside.

κοπανίζω [kopaneezo] beat, pound, grind.

κόπανος, ο [kopanos] pestle, crusher || (μεταφ) fool, idiot.

κοπέλλα, η [kopela] girl || (υπηρεσίας) servant, maid.

κοπή, η [kopee] cutting || stoppage.

κόπια, η [kopeea] copy, transcript.

κοπιάζω [kopeeazo] labour, toil || take the trouble (to).

κοπιαστικός [kopeeasteekos] wearisome, hard, fatiguing, troublesome.

κοπίδι, το [kopeeðee] chisel.

κόπος, ο [kopos] fatigue, toil, labour, trouble, effort.

κόπρανα, τα [koprana] πλ excrement.

κοπριά, η [kopreea] dung, manure.

κοπρόσκυλο, το [koproskeelo] (μεταφ) worthless person, scoundrel.

κοπτήρας, ο [kopteeras] incisor || (χαρτοκοπτήρας) cutter.

κοπτική, η [kopteekee] cutting, tailoring.

κόπτω [kopto] βλ κόβω.

κόπωση, η [koposee] fatigue, weariness, toil.

κόρακας, ο [korakas] crow, raven.

κοράλλι, το [koralee] coral.

κορδέλλα, η [kordela] ribbon, band, tape || (μεταφ) zigzag, twist and turn.

κορδόνι, το [kordonee] cord, string.

κορδώνομαι [kordonome] strut, swagger, put on airs.

κορδώνω [kordono] tighten, stretch, extend.

κορεσμός, ο [koresmos] satisfaction, satiety.

κόρη, η [koree] girl || (παρθένα) virgin || (παιδί) daughter || (οφθαλμού) pupil.

κοριός, ο [korios] bedbug.

κοριτσάκι, το [koreetsakee] little girl.

κορίτσι, το [koreetsee] girl || virgin.

κορμί, το [kormee] body || trunk.

κορμός, ο [kormos] trunk.

κορμοστασιά, η [kormostasia] stature, bearing, figure.

κορνάρω [kornaro] sound one's horn, hoot.

κορνίζα, η [korneeza] frame || cornice.

κοροϊδεύω [koroeedevo] scoff at, laugh at, ridicule || deceive.

κορόιδο, το [koroeedo] laughing stock, butt, scapegoat.

κορσές, ο [korses] corset.

κορτάρω [kortaro] flirt, court.

κορυδαλλός, ο [koreedalos] skylark, lark.

κορυφαίος, ο [koreefeos] leader, chief.

κορυφή, η [koreefee], κορφή, η [korfee] top || (όρους) top, peak || (γωνίας) vertex || (μεταφ) leading person, outstanding person.

κόρφος, ο [korfos] bosom.

κορώνα, η [korona] crown, coronet || ~ γράμματα heads or tails.

κοσκινίζω [koskeeneezo] sift, screen || (μεταφ) sift carefully.

κόσκινο, το [koskeeno] sieve, sifter.

κοσμάκης, ο [kosmakees] the man in the street.

κόσμημα, το [kosmeema] decoration, jewel || κοσμήματα πλ jewellery.

κοσμήτορας, ο [kosmeetoras] dean (of university).

κοσμικός [kosmeekos] lay || mundane || (γεγονός) social.

κόσμιος [kosmeeos] decent, modest, proper.

κόσμος, ο [kosmos] universe, world || (άνθρωποι) people || (στόλισμα) embellishment.

κοσμώ [kosmo] adorn, embellish.

κοστίζω [kosteezo] cost, be expensive.

κόστος, το [kostos] cost, price.

κοστούμι, το [kostoumee] suit.

κότερο, το [kotero] sailboat, yacht || (ναυτ) cutter.

κοτέτσι, το [kotetsee] hen coop.

κοτόπουλο, το [kotopoulo] chicken.

κοτρώνι, το [kotronee] large stone, boulder.

κοτσάνι, το [kotsanee] stem, stalk.

κότσι, το [kotsee] anklebone.

κότσια, τα [kotseea] πλ guts, strength.

κοτσίδα, η [kotseeda] tress, braid, pigtail.

κότσυφας, ο [kotseefas] blackbird.

κότ(τ)α, η [kota] hen || fowl.

κουβαλώ [kouvalo] carry, bring, transport.

κουβάρι, το [kouvaree] ball.

κουβαριάζω [kouvareeazo] wind into a ball || crumple || (μεταφ) cheat.

κουβαρίστρα, η [kouvareestra] bobbin, spool.

κουβάς, ο [kouvas] bucket, pail.

κουβέντα, η [kouventa] conversation, chat.

κουβεντιάζω [kouventeeazo] converse, discuss, chat.

κουβέρ, το [kouver] service charge, cover charge.

κουβέρτα, η [kouverta] blanket, coverlet || (ναυτ) deck.

κουδούνι, το [koudhounee] bell || (εισόδου) doorbell.

κουδουνίζω [koudhouneezo] ring, tinkle, jingle.

κουδουνίστρα, η [koudhouneestra] rattle.

κουζίνα, η [kouzeena] kitchen || (για μαγείρευμα) stove.

κουκέτα, η [kouketa] berth.

κουκί, το [koukee] broad bean || grain.

κούκλα, η [koukla] doll || (ράφτη) dummy || (καλαμποκιού) corn cob || (μεταφ) lovely child || pretty woman.

κούκος, ο [koukos] cuckoo || bonnet, cap.

κουκουβάγια, η [koukouvaya] owl.

κουκούλα, η [koukoula] cowl, hood || (τσαγιού) tea cosy.

κουκούλι, το [koukoulee] cocoon.

κουκουλώνω [koukoulono] keep secret || bury || wrap warmly.

κουκουνάρι, το [koukounaree] pine cone || seed of pine cone.

κουκούτσι, το [koukoutsee] stone, kernel, pip || (μεταφ) morsel, scrap.

κουλούρα, η [kouioura] roll, French roll || (ναυτ) lifebuoy.

κουλούρι, το [koulouree] ring-shaped biscuit.

κουλουριάζω [kouloureeazo] coil, roll up, fold.

κουμάντο, το [koumanto] order, control.

κουμπάρα, η [koumbara] godmother || matron of honour.

κουμπαράς, ο [koumbaras] moneybox, piggy bank.

κουμπάρος, ο [koumbaros] godfather || (σε γάμο) best man.

κουμπί, το [koumbee] button, stud || (φώτων) switch.

κουμπότρυπα, η [koumbotreepa] buttonhole.

κουμπώνω [koumbono] button up, fasten.

κουνάβι, το [kounavee] marten, ferret.

κουνέλι, το [kounelee] rabbit.

κούνημα, το [kouneema] shaking, swinging, wagging || (μεταφ) swaying.

κούνια, η [kounea] cradle, cot, crib || (κήπου) swing.

κουνιάδα, η [kouneeadha] sister-in-law.

κουνιάδος, ο [kouneeadhos] brother-in-law.

κουνιστός [kouneestos] rocking || (μεταφ) swaying.

κουνούπι, το [kounoupee] mosquito.

κουνουπίδι, το [kounoupeedhee] cauliflower.

κουνιέμαι [kounieme] move, shake || get moving.

κουνώ [kouno] move, shake || (μαντήλι) wave || (ουρά) wag || (μωρό) rock || (κεφάλι) shake.

κούπα, η [koupa] cup, bowl, glass || (σε χαρτιά) heart.

κουπί, το [koupee] oar || **τραβώ ~** to row.

κούρα, η [koura] cure || medical attendance.

κουράγιο, το [kourayo] bravery, fearlessness.

κουράζομαι [kourazome] get tired, tire o.s.

κουράζω [kourazo] tire, weary || bore || (όραση) strain.

κουράση, η [kourasee] weariness, fatigue || (μηχανής) wear and tear.

κουρασμένος [kourasmenos] tired, weary || (πρόσωπο) drawn.

κουραστικός [kourasteekos] tiresome, trying, troublesome.

κουραφέξαλα, τα [kourafeksala] πλ bullshit (col), balls (col).

κουρδίζω [kourŏeezo] wind up || (βιολί) tune || (μεταφ) stir up, incite.

κουρέας, ο [koureas] barber.

κουρείο, το [koureeo] barber's shop.

κουρέλι, το [kourelee] rag, tatter, shred.

κούρεμα, το [kourema] haircut || shearing, clipping.

κουρεύω [kourevo] cut the hair of, trim, clip || (πρόβατο) shear || (χλόη) mow.

κουρκούτι, το [kourkootee] batter || pap.

κούρσα, η [koursa] race || (διαδρομή) ride || (αμάξι) car.

κουρσάρος, ο [koursaros] pirate.

κουρσεύω [koursevo] plunder, raid.

κουρτίνα, η [kourteena] curtain.

κουσούρι, το [kousouree] defect, fault.

κουτάβι, το [koutavee] puppy.

κουτάλι, το [koutalee] spoon.

κουταμάρα, η [koutamara] foolishness, nonsense.

κούτελο, το [koutelo] forehead.

κουτί, το [koutee] box, case || (σπίρτων) matchbox || (κονσέρβας) tin.

κουτός [koutos] silly, foolish, slow-witted.

κουτουλώ [koutoulo] nod drowsily || butt.

κουτουρού [koutourou]: στα ~ heedlessly, haphazardly, by chance.

κουτρουβάλα, η [koutrouvala] somersault.

κουτσαίνω [koutseno] limp || cripple.

κουτσομπολεύω [koutsombolevo] gossip, spread reports, tittle-tattle.

κουτσομπολιό, το [koutsombolio] gossip, tittle-tattle.

κουτσός [koutsos] crippled, limping.

κούτσουρο, το [koutsouro] log, stump.

κουφαίνομαι [koufenome] go deaf.

κουφαίνω [koufeno] deafen, make deaf.

κουφαμάρα, η [koufamara] deafness.

κουφάρι, το [koufaree] body || corpse.

κουφέτο, το [koufeto] sugared almond.

κούφιος [koufeeos] hollow, empty || (δόντι) decayed || (ήχος) muffled || (άνθρωπος) not serious, frivolous.

κουφόβραση, η [koufovrasee] sweltering heat.

κουφός [koufos] hard of hearing.

κούφωμα, το [koufoma] hollow, cavity || opening.

κοφίνι, το [kofeenee] basket, hamper, pannier.

κοφτά [kofta]: ορθά ~ frankly, categorically.

κοφτερός [kofteros] sharp, cutting.

κόφτω [kofto] βλ **κόβω**.

κόχη, η [kohee] βλ **κώχη**.

κοχλάζω [kohlazo] boil, bubble || (μεταφ) seethe.

κοχλίας, ο [kohleeas] snail || (ήλος) screw.

κοχύλι, το [koheelee] sea shell.

κόψη, η [kopsee] cutting, slicing, clipping || edge.

κόψιμο, το [kopseemo] cut, gash || cutting || (ασθένια) bellyache (col).

κραγιόν, το [krayon] crayon || lipstick.

κραδαίνω [kradeno] flourish, wave, vibrate.

κράζω [krazo] croak, caw || cry out || call.

κραιπάλη, η [krepalee] riot, orgy || drunkenness.

κράμα, το [krama] mixture, blend || alloy, amalgam.

κρανίο, το [kraneeo] cranium || skull.

κράνος, το [kranos] helmet.

κράξιμο, το [krakseemo] crowing, cawing.

κρασί, το [krasee] wine.

κράση, η [krasee] (σώματος) temperament, make-up.

κράσπεδο, το [kraspedo] (λόφου) foot || (πεζοδρομίου) kerb || curb (US).

κρατήρας, ο [krateeras] crater.

κράτηση, η [krateese] confinement, arrest || (μισθού) deduction(s).

κρατιέμαι [kratieme] hold one's own, be well preserved.

κρατικοποίηση, η [krateekopieesee] nationalization.

κρατικός [krateekos] national.

κράτος, το [kratos] influence, power, authority || the state.

κρατώ [krato] last, keep || (επιβάλλομαι) hold in check, rule || (κατάγομαι) be descended from || (βαστώ) have, hold || (υποβαστώ) support.

κραυγάζω [kravgazo] cry, howl, shout, scream.

κραυγή, η [kravyee] shout, cry, outcry.

κρέας, το [kreas] meat, flesh.

κρεββάτι, το [krevatee] bed.

κρεββατοκάμαρα, η [krevatokamara] bedroom.

κρεββατώνω [krevatono] confine to bed, lay up.

κρέμα, η [krema] cream.

κρεμάζω [kremazo] hang, suspend.

κρεμάλα, η [kremala] gallows, gibbet.

κρέμασμα, το [kremasma] suspension, hooking on || hanging.

κρεμαστός [kremastos] suspended.

κρεμάστρα, η [kremastra] hanger || hat rack || portmanteau.

κρεμιέμαι [kremieme] hang, be suspended.

κρεμμύδι, το [kremeedee] onion.

κρεμ(ν)ώ [krem(n)o] hang, hook up, suspend.

κρεοπώλης, ο [kreopolees] butcher.

κρεουργώ [kreourgo] butcher || massacre.

κρεπ, το [krep] crêpe rubber || crape.

κρημνίζομαι [kreemneezome] fall, crumble, collapse.

κρημνίζω [kreemneezo] hurl down, pull down, wreck.

κρήνη, η [kreenee] fountain.

κρηπίδωμα, το [kreepeedoma] foundation, base, groundwork || (ναυτ) breakwater || (σταθμού) railway platform.

κρησφύγετο, το [kreesfeeyeto] hideaway, retreat.

κριάρι, το [kreearee] ram.

κριθαράκι, το [kreetharakee] barley-shaped noodle || (ματιού) stye.

κριθάρι, το [kreetharee] barley.

κρίκος, ο [kreekos] link, buckle, ring || (συνцήσεως) jack.

κρίμα, το [kreema] sin, guilt || pity, misfortune || τι ~! what a pity!, what a shame!

κρίνος, ο [kreenos] lily.

κρίνω [kreeno] judge, consider || (αποφασίζω) decide.

κριός, ο [krios] ram.

κρίσιμος [kreeseemos] critical, grave, momentous || trying.

κρίση, η [kreesee] judgment, view || (οικονομική) crisis, depression || (έλλειψη) deficiency, shortage || (πνεύματος) judgment.

κριτήριο, το [kreeteereeo] criterion, test.

κριτής, ο [kreetees] judge.

κριτική, η [kreeteekee] criticism, review.

κριτικός [kreeteekos] discerning, critical || (ουσ) critic.

κροκόδειλος, ο [krokoðeelos] crocodile.

κρόκος, ο [krokos] crocus || (αυγού) yolk.

κρόσσι, το [krosee] fringe.

κρόταφος, ο [krotafos] (ανατ) temple.

κρότος, ο [krotos] crash, bang, noise || (μεταφ) sensation.

κρουαζιέρα, η [krouaziera] cruise.

κρούση, η [krousee] striking, sounding || (στρατ) encounter.

κρούσμα, το [krousma] (ιατρ, νομ) case.

κρούστα, η [krousta] crust, rind || scab.

κρούω [krouo] strike, sound || knock on || (κουδούνι) ring.

κρυάδα, η [kreeaða] cold, chill.

κρύβομαι [kreevome] go into hiding.

κρύβω [kreevo] βλ κρύπτω.

κρυμμένος [kreemenos] concealed.

κρύο, το [kreeo] cold.

κρυολόγημα, το [kreeoloyeema] (ιατρ) cold.

κρυοπάγημα, το [kreeopayeema] frostbite.

κρύος [kreeos] cold || indifferent, phlegmatic, cool.

κρύπτω [kreepto] hide, conceal || cover, screen || (μεταφ) withhold, hold back.

κρυστάλλινος [kreestaleenos] like crystal, very clear.

κρύσταλλο, το [kreestalo] crystal (glass).

κρυφά [kreefa] secretly, clandestinely, stealthily.

κρυφός [kreefos] private, secluded || (χαρά) secret, inner || (άνθρωπος) discreet, reticent.

κρύψιμο, το [kreepseemo] concealing, hiding.

κρυψίνους [kreepseenous] deceitful, underhand, sneaky.

κρυψώνας, ο [kreepsonas] hideout, lurking place.

κρυώνω [kreeono] grow cold, feel cold || cool down, chill.

κτένι, το [ktenee] comb || (τσουγκράνα) rake || κτενίζω to comb || (μεταφ) brush up, finish in detail || ~σμα combing || hair-dressing.

κτήμα, το [kteema] estate, land || κτηματίας, ο landowner, proprietor.

κτηνίατρος, ο [kteeneeatros] veterinary surgeon.

κτήνος, το [kteenos] brute, beast, animal || κτήνη cattle.

κτηνοτροφία, η [kteenotrofeea] stockbreeding.

κτηνώδης [kteenoðees] beastly, bestial || (όρεξη) hoggish.

κτήση, η [kteesee] acquisition, occupation, occupancy.

κτητικός [kteeteekos] (γραμμ) possessive || acquisitive.

κτίζω [kteezo] construct, erect, build.

κτίριο, το [kteereeo] building, edifice.

κτίσιμο, το [kteeseemo] building, erection.

κτίστης, ο [kteestees] builder, mason.

κτυπώ [kteepo] beat, strike, flog, thrash.

κυάνιο, το [keeaneeo] cyanide.

κυβέρνηση, η [keeverneesee] government, management.

κυβερνήτης, ο [keeverneetees] governor || (ναυτ) commander.

κυβερνητικός [keeverneeteekos] governmental.

κυβερνώ [keeverno] govern || (πλοίο) steer || (σπίτι) manage, direct.

κύβος, ο [keevos] cube || die.

κυδώνι, το [keedonee] quince || (όστρακο) kind of shellfish.

κύηση, η [kieesee] pregnancy || gestation.

κυκλάμινο, το [keeklameeno] cyclamen.

κυκλικός [keekleekos] circular.

κύκλος, ο [keeklos] circle || (ηλιακός κτλ) cycle, period || (προσώπων) set.

κυκλοφορία, η [keekloforeea] circulation || (αυτοκινήτων) traffic flow.

κυκλοφορώ [keekloforo] put into circulation, spread || go about.

κύκλωμα, το [keekloma] electric circuit || encirclement.

κυκλώνας, ο [keeklonas] cyclone.

κυκλώνω [keeklono] surround, encircle, envelop.

κύκνος, ο [keeknos] swan.

κυλάω [keelao] roll.

κυλιέμαι [keelieme] roll over || (χοίρος) wallow.

κυλικείο, το [keeleekeeo] buffet, sideboard || refreshment room.

κύλινδρος, ο [keeleenðros] cylinder || roller, barrel.

κυλότα, η [keelota] panties.

κύμα, το [keema] wave.

κυμαίνομαι [keemenome] undulate, wave, ripple || (μεταφ) fluctuate, waver, hesitate.

κυματίζω [keemateezo] wave, flutter || ripple.

κυματοθραύστης, ο [keematothravstees] breakwater.

κύμινο, το [keemeeno] cumin.

κυνήγι, το [keeneeyee] hunting, shooting, chase || game.

κυνηγός, ο [keeneegos] hunter, shooter.

κυνηγώ [keeneego] hunt, chase, run after || go shooting.

κυνικός [keeneekos] cynic(al).

κυοφορώ [keeoforo] be pregnant.

κυπαρίσσι, το [keepareesee] cypress tree.

κύπελλο, το [keepelo] cup, goblet, tumbler.

κυπριακός [keepreeakos] Cypriot.

Κύπριος, ο [keepreeos] Cypriot.

Κύπρος, η [keepros] Cyprus.

κύπτω [keepto] bend, bow || slant || (μεταφ) give way.

κυρά, η [keera] missus (col).

κυρία, η [keereea] lady, mistress || Mrs.

Κυριακή, η [keereeakee] Sunday.

κυριαρχία, η [keereearheea] sovereignty, dominion.

κυριαρχώ [keereearho] dominate, exercise authority || be sovereign.

κυριεύω [keerievo] subjugate, capture, dominate || (πάθος) seize, possess.

κυριολεκτικώς [keereeolekteekòs] exactly, precisely, to the letter.

κύριος, ο [keereeos] master, sir, gentleman || Mr.

κύριος [keereeos] essential, vital || main, chief, leading.

κυριότητα, η [keereeoteeta] ownership.

κυρίως [keereeos] principally, chiefly, mainly, especially.

κύρος, το [keeros] authority, power || validity, weight.

κυρτός [keertos] bent, crooked || convex, bulging.

κυρώνω [keerono] confirm || (νόμο)

sanction, approve || (απόφαση)
ratify, validate.
κύρωση, η [keerosee]
confirmation, sanction || penalty.
κύστη, η [keestee] bladder, cyst.
κύτος, το [keetos] (ναυτ) hold.
κυττάζω βλ **κοιτάζω.**
κύτταρο, το [keetaro] cell.
κυψέλη, η [keepselee] swarm (of bees) || beehive || (αυτιού) earwax.
κώδικας, ο [kοδeekas] code || codex.
κωδωνοκρουσία, η [kοδonokrouseea] chiming, ringing, pealing.
κωδωνοστάσιο, το [kοδonostaseeo] belfry, church steeple.
κώκ, το [kok] coke.
κώλος, ο [kolos] arse (col), bottom, backside (col) || ~ **και βρακί** intimate.
κωλοφωτιά, η [kolofotia] glow-worm.
κώλυμα, το [koleema] obstacle, impediment.
κωλυσιεργώ [koleesiergo] obstruct, hinder.
κωλύω [koleeo] stop, prevent, hinder.
κώμα, το [koma] coma.
κωματώδης [komatοδees] comatose, lethargic.
κωμικός [komeekos] comic(al), funny || (ουσ) comedian.
κωμόπολη, η [komopolee] market town.
κωμωδία, η [komοδeea] comedy.
κώνος, ο [konos] cone.
κωπηλασία, η [kopeelaseea] rowing.
κωπηλάτης, ο [kopeelatees] rower.
κωφάλαλος [kofalalos] deaf-and-dumb.
κώχη, η [kohee] corner, nook, recess || (πανταλονιού) crease.

Λ, λ

λάβα, η [lava] lava.
λαβαίνω [laveno] βλ **λαμβάνω.**
λάβαρο, το [lavaro] banner, standard.
λαβείν, το [laveen] credit || **δούναι και** ~ debit and credit.
λαβή, η [lavee] handle, grip || pretext, excuse, reason.
λαβίδα, η [laveeδa] grip, nippers, hold || (χειρουργική) forceps.
λάβρα, η [lavra] excessive heat, suffocating heat.
λαβράκι, το [lavrakee] bass fish.
λαβύρινθος, ο [laveereenthos] labyrinth.
λαβωματιά, η [lavomatia] wound.
λαβώνω [lavono] wound.
λαγάνα, η [lagana] unleavened bread.
λαγκάδι, το [langaδee] ravine, narrow valley, defile.
λάγνος [lagnos] lewd, lascivious, wanton.
λαγός, ο [lagos] hare.
λαγωνικό, το [lagoneeko] hunting dog || greyhound, pointer.
λαδερός [laδeros] oily, greasy || cooked with oil.
λάδι, το [laδee] olive oil.
λαδομπογιά, η [laδomboya] oil paint.
λαδόχαρτο, το [laδoharto] greaseproof paper.
λαδώνω [laδono] apply oil || lubricate || (μεταφ) bribe.
λαδωτήρι, το [laδoteeree] cruet stand.
λάθος, το [lathos] error, mistake, slip, fault || **κατά** ~ by mistake.
λαθραίος [lathreos] furtive, clandestine, secret.
λαθραίως [lathreos] secretly, furtively, stealthily.

λαθρεμπόριο, το [lathremboreeo] smuggling || contraband.

λαθρέμπορος, ο [lathremboros] smuggler, contrabandist.

λαθρεπιβάτης, ο [lathrepeevatees] stowaway.

λαίδη, η [ieðee] (τίτλος) lady.

λαϊκός [laeekos] popular, familiar, vulgar || current, common || lay.

λαίμαργος [lemargos] gluttonous, greedy || (ουσ) gourmand.

λαιμός, ο [lemos] neck, throat, gullet || (μεταξύ βουνών) gorge, pass.

λακέρδα, η [lakerða] salted tunny fish.

λακές, ο [lakes] lackey, flunkey.

λακκάκι, το [lakakee] dimple.

λάκκος, ο [lakos], **λακκούβα, η** [lakouva] hole, pit || grave.

λακτίζω [lakteezo] kick, boot, lash out.

λακωνικός [lakoneekos] laconic, terse, brief.

λαλιά, η [lalia] voice || speech || (για πουλιά) singing, warbling.

λαλώ [lalo] speak, talk || crow || sing.

λάμα, η [lama] sheet, thin plate || (μαχαιριού) blade.

λαμαρίνα, η [lamareena] sheet iron, iron plate.

λαμβάνω [lamvano] take hold of, take || receive, obtain || ~ την τιμή I have the honour || ~ χώρα to take place, occur.

λάμδα, το [lamða] the letter Λ.

λάμπα, η [lamba] lamp || (ηλεκτρική) electric lamp, bulb.

λαμπάδα, η [lambaða] torch || candle, taper.

λαμποκοπώ [lambokopo] shine, gleam.

Λαμπρή, η [lambree] Easter.

λαμπρός [lambros] brillant, splendid, excellent, superb.

λαμπρώς [lambros] (επιρ) splendid!, excellent! || (επίρ) brilliantly.

λαμπτήρας, ο [lambteeras] βλ **λάμπα.**

λάμπω [lambo] shine, glitter, gleam || (μεταφ) excel.

λάμψη, η [lampsee] brightness, brilliance || glaze.

λανθάνω [lanthano] be latent || escape notice.

λανθασμένος [lanthasmenos] mistaken, wrong.

λανσάρω [lansaro] launch, advertise, present.

λαξεύω [laksevo] hew, chisel, carve.

λαογραφία, η [laografeea] folklore.

λαός, ο [laos] people, multitude, masses.

λαούτο, το [laouto] lute.

λαπάς, ο [lapas] pap, boiled rice || poultice || (μεταφ) indolent person.

λαρδί, το [larðee] lard, fat.

λαρύγγι, το [lareengee] throat, larynx, windpipe, gullet.

λαρυγγίτιδα, η [lareengeeteeða] laryngitis.

λαρυγγολόγος, ο [lareengologos] throat specialist.

λασκάρω [laskaro] slacken, loosen || (ναυτ) cast off.

λάσπη, η [laspee] mud, mire || mortar || **έκοψε** ~ he escaped || he disappeared.

λασπώνω [laspono] cover with mud, dirty, soil.

λαστιχένιος [lasteeheneeos] rubber || elastic.

λάστιχο, το [lasteeho] rubber || elastic || rubber band || (αυτοκινήτου) tyre || (παιδιού) catapult, sling.

λατέρνα, η [laterna] barrel organ.

λατινικά, τα [lateeneeka] πλ Latin.

λατινικός [lateeneekos] Latin.

λατομείο, το [latomeeo] quarry.

λατρεία, η [latreea] adoration, worship || (αγάπη) fervent love.

λατρευτός [latrevtos] adorable, adored.

λατρεύω [latrevo] adore || idolize.

λάτρης, ο [latrees] worshipper || fan.

λάφυρο, το [lafeero] booty, spoils, loot.

λαχαίνω [laheno] meet, come across || (συμβαίνω) happen, occur || (στον κλήρο) fall to, win.

λαχαναγορά, η [lahanagora] vegetable market.

λαχανιάζω [lahaneeazo] pant, gasp.

λαχανικό, το [lahaneeko] vegetable, green.

λάχανο, το [lahano] cabbage.

λαχείο, το [laheeo] lottery, raffle.

λαχνός, ο [lahnos] lot, chance || prize, share.

λαχτάρα, η [lahtara] anxiety || (επιθυμία) yearning || (φόβος) dread, fright.

λαχταρώ [lahtaro] be impatient || (επιθυμώ) yearn, desire || (φοβάμαι) be frightened.

λέαινα, η [layena] lioness.

λεβάντα, η [levanta] lavender.

λεβέντης, ο [leventees] fine man, gentleman || brave man.

λεβεντιά, η [leventia] manliness.

λέβητας, ο [leveetas] cauldron || boiler.

λεβιές, ο [levies] lever.

λεγάμενος [legamenos] **ο ~** you know who || the so-called.

λεγεώνα, η [leyeona] legion || great number.

λέγω [lego] say, tell, speak || (πιστεύω) think || (εννοώ) mean || **δεν σου ~** I do not deny it, but || **τι λες** (επιφ) you don't say!, fancy that! || **που λες** well! || **λες και** as if.

λεπλασία, η [leyeelaseea] plundering, looting, pillage.

λεπλατώ [leyeelato] plunder, loot.

λεία, η [leea] prey || booty, loot.

λειαίνω [lieno] smooth, level, plane, polish.

λειβάδι, το [leevaðee] pasture land, meadow.

λείος [leeos] smooth, even, level.

λείπω [leepo] be absent, be missing, want, lack || **μου λείπει** I am missing, I lack || **μας έλειψες** we missed you || **λίγο έλειψε να** he nearly, he almost.

λειρί, το [leeree] cockscomb, crest.

λειτουργία, η [leetouryeea] function, operation || (εκκλ) mass, liturgy.

λειτουργός, ο, η [leetourgos] officer, official, civil servant.

λειτουργώ [leetourgo] function, work || (εκκλ) celebrate mass.

λείψανα, τα [leepsana] πλ remnants, remains || (εκκλ) relics.

λειψός [leepsos] deficient, defective.

λειώνω [leeono] melt, liquefy || (συνθλίβω) crush, smash || (διαλύω) dissolve || (ναθαίνω φθορά) wear out, spoil.

λεκάνη, η [lekanee] basin, washbowl || pan.

λεκές, ο [lekes] stain, splash, spot || (μελάνης) blot.

λεκιάζω [lekeeazo] stain, soil, spot.

λελέκι, το [lelekee] stork || (μεταφ) tall person.

λεμβοδρομία, η [lemvoðromeea] regatta, boat race.

λέμβος, η [lemvos] rowboat || launch.

λεμονάδα, η [lemonaða] lemonade.

λεμόνι, το [lemonee] lemon || **λεμονιά** lemon tree.

λεξικογραφία, η [lekseekografeea] lexicography.

λεξικό, το [lekseeko] lexicon, dictionary.

λεξιλόγιο, το [lekseeloyo] vocabulary || glossary.

λέξη, η [leksee] word.

λεοντάρι, το [leontaree] lion.

λεοπάρδαλη, n [leopardalee] leopard.

λέπι, το [lepee] (ψαριού) scale (of fish).

λεπίδα, n [lepeeδa] blade.

λέπρα, n [lepra] leprosy.

λεπρός [lepros] leprous.

λεπτά, τα [lepta] πλ money.

λεπταίνω [lepteno] thin, make slender || refine.

λεπτοκαμωμένος [leptokamomenos] delicate, frail || thin, slim.

λεπτολογώ [leptologo] scrutinize, examine carefully, sift.

λεπτομέρεια [leptomereea] detail, particular || λεπτομερειακός detailed, of detail.

λεπτομερώς [leptomeros] minutely, closely, in detail.

λεπτό, το [lepto] (της ώρας) minute || (νόμισμα) lepton (one hundredth of a drachma).

λεπτός [leptos] thin, fine, slight, slim || (στη σκέψη) subtle || (ρουχισμός) light || (των αισθήσεων) keen.

λεπτότητα, n [leptoteeta] delicacy, weakness || tactfulness, tact || subtlety.

λέρα, n [lera] dirt, filth || (άνθρωπος) rogue, rascal.

λερωμένος [leromenos] dirty, filthy, grubby, grimy.

λερώνομαι [leronome] get dirty.

λερώνω [lerono] dirty, soil, stain || (μεταφ) tarnish, taint.

λέσχη, n [leshee] club || casino.

λεύκα, n [levka] poplar.

λευκαίνω [levkeno] whiten || bleach || (τοίχο) whitewash.

λευκός [levkos] white, clean || blank.

λευκοσίδηρος [levkoseeδeeros] tin.

λευκόχρυσος, ο [levkohreesos] platinum.

λεύκωμα, το [levkoma] album || (ιατρ) albumin.

λευτεριά, n [levteria] freedom, liberty.

λευχαιμία, n [levhemeea] leukaemia.

λεφτά [lefta] βλ λεπτά.

λεφτό [lefto] βλ λεπτό.

λεχώνα, n [lehona] woman who has just given birth.

λέω [leo] βλ λέγω.

λεωφορείο, το [leoforeeo] bus, omnibus, coach.

λεωφόρος, n [leoforos] avenue, boulevard.

λήγω [leego] come to an end, terminate || (οίκο) mature, fall due.

λήθαργος, ο [leethargos] lethargy, drowsiness, stupor.

λήθη, n [leethee] forgetfulness, forgetting, oversight.

λημέρι, το [leemeree] retreat, hiding place, hideout, den.

ληξιαρχείο, το [leekseearheeo] registry office, parish register.

λήξη, n [leeksee] termination, conclusion || expiration date.

λησμονώ [leesmono] forget, neglect, omit.

ληστεία, n [leesteea] holdup, robbery.

ληστεύω [leestevo] rob, hold up.

ληστής, ο [leestees] brigand, bandit, robber.

λήψη, n [leepsee] receipt, reception.

λιάζομαι [leeazome] sunbathe, lie in the sun.

λιακάδα, n [leeakaδa] sunshine.

λίαν [leean] much, very much, too.

λιανίζω [leeaneezo] cut to pieces, mince.

λιανικός [leeaneekos] retail.

λιανός [leeanos] thin, slender.

λιβάδι, το [leevaδee] βλ λειβάδι.

λιβανέζικος [leevanezeekos] Lebanese.

Λιβανέζος, ο [leevanezos] Lebanese.

λιβάνι, το [leevanee] incense, frankincense.

λιβανίζω [leevaneezo] burn incense || (μεταφ) flatter basely.

Λίβανο, το [leevano] Lebanon.

λίβρα, η [leevra] pound.

Λιβύη, η [leeviee] Libya.

λιβυκός [leeveekos] Libyan.

Λίβυος, ο [leeveeos] Libyan.

λιγάκι [leegakee] a little, a bit.

λίγδα, η [leegδa] fat, grease || dirt, stain.

λιγνίτης, ο [leegneetees] lignite.

λιγνός [leegnos] skinny, thin, slim.

λίγο [leego] a little, a bit || ~ πολύ more or less.

λίγος [leegos] a little, a bit || παρά λίγο nearly, almost.

λιγοστεύω [leegostevo] lessen, decrease.

λιγοστός [leegostos] very little, hardly enough.

λιγότερος [leegoteros] less.

λιγούρα, η [leegoura] nausea || faintness from hunger.

λιγοψυχία, η [leegopseeheea] faintheartedness || faintness.

λιγώνομαι [leegonome] long for, be impatient || be faint from desire.

λιγώνω [leegono] nauseate || make faint.

λιθάρι, το [leetharee] stone.

λίθινος [leetheenos] of stone.

λιθοβολώ [leethovolo] pelt with stones, stone.

λιθογραφία, η [leethografeea] lithography.

λιθόκτιστος [leethokteestos] built in stone.

λίθος, ο, η [leethos] stone || (ιατρ) calculus.

λιθόστρωτο, το [leethostroto] pavement, paved way.

λιθόστρωτος [leethostrotos] paved with stones.

λικέρ, το [leeker] liqueur.

λικνίζω [leekneezo] rock, lull to sleep || swing.

λίκνο, το [leekno] cradle, cot, crib.

λίμα, η [leema] (εργαλείο) file.

λιμάνι, το [leemanee] port, harbour.

λιμάρω [leemaro] file || chatter, gossip.

λιμενάρχης, ο [leemenarhees] harbour master.

λιμενικός [leemeneekos] of the port, of the harbour.

λιμήν, ο [leemeen] βλ **λιμάνι**.

λίμνη, η [leemnee] lake.

λιμνοθάλασσα, η [leemnothalasa] lagoon.

λιμοκτονώ [leemoktono] starve, famish.

λινάρι, το [leenaree] flax.

λινάτσα, η [leenatsa] sacking.

λινέλαιο, το [leeneleo] linseed oil.

λινός [leenos] linen.

λιοντάρι, το [leeontaree] lion.

λιπαίνω [leepeno] lubricate, grease || (με λίπασμα) manure, fertilize.

λιπαρός [leeparos] greasy, fatty || (γόνιμος) fat, rich.

λίπασμα, το [leepasma] fertilizer, manure.

λιποθυμία, η [leepotheemeea] faint(ing), swooning.

λιποθυμώ [leepotheemo] faint, lose consciousness.

λίπος, το [leepos] fat, lard || grease.

λιποτάκτης, ο [leεpotaktees] deserter.

λίρα, η [leera] pound, sovereign.

λιρέττα, η [leereta] Italian lira.

λίστα, η [leesta] list, catalogue.

λιτανεία, η [leetaneea] religious procession.

λιτός [leetos] temperate, frugal || plain.

λιτότητα, η [leetoteeta] temperance, moderation || (οικον) austerity.

λίτρα, n [leetra] (βάρος) pound || litre.

λίτρο, το [leetro] βλ **λίτρα.**

λιχουδιά, n [leehoudia] titbit || appetizer.

λοβός, ο [lovos] lobe || husk || (αρχιτεκ) foil.

λογαριάζω [logareeazo] count, measure, compute || rely on, look to || (λαμβάνω υπόψη) consider || (πρόθεση να) count on, aim to, mean to.

λογαριασμός, ο [logareeasmos] count, calculation, computation || bill || accounts.

λογάριθμος, ο [logareethmos] logarithm.

λογάς, ο [logas] gossip, babbler, longwinded talker.

λόγγος, ο [longos] thicket.

λόγια, τα [loya] πλ words.

λογιάζω [loyazo] take into consideration.

λογική, n [loyeekee] logic.

λογικός [loyeekos] rational, logical, sensible || right, fair.

λόγιος, ο [loyos] scholar, man of letters.

λογισμός, ο [loyeesmos] reasoning, thought || reckoning || (μαθημ) calculus.

λογιστήριο, το [loyeesteereeo] bursar's office || bursary.

λογιστής, ο [loyeestees] accountant, bookkeeper || (ναυτ) purser.

λογιστική, n [loyeesteekee] accountancy.

λογοδιάρροια, n [logodeeareea] unrestrained talkativeness, chattering.

λογοδοτώ [logodoto] give an account, account for.

λογοκρισία, n [logokreeseea] censorship.

λογομαχία, n [logomaheea] dispute, wrangle, controversy.

λογοπαίγνιο, το [logopegneeo] pun.

λόγος, ο [logos] (ομιλία) speech || (φράση κτλ) word, saying || (μνεία) mention || rumour || (αίτιο) cause, reason, purpose || (παράδειγμα) instance, supposition || (αγόρευση) speech, discourse || (λογοδοσία) explanation, account || (υπόσχεση) promise || (αναλογία) ratio, proportion.

λογοτέχνης, ο [logotehnees] author, writer.

λογοτεχνία, n [logotehneea] literature.

λόγχη, n [longhee] bayonet || spear, lance.

λοιμός, ο [leemos] pestilence, pest, plague.

λοιμώδης [leemodees] contagious.

λοιπόν [leepon] then, thus, and so || well!, what then!

λοιπός [leepos] left, remaining || **και τα λοιπά** and so forth, and so on.

λόξα, n [loksa] whim, mania, fancy.

λοξά [loksa] on the slant, obliquely || in an underhand way.

λοξοδρομώ [loksodromo] shift course, deviate || (ναυτ) tack || (μεταφ) go astray.

λοξός [loksos] oblique, slanting, inclined.

λόξυγγας, ο [lokseengas] hiccup.

λόρδος, ο [lordos] lord.

λοσιόν, n [losion] lotion.

λοστός, ο [lostos] crowbar, iron bar.

λοστρόμος, ο [lostromos] boatswain.

λούζομαι [louzome] wash one's hair.

λούζω [louzo] wash, bathe || (μεταφ) reproach severely.

λουκάνικο, το [loukaneeko] sausage, hot dog, frankfurter.

λουκέτο, το [louketo] padlock.

λούκι, το [loukee] pipe, conduit || gutter.

λουκούμι, το [loukoumee] Turkish delight || (μεταφ) delicious (attr).

λουλάκι, το [loulakee] indigo.

λουλούδι, το [loulouδee] flower, blossom.

λουξ [louks] luxurious, posh.

Λουξεμβούργο, το [louksemvourgo] Luxembourg.

λουρί, το [louree] strap || (μηχανής) belt, band.

λουρίδα, η [loureeδa] strip, belt, band.

λούσιμο, το [louseemo] washing one's hair || (μεταφ) reprimanding.

λούσο, το [louso] smart clothes || sumptuousness, luxury.

λουστράρω [loustraro] gloss, glaze || (ναπούτσια) polish.

λουστρίνια, τα [loustreeneea] πλ patent leather shoes.

λούστρος, ο [loustros] shoeblack, boot black.

λουτρά, τα [loutra] πλ baths, hot springs.

λουτρό, το [loutro] bath || (δωμάτιο) bathroom.

λουτρόπολη, η [loutropolee] bathing resort, spa.

λουφάζω [loufazo] remain silent || cringe with fear.

λοφίο, το [lofeeo] plume || (πτηνού) tuft, crest || (στρατ) pompom.

λόφος, ο [lofos] hill, height.

λοχαγός, ο [lohagos] captain.

λοχίας, ο [loheeas] sergeant.

λόχος, ο [lohos] company.

λυγερός [leeyeros] slim, lithe, graceful.

λυγίζω [leeyeezo] bend, curve || yield.

λυγμός, ο [leegmos] sob, sobbing.

λύκειο, το [leekeeo] private secondary school, lyceum.

λύκος, ο [leekos] wolf.

λυκόφως, το [leekofos] evening twilight, dusk.

λυμαίνομαι [leemenome] ravage, devastate, lay waste.

λυντσάρω [leentsaro] lynch.

λύνω [leeno] βλ **λύω.**

λύομαι [leeome] come undone.

λυπάμαι [leepame] be sorry, regret || pity.

λύπη, η [leepee] grief, chagrin, sorrow || pity, commiseration.

λυπημένος [leepeemenos] sad, grieved, distressed.

λυπούμαι [leepoume] βλ **λυπάμαι.**

λύσιμο, το [leeseemo] undoing, loosening || solution, solving || taking to pieces.

λύση, η [leesee] answer, solution || untying || dismantling.

λύσσα, η [leesa] rabies || (μεταφ) rage, fury, wrath.

λυσσά(ζ)ω [leesa(z)o] rage, go mad.

λυσσώ [leeso] (μεταφ) be furious.

λυτός [leetos] loose, untied, unfastened.

λύτρα, τα [leetra] πλ ransom money.

λυτρώνω [leetrono] deliver, free, set free.

λυτρωτής, ο [leetrotees] liberator, redeemer, rescuer.

λύω [leeo] unloose || (δεσμό κτλ) untie, unfasten || (διαλύω) dismantle || (βρίσκω λύση) resolve || (παύω) close, discharge || (καταργώ) annul, break off.

λυώνω [leeono] βλ **λειώνω.**

λωλαίνω [loleno] drive mad, bewilder.

λωλός [lolos] foolish, crazy, mad.

λωποδύτης, ο [lopoδeetees] thief, blackleg.

λωρίδα, η [loreeδa] strip, band, belt.

M, μ

μα [ma] but || by || ~ **το Θεό** by God!, God be witness!

μαγαζί, το [magazee] shop, store.

μαγγάνι, το [manganee] (εργαλείο) tool, vice || (πηγαδιού) wheel || winch.

μαγγάνιο, το [manganeeo] manganese.

μαγγανοπήγαδο, το [manganopeegaðo] wheel well (for water).

μαγγώνω [mangono] grip, squeeze, clip.

μαγεία, η [mayeea] sorcery, witchcraft, magic || charm, fascination.

μάγειρας, ο [mayeeras] cook.

μαγειρεύω [mayeerevo] cook || (μεταφ) plot, manipulate.

μαγειρική, η [mayeereekee] cooking, cookery.

μαγευτικός [mayevteekos] charming, enchanting, delightful.

μαγεύω [mayevo] charm, fascinate, delight, attract.

μάγια, τα [maya] πλ witchcraft, spell, charm.

μαγιά, η [maya] yeast, leaven.

μαγικός [mayeekos] magic(al), fascinating, bewitching.

μαγιό, το [mayo] bathing suit, swimsuit.

μαγιονέζα, η [mayoneza] mayonnaise.

μάγισσα, η [mayeesa] witch, enchantress.

μαγκάλι, το [mangalee] brazier, firepan.

μάγκας, ο [mangas] urchin, rascal, bum.

μαγκούρα, η [mangoura] crook, heavy stick.

μαγνήσιο, το [magneeseeo] magnesium.

μαγνήτης, ο [magneetees] magnet.

μαγνητίζω [magneeteezo] magnetize || attract, captivate.

μαγνητικός [magneeteekos] magnetic || attractive.

μαγνητισμός, ο [magneeteesmos] magnetism.

μαγνητόφωνο, το [magneetofono] tape recorder.

μάγος, ο [magos] magician, wizard.

μαγουλάδες, οι [magoulaðes] mumps.

μάγουλο, το [magoulo] cheek (of face).

μάδημα, το [maðeema] plucking, depilation || (μεταφ) fleecing.

μαδώ [maðo] pluck, pluck off, remove the hair || (μεταφ) fleece.

μαέστρος, ο [maestros] conductor || (μεταφ) authority.

μάζα, η [maza] paste || lump || (ανθρώπων) mass, crowd.

μάζεμα, το [mazema] collecting, gathering || (υφάσματος) shrinking.

μαζεύομαι [mazevome] collect || nestle || settle down.

μαζεύω [mazevo] gather, collect || (μαλλί) wind || (για ρούχα) shrink.

μαζί [mazee] together, with, in one lot, jointly.

μαζικός [mazeekos] of the mass, collective.

Μάης, ο [maees] May.

μαθαίνω [matheno] learn || teach, train || (νέα) hear || learn.

μάθημα, το [matheema] lesson.

μαθηματικά, τα [matheemateeka] πλ mathematics.

μαθηματικός [matheemateekos] mathematical || (ουσ) mathematician.

μαθημένος [matheemenos] used to.

μάθηση, η [matheesee] learning, education.

μαθητευόμενος

[matheetevomenos] apprentice, novice.

μαθητής, ο [matheetees] student, pupil || (φιλοσόφου) disciple.

μαία, η [mea] midwife.

μαίανδρος, ο [meandros] meander, in-and-out.

μαιευτήρας, ο [mayevteeras] obstetrician.

μαιευτήριο, το [mayevteereeo] maternity hospital.

μαιευτική, η [mayevteekee] obstetrics.

μαϊμού, η [maeemou] monkey, ape.

μαίνομαι [menome] rage, be furious.

μαϊντανός, ο [maeentanos] parsley.

Μάιος, ο [maeeos] May.

μακάβριος [makavreeos] macabre, gruesome, ghastly.

μακάρι [makaree] (επιφ) would to God!

μακαρίζω [makareezo] regard as fortunate, envy.

μακάριος [makareeos] happy, fortunate, blessed || calm, serene.

μακαρίτης [makareetees] late, deceased.

μακαρόνια, τα [makaroneea] πλ macaroni.

μακελειό, το [makelio] (μεταφ) slaughter, massacre.

μακέτα, η [maketa] model, drawing, plan.

μακραίνω [makreno] make longer || grow taller.

μακριά [makria] (a)far, far off, at a distance.

μακρινός [makreenos] far distant, far off || (ταξίδι) long.

μακρόβιος [makroveeos] long-lived.

μάκρος, το [makros] length || duration.

μακρύνω [makreeno] βλ μακραίνω.

μακρύς [makrees] long, lengthy, extensive.

μαλάζω [malazo] massage, knead || soften, mollify, pacify || (πόνο) alleviate.

μαλάκιο, το [malakeeo] mollusc.

μαλακός [malakos] soft || mild, gentle || (κλίμα) genial.

μαλάκυνση, η [malakeensee] softening, enervation.

μαλακώνω [malakono] soften, get milder || assuage || become calmer.

μάλαμα, το [malama] gold.

μαλάσσω [malaso] βλ **μαλάζω**.

μαλθακός [malthakos] soft, effeminate, delicate.

μάλιστα [maleesta] more especially, particularly || yes, indeed || even.

μαλλί, το [malee] wool, fleece || hair.

μαλλιά, τα [malia] πλ hair (of the head) || ~ **κουβάρια** upside down.

μαλλιαρός [maleearos] hairy, long-haired || woolly.

μάλλινος [maleenos] woollen.

μάλλον [malon] more, better, rather.

μαλώνω [malono] argue || chide, reprimand, rebuke.

μαμά, η [mama] mother, mummy.

μάμμη, η [mamee] grandmother.

μαμμή, η [mamee] midwife.

μαμμούνι, το [mamounee] small insect, grub.

μάνα, η [mana] mother, mamma.

μανδύας, ο [mandeeas] mantle, cloak || (στρατ) greatcoat.

μάνι μάνι [maneemanee] quickly, in a jiffy.

μανία, η [maneea] fury, passion, mania || whim, fancy || **έχω ~ με** to be crazy about.

μανιακός [maneeakos] raving, frenzied || (ποιότης) inveterate.

μανιβέλλα, η [maneevela] starting handle || lever, bar.

μανικέτι, το [maneeketee] cuff.

μανίκι, το [maneekee] sleeve.

μανιτάρι, το [maneetaree] mushroom.

μανιώδης [maneeodees] passionate, inveterate || furious, raging.

μανούλα, n [manoula] mummy || mom (US).

μανουάλιο, το [manoualeeo] candelabrum.

μανούβρα, n [manouvra] manoeuvre.

μανούρι, το [manouree] kind of white cheese.

μανταλάκι, το [mantalakee] clothes peg.

μάνταλο, το [mantalo] latch, bolt, bar.

μανταλώνω [mantalono] latch, lock up, bolt.

μανταρίνι, το [mantareenee] tangerine.

μαντάρισμα, το [mantareesma] darning || (υφάσματος) mending.

μαντάρω [mantaro] darn, mend.

μαντάτο, το [mantato] information, news.

μαντείο, το [manteeo] oracle.

μαντεύω [mantevo] foretell || guess || find out, fathom.

μαντήλι, το [manteelee] handkerchief.

μάντης, ο [mantees] wizard, prophet.

μαντινάδα, n [manteenaδa] rhyming couplet.

μάντρα, n [mantra] pen, fold, sty || (περίφραγμα) enclosure, wall || yard.

μανταχάλος, ο [mantrahalos] lanky fellow.

μαξιλάρι, το [makseelaree] pillow, cushion.

μάππας, ο [mapas] stupid fellow, imbecile.

μαραγκός, ο [marangos] carpenter || joiner.

μαράζι, το [marazee] pining,

depression, languor.

μάραθ(ρ)ο, το [marath(r)o] fennel.

μαραίνομαι [marenome] fade, wither away, shrivel || (μεταφ) waste away.

μαραίνω [mareno] wither, dry up, fade.

μαρασμός, ο [marasmos] withering, fading away || (μεταφ) decay.

μαργαρίνη, n [margareenee] margarine.

μαργαρίτα, n [margareeta] daisy.

μαργαριτάρι, το [margareetaree] pearl.

μαρίδα, n [mareeδa] whitebait, small fry.

μάρκα, n [marka] (εμπορ) make || (αυτοκινήτου) model || (νόμισμα) mark || (μεταφ) cunning fellow.

μαρμαρένιος [marmareneeos] of marble.

μάρμαρο, το [marmaro] marble.

μαρμελάδα, n [marmelaδa] marmalade.

Μαροκινός, ο [marokeenos] Moroccan || μ~ (επιθ) Moroccan.

Μαρόκο, το [maroko] Morocco.

μαρούλι, το [maroulee] lettuce.

Μάρτης, ο [martees] March.

μαρτυρία, n [marteereea] deposition, giving of evidence || proof, token.

μαρτυρικός [marteereekos] insufferable, unbearable.

μαρτύριο, το [marteereeo] torment, suffering.

μαρτυρώ [marteero] give evidence, testify || (προδίδω) betray, inform against || (ενδεικνύω) show, indicate || (γίνομαι μάρτυς) suffer martyrdom (for Christ).

μάρτυς, ο [martees] witness || (εκκλ) martyr.

μας [mas] us || our.

μασέλα, n [masela] false teeth.

μασιά, η [masia] πλ tongs, fire-tongs || pincers.

μάσκα, η [maska] mask || **μασκαράς, ο** masquerader || (μεταφ) impostor, rascal, scoundrel.

μασόνος, ο [masonos] freemason.

μασουλώ [masoulo] chew, munch.

μασούρι, το [masouree] spool, bobbin || tube.

μάστιγα, η [masteega] whip || (μεταφ) curse, plague.

μαστίγιο, το [masteeyo] whip || switch.

μαστιγώνω [masteegono] whip, lash, flog.

μαστίζω [masteezo] infest, devastate, desolate.

μαστίχα, η [masteeha] mastic || (ποτό) mastic brandy.

μάστορας, ο [mastoras] artisan, workman || (μεταφ) expert, skilful person.

μαστορεύω [mastorevo] work || mend, repair.

μαστός, ο [mastos] breast || (μεταφ) hillock.

μαστροπός, ο, η [mastropos] procurer, procuress, pimp.

μασχάλη, η [mashalee] armpit.

μασώ [maso] chew, masticate || (το λόγια) stammer.

ματαιόδοξος [mateeodoksos] vain, self-conceited.

μάταιος [mateos] vain, useless, unavailing || conceited.

ματαιώνω [mateono] frustrate, foil, cancel, stop.

μάτι, το [matee] eye || (φύλλου κτλ) bud || αυγό ~ fried egg (sunny-side up) || βάζω στο ~ to set one's heart on || έχω στο ~ to covet || κλείνω το ~ to wink || μάτια μου! my darling!

ματιά, η [matia] glance, gaze, eye, look || ~ζω cast an evil eye on, bewitch.

ματόκλαδο, το [matoklaðo] eyelash, lash.

ματόφυλλο, το [matofeelo] eyelid.

μάτσο, το [matso] truss, bunch, bundle || (ξύλων) faggot.

ματσούκα, η [matsouka] club, cudgel.

ματώνω [matono] bleed.

μαυραγορίτης, ο [mavragoreetees] black marketeer.

μαυρειδερός [mavreeðeros] blackish || brown.

μαυρίζω [mavreezo] blacken, darken || (από ήλιο) get tanned || (μεταφ) blackball, vote against.

μαυρίλα, η [mavreela] blackness, darkness, gloominess.

μαυροδάφνη, η [mavroðafnee] kind of sweet wine.

μαυροπίνακας, ο [mavropeenakas] blackboard || blacklist.

μαύρος [mavros] black || brown || (νέγρος) negro || (μεταφ) miserable, luckless.

μαχαίρι, το [maheree] knife || στα ~ α at loggerheads.

μαχαιριά, η [maheria] stab.

μαχαιροβγάλτης, ο [maherovgaltees] cut-throat || bully.

μαχαιροπήρουνα, τα [maheropeerouna] πλ cutlery.

μαχαιρώνω [maherono] stab.

μαχαλάς, ο [mahalas] quarter, district, neighbourhood.

μάχη, η [mahee] battle, combat || struggle, fight.

μαχητής, ο [maheetees] combatant, fighter, soldier.

μαχητικός [maheeteekos] warlike, martial || combative, ready to fight.

μάχομαι [mahome] fight, combat, struggle || hate, abhor.

με [me] with, by, through, by means of, on, of || ~ το νόδια on foot || ~ το καλό God willing || ~ το μήνα by the month || δύο ~ τρία two by

three (*feet etc*) || ~ τον καιρό eventually, in the course of time || δύο ~ τρεις between two and three o'clock || έχω μανία ~ το to be mad on, be crazy about || γελώ ~ to laugh at || ~ τη σειρά in turn || ανάλογα ~ according to whether.

μεγάθυμος [megatheemos] generous, magnanimous.

μεγαλείο, το [megaleeo] splendour, grandeur || (μεταφ) splendid.

μεγαλειότητα, η [megaleeoteeta] majesty, grandeur || **η Αυτού** ~ His Majesty.

μεγαλειώδης [megaleeodees] magnificent, superb, majestic.

μεγαλέμπορος, ο [megalemboros] wholesaler.

μεγαλεπήβολος [megalepeevolos] grandiose, imposing.

μεγαλοποιώ [megalopeeo] magnify, exaggerate, overdo.

μεγαλοπρεπής [megaloprepees] majestic, stately, splendid, magnificent.

μεγάλος [megalos] great, large, big, long.

μεγαλουργώ [megalourgo] achieve great things.

μεγαλόφρονας [megalofronas] generous, magnanimous || boastful, arrogant.

μεγαλοφυής [megalofiees] gifted, ingenious.

μεγαλόψυχος [megalopseehos] magnanimous, generous.

μεγαλύνω [megaleeno] magnify, exalt.

μεγαλώνω [megalono] increase, enlarge || (ανατρέφω) bring up, raise || (μεγαλοποιώ) magnify, exaggerate || grow up.

μέγαρο, το [megaro] mansion, palace, imposing building.

μέγας [megas] βλ **μεγάλος**.

μεγάφωνο, το [megafono]

(ραδιοφώνου) loudspeaker || megaphone.

μέγγενη, η [mengenee] (εργαλείο) vice.

μέγεθος, το [meyethos] size, greatness, height, magnitude, extent, length.

μεγέθυναn, η [meyetheensee] enlargement, increase, extension.

μεγιστάνας, ο [meyeestanas] magnate, seigneur.

μέγιστος [meyeestos] greatest, largest || enormous, colossal.

μεδούλι, το [medoulee] marrow.

μέδουσα, η [medousa] kind of jellyfish.

μεζές, ο [mezes] titbit, snack.

μεζούρα, η [mezoura] tape measure.

μεθαύριο [methavreeo] the day after tomorrow.

μέθη, η [methee] intoxication, drunkenness || (μεταφ) enthusiasm.

μεθοδικός [methodeekos] systematic, methodical.

μέθοδος, η [methodos] method, system, process.

μεθόριος, η [methoreeos] boundary, frontier.

μεθύσι, το [metheesee] βλ **μέθη**.

μεθυσμένος [metheesmenos] drunk.

μεθώ [metho] make drunk, intoxicate || get drunk.

μειδίαμα, το [meedeeama] smile.

μείζων [meezon] larger, greater || (μουσ) major.

μειοδοτώ [meeodoto] bid the lowest price.

μείον [meeon] less, minus.

μειονέκτημα, το [meeonekteema] disadvantage, inconvenience.

μειονότητα, η [meeonoteeta] minority.

μειοψηφία, η [meeopseefeea] minority of votes.

μειώνω [meeono] lessen, diminish, reduce, decrease.

μείωση, η [meeosee] decrease, reduction || (μεταφ) humiliation.

μελαγχολία, η [melangholeea] melancholy, dejection, gloominess.

μελαγχολικός [melangholeekos] sad, depressed, gloomy.

μελαγχολώ [melangholo] become sad.

μελάνη, η [melanee] ink.

μελανιά, η [melania] inkstain | bruise || ~ζω bruise || turn blue with cold.

μελανοδοχείο, το [melanoðoheeo] inkstand, inkpot.

μελάτος [melatos] (αυγό) soft-boiled.

μελαχροινός [melahreenos] dark, brown, swarthy.

μελαψός [melapsos] dark-skinned, swarthy.

μέλει [melee]: **δεν με** ~ I don't care, I'm not interested.

μελέτη, η [meletee] (πραγματεία) treatise || study || (κτιρίου) plan, design || mediation, contemplation.

μελετηρός [meleteeros] studious.

μελετώ [meleto] study || (ερευνώ) search, investigate || (σκοπεύω) have in mind, intend || (πιάνο) practise.

μέλημα, το [meleema] concern, care, solicitude, duty.

μέλι, το [melee] honey.

μελίγγι, το [meleengee] (ανατ) temple.

μέλισσα, η [meleesa] bee.

μελίσσι, το [meleesee] beehive || swarm.

μελισσοκομία, η [meleesokomeea] beekeeping.

μελιτζάνα, η [meleedzana] eggplant.

μέλλον, το [melon] future || outlook.

μελλόνυμφος, ο, η [meloneemfos] husband-/wife-to-be.

μέλλω [melo] intend, be about to.

μέλλων [melon] future || ο ~ (γραμμ) future tense.

μέλος, το [melos] member || (μουσ) melody, air || (του σώματος) member, limb.

μελτέμι, το [meltemee] north wind, trade wind.

μελωδία, η [meloðeea] melody, tune.

μελωδικός [meloðeekos] melodious, tuneful.

μεμβράνη, η [memvranee] membrane || (χαρτί) parchment.

μεμονωμένος [memonomenos] isolated, lonely, alone.

μεν [men] on the one hand || **οι** ~ ... **οι δε** some ... others.

μενεξές, ο [menekses] violet.

μένος [menos] fervour, zeal, eagerness || wrath, anger, fury.

μέντα, η [menta] mint, peppermint.

μένω [meno] remain, stop, stay || (απομένω) be left, survive || (διαμένω) reside, live || ~ **από** run out of, be short of.

μέρα, η [mera] βλ **ημέρα**.

μεράκι, το [merakee] ardent desire, yearning || (λύπη) regret, sorrow.

μεραρχία, η [merarheea] division.

μεριά, η [meria] place || side.

μερίδα, η [mereeða] ration, portion, helping.

μερίδιο, το [mereeðeeo] share, portion.

μερικός [mereekos] partial, some, a few || **μερικά** πλ some, certain, a few.

μέριμνα, η [mereemna] care, anxiety, solicitude, concern.

μεριμνώ [mereemno] look after, care for, be anxious about.

μέρισμα, το [mereesma] dividend || allotment, part.

μερμήγκι, το [mermeengee] ant.

μεροκάματο, το [merokamato] day's wages.

μερολιπτώ [meroleepto] take sides, be partial, be one-sided.

μέρος, το [meros] part, party || (μερίδα) portion, share || (τόπος) place, spot || (πλευρά) side || (ρόλος) role || (γραμμ) part of speech || (αποχωρητήριο) W.C. || κατά ~ aside, apart.

μέσα [mesa] in(to) || inside || within || among || (πολιτ) means || ~ σε inside, within || in, into.

μεσάζω [mesazo] mediate, intercede.

μεσαίος [meseos] middle.

μεσαίωνας, ο [meseonas] Middle Ages || μεσαιωνικός medieval.

μεσάνυχτα, τα [mesaneehta] πλ midnight.

μέση, η [mesee] middle || (σώματος) waist || αφήνω στη ~ to leave incomplete, leave undone.

μεσήλικας [meseeleekas] middle-aged.

μεσημβρινός [meseemvreenos] of noon || (νότιος) southern || (ουσ) meridian.

μεσημέρι, το [meseemeree] noon || μέρα ~ in broad daylight || μεσημεριανός midday || μεσημεριανός ύπνος siesta.

μεσίστιος [meseesteeos] half-mast.

μεσιτεύω [meseeteevo] intercede, intervene || be a broker.

μεσίτης, ο [meseetees] mediator || agent, broker.

μεσιτικό [meseeteeko]: ~ γραφείο house agency.

μεσογειακός [mesoyakos] Mediterranean.

Μεσόγειος, η [mesoyos] the Mediterranean.

μεσόκοπος [mesokopos] βλ μεσήλικας.

μεσολαβώ [mesolavo] intercede,

intervene || (σε χρόνο) come between.

μέσο, το [meso] middle, midst || (τρόπος) method, means, way || μέσα πλ influence, pull, power.

μέσος [mesos] middle || medium || (όρος) mean, average.

μεσοφόρι, το [mesoforee] petticoat, underskirt.

μεστός [mestos] full, replete, crammed with || (ώριμος) ripe.

μεστώνω [mestono] mature, ripen, mellow.

μέσω [meso] through, via.

μετά [meta] with || after, in || (επίρ) afterwards.

μεταβαίνω [metaveno] go, proceed.

μεταβάλλω [metavalo] change, convert, transform.

μετάβαση, η [metavasee] going, passage, transference.

μεταβατικός [metavateekos] transitional, provisory || (γραμμ) transitive (verb).

μεταβιβάζω [metaveevazo] (διαταγή) transmit, hand on || (μεταφέρω) transport || (ιδιοκτησία) transfer, hand over.

μεταβλητός [metavleetos] variable, unsettled, changeable.

μεταβολή, η [metavolee] alteration, change || (στρατ) about-turn, half-turn.

μετάγγιση, η [metangeesee] transfusion, drawing off || (κρασιού κτλ) decanting.

μεταγενέστερος [metayenesteros] posterior, subsequent, later.

μεταγραφή, η [metagrafee] transfer.

μεταγωγικό, το [metagoyeeko] (ναυτ) transport ship.

μεταδίδω [metadeedo] impart, transmit || (ραδιοφωνία) broadcast || (αρρώστια) infect.

μετάδοση, η [metadosee] transmission || (αρρώστιας)

contagion, spreading || αγία ~ Holy Communion.

μεταδοτικός [metadoteekos] contagious, infectious.

μετάθεση, η [metathesee] transfer, removal.

μεταθέτω [metatheto] transpose, transfer, remove, move.

μετακινώ [metakeeno] move, shift, displace.

μετακομίζω [metakomeezo] transport, transfer, remove || (σπίτι) move, change residence, move out.

μεταλλείο, το [metaleeo] mine.

μετάλλευμα, το [metalevma] ore.

μεταλλικός [metaleekos] metallic || mineral.

μετάλλινος [metaleenos] of metal.

μετάλλιο, το [metaleeo] medal.

μέταλλο, το [metalo] metal.

μεταμέλεια, η [metameleea] repentance, regrets.

μεταμόρφωση, η [metamorfosee] transformation, reformation || (εκκλ) transfiguration.

μεταμόσχευση, η [metamoshevsee] transplantation.

μεταμφίεση, η [metamfiesee] disguise, masquerade.

μεταμφιεσμένος [meemfiesmenos] disguised.

μετανάστευση, η [metanastevsee] emigration, (im)migration.

μεταναστεύω [metanastevo] (e)migrate, immigrate.

μετανάστης, ο [metanastees] (e)migrant, immigrant.

μετάνοια, η [metaneea] repentance, regret || (εκκλ) penance || (γονυκλισιά) genuflexion.

μετανοώ [metanoo] repent, regret, be sorry (for).

μετάξι, το [metaksee] silk.

μεταξοσκώληκας, ο [metaksoskoleekas] silkworm.

μεταξύ [metaksee] between, among, amongst, amid(st) || ~ μας

between ourselves, between you and me || εν τω ~ meanwhile.

μεταξωτό, το [metaksoto] silk material, silk stuff.

μεταπείθω [metapeetho] dissuade, prevail upon.

μεταποιώ [metapeeo] transform, alter, convert.

μεταπολεμικός [metapolemeekos] postwar.

μετάπτωση, η [metaptosee] change, relapse.

μεταπωλώ [metapolo] resell, sell again.

μεταρρυθμίζω [metareethmeezo] reform, rearrange.

μετασχηματιστής, ο [metashemateestees] transformer.

μετατοπίζω [metatopeezo] shift, displace.

μετατόπιση, η [metatopeesee] shifting || displacement.

μετατρέπω [metatrepo] transform, turn, change, alter || (για ποινή) commute.

μεταφέρω [metafero] transport, carry, convey || (οίκον) transfer, carry over.

μεταφορά, η [metafora] transportation, conveyance || (γραμμ) metaphor.

μεταφορικά, τα [metaforeeka] πλ carriage fees.

μεταφράζω [metafrazo] translate.

μετάφραση, η [metafrasee] translation.

μεταφραστής, ο [metafrastees] translator.

μεταφυτεύω [metafeetevo] transplant.

μεταχειρίζομαι [metaheereezome] use, employ || treat, behave towards.

μεταχειρισμένος [metaheereesmenos] worn, used || (δεύτερο χέρι) secondhand.

μετεκπαίδευση, η

[metekpeðevsee] postgraduate study.

μετέπειτα [metepeeta] after, afterwards, subsequently || **οι ~** posterity, the descendants.

μετέχω [meteho] take part, participate || partake.

μετέωρο, το [meteoro] meteor, shooting star.

μετέωρος [meteoros] dangling, in the air || (μεταφ) hesitant, undecided || in suspense.

μετοικώ [meteeko] emigrate || (σπίτι) move house.

μετόπισθεν [metopeesthen]: **τα ~** the rear.

μετοχή, η [metohee] (οικον) stock, share || (γραμμ) participle.

μετοχικός [metoheekos] (οικον) of a share, of joint stock || (γραμμ) participial.

μέτοχος, ο [metohos] participant, sharer || (οικον) shareholder.

μέτρα, τα [metra] πλ measurements || proceedings, steps || **λαμβάνω ~** to take measures.

μέτρημα, το [metreema] measuring, mensuration || counting, numbering.

μετρημένος [metreemenos] measured, limited || (άνθρωπος) temperate, discreet, moderate.

μετρητά, τα [metreeta] πλ: **τα ~** cash, money || **τοις μετρητοίς** in cash, (for) ready money.

μετρητής, ο [metreetees] meter, counter, gauge.

μετρητός [metreetos] measurable, calculable.

μετριάζω [metreeazo] moderate, diminish, slacken, lessen.

μετρικός [metreekos] metric(al).

μετριοπάθεια, η [metreeopatheea] moderation, temperance.

μετριοπαθής [metreeopathees] moderate, sober, temperate.

μέτριος [metreeos] ordinary,

moderate || mediocre || (καφές) semi-sweetened.

μετριόφρονας [metreeofronas] modest, unassuming, decent, retiring.

μετριοφροσύνη, η [metreeofroseenee] modesty, decency.

μέτρο, το [metro] measure, metre || (μεταφ) measure, step || (μουσ) bar, measure || (ποιητικό) metre, foot.

μετρώ [metro] measure, count, number, gauge.

μέτωπο, το [metopo] forehead, brow || (πρόσοψη) face, front, facade || (μάχη) front, battlefront.

μέχρι(ς) [mehree(s)] till, until, down to, up to || as far as || **~ ενός** to the last man || **~ τούδε** until now.

μη [mee] don't || not, no || lest.

μηδαμινός [meeðameenos] worthless, of no account, insignificant, trivial.

μηδέν, το [meeðen] nothing || zero || cipher.

μηδενίζω [meeðeneezo] nullify || mark with a zero.

μηδενικό, το [meeðeneeko] zero || cipher.

μηδενιστής, ο [meeðeneestees] nihilist.

μήκος, το [meekos] length || (γεωγραφικό) longitude || **κατά ~** in length, lengthwise.

μηλίγγι, το [meeleengee] (ανατ) temple.

μήλο, το [meelo] apple || (πρόσωπο) cheekbone || **μηλίτης** cider.

μηλόπιττα, η [meelopeeta] apple pie.

μην, ο [meen], **μήνας, ο** [meenas] month.

μηνιαίος [meenieos] monthly || month's.

μηνιάτικο, το [meeniateeko] month's wages || month's rent.

μηνίγγι, το [meeneengee] βλ **μηλίγγι**.

μηνιγγίτιδα, η [meeneengeeteeδa] meningitis.

μήνις, η [meenees] rage, anger, fury, wrath.

μήνυμα, το [meeneema] message, notice, announcement.

μήνυση, η [meeneesee] summons, charge.

μηνυτής, ο [meeneetees] plaintiff, complainant.

μηνύω [meeneeo] give notice || bring a charge against.

μήπως [meepos] lest in any way, in case || I wonder if.

μπρός, ο [meeros] thigh, leg.

μηρυκάζω [meereekazo] chew the cud, ruminate.

μήτε [meete] βλ **ούτε**.

μητέρα, η [meetera] mother.

μήτρα, η [meetra] uterus, womb || (χυτηρίου) mould, matrix, form.

μητρική [meetreekee]: ~ **γλώσσα** mother tongue, native language.

μητρόπολη, η [meetropolee] metropolis, capital || (εκκλ) cathedral.

μητροπολιτικός [meetropoleeteekos] metropolitan.

μητροπολίτης, ο [meetropoleetees] metropolitan bishop.

μητρότητα, η [meetroteeta] motherhood.

μητρυιά, η [meetria] stepmother.

μητρυιός, ο [meetrios] stepfather.

μητρώο, το [meetroo] register, roll, official list of names.

μηχανεύομαι [meehanevome] contrive, engineer, plot, bring about.

μηχανή, η [meehanee] machine, engine, works || (μεταφ) typewriter || camera.

μηχάνημα, το [meehaneema] machine, apparatus, contrivance.

μηχανική, η [meehaneekee] engineering, mechanics.

μηχανικός [meehaneekos] mechanical || (ουσ) engineer || mechanic || architect.

μηχανισμός, ο [meehaneesmos] mechanism, machinery.

μηχανοκίνητος [meehanokeeneetos] motorized || machine-operated.

μηχανοποιώ [meehanopeeo] mechanize.

μηχανορραφία, η [meehanorafeea] machination || intrigue.

μία, μια [meea, mia] one || a, an || ~ **και** since, seeing that || ~ **που** as, since.

μίασμα, το [meeasma] miasma, infection.

μιγάδας, ο [meegaδas] half-caste, mulatto || hybrid.

μίγμα, το [meegma] mixture, blend.

μίζα, η [meeza] (μηχανής) self-starter || (στα χαρτιά) stake.

μιζέρια, η [meezereea] misery, wretchedness || (τσιγγουνιά) meanness.

μικραίνω [meekreno] curtail, lessen || shorten, grow smaller.

μικρόβιο, το [meekroveeo] microbe.

μικρογραφία, η [meekrografeea] miniature.

μικροπρά(γ)ματα, τα [meekropra(g)mata] πλ trifles.

μικροπρεπής [meekroprepees] mean, base.

μικρός [meekros] small, little || short || young || (διαφορά) trivial.

μικροσκοπικός [meekroskopeekos] minute.

μικροσκόπιο, το [meekroskopeeo] microscope.

μικρόφωνο, το [meekrofono] microphone.

μικρόψυχος [meekropseehos] faint-hearted.

μικρύνω [meekreeno] βλ μικραίνω.

μικτό [meekto]: ~ βάρος gross weight.

μικτός [meektos] mixed, composite || (σχολείο) coeducational.

μιλιά, η [meelia] speech, word.

μίλι, το [meelee] mile.

μιλώ [meelo] speak.

μίμηση, η [meemeesee] imitation.

μιμητής, ο [meemeetees] imitator.

μιμητικός [meemeeteekos] imitative.

μιμόζα, η [meemoza] mimosa.

μίμος, ο [meemos] mimic, jester.

μιμούμαι [meemoume] imitate, copy, mimic.

μινιατούρα, η [meeneeatoura] miniature.

μίξη, η [meeksee] mixing, mixture, blend.

μισαλλόδοξος [meesalodoksos] intolerant.

μισάνθρωπος, ο [meesanthropos] misanthrope.

μισητός [meeseetos] hated, hateful, odious.

μισθοδοτώ [meesthodhoto] pay a salary to, hire.

μισθολόγιο, το [meestholoyo] payroll || rate of pay.

μισθός, ο [meesthos] salary, wages, pay.

μισθοφόρος, ο [meesthoforos] mercenary, hired man.

μισθώνω [meesthono] hire, rent || let out, hire out.

μισθωτής, ο [meesthotees] tenant || hirer.

μισθωτός [meesthotos] salaried, paid.

μισό, το [meeso] half || στα μισά halfway, in the middle.

μισογύνης, ο [meesoyeenees] woman-hater, misogynist.

μίσος, το [meesos] hatred, aversion.

μισός [meesos] half.

μισοφέγγαρο, το [meesofengaro] halfmoon, crescent.

μίσχος, ο [meeshos] stalk (of leaf).

μισώ [meeso] hate, detest, loathe.

μίτρα, η [meetra] mitre.

μνεία, η [mnea] mention.

μνήμα, το [mneema] grave, tomb, sepulchre.

μνημείο, το [mneemeeo] monument, cenotaph.

μνήμη, η [mneemee] memory, mind, recollection.

μνημονεύω [mneemonevo] celebrate, commemorate || quote, mention || learn by heart.

μνημονικό, το [mneemoneeko] βλ μνήμη.

μνημόσυνο, το [mneemoseeno] requiem.

μνησίκακος [mneeseekakos] spiteful, vindictive.

μνηστεύομαι [mneestevome] get engaged.

μνηστή, η [mneestee] fiancée.

μνηστήρας, ο [mneesteeras] fiancé || (μεταφ) claimant.

μόδα, η [moða] fashion, custom, habit, way || της ~ς fashionable.

μοδίστρα, η [moðeestra] dressmaker, seamstress.

μοιάζω [meeazo] look like.

μοίρα, η [meera] fate, destiny, fortune || (αερο) squadron || (γεωμ) degree.

μοιράζομαι [meerazome] share with.

μοιράζω [meerazo] share out, divide, distribute || (ρόλους) allot, assign || (διανέμω) deliver || (χαρτιά) deal || ~ τη διαφορά to split the difference.

μοιραίος [meereos] unavoidable || fatal, deadly.

μοιραίως [meereos] inevitably, fatally.

μοίραρχος, ο [meerarhos] captain of the gendarmerie.

μοιρολατρεία, η [meerolatreea] fatalism.

μοιρολόγι, το [meeroloyee] dirge, lamentation.

μοιρολογώ [meerologo] lament, mourn.

μοιχεία, η [meeheea] adultery.

μολαταύτα [molatavta] nevertheless, yet, still.

μόλη [molee] barely, hardly, scarcely || as soon as.

μολονότι [molonotee] although, though.

μόλυβδος, ο [moleevðos] lead.

μολύβι, το [moleevee] lead || pencil.

μόλυνση, η [moleensee] contamination, infection, pollution.

μολύνω [moleeno] infect, contaminate, pollute.

μόλυσμα, το [moleesma] infection, contagion.

μομφή, η [momfee] blame, reproach, reprimand.

μονάδα, η [monaða] unit.

μοναδικός [monaðeekos] unique, singular, only.

μοναξιά, η [monaksia] solitude, isolation, loneliness.

μονάρχης, ο [monarhees] monarch, sovereign.

μοναρχία, η [monarheea] monarchy.

μοναρχικός, ο [monarheekos] monarchist.

μοναστήρι, το [monasteeree] monastery.

μονάχα [monaha] only.

μοναχή, η [monahee] nun.

μοναχικός [monaheekos] monastic || (ερημικός) isolated, solitary, lonely.

μοναχοπαίδι, το [monahopeðee] only child.

μοναχός [monahos] alone, single, only, sole || real, authentic.

μοναχός, ο [monahos] monk.

μονή, η [monee] βλ μοναστήρι.

μόνιμος [moneemos] permanent, lasting, durable, fixed.

μονογαμία, η [monogameea] monogamy.

μονογενής [monoyenees] one and only.

μονόγραμμα, το [monograma] monogram, initials.

μονογραφή, η [monografee] initials.

μονόδρομος, ο [monoðromos] one-way street.

μονοιάζω [moneeazo] agree with, get on well with || reconcile.

μονοκατοικία, η [monokateekeea] one-family house.

μονοκόμματος [monokomatos] in one piece || stiff || forthright || massive.

μονομαχία, η [monomaheea] duel.

μονομερής [monomerees] one-sided, partial.

μονομιάς [monomias] all at once.

μόνο [mono] only, alone, solely, merely, nothing but || ~ που except that || ~ να provided that.

μονοπάτι, το [monopatee] footpath, pathway.

μονόπλευρος [monoplevros] one-sided, partial.

μονοπώλιο, το [monopoleeo] monopoly.

μονοπωλώ [monopolo] monopolize.

μόνος [monos] alone, single, by o.s., apart || ~ μου of my own accord, by myself.

μονός [monos] single || simple || (αριθμός) odd.

μονότονος [monotonos] monotonous, unvaried || (μεταφ) wearisome.

μονόφθαλμος [monofthalmos] one-eyed.

μοντέλο, το [montelo] model.

μοντέρνος [monternos] modern, up-to-date.

μονώνω [monono] set apart, cut off || insulate.

μόνωση, η [monosee] insulation || solitude, isolation.

μονωτικός [monoteekos] insulating.

μόριο, το [moreeo] particle || molecule.

μόρτης, ο [mortees] hooligan, blackguard

μορφάζω [morfazo] grimace, make faces || (από πόνο) wince.

μορφασμός, ο [morfasmos] grimace || wince.

μορφή, η [morfee] shape, form || look, face, aspect || phase.

μορφίνη, η [morfeenee] morphine.

μορφολογία, η [morfoloyeea] morphology.

μορφώνω [morfono] shape, form || (εκπαιδεύω) train, educate, teach.

μόρφωση, η [morfosee] education, learning.

μορφωτικός [morfoteekos] cultural || instructive.

μόστρα, η [mostra] shop window, display || specimen, sample.

μοσχάρι, το [mosharee] calf || veal.

μοσχοβολώ [moshovolo] smell sweetly, be fragrant.

μοσχοκάρυδο, το [moshokareedo] nutmeg.

μοσχολίβανο, το [mosholeevano] frankincense.

μοτοσυκλέτα, η [motoseekleta] motorbike, motorcycle.

μου [mou] me || my.

μουγγός [moungos] dumb, mute.

μουγγρίζω [moungreezo] roar, bellow || (άνεμος) howl, wail || (από πόνο) moan, groan.

μουδιάζω [moudeeazo] become numb.

μουλάρι, το [moularee] mule.

μούμια, η [moumeea] mummy || shrivelled person.

μουντζούρα, η [mountzoura] smudge, stain, smear || (μεταφ) blemish.

μουντός [mountos] dull, dim.

μούρη, η [mouree] face || snout.

μούρλια, η [mourleea] madness || είναι ~ it's perfect!, it's a dream!

μουρλός [mourlos] mad, insane || bewildered.

μουρμουρητό, το [mourmoureeto] murmuring || grumbling.

μουρμουρίζω [mourmoureezo] mutter, murmur || (μεταφ) whisper || babble.

μούρο, το [mouro] mulberry ||

μουριά, η [mouria] mulberry tree.

μουρούνα, η [mourouna] codfish.

μούσα, η [mousa] muse.

μουσακάς, ο [mousakas] moussaka, minced meat with vegetables.

μουσαμάς, ο [mousamas] oilcloth, linoleum || mackintosh.

μουσαφίρης, ο [mousafeerees] guest, visitor.

μουσείο, το [mouseeo] museum.

μούσι, το [mousee] beard, goatee.

μουσική, η [mouseekee] music.

μουσικός [mouseekos] musical || (ουσ) musician.

μούσκεμα, το [mouskema] wetting, soaking || τα κάνω ~ to make a mess of.

μουσκεύω [mouskevo] soak, wet, damp || get wet.

μούσμουλο, το [mousmoulo] loquat.

μουσουργός, ο, η [mousourgos] composer.

μουστάκι, το [moustakee] moustache.

μουστάρδα, η [moustarda] mustard.

μούστος, ο [moustos] must.

μούτρα, τα [moutra] πλ: **έχω ~ να** I dare to || **πέφτω με τα ~** to apply o.s. enthusiastically || to tuck in.

μούτρο [moutro]: **είναι ~** he's a thief, he's deceitful.

μούτσος, ο [moutsos] cabin boy.

μούχλα, η [mouhla] mould, mildew.

μουχλιάζω [mouhleeazo] make mouldy || become mouldy.

μοχθηρός [mohtheeros] wicked, mischievous, malicious.

μόχθος, ο [mohthos] pains, fatigue, trouble.

μοχλός, ο [mohlos] lever, (crow)bar || (μεταφ) promoter, instigator.

μπαγιάτικος [bayateekos] (ψωμί) stale || rancid.

μπάγκος, ο [bangos] bench || counter.

μπάζα, τα [baza] πλ debris, rubble.

μπάζω [bazo] usher in, thrust || (συμμαζεύομαι) shrink.

μπαίνω [beno] go into, get in, enter || (ύφασμα) shrink || (μεταφ) catch on, understand || **~ μέσα** to fall into debt || **~ σε μια σειρά** to settle down, fall into line.

μπακάλης, ο [bakalees] grocer.

μπακάλικο, το [bakaleeko] grocer's shop || grocery (US).

μπακαλιάρος, ο [bakaleearos] salted codfish.

μπακίρι, το [bakeeree] copper.

μπακλαβάς, ο [baklavas] pastry of almonds and honey.

μπαλαντέρ, ο [balander] (στα χαρτιά) joker.

μπαλκόνι, το [balkonee] balcony.

μπάλα, η [bala] ball || bullet.

μπαλέτο, το [baleto] ballet.

μπαλόνι, το [balonee] balloon.

μπαλντάς, ο [baltas] axe, hatchet.

μπάλωμα, το [baloma] mending, patching, repairing.

μπαλώνω [balono] patch, mend, repair || **τα ~** to make excuses || to make up.

μπάμιες, οι [bamies] πλ okra, gumbo, lady's fingers.

μπαμπάκι, το [bambakee] cotton.

μπαμπάς, ο [bambas] daddy, papa.

μπάμπουρας, ο [bambouras] hornet.

μπανάνα, η [banana] banana.

μπανιέρα, η [baniera] bathtub.

μπάνιο, το [banio] bath || bathing, swimming || (λεκάνη) tub || (δωμάτιο) bathroom.

μπάντα, η [banta] (ήσυχη γωνιά) corner || (πλευρά) side || (μουσ) band || (συμμορία) gang, band || **βάζω στη ~** to save || **κάνε στη ~** make room, stand aside.

μπαντιέρα, η [bantiera] banner, standard.

μπαξές, ο [bakses] garden.

μπασούλο, το [baoulo] trunk, chest.

μπαρκάρω [barkaro] go on board || ship.

μπάρμπας, ο [barbas] old man || uncle.

μπαρμπούνι, το [barbounee] red mullet.

μπαρούτι, το [baroutee] gunpowder || **έγινε ~** he got furious.

μπάρρα, η [bara] bar, crowbar.

μπασμένος [basmenos] aware || knowledgeable || (ρούχα) shrunk.

μπάσταρδος, ο [bastardos] bastard.

μπαστούνι, το [bastounee] walking stick, cane || (χαρτιά) club.

μπαταρία, η [batareea] battery.

μπατζανάκης, ο [batzanakees] brother-in-law.

μπάτσος, ο [batsos] slap, smack || (sl) policeman.

μπαχαρικό, το [bahareeko] spice.

μπεζ [bez] beige.

μπεκάτσα, η [bekatsa] woodcock.

μπεκρής, ο [bekrees] drunkard, tippler, boozer.

μπελάς, ο [belas] trouble, embarrassment, annoyance.

μπέμπης, ο [bembees] baby.

μπενζίνα, η [benzeena] petrol || (πλοιάριο) motorboat.

μπέρδεμα, το [berðema] tangle, entanglement, confusion, disorder.

μπερδεύομαι [berðevome] get implicated, become entangled || be confused.

μπερδεύω [berðevo] involve || confuse, make a muddle of || entangle.

μπερμπάντης, ο [bermbantees] rascal, scoundrel.

μπετό, το [beto] concrete.

μπετούγια, η [betouya] latch, catch.

μπήζω [beezo] drive in, hammer in || (βελόνα) stick in, thrust in.

μπιζέλι, το [beezelee] pea.

μπίρα, η [beera] beer.

μπισκότο, το [beeskoto] biscuit.

μπήτ(ι) [beet(ee)] entirely || not in the least.

μπιφτέκι, το [beeftekee] hamburger, steak.

μπλάστρι, το [blastree] plaster.

μπλε [ble] blue.

μπλέκω [bleko] complicate, perplex || get implicated.

μπλέξιμο, το [blekseemo] entanglement, involvement, complication.

μπλοκάρω [blokaro] blockade || block.

μπλούζα, η [blouza] blouse.

μπλόφα, η [blofa] bluff, deception.

μπογιά, η [boya] paint, dye || (παπουτσιών) boot polish.

μπόγιας, ο [boyas] dog-catcher || hangman.

μπογιατζής, ο [boyadzees] painter || polisher.

μπογιατίζω [boyateezo] paint, colour, coat || polish.

μπόι, το [boee] height, size.

μπόλι, το [bolee] graft || **μπολιάζω** vaccinate, inoculate || graft.

μπόλικος [boleekos] plentiful, abundant, numerous.

μπόμπα, η [bomba] bomb.

μπόρα, η [bora] rain squall, shower, storm.

μπορώ [boro] can, be able, may.

μπόσικος [boseekos] loose, slack || (μεταφ) trifling || unreliable.

μποστάνι, το [bostanee] melon field.

μποτίλια, η [boteeleea] bottle || **μποτιλιάρω** bottle || (μεταφ) block up, jam.

μπότα, η [bota] boot.

μπουγάδα, η [bougaða] family wash, washing.

μπουζί, το [bouzee] spark plug.

μπουζούκι, το [bouzoukee] kind of mandolin, bouzouki.

μπούκα, η [bouka] hole, mouth, entrance || muzzle.

μπουκάλα, η [boukala] big bottle || έμεινε ~ he was left in the lurch.

μπουκάλι, το [boukalee] bottle.

μπουκιά, η [boukia] mouthful.

μπουκώνω [boukono] fill the mouth || (μεταφ) bribe.

μπουλούκι, το [bouloukee] crowd || band, troop.

μπουμπούκι, το [boumboukee] bud, sprout.

μπουμπουνητό, το [boumbouneeto] thundering, roll of thunder, rumble.

μπουνάτσα, η [bounatsa] fine weather || calm sea.

μπουνιά, η [bounia] punch, blow with the fist.

μπούρδα, η [bourða] rubbish, hot air.

μπουρμπουλήθρα, n [bourmbouleethra] bubble.

μπουσουλώ [bousoulo] crawl.

μπούστος, ο [boustos] bust.

μπούτι, το [boutee] thigh || (αρνήσιο) leg of lamb.

μπουφές, ο [boufes] sideboard || buffet.

μπούφος, ο [boufos] horned owl || (μεταφ) booby.

μπουχτίζω [bouhteezo] have enough of || eat one's fill.

μπόχα, n [boha] stink, foul smell.

μπράβο [bravo] (επιφ) good show!, bravo!, good for you!

μπράτσο, το [bratso] arm.

μπριζόλα, n [breezola] chop, cutlet.

μπρίκι, το [breekee] coffee pot.

μπρος [bros] forward(s), in front of || βλ και εμπρός.

μπροστινός [brosteenos] in front || former.

μπρούμυτα [broumeeta] flat on one's face.

μπρούντζος, ο [broundzos] bronze, brass.

μπύρα, n [beera] βλ μπίρα.

μυ, το [mee] the letter M.

μυαλό, το [meealo] brain(s) || (γνώση) mind, intellect.

μυαλωμένος [meealomenos] learned, wise.

μύγα, n [meega] fly.

μύδι, το [meedee] mussel.

μυελός, ο [mielos] marrow (of bone).

μυζήθρα, n [meezeethra] kind of white soft cheese.

μύηση, n [mieesee] initiation.

μυθικός [meetheekos] mythical, legendary || incredible.

μυθιστόρημα, το [meetheestoreema] novel, romance, story.

μυθιστοριογράφος, ο [meetheestoreeografos] novelist.

μυθολογία, n [meetholoyeea] mythology.

μύθος, ο [meethos] fable || myth || legend.

μυθώδης [meethodees] fabled, legendary || untrue || incredible.

μυϊκός [mieekos] muscular.

μυκηθμός, ο [meekeethmos] bellowing, howling || lowing.

μύκητας, ο [meekeetas] fungus, mushroom.

μύλος, ο [meelos] mill || (ανεμόμυλος) windmill.

μυλωνάς, ο [meelonas] miller.

μύξα, n [meeksa] snot || mucus.

μυρίζω [meereezo] smell.

μύριοι [meeriee] ten thousand || (μεταφ) numberless.

μυρμήγκι, το [meermeengee] ant.

μυρτιά, n [meertia] myrtle.

μυρωδάτος [meerodatos] aromatic, fragrant.

μυρωδιά, n [meerodia] smell, scent, odour || (αρωματικό) fragrance, perfume || παίρνω ~ to get wind of.

μυς, ο [mees] muscle.

μυσαρός [meesaros] abominable, detestable, odious.

μυσταγωγία, n [meestagoyeea] initiation || holy ceremony.

μυστήριο, το [meesteereeo] mystery, secret.

μυστήριος [meesteereeos] mysterious, inexplicable.

μυστηριώδης [meesteereeodees] mysterious, dark.

μυστικιστής, ο [meesteekeestees] mystic.

μυστικό, το [meesteeko] secret.

μυστικός [meesteekos] secret(ive) || reticent, discreet || (αστυνομικός) undercover man || ~ δείπνος Last Supper.

μυστικότητα, n [meesteekoteeta] secrecy, discretion.

μυστρί, το [meestree] trowel.

μυτερός [meeteros] pointed.

μύτη, η [meetee] nose || (άκρη) tip || (παπουτσιού) toe || (νένας) nib || (βελόνας) point.

μυώ [meeo] initiate into, admit into.

μυώδης [meeodees] muscular, brawny, powerful.

μύωπας [meeopas] near-sighted, short-sighted.

μωαμεθανός, ο [moamethanos] Mohammedan.

μωβ [mov] mauve.

μώλος, ο [molos] mole, jetty, pier.

μωλωπίζω [molopeezo] bruise, contuse.

μώλωπας, ο [molopas] bruise, contusion.

μωρέ [more] (επιφ) hey you!, you!, I say!

μωρία, η [moreea] stupidity, foolishness.

μωρό, το [moro] baby, infant.

μωσαϊκό, το [mosaeeko] mosaic.

N, ν

να [na] that, to, in order to, so as to || here it is!

ναι [ne] yes, indeed, certainly.

νάιλον, το [naeelon] nylon.

νάνος, ο [nanos] dwarf.

νανουρίζω [nanoureezo] lull to sleep || (στην κούνια) rock || (στην αγκαλιά) nurse.

νανούρισμα, το [nanoureesma] lullaby || rocking to sleep.

ναός, ο [naos] church || temple.

ναργιλές, ο [naryeelees] hubble-bubble, hookah.

νάρθηκας, ο [nartheekas] (εκκλ) nave, narthex || (βοτ) fennel.

ναρκαλιευτικό, το [narkalievteeko] minesweeper.

νάρκη, η [narkee] numbness, torpor || (ναυτ) mine || (πνεύματος) sluggishness.

νάρκισσος, ο [narkeesos] narcissus.

ναρκώνω [narkono] numb || (μεταφ) dull, stupefy.

νάρκωση, η [narkosee] numbness || torpidity, sluggishness.

ναρκωτικά, τα [narkoteeka] πλ drugs, narcotics.

νάτριο, το [natreeo] sodium.

ναυάγιο, το [navayo] shipwreck || (μεταφ) wreck.

ναυαγός, ο [navagos] shipwrecked person.

ναυαρχείο, το [navarheeo] admiralty.

ναύαρχος, ο [navarhos] admiral.

ναύκληρος, ο [navkleeros] boatswain.

ναύλα, τα [navla] πλ fare, passage money.

ναυλώνω [navlono] charter, freight.

ναυμαχία, η [navmaheea] sea battle, naval action.

ναυπηγείο, το [navpeeyeeo] shipyard, dockyard.

ναυσιπλοΐα, η [navseeploeea] sailing, shipping || navigation.

ναύσταθμος, ο [navstathmos] dockyard, naval arsenal.

ναύτης, ο [navtees] sailor, seaman, mariner.

ναυτία, η [navteea] seasickness || nausea.

ναυτικό, το [navteeko] navy.

ναυτικός [navteekos] maritime || nautical || (άνδρας) seafarer.

ναυτιλία, η [navteeleea] navigation || shipping || **ναυτιλιακός** marine, naval, nautical.

ναυτολογώ [navtologo] enlist a crew, muster seamen.

νέα, η [nea] girl.

νέα, τα [nea] πλ news.

νεανικός [neaneekos] youthful, juvenile.

νεαρός [nearos] young || youthful, juvenile.

νέγρος, ο [negros] negro.

νέκρα, η [nekra] dead silence, stagnation.

νεκρικός [nekreekos] of death, funereal || gloomy.

νεκροθάπτης, ο [nekrothaptees] gravedigger.

νεκροκεφαλή, η [nekrokefalee] skull.

νεκρολογία, η [nekroloyeea] obituary.

νεκρός [nekros] dead, lifeless || (ουσ) ο ~ dead person.

νεκροταφείο, το [nekrotafeeo] cemetery, graveyard.

νεκροτομείο, το [nekrotomeeo] mortuary, morgue.

νεκροφόρα, η [nekrofora] hearse.

νεκροψία, η [nekropseea] autopsy, post-mortem.

νεκρώνω [nekrono] deaden || (τα πάθη) subdue.

νεκρώσιμος [nekroseemos] funeral.

νέκταρ, το [nektar] nectar.

νέμω [nemo] distribute, share.

νέο, το [neo] piece of news.

νεογέννητος [neoyeneetos] newborn.

νεογνό, το [neogno] newborn animal || newborn baby.

νεοελληνικά, τα [neoeleeneeka] πλ modern Greek (language).

νεοελληνικός [neoeleeneekos] of modern Greece.

νεόκτιστος [neokteestos] newly constructed.

νεολαία, η [neolea] youth.

νεόνυμφος, ο, η [neoneemfos] recently married man or woman.

νεόπλουτος [neoploutos] nouveau riche, parvenu.

νέος [neos] young || (καινούργιο) new, fresh || (επιπρόσθετο) further, additional || (σύγχρονος) modern || (ουσ) a young man.

νεοσσός, ο [neosos] nestling, chick.

νεοσύλλεκτος, ο [neoseelektos] recruit.

νεοσύστατος [neoseestatos] newly-established, newly-founded.

νεότητα, η [neoteeta] βλ **νεολαία**.

νεράιδα, η [neraeeda] fairy, Nereid.

νεράντζι, το [nerandzee] bitter orange.

νερό, το [nero] water || urine.

νερόβραστος [nerovrastos] boiled in water || (μεταφ) insipid, tasteless.

νερομπογιά, η [neromboya] watercolour.

νεροποντή, η [neropontee] shower of rain, downpour.

νερουλός [neroulos] watery, thin.

νεροχύτης, ο [neroheetees] kitchen sink.

νερώνω [nerono] mix with water.

νέτα σκέτα [netasketa] frankly, flatly.

νέτος [netos] net || (μεταφ) done, finished, completed.

νεύμα, το [nevma] sign, nod, wink, beckoning.

νευραλγία, η [nevralyeea] neuralgia.

νευραλγικός [nevralyeekos]: **νευραλγικό σημείο** weak spot.

νευριάζω [nevreeazo] make angry, irritate, vex || become angry.

νευρικός [nevreekos] nervous || excitable, highly strung.

νεύρο, το [nevro] nerve || muscle || vigour.

νευρόσπαστος, ο [nevrospastos] (μεταφ) nervous person.

νευρώδης [nevrodees] sinewy || nervous || (μεταφ) strong, spirited.

νευρωτικός [nevroteekos] neurotic.

νεύω [nevo] nod, make a sign, beckon, wink.

νεφελώδης [nefelodees] cloudy, nebulous || (μεταφ) vague, hazy.

νέφος, το [nefos] cloud || (μεταφ) gloom, shadow.

νεφοσκεπής [nefoskepees] cloudy, overcast.

νεφρό, το [nefro] kidney.

νέφτι, το [neftee] turpentine, turps.

νεώριο, το [neoreeo] dry dock, dockyard.

νεωτερισμός, ο [neotereesmos] innovation || novelty, fashion.

νεώτερα, τα [neotera] πλ latest news.

νεώτερος [neoteros] younger || (γεγονός) recent, later || (νέα) fresh.

νήμα, το [neema] thread || (βαμβακερό) cotton thread || (μάλλινο) yarn.

νηνεμία, η [neenemeea] calmness, stillness.

νηολόγιο, το [neeoloyo] register of merchant shipping.

νηοπομπή, η [neeopombee] convoy, escort of ships.

νηπιαγωγείο, το [neepeeagoyeeo] kindergarten.

νήπιο, το [neepeeo] infant, baby, newborn child.

νησί, το [neesee] island.

νησιώτης, ο [neeseeotees] islander.

νήσος, η [neesos] βλ **νησί**.

νηστεία, η [neesteea] fast, fasting.

νηστεύω [neestevo] fast.

νηστικός [neesteekos] hungry.

νηφάλιος [neefaleeos] sober || (μεταφ) calm, cool, composed.

νιαουρίζω [neeaoureezo] miaow, mew.

νιάτα, τα [neeata] πλ youth.

νικέλιο, το [neekeleeo] nickel.

νίκη, η [neekee] victory, triumph.

νικητής, ο [neekeetees] victor || (σε παιχνίδι) winner.

νικηφόρος [neekeeforos] victorious, triumphant.

νικώ [neeko] (τον εχθρό) defeat, vanquish || (ανταγωνιστή) beat,

surpass || (εμπόδια κτλ) surmount, overcome.

νίλα, η [neela] practical joke || calamity, ruin.

νιπτήρας, ο [neepteeras] washbasin, washstand.

νίπτω [neepto] wash || (μεταφ) wash out.

νισάφι, το [neesafee] mercy, compassion, pity.

νιφάδα, η [neefaδa] snowflake.

Νοέμβρης, ο [noemvrees], **Νοέμβριος, ο** [noemvreeos] November.

νοερός [noeros] mental, intellectual.

νόημα, το [noeema] reflection, thought || (έννοια) sense, meaning || (νεύμα) sign, wink.

νοημοσύνη, η [noeemoseenee] intelligence, intellect.

νοήμων [noeemon] intelligent, smart.

νόηση, η [noeesee] understanding, intellect || mind, wit.

νοητός [noeetos] comprehensible, conceivable.

νοθεία, η [notheea] falsification, adulteration.

νόθευση, η [nothevsee] adulteration, forgery.

νοθεύω [nothevo] falsify, forge, adulterate.

νόθος [nothos] bastard || (για ζώα κτλ) hybrid || (μεταφ) unstable.

νοιάζει [neeazee]: **με ~** I care, I am anxious about.

νοιάζομαι [neeazome] care about, look after || be anxious about.

νοίκι, το [neekee] rent || **νοικιάζω** [neekeeazo] rent, hire, let out || **νοικάρης, ο** [neekarees] tenant.

νοικοκυρά, η [neekokeera] housewife, mistress of the house || landlady.

νοικοκύρης, ο [neekokeerees]

landlord || owner || (αυτεξούσιος) independent || wise.

νοικοκυριό, το [neekokeerio] housekeeping.

νοιώθω [neeotho] understand || feel, perceive || know.

νομαδικός [nomadeekos] nomadic, roving.

νομαρχείο, το [nomarheeo] prefecture.

νομάρχης, ο [nomarhees] prefect, governor.

νομίζω [nomeezo] believe, think || suppose, presume.

νομικά, τα [nomeeka] πλ law studies, jurisprudence.

νομική, η [nomeekee] law.

νομικός [nomeekos] of the law, legal, lawful.

νομιμοποιώ [nomeemopeeo] legitimize, legalize, validate.

νόμιμος [nomeemos] legal, lawful, rightful.

νομιμότητα, η [nomeemoteeta] legitimacy, legality.

νομιμόφρονας [nomeemofronas] law-abiding, obedient, loyal.

νόμισμα, το [nomeesma] money, coin, currency.

νομοθεσία, η [nomotheseea] legislation, law-making.

νομοθέτης, ο [nomothetees] legislator, lawgiver.

νομομαθής, ο [nomomathees] jurist, legist.

νομός, ο [nomos] prefecture, province.

νόμος, ο [nomos] law, act (of Parliament), enactment.

νομοσχέδιο, το [nomosheðeeo] bill, draft of a law.

νομοταγής [nomotayees] law-abiding, loyal.

νονός, ο [nonos] godfather, sponsor.

νοοτροπία, η [nootropeea] mentality, mental character.

Νορβηγία, η [norveeyeea] Norway.

νορβηγικός [norveeyeekos] Norwegian.

Νορβηγός, ο [norveegos] Norwegian.

νοσηλεία, η [noseeleea] nursing, treatment, care of the sick.

νοσηλεύω [noseelevo] treat, tend, nurse.

νοσηρός [noseeros] unhealthy, sickly, weakly || (περιέργεια) morbid.

νοσοκομείο, το [nosokomeeo] hospital, infirmary.

νοσοκόμος, ο, η [nosokomos] nurse || (στρατ) hospital orderly.

νόσος, η [nosos] illness, disease, sickness.

νοσταλγία, η [nostalyeea] nostalgia || homesickness.

**νοσταλγικός, [nostalyeekos] nostalgic || homesick.

νοσταλγώ [nostalgo] feel nostalgic for || crave for || be homesick.

νοστιμάδα, η [nosteemaða] tastiness || prettiness || piquancy.

νοστιμεύω [nosteemevo] flavour, make tasty || make attractive.

νόστιμος [nosteemos] tasty || attractive, charming.

νότα, η [nota] (διπλωματική) note || (μουσ) note.

νοτιά, η [notia] south || south wind.

νοτίζω [noteezo] moisten, dampen || become damp.

νοτιοανατολικός [noteeoanatoleekos] south-eastern.

νοτιοδυτικός [noteeoðeeteekos] south-western.

νότιος [noteeos] southern.

νότος, ο [notos] south.

νουθεσία, η [noutheseea] admonition, advice, counsel.

νουθετώ [noutheto] admonish, advise, give advice to.

νούμερο, το [noumero] number || (θεάτρου) act || odd character.

νουνός, ο [nounos] godfather, sponsor.

νους, ο [nous] mind, wit, intelligence, sense.

νούφαρο, το [noufaro] water lily.

νοώ [noo] comprehend, understand || think, reflect.

ντάης, ο [daees] bully, ruffian.

ντάμα, η [dama] lady || partner || (στα χαρτιά) queen || (παιχνίδι) game of draughts.

νταμιτζάνα, η [dameedzana] demijohn.

νταμπλάς, ο [damblas] apoplexy || (μεταφ) amazement, stupefaction.

νταντά, η [danda] child's nurse, nanny.

νταντέλα, η [dantela] lace.

νταούλι, το [daoulee] drum.

νταραβέρι, το [daraveree] relation, dealing || (φασαρία) fuss, trouble.

ντε [de]: έλα ~ (επιφ) come on!, hurry up!

ντεπόζιτο, το [depozeeto] cistern || tank.

ντέρτι, το [dertee] regret, pain, sorrow || longing, yearning.

ντιβάνι, το [deevanee] divan.

ντολμάς, ο [dolmas] stuffed vine or cabbage leaves.

ντομάτα, η [domata] tomato.

ντόμπρος [dombros] sincere, candid, frank, honest.

ντόπιος [dopeeos] local, native.

ντόρος, ο [doros] trouble, din || (μεταφ) sensation.

ντουβάρι, το [douvaree] wall || (μεταφ) fool.

ντουέτο, το [doueto] duet.

ντουζίνα, η [douzeena] dozen.

ντουλάπα, η [doulapa] wardrobe.

ντουλάπι, το [doulapee] cupboard.

ντουνιάς, ο [dounias] people, mankind, humanity.

ντους, το [dous] shower bath.

ντρέπομαι [drepome] be bashful || be ashamed.

ντροπαλός [dropalos] shy, modest, timid.

ντροπή, η [dropee] shame || modesty, bashfulness.

ντροπιάζω [dropeeazo] shame.

ντυμένος [deemenos] dressed.

ντύνομαι [deenome] get dressed.

ντύνω [deeno] dress || (έπιπλα) upholster.

ντύσιμο, το [deeseemo] dressing || attire, outfit, dress.

νυ, το [nee] the letter N.

νυκτερινός [neektereenos] of night, nocturnal.

νυκτόβιος [neektoveeos] living by night.

νυκτοφύλακας, ο [neektofeelakas] night watchman.

νυμφεύω [neemfevo] marry, wed.

νύμφη, η [neemfee] bride || (μυθολογία) nymph || (ζώου) larva.

νύξη, η [neeksee] hint, allusion.

νύστα, η [neesta] sleepiness, drowsiness.

νυστάζω [neestazo] be sleepy, feel sleepy.

νυσταλέος [neestaleos] sleepy || (μεταφ) dull, sluggish.

νύφη, η [neefee] βλ νύμφη.

νυφικός [neefeekos] bridal, nuptial.

νυφίτσα, η [neefeetsa] weasel.

νυχθημερόν [neehtheemeron] day and night.

νύχι, το [neehee] nail || (ποδιών) toenail || (ζώου) claw, talon || **νύχια** πλ clutches.

νύχτα, η [neehta] night, darkness || (επιρ) at night, by night.

νυχτερίδα, η [neehtereeða] bat.

νυχτικό, το [neehteeko] nightgown.

νυχτώνω [neehtono]: **νυχτώνει** night falls.

νωθρός [nothros] sluggish, lazy, slothful.

νωπός 151 ξεβράκωτος

νωπός [nopos] fresh, new, recent || (για ρούχα) still damp.

νωρίς [norees] early.

νώτα, τα [nota] πλ back || (στρατ) rear.

νωχελής [nohelees] indolent, idle, slothful.

Ξ, ξ

ξαγρυπνώ [ksagreepno] stay awake || watch over || burn the midnight oil.

ξαδέρφη, η [ksaderfee] cousin.

ξάδερφος, ο [ksaderfos] cousin.

ξακουστός [ksakoustos] renowned, celebrated, famous.

ξαλαφρώνω [ksalafrono] lighten the load of, help || (μεταφ) relieve || relieve one's mind.

ξανά [ksana] again, afresh, anew.

ξαναβάζω [ksanavazo] put back again, replace.

ξανάβω [ksanavo] irritate || become annoyed, get furious.

ξαναγυρίζω [ksanayeereezo] return, send back || turn again.

ξανακάνω [ksanakano] redo, remake, repeat.

ξαναλέω [ksanaleo] repeat, reiterate.

ξανανιώνω [ksananeeono] rejuvenate || become young again.

ξαναπαθαίνω [ksanapatheno] be taken in again || suffer again.

ξαναπαίρνω [ksanaperno] take again || (θάρρος) pluck up again || (υπάλληλος) take on again, rehire || (θέση) go back to.

ξαναπαντρεύομαι [ksanapandrevome] remarry.

ξανασαίνω [ksanaseno] recover, refresh o.s., relax.

ξαναφορτώνω [ksanafortono] reload.

ξανθίζω [ksantheezo] become fairer.

ξανθομάλλης [ksanthomalees] fair-haired.

ξανθός [ksanthos] blond, fair, light || (στάχυ) yellow, golden.

ξάνοιγμα, το [ksaneegma] clearing up, brightening || launching out.

ξανοίγομαι [ksaneegome] confide one's secrets || spend freely.

ξανοίγω [ksaneego] (μεταφ) look, see || clear up.

ξάπλα, η [ksapla] sprawling around || lying down.

ξάπλωμα, το [ksaploma] lying down || stretching out, spreading.

ξαπλώνομαι [ksaplonome] spread || lie down.

ξαπλώνω [ksaplono] spread out || lie down.

ξαποσταίνω [ksaposteno] rest, relax.

ξαποστέλνω [ksapostelno] send off, forward || dismiss.

ξασπρίζω [ksaspreezo] whiten || blanch, pale, fade.

ξάστερα [ksastera] frankly, flatly, categorically.

ξάστερος [ksasteros] cloudless, bright || (μεταφ) lucid, clear.

ξαφνιάζομαι [ksafneeazome] be taken by surprise, be frightened.

ξαφνιάζω [ksafneeazo] startle, surprise, frighten, scare.

ξαφνικά [ksafneeka] all of a sudden.

ξαφνικό, το [ksafneeko] surprise || accident, mishap.

ξαφρίζω [ksafreezo] skim || (μεταφ) steal.

ξάφρισμα, το [ksafreesma] skimming || frothing.

ξεβάφω [ksevafo] fade || lose colour, discolour.

ξεβγάζω [ksevgazo] wash out || (προπέμπω) show out, get rid of.

ξεβράκωτος [ksevrakotos] trouserless || (μεταφ) penniless.

ξεγελώ [kseyelo] cheat, dupe, deceive.

ξεγεννώ [kseyeno] deliver a child || be delivered of.

ξεγνοιάζω [ksegneeazo] be free from care.

ξεγράφω [ksegrafo] efface, strike out || (μεταφ) wipe out || write off.

ξεδιαλέγω [ksedeealego] select, choose, sort.

ξεδιαλύνω [ksedeealeeno] get to the bottom of, unravel.

ξεδιάντροπος [ksedeeantropos] immodest, brazen.

ξεδιπλώνω [ksedeeplono] unfurl, open out, spread.

ξεδιψώ [ksedeepso] quench one's thirst || refresh.

ξεθαρρεύω [ksetharevo] become too bold.

ξεθεώνω [ksetheono] wear out, exhaust, harass, worry.

ξεθυμαίνω [ksetheemeno] escape, leak out || (μεταφ) calm down, abate.

ξεθωριάζω [ksethoreeazo] fade || lose colour, discolour.

ξεκαθαρίζω [ksekathareezo] liquidate, settle accounts || elucidate || kill off.

ξεκάνω [ksekano] sell off || kill, exterminate.

ξεκαρδίζομαι [ksekardeezome] burst out laughing.

ξεκάρφωτος [ksekarfotos] (μεταφ) unconnected, irrelevant.

ξεκινώ [ksekeeno] set off, start, depart || drive off.

ξεκλείδωτος [ksekleedotos] unlocked.

ξεκοκκαλίζω [ksekokaleezo] eat to the bone || (μεταφ) spend foolishly.

ξεκομμένα [ksekomena] to the point, frankly.

ξεκουμπώνω [ksekoumbono] unbutton, unfasten.

ξεκουράζομαι [ksekourazome] relax, rest.

ξεκουράζω [ksekourazo] rest, relieve, refresh, repose.

ξεκουφαίνω [ksekoufeno] deafen, stun.

ξελιγωμένος [kseleegomenos] hungry for, hunger for.

ξελιγώνω [kseleegono] (μεταφ) wear o.s. out, tire.

ξελογιάζω [kseloyazo] seduce, lead astray, fascinate.

ξεμαλλιασμένος [ksemaleeasmenos] dishevelled.

ξεμοναχιάζω [ksemonaheeazo] take aside.

ξεμπαρκάρω [ksembarkaro] land || unload.

ξεμπερδεύω [ksemberdevo] unravel, disentangle || get clear of, get rid of.

ξεμπλέκω [ksembleko] free o.s. || ~ από get free of.

ξεμυαλίζω [ksemeealeezo] infatuate, turn the head of, lead astray.

ξένα, τα [ksena] πλ foreign parts.

ξεναγός, ο, η [ksenagos] tourist guide.

ξενητειά, η [kseneetia] foreign parts, foreign country.

ξενητεύομαι [kseneetevome] live abroad.

ξενίζω [kseneezo] surprise, astonish.

ξενικός [kseneekos] foreign, alien, outlandish.

ξενοιάζω [kseneeazo] be free from cares.

ξενοδοχείο, το [ksenodoheeo] hotel.

ξενοδόχος, ο [ksenodohos] hotelier, innkeeper.

ξενοικιάζομαι [kseneekeeazome] become vacant.

ξένος [ksenos] foreign, strange,

unfamiliar || (ουσ) ~ foreigner, stranger || visitor.

ξενοφοβία, η [ksenofoveea] xenophobia.

ξενόφωνος [ksenofonos] foreign-speaking.

ξεντύνω [ksenteeno] undress, disrobe.

ξενυχτώ [kseneehto] stay up late, stay out all night.

ξενώνας, ο [ksenonas] spare room, guest room.

ξεπαγιάζω [ksepayazo] freeze || get frozen.

ξεπαστρεύω [ksepastrevo] exterminate, wipe out.

ξεπερασμένος [kseperasmenos] out-of-date, old-fashioned.

ξεπερνώ [kseperno] surpass, overtake || (σε δρόμο) outrun || (σε ύψος) be taller.

ξεπεσμός, ο [ksepesmos] decay, decline || (τιμών) fall || (νομίσματος) depreciation.

ξεπετιέμαι [ksepetieme] jump up suddenly, shoot up.

ξεπέφτω [ksepefto] reduce, abate || (τιμών) fall || (μεταφ) fall into disrepute.

ξεπλένω [ksepleno] rinse.

ξεπληρώνω [ksepleerono] pay off, discharge (a debt).

ξεπούλημα, το [ksepouleema] sale, sellout, liquidation || fire sale (US).

ξεπουλώ [ksepoulo] sell off || sell out, liquidate.

ξεπροβοδίζω [kseprovodeezo] escort off, say goodbye to.

ξέρα, η [ksera] (θάλασσας) rock, reef || (ξηρασία) drought, dryness.

ξεραΐλα, η [kseraeela] aridity, dryness, drought.

ξεραίνομαι [kserenome] dry up, wither, get parched.

ξεραίνω [ksereno] dry up || parch, bake || (φυτά) wither.

ξερνώ [kserno] vomit, bring up || belch out.

ξερόβηχας, ο [kseroveehas] dry cough.

ξεροκατανίνω [kserokatapeeno] swallow with embarrassment.

ξεροκέφαλος [kserokefalos] thickheaded || obstinate, stubborn.

ξερονήσι, το [kseroneesee] barren island, desert island.

ξερός [kseros] arid, dry, barren || (γλώσσα) parched || (ύφος) curt, snappish || **έμεινε ~** he was stumped || he dropped dead || **έπεσε ~ στον ύπνο** he dropped off to sleep.

ξεριζώνω [ksereezono] pull up, uproot || root out, wipe out.

ξέρω [ksero] know how to, understand, be aware of.

ξεσηκώνω [kseseekono] rouse, excite || (σχέδιο) transfer, copy.

ξεσκάζω [kseskazo] refresh o.s., relax.

ξεσκεπάζω [kseskepazo] unveil, uncover || reveal, disclose, let out.

ξεσκίζω [kseskeezo] rip up.

ξεσκονίζω [kseskoneezo] dust, give a dusting to.

ξεσκονόπανο, το [kseskonopano] duster, dust rag.

ξεσπάζω [kseskazo] (μεταφ) burst into, burst out.

ξεσπαθώνω [ksespathono] unsheathe one's sword || (μεταφ) speak out.

ξεστομίζω [ksestomeezo] utter, launch, hurl.

ξεστρατίζω [ksestravono] straighten out || become straight.

ξεστρώνω [ksestrono] take up, remove || (τραπέζι) clear away.

ξεσχίζω [kseskeezo] tear to pieces, lacerate.

ξετινάζω [kseteenazo] toss, shake, beat || (μεταφ) reduce to poverty.

ξετρελαίνω [ksetreleno] drive mad, bewilder || (από έρωτα) bewitch.

ξετρυπώνω [ksetreepono] appear suddenly, crop up.

ξετσίπωτος [ksetseepotos] shameless.

ξεύρω [ksevro] βλ **ξέρω**.

ξεφαντώνω [ksefantono] live fast, feast, revel.

ξεφεύγω [ksefevgo] elude || slip out.

ξεφλουδίζω [ksefloudeezo] peel || pare || shell || (το δέρμα) lose the skin.

ξεφορτώνομαι [ksefortonome] get rid of, shake off.

ξεφορτώνω [ksefortono] unload || (μεταφ) get rid of.

ξεφτέρι, το [ksefteree] sharp person, witty person.

ξεφτίζω [ksefteezo] fray out || (νήμα) pull out, unweave.

ξεφυλλίζω [ksefeeleezo] skim over, run through || strip the leaves, pluck.

ξεφυτρώνω [ksefeetrono] sprout, shoot up || appear suddenly.

ξεφωνητό, το [ksefoneeto] yell, shout, outcry, scream.

ξεφωνίζω [ksefoneezo] shout, bawl, yell, scream.

ξεχαρβαλωμένος [kseharvalomenos] shaky, loose, falling apart.

ξεχασμένος [ksehasmenos] forgotten.

ξεχειλίζω [kseheeleezo] overflow, run over.

ξεχειμωνιάζω [kseheemoneeazo] pass the winter, winter.

ξεχνώ [ksehno] forget, leave out, neglect.

ξεχρεώνω [ksehreono] pay up, discharge || settle, fulfil.

ξεχύνομαι [kseheenome] overflow.

ξεχύνω [kseheeno] pour out, overflow.

ξέχωρα [ksehora] apart, separately || ~ από apart from.

ξεχωρίζω [ksehoreezo] separate || single out || distinguish, discern || make one's mark.

ξεχωριστά [ksehoreesta] separately.

ξεχωριστός [ksehoreestos] separate || distinct, peculiar || distinguished, exceptional.

ξεψυχώ [ksepseeho] die, expire, give up the ghost.

ξηλώνω [kseelono] take apart, unstitch.

ξημερώματα [kseemeromata] πλ daybreak, dawn.

ξημερώνομαι [kseemeronome] stay awake till morning.

ξηρά, η [kseera] dry land, mainland.

ξηραίνω [kseereno] dry, drain.

ξηραντήριο, το [kseeranteereeo] drier.

ξηρασία, η [kseeraseea] aridity || drought.

ξηροί [kseeree]: ~ καρποί πλ dried fruit and nuts.

ξι, το [ksee] the letter Ξ.

ξινίζω [kseeneezo] turn sour, get sour.

ξινίλα, η [kseeneela] bitterness, acidity, tartness, sharpness.

ξινός [kseenos] sour, acid, sharp || (για φρούτα) unripe, green.

ξιπασμένος [kseepasmenos] vain, conceited.

ξιφασκία, η [kseefaskia] fencing, swordplay.

ξιφίας, ο [kseefeeas] swordfish.

ξιφολόγχη, η [kseefolonghee] bayonet.

ξιφομαχώ [kseefomaho] fence.

ξίφος, το [kseefos] sword.

ξοδεύομαι [ksodevome] spend, incur expenses.

ξοδεύω [ksodevo] spend, use up, consume, expend.

ξόρκι, το [ksorkee] exorcism ||
entreaty.

ξύγκι, το [kseengee] fat, lard,
grease, tallow.

ξυδάτος [kseedatos] pickled.

ξύδι, το [kseedee] vinegar.

ξυλάνθρακας, ο [kseelanthrakas]
charcoal.

ξυλεία, η [kseeleea] timber,
lumber.

ξύλινος [kseeleenos] wooden, wood.

ξύλο, το [kseelo] wood || τρώω ~
to receive a beating || έπεσε ~
there was a fight.

ξυλοκάρβουνο, το
[kseelokarvouno] charcoal.

ξυλοκόπος, ο [kseelokopos]
woodcutter, lumberjack.

ξυλοκοπώ [kseelokopo] thrash,
beat soundly.

ξυλοπόδαρο, το [kseelopodaro]
stilt.

ξυλουργική, η [kseelouryeekee]
joinery, carpentry.

ξυλουργός, ο [kseelourgos] joiner,
carpenter.

ξυλοφορτώνω [kseelofortono]
thrash, leather, lick.

ξύνομαι [kseenome] scratch (o.s.).

ξύνω [kseeno] scratch, scrape ||
(μολύβι) sharpen || scrape off.

ξύπνημα, το [kseepneema]
awakening, waking up.

ξυπνητήρι, το [kseepneeteeree]
alarm clock.

ξύπνιος [kseepneeos] wakeful,
awake || (μεταφ) alert, clever,
intelligent.

ξυπνώ [kseepno] wake up, rouse.

ξυπόλυτος [kseepoleetos]
barefooted, shoeless.

ξυράφι, το [kseerafee] razor.

ξυραφάκι, το [kseerafakee] razor
blade.

ξυρίζομαι [kseereezome] shave, get
shaved, have a shave.

ξυρίζω [kseereezo] shave.

ξύρισμα, το [kseereesma] shave,
shaving.

ξυριστική [kseereesteekee]: ~
μηχανή safety razor.

ξύσιμο, το [kseeseemo] scratching,
scraping || rubbing, erasing ||
sharpening.

ξυστός [kseestos] grated,
scratched.

ξύστρα, η [kseestra] grater,
scraper, rasp || pencil sharpener.

ξωκκλήσι, το [ksokleesee] country
chapel.

ξωτικό, το [ksoteeko] ghost, spirit,
goblin.

ξώφυλλο, το [ksofeelo] book cover
|| (παραθύρου) outside shutter.

Ο, ο

ο [o] the.

όαση, η [oasee] oasis.

οβελίας, ο [oveleeas] lamb on the
spit.

οβίδα, η [oveeda] explosive shell.

οβολός, ο [ovolos] mite,
contribution.

ογδόντα [ogdonda] eighty.

ογδοηκοστός [ogdoeekostos]
eightieth.

ογδοντάρης, ο [ogdontarees]
octogenarian.

όγδοος [ogdoos] eighth.

ογκόλιθος, ο [ongoleethos] block
of stone.

όγκος, ο [ongos] volume, mass,
bulk, lump || (ιατρ) tumour.

ογκούμαι [ongoume] swell, grow
fatter || (μεταφ) increase, swell.

ογκώδης [ongodees] voluminous,
massive || (άτομο) stout, portly.

οδεύω [odevo] walk, tramp, trudge ||
accompany || (προς) proceed,
advance.

οδηγητής, ο [odeeyeetees] guide.

οδηγία, η [odeeyeea] direction,

guidance || instruction, directions, orders.'

οδηγός, ο [odeegos] guide, conductor || (αυτοκινήτου) driver, chauffeur.

οδηγώ [odeego] guide, lead || (αυτοκίνητο κτλ) drive || show how to, instruct.

οδοιπορία, η [odeeporeea] walk, journey || march.

οδοιπορικά, τα [odeeporeeka] πλ: ~ έξοδα travelling expenses.

οδοιπόρος, ο, η [odeeporos] traveller, voyager.

οδοιπορώ [odeeporo] walk, tramp || march || travel.

οδοκαθαριστής, ο [odokathareestees] street sweeper.

οδοντιατρείο, το [odonteeatreeo] dentist's surgery, dental clinic.

οδοντιατρική, η [odonteeatreekee] dentistry.

οδοντίατρος, ο, η [odonteeatros] dentist.

οδοντόβουρτσα, η [odontovourtsa] toothbrush.

οδοντογλυφίδα, η [odontogleefeeda] toothpick.

οδοντόπαστα, η [odontopasta] dentifrice, toothpaste.

οδοντοστοιχία, η [odontosteeheea] (set of) false teeth.

οδοντωτός [odontotos] toothed, jagged, cogged || ~ σιδηρόδρομος funicular railway.

οδοποιία, η [odopieea] road construction, roadmaking.

οδός, η [odos] street || (ευρεία) main street, thoroughfare || (εθνική) state highway || (εμπορική) trade route || **καθ' οδόν** on the way, along the road.

οδόστρωμα, το [odostroma] road surface.

οδοστρωτήρας, ο [odostroteeras] steamroller.

οδόφραγμα, το [odofragma] barricade, roadblock, barrier.

οδύνη, η [odeenee] pain, suffering || (ηθική) grief || affliction.

οδυνηρός [odeeneeros] (πληγή) painful || (μέρος) sore || (θέαμα) harrowing.

οδυρμός, ο [odeermos] lamentation, wailing.

οδύρομαι [odeerome] lament, complain, moan.

όζον, το [ozon] ozone.

όζος, ο [ozos] knot || (των δακτύλων) knuckles.

οζώδης [ozodees] knotty, gnarled.

οθόνη, η [othonee] screen.

Οθωμανός, ο [othomanos] Ottoman.

οίδημα, το [eedeema] swelling.

οικειοθελώς [eekeeeothelos] (υποκούω) voluntarily || (κάνω κάτι) purposely, wilfully.

οικειοποίηση, η [eekeeopieesee] appropriation.

οικειοποιούμαι [eekeeopeeoume] appropriate to o.s., usurp.

οικείος [eekeeos] intimate, familiar || sociable, affable || **οι οικείοι** relatives, close relations.

οικειότητα, η [eekeeoteeta] familiarity, closeness.

οίκημα, το [eekeema] dwelling, lodging, habitation.

οικία, η [eekeea] house, home.

οικιακός [eekeeakos] domestic, home || (ζώο) domesticated.

οικίζω [eekeezo] inhabit, colonize, settle.

οικισμός, ο [eekeesmos] settling, colonizing.

οικογένεια, η [eekoyeneea] family.

οικογενειακός [eekoyeneeakos] of the family.

οικογενειακώς [eekoyeneeakos] with the entire family.

οικοδέσποινα, η [eekodespeena] lady of the house, hostess.

οικοδεσπότης, ο [eekodespotees] master of the house, host.

οικοδομή, η [eekodomee] construction, act of building || building under construction.

οικοδόμημα, το [eekodomeema] building, structure.

οικοδόμηση, η [eekodomeesee] construction, building, erection.

οικοδομική, η [eekodomeekee] building.

οικοδομικός [eekodomeekos] constructive.

οικοδομώ [eekodomo] build, construct, raise.

οικοκυρά [eekokeera] βλ **νοικοκυρά**.

οικοκύρης [eekokeerees] βλ **νοικοκύρης**.

οίκον [eekon] **κατ' ~** at home.

οικονομία, η [eekonomeea] economy, husbandry, thrift || saving.

οικονομικά, τα [eekonomeeka] πλ finances || (επιρ) reasonably, cheaply.

οικονομικός [eekonomeekos] economic, financial || (φθηνά) reasonable, cheap.

οικονόμος, ο, η [eekonomos] steward, stewardess || (μεταφ) thrifty person.

οικονομώ [eekonomo] save, economize || (βρω, get hold of) || **τα ~** make ends meet, make money.

οικόπεδο, το [eekopedo] building site, plot.

οίκος, ο [eekos] house || business house.

οικοτροφείο, το [eekotrofeeo] boarding school.

οικότροφος, ο, η [eekotrofos] boarder.

οικουμένη, η [eekoumenee] world, universe.

οικουμενικός [eekoumeneekos] ecumenical.

οικτείρω [eekteero] feel compassion for, pity || despise, scorn.

οίκτος, ο [eektos] compassion, pity || contempt, scorn.

οικτρός [eektros] deplorable || wretched, miserable.

οινόπνευμα, το [eenopnevma] alcohol || **οινοπνευματώδης** alcoholic.

οίνος, ο [eenos] wine.

οιοσδήποτε [eeosdeepote] any(body) || any kind of, whoever, whichever.

οισοφάγος, ο [eesofagos] oesophagus.

οίστρος, ο [eestros] gadfly || (μεταφ) inspiration, goading.

οιωνός, ο [eeonos] omen, presage, portent.

οκνηρός [okneeros] lazy, idle, sluggish.

οκνός [oknos] nonchalant, languid, slack.

οκρίβαντας, ο [okreevantas] easel.

οκτάγωνος [oktagonos] octagonal.

οκτακόσιοι [oktakosiee] eight hundred.

οκταπόδι, το [oktapodee] octopus.

οκτώ [okto] eight.

Οκτώβριος, ο [oktovreeos] October.

όλα, τα [ola] πλ everything || **~ κι ~** anything else but.

ολάκερος [olakeros] whole, entire, total, complete.

ολέθριος [olethreeos] ominous, disastrous, destructive.

όλεθρος, ο [olethros] calamity, destruction, ruin.

ολημερίς [oleemerees] all day long.

ολιγάριθμος [oleegareethmos] few in number, a few.

ολιγαρκής [oleegarkees] temperate, frugal, moderate.

ολιγαρχία, η [oleegarheea] oligarchy.

ολιγόλογος [oleegologos] concise, succinct || taciturn.

ολίγο [oleego] (a) little.

ολίγος [oleegos] short, a little, a few || ολίγον κατ' ολίγον gradually || παρ' ολίγο να nearly, almost.

ολιγοστεύω [oleegostevo] diminish, decrease, lessen.

ολιγοστός [oleegostos] scarcely enough, scanty, inconsiderable.

ολιγοψυχία, η [oleegopseeheea] timidity.

ολιγωρία, η [oleegoreea] negligence, neglect, indifference.

ολικός [oleekos] total, whole, complete.

ολικώς [oleekos] totally, utterly.

ολισθαίνω [oleestheno] slip, slide || (μεταφ) lapse into, slip into.

ολίσθημα, το [oleestheema] slip(ping), slide || mistake, fault.

ολισθηρός [oleestheeros] slippery, greasy.

ολκή, η [olkee] attraction, pull, weight || calibre, bore.

Ολλανδέζος, ο [olandezos] Dutchman.

Ολλανδία, η [olandeea] Holland.

ολλανδικός [olandeekos] Dutch.

όλμος, ο [olmos] mortar.

όλο [olo] all || ~ και περισσότερο more and more, always.

ολογράφως [olografos] written in full.

ολόγυρα [oloyeera] all round, in a circle.

ολοένα [oloena] incessantly, constantly.

ολοήμερος [oloeemeros] lasting a whole day.

ολόιδιος [oloeedeeos] the spitting image.

ολόισιος [oloeeseeos] direct, straight || upright.

ολοκαύτωμα, το [olokavtoma] holocaust || sacrifice.

ολόκληρος [olokleeros] entire, whole, full, complete.

ολοκληρώνω [olokleerono] complete, finish || (μαθημ) integrate.

ολοκληρωτικός [olokleeroteekos] full, entire, complete || totalitarian || (μαθημ) integral.

ολόμαλλος [olomalos] all wool, pure wool.

ολομέλεια, η [olomeleea] total membership, all members present.

ολομερής [olomerees] entire, whole, complete.

ολομόναχος [olomonahos] quite alone.

ολονυχτίς [oloneehtees] the whole night long.

ολόρθος [olorthos] straight, upright, standing.

όλος [olos] all, whole || όλοι everyone, everybody || όλοι μας all of us, altogether || όλα όλα altogether, the total.

ολοσχερής [olosherees] utter, complete, full, entire.

ολοταχώς [olotahos] at full speed, at top speed.

ολότελα [olotela] entirely, altogether, completely.

ολοφάνερος [olofaneros] obvious, plain, clear.

ολόχαρος [oloharos] joyful, happy.

ολόχρυσος [olohreesos] all gold, solid gold.

ολόψυχος [olopseehos] wholeheartedly.

Ολυμπιακός [oleembeeakos] Olympic.

όλως [olos] wholly, altogether, totally || ~ διόλου completely, wholly || ~ υμέτερος yours truly.

ομάδα, η [omaδa] group, company, band, gang || (αθλητική) team.

ομαδικός [omaδeekos] collective.

ομαδικώς [omaδeekos] in a body, collectively.

ομαλός [omalos] even || level || smooth, regular || (βίος) uneventful || flat.

ομαλότητα, η [omaloteeta] regularity, smoothness, evenness.

ομελέτα, η [omeleta] omelette.

ομήγυρη, η [omeeyeeree] party, meeting, assembly, circle.

όμηρος, ο [omeeros] hostage.

όμικρο, το [omeekro] the letter O.

ομιλητής, ο [omeeleetees] speaker, lecturer.

ομιλητικός [omeeleeteekos] sociable, affable.

ομιλία, η [omeeleea] talk, conversation || speech, lecture.

όμιλος, ο [omeelos] company, group, club.

ομιλώ [omeelo] speak, talk.

ομίχλη, η [omeehlee] fog, mist.

ομιχλώδης [omeehlodees] foggy, misty.

ομβροντία, η [omvronteea] salvo, volley.

ομογένεια, η [omoyeneea] homogeneity || fellow Greeks.

ομογενής [omoyenees] similar || of the same race || expatriate Greek.

ομοεθνής [omoethnees] of the same nation, fellow (*countryman*).

ομοειδής [omoeedees] of the same kind || uniform, similar.

ομόθρησκος [omothreeskos] of the same religion.

ομόθυμος [omotheemos] unanimous.

ομοιάζω [omeeazo] resemble, look like || be like.

ομοιογενής [omeeoyenees] homogeneous || uniform.

ομοιοκαταληξία, η [omeeokataleekseea] rhyme, rime.

ομοιόμορφος [omeeomorfos] uniform, unvarying.

ομοιοπαθής [omeeopathees] fellow (*sufferer*), in the same boat.

όμοιος [omeeos] similar, (a)like, same, in conformity with.

ομοιότητα, η [omeeoteeta] resemblance, similarity, likeness.

ομοίωμα, το [omeeoma] likeness, image || effigy.

ομοιωματικά, τα [omeeomateeka] πλ ditto marks.

ομόκεντρος [omokentros] concentric.

ομολογία, η [omoloyeea] confession, avowal, acknowledgement, admission || (οικον) bond, share.

ομόλογο, το [omologo] bond, promissory note, obligation.

ομολογουμένως [omologoumenos] avowedly, admittedly.

ομολογώ [omologo] acknowledge, confess, admit.

ομόνοια, η [omoneea] concord, agreement, accord, peace.

ομόρρυθμος [omoreethmos]: ~ **εταιρεία** partnership (*in business*).

ομορφαίνω [omorfeno] beautify || become beautiful.

ομορφιά, η [omorfia] beauty, handsomeness.

όμορφος [omorfos] handsome, beautiful, nice.

ομοσπονδία, η [omospondeea] federation, confederacy.

ομότιμος [omoteemos]: ~ **καθηγητής** professor emeritus.

ομόφρονας [omofronas] having the same ideas, thinking alike.

ομοφυλοφιλία, η [omofeelofeeleea] homosexuality.

ομοφωνία, η [omofoneea] unanimity.

ομόφωνος [omofonos] unanimous.

ομπρέλλα, η [ombrella] umbrella.

ομφαλός, ο [omfalos] navel || (μεταφ) centre.

ομώνυμος [omoneemos] having the same name.

όμως [omos] yet, nevertheless, but, however.

ον, το [on] creature, being.

ονειρεύομαι [oneerevome] dream, have visions.

ονειροκρίτης, ο [oneerokreetees] dream interpreter.

όνειρο, το [oneero] dream || vision, imagination.

ονειροπολώ [oneeropolo] daydream || dream (of), build castles in the air.

ονειρώδης [oneeroodees] dreamlike, fantastic || grand.

όνομα, το [onoma] name || (γραμμ) noun || fame, reputation || **βγάζω** ~ gain renown, become famous || ~ **και πράμα** in every sense || **ονόματι** by name of.

ονομάζω [onomazo] name, call || appoint.

ονομασία, η [onomaseea] name, appellation || designation, appointment.

ονομαστική, η [onomasteekee] (γραμμ) nominative (case) || ~ **εορτή** name day.

ονομαστικός [onomasteekos] nominal.

ονομαστός [onomastos] famous, famed, celebrated.

ονοματεπώνυμο, το [onomatepoeneemo] name and surname.

ονοματολογία, η [onomatoloyeea] nomenclature, terminology.

οντότητα, η [ontoteeta] entity, being || personality.

όντως [ontos] really, truly, in truth.

οξεία, η [okseea] (γραμμ) acute accent.

οξείδιο, το [okseedeeo] oxide.

οξείδωση, η [okseedosee] oxidation || corrosion, rusting.

οξικός [okseekos] acetic.

όξινος [okseenos] sour, bitter, acid.

οξύ, το [oksee] acid.

οξιά, η [oksia] beech tree || beech.

οξυγονοκόλληση, η [okseegonokoleesee] oxyacetylene welding.

οξυγόνο, το [okseegono] oxygen.

οξυδέρκεια, η [okseederkeea] perspicacity, acumen || (μεταφ) discernment.

οξύθυμος [okseetheemos] irritable, touchy.

οξύνους [okseenous] sagacious, acute, keen, clever.

οξύνω [okseeno] sharpen, whet || (το νου) sharpen || (αισθήματα) stir up, arouse, provoke.

οξύς [oksees] sharp, pointed || piercing, shrill || (γεύση) sour, strong.

οξύτητα, η [okseeteeta] sharpness || keenness, acuteness.

οξύφωνος, ο [okseefonos] (μουσ) tenor.

όξω [okso] βλ έξω.

οπαδός, ο, η [opados] adherent, partisan, supporter.

όπερα, η [opera] opera.

οπή, η [opee] opening, aperture, hole, gap.

όπιο, το [opeeo] opium.

όπισθεν [opeesthen] behind, in the rear || **κάνω** ~ go backwards, put in reverse.

οπίσθιος [opeestheeos] hind, posterior, back.

οπισθογραφώ [opeesthografo] endorse (a cheque).

οπισθοδρομικός [opeesthodromeekos] retrogressive || (στις απόψεις) reactionary.

οπισθοφυλακή, η [opeesthofeelakee] rearguard.

οπισθοχώρηση, η [opeesthohoreesee] retreat, withdrawal.

οπίσω [opeeso] behind, back || again.

όπλα, τα [opla] βλ arms.

οπλή, η [oplee] hoof.

οπλίζω [opleezo] arm || (μεταφ) reinforce, strengthen.

οπλισμός, ο [opleesmos] armament, equipment || (καλωδίου) sheathing.

οπλιταγωγό, το [opleetagogo] troopship.

οπλίτης, ο [opleetees] soldier.

όπλο, το [oplo] arm, weapon || rifle || (αμύνης) branch of army.

οπλοπολυβόλο, το [oplopoleevolo] light machine gun.

οπλοστάσιο, το [oplostaseeo] arsenal, armoury.

οπλοφορία, η [oploforeea] carrying of arms.

όποιος [opeeos] whoever, whichever || ~ **κι'** whosoever, anybody.

οποίος [opeeos] of what kind || **ο** ~ who, which.

οποιοσδήποτε [opeeosdeepote] whoever, whatsoever.

οπόταν [opotan] whenever, when.

οπότε [opote] whenever, at any time.

οπότε [opote] at which time, when.

όπου [opou] where, wherever.

οπουδήποτε [opoudeepote] wheresoever, wherever.

οπτασία, η [optaseea] vision, apparition.

οπτική, η [opteekee] optics.

οπτικός [opteekos] optic(al) || (ουσ) optician.

οπωρικά, τα [oporeeka] πλ fruit.

οπωροπωλείο, το [oporopoleeo] fruit market.

οπωροφόρος [oporoforos] bearing fruit, fruit-producing.

όπως [opos] as, like || ~ ~ somehow or other, after a fashion || (συνδ) in order that, so as.

οπωσδήποτε [oposdeepote] howsoever, anyway, without fail || definitely.

όραμα, το [orama] vision ||

οραματίζομαι [oramateezome] have visions, visualize.

όραση, η [orasee] sense of sight, vision.

ορατός [oratos] visible, perceptible.

ορατότητα, η [oratoteeta] visibility.

οργανικός [organeekos] organic.

οργανισμός, ο [organeesmos] organism || organization.

όργανο, το [organo] organ || (μουσ) instrument || implement, tool || (κατασκοπείας) agent.

οργανώνω [organono] organize, constitute, form.

οργάνωση, η [organosee] organization, arranging.

οργασμός, ο [orgasmos] orgasm, heat || (μεταφ) feverish activity.

οργή, η [oryee] anger, rage || **να πάρει η** ~ damn it!, damnation!

όργια, τα [orya] πλ orgies || (μεταφ) corrupt practices || **οργιάζω** revel, debauch.

οργίζω [oryeezo] anger, enrage, irritate.

οργυιά, η [orya] fathom.

όργωμα, το [orgoma] ploughing, tilling, tillage.

οργώνω [orgono] plough, till, furrow.

ορδή, η [ordee] horde, host, rabble.

ορειβασία, η [oreevaseea] mountain climbing.

ορειβάτης, ο [oreevatees] mountain climber.

ορειβατικός [oreevateekos] of climbing, of mountaineering.

ορεινός [oreenos] mountainous, hilly || of the mountains.

ορείχαλκος, ο [oreehalkos] brass, bronze.

ορεκτικό, το [orekteeko] appetizer, titbit || drink.

ορεκτικός [orekteekos] appetizing savoury || tempting.

όρεξη, η [oreksee] appetite || desire, liking.

ορθά [ortha] right, rightly || upright || ~ **κοφτά** flatly, frankly.

ορθάνοιχτος [orthaneehtos] wide open.

όρθιος [ortheeos] on end, upright, erect, standing.

ορθογραφία, η [orthografeea] spelling, orthography || dictation.

ορθογώνιο, το [orthogoneeo] rectangle.

ορθογώνιος [orthogoneeos] right-angled || rectangular.

ορθοδοξία, η [orthodokseea] orthodoxy.

ορθόδοξος [orthodoksos] orthodox.

ορθολογισμός, ο [ortholoyeesmos] rationalism.

ορθοπεδική, η [orthopedeekee] orthopaedics.

ορθοποδώ [orthopodo] walk straight || stand on sure ground, thrive.

ορθός [orthos] light || correct || proper || upright, erect, standing.

ορθοστασία, η [orthostaseea] standing.

ορθότητα, η [orthoteeta] accuracy || soundness || aptness.

όρθρος, ο [orthros] (εκκλ) matins || dawn, daybreak.

υρθώνομαι [orthonome] rise, get up || (άλογο) rear up.

ορθώνω [orthono] raise, pull up, lift up || redress.

ορθώς [orthos] βλ **ορθά.**

οριζόντιος [oreezonteeos] horizontal, level.

ορίζω [oreezo] mark, bound, delimit || fix, settle, define || rule, control, govern.

ορίζων, ο [oreezon] horizon.

όριο, το [oreeo] boundary, limit, border || (μεταφ) scope, boundary.

ορισμένος [oreesmenos] defined, fixed || certain, special.

ορισμός, ο [oreesmos] designation, fixing || definition || order, instruction.

ορίστε [oreeste] I beg your pardon? || come in, take a seat || may I help you? || **καλώς ορίσατε** (επιφ) welcome!

οριστική, η [oreesteekee] (γραμμ) indicative (mood).

οριστικός [oreesteekos] definitive, final.

ορκίζομαι [orkeezome] swear, take the oath.

ορκίζω [orkeezo] put on oath, swear in.

όρκος, ο [orkos] oath || vow.

ορκωμοσία, η [orkomoseea] swearing (in).

ορκωτός [orkotos] sworn || **οι ορκωτοί** the jury.

ορμή, η [ormee] vehemence || impulse, impetus || passion.

ορμητήριο, το [ormeeteereeo] starting place || motive.

ορμητικός [ormeeteekos] impetuous, hot-tempered, fiery.

ορμόνη, η [ormonee] hormone.

όρμος, ο [ormos] bay, inlet.

ορμώ [ormo] dash, rush || ~ **μαι** be urged || come from.

όρνεο, το [orneo] bird of prey.

όρνιθα, η [orneetha] hen, chicken, fowl.

ορνιθοσκαλίσματα, τα [orneethoskaleesmata] πλ scrawl, scribble.

ορνιθοτροφείο, το [orneethotrofeeo] poultry farm.

ορνιθώνας, ο [orneethonas] chicken coop, henhouse, hen roost.

όρνιο, το [orneeo] bird of prey || (μεταφ) dullard, dolt.

οροθεσία, η [orotheseea] fixing of boundaries.

ορολογία, η [oroloyeea] terminology.

οροπέδιο, το [oropedeeo] plateau, tableland.

όρος, το [oros] mountain.

όρος, ο [oros] term, condition, stipulation, proviso || limit, end || (επιστημονικός) term, definition.

ορρός, ο [oros] serum.

οροσειρά, η [oroseera] mountain range, mountain chain.

ορόσημο, το [oroseemo] boundary mark, boundary stone.

οροφή, η [orofee] ceiling, roof.

όροφος, ο [orofos] floor, storey.

ορτύκι, το [orteekee] quail.

όρυζα, η [oreeza] rice.

ορυκτέλαιο, το [oreekteleo] petroleum || lubricant.

ορυκτολογία, η [oreektoloyeea] mineralogy.

ορυκτό, το [oreekto] mineral, ore.

ορυκτός [oreektos] mineral, dug-up.

ορύσσω [oreeso] dig, excavate || (πηγάδι) bore, sink.

ορυχείο, το [oreeheeo] mine.

ορφανός [orfanos] orphan.

ορφανοτροφείο, το [orfanotrofeeo] orphanage.

όρχης, η [orhees] testicle || (λουλούδι) orchid.

ορχήστρα, η [orheestra] orchestra.

όσιος [oseeos] holy, blessed || saint.

οσμή, η [osmee] odour, smell, scent.

όσο [oso] as, as far as, as long as || ~ για as for || ~ αφορά as regards, with regard to || εφ ~ as long as, inasmuch as || ~ νάρθει until he comes || ~ νάναι nevertheless.

όσος [osos] as much as, as many as, all.

όσπριο, το [ospreeo] pulse, legume.

οστούν, το [ostoun] bone.

οστρακιά, η [ostrakia] scarlet fever.

όστρακο, το [ostrako] shell || (αρχαιολογία) potsherd.

οσφραίνομαι [osfrenome] smell, scent || (μεταφ) feel.

όσφρηση, η [osfreesee] sense of smell.

οσφύς, η [osfees] waist, loins, haunches.

όταν [otan] when, at the time when, whenever.

ότι [otee] (συνδ) that || (επιρ) as soon as || just (now).

ό, τι [otee] what(ever).

οτιδήποτε [oteedeepote] whatsoever || anything at all.

ότου [otou] έως ~ until || μέχρις ~ until || αφ ~ since.

Ουγγαρία, η [oungareea] Hungary.

ουγγιά, η [oungia] ounce.

ουγγρικός [oungreekos] Hungarian.

Ούγγρος, ο [oungros] Hungarian.

ουδέ [oude] βλ ούτε.

ουδείς [oudees] no(body), no one, none.

ουδέποτε [oudepote] never.

ουδέτερος [oudeteros] neither || (επιθ) neutral || (γραμμ) neuter.

ουδόλως [oudolos] by no means, no wise, by no manner of means.

ούζο, το [ouzo] ouzo.

ουλή [oulee] scar.

ούλο, το [oulo] (ανατ) gum.

ούρα, τα [oura] πλ urine, piss (col).

ουρά, η [oura] tail || train of dress || queue || (φάλαγγος) rear || λεφτά με ~ loads of money.

ουραγός, ο [ouragos] person bringing up the rear, the last one.

ουρανής [ouranees] sky-blue.

ουράνιο, το [ouraneeo] uranium.

ουράνιο, το [ouraneeo]: ~ τόξο rainbow.

ουράνιος [ouraneeos] heavenly, celestial.

ουρανίσκος, ο [ouraneeskos] palate.

ουρανοκατέβατος

[ouranokatevatos] heaven-sent ||
(μεταφ) unexpected.

ουρανοξύστης, ο
[ouranokseestees] skyscraper.

ουρανός, ο [ouranos] sky, heaven ||
canopy.

ουρητήριο, το [oureeteereeo]
urinal, john (col).

ουρικός [oureekos] uric, urinary.

ούριος [oureeos] (άνεμος) tail,
favourable, fair.

ουρλιάζω [ourleeazo] howl, roar ||
(από πόνο) yell, scream || (από
θυμό) bellow.

ούρλιασμα, το [ourleeasma]
howl(ing), bellowing, yelling.

ουρώ [ouro] urinate.

ους, το [ous] ear.

ουσία, η [ousea] matter, substance
|| essence || (μεταφ) gist, main point.

ουσιαστικό, το [ouseeasteeko]
(γραμμ) substantive, noun.

ουσιαστικός [ouseeasteekos]
substantial, essential.

ουσιώδης [ouseeoδees] essential,
vital, indispensable, capital.

ούτε [oute] not even || ~ ... ~
neither ... nor.

ουτοπία, η [outopeea] Utopia.

ούτω(ς) [outo(s)] so, such, thus || ~
ώστε so that, in order that.

ουχί [ouhee] βλ **όχι.**

οφειλέτης, ο [ofeeletees] debtor.

οφειλή, η [ofeelee] debt, sum due ||
(μεταφ) obligation, duty.

οφείλομαι [ofeelome] be due.

οφείλω [ofeelo] owe || be obliged to ||
~ **να πάω** I should go.

όφελος, το [ofeios] profit,
advantage, benefit.

οφθαλμαπάτη, η [ofthalmapatee]
optical illusion.

οφθαλμίατρος, ο, η
[ofthalmeeatros] eye specialist,
oculist.

οφθαλμός, ο [ofthalmos] eye ||
(βιολ) bud.

οφθαλμοφανής [ofthalmofanees].
obvious, manifest, evident.

όφις, ο [ofees] snake, serpent.

όχεντρα, η [ohentra] βλ **οχιά.**

οχέτευση, η [ohetevsee] drainage.

οχετός, ο [ohetos] drain, sewer ||
conduit, pipe.

όχημα, το [oheema] vehicle,
carriage, coach.

όχθη, η [ohthee] (ποταμού) bank ||
(λίμνης) shore.

όχι [ohee] no || not.

οχιά, η [ohia] viper.

οχλαγωγία, η [ohlagoyea]
disturbance, riot, tumult.

οχληρός [ohleeros] tiresome,
unpleasant, burdensome.

οχλοβοή, η [ohlovoee] uproar, din,
hubbub.

οχλοκρατία, η [ohlokrateea] mob
rule.

όχλος, ο [ohlos] populace, mob,
crowd, rabble.

οχυρό, το [oheero] strong point,
fort, stronghold.

οχυρώνομαι [oheeronome] (μεταφ)
find an excuse, justify.

οχυρώνω [oheerono] fortify,
entrench.

όψη, η [opsee] aspect, appearance,
look || view, sight || countenance ||
face || **λαμβάνω υπ** ~ take into
account || **εξ όψεως** by sight || **εν
όψει** in view of || in view.

οψιγενής [opseeyenees]
posthumous || late, belated.

όψιμος [opseemos] tardy, late, of a
late season.

Π, π

παγανισμός, ο [paganeesmos]
paganism.

παγερός [payeros] icy cold,
freezing || (μεταφ) chilly, frigid.

παγετός, ο [payetos] frost.

παγετώδης [payetodees] icy, icy cold, freezing.

παγετώνας, ο [payetonas] glacier.

παγίδα, η [payeeδa] trap, snare || (τάφρος) pitfall.

παγίδευμα, το [payeeδevma] ensnaring, trapping.

παγιδεύω [payeeδevo] snare, catch, entice.

πάγιος [payos] fixed, stable, firm || (καθεστώς) secure, durable || (δάνειο) consolidated loan || (πρόσοδος) steady income.

παγιώνω [payono] consolidate, make secure.

παγίως [payeeos] firmly, securely.

πάγκος, ο [pangkos] bench, seat.

παγκόσμιος [pangkosmeeos] universal,world-wide.

πάγκρεας, το [pangkreas] pancreas.

παγόβουνο, το [pagovouno] iceberg.

παγόδα, η [ragoδa] pagoda.

παγοδρομία, η [pagoδromeea] skating.

παγοθραύστης, ο [pagothravstees] icebreaker.

παγοπέδιλο, το [pagopeδeelo] iceskate.

πάγος, ο [pagos] ice, frost.

παγούρι, το [pagouree] can, tin, flask || (στρατ) canteen.

παγωμένος [pagomenos] frozen, frostbitten.

παγώνι, το [pagonee] peacock.

παγωνιά, η [pagonia] frost.

παγώνω [pagono] freeze, congeal, frost.

παγωτό, το [pagoto] ice cream.

παζαρεύω [pazarevo] haggle over, bargain for.

παζάρι, το [pazaree] market, bazaar || bargaining, haggling.

παθαίνω [patheno] undergo, suffer, be injured.

πάθημα, το [patheema] mishap, accident.

πάθηση, η [patheesee] complaint, sickness, affliction.

παθητικός [patheeteekos] passive, submissive || (γραμμ) passive (voice) || charged with passion || (οικ) debit.

παθολογία, η [patholoyeea] pathology.

παθολογικός [patholoyeekos] pathological.

παθολόγος, ο [pathologos] general practitioner.

πάθος, το [pathos] illness, passion || suffering || (έχθρα) animosity.

παιδαγωγείο, το [peδagoyeeo] children's school.

παιδαγωγία, η [peδagoyeea] education, pedagogy.

παιδαγωγικός [peδagoyeekos] educational, pedagogical.

παιδαγωγός, ο, η [peδagogos] tutor, preceptor, pedagogue.

παιδαγωγώ [peδagogo] educate, instruct, teach.

παιδάκι, το [peδakee] little child.

παιδαριώδης [peδareeoδees] puerile, childish || (εύκολο) quite simple, trivial.

παιδεία, η [peδeea] education, learning, instruction, culture.

παίδεμα, το [peδema] torture, trial, ordeal.

παιδεύομαι [peδevome] try hard, struggle.

παιδεύω [peδevo] pester, torture, torment.

παιδί, το [peδee] child, boy || chap.

παιδιαρίζω [peδeeareezo] act like a child.

παιδίατρος, ο, η [peδeeatros] paediatrician, child specialist.

παιδικός [peδeekos] child's, of children || childish || ~ σταθμός day nursery.

παίζω [pezo] play || (παιχνίδι)

speculate, gamble || (μεταφ) swing, sway.

παίκτης, ο [pektees] player || gambler, gamester.

παινεύω [penevo] βλ **επαινώ.**

παίξιμο, το [pekseemo] playing || (με κάτι) toying with || (θεάτρου) performance || (παιχνίδι) gaming, gambling.

παίρνω [perno] receive, take hold of, get, contain || (πόλη κτλ) capture || (διά της βίας) wrench from || (υπηρέτη) hire, take on || (καφέ κτλ) take, have || (κρύο κτλ) catch, get || (σαν παράδειγμα) take, draw || (σημείωση) take (a note) || (κάτι για κάτι) take for, consider (as) || (με κάποια έννοια) understand, interpret || (χρήματα) be paid, draw, receive || (για γυναίκα) marry, wed || **τον ~** fall asleep || **~ από πίσω** follow closely.

παιχνίδι, το [pehneedee] play, game, sport || (για παιδιά) toy, plaything.

παιχνιδιάρης [pehneedeearees] playful, gay, mirthful.

πακετάρω [paketaro] pack, box.

πακέτο, το [paketo] pack, packet, parcel, box, bundle.

παλαβομάρα, η [palavomara] madness, lunacy, foolish act.

παλαβός [palavos] mad, insane, stupid || (παράτολμος) foolhardy.

παλαίμαχος [palemahos] veteran.

παλαιογραφία, η [paleografeea] pal(a)eography.

παλαιοπωλείο, το [paleopoleeo] secondhand shop, antique shop.

παλαιοπώλης, ο [paleopolees] secondhand dealer.

παλαιός [paleos] old || (μνημείο κτλ) ancient, old || (άλλοτε) former.

παλαιστής, ο [palestees] wrestler.

παλαίστρα, η [palestra] arena, ring.

παλαιώνω [paleono] wear out, become antiquated.

παλαμάκια, τα [palamakeea] πλ clapping, applause.

παλαμάρι, το [palamaree] (ναυτ) cable, mooring line.

παλάμη, η [palamee] palm || (μέτρο) span.

παλάτι, το [palatee] palace || mansion.

παλεύω [palevo] wrestle, struggle, fight.

πάλη, η [palee] wrestling || (μεταφ) struggle, strife, contest.

παλιανθρωπιά, η [palianthropia] villainy, meanness, roguery.

παλιάνθρωπος, ο [palianthropos] rogue, rascal, scamp.

παλιάτσος, ο [paliatsos] clown, buffoon.

πάλι [palee] again, once more, over again.

παλινδρομικός [paleenδromeekos] alternating, reciprocating, recoiling.

παλινόρθωση, η [paleenorthosee] restoration, re-establishment.

παλιόπαιδο, το [paliopeδo] bad boy, young scamp.

παλίρροια, η [paleerreea] tide, floodtide.

παλληκαράς, ο [paleekaras] bully.

παλληκάρι, το [paleekaree] young man, brave person || (εργένης) bachelor.

παλληκαρίσια [paleekareeseea] boldly, bravely.

πάλλω [palo] throb, beat, palpitate || (πλεκτ) vibrate.

παλμός, ο [palmos] oscillation, vibration || palpitation, throbbing || (ενθουσιασμού) feeling, eagerness.

παλούκι, το [paloukee] stake, pole || (μεταφ) difficulty.

παλτό, το [palto] overcoat.

παμπάλαιος [pampaleos] ancient || out-of-date.

πάμπλουτος [pamploutos] extremely wealthy.

παμπόνηρος [pamponeeros] very cunning, very sly.

πάμπτωχος [pamptohos] very poor, very needy.

πάμφθηνος [pamftheenos] very cheap, extremely cheap.

παμψηφεί [pampseefee] unanimously.

παν, το [pan] the whole world || (το κεφαλαιώδες) essentials, everything.

πανάγαθος [panagathos] merciful || extremely virtuous.

Παναγία, η [panayeea] the Virgin Mary.

πανάδα, η [panaδa] brown patch, freckle.

πανάθλιος [panathleeos] wretched, miserable.

πανάκεια, η [panakeea] panacea.

πανάρχαιος [panarheos] very ancient.

πανδαιμόνιο, το [panδemoneeo] pandemonium.

πάνδεινος [panδeenos] disastrous, most terrible.

πανδοχείο, το [panδoheeo] inn.

πανδρειά, η [panδria] marriage, matrimony.

πανδρεύω [panδrevo] marry.

πανελλήνιος [paneleeneeos] panhellenic.

πανεπιστημιακός [panepeesteemeeakos] of the university.

πανεπιστήμιο, το [panepeesteemeeo] university.

πανέρι, το [paneree] wide basket.

πανευτυχής [panefteehees] very happy.

πανηγυρίζω [paneeyeereezo] celebrate, fête.

πανηγυρικός [paneeyeereekos] festive || (ουσ) oration, panegyric.

πανηγύρι, το [paneeyeeree] festival, festivity || (εμπορικό) fair.

πανηγυρισμός, ο [paneeyeereesmos] celebration.

πάνθηρας, ο [pantheeras] panther.

πανί, το [panee] cloth, linen || (ναυτ) sail.

πανίδα, η [paneeδa] fauna.

πανικόβλητος [paneekovleetos] panic-stricken.

πανικός, ο [paneekos] panic.

πανίσχυρος [paneesheeros] all-powerful.

πάνινος [paneenos] of cloth, of linen, of cotton.

πανόμοιος [panomeeos] similar, alike.

πανομοιότυπο, το [panomeeooteepo] facsimile.

πανοπλία, η [panopleea] arms, armour.

πανόραμα, το [panorama] panorama.

πανούκλα, η [panoukla] plague, pestilence.

πανουργία, η [panouryeea] ruse, trick, cunning.

πανούργος [panourgos] malicious, tricky, wily, cunning.

πανσέληνος, η [panseleenos] full moon.

πανσές, ο [panses] pansy.

πάντα [panta] forever, always || anyway, in any case.

πανταλόνι, το [pantalonee] trousers || pants, knickers.

πανταχού [pantahoo] everywhere.

παντελής [pantelees] complete, absolute, entire.

παντελώς [pantelos] utterly, absolutely, totally.

παντζάρι, το [pandzaree] beetroot.

παντιέρα, η [pantiera] banner, flag.

παντοδύναμος [pantoδeenamos] omnipotent, all-powerful.

παντοειδώς [pantoeeδos] in every way.

παντοιοτρόπως [panteeotropos] in every way, by every means.

Παντοκράτορας, ο
[pantokratoras] the Almighty.

παντομίμα, η [pantomeema]
pantomime.

παντοπωλείο, το [pantopoleeo]
grocer's shop || grocery (US).

παντοπώλης, ο [pantopolees]
grocer.

πάντοτε [pantote] always, at all
times, forever.

παντοτεινά [pantoteena]
perpetually, everlastingly.

παντού [pantou] everywhere.

παντούφλα, η [pantoufla] slipper.

παντρειά, η [pantria] βλ
πανδρειά.

παντρεύω [pantrevo] βλ
πανδρεύω.

πάντως [pantos] anyhow, in any
case, at any rate.

πανωλεθρία, η [panolethreea]
heavy loss, total ruin.

πανώλη, η [panolee] plague,
pestilence.

πανωφόρι, το [panoforee]
overcoat.

παξιμάδι, το [paksemaδee] rusk ||
(για βίδα) nut (of screw).

παπαδιά, η [paρaδia] priest's wife.

παπάκι, το [papakee] duckling.

παπαρούνα, η [paparouna] poppy.

Πάπας, ο [papas] Pope.

παπάς, ο [papas] priest.

παπί, το [papee] young duck ||
γίνομαι ~ get wet to the skin.

πάπια, η [papeea] duck || bedpan ||
κάνω την ~ to act the innocent.

πάπλωμα, το [paploma] cotton
quilt.

παπουτσάδικο, το
[papoutsaδeeko] shoemaker's shop.

παπουτσής, ο [papoutsees]
shoemaker, bootmaker.

παπούτσι, το [papoutsee] shoe.

παππούς, ο [papoos] grandfather.

παρά [para] than || but || (προθ) near,
close, by || (προσθήκη) in spite of,

against my will || (αντίθεση) against,
contrary to || (αφαίρεση) by, almost,
nearly.

παραβαίνω [paraveno] break,
violate, infringe.

παραβάλλω [paravalo] compare.

παραβάν, το [paravan] (folding)
screen.

παραβαρύνω [paravareeno]
overload, overburden || become
very heavy.

παράβαση, η [paravasee] violation,
transgression, breach.

παραβάτης, ο [paravatees]
violator, transgressor.

παραβιάζω [paraveeazo] (πόρτα
κτλ) force entry, break open ||
(νόμο) violate, infringe.

παραβλέπω [paravlepo] neglect,
omit || turn a blind eye (to), ignore.

παραβολή, η [paravolee]
comparison, collation || (εκκλ)
parable || (μαθημ) parabola.

παράβολο, το [paravolo] fee,
deposit.

παραγάδι, το [paragaδee] large
fishing net.

παραγγελία, η [parangeleea]
command, commission, order ||
(μήνυμα) message || **επί** ~ made to
order.

παραγγέλω [parangelo] order,
command || inform.

παραγεμίζω [parayemeezo] fill up ||
become too full || (μαγειρική) stuff ||
cram.

παραγίνομαι [parayeenome] grow
too much || go too far || get overripe
|| ~ **χοντρός** grow too fat.

παράγκα, η [paranga] wooden hut,
shack.

παραγκωνίζω [parangoneezo]
elbow, thrust aside.

παραγνωρίζω [paragnoreezo]
ignore || misinterpret || mistake
identity of.

παράγομαι [paragome] be derived from.

παράγοντας, ο [paragontas] βλ **παράγων**.

παράγραφος, ο [paragrafos] paragraph.

παράγω [parago] produce, bear || derive.

παραγωγή, η [paragoyee] production || output, generation || (γραμμ) derivation.

παραγωγικός [paragoyeekos] productive.

παραγωγός, ο [paragogos] producer, grower.

παράγων, ο [paragon] agent, factor || (μαθημ) factor.

παράδειγμα, το [paradeegma] example || **παραδείγματος χάρη** for example, for instance.

παραδειγματίζω [paradeegmateezo] set an example, exemplify.

παράδεισος, ο [paradeesos] paradise.

παραδεκτός [paradektos] admitted, accepted || acceptable, admissible.

παραδέχομαι [paradehome] admit, acknowledge, confess, allow.

παραδίδομαι [paradeedome] surrender, submit, yield.

παραδίδω [paradeedo] hand over || surrender || (μάθημα) teach, give lessons.

παράδοξος [paradoksos] peculiar, odd, singular || unusual.

παραδόπιστος [paradopeestos] greedy, extremely fond of money.

παράδοση, η [paradosee] delivery, surrender || (της χώρας) tradition || (μαθήματος) teaching.

παραδουλεύτρα, η [paradoulevtra] charwoman.

παραδρομή, η [paradromee] carelessness, oversight.

παραείμαι [paraeeme] be beyond measure, be too much.

παραζάλη, η [parazalee] confusion, agitation, turmoil.

παραθαλάσσιος [parathalaseeos] by the sea, coastal.

παραθερίζω [parathereezo] spend the summer.

παραθεριστής, ο [parathereestees] summer holidaymaker.

παραθέτω [paratheto] contrast, compare || (αναφέρω) cite, quote.

παράθυρο, το [paratheero] window.

παραθυρόφυλλο, το [paratheerofeelo] shutter.

παραίσθηση, η [parestheesee] hallucination, illusion.

παραίτηση, η [pareeteesee] resignation, renunciation || abdication.

παραιτούμαι [paretoume] resign, give up || (αποφεύγω) avoid.

παραιτώ [pareto] give up, leave, desert.

παράκαιρος [parakeros] unseasonable, inopportune, untimely.

παρακάλια, τα [parakaleea] πλ supplications, pleading.

παρακαλώ [parakalo] ask, beg, entreat || ~! don't mention it!, please!, a pleasure!

παρακάμπτω [parakampto] get round, surpass || (ένα θέμα) evade.

παρακάνω [parakano] exaggerate, go too far.

παρακαταθήκη, η [parakatatheekee] consignment, deposit || stock || provisions || (παράδοση) heritage.

παρακάτω [parakato] lower down || at a lower price.

παρακείμενος [parakeemenos] adjoining, adjacent || ο ~ (γραμμ) perfect tense.

παρακινώ [parakeeno] exhort, urge || instigate.

παρακλάδι, το [paraklaðee] shoot, bough || (ποταμού) branch.

παράκληση, η [parakleesee] request, plea || (εκκλ) prayer.

παρακμή, η [parakmee] decay, decline.

παρακοή, η [parakoee] disobedience, insubordination.

παρακολουθώ [parakolootho] follow, come behind || watch || go after || (την έννοια) understand.

παρακούω [parakouo] hear wrongly || (απειθαρχώ) disobey.

παρακρατώ [parakrato] retain || keep back || (για χρόνο) last too long.

παράκτιος [parakteeos] coastal, inshore.

παραλαβή, η [paralavee] receipt, receiving, delivery.

παραλαμβάνω [paralamvano] receive, take delivery of || take possession of.

παραλείπω [paraleepo] leave out, miss, neglect, omit.

παράλειψη, η [paraleepsee] omission, neglect(ing).

παραλέω [paraleo] exaggerate, overcolour.

παραλήπτης, ο [paraleeptees] payee, addressee, consignee.

παραλήρημα, το [paraleereema] delirium, frenzy.

παραλία, η [paraleea] seashore, shore, coast, beach || **παραλιακός** of the seashore, of the coast.

παραλλαγή, η [paralayee] change, variation || (αστρον) deviation.

παράλληλος [paraleelos] parallel.

παραλογίζομαι [paraloyeezome] talk irrationally, rave.

παράλογος [paralogos] illogical, absurd, foolish.

παράλυση, η [paraleesee] paralysis || helplessness.

παράλυτος [paraleetos] paralytic, stiff, crippled || (ιατρ) paralyzed.

παραλύω [paraleeo] make loose, make shaky || slacken, relax || (ιατρ) paralyze.

παραμάνα, η [paramana] nurse, nanny || (καρφίτσα) safety pin.

παραμελώ [paramelo] neglect, leave undone, disregard.

παραμένω [parameno] stay by || remain, continue to exist || sojourn.

παράμερα [paramera] out of the way, apart.

παραμερίζω [paramereezo] set aside || get out of the way || fend off.

παραμιλώ [parameelo] speak too much || rave.

παραμονεύω [paramonevo] watch for, waylay.

παραμονή, η [paramonee] stay || eve.

παραμορφώνω [paramorfono] deform, disfigure, twist.

παραμύθι, το [parameethee] fable, story, fairy tale.

παρανόηση, η [paranoeesee] misunderstanding.

παρανομία, η [paranomeea] illegality || breach of the law.

παράνομος [paranomos] illegal, unlawful.

παρανομώ [paranomo] transgress a law.

παρανοώ [paranoo] misunderstand.

παράνυμφος, η [paraneemfos] bridesmaid.

παρανυχίδα, η [paraneeheeða] hangnail.

παράξενα [paraksena] oddly, strangely.

παραξενεύομαι [paraksenevome] be astonished, be amazed (at).

παραξενιά, η [parakseneea] caprice, fancy, whim.

παράξενος [paraksenos] peculiar, singular, odd.

παραξηλώνω [parakseelono] unsew, unstitch || **το** ~ I go too far, I exaggerate.

παραπανήσιος [parapaneeseeos] superfluous, to spare || (τιμή) excess, overly much.

παραπάνω [parapano] higher up || (επιπρόσθετα) in addition || **με το ~** enough and to spare || **~ από** over, more than, greater than.

παραπάτημα, το [parapateema] false step || (μεταφ) misconduct.

παραπατώ [parapato] slip, stumble || stagger.

παραπέμπω [parapembo] refer to || send, hand over.

παραπέρα [parapera] further on, over there.

παραπεταμένος [parapetamenos] thrown away || (μεταφ) disdained, scorned.

παραπέτασμα, το [parapetasma] curtain || (πολιτ) Iron Curtain.

παραπέτο, το [parapeto] parapet, breastwork.

παράπηγμα, το [parapeegma] wooden hut, shack, shanty.

παραπλανώ [paraplano] seduce, mislead, lead astray.

παραπλεύρως [paraplevros] next door || next to, beside.

παραπλήσιος [parapleeseeos] next to, nearby || (όμοιος) very like, similar.

παραποιώ [parapeeo] counterfeit || forge, tamper with.

παραπομπή, η [parapombee] referring || (σε βιβλίο) reference, footnote.

παραπονετικός [paraponeteekos] doleful, whining.

παραπονιάρης [paraponeearees] grumbling, grousing.

παραπονιέμαι [paraponieme] complain, grumble.

παράπονο, το [parapono] complaint, grievance.

παράπτωμα, το [paraptoma] fault, mistake || breach.

παράρτημα, το [pararteema]

annexe, supplement || outbuilding || (τράπεζας) branch || (εφημερίδας) special edition, extra.

παράς, ο [paras] money, cash.

παράσημο, το [paraseemo] decoration, medal, order, insignia.

παρασημοφορώ [paraseemoforo] decorate, invest with an order.

παράσιτα, τα [paraseeta] πλ atmospherics || parasites.

παράσιτος, ο [paraseetos] sponger, hanger-on, parasite.

παρασιωπώ [paraseeopo] pass over in silence.

παρασκευάζω [paraskevazo] prepare, get ready, arrange.

παρασκεύασμα, το [paraskevasma] substance prepared, preparation.

παρασκευή, η [paraskevee] preparation || (ημέρα) Friday.

παρασκήνια, τα [paraskeeneea] πλ (θέατρο) wings || **παρασκηνιακός** behind the scenes.

παράσταση, η [parastasee] representation, portrayal || (παρουσία) presence, demeanour || (θεάτρου) show, performance || (νομ) appearance.

παραστατικός [parastateekos] expressive, descriptive, vivid.

παραστέκω [parasteko] assist, help, support.

παράστημα, το [parasteema] carriage, bearing, figure.

παραστράτημα, το [parastrateema] straying, misconduct.

παρασύνθημα, το [paraseentheema] password.

παρασύρω [paraseero] drag along, sweep away || run over || (σε σφάλμα) lead astray, carry away.

παράταξη, η [parataksee] array, parade, order || pomp, ceremony || (πολιτ) political party.

παράταση, η [paratasee] extension, protraction || renewal.

παρατάσσω [parataso] arrange, set in order, line up.

παρατατικός, ο [paratateekos] (γραμμ) imperfect tense.

παρατείνω [parateeno] prolong, lengthen || extend, defer.

παρατήρηση, η [parateereesee] observation, remark || (κουβέντα) comment || reproach, reprimand.

παρατηρητής, ο [parateereetees] observer, watcher, spotter.

παρατηρητικός [parateereeteekos] observing, keen || reproachful.

παρατηρώ [parateero] observe, perceive, notice || (επιπλ) reproach, blame.

παράτολμος [paratolmos] reckless, audacious, bold.

παρατραβώ [paratravo] draw out, prolong || last too long || (μεταφ) go too far.

παρατράγουδο, το [paratragouđo] untoward incident.

παρατσούκλι, το [paratsouklee] nickname.

παρατυπία, η [parateepeea] breach of formalities || irregularity.

πάραυτα [paravta] immediately, at once, forthwith.

παραφέρνω [paraferno] carry more than necessary || resemble.

παραφέρομαι [paraferome] flare up, lose one's temper.

παραφθορά, η [parafthora] alteration, corruption, change.

παραφορά, η [parafora] frenzy, outburst || rage.

παράφορος [paraforos] hotheaded, hasty, furious.

παραφορτώνω [parafortono] overload, overburden || (μεταφ) drive too hard.

παράφραση, η [parafrasee] paraphrase, free translation.

παραφρονώ [parafrono] become insane, go mad.

παραφροσύνη, η [parafroseenee] madness, insanity, foolish act.

παραφυάδα, η [parafiada] sprout, shoot.

παραφυλάω [parafeelao] lie in wait for || be on the watch for.

παραφωνία, η [parafoneea] dissonance || (μεταφ) discord, disagreement.

παραχαράκτης, ο [paraharaktees] forger, counterfeiter.

παραχωρώ [parahoro] grant, yield, concede || (παραδίδω) surrender, resign.

παρδαλός [parđalos] spotted || multicoloured, gaudy.

παρέα, η [parea] company, set, party || κάνω ~ με keep company with.

παρειά, η [paria] cheek || (μεταφ) wall.

παρείσακτος [pareesaktos] intrusive, intruding.

παρέκβαση, η [parekvasee] digression.

παρέκει [parekee] further on, a little further.

παρεκκλήσι, το [parekleesee] chapel.

παρεκκλίνω [parekleeno] deviate from, turn aside from || diverge.

παρεκτείνω [parekteeno] prolong, extend.

παρεκτός [parektos] except, save, besides.

παρεκτροπή, η [parektropee] aberration, deviation || (ηθική) misconduct, dissoluteness.

παρέλαση, η [parelasee] parade, march-past, procession.

παρελαύνω [parelavno] march past, parade.

παρέλευση, η [parelevsee] passage of time, passing.

παρελθόν, το [parelthon] the past.

παρεμβαίνω [paremveno] interfere, intervene, meddle with.

παρεμβάλλω [paremvalo] insert, interpose.

παρέμβαση, η [paremvasee] intervention, mediation.

παρεμβολή, η [paremvolee] insertion.

παρεμπιπτόντως [parempeeptontos] by the way.

παρεμφερής [paremferees] similar, of the same nature, resembling.

παρενέργεια, η [parenerya] side effect.

παρένθεση, η [parenthesee] insertion || (γραμμ) parenthesis.

παρενοχλώ [parenohlo] inconvenience, trouble, harass.

παρεξήγηση, η [parekseeyeesee] misunderstanding.

παρεξηγώ [parekseego] misunderstand, misinterpret, misconstrue.

παρεπόμενα, τα [parepomena] πλ consequences, issues.

παρερμηνεία, η [parermeeneea] misinterpretation.

παρέρχομαι [parerhome] elapse, pass || (τελειώνω) come to an end || (πηδώ) pass over || omit.

παρευρίσκομαι [parevreeskome] be present at, attend.

παρεφθαρμένος [pareftharmenos] defective (linguistically).

παρέχω [pareho] procure || give, supply || (ευκαιρία) occasion, bring about.

παρηγορία, η [pareegoreea] consolation, comfort, solace.

παρηγορώ [pareegoro] console, comfort.

παρθενία, η [partheneea] virginity, maidenhood || chastity.

παρθενικός [partheneekos] virginal || (μεταφ) pure || maiden.

παρθένος, η [parthenos] virgin, maiden.

Παρθενώνας, ο [parthenonas] Parthenon.

παρίσταμαι [pareestame] be present at, assist (at) || arise.

παριστάνω [pareestano] represent, portray, depict || (ρόλο) perform || pretend to be.

πάρκο, το [parko] park.

παρμπρίζ, το [parbreez] (αυτοκινήτου) windscreen.

παρντόν [parnton] pardon me!

παροδικός [parodeekos] passing, fleeting, momentary.

πάροδος, η [parodos] side street || (χρόνου κτλ) passing, course.

παροικία, η [pareekeea] colony, quarter.

παροιμία, η [pareemeea] proverb, adage, saying.

παροιμιώδης [pareemeeodees] proverbial || famous, renowned.

παρομοιάζω [paromeeazo] compare, liken || resemble, be similar.

παρόμοιος [paromeeos] similar, alike.

παρόν, το [paron] the present.

παρονομαστής, ο [paronomastees] (μαθημ) denominator.

παροξυσμός, ο [parokseesmos] fit, attack || incitement.

παρόρμηση, η [parormeesee] prompting, instigation || stimulation, exhortation.

παροτρύνω [parotreeno] βλ παρακινώ.

παρουσία, η [parouseea] presence, attendance || δευτέρα ~ second coming, doomsday.

παρουσιάζομαι [parouseeazome] appear || introduce o.s.

παρουσιάζω [parouseeazo] present, show, introduce.

παρουσιαστικό, το

παροχή [parouseeasteeko] presence, demeanour, bearing.

παροχή, n [parohee] furnishing || contribution, donation || granting.

παρρησία, n [pareeseea] frankness, candour.

πάρσιμο, το [parseemo] capture, taking || (ελάττωση) trimming, lessening.

παρτέρι, το [parteree] flower bed.

παρτίδα, n [parteeδa] part, portion || (παιγνιδιού) game (of cards).

παρωδία, n [paroδeea] parody, farce, travesty.

παρών [paron] present, actual.

παρωνυμία, n [paroneemeea] nickname || surname.

παρωνίδα, n [paropeeδa] blinker, blind.

παρωχημένος [paroheemenos] past, gone by.

πας [pas] any, all, every || (οι πάντες) everybody, everyone.

πασαλείβομαι [pasaleevome] be smeared || get a smattering of knowledge.

πασαλείβω [pasaleevo] smear, daub || smudge.

πασάς, ο [pasas] pasha.

πασίγνωστος [paseegnostos] well-known, notorious.

πασιέντζα, n [pasiendza] patience, solitaire (card game).

πασπαλίζω [paspaleezo] sprinkle, powder (with).

πασπατεύω [paspatevo] pry about, feel, finger.

πάσσαλος, ο [passalos] stake, post, pole.

πάσσο, το [passo] stride, step || πάω ~ (στα χαρτιά) pass (at cards).

πάστα, n [pasta] dough, paste || (γλυκό) pastry, cake || (χαρακτήρας) character, sort.

παστέλι, το [pastelee] concoction of honey and sesame.

παστίτσιο, το [pasteetseeo] baked macaroni.

παστός [pastos] salted.

παστουρμάς, ο [pastourmas] seasoned cured meat.

παστρεύω [pastrevo] clean, cleanse || (μεταφ) destroy, exterminate.

παστρικός [pastreekos] clean, neat || (μεταφ) dishonest, depraved.

Πάσχα, το [pasha] Easter.

πασχαλιά, n [pashalia] lilac.

πασχίζω [pasheezo] try hard to, strive, endeavour.

πάσχω [pasho] be ill, suffer || ο πάσχων the patient, the sufferer.

πάταγος, ο [patagos] din, noise, bang || (μεταφ) sensation, stir.

παταγώδης [patagoδees] uproarious, noisy, loud.

πατάρι, το [pataree] loft, attic.

πατάτα, n [patata] potato.

πατέρας, ο [pateras] father.

πατερίτσα, n [patereetsa] crook, crutch || bishop's staff.

πατικώνω [pateekono] press down, crush, compress.

πάτημα, το [pateema] step, footstep || (ίχνος) footprint || (σταφυλιών) treading, pressing || excuse.

πατημασιά, n [pateemasia] footprint, trace, track.

πατινάρω [pateenaro] skate.

πάτος, ο [patos] bottom.

πατούσα, n [patousa] (ανατ) sole.

πατριάρχης, ο [patreearhees] patriarch.

πατριαρχείο, το [patreearheeo] patriarchate.

πατρίδα, n [patreeδa] native country, birthplace.

πατρικός [patreekos] paternal || fatherly.

πάτριος [patreeos] paternal, ancestral || native.

πατριώτης, ο [patreeotees] compatriot || patriot.

πατριωτικός [patreeoteekos] patriotic.

πατριωτισμός, ο [patreeoteesmos] patriotism.

πατρόν, το [patron] pattern (*in dressmaking*).

πατροπαράδοτος [patroparadotos] usual, customary, traditional || hereditary.

πατρυιός, ο [patreeos] stepfather.

πατσαβούρα, η [patsavoura] dish cloth, rag || (μεταφ) rag (*newspaper*).

πατσάς, ο [patsas] (soup of) tripe.

πάτσι [patsee] even, quits.

πατώ [pato] step on || (κουδούνι κτλ) press || press down || (μεταφ) violate || run over || ~ πόδι I put my foot down.

πάτωμα, το [patoma] floor, ground || storey.

πατώνω [patono] lay a floor || touch bottom, reach bottom.

παύλα, η [pavla] dash (*punctuation*).

παύση, η [pavsee] stoppage, cessation, discharge || (μουσ) rest, pause.

παύω [pavo] cease, stop || cause to cease || (απολύω) dismiss || (σταματώ) stop, finish, give up.

παφλασμός, ο [paflasmos] splashing, gushing || bubbling up.

παχαίνω [paheno] βλ **παχύνω**.

παχιά [pahia] πλ: ~ λόγια empty words, empty promises.

πάχνη, η [pahnee] hoarfrost, rime.

παχνί, το [pahnee] manger, crib.

πάχος, το [pahos] plumpness || thickness || (λίπος) fat, grease || (στρώματος) depth.

παχουλός [pahoulos] plump, chubby.

παχύδερμος [paheedermos] (μεταφ) insensitive.

παχύνω [paheeno] fatten || grow fat.

παχύς [pahees] trick || fleshy, fat || (σε λίπος) rich in fat || (λειβάδι) rich.

παχύσαρκος [paheesarkos] fat, stout, obese.

πάω [pao] go || take || carry || τα ~ καλά I get along well with || ~ περίπατο it's a washout || I go for a walk || ~ να σκάσω I'm ready to burst.

πεδιάδα, η [pedeeada] plain, flat country.

πεδίλο, το [pedeelo] sandal.

πεδινός [pedeenos] flat, level || (έδαφος) even, smooth.

πεδίο, το [pedeeo] plain, flat country, ground || (μάχης) field of battle || (οπτικό) field.

πεζεύω [pezevo] dismount.

πεζή [pezee] on foot.

πεζικό, το [pezeeko] infantry.

πεζογραφία, η [pezografeea] prose.

πεζογράφος, ο, η [pezografos] prose writer, novelist.

πεζοδρόμιο, το [pezodromeeo] pavement || sidewalk (*US*).

πεζοναύτης, ο [pezonavtees] marine.

πεζοπορία, η [pezoporeea] walking, walk || (στρατ) march.

πεζός [pezos] pedestrian || (της πρόζας) in prose || (μεταφ) banal, trivial, common.

πεζούλι, το [pezoulee] parapet || bench || (σε λόφο) terrace.

πεθαίνω [petheno] die || (μεταφ) perish || be fond of, be mad about.

πεθερά, η [pethera] mother-in-law.

πεθερικά, τα [pethereeka] πλ in-laws.

πεθερός, ο [petheros] father-in-law.

πειθαρχία, η [peetharheea] discipline.

πειθαρχικός [peetharheekos] disciplinary || (υπάκουος) obedient, docile, submissive.

πειθαρχώ [peetharho] be obedient, obey one's superiors.

πειθήνιος [peetheeneeos] docile, obedient, submissive.

πείθω [peetho] convince, persuade.

πειθώ, η [peetho] persuasion, conviction.

πείνα, η [peena] hunger, famine, starvation || πειναλέος starving, famished, ravenous || πεινασμένος hungry, famished.

πεινώ [peeno] be hungry, be starving.

πείρα, η [peera] experience, background.

πείραγμα, το [peeragma] teasing || annoyance || (ασθένεια) malady.

πειραγμένος [peeragmenos] hurt, offended || (κρέας) tainted, spoilt.

πειράζει [peerazee]: ~; is it all right?, is it important?

πειράζω [peerazo] trouble, anger, annoy || tease || (την υγεία) be bad for || (ενοχλώ) disturb.

πειρακτικός [peerakteekos] irritating, offensive, cutting.

πείραμα, το [peerama] experiment || trial, test || πειραματικός experimental.

πειρασμός, ο [peerasmos] temptation.

πειρατής, ο [peeratees] pirate, corsair || πειρατικό ταξί pirate taxi.

πείσμα, το [peesma] obstinacy, stubbornness || πεισματάρης obstinate, stubborn || πεισματωδώς headstrong, stubborn || πεισματώνομαι be unyielding || πεισματώνω make obstinate, irritate || become obdurate.

πειστήριο, το [peesteereeo] proof.

πειστικός [peesteekos] convincing, persuasive.

πέλαγος, το [pelagos] open sea.

πελαγώνω [pelagono] lose one's way, be at a loss, feel at sea.

πελαργός [pelargos] stork.

πελατεία, η [plateea] clientèle, customers, patronage.

πελάτης, ο [pelatees] customer, patron, client || (ξενοδοχείου) guest.

πελεκάνος, ο [pelekanos] pelican.

πελεκούδι, το [pelekoudee] chip, paring, shaving.

πελεκώ [peleko] axe, hew, cut into shape, carve || (μεταφ) thrash.

πέλμα, το [pelma] (ανατ) sole || (τεχνική) shoe, flange.

Πελοπόννησος, η [peloponeesos] the Peloponnese.

πελτές, ο [peltes] tomato purée || (φρούτων) jelly.

πελώριος [peloreeos] enormous, mammoth || (σφάλμα) gross.

Πέμπτη, η [pemptee] Thursday.

πέμπτος [pemptos] fifth.

πενήντα [peneenta] fifty.

πενηνταριά, η [peeneentaria]: καμιά ~ about fifty.

πενθήμερος [pentheemeros] of five days.

πένθιμος [pentheemos] sorrowful, mournful, dismal || in mourning.

πένθος, το [penthos] bereavement || mourning.

πενθώ [pentho] lament, mourn || be in mourning.

πενία, η [peneea] poverty, want.

πενιχρός [peneehros] poor, mean || (γεύμα) poor, scant || paltry.

πέννα, η [pena] pen || (μουσ) plectrum || (νόμισμα) penny.

πένσα, η [pensa] tweezers, forceps || (ραπτικής) dart.

πεντάγραμμο, το [pentagramo] (μουσ) stave, staff.

πεντακόσιοι [pentakosiee] five hundred.

πεντάμορφος [pentamorfos] extremely beautiful.

πεντάρα, η [pentara] (μεταφ) farthing || nickel (US).

πεντάρι, το [pentaree] figure 5 || (στα χαρτιά) five (at cards).

πέντε [pente] five.

Πεντηκοστή, η [penteekostee] Whit Sunday.

πέος, το [peos] penis.

πεπειραμένος [pepeeramenos] experienced, versed in.

πεπεισμένος [pepeesmenos] convinced, certain, sure.

πέπλο, το [peplo] veil.

πεποίθηση, η [pepeetheesee] conviction, certainty, assurance.

πεπόνι, το [peponee] melon.

πεπτικός [pepteekos] digestive, peptic.

πέρα [pera] beyond, over, on the other side, over there || εκεί ~ yonder || ~ για ~ through and through || εδώ ~ here || ~ από beyond, across || τα βγάζω ~ manage, make out.

περαιτέρω [peretero] further || moreover.

πέραμα, το [perama] passage, ford || ferry.

πέρας, το [peras] end, extremity || completion, close.

πέρασμα, το [perasma] crossing, passage || (βελόνας) threading || (ασθενείας) passing || (τόπος) much-visited spot.

περασμένος [perasmenos] past, gone, last, by.

περαστικά [perasteeka]: ~! get well soon!

περαστικός [perasteekos] passing by || transient, transitory || (δρόμος) frequented, busy.

περατώνω [peratono] finish, bring to an end, complete.

περβάζι, το [pervazee] doorframe, frame, cornice.

περγαμηνή, η [pergameenee] parchment.

πέρδικα, η [perdeeka] partridge.

πέρδομαι [perdome] fart (col), break wind.

περηφάνεια, η [pereefaneea] βλ υπερηφάνεια.

περηφανεύομαι [pereefanevome] βλ υπερηφανεύομαι.

περήφανος [pereefanos] βλ υπερήφανος.

περί [peree] about, concerning, regarding, of || (με απ) round, near || round about, approximately || ~ τίνος πρόκειται; what's it all about?

περιαυτολογία, η [pereeavtologeea] boasting, bragging.

περιαυτολογώ [pereeavtologo] boast.

περιβάλλον, το [pereevalon] environment, surroundings.

περιβάλλω [pereevalo] encircle, surround || (ρούχα) clothe, dress.

περίβλημα, το [pereevleema] wrapper || (καρπού) shell, husk || casing.

περιβόητος [pereevoeetos] famous, renowned, infamous.

περιβολάρης, ο [pereevolarees] gardener.

περιβολή, η [pereevolee] garment, dress || surrounding.

περιβόλι, το [pereevolee] garden, orchard.

περίβολος, ο [pereevolos] enclosure, yard || (τοίχος) surrounding wall || park.

περιβρέχω [pereevreho] bathe, wash.

περίγελος, ο [pereeyelos] laughing stock.

περιγελώ [pereeyelo] mock, ridicule, derive || dupe, trick.

περιγιάλι, το [pereeyalee] seashore, coast.

περιγραφή, η [pereegrafee] description, account.

περιγράφω [pereegrafo] describe, portray.

περίδοξος [pereedoksos] illustrious, famous.

περιεκτικός [periekteekos] capacious || (τροφή) substantial || (λόγος) comprehensive, concise, succinct.

περιεργάζομαι [periergazome] examine carefully.

περιέργεια, η [perierya] curiosity.

περίεργος [periergos] curious, strange, inquiring.

περιεχόμενο, το [periehomeno] contents || (σημασία) meaning.

περιέχω [perieho] contain, hold.

περιζήτητος [pereezeeteetos] in great demand, greatly prized.

περιηγητής, ο [perieeyeetees] tourist, traveller.

περιθάλπω [pereethalpo] attend, look after, treat.

περίθαλψη, η [pereethalpsee] attendance, care, relief.

περιθώριο, το [pereethoreeo] margin, room.

περικάλυμμα, το [pereekaleema] wrapper, covering, shell.

περικεφαλαία, η [pereekefalea] helmet.

περικλείω [pereekleeo] enclose, include.

περικοκλάδα, η [pereekoklaδa] climbing plant || convolvulus.

περικοπή, η [pereekopee] cutting off, deduction || (από βιβλίο) extract, passage.

περικυκλώνω [pereekeeklono] surround.

περιλαίμιο, το [pereelemeeo] animal's collar || necklace.

περιλάλητος [pereelaleetos] celebrated, famous, renowned.

περιλαμβάνω [pereelamvano] contain, have, hold || (περιέχω) include, comprise.

περιληπτικός [pereeleepteekos] comprehensive || concise, succinct.

περίληψη, η [pereeleepsee] summary, précis, résumé.

περίλυπος [pereeleepos] sad, sorrowful || (έκφραση) gloomy, doleful.

περιμαζεύω [pereemazevo] gather up || (από τον δρόμο) rescue, harbour || (περιορίζω) check, control.

περιμένω [pereemeno] wait || wait for, expect.

περίμετρος, η [pereemetros] circumference, perimeter.

πέριξ [pereeks] about, round || τα ~ the environs, suburb.

περιοδεία, η [pereeoδeea] tour, travelling, trip.

περιοδικό, το [pereeoδeeko] magazine, periodical.

περιοδικός [pereeoδeekos] periodic(al).

περίοδος, η [pereeoδos] period, era, age || season || (γυναικών) (menstrual) period.

περίοπτος [pereeoptos] overlooking, rising, conspicuous || noticeable.

περιορίζω [pereeoreezo] limit, restrict || (ελέγχω) control || (ελαττώνω) reduce, cut down, curtail.

περιορισμός, ο [pereeoreesmos] limitation || detention, restriction || (ελάττωση) reduction.

περιουσία, η [pereeouseea] property, estate || (πλούτη) fortune, wealth.

περιοχή, η [pereeohee] area, region, district || extent, expanse.

περιπαίζω [pereepezo] ridicule, mock || dupe, trick, take in.

περίπατο [pereepato]: πάω ~ go for a stroll || (μεταφ) be a failure.

περίπατος, ο [pereepatos] walk, ride, drive, spin.

περιπέτεια, η [pereepeteea]

adventure || (μεταφ) misadventure, incident.

περιπετειώδης [pereepeteeodees] full of adventures || (ιστορία) of adventure.

περιπλανώ [pereeplano] send long way round || ~ μαι wander, rove, lose one's way.

περιπλέκω [pereepleko] interlace, entangle || complicate, confuse, muddle.

περιπλέω [pereepleo] circumnavigate.

περιπλοκή, η [pereeplokee] complication, complexity, intricacy.

περίπλοκος [pereeplokos] complex, involved.

περιποίηση, η [pereepieesee] care, attendance, looking after.

περιποιητικός [pereepieeteekos] considerate, obliging.

περιποιούμαι [pereepeeoume] take care of || (ασθενή) nurse.

περίπολος, η [pereepolos] patrol.

περίπου [pereepou] about, nearly, almost.

περίπτερο, το [pereeptero] pavilion, kiosk.

περιπτώσει [pereeptosee]: εν πάσει ~ in any case, anyway.

περίπτωση, η [pereeptosee] case, condition, circumstance.

περίσκεψη, η [pereeskepsee] prudence, caution, discretion.

περισπασμός, ο [pereespasmos] diversion, distraction.

περίσσεια, η [pereeseea] excess, superabundance.

περίσσευμα, το [pereesevma] surplus, excess.

περισσεύω [pereesevo] be in excess, be left over.

περίσσιος [pereeseeos] (άφθονος) abundant || (περιττός) unnecessary.

περισσότερο [pereesotero] more.

περισσότερος [pereesoteros] more || ο ~ most.

περίσταση, η [pereestasee] circumstance, event, fact, occasion, situation.

περιστατικό, το [pereestateeko] incident, event.

περιστέλλω [pereestelo] repress, check, restrain, reduce.

περιστέρι, το [pereesteree] pigeon, dove.

περιστοιχίζω [pereesteeheezo] surround, encircle.

περιστολή, η [pereestolee] limitation, decrease, restriction, checking.

περιστρέφομαι [pereestrefome] revolve, spin, turn.

περιστρέφω [pereestrefo] (ρόδα κτλ) turn, rotate || (κλειδί) turn, twist.

περιστροφή, η [pereestrofee] revolution, turn, rotation.

περίστροφο, το [pereestrofo] revolver.

περισυλλέγω [pereeseelego] collect, gather.

περιτειχίζω [pereeteeheezo] build a wall round.

περιτομή, η [pereetomee] circumcision.

περίτρανος [pereetranos] obvious, clear, evident.

περιτριγυρίζω [pereetreeyeereezo] surround, encircle, border.

περίτρομος [pereetromos] terrified, frightened.

περιτροπή, η [pereetropee]: εκ περιτροπής by turns, in turn.

περιττός [pereetos] (προσπάθεια) useless, unavailing || superfluous, unnecessary, needless || ~ αριθμός odd number.

περιτύλιγμα, το [pereeteeleegma] wrapper, wrapping.

περιτυλίσσω [pereeteeleeso] wrap up || roll up.

περιφέρεια, η [pereefereea] (δένδρου) girth || (γεωμ) circumference || (χώρος) district, region.

περιφέρομαι [pereeferome] stroll, walk up and down, hang about || (η γη κτλ) turn round, rotate.

περιφέρω [pereefero] turn, revolve, rotate.

περίφημος [pereefeemos] famous, admirable, celebrated.

περίφραγμα, το [pereefragma] enclosure, hedge, fencing.

περίφραξη, η [pereefraksee] enclosing, fencing.

περιφραστικός [pereefrasteekos] periphrastic(al).

περιφρόνηση, η [pereefroneesee] contempt, scorn.

περιφρονητικός [pereefroneeteekos] disdainful, contemptuous, haughty.

περιφρονώ [pereefrono] hold in contempt, despise, spurn.

περιχαρής [pereeharees] cheerful, merry, joyful, gay.

περίχωρα, τα [pereehora] πλ neighbourhood, environs || (πόλη) suburb, outskirts.

περιωπή, η [pereeopee] eminence || (μεταφ) importance.

περνώ [perno] (ποτάμι, γέφυρα κτλ) pass, cross, go over || (κάτι σε κάποιο) pass, hand over || (κάτι μέσα σε κάτι) pass through || (τον καιρό) spend || (βελόνα) thread (*a needle*) || (υγρό από φίλτρο) filter, strain || (νόμο) get voted, pass || (στο δρόμο) pass, leave behind || ~ **για** mistake for || ~ **από** call at, go via.

περονιάζω [peroneeazo] pierce, go through.

περονόσπορος, ο [peronosporos] mildew.

περούκα, η [perouka] wig.

περπάτημα, το [perpateema] walking || gait.

περπατώ [perpato] walk || go across || (σκύλο κτλ) take for a walk.

Πέρσης, ο [persees] Iranian.

Περσία, η [perseea] Iran.

περσικός [perseekos] Iranian.

πέρ(υ)σι [per(ee)see] last year || **περ(υ)σινός** of last year.

πέσιμο, το [peseemo] falling, fall.

πεσμένος [pesmenos] fallen || impaired, worsened.

πέστροφα, η [pestrofa] trout.

πέταγμα, το [petagma] flying, flight || throwing away, casting.

πετάγομαι [petagome] fly up || rush || butt in.

πετάλι, το [petalee] pedal.

πεταλίδα, η [petaleeda] limpet.

πέταλο, το [petalo] petal || (αλόγου) horseshoe.

πεταλούδα, η [petalouda] butterfly || (λαμπαδέτου) bow, bow tie.

πεταλώνω [petalono] shoe (a horse).

πέταμα [petama] βλ **πέταγμα**.

πεταχτά [petahta]: **στα** ~ hastily, hurriedly, quickly.

πεταχτός [petahtos] nimble || sticking out.

πετεινός, ο [peteenos] cock || (έπιπλου) hammer.

πετ(ι)μέζι, το [pet(ee)mezee] must turned into syrup || (επίθ, μεταφ) very sweet.

πέτο, το [peto] lapel.

πετονιά, η [petonia] fishing line.

πέτρα, η [petra] stone, rock || precious stone.

πετράδι, το [petradee] pebble || precious stone.

πετρέλαιο, το [petreleo] petroleum, oil || (ακάθαρτο) crude oil.

πετρελαιοπηγή, η [petreleopeeyee] oil well.

πετρελαιοφόρο, το [petreleoforo] oil tanker.

πέτρινος [petreenos] made of stone.

πετροβολώ [petrovolo] pelt with stones.

πέτσα, η [petsa] skin || (γάλακτος) cream.

πετσέτα, η [petseta] table napkin || towel.

πετσί, το [petsee] skin, pelt, hide || leather, dressed skin.

πέτσινος [petseenos] leather.

πετσοκόβω [petsokovo] cut up, carve || cut badly, butcher.

πετυχαίνω [peteeheno] βλ επιτυγχάνω.

πετώ [peto] fly || (από χαρά) jump for joy || (στα σκουπίδια) throw away || ~ **έξω** throw out || kick out (col).

πεύκο, το [pefko] pine.

πέφτει [peftee]: **δε σου ~ λόγος** you've got no say in the matter.

πέφτω [pefto] tumble, fall || drop, come down, subside || come off || occur || ~ **στο κρεββάτι** I go to bed || ~ **έξω** make a mistake || (ναυτ) run aground || ~ **δίπλα** make up to || ~ **με τα μούτρα** apply o.s., take up eagerly.

πέψη, η [pepsee] digestion.

πηγάδι, το [peegadee] well.

πηγάζω [peegazo] spring from, originate, emanate.

πηγαινοέρχομαι [peeyenoerhome] go to and fro.

πηγαίνω [peeyeno] go || escort, take || βλ και **πάω**.

πηγή, η [peeyee] spring, source || (μεταφ) origin, cause.

πηγούνι, το [peegounee] chin.

πηδάλιο, το [peedaleeo] rudder || helm || wheel.

πηδαλιούχος, ο [peedaleeouhos] helmsman.

πήδημα, το [peedeema] jump(ing), spring || sudden rise.

πηδώ [peedo] leap, jump, vault || jump over || (παραλείπω) skip, leave out.

πήζω [peezo] coagulate, thicken, curdle.

πηκτός [peektos] coagulated, thick, curdled.

πηλάλα, η [peelala] quick running || (επιρ) at full speed.

πηλίκο, το [peeleeko] quotient.

πήλινος [peeleenos] earthen, of clay.

πηλός, η [peelos] clay || mud, slime, sludge.

πηνίο, το [peeneeo] bobbin, spool || (ηλεκ) coil.

πήξη, η [peeksee] coagulation, congealing || sticking in.

πηρούνι, το [peerounee] fork.

πήχη, η [peehee] measure of length (0.46 m).

πηχτός [peehtos] coagulated, jellied || thick.

πήχυς, ο [peehees] cubit || ell.

πι, το [pee] the letter Π || **στο ~ και φι** in two shakes of a lamb's tail.

πια [pia] not any longer || now, finally, at last, at long last.

πιάνο, το [peeano] piano.

πιάνομαι [peeanome] be caught at, be paralyzed || (τσακώνομαι) quarrel with.

πιάνω [peeano] take hold of, catch || occupy || (συζήτηση) engage || (περιέχω) contain, hold || (λιμάνι) land || ~ **σπίτι** rent a house || ~ **τόπο** come in useful || ~ **κουβέντα** get into conversation || ~ **δουλειά** start a job, find a job.

πιάσιμο, το [peeaseemo] hold, grasp || catching || (αφή) feeling, touch || (φυτού κτλ) taking root || (σώματος) stiffness, paralysis.

πιασμένος [peeasmenos] occupied, taken || (στο σώμα) cramped, (feeling) stiff.

πιατέλα, n [peeatela] large dish, flat dish.

πιατικά, τα [peeateeka] πλ crockery, earthenware.

πιάτσα, n [peeatsa] market || (ταξί) taxi rank.

πιέζω [piezo] press, squeeze, compress || oppress, force.

πίεση, n [piesee] pressure, oppression || (αίματος) blood pressure.

πιεστήριο, το [piesteereeo] press || (ελιών) oil press.

πιεστικός [piesteekos] pressing, oppressive || urgent.

πιέτα, n [pieta] pleat.

πιθαμή, n [peethamee] span of hand.

πιθανός [peethanos] probable, likely.

πιθανότητα, n [peethanoteeta] likelihood, probability.

πιθανώς [peethanos] probably, likely, in all likelihood.

πίθηκος, ο [peetheekos] ape.

πιθάρι, το [peetharee] jar.

πίκα, n [peeka] umbrage, pique || (στα χαρτιά) spade.

πικάντικος [peekanteekos] piquant, spicy.

πίκρα, n [peekra] grief, bitterness, affliction.

πικραίνομαι [peekrenome] be grieved, be embittered.

πικραίνω [peekreno] render bitter || grieve, distress.

πικροδάφνη, n [peekroδafnee] oleander.

πικρός [peekros] bitter || biting, harsh.

πικρόχολος [peekroholos] (μεταφ) touchy, irritable, snappy.

πιλάφι, το [peelafee] pilaf, rice dish.

πιλότος, ο [peelotos] pilot.

πίνακας, ο [peenakas] list, table || (του τείχου) notice board ||

(σχολείου) blackboard || (περιεχομένων) table of contents.

πινακίδα, n [peenakeeδa] nameplate || (αυτοκινήτου) licence plate, number plate.

πινακοθήκη, n [peenakotheekee] picture gallery, art gallery.

πινέζα, n [peeneza] drawing pin.

πινέλο, το [peenelo] artist's paintbrush.

πίνω [peeno] drink, take in || (τσιγάρο) smoke.

πιο [pio] more, greater.

πιοτό, το [pioto] drinking || liquor.

πίπα, n [peepa] pipe || cigarette holder.

πιπεράτος [peeperatos] peppery || biting, caustic, piquant.

πιπέρι, το [peeperee] pepper.

πιπεριά, n [peeperia] pepper || (δένδρο) pepper tree.

πιπιλίζω [peepeeleezo] suck, sip.

πισίνα, n [peeseena] swimming pool.

πισινός [peeseenos] back, posterior || ο ~ backside (col), arse (col), bum (col).

πίσσα, n [peesa] pitch, tar, asphalt.

πισσώνω [peesono] tar, pitch.

πίστα, n [peesta] ring || racetrack || (χορού) dance floor.

πιστευτός [peestevtos] trustworthy || credible.

πιστεύω [peestevo] believe, have faith in || suppose, fancy, think.

πίστη, n [peestee] faith, confidence, trust || fidelity || (οίκον) credit, trustworthiness.

πιστόλι, το [peestolee] pistol.

πιστοποιητικό, το [peestopieeteeko] certificate.

πιστοποιώ [peestopieo] certify, guarantee, vouch for.

πιστός [peestos] faithful, loyal, devoted || accurate.

πιστώνω [peestono] (οίκον) credit with, give credit.

πίστωση, η [peestosee] credit, trust.

πιστωτής, ό [peestotees] creditor.

πίσω [peeso] behind || back || over again || **πάει** ~ **το ρολόι** the clock is slow || **κάνω** ~ move back || ~ **μου** behind me || ~ **από** behind, following.

πίτα, η [peeta] kind of cake, pie.

πίτουρο, το [peetouro] bran.

πιτσιλίζω [peetseeleezo] splash, sprinkle, dash (with).

πιτσιρίκος, ό [peetseereekos] small boy || kid (col).

πιτυρίδα, η [peeteereeδa] scurf, dandruff.

πιωμένος [piomenos] drunk, tipsy.

πλά(γι)η, το [pla(γi)ee] side || **στο πλάι** close by, near, beside.

πλαγιά, η [playa] slope of hill, hillside.

πλαγιάζω [playazo] go to bed || lie down || put to bed.

πλαγιαστός [playiastos] lying down, reclining.

πλάγιος [playeos] oblique || indirect || crooked, dishonest.

πλαγίως [playeos] indirectly || next door.

πλαδαρός [plaδaros] flabby, soft || (προσπάθεια) feeble, ineffective.

πλάζ, η [plaz] bathing beach.

πλάθω [platho] mould, create, fashion.

πλάι [plaee] alongside, next door || ~ ~ side by side || ~ **σε** next to, along with.

πλαϊνός [plaeenos] adjoining, next door.

πλαίσιο, το [pleseeo] frame, framework || chassis || (μεταφ) scope, range.

πλαισιώνω [pleseeono] border, surround, frame, encircle.

πλάκα, η [plaka] slab, plate, paving stone || plaque || (σχολική) slate || (σαπούνι) cake || (γραμμοφώνου)

record || (φωτογραφική) plate || **σπάσαμε** ~ we had a lot of fun || **έχει** ~ it's funny, it's hilarious.

πλακάκι, το [plakakee] floor tile, wall tile.

πλακόστρωτος [plakostrotos] paved, laid with tiles.

πλάκωμα, το [plakoma] pressure, crush || unexpected arrival.

πλακώνω [plakono] crush, press down || happen unexpectedly || come suddenly.

πλάνη, η [planee] mistake, delusion || (εργαλείο) plane.

πλανήτης, ό [planeetees] planet.

πλανίζω [planeezo] plane, smooth down.

πλανόδιος [planoδeos] travelling || ~ **έμπορος** pedlar, hawker.

πλαντάζω [plantazo] be furious, fume, be enraged.

πλανώμαι [planome] ramble, wander || (κάνω λάθος) be mistaken, delude o.s.

πλασιέ, ό [plasie] commercial traveller, salesman.

πλάση, η [plasee] foundation, creation || moulding, formation.

πλάσμα, το [plasma] creature, being || invention, fiction || beauty.

πλάστιγγα, η [plasteenga] weighing machine, balance.

πλαστικός [plasteekos] plastic || comely.

πλαστογραφώ [plastografo] counterfeit || falsify.

πλαστός [plastos] false, forged || artificial, fictitious.

πλαταίνω [plateno] βλ **πλατύνω**.

πλάτανος, ό [platanos] plane tree.

πλατεία, η [plateea] town square || (θεάτρου) pit.

πλάτη, η [platee] back || shoulder blade.

πλατιά [platia] widely.

πλάτος, το [platos] width,

broadness, breadth || (γεωγραφικό) **latitude**.

πλατύνω [plateeno] **make wider, stretch, let out** || **become wider, broaden**.

πλατύς [platees] **wide, broad, large, ample** || (μεταφ) **far-reaching**.

πλέγμα, το [plegma] **network**.

πλειοδοτώ [pleeodoto] **make highest offer** *or* **bid**.

πλειονότητα, η [pleeonoteeta] **majority**.

πλειοψηφία, η [pleeopseefeea] **majority** (**of votes**).

πλειστηριασμός, ο [pleesteereeasmos] **auction**.

πλεκτός [plektos] **knitted, plaited, woven**.

πλέκω [pleko] **plait, weave** || (κάλτσες) **knit**.

πλεμόνι, το [plemonee] **lung**.

πλένω [pleno] βλ **πλύνω**.

πλέξιμο, το [plekseemo] **knitting** || **braiding** || (σε υπόθεση) **involvement**.

πλεξούδα, η [pleksouδa] **plait, braid, tress**.

πλέον [pleon] **more** || **επί ~ in addition** || **not any longer** || **moreover** || **now**.

πλεονάζω [pleonazo] **abound, be plentiful** || **exceed, be superfluous**.

πλεόνασμα, το [pleonasma] **surplus, excess** || (βάρους) **overweight**.

πλεονέκτημα, το [pleonekteema] **advantage, benefit** || **gift, quality, merit**.

πλεονέκτης, ο [pleonektees] **greedy person, covetous person**.

πλεονεκτώ [pleonekto] **have the advantage** || **be greedy**.

πλεονεξία, η [pleonekseea] **cupidity, greed, avidity**.

πλευρά, η [plevra] **side** || **rib** || (όρους) **slope, declivity** || (μεταφ) **point of view**.

πλευρίζω [plevreezo] (ναυτ) **come alongside**.

πλευρίτιδα, η [plevreeteeδa] **pleurisy**.

πλευρό, το [plevro] **side** || **rib** || (στρατ) **flank**.

πλεχτό, το [piehto] **pullover** || **knitted article**.

πλέω [pleo] **navigate, sail** || **float** || (μεταφ) **wade, wallow**.

πληγή, η [pleeyee] **wound, injury, sore** || (μεταφ) **plague, evil, sore**.

πλήγμα, το [pleegma] **blow** || **wound**.

πληγώνω [pleegono] **wound, injure** || **offend, hurt**.

πλήθη, τα [pleethee] πλ **the masses**.

πλήθος, το [pleethos] **crowd** || **mass** || **great number**.

πληθυντικός, ο [pleetheenteekos] (γραμμ) **plural**.

πληθύνω [pleetheeno] **multiply, increase** || **augment**.

πληθυσμός, ο [pleetheesmos] **population**.

πληθώρα, η [pleethora] **abundance, excess, plenitude**.

πληθωρισμός, ο [pleethoreesmos] **inflation** || **plenitude**.

πληκτικός [pleekteekos] **boring, tiresome, irksome, dull, trying**.

πλήκτρο, το [pleektro] (πιάνο κτλ) **key** || **plectrum** || **drumstick**.

πλημμέλημα, το [pleemeleema] **misdemeanour, offence**.

πλημμύρα, η [pleemeera] **flood, inundation** || (μεταφ) **plenitude**.

πλημμυρίζω [pleemeereezo] **inundate, overflow** || (μεταφ) **swarm**.

πλην [pleen] **except, save** || (επίρ) **unless, except that** || (συνδ) **but** || (μαθημ) **minus** || **~ τούτου besides, moreover**.

πλήξη, η [pleeksee] **tedium, weariness, boredom**.

πληρεξούσιο, το [pleereksouseeo] power of attorney.

πληρεξούσιος, ο, η [pleereksouseeos] representative, proxy || plenipotentiary, deputy.

πλήρης [pleerees] full, complete, whole || swarming, teeming, packed.

πληροφορία, η [pleeroforeea] information, report.

πληροφορίες, οι [pleerofories] πλ information.

πληροφορική, η [pleeroforeekee] informatics, computer science.

πληροφορούμαι [pleeroforoume] learn, discover.

πληροφορώ [pleeroforo] inform, notify.

πληρώ [pleero] fill || fulfil, perform.

πλήρωμα, το [pleeroma] crew || fullness || filling, completion.

πληρωμή, η [pleeromee] payment, reward || salary, wages.

πληρώνω [pleerono] pay, settle || (μεταφ) pay up, discharge.

πληρωτής [pleerotees] payer.

πλησιάζω [pleeseeazo] approach, go near, put near, draw near.

πλησιέστερος [pleesiesteros] closer || ο ~ the nearest.

πλησίον [pleeseeon] near, close by || ο ~ neighbour.

πλήττω [pleeto] strike, hit, wound, afflict || (παθαίνω πλήξη) be bored, be weary.

πλινθόκτιστος [pleenthokteestos] built of bricks.

πλίνθος, η [pleenthos] brick, firebrick.

πλόηγος, ο [ploeegos] (ναυτ) pilot.

πλοιάριο, το [pleeareeo] small boat, launch.

πλοίαρχος, ο [pleearhos] (ναυτ) captain || (εμπορικού) master, skipper.

πλοίο, το [pleeo] ship, vessel, boat.

πλοκάμι, το [plokamee] tress, braid, plait || (χταποδιού) tentacle.

πλοκή, η [plokee] plot (of play).

πλους, ο [plous] sailing, passage || navigating.

πλουσιοπάροχος [plouseeoparohos] copious, generous, abundant.

πλούσιος, ο [plouseeos] rich, wealthy || splendid, magnificent.

πλουτίζω [plouteezo] make rich || get rich.

πλούτη, τα [ploutee] πλ riches, wealth.

πλούτος, ο [ploutos] opulence, wealth || richness || (εδάφους) fertility.

πλυντήριο, το [pleenteereeo] laundry room || washing machine.

πλύνω [pleeno] wash, clean || brush || scrub.

πλύσιμο, το [pleeseemo] wash(ing).

πλυσταριό, το [pleestario] laundry room.

πλύστρα, η [pleestra] washerwoman || wash-board.

πλώρη, η [ploree] prow || **βάζω** ~ set sail (for).

πλωτάρχης, ο [plotarhees] lieutenant-commander.

πλωτός [plotos] navigable || floating || (γέφυρα) pontoon bridge.

πνεύμα, το [pnevma] ghost, soul, breath of life || mind || genius, spirit || (γραμμ) breathing || **Άγιο** ~ Holy Ghost.

πνευματικός [pnevmateekos] spiritual || intellectual, mental || pneumatic.

πνευμονία, η [pnevmoneea] pneumonia.

πνεύμονας, ο [pnevmonas] lung.

πνευστός [pnevstos] blown, wind (instrument).

πνέω [pneo] blow || ~ τα λοίσθια I breathe my last.

πνιγηρός [pneeyeeros] stifling, suffocating, choking.

πνιγμός, ο [pneegmos] suffocation, choking || drowning || throttling.

πνίγω [pneego] drown || stifle, suffocate || choke, throttle.

πνίξιμο, το [pneekseemo] drowning || strangulation.

πνοή, η [pnoee] breath(ing) || (μεταφ) inspiration.

ποδήλατο, το [poðeelato] bicycle.

ποδηλατώ [poðeelato] cycle, pedal.

πόδι, το [poðee] foot, leg || (μέτρο) foot || (ποτηριού) stem || στο ~ standing || on the go || σηκώνω στο ~ cause a commotion.

ποδιά, η [poðia] apron, overall || (παραθύρου) windowsill.

ποδόγυρος, ο [poðoyeeros] border, hem.

ποδοπατώ [poðopato] tread on, trample on, trample underfoot.

ποδοσφαιριστής, ο [poðosfereestees] football player.

ποδόσφαιρο, το [poðosfero] game of football.

πόζα, η [poza] pose, affectation.

ποζάρω [pozaro] pose, sit for || put on.

πόθος, ο [pothos] desire, wish, yearning.

ποθώ [potho] desire, long for, wish, be eager for.

ποίημα, το [pieema] poem.

ποίηση, η [pieese] poetry.

ποιητής, ο [pieetees] poet || creator, maker.

ποιητικός [pieeteekos] poetic.

ποικιλία, η [peekeeleea] variety, diversity, assortment.

ποικίλλω [peekeelo] embellish, adorn || vary, change.

ποικίλος [peekeelos] varied, diverse, different || miscellaneous.

ποιμένας, ο [peemenas] shepherd, herdsman.

ποίμνιο, το [peemneeo] flock, herd, drove || (εκκλ) flock.

ποινή, η [peenee] penalty, punishment, pain.

ποινικός [peeneekos] penal, criminal, felonious.

ποιόν, το [peeon] quality, property, attribute, nature.

ποιος [peeos] who?, which?, what?

ποιότητα, η [peeoteeta] quality, property.

πολεμικό, το [polemeeko] warship.

πολεμικός [polemeekos] warlike, bellicose || of war, martial.

πολέμιος, ο [polemeeos] unfriendly, hostile || o ~ enemy, adversary.

πολεμιστής, ο [polemeestees] fighter, warrior, combatant.

πόλεμος, ο [polemos] war, warfare.

πολεμοφόδια, τα [polemofoðeea] nλ munitions, ammunition.

πολεμώ [polemo] fight, make war against || contend, strive (to).

πολεοδομία, η [poleoðomeea] town planning.

πόλη, η [polee] city, town.

πολικός [poleekos] polar.

πολιορκία, η [poleeorkeea] siege, blockade.

πολιορκώ [poleeorko] besiege, surround || invest.

πολιτεία, η [poleeteea] state, government || country, nation || town.

πολίτευμα, το [poleetevma] system of government, regime.

πολιτεύομαι [poleetevome] go into politics, meddle in politics.

πολιτευτής, ο [poleetevtees] politician, statesman.

πολιτικά, τα [poleeteeka] nλ politics.

πολίτης, ο [poleetees] citizen || civilian.

πολιτική, η [poleeteekee] politics || policy.

πολιτικός [poleeteekos] civic,
civilian || political || (ουσ) politician.
πολιτισμένος [poleeteesmenos]
civilized, cultured.
πολιτισμός, ο [poleeteesmos]
civilization, culture.
πολιτογραφώ [poleetografo]
naturalize (as citizen).
πολιτοφυλακή, η
[poleetofeelakee] militia, civil
guard || national guard (US).
πολλαπλασιάζω [polaplaseeazo]
multiply || propagate, increase.
πολλαπλασιασμός, ο
[polaplaseeasmos] multiplication ||
increase.
πολλαπλάσιο, το [polaplaseeo]
multiple.
πολλοί [polee] πλ many.
πόλο, το [polo] polo.
πόλος, ο [polos] pole.
πολτός, ο [poltos] pap || purée || rag
pulp.
πολύ [polee] much || numerous,
several || great, a lot || **το** ~ at the
most.
πολυάνθρωπος [poleeanthropos]
populous, crowded.
πολυάριθμος [poleeareethmos]
numerous.
πολυάσχολος [poleeasholos] very
busy, very occupied.
πολυβόλο, το [poleevolo] machine
gun.
πολυγαμία, η [poleegameea]
polygamy.
πολύγλωσσος [poleeglosos]
polyglot.
πολυγράφος, ο [poleegrafos]
duplicator.
πολυέλαιος, ο [polieleos]
chandelier.
πολυζήτητος [poleezeeteetos]
much sought-after.
πολυθρόνα, η [poleethrona]
armchair.

πολυκατοικία, η [poleekateekeea]
block of flats, apartment building.
πολυκοσμία, η [poleekosmeea]
crowds of people.
πολύκροτος [poleekrotos] causing
a commotion.
πολυλογάς, ο [poleelogas]
chatterbox, babbler, gossip.
πολυλογία, η [poleeloyeea]
loquacity, garrulity, babble.
πολυμελής [poleemelees] having
many members, numerous.
πολυμερής [poleemerees] varied,
diversified.
πολυμήχανος [poleemeehanos]
very ingenious || cunning, crafty.
πολυπληθής [poleepleethees] very
numerous, crowded.
πολύπλοκος [poleeplokos]
intricate, complicated, very
involved.
πολύπους, ο [poleepous] polyp ||
(ιατρ) polypus.
πολύπτυχος [poleepteehos] with
many folds, many-pleated.
πολύς [polees] much, numerous,
many, great || (χρόνος) long.
πολυσύνθετος [poleeseenthetos]
very complex || compound.
πολυτέλεια, η [poleeteleea] luxury.
πολυτελής [poleetelees]
sumptuous, splendid, rich.
πολυτεχνείο, το [poleetehneeo]
Polytechnic, National Technical
School.
πολύτιμος [poleeteemos] valuable,
precious, priceless.
πολυφαγία, η [poleefayeea]
gluttony, voracity, greediness.
πολύχρωμος [poleehromos]
multicoloured, variegated.
πολύωρος [poleeoros] lasting many
hours, long-drawn-out.
Πολωνία, η [poloneea] Poland.
πολωνικός [poloneekos] Polish.
πόμολο, το [pomolo] door knob,
handle.

πομπή, η [pompee] procession, parade || shame, stigma.

πομπός, ο [pompos] transmitter.

πομπωδης [pompodees] pompous, bombastic.

πονεμένος [ponemenos] in distress || sad, hurt.

πονηρεύομαι [poneerevome] employ cunning, use wiles || become suspicious.

πονηρεύω [poneerevo] rouse suspicions of || make suspicious || become cunning.

πονηρία, η [poneereea] ruse, trick, guile || suspicion, slyness.

πονηρός [poneeros] cunning, wily, crafty || suspicious, distrustful || diabolical.

πονόδοντος, ο [ponodontos] toothache.

πονοκέφαλος, ο [ponokefalos] headache.

πονόλαιμος, ο [ponolemos] sore throat.

πόνος, ο [ponos] suffering, pain || (τοκετού) labour || compassion, pity, sympathy.

ποντάρω [pontaro] punt || back, bet on.

ποντικός, ο [ponteekos] mouse, rat || (ανατ) muscle.

πόντος, ο [pontos] sea || (παιχνιδιού) point || (μέτρο) centimetre || (πλέξιμο) stitch || **Εύξεινος ~** Black Sea.

πονώ [pono] feel compassion for, sympathize with || hurt, pain || (αμετ) feel pain, suffer.

πορδή, η [pordee] fart (col).

πορεία, η [poreea] march, route || course, run.

πορεύομαι [porevome] proceed, go, walk, march.

πορθείο, το [porthmeeo] ferry (boat).

πορθμός, ο [porthmos] strait, sound, channel.

πόρισμα, το [poreesma] deduction, inference, conclusion || finding || (μαθημ) corollary.

πορνείο, το [porneeo] brothel || whorehouse (US).

πόρνη, η [pornee] prostitute, whore.

πόρος, ο [poros] passage, ford || (του σώματος) pore || πλ means, income, resources.

πόρπη, η [porpee] buckle, clasp, brooch.

πορσελάνη, η [porselanee] china, porcelain.

πόρτα, η [porta] door, gate, doorway, gateway.

Πορτογαλία, η [portogaleea] Portugal.

πορτογαλικός [portogaleekos] Portuguese.

Πορτογάλος, ο [portogalos] Portuguese man.

πορτοκαλάδα, η [portokalaða] orangeade.

πορτοκάλι, το [portokalee] orange.

πορτοκαλιά, η [portokalia] orange tree.

πορτοφολάς, ο [portofolas] pickpocket.

πορτοφόλι, το [portofolee] wallet.

πορτραίτο, το [portreto] portrait.

πορφύρα, η [porfeera] purple.

πορώδης [poroðees] porous.

πόσιμο [poseemo] **~ νερό** drinking water.

πόσιμος [poseemos] drinkable.

ποσό, το [poso] quantity, amount || (χρήματος) sum.

πόσο [poso] how much.

πόσος [posos] how much?, how many?, how large?, how great?

ποσοστό, το [pososto] percentage, share, quota.

ποσότητα, η [posoteeta] quantity, amount.

πόστο, το [posto] strategic position.

ποσώς [posos] not at all, in nc way, by no means.

ποτάμι, το [potamee] **ποταμός, ο** [potamos] river.

πότε [pote] when? || ~ ~ sometimes, from time to time || ~ ... ~ sometimes... sometimes.

ποτέ [pote] once, formerly || ever || (μετά από αρνητ) never || ~ **πλέον** never again.

ποτήρι, το [poteeree] drinking glass.

πότης, ο [potees] heavy drinker, boozer.

ποτίζω [poteezo] water, irrigate || become damp, become saturated.

πότισμα, το [poteesma] watering, irrigation.

ποτιστήρι, το [poteesteeree] watering can.

ποτό, το [poto] drink, beverage.

πού [pou] where?, whither? || **για** ~; where are you going? || ~ **να ξέρω;** how should I know? || ~ **και** ~ once in a while, now and then.

που [pou] who, whom, which, that || when || (συνδ) that || (επίρ) somewhere, where.

πουγγί, το [poungee] purse, bag || money.

πούδρα, η [pouðra] powder.

πουθενά [pouthena] not anywhere || nowhere.

πουκάμισο, το [poukameeso] shirt.

πουλάκι, το [poulakee] little bird || ~ **μου** my darling, my pet.

πουλάρι, το [poularee] foal, colt.

πουλερικά, τα [poulereeka] πλ poultry.

πουλί, το [poulee] bird.

πούλμαν, το [poulman] (motor) coach.

πουλώ [poulo] βλ **πωλώ.**

πούντα, η [pounda] cold, pleurisy.

πουντιάζω [pounteeazo] cool, chill || feel very cold.

πούπουλο, το [poupoulo] down, plume, feather.

πουρές, ο [poures] purée.

πουρμπουάρ, το [pourbouar] gratuity, tip.

πουρνάρι, το [pournaree] evergreen oak.

πούρο, το [pouro] cigar.

πούσι, το [pousee] mist, fog.

πούστης, ο [poustees] bugger, queen (col), queer (col).

πουτάνα, η [poutana] whore.

πράγμα, το [pragma] thing, object || matter, business, affair || (προϊόντα) goods || (ύφασμα) cloth.

πράγματι [pragmatee] in fact, actually.

πραγματεύομαι [pragmatevome] deal with, treat, handle || negotiate.

πραγματικός [pragmateekos] real, actual, substantial, authentic.

πραγματικότητα, η [pragmateekoteeta] reality, fact, truth.

πραγματογνώμονας, ο [pragmatognomonas] assessor, valuer || expert.

πραγματοποιώ [pragmatopeeo] carry out, realize, fulfil, work out.

πρακτικά, τα [prakteeka] πλ records, minutes, proceedings.

πρακτικός [prakteekos] useful, practical || vocational.

πρακτορείο, το [praktoreeo] agency, travel agency.

πράκτορας, ο [praktoras] agent || **μυστικός** ~ secret agent.

πραμάτεια, η [pramateea] goods, commodities.

πράξη, η [praksee] action, act || practice, experience || (γεννήσεως κτλ) certificate, registration || (οικον) deal, transaction || (μαθημ) operation.

πραξικόπημα, το [prakseekopeema] coup d'état.

πράος [praos] affable, gentle, kind.

πρασιά, η [prasia] flower bed or lawn round house.

πρασινάδα, η [praseenaδa] verdure, greenery || green colour.

πράσινος [praseenos] green, verdant || unripe.

πράσο, το [praso] leek.

πρατήριο, το [prateereeo] specialist shop || ~ **βενζίνης** petrol station.

πράττω [prato] perform, act || do.

πραΰνω [praeeno] appease, calm, soothe, pacify.

πρέζα, η [preza] pinch.

πρέπει [prepee] it is necessary, it is proper that || ~ **να πάω** I must go || **καθώς** ~ decent, honourable, a gentleman.

πρέπων [prepon] suitable, fitting, proper || decent, correct.

πρεσβεία, η [presveea] embassy, legation || delegation.

πρεσβευτής, ο [presvevtees] ambassador, minister || representative.

πρεσβεύω [presvevo] profess, avow, affirm, represent.

πρεσβυωπία, η [presveeopeea] long-sightedness.

πρέφα, η [prefa] card game || **το πήρε** ~ he smelt a rat.

πρήζομαι [preezome] become swollen, swell.

πρήζω [preezo] (μεταφ) infuriate.

πρήξιμο, το [preekseemo] swelling, tumour.

πρίγκηπας, ο [preengkeepas] prince.

πρίζα, η [preeza] plug, socket.

πριν [preen] before, previously, prior to || ~ **από μένα** ahead of me, in front of me || ~ **τον πόλεμο** before the war.

πριόνι, το [preeonee] saw, handsaw, hacksaw.

πριονίζω [preeoneezo] saw.

πρίσμα, το [preesma] prism.

προ [pro] before, in front of, ahead of, in the face of || ~ **ημερών** a few days ago || ~ **παντός** especially, above all.

προαγγέλλω [proangelo] predict, prophesy.

προάγω [proago] put forward, promote, advance || speed up, further || **η προαγωγή** (ουσ) advancement, promotion || **ο προαγωγός** (ουσ) pimp, pander.

προαίρεση, η [proeresee] intention, purpose || bent, bias.

προαιρετικός [proereteekos] optional || voluntary.

προαίσθηση, η [proestheesee] presentiment, foreboding.

προάλλες [proales] **τις** ~ just the other day, recently.

προαναφερθείς [proanafertheees] above-mentioned.

προασπίζω [proaspeezo] defend, protect, guard.

προάστειο, το [proasteeo] suburb.

προαύλιο, το [proavleeo] forecourt, courtyard.

πρόβα, η [prova] fitting of clothes || trial, rehearsal.

προβάδισμα, το [provaδeesma] precedence, priority.

προβαίνω [proveno] advance, move forward || proceed, make || ~ **σε** carry out, make.

προβάλλω [provalo] project, further || (σκιά) cast || (φιλμ) project, show || (αντίσταση) offer resistance || (αντίρρηση) raise || (δικαιολογία) put forward an excuse || (σμετ) appear suddenly in view.

προβάρω [provaro] try on, go for a fitting.

προβατίνα, η [provateena] ewe, lamb.

πρόβατο, το [provato] sheep.

προβιά, η [provia] animal's skin.

προβιβάζω [proveevazo] promote, push forward.

πρόβιος [proveeos] of a sheep.

προβλέπω [provlepo] foresee, forecast || prepare for, provide.

πρόβλεψη, η [provlepsee] forecast, anticipation.

πρόβλημα, το [provleema] problem || (μεταφ) riddle, puzzle.

προβλήτα, η [provleeta] jetty, mole.

προβολέας, ο [provoleas] searchlight, headlight || (σινεμά) projector.

προβολή, η [provolee] projection || (προϊόντος) promotion.

προβοσκίδα, η [provoskeeδa] trunk || (εντόμου) proboscis.

προγενέστερος [proyenesteros] anterior, previous, former || (ουσ) precursor.

πρόγευμα, το [proyevma] breakfast.

προγνωστικό, το [prognosteeko] prediction, forecast || tip.

πρόγονος, ο [progonos] ancestor, forefather, forebear.

προγονός, ο, η [progonos] stepson, stepdaughter.

πρόγραμμα, το [programa] programme, plan, schedule.

προγράφω [prografo] proscr:be, outlaw.

προγυμνάζω [proyeemnazo] exercise, train || tutor.

προδιαγράφω [proδeeagrafo] prearrange.

προδιάθεση, η [proδeeathesee] predisposition, liability (to), prejudice (against).

προδιαθέτω [proδeeatheto] predispose, forewarn, influence, prejudice.

προδίδω [proδeeδo] reveal, betray || denounce, inform.

προδοσία, η [proδoseea] betrayal || treachery.

προδότης, ο [proδotees] traitor, informer.

πρόδρομος, ο [proδromos] forerunner, precursor || herald.

προεδρεία, η [proeδreea] presidency, chairmanship.

προεδρεύω [proeδrevo] preside, chair.

πρόεδρος, ο, η [proeδros] president, chairman || presiding judge.

προειδοποίηση, η [proeeδopieesee] previous warning, premonition.

προειδοποιώ [proeeδopeeo] let know || warn.

προεισαγωγή, η [proeesagoyee] introduction, preface.

προεκλογικός [proekloyeekos] pre-election.

προέκταση, η [proektasee] extension, prolongation.

προέλαση, η [proelasee] advance, forward movement.

προελαύνω [proelavno] advance, move forward.

προέλευση, η [proelevsee] provenance, place of origin.

προεξέχω [proekseho] jut out, project, protrude.

προεξοφλώ [proeksoflo] (χρέος) pay off in advance || receive in advance || take for granted, rely on.

προεξοχή, η [proeksohee] projection, protrusion, prominence.

προεργασία, η [proergaseea] preliminary work.

προέρχομαι [proerhome] originate, come from, issue from.

προετοιμάζω [proeteemazo] prepare, fit for, train for.

προετοιμασία, η [proeteemaseea] preparation.

προέχω [proeho] jut out || surpass || predominate.

πρόζα, η [proza] prose.

προηγούμαι [proeegoume] surpass, be ahead || precede, come before.

προηγούμενο, το [proeegoumeno] precedent.

προηγούμενος [proeegoumenos] preceding, previous, earlier.

προηγουμένως [proeegoumenos] previously, beforehand.

προθάλαμος, ο [prothalamos] anteroom, antechamber, waiting room.

πρόθεση, η [prothesee] purpose, design, intention || (γραμμ) preposition, prefix.

προθεσμία, η [prothesmeea] time limit, delay, term, option.

προθήκη, η [protheekee] shop window || showcase.

προθυμία, η [protheemeea] eagerness, readiness, alacrity.

πρόθυμος [protheemos] eager, willing, ready || obliging.

πρόθυρα, τα [protheera] πλ gates, approach || (μεταφ) verge, eve, threshold.

προίκα, η [preeka] dowry, marriage portion.

προικίζω [preekeezo] dower || endow (with), equip (with).

προικοθήρας, ο [preekotheeras] fortune hunter, dowry hunter.

προικοσύμφωνο, το [preekoseemfono] marriage contract.

προϊόν, το [proeeon] product, production || proceeds.

προϊόντα, τα [proeeonta] πλ produce, articles, products.

προΐσταμαι [proeestame] direct, manage, supervise.

προϊστάμενος, ο [proeestamenos] superior, chief, supervisor.

πρόκα, η [proka] nail, tack.

προκαλώ [prokalo] challenge || provoke, incite.

προκαταβολή, η [prokatavolee] prepayment, advance payment || deposit.

προκαταβολικώς [prokatavoleekos] in advance, beforehand.

προκαταλαμβάνω [prokatalamvano] forestall, occupy beforehand.

προκατάληψη, η [prokataleepsee] bias, prejudice.

προκαταρκτικός [prokatarkteekos] preliminary, preparatory.

προκατειλημμένος [prokateeleemenos] biased, prejudiced.

προκάτοχος, ο [prokatohos] predecessor || previous holder, previous occupant.

πρόκειται [prokeete] it's a matter of || it's a question of || περί τίνος ~; what's it all about? || ~ να έλθω I am due to come.

προκήρυξη, η [prokeereeksee] proclamation, announcement || manifesto.

πρόκληση, η [prokleesee] affront, challenge || provocation, instigation.

προκλητικός [prokleeteekos] provocative, provoking || seductive.

προκόβω [prokovo] progress, succeed, prosper, make good.

προκομμένος [prokomenos] hardworking, diligent.

προκοπή, η [prokopee] progress || industry || success.

προκρίνω [prokreeno] prefer, choose || predetermine.

προκυμαία, η [prokeemea] quay, pier, jetty.

προκύπτω [prokeepto] arise || result, ensue.

προλαβαίνω [prolaveno] get a start on, forestall || catch, overtake || (σε χρόνο) be on time, manage || have enough time for.

προλεγόμενα, τα [prolegomena]
πλ preface, foreword.

προλέγω [prolego] forecast, predict
|| say previously.

προλετάριος [proletareeos]
proletarian.

προληπτικός [proleepteekos]
precautionary, preventive ||
superstitious.

πρόληψη, η [proleepsee]
prevention || superstition.

πρόλογος, ο [prologos] prologue,
preface, preamble.

προμαντεύω [promantevo]
prophesy, foretell, predict.

πρόμαχος, ο [promahos]
champion, defender, protector.

προμελέτη, η [promeletee]
preliminary study || premeditation ||
εκ προμελέτης deliberately ||
premeditated.

προμεσημβρία, η
[promeseemvreea] forenoon,
morning.

προμήθεια, η [promeetheea]
supply, provision, supplying,
victualling || (ποσοστό) commission,
brokerage.

προμηθευτής, ο [promeethevtees]
provider, purveyor, supplier.

προμηθεύομαι [promeethevome]
get, supply o.s. with.

προμηθεύω [promeethevo] supply,
provide, furnish.

προμηνύω [promeeneeo] portend,
presage, foretell.

προνοητικός [pronoeeteekos]
having foresight, provident, careful.

πρόνοια, η [proneea] care,
concern, precaution || providence,
welfare.

προνόμιο, το [pronomeeo]
privilege, advantage || gift, talent.

προνομιούχος [pronomeeouhos]
privileged, favoured.

προνοώ [pronoo] foresee, forecast ||
provide for, think of.

προξενείο, το [prokseneeo]
consulate.

προξενητής, ο [proksenetees]
intermediary, matchmaker.

προξενιά, η [proksenia]
matchmaking.

πρόξενος, ο [proksenos]
(διπλωμάτης) consul.

προξενώ [prokseno] cause,
occasion, inflict, bring about.

προοδευτικός [proodevteekos]
progressive, forward || gradual.

προοδεύω [proodevo] progress,
make headway || develop.

πρόοδος, η [proodos] advance,
progress || development,
improvement || (μάθημ)
progression.

προοίμιο, το [proeemeeo] preface,
prelude, preamble.

προοπτική, η [proopteekee]
perspective || prospect in view.

προορίζω [prooreezo] destine,
intend, foreordain.

προορισμός, ο [prooreesmos] end,
intention || destination.

προπαγάνδα, η [propaganda]
propaganda.

προπαρασκευή, η
[proparaskevee] preparation ||
coaching.

προπέλα, η [propela] propeller.

πρόπερσι [propersee] two years
ago.

προπέτασμα, το [propetasma]
screen || ~ **καπνού** smoke screen.

προπληρώνω [propleerono] pay in
advance.

πρόποδες, οι [propodes] πλ foot of
mountain.

προπολεμικός [propolemeekos]
prewar.

προπόνηση, η [proponeesee]
training, coaching.

πρόποση, η [propose] toast
(drink).

προπύλαια, τα [propeelea] πλ propylaea.

προπύργιο, το [propeeryo] rampart, bulwark, bastion.

προς [pros] towards || (για) for || at || in || ~ όφελός μου to my advantage, to my good || ~ τιμή του in his honour, for his sake || ~ το παρόν for the present || ένα ~ ένα one by one || ως ~ εμέ as far as I am concerned || ~ Θεού! for God's sake! || ~ τούτοις moreover || ~ δε in addition, furthermore.

προσάγω [prosago] put forward, exhibit, produce.

προσάναμα, το [prosanama] tinder, firewood || fuel.

προσανατολίζομαι [prosanatoleezome] find one's bearings.

προσανατολίζω [prosanatoleezo] orientate || direct, guide.

προσαράσσω [prosaraso] run aground, be stranded.

προσαρμογή, η [prosarmoyee] adaptation, accommodation || adjustment.

προσαρμόζω [prosarmozo] fit to || adapt, adjust, apply.

προσάρτημα, το [prosarteema] accessory, annexe, addition.

προσάρτηση, η [prosarteesee] annexation.

προσαρτώ [prosarto] append, attach || annex.

προσβάλλω [prosvalo] assail, attack || (υγεία) harm, injure || (δυσαρεστώ) hurt, offend || (διαθήκη) challenge.

προσβλητικός [prosvleeteekos] offensive, abusive, insolent.

προσβολή, η [prosvolee] onset, attack || (υγείας) fit, stroke || offence, insult.

προσγειώνομαι [prosyeeonome] land.

προσγείωση, η [prosyeeosee] landing, alighting.

προσδίδω [prosdeedo] lend, add to, give.

προσδιορίζω [prosdeeoreezo] determine, define, fix || allocate, assign.

προσδοκώ [prosdoko] hope, expect, anticipate.

προσεγγίζω [prosengeezo] put near || approach, come near || (κατά προσέγγιση) approximate || (ναυτ) put in at, land at.

προσεκτικός [prosekteekos] attentive, heedful, mindful || careful.

προσέλευση, η [proselevsee] arrival, approach.

προσελκύω [proselkeeo] (προσοχή) attract, win, draw, catch || (υποστηρικτές) gain, win over.

προσέρχομαι [proserhome] attend, present o.s. || apply for.

προσευχή, η [prosevhee] prayer.

προσεύχομαι [prosevhome] pray, say one's prayers.

προσεχής, η [proseehees] next || forthcoming.

προσέχω [proseho] pay attention to, notice || be attentive, be mindful || (κόπιο) take care of.

προσεχώς [prosehos] shortly, soon, in a short time.

προσηλυτίζω [proseeleeteezo] convert, proselytize.

προσηλωμένος [proseelomenos] attached to, devoted to, absorbed in.

προσηλώνω [proseelono] nail, fix || (μεταφ) look fixedly (at).

πρόσθεση, η [prosthesees] addition, increase.

πρόσθετος [prosthetos] additional, extra.

προσθέτω [prostheto] add, sum up || mix with.

προσθήκη, η [prostheekee] addition, increase.

πρόσθιος [prostheeos] front, fore.

προσιτός [proseetos] attainable, accessible || (τιμή) reasonable, within one's means.

πρόσκαιρος [proskeros] transitory, passing, momentary.

προσκαλώ [proskalo] call, send for || (νομ) summon, subpoena || (σε γεύμα κτλ) invite.

προσκεκλημένος [proskeklemenos] invited.

προσκέφαλο, το [proskefalo] pillow, cushion.

πρόσκληση, η [proskleesee] call, summons || (σε δεξίωση κτλ) invitation || (στρατ) calling up || (εισιτήριο δωρεάν) complimentary ticket.

προσκλητήριο, το [proskleeteereeo] invitation (card) || (στρατ) call, roll call || (ναυτ) muster roll.

προσκόλληση, η [proskoleesee] adherence, attaching || fidelity.

προσκολλώ [proskolo] stick, attach, paste on || second, attach.

προσκομίζω [proskomeezo] bring forward, bring || offer.

πρόσκοπος, ο [proskopos] scout || boy scout.

προσκρούω [proskrouo] crash || strike (against) || be opposed to.

προσκύνημα, το [proskeeneema] adoration || submission || place of pilgrimage.

προσκυνητής, ο [proskeeneetees] pilgrim.

προσκυνώ [proskeeno] adore, worship || pay homage to, yield.

προσλαμβάνω [proslamvano] take on, engage, employ.

προσμένω [prosmeno] wait for, hope for.

πρόσμειξη, η [prosmeeksee] blending, mixing.

πρόσοδος, η [prosodos] income, revenue || (εμπόριο) profit || yield.

προσοδοφόρος [prosodoforos] productive, profitable, lucrative.

προσόν, το [proson] aptitude, fitness, qualification || advantage.

προσοχή, η [prosohee] attention, notice || caution, precaution, care.

πρόσοψη, η [prosopsee] façade, front(age).

προσόψι, το [prosopsee] towel.

προσπάθεια, η [prospatheea] endeavour, effort, attempt, labour.

προσπαθώ [prospatho] try, attempt.

προσπερνώ [prosperno] overtake || (μεταφ) surpass.

προσποίηση, η [prospieesee] pretence, sham.

προσποιητός [prospieetos] affected, assumed, feigned.

προσποιούμαι [prospeeoume] affect, put on || pretend.

προσταγή, η [prostayee] order, ordering, command.

προστάζω [prostazo] order, direct, command.

προστακτική, η [prostakteekee] (γραμμ) imperative (mood).

προστασία, η [prostaseea] protection, defence.

προστατευόμενος, ο [prostatevomenos] protégé.

προστατευτικός [prostatevteekos] protecting || condescending.

προστατεύω [prostatevo] defend, protect || extend patronage to.

προστάτης, ο [prostates] protector, patron || (ανατ) prostate.

προστίθεμαι [prosteetheme] be added, be mixed (with).

πρόστιμο, το [prosteemo] fine, penalty.

προστρέχω [prostreho] rush up, run up || resort to, turn to.

προστριβή, η [prostreevee] friction, rubbing || (μεταφ) dispute.

προστυχιά, η [prosteehia] vulgarity, rudeness, contemptible act.

πρόστυχος [prosteehos] vile, rude, ill-mannered || of bad quality.

προσύμφωνο, το [proseemfono] preliminary agreement, draft agreement.

πρόσφατος [prosfatos] recent, new || (μόδα) modern.

προσφέρομαι [prosferome] offer || be appropriate, be fitting.

προσφέρω [prosfero] offer, present, give.

προσφεύγω [prosfevgo] have recourse to, turn to.

προσφιλής [prosfeelees] dear, loved, precious.

προσφορά, η [prosfora] offer, offering, proposal, bid || thing offered.

πρόσφορος [prosforos] convenient, opportune, suitable.

πρόσφυγας, ο [prosfeegas] refugee.

προσφυγή, η [prosfeeyee] recourse, resort || (νομ) legal redress, appeal.

προσφυής [prosfiees] suitable, well-adapted, fitting.

πρόσχαρος [prosharos] cheerful, lively, merry, gay.

προσχέδιο, το [proshedeeo] rough draft, sketch.

πρόσχημα, το [prosheema] pretext, excuse.

προσχωρώ [proshoro] join, go over (to) || cleave (to), adhere (to).

προσωδία, η [prosodeea] prosody.

προσωνυμία, η [prosoneemeea] nickname, name.

προσωπάρχης, ο [prosoparhees] personnel officer, staff manager.

προσωπείο, το [prosopeeo] mask.

προσωπικό, το [prosopeeko] personnel, staff || (σπιτιού) servants.

προσωπικός [prosopeekos] personal.

προσωπικότητα, η [prosopeekoteeta] personality, individuality.

προσωπικώς [prosopeekos] personally.

προσωπίδα, η [prosopeeda] mask.

πρόσωπο, το [prosopo] face, visage || person || (θεάτρου) role, character, part.

προσωπογραφία, η [prosopografeea] portrait painting, portrait.

προσωποποίηση, η [prosopopieesee] personification || impersonation.

προσωρινός [prosoreenos] provisional, passing, fleeting.

πρόταση, η [protasee] proposal, suggestion, offer, motion || (γραμμ) sentence || clause.

προτείνω [proteeno] extend, stretch out, put forward || propose, suggest.

προτελευταίος [protelevteos] last but one.

προτεραιότητα, η [protereoteeta] priority, primacy.

προτέρημα, το [protereema] gift, faculty, advantage, talent.

πρότερος [proteros] earlier, previous to, prior (to).

προτέρων [proteron]: εκ των ~ beforehand.

προτεσταντισμός, ο [protestanteesmos] Protestantism.

προτίθεμαι [proteetheme] intend, propose, mean, think.

προτίμηση, η [proteemeesee] preference, predilection.

προτιμότερος [proteemoteros] preferable to.

προτιμώ [proteemo] prefer, like better.

προτομή, η [protomee] bust.

προτού [protou] before || previously.

προτρέπω [protrepo] exhort, instigate, incite.

προτροπή, η [protropee] exhortation, prompting.

πρότυπο, το [proteepo] original, pattern, model, example || mould.

πρότυπος [proteepos] model.

προϋπαντώ [prooepanto] go to meet.

προϋπάρχω [prooeparho] pre-exist || (σε χρόνο) come before.

προϋπόθεση, η [prooeepothesee] assumption, presumption.

προϋποθέτω [prooeepotheto] presuppose, presume.

προϋπολογίζω [prooeepoloyeezo] estimate, compute beforehand.

προϋπολογισμός, ο [prooeepoloyeesmos] estimate || budget.

προφανής [profanees] obvious, evident, plain, clear.

προφανώς [profanos] obviously, evidently, manifestly.

πρόφαση, η [profasee] pretext, excuse, pretence.

προφέρ(ν)ω [profer(n)o] pronounce, utter, articulate.

προφητεία, η [profeeteea] prophecy, prophetic utterance.

προφητεύω [profeeteevo] prophesy, predict.

προφήτης, ο [profeetees] prophet.

προφητικός [profeeteekos] prophetic.

προφθάνω [profthano] anticipate, forestall || catch, overtake, overhaul || (σε χρόνο) be in time for, have the time to.

προφορά, η [profora] pronunciation, accent.

προφτάνω [proftano] βλ **προφθάνω**.

προφυλακή, η [profeelakee] vanguard, outpost.

προφυλακίζω [profeelakeezo] hold in custody, detain.

προφυλακτήρας, ο [profeelakteeras] bumper (AUT).

προφυλακτικός [profeelakteekos] wary, careful || precautionary, preventive.

προφύλαξη, η [profeelaksee] precaution, cautiousness.

προφυλάσσομαι [profeelasome] take precautions, protect o.s.

προφυλάσσω [profeelaso] protect, preserve (from), defend.

πρόχειρος [proheeros] ready, handy || impromptu.

προχθές [prohthes] the day before yesterday.

προχωρώ [prohoro] go forward, advance || progress, gain ground.

προωθώ [prootho] impel || push forward, urge on.

πρόωρος [prooros] premature, untimely, hasty.

πρύμ(ν)η [preem(n)ee] stern, poop.

πρύτανης, ο [preetanees] head of university, dean.

πρώην [proeen] former, ex-.

πρωθυπουργός, ο [protheepourgos] prime minister, premier.

πρωί [proee] in the morning || (ουσ) morning.

πρώιμος [proeemos] untimely, premature || (για φυτά) precocious, early.

πρωινός [proeenos] morning || rising early.

πρωινό, το [proeeno] morning || (πρόγευμα) breakfast.

πρωκτός, ο [proktos] anus.

πρώρα, η [prora] prow, bows.

πρώτα [prota] first, at first || before, formerly, once.

πρωταγωνιστής, ο [protagoneestees] protagonist, hero.

πρωτάθλημα, το [protathleema] championship.

πρωτάκουστος [protakoustos] unheard-of, unprecedented.

πρωταρχικός [protarheekos] most important.

πρωτεία, τα [proteea] πλ first place, primacy, precedence.

πρωτεργάτης, ο [protergatees] perpetrator, pioneer, cause.

πρωτεύουσα, η [protevousa] capital, metropolis.

πρωτεύω [protevo] be first, lead, surpass, triumph (over).

πρωτοβάθμιος [protovathmeeos] of the first degree.

πρωτοβουλία, η [protovouleea] initiative.

πρωτοβρόχια, τα [protovroheea] πλ first rains in autumn.

πρωτόγονος [protogonos] primitive || (ήθη) rough, rude, unpolished.

πρωτοδικείο, το [protoδeekeeo] court of first instance.

πρωτοετής [protoetees] first-year.

πρωτόκολλο, το [protokolo] register, record || protocol, etiquette.

Πρωτομαγιά, η [protomaya] May Day.

πρωτομηνιά, η [protomeenia] first day of month.

πρώτο [proto] first, firstly, in the first place, to start with.

πρωτοπορεία, η [protoporeea] vanguard.

πρωτόπορος, ο [protoporos] pioneer, forerunner, innovator.

πρώτος [protos] first, foremost || best, top || initial, elementary || (αριθμός) prime.

πρωτοστατώ [protostato] lead.

πρωτότοκος, ο [prototokos] first-born, oldest.

πρωτοτυπία, η [prototeepeea] originality || eccentricity.

πρωτότυπο, το [prototeepo] original, pattern, model.

πρωτότυπος [prototeepos] original, novel, singular.

πρωτοφανής [protofanees] new, fresh || astonishing.

Πρωτοχρονιά, η [protohronia] New Year's Day.

πρωτύτερα [proteetera] earlier on, at first, before.

πταισματοδικείο, το [ptesmatoδeekeeo] police court.

πτέρυγα, η [ptereega] wing.

πτερύγιο, το [ptereeyo] fin || aileron, wing flap.

πτερωτός [pterotos] winged.

πτηνό, το [pteeno] bird, fowl.

πτηνοτροφεία, η [pteenotrofeea] poultry farming.

πτήση, η [pteesee] flight, flying.

πτοώ [ptoo] intimidate, frighten, browbeat.

πτυχή, η [pteehee] fold, pleat || wrinkle || (πανταλονιού) crease.

πτυχίο, το [pteeheeo] diploma, certificate.

πτυχιούχος [pteeheeouhos] graduate, holding a diploma.

πτώμα, το [ptoma] corpse, dead body || (ζώου) carcass.

πτώση, η [ptosee] fall, tumble || collapse || drop || (γραμμ) case.

πτώχευση, η [ptohevsee] bankruptcy, failure, insolvency.

πτωχεύω [ptohevo] go bankrupt || become poor.

πτωχοκομείο, το [ptohokomeeo] poorhouse.

πτωχός [ptohos] poor, needy.

πυγμαχία, η [peegmaheea] boxing, pugilism.

πυγμή, η [peegmee] fist || (μεταφ) vigour, determination.

πυγολαμπίδα, η [peegolampeeδa] glow-worm, firefly.

πυθμένας, ο [peethmenas] bottom.

πυκνά [peekna] closely, densely, thickly.

πυκνός [peeknos] thick, dense, closely-packed, close || (γένεια) bushy.

πυκνότητα, η [peeknoteeta] density, compactness, thickness || (κυμάτων) frequency.

πυκνώνω [peeknono] thicken, condense, grow thick || make more frequent.

πυκνωτής, ο [peeknotees] (ηλεκ) condenser.

πύλη, η [peelee] gate, gateway.

πυξίδα, η [peekseeða] (mariner's) compass || box.

πύο, το [peeo] pus, matter.

πυρ, το [peer] fire, firing.

πυρά, η [peera] fire || (μεταφ) sensation of burning.

πυρακτώνω [peeraktono] make red-hot, glow.

πυραμίδα, η [peerameeða] pyramid.

πύραυλος, ο [peeravlos] rocket.

πύργος, ο [peergos] tower || castle, palace || (ναυτ) bridge house.

πυρετός, ο [peeretos] high temperature, fever || (μεταφ) activity, energy.

πυρετώδης [peeretoðees] feverish || (μεταφ) restless, feverish.

πυρήνας, ο [peereenas] stone, pip || centre, core || nucleus.

πυρηνέλαιο, το [peereeneleo] oil from stones || seed oil.

πυρηνικός [peereeneekos] nuclear.

πύρινος [peereenos] burning, fiery, red-hot || (μεταφ) ardent, fervent.

πυρίτης, ο [peereetees] pyrites, flint.

πυρίτιδα, η [peereeteeða] gunpowder, powder.

πυρκαϊά, η [peerkaeea] fire, burning, conflagration.

πυροβολητής, ο [peerovoleetees] gunner.

πυροβολικό, το [peerovoleeko] artillery.

πυροβολισμός, ο [peerovoleesmos] firing, shot.

πυροβολώ [peerovolo] fire || shoot at || shell.

πυρομαχικά, τα [peeromaheeka] πλ munitions || ammunition.

πυροσβέστης, ο [peerosvestees] fireman.

πυροσβεστική [peerosvesteekee]: ~ υπηρεσία fire brigade.

πυροτέχνημα, το [peerotehneema] firework, cracker.

πυρπολικό, το [peerpoleeko] fire ship.

πυρπολώ [peerpolo] set on fire, burn down, consume by fire.

πυρσός, ο [peersos] torch, brand || beacon.

πυρώνω [peerono] get red-hot, heat.

πυτζάμα, η [peedzama] pyjamas.

πυώδης [peeoðees] full of pus.

πωλείται [poleete] ' ~ ' 'for sale'.

πώληση, η [poleesee] sale, selling.

πωλητής, ο [poleetees] seller || salesman || shop assistant.

πωλήτρια, η [poleetreea] seller || saleswoman.

πωλώ [polo] sell || (μεταφ) sell, betray.

πώμα, το [poma] stopper, plug || (μποτίλιας) cork || lid, cover.

πωρόλιθος, ο [poroleethos] porous stone.

πώρωση, η [porosee] hardening || (μεταφ) insensibility, callousness.

πώς [pos] how?, what? || ~ όχι; why not? || ~! yes, certainly.

πως [pos] that.

πως [pos] somewhat, somehow, in any way.

Ρ, ρ

ραββίνος, ο [raveenos] rabbi.

ραβδί, το [ravðee] cane, stick.

ραβδίζω [ravðeezo] flog, thrash, cane.

ράβδος, η [ravδos] stick, staff || (μαγική) wand || (εκκλ) pastoral staff || (σιδηροδρομική) rail.

ράβδωση, η [ravδosee] stripe || (αρχιτεκτονική) fluting || groove.

ραβδωτός [ravδotos] striped || fluted || lined, ruled.

ράβω [ravo] sew up, sew on || stitch || (κοστούμι) have a suit made.

ραγάδα, η [ragaδa] crack, fissure, chink.

ραγδαίος [ragδeos] violent, turbulent || (πτώση) rapid, headlong || (πρόοδος) rapid, speedy.

ραγδαίως [ragδeos] violently, impetuously, swiftly.

ραγίζω [rayeezo] crack, split.

ράγισμα, το [rayeesma] crack, fissure, split.

ραδιενέργεια, η [raδienerya] radioactivity.

ραδιενεργός [raδienergos] radioactive.

ραδίκι, το [raδeekee] chicory, dandelion.

ραδιογραφία, η [raδeeografeea] X-ray photography.

ραδιοθεραπεία, η [raδeeotherapeea] X-ray treatment.

ραδιολογία, η [raδeeoloyeea] radiology.

ράδιο, το [raδeeo] radium.

ραδιοτηλεγράφημα, το [raδeeoteelegrafeema] radiotelegram.

ραδιοτηλεγραφία, η [raδeeoteelegrafeea] radiotelegraphy.

ραδιοτηλεφωνία, η [raδeeoteelefoneea] radiotelephony.

ραδιουργία, η [raδiouryeea] intrigue, machination.

ραδιούργος [raδiourgos] scheming, intriguing, plotting.

ραδιόφωνο, το [raδeeofono] radio.

ράθυμος [ratheemos] languid, listless, lazy.

ραίνω [reno] sprinkle, scatter, spread.

ράισμα [raeesma] βλ **ράγισμα**.

ρακένδυτος [rakenδeetos] in rags, tattered.

ρακί, το [rakee] kind of spirit.

ράκος, το [rakos] rag, tatters || (μεταφ) physical wreck.

ράμμα, το [rama] stitch, thread.

ραμμένος [ramenos] sewn.

ραμολής, ο [ramolees] imbecile, half-wit.

ραμφίζω [ramfeezo] peck at, pick up.

ράμφος, το [ramfos] (μεγάλων πουλιών) bill, beak || (μεταφ) burner, jet.

ρανίδα, η [raneeδa] drop, blob.

ραντεβού, το [rantevou] meeting, engagement, rendezvous.

ραντίζω [ranteezo] sprinkle, spray, water.

ράντισμα, το [ranteesma] sprinkling, watering.

ραντιστήρι, το [ranteesteeree] watering can || (εκκλ) sprinkler.

ράντσο, το [rantso] campbed.

ρανάνι, το [rapanee] radish.

ραπίζω [rapeezo] slap or smack in the face.

ράπισμα, το [rapeesma] clout, slap.

ραπτάδικο, το [raptaδeeko] βλ **ραφτάδικο**.

ράπτης, ο [raptees] tailor.

ραπτικά, τα [rapteeka] πλ fees for tailoring, fees for sewing.

ραπτική, η [rapteekee] βλ **ραφτική**.

ραπτομηχανή, η [raptomeehanee] sewing machine.

ράπτρια, η [raptreea] dressmaker.

ράπτω [rapto] βλ **ράβω**.

ράσο, το [raso] frock, cassock.

ρασοφόρος, ο [rasoforos] priest, monk.

ράτσα, η [ratsa] race, generation, breed || από ~ thoroughbred.

ραφείο, το [rafeeo] tailor's shop.

ραφή, η [rafee] dressmaking || stitching, seam.

ράφι, το [rafee] shelf || (τοίχου) bracket || μένω στο ~ be left on the shelf, be an old maid.

ραφινάρισμα, το [rafeenareesma] refinement.

ραφινάρω [rafeenaro] refine || purify, polish.

ραφτάδικο, το [raftaδeeko] tailor's shop.

ράφτης [raftees] βλ ράπτης.

ραφτικά, τα [rafteeka] βλ ραπτικά.

ραφτική, η [rafteekee] dressmaking, sewing, tailoring.

ραχάτι, το [rahatee] lazing about, idling, leisure.

ράχη, η [rahee] back, backbone || (βιβλίου) spine || (βουνού) crest, ridge.

ραχιτικός [raheeteekos] suffering from rickets.

ραχοκοκκαλιά, η [rahokokalia] backbone, spine.

ράψιμο, το [rapseemo] sewing, stitching || tailoring, dressmaking.

ραψωδία, η [rapsoδeea] rhapsody.

ρεαλισμός, ο [realeesmos] realism.

ρεαλιστής, ο [realeestees] realist.

ρεβεγιόν, το [reveyon] midnight supper.

ρεβίθι, το [reveethee] chickpea.

ρέγγα, η [renga] herring.

ρέγουλα, η [regoula] order, regular arrangement || moderation, measure.

ρεζέρβα, η [rezerva] stock || (λάστιχου κτλ) spare wheel.

ρεζιλεύω [rezeelevo] ridicule, make a fool of || humiliate.

ρεζίλι, το [rezeelee] shame, derision, object of ridicule ||

γίνομαι ~ become a laughing stock.

ρεζιλίκι [rezeeleekee] βλ ρεζίλι.

ρείθρο, το [reethro] watercourse, rivulet || ditch, gutter (of street).

ρεκλάμα, η [reklama] advertisement || show, display.

ρεκλαμάρω [reklamaro] advertise.

ρεκόρ, το [rekor] record.

ρεμάλι, το [remalee] worthless person.

ρεματιά, η [rematia] ravine, torrent, riverbed.

ρεμβάζω [remvazo] muse, daydream, be in a reverie.

ρεμβασμός, ο [remvasmos] musing, reverie.

ρέμπελος [rembelos] lazy, sluggish || disorderly.

ρεπάνι, το [repanee] radish.

ρεπερτόριο, το [repertoreeo] repertoire.

ρεπό, το [repo] time off, break, rest period, rest.

ρέπω [repo] lean, incline, slope || (μεταφ) tend towards.

ρεσιτάλ, το [reseetal] recital.

ρέστα, τα [resta] πλ change.

ρετάλι, το [retalee] remnant.

ρετσίνα, η [retseena] resinated wine.

ρετσινόλαδο, το [retseenolaδo] castor oil.

ρεύμα, το [revma] current, stream, flow || (αέρος) draught.

ρευματισμός, ο [revmateesmos] rheumatism.

ρεύομαι [revome] belch.

ρεύση, η [revsee] outflow, flowing || emission.

ρευστοποιώ [revstopeeo] liquefy.

ρευστός [revstos] fluid, liquid || (μεταφ) fickle, inconstant, changeable.

ρευστότητα, η [revstoteeta] fluidity || (μεταφ) inconstancy.

ρεφενές, ο [refenes] share, quota.

ρεφορμιστής, ο [reformeestees] reformist.

ρέψιμο, το [repseemo] belching || decay.

ρέω [reo] flow, stream || (σταγόνες) trickle || (δάκρυα) fall.

ρήγας, ο [reegas] (χαρτιά) king.

ρήγμα, το [reegma] crack, breach, fissure, hole || (μεταφ) rupture.

ρήμα, το [reema] word, saying || (γραμμ) verb.

ρημάδι, το [reemadee] ruin || wreckage, derelict || **κλείσ' το ~** shut the blooming thing!

ρημάζω [reemazo] ruin, destroy || fall into ruins.

ρήξη, η [reeksee] rupture, breach || conflict, quarrel, dispute.

ρητίνη, η [reeteenee] resin.

ρητό, το [reeto] maxim, saying, motto.

ρητορεύω [reetorevo] make speeches, harangue.

ρητορική, η [reetoreekee] oratory.

ρητός [reetos] formal, explicit, flat, positive.

ρήτρα, η [reetra] clause, proviso, provision.

ρήτορας, ο [reetoras] orator.

ρητώς [reetos] explicitly, expressly, flatly.

ρηχά, τα [reeha] πλ shallows.

ρίγα, η [reega] ruler, measuring rule || line, stripe.

ρίγανη, η [reeganee] origanum.

ριγέ [reeye] striped.

ρίγος, το [reegos] shiver || thrill.

ριγώ [reego] shiver, tremble, thrill.

ριγωτός [reegotos] (χάρτης) lined, ruled || (ύφασμα) striped.

ρίζα, η [reeza] root || (βουνού) foot, base || (μεταφ) origin, source, cause.

ριζικό, το [reezeeko] destiny, fortune, lot, fate.

ριζικός [reezeekos] radical, fundamental.

ριζόγαλο, το [reezogalo] rice pudding.

ριζόνερο, το [reezonero] rice water.

ριζοσπάστης, ο [reezospastees] radical.

ριζοσπαστικός [reezospasteekos] radical.

ριζώνω [reezono] become established, become fixed, take root, grow.

ρίμα, η [reema] rhyme.

ρινικός [reeneekos] nasal.

ρινίσματα, τα [reeneesmata] πλ filings.

ρινόκερος, ο [reenokeros] rhinoceros.

ριξιά, η [reeksia] throw, cast(ing) || (όπλου) charge || shot, firing.

ρίξιμο, το [reekseemo] casting, throwing || dropping || (όπλου) firing, shooting.

ριπή, η [reepee] burst of firing, throwing || (ανέμου) gust, blast.

ρίπτω [reepto] βλ **ρίχνω**.

ρίχνομαι [reehnome] fling o.s., rush || (στο νερό) plunge.

ρίχνω [reehno] throw, fling, cast || (βόμβα) drop || (όπλο) shoot, fire || (ανατρέπω) overthrow, defeat || (τοίχο) pull down, demolish || (δένδρο) hew, fell || **ρίχνει βροχή** it's raining.

ριψοκινδυνεύω [reepsokeendeenevo] risk, endanger || take risks.

ρόγχος, ο [ronghos] rattle, blowing || death rattle.

ρόδα, η [roda] wheel.

ροδάκινο, το [rodakeeno] peach.

ροδαλός [rodalos] rosy, light pink.

ροδέλα, η [rodela] washer.

ρόδι, το [rodee] pomegranate.

ροδινός [rodeenos] rosy || (μεταφ) rose-coloured, bright.

ροδίτης, ο [rodeetees] kind of pink grape.

ροδοδάφνη, η [rododafnee]
oleander.

ροδοκόκκινος [rodokokeenos]
ruddy, rose-red.

ρόδο, το [rodo] rose.

ροζ [roz] pink.

ροζιάρικος [rozeareekos] gnarled.

ρόζος, ο [rozos] knot, node ||
(δακτύλων) knuckle.

ροή, η [roee] flow, flood || (νέου)
discharge, running.

ρόκα, η [roka] distaff || (χόρτο)
rocket.

ροκάνα, η [rokana] (παιχνίδι) rattle.

ροκάνι, το [rokanee] plane.

ροκανίδι, το [rokaneedee] chip,
shaving.

ροκανίζω [rokaneezo] plane ||
(μεταφ) gnaw, crunch.

ροκέτα, η [roketa] rocket.

ρολό, το [rolo] cylindrical roll ||
shutter.

ρολογάς, ο [rologas] watchmaker,
clockmaker.

ρολόι, το [roloee] (τοίχου) clock ||
(χεριού) watch || (μετρητής) meter ||
πάει ~ it's going smoothly.

ρόλος, ο [rolos] roll || (θεατρικός)
part, role || (μεταφ) part || δεν
παίζει ρόλο it's not important.

ρομάντζο, το [romantzo] romance.

ρομαντικός [romanteekos]
romantic.

ρομαντικότητα, η
[romanteekoteeta] romanticism.

ρόμβος, ο [romvos] rhombus.

ρόμπα, η [romba] dressing gown.

ρόπαλο, το [ropalo] club.

ροπή, η [ropee] inclination,
propensity || (μηχανής) momentum.

ρουζ, το [rouz] rouge.

ρουθούνι, το [routhounee] nostril.

ρουθουνίζω [routhouneezo] snort,
sniff, snuffle.

ρουκέτα [rouketa] βλ ροκέτα.

ρουλεμάν, το [rouleman] ball
bearings, roller bearings.

ρουλέτα, η [rouleta] roulette.

Ρουμανία, η [roumaneea]
Rumania.

ρουμανικός [roumaneekos]
Rumanian.

Ρουμάνος, ο [roumanos]
Rumanian.

ρούμι, το [roumee] rum.

ρουμπίνι, το [roumbeenee] ruby.

ρούπι, το [roupee] measure of
length (.08 m) || δεν το κουνάω
~ I refuse to move.

ρους, ο [rous] βλ ροή.

ρουσφέτι, το [rousfetee] favour,
string pulling, political favour.

ρουτίνα, η [routeena] routine.

ρούφηγ(μ)α, το [roufee(g)ma]
noisy sipping, gulp, sucking in.

ρουφηξιά, η [roufeeksia] mouthful,
sip || (πίπας κτλ) puff.

ρουφήχτρα, η [roufeehtra]
whirlpool.

ρουφιάνος, ο [roufeeanos] pimp ||
schemer.

ρουφώ [roufo] draw in, suck up,
absorb, sip.

ρουχικά, το [rouheeka] πλ clothing,
garments.

ρούχο, το [rouho] cloth, stuff,
material || (φόρεμα) dress, attire.

ρόφημα, το [rofeema] hot drink.

ροχαλητό, το [rohaleeto] snore,
snoring.

ροχαλίζω [rohaleezo] snore.

ρόχαλο, το [rohalo] phlegm, spit.

ρυάκι, το [reeakee] stream, brook,
rivulet.

ρύγχος, το [reenghos] muzzle,
nose, snout || nozzle.

ρύζι, το [reezee] rice.

ρυζόγαλο, το [reezogalo] rice
pudding.

ρυθμίζω [reethmeezo] (ρολόι)
regulate, set right || (τα του σπιτιού)
manage || (υποθέσεις) settle ||
(λογαριασμούς) close, make up.

ρυθμικός [reethmeekos] rhythmical.

ρύθμιση, η [reethmeesee] regulating, adjusting.

ρυθμιστής, ο [reethmeestees] regulator.

ρυθμός, ο [reethmos] rhythm, rate || (μουσ) cadence || (αρχιτεκτονική) order, style.

ρυμοτομία, η [reemotomeea] street plan, roadmaking.

ρυμούλκα, η [reemoulka] trailer.

ρυμούλκηση, η [reemoulkeesee] towing, dragging.

ρυμουλκό, το [reemoulko] tugboat, steam tug || (τρακτέρ) tractor.

ρυμουλκώ [reemoulko] tow, tug, drag, pull || (μεταφ) drag by the nose.

ρυπαίνω [reepeno] make dirty, soil || (μεταφ) defile, tarnish.

ρύπανση, η [reepansee] dirtying, blemishing, defiling || pollution.

ρύπος, ο [reepos] filth, dirt || (μεταφ) disgrace, shame.

ρυτίδα, η [reeteeda] wrinkle, seam, line || (της θάλασσας) ripple.

ρυτιδώνω [reeteedono] wrinkle, line || get wrinkled.

ρω, το [ro] the letter P.

ρώγα, η [roga] nipple.

ρωγμή, η [rogmee] crack, split, cleft, crevice.

ρωμαίικα, τα [romeika] Modern Greek, Demotic Greek || μίλα ~! come to the point!

ρωμαϊκός [romaeekos] Roman.

Ρωμαίος, ο [romeos] Roman.

ρωμαλέος [romaleos] robust, strong, vigorous, sturdy.

ρώμη, η [romee] vigour, strength, force, robustness.

Ρώμη, η [romee] Rome.

Ρωμιός, ο [romios] modern Greek.

Ρωμιοσύνη, η [romioseenee] the modern Greek people.

Ρωσία, η [roseea] Russia.

Ρώσος, ο [rosos] Russian (person).

ρωτώ [roto] βλ ερωτώ.

Σ, σ

σα [sa] βλ σαν.

σάβανο, το [savano] winding sheet, shroud.

σάββατο, το [savato] Saturday.

σαββατοκύριακο, το [savatokeereeako] weekend.

σαβούρα, η [savoura] rubbish, junk, trash || ballast.

σαγανάκι, το [saganakee] frying pan || (φαγητό) dish of fried cheese.

σαγή, η [sayee] harness.

σαγηνεύω [sayeenevo] seduce, charm, attract.

σαγήνη, η [sayeenee] fascination, enchantment.

σαγόνι, το [sagonee] chin.

σαδισμός, ο [sadeesmos] sadism.

σαδιστής, ο [sadeestees] sadist.

σαθρός [sathros] rotted, decayed, rotten || (μεταφ) groundless.

σαιζόν, η [sezon] season.

σαΐτα, η [saeeta] arrow, dart || weaver's shuttle.

σάκα, η [saka] (μαθητική) satchel || (κυνηγού) game pouch, gamebag || briefcase.

σακάκι, το [sakakee] jacket, coat.

σακαράκα, η [sakaraka] tin lizzie (col), old motorcar, old bike.

σακατεύω [sakatevo] cripple, mutilate, maim || (μεταφ) wear out, exhaust.

σακάτης, ο [sakatees] cripple, maimed person.

σακί, το [sakee] sack, bag.

σακίδιο, το [sakeedeeo] haversack, satchel, small bag.

σακοράφα, η [sakorafa] sack needle, packing needle.

σάκος, ο [sakos] sack, bag, sackful || (ταχυδρομικός) mailbag || kitbag.

σακούλα, η [sakoula] sack, bag || paper bag.

σακούλι, το [sakoulee] sack, small bag.

σακουλιάζω [sakouleeazo] put into a bag, put into a sack, pocket || (για ρούχα) be loose-fitting, not fit well.

σαλάμι, το [salamee] sausage, salami.

σαλαμούρα, η [salamoura] brine.

σαλάτα, η [salata] salad || **τα κάνω ~** make a muddle of it, foul up the works.

σάλεμα, το [salema] moving, stirring, shaking.

σαλεύω [salevo] move, stir, shake || budge.

σάλι, το [salee] shawl.

σάλιαγκας, ο [saleeangas] snail.

σαλιάζω [saleeazo] salivate.

σαλιάρα, η [saleeara] baby's bib.

σαλιαρίζω [saleeareezo] chatter, prattle.

σαλιγκάρι [saleengaree] βλ **σάλιαγκας**.

σάλιο, το [saleeo] saliva, spittle.

σαλιώνω [saleeono] lick, moisten, dampen, wet.

σαλόνι, το [salonee] drawing room || (πλοίου) saloon.

σάλος, ο [salos] swell, surge || (πλοίου) rolling || (μεταφ) disturbance || tumult.

σαλπάρω [salparo] weigh anchor.

σάλπιγκα, η [salpeenga] trumpet, bugle || (ανατ) tube.

σαλπίζω [salpeezo] sound the trumpet.

σάλπισμα, το [salpeesma] trumpet call.

σαλτάρω [saltaro] jump, leap.

σαλτιμπάγκος, ο [salteembangos] fairground acrobat || (μεταφ) charlatan, buffoon.

σάλτος, ο [saltos] jump, leap, bound.

σάλτσα, η [saltsa] gravy, sauce.

σαμάρι, το [samaree] packsaddle.

σαμαρώνω [samarono] saddle, pack.

σαματάς, ο [samatas] (φασαρία) noise, din, roar || fight.

σάματι(ς) [samatee(s)] as though.

σαμπάνια, η [sampaneea] champagne.

σαμποτάζ, το [sampotaz] sabotage.

σαμποτάρω [sampotaro] sabotage.

σαμπρέλα, η [sambrela] inner tube.

σάμπως [sambos] as though || it appears that.

σαν [san] when, as soon as, if || like, as if || **~ σήμερα πέρου** about a year ago today || **~ τι**; like what? || **~ να** as though.

σανατόριο, το [sanatoreeo] sanatorium.

σανδάλι, το [sanðalee] sandal.

σανίδα, η [saneeða] board, beam, plank || (σιδερώματος) ironing board.

σανιδώνω [saneeðono] floor, plank, cover with board.

σανός, ο [sanos] hay, fodder.

σαντιγύ, το [santeeyee] chantilly.

σάντουιτς, το [santoueets] sandwich.

σαντούρι, το [santouree] kind of string instrument.

σαπίζω [sapeezo] rot, spoil, decompose, decay.

σαπίλα, η [sapeela] decay, putridity || (μεταφ) corruption, dishonesty.

σάπιος [sapeeos] decomposed, rotten || corrupt, depraved, wicked.

σαπουνάδα, η [sapounaða] soapsuds, lather.

σαπούνι, το [sapounee] soap || (ξυρίσματος) shaving soap.

σαπουνίζω [sapouneezo] soap || lather.

σαπουνόφουσκα, η
[sapounofouska] soap bubble.

σαπωνοποιός, ο [saponopeeos]
soap manufacturer.

σάρα, η [sara]: n ~ και η μάρα
rabble.

σαράβαλο, το [saravalo] ruin,
wreck || sickly person.

σαράκι, το [sarakee] woodworm ||
(μεταφ) remorse, prick of
conscience.

σαρακοστή, η [sarakostee] Lent.

σαράντα [saranta] forty.

σαρανταποδαρούσα, η
[sarantapoðarousa] centipede.

σαρανταριά, η [sarantaria] forty.

σαραντίζω [saranteezo] become
forty || be forty days since.

σαράφης, ο [sarafees]
moneychanger.

σαρδέλα, η [sarðela] anchovy ||
sardine.

σαρδόνιος [sarðoneeos] sardonic,
sarcastic.

σαρίκι, το [sareekee] turban.

σάρκα, η [sarka] flesh.

σαρκασμός, ο [sarkasmos]
derision, raillery, sarcasm.

σαρκαστικός [sarkasteekos]
sarcastic, jeering, mocking.

σαρκικός [sarkeekos] carnal,
fleshy, sensual.

σαρκοβόρος [sarkovoros],
σαρκοφάγος [sarkofagos]
carnivorous, flesh-eating || η
σαρκοφάγος sarcophagus.

σαρκώδης [sarkoðees] fleshy ||
(φρούτο) pulpy.

σάρκωμα, το [sarkoma] sarcoma,
fleshy growth.

σάρπα, η [sarpa] scarf.

σάρωμα, το [saroma] sweeping.

σαρώνω [sarono] (δωμάτιο) sweep ||
(δρόμο) scavenge || (μεταφ) rake.

σας [sas] you || your.

σασ(σ)ί, το [sasee] chassis.

σαστίζω [sasteezo] disconcert,

embarrass, confuse || get
disconcerted.

σατανάς, ο [satanas] Satan ||
(μεταφ) devilish person.

σατανικός [sataneekos] devilish,
satanical, fiendish.

σατέν, το [saten] satin.

σατράπης, ο [satrapees] satrap ||
(μεταφ) tyrant.

σάτυρα, η [sateera] satire, skit,
lampoon.

σατυρίζω [sateereezo] satirize,
ridicule.

σατυρικός [sateereekos] satirical.

σάτυρος, ο [sateeros] satyr ||
(μεταφ) debauchee.

σαύρα, η [savra] lizard.

σαφήνεια, η [safeeneea] clearness,
distinctness, lucidity.

σαφηνίζω [safeeneezo] clarify,
elucidate, explain.

σαφής [safees] clear, obvious, plain.

σαφώς [safos] clearly, obviously.

σαχλαμάρα, η [sahlamara]
nonsense, rubbish.

σαχλός [sahlos] flat, flabby || stupid.

σβάρνα, η [svarna] harrow.

σβέλτος [sveltos] nimble || slim,
slender.

σβέρκος, ο [sverkos] nape of neck,
scruff.

σβήνω [sveeno] extinguish, quench,
put out || (γράμματα) erase || (διά
τριβής) rub out || (με πένα κτλ) strike
out || (φωτιά) die out || (χρώμα) fade ||
(ενθουσιασμός) subside, die down.

σβήσιμο, το [sveeseemo]
extinction || erasure, rubbing out.

σβηστός [sveestos] put out,
extinguished, switched off.

σβούρα, η [svoura] spinning top.

σβύνω [sveeno] βλ σβήνω.

σβώλος, ο [svolos] lump (of earth) ||
ball, clod.

σγουραίνω [sgoureno] curl ||
become curly.

σγουρός [sgouros] curly, fuzzy, curled || curly-haired.

σε [se] you || to, at, in.

σέβας, το [sevas], **σεβασμός, ο** [sevasmos] regard, reverence, deference.

σεβάσμιος [sevasmeeos] venerable, respectable, reverend.

σεβαστός [sevastos] respected || respectable, considerable.

σέβη, τα [sevee] πλ respects.

σεβντάς, ο [sevntas] love, yearning.

σέβομαι [sevome] respect, venerate, admire, esteem.

σειρά, η [seera] series, succession || row, line, rank || (στην τάξη) turn || sequence, order || **με τη** ~ in turn, in order || **μπαίνω σε** ~ settle down.

σειρήνα, η [seereena] siren, enchantress || hooter, buzzer, alarm.

σειρήτι, το [seereetee] stripe, ribbon, braid.

σεισμικός [seesmeekos] seismic.

σεισμογράφος, ο [seesmografos] seismograph.

σεισμόπληκτος [seesmopleektos] struck by earthquake.

σεισμός, ο [seesmos] earthquake.

σείω [seeo] move, shake, wave.

σέλα, η [sela] saddle.

σέλας, το [selas] brightness, brilliance, radiance || **βόρειο** ~ northern lights, aurora borealis.

σελάχι, το [selahee] gun belt || (ψάρι) ray.

σελήνη, η [seleenee] moon.

σεληνιασμός, ο [seleeneeasmos] epilepsy.

σεληνόφως, το [seleenofos] moonlight.

σελίδα, η [seleeda] page (of book).

σελίνι, το [seleenee] shilling.

σέλινο, το [seleeno] celery.

σελώνω [selono] saddle.

σεμινάριο, το [semeenareeo] seminary.

σεμνός [semnos] decent, unassuming, modest || (ενδυμασία) simple, plain.

σεμνότητα, η [semnoteeta] dignity, modesty, decency.

σεμνότυφος [semnoteefos] prudish, demure, priggish.

σένα [sena] you.

σεντόνι, το [sentonee] sheet.

σεντούκι, το [sentookee] linen closet || box, chest.

σεξ, το [seks] sex.

σεξουαλικότητα, η [seksoualeekoteeta] sexual instinct, sexuality.

Σεπτέμβρης, ο [septemvrees], **Σεπτέμβριος, ο** [septemvreeos] September.

σέρα, η [sera] greenhouse, glasshouse.

σερβίρισμα, το [serveereesma] waiting on, serving.

σερβίρω [serveero] wait at table, serve.

σερβιτόρα, η [serveetora] waitress.

σερβιτόρος, ο [serveetoros] waiter.

σερβίτσιο, το [serveetseeo] dinner service || place setting.

σεργιάνι, το [seryanee] walk, promenade.

σερμπέτι, το [sermbetee] sherbet, syrup.

σέρνομαι [sernome] creep, crawl, drag || drag o.s. along.

σέρνω [serno] draw, pull, drag || (βαρύ πράγμα) haul || (χορό) lead || ~ **φωνή** scream, shriek, cry out.

σεσημασμένος [seseemasmenos] criminal.

σεφτές, ο [seftes] first sale (of a day).

σήκωμα, το [seekoma] raising, lifting || getting out of bed.

σηκωμός, ο [seekomos] rising, rebellion.

σηκώνομαι [seekonome] rise, stand up, get up || (επαναστατώ) rebel.

σηκώνω [seekono] raise, hoist, pick up, lift up || (μεταφέρω) carry || (αφηνίζω) get up || (ανέχομαι) bear, tolerate || ~ **το τραπέζι** clear the table || ~ **στο πόδι** incite, rouse, disturb || ~ **κεφάλι** become arrogant, rebel.

σηκώτι, το [seekotee] liver.

σήμα, το [seema] signal, sign, mark, badge || ~ **κατατεθέν** trademark, registration mark.

σημαδεμένος [seemaδemenos] marked || maimed, scarred.

σημαδεύω [seemaδevo] mark || aim at, take aim at.

σημάδι, το [seemaδee] trace, scar, spot || (ένδειξη) sign, mark, indication.

σημαδούρα, η [seemaδoura] buoy.

σημαία, η [seemea] flag, ensign, colours, standard.

σημαίνω [seemeno] mean, be a sign of, signify || (καμπάνα κτλ) ring, strike, sound, signal || (έχων σημασία) matter, be of consequence.

σημαιοφόρος, ο [seemeoforos] standard bearer || (ναυτ) ensign, sub-lieutenant || (μεταφ) leader.

σήμανση, η [seemansee] marking, stamping || noting of details.

σημαντικός [seemanteekos] important, significant || (πρόσωπο) remarkable, considerable || momentous.

σήμαντρο, το [seemantro] stamp, seal || (εκκλ) special monastery bell.

σημασία, η [seemasea] sense, meaning || importance, gravity, significance.

σημείο, το [seemeeo] sign, mark, proof, indication || (θέση, βαθμός) stage, point || (μαθημ) symbol, sign ||

~ **του ορίζοντος** point of the compass.

σημείωμα, το [seemeeoma] written note, memorandum, record.

σημειωματάριο, το [seemeeomatareeo] notebook, agenda, diary.

σημείωση, η [seemeeosee] written note || remark, comment.

σημειωτέος [seemeeoteos] to be noted || noticeable, noteworthy.

σήμερα [seemera] today || ~ **το απόγευμα** this evening, this afternoon.

σήπομαι [seepome] rot, decay, decompose.

σηπτικός [seepteekos] septic.

σήραγγα, η [seeranga] tunnel.

σηψαιμία, η [seepsemea] septicaemia, blood poisoning.

σήψη, η [seepsee] decay, putrefaction || (ιατρ) sepsis.

σθεναρός [sthenaros] sturdy, strong, vigorous, powerful, robust.

σθένος, το [sthenos] vigour, strength, energy || courage, pluck.

σιαγώνα, η [seeagona] jaw || (ανατ) jawbone.

σιάζω [seeazo] arrange, set in order, straighten, tidy || (επισκευάζω) repair, mend, patch.

σίαλος, ο [seealos] saliva, spittle.

σιάξιμο, το [δecaksecmo] tidying.

σιγά [seega] softly, lightly, gently, slowly || ~ ~ carefully, by degrees.

σιγαλός [seegalos] silent, quiet, gentle, still || (επίρ) slowly.

σιγανός [seeganos] βλ **σιγαλός**.

σιγαρέτο, το [seegareto] cigarette.

σιγή, η [seeyee] silence, hush.

σίγμα, το [seegma] the letter Σ.

σιγοβράζω [seegovrazo] simmer.

σίγουρα [seegoura] for certain, for sure.

σίγουρος [seegouros] certain, assured, sure || (φάρμακο) infallible.

σιγώ [seego] keep quiet, remain silent || die down.

σίδερα, τα [seedera] πλ ironwork || (γραμμές) railway lines || (φυλακή) irons, fetters.

σιδεράς, ο [seederas] blacksmith, ironmonger.

σιδερένιος [seedereneeos] of iron.

σιδερικά, τα [seedereeka] πλ scrap iron || ironware.

σίδερο, το [seedero] iron || (σιδερώματος) flatiron || (μαλλιών) curling tongs.

σιδέρωμα, το [seederoma] ironing, pressing.

σιδερώνω [seederono] iron.

σιδηροδρομικός [seedheeroðromeekos] of railways.

σιδηροδρομικώς [seedheeroðromeekos] by rail, by train.

σιδηρόδρομος, ο [seedheeroðromos] railway, railroad.

σιδηροπυρίτης, ο [seedheeropeereetees] pyrites.

σίδηρος, ο [seedheeros] iron.

σιδηροτροχιά, η [seedheerotrohia] railway track.

σιδηρουργείο, το [seedheerouryeeo] forge, smithy.

σιδηρουργός, ο [seedheerourgos] blacksmith.

σιδηρωρυχείο, το [seedheeroreeheeo] iron mine.

σίελος, ο [sielos] βλ σίαλος.

σικ [seek] chic, stylishness || (επίθ) smart, stylish.

σίκαλη, η [seekalee] rye.

σιλό, το [seelo] silo.

σιλουέτα, η [seeloueta] silhouette, figure.

σιμά [seema] near, close by.

σιμιγδάλι, το [seemeegðalee] semolina.

σιμώνω [seemono] approach, draw near.

σινάπι, το [seenapee] mustard, mustard seed.

σινιάλο, το [seeneealo] βλ σήμα.

σινικός [seeneekos]: σινική μελάνη India ink.

σιντριβάνι, το [seentreevanee] fountain.

σιρόκος, ο [seerokos] south-east wind.

σιρόπι, το [seeropee] syrup.

σιταρένιος [seetareneeos] wheaten, of wheat.

σιτάρι, το [seetaree] wheat, grain.

σιτεύω [seetevo] fatten || (το κρέας) hang, make tender.

σιτηρά, τα [seeteera] πλ cereals.

σιτίζω [seeteezo] feed, nurture, nourish.

σιτοβολώνας, ο [seetovolonas] granary, barn.

σίτος, ο [seetos] βλ σιτάρι.

σιφόνι, το [seefonee] siphon.

σιφονιέρα, η [seefoniera] chest of drawers.

σίφουνας, ο [seefounas] waterspout, whirlwind.

σιχαίνομαι [seehenome] loathe, detest, feel disgust for.

σιχαμένος [seehamenos] loathsome, sickening.

σιχαμερός [seehameros] disgusting, repulsive.

σιωπή η [seeopee] silence.

σιωπηλός [seeopeelos] silent, quiet, noiseless.

σιωπηρός [seeopeeros] tacit.

σιωπώ [seeopo] remain silent || hold one's tongue.

σκάβω [skavo] βλ σκάπτω.

σκάγι, το [skayee] small shot, pellet.

σκάζω [skazo] burst, open, split, crack || (ξύλο κτλ) split, splinter || (οβίδα) burst, explode || be exasperated, be infuriated (by) || το ~ make off || σκάσε! shut up!

σκαθάρι, το [skatharee] scarab(ee).

σκάκι, το [skakee] chess.

σκάλα, η [skala] stairs, staircase, flight, ladder || (υππρεσίας) backstairs || (αποβάθρα) wharf, landing stage || (λιμάνι) port || (μους) scale || (μαλλιών) wave.

σκαλί, το [skalee] step, flight, rung || grade.

σκαλίζω [skaleezo] hoe, weed, dig || (μέταλλο) chisel || (πέτρα κτλ) sculpture || (ξύλο) carve || (φωτιά) stir, poke || (βιβλιοθήκη κτλ) rummage, seek, search.

σκάλισμα, το [skaleesma] weeding, hoeing || searching || carving, sculpting.

σκαλιστήρι, το [skaleesteeree] hoe, weeding fork.

σκαλιστής, ο [skaleestees] carver, engraver, chiseller.

σκαλιστός [skaleestos] engraved, carved, chiselled, sculptured.

σκαλοπάτι, το [skalopatee] step, rung.

σκάλωμα, το [skaloma] scaling || (μεταφ) hitch, impediment.

σκαλώνω [skalono] climb, mount || (μεταφ) get held up, meet with an obstacle.

σκαλωσιά, η [skalosia] scaffolding.

σκαμνί, το [skamnee] stool || chair.

σκαμπίλι, το [skambeelee] slap, smack.

σκαμπιλίζω [skambeeleezo] slap.

σκανδάλη, η [skandalee] trigger.

σκανδαλιάρης, ο [skandaliarees] unruly or muddled or mischievous person.

σκανδαλίζομαι [skandaleezome] be tempted || be shocked.

σκανδαλίζω [skandaleezo] intrigue, allure || scandalize, shock, offend.

σκάνδαλο, το [skandalo] scandal || intrigue.

σκανδαλωδώς [skandaloðees] scandalous, disgraceful.

σκαντζόχοιρος, ο [skandzoheeros] hedgehog.

σκαπάνη, η [skapanee] mattock, pickaxe, pick.

σκαπουλάρω [skapoularo] escape from, elude.

σκάπτω [skapto] dig up, scoop out || (τάφρο) excavate || (χαράσσω) engrave, carve, chisel.

σκάρα [skara] βλ **εσχάρα**.

σκαρί, το [skaree] slipway || (μεταφ) character, make-up, idiosyncrasy.

σκαρλατίνα, η [skarlateena] scarlet fever.

σκαρπίνι, το [skarpeenee] lace-up shoe.

σκάρτος [skartos] defective, useless, unserviceable.

σκαρφάλωμα, το [skarfaloma] climbing up, scrambling up.

σκαρφαλώνω [skarfalono] climb, clamber up, scramble up.

σκάρωμα, το [skaroma] (μεταφ) fabrication, invention.

σκαρώνω [skarono] (μεταφ) fabricate, invent.

σκασίλα, η [skaseela] chagrin, spite, vexation, distress || **σκασίλα μου!** I couldn't care less!

σκάσιμο, το [skaseemo] fissure, cracking || (ρήγματος) chap || (διαφυγή) desertion, escape || (μαθήματος) playing truant.

σκασμός, ο [skasmos] suffocation || resentment || ~! shut up!, hold your tongue!

σκαστός [skastos] noisy || loud || (στρατ) AWOL || (μαθητής) playing truant.

σκατά, τα [skata] πλ shit (col).

σκάφανδρο, το [skafanðro] diving suit.

σκάφη, η [skafee] trough, tub.

σκαφή, η [skafee] digging.

σκάφος, το [skafos] hull || ship, vessel, boat.

σκάψιμο, το [skapseemo] digging, ploughing || carving.

σκάω [skao] βλ **σκάζω**.

σκεβρός [skevros] crooked, warped, deformed.

σκεβρώνω [skevrono] warp, twist || get warped.

σκέλεθρο, το [skelethro], **σκελετός, ο** [skeletos] skeleton || framework, shape || (αυτοκινήτου) chassis.

σκελετώδης [skeletoδees] bony, emaciated.

σκελίδα, η [skeleeδa] clove of garlic.

σκέλος, το [skelos] leg || side.

σκεπάζω [skepazo] cover || protect || hide.

σκεπάρνι, το [skeparnee] adze.

σκέπασμα, το [skepasma] roofing, covering || blanket || lid.

σκεπαστά [skepasta] secretly, on the quiet.

σκεπαστός [skepastos] covered in, veiled, roofed || (μεταφ) secret.

σκέπη, η [skepee] shelter, cover || (μεταφ) protection.

σκεπή, η [skepee] roof.

σκεπτικιστής, ο [skepteekeestees] sceptic, doubtful person.

σκεπτικός [skepteekos] sceptical || pensive, engrossed.

σκέπτομαι [skeptome] think, reflect || contemplate (doing).

σκέρτσα, τα [skertsa] πλ flirtatious ways.

σκέρτσο, το [skertso] charm || jesting, playfulness.

σκέτος, το [sketos] plain, simple || (καφές) without sugar.

σκεύος, το [skevos] utensil, implement || (εκκλ) vessel.

σκευοφόρος, ο [skevoforos] luggage van, baggage cart.

σκευωρία, η [skevoreea] scheme, machination, intrigue.

σκέψη, η [skepsee] thought, consideration || concern.

σκηνή, η [skeenee] scene, trouble, quarrel || (θεάτρου) action, stage || (τέντα) tent.

σκηνικά, τα [skeeneeka] πλ (stage) scenery.

σκηνικός [skeeneekos] of the stage, theatrical.

σκηνογραφία, η [skeenografeea] stage designing.

σκηνοθεσία, η [skeenotheseea] stage production || (μεταφ) fabrication.

σκηνοθέτης, ο [skeenothetees] stage manager.

σκήπτρο, το [skeeptro] sceptre || (μεταφ) superiority, prevalence.

σκήτη, η [skeetee] small monastery, cloister.

σκιά, η [skia] shade, shadow || phantom.

σκιαγραφώ [skeeagrafo] sketch, line.

σκιάδι, το [skeeaδee] straw hat || sunshade.

σκιάζομαι [skeeazome] be scared, take fright (at).

σκιάζω [skeeazo] shade || conceal the sun || veil, hide || (φοβίζω) frighten || (μεταφ) overshadow.

σκιάχτρο, το [skeeahtro] scarecrow || bogey.

σκιερός [skieros] shady, shadowy.

σκίζομαι [skeezome] struggle.

σκίζω [skeezo] split, cleave, tear, rip || ~ τα ρούχα μου I swear I'm innocent.

σκίουρος, ο [skeeouros] squirrel.

σκιρτώ [skeerto] bound, leap, bounce, hop.

σκίσιμο, το [skeeseemo] tear, rent, laceration || crack.

σκίτσο, το [skeetso] sketch, cartoon.

σκιώδης [skeeodees] βλ **σκιερός**.

σκλαβιά, η [sklavia] servitude, slavery || (μεταφ) obligation, drudgery.

σκλάβος, ο [sklavos] slave || captive.

σκλαβώνω [sklavono] subjugate, enslave || (μεταφ) put under obligation.

σκληραγωγώ [skleeragogo] accustom to hardship, season, toughen.

σκληραίνω [skleereno] harden, make hard || become callous.

σκληρός [skleeros] hard, tough || cruel, heartless.

σκληροτράχηλος [skleerotraheelos] opinionated, headstrong, obstinate.

σκληρύνω [skleereeno] βλ **σκληραίνω**.

σκνίπα, η [skneepa] gnat, midge || (μεταφ) drunk as a lord.

σκοινί, η [skeenee] βλ **σχοινί**.

σκόλη, η [skolee] holiday, feast day.

σκολίωση, η [skoleeosee] scoliosis.

σκολνώ [skolno] repose || get off (work), leave.

σκόνη, η [skonee] dust, powder || (για δόντια) tooth powder.

σκονίζω [skoneezo] coat with dust.

σκοντάφτω [skontafto] knock against, stumble || come up against an obstacle.

σκόντο, το [skonto] discount, deduction.

σκόπελος, ο [skopelos] reef, rock, shoal || (μεταφ) stumbling block, danger.

σκοπευτήριο, το [skopevteereeo] shooting gallery, shooting range.

σκοπεύω [skopevo] take aim at || (με όπλο) take aim || (έχω σκοπό) intend, propose, plan.

σκοπιά, η [skopia] lookout || sentry box || (σιδηροδρομική) signal box.

σκόπιμος [skopeemos] opportune,

convenient, expedient || intentional, deliberate.

σκοπίμως [skopeemos] intentionally, deliberately.

σκοποβολή, η [skopovolee] target practice, shooting.

σκοπός, ο [skopos] purpose, intent, intention || aim, goal || (φρουρός) sentinel || (στόχος) mark, target || (ήχος) tune, air.

σκορβούτο, το [skorvouto] scurvy.

σκορδαλιά, η [skorðalia] garlic sauce.

σκόρδο, το [skorðo] garlic.

σκόρος, ο [skoros] moth.

σκοροφαγωμένος [skorofagomenos] moth-eaten.

σκορπίζω [skorpeezo] scatter, disperse || (περιουσία) dissipate, waste || (φως) shed, spread || disintegrate, melt away.

σκόρπιος [skorpeeos] dispersed.

σκορπιός, ο [skorpios] scorpion.

σκορπώ [skorpo] βλ **σκορπίζω**.

σκοτάδι, το [skotaðee] darkness, obscurity || gloom.

σκοτεινιάζω [skoteeneeazo] darken, become overcast || cloud over.

σκοτεινός [skoteenos] dark, dismal, gloomy || (ουρανός) overcast || (νύχτα) murky || (χαρακτήρας) sombre, melancholy || (προθέσεις) underhand, sinister || (λόγια) obscure, abstruse.

σκοτίζομαι [skoteezome] worry, trouble o.s. || care for.

σκοτίζω [skoteezo] darken, obscure || worry, annoy, vex.

σκοτοδίνη, η [skotoðeenee] dizziness, vertigo.

σκότος, το [skotos] darkness, obscurity, gloom.

σκοτούρα, η [skotoura] (μεταφ) care, nuisance || dizziness.

σκοτωμός, ο [skotomos] massacre, killing || (μεταφ) hustle, jostle.

σκοτώνομαι [skotonome] hurt o.s. seriously || (μεταφ) work o.s. to death.

σκοτώνω [skotono] kill || while away (the time), kill time.

σκούζω [skouzo] howl, yell, scream.

σκουλαρίκι, το [skoulareekee] earring.

σκουλήκι, το [skouleekee] worm || maggot, mite.

σκουντουφλώ [skountouflo] stumble, bump against.

σκουντώ [skounto] push, jostle, shove.

σκούπα, η [skoupa] broom.

σκουπιδιαριό, το [skoupeedario] rubbish dump.

σκουπίδι, το [skoupeedee] rubbish, garbage, refuse.

σκουπιδιάρης, ο [skoupeedeearees] dustman, garbage collector.

σκουπίζω [skoupeezo] sweep, wipe, mop, dust, clean.

σκούρα [skoura] **τα βρήκα ~** I found things difficult.

σκουριά, η [skouria] rust || **~ζω** rust, corrode.

σκούρος [skouros] dark-coloured, brown.

σκούφια, η [skoufeea] cap, baby's bonnet.

σκούφος, ο [skoufos] cap, beret, bonnet.

σκύβαλα, τα [skeevala] πλ (μεταφ) grain siftings || refuse.

σκύβω [skeevo] bend, lean, bow, incline.

σκυθρωπός [skeethropos] sullen, sulky, surly || (όψος) morose.

σκύλα, η [skeela] bitch || (μεταφ) cruel woman.

σκυλί, το [skeelee] dog || **έγινε ~** he got furious.

σκυλιάζω [skeeleeazo] infuriate || become enraged.

σκυλοβρίζω [skeelovreezo] berate rudely.

σκυλολόι, το [skeeloloee] rabble, mob, riffraff.

σκύλος, ο [skeelos] βλ **σκυλί**.

σκυλόψαρο, το [skeelopsaro] dogfish || shark.

σκυταλοδρομία, η [skeetalοδromeea] relay race.

σκυφτός [skeeftos] bending, stooping.

σκωληκοειδίτιδα, η [skoleekoeeδeeteeδa] appendicitis.

σμάλτο, το [smalto] enamel.

σμαράγδι, το [smaragδee] emerald.

σμέουρο, το [smeouro] raspberry.

σμηναγός, ο [smeenagos] (αερο) flight lieutenant.

σμήναρχος, ο [smeenarhos] group captain || colonel (US).

σμηνίας, ο [smeeneeas] sergeant.

σμηνίτης, ο [smeeneetees] airman.

σμήνος, το [smeenos] swarm || (αερο) flight, squadron || crowd.

σμίγω [smeego] mingle, mix || meet, come face to face with || join.

σμίκρυνση, η [smeekreensee] reduction, diminution, decrease.

σμίλη, η [smeelee] chisel.

σμίξιμο, το [smeekseemo] mixing, meeting, mating, joining.

σμόκιν, το [smokeen] dinner jacket.

σμπαράλια, τα [smbaraleea] πλ tiny pieces.

σμπάρο, το [smbaro] shot.

σμύρη, η [smeeree] emery.

σνομπαρία, η [snombareea] snobbishness.

σοβαρεύομαι [sovarevome] look serious, speak seriously.

σοβαρό [sovaro] **~ ποσό** a substantial sum.

σοβαρός [sovaros] serious, grave, solemn.

σοβάς, ο [sovas] wall plaster.

σοβατίζω [sovateezo] plaster.

σόδα, η [soda] soda water ||
bicarbonate of soda.

σοδειά, η [sodia] βλ εσοδεία.

σόι [soee] lineage, breed || sort, kind
|| από ~ from a good family.

σοκάκι, το [sokakee] narrow street,
lane, alley.

σοκάρω [sokaro] shock, upset.

σόκιν [sokeen] shocking, suggestive.

σοκολάτα, η [sokolata] chocolate.

σόλα, η [sola] sole (of shoe).

σόλοικος [soleekos] incorrect,
ungrammatical || (μεταφ) improper.

σολομός, ο [solomos] salmon.

σόμπα, η [somba] heater, heating
stove.

σορός, ο [soros] bier, coffin || the
dead (person).

σοσιαλιστής, ο [soseealeestees]
socialist.

σου [sou] your.

σούβλα, η [souvla] skewer.

σουβλάκια, τα [souvlakeea] πλ
meat on a skewer.

σουβλερός [souvleros] sharp,
pointed.

σουβλί, το [souvlee] awl || spit.

σουβλιά, η [souvlia] injury from a
pointed object || (πόνος) acute pain.

σουβλίζω [souvleezo] run through,
pierce || (ψήνω) skewer || (πονώ)
cause pain.

σουγιάς, ο [souyas] penknife.

σούζα [souza] στέκομαι ~ obey
blindly || (μεταφ) fawn.

Σουηδία, η [soueedeea] Sweden.

σουηδικός [soueedeekos] Swedish.

Σουηδός, ο [soueedos] Swede.

σουλατσάρω [soulatsaro] wander
about, loaf.

σουλούπι, το [souloupee] outline,
cut, contour.

σουλτανίνα, η [soultaneena] sort
of seedless grape, sultana.

σουλτάνος, ο [soultanos] sultan.

σουμιές, ο [soumies] spring
mattress.

σούπα, η [soupa] soup.

σουπιά, η [soupia] cuttlefish ||
(μεταφ) sneaky person.

σούρα, η [soura] fold, wrinkle,
crease, pleat.

σουραύλι, το [souravlee] pipe,
reed, flute.

σούρουπο, το [souroupo] dusk,
nightfall.

σουρτούκης, ο [sourtoukees]
gadabout.

σουρωμένος [souromenos]
intoxicated.

σουρώνω [sourono] strain, filter ||
fold, pleat, crease || (αδυνατίζω) lose
weight, grow thin || get drunk.

σουρωτήρι, το [souroteeree]
strainer.

σουσάμι, το [sousamee] sesame.

σούσουρο, το [sousouro] noise, din
|| rustle || (μεταφ) scandal.

σούστα, η [sousta] spring (of seat) ||
(όχημα) cart || clasp, clip.

σουτ [sout] (επιφ) hush!, shut up!

σουτζουκάκια, τα [soutzoukakeea]
πλ meatballs.

σουτιέν, το [soutien] bra(ssiere).

σούφρα, η [soufra] pleat, crease,
fold || (μεταφ) theft.

σουφρώνω [soufrono] fold, pleat,
crease || (μεταφ) pinch, steal.

σοφία, η [sofeea] wisdom, learning
|| erudition.

σοφίζομαι [sofeezome] devise.

σοφίτα, η [sofeeta] attic, garret.

σοφός [sofos] wise || learned,
lettered.

σπαγγοραμένος [spangoramenos]
mean, tight-fisted.

σπάγγος, ο [spangos] twine, string
|| (μεταφ) mean person.

σπάζω [spazo] break, shatter, smash
|| ~ το κεφάλι μου think hard ||
~ στο ξύλο beat.

σπαθί, το [spathee] sabre, sword ||
(στα χαρτιά) spade.

σπαθιά, η [spathia] sword stroke.

σπανάκι, το [spanakee] spinach.

σπάνη, η [spanee] rarity, shortage.

σπανίζω [spaneezo] become rare,
be exceptional, be scarce.

σπάνιος [spaneeos] few and far
between, uncommon.

σπανιότητα, η [spaneeoteeta]
rarity, rareness, scarcity.

σπανίως [spaneeos] rarely.

σπανός [spanos] smooth-faced,
beardless || raw, very young.

σπαράγγι, το [sparangee]
asparagus.

σπαραγμός, ο [sparagmos] tearing
|| heartbreak, anguish.

σπαρακτικός [sparakteekos]
heartbreaking, agonizing || (θέαμα)
harrowing.

σπάραχνα, το [sparahna] πλ gills.

σπάργανα, τα [spargana] πλ
swaddling clothes.

σπαρμένος [sparmenos] spread ||
strewn, sown.

σπαρτά, τα [sparta] πλ crops.

σπαρταριστός [spartareestos]
(ψάρι) fresh || (κορίτσι) beautiful ||
vivid, very descriptive.

σπαρταρώ [spartaro] throb,
palpitate, jump.

σπαρτός [spartos] βλ σπαρμένος.

σπάσιμο, το [spaseemo] break,
fracture.

σπασμός, ο [spasmos] convulsion,
twitching.

σπασμωδικός [spasmodeekos]
spasmodic || hasty.

σπατάλη, η [spatalee] lavishness,
extravagance, waste.

σπάταλος [spatalos] wasteful,
extravagant.

σπαταλώ [spatalo] waste, lavish,
squander.

σπάτουλα, η [spatoula] spatula.

σπείρα, η [speera] coil, spiral ||
(ομάδα) band, gang, clique.

σπείρω [speero] sow || propagate.

σπεκουλάρω [spekoularo]
speculate.

σπέρμα, το [sperma] seed, germ ||
semen, sperm || (μεταφ) offspring ||
cause, motive.

σπερμολογία, η [spermologeea]
spreading of rumours.

σπέρνω [sperno] βλ σπείρω.

σπεύδω [spevdo] hurry, make haste.

σπήλαιο, το [speeleo], σπηλιά, η
[speelia] cave, cavern, lair.

σπίθα, η [speetha] spark, flash.

σπιθαμή, η [speethamee] span.

σπιθοβολώ [speethovolo] sparkle,
spark || gleam, glitter.

σπιθούρι, το [speethouree] pimple.

σπινθήρας, ο [speentheeras] spark.

σπινθηρίζω [speetheereezo] sparkle,
emit sparks, flash, glitter.

σπιούνος, ο [speeounos] spy || stool
pigeon.

σπιρούνι, το [speerounee] spur.

σπιρτάδα, η [speertaða] pungency ||
(μεταφ) wit, intelligence.

σπίρτο, το [speerto] match ||
alcohol.

σπιρτόζος [speertozos] witty,
clever, ingenious.

σπιτήσιος [speeteeseeos] home-
made, domestic.

σπίτι, το [speetee], σπιτικό, το
[speeteeko] house, home || (μεταφ)
family || από ~ wellborn.

σπιτικός [speeteekos] βλ
σπιτήσιος.

σπιτονοικοκύρης, ο
[speetoneekokeerees] householder,
landlord.

σπιτώνω [speetono] lodge, house ||
(μεταφ) keep (a woman).

σπλάχνα, τα [splahna] πλ entrails,
innards || (μεταφ) feelings ||
offspring.

σπλαχνικός [splahneekos]
merciful, sympathetic.

σπλάχνο, το [splahno] offspring,
child.

σπλήνα, η [spleena] spleen.

σπογγαλιεία, η [spongalieea]
sponge fishing.

σπογγίζω [spongeezo] sponge up ||
mop up, wipe away.

σπόγγος, ο [spongos] sponge.

σπογγώδης [spongodees] spongy.

σπονδή, η [spondee] libation.

σπονδυλική [spondeeleekee]: ~
στήλη spine, backbone.

σπονδυλικός [spondeeleekos]
vertebral.

σπόνδυλος, ο [spondeelos]
vertebra || (κίονος) drum.

σπονδυλωτός [spondeelotos]
vertebrate.

σπορ, το [spor] sport, games,
pastime.

σπορά, η [spora] sowing || seed time
|| (μεταφ) generation.

σποραδικός [sporadeekos]
dispersed, scanty.

σπορέλαιο, το [sporeleo] seed oil.

σπόρια, τα [sporeea] πλ seeds.

σπόρος, ο [sporos] seed, germ ||
semen.

σπουδάζω [spoudazo] study, attend
school.

σπουδαίος [spoudeos] serious,
important || exceptional.

σπουδασμένος [spoudasmenos]
learned, educated.

σπουδαστής, ο [spoudastees]
student.

σπουδή, η [spoudee] haste,
keenness || (μελέτη) study.

σπουργίτης, ο [spouryeetees]
sparrow.

σπρωξιά, η [sproksia] push, hustle,
jostle, shoving.

σπρώξιμο, το [sprokseemo]
pushing || encouraging.

σπρώχνω [sprohno] push, thrust,
shove || encourage, incite.

σπυρί, το [speeree] grain ||
(εξάνθημα) pimple || boil.

σπυρωτός [speerotos] granular,
granulated.

στάβλος, ο [stavlos] stable ||
cowshed.

σταγόνα, η [stagona] drop, dash.

σταγονόμετρο, το [stagonometro]
dropper || με το ~ in small doses,
little by little.

σταδιοδρομία, η [stadeeodromeea]
career, course.

στάδιο, το [stadeeo] stadium,
athletic ground || (μεταφ) career,
vocation.

στάζω [stazo] trickle, dribble, drip,
leak.

σταθεροποίηση, η
[statheropieesee] stabilization,
steadying down.

σταθερός [statheros] stable, firm,
steadfast, secure.

σταθμά, τα [stathma] πλ weights.

σταθμάρχης, ο [stathmarhees]
station master.

στάθμευση, η [stathmevsee]
stopping, waiting, parking ||
stationing.

σταθμεύω [stathmevo] stop, wait,
stand, camp, park.

στάθμη, η [stathmee] level,
plumbline || (νερού) water level.

σταθμίζω [stathmeezo] weigh, level
|| (μεταφ) appreciate, calculate.

σταθμός, ο [stathmos] station,
halting place || (αυτοκινήτου) garage
|| parking lot (US) || (ταξί) taxi rank ||
stop, stay, wait || (στην ιστορία)
landmark, stage.

στάκτη, η [staktee] ash, ashes,
cinders.

σταλα(γ)ματιά, η [stala(g)matia]
drop, dash.

σταλάζω [stalazo] drip, dribble,
trickle.

σταλακτίτης, ο [stalakteetees]
stalactite.

στᾰμάτημα, το [stamateema] stop, halting, checking || pause || block.

σταμᾰτώ [stamato] stop (working), check.

στάμνα, η [stamna] pitcher, jug.

στάμπα, η [stampa] stamp, seal || impression.

στάνη, η [stanee] sheepfold, pen.

στᾰνιό, το [stanio]: **με το ~** against one's will, involuntarily.

στάξιμο, το [stakseemo] dripping, trickling.

στάση, η [stasee] halt, stop, bus stop, station || (εργασίας) suspension, stoppage || (τρόπος) posture, position || (ιατρ) retention || (εξέγερση) revolt, rebellion || (μεταφ) behaviour, attitude.

στᾰσιάζω [staseeazo] mutiny, rebel.

στᾰσίδι, το [staseedee] pew, stall.

στάσιμος [staseemos] motionless, stationary || (νερό) stagnant.

στᾰτήρας, ο [stateeras] hundredweight.

στᾰτική, η [stateekee] statics.

στᾰτικός [stateekos] static(al).

στᾰτιστική, η [stateesteekee] statistics.

σταυλάρχης, ο [stavlarhees] stable master.

σταύλος, ο [stavlos] stable || cowshed || (χοίρων) pig sty.

σταυροδρόμι, το [stavroðromee] crossroads || crossing.

σταυροειδής [stavroeeðees] cruciform, crosslike.

σταυροκοπιέμαι [stavrokopieme] cross o.s. over and over again.

σταυρόλεξο, το [stavrolekso] crossword puzzle.

σταυροπόδι [stavropoðee] cross-legged.

σταυρός, ο [stavros] cross, crucifix || stake, pale.

σταυροφορία, η [stavroforeea] crusade.

σταυρώνω [stavrono] crucify || (τα

χέρια) cross || (διασταυρούμαι) cross, meet and pass, cut across.

σταυρωτός [stavrotos] crossways, crosswise || (σακάκι) double-breasted.

στᾰφίδα, η [stafeeða] raisin || (σμυρναϊκή) sultana || **κορινθιακή ~** currant || **γίνομαι ~** get intoxicated.

στᾰφύλη, η [stafeelee] grapes || (ανατ) uvula.

στᾰφύλι, το [stafeelee] grape.

στᾰφυλόκοκκος, ο [stafeelokokos] staphylococcus.

στάχι, το [stahee] ear of corn, ear of wheat.

στάχτη, η [stahtee] βλ **στάκτη**.

στᾰχτής [stahtees] ashen, pale.

στᾰχτόνερο, το [stahtonero] lye.

στεγάζω [stegazo] roof || cover, house, shelter.

στεγανός [steganos] airtight, hermetical, waterproof.

στέγαση, η [stegasee] housing, sheltering.

στέγασμα, το [steyasma] roof || cover, shelter.

στέγη, η [steyee] roof || (μεταφ) house, dwelling.

στεγνός [stegnos] dry || (μεταφ) skinny, spare.

στεγνώνω [stegnono] dry, become dry.

στείρος [steeros] barren, unproductive || (προσπάθεια) vain.

στέκα, η [steka] billiard cue || (μεταφ) woman as thin as a rake.

στέκει [stekee]: **~ καλά** he is well-off || he is fit and well.

στέκομαι [stekome] stand up || come to a standstill, stop || (μεταφ) prove to be || happen.

στέκω [steko] stand, stand still, come to a stop.

στελέχη, τα [stelehee] πλ cadres, management staff.

στέλεχος, το [stelehos] stalk, stem

στέλλω 218 στπλώνω

|| shank, rod || (τοεκ) counterfoil || (χερούλι) handle.

στέλλω [stelo], **στέλνω** [stelno] send, direct, dispatch, forward.

στέμμα, το [stema] crown, diadem.

στεναγμός, ο [stenagmos] sigh, sighing || moan, groan.

στενάζω [stenazo] sigh, heave a sigh || (μεταφ) moan.

στενεύω [stenevo] narrow down, take in, tighten || shrink, get narrow.

στενογραφία, η [stenografeea] shorthand, stenography.

στενοκέφαλος [stenokefalos] narrow-minded, strait-laced.

στενόμακρος [stenomakros] long and narrow, oblong.

στενό, το [steno] strait || (οροσειράς) pass, gorge.

στενός [stenos] narrow || tight-fitting || (μεταφ) close, intimate || (φίλος) dear.

στενότητα, η [stenoteeta] tightness, closeness || narrowness || ~ χρήματος lack of money.

στενοχωρημένος [stenohoreemenos] upset, sad || hard-up || ill at ease.

στενοχώρια, η [stenohoreea] lack of room || (δυσκολία) difficulty, inconvenience, discomfort.

στενόχωρος [stenohoros] narrow, limited, tight || troublesome.

στενοχωρώ [stenohoro] worry, embarrass, annoy.

στενωπός, η [stenopos] narrow street, back street || defile, pass.

στερεά, η [sterea] mainland || ~ Ελλάδα central Greece.

στερεοποιώ [stereopeeo] solidify.

στερεός [stereos] firm, compact, well-built || solid, substantial || (χρώμα) fast.

στερεότυπος [stereoteepos] stereotyped, invariable.

στερεύω [sterevo] dry up || stop, cease.

στερέωμα, το [stereoma] consolidation || support, fastening || (ουρανός) firmament.

στερεώνω [stereono] consolidate || make secure || ~ σε μια δουλειά settle down to one job.

στερήσεις, οι [stereesees] πλ privation, want, loss.

στέρηση, η [stereese] deprivation || shortage, absence.

στεριά, η [steria] terra firma.

στερλίνα, η [sterleena] pound sterling.

στέρνα, η [sterna] cistern, tank.

στέρνο, το [sterno] breastbone, chest.

στερνός [sternos] later, last.

στερούμαι [steroume] go without, lack || (φτώχεια) be needy.

στερώ [stero] deprive of, take away.

στέφανα, τα [stefana] πλ marriage wreaths.

στεφάνη, η [stefanee] crown || (αγγείου) brim || (βαρελιού) hoop || (άνθους) corolla || ring, band || (τροχού) tyre.

στεφάνι, το [stefanee] garland, wreath || (βαρελιού) hoop, band.

στεφανώνομαι [stefanonome] marry, get married.

στεφανώνω [stefanono] crown || be the best man at a wedding.

στέψη, η [stepsee] coronation || wedding ceremony.

στηθόδεσμος, ο [steethodesmos] βλ σουτιέν.

στήθος, το [steethos] chest, breast || (γυναικός) bosom.

στηθοσκοπώ [steethoskopo] examine with a stethoscope.

στήλη, η [steelee] staff, pillar, column || (μπαταρία) electric battery || (εφημερίδας) column.

στηλώνω [steelono] prop up, support || bolster up.

στημόνι, το [steemonee] warp.

στήνω [steeno] raise, hold up, erect, put up || ~ παγίδα lay a trap.

στήριγμα, το [steereegma] prop, support, stay.

στηρίζομαι [steereezome] lean on, rely on || be based on.

στηρίζω [steereezo] support || prop || base on, reckon on.

στητός [steetos] standing, upright.

στιβαρός [steevaros] strong, robust, steady, firm.

στιβάδα, η [steevaδa] pile, heap, mass.

στίβος, ο [steevos] track, ring, racetrack.

στίγμα, το [steegma] spot, brand, stain, stigma || disgrace || position, fix.

στιγμή, η [steegmee] instant, moment || (τυπογραφικό) dot, point || τελεία ~ full stop || άνω ~ colon.

στιγμιαίος [steegmieos] instantaneous || momentary, temporary.

στιγμιότυπο, το [steegmeeoteepo] snapshot, snap.

στίλβω [steelvo] shine, glitter, sparkle.

στιλβώνω [steelvono] polish, varnish, burnish.

στιλβωτήριο, το [steelvoteereeo] shoe shine parlour.

στιλέτο, το [steeleto] stiletto, dagger.

στιλπνός [steelpnos] brilliant, polished, bright.

στίξη, η [steeksee] punctuation || dot, spot, speckle.

στιφάδο, το [steefaδo] meat stew with onions.

στίφος, το [steefos] crowd, horde, throng || rabble, gang.

στιχομυθία, η [steehomeetheea] vivid dialogue.

στίχος, ο [steehos] line, row, file || verse.

στιχουργός, ο [steehourgos] rhymester, versifier.

στοά, η [stoa] colonnade, portico, arcade || passage || (ορυχείου) gallery || (μασωνική) (masonic) lodge.

στοίβα, η [steeva] pile, stack, mass.

στοιβάζω [steevazo] stack, pile up || crowd, squeeze.

στοιχεία, τα [steeheea] πλ elements, rudiments || (τυπογραφείου) printing types.

στοιχειό, το [steeheio] ghost, phantom.

στοιχείο, το [steeheeo] component, element || (νομ) piece of evidence || (αλφαβήτου) letter || (ηλεκτ) cell || (μεταφ) factor.

στοιχειοθεσία, η [steeheeotheseea] typesetting.

στοιχειώδης [steeheeoδees] elementary, rudimentary || essential, capital.

στοιχειωμένος [steeheeomenos] haunted.

στοιχειώνω [steeheeono] become haunted, haunt.

στοίχημα, το [steeheema] bet, wager || stake || βάζω ~ lay a bet, wager.

στοιχηματίζω [steeheemateezo] bet, wager.

στοιχίζω [steeheezo] cost || (μεταφ) pain, grieve.

στοίχος, ο [steehos] row, line, rank.

στόκος, ο [stokos] putty, stucco.

στολή, η [stolee] uniform || costume.

στολίδι, το [stoleeδee] jewellery || (στόλισμα) adornment, decoration.

στολίζω [stoleezo] adorn, decorate, deck, trim, embellish.

στολισμός, ο [stoleesmos] ornamenting, decoration, embellishing.

στόλος, ο [stolos] navy, fleet.

στόμα, το [stoma] mouth || lips.

στομάχι, το [stomahee] stomach.

στομαχιάζω [stomaheeazo] suffer from indigestion.

στόμιο, το [stomeeo] mouth, opening, aperture, entrance || muzzle.

στόμφος, ο [stomfos] boast, declamation.

στομώνω [stomono] blunt || temper, harden.

στορ, το [stor], στόρι, το [storee] blind, roller blind.

στοργή, η [storyee] affection, tenderness, love.

στουμπώνω [stoumbono] stuff, pad, plug || become stuffed.

στουνί, το [stoupee] oakum, wad, tow || (μεταφ) drunk as a lord.

στουπόχαρτο, το [stoupoharto] blotting paper.

στουρνάρι, το [stournaree] flint, gun flint.

στοχάζομαι [stohazome] think, meditate (on) || consider.

στοχασμός, ο [stohasmos] thought, meditation.

στοχαστικός [stohasteekos] thoughtful || discreet, wise.

στόχαστρο, το [stohastro] front sight (of gun).

στόχος, ο [stohos] mark, target, objective || aim, end.

στραβά [strava] obliquely, crookedly || wrongly, amiss || τόβαλε ~ he doesn't give a damn.

στραβισμός, ο [straveesmos] squinting.

στραβοκάνης [stravokanees] bandy-legged.

στραβομάρα, η [stravomara] blindness || (κακοτυχία) bad luck, mischance || (μεταφ) blunder, gross mistake, howler.

στραβόξυλο, το [stravokseelo] obstinate person, contrary fellow.

στραβοπάτημα, το [stravopateema] staggering || false step.

στραβός [stravos] crooked, awry, twisted || (λοξός) slanting || (ελαπτωματικός) faulty || (τυφλός) blind.

στραβώνομαι [stravonome] go blind.

στραβώνω [stravono] bend, distort || make a mess of || spoil || (τυφλώνω) blind || (λυγίζω) become twisted.

στραγάλια, τα [stragaleea] πλ roasted chickpeas.

στραγγαλίζω [strangaleezo] strangle, throttle || stifle.

στραγγαλιστής, ο [strangaleestees] strangler.

στραγγίζω [strangeezo] drain, filter, press out, wring out || (κουράζομαι) get exhausted.

στραγγιστήρι, το [strangeesteeree] strainer, filter, colander.

στραμπουλίζω [strambouleezo] sprain, twist.

στραπατσάρω [strapatsaro] harm, damage || ruffle || (ταπεινώνω) humiliate.

στραπάτσο, το [strapatso] maltreatment || humiliation.

στράτα, η [strata] way, street, road.

στρατάρχης, ο [stratarhees] (field) marshal.

στράτευμα, το [stratevma] army, troops, forces.

στρατεύματα, τα [stratevmata] πλ troops.

στρατεύομαι [stratevome] serve in the army.

στρατεύσιμος [stratevseemos] subject to conscription.

στρατηγείο, το [strateeyeeo] headquarters.

στρατήγημα το [strateeyeema] stratagem || trick, ruse.

στρατηγία, η [strateeyeea] generalship.

στρατηγική, η [strateeyeekee] strategy.

στρατηγικός [strateeyeekos] strategic.

στρατηγός, ο [strateegos] general.

στρατί, το [stratee] βλ στράτα.

στρατιά, η [stratia] army, force.

στρατιώτης, ο [strateeotees] soldier, private || warrior.

στρατιωτικό, το [strateeoteeko] military service.

στρατιωτικός [strateeoteekos] military || ~ νόμος martial law.

στρατοδικείο, το [stratodeekeeo] court-martial.

στρατοκρατία, η [stratokrateea] militarism, military government.

στρατολογία, η [stratoloyeea] conscription, call-up.

στρατόπεδο, το [stratopedo] camp, encampment || side, party.

στρατός, ο [stratos] army, troops, forces.

στρατόσφαιρα, η [stratosfera] stratosphere.

στρατώνας, ο [stratonas] barracks.

στρεβλός [strevlos] crooked, deformed, twisted || (μεταφ) rough, difficult.

στρείδι, το [streedee] oyster.

στρέμμα, το [strema] (approx) quarter of an acre.

στρέφομαι [strefome] turn, rotate || revolve.

στρέφω [strefo] turn, turn about || rotate, revolve.

στρεψοδικία, η [strepsodeekeea] chicanery, quibbling, pettifoggery.

στρίβω [streevo] twist, rotate, turn || το ~ slip away, slip off.

στρίγγ(γ)λα, η [stree(n)gla] witch, sorceress, shrew.

στριγγ(γ)λιά, η [stree(n)glia] wickedness, shrewishness || (κραυγή) shrill cry, shriek.

στριμμένος [streemenos] twisted || ill-humoured, wicked, malicious.

στριφογυρίζω [streefoyeereezo] move round, turn round || whirl, spin.

στρίφωμα, το [streefoma] hemming.

στρίψιμο, το [streepseemo] twisting, turning.

στροβιλίζω [stroveeleezo] whirl, turn round, twirl.

στρόβιλος, ο [stroveelos] spinning top, peg top || (άνεμος) whirlwind || (χιόνι) eddying, swirling || (μηχανή) turbine || (σκόνης) whirling cloud.

στρογγυλεύω [strongeelevo] make round || grow plump, get stout.

στρογγυλός [strongeelos] round(ed) || (πρόσωπο) full || (αριθμός) round, even.

στρουθοκάμηλος, η [strouthokameelos] ostrich.

στρουμπουλός [stroumboulos] plump.

στρόφαλος, ο [strofalos] crank, handle || (αυτοκινήτου) starting handle.

στροφή, η [strofee] turn, revolution || (οδού) twist, bend || (κατευθύνσεως) detour, change of direction || (ποίηση) stanza || (μουσ) ritornello.

στρόφιγγα, η [strofeenga] hinge, pivot || tap.

στρυμώ(χ)νω [streemo(h)no] squeeze, crowd, cram || press hard, oppress, annoy.

στρυφνός [streefnos] harsh || peevish || (χαρακτήρας) crabbed || (ύφος κτλ) obscure, difficult || (γεύση) sharp, biting.

στρώμα, το [stroma] couch, bed, mattress || (γεωλογίας) bed, layer, stratum || στο ~ ill in bed.

στρώνομαι [stronome] apply o.s. || install o.s.

στρώνω [strono] spread, lay || (κρεβάτι) make || (δρόμο) pave ||

(μεταφ) be well under way || ~ το κρεβάτι mε ke the bed.

στρώση, η [strosee] layer || strewing || paving, flooring.

στρωσίδι, το [stroseedee] carpet || bedding.

στρωτός [strotos] strewn || paved || (ζωή) even, normal, regular.

στύβω [steevo] squeeze, wring, press || (μεταφ) rack one's brains || (στειρεύω) dry up, run dry.

στυγερός [steeyeros] abominable, heinous, horrible.

στυγνός [steegnos] doleful, despondent, gloomy.

στυλό, το [steelo] fountain pen.

στυλοβάτης, ο [steelovatees] pedestal, base || (μεταφ) pillar, founder.

στύλος, ο [steelos] pillar, column, pole || (μεταφ) prop, mainstay, breadwinner.

στυλώνω [steelono] support, prop up || fix.

στυπτικός [steepteekos] binding, styptic.

στυφός [steefos] sour, acrid, bitter.

στύψη, η [steepsee] alum.

στύψιμο, το [steepseemo] squeezing, pressing, wringing.

στωικός [stoeekos] stoic(al).

συ [see] you.

σύγγαμβρος, ο [seengamvros] brother-in-law.

συγγένεια, η [seengeneea] relationship, kinship || affinity, relation, connection.

συγγενής [seengenees] connected, related || (ουσ) relation, kinsman.

συγγενολό(γ)ι, το [seengenolo(y)ee] relations, relatives, kindred.

συγγνώμη, η [seengnomee] pardon, excuse || forgiveness.

σύγγραμμα, το [seengrama] work (of writing), treatise.

συγγραφέας, ο [seengrafeas] author, writer.

συγγράφω [seengrafo] write a work, compose.

συγκαίομαι [seengkeome] be chafed, be galled.

σύγκαλα, τα [seengkala] πλ: στα ~ μου normal, in good health.

συγκαλύπτω [seengkaleepto] hide, cloak, hush up, cover.

συγκαλώ [seengkalo] convene, convoke || (πρόσωπα) assemble, call together.

συγκαταβατικός [seengkatavateekos] accommodating || (τιμή) moderate, reasonable.

συγκατάθεση, η [seengkatathesee] assent, consent, acquiescence.

συγκαταλέγω [seengkatalego] include, number among || consider, regard.

συγκατανεύω [seengkatanevo] consent, assent, adhere to.

συγκατοικώ [seengkateeko] cohabit, live together.

συγκεκριμένος [seengkekreemenos] concrete, positive, clear, specific.

συγκεκριμένως [seengkekreemenos] plainly, concretely, actually.

συγκεντρώνομαι [seengkentronome] concentrate.

συγκεντρώνω [seengkentrono] collect, bring togther, concentrate || centralize.

συγκέντρωση, η [seengkentrosee] crowd, gathering, assembly || concentration || centralization.

συγκερασμός, ο [seengkerasmos] mixing, mingling || compromise.

συγκεχυμένος [seengkeheemenos] confused, jumbled || (ήχος) indistinct || (φήμες) vague || (ιδέες)

hazy, dim || (λόγοι) imprecise, obscure.

συγκίνηση, n [seengkeeneesee] emotion, sensation.

συγκινητικός [seengkeeneeteekos] moving, touching, stirring.

συγκινούμαι [seengkeenoume] be excited || be touched.

συγκινώ [seengkeeno] move, affect, touch || excite.

σύγκληση, n [seengkleesee] convocation, calling together.

σύγκλητος, η [seengkleetos] senate.

συγκλίνω [seengkleeno] converge, concentrate.

συγκλονίζω [seengkloneezo] shake, excite, stir up, shock.

συγκοινωνία, n [seengkeenoneea] communications || means of transport.

συγκοινωνώ [seengkeenono] communicate, be connected.

συγκολλώ [seengkolo] glue, join together || (μέταλλα) weld, solder || ~ σαμπρέλα mend a puncture.

συγκομιδή, n [seengkomeedee] harvest, crop.

συγκοπή, n [seengkopee] syncopation || (ιατρ) heart failure || (γραμμ) contraction.

συγκράτηση, n [seengkrateesee] containing, bridling, restraining.

συγκρατούμαι [seengkratoume] control o.s., contain o.s.

συγκρατώ [seengkrato] check || (πάθη) govern || (θυμό) contain, control, suppress || (τα πλήθη) restrain.

συγκρίνω [seengkreeno] compare (with), liken (to).

σύγκριση, n [seengkreesee] comparison, parallel.

συγκριτικός [seengkreeteekos] comparative, compared (to).

συγκρότημα, το [seengkroteema] group, cluster || (κτίρια) complex || (μουσ) group, band.

συγκροτώ [seengkroto] form, compose || convoke, convene.

συγκρούομαι [seengkrouome] bump into, collide || clash, come to blows.

σύγκρουση, n [seengkrousee] collision, clash, fight, engagement.

σύγκρυο, το [seengkreeo] shivering, trembling.

συγκυρία, n [seengkeereea] coincidence, occurrence, chance || (οίκον) conjuncture.

συγυρίζω [seeyeereezo] tidy up, arrange || (μεταφ) ill-treat.

συγχαίρω [seenghero] congratulate, compliment.

συγχαρητήρια, τα [seenghareeteereea] πλ congratulations.

συγχέω [seengheo] confound, confuse, perplex.

συγχορδία, n [seenghordeea] harmony of sounds, accord.

συγχρονίζω [seenghroneezo] modernize, bring up to date.

σύγχρονος [seenghronos] contemporary || simultaneous || contemporaneous.

συγχύζω [seengheezo] get mixed up || worry, confound, harass.

σύγχυση, n [seengheesee] confusion, disorder || chaos, commotion.

συγχωνεύω [seenghonevo] amalgamate, blend, merge.

συγχώρηση, n [seenghoreesee] remission, pardon.

συγχωρητέος [seenghoreeteos] pardonable, excusable.

συ(γ)χωρείτε [see(ng)horeete] **με ~** excuse me, I beg your pardon.

συγχωρώ [seenghoro] pardon, forgive, excuse || tolerate, permit.

συζήτηση, n [seezeeteesee]

22

discussion, debate || ούτε ~ it's out of the question.
συζητώ [seezeeto] discuss, argue, debate.
συζυγικός [seezeeyeekos] conjugal, marital.
σύζυγος, o, n [seezeegos] consort, spouse, husband, wife.
συζώ [seezo] live together, cohabit.
συκιά, n [seekia] fig tree.
σύκο, το [seeko] fig.
συκοφάντης, o [seekofantees] slanderer.
συκοφαντώ [seekofanto] slander.
συκώτι, το [seekotee] liver.
σύληση, n [seeleesee] spoliation, sacking.
συλλαβή, n [seelavee] syllable.
συλλαλητήριο, το [seelaleeteereeo] mass meeting, demonstration.
συλλαμβάνω [seelamvano] catch, lay hold of, capture, seize, arrest || (ιδέες) conceive.
συλλέγω [seelego] collect, gather.
συλλέκτης, o [seelektees] collector.
σύλληψη, n [seeleepsee] capture, arrest, seizure || (ιδέας) conception.
συλλογή, n [seeloyee] set, assortment, collection || (σκέψη) thought, concern.
συλλογίζομαι [seeloyeezome] think out, reflect about, consider, reason (out).
συλλογικός [seeloyeekos] collective.
συλλογισμένος [seeloyeesmenos] pensive, thoughtful, absorbed (in).
συλλογισμός, o [seeloyeesmos] thought, reflection || reasoning, syllogism.
σύλλογος, o [seelogos] society, club, association.
συλλυπητήρια, τα [seeleepeeteereea] πλ condolences, sympathy.

συλλυπούμαι [seeleepoume] offer condolence || feel sorry for.
συμβαδίζω [seemvadeezo] keep up with || go together, coexist.
συμβαίνω [seemveno] happen, take place, come about.
συμβάλλομαι [seemvalome] contract, enter into an agreement.
συμβάλλω [seemvalo] contribute to, pay one's share || (ποτάμι) meet, join, unite.
συμβάν, το [seemvan] event, accident, occurrence.
σύμβαση, n [seemvasee] agreement, contract, treaty, pact.
συμβία, n [seemvea] wife, consort.
συμβιβάζομαι [seemveevazome] compromise, agree with || be compatible with.
συμβιβάζω [seemveevazo] reconcile, arrange, adjust.
συμβιβασμός, o [seemveevasmos] compromise, accommodation, adjustment, settlement.
συμβίωση, n [seemveeosee] living together, cohabitation.
συμβόλαιο, το [seemvoleo] contract, agreement.
συμβολαιογράφος, o [seemvoleografos] notary public.
συμβολή, n [seemvolee] contribution || (ποταμών) confluence, junction.
συμβολίζω [seemvoleezo] symbolize, represent.
σύμβολο, το [seemvolo] symbol, mark, sign, emblem, token.
συμβουλεύομαι [seemvoulevome] consult, refer to, take advice.
συμβουλεύω [seemvoulevo] advise, recommend.
συμβουλή, n [seemvoulee] advice, counsel.
συμβούλιο, το [seemvouleeo] council, board, committee.
σύμβουλος, o [seemvoulos] adviser, counsellor || councillor.

συμμαζεύω [seemazevo] tidy up, collect, assemble, gather together || (ελέγχω) restrain, check, hold.

συμμαχία, η [seemaheea] alliance, coalition.

σύμμαχος [seemahos] allied || (ουσ) ally.

συμμερίζομαι [seemereezome] share, have a part (in).

συμμετέχω [seemeteho] participate in, take part in, be a party to.

συμμετοχή, η [seemetohee] participation || sharing.

συμμετρία, η [seemetreea] symmetry, proportion.

συμμετρικός [seemetreekos] symmetrical || well-proportioned.

συμμορία, η [seemoreea] gang, band, body.

συμμορφώνομαι [seemorfonome] comply, conform, agree with, adapt to.

συμμορφώνω [seemorfono] adapt, conform || bring to heel.

συμπαγής [seembayees] solid, firm, compact, close.

συμπάθεια, η [seempatheea] compassion, sympathy || weakness (for) || favourite.

συμπαθής [seempathees] likeable, lovable.

συμπαθητικός [seempatheeteekos] likeable, lovable || sympathetic.

συμπάθιο, το [seempatheeo] **με το ~** begging your pardon.

συμπαθώ [seempatho] feel compassion for || have a liking for.

σύμπαν, το [seempan] universe || everything, all, everybody.

συμπατριώτης, ο [seempatreeotees] compatriot, fellow countryman.

συμπεθεριά, η [seempetheria] relationship by marriage.

συμπέθεροι, οι [seempetheree] πλ

fathers-in-law || relations by marriage.

συμπεραίνω [seempereno] conclude, presume, infer, surmise.

συμπέρασμα, το [seemperasma] conclusion, inference, end.

συμπεριλαμβάνω [seempereelamvano] include, contain, comprise.

συμπεριφέρομαι [seempereeferome] behave, conduct o.s.

συμπεριφορά, η [seempereefora] behaviour, conduct.

συμπίεση, η [seempiesee] compression, squeezing.

συμπίπτω [seempeepto] coincide, concur, converge || happen, change.

σύμπλεγμα, το [seemplegma] tangle || cluster || network.

συμπλέκομαι [seemplekome] come to blows, quarrel || fight.

συμπλέκτης, ο [seemblektees] (μηχαν) clutch.

συμπλήρωμα, το [seempleeroma] complement || supplement, addition.

συμπληρωματικός [seempleeromateekos] complementary, further || supplementary.

συμπληρώνω [seempleerono] complete, complement, finish || (θέση) fill || (φόρμα) fill in.

συμπλήρωση, η [seempleerosee] completion, filling, achievement.

συμπλοκή, η [seemplokee] fight, engagement, clash, brawl.

σύμπνοια, η [seempneea] harmony, agreement, understanding.

συμπολιτεία, η [seempoleeteea] confederation, confederacy.

συμπολίτης, ο [seempoleetees] fellow citizen, fellow countryman.

συμπονώ [seempono] feel compassion for, sympathize with.

συμπόσιο, το [seemposeeo] banquet, feast.

συμποσούμαι [seemposoume] come to, run (to).

σύμπραξη, n [seempraksee] cooperation, contribution.

συμπτύσσομαι [seempteesome] fall back, shorten.

συμπτύσσω [seempteeso] shorten, abridge, abbreviate, cut short.

σύμπτωμα, το [seemptoma] symptom || sign, indication.

σύμπτωση, n [seemptosee] coincidence, accident, chance.

συμπυκνώνω [seempeeknono] condense, compress.

συμπυκνωτής, ο [seempeeknotees] condenser.

συμφέρει [seemferee] it's worth it, it's to one's advantage.

συμφέρον, το [seemferon] advantage, interest, profit, benefit.

συμφεροντολογία, n [seemferontoloyeea] self-interest.

συμφιλιώνω [seemfeeleeono] reconcile, restore friendship, make up.

συμφορά, n [seemfora] calamity, disaster, misfortune.

συμφόρηση, n [seemforeesee] traffic jam, congestion || (ιατρ) stroke.

σύμφορος [seemforos] advantageous, profitable, useful.

συμφύρω [seemfeero] confuse, mingle, mix, jumble.

σύμφωνα [seemfona]: ~ με according to, in conformity with.

συμφωνητικό, το [seemfoneeteeko] agreement, deed of contract.

συμφωνία, n [seemfoneea] agreement, convention || accord, consent || (μουσ) symphony.

σύμφωνο, το [seemfono] (γράμμα) consonant || compact, agreement, pact.

σύμφωνος [seemfonos] in accord, in conformity with.

συμφωνώ [seemfono] concur, agree || match, go well together.

συμψηφίζω [seempseefeezo] counterbalance, make up for.

συν [seen] together, with || (μαθημ) plus || ~ τω χρόνω in time, gradually, eventually || ~ τοις άλλοις moreover, in addition.

συναγερμός, ο [seenayermos] alarm, call to arms, alert || (πολιτικός) rally, mass meeting.

συναγρίδα, n [seenagreeða] kind of sea bream.

συνάγω [seenago] assemble, collect, bring together || (συμπεραίνω) infer, conclude, deduce.

συναγωγή, n [seenagoyee] collection, gathering, assembly || (εβραίων) synagogue.

συναγωνίζομαι [seenagoneezome] rival, compete || fight together.

συναγωνιστής, ο [seenagoneestees] rival, competitor || (συμπολεμιστής) brother in arms || (ανταγωνιστής) rival.

συνάδελφος, ο [seenaðelfos] colleague, fellow member.

συναινώ [seeneno] consent to, agree to, acquiesce.

συναίρεση, n [seeneresee] (γραμμ) contraction.

συναισθάνομαι [seenesthanome] become aware of, be conscious of, feel.

συναίσθημα, το [seenestheema] sentiment, feeling, sensation.

συναισθήματα, τα [seenestheemata] πλ emotions, feelings.

συναισθηματικός [seenestheemateekos] emotional, sentimental.

συναίσθηση, n [seenestheesee]

feeling, sense, appreciation, consciousness.

συναλλαγή, η [seenalayee] exchange, dealings, trade || ελεύθερη ~ free trade.

συνάλλαγμα, το [seenalagma] foreign currency || draft, bill || τιμή συναλλάγματος rate of exchange.

συναλλαγματική, η [seenalagmateekee] bill of exchange.

συναλλάσσομαι [seenalasome] deal, trade, traffic || (συναναστρέφομαι) associate with.

συνάμα [seenama] together, in one lot, at the same time, at once.

συναναστρέφομαι [seenanastrefome] consort with, mix with.

συναναστροφή, η [seenanastrofee] association, company || party, reception.

συνάντηση, η [seenanteesee] falling in with, meeting || encounter.

συναντώ [seenanto] meet, happen (upon), run across.

συναντώμαι [seenantome] meet, come together.

σύναξη, η [seenaksee] concentration, meeting || collecting, receipts.

συναπτός [seenaptos] consecutive, successive || annexed, tied, appended.

συνάπτω [seenapto] annex, attach || (συμμαχία) contract, form || (δάνειο) incur || (ειρήνη) conclude || (μάχη) join, give battle || ~ σχέσεις make friends.

συναρμολογώ [seenarmologo] fit together || join || make up, piece together.

συναρπάζω [seenarpazo] carry away, enrapture, entrance.

συνάρτηση, η [seenarteesee] attachment, connection || cohesion.

συνασπισμός, ο [seenaspeesmos] coalition, alliance, league.

συναυλία, η [seenavleea] concert.

συνάφεια, η [seenafeea] connection, link, reference.

συναφής [seenafees] adjacent (to) || linked, connected || like.

συνάχι, το [seenahee] cold (in the head), catarrh.

σύναψη, η [seenapsee] conclusion, arrangement || contraction || joining.

συνδεδεμένος [seendeðemenos] closely associated with, having ties with.

σύνδεση, η [seendesee] joining, binding together.

σύνδεσμος, ο [seendesmos] bond, union || (στρατ) liaison || relationship, affinity || (γραμμ) conjunction.

συνδετήρας, ο [seendeteeras] clip, paper clip.

συνδετικός [seendeteekos] joining, connective || (γραμμ) copulative.

συνδέω [seendeo] bind together, unite || (μεταφ) join, link, bind.

συνδιαλέγομαι [seendeealegome] converse (with), talk (to).

συνδιάσκεψη, η [seendeeaskepsee] deliberation || conference.

συνδικάτο, το [seendeekato] syndicate || (εργατών) trade union.

συνδράμω [seendramo] support, help || contribute to.

συνδρομή, η [seendromee] coincidence, conjunction || (βοήθεια) help, assistance || subscription, contribution.

συνδρομητής, ο [seendromeetees] subscriber.

σύνδρομο, το [seendromo] syndrome.

συνδυάζομαι [seendeeazome] harmonize, go together, match.

συνδυάζω [seenδeeazo] unite, combine || match, pair || arrange.

συνδυασμός, ο [seenδeeasmos] combination, arrangement || matching.

συνεδριάζω [seeneδreeazo] meet, be in session.

συνέδριο, το [seeneδreeo] congress, convention, council.

σύνεδρος, ο [seeneδros] delegate || councillor || (δικαστηρίου) judge.

συνείδηση, η [seeneeδeesee] conscience.

συνειδητός [seeneeδeetos] conscious, wilful.

συνειρμός, ο [seeneermos] coherence, order, sequence.

συνεισφέρω [seeneesfero] contribute, subscribe.

συνεκτικός [seenekteekos] cohesive, binding, tenacious.

συνέλευση, η [seenelevsee] meeting, assembly.

συνεννόηση, η [seenenoeesee] understanding, concert, concord, agreement || exchange of views.

συνεννοούμαι [seenenooume] agree, come to an agreement || exchange views.

συνενοχή, η [seenenohee] complicity, abetment, connivance.

συνέντευξη, η [seenentevksee] interview, appointment, rendezvous.

συνενώ [seeneno] unite, join together.

συνεπάγομαι [seenepagome] lead to, involve, have as consequence, call for.

συνεπαίρνω [seeneperno] transport, carry away.

συνέπεια, η [seenepeea] result, outcome, consequence || consistency || **κατά ~** consequently.

συνεπής [seenepees] true, in keeping with, consistent || punctual.

συνεπώς [seenepos] consequently, accordingly.

συνεπτυγμένος [seenepteegmenos] compact, succinct, brief.

συνεργάζομαι [seenergazome] cooperate, collaborate || contribute.

συνεργάτης, ο [seenergatees] collaborator || contributor.

συνεργείο, το [seeneryeeo] workroom, workshop || gang, shift, team of workers || repair shop.

συνεργία, η [seeneryeea] complicity, abetment, confederacy.

σύνεργο, το [seenergo] implement, tool, instrument.

συνεργός, ο [seenergos] accessary, accomplice, abettor, party (to).

συνερίζομαι [seenereezome] heed, take into account, keep up rivalry with.

συνέρχομαι [seenerhome] get over, recover || come together, meet, assemble.

σύνεση, η [seenesee] caution, good sense, prudence, judgment.

συνεσταλμένος [seenestalmenos] shy, modest, timid, circumspect.

συνεταιρισμός, ο [seenetereesmos] cooperative, association.

συνέταιρος, ο [seeneteros] partner, associate, colleague, co-partner.

συνετός [seenetos] wise, discreet, prudent, sensible, cautious.

συνεφέρνω [seeneferno] revive, bring round || come to.

συνέχεια, η [seeneheea] continuity || continuation, outcome || (επίρ) continuously, successively.

συνεχής [seenehees] continuous, incessant, unceasing, continual || successive || adjacent.

συνεχίζω [seeneheezo] continue, keep on, go on.

συνεχώς [seenehos] continually, endlessly.

συνήγορος, ο [seeneegoros] advocate, defender, counsel.

συνήθεια, η [seeneetheea] habit, custom, practice, use.

συνήθης [seeneethees] habitual, customary, usual, common, ordinary.

συνηθίζεται [seeneetheezete] it is usual, it is the fashion.

συνηθίζω [seeneetheezo] accustom to || get accustomed to || be in the habit of.

συνηθισμένος [seeneetheesmenos] accustomed, familiar || habitual, customary.

συνημμένος [seeneemenos] attached, connected, annexed, enclosed.

σύνθεση, η [seenthesee] mixture, composition || collocation || structure, synthesis.

συνθέτης, ο [seenthetees] composer || compositor.

συνθετικό, το [seentheteeko] component, constituent.

συνθετικός [seentheteekos] constituent, component || artificial, synthetic.

σύνθετος [seenthetos] compound, composite || intricate.

συνθέτω [seentheto] compose, make up.

συνθήκες, οι [seentheekes] πλ conditions, circumstances, situation.

συνθήκη, η [seentheekee] treaty, agreement, pact || convention.

συνθηκολογώ [seentheekologo] surrender, capitulate || negotiate a treaty.

σύνθημα, το [seentheema] signal, sign, password, watchword.

συνθηματικός [seentheemateekos] symbolic || in code.

συνθλίβω [seenthleevo] squeeze, compress, crush.

συνίσταμαι [seeneestame] consist of, be composed of.

συνιστώ [seeneesto] advise, recommend || (επιτροπή) establish, set up, form || (γνωρίζω) introduce.

συννεφιά, η [seenefia] cloudy weather || ~ ζω become cloudy || (μεταφ) look sullen.

σύννεφο, το [seenefo] cloud.

συννυφάδα, η [seeneefada] wife of one's brother-in-law.

συνοδ(ε)ία η [seenodeea] escort, retinue, suite, convoy, procession || (μουσ) accompaniment.

συνοδεύω [seenodevo] accompany, go with, escort || (ναυτ) convoy.

συνοδοιπόρος, ο [seenodeeporos] fellow traveller.

σύνοδος, η [seenodos] congress, sitting, assembly || (εκκλ) synod.

συνοδός, ο, η [seenodos] steward, escort || ιπτάμενη ~ air hostess.

συνοικέσιο, το [seeneekeseeo] arranged marriage, match.

συνοικία, η [seeneekeea] quarter, neighbourhood, ward.

συνοικιακός [seeneekeeakos] local, suburban.

συνοικισμός, ο [seeneekeesmos] settlement || colonization || quarter.

συνολικός [seenoleekos] total, whole.

σύνολο, το [seenolo] total, entirety.

συνομήλικος [seenomeeleekos] of the same age.

συνομιλητής, ο [seenomeeleetees] interlocutor.

συνομιλία, η [seenomeeleea] conversation, chat, talk || interview.

συνομοταξία, η [seenomotakseea] branch, group, class.

συνονόματος [seenonomatos] namesake, having the same name.

συνοπτικός [seenopteekos] summary, brief, synoptic, concise.

σύνορα, τα [seenora] πλ frontier, boundaries.

συνορεύω [seenorevo] have a common frontier, border on.

σύνορο, το [seenoro] boundary, border, frontier.

συνουσία, n [seenouseea] coition, intercourse, copulation.

συνοφρυόνομαι [seenofreeonome] frown, scowl || look sullen.

συνοχή, n [seenohee] coherence, cohesion || (ιδεών) sequence, chain.

σύνοψη, n [seenopsee] summary, compendium, synopsis || (εκκλ) prayer book, breviary.

συνταγή, n [seentayee] formula, prescription || recipe.

σύνταγμα, το [seentagma] constitution, charter || (στρατ) regiment.

συνταγματάρχης, ο [seentagmatarhees] colonel.

συνταγματικός [seentagmateekos] constitutional.

συντάκτης, ο [seentaktees] author, writer || (εφημερίδας) editor || (συνθήκης) drafter, framer.

συντακτικός [seentakteekos] component, constituent || (εφημερίδας) editorial || (γραμμ) syntactic(al).

σύνταξη, n [seentaksee] compilation || wording, writing || organization || (εφημερίδας) editing, editorial staff || pension || (γραμμ) construction, syntax.

συνταξιούχος, ο, n [seentaksiouhos] pensioner || retired officer.

συνταράσσω [seentaraso] agitate, shake, disturb, trouble || (μεταφ) disconcert.

συντάσσω [seentaso] arrange, compile || write, draft, draw up || (γραμμ) construe || constitute, form, organize || (νόμο) frame || (εφημερίδα) edit.

συνταυτίζω [seentavteezo] identify, regard as the same.

συντείνω [seenteeno] contribute to, concur.

συντέλεια, n [seenteleea]: ~ του κόσμου end of the world.

συντελεστής, ο [seentelestees] factor, component, contributor || (μαθημ) coefficient.

συντελώ [seentelo] finish, complete || contribute, to conduce to.

συντεταγμένη, n [seentetagmenee] coordinate.

συντετριμμένος [seentetremenos] deeply afflicted, crushed.

συντεχνία, n [seentehneea] guild, fellowship, confraternity || trade union.

συντήρηση, n [seenteereesee] preservation, conservation || (μηχανής) maintenance.

συντηρητικός [seenteereeteekos] conservative, preserving.

συντηρώ [seenteero] preserve, conserve || keep up, maintain || (διατρέφω) maintain, support.

σύντομα [seentoma] in short, briefly || soon, at once, immediately.

συντομεύω [seentomevo] shorten, curtail, abridge.

συντομία, n [seentomeea] shortness, brevity || terseness.

σύντομος [seentomos] short, succinct, brief.

συντονίζω [seentoneezo] coordinate, harmonize, tune together.

συντρέχω [seentreho] help || meet, converge || contribute.

συντριβή, n [seentreevee] ruin || crushing, smashing.

συντρίβω [seentreevo] shatter, break, crush, smash || ruin, wear out.

συντρίμια, τα [seentreemeea] πλ debris, fragments, wreckage.

συντριπτικός [seentreepteekos] (μεταφ) crushing, overwhelming.

συντροφιά, η [seentrofia] companionship, company || gathering, society || (επίρ) together.

σύντροφος, ο, η [seentrofos] companion, mate, comrade || (εμπορ) associate, partner.

συνύπαρξη, η [seeneeparksee] coexistence.

συνυπάρχω [seeneeparho] coexist.

συνυπεύθυνος [seeneepevtheenos] jointly liable.

συνυφαίνω [seeneefeno] entwine || (μεταφ) conspire, intrigue.

συνωμοσία, η [seenomoseea] conspiracy, plot.

συνωμοτώ [seenomoto] conspire, plot.

συνώνυμο, το [seenoneemo] synonym.

συνωστισμός, ο [seenosteesmos] jostle, crush, scramble.

σύξυλος [seekseelos] with crew and cargo || **έμεινε ~** he was amazed, he was speechless.

Συρία, η [seereea] Syria.

συριακός [seereeakos] Syrian.

σύριγγα, η [seereenga] pan pipes || syringe, tube.

Σύριος, ο [seereeos] Syrian.

σύρμα, το [seerma] wire.

συρματόπλεγμα, το [seermatoplegma] barbed wire || wire netting.

σύρραξη, η [seeraksee] clash, collision, shock, conflict.

συρρέω [seereo] crowd, throng, flock || flow into.

σύρριζα [seereeza] by the root, root and branch || very closely.

συρροή, η [seeroee] crowd, throng || inflow, influx || abundance, profusion.

συρτάρι, το [seertaree] drawer.

σύρτης, ο [seertees] bolt, bar.

συρτός [seertos] dragged || listless, drawling || (νότα) sliding || (ουσ) kind of circular dance.

συρφετός, ο [seerfetos] mob, populace, common people.

σύρω [seero] βλ **σέρνω.**

συσκέπτομαι [seeskeptome] confer, deliberate, take counsel.

συσκευάζω [seeskevazo] pack, box, wrap, parcel.

συσκευασία, η [seeskevaseea] wrapping up, packing || (φαρμακευτική) preparation.

συσκευή, η [seeskevee] apparatus, contrivance.

σύσκεψη, η [seeskepsee] discussion, deliberation || conference, consultation.

συσκοτίζω [seeskoteezo] obscure, darken, black out || (μεταφ) confuse.

συσκότιση, η [seeskoteesee] blackout || confusion.

σύσπαση, η [seespasee] contraction, writhing, shrinking.

συσπειρούμαι [seespeeroume] roll into a ball, coil || (μεταφ) snuggle.

συσσίτιο, το [seeseeteeo] mess, common meal || soup kitchen.

σύσσωμος [seesomos] all together, entire, united, in a body.

συσσωρευτής, ο [seesorevtees] accumulator.

συσσωρεύω [seesorevo] accumulate, collect, pile up || amass.

συσταίνω [seesteno] βλ **συστώ.**

συστάδα, η [seestada] clump of trees, cluster, grove.

συστάσεις, οι [seestasees] πλ references, advice || recommendation, introductions.

σύσταση, η [seestasee] address.

σύσταση, η [seestasee] composition, structure || (πάχος) consistency || (σχηματισμός) formation, creation, setting up ||

(πρόταση) recommendation, recommending || (συμβουλή) advice, counsel.

συστατικά, τα [seestateeka] πλ component parts, ingredients || references, recommendations.

συστατική [seestateekee]: ~ επιστολή letter of introduction, letter of reference.

συστατικός [seestateekos] component, essential, constituent.

συστέλλομαι [seestelome] shrink, contract || feel shy, be timid.

συστέλλω [seestelo] contract, shrink, shrivel.

σύστημα, το [seesteema] method, system, plan || custom, habitude.

συστηματικός [seesteemateekos] systematic, methodical.

συστημένο [seesteemeno]: ~ γράμμα registered letter.

συστήνω [seesteeno] βλ συνιστώ.

συστολή, η [seestolee] shrinking, contraction || modesty, shame, bashfulness.

συσφίγγω [seesfeengo] tighten, constrict, draw tighter, grasp.

συσχετίζω [seesheteezo] compare, relate, put together.

σύφιλη, η [seefeelee] syphilis.

συχνά [seehna] often, frequently.

συχνάζω [seehnazo] frequent, haunt, resort.

συχνός [seehnos] frequent, repeated.

συχνότητα, η [seehnoteeta] frequency.

συχωράω [seehorao] forgive, tolerate.

σφαγείο, το [sfayeeo] slaughterhouse || butchery, slaughter.

σφαγή, η [sfayee] slaughter, carnage, massacre.

σφάγιο, το [sfayo] victim, animal for slaughter.

σφαδάζω [sfadazo] writhe, jerk, squirm.

σφάζω [sfazo] slaughter, kill, massacre, murder.

σφαίρα, η [sfera] globe, sphere || ball || (όπλου) bullet || (μεταφ) sphere, field.

σφαλιάρα, η [sfaleeara] slap in the face || smack.

σφαλίζω [sfaleezo] enclose, shut in || (κλείνω) close, lock, bolt.

σφάλλω [sfalo] be wrong, make a mistake || misfire.

σφάλμα, το [sfalma] wrong act, fault || error, blunder, slip.

σφάχτης, ο [sfahtees] twinge, sharp pain.

σφενδόνη, η [sfendonee] sling.

σφετερίζομαι [sfetereezome] purloin, embezzle || appropriate, usurp.

σφήκα, η [sfeeka] wasp.

σφην, η [sfeen)], σφήνα, η [sfeena] wedge.

σφηνώνω [sfeenono] push in, thrust in between || wedge.

σφίγγα, η [sfeenga] sphinx || (μεταφ) enigmatic.

σφίγγομαι [sfeengome] squeeze together || endeavour, try hard.

σφίγγω [sfeengo] squeeze, press || tighten, pull tighter || (σκληρύνω) become tight, stick.

σφίξη, η [sfeeksee] urgency, necessity.

σφίξιμο, το [sfeekseemo] pressing, tightening, squeezing || pressure, squeeze.

σφιχτός [sfeehtos] tight, hard, thick || stingy, tight-fisted.

σφοδρός [sfoðros] violent, wild, strong, severe, sharp.

σφοδρότητα, η [sfoðroteeta] violence, vehemence, wildness.

σφουγγάρι, το [sfoungaree] sponge.

σφουγγαρόπανο, το [sfoungaropano] mop, floorcloth.

σφραγίζω [sfrayeezo] set one's seal to, stamp || (μπουκάλι) cork || (δόντι) fill.

σφραγίδα, η [sfrayeeða] seal, signet, stamp || (μεταφ) impression.

σφρίγος, το [sfreegos] youthful exuberance, vigour, pep.

σφυγμός, ο [sfeegmos] pulse || (μεταφ) caprice, whim.

σφύζω [sfeezo] throb, beat violently, pulsate.

σφύξη, η [sfeeksee] pulsation, throbbing, throb.

σφυρηλατώ [sfeereelato] hammer, batter, forge, pound away || trump up.

σφυρί, το [sfeeree] hammer.

σφύριγμα, το [sfeereegma] whistling, hissing.

σφυρίζω [sfeereezo] whistle, hiss, boo.

σφυρίχτρα, η [sfeereehtra] whistle || (ναυτ) pipe.

σφυροκοπώ [sfeerokopo] hammer || pound away.

σχεδία, η [sheðeea] raft, float.

σχεδιάγραμμα, το [sheðeeagrama] sketch, outline, draft.

σχεδιάζω [sheðeeazo] sketch, outline, design, draw || plan, intend, mean.

σχεδιαστής, ο [sheðeeastees] draughtsman, designer.

σχέδιο, το [sheðeeo] plan, design || sketch, outline || scheme || ~ πόλεως town planning.

σχεδόν [sheðon] almost, nearly, all but || not much, scarcely.

σχέση, η [shesee] relation, connection, reference || intercourse, relations.

σχετίζομαι [sheteezome] be intimate with, get acquainted with, make friends with.

σχετίζω [sheteezo] put side by side, connect, compare.

σχετικά [sheteeka] relative to, relatively || ~ με with reference to, regarding, referring to.

σχετικός [sheteekos] relative, pertinent.

σχετικότητα, η [sheteekoteeta] relativity.

σχήμα, το [sheema] form, shape || (μέγεθος) format, size || (ιερατικό) cloth || gesture || ~ λόγου figure of speech.

σχηματίζω [sheemateezo] form, model, shape || create, produce || constitute.

σχηματισμός, ο [sheemateesmos] forming, formation, fashioning, construction.

σχίζομαι [sheezome] crack, tear || fork.

σχίζω [sheezo] split, cleave || tear, rend, fissure.

σχίσμα, το [sheesma] crack || schism, dissension, breach.

σχισμάδα, η [sheesmaða] crack, split, fissure.

σχισμή, η [sheesmee] crack, fissure, split.

σχιστόλιθος, ο [sheestoleethos] schist, slate.

σχιστός [sheestos] split, slit, torn, open.

σχοινί, το [sheenee] rope, cord || clothes line.

σχοινοβάτης, ο [sheenovatees] acrobat, rope dancer.

σχολάω [sholao] stop work || rest, be on vacation || (από σχολείο) let out || (από εργασία) dismiss, discharge.

σχολαστικός [sholasteekos] pedantic, scholastic.

σχολείο, το [sholeeo] school.

σχολή, η [sholee] school, academy || free time, leisure.

σχολιάζω [sholeeazo] comment on,

pass remarks (on), criticize || annotate, edit.

σχολιαστής, ο [sholeeastees] commentator || editor, annotator, scholiast.

σχολικός [sholeekos] of school, scholastic, educational.

σχόλιο, το [sholeeo] comment, commentary, annotation.

σώβρακο, το [sovrako] pants, drawers.

σώζομαι [sozome] escape || remain in existence.

σώζω [sozo] save, rescue || preserve, keep.

σωθικά, τα [sotheeka] πλ entrails, bowels, intestines, innards.

σωλήνας, ο [soleenas] pipe, tube, conduit || hose.

σωληνάριο, το [soleenareeo] small tube.

σώμα, το [soma] body, corpse || corps || ~ στρατού army corps, armed force, army.

σωματείο, το [somateeo] guild, association.

σωματέμπορος, ο [somatemboros] white slaver || pimp.

σωματικός [somateekos] of the body, physical.

σωματοφυλακή, η [somatofeelakee] bodyguard.

σωματώδης [somatodees] corpulent, stout, portly.

σώνει [sonee] ~ **και καλά** with stubborn insistence.

σώνω [sono] save, rescue, preserve || use up, consume || attain, reach || be enough, be sufficient.

σώος [soos] safe, entire, whole, unharmed || intact || ~ **κι αβλαβής** safe and sound.

σωπαίνω [sopeno] keep silent, say nothing.

σωριάζομαι [soreeazome] collapse, fall in.

σωρός, ο [soros] heap, mass, pile || a lot of, a stack of.

σωσίας, ο [soseeas] living image, double || stand-in.

σωσίβιο, το [soseeveeo] lifebelt, life jacket.

σώσιμο, το [soseemo] saving || finishing up, eating.

σωστά [sosta]: **με τα ~ του** in his right mind, in earnest.

σωστά [sosta] correctly, precisely, rightly, exactly, absolutely.

σωστός [sostos] correct, just, right || whole, entire || absolute.

σωτήρας, ο [soteeras] saviour, liberator, rescuer.

σωτηρία, η [soteereea] safety, security || salvation, deliverance, saving.

σωφέρ, ο [sofer] chauffeur, driver.

σώφρονας, ο [sofronas] wise, sensible, prudent || moderate, sober, temperate.

σωφρονίζω [sofroneezo] reform, chastise, correct, bring to reason, render wise.

σωφροσύνη, η [sofroseenee] wisdom, prudence, sense, judgment || moderation, composure.

Τ, τ

τα [ta] πλ the || them.

ταβάνι, το [tavanee] ceiling.

ταβέρνα, η [taverna] tavern, inn, eating house.

τάβλα, η [tavla] board, plank || table || ~ **στο μεθύσι** dead drunk.

τάβλι, το [tavlee] backgammon.

ταγάρι, το [tagaree] bag, sack, wallet.

ταγγός [tangos] rancid, rank.

ταγή, η [tayee] fodder.

ταγιέρ, το [tayier] woman's suit.

τάγμα, το [tagma] order || (στρατ) battalion.

ταγματάρχης, ο [tagmatarhees] major.

τάδε [taðe] as follows, the following, this, that || ο ~ Mr so and so || such.

τάζω [tazo] promise, dedicate, vow.

ταΐζω [taeezo] feed || (μωρό) nurse.

ταινία, η [teneea] band, stretch, strip, ribbon || (κινηματογράφου) strip, film || (μηχανής) tape, ribbon || (ιατρ) tapeworm || (μετρήσεως) tape measure.

ταίρι, το [teree] helpmate, partner, mate || one of two || match, equal.

ταιριάζει [tereeazee]: δεν ~ it's not fitting, it's not proper.

ταιριάζω [tereeazo] match, pair, suit, harmonize.

ταιριαστός [tereeastos] well-suited, matched.

τάκος, ο [takos] wooden fixing block, stump.

τακούνι, το [takounee] heel.

τακτ, το [takt] tact.

τακτικά [takteeka] regularly, frequently.

τακτική, η [takteekee] tactics, strategy || method, regularity.

τακτικός [takteekos] regular || orderly, settled, quiet || fixed || (αριθμός) ordinal.

τακτοποίηση, η [taktopeeesee] arrangement, accommodation || compromise.

τακτοποιώ [taktopeeo] arrange, set in order || settle, fix up.

τακτός [taktos] fixed, appointed, settled.

ταλαιπωρία, η [taleporeea] torment, hardship, pain, adversity.

ταλαίπωρος [taleporos] miserable, wretched, unfortunate.

ταλαιπωρούμαι [taleporoume] suffer, toil, labour.

ταλαιπωρώ [taleporo] harass, pester, torment.

ταλαντεύομαι [talantevome] swing, sway, rock || waver, hesitate.

τάλέντο, το [talento] talent, gift, faculty.

τάλιρο, το [taleero] coin of five drachmas.

τάμα, το [tama] βλ τάξιμο.

ταμείο, το [tameeo] cashier's office, booking office, cash desk || treasury, pension fund.

ταμίας, ο [tameeas] cashier, teller, treasurer.

ταμιευτήριο, το [tamievteereeo] savings bank.

ταμπακιέρα, η [tambakiera] cigarette case || snuff box.

ταμπέλα, η [tambela] nameplate, bill || registration plate.

ταμπλό, το [tamblo] painting, picture || (αυτοκινήτου) dashboard || switchboard || instrument panel.

ταμπούρλο, το [tambourlo] drum || (παιδικό) side drum.

τανάλια, τα [tanaleea] πλ pliers, tongs, tweezers.

τανκ, το [tank] (στρατ) tank.

τάξη, η [taksee] order, succession, regularity || class, rank, grade || (σχολείου) form || εντάξει O.K., all right || τάξεις πλ ranks || πρώτης τάξεως first-rate, first-class.

ταξί, το [taksee] taxi (cab).

ταξιάρχης, ο [takseearhees] brigadier || (εκκλ) archangel.

ταξιαρχία η [takseearheea] brigade.

ταξιδεύω [takseeðevo] travel, journey.

ταξίδι, το [takseeðee] trip, journey, travel, voyage.

ταξιδιώτης, ο [takseeðeeotees] traveller.

ταξιθέτρια, η [takseethetreea] theatre attendant, usher.

ταξικός [takseekos] class.

ταξίμετρο, το [takseemetro] taximeter.

τάξιμο, το [takseemo] vow, promise.

ταξινομώ [takseenomo] classify, class, arrange || grade.

τάπα, n [tapa] plug, cork, stopper || ~ στο μεθύσι dead drunk.

ταπεινός [tapeenos] modest, humble || abject, vile, base.

ταπεινοφροσύνη, n [tapeenofroseenee] humility, modesty.

ταπεινώνομαι [tapeenonome] be humiliated || lower o.s.

ταπεινώνω [tapeenono] humble, humiliate, mortify, embarrass.

ταπέτο, το [tapeto] carpet, rug.

ταπετσαρία, n [tapetsareea] tapestry, wall covering || upholstery.

ταπητουργία, n [tapeetouryeea] carpet-making.

τάραγμα, το [taragma] agitation, shaking.

ταράζω [tarazo] shake || disturb, upset.

ταραμάς, ο [taramas] preserved roe.

ταραξίας, ο [tarakseeas] rowdy person, agitator, noisy person.

ταράτσα, n [taratsa] flat roof, terrace.

ταραχή, n [tarahee] agitation, disturbance || upset.

ταραχοποιός, ο [tarahopeeos] βλ **ταραξίας**.

ταρίφα, n [tareefa] scale of charges, price list, rates.

ταριχεύω [tareehevo] embalm || preserve, cure, smoke.

ταρσανάς, ο [tarsanas] boatbuilder's yard.

τάρταρα, τα [tartara] πλ bowels of the earth.

τασάκι, το [tasakee] saucer || ashtray.

τάση, n [tasee] tension, strain || (ηλεκτ) voltage || (μεταφ) inclination, proclivity, tendency.

τάσι, το [tasee] shallow bowl, goblet.

τάσσομαι [tasome] place o.s. || (μεταφ) support.

τάσσω [taso] place, put || post, set || marshal || assign, fix.

ταυ, το [tav] the letter T.

ταυρομαχία, n [tavromaheea] bullfight.

ταύρος, ο [tavros] bull.

ταύτα [tavta] πλ these || μετά ~ afterwards.

ταυτίζω [tavteezo] identify, regard as same.

ταυτόσημος [tavtoseemos] equivalent, synonymous.

ταυτότητα, n [tavtoteeta] identity, sameness || identity card.

ταυτόχρονος [tavtohronos] simultaneous.

ταφή, n [tafee] burial, interment.

τάφος, ο [tafos] grave, tomb, vault.

τάφρος, ο [tafros] ditch, trench, drain || (οχυρού) moat.

τάχα(τες) [taha(tes)] perhaps, apparently, supposedly || as if.

ταχεία, n [taheea] express train.

ταχίνι, το [taheenee] ground sesame.

ταχυδακτυλουργία, n [taheeδakteelouryeea] conjuring trick, juggling.

ταχυδρομείο, το [taheeδromeeo] post, mail || post office.

ταχυδρομικώς [taheeδromeekos] by post, by mail.

ταχυδρόμος, ο [taheeδromos] postman.

ταχυδρομώ [taheeδromo] mail, post.

ταχύνω [taheeno] quicken, speed up, accelerate || hasten, push forward.

ταχυπαλμία, n [taheepalmeea] palpitation.

ταχύς [tahees] quick, brisk, rapid, fleet, swift, fast || prompt, speedy.

ταχύτητα, η [taheeteeta] swiftness, speed, rapidity || promptness || velocity, rate.

ταμί, το [tapsee] large shallow baking pan.

τέζα [teza] stretched, spread, tight || έμεινε ~ he kicked the bucket (col) || ~ στο μεθύσι dead drunk.

τεθλασμένη, η [tethlasmenee] zigzag line, broken line.

τεθλασμένος [tethlasmenos] broken.

τεθλιμμένος [tethleemenos] grief-stricken, heartbroken.

τείνω [teeno] tighten, stretch out || strain || tend (to), lead (to), be inclined (to).

τείχος, το [teehos] wall, high wall.

τεκμήριο, το [tekmeereeo] sign, token, mark, clue, indication.

τεκτονισμός, ο [tektoneesmos] freemasonry.

τελάρο, το [telaro] embroidery frame || (θύρας) doorframe || (πίνακα) frame.

τελεία, η [teleea] full stop || άνω ~ semicolon.

τελεσίγραφο, το [teleseegrafo] ultimatum.

τελεσίδικος [teleseeδeekos] final, irrevocable, decisive.

τέλεση, η [telesee] ceremony || perpetration || completion.

τελετάρχης, ο [teletarhees] master of ceremonies.

τελετή, η [teletee] celebration, rite || feast, festival.

τελευταίος [televteos] last || most recent.

τελευταίως [televteos] of late, recently.

τέλι, το [telee] thin wire.

τελικά [teleeka] in the end, finally.

τέλμα, το [telma] swamp, marsh, bog.

τέλος, το [telos] end || (φόρος) tax, duty || expiration, close || ~ πάντων after all, at all events, finally || επί τέλους at last, at long last || στο ~ at the end, finally || εν τέλει in the end, finally.

τελούμαι [teloume] happen, take place.

τελωνείο, το [teloneeo] customs house.

τελώνης, ο [telonees] customs officer.

τεμαχίζω [temaheezo] cut into pieces, separate, break up.

τεμάχιο, το [temaheeon] piece, parcel, bit, fragment, chunk.

τέμενος, το [temenos] temple, shrine, mosque, house of worship.

τέμνω [temno] cut, divide, open.

τεμπέλης [tembelees] lazy, indolent, idle.

τεμπελιάζω [tembeleeazo] loaf, get lazy, idle.

τέμπλο, το [templo] iconostasis, reredos.

τενεκεδένιος [tenekeδeneeos] made of tin.

τενεκές, ο [tenekes] tin || large can || (μεταφ) good-for-nothing.

τέλειος [teleeos] perfect, faultless || ideal || accomplished.

τελειότητα, η [teleeoteeta] perfection, faultlessness.

τελειόφοιτος [teleeofeetos] final-year (student) || graduate.

τελειωμός, ο [teleeomos] end, finish || τελειωμό δεν έχει it is interminable, it is inexhaustible.

τελειώνω [teleeono] exhaust, finish up || end, conclude, finish || (μεταφ) die, be exhausted.

τελείως [teleeos] faultlessly, perfectly || completely, fully, entirely, utterly.

τελειωτικός [teleeoteekos] definitive, decisive, final, conclusive.

τένις, το [tenees] tennis.

τένοντας, ο [tenontas] tendon.

τενόρος, ο [tenoros] tenor.

τέντα, η [tenta] tent || marquee.

τέντζερες, ο [tendzeres] cooking pot, kettle, casserole.

τεντώνω [tentono] stretch, tighten, bend || (μεταφ) strain.

τέρας, το [teras] monster, abortion, freak || (μεταφ) terror.

τεράστιος [terasteeos] prodigious, enormous, huge, vast.

τερατούργημα, το [teratouryeema] monstrosity || atrocious deed.

τερατώδης [teratodees] prodigious, monstrous || ugly, frightful.

τέρμα, το [terma] extremity, terminus, end || (αθλητ) goal.

τερματίζω [termateezo] finish, put an end to, terminate, end.

τερματικό, το [termateeko] computer terminal.

τερματοφύλακας, ο [termatofeelakas] goalkeeper.

τερπνός [terpnos] delightful, agreeable, pleasing.

τερτίπι, το [terteepee] trick.

τέρψη, η [terpsee] delight, pleasure, amusement.

τέσσαρα [tessara] four || **με τα ~** on all fours.

τέσσερις [tesserees] four.

τεταμένος [tetamenos] stretched, extended, strained.

τέτανος, ο [tetanos] tetanus.

Τετάρτη, η [tetartee] Wednesday.

τέταρτο, το [tetarto] quarter of an hour || quarto.

τέταρτος [tetartos] fourth.

τετελεσμένος [tetelesmenos] accomplished, achieved, done || **τετελεσμένο ~ μέλλων** (γραμμ) future perfect tense.

τέτοιος [teteeos] similar, alike, such || **ο ~** what's-his-name.

τετραγωνικός [tetragoneekos] square, quadrangular.

τετράγωνο, το [tetragono] (γεωμ) square, quadrangle || (πόλης) block.

τετράγωνος [tetragonos] square || (μεταφ) well-grounded, reasonable.

τετράδιο, το [tetradeeo] exercise book, copybook.

τετρακόσιοι [tetrakosiee] four hundred.

τετράπαχος [tetrapahos] very stout, very fat, corpulent.

τετραπέρατος [tetraperatos] very clever, shrewd.

τετραπλάσιος [tetraplaseeos] four times as much.

τετράποδο, το [tetrapodo] quadruped || (μεταφ) beast, brute.

τετράδα, η [tetrada] set of four.

τετράτροχος [tetratrohos] four-wheeled.

τετριμμένος [tetreemenos] worn-out || (μεταφ) hackneyed.

τεύτλο, το [tevtlo] beetroot, beet.

τεύχος, το [tevhos] issue (of a publication).

τέφρα, η [tefra] ashes, cinders.

τεφτέρι, το [tefteree] notebook || account book.

τέχνες, οι [tehnes] πλ: **καλές ~** fine arts.

τέχνασμα, το [tehnasma] ruse, artifice, trick, device.

τέχνη, η [tehnee] art || profession || dexterity || (πολεμική) stratagem.

τεχνητός [tehneetos] sham, false, artificial || simulated, affected.

τεχνική, η [tehneekee] technique, means.

τεχνικός [tehneekos] technical, professional || (ουσ) technician.

τεχνίτης, ο [tehneetees] professional, craftsman || technician, mechanic || (μεταφ) specialist, expert.

τεχνολογία, η [tehnoloyeea]

technology || (γραμμ) grammatical analysis.

τεχνοτροπία, η [tehnotropeea] artistic style.

τέως [teos] formerly, former, late || ο ~ **πρόεδρος** the ex-president.

τζάκι, το [dzakee] fireplace || heating range.

τζάμι, το [dzamee] window pane, pane of glass.

τζαμί, το [dzamee] mosque.

τζάμπα [dzamba] free, gratis, for nothing || to no purpose, wantonly.

τζαναμπέτης, ο [dzanambetees] peevish person || wicked person.

τζελατίνα, η [dzelateena] gelatine || celluloid holder.

τζίρος, ο [dzeeros] business turnover.

τζίτζικας, ο [dzeedzeekas] cicada.

τζίφρα, η [dzeefra] cipher || initial, monogram.

τζόγος, ο [dzogos] gambling.

τζόκεϋ, ο [dzokey] jockey.

τήβεννος, η [teevennos] toga || gown, robe.

τηγανητός [teeganeetos] fried.

τηγάνι, το [teeganee] frying pan.

τηγανίζω [teeganeezo] fry.

τήκομαι [teekome] thaw, melt || wither, pine, languish.

τήκω [teeko] melt, thaw.

τηλεβόας, ο [teelevoas] loudhailer, loudspeaker.

τηλεβόλο, το [teelevolo] cannon.

τηλεγράφημα, το [teelegrafeema] telegram, cable.

τηλέγραφος, ο [teelegrafos] telegraph.

τηλεγραφώ [teelegrafo] telegraph, wire.

τηλεόραση, η [teeleorasee] television.

τηλεπάθεια, η [teelepatheea] telepathy.

τηλεπικοινωνία, η

[teelepeekeenoneea] telecommunications.

τηλεσκόπιο, το [teeleskopeeo] telescope.

τηλεφώνημα, το [teelefoneema] telephone call.

τηλεφωνητής, ο [teelefoneetees] telephone operator.

τηλέφωνο, το [teelefono] telephone, phone.

τηλεφωνώ [teelefono] telephone, call up.

τήξη, η [teeksee] melting, thawing || casting.

τήρηση, η [teereesee] observance || maintenance, keeping.

τηρώ [teero] keep, observe, follow, maintain.

τι [tee] what || what, how.

τι [tee] something || a bit.

τίγρη, η [teegree] tiger, tigress.

τιθασεύω [teethasevo] tame, domesticate.

τίθεμαι [teetheme] be arranged, be placed, be imposed.

τίλιο, το [teeleeo] infusion of lime flowers.

τιμαλφή, τα [teemalfee] πλ jewellery, jewels.

τιμάριθμος, ο [teemareethmos] cost of living.

τιμή, η [teemee] respect, honour || rate, price || value, worth.

τίμημα, το [teemeema] cost, price || value.

τιμητικός [teemeeteekos] honorary || honouring.

τίμιος [teemeeos] honest, upright || precious, valuable.

τιμιότητα, η [teemeeoteeta] honesty.

τιμοκατάλογος, ο [teemokatalogos] price list, tariff.

τιμολόγιο, το [teemoloyo] invoice, bill.

τιμόνι, το [teemonee] helm, rudder || tiller, wheel || (αυτοκινήτου)

steering wheel || (ποδηλάτου) handlebars.

τιμονιέρης, ο [teemonierees] steersman, helmsman.

τιμώ [teemo] honour, respect, venerate, do honour to.

τιμώμαι [teemome] cost, be worth || be honoured.

τιμωρία, η [teemoreea] punishment, chastisement, penalty.

τιμωρώ [teemoro] punish, chastise || fine.

τινάζομαι [teenazome] leap, spring, start || brush one's clothes.

τινάζω [teenazo] shake off, shake || (πετώ) hurl, toss || (φτερουγίζω) flap || ~ στον αέρα blow up.

τίποτα [teepota] any, anything || nothing || —! don't mention it!, forget it!

τιποτένιος [teepoteneeos] mean, trivial, trifling, worthless.

τιράντες, οι [teerantes] πλ pair of braces.

τιρμπουσόν, το [teermbouson] corkscrew.

τίτλος, ο [teetlos] title, right, claim || certificate.

τιτλοφορώ [teetloforo] entitle, confer a title.

τμήμα, το [tmeema] part, segment, section || (υπουργείου) branch, department || (αστυνομίας) police station.

τμηματάρχης, ο [tmeematarhees] chief of a department.

το [to] the || it.

τοιούτος [teeoutos] such || (μεταφ) homosexual.

τοιχογραφία, η [teehografeea] fresco, wall painting.

τοιχοκόλληση, η [teehokoleesee] bill posting, bill sticking.

τοίχος, ο [teehos] wall.

τοίχωμα, το [teehoma] inner wall, partition wall || inner surface.

τοκετός, ο [toketos] childbirth, confinement.

τοκίζω [tokeezo] lend at interest, invest.

τοκογλύφος, ο [tokogleefos] usurer.

τοκομερίδιο, το [tokomereedheeo] dividend coupon.

τόκος, ο [tokos] interest, rate.

τόλμη, η [tolmee] daring, audacity.

τολμηρός [tolmeeros] bold, courageous, daring, venturesome.

τολμώ [tolmo] dare, risk, hazard.

τομάρι, το [tomaree] hide, skin, leather.

τομέας, ο [tomeas] sector || incisor, chisel.

τομή, η [tomee] cut, gash, incision || (διαγράμματος) section.

τόμος, ο [tomos] volume, tome.

τονίζω [toneezo] accent || accentuate, stress, lay emphasis on || tone up.

τονισμός, ο [toneesmos] accentuation || emphasizing.

τόνος, ο [tonos] ton || (ψάρι) tuna fish || accent, tone || (γραμμ) accent || (μουσ) key || μιλώ με τόνο raise one's voice || δίνω ~ σε brighten up.

τονώνω [tonono] fortify, invigorate, brace up.

τονωτικός [tonoteekos] bracing, invigorating, tonic.

τοξικομανής, ο, η [tokseekomanees] drug addict.

τοξικός [tokseekos] toxic || poisonous.

τοξοειδής [toksoeedhees] bowed, arched, curved, bow-shaped.

τόξο, το [tokso] bow || (κτιρίου) arch || (γεωμ) arc, curve.

τοπίο, το [topeeo] landscape || site, locality.

τόπι, το [topee] ball || (υφάσματος) roll of cloth || (κανονιού) cannonball.

τοπικός [topeekos] local.

τοπογραφία, η [topografeea] topography.

τοποθεσία, η [topotheseea] location, site, position, place.

τοποθέτηση, η [topotheteesee] putting, placing || (οικον) investment, investing.

τοποθετώ [topotheto] place, set, put || (οικον) invest.

τόπος, ο [topos] place, position, site || (χώρα) country || (χώρος) space, room || (μαθημ) locus || **πιάνω τόπο** have effect, be of use || **έμεινε στον τόπο** he died suddenly.

τοπωνυμία, η [toponeemeea] place name.

τορνευτός [tornevtos] well-turned, turned.

τορνεύω [tornevo] turn a lathe, work a lathe || (μεταφ) give fine shape to.

τόρνος, ο [tornos] lathe.

τορπίλη, η [torpeelee] torpedo.

τορπιλίζω [torpeeleezo] torpedo.

τόσο [toso] so much || ~ ... **όσο** as much ... as, both ... and || **όχι και** ~ not so much.

τόσος [tosos] so big, so large, so great || so much, so many || ~ **δα** very little, very small, only so small || **άλλοι τόσοι** as many again || **κάθε τόσο** every now and again || **εκατόν τόσα** a hundred odd.

τότε [tote] then, at that time || in that case, therefore, thereupon || ~ **που** when.

τουαλέτα, η [toualeta] toilet || (γυναίκας) dress || (αίθουσα) dressing room || (τραπέζι) dressing table || (αποχωρητήριο) lavatory.

τούβλο, το [touvlo] brick || (μεταφ) simpleton.

τουλάχιστον [toulaheeston] at least, at all events.

τούλι, το [toulee] tulle.

τουλίπα, η [touleepa] tulip.

τουλούμι, το [touloumee] goatskin bottle || **βρέχει με το** ~ it's raining cats and dogs.

τούμπα, η [toumba] somersault, fall || (mound) || **κάνω τούμπες κωντω** fall head over heels.

τούμπανο, το [toumbano] drum.

τουμπάρω [toumbaro] overturn, upset || (μεταφ) persuade || reverse.

τουναντίο(ν) [tounanteeo(n)] on the contrary.

τουπέ, ο [toupe] cheek, audacity, nerve.

τουρισμός, ο [toureesmos] tourism, touring.

τουρίστας, ο [toureestas] tourist.

Τουρκία, η [tourkeea] Turkey.

τουρκικός [tourkeekos] Turkish.

τουρκοκρατία, η [tourkokrateea] Turkish domination of Greece.

Τούρκος, ο [tourkos] Turk || **γίνομαι** ~ get angry.

τουρλώνω [tourlono] pile up || swell out, become round.

τουρλωτός [tourlotos] piled up || rounded, bulging.

τουρνέ, η [tourne] theatrical tour.

τουρσί, το [toursee] pickle, brine.

τούρτα, η [tourta] gateau, layer cake, tart.

τουρτουρίζω [tourtoureezo] shiver, tremble, shudder.

τούτος [toutos] this one.

τούφα, η [toufa] tuft, bunch, cluster.

τουφέκι, το [toufekee] rifle, musket, gun.

τουφεκιά, η [toufekia] gunshot, rifle shot.

τουφεκίζω [toufekeezo] shoot, fire || execute.

τράβηγμα, το [traveegma] pulling, dragging, tug || (υγρού) drawing off.

τραβώ [travo] pull, drag, heave, haul || ~ **το δρόμο μου** go my own way || (όπλο, χρήματα κτλ) draw || **το τραβάει** he imbibes ||

(απορροφώ) absorb || (τουφεκιά) fire, shoot || (ταχύτητα) reach distance of || (προσελκύω) entice, attract || **δε με τραβάει** it doesn't attract me || (ζητώ) ask for, want || **ο καιρός τραβάει πανωφόρι** the weather calls for a coat || **η καρδιά μου ~ τσιγάρο** I need a smoke || (υποφέρω) undergo, endure, bear || (αμετ) make towards, head for || move on || (συνεχίζω) last, go on || (τσιμπούκι κτλ) suck, draw || **τραβιέμαι** (αμετ) draw back, leave || (εμπόριο) be in demand || (δεν υποφέρεται) it's unbearable.

τραγανίζω [traganeezo] crunch, munch, grind.

τραγανό, το [tragano] cartilage, grist.

τραγανός [traganos] crisp, brittle.

τραγί, το [trayee] kid.

τραγικός [trayeekos] calamitous, tragic || (ποιητής) tragic poet.

τράγος, ο [tragos] goat.

τραγούδι, το [tragoudee] song, air, tune.

τραγουδιστής, ο [tragoudeestees] singer, vocalist.

τραγουδιστός [tragoudeestos] sung || (φωνή) tuneful.

τραγουδώ [tragoudo] sing, chant || (σιγά) hum.

τραγωδία, η [tragodeea] tragedy.

τραγωδός, ο, η [tragodos] tragic actor, tragedian, tragic actress.

τραίνο, το [treno] railway train || (επιβατικό) passenger train.

τρακ, το [trak] stage fright.

τρακάρισμα, το [trakareesma] crash, collision || unexpected meeting.

τρακάρω [trakaro] knock against, collide with || meet by accident || (μεταφ) touch for a loan.

τρακατρούκα, η [trakatrouka] firecracker.

τράκο, το [trako], **τράκος, ο**

[trakos] collision || (μεταφ) attack, assault.

τρακτέρ, το [trakter] farm tractor.

τραμ, το [tram] tram, tramcar, tramway.

τραμπούκος, ο [tramboukos] out-and-out rascal, scoundrel, rotter.

τρανός [tranos] powerful || large, grand || important, weighty.

τράνταγμα, το [trantagma] jolting, shake, shaking || jolt, jerk.

τραντάζω [trantazo] jolt, shake up and down.

τράπεζα, η [trapeza] table || (εμπορ) bank || **αγία ~** altar.

τραπεζαρία, η [trapezareea] dining room.

τραπέζι, το [trapezee] table || dinner || **στρώνω ~** set the table || **τους είχαμε ~** we invited them to dinner.

τραπεζίτης, ο [trapezeetees] banker || (δόντι) molar.

τραπεζιτικός [trapezeeteekos] banking || (υπάλληλος) bank employee.

τραπεζομάντηλο, το [trapezomanteelo] tablecloth.

τράπουλα, η [trapoula] pack of cards.

τράτα, η [trata] seine || fishing boat.

τρατάρω [trataro] regale || pay for, offer.

τραυλίζω [travleezo] stammer, stutter, lisp.

τραυλός [travlos] stammering, stuttering.

τραύμα, το [travma] wound, hurt, injury || (μεταφ) wound, sore.

τραυματίας, ο [travmateeas] casualty, wounded person.

τραυματίζω [travmateezo] wound, hurt, injure.

τραχεία, η [traheea] trachea, windpipe.

τραχηλιά, η [traheelia] collar, collarette || bib.

τράχηλος, ο [traheelos] neck.
τραχύνω [traheeno] make harsh, make rough || irritate.
τραχύς [trahees] harsh, rough || (στη γεύση) tart, sharp || (στην ακοή) harsh, grating || (χαρακτήρας) sour, crabbed.
τρεις [trees] three.
τρέλα, n [trela] madness, insanity || folly || (ιατρ) mania || (μεταφ) anything pleasing.
τρελαίνομαι [trelenome] go insane || be driven mad || be mad about.
τρελαίνω [treleno] drive mad, bewilder.
τρελοκομείο, το [trelokomeeo] madhouse.
τρελός [trelos] insane, mad || (ουσ) madman || (μωρό) mischievous.
τρεμοσβήνω [tremosveeno] flicker, sparkle.
τρεμούλα, n [tremoula] shivering, trembling || (φωνής) quiver || (από κρύο) shivering || scare.
τρέμω [tremo] tremble || (από κρύο) shiver || (από φόβο) shake || (το φως) flicker, waver || (φωνή) quiver.
τρέξιμο, το [trekseemo] running || (υγρού) flowing || (αίματος) flow, gush.
τρέπω [trepo] change, convert || turn, translate || ~ δε φυγή put to flight.
τρέφω [trefo] nourish, nurture || (ελπίδα) cherish, foster || (γένια) grow || support, keep.
τρεχάλα, n [trehala] running || (σαν επίρ) at full speed.
τρεχάματα, τα [trehamata] πλ running about || (μεταφ) cares.
τρεχάμενος [trehamenos] running.
τρεχαντήρι, το [trehanteeree] small sailing boat.
τρεχάτος [trehatos] running, hasty.
τρέχω [treho] run, race, hurry || (για υγρά) flow || leak || **τι τρέχει;**

what's happening?, what's the matter?
τρεχούμενος [trehoumenos] (λογαριασμός) current.
τρία [treea] three.
τριάδα, n [treeaδa] trinity || trio.
τρίαινα, n [triena] trident.
τριακόσιοι [treeakosiee] three hundred.
τριανδρία, n [treeanδreea] triumvirate.
τριάντα [treeanta] thirty.
τριαντάφυλλο, το [treeantafeelo] rose.
τριάρι, το [treearee] figure 3 || three at cards || (διαμέρισμα) three-room apartment.
τριάδα, n [treeaδa] trinity || trio.
τριβή, n [treevee] friction, chafing, rubbing || wear and tear || (μεταφ) practice, use, experience.
τρίβομαι [treevome] wear out || disintegrate || (μεταφ) get experienced, get practice in.
τρίβω [treevo] rub || polish up || grate || (το σώμα) massage.
τριγμός, ο [treegmos] crackling, creaking || (δοντιών) grinding, gnashing.
τριγυρίζω [treeyeereezo] encircle || roam, hang about.
τριγυρνώ [treeyeerno] encircle || roam, hang about.
τριγωνικός [treegoneekos] triangular.
τριγωνομετρία, n [treegonometreea] trigonometry.
τρίγωνο, το [treegono] triangle.
τρίδυμα, τα [treeδeema] πλ triplets.
τριετής [trietees] of three years || (ηλικία) three years old || (φοιτητής) third-year.
τρίζω [treezo] crackle, crack, creak, squeak || (δόντια) grind, gnash, grit.
τριήρης, n [trieerees] trireme.
τρικαντό, το [treekanto] three-cornered hat, cocked hat.

τρικλίζω [treekleezo] stagger, totter, wobble, reel.

τρίκλωνος [treeklonos] three-stranded.

τρικούβερτος [treekouvertos] (μεταφ) splendid, terrific, wonderful.

τρικυμία, η [treekeemeea] storm, tempest, hurricane.

τρικυμιώδης [treekeemeeoðees] stormy, tempestuous, rough.

τρίλια, η [treeleea] trill.

τριμελής [treemelees] of three members.

τριμερής [treemerees] tripartite.

τριμηνία, η [treemeeneea] quarter of a year || quarter's rent.

τριμηνιαίος [treemeeneeos] of three months, quarterly.

τρίμηνο, το [treemeeno] βλ **τριμηνία.**

τρίμηνος [treemeenos] βλ **τριμηνιαία.**

τρίμμα, το [treema] fragment, morse, chip, particle.

τριμμένος [treemenos] showing signs of wear and tear || ground.

τρίξιμο, το [treekseemo] gnashing, grinding.

τρίπατος [treepatos] three-storeyed.

τριπλασιάζω [treeplaseeazo] treble, triple, triplicate.

τριπλάσιος [treeplaseeos] threefold, triple, treble.

τριποδίζω [treepoðeezo] trot.

τρίποδο, το [treepoðo] tripod || easel || three-legged support.

τρίπτυχο, το [treepteeho] triptych.

τρισδιάστατος [treesðeeastatos] three-dimensional.

τρισέγγονο, το [treesengono] great-great-grandchild.

τρισκατάρατος [treeskataratos] thrice-cursed || abominable.

Τρίτη, η [treetee] Tuesday.

τρίτο, το [treeto] third || (επίρ) thirdly.

τρίτος [treetos] third || third-party.

τρίφτης, ο [treeftees] grater, rasp.

τριφύλλι, το [treefeelee] clover, trefoil.

τρίχα, η [treeha] hair || bristle || fur || στην ~ spruced up || παρά ~ nearly.

τρίχες, οι [treehes] πλ nonsense, rubbish.

τριχιά, η [treehia] rope.

τριχοειδής [treehoeeðees] capillary.

τρίχωμα, το [treehoma] fur || (σώματος) hair.

τριχωτός [treehotos] hairy, shaggy.

τρίψιμο, το [treepseemo] chafing, massage, rubbing, friction || (στίλβωμα) polishing || grating, grinding, crushing.

τρίωρος [treeoros] of three hours.

τρόλλεϋ, το [troley] trolley bus.

τρόραγμα, το [tromagma] fright, scare.

τρομάζω [tromazo] terrify, frighten || get scared.

τρομακτικός [tromakteekos] fearful, awful, frightening || (μεταφ) terrific.

τρομάρα, η [tromara] dread, fright, fear.

τρομερός [tromeros] terrible, dreadful, frightful || (μεταφ) terrific, astonishing.

τρομοκρατία, η [tromokrateea] terrorism || terror.

τρομοκρατώ [tromokrato] terrorize.

τρόμος, ο [tromos] trembling, shaking || dread, fright.

τρόμπα, η [trompa] pump.

τρομπέτα, η [trompeta] trumpet.

τρομπόνι, το [tromponee] trombone.

τρόπαιο, το [tropeo] trophy || triumph.

τροπάριο, το [tropareeo] (εκκλ) hymn || (μεταφ) same old refrain.

τροπή, η [tropee] change || turn || (μαθημ) conversion.

τροπικός [tropeekos] tropical || (γραμμ) of manner.

τροπολογία, η [tropoloyeea] amendment, alteration, change, modification.

τροποποίηση, η [tropopieesee] modification, alteration, change.

τρόποι, οι [tropee] πλ manners, behaviour.

τρόπος, ο [tropos] way, manner, method || behaviour, conduct || (μουσ) mode || ~ του λέγειν so to speak.

τρούλλος, ο [troulos] dome, cupola.

τρουλλωτός [troulotos] domed, dome-shaped.

τροφή, η [trofee] food, nutrition || (ζώων) pasture, fodder || sustenance.

τρόφιμα, τα [trofeema] πλ provisions, food, victuals.

τρόφιμος, ο, η [trofeemos] lodger, boarder || paying guest || inmate || (μεταφ) nursling.

τροφοδοσία, η [trofodoseea] provisioning, supplying || supply.

τροφοδότης, ο [trofodotees] caterer, purveyor, provider, supplier.

τροφοδοτώ [trofodoto] feed, provision, keep supplied, supply, serve.

τροχάδην [trohadeen] hurriedly, hastily, at full speed || (μεταφ) fluently.

τροχαία [trohea]: ~ κίνηση traffic || η ~ traffic police.

τροχαίο [troheo]: ~ υλικό rolling stock.

τροχαίος, ο [troheos] trochee || (επίθ) wheeled, rolling.

τροχαλία, η [trohaleea] pulley, block.

τροχιά, η [trohia] track, groove, rut || (σιδηροδρόμου) track, rail || (δορυφόρου κτλ) orbit, trajectory.

τροχίζω [troheezo] sharpen, whet, grind || (μεταφ) train, exercise.

τρόχισμα, το [troheesma] sharpening, whetting, grinding || (μεταφ) exercising.

τροχονόμος, ο [trohonomos] traffic policeman.

τροχοπέδη, η [trohopedee] brake, skid, wheel brake.

τροχός, ο [trohos] wheel || grindstone, whetstone.

τροχοφόρο, το [trohoforo] vehicle.

τρυγητής, ο [treeyeetees] grape harvester, vintager.

τρυγητός, ο [treeyeetos] grape harvest, vintage.

τρυγόνι, το [treegonee] turtledove.

τρύγος, ο [treegos] βλ **τρυγητός**.

τρυγώ [treego] gather grapes || (μεταφ) loot, fleece.

τρύπα, η [treepa] hole || (βελόνας) eye || (μεταφ) den, lair.

τρυπάνι, το [treepanee] drill, drilling machine.

τρύπημα, το [treepeema] perforating, boring, piercing || prick, punch.

τρυπητήρι, το [treepeeteeree] awl, punch, drill.

τρυπητό, το [treepeeto] strainer, colander.

τρύπιος [treepeeos] with holes, perforated, holed, riddled.

τρυπητός [treepeetos] perforated, holed, riddled.

τρυπώ [treepo] bore, make a hole, pierce || prick, punch.

τρυπώνω [treepono] hide, conceal || squeeze in || take refuge.

τρυφερός [treeferos] tender, soft || affectionate, affable, mild.

τρυφερότητα, η [treeferoteeta] tenderness, softness || affection, kindness.

τρώγλη, η [troglee] hole, lair, den || hovel, shack.

τρώγομαι [trogome] be edible || (μεταφ) be tolerable || **τρώγονται** they are quarrelling.

τρώγω [trogo] eat, bite || **με τρώει** it itches || ~ **ξύλο** get a beating || ~ **το κόσμο** look everywhere.

τρωκτικό, το [trokteeko] rodent.

τρωτός [trotos] vulnerable.

τρώω [troo] βλ **τρώγω**.

τσαγιέρα, η [tsayera] teapot.

τσαγκάρης, ο [tsangarees] shoemaker.

τσάι, το [tsaee] tea.

τσακάλι, η [tsakalee] jackal.

τσακίζομαι [tsakeezome] strive, struggle || (διπλώνω) fold.

τσακίζω [tsakeezo] break, shatter, smash || (μεταφ) weaken, wear out, enfeeble.

τσάκιση, η [tsakeesee] crease, pleat.

τσάκισμα, το [tsakeesma] breaking, shattering, smashing.

τσακμάκι, το [tsakmakee] tinderbox || cigarette lighter.

τσάκωμα, το [tsakoma] seizing, catching || quarrelling, dispute.

τσακώνομαι [tsakonome] quarrel.

τσακώνω [tsakono] catch in the act.

τσαλαβουτώ [tsalavouto] flounder, wallow, splash about || (μεταφ) do a sloppy job.

τσαλακώνω [tsalakono] crease, crumple, wrinkle.

τσαλαπατώ [tsalapato] trample underfoot, tread over.

τσαμπί, το [tsambee] bunch (of grapes), cluster.

τσάντα, η [tsanta] pouch || handbag || briefcase || (γωνίσματος) shopping bag || (ταχυδρόμου) satchel.

τσάπα, η [tsapa] hoe, pickaxe.

τσαπατσούλης [tsapatsoulees] untidy in one's work.

τσαπί, το [tsapee] βλ **τσάπα**.

τσάρκα, η [tsarka] walk, promenade, stroll.

τσαρούχι, το [tsarouhee] rustic shoe with pompom.

τσατσάρα, η [tsatsara] comb.

τσαχπινιά, η [tsahpeenia] coquetry, roguery, trickery.

τσεκ, το [tsek] cheque || check (US).

τσεκούρι, το [tsekouree] axe, hatchet.

τσέλιγκας, ο [tseleengas] chief shepherd.

τσεμπέρι, το [tsemberee] kerchief, veil.

τσέπη, η [tsepee] pocket || pocketful.

τσεπώνω [tsepono] pocket || (μεταφ) filch, swipe.

τσευδίζω [tsevdeezo] lisp, stammer, falter.

τσευδός [tsevdos] lisping, stammering.

τσεχικός [tseheekos] Czech.

Τσέχος, ο [tsehos] Czech.

Τσεχοσλοβακία, η [tsehoslovakeea] Czechoslovakia.

τσιγαρίζω [tseegareezo] fry lightly, brown, roast brown.

τσιγάρο, το [tseegaro] cigarette.

τσιγαροθήκη, η [tseegarotheekee] cigarette case.

τσιγαρόχαρτο, το [tseegaroharto] tissue paper.

τσιγγάνος, ο [tseenganos] gipsy.

τσιγγούνης [tseengounees] miserly, stingy || (ουσ) miser.

τσιγκέλι, το [tseengelee] meat hook.

τσιγκλώ [tseenglo] goad, prick, spur.

τσίγκος, ο [tseengos] zinc.

τσίκνα, η [tseekna] smell of burning meat.

τσικνίζω [tseekneezo] scorch, burn || have a burnt smell.

τσικουδιά, η [tseekouδia] terebinth || (ποτό) kind of spirit.

τσίμα [tseema]: ~ ~ scarcely || on the brink of.

τσιμέντο, το [tseemento] cement.

τσιμουδιά, η [tseemouδia]: δεν έβγαλε ~ he remained speechless || ~! not a word!, mum's the word!

τσίμπημα, το [tseembeema] prick, sting, pinch || bite, peck.

τσιμπιά, η [tseembia] pinch.

τσιμπίδα, η [tseembeeδa] nippers, tongs, forceps, pincers.

τσιμπιδάκι, το [tseembeeδakee] tweezers || hairclip.

τσίμπλα, η [tseembla] mucus of eyes.

τσιμπούκι, το [tseemboukee] tobacco pipe.

τσιμπούρι, το [tseembouree] (έντομο) tick || (μεταφ) troublesome or bothersome person, pest.

τσιμπούσι, το [tseembousee] spread, repast, regalement, feast.

τσιμπώ [tseembo] prick, pinch, sting || (δαγκώνω) bite, peck || (φαγητό) nibble || (μεταφ) cadge || (συλλαμβάνω) seize, collar.

τσίνορο, το [tseenoro] eyelash.

τσίπα, η [tseepa] thin skin, crust || (μεταφ) shame.

τσιπούρα, η [tseepoura] gilthead.

τσίπουρο, το [tseepouro] kind of spirit.

τσιρίζω [tseereezo] screech, shriek, scream.

τσίρκο, το [tseerko] circus.

τσίρλα, η [tseerla] diarrhoea.

τσίρος, ο [tseeros] dried mackerel || (μεταφ) skinny person.

τσιρότο, το [tseeroto] sticking plaster.

τσίτα [tseeta] very tight || ~ ~ scarcely.

τσιτσίδι [tseetseeδee] stark naked.

τσιτσιρίζω [tseetseereezo] sizzle.

τσιτώνω [tseetono] stretch, tighten, strain.

τσιφλίκι, το [tseefleekee] large country estate, farm, ranch.

τσίχλα, η [tseehla] thrush || (αδύνατος) skinny person.

τσόκαρο, το [tsokaro] wooden shoe.

τσολιάς, ο [tsolias] evzone, kilted soldier.

τσο(μ)πάνης, ο [tso(m)panees] shepherd.

τσοντάρω [tsontaro] join on.

τσουβάλι, το [tsouvalee] sackful || sack.

τσουγκράνα, η [tsoungrana] rake.

τσουγκρανίζω [tsoungraneezo] scratch, rake.

τσουγκρίζω [tsoungreezo] strike against || clink glasses, touch glasses.

τσούζω [tsouzo] smart, sting, hurt.

τσουκάλι, το [tsoukalee] jug, pot || chamberpot.

τσουκνίδα, η [tsoukneeδa] nettle.

τσούλα, η [tsoula] loose-living woman, whore.

τσουλάω [tsoulao] slip along, slide along || (όχημα) push.

τσουλούφι, το [tsouloufee] lock of hair.

τσουρέκι, το [tsourekee] bun, brioche.

τσούρμο, το [tsourmo] throng || band, troop.

τσουρουφλίζω [tsouroufleezo] grill brown, scorch.

τσουχτερός, ο [tsouhteros] keen, smart, sharp || (κρύο) biting || harsh.

τσούχτρα, η [tsouhtra] jellyfish.

τσόφλι, το [tsoflee] shell || rind.

τσόχα, η [tsoha] felt.

τυγχάνω [teenghano] happen to be || obtain, attain.

τύλιγμα, το [teeleegma] winding, rolling, coiling, wrapping.

τυλίγω [teeleego] roll up, wind, coil || wrap up, fold round, twist.

τυλώνω [teelono] fill up.

τύμβος, ο [teemvos] grave, tomb.

τύμπανο, το [teembano] drum, tambour || (αυτιού) || eardrum || tympanum.

Τυνησία, η [teeneeseea] Tunisia.

τυνησιακός [teeneeseeakos] Tunisian.

Τυνήσιος, ο [teeneeseeos] Tunisian.

τυπικός [teepeekos] usual, conventional || typical.

τυπικότητα, η [teepeekoteeta] formality.

τυπογραφείο, το [teepografeeo] printing press, printer's.

τυπογραφία, η [teepografeea] printing.

τυπογράφος, ο [teepografos] printer.

τύποι, οι [teepee] πλ conventions, form.

τυποποίηση, η [teepopieesee] standardization.

τύπος, ο [teepos] print, imprint, stamp || (καλούπι) mould, matrix, form || (υπόδειγμα) model, type || (συμπεριφοράς) formality, rule of procedure || (οικίας) type, kind of || (μαθημ) formula || (εφημερίδες) the press || (για άνθρωπο) figure, character.

τυπώνω [teepono] print, stamp.

τυραννία, η [teeraneea] tyranny, oppression || torment, torture.

τύραννος, ο [teeranos] oppressor, tyrant.

τυραννώ [teerano] oppress || torture, harass.

τυρί, το [teeree] cheese.

τυροκομία, η [teerokomeea] cheese-making.

τυρόπιτα, η [teeropeeta] cheese pie || cheesecake.

τύρφη, η [teerfee] peat.

τύφλα, η [teefla] blindness || ~ στο μεθύσι dead drunk.

τυφλοπόντικας, ο [teefloponteekas] mole.

τυφλός [teeflos] blind.

τυφλώνομαι [teeflonome] grow blind, blind o.s.

τυφλώνω [teeflono] blind || (φως) dazzle || (μεταφ) deceive, hoodwink.

τύφος, ο [teefos] εξανθηματικός ~ typhus || κοιλιακός ~ typhoid fever.

τυφώνας, ο [teefonas] typhoon, hurricane, cyclone.

τυχαίνω [teeheno] βλ τυγχάνω.

τυχαίος [teeheos] casual, fortuitous, chance.

τυχαίως [teeheos] by chance, by accident.

τυχερά [teehera] πλ casual profits, tips, perks.

τυχερό, το [teehero] fortune, destiny.

τυχερός [teeheros] fortunate, lucky.

τύχη, η [teehee] destiny, chance, fortune, lot, fate || (καλή) good luck || στην ~ haphazard, at random.

τυχοδιώκτης, ο [teehoδeeoktees] adventurer, opportunist.

τυχόν [teehon] by chance || τα ~ έξοδα incidental expenses.

τυχών [teehon] ο ~ the first comer, anyone.

τύψη, η [teepsee] remorse, prick of conscience.

τώρα [tora] nowadays, at present, now || this minute || at once.

τωρινός [toreenos] present-day, contemporary, of today.

Υ, υ

ύαινα, η [iena] hyena.

υάκινθος, ο [yakeenthos] hyacinth.

ύαλος, η [eealos] glass.

υαλουργία, η [yalouryeea] glassmaking.

υαλουργός, ο [yalourgos] glassmaker.

υάρδα, η [yarða] yard.

ύβος, ο [eevos] hump.

υβρεολόγιο, το [eevreoloyo] volley of abuse, tirade.

υβρίζω [eevreezo] insult, abuse, swear at.

ύβρη, η [eevree] insult, injury || oath.

υβριστικός [eevreesteekos] insulting, rude.

υγεία, η [eeyeea] health.

υγειονομικός [eeyonomeekos] sanitary.

υγιαίνω [eeyeno] be healthy.

υγιεινός [eeyeenos] healthy || wholesome.

υγιής [eeyees] healthy || (μεταφ) sound.

υγραίνω [eegreno] moisten, dampen, wet.

υγρασία, η [eegraseea] moisture, moistness, humidity.

υγροποιώ [eegropeeo] liquefy.

υγρός [eegros] fluid, liquid || humid, damp || watery.

υδαταγωγός, ο [eeðatagogos] water pipe.

υδατάνθρακας, ο [eeðatanthrakas] carbohydrate.

υδατοστεγής [eeðatosteyees] watertight, waterproof.

υδατοφράκτης, ο [eeðatofraktees] dam, weir.

υδραγωγείο, το [eeðragoyeeo] aqueduct.

υδραντλία, η [eeðrantleea] water pump.

υδράργυρος, ο [eeðraryeeros] mercury, quicksilver.

υδρατμός, ο [eeðratmos] vapour, steam!

υδραυλική, η [eeðravleekee] hydraulics.

υδραυλικός [eeðravleekos] hydraulic || (ουσ) plumber.

ύδρευση, η [eeðrevsee] water supply, drawing of water.

υδρόβιος [eeðroveeos] aquatic.

υδρόγειος, η [eeðroyos] earth.

υδρογόνο, το [eeðrogono] hydrogen.

υδρογραφία, η [eeðrografeea] hydrography.

υδροηλεκτρικός [eeðroeelektreekos] hydroelectric.

υδροκέφαλος [eeðrokefalos] hydrocephalous.

υδροκίνητος [eeðrokeeneetos] waterpowered.

υδροκυάνιο, το [eeðrokeeaneeo] prussic acid.

υδρόμυλος, ο [eeðromeelos] water mill.

υδροπλάνο, το [eeðroplano] seaplane.

υδρορρόη, η [eeðroroee] (στη στέγη) gutter.

υδροστάθμη, η [eeðrostathmee] water level.

υδροστατικός [eeðrostateekos] hydrostatic.

υδροστρόβιλος, ο [eeðrostroveelos] water turbine || whirlpool.

υδροφοβία, η [eeðrofoveea] rabies, hydrophobia.

υδροφόρος [eeðroforos] water-carrying || (ουσ) water carrier.

υδροχαρής [eeðroharees] water-loving.

υδροχλωρικός [eeðrohloreekos] hydrochloric.

υδρόχρωμα, το [eeðrohroma] whitewash.

υδρόψυκτος [eeðropseektos] water-cooled.

υδρωπικία, η [eeðropeekeea] dropsy.

ύδωρ, το [eeðor] water.

υιοθεσία, η [yotheseea] adoption.

υιοθετώ [yotheto] adopt, accept, support.

υιός, ο [yos] son.

ύλη, η [eelee] material, matter, stuff.

υλικό, το [eeleeko] material, stuff || element, ingredient.

υλικός [eeleekos] material, real.

υλισμός, ο [eeleesmos] materialism.

υλιστής, ο [eeleestees] materialist.

υλοτομία, η [eelotomeea] woodcutting, timber-felling.

υμένας, ο [eemenas] membrane || tissue, hymen.

ύμνος, ο [eemnos] hymn || anthem.

υμνώ [eemno] celebrate, praise, eulogize.

υνί, το [eenee] ploughshare.

υπάγομαι [eepagome] belong, be dependent || be answerable.

υπαγόρευση, η [eepagorevsee] dictation || (μεταφ) suggestion.

υπαγορεύω [eepagorevo] dictate || (μεταφ) inspire, suggest.

υπάγω [eepago] go || go under, rank.

υπαίθριος [eepethreeos] outdoor, in the open air || field.

ύπαιθρο, το [eepethro] open air, open country.

ύπαιθρος, η [eepethros] (χώρα) countryside

υπαινιγμός, ο [eepeneegmos] hint, allusion, intimation.

υπαινίσσομαι [eepeneesome] hint at, allude to.

υπαίτιος [eepeteeos] responsible, culpable.

υπακοή, η [eepakoee] obedience || submission.

υπάκουος [eepakouos] obedient || submissive.

υπακούω [eepakouo] obey.

υπάλληλος, ο, η [eepaleelos] employee, clerk || (υπουργείου) official, functionary || **δημόσιος ~**

civil servant, government employee.

υπαξιωματικός, ο [eepakseeomateekos] non-commissioned officer.

υπαρκτός [eeparktos] existent || subsisting || real.

ύπαρξη, η [eeparksee] existence || being, life.

υπαρχηγός, ο [eeparheegos] deputy commander.

υπάρχω [eeparho] exist, be || live || **υπάρχει** there is || **τα υπαρχοντά μου** my possessions, my things.

υπασπιστής, ο [eepaspeestees] aide-de-camp || (στρατ) adjutant.

ύπατος, ο [eepatos] consul || (επίθ) highest, supreme.

υπέδαφος, το [eepedafos] subsoil.

υπεισέρχομαι [eepeeserhome] enter secretly || glide into.

υπεκφεύγω [eepekfevgo] escape, avoid || slip away.

υπεκφυγή, η [eepekfeeyee] escape, subterfuge || evasion.

υπενθυμίζω [eepentheemeezo] remind of, call to mind || allude to.

υπενοικιάζω [eepeneekeeazo] sublet, rent from a tenant.

υπεξαίρεση, η [eepekseresee] pilfering, taking away.

υπέρ [eeper] over, upwards, above || (για) for, on behalf of || **τα ~ και τα κατά** pros and cons, for and against.

υπεραιμία, η [eepereemeea] excess of blood.

υπεραμύνομαι [eeperameenome] defend, support.

υπεράνθρωπος [eeperanthropos] superhuman || (ουσ) superman.

υπεράνω [eeperano] above, beyond, over.

υπερασπίζομαι [eeperaspeezome] defend o.s.

υπερασπίζω [eeperaspeezo] defend, protect || maintain.

υπεράσπιση, η [eeperaspeesee]
 defence || protection || the
 defendants.

υπεραστικός [eeperasteekos] long-
 distance.

υπερβαίνω [eeperveno] cross,
 surmount || exceed, go beyond,
 overdo.

υπερβάλλω [eepervalo] surpass,
 outdo, exceed || exaggerate, overdo,
 magnify.

υπέρβαση, η [eepervasee]
 exceeding || (traffic) violation ||
 trespass.

υπερβολή, η [eepervolee]
 exaggeration || (γεωμ) hyperbola.

υπερβολικός [eepervoleekos]
 excessive || exaggerated ||
 exaggerating.

υπέργηρος [eeperyeeros]
 extremely old, very old.

υπερδιέγερση, η [eeperðieyersee]
 over-excitement.

υπερένταση, η [eeperentasee]
 overstrain, overstress.

υπερευαίσθητος
 [eeperevestheetos] over-sensitive,
 hypersensitive.

υπερέχω [eepereho] excel, surpass,
 exceed.

υπερηλικος/κη [eepereeleekas]
 elderly person, very old person.

υπερηφάνεια, η [eepereefaneea]
 pride || haughtiness.

υπερηφανεύομαι
 [eepereefanevome] pride o.s. || be
 proud.

υπερήφανος [eepereefanos] proud
 || haughty.

υπερθεματίζω [eeperthemateezo]
 make higher bid || (μεταφ) outdo.

υπερθετικός [eepertheteekos]
 superlative.

υπερίπταμαι [eepereeptame] fly
 over, fly above.

υπερισχύω [eepereeshseeo]
 predominate, prevail over ||
 overcome, triumph.

υπεριώδης [eepereeoðees]
 ultraviolet.

υπερκόπωση, η [eeperkoposee]
 overwork, breakdown.

υπέρμαχος, ο, η [eepermahos]
 champion, defender.

υπέρμετρος [eepermetros]
 excessive, huge.

υπερνικώ [eeperneeko] overcome ||
 subdue, master.

υπέρογκος [eeperongos] colossal,
 enormous || outrageous.

υπεροπτικός [eeperopteekos]
 haughty, presumptuous, arrogant.

υπεροχή, η [eeperohee]
 superiority, predominance.

υπέροχος [eeperohos] superior,
 excellent, eminent.

υπεροψία, η [eeperopseea]
 arrogance, disdain, haughtiness.

υπερπέραν, το [eeperperan] the
 beyond, afterlife.

υπερπηδώ [eeperpeeðo] surmount ||
 jump over.

υπερπόντιος [eeperponteeos]
 overseas || transmarine.

υπέρταση, η [eepertasee] high
 blood pressure.

υπέρτατος [eepertatos] highest,
 greatest, supreme.

υπερτερώ [eepertero] excel,
 exceed, surpass || outnumber.

υπερτίμηση, η [eeperteemeesee]
 overestimation || (οικ) rise in price,
 increase in value.

υπερτιμώ [eeperteemo] overvalue,
 overestimate || (οικ) raise price of.

υπερτροφία, η [eepertrofeea]
 (ιατρ) hypertrophy.

υπέρυθροι [eepereethree] πλ: ~
 ακτίνες infrared rays.

υπέρυθρος [eepereethros] reddish.

υπερύψηλος [eepereepseelos]
 very high, exceedingly high.

υπερυψώνω [eepereepsono] raise up || exalt.

υπερφυσικός [eeperfeeseekos] supernatural || (μεταφ) extraordinary, prodigious.

υπερωκεάνειο, το [eeperokeaneeo] liner.

υπερωρία, η [eeperoreea] overtime.

υπεύθυνος [eepevtheenos] responsible, answerable.

υπήκοος [eepeekoos] submissive, obedient || (ουσ) subject of state.

υπηκοότητα, η [eepeekooteeta] nationality, citizenship.

υπηρεσία, η [eepereseea] service, attendance || duty, employ || (οικίας) domestic servant.

υπηρεσιακή [eepereseeakee]: ~ **κυβέρνηση** caretaker government.

υπηρεσιακός [eepereseeakos] of service.

υπηρέτης, ο [eepeeretees] servant.

υπηρέτρια, η [eepeeretreea] maid.

υπηρετώ [eepeereto] serve || do one's military service.

υπναλέος [eepnaleos] drowsy, sleepy.

υπναράς, ο [eepnaras] person who enjoys sleeping.

υπνοβάτης, ο [eepnovatees] sleepwalker.

ύπνος, ο [eepnos] sleep.

ύπνωση, η [eepnosee] hypnosis.

υπνωτίζω [eepnoteezo] hypnotize.

υπνωτικό, το [eepnoteeko] soporific drug, sleeping pill.

υπνωτισμός, ο [eepnoteesmos] hypnotism.

υπό [eepo] below, beneath || (μέσο) by, with.

υπόβαθρο, το [eepovathro] base, pedestal, stand.

υποβάλλω [eepovalo] submit, hand in || (υποτάσσω) subject || suggest, propose.

υποβαστάζω [eepovastazo] support, prop up, bear.

υποβιβάζω [eepoveevazo] lower || reduce, diminish || demote.

υποβλέπω [eepovlepo] suspect || cast glances at, leer.

υποβλητικός [eepovleeteekos] evocative.

υποβοηθώ [eepovoeetho] assist, back up, support.

υποβολέας, ο [eepovoleas] prompter || instigator.

υποβολή, η [eepovolee] submission, presentation || prompting, instigation.

υποβόσκω [eepovosko] smoulder || lie hidden.

υποβρύχιο, το [eepovreeheeo] submarine || (μεταφ) kind of sweet.

υπόγειο, το [eepoyeeo] basement, cellar.

υπόγειος [eepoyeeos] underground.

υπογραμμίζω [eepogrameezo] underline, emphasize.

υπογραφή, η [eepografee] signature.

υπογράφω [eepografo] sign || (μεταφ) approve, subscribe.

υποδαυλίζω [eepodavleezo] fan the flame || (μεταφ) foment, excite.

υποδεέστερος [eepodeesteros] inferior, lower.

υπόδειγμα, το [eepodeegma] model, example, specimen || sample.

υποδειγματικός [eepodeegmateekos] exemplary, representative.

υποδεικνύω [eepodeekneeo] indicate || suggest, propose.

υπόδειξη, η [eepodeeksee] indication || recommendation.

υποδέχομαι [eepodehome] receive, welcome, greet.

υποδηλώ [eepodeelo] convey, indicate, hint at.

υποδηματοποιείο, το

[eepodeematopieeo] shoemaker's shop.

υποδιαίρεση, η [eepodieresee] subdivision.

υποδιαιρώ [eepodiero] subdivide.

υποδιαστολή, η [eepodeeastolee] decimal point || (γραμμ) comma.

υποδιευθυντής, ο [eepodiefthendees] assistant director, vice-principal, deputy manager.

υπόδικος, ο [eepodeekos] the accused.

υπόδουλος [eepodoulos] enslaved.

υποδουλώνω [eepodoulono] subjugate, enslave, subdue.

υποδοχή, η [eepodohee] reception.

υποδύομαι [eepodeome] play the part, assume a role.

υποζύγιο, το [eepozeeyo] beast of burden.

υποθάλπω [eepothalpo] foment || protect, maintain || entertain, harbour.

υπόθεση, η [eepothesee] conjecture, supposition || matter, affair, business || (δικαστηρίου) case, action || (θεατρικού έργου κτλ) subject, plot, matter, theme.

υποθετικός [eepotheteekos] hypothetical, speculative || imaginary || (γραμμ) conditional.

υπόθετο, το [eepotheto] suppository.

υποθέτω [eepotheto] suppose, assume.

υποθηκεύω [eepotheekevo] mortgage.

υποθήκη, η [eepotheekee] mortgage.

υποκαθιστώ [eepokatheesto] replace, substitute.

υποκατάσταση, η [eepokatastasee] replacement, substitution.

υποκατάστημα, το

[eepokatasteema] branch office || chain store (US).

υπόκειμαι [eepokeeme] be subject, be liable || lie under.

υποκειμενικός [eepokeemeneekos] subjective.

υποκείμενο, το [eepokeemeno] subject || individual || scamp.

υποκινώ [eepokeeno] stir up, excite, incite.

υποκλέπτω [eepoklepto] purloin, pilfer.

υποκλίνομαι [eepokleenome] bow, bend || yield.

υπόκλιση, η [eepokleesee] bow, curtsy.

υποκοριστικό, το [eepokoreesteeko] diminutive.

υπόκοσμος, ο [eepokosmos] underworld.

υποκρίνομαι [eepokreenome] act, play the part of, impersonate || dissemble.

υπόκριση, η [eepokreesee] pretending, acting || dissembling.

υποκρισία, η [eepokreeseea] hypocrisy.

υποκριτής, ο [eepokreetees] actor || hypocrite.

υποκριτικός [eepokreeteekos] feigned, insincere.

υπόκρουση, η [eepokrousee] accompaniment.

υποκύπτω [eepokeepto] bend, submit, succumb || yield.

υπόκωφος [eepokofos] hollow, deep || smothered.

υπόλειμμα, το [eepoleema] residue, remnant, rest.

υπολείπομαι [eepoleepome] be left || be inferior to.

υπόληψη, η [eepoleepsee] esteem || credit, reputation.

υπολογίζω [eepoloyeezo] estimate, calculate || consider.

υπολογισμός, ο [eepoloyeesmos] calculation, estimate || account.

υπολογιστής, ο [eepoloyeestees]: (ηλεκτρονικός) ~ computer.

υπόλογος [eepologos] responsible, accountable, liable.

υπόλοιπο, το [eepoleepo] remainder, balance.

υπόλοιπος [eepoleepos] remaining, rest of.

υπολοχαγός, ο [eepolohagos] lieutenant.

υπομένω [eepomeno] endure, tolerate.

υπόμνημα, το [eepomneema] memorandum.

υπόμνηση, η [eepomneesee] reminder || suggestion.

υπομονεύω [eepomonevo] be patient || endure.

υπομονή, η [eepomonee] patience, endurance.

υπομονητικός [eepomoneeteekos] patient, enduring.

υπόνοια, η [eeponeea] suspicion || surmise.

υπονομεύω [eeponomevo] undermine, sabotage.

υπόνομος, ο, η [eeponomos] sewer || (στρατ) mine.

υπονοώ [eeponoo] infer, mean.

υποπίπτω [eepopeepto] commit, fall into || come to the notice of.

υποπροϊόν, το [eepoproeeon] by-product.

υποπρόξενος, ο [eepoproksenos] vice-consul.

υποπτεύομαι [eepoptevome] suspect, have an idea.

ύποπτος [eepoptos] suspect, suspicious, suspected.

υποσημείωση, η [eeposeemeeosee] footnote, annotation.

υποσιτισμός, ο [eeposeeteesmos] undernourishment, malnutrition.

υποσκάπτω [eeposkapto] undermine, sabotage.

υποσκελίζω [eeposkeleezo] upset || supplant.

υποστάθμη, η [eepostathmee] dregs, sediment, residue.

υπόσταση, η [eepostasee] existence || foundation, basis || (ιατρ) hypostasis.

υπόστεγο, το [eepostego] shed, hangar || shelter.

υποστέλλω [eepostelo] strike, lower || slow down, reduce.

υποστήριγμα, το [eeposteereegma] support, prop.

υποστηρίζω [eeposteereezo] prop up, support || second, back || maintain.

υποστήριξη, η [eeposteereeksee] prop, support || backing.

υπόστρωμα, το [eepostroma] substratum || saddlecloth.

υποσυνείδητο, το [eeposeeneedeeto] subconscious.

υπόσχεση, η [eeposhesee] promise, pledge, engagement.

υπόσχομαι [eeposhome] promise, pledge.

υποταγή, η [eepotayee] obedience, subjection, submission.

υποτακτική, η [eepotakteekee] subjective.

υποτακτικός [eepotakteekos] obedient, submissive.

υπόταση, η [eepotasee] low blood pressure.

υποτάσσομαι [eepotasome] submit, give in.

υποτάσσω [eepotaso] subjugate, subdue.

υποτείνουσα, η [eepoteenousa] hypotenuse.

υποτελής [eepotelees] subordinate, tributary, vassal.

υποτίθεμαι [eepoteetheme] be supposed || suppose, consider.

υποτίμηση, η [eepoteemeesee] reduction in price, depreciation || underestimation.

υποτιμώ [eepoteemo] underestimate || lower the price of, depreciate.

υποτροπή, n [eepotropee] relapse, deterioration.

υποτροφία, n [eepotrofeea] scholarship.

υποτυπώδης [eepoteepodees] sketchy, imperfectly formed.

ύπουλος [eepoulos] shifty, underhand, cunning.

υπουργείο, το [eepouryeeo] ministry.

υπουργικός [eepouryeekos] ministerial.

υπουργός, ο [eepourgos] minister || secretary (US).

υποφαινόμενος [eepofenomenos]: **ο ~** the undersigned.

υποφερτός [eepofertos] tolerable || passable.

υποφέρω [eepofero] bear, support, endure || feel pain, suffer.

υποχθόνιος [eepohthoneeos] infernal, subterranean.

υποχονδρία, n [eepohonðreea] hypochondria || obsession.

υπόχρεος [eepohreos] obliged.

υποχρεώνω [eepohreono] oblige || compel.

υποχρέωση, n [eepohreosee] obligation, duty.

υποχρεωτικός [eepohreoteekos] obligatory || compulsory.

υποχώρηση, n [eepohoreesee] withdrawal, yielding || subsidence.

υποχωρώ [eepohoro] withdraw, give way || fall in, cave in.

υποψήφιος, ο [eepopseefeeos] candidate, applicant.

υποψηφιότητα, n [eepopseefeeoteeta] candidature, application.

υποψία, n [eepopseea] suspicion, misgiving.

υποψιάζομαι [eepopseeazome] suspect, have suspicions.

ύπτιος [eepteeos] lying on one's back.

ύστατος [eestatos] last, final.

ύστερα [eestera] afterwards, then, later || furthermore || **~ από** after, following (this).

υστέρημα, το [eestereema] shortage, deficiency || small savings.

υστερία, n [eestereea] hysteria.

υστερικός [eestereekos] hysterical.

υστερισμός, ο [eestereesmos] hysteria, hysterics.

υστεροβουλία, n [eesterovouleea] afterthought || deceit.

υστερόγραφο, το [eesterografo] postscript.

ύστερος [eesteros] later || inferior || **εκ των υστέρων** on second thoughts, looking back.

υστερώ [eestero] come after || be inferior || deprive.

υφαίνω [eefeno] weave, spin || (μεταφ) plot.

ύφαλα, τα [eefala] πλ beam || part below waterline.

υφαλοκρηπίδα, n [eefalokreepeeða] continental shelf.

ύφαλος, n [eefalos] reef, shoal.

ύφανση, n [eefansee] weaving || weave.

υφαντός [eefandos] woven.

υφαντουργία, n [eefandouryeea] textile industry, weaving industry.

υφαρπάζω [eefarpazo] obtain by fraud.

ύφασμα, το [eefasma] cloth, fabric, stuff, material || **υφάσματα** textiles.

ύφεση, n [eefesee] decrease, abatement || (βαρομέτρου) depression || (μουσ) flat (note).

υφή, n [eefee] texture, web, weave.

υφηγητής, ο [eefeeyeetees] lecturer || assistant professor (US).

υφήλιος, n [eefeeleeos] earth, world, globe.

υφίσταμαι [eefeestame] bear, undergo, sustain || (είμαι) exist, be in force.

υφιστάμενος, το [eefeestamenos] subordinate, inferior.

ύφος, το [eefos] style || air, look, tone.

υφυπουργός, ο [eefeepourgos] undersecretary of state.

υψηλός [eepseelos] high, towering, tall || (μεταφ) lofty, great.

υψηλότητα, η [eepseeloteeta] Highness || **η Αυτού** ~ His Royal Highness.

υψηλόφρονας [eepseelofronas] generous || highminded, haughty.

υψικάμινος, η [eepseekameenos] blast furnace.

ύψιλον, το [eepseelon] the letter Υ.

υψίπεδο, το [eepseepeδo] plateau.

ύψιστος [eepseestos] highest || (ουσ) God.

υψίφωνος, ο, η [eepseefonos] tenor || soprano.

υψόμετρο, το [eepsometro] altitude.

ύψος, το [eepsos] height, altitude || (μουσ) pitch.

ύψωμα, το [eepsoma] height, elevation || hillock.

υψώνω [eepsono] raise, elevate || increase || hoist.

ύψωση, η [eepsosee] raising, lifting, elevation || rise in price.

Φ, φ

φάβα, η [fava] yellow pea || pea purée.

φαγάς, ο [fagas] glutton, gourmand.

φαγγρί, το [fangree] sea bream.

φαγητό, το [fayeeto] meal, dish, food || dinner.

φαγκότο, το [fangoto] bassoon.

φαγοπότι, το [fagopotee] revel, eating and drinking.

φαγούρα, η [fagoura] itching, irritation.

φάγωμα, το [fagoma] corrosion, disintegration || (τσακωμός) quarrel, dispute, wrangling.

φαγωμάρα, η [fagomara] itch, irritation || (τσακωμός) arguing, dispute.

φαγωμένος [fagomenos] eaten || eroded || **είμαι** ~ I've eaten.

φαγώσιμα, τα [fagoseema] πλ provisions, victuals.

φαγώσιμος [fagoseemos] eatable, edible.

φαεινή [faeenee]: ~ **ιδέα** brainwave, bright idea.

φαΐ, το [faee] food, meal.

φαιδρός [feδros] merry, cheerful || (μεταφ) ridiculous.

φαίνομαι [fenome] appear, come in sight || seem, look || show o.s. to be.

φαινόμενα, τα [fenomena] πλ: **κατά τα** ~ judging by appearances.

φαινομενικώς [fenomeneekos] apparently, outwardly.

φαινόμενο, το [fenomeno] wonder, prodigy || phenomenon.

φάκα, η [faka] mousetrap || snare.

φάκελος, ο [fakelos] envelope || file, cover, dossier, record.

φακή, η [fakee] lentils.

φακίδα, η [fakeeδa] freckle.

φακός, ο [fakos] lens || magnifying glass, magnifier.

φάλαγγα, η [falanga] phalanx || (στρατ) column || (στοίχος) row.

φάλαινα, η [falena] whale.

φαλάκρα, η [falakra] baldness || bald head.

φαλακραίνω [falakreno] go bald.

φαλακρός [falakros] bald(-headed) || bare.

φαλλός, ο [falos] phallus.

φάλτσο, το [faltso] wrong note, dissonance || (μεταφ) mistake, fault, error.

φαμίλια, η [fameeleea] family.

φάμπρικα, η [fambreeka] factory || fabrication, device, artifice.

φανάρι, το [fanaree] lamp, light, lantern || (αυτοκινήτου) headlamp || (φόρου) lighthouse.

φαναρτζής, ο [fanardzees] tinsmith || lampmaker.

φανατίζω [fanateezo] make fanatical, fanaticize.

φανατικός [fanateekos] overzealous, fanatical || (ουσ) fanatic, zealot.

φανατισμός, ο [fanateesmos] fanaticism.

φανέλα, η [fanela] flannel || vest || woollen cloth.

φανερός [faneros] clear, plain, evident, certain.

φανερώνω [fanerono] reveal, make plain.

φαντάζομαι [fandazome] imagine, fancy, think || (πιστεύω) believe.

φαντάζω [fandazo] make an impression, stand out || look glamorous.

φάνταρος, ο [fandaros] infantryman.

φαντασία, η [fandaseea] imagination || illusion || (υπερηφάνεια) vanity, pride || (μους) fantasia.

φαντασιοπληξία, η [fandaseeopleekseea] extravagant notion || caprice, whim.

φάντασμα, το [fandasma] phantom, ghost, spirit.

φαντασμαγορία, η [fandasmagoreea] phantasmagoria.

φαντασμένος [fandasmenos] presumptuous, vain.

φανταστικός [fandasteekos] illusory, imaginary || fantastic, extravagant.

φανταχτερός [fandahteros] showy, bright || gaudy, glaring.

φάντης, ο [fandees] (στα χαρτιά) knave.

φανφαρόνος, ο [fanfaronos] braggart, boaster, blusterer.

φάπα, η [fapa] slap, box on the ear, smack.

φάρα, η [fara] race, progeny, breed || crew.

φαράγγι, το [farangee] gorge, gully, precipice, ravine.

φαράσι, το [farasee] dustpan.

φαρδαίνω [farðeno] widen, broaden, become wider || stretch, extend.

φάρδος, το [farðos] width, breadth.

φαρδύς [farðees] wide, large, broad, ample.

φαρέτρα, η [faretra] quiver.

φαρμακείο, το [farmakeeo] chemist shop.

φαρμακερός [farmakeros] venomous || spiteful, bitter.

φαρμάκι, το [farmakee] poison || (μεταφ) anything bitter.

φάρμακο, το [farmako] drug, medicine, remedy.

φαρμακοποιός, ο [farmakopeeos] pharmacist, chemist || druggist (US).

φαρμακώνω [farmakono] poison || (μεταφ) cause grief || mortify.

φάρος, ο [faros] lighthouse, beacon.

φάρσα, η [farsa] trick, farce || practical joke.

φάρυγγας, ο [fareengas] pharynx, windpipe.

φασαρία, η [fasareea] disturbance || fuss, noise, bustle.

φασιανός, ο [faseeanos] pheasant.

φάση, η [fasee] phase || change, turn || aspect.

φασισμός, ο [faseesmos] fascism.

φασιστικός [faseesteekos] fascist.

φασκιά, η [faskia] swaddling band, swaddling clothes.

φασκόμπλο, το [faskomeelo] sage || sage tea.

φάσκω [fasko]: ~ και αντιφάσκω contradict o.s.

φάσμα, το [fasma] ghost, spirit || (φυσική) spectrum.

φασματοσκόπιο, το [fasmatoskopeeo] spectroscope.

φασόλι, το [fasolee] haricot bean, kidney bean.

φασο(υ)λάδα, η [faso(u)laδa] bean soup.

φασο(υ)λάκια, τα [faso(u)lakeea] πλ green beans.

φάτνη, η [fatnee] manger, crib, stall.

φατρία, η [fatreea] faction, clique, gang.

φατριάζω [fatreeazo] form factions, be factious.

φάτσα, η [fatsa] face || front || (επίρ) opposite.

φαυλοκρατία, η [favlokrateea] political corruption.

φαύλος [favlos] wicked, depraved || ~ κύκλος vicious circle.

φαφλατάς, ο [faflatas] chatterer, mumbler.

Φεβρουάριος, ο [fevrouareeos] February.

φεγγάρι, το [fengaree] moon.

φεγγίτης, ο [fengeetees] skylight, fanlight, garret window.

φεγγοβολώ [fengovolo] shine brightly.

φέγγω [fengo] shine, give light.

φείδομαι [feeδome] save, spare || be sparing of, be stingy.

φειδωλός [feeδolos] sparing, thrifty || stingy, mean, niggardly.

φελλός, ο [felos] cork.

φεουδαρχικός [feouδarheekos] feudal.

φέουδο, το [feouδo] fief.

φερέγγυος [ferengeeos] solvent, trustworthy.

φερέλπις [ferelpees] full of promise || hopeful.

φερετζές, ο [feredzes] veil (of a Moslem woman).

φέρετρο, το [feretro] coffin, bier.

φερμένος [fermenos] arrived, brought, imported.

φερμουάρ, το [fermouar] zip fastener.

φέρνω [ferno] βλ φέρω.

φέρομαι [ferome] conduct, behave || be reputed, be held as.

φέρσιμο, το [ferseemo] behaviour, conduct.

φέρω [fero] bring, carry, support || (στέλλω) fetch || (έχω πάνω μου) carry, have || (προξενώ) cause || (παράγω) bear, bring forth, bring in, yield || (φορώ) wear || (κατευθύνω) lead, conduct || ~ αντιρρήσεις protest || φερ' ειπείν for example.

φέσι, το [fesee] fez || γίνομαι ~ get dead drunk.

φέτα, η [feta] slice || (τυρί) kind of white cheese.

φετινός [feteenos] of this year.

φέτος [fetos] this year.

φευγάλα, η [fevgala] flight, escape, stampede.

φευγαλέος [fevgaleos] fleeting.

φευγατίζω [fevgateezo] help to escape.

φευγάτος [fevgatos] gone, fled, run away, left.

φεύγω [fevgo] leave, depart, get away || escape, flee || run away from, shun.

φήμη, η [feemee] report, rumour || reputation || renown, repute || fame.

φημίζομαι [feemeezome] be well-known.

φθάνω [fthano] catch, overtake, attain || (μεταφ) equal, be equal to || arrive, reach || draw near || ~ σε reach the point of, be reduced to || **φθάνει να** provided that.

φθαρτός [thartos] perishable, destructible, liable to decay.

φθείρομαι [theerome] decay, wash away || (μεταφ) lose importance.

φθείρω [ftheero] damage, spoil || corrupt, pervert, taint.

φθινόπωρο, το [ftheenoporo] autumn.

φθίνω [theeno] pine away || decay || decline, fail.

φθισικός [ftheeseekos] consumptive, tubercular.

φθίση, η [ftheesee] consumption || decline.

φθόγγος, ο [fthongos] voice, sound || (μουσ) note.

φθονερός [fthoneros] envious, jealous.

φθόνος, ο [fthonos] malicious envy, jealousy.

φθονώ [fthono] be envious of, begrudge.

φθορά, η [fthora] deterioration, damage, destruction || decay || loss.

φθορισμός, ο [fthoreesmos] fluorescence.

φι, το [fee] the letter Φ.

φιάλη, η [feealee] bottle, flagon, flask.

φιγούρα, η [feegoura] figure, image || (μεταφ) expression, air || **κάνω ~** cut a fine figure.

φιγουράρω [feegouraro] show off, appear.

φίδι, το [feeðee] snake, serpent.

φιδωτός [feeðotos] winding, twisting.

φίλαθλος, ο, η [feealthlos] sports fan.

φιλαλήθης [feelaleethees] truthful.

φιλάνθρωπος, ο, η [feelanthropos] philanthropist, charitable person.

φιλαράκος, ο [feelarakos] beau || chum, pal || scoundrel, rascal.

φιλάργυρος, ο [feelaryeeros] niggardly, miserly || (ουσ) miser.

φιλάρεσκος [feelareskos] coquettish, spruce.

φιλαρμονική, η [feelarmoneekee] (musical) band.

φιλαρχία, η [feelarheea] love of authority.

φιλάσθενος [feelasthenos] sickly, weakly, puny.

φιλελευθερισμός, ο [feelelevthereesmos] liberalism.

φιλελεύθερος, ο [feelelevtheros] liberal.

φιλέλληνας, ο, η [feelelleenas] philhellene.

φιλενάδα, η [feelenaða] girlfriend || (μεταφ) mistress.

φιλές, ο [feeles] hairnet.

φιλέτο, το [feeleto] fillet of meat.

φιλεύω [feelevo] make a present || entertain.

φίλη, η [feelee] friend.

φιλήδονος [feeleeðonos] sensual, voluptuous.

φίλημα, το [feeleema] kiss.

φιλήσυχος [feeleeseehos] peace-loving, calm, quiet, serene.

φιλί, το [feelee] βλ **φίλημα**.

φιλία, η [feeleea] friendship.

φιλικός [feeleekos] friendly || of a friend.

φίλιππος, ο, η [feeleepos] horse lover || racegoer.

φιλιστρίνι, το [feeleestreenee] porthole.

φιλμ, το [feelm] film.

φίλντισι, το [feelnteesee] mother-of-pearl || ivory.

φιλόδοξος [feeloðoksos] ambitious || pretentious, showy.

φιλοδοξώ [feeloðokso] be ambitious || aspire to, desire strongly.

φιλοδώρημα, το [feeloðoreema] tip || gratuity.

φιλοκερδής [feelokerðees] greedy, covetous, eager for gain.

φιλολογία, η [feeloloyeea] literature || philology.

φιλόλογος, ο [feelologos] man of letters, philologist || scholar.

φιλομαθής [feelomathees] fond of learning.

φιλόμουσος [feelomousos] lover of music || fond of learning.

φιλονικία, η [feeloneekeea] dispute, wrangle.

φιλονικώ [feeloneeko] quarrel,wrangle.

φιλοξενία, η [feelokseneea] hospitality.

φιλόξενος [feeloksenos] hospitable.

φιλοξενώ [feelokseno] entertain, give hospitality, receive.

φιλοπατρία, η [feelopatreea] patriotism.

φιλοπόλεμος [feelopolemos] warlike, martial.

φιλόπονος [feeloponos] assiduous, diligent, industrious.

φιλοπονώ [feelopono] prepare assiduously.

φίλος, ο [feelos] friend || (επιθ) dear, friendly.

φιλοσοφία, η [feelosofeea] philosophy.

φιλοσοφικός [feelosofeekos] philosophical.

φιλόσοφος, ο, η [feelosofos] philosopher.

φιλόστοργος [feelostorgos] loving, affectionate.

φιλοτελισμός, ο [feeloteleesmos] philately.

φιλοτέχνημα, το [feelotehneema] work of art.

φιλότεχνος [feelotehnos] art lover || artistic, skilful.

φιλοτιμία, η [feeloteemeea] sense, **φιλότιμο, το** [feeloteemo] sense of honour, pride, self-respect, dignity.

φιλότιμος [feeloteemos] eager to excel || obliging || having a sense of pride and honour || generous.

φιλοτιμούμαι [feeloteemoume] make it a point of honour.

φιλοτιμώ [feeloteemo] put s.o. on his dignity.

φιλοφρόνηση, η [feelofroneesee] compliment, courtesy.

φίλτατος [feeltatos] dearest, most beloved.

φίλτρο, το [feeltro] filter || philtre.

φιλύποπτος [feeleepoptos] distrustful, suspicious.

φιλώ [feelo] kiss, embrace.

φιμώνω [feemono] muzzle, gag || (μεταφ) silence, hush.

φίμωτρο, το [feemotro] muzzle, gag.

Φινλανδία, η [feenlandeea] Finland.

φινλανδικός [feenlandeekos] Finnish.

Φινλανδός, ο [feenlandos] Finn.

φίνος [feenos] fine.

φιόγκος, ο [feeongos] knot, bow.

φίρμα, η [feerma] firm || trade name.

φίσα, η [feesa] filing slip || gambling chip.

φίσκα [feeska] brimming over.

φιστίκι, το [feesteekea] pistachio nut || ~ αράπικο monkey nut, peanut.

φιτίλι, το [feeteelee] wick || (δυναμίτιδας) fuse.

φλάμπουρο, το [flambouro] pennon, standard.

φλάουτο, το [flaouto] flute.

φλέβα, η [fleva] vein || (μεταλλεύματος) lode || (μεταφ) talent.

Φλεβάρης, ο [flevarees] February.

φλέγμα, το [flegma] phlegm, mucus || (μεταφ) coolness, unconcern.

φλεγματικός [flegmateekos] phlegmatic || stolid.

φλεγμονή, η [flegmonee] inflammation, soreness.

φλέγομαι [flegome] burn, ignite || (μεταφ) flare up.

φλέγον [flegon]: ~ ζήτημα topical problem.

φλερτάρω [flertaro] flirt with.

φλυναφώ [fleenafo] prate, babble, prattle.

φλιτζάνι, το [fleedzanee] cup.

φλόγα, η [floga] flame, blaze || (μεταφ) passion, ardour.

φλογέρα, η [floyera] shepherd's pipe, reed.

φλογερός [floyeros] burning, flaming || (μεταφ) ardent, fervent.

φλογίζω [floyeezo] inflame, kindle.

φλόγωση, η [flogosee] inflammation, soreness.

φλοιός, ο [fleeos] peel, rind || (φυστικιού) shell || (δένδρου) bark || (γης) crust.

φλοίσβος, ο [fleesvos] rippling of waves || babbling.

φλοκάτη, η [flokatee] thick blanket, peasant's cape.

φλόκος, ο [flokos] jib.

φλομώνω [flomono] stun || grow wan.

φλούδα, η [flouda] βλ φλοιός.

φλουρί, το [flouree] gold coin.

φλυαρία, η [fleeareea] gossiping, chatter, prattle.

φλύαρος, ο [fleearos] talkative.

φλυαρώ [fleearo] chatter, tattle, prattle.

φλυτζάνι, το [fleedzanee] cup.

φοβάμαι [fovame] be afraid.

φοβέρα, η [fovera] threat, menace, intimidation.

φοβερίζω [fovereezo] threaten, menace, intimidate.

φοβερός [foveros] terrible, frightful || amazing, formidable.

φόβητρο, το [foveetro] scarecrow || bogey || fright.

φοβητσιάρης [foveetseearees] fearful, timid, timorous.

φοβία, η [foveea] fear, phobia.

φοβίζω [foveezo] frighten || menace, threaten, intimidate.

φόβος, ο [fovos] fear, dread, fright.

φόδρα, η [fodra] lining.

φοίνικας, ο [feeneekas] palm tree || (καρπός) date || phoenix.

φοίτηση, η [feeteesee] attendance (at school).

φοιτητής, ο [feeteetees] student.

φοιτώ [feeto] be a student, attend a course of studies.

φόλα, η [fola] dog poison.

φονεύω [fonevo] murder, kill.

φονιάς, ο [fonias] murderer.

φονικό, το [foneeko] murder, homicide, carnage.

φόνος, ο [fonos] murder, homicide.

φόντο, το [fonto] bottom, base, back || (ζωγραφιάς) background || (κεφάλαιο) capital.

φόρα, η [fora] impulse, impetus || force || βγάζω στη ~ bring into the open, uncover.

φορά, η [fora] force || course, run, impetus || (κατεύθυνση) direction || (ευκαιρία) time || άλλη ~ another time || άλλη μια ~ once again || μια ~ once, only once.

φοράδα, η [forada] mare.

φορατζής, ο [foradzees] tax collector.

φορβή, η [forvee] fodder, forage.

φορείο, το [foreeo] stretcher, litter.

φόρεμα, το [forema] dress, garment.

φορεσιά, η [foresia] dress, suit of clothes || attire.

φορέας, ο [foreas] carrier, porter || (οικον) agent, body.

φορητός [foreetos] portable, easy to carry.

φόρμα, η [forma] form, shape || mould, matrix || (εργάτη) overall || (ντοκουμέντο) form, document || σε ~ in good form, in tiptop shape.

φοροδιαφυγή, η [forodeeafeeyee] tax evasion.

φορολογία, η [foroloyeea] taxation || tax, rate.

φορολογούμενος, ο [forologoumenos] taxpayer, ratepayer.

φορολογώ [forologo] tax, put a tax on.

φόρος, ο [foros] tax, rate, duty.

φορτηγό, το [forteego] lorry || truck (US) || (ναυτ) cargo vessel.

φορτίζω [forteezo] charge with electricity.

φορτικός [forteekos] intrusive, importunate || troublesome.

φορτίο, το [forteeo] cargo, load || burden, charge, weight.

φορτοεκφορτωτής, ο [fortoekfortotees] stevedore.

φόρτος, ο [fortos] burden, heavy load.

φορτσάρω [fortsaro] force || intensify || (ανέμου) increase, strengthen.

φόρτωμα, το [fortoma] loading || (μεταφ) burden, care.

φορτώνομαι [fortonome] pester, annoy, bother.

φορτώνω [fortono] load, pile (on) || take on cargo.

φορτωτική, η [fortoteekee] bill of lading.

φορώ [foro] wear || put on, get into || carry.

φουγάρο, το [fougaro] funnel, flue, tall chimney, smokestack.

φουκαράς, ο [foukaras] poor devil || unfortunate fellow.

φουμάρω [foumaro] smoke.

φούμος, ο [foumos] soot || lampblack.

φούντα, η [founta] tassel || tuft, crest.

φουντάρω [fountaro] (ναυτ) sink || cast anchor.

φουντούκι, το [fountoukee] hazelnut.

φουντώνω [fountono] become bushy || stretch out, spread || expand.

φουντωτός [fountotos] bushy, thick.

φούρια, η [foureea] haste.

φούρκα, η [fourka] rage, anger || (κρεμάλα) gallows, gibbet.

φουρκέτα, η [fourketa] hairpin.

φουρκίζω [fourkeezo] vex, harass.

φούρναρης, ο [fournarees] baker.

φουρνέλο, το [fournelo] grid || blasting charge.

φουρνιά, η [fournia] ovenful || (μεταφ) batch.

φούρνος, ο [fournos] oven || bakery || kiln, furnace.

φουρτούνα, η [fourtouna] tempest, storm || rough sea || (μεταφ) calamity, misfortune.

φούσκα, η [fouska] bladder || (παιχνίδι) balloon || blister || soap bubble.

φουσκάλα, η [fouskala] blister || bubble.

φουσκοθαλασσιά, η [fouskothalasia] surge of sea.

φούσκωμα, το [fouskoma] inflation, swelling || swaggering.

φουσκωμένος [fouskomenos] swollen, inflated, puffed up

φουσκώνω [fouskono] swell, inflate, blow up || (λάστιχο) pump || (μεταφ) exaggerate || (ενοχλώ) irritate || (ζύμη) rise || (ενοχλώ) puff, pant || (μεταφ) puff o.s. up.

φουσκωτός [fouskotos] puffed, inflated || curved.

φούστα, η [fousta] skirt.

φουστανέλα, η [foustanela] kind of kilt worn as part of the Greek national costume.

φουστάνι, το [foustanee] gown, dress, frock.

φούχτα, η [fouhta] handful || hollow of hand.

φράγκο, το [frango] franc || drachma.

φραγκοστάφυλο, το [frangostafeelo] redcurrant.

φραγκόσυκο, το [frangoseeko] prickly pear.

φράγμα, το [fragma] enclosure, fence || barrage, dam || barrier.

φραγμός, ο [fragmos] fence, barrier || (στρατ) barrage.

φράζω [frazo] surround, hedge || bar, block up, stop, obstruct.

φράκο, το [frako] dress coat, tails.

φράκτης, ο [fraktees] fence, enclosure, fencing.

φραμπαλάς, ο [frambalas] furbelow.

φράντζα, η [frandza] fringe.

φραντζόλα, η [frandzola] long loaf.

φράξιμο, το [frakseemo] enclosing, fencing || stopping up, blockage.

φράουλα, η [fraoula] strawberry.

φράπα, η [frapa] kind of large citrus fruit, grapefruit.

φρασεολογία, η [fraseoloyeea] phraseology.

φράση, η [frasee] phrase || period.

φράσσω [fraso] βλ **φράζω**.

φράχτης, ο [frahtees] fence, enclosure, fencing, hedge.

φρέαρ, το [frear] well || (μεταλλείο) pit, shaft.

φρεάτιο, το [freateeo] small well.

φρεγάδα, η [fregaða] frigate.

φρένα, τα [frena] πλ reason, senses || brakes.

φρεναρισμα, το [frenareesma] braking.

φρενάρω [frenaro] brake || (μεταφ) check.

φρένες, οι [frenes] πλ mind, reason, wits || **έξω φρενών** off one's head, enraged || unbelievable.

φρενιάζω [freneeazo] get furious, fret and fume.

φρένο, το [freno] brake.

φρενοβλαβής [frenovlavees] mentally disturbed.

φρενοκομείο, το [frenokomeeo] madhouse, lunatic asylum.

φρενολογία, η [frenoloyeea] phrenology.

φρεσκάδα, η [freskaða] freshness || coolness, chilliness.

φρεσκάρω [freskaro] freshen, cool || (ο καιρός) become worse.

φρέσκο, το [fresko] fresco || coolness, freshness, chilliness || **στο ~** in prison.

φρέσκος [freskos] fresh, new, recent || cool.

φρικαλέος [freekaleos] horrible, hideous, ghastly.

φρίκη, η [freekee] terror, horror || (επιφ) frightful.

φρικιάζω [freekeeazo] shiver, shudder || be disgusted.

φρικτός [freektos], **φρικώδης** [freekoðees] (θέμα) horrible, ghastly || (εμφάνιση) hideous || (καιρός) horrid, vile || awful.

φρόκαλο, το [frokalo] sweepings, rubbish || broom.

φρόνημα, το [froneema] opinion, sentiment, morale || **φρονήματα** political convictions.

φρονηματίζω [froneemateezo] inspire self-confidence, render self-confident.

φρόνηση, η [froneesee] prudence, wariness, circumspection.

φρόνιμα [froneema] (επιρ) behave yourself.

φρονιμάδα, η [froneemaða] wisdom, prudence || moderation || (παιδιού) quietness, good behaviour || (γυναίκας) modesty, chastity.

φρονιμεύω [froneemevo] become prudent, grow wise, be well-behaved.

φρονιμίτης, ο [froneemeetees] wisdom tooth.

φρόνιμος [froneemos] reasonable, sound, well-behaved || virtuous, wise.

φροντίζω [fronteezo] look after, care for || see to.

φροντίδα, η [fronteeda] concern, care, anxiety.

φροντίδες, οι [fronteedes] πλ things to do, cares.

φροντιστήριο, το [fronteesteereeo] coaching school || prep school.

φρονώ [frono] think, suppose, believe, consider.

φρουρά, η [froura] lookout, guard || garrison.

φρούριο, το [froureeo] fortress, stronghold.

φρουρός, ο [frouros] guard, sentinel, sentry || (μεταφ) guardian.

φρουρώ [frouro] guard, keep watch, stand sentry.

φρούτο, το [frouto] fruit, dessert.

φρυγανιά, η [freegania] toast.

φρύδι, το [freedee] eyebrow.

φταίξιμο, το [ftekseemo] fault, error, mistake, blame.

φταίχτης, ο [ftehtees] person responsible, culprit.

φταίω [fteo] be responsible, be to blame || make a mistake.

φτάνω [ftano] βλ **φθάνω**.

φτέρη, η [fteree] fern.

φτέρνα, η [fterna] heel.

φτερνίζομαι [fterneezome] sneeze.

φτέρνισμα, το [fterneesma] sneeze, sneezing.

φτερό, το [ftero] feather, plume || wing || (ξεσκονίσματος) feather duster || (αυτοκινήτου) mudguard || fender (US).

φτερούγα, η [fterouga] wing.

φτερουγίζω [fterouyeezo] flutter, flap.

φτηναίνω [fteeneno] cheapen, become cheaper, go down.

φτήνεια, η [fteeneea] cheapness, low price.

φτηνός [fteenos] cheap.

φτιά(χ)νομαι [ftiea(h)nome] make up one's face || look better.

φτιά(χ)νω [ftiea(h)no] arrange,

tidy up, correct || (κατασκευάζω) make || have made || do.

φτιαχτός [fteeahtos] fabricated, affected.

φτυάρι, το [fteearee] shovel, spade, scoop.

φτύνω [fteeno] spit, expectorate || spit out.

φτύσιμο, το [fteeseemo] spitting.

φτυστός [fteestos]: ~ ο πατέρας του the spitting image of his father.

φτωχαίνω [ftoheno] impoverish, make poor || become poor.

φτώχεια, η [ftoheea] poverty, destitution.

φτωχεύω [ftohevo] become poor || go bankrupt.

φτωχικό, το [ftoheeko] humble abode.

φτωχικός [ftoheekos] poor, mean, scant || shabby.

φτωχός [ftohos] poor, needy, penniless.

φυγαδεύω [feegadevo] help to escape.

φυγάδας, ο [feegadas] runaway, deserter, fugitive, renegade.

φυγή, η [feeyee] escape, fleeing, flight.

φυγοδικία, η [feegodeekeea] default.

φυγόδικος/κη [feegodeekos] defaulter.

φυγόκεντρος [feegokentros] centrifugal.

φυγόπονος [feegoponos] lazy || (ουσ) slacker, shirker.

φύκια, τα [feekeea] πλ seaweed.

φυλάγομαι [feelagome] take precautions, take care.

φυλάγω [feelago] guard, protect || mind, tend || (αντικείμενο) keep, lay aside || lie in wait for.

φύλακας, ο [feelakas] keeper, guardian, watchman, guard, caretaker.

φυλακή, η [feelakee] prison, jail.

φυλακίζω [feelakeezo] incarcerate, imprison.

φυλάκιο, το [feelakeeo] guardhouse, post.

φυλάκιση, η [feelakeesee] imprisonment.

φυλακισμένος, ο [feelakeesmenos] prisoner.

φυλαχτό, το [feelahto] talisman, amulet, charm.

φυλετικός [feeleteekos] tribal, racial.

φυλή, η [feelee] race, tribe, line.

φυλλάδα, η [feelaδa] booklet, pamphlet, brochure.

φυλλάδιο, το [feelaδeeo] pamphlet || instalment, issue, part.

φυλλοκάρδια, τα [feelokarδeea] πλ bottom of one's heart.

φυλλομετρώ [feelometro] turn pages of, skim over, run through.

φύλλο, το [feelo] leaf || (λουλουδιού) petal || (χαρτιού κτλ) sheet || (σελίδα) page || (πόρτας κτλ) shutter, leaf || (χαρτοπαιξίας) (playing) card || (εφημερίδα) newspaper || ~ **πορείας** marching orders.

φυλλοξήρα, η [feelokseera] phylloxera.

φύλλωμα, το [feeloma] foliage.

φύλο, το [feelo] sex || race.

φυματικός [feemateekos] consumptive, tubercular.

φυμάτίωση, η [feemateeosee] tuberculosis, consumption.

φύομαι [feeome] grow, bud, sprout.

φύρα, η [feera] loss of weight, waste.

φυραίνω [feereno] shorten, shrink || lose weight, lose volume.

φύραμα, το [feerama] paste, dough || blend || (μεταφ) character, sort.

φύρδην [feerδeen]: ~ **μίγδην** pell-mell, helter-skelter.

φυσαλίδα, η [feesaleeδa] bubble || blister.

φυσαρμόνικα, η [feesarmoneeka] accordion || mouth organ.

φυσέκι, το [feesekee] cartridge.

φυσερό, το [feesero] bellows.

φύση, η [feesee] nature.

φύσημα, το [feeseema] breath || puff || breathing.

φυσίγγιο, το [feeseengeeo] cartridge.

φυσικά, τα [feeseeka] πλ physics.

φυσικά [feeseeka] naturally, as a matter of fact.

φυσική, η [feeseekee] physics, natural philosophy.

φυσικό, το [feeseeko] custom, habit.

φυσικός [feeseekos] natural || physical || (ουσ) physicist.

φυσικότητα, η [feeseekoteeta] naturalness, artlessness.

φυσιογνωμία, η [feeseeognomeea] cast of features || countenance || well-known person.

φυσιολάτρης, ο [feeseeolatrees] lover of nature.

φυσιολογία, η [feeseeoloyeea] physiology.

φυσιολογικός [feeseeoloyeekos] physiological || (μεταφ) normal.

φύση, η [feesee] nature || character, temper || **φύσει** by nature.

φυσομανώ [feesomano] rage.

φυσώ [feeso] blow up || puff, blow out || pant || (μεταφ) it's windy.

φυτεία, η [feeteea] plantation || vegetation, bed of vegetables.

φύτεμα, το [feetema] planting.

φυτεύω [feetevo] plant, lay out || (μεταφ) lodge, stick.

φυτικός [feeteekos] vegetable.

φυτοζωώ [feetozoo] live in poverty, scrape through.

φυτοκομία, η [feetokomeea] horticulture.

φυτολογία, η [feetoloyeea] botany.

φυτό, το [feeto] plant, vegetable.

φύτρα, η [feetra] germ, embryo || (μεταφ) lineage, origin.

φυτρώνω [feetrono] grow, germinate, sprout.

φυτώριο, το [feetoreeo] nursery, plantation, seedbed.

φώκια, η [fokeea] seal.

φωλιά, η [foleea] nest, den, lair, hole || (μεταφ) hovel.

φωλιάζω [foleeazo] nestle, nest.

φωνάζω [fonazo] shout, call, summon || cry, scream, shriek.

φωνακλάς, ο [fonaklas] loud talker, noisy talker.

φωνή, η [fonee] sound || voice || cry, shout, scream.

φωνήεν, το [fonien] vowel.

φωνητική, η [foneeteekee] phonetics.

φωνητικός [foneeteekos] vocal || phonetic, phonic.

φως, το [fos] light || (μεταφ) sight || knowledge, illumination.

φωστήρ(ας), το [fosteer(as)] luminary || (μεταφ) learned, erudite person.

φωσφόρος, ο [fosforos] phosphorus.

φώτα, τα [fota] πλ lights || (μεταφ) knowledge, learning || (εκκλ) Epiphany.

φωταγωγός, ο [fotagogos] light well, skylight.

φωταγωγώ [fotagogo] illuminate.

φωταέριο, το [fotaereeo] gas (lighting).

φωταψία, η [fotapseea] illumination.

φωτεινός [foteenos] luminous, light, bright || clear, lucid.

φωτιά, η [fotia] fire || (καπνιστού) light || (μεταφ) great heat || fury || (σε τιμή) costliness.

φωτίζω [foteezo] illuminate, light up, light || enlighten, inform.

φώτιση, η [foteesee] enlightenment || inspiration.

φωτισμός, ο [foteesmos] lighting, illumination.

φωτοβολίδα, η [fotovoleeδa] flare.

φωτογενής [fotogenees] photogenic.

φωτογραφείο, το [fotografeeo] photographic studio.

φωτογραφία, η [fotografeea] photograph || photography.

φωτογραφική, η [fotografeekee] photography || ~ μηχανή camera.

φωτογράφος, ο [fotografos] photographer.

φωτόμετρο, το [fotometro] light meter.

φωτοσκίαση, η [fotoskeeasee] shading, light and shade.

φωτοστέφανος, ο [fotostefanos] halo || (μεταφ) glory, prestige.

φωτοτυπία, η [fototeepeea] photocopy.

φωτοχυσία, η [fotoheeseea] illumination.

Χ, χ

χαβάς, ο [havas] tune, air, melody.

χαβιάρι, το [haviaree] caviar.

χαβούζα, η [havouza] cistern, reservoir.

χαγιάτι, το [hayiatee] upper gallery round courtyard.

χάδια, τα [haδeea] πλ petting, cajolery.

χαζεύω [hazevo] gape || idle about, loiter.

χάζι, το [hazee] pleasure, delight || το κάνω ~ it entertains me.

χαζός [hazos] stupid, silly, foolish.

χαϊβάνι, το [haeevanee] beast || (μεταφ) jackass.

χάϊδεμα, το [haeeδema] caressing, pat, stroke || (μεταφ) cajolery.

χαϊδευτικός [haeeδevteekos]

caressing, affectionate || (άνεμος) soft.

χαϊδεμένος [haeedemenos] spoilt.

χαϊδεύομαι [haeedevome] nuzzle, cuddle || seek attention.

χαϊδεύω [haeedevo] caress, fondle, pat || pet, spoil || fawn upon.

χαιρέκακος [herekakos] malicious, mischievous.

χαίρετε [herete] (επιφ) hello, good day || be seeing you.

χαιρετίζω [hereteezo] hail, greet || salute.

χαιρέτισμα, το [hereteesma] salute, greeting, salutation, bow.

χαιρετισμός, ο [hereteesmos] βλ **χαιρέτισμα.**

χαιρετώ [hereto] βλ **χαιρετίζω.**

χαίρομαι [herome] be happy || enjoy.

χαίρω [hero] be pleased || ~ **άκρας υγείας** be in tiptop shape.

χαίτη, η [hetee] mane, shock of hair.

χακί, το [hakee] khaki.

χαλάζι, το [halazee] hail.

χαλάλι [halalee]: ~ **σου** you merit it, you can have it.

χαλαρός [halaros] relaxed, slack, loose.

χαλαρώνω [halarono] unbend || (σχοινί) loosen, slacken || (μεταφ) relax || (προσπάθεια) abate, ease up || (ζήλο) cool.

χάλασμα, το [halasma] ruin, demolition || (μηχανής) putting out of order || ruin.

χαλασμένος [halasmenos] rotten, turned bad || broken, not working || damaged, demolished.

χαλασμός, ο [halasmos] demolition, destruction || (μεταφ) disturbance, storm, excitement || catastrophe.

χαλάστρα, η [halastra]: **μου κάνουν** ~ they foiled my plans, they cramped my style.

χαλβάς, ο [halvas] halva || (μεταφ) indolent person, silly fellow.

χαλί, το [halee] carpet, rug.

χάλια, τα [haleea] πλ bad condition, sad plight.

χαλίκι, το [haleekee] pebble, small stone, gravel.

χαλιναγωγώ [haleenagogo] lead by the bridle || (μεταφ) check, curb || (πάθη) control, curb.

χαλινάρι, το [haleenaree] bridle, bit, rein || (μεταφ) curbing, holding back.

χαλκάς, ο [halkas] ring, link.

χάλκινος [halkeenos] of copper.

χαλκογραφία, η [halkografeea] copperplate engraving, art of copperplating.

χαλκομανία, η [halkomaneea] transfer design.

χαλκός, ο [halkos] copper, brass, bronze.

χαλνώ [halno] βλ **χαλώ.**

χάλυβας, ο [haleevas] steel.

χαλύβδινος [haleevdeenos] made of steel.

χαλώ [halo] demolish, break, ruin, spoil || (φθείρω) wear out || (νεύρα) fret || (υγεία) break down || (δαπανώ) spend, consume || (διαφθείρω) corrupt, pervert || (νόμισμα) change || (δόντι) decay || (κρέας) taint, go bad || ~ **τον κόσμο** move heaven and earth, make a fuss.

χαμαιλέοντας, ο [hameleondas] chameleon || (βοτ) thistle.

χαμάλης, ο [hamalees] porter || (μεταφ) vulgar fellow, scoundrel.

χαμάμι, το [hamamee] Turkish bath.

χαμένα [hamena]: **τα έχω** ~ be mixed up, be bewildered.

χαμένος [hamenos] lost, disappeared || (ουσ: στα χαρτιά) loser || (μεταφ) scoundrel, rascal || scatterbrain.

χαμηλός [hameelos] low || (φωνή) gentle, soft, subdued.

χαμηλόφωνα [hameelofona] in an undertone, softly.

χαμηλώνω [hameelono] lower, reduce, bring down || subside.

χαμίνι, το [hameenee] street urchin, mischievous youngster.

χαμόγελο, το [hamoyelo] smile.

χαμογελώ [hamoyelo] smile.

χαμόκλαδο, το [hamoklaδo] shrub.

χαμομήλι, το [hamomeelee] camomile.

χαμός, ο [hamos] loss, destruction, ruin || death.

χάμουρα, τα [hamoura] πλ harness, trappings.

χαμπάρι, το [hambaree] piece of news || **παίρνω** ~ become aware, perceive.

χάμω [hamo] down, on the ground.

χάνι, το [hanee] country inn, lodging house.

χανούμισσα, η [hanoumeesa] Turkish lady.

χαντάκι, το [hantakee] ditch, drain, trench || (οχυρού) moat.

χαντακώνω [hantakono] (μεταφ) destroy, ruin.

χάντρα, η [hantra] bead.

χάνομαι [hanome] lose o.s., get lost || **να χαθείς!** go to hell! || **χάσου** get out of my sight!

χάνω [hano] lose, go astray || (ευκαιρία) let slip || (καιρό) waste time || (τραίνο) lose, miss || become disconcerted, get confused.

χάος, το [haos] chaos, wild disorder || bottomless pit.

χάπι, το [hapee] pill.

χαρά, η [hara] joy || (υπερβολική) delight, glee || pleasure, enjoyment || ~ **θεού** delight || **μια** ~ very well, splendidly || **γεια** ~ so long!, goodbye! || hello! || ~ **στο πράμα** wonderful!, it's nothing! (ironic).

χάραγμα, το [haragma] tracing, engraving || incision, cut.

χαράδρα, η [haraδra] ravine, gorge, gully.

χαράζω [harazo] cut, engrave || rule lines || trace || (δρόμο κτλ) mark out, lay out.

χάρακας, ο [harakas] straight edge, ruler.

χαρακιά, η [harakia] scratch, incision, mark || groove || (γραμμή) line, stroke.

χαράκτηρας, ο [harakteeras] character, letter || temper, nature.

χαρακτηρίζω [harakteereezo] define, qualify || characterize.

χαρακτηριστικά, τα [harakteereesteeka] πλ person's features.

χαρακτηριστικός [harakteereesteekos] typical, distinctive, characteristic.

χαράκτης, ο [haraktees] engraver, carver.

χαρακτική, η [harakteekee] art of engraving.

χαράκωμα, το [harakoma] trench || (γραμμών) ruling.

χαραμάδα, η [haramaδa] fissure, crack, crevice.

χαράματα, τα [haramata] πλ dawn, daybreak.

χαραματιά, η [haramatia] incision, crack || (επιφάνειας) scratch, trace, engraving.

χαραμίζω [harameezo] waste, spend uselessly.

χάραξη, η [haraksee] engraving, tracing, incision || (δρόμου) laying out.

χαράσσω [harasso] engrave, carve || (γραμμές) rule || map out, trace || (δρόμο) lay out.

χαράτσι, το [haratsee] (μεταφ) oppressive tax.

χαρατσώνω [haratsono] exact money from || tax oppressively.

χαραυγή, n [haravyee] daybreak, dawn.

χαρέμι, το [haremee] harem.

χάρη, n [haree] grace, charm || good point || favour || gratitude || (ποινής) remittance, pardon || ~ σε σένα thanks to you || λόγου ~ for instance || χάριν του for, on behalf of || παραδείγματος ~ for example, for instance || για ~ σου for your sake, on your behalf.

χαριεντίζομαι [harienteezome] be in a teasing mood, jest || become very charming.

χαρίζω [hareezo] give, donate, present || (χρέος κτλ) remit.

χάρισμα, το [hareesma] talent, gift || accomplishment || (επιρ) free, gratis, for nothing.

χαριστική [hareesteekee]: ~ βολή coup de grace.

χαριστικός [hareesteekos] prejudiced, partial.

χαριτολογώ [hareetologo] jest, speak wittily, speak amusingly.

χαριτωμένος [hareetomenos] charming, enchanting.

χάρμα, το [harma] delight, source of joy.

χαρμάνι, το [harmanee] mixture, blend.

χαρμόσυνος [harmoseenos] cheerful, glad.

χαροκόπος, ο [harokopos] pleasure-loving person, rake.

χάρος, ο [haros] death.

χαρούμενος [haroumenos] cheerful, joyful, happy.

χαρούπι, το [haroupee] carob.

χαρταετός, ο [hartaetos] kite.

χαρτζιλίκι, το [hardzeeleekee] pocket money.

χάρτης, ο [hartees] paper || (γεωγραφικός) map || (συνταγματικός) charter.

χαρτί, το [hartee] paper ||

(χαρτοπαιξίας) playing card || ~ υγείας toilet paper.

χάρτινος [harteenos] of paper.

χαρτοκόπτης, ο [hartokoptees] paper knife.

χαρτόνι, το [hartonee] cardboard, pasteboard.

χαρτονόμισμα, το [hartonomeesma] banknote || bill (US) || paper money.

χαρτοπαίκτης, ο [hartopektees] gambler, card player.

χαρτοπαιξία, n [hartopekseea] gambling, card playing.

χαρτοπόλεμος, ο [hartopolemos] confetti throwing.

χαρτοπώλης, ο [hartopolees] stationer, paper merchant.

χαρτόσημο, το [hartoseemo] stamp tax.

χαρτοφύλακας, ο [hartofeelakas] briefcase || (εκκλ) archivist.

χαρτοφυλάκιο, το [hartofeelakeeo] letter-case, briefcase || (μεταφ) portfolio.

χαρωπός [haropos] cheerful, happy.

χασάπης, ο [hasapees] butcher.

χασάπικο, το [hasapeeko] butcher's shop.

χάση, n [hasee]: στη ~ και στη φέξη once in a blue moon.

χάσιμο, το [haseemo] loss.

χασίσι, το [haseesee] hashish.

χάσκω [hasko] yawn, gape || stand ajar.

χάσμα, το [hasma] abyss, pit || lacuna, gap.

χασμουρητό, το [hasmoureeto] yawning, yawn.

χασμουριέμαι [hasmourieme] yawn.

χασμωδία, n [hasmodeea] hiatus || disorder, confusion.

χασομερώ [hasomero] be idle || hang around, linger.

χασούρα, n [hasoura] loss.

χαστούκι, το [hastookee] slap, smack, clout.

χατίρι, το [hateeree] favour, good turn || **για το ~ σου** for your sake.

χαυλιόδοντας, ο [havleeodondas] tusk.

χαύνος [havnos] slack, indolent || faint-hearted.

χαφιές, ο [hafies] stool, nark, agent, informer.

χάφτω [hafto] swallow, gobble down || (μεταφ) take in.

χαχανίζω [hahaneezo] burst into laughter, laugh loudly.

χάχας, ο [hahas] moron, idiot.

χαψιά, η [hapsia] mouthful.

χαώδης [haodees] chaotic, confused.

χέζομαι [hezome] be in a fright, be scared || **χέστηκα** I don't give a damn.

χέζω [hezo] defecate || (μεταφ) send to the devil.

χείλι, το [heelee], **χείλος, το** [heelos] lip || (μεταφ) brink, verge || (ποτηριού) brim, rim.

χείμαρρος, ο [heemaros] torrent, torrent bed.

χειμερινός [heemereenos] winter, wintry.

χειμώνας, ο [heemonas] winter.

χειμωνιάτικος [heemoneeateekos] βλ **χειμερινός.**

χειραφετώ [heerafeto] liberate, emancipate || manumit.

χειραψία, η [heerapseea] shake of the hand.

χειρίζομαι [heereezome] handle, manipulate, manage || (μηχανή) drive.

χειρισμός, ο [heereesmos] manipulation, working, driving || (υποθέσεως) handling, management.

χειριστήρια, τα [heereesteereea] πλ controls of a machine.

χειριστής, ο [heereestees] operator || pilot.

χειροβομβίδα, η [heerovomveeda] grenade.

χειρόγραφο, το [heerografo] manuscript.

χειροκίνητος [heerokeeneetos] hand-operated.

χειροκρότημα, το [heerokroteema] clapping, applause.

χειροκροτώ [heerokroto] applaud, cheer, clap.

χειρομαντεία, η [heeromandeea] palm reading.

χειρονομία, η [heeronomeea] flourish, gesture || gesticulation.

χειροπέδες, οι [heeropedes] πλ pair of handcuffs.

χειροπιαστός [heeropeeastos] tangible.

χειροπόδαρα [heeropodara] hand and foot.

χειροποίητος [heeropieetos] handmade.

χειρότερα [heerotera] worse.

χειροτερεύω [heeroterevo] worsen, deteriorate.

χειρότερος [heeroteros] worse || **ο ~** the worst.

χειροτεχνία, η [heerotehneea] handicraft.

χειροτονία, η [heerotoneea] ordination, consecration.

χειρουργείο, το [heerouryeeo] operating theatre.

χειρουργική, η [heerouryeekee] surgery.

χειρουργικός [heerouryeekos] surgical.

χειρουργός, ο [heerourgos] surgeon.

χειροφίλημα, το [heerofeeleema] kissing of the hand.

χειρωνακτικός [heeronakteekos] manual.

χέλι, το [helee] eel.

χελιδόνι, το [heeleedonee] (ζωολ) swallow.

χελώνα, η [helona] tortoise, turtle.

χεράκι, το [herakee] tiny hand.

χέρι, το [heree] hand || arm || (χειρολαβή) handle || (μπογιάς) coat || (στο πλύσιμο) treatment, going-over || ~ ~ hand-in-hand || ~ με ~ quickly, directly || βάζω ένα ~ give a hand || βάζω ~ lay hands on, fondle || από πρώτο ~ at first hand.

χερούλι, το [heroulee] handle, haft || (στάμνας) ear.

χεραίος [herseos] terrestrial || (κλίμα) continental.

χερσόνησος, η [hersoneesos] peninsula.

χέρσος [hersos] uncultivated, fallow, waste,

χέσιμο, το [heseemo] defecation || (μεταφ) fright, terror || volley of abuse.

χημεία, η [heemeea] chemistry.

χημικός [heemeekos] chemical || (ουσ) chemist.

χήνα, η [heena] goose.

χήρα, η [heera] widow.

χηρεύω [heerevo] become widowed || (θέση) be unoccupied, be vacant.

χήρος, ο [heeros] widower.

χθες [hthes] yesterday.

χθεσινός [hthseenos] of yesterday || (πρόσφατος) latest, recent.

χι, το [hee] the letter X.

χιαστί [heeastee] crossways, crosswise, diagonally.

χίλια [heeleea]: ~ δυο a thousand and two.

χιλιάδα, η [heeleeaða] thousand.

χιλιάρικο, το [heeleeareeko] thousand-drachma note.

χιλιετηρίδα, η [heelieteereeða], χιλιετία, η [heelieteea] millenium.

χιλιόγραμμο, το [heeleeogramo] kilogramme.

χίλιοι [heeliee] thousand.

χιλιόμετρο, το [heeleeometro] kilometre.

χιλιοστό, το [heeleeosto] millimetre || thousandth part.

χιλιοστός [heeleeostos] thousandth.

χίμαιρα, η [heemera] chimera || (μεταφ) illusion.

χιμπαντζής, ο [heempandzees] chimpanzee.

χιονάνθρωπος, ο [heeonanthropos] snowman.

χιονάτος [heeonatos] snow-white, snowy.

χιόνι, το [heeonee] snow.

χιονιά, η [heeonia] snowy weather || snowball.

χιονίζει [heeoneezee] it is snowing.

χιονίστρα, η [heeoneestra] chilblain.

χιονοδρομία, η [heeonoðromeea] skiing.

χιονοθύελλα, η [heeonothiela] snowstorm, blizzard.

χιονόνερο, το [heeononero] sleet, melted snow.

χιονοστιβάδα, η [heeonosteevaða] avalanche, snowdrift.

χιούμορ, το [heeoumor] wit, humour || χιουμοριστικός humorous, humoristic.

χιτώνας, ο [heetonas] robe, tunic || (μππιού) cornea.

χλαίνη, η [hlenee] greatcoat || (ναυτ) duffel coat || cloak, capote.

χλαμύδα, η [hlameeða] mantle.

χλευάζω [hlevazo] mock, scoff at, make fun of.

χλευαστικός [hlevasteekos] mocking, sarcastic, derisive.

χλιαρός [hleearos] tepid, lukewarm || (άνεμος) mild || (μεταφ) weak, lax.

χλιδή, η [hleeðee] luxury, voluptuousness.

χλιμιντρίζω [hleemeendreezo] neigh, whinny.

χλοερός [hloeros] green, fresh, verdant.

χλόη, n [hloee] grass, turf, lawn || greenness, verdure.

χλωμιάζω [hlomeeazo] (go) pale || blanch.

χλωμός [hlomos] pale, pallid, wan.

χλώριο, το [hloreeo] chlorine, chloride.

χλωρίδα, n [hloreeða] flora.

χλωρός [hloros] green, unseasoned || fresh.

χλωροφόρμιο, το [hloroformeeo] chloroform.

χλωροφύλλη, n [hlorofeelee] chlorophyll.

χνάρι, το [hnaree] pattern, model || track.

χνούδι, το [hnouðee] down, fuzz, fluff.

χνουδωτός [hnoudotos] downy, fluffy.

χνώτο, το [hnoto] breath.

χόβολη, n [hovolee] embers, burning charcoal.

χοιρινό, το [heereeno] pork.

χοιρομέρι, το [heeromeree] ham, bacon.

χοίρος, ο [heeros] pig, hog, swine.

χολέρα, n [holera] cholera.

χολή, n [holee] bile || (ζώου) gall || (μεταφ) rancour, bitterness.

χολιάζω [holeeazo] get irritated || irritate || lose one's temper.

χολοσκάω [holoskao] afflict, grieve, exasperate || get riled.

χονδρικός [honðreekos] wholesale.

χονδροειδής [honðroeeðees] rough, clumsy, coarse || (ψεύδος) flagrant || vulgar.

χόνδρος, το [honðros] cartilage || grit.

χονδρός [honðros] big, fat, stout, thick || (σε τρόπους) vulgar, unpolished || (οστείο) coarse.

χοντραίνω [hondreno] become fat, make thicker, put on weight.

χοντροκέφαλος [hondrokefalos] stupid, thickheaded || obstinate, headstrong.

χοντροκοπιά, n [hondrokopia] clumsy job of work.

χοντρός [hondros] βλ **χονδρός**.

χορδή, n [horðee] chord, string || (ανατ) cord.

χορευτής, ο [horevtees] dancer || partner.

χορευτικός [horevteekos] for dancing, of dancing.

χορεύω [horevo] dance || dance with.

χορήγηση, n [horeeyeesee] granting, giving, supplying.

χορηγώ [horeego] provide, allocate, supply, grant.

χορογραφία, n [horografeea] choreography.

χοροδιδάσκαλος, ο [horoðeeðaskalos] dancing master.

χοροπηδώ [horopeeðo] leap about, gambol, caper.

χορός, ο [horos] dancing, dance || chorus, choir.

χοροστατώ [horostato] conduct divine service.

χόρτα, τα [horta] πλ green vegetables, wild greens.

χορταίνω [horteno] have enough, satiate || satisfy || (βαριέμαι) get bored with.

χορτάρι, το [hortaree] grass.

χορταρικά, τα [hortareeka] πλ vegetables, greens.

χορτασμός, ο [hortasmos] satisfaction, satiety.

χορταστικός [hortasteekos] satisfying, substantial, filling || abundant.

χορτάτος [hortatos] satisfied, satiated.

χόρτο, το [horto] grass, herb || (άγριο) weed.

χορτοφάγος [hortofagos] vegetarian || (ζώο) herbivorous.

χορωδία, η [horodeea] choir, chorus.

χουζούρι, το [houzouree] rest, idleness, leisure.

χουρμάς, ο [hourmas] (βοτ) date.

χούφτα, η [houfta] handful || hollow of hand.

χουφτιά, η [houftia] handful.

χρειάζομαι [hreeazome] lack, want, require || be necessary, be useful.

χρεόγραφο, το [hreografo] security, debenture, bond.

χρέος, το [hreos] debt || obligation.

χρεωκοπία, η [hreokopeea] bankruptcy, failure.

χρεωκοπώ [hreokopo] go bankrupt, break.

χρεωλυσία, η [hreoleesea] amortization, sinking fund.

χρεώνομαι [hreonome] get into debt.

χρεώνω [hreono] debit, charge.

χρεωστάσιο, το [hreostaseeo] moratorium.

χρεώστης, ο [hreostees] debtor.

χρεωστώ [hreosto] be in debt, owe, be indebted (to) || be obliged.

χρήμα, το [hreema] money.

χρηματίζομαι [hreemateezome] take bribes || hoard up money.

χρηματίζω [hreemateezo] serve as, be.

χρηματικός [hreemateekos] of money, monetary.

χρηματιστήριο, το [hreemateesteereeo] stock exchange.

χρηματιστής, ο [hreemateestees] stockbroker.

χρηματοδοτώ [hreematodoto] finance, invest.

χρηματοκιβώτιο, το [hreematokeevoteeo] safe, strong-box, cash box.

χρήση, η [hreesee] use, usage, employment || enjoyment || application || (οικον) financial year

|| προς ~ for the use || εν χρήσει in use, used.

χρησιμεύω [hreeseemevo] be useful || be good for, serve.

χρησιμοποίηση, η [hreeseemopieesee] employment, utilization.

χρησιμοποιώ [hreeseemopeeo] use, utilize, make use of.

χρήσιμος, ο [hreeseemos] useful, handy.

χρησιμότητα, η [hreeseemoteeta] usefulness, utility, benefit.

χρησμός, ο [hreesmos] oracle, divination.

χρηστός [hreestos] honourable, upright, virtuous.

χρίζω [hreezo] βλ χρίω.

χρίσμα, το [hreesma] chrism, unction || anointing.

χριστιανικός [hreesteeaneekos] Christian.

χριστιανισμός, ο [hreesteeaneesmos] Christianity.

χριστιανός, ο [hreesteeanos] Christian.

χριστιανοσύνη, η [hreesteeanoseenee] Christendom.

Χριστός, ο [hreestos] Christ.

Χριστούγεννα, τα [hreestouyena] πλ Christmas.

χρίω [hreeo] anoint || plaster.

χροιά, η [hreea] complexion, colour || shade, tone, nuance.

χρονιά, η [hroneea] year.

χρονικά, τα [hroneeka] πλ annals.

χρονικογράφος, ο [hroneekografos] chronicler.

χρονικό, το [hroneeko] chronicle.

χρονικός [hroneekos] of time, temporal.

χρόνιος [hroneeos] chronic, enduring, lasting.

χρονογράφημα, το [hronografeema] newspaper leader article.

χρονογράφος, ο [hronografos] leader writer.

χρονολογία, η [hronoloyeea] date || chronology.

χρονολογούμαι [hronologoume] date from, be dated.

χρονόμετρο, το [hronometro] chronometer.

χρόνος, ο [hronos] time, duration || age, period || (γραμμ) tense, quantity || **ο ~ year** || **προ χρόνων** some years ago || **του χρόνου** next year || **χρόνια πολλά!** happy name day!, happy birthday!, many happy returns!

χρονοτριβώ [hronotreevo] linger, loiter.

χρυσαλλίδα, η [hreesaleeða] chrysalis.

χρυσάνθεμο, το [hreesanthemo] chrysanthemum.

χρυσάφι, το [hreesafee] gold.

χρυσαφικά, τα [hreesafeeka] πλ jewellery.

χρυσή, η [hreesee] jaundice.

χρυσικός, ο [hreeseekos] goldsmith || jeweller.

χρυσόδετος [hreesoðetos] mounted in gold.

χρυσοθήρας, ο [hreesotheeras] gold-digger, prospector.

χρυσόμαλλο [hreesomalo]: **~ δέρας** golden fleece.

χρυσός, ο [hreesos] gold || (επίθ) golden || (μεταφ) kind-hearted, adorable.

χρυσοχοείο, το [hreesohoeeo] jeweller's shop, goldsmith's shop.

χρυσοχόος, ο [hreesohoos] goldsmith || jeweller.

χρυσόψαρο, το [hreesopsaro] goldfish.

χρυσώνω [hreesono] gild, gold-plate.

χρυσωρυχείο, το [hreesoreeheeo] gold mine.

χρώμα, το [hroma] colour, tint, hue || (μπογιά) paint, dye || complexion.

χρωματίζω [hromateezo] colour, paint, dye, tint.

χρωματικός [hromateekos] chromatic || of colour.

χρωματισμός, ο [hromateesmos] colouring, painting.

χρωματιστός [hromateestos] coloured.

χρώμιο, το [hromeeo] chromium, chrome.

χρωστικός [hrosteekos] colouring.

χρωστώ [hrosto] βλ **χρεωστώ**.

χταπόδι, το [htapoðee] octopus.

χτένα, η [htena] βλ **χτένι**.

χτένι, το [htenee] comb.

χτενίζω [hteneezo] comb || (ομιλία κτλ) polish up.

χτένισμα, το [hteneesma] combing || hairstyle.

χτες [htes] βλ **χθές**.

χτεσινός [hteseenos] βλ **χθεσινός**.

χτήμα, το [hteema] βλ **κτήμα**.

χτίζω [hteezo] βλ **κτίζω**.

χτικιό, το [hteekio] tuberculosis || (μεταφ) torture, anguish.

χτίστης, ο [hteestees] bricklayer, builder.

χτυπάω [hteepao] βλ **χτυπώ**.

χτύπημα, το [hteepeema] blow, punch, kick, hit, knock || bruise, wound.

χτυπητός [hteepeetos] beaten || tawdry, garish, loud, striking.

χτυποκάρδι, το [hteepokarðee] rapid beating of the heart.

χτύπος, ο [hteepos] blow, stroke || (καρδιάς) throb, beat || (ρολογιού) tick(ing).

χτυπώ [hteepo] knock, thrash, hit, beat, strike || hurt o.s. || (χέρια) clap || (πόδια) stamp || (αυγά κτλ) whisk || (ρολογιού κτλ) peal, strike, sound || **χτυπάει άσχημα** it jars, it looks bad || **μου χτυπάει στα νεύρα** it gets on my

nerves || **χτυπιέμαι** come to blows || feel sorry, repent.

χυδαίος [heedeos] vulgar, trivial, crude, rude, coarse.

χυδαιότητα, η [heedeoteeta] vulgarity, coarseness, foul language.

χυλόπιτα, ο [heelopeeta] kind of macaroni || (μεταφ) failure in love.

χυλός, ο [heelos] pap, liquid paste.

χύμα [heema] confusedly, pell-mell || loose, unpacked, unbottled.

χυμός, ο [heemos] sap, juice.

χυμώ [heemo] rush upon, charge.

χυμώδης [heemoðees] juicy, sappy.

χύνομαι [heenome] overflow, pour out || flow out || (μεταφ) charge against, rush upon.

χύνω [heeno] spill, tip over, pour out || (δάκρυα) shed || (μέταλλο) cast.

χύσιμο, το [heeseemo] discharge, pouring out, spilling || casting, moulding.

χυτήριο, το [heeteereeo] foundry, smelting works.

χυτός [heetos] moulded, cast || (σκορπισμένος) dispersed, scattered || (μαλλιά) flowing, loose || (ρούχα) tight-fitting.

χυτοσίδηρος, ο [heetoseeðeeros] cast iron.

χύτρα, η [heetra] cooking pot, pot, porridge pot.

χωλ, το [hol] hall.

χωλαίνω [holeno] limp, be lame || (μεταφ) halt, hobble, move slowly.

χώμα, το [homa] soil, dust, earth || ground.

χωματένιος [homateneeos] earthen.

χώνευση, η [honevsee] digestion || (μετάλλων) casting, founding.

χωνευτήριο, το [honevteereeo] crucible, melting pot.

χωνευτικός [honevteekos] digestible, digestive.

χωνεύω [honevo] digest || (μέταλλο)

cast, smelt || (μεταφ) tolerate, endure.

χωνί, το [honee] funnel, horn || (παγωτού) cone.

χώνομαι [honome] squeeze in || hide || (μεταφ) interfere.

χώνω [hono] thrust, force || bury || (κρύβω) hide.

χώρα, η [hora] country, place || chief town || (ανατ) region || **λαμβάνω ~** happen.

χωρατεύω [horatevo] joke.

χωρατό, το [horato] joke, jest, witticism.

χωράφι, το [horafee] field, land.

χωράω [horao] βλ **χωρώ**.

χωρητικότητα, η [horeeteekoteeta] volume, capacity || (ναυτ) tonnage.

χώρια [horeea] βλ **χωριστά**.

χωριανός, ο [horeeanos] fellow villager, countryman.

χωριάτης, ο [horeeatees] peasant, villager, countryman || (μεταφ) ill-mannered person, unpolished person.

χωριάτικος [horeeateekos] peasant, of the village || rustic.

χωρίζομαι [horeezome] leave, part from.

χωρίζω [horeezo] separate, disconnect, part, split || (δρόμοι) branch off || (ζεύγος) get a divorce || **~ με** break up with, part from.

χωριό, το [horeeo] village, rural, country || (ουσ) peasant, villager.

χωριό, το [horio] village, hamlet || (μεταφ) hometown.

χωρίς [horees] without, apart from || not including || **~ άλλο** without fail || **με ~** without.

χώρισμα, το [horeesma] sorting, separation || (δωματίου) wall, partition || compartment.

χωρισμένος [horeesmenos] divided || separated, divorced.

χωρισμός, ο [horeesmos]

separation || partition || separating || divorce.

χωριστά [horeesta] apart, individually || (προθ) not counting, apart from, not including.

χωριστός [horeestos] separate, different, distinct, isolated.

χωρίστρα, n [horeestra] parting of hair.

χώρος, ο [horos] space, area, room || interval, distance.

χωροφύλακας, ο [horofeelakas] gendarme.

χωροφυλακή, n [horofeelakee] gendarmerie.

χωρώ [horo] fit into, have room || (περιέχω) hold, contain || **δε χωράει αμφιβολία** there's no doubt, undoubtedly.

χώσιμο, το [hoseemo] driving in, burying || hiding.

Ψ, ψ

ψάθα, n [psatha] straw, cane || (χαλί) rush mat || (καπέλο) straw hat || **στη** ~ penniless.

ψάθινος [psatheenos] made of straw.

ψαλίδα, n [psaleeða] shears || centipede.

ψαλίδι, το [psaleeðee] scissors, pruning scissors || curling tongs.

ψαλιδίζω [psaleeðeezo] cut, trim || (μεταφ) reduce, cut down.

ψάλλω [psalo] sing, chant || extol, celebrate.

ψαλμός, ο [psalmos] psalm, chant.

ψαλμωδία, n [psalmoðeea] chanting of psalms || monotonous delivery.

ψάλτης, ο [psaltees] chorister, singer, chanter.

ψάξιμο, το [psakseemo] searching, quest, search.

ψαράδικο, το [psaraðeeko] fishing boat || fishmonger's shop.

ψαράδικος [psaraðeekos] of a fisherman.

ψαράς, ο [psaras] fisherman || fishmonger.

ψάρεμα, το [psarema] fishing, angling, netting.

ψαρεύω [psarevo] fish || sound, fish for information.

ψάρι, το [psaree] fish.

ψαρόβαρκα, n [psarovarka] fishing boat.

ψαροκόκαλο, το [psarokokalo] fish bone || (σχέδιο) herringbone.

ψαρόκολλα, n [psarokola] fish glue.

ψαρομάλλης, ο [psaromalees] grey-haired person.

ψαρονέφρι, το [psaronefree] fillet of meat.

ψαρός [psaros] grey, grizzled.

ψαύση, n [psavsee] touching, feeling, light touch.

ψαχνό, το [psahno] lean meat.

ψάχνομαι [psahnome] look through one's pockets.

ψάχνω [psahno] search for, look for || seek, rummage.

ψαχουλεύω [psahoulevo] search for, grope for, fumble around for.

ψεγάδι, το [psegaðee] fault, failing, shortcoming.

ψέγω [psego] blame, reprove, censure.

ψείρα, n [pseera] louse || vermin.

ψειριάζω [pseereeazo] get lousy.

ψειρίζω [pseereezo] delouse || (μεταφ) examine in great detail.

ψεκάζω [psekazo] spray.

ψεκαστήρας, ο [psekasteeras] spray, vapourizer || scent sprayer.

ψελλίζω [pseleezo] stammer, stutter.

ψέλνω [pselno] βλ **ψάλλω**.

ψέμα, το [psema] lie, falsehood, fib.

ψες [pses] last night.

ψευδαίσθηση, η [psevdestheesee] delusion, hallucination.

ψευδάργυρος, ο [psevdaryeeros] zinc.

ψευδής [psevdees] untrue, false || artificial, sham, fictitious || deceptive.

ψευδίζω [psevdeezo] βλ **ψελλίζω**.

ψευδολογώ [psevdologo] tell lies, tell stories, fib.

ψεύδομαι [psevdome] lie, fib.

ψευδομάρτυρας, ο, η [psevdomarteeras] false witness, perjurer.

ψευδομαρτυρώ [psevdomarteero] give false witness, commit perjury.

ψευδορκία, η [psevdorkeea] perjury.

ψευδορκώ [psevdorko] commit perjury, perjure.

ψευδός [psevdos] lisping, stammering, stuttering.

ψευδώνυμο, το [psevdoneemo] pseudonym, assumed name.

ψεύτης, ο [psevtees] liar, fibber || cheat, impostor.

ψευτιά, η [psevtia] untruth, lie.

ψευτίζω [psevteezo] adulterate || become adulterated.

ψεύτικος [psevteekos] false, untrue || artificial || (σε ποιότητα) inferior.

ψήγμα, το [pseegma] filings, shavings, chips.

ψηλά [pseela] high up, aloft.

ψηλαφώ [pseelafo] feel, touch, finger || (ψάχνω) feel one's way, grope.

ψηλομύτης [pseelomeetees] haughty, overbearing.

ψηλός [pseelos] high, tall, lofty, great.

ψήλωμα, το [pseeloma] eminence, elevation || making taller, growing.

ψηλώνω [pseelono] make taller, make higher || grow taller.

ψήνομαι [pseenome] become very

hot || (στη δουλειά) become broken in.

ψήνω [pseeno] bake, roast, cook || (μεταφ) torture, worry, pester.

ψήσιμο, το [pseeseemo] baking, broiling, roasting, cooking, frying.

ψησταριά, η [pseestaria] barbecue apparatus.

ψητό, το [pseeto] roast meat, grilled meat || (μεταφ) the main point.

ψητός [pseetos] roast, baked, roasted.

ψηφιδωτό, το [pseefeedoto] mosaic.

ψηφίζω [pseefeezo] vote || (νόμο) pass, carry.

ψηφίο, το [pseefeeo] cipher, figure || (αλφαβήτου) letter, character.

ψήφισμα, το [pseefeesma] decree, enactment, edict.

ψηφοδέλτιο, το [pseefoδelteeo] ballot paper.

ψηφοδόχος, η [pseefoδohos] ballot box.

ψηφοθηρώ [pseefotheero] solicit votes, canvass for votes.

ψήφος, ο, η [pseefos] vote, voting, suffrage.

ψηφοφορία, η [pseefoforeea] voting, ballot(ting).

ψι, το [psee] the letter Ψ.

ψιθυρίζω [pseetheereezo] mutter, murmur, whisper.

ψιθύρισμα, το [pseetheereesma] whisper(ing), muttering, murmuring.

ψίθυρος, ο [pseetheeros] murmur, whisper, mutter, growl.

ψιλά, τα [pseela] πλ small change || (μεταφ) cash, money.

ψιλικά, τα [pseeleeka] πλ haberdashery || small wares.

ψιλικαντζήδικο, το [pseeleekandzeeδeeko] haberdashery.

ψιλολογώ [pseelologo] examine carefully, sift.

ψιλός [pseelos] fine, slender, thin || shrill.

ψιλοτραγουδώ [pseelotragoudo] hum.

ψίχα, η [pseeha] kernel, crumb || (καρυδιού) edible part of nut || (μεταφ) bit, scrap.

ψιχάλα, η [pseehala] drizzle.

ψιχαλίζει [pseehaleezee] it's drizzling.

ψίχουλο, το [pseehoulo] crumb.

ψόγος, ο [psogos] blame, reproach.

ψοφίμι, το [psofeemee] carcass, carrion.

ψόφιος [psofeeos] (για ζώα) dead || (μεταφ) worn-out || ~ στην κούραση dead tired.

ψόφος, ο [psofos] noise, tumult || (θάνατος) death || (μεταφ) freezing cold.

ψοφώ [psofo] die || (μεταφ) ~ για yearn for, be mad on.

ψυγείο, το [pseeyeeo] refrigerator, icebox || (αυτοκινήτου) radiator.

ψυκτικός [pseekteekos] cooling.

ψύλλος, ο [pseelos] flea || (μεταφ) trifle.

ψύξη, η [pseeksee] refrigeration || chill, chilling.

ψυχαγωγία, η [pseehagoyeea] recreation, amusement, diversion, entertainment.

ψυχαγωγικός [pseehagoyeekos] recreational, entertaining.

ψυχανάλυση, η [pseehanaleesee] psychoanalysis.

ψυχή, η [pseehee] soul, ghost || heart, core || (θάρρος) energy, spirit.

ψυχιατρείο, το [pseeheeatreeo] mental hospital, asylum.

ψυχιατρική, η [pseeheeatreekee] psychiatry.

ψυχίατρος, ο [pseeheeatros] psychiatrist.

ψυχικό, το [pseeheeko] act of charity || alms, charity.

ψυχικός [pseeheekos] psychical || ψυχική διάθεση humour, mood, disposition || ψυχική οδύνη mental stress.

ψυχογιός, ο [pseehoyos] adopted son.

ψυχολογία, η [pseeholoyeea] psychology.

ψυχολογικός [pseeholoyeekos] psychological.

ψυχολόγος, ο [pseehologos] psychologist.

ψυχολογώ [pseehologo] read mind of || psychoanalyse.

ψυχομαχώ [pseehomaho] be at the last gasp.

ψυχοπαθής [pseehopathees] psychopath(ic).

ψυχοπαίδι, το [pseehopedee] adopted child.

ψυχοπόνια, η [pseehoponeea] commiseration, pity.

ψυχορραγώ [pseehorago] βλ ψυχομαχώ.

ψύχος, το [pseehos] cold, chilliness.

ψυχοσύνθεση, η [pseehoseenthesee] person's psychological make-up.

ψύχρα, η [pseehra] chilly weather, cold.

ψυχραιμία, η [pseehremeea] self-control, sangfroid, coolness.

ψύχραιμος [pseehremos] cool, cool-headed.

ψυχραίνομαι [pseehrenome] be on bad terms with.

ψυχραίνω [pseehreno] cool, chill, make cold || (μεταφ) cool off.

ψυχρολουσία, η [pseehrolouseea] (μεταφ) telling off, rebuke.

ψυχρός [pseehros] cold || (μεταφ) indifferent, apathetic.

ψυχρότητα, η [pseehroteeta] coldness || indifference.

ψύχω [pseeho] freeze, chill, make cold.

ψύχωση, η [pseehosee] psychosis || craze, complex.

ψωμάκι, το [psomakee] roll, piece of bread.

ψωμάς, ο [psomas] baker.

ψωμί, το [psomee] bread || loaf || (μεταφ) living.

ψωμοζώ [psomozo] eke out one's living, live scantily.

ψωμοτύρι, το [psomoteeree] bread and cheese.

ψώνια, τα [psoneea] nλ provisions, shopping, purchases.

ψωνίζω [psoneezo] buy, purchase || go shopping || την ~ become queer, go mad.

ψώνιο, το [psoneeo] purchase || (μεταφ) mania.

ψώρα, η [psora] scabies, itch, mange || (μεταφ) pest.

ψωριάζω [psoreeazo] become itchy, be mangy.

ψωριάρης [psoreearees] mangy || (μεταφ) beggar, ragamuffin.

ψωρίαση, η [psoreeasee] psoriasis, itch(ing).

ψωροκώσταινα, η [psorokostena] poverty-stricken Greece, poor Greece.

ψωροπερηφάνεια, η [psoropereefaneea] pretensions, stupid pride.

ωδίνες, οι [odeenes] nλ childbirth pains || (μεταφ) difficulties.

ώθηση, η [otheesee] push, pushing, thrust, impulsion.

ωθώ [otho] push, thrust, impel || incite, urge.

ωκεανός, ο [okeanos] ocean.

ωλένη, η [olenee] forearm.

ωμέγα, το [omega] the letter Ω.

ωμοπλάτη, η [omoplatee] shoulder blade.

ώμος, ο [omos] shoulder.

ωμός [omos] uncooked, raw || hard, cruel, unrelenting.

ωμότητα, η [omoteeta] cruelty, ferocity.

ωμότητες, οι [omoteetes] nλ outrages, atrocities.

ωοειδής [ooeedees] oval, egg-shaped.

ωοθήκη, η [ootheekee] ovary || egg cup.

ωοτόκος [ootokos] oviparous, egg-laying.

ώρα, η [ora] hour, time || με την ~ on the hour || ~ με την ~ any minute || με τις ώρες for hours || στην ~ at the right time, on the dot, on time || της ώρας fresh, cooked to order.

ωραία [orea] beautiful || very well, perfectly, good.

ωραίος [oreos] handsome, comely, lovely || fine, good.

ωραιότητα, η [oreoteeta] beauty, good looks.

ωράριο, το [orareeo] working hours, timetable.

ωριαίος [orieos] hourly || lasting an hour.

ωριμάζω [oreemazo] become ripe, mature, mellow.

ωρίμανση, η [oreemansee] ripening, maturity.

ώριμος [oreemos] ripe, mature, mellow.

Ω, ω

ω [o] (επιφ) oh!, ah!, aha!

ωάριο, το [oareeo] ovum.

ωδείο, το [odeeo] conservatory.

ωδή, η [odee] ode, song.

ωδική, η [odeekee] singing lesson || art of singing.

ωδικός [odeekos] singing, melodious.

ωριμότητα, η [oreemoteeta]
ripeness, maturity, full growth.

ωροδείκτης, ο [orodeektees] hour
hand.

ωροσκόπιο, το [oroskopeeo]
horoscope.

ωρύομαι [oreeome] howl, roar ||
yell, scream.

ως [os] until, till, down to, up to, as
far as || (επίρ) about || ~ ότου να
until.

ως [os] as, for, like, just as, such as ||
(συνδ) as, while, as soon as || βλ και
ως.

ωσότου [osotou] until, by the time.

ώσπου [ospou] until.

ώστε [oste] thus, and so, so,
accordingly, therefore || that ||
ούτως ~ thereby.

ωστόσο [ostoso] nevertheless ||
meanwhile.

ωτακουστής, ο [otakoustees]
eavesdropper.

ωτομοτρίς, η [otomotrees] railcar.

ωτορινολαρυγγολόγος, ο
[otoreenolareengologos] ear, nose
and throat doctor.

ωφέλεια, η [ofeleea] benefit, utility,
usefulness, profit, advantage || είδα
~ I benefited.

ωφέλημα, το [ofeleema] benefit,
gain, particular profit, advantage.

ωφέλιμος [ofeleemos] beneficial,
useful, of use, advantageous.

ωφελούμαι [ofeloume] benefit,
profit from, turn to good account.

ωφελώ [ofelo] do good to, be useful
to, benefit, aid.

ώχρα, η [ohra] ochre.

ωχριώ [ohreeo] become pale, make
wan.

ωχρός [ohros] pallid, pale || (μεταφ)
indistinct, dim.

ωχρότητα, η [ohroteeta] pallor,
paleness.

ENGLISH–GREEK
ΑΓΓΛΙΚΑ-ΕΛΛΗΝΙΚΑ

A

a, an [ei,æn] *indefinite article* ένας, μια, ένα.

A.A. *n. abbr of* Automobile Association; *abbr of* Alcoholics Anonymous.

aback [ə'bæk] *ad:* **to be taken ~** ξαφνιάζομαι, σαστίζω.

abandon [ə'bændən] *vt* εγκαταλείπω, αφήνω.

abash [ə'bæʃ] *vt* ξεφτελίζω, ντροπιάζω.

abate [ə'beit] *vi* μειώνομαι, κοπάζω, καταργούμαι.

abbey ['æbi] *n* μονή, μοναστήρι.

abbot ['æbət] *n* ηγούμενος, αββάς.

abbreviate [ə'bri:vieit] *vt* συντομεύω.

abbreviation [əbri:vi'eiʃən] *n* σύντμηση, συντετμημένη λέξη.

abdicate ['æbdikeit] *vi* παραιτούμαι, εγκαταλείπω.

abdication [æbdi'keiʃən] *n* παραίτηση.

abdomen ['æbdəmən] *n* κοιλία.

abduction [æb'dʌkʃən] *n* απαγωγή.

aberration [æbə'reiʃən] *n* παρέκκλιση, παρεκτροπή.

abet [ə'bet] *vt* υποκινώ, παρακινώ.

abeyance [ə'beiəns] *n:* **in ~** εκκρεμώ, αχρηστεύομαι.

abhor [əb'hɔ:] *vt* απεχθάνομαι, σιχαίνομαι || **~rent** a απεχθής.

abide [ə'baid] *(irreg v) vt* ανέχομαι, αντέχω ♦ *vi* εμμένω, τηρώ || **to ~ by** τηρώ, συμμορφούμαι.

ability [ə'biliti] *n* ικανότητα, επιδεξιότητα, δύναμη.

ablaze [ə'bleiz] *a* φλεγόμενος, λάμπων.

able ['eibl] *a* ικανός, επιτήδειος.

ably ['eibli] *ad* επιδέξια, προκομμένα.

abnormal [æb'nɔ:məl] *a* ανώμαλος || **~ity** *n* ανωμαλία || *(BIOL)* τερατωδία, δυσμορφία.

aboard [ə'bɔ:d] *ad:* **to go ~** επιβιβάζομαι || **to be ~** ευρίσκομαι επί.

abode [ə'bəud] *n* διαμονή, κατοικία.

abolish [ə'bɔliʃ] *vt* καταργώ.

abolition [æbə'liʃən] *n* κατάργηση.

abominable [ə'bɔminəbl] *a* αποτρόπαιος, απαίσιος.

abominably [ə'bɔminəbli] *ad* απαίσια.

aborigines [æbə'ridʒiniz] *npl* ιθαγενείς.

abort [ə'bɔ:t] *vt* αποβάλλω, διακόπτω ♦ *vi* αποβάλλομαι, ματαιούμαι.

abortion [ə'bɔ:ʃən] *n* έκτρωση, αποβολή.

abortive [ə'bɔ:tiv] *a* αποτυχημένος, πρόωρος, ανεπιτυχής.

abound [ə'baund] *vi* αφθονώ, βρίθω.

about [ə'baut] *prep* περί, γύρω από, κοντά ♦ *ad* (τρι)γύρω, κοντά || *(estimate)* περίπου || **to be ~ to** μόλις πρόκειται να.

above [ə'bʌv] prep πάνω από, πέρα από || (in rank) ανώτερος από, μεγαλύτερος από ♦ ad επάνω, στους ουρανούς || ~**board** a τίμια και ειλικρινή, άψογα || ~ **ground** επιφανειακός.

abrasion [ə'breɪʒən] n φθορά, (εκ)τριβή, γδάρσιμο.

abrasive [ə'breɪzɪv] a αποξεστικός || ~ **material** μέσον λειάνσεως.

abreast [ə'brɛst] ad παραπλεύρως, μαζί.

abridge [ə'brɪdʒ] vt συντομεύω, συντέμνω.

abroad [ə'brɔːd] ad στο εξωτερικό, στα ξένα.

abrupt [ə'brʌpt] a απότομος, ξαφνικός, αγενής.

abscess ['æbsɪs] n απόστημα nt.

abscond [əb'skɒnd] vi φυγοδικώ, δραπετεύω, φεύγω κρυφά.

absence ['æbsəns] n απουσία || (lack of) έλλειψη, ανυπαρξία || (of mind) αφηρημάδα.

absent ['æbsənt] a απών, απουσιάζων ♦ [æb'sɛnt] vt: **he ~ed himself** απουσίαζε || ~**ee** n απών m, απουσιάζων m || ~**eeism** n απουσία || ~-**minded** a αφηρημένος.

absolute ['æbsəluːt] a απόλυτος, τέλειος, απεριόριστος || ~**ly** ad τελείως.

absolve [əb'zɒlv] vt απαλλάσσω, αθωώνω.

absorb [əb'zɔːb] vt απορροφώ.

absorbent [əb'zɔːbənt] a, n απορροφητικός || ~ **cotton** (US) n απορροφητικό βαμβάκι.

absorbing [əb'zɔːbɪŋ] a ενδιαφέρων.

abstain [əb'steɪn] vi απέχω, συγκρατούμαι || **to ~ from** αποφεύγω.

abstinence ['æbstɪnəns] n αποχή, εγκράτεια.

abstract ['æbstrækt] a αφηρημένος ♦ n το αφηρημένο || (summary) περίληψη || (excerpt) απόσπασμα nt ♦ [æb'strækt] vt (remove) αφαιρώ.

abstruse [æb'struːs] a ασαφής, δυσνόητος.

absurd [əb'sɜːd] a γελοίος, παράλογος || ~**ity** n παραλογισμός.

abundance [ə'bʌndəns] n αφθονία, περίσσευμα nt.

abundant [ə'bʌndənt] a άφθονος, πλούσιος.

abuse [ə'bjuːz] vt (misuse) κακομεταχειρίζομαι, καταχρώμαι || (speak harshly) βρίζω ♦ [ə'bjuːs] n κακομεταχείριση, κατάχρηση || (swearing) βρισιές fpl.

abusive [əbjuːsɪv] a υβριστικός.

abut [ə'bʌt] vi συνορεύω με.

abysmal [ə'bɪzml] a φοβερός, απερίγραπτος.

abyss [ə'bɪs] n άβυσσος.

academic [ækə'dɛmɪk] n, a ακαδημαϊκός.

academy [ə'kædəmɪ] n ακαδημία.

accede [æk'siːd] vi (agree) συμφωνώ, προσχωρώ || (to throne) ανέρχομαι.

accelerate [æk'sɛləreɪt] vt επιταχύνω, επισπεύδω ♦ vi επιταχύνομαι.

acceleration [æksɛlə'reɪʃən] n επιτάχυνση.

accelerator [ək'sɛləreɪtə*] n (AUT) γκάζι.

accent ['æksɛnt] n τόνος || (of speech) προφορά ♦ [æk'sɛnt] vt τονίζω || ~**uate** vt τονίζω.

accept [ək'sɛpt] vt (gift etc) δέχομαι || (agree) παραδέχομαι || ~**able** a (απο)δεκτός, ευπρόσδεκτος, παραδεκτός || ~**ance** n αποδοχή, παραδοχή.

access ['æksɛs] n (entrance) είσοδος f|| (COMPUT) πρόσβαση || ~ **time**

(COMPUT) χρόνος προσπέλασης || ~**ible** a προσιτός, ευπρόσιτος.

accessories [æk'sɛsərɪz] npl εξαρτήματα ntpl, συμπληρώματα ntpl || (toilet) είδη ntpl τουαλέτας.

accessory [æk'sɛsərɪ] a συμπληρωματικός ♦ n (to a crime etc) συνένοχος || (part) εξάρτημα nt.

accident ['æksɪdənt] n (mishap) δυστύχημα nt, ατύχημα nt || (chance) τύχη || **by** ~ κατά τύχη || ~**ally** ad τυχαία.

acclaim [ə'kleɪm] vt επευφημώ, ζητωκραυγάζω, αναφωνώ ♦ n ζητωκραυγή.

acclimatize [ə'klaɪmətaɪz] vt: **to become** ~**d to** εγκλιματίζομαι.

accommodate [ə'kɒmədeɪt] vt (be suitable for) εξοικονομώ, διευθετώ, προσαρμόζω || (lodge) στεγάζω, παρέχω κατάλυμα || (supply etc) εξοικονομώ, εφοδιάζω.

accommodating [ə'kɒmədeɪtɪŋ] a εξυπηρετικός, πρόθυμος.

accommodation [əkɒmə'deɪʃən] n (lodging) κατάλυμα nt, στέγαση || (loan) δάνειο || (adjustment) προσαρμογή.

accompaniment [ə'kʌmpənɪmənt] n συνοδεία || (MUS) ακομπανιαμέντο.

accompany [ə'kʌmpənɪ] vt συνοδεύω, συντροφεύω.

accomplice [ə'kʌmplɪs] n συνένοχος, συνεργός.

accomplish [ə'kʌmplɪʃ] vt περατώνω, συμπληρώνω || ~**ed** a (skilled) τέλειος || ~**ment** n (ability) ικανότητα, προσόντα ntpl || (completion) εκπλήρωση.

accord [ə'kɔːd] n συμφωνία, ομοφωνία || **of my own** ~ αυθόρμητα ♦ vt (grant) παρέχω, χορηγώ || (agree with) συμφωνώ || ~**ance** n συμφωνία || **in** ~**ance with** σύμφωνα με || ~**ing to** prep

σύμφωνα με, κατά τον || ~**ingly** ad επομένως.

accordion [ə'kɔːdɪən] n ακορντεόν nt inv.

accost [ə'kɒst] vt πλησιάζω, πλευρίζω.

account [ə'kaʊnt] n (bill) λογαριασμός, υπολογισμός || (credit) λογαριασμός || (story) αφήγηση, περιγραφή || (financial report) ανάλυση, έκθεση || **on no** ~ για κανένα λόγο || **on** ~ **of** εξαιτίας || **to** ~ **for** vt εξηγώ || **to take into** ~ λαμβάνω υπόψη || ~**able** a υπόλογος, υπεύθυνος || (explicable) ευεξήγητος.

accountant [ə'kaʊntənt] n λογιστής.

accumulate [ə'kjuːmjʊleɪt] vt συσσωρεύω, μαζεύω ♦ vi συσσωρεύομαι.

accumulation [əkjuːmjʊ'leɪʃən] n συσσώρευση, μάζεμα nt.

accuracy ['ækjʊrəsɪ] n ακρίβεια.

accurate ['ækjʊrɪt] a ακριβής, ορθός || ~**ly** ad με ακρίβεια, σωστά.

accusation [ækjuː'zeɪʃən] n κατηγορία.

accuse [ə'kjuːz] vt κατηγορώ || ~**d** n κατηγορούμενος || ~**r** n εναγων m, μηνυτής, κατήγορος.

accustom [ə'kʌstəm] vt συνηθίζω, εθίζω || ~**ed** a συνηθισμένος.

ace [eɪs] n άσσος.

ache [eɪk] vi πονώ.

achieve [ə'tʃiːv] vt κατορθώνω, επιτυγχάνω, φθάνω || ~**ment** n κατόρθωμα, επίτευξη.

acid ['æsɪd] a οξύς, ξινός ♦ n (CHEM) οξύ nt || ~ **test** n αποφασιστική δοκιμασία, τελικό κριτήριο || ~**ity** n (CHEM) οξύτητα, ξινίλα.

acknowledge [ək'nɒlɪdʒ] vt (admit) αναγνωρίζω, παραδέχομαι || (letter) είμαι ευγνώμων, απαντώ || ~**ment** n

αναγνώριση, παραδοχή || (of letter etc) βεβαίωση.

acne ['ækni] n ακμή, σπυράκια *ntpl.*

acorn ['eikɔ:n] n βαλανίδι.

acoustic [ə'ku:stik] a ακουστικός || ~ **s** npl ακουστική.

acquaint [ə'kweint] vt γνωρίζω, πληροφορώ || ~ **ance** n (person) γνωριμία, γνωστός/ή m/f || (knowledge) γνώση, αντίληψη.

acquiesce [ækwi'es] vi συναινώ, συγκατατίθεμαι, δέχομαι.

acquire [ə'kwaiə*] vt αποκτώ.

acquisition [ækwi'ziʃən] n απόκτημα nt, απόκτηση.

acquisitive [ə'kwizitiv] a πλεονέκτης, αρπακτικός.

acquit [ə'kwit] vt (free from accusation) απαλλάσσω, αθωώνω || (conduct o.s.) εκπληρώ, καταφέρνω || ~ **tal** n αθώωση, απαλλαγή.

acre ['eikə*] n 4 στρέμματα ntpl.

acrobat ['ækrəbæt] n ακροβάτης.

across [ə'krɒs] prep (through) δια μέσου ♦ ad (crosswise) εγκάρσια, λοξά, σταυρωτά || (distance) πλάτος, μήκος || ~ **the road** (στο δρόμο) απέναντι.

act [ækt] n (deed) πράξη, ενέργεια || (law or decree) νόμος, νομοθέτημα nt || (of play) πράξη (έργου) ♦ vti (take action) ενεργώ, δρω, πράττω || (part) παίζω, παριστάνω, κάνω || (pretend) προσποιούμαι, υποκρίνομαι, υποδύομαι || ~ **ing** n (THEAT) ηθοποιία, παίξιμο ♦ a αναπληρωματικός.

action ['ækʃən] n (deed) πράξη || (motion) λειτουργία, ενέργεια || (battle) μάχη || **to bring an** ~ **against** κάνω αγωγή κατά || **naval** ~ ναυμαχία || **to take** ~ ενεργώ.

active ['æktiv] a (lively) ενεργητικός, ζωηρός || (working) δραστήριος, ενεργός || (GRAM)

ενεργητικός || **on** ~ **service** εν ενεργεία.

activity [æk'tiviti] n δραστηριότητα, δράση.

actor ['æktə*] n ηθοποιός.

actress ['æktris] n ηθοποιός f, θεατρίνα.

actual ['æktjuəl] a πραγματικός, αληθινός || ~ **ly** ad πράγματι.

acumen ['ækjumen] n οξύνοια, ευφυΐα.

acute [ə'kju:t] a οξύς, διαπεραστικός || ~ **ly** ad έντονα || ~ **accent** n οξεία.

ad [æd] abbr of **advertisement.**

A.D. ad (abbr of Anno Domini) μ.Χ.

Adam ['ædəm] n Αδάμ || ~ **'s apple** n καρύδι του λαιμού.

adamant ['ædəmənt] a αμετάπειστος, άκαμπτος.

adapt [ə'dæpt] vt προσαρμόζω, εναρμόζω ♦ vi: **to** ~ προσαρμόζομαι || ~ **able** a προσαρμόσιμος, ευπροσάρμοστος || ~ **ation** n προσαρμογή || (of play etc) διασκευή || ~ **er** n (ELEC) προσαρμοστής.

add [æd] vt προσθέτω, αθροίζω || **to** ~ **up** vt προσθέτω.

adder ['ædə*] n (snake) οχιά, όχεντρα.

addict ['ædikt] n: **drug** ~ ναρκομανής ♦ [ə'dikt] vt αφοσιώνω, παραδίδω || **to be** επιρρεπής σε || ~ **ion** n ροπή προς, εθισμός.

adding machine ['ædiŋməʃi:n] n αθροιστική μηχανή.

addition [ə'diʃən] n πρόσθεση, προσθήκη || **in** ~ επί πλέον, επιπροσθέτως || ~ **al** a πρόσθετος.

address [ə'dres] n διεύθυνση || (speech) προσφώνηση, λόγος || (manners) συμπεριφορά || (COMPUT) διεύθυνση vt απευθύνω || (speak) προσφωνώ || (envelope) γράφω διεύθυνση.

addressee [ædre'si:] n
παραλήπτης.

adenoids ['ædinɔidz] npl κρεατάκια.

adept ['ædept] a: ~ **at** έμπειρος σε,
ικανός σε.

adequate ['ædikwit] a επαρκής,
ικανός.

adhere [əd'hiə*] vi (stick to)
προσκολλώμαι || (support) εμμένω,
προσχωρώ || **to ~ to** προσχωρώ,
εμμένω.

adhesive [əd'hi:ziv] a
συγκολλητικός, κολλώδης ♦ n
κολλητική ουσία || ~ **tape** ||
λευκοπλάστης.

adjacent [ə'dʒeisənt] a
παρακείμενος, γειτονικός,
συνορεύων.

adjective ['ædʒektiv] n επίθετο.

adjoin [ə'dʒɔin] vi γειτονεύω,
συνορεύω με, συνάπτω || ~**ing** a
συνεχόμενος, παρακείμενος.

adjourn [ə'dʒɜːn] vt (postpone)
αναβάλλω ♦ vi αναβάλλομαι,
διακόπτομαι.

adjudicator [ə'dʒu:dikeitə*] n
διαιτητής, δικαστής.

adjust [ə'dʒʌst] vt (put right)
ρυθμίζω, κανονίζω || (to fit)
προσαρμόζω, εφαρμόζω || ~**able** a
ρυθμιζόμενος, ρυθμιστός || ~**ment**
n ρύθμιση, τακτοποίηση.

adjutant ['ædʒətənt] n υπασπιστής.

ad lib [æd'lib] ad κατά βούληση ♦
ad-lib vi αυτοσχεδιάζω.

administer [əd'ministə*] vt
(manage) διευθύνω, διαχειρίζομαι,
διοικώ || (dispense) απονέμω ||
(medicine) παρέχω, δίνω.

administration [ədminis'treifən]
n διοίκηση, διαχείριση, διεύθυνση ||
~ **of justice** απονομή δικαιοσύνης.

administrative [əd'ministrativ] a
διοικητικός.

administrator [əd'ministreitə*] n

διευθυντής, διοικητής || (of will)
εκτελεστής.

admirable ['ædmərəbl] a
θαυμαστός, θαυμάσιος.

admiral ['ædmərəl] n ναύαρχος.

Admiralty ['ædmərəlti] n
ναυαρχείο.

admiration [ædmə'reifən] n
θαυμασμός, κατάπληξη.

admire [əd'maiə*] vt θαυμάζω ||
~**r** n θαυμαστής.

admission [əd'mifən] n (entrance)
είσοδος f, εισαγωγή || (fee) τιμή
εισιτηρίου || (confession) παραδοχή,
αναγνώριση.

admit [əd'mit] vt (let in) επιτρέπω
την είσοδο, εισέρχομαι || (confess)
παραδέχομαι, αναγνωρίζω || (receive
as true) (επι)δέχομαι || ~ **tance** n
εισδοχή, είσοδος f || ~ **tedly** ad
ομολογουμένως.

ado [ə'du:] n: **without more** ~
χωρίς περισσότερη φασαρία.

adolescence [ædəu'lesns] n
εφηβική ηλικία.

adolescent [ædəu'lesnt] a, n
έφηβος.

adopt [ə'dɔpt] vt υιοθετώ || (accept)
παραδέχομαι, αποδέχομαι || ~**ed
son** n θετός || ~**ion** n υιοθεσία || (of
idea etc) αποδοχή, έγκριση.

adore [ə'dɔ:*] vt λατρεύω,
υπεραγαπώ.

adorn [ə'dɔ:n] vt κοσμώ, στολίζω,
καλλωπίζω.

adrenalin [ə'drenəlin] n
αδρεναλίνη.

Adriatic [eidri'ætik] n Αδριατική.

adrift [ə'drift] ad έρμαιο || (col) τα
έχω χαμένα.

adult ['ædʌlt] a, n ενήλικος, έφηβος
|| (LAW) ενήλικος.

adulterate [ə'dʌltəreit] vt νοθεύω,
αλλοιώνω, νερώνω.

adultery [ə'dʌltəri] n μοιχεία.

advance [əd'va:ns] n πρόοδος f,

προχώρηση || *(money)* προκαταβολή, πίστωση || *(in prices)* αύξηση, ύψωση ♦ *vi* προχωρώ || *(MIL)* προελαύνω || *(price)* ανατιμώμαι, ανεβαίνω || ~**d** a προχωρημένος || *(ideas)* προοδευτικός || *(study etc)* ανώτερος || ~ **d ignition** n προανάφλεξη || **in** ~ προκαταβολικά || **in** ~ **of** πριν από, (ε)νωρίτερα || ~ **booking** n: **to make an** ~ **booking** κλείνω θέση.

advantage [ədˈvɑːntɪdʒ] n πλεονέκτημα nt, προτέρημα nt || **to take** ~ **of** *(profit by)* επωφελούμαι από, εκμεταλλεύομαι || *(misuse)* καταχρώμαι || ~ **over** υπεροχή.

advantageous [ædvənˈteɪdʒəs] a επωφελής, ευτελής.

advent [ˈædvənt] n έλευση, εμφάνιση || *(REL)* σαραντάμερο || **the Second A** ~ η Δευτέρα Παρουσία.

adventure [ədˈvɛntʃə*] n περιπέτεια || *(bold undertaking)* τόλμημα nt || ~ **r** n τολμηρός || *(in bad sense)* τυχοδιώκτης.

adventurous [ədˈvɛntʃərəs] a ριψοκίνδυνος, τυχοδιωκτικός.

adverb [ˈædvɜːb] n επίρρημα nt.

adversary [ˈædvəsərɪ] n αντίπαλος, ανταγωνιστής.

adverse [ˈædvɜːs] a αντίθετος, ενάντιος, δυσμενής.

adversity [ədˈvɜːsɪtɪ] n ατυχία, αναποδιά.

advertise [ˈædvətaɪz] vt διαφημίζω, ρεκλαμάρω.

advertisement [ədˈvɜːtɪsmənt] n διαφήμιση, ρεκλάμα || *(poster)* αφίσα.

advertiser [ˈædvətaɪzə*] n διαφημιστής.

advertising [ˈædvətaɪzɪŋ] n διαφήμιση, ρεκλάμα || ~ **agency** n διαφημιστικό γραφείο.

advice [ədˈvaɪs] n συμβουλή || *(information)* πληροφορία, είδηση.

advisable [ədˈvaɪzəbl] a φρόνιμος, σκόπιμος.

advise [ədˈvaɪz] vt συμβουλεύω, συνιστώ || *(apprise)* ειδοποιώ || ~ **r** n σύμβουλος.

advisory [ədˈvaɪzərɪ] a συμβουλευτικός.

advocate [ˈædvəkɪt] n *(LAW)* δικηγόρος, συνήγορος || *(supporter)* υποστηρικτής ♦ [ˈædvəkeɪt] vt υποστηρίζω, συνιστώ || *(LAW)* συνηγορώ.

aerial [ˈɛərɪəl] a εναέριος ♦ n κεραία || ~ **photograph** n εναέριος φωτογραφία.

aeroplane [ˈɛərəpleɪn] n αεροπλάνο.

aerosol [ˈɛərəsɒl] n αερόζολ nt inv.

aesthetic [iːsˈθɛtɪk] a αισθητικός || *(artistic)* καλαίσθητος.

afar [əˈfɑː*] ad: **from** ~ από μακριά.

affable [ˈæfəbl] a προσηνής, γλυκομίλητος, καταδεκτικός.

affair [əˈfɛə*] n υπόθεση, δουλειά || *(matter)* πράγμα nt.

affect [əˈfɛkt] vt *(influence)* θίγω, επηρεάζω || *(feign)* προσποιούμαι, κάνω τον || ~**ation** n προσποίηση || ~**ed** a προσποιητός || *(moved)* συγκινημένος || *(MED)* προσβλημένος.

affection [əˈfɛkʃən] n αγάπη, στοργή || ~**ate** a φιλόστοργος.

affiliate [əˈfɪlɪeɪt] vt εισάγω, συνεργάζομαι.

affinity [əˈfɪnɪtɪ] n συγγένεια.

affirmation [æfəˈmeɪʃən] n *(δια)*βεβαίωση || *(assent)* κατάφαση.

affirmative [əˈfɜːmətɪv] a καταφατικός, βεβαιωτικός ♦ n κατάφαση || **in the** ~ καταφατικά.

affix [əˈfɪks] vt επισυνάπτω, προσαρτώ, θέτω.

afflict [əˈflɪkt] vt θλίβω, πικραίνω || *(MED)* προσβάλλω || ~**ion** n θλίψη, λύπη || *(misfortune)* ατύχημα nt, συμφορά.

affluence ['æfluəns] n (abundance) αφθονία || (wealth) πλούτος.

affluent ['æfluənt] a πλούσιος.

afford [ə'fɔːd] vt (have the means) δύναμαι, έχω τα μέσα || (provide) παρέχω, προσφέρω.

affront [ə'frʌnt] vt προσβάλλω, ντροπιάζω ♦ n προσβολή.

Afghanistan [æf'gænistæn] n Αφγανιστάν n.

afield [ə'fiːld] ad: far ~ μακριά.

afloat [ə'fləut] ad: I am ~ επιπλέω.

afraid [ə'freid] a έμφοβος, φοβισμένος || to be ~ of φοβούμαι || to be ~ to δεν τολμώ || that φοβούμαι ότι.

afresh [ə'freʃ] ad από την αρχή, πάλι.

Africa ['æfrikə] n Αφρική || ~ n n Αφρικανός/n m/f ♦ a αφρικάνικος.

aft [aːft] ad προς την πρύμνη, προς τα πίσω.

after ['aːftə*] prep μετά, ύστερα από || (according to) κατά ♦ ad έπειτα, ύστερα ♦ a επόμενος || cj αφού || some time ~ λίγο αργότερα || what is he ~? τι ζητά; || τι ψάχνει; || ~ all τέλος πάντων, επί τέλους || ~ five (o'clock) περασμένες πέντε || ~ you, sir! παρακαλώ!, περάτε!

after- ['aːftə*] (in compds) a μετά, μέλλων.

aftermath ['aːftəmæθ] n συνέπεια, επακόλουθο.

afternoon ['aːftə'nuːn] n απόγευμα nt || good ~! χαίρετε!

afterthought ['aːftəθɔːt] n μεταγενέστερη σκέψη.

afterwards ['aːftəwədz] ad αργότερα, στη συνέχεια.

again [ə'gen] ad πάλι, ξανά || ~ and ~ επανειλημμένως, πάλι και πάλι.

against [ə'genst] prep κατά, εναντίον.

age [eid3] n ηλικία || (generation) γενεά || (period) εποχή || (century)

αιώνας m ♦ vti γερνώ || (wine etc) ωριμάζω || of ~ ενηλικιωμένος, ενήλικος || ~ d a πλικιωμένος, γέρος || ~ d 20 (years) ηλικίας 20 ετών || ~less a αγέραστος, αιώνιος.

agency ['eid3ənsi] n, a (επί)δραση, ενέργεια || (factor) παράγοντας, αίτιο || (intervention) υπηρεσία, οργανισμός || (office) πρακτορείο, αντιπροσωπεία.

agenda [ə'd3endə] n ημερησία διάταξη || (notebook) ατζέντα, σημειωμάτριο.

agent ['eid3ənt] n πράκτορας, αντιπρόσωπος || (cause) παράγοντας, συντελεστής.

aggravate ['ægrəveit] vt επιδεινώνω, χειροτερεύω || (provoke) εντείνω, ερεθίζω.

aggregate ['ægrigit] n άθροισμα nt, σύνολο ♦ a συνολικός.

aggression [ə'greʃən] n επίθεση, επιδρομή.

aggressive [ə'gresiv] a επιθετικός || (vigorous) δραστήριος.

aggrieved [ə'griːvd] a θλιμμένος, πικραμένος.

aghast [ə'gaːst] a κατάπληκτος, εμβρόντητος.

agile ['æd3ail] a ευκίνητος, ελαφρός.

agitate ['æd3iteit] vt (set in motion) (ανα)ταράσσω || (excite) ταράσσω, ανησυχώ || (POL) κινούμαι, κάνω κίνηση || to ~ for δημιουργώ κίνηση για.

agitation [æd3i'teiʃən] n αναταραχή.

agitator ['æd3iteitə*] n υποκινητής, ταραξοπούλης.

agnostic [æg'nɒstik] a, n αγνωστικός.

ago [ə'gəu] ad περασμένος, πριν, από πριν || long ~ προ πολλού || some time ~ προ καιρού.

agog [ə'gɒg] a ανυπόμονος.

agonizing ['ægənaɪzɪŋ] *a*
σπαρακτικός, φρικτός.

agony ['ægənɪ] *n* αγωνία, βάσανο.

agree [ə'griː] *vti* (consent)
συγκατατίθεμαι, αποδέχομαι || (have
same opinion) συμφωνώ, είμαι
σύμφωνος || (of climate etc) ταιριάζω,
ωφελώ || (come to an agreement)
συμβιβάζομαι || **It does not** ~ **with**
me με πειράζει, με ενοχλεί, δεν μου
ταιριάζει || ~ **d** *a* (of persons) είμαι
σύμφωνος || (of things) εγκρίνεται,
σύμφωνοι! || ~ **ment** *n* συμφωνία ||
(formal) σύμβαση, συνθήκη.

agricultural [ægrɪ'kʌltʃərəl] *a*
γεωργικός.

agriculture ['ægrɪkʌltʃə*] *n*
γεωργία.

aground [ə'graʊnd] *ad* (NAUT) στη
στεριά || **to run** ~ προσαράσσω,
καθίζω, εξοκέλλω.

ahead [ə'hed] *ad* εμπρός, προ || **to**
get ~ προχωρώ, προηγούμαι || ~
of μπρος από.

A.I. *n* (abbr of artificial intelligence)
Τ.Ν.

aid [eɪd] *n* βοήθεια, συνδρομή ||
(assistant) βοηθός ♦ *vt* βοηθώ,
συντρέχω.

ailment ['eɪlmənt] *n* αδιαθεσία,
αρρώστια.

aim [eɪm] *n* (point) σκόπευση ||
(target) στόχος || (purpose) σκοπός,
αντικείμενο ♦ *vti* (throw) ρίχνω,
κτυπώ || (point) σκοπεύω || (intend)
επιδιώκω || ~ **less** *a* άσκοπος,
ασυνάρτητος.

air [εə*] *n* ο αέρας *m* || (tune) μέλος *nt*,
σκοπός, ήχος || (appearance)
παρουσιαστικό, αέρας, ύφος ♦ *vt*
αερίζω || (question) εκθέτω, ανακινώ ||
(opinions) επιδεικνύω, αποκαλύπτω ||
~ **borne** *a* αεροφερόμενος || ~
conditioning *n* κλιματισμός ||
~ **craft** *n* αεροσκάφος *nt*,
αεροπλάνο || ~ **craft carrier** *n*

αεροπλανοφόρο || ~ **force** *n*
(πολεμική) αεροπορία || ~ **gun** *n*
αεροβόλο || ~ **hostess** *n*
αεροσυνοδός || ~ **line** *n*
αεροπορική γραμμή || ~ **liner** *n*
επιβατικό αεροπλάνο || ~ **mail** *n*: by
~ **mail** αεροπορικώς || ~ **plane** *n*
(US) αεροπλάνο || ~ **pocket** *n* κενόν
nt αέρος || ~ **port** *n* αερολιμήν *m* ||
~ **raid** *n* αεροπορική επιδρομή ||
~ **tight** *a* αεροστεγής, ερμητικός.

aisle [aɪl] *n* διάδρομος || (of church)
πτέρυγα.

ajar [ə'dʒɑː*] *ad* μισοανοιγμένος.

akin [ə'kɪn] *a* συγγενεύων.

à la carte [ælæ'kɑːt] *ad* α-λα-καρτ.

alarm [ə'lɑːm] *n* (of danger)
συναγερμός, κραυγή κινδύνου ||
(device) σύστημα ειδοποίησης ||
(fright) φόβος, αναταραχή ♦ *vt*
τρομάζω, φοβίζω, ταράσσω || ~
clock *n* ξυπνητήρι.

Albania [æl'beɪnɪə] *n* Αλβανία || ~ **n**
n Αλβανός/ίδα *m/f* ♦ *a* αλβανικός.

album ['ælbəm] *n* λεύκωμα *nt*,
άλμπουμ *nt inv*.

alcohol ['ælkəhɒl] *n* αλκοόλ *nt inv*,
οινόπνευμα *nt* || ~ **ic** *a, n*
αλκοολικός.

alcove ['ælkəʊv] *n* παστός, αλκόβα
|| (of wall) οικός, αχιβάδα.

alderman ['ɔːldəmən] *n* δημοτικός
σύμβουλος.

ale [eɪl] *n* μπύρα.

alert [ə'lɜːt] *a* άγρυπνος,
προσεκτικός || (nimble) ευκίνητος,
σβέλτος ♦ *n* επιφυλακή,
συναγερμός.

algebra ['ældʒɪbrə] *n* άλγεβρα.

Algeria [æl'dʒɪərɪə] *n* Αλγερία ||
Algerian *a* αλγερίνικος ♦ *n*
Αλγερίνος/ή *m/f*.

alias ['eɪlɪæs] *ad* άλλως ♦ *n*
ψευδώνυμο, πλαστό όνομα *nt*.

alibi ['ælɪbaɪ] *n* άλλοθι || (col)
δικαιολογία.

alien ['eiliən] n, a ξένος, αλλοδαπός || ~**ate** vt (turn away) αποσπώ, αποξενώ || ~**ation** n αποξένωση.

alight [ə'lait] a αναμμένος, φλεγόμενος ♦ vi κατέρχομαι, κατεβαίνω || (of birds) κάθομαι.

align [ə'lain] vt ευθυγραμμίζω || ~**ment** n ευθυγράμμιση.

alike [ə'laik] a όμοιος, παρόμοιος, ίδιος ♦ ad ομοίως, ίδια.

alive [ə'laiv] a ζωντανός || (lively) ζωηρός || (teeming) βρίθων, γεμάτος.

alkali ['ælkəlai] n άλκαλι.

all [ɔːl] a, pron πας, όλος, όλοι, πάντες ♦ n όλο, σύνολο, ολότητα ♦ ad τελείως, τελείως, όλο || after ~ στο κατω-κάτω || ~ **in** ~ στο σύνολο || **above** ~ προπαντός.

all- ['ɔːl] (in compds) a ολο-, παν-, παντο-, τελείως.

allay [ə'lei] vt καταπραΰνω, γλυκαίνω || (lessen) καθησυχάζω, ανακουφίζω.

allegation [ælɪ'geiʃən] n ισχυρισμός, υπόνοια.

allege [ə'ledʒ] vt ισχυρίζομαι, επικαλούμαι || ~**dly** ad δήθεν.

allegiance [ə'liːdʒəns] n πίστη, υπακοή.

allegory ['æligəri] n αλληγορία.

allergic [ə'lɜːdʒik] a αλλεργικός.

allergy ['ælədʒi] n αλλεργία.

alleviate [ə'liːvieit] vt ελαφρύνω, ανακουφίζω.

alley ['æli] n δρομίσκος, πάροδος f, δρομάκος.

alliance [ə'laiəns] n συμμαχία || (marriage) επιγαμία, επισυμμαχία.

allied ['ælaid] a: ~ **to** συγγενεύω με.

alligator ['æligeitə*] n αλλιγάτορας.

all-in [ɔːl'in] a (exhausted) εξαντλημένος.

alliteration [ə'litə'reiʃən] n παρήχηση.

all-night ['ɔːl'nait] a (café etc) ολονύκτιος, διανυκτερεύων.

allocate ['æləkeit] vt διαθέτω, παραχωρώ || (for special purpose) κατανέμω, αναθέτω.

allocation [æləu'keiʃən] n εκχώρηση, απονομή.

allot [ə'lɒt] vt παραχωρώ, διαθέτω, κατανέμω || ~**ment** n (share) μερίδιο, τμήμα nt.

all-out [ɔːl'aut] ad με όλες τις δυνάμεις.

allow [ə'lau] vt επιτρέπω || (grant) παρέχω, δίδω || (acknowledge) αναγνωρίζω, (παρα)δέχομαι || **to** ~ **for** αφήνω περιθώριο για || ~**ance** n επίδομα nt, εισόδημα nt.

alloy ['ælɔi] n κράμα nt ♦ vt αναμιγνύω, συντήκω || (fig) νοθεύω.

all-round ['ɔːl'raund] a τελειότατος, αρτιότατος.

all-time ['ɔːl'taim] a παντοτινός.

allude [ə'luːd] vi: **to** ~ **to** εννοώ, υπονοώ, υπαινίσσομαι.

alluring [ə'ljuəriŋ] a δελεαστικός, γοητευτικός.

allusion [ə'luːʒən] n υπαινιγμός, νύξη.

ally ['ælai] n σύμμαχος ♦ [ə'lai] vi συνδέω, ενώνω ♦ vi συμμαχώ, συνδέομαι.

almighty [ɔːl'maiti] a: **the A** ~ ο Παντοδύναμος.

almond ['ɑːmənd] n αμύγδαλο || (tree) αμυγδαλιά.

almost [ɔːlməust] ad σχεδόν, περίπου.

alms [ɑːmz] npl ελεημοσύνη, ψυχικό.

alone [ə'ləun] a μόνος, μονάχος, μοναχός ♦ ad μόνο.

along [ə'lɒŋ] ad: move ~ προχωρώ, βηματίζω || εμπρός!, έλα λοιπόν! ♦ prep κατά μήκος || ~**side** ad, prep πλευρισμένος, πλάι-πλάι || **all** ~ από καιρό, απ' την αρχή.

aloof [ə'luːf] a, ad μακριά, σε απόσταση.

aloud [ə'laʊd] ad μεγαλοφώνως, φωναχτά, δυνατά.

alphabet ['ælfəbet] n αλφάβητο || ~ical a αλφαβητικός.

alpine ['ælpaɪn] a αλπικός.

Alps [ælps] npl: **the** ~ οι 'Αλπεις.

already [ɔːl'redɪ] ad ήδη, κιόλας.

alright [ɔːl'raɪt] = **all right** || see **right.**

also ['ɔːlsəʊ] ad επίσης, ακόμη και.

altar ['ɒltə*] n βωμός, θυσιαστήριο || (church) Αγία Τράπεζα.

alter ['ɒltə*] vt μεταβάλλω, τροποποιώ, μετανοώ ♦ vi μεταβάλλομαι || ~**ation** n μεταβολή, αλλαγή, αλλοίωση.

alternate [ɒl'tɜːnɪt] a εναλλάσσων, εναλλασσόμενος ♦ ['ɒltɜːneɪt] vt εναλλάσσω, χρησιμοποιώ εναλλάξ ♦ vi εναλλάσσομαι (with μɛ) || ~**ly** ad εναλλάξ, αλληλοδιαδόχως.

alternative [ɒl'tɜːnətɪv] n εκλογή, λύση || ~**ly** ad εναλλάξ.

alternator ['ɒltɜːneɪtə*] n (ELEC) εναλλάκτης.

although [ɔːl'ðəʊ] cj αν και, μολονότι, καίτοι.

altitude ['æltɪtjuːd] n ύψος, υψόμετρο.

alto ['æltəʊ] n (male) οξύφωνος || (female) κοντράλτο.

altogether [ɔːltə'geðə*] ad τελείως, ολοσχερώς, εντελώς.

aluminium [æljʊ'mɪnɪəm], (US) **aluminum** [ə'luːmɪnəm] n αλουμίνιο, αργίλιο.

always ['ɔːlweɪz] ad πάντα, πάντοτε, διαρκώς.

am [æm] see **be.**

a.m. ad (abbr of ante meridiem) π.μ.

amass [ə'mæs] vt συσσωρεύω, μαζεύω.

amateur ['æmətə*] n ερασιτέχνης ♦ a ερασιτεχνικός.

amaze [ə'meɪz] vt εκπλήσσω, καταπλήσσω, θαμπώνω || ~**ment** n κατάπληξη, έκπληξη, ξάφνιασμα nt.

amazing [ə'meɪzɪŋ] a καταπληκτικός, απίστευτος.

ambassador [æm'bæsədə*] n πρεσβευτής, πρέσβυς m.

ambiguity [æmbɪ'gjuːtɪ] n αμφιλογία, ασάφεια, διφορούμενο.

ambiguous [æm'bɪgjʊəs] a αμφίλογος, αβέβαιος, ασαφής.

ambition [æm'bɪʃən] n φιλοδοξία.

ambitious [æm'bɪʃəs] a φιλόδοξος.

amble ['æmbl] vi βαδίζω ήρεμα.

ambulance ['æmbjʊləns] n ασθενοφόρο αυτοκίνητο.

ambush ['æmbʊʃ] n ενέδρα, καρτέρι ♦ vt παρασύρω σε ενέδρα.

amenable [ə'miːnəbl] a υπάκουος, πρόθυμος.

amend [ə'mend] vt διορθώνω, τροποποιώ ♦ vi διορθώνομαι ♦ n: **to make** ~**s** επανορθώνω, αποζημιώνω || ~**ment** n τροποποίηση, διόρθωση.

amenity [ə'miːnɪtɪ] n χάρη, ομορφιά, άνεση.

America [ə'merɪkə] n Αμερική.

American [ə'merɪkən] a αμερικανικός ♦ n Αμερικανός/ίδα m/f.

amiable ['eɪmɪəbl] a ευγενικός, φιλόφρων.

amicable ['æmɪkəbl] a φιλικός || ~ **settlement** n συμβιβασμός.

amid(st) [ə'mɪd(st)] prep ανάμεσα, αναμεταξύ.

amiss [ə'mɪs] a, ad εσφαλμένα, κακά, στραβά || **to take** ~ παίρνω στραβά, παρεξηγώ.

ammunition [æmjʊ'nɪʃən] n πολεμοφόδια ntpl, πυρομαχικά ntpl.

amnesia [æm'niːzɪə] n αμνησία.

amnesty ['æmnɪstɪ] n αμνηστία.

amok [ə'mɒk] ad = **amuck.**

among(st) [ə'mʌŋ(st)] *prep* μεταξύ, μέσα, ανάμεσα.

amoral [æ'mɒrəl] *a* άσχετος με την ηθική.

amorous ['æmərəs] *a* ερωτόληπτος, ερωτιάρης.

amount [ə'maunt] *n* ποσό, σύνολο, ποσότητα ♦ *vi* ανέρχομαι, ισοδυναμώ || to — **to** ανέρχομαι.

ampere ['æmpɛə*] *n* αμπέρ *nt inv.*

amphibious [æm'fɪbɪəs] *a* αμφίβιος.

amphitheatre ['æmfɪθɪətə*] *n* αμφιθέατρο.

ample ['æmpl] *a* (enough) αρκετός, πλήρης || (big) ευρύς, πλατύς || (abundant) άφθονα, πλούσια.

amplifier ['æmplɪfaɪə*] *n* ενισχυτής.

amputate ['æmpjuteit] *vt* αποκόπτω, ακρωτηριάζω.

amuck [ə'mʌk] *ad*: to run ~ παθαίνω αμόκ, καταστρέφω.

amuse [ə'mjuːz] *vt* διασκεδάζω, ξεκουράζω || ~**ment** *n* διασκέδαση, θέαμα *nt*, αναψυχή.

amusing [ə'mjuːzɪŋ] *a* διασκεδαστικός, ξεκαρδιστικός.

an [æn] *see* **a**.

anaemia [ə'niːmɪə] *n* αναιμία.

anaemic [ə'niːmɪk] *a* αναιμικός.

anaesthetic [ænɪs'θetɪk] *n* αναισθητικό.

analgesic [ænæl'dʒiːsɪk] *a, n* αναλγητικός.

analogy [ə'nælədʒɪ] *n* αναλογία.

analyse [ə'nəlaɪz] *vt* αναλύω.

analysis [ə'næləsɪs] *n* ανάλυση.

anarchist ['ænəkɪst] *n* αναρχικός.

anarchy ['ænəkɪ] *n* αναρχία.

anatomy [ə'nætəmɪ] *n* ανατομία.

ancestor ['ænsɪstə*] *n* πρόγονος, προπάτορας.

ancestry ['ænsɪstrɪ] *n* καταγωγή.

anchor ['æŋkə*] *n* άγκυρα ♦ *vi* αγκυροβολώ, ρίχνω άγκυρα, αράζω.

anchovy ['æntʃəvɪ] *n* αντσούγια, χαμψί.

ancient ['eɪnʃənt] *a* αρχαίος, παλαιός.

and [ænd, ənd] *cj* και.

anecdote ['ænɪkdəut] *n* ανέκδοτο.

anew [ə'njuː] *ad* πάλι, ξανά.

angel ['eɪndʒəl] *n* άγγελος, αγγελούδι.

anger ['æŋgə*] *n* οργή, θυμός, παραφορά ♦ *vt* εξοργίζω, θυμώνω.

angle ['æŋgl] *n* γωνία || (viewpoint) άποψη ♦ *vt* ψαρεύω || ~**r** *n* ψαράς (με καλάμι).

Anglican ['æŋglɪkən] *n* Αγγλικανός.

angling ['æŋglɪŋ] *n* ψάρεμα *nt.*

Anglo- ['æŋgləu] *prefix* αγγλο-.

angrily ['æŋgrɪlɪ] *ad* οργισμένα, θυμωμένα.

angry ['æŋgrɪ] *a* οργισμένος, θυμωμένος.

anguish ['æŋgwɪʃ] *n* αγωνία, αδημονία, πόνος.

angular ['æŋgjulə*] *a* γωνιακός, γωνιώδης.

animal ['ænɪməl] *n* ζώο ♦ *a* ζωικός.

animate ['ænɪmeɪt] *a* έμψυχος, ζωντανός ♦ ['ænɪmeɪt] *vt* ζωογονώ, δίδω κίνηση || ~**d** *a* ζωντανός, ζωηρός.

animosity [ænɪ'mɒsɪtɪ] *n* εχθρότητα, έχθρα.

aniseed ['ænɪsiːd] *n* γλυκάνισο.

ankle ['æŋkl] *n* αστράγαλος.

annex ['æneks] *n* (also: **annexe**) παράρτημα *nt* ♦ [ə'neks] *vt* προσαρτώ.

annihilate [ə'naɪəleɪt] *vt* εκμηδενίζω, εξαφανίζω.

anniversary [ænɪ'vɜːsərɪ] *n* επέτειος *f.*

annotate ['ænəuteit] *vt* σχολιάζω.

announce [ə'nauns] *vt* (αν)αγγέλλω, ανακοινώ || ~**ment** *n*

αναγγελία, ανακοίνωση || ~r n εκφωνητής.

annoy [ə'nɔɪ] vt ενοχλώ, πειράζω || ~ance n ενόχληση, μπελάς || ~ing a ενοχλητικός, οχληρός.

annual ['ænjuəl] a ετήσιος, χρονιάρικος, ♦ n (book) επετηρίδα, ημερολόγιο || ~ly ad ετησίως.

annuity [ə'njuːɪtɪ] n πρόσοδος f, επίδομα nt.

annul [ə'nʌl] vt ακυρώνω, διαλύω, καταργέλλω || ~ment n ακύρωση, κατάργηση.

annum ['ænəm] see **per**.

anoint [ə'nɔɪnt] vt χρίω, αλείφω.

anomaly [ə'nɔməlɪ] n ανωμαλία.

anonymous [ə'nɔnɪməs] a ανώνυμος.

another [ə'nʌðə*] a, pron άλλος (ένας), ακόμη (ένας) || **one** ~ ο ένας τον άλλο.

answer ['ɑːnsə*] n απάντηση || (solution) λύση ♦ vt απαντώ || (suit) ανταποκρίνομαι || **to** ~ **for** vt εγγυούμαι για || ~**able** a υπεύθυνος, υπόλογος.

ant [ænt] n μυρμήγκι.

antagonist [æn'tægənɪst] n ανταγωνιστής, αντίπαλος || ~**ic** a εχθρικός, ανταγωνιστικός.

antagonize [æn'tægənaɪz] vt προκαλώ ανταγωνισμό, προκαλώ εχθρότητα.

Antarctic [ænt'ɑːktɪk] a ανταρκτικός.

antelope ['æntɪləʊp] n αντιλόπη.

antenatal ['æntɪ'neɪtl] a πριν τη γέννηση.

antenna [æn'tɛnə] n κεραία.

anthem ['ænθəm] n ύμνος.

anthology [æn'θɔlədʒɪ] n ανθολογία.

anthropologist [ænθrə'pɔlədʒɪst] n ανθρωπολόγος.

anthropology [ænθrə'pɔlədʒɪ] n ανθρωπολογία.

anti-aircraft ['æntɪ'ɛəkrɑːft] a αντιαεροπορικός.

antibiotic ['æntɪbaɪ'ɔtɪk] n αντιβιοτικό.

anticipate [æn'tɪsɪpeɪt] vt προλαμβάνω || (foresee) προβλέπω, προσδοκώ.

anticipation [æntɪsɪ'peɪʃən] n πρόληψη, πρόβλεψη || (expectation) προσδοκία.

anticlimax ['æntɪ'klaɪmæks] n αντικλίμακα, κατάπτωση, παρακμή.

anticlockwise ['æntɪ'klɒkwaɪz] ad αριστερόστροφα.

antics ['æntɪks] npl κόλπα ntpl, αστεία ntpl.

anticyclone ['æntɪ'saɪkləʊn] n αντικυκλώνας.

antidote ['æntɪdəʊt] n αντίδοτο.

antifreeze ['æntɪ'friːz] n αντιψυκτικό, αντιπηκτικό.

antiquarian [æntɪ'kwɛərɪən] n αρχαιοδίφης, αρχαιόφιλος.

antiquated ['æntɪkweɪtɪd] a αρχαϊκός, απηρχαιωμένος, πεπαλαιωμένος.

antique [æn'tiːk] n αρχαίο, παλιό, αντίκα || ~s npl αρχαιότητες, αντίκες.

antiquity [æn'tɪkwɪtɪ] n αρχαιότητα.

antiseptic [æntɪ'sɛptɪk] a, n αντισηπτικό.

antisocial ['æntɪ'səʊʃəl] a αντικοινωνικός.

antlers ['æntləz] npl κέρατα (ελαφιού).

anus ['eɪnəs] n δακτύλιος, έδρα.

anvil ['ænvɪl] n άκμονας, αμόνι.

anxiety [æŋ'zaɪətɪ] n ανησυχία, φόβος.

anxious ['æŋkʃəs] a ανήσυχος, στενοχωρημένος || (impatient) ανυπόμονος || ~ly ad ανήσυχα, ανυπόμονα.

any ['ɛnɪ] pron, a κανείς, καμμία,

κανένα || (whosoever) οποιοσδήποτε, κάθε ♦ ad καθόλου, πια || ~body pron κανείς, καμμιά, οποιοσδήποτε, καθένας || ~how ad οπωσδήποτε, όπως κι αν είναι || ~one pron οποιοσδήποτε, καθένας, όλοι || ~thing pron τίποτε, κάτι, οτιδήποτε || ~way ad οπωσδήποτε, πουθενά || ~where ad οπωσδήποτε, πουθενά.

apart [ə'pɑːt] ad χωριστά, κατά μέρος || ~ **from** εκτός του ότι.

apartheid [ə'pɑːteit] n φυλετική διάκριση.

apartment [ə'pɑːtmənt] n (flat) διαμέρισμα nt.

apathetic [æpə'θetik] a απαθής, αδιάφορος.

apathy ['æpəθi] n απάθεια, αδιαφορία.

ape [eip] n πίθηκος, μαϊμού f ♦ vt μιμούμαι.

aperitif [ə'peritiv] n ορεκτικό.

aperture ['æpətjuə*] n άνοιγμα nt, οπή, σχισμή.

apex ['eipeks] n κορυφή.

apologetic [əpɔlə'dʒetik] a απολογητικός.

apologize [ə'pɔlədʒaiz] vi ζητώ συγγνώμη.

apology [ə'pɔlədʒi] n απολογία, συγγνώμη.

apostle [ə'pɔsl] n απόστολος.

apostrophe [ə'pɔstrəfi] n απόστροφος.

appal [ə'pɔːl] vt τρομάζω, προκαλώ φρίκη || ~**ling** a τρομερός, φρικτός.

apparatus [æpə'reitəs] n συσκευή, μηχάνημα nt.

apparent [ə'pærənt] a φαινόμενος, εμφανής, φανερός || ~**ly** ad προφανώς, όπως φαίνεται.

apparition [æpə'riʃən] n φάντασμα nt.

appeal [ə'piːl] n έκκληση, κλήση προσφυγή || (LAW) κλήση, έφεση ||

(charm) γοητευτική, ελκυστική ♦ vi προσφεύγω, απευθύνομαι || ~**ing** a συγκινητικός, συμπαθητικός.

appear [ə'piə*] vi φαίνομαι, εμφανίζομαι || ~**ance** n εμφάνιση, παρουσία, παρουσιαστικό || **to put in** or **make an** ~**ance** εμφανίζομαι, παρουσιάζομαι.

appease [ə'piːz] vt κατευνάζω, ικανοποιώ.

appendicitis [əpendi'saitis] n σκωληκοειδίτιδα.

appendix [ə'pendiks] n παράρτημα nt, εξάρτημα nt || (ANAT) σκωληκοειδής απόφυση.

appetite ['æpitait] n όρεξη || **loss of** ~ n ανορεξία.

appetizing ['æpitaiziŋ] a ορεκτικός, ελκυστικός.

applaud [ə'plɔːd] vt χειροκροτώ, επευφημώ.

applause [ə'plɔːz] n χειροκρότημα ntpl, επιδοκιμασία.

apple ['æpl] n μήλο || ~ **pie** n μηλόπιττα || ~ **tree** n μηλιά.

appliance [ə'plaiəns] n όργανο, μηχάνημα nt, εργαλείο.

applicable [ə'plikəbl] a εφαρμόσιμος, κατάλληλος.

applicant ['æplikənt] n υποψήφιος, αιτητής.

application [æpli'keiʃən] n (request) αίτηση || (hard work) επιμέλεια, προσοχή, προσήλωση || (putting into practice) εφαρμογή, χρήση.

apply [ə'plai] vi εφαρμόζω || (place on) επιθέτω, βάζω || (for job etc) απευθύνομαι, υποβάλλω αίτηση || **to** ~ **the brake** πατώ φρένο, φρενάρω || **to** ~ **o.s.** προσηλούμαι, αφοσιώνομαι.

appoint [ə'pɔint] vt (δι)ορίζω, ονομάζω || ~**ment** n συνάντηση, ραντεβού nt inv.

apportion [ə'pɔːʃən] vt κατανέμω, διανέμω, μοιράζω.

appreciable [ə'priːʃəbl] a υπολογίσιμος, αισθητός.
appreciate [ə'priːʃieit] vt εκτιμώ, υπολογίζω, αποδίδω σημασία ♦ vi (ECON) ανατιμούμαι, υπερτιμούμαι.
appreciation [əpriːʃi'eiʃən] n εκτίμηση || (ECON) υπερτίμηση, ανατίμηση.
apprehend [æpri'hend] vt συλλαμβάνω, αντιλαμβάνομαι.
apprehension [æpri'henʃən] n (fear) φόβος, ανησυχία || (understanding) αντίληψη, νόηση || (arrest) σύλληψη.
apprehensive [æpri'hensiv] a (worried) ανήσυχος, φοβισμένος.
apprentice [ə'prentis] n μαθητευόμενος ♦ vt τοποθετώ σαν μαθητευόμενο || ~**ship** n μαθητεία, μαθήτευση.
approach [ə'prəutʃ] n προσέγγιση, πλησίασμα nt|| (path) είσοδος f, οδός f|| (GOLF) κτύπημα nt ♦ vti πλησιάζω, προσεγγίζω || ~**able** a ευπρόσιτος, προσιτός.
appropriate [ə'prəupriit] a κατάλληλος, αρμόδιος, ταιριαστός ♦ [ə'prəuprieit] vt οικειοποιούμαι, ιδιοποιούμαι, παίρνω.
approval [ə'pruːvəl] n έγκριση.
approve [ə'pruːv] vti εγκρίνω, επιδοκιμάζω, επικυρώνω || ~**d** a εγκριθείς, εγκεκριμένος.
approximate [ə'prɒksimit] a κατά προσέγγιση ♦ [ə'prɒksimeit] vt προσεγγίζω, πλησιάζω.
approximation [əprɒksi'meiʃən] n προσέγγιση, εγγύτητα.
apricot ['eiprikɒt] n βερύκοκκο.
April ['eiprəl] n Απρίλιος.
apron ['eiprən] n ποδιά.
apt [æpt] a (suitable) κατάλληλος, αρμόζων || (ready) υποκείμενος σε.
aptitude ['æptitjuːd] n ικανότητα.
aqualung ['ækwʌlʌŋ] n συσκευή καταδύσεως, ακουαλάγκ nt inv.

aquarium [ə'kwɛəriəm] n ενυδρείο, ακουάριο.
aquatic [ə'kwætik] a υδρόβιος || ~ **sports** npl θαλάσσια σπορ nt inv.
aqueduct ['ækwidʌkt] n υδραγωγείο.
Arab ['ærəb] a αραβικός.
Arabia [ə'reibiə] n Αραβία || ~ **n** a άραβας, αραβικός ♦ n 'Αραβας, Αράπης/ίνα m/f.
Arabic ['ærəbik] a αραβικός ♦ n αραβική γλώσσα.
arable ['ærəbl] a καλλιεργήσιμος.
arbitrary ['aːbitrəri] a αυθαίρετος.
arbitration [aːbi'treiʃən] n διαιτησία || ~ **court** n διαιτητικό δικαστήριο.
arbitrator ['aːbitreitə*] n διαιτητής.
arc [aːk] n τόξο.
arcade [aː'keid] n στοά, καμάρα.
arch [aːtʃ] n αψίδα, καμάρα ♦ a (chief) αρχι- ♦ vt (bend) λυγίζω, καμπουριάζω.
archaeologist [aːki'ɒlədʒist] n αρχαιολόγος.
archaeology [aːki'ɒlədʒi] n αρχαιολογία.
archaic [aː'keiik] a αρχαϊκός.
archbishop ['aːtʃ'biʃəp] n αρχιεπίσκοπος.
archer ['aːtʃə*] n τοξότης || ~ **y** n τοξοβολία.
archetype ['aːkitaip] n αρχέτυπο.
archipelago [aːki'peligəu] n αρχιπέλαγος nt.
architect ['aːkitekt] n αρχιτέκτονας || ~**ural** a αρχιτεκτονικός || ~**ure** n αρχιτεκτονική.
archives ['aːkaivz] npl αρχεία ntpl, έγγραφα ntpl.
archway ['aːtʃwei] n στοά, αψιδωτή είσοδος.
Arctic ['aːktik] a αρκτικός.

ardent [ˈɑːdənt] a φλογερός, ζωηρός.

ardour [ˈɑːdə*] n ζέση, μανία, πόθος.

arduous [ˈɑːdjuəs] a τραχύς, δύσκολος, κοπιώδης.

are [ɑː*] see be.

area [ˈɛərɪə] n περιοχή, έκταση, χώρος || (MATH) εμβαδόν.

arena [əˈriːnə] n παλαίστρα, κονίστρα, αρένα.

aren't [ɑːnt] = are not || see be.

argue [ˈɑːgjuː] vti (discuss) συζητώ, πραγματεύομαι || (prove) (απο)δεικνύω || (reason) φέρω επιχειρήματα, παρατάσσω.

argument [ˈɑːgjəmənt] n επιχείρημα nt, συζήτηση || (dispute) φιλονικία, λογομαχία || (of play) σύνοψη, περίληψη || **~ative** a συζητητικός.

aria [ˈɑːrɪə] n σκοπός, άρια.

arid [ˈærɪd] a ξηρός, άνυδρος.

arise [əˈraɪz] (irreg v) vi σηκώνομαι || (appear) εμφανίζομαι, απορρέω.

aristocracy [ærɪsˈtɒkrəsɪ] n αριστοκρατία.

aristocrat [ˈærɪstəkræt] n αριστοκράτης.

arithmetic [əˈrɪθmətɪk] n αριθμητική.

arm [ɑːm] n βραχίονας, μπράτσο || (hand) χέρι || (weapon) όπλο ♦ vt (εξ)οπλίζω, αρματώνω || **~s** npl όπλα ntpl || **~ed forces** npl ένοπλες δυνάμεις.

armchair [ˈɑːmtʃɛə*] n πολυθρόνα.

armful [ˈɑːmful] n αγκαλιά.

armistice [ˈɑːmɪstɪs] n ανακωχή.

armour, (US) **armor** [ˈɑːmə*] n θωράκιση || (panoply) αρματωσιά || **~ed car** n τεθωρακισμένο άρμα μάχης.

armoury [ˈɑːmərɪ] n οπλοστάσιο, οπλαποθήκη.

armpit [ˈɑːmpɪt] n μασχάλη.

army [ˈɑːmɪ] n στρατός || (of people etc) πλήθος nt.

aroma [əˈrəumə] n άρωμα nt, μυρωδιά || **~tic** a αρωματικός.

around [əˈraund] ad (τρι)γύρω, ολόγυρα || (about) περίπου ♦ prep περί, γύρω.

arouse [əˈrauz] vt διεγείρω, αφυπνίζω, ξυπνώ.

arrange [əˈreɪndʒ] vt τακτοποιώ, διαρρυθμίζω, διευθετώ, κανονίζω || **~ment** n τακτοποίηση, ρύθμιση, διευθέτηση.

arrears [əˈrɪəz] npl καθυστερούμενα ntpl, εκπρόθεσμος || **in ~** καθυστερούμενα.

arrest [əˈrɛst] n (making prisoner) σύλληψη, κράτηση || (halt) ανακαίτηση, σταμάτημα nt ♦ vt σταματώ, ανακαιτίζω || (LAW) συλλαμβάνω.

arrival [əˈraɪvl] n άφιξη, ερχομός || **new ~** n νεοαφιχθείς/ίσα m/f || (baby) νεογέννητο.

arrive [əˈraɪv] vi αφικνούμαι, φθάνω (at σε) || (at a conclusion) καταλήγω.

arrogance [ˈærəgəns] n αλαζονεία, έπαρση, αυθάδεια.

arrogant [ˈærəgənt] a αλαζόνας, υπερόπτης, αυθάδης.

arrow [ˈærəu] n βέλος nt, σαΐτα.

arsenal [ˈɑːsɪnl] n οπλοστάσιο.

arsenic [ˈɑːsnɪk] n αρσενικό.

arson [ˈɑːsn] n εμπρησμός.

art [ɑːt] n τέχνη || **~ gallery** n πινακοθήκη.

artery [ˈɑːtərɪ] n αρτηρία.

artful [ˈɑːtful] a (a person) επιδέξιος, εφευρετικός || (crafty) πονηρός, δόλιος.

arthritis [ɑːˈθraɪtɪs] n αρθρίτιδα.

artichoke [ˈɑːtɪtʃəuk] n αγκινάρα.

article [ˈɑːtɪkl] n (of agreement etc) άρθρο, όρος || (GRAM) άρθρο

(newspaper etc) άρθρο || *(items)* είδος nt, αντικείμενο.

articulate [α:'tιkjulιt] *a* αρθρωτός, έναρθρος || *(in expression)* σαφής, ευκρινής || ~ **d** *a* έναρθρος.

artificial [α:tι'fιʃəl] *a* τεχνητός, ψεύτικος || ~ **intelligence (A.I.)** *(COMPUT)* τεχνητή νοημοσύνη (T.N.) || ~ **respiration** *n* τεχνητή αναπνοή.

artillery [α:'tιlərι] *n* πυροβολικό.

artisan ['α:tιzæn] *n* τεχνίτης, βιοτέχνης, εργάτης.

artist ['α:tιst] *n* καλλιτέχνης/ιδα *m/f* || *(painter)* ζωγράφος || ~ **ic** *a* καλλιτεχνικός.

artless ['α:tlιs] *a* άτεχνος || *(natural)* απέριττος, φυσικός || *(naive)* αφελής, απονήρευτος.

as [æz, əz] *ad (in main clause)* επίσης, εξίσου, τόσο ... όσο || ~ **regards** όσο για || *cj (in subject clause)* όσο, τόσο ... όσο, όσον || *(time)* ενώ, καθώς || *(because)* επειδή || *(manner)* do ~ **you like** κάμετε όπως σας αρέσει || ~ **is** όπως είναι.

asbestos [æz'bεstɒs] *n* αμίαντος, άσβεστος.

ascend [ə'sεnd] *vi* ανέρχομαι, ανεβαίνω.

ascension [ə'sεnʃən] *n* ανάβαση, άνοδος *f*, ανάληψη || **A~ Day** *n* της Αναλήψεως.

ascent [ə'sεnt] *n* άνοδος *f*, ανάβαση || *(incline)* ανήφορος, ανωφέρεια, κλίση.

ascertain [æsə'tein] *vt* διαπιστώνω, εξακριβώνω.

ascetic [ə'sεtιk] *a* ασκητικός.

ash [æʃ] *n* τέφρα, στάχτη || *(tree)* μελία, φλαμούρι.

ashamed [ə'feimd] *a:* to be ~ είμαι ντροπιασμένος, ντρέπομαι.

ashen ['æʃən] *a* σταχτής || *(person)* ωχρός, κίτρινος.

ashore [ə'ʃɔ:*] *ad* στην ξηρά, προσαραγμένος.

ashtray ['æʃtrei] *n* στακτοδοχείο.

Asia ['eiʒə] *n* Ασία || ~ *n a* ασιατικός || ~ **tic** *a* ασιατικός || ~ **Minor** *n* Μικρά Ασία.

aside [ə'said] *ad* κατά μέρος, πλάι, παράμερα || ~ **from** εκτός, πέρα.

ask [α:sk] *vt* (ε)ρωτώ, ζητώ, προσκαλώ || *vi* ~ **a question** υποβάλλω ερώτηση.

askance [ə'skα:ns] *ad:* to look at s.o. ~ κοιτάζω με δυσπιστία.

askew [ə'skju:] *ad* λοξά, στραβά.

asleep [ə'sli:p] *a, ad* κοιμισμένος || *(foot)* μουδιασμένος || **to fall** ~ αποκοιμιέμαι.

asparagus [əs'pærəgəs] *n* σπαράγγι.

aspect ['æspεkt] *n* θέα, όψη, προσανατολισμός.

asphalt ['æsfælt] *n* άσφαλτος *f* || ~ **road** *n* ασφαλτοστρωμένος (δρόμος).

asphyxiate [æs'fιksιeιt] *vt* πνίγω.

aspiration [æspə'reiʃən] *n* φιλοδοξία, βλέψη || *(GRAM)* δασεία προφορά.

aspire [əs'paιə*] *vt:* to ~ to φιλοδοξώ, αποβλέπω.

aspirin ['æsprιn] *n* ασπιρίνη.

ass [æs] *n* γάιδαρος.

assailant [ə'seιlənt] *n* επιτιθέμενος.

assassin [ə'sæsιn] *n* δολοφόνος || ~ **ate** *vt* δολοφονώ || ~ **ation** *n* δολοφονία.

assault [ə'sɔ:lt] *n* έφοδος, επίθεση ♦ *vt* επιτίθεμαι, εξορμώ || *(person)* βιάζω.

assemble [ə'sεmbl] *vt* συγκεντρώνω, συναθροίζω || *(machine etc)* ενώνω, συναρμολογώ ♦ *vi* συγκεντρώνομαι, συγκεντρώνομαι.

assembly [ə'sεmblι] *n* συνέλευση, συγκέντρωση || *(machines)*

συναρμολόγηση, συγκρότημα *nt* ‖ ~ **line** *n* τράπεζα συναρμολογήσεως, αλυσίδα.

assent [ə'sɛnt] *n* συγκατάθεση, έγκριση ♦ *vi* συγκατατίθεμαι, συναινώ, επικυρώ.

assert [ə'sɜːt] *vt* επιβάλλω, διεκδικώ ‖ (*ascertain*) βεβαιώ, υποστηρίζω ‖ ~**ion** *n* ισχυρισμός, υποστήριξη.

assess [ə'sɛs] *vt* καταλογίζω, υπολογίζω, επιβάλλω (φόρο) ‖ (*property*) εκτιμώ, φορολογώ ‖ ~**ment** *n* καταλογισμός, εκτίμηση ‖ (*tax*) φόρος ‖ ~**or** *n* ελεγκτής (εφοριακός).

asset ['æsɛt] *n* περιουσιακό στοιχείο ‖ (*qualities*) προσόν *nt*, αξία, ατού *nt* *inv*‖ ~**s** *npl* περιουσία ‖ (*ECON*) ενεργητικό.

assiduous [ə'sidjuəs] *a* επιμελής, προσεκτικός.

assign [ə'sain] *vt* προορίζω, παρέχω, παραχωρώ, δίδω ‖ ~**ment** *n* ανατιθεμένη εργασία.

assimilate [ə'simileit] *vt* εξομοιώνω ‖ (*food*) αφομοιώνω.

assist [ə'sist] *vt* βοηθώ, συντρέχω, μετέχω ‖ ~**ance** *n* βοήθεια, αρωγή ‖ ~**ant** *n* βοηθός *m/f* ♦ *a* βοηθητικός, αναπληρωματικός.

assizes [ə'saiziz] *npl*: **court of** ~ ορκωτό δικαστήριο.

associate [ə'səuʃiit] *n* εταίρος, συνέταιρος, συνεργάτης ♦ [ə'səuʃieit] *vti*: **to** ~ **with** συνδέω, συνεταιρίζω, συνεργάζομαι, συναναστρέφομαι.

association [əsəusi'eiʃən] *n* (*club*) εταιρεία, οργανισμός, σωματείο ‖ (*keeping company*) συναναστροφή, σχέση ‖ ~ **football** *n* ποδόσφαιρο.

assorted [ə'sɔːtid] *a* ταιριασμένος.

assortment [ə'sɔːtmənt] *n* συλλογή ‖ (*arrangement*) τακτοποίηση, ταξινόμηση.

assume [ə'sjuːm] *vt* (*take for granted*) υποθέτω, θεωρώ ‖ (*duty*) αναλαμβάνω, αναδέχομαι ‖ ~**d name** *n* ψευδώνυμο.

assumption [ə'sʌmpʃən] *n* (*supposition*) υπόθεση, εικασία.

assurance [ə'ʃuərəns] *n* (*certainty*) βεβαιότητα ‖ (*confidence*) διαβεβαίωση, υπόσχεση ‖ (*insurance*) ασφάλεια (ζωής).

assure [ə'ʃuə*] *vt* (δια)βεβαιώ, εξασφαλίζω ‖ ~**d** *a* βέβαιος.

asterisk ['æstərisk] *n* αστερίσκος.

astern [ə'stɜːn] *ad* πίσω, προς τα πίσω.

asthma ['æsmə] *n* άσθμα *nt*‖ ~**tic** *a* ασθματικός.

astonish [ə'stɔniʃ] *vt* εκπλήσσω, καταπλήσσω ‖ ~**ment** *n* έκπληξη, κατάπληξη.

astound [ə'staund] *vt* καταπλήσσω.

astray [ə'strei] *ad*: **to go** ~ περιπλανώμαι, παραστρατίζω, ξεστρατίζω.

astride [ə'straid] *a*, *prep* καβάλλα, ασεβάλ.

astrologer [əs'trɔlədʒə*] *n* αστρολόγος.

astrology [əs'trɔlədʒi] *n* αστρολογία.

astronaut ['æstrənɔːt] *n* αστροναύτης.

astronomer [əs'trɔnəmə*] *n* αστρονόμος.

astronomy [əs'trɔnəmi] *n* αστρονομία.

astute [əs'tjuːt] *a* έξυπνος, τετραπέρατος ‖ (*crafty*) πανούργος, πονηρός.

asunder [ə'sʌndə*] *ad* χωριστά, κομματιαστά.

asylum [ə'sailəm] *n* (*refuge*) άσυλο, καταφύγιο ‖ (*for insane*) ψυχιατρείο.

at [æt] *prep* (*of place*) σε ‖ (*of time*) σε, κατά, περί ‖ ~ **six o'clock** στις έξι ‖ ~ **first** στην αρχή ‖ ~ **home** στο

σπίτι|| ~ least τουλάχιστο || ~ last επί τέλους || (of cause) για || ~ all καθόλου || not ~ all καθόλου.

ate [eɪt] pt of **eat.**

atheist ['eɪθɪɪst] n άθεος, αθεϊστής.

athlete ['æθliːt] n αθλητής/τρια m/f.

athletic [æθ'letɪk] a αθλητικός || ~**s** n αθλητισμός, απορ nt inv.

Atlantic [ɒt'læntɪk] n Ατλαντικός.

atlas ['ætləs] n άτλας.

atmosphere ['ætməsfɪə*] n ατμόσφαιρα.

atmospheric [ætməs'ferɪk] a ατμοσφαιρικός.

atom ['ætəm] n άτομο || ~**ic bomb** n ατομική βόμβα || ~**ic energy** n ατομική ενέργεια.

atonement [ə'təʊnmənt] n έκτιση, επανόρθωση.

atrocious [ə'trəʊʃəs] a φρικτός, φρικαλέος.

atrocity [ə'trɒsɪtɪ] n αγριότητα, φρίκη (εγκλήματος).

attach [ə'tætʃ] vt συνδέω, προσαρτώ, (επι)συνάπτω || **to ~ importance to** δίνω σημασία σε || ~**ed** a αποσπασμένος, προσαρτημένος || ~**ment** n προσάρτηση, προσκόλληση || (devotion to) αφοσίωση, στοργή.

attaché [ə'tæʃeɪ] n ακόλουθος || ~ **case** n χαρτοφύλακας.

attack [ə'tæk] n επίθεση, προσβολή ♦ vt επιτίθεμαι, προσβάλλω || ~**er** n επιτιθέμενος.

attain [ə'teɪn] vt φθάνω, κατορθώνω || ~**ment** n επίτευξη, πραγματοποίηση || (learning) γνώση, προσόν nt.

attempt [ə'tempt] n απόπειρα, προσπάθεια, δοκιμή ♦ vt αποπειρώμαι, προσπαθώ.

attend [ə'tend] vt (be present) παρευρίσκομαι || (visit) επισκέπτομαι, συχνάζω || (wait on) υπηρετώ ♦ vi (listen) εισακούω || (look after)

ασχολούμαι || **to ~ to** προσέχω, φροντίζω || ~**ance** n (presence) συμμετοχή, παρουσία || ~**ant** n ακόλουθος, υπηρέτης/τρια m/f ♦ a συνοδεύων.

attention [ə'tenʃən] n προσοχή || (care) περιποίηση, φροντίδα.

attentive [ə'tentɪv] a προσεκτικός, περιποιητικός.

attest [ə'test] vt επικυρώ, βεβαιώ, καταθέτω σαν μάρτυρας.

attic ['ætɪk] n σοφίτα.

attitude ['ætɪtjuːd] n στάση.

attorney [ə'tɜːnɪ] n δικηγόρος, πληρεξούσιος || **district** ~ n εισαγγελέας || **A ~ general** n γενικός εισαγγελέας || **power of** ~ n πληρεξούσιο.

attract [ə'trækt] vt ελκύω, έλκω, τραβώ, γοητεύω || ~**ion** n (PHYS) έλξη || (of person) γοητεία || (THEAT) ατραξιόν f inv || ~**ive** a ελκυστικός, γοητευτικός.

attribute ['ætrɪbjuːt] n χαρακτηριστικό γνώρισμα nt|| (GRAM) επίθετο ♦ [ə'trɪbjuːt] vt: **to ~ to** αποδίδω (σε).

auburn ['ɔːbən] a πυρόξανθος.

auction ['ɔːkʃən] n πλειστηριασμός, δημοπρασία ♦ vt πλειστηριάζω, βγάζω στο σφυρί || ~**eer** n προϊστάμενος δημοπρασιών.

audacious [ɔː'deɪʃəs] a τολμηρός, παράτολμος || (insolent) θρασύς, αναιδής.

audacity [ɔː'dæsɪtɪ] n τόλμη, θάρρος nt|| (insolence) αναίδεια.

audible ['ɔːdɪbl] a ακουστός, ακουόμενος.

audience ['ɔːdɪəns] n (formal interview) ακρόαση || (gathering) ακροατήριο || (THEAT) θεατές mpl.

audit ['ɔːdɪt] n έλεγχος, επαλήθευση ♦ vt ελέγχω || ~**or** n ελεγκτής || (student) ακροατής.

audition [ɔːˈdɪʃən] n ακρόαση (τραγουδιστού κτλ).

auditorium [ɔːdɪˈtɔːrɪəm] n αίθουσα, θέατρο.

augment [ɔːgˈment] vt (επ)αυξάνω, μεγαλώνω.

augur [ˈɔːgə*] vi προοιωνίζομαι, προβλέπω.

August [ˈɔːgəst] n Αύγουστος.

aunt [ɑːnt] n θεία || ~y, ~ie n θείτσα.

aura [ˈɔːrə] n ατμόσφαιρα, φωτοστέφανος.

auspices [ˈɔːspɪsɪz] npl αιγίδα || (omens) οιωνοί || **under the ~ of** υπό την αιγίδα του.

auspicious [ɔːsˈpɪʃəs] a ευνοϊκός, ευοίωνος.

austere [ɒsˈtɪə*] a αυστηρός.

austerity [ɒsˈterɪtɪ] n αυστηρότητα || (of habits etc) λιτότητα.

Australia [ɒsˈtreɪlɪə] n Αυστραλία || ~n n Αυστραλός/ίδα m/f ♦ a αυστραλιακός.

Austria [ˈɒstrɪə] n Αυστρία || ~n n Αυστριακός/ή m/f ♦ a αυστριακός.

authentic [ɔːˈθentɪk] a αυθεντικός, γνήσιος.

author [ˈɔːθə*] n συγγραφέας || (cause) δημιουργός, πρωταίτιος.

authoritarian [ɔːθɔrɪˈteərɪən] a απολυταρχικός.

authority [ɔːˈθɒrɪtɪ] n εξουσία, άδεια, εντολή || (specialist) αυθεντία || (POL.) υπηρεσία.

authorize [ˈɔːθəraɪz] vt εξουσιοδοτώ, επιτρέπω.

auto [ˈɔːtəu] n (US) = **automobile**.

autobiography [ɔːtəubaɪˈɒgrəfɪ] n αυτοβιογραφία.

autograph [ˈɔːtəgrɑːf] n αυτόγραφο.

automatic [ɔːtəˈmætɪk] a αυτόματος.

automation [ɔːtəˈmeɪʃən] n αυτοματοποίηση.

automaton [ɔːˈtɒmətən] n αυτόματο.

automobile [ˈɔːtəməbiːl] n (US) αυτοκίνητο, αμάξι.

autonomous [ɔːˈtɒnəməs] a αυτόνομος.

autopsy [ˈɔːtɒpsɪ] n νεκροψία.

autumn [ˈɔːtəm] n φθινόπωρο.

auxiliary [ɔːgˈzɪlɪərɪ] a βοηθητικός, επικουρικός.

avail [əˈveɪl] n χρησιμότητα, ωφέλεια, όφελος ♦ vti ωφελώ, βοηθώ, εξυπηρετώ.

availability [əveɪlə·bɪlɪtɪ] n διαθεσιμότητα.

available [əˈveɪləbl] a διαθέσιμος, προσιτός.

avalanche [ˈævəlɑːnʃ] n χιονοστιβάδα || (fig) συρροή, πλημμύρα.

avant-garde [ˈævɑ̃ːˈgɑːd] n προφυλακή.

Ave. abbr of **Avenue**.

avenge [əˈvendʒ] vt εκδικούμαι.

avenue [ˈævənjuː] n λεωφόρος f.

average [ˈævərɪdʒ] n μέσο, μέσος όρος || (NAUT) αβαρία ♦ a μέσος, μέτριος ♦ vti εξάγω το μέσο όρο.

averse [əˈvɜːs] a αντίθετος εναντίος || **to be ~ to** εναντιούμαι σε.

aversion [əˈvɜːʃən] n αποστροφή, απέχθεια || (col) αντιπάθεια.

avert [əˈvɜːt] vt αποστρέφω || (prevent) αποτρέπω, απομακρύνω.

aviary [ˈeɪvɪərɪ] n πτηνοτροφείο.

aviation [eɪvɪˈeɪʃən] n αεροπορία.

avid [ˈævɪd] a: ~ **for** άπληστος αχόρταγος || ~**ly** ad άπληστα.

avocado [ævəˈkɑːdəu] n αβοκάντο.

avoid [əˈvɔɪd] vt αποφεύγω || ~**able** a αποφευκτός || ~**ance** n αποφυγή.

await [əˈweɪt] vt αναμένω, περιμένω.

awake [ə'weɪk] (irreg v) vti ξυπνώ, αφυπνίζω, εφυπνίζομαι ♦ a ξύπνιος, άγρυπνος.

awakening [ə'weɪknɪŋ] n αφύπνιση, ξύπνημα nt.

award [ə'wɔːd] n βραβείο || (LAW) διαιτησία ♦ vt επιδικάζω || (reward) απονέμω.

aware [ə'weə*] a: ~ (of) πληροφορημένος, γνώστης || ~ness n συνείδηση.

away [ə'weɪ] ad μακριά || (absent) απουσιάζω, λείπω.

awe [ɔː] n φόβος, τρόμος || (deep respect) σεβασμός ♦ vt τρομάζω || ~-inspiring a επιβλητικός.

awful ['ɔːfəl] a (very bad) τρομερός, φοβερός || ~ly ad τρομερά, τρομακτικά.

awhile [ə'waɪl] ad για λίγο, μια στιγμή.

awkward ['ɔːkwəd] a αδέξιος, ανεπιτήδειος.

awning ['ɔːnɪŋ] n σκηνή, τέντα.

awoke [ə'wəʊk] pt, pp of **awake**.

awry [ə'raɪ] ad λοξός, στραβός || to go ~ πηγαίνω στραβά.

ax [æks] (US) = **axe**.

axe [æks] n τσεκούρι ♦ vt περιορίζω || (dismiss) απολύω.

axiom ['æksɪəm] n αξίωμα nt.

axle ['æksl] n άξονας.

ay(e) [aɪ] interj (yes) ναι || the ~es npl τα ναι, τα υπέρ.

B

B.A. see **bachelor**.

babble ['bæbl] n μωρολογία, τραύλισμα nt ♦ vi τραυλίζω, φλυαρώ.

babe [beɪb] n μωρό, μπέμπης.

baboon [bə'buːn] n μπαμπουίνος.

baby ['beɪbɪ] n βρέφος nt, νήπιο, μωρό || ~ carriage n (US)

καροτσάκι μωρού || ~ish a μωρουδίστικος || ~-sit vi μπέιμπισιτ, φυλάω νήπιο, προσέχω μωρό || ~-sitter n φύλακας νηπίων, μπέιμπισιτερ.

bachelor ['bætʃələ*] n άγαμος, εργένης || B~ of Arts (B.A.) n πτυχιούχος πανεπιστημίου (θεωρητικών επιστημών) || B~ of Science (B.Sc.) n πτυχιούχος πανεπιστημίου (θετικών επιστημών).

back [bæk] n (person, horse) πλάτη, νώτα ntpl || (house etc) το πίσω μέρος || (SPORT) μπακ nt inv ♦ vt (support) υποστηρίζω || (movement) κάνω πίσω || (SPORT) ποντάρω ♦ vi (go backwards) οπισθοχωρώ, κάνω πίσω ♦ a οπίσθιος, πισινός ♦ ad πίσω, προς τα πίσω || (again) πάλι || (in time) εδώ και λίγα χρόνια || to ~ out vt ανακαλώ, αποσύρομαι || (col) το σκάω || to ~ up vt (COMPUT) εξασφαλίζω || ~biting n κουτσομπολιό || ~bone n ραχοκοκαλιά || (firmness) θάρρος nt, κουράγιο || ~-cloth n φόντο || ~er n (SPORT) παίκτης || (COMM) χρηματοδότης || ~fire n πρόωρη έκρηξη || ~ground n (scene) βάθος nt, φόντο || (information) προϊστορία, το ιστορικό || (education etc) προσόντα ntpl || ~hand n (blow) ανάποδη καρπαζιά || ~handed a ύπουλος || ~handed compliment διφορούμενο κομπλιμέντο, διφορούμενη φιλοφρόνηση || ~ing n υποστήριξη || (movement) οπισθοδρόμηση || ~ number n (newspaper etc) παληό φύλλο || ~pay n καθυστερούμενος μισθός|||| ~side n (col) πισινός || ~up disk n (COMPUT) εφεδρικός δίσκος || ~ward a οπίσθιος, προς τα πίσω || (child etc) καθυστερημένος || ~wards ad προς τα πίσω || (flow) αντίθετα || ~ yard n πίσω αυλή.

bacon ['beɪkən] *n* καπνιστό χοιρινό, μπέικον *nt inv.*

bacteria [bæk'tɪərɪə] *npl* μικρόβια *ntpl.*

bad [bæd] *a* κακός, άσχημος.

badge [bædʒ] *n* διακριτικό, σήμα *nt*, έμβλημα *nt.*

badger ['bædʒə*] *n* ασβός ♦ *vt* παρενοχλώ, βασανίζω.

badly ['bædlɪ] *ad* κακά, άσχημα || ~ **off** σε δύσκολη οικονομική κατάσταση φτωχός.

bad-tempered ['bæd'tempəd] *a* δύστροπος, γκρινιάρης.

baffle ['bæfl] *vt* (*puzzle*) ματαιώνω, τα χάνω.

bag [bæg] *n* σάκκος, σακκούλα || (*handbag*) τσάντα ♦ *vt* σακκουλιάζω || (*capture etc*) σκοτώνω, πιάνω || ~**ful** *n* σακκουλιά.

baggage ['bægɪdʒ] *n* αποσκευές *fpl*, βαλίτσες *pl.*

bagpipes ['bægpaɪps] *npl* γκάιντα.

bail [beɪl] *n* εγγύηση ♦ *vt* (*prisoner*) ελευθερώνω με εγγύηση || **to ~ out** (*boat*) βγάζω τα νερά, αδειάζω || *see also* **bale.**

bailiff ['beɪlɪf] *n* δικαστικός κλητήρας.

bait [beɪt] *n* δόλωμα *nt* ♦ *vt* δελεάζω, δολώνω || (*harass*) βασανίζω.

bake [beɪk] *vt* ψήνω σε φούρνο ♦ *vi* ψήνομαι || ~**r** *n* φούρναρης || ~**ry** *n* φουρνάρικο.

baking ['beɪkɪŋ] *n* ψήσιμο.

balance ['bæləns] *n* ζυγός, ζυγαριά || (*equilibrium*) ισορροπία || (*of account*) υπόλοιπο|| (ECON) ισολογισμός || *vt* ζυγίζω, σταθμίζω|| (*counterbalance*) ισορροπώ, ισοζυγίζω || ~**d** *a* ισορροπημένος || (*equal*) ίσος, ισοδύναμος || ~ **sheet** *n* ισολογισμός.

balcony ['bælkənɪ] *n* εξώστης, μπαλκόνι.

bald [bɔːld] *a* φαλακρός || (*plain*) γυμνός, ξηρός.

bale [beɪl] *n* δέμα *nt*, μπάλα, κόλος || **to ~** *or* **bail out** (AVIAT) πηδώ με αλεξίπτωτο.

Balkan ['bɔːlkən] *a* Βαλκανικός.

ball [bɔːl] *n* σφαίρα, μπάλα, τόπι || (*dance*) χοροεσπερίδα, χορός.

ballad ['bæləd] *n* μπαλάντα.

ballast ['bæləst] *n* έρμα, σαβούρα.

ball bearing ['bɔːl'bɛərɪŋ] *n* σφαιροτριβέας, ρουλεμάν *nt inv.*

ballerina [bælə'riːnə] *n* μπαλαρίνα.

ballet ['bæleɪ] *n* μπαλέτο.

balloon [bə'luːn] *n* αερόστατο, μπαλόνι.

ballot ['bælət] *n* ψηφοδέλτιο.

ballpoint (pen) ['bɔːlpɔɪnt (pɛn)] *n* στυλό, πένα διαρκείας.

ballroom ['bɔːlrum] *n* αίθουσα χορού.

balmy ['bɑːmɪ] *a* γλυκός, κατευναστικός || (*col*) παλαβός.

balustrade [bæləs'treɪd] *n* κιγκλίδωμα *nt*, κάγκελλα *ntpl.*

bamboo [bæm'buː] *n* μπαμπού *nt inv*, καλάμι.

ban [bæn] *n* απαγόρευση || (*church*) αφορισμός ♦ *vt* απαγορεύω.

banal [bə'nɑːl] *a* κοινός, χυδαίος.

banana [bə'nɑːnə] *n* μπανάνα.

band [bænd] *n* δεσμός, δέσιμο, στεφάνι || (*group*) ομάδα, συντροφιά || (MUS) ορχήστρα, μπάντα ♦ *vi* (+ *together*) συνασπίζομαι ♦ *vt* (*tie*) δένω.

bandage ['bændɪdʒ] *n* επίδεσμος, φασκιά.

bandit ['bændɪt] *n* ληστής.

bandy(-legged) ['bændɪ('lɛgd] *a* στραβοπόδης, στραβοκάνης.

bang [bæŋ] *n* (*blow*) κτύπημα *nt*|| (*noise*) θόρυβος, κρότος ♦ *vti* κτυπώ, κρούω.

banish ['bænɪʃ] *vt* εξορίζω, εκτοπίζω.

banister(s) ['bænɪstə*(z)] *n(pl)*
κιγκλίδωμα *nt*, κάγκελλα *ntpl*.

banjo ['bændʒəʊ] *n* μπάντζο.

bank [bæŋk] *n* τράπεζα || *(ground)*
ανάχωμα *nt*, ύψωμα *nt* || *(of river)*
όχθη ♦ *vt (tilt)* κλίνω, στρέφω || *(pile
up)* σωριάζω || *(money)* καταθέτω,
βάζω || ~ **account** *n* τραπεζιτικός
λογαριασμός || ~**er** *n* τραπεζίτης ||
~ **holiday** *n* αργία τραπεζών ||
~**note** *n* τραπεζογραμμάτιο,
μπανκνότα.

bankrupt ['bæŋkrʌpt] *n*
πτωχεύσας, χρεωκοπημένος ♦ *vt*
πτωχεύω || ~**cy** *n* πτώχευση,
χρεωκοπία.

banner ['bænə*] *n* σημαία,
μπαντιέρα.

banns [bænz] *npl* αγγελία γάμου.

banquet ['bæŋkwɪt] *n* συμπόσιο,
γλέντι, τσιμπούσι.

baptism ['bæptɪzəm] *n* βάφτισμα *nt*.

baptize [bæp'taɪz] *vt* βαφτίζω.

bar [baː*] *n (rod)* ράβδος *f*, κοντάρι ||
(of soap etc) κομμάτι, πλάκα || *(pub)*
μπάρ *nt inv*, ποτοπωλείο || *(obstacle)*
φραγμός, εμπόδιο || *(in court)* εδώλιο
|| *(MUS)* μπάρα ♦ *vt (fasten)* κλείνω,
αμπαρώνω, κιγκλιδώνω || *(hinder)*
φράσσω, εμποδίζω || *(exclude)*
απαγορεύω, αποκλείω || **the B** ~
δικηγορικό επάγγελμα *nt*.

barbaric [baː'bærɪk] *a* βάρβαρος,
αγροίκος.

barbarity [baː'bærɪtɪ] *n*
βαρβαρότητα, αγριότητα.

barbarous ['baːbərəs] *a* βάρβαρος.

barbecue ['baːbɪkjuː] *n* σχάρα.

barbed wire ['baːbd'waɪə*] *n*
συρματόπλεγμα *nt*.

barber ['baːbə*] *n* κουρέας,
μπαρμπέρης.

barbiturate [baː'bɪtjurɪt] *n*
βαρβιτουρικό.

bare [bɛə*] *a* γυμνός || *(living etc)*
λιγοστός ♦ *vt* γυμνώνω || *(reveal)*

αποκαλύπτω || ~**back** *ad* χωρίς
σέλλα || ~**faced** *a* ξεδιάντροπος,
αναιδής || ~**foot** *a* ξυπόλητος || ~**ly**
ad μόλις.

bargain ['baːgɪn] *n* συναλλαγή,
αγορά || *(bought cheaply)* ευκαιρία ||
into the ~ επί πλέον, από πάνω.

barge [baːdʒ] *n* φορτηγίδα, μαούνα
|| **to** ~ **in** *vi* επεμβαίνω.

baritone ['bærɪtəʊn] *n* βαρύτονος.

bark [baːk] *n (tree)* φλοιός, φλούδα
|| *(dog)* γαύγισμα *nt* ♦ *vi (dog)*
γαυγίζω.

barley ['baːlɪ] *n* κριθάρι.

barmaid ['baːmeɪd] *n* σερβιτόρα
του μπαρ.

barman ['baːmən] *n* μπάρμαν *m
inv*.

barn [baːn] *n (σιτ)*αποθήκη || *(US)*
στάύλος.

barnacle ['baːnəkl] *n* ανατίφη,
στρειδόνι.

barometer [bə'rɒmɪtə*] *n*
βαρόμετρο.

baron ['bærən] *n* βαρώνος || ~**ess** *n*
βαρώνη.

barracks ['bærəks] *npl* στρατώνας,
μπαράκα.

barrage ['bæraːʒ] *n (dam)* φράγμα
nt || *(MIL)* πυρ *nt* φραγμού, μπαράζ
nt inv.

barrel ['bærəl] *n* βυτίο, βαρέλι ||
(measure) βαρέλι || *(gun)* κάννη.

barren ['bærən] *a* στείρος, άγονος.

barricade [bærɪ'keɪd] *n*
προπέτασμα *nt* φράγμα *nt* ♦ *vt*
φράσσω.

barrier ['bærɪə*] *n* φραγμός ||
(obstruction) εμπόδιο.

barrister ['bærɪstə*] *n* δικηγόρος
m/f.

barrow ['bærəʊ] *n (cart)*
μονότροχο, χειράμαξα.

bartender ['baːtendə*] *n (US)* =
barman.

base [beɪs] *n* βάση ♦ *vt* βασίζω,

στηρίζω ♦ a ταπεινός, πρόστυχος || *(inferior)* φθηνός || ~**ball** n μπέιζ-μπωλ *nt inv* || ~**ment** n υπόγειο.

bash [bæʃ] *vt (col)* κτυπώ, τσακίζω.

bashful ['bæʃful] a ντροπαλός.

basic ['beisik] a βασικός, θεμελιώδης || ~**ally** ad βασικά.

basilica [bə'zilikə] n βασιλική.

basin ['beisn] n λεκάνη || *(NAUT)* νεωδόχος f, δεξαμενή.

basis ['beisis] n βάση.

bask [baːsk] vi λιάζομαι.

basket ['baːskit] n καλάθι, πανέρι || ~**ball** n καλαθόσφαιρα, μπάσκετ *nt inv*.

bass [beis] n *(MUS)* βαθύφωνος, μπάσος.

bassoon [bə'suːn] n φαγκότο.

bastard ['baːstəd] n νόθος/n m/f, μπάσταρδος.

baste [beist] vt *(sewing)* παρραράβω, ξυλίζω, ραβδίζω || *(cooking)* βουτυρώνω.

bastion ['bæstiən] n *(stronghold)* προμαχώνας.

bat [bæt] n *(SPORT)* ρόπαλο, μαγγούρα || *(ZOOL)* νυκτερίδα ♦ vi κτυπώ με το ρόπαλο || **off one's own** ~ εξ ιδίας πρωτοβουλίας.

batch [bætʃ] n φουρνιά (ψωμί) || *(set)* σωρός, ομάδα.

bath [baːθ] n λουτρό, μπάνιο || *(tub)* λουτήρας, μπανιέρα ♦ vt λούω, μπανιαρίζω || ~ npl δημόσια λουτρά *ntpl*, μπάνια *ntpl*, χαμάμ *nt inv* || ~**chair** n καροτσάκι (αναπήρων), αναπηρική καρέκλα.

bathe [beið] vi λούομαι, κάνω μπάνιο ♦ vt λούω, πλένω || ~**r** n κολυμβητής/τρια m/f, λουόμενος/η m/f.

bathing ['beiðiŋ] n κολύμπι || ~**cap** n σκούφος του μπάνιου || ~**costume** n μπανιερό, μαγιό *nt inv*.

bathmat ['baːθmæt] n ψάθα του μπάνιου.

bathroom ['baːθrum] n λουτρό.

bath towel ['baːθtauəl] n πετσέτα του μπάνιου.

baton ['bætən] n ράβδος f|| *(conductor's)* μπαγκέτο || *(truncheon)* γκλόμπ *nt inv*.

battalion [bə'tæliən] n τάγμα *nt*.

batter ['bætə*] n κουρκούτι ♦ vt κτυπώ, κοπανίζω.

battery ['bætəri] n *(cell)* συστοιχία, πυροβολαρχία || *(MIL)* πυροβολαρχία || *(cell)* συστοιχία.

battle ['bætl] n μάχη ♦ vi μάχομαι, πολεμώ || ~**field** n πεδίο μάχης, πολεμίστρες fpl || ~**ments** npl επάλξεις fpl, παραπέτο, πολεμίστρες fpl || ~**ship** n θωρηκτό.

bawdy ['bɔːdi] a ασελγής, αισχρός.

bawl [bɔːl] vi κραυγάζω, σκούζω.

bay [bei] n *(of sea)* κόλπος, κόρφος || *(tree)* δάφνη || **at** ~ σε δύσκολη θέση, στα στενά.

bayonet ['beiənit] n ξιφολόγχη, μπαγιονέττα.

bay window ['bei'windəu] n παράθυρο σε προεξοχή τοίχου.

bazaar [bə'zaː*] n παζάρι || *(for charity)* φιλανθρωπική αγορά.

B.B.C. abbr of British Broadcasting Corporation.

B.C. ad *(abbr of before Christ)* π.Χ.

be [biː] *(irreg v)* vi *(exist)* είμαι, υπάρχω || *(live)* είμαι, ζω, κατοικώ || *(stay)* είμαι, κάνω || *(cost)* είμαι, κοστίζω || *(location)* είμαι, ευρίσκομαι || *(visit)* είμαι, επισκέπτομαι || *(take place)* είμαι, γίνομαι.

beach [biːtʃ] n παραλία, ακρογιαλιά ♦ vt προσγιαλώ, αράζω || *(run aground)* προσαράσσω.

beacon ['biːkən] n φάρος, φανάρι.

bead [biːd] n χάντρα, πέρλα || *(perspiration)* σταγονίδι.

beak [biːk] n ράμφος *nt*, μύτη.

beaker ['biːkə*] n γυάλινο ποτήρι.

beam [biːm] n δοκός f, δοκάρι || *(of*

balance) ζυγοστάτης, μπάτσο || *(of light)* αχτίδα, δέσμη || *(smile)* λάμψη, ακτινοβολία ♦ vi ακτινοβολώ, λάμπω.

bean [biːn] n *(broad)* κουκί || *(kidney* φασόλι || *(string)* φασολάκι.

bear [bɛə*] *(irreg v)* n αρκούδα ♦ vt *(carry)* φέρω, βαστώ, σηκώνω || *(support)* υποβαστάζω, στηρίζω || *(put up with)* υποφέρω, αντέχω, ανέχομαι || *(produce)* γεννώ, παράγω || ~**able** a υποφερτός, ανεκτός.

beard [biəd] n γένι, μούσι || ~**ed** a με γένεια.

bearing ['bɛəriŋ] n *(behaviour)* συμπεριφορά, ύφος nt || *(relation)* σχέση, έννοια || ~**s** npl: **I lose my** ~**s** χάνω τον προσανατολισμό.

beast [biːst] n ζώο, κτήνος nt, θηρίο || *(person)* ζώο, παλιάνθρωπος || ~**ly** a κτηνώδης, βρώμικος.

beat [biːt] *(irreg v)* n *(stroke)* κτύπημα nt || *(pulsation)* σφυγμός, παλμός || *(of policeman)* περιπολία || *(MUS)* χρόνος, μέτρο ♦ vt κτυπώ, δέρνω, ματσουκώνω || *(defeat)* υπερτερώ, νικώ || **to** ~ **about the bush** γυρίζω γύρω-γύρω από ένα θέμα || **to** ~ **time** κρατώ το χρόνο || **to** ~ **off** vt διώχνω, απωθώ || **to** ~ **up** vt σπάζω στο ξύλο || ~**en track** n πεπατημένη || ~**er** n *(for eggs, cream)* κτυπητήρι.

beautiful ['bjuːtiful] a ωραίος, εξαίσιος, υπέροχος || ~**ly** ad θαυμάσια, υπέροχα.

beauty ['bjuːti] n ομορφιά || *(woman)* καλλονή.

beaver ['biːvə*] n κάστορι, κάστορας.

because [bi'kɔz] cj διότι, γιατί, επειδή || ~ **of** εξαιτίας (+ *genitive*).

beckon ['bekən] vt νεύω, κάνω νόημα.

become [bi'kʌm] vt *(befit)* αρμόζω, ταιριάζω ♦ vi γίνομαι, καταντώ.

becoming [bi'kʌmiŋ] a αρμόζων *(dress etc)* ταιριαστός, που πηγαίνει.

bed [bed] n κρεββάτι || *(of river)* κοίτη || *(foundation)* στρώμα nt, στρώση || *(garden)* πρασιά || ~ **and breakfast** n δωμάτιο με πρωινό || ~ **clothes** npl σεντόνια ntpl και κουβέρτες fpl || ~**ding** n στρώματα ntpl.

bedlam ['bedləm] n *(uproar)* φασαρία, θόρυβος.

bedraggled [bi'drægld] a κουρελιασμένος.

bedridden ['bedridn] a κρεββατωμένος, κατάκοιτος.

bedroom ['bedrum] n υπνοδωμάτιο, κρεββατοκάμαρα.

bed-sitter ['bed'sitə*] n υπνοδωμάτιο.

bee [biː] n μέλισσα.

beech [biːtʃ] n οξυά.

beef [biːf] n βωδινό.

beehive ['biːhaiv] n κυψέλη.

beeline ['biːlain] n: **to make a** ~ **for** πηγαίνω κατ, ευθείαν.

been [biːn] pp of **be**.

beer [biə*] n μπύρα.

beetle ['biːtl] n σκαθάρι.

beetroot ['biːtruːt] n πατζάρι, κοκκινογούλι.

befall [bi'fɔːl] vti συμβαίνω, τυχαίνω.

before [bi'fɔː*] prep *(in place)* προ, εμπρός, ενώπιον || *(of time)* πριν, προ ♦ cj προ, πριν, πριν να ♦ ad *(of place)* εμπρός, προ, μπροστά || *(of time)* πριν, πρωτύτερα, προτού.

befriend [bi'frend] vt βοηθώ, προστατεύω.

beg [beg] vti ζητώ, παρακαλώ || *(for alms)* ζητιανεύω.

began [bi'gæn] pt of **begin**.

beggar ['begə*] n ζητιάνος/α m/f, επαίτης.

begin [bi'gin] *(irreg v)* vti αρχίζω, αρχινώ || **to** ~ **with** πρώτα-πρώτα, πριν ν'αρχίσουμε || ~**ner** n

αρχάριος/α m/f, πρωτάρης/α m/f||
~ning η αρχή.

begrudge [bɪ'grʌdʒ] vt δίνω με το
ζόρι, λυπούμαι.

begun [bɪ'gʌn] pp of **begin**.

behalf [bɪ'hɑːf] η εκ μέρους, υπέρ ||
on ~ of για λογαριασμό του, εκ
μέρους.

behave [bɪ'heɪv] vi
(συμπερι)φέρομαι.

behaviour, (US) **behavior**
[bɪ'heɪvjə*] η συμπεριφορά,
φέρσιμο.

behind [bɪ'haɪnd] prep πίσω από ||
(time) καθυστερημένος ♦ ad
όπισθεν, πίσω από ♦ η πισινός.

behold [bɪ'həʊld] vt βλέπω,
αντικρύζω.

beige [beɪʒ] a μπεζ.

being ['biːɪŋ] η ύπαρξη, γέννηση ||
(person) ον vt, είναι et inv.

belch [beltʃ] vti ρεύομαι.

belfry ['belfrɪ] η καμπαναριό.

Belgian ['beldʒən] η
Βέλγος/Βελγίδα m/f ♦ a βελγικός.

Belgium ['beldʒəm] η Βέλγιο.

belie [bɪ'laɪ] vt διαψεύδω, ξεγελώ.

belief [bɪ'liːf] η (trust) πίστη || (idea)
γνώμη, δοξασία.

believable [bɪ'liːvəbl] a πιστευτός.

believe [bɪ'liːv] vt πιστεύω, δέχομαι
♦ vi πιστεύω, έχω εμπιστοσύνη ||
~r η πιστός/ή m/f.

belittle [bɪ'lɪtl] vt υποτιμώ,
περιφρονώ.

bell [bel] η καμπάνα || (in house)
κουδούνι.

belligerent [bɪ'lɪdʒərənt] a (fig)
καυγατζής.

bellow ['beləʊ] vti μουγγρίζω,
μουγκαρίζω ♦ μουγκρητό.

bellows ['beləʊz] npl φυσερό.

belly ['belɪ] η κοιλιά.

belong [bɪ'lɒŋ] vi ανήκω || **it does
not ~ here** δεν ανήκει εδώ || **to ~
to** vt ανήκω σε || (a place)

kατάγομαι από||~ings npl
περιουσία, υπάρχοντα ntpl.

beloved [bɪ'lʌvɪd] a
πολυαγαπημένος ♦ η αγαπητός.

below [bɪ'ləʊ] prep υπό, κάτω από,
κάτω θεν ♦ ad από κάτω.

belt [belt] η ζώνη, ταινία || (round
waist) ζωνάρι, λουρί ♦ vt ζώνω ||
(beat) δέρνω με λουρί.

bench [bentʃ] η κάθισμα nt, πάγκος ||
(workshop) τεζάκι, πάγκος || (of judge)
έδρα.

bend [bend] (irreg v) η καμπή,
στροφή, γωνία ♦ vt κάμπτω, λυγίζω
|| (NAUT) δένω ♦ vi (stoop) σκύβω.

beneath [bɪ'niːθ] prep κάτωθεν,
χαμηλότερα, υπό ♦ ad από κάτω.

benefactor ['benɪfæktə*] η
ευεργέτης, δωρητής.

beneficial [benɪ'fɪʃəl] a ωφέλιμος,
χρήσιμος.

benefit ['benɪfɪt] η όφελος nt,
ωφέλεια ♦ vt ωφελώ ♦ vi
επωφελούμαι.

benevolent [bɪ'nevələnt] a
αγαθοεργός, καλοπροαίρετος.

bent [bent] η (inclination) κλίση, ροπή
♦ a: **to be ~ on** αποφασισμένος να
♦ pt, pp of **bend**.

bequeath [bɪ'kwiːð] vt κληροδοτώ,
αφήνω.

bequest [bɪ'kwest] η κληροδότημα.

bereaved [bɪ'riːvd] η (person)
τεθλιμμένος.

bereavement [bɪ'riːvmənt] η
απώλεια, πένθος nt.

beret ['bereɪ] η μπερέ nt inv,
σκούφος.

berry ['berɪ] η ρόγα, μούρο.

berserk [bə'sɜːk] a: **to go ~**
γίνομαι έξω φρενών.

berth [bɜːθ] η (anchoring) όρμος ||
(ship, train) κλίνη, καμπίνα ♦ vt
προσορμίζω, πλευρίζω ♦ vi
αγκυροβολώ, πλευρίζω.

beseech [bɪ'siːtʃ] (irreg v) vt
ικετεύω, εκλιπαρώ.

beset [bɪ'set] vt κυκλώνω,
περισφίγγω.

beside [bɪ'saɪd] prep πλάι, κοντά,
δίπλα || **to be ~ o.s.** είμαι εκτός
εαυτού.

besides [bɪ'saɪdz] prep εκτός από ♦
ad εκτός αυτού, ακόμη, άλλωστε.

besiege [bɪ'siːdʒ] vt πολιορκώ.

best [best] a καλύτερος ♦ ad
καλύτερα || **at ~** το καλύτερο,
ακόμα και || **to make the ~ of it**
όσο μπορώ καλύτερα || **~ man** n
παράνυμφος, κουμπάρος.

bestow [bɪ'stəʊ] vt παρέχω,
απονέμω.

bestseller ['best'selə*] n βιβλίο
μεγάλης κυκλοφορίας.

bet [bet] (irreg v) n στοίχημα nt ♦ vt
στοιχηματίζω, βάζω στοίχημα.

betray [bɪ'treɪ] vt προδίδω,
αποκαλύπτω || (be false) εξαπατώ ||
~al n προδοσία.

better ['betə*] a καλύτερος ♦ ad
καλύτερα ♦ vt καλυτερεύω,
βελτιώνω ♦ n: **to get the ~** of νικώ
κάποιο, υπερέχω || **he thought ~** of
it άλλαξε γνώμη || **~ off** a (richer)
πιο εύπορος, πλουσιότερος.

betting ['betɪŋ] n στοίχημα(τα) nt.

between [bɪ'twiːn] prep μεταξύ,
ανάμεσα ♦ ad ανάμεσα.

beverage ['bevərɪdʒ] n ποτό.

beware [bɪ'weə*] vt προσέχω,
φοβούμαι || **'~ of the dog'**
'προσοχή, σκύλος'.

bewildered [bɪ'wɪldəd] a
ζαλισμένος, χαμένος.

bewitching [bɪ'wɪtʃɪŋ] a
γοητευτικός, μαγευτικός.

beyond [bɪ'jɒnd] prep (of place) πέρα
από || (of time) πέραν του || (in
addition) εκτός, πέρα από ♦ ad πέρα
από, εκεί κάτω.

bias ['baɪəs] n (slant) λοξότητα ||

(prejudice) προκατάληψη, συμπάθεια
|| **~(s)ed** a προκατειλημμένος,
επηρεασμένος.

bib [bɪb] n σαλιάρα, μπούστο.

Bible ['baɪbl] n Βίβλος f, Ευαγγέλιο.

bibliography [bɪblɪ'ɒgrəfɪ] n
βιβλιογραφία.

bicker ['bɪkə*] vi καυγαδίζω || **~ing**
n καυγάς.

bicycle ['baɪsɪkl] n ποδήλατο.

bid [bɪd] (irreg v) n προσφορά ||
(CARDS) δήλωση ♦ vt (command)
διατάσσω, προστάζω || (offer)
προσφέρω, πλειοδοτώ || (greeting)
χαιρετώ || (goodbye) αποχαιρετώ ||
~der n (person) πλειοδότης ||
~ding n (order) εντολή, παραγγελία
|| (offer) πλειοδοσία.

bidet ['biːdeɪ] n μπιντέ nt inv.

big [bɪg] a μεγάλος, σπουδαίος.

bigamy ['bɪgəmɪ] n διγαμία.

bigot ['bɪgət] n στενοκέφαλος,
φανατικός || **~ed** a στενοκέφαλος ||
~ry n μισαλλοδοξία.

bike [baɪk] n ποδήλατο.

bikini [bɪ'kiːnɪ] n μπικίνι nt inv.

bile [baɪl] n χολή.

bilingual [baɪ'lɪŋgwəl] a
δίγλωσσος.

bill [bɪl] n (notice) αγγελία, αφίσα ||
(account) λογαριασμός || (law)
νομοσχέδιο || (note) χαρτονόμισμα ||
(beak) ράμφος nt, μύτη || (US)
χαρτονόμισμα nt.

billet ['bɪlɪt] n (MIL) κατάλυμα nt ||
(job) θέση.

billfold ['bɪlfəʊld] n (US) πορτοφόλι.

billiards ['bɪlɪədz] n μπιλιάρδο.

billion ['bɪlɪən] n (Brit)
τρισεκατομμύριο || (US)
δισεκατομμύριο.

billy goat ['bɪlɪgəʊt] n τράγος.

bin [bɪn] n κασέλα, κασόνι, κιβώτιο.

bind [baɪnd] (irreg v) vt (tie) δένω ||
(together) προσδένω || (a book) δένω ||
(oblige) δεσμεύω, δένω || **~ing** n

σύνδεση, δέση, δέσιμο || (book) βιβλιοδεσία.

binoculars [bɪˈnɒkjʊləz] npl κιάλια ntpl.

biochemistry [ˈbaɪəʊˈkɛmɪstrɪ] n βιοχημεία.

biography [baɪˈɒɡrəfɪ] n βιογραφία.

biological [baɪəˈlɒdʒɪkəl] a βιολογικός.

biology [baɪˈɒlədʒɪ] n βιολογία.

birch [bɜːtʃ] n (tree) σημύδα || (for whipping) βέργα.

bird [bɜːd] n πουλί || ~'s-eye view n θέα από ψηλά.

birth [bɜːθ] n γέννα, τοκετός || (beginning) γέννηση || **of good** ~ καλής καταγωγής || ~ **certificate** n πιστοποιητικό γεννήσεως || ~ **control** n έλεγχος γεννήσεων || ~ **day** n γενέθλια ntpl || ~ **place** n τόπος γεννήσεως || ~ **rate** n γεννήσεις fpl.

biscuit [ˈbɪskɪt] n παξιμάδι, μπισκότο.

bisect [baɪˈsɛkt] vt διχοτομώ.

bishop [ˈbɪʃəp] n επίσκοπος, δεσπότης.

bit [bɪt] n (piece) κομμάτι || (of tool) τρυπάνι || (of horse) στομίδα, χαβιά, χαλινάρι || (COMPUT) bit nt inv.

bitch [bɪtʃ] n (dog) σκύλα || (unpleasant woman) παλιοθήλυκο.

bite [baɪt] (irreg v) n δάγκωμα nt || (mouthful) μπουκιά ♦ vti δαγκώνω || (insect) τσιμπώ || **a** ~ **to eat** μπουκιά, λίγο φαγητό.

biting [ˈbaɪtɪŋ] a δηκτικός.

bitter [ˈbɪtə*] a πικρός || (feeling) φαρμακερός, δηκτικός, πικρός ♦ n (beer) πικρή μπύρα || **to the** ~ **end** μέχρι τέλους, μέχρι εσχάτων || ~**ness** n πικρία, πίκρα || ~**sweet** a γλυκόπικρος.

bizarre [bɪˈzɑː*] a παράξενος, αλλόκοτος.

blab [blæb] vti τα λέω όλα, προδίδω.

black [blæk] a μαύρος || (without light) σκοτεινός ♦ vt (shoes) βάφω, λουστράρω || (eye) μαυρίζω || ~ **and blue** γεμάτος σημάδια, καταμαυρισμένος || ~**berry** n βατόμουρο || ~**bird** n κότσυφας || ~**board** n πίνακας, μαυροπίνακας || ~**currant** n μαύρο φραγκοστάφυλλο || ~**en** vt μαυρίζω, λερώνω || ~**leg** n απεργοσπάστης || ~**list** n μαύρος πίνακας || ~**mail** vt εκβιάζω || ~**mailer** n εκβιαστής || ~ **market** n μαύρη αγορά || ~**out** n (MIL) συσκότιση || (ELEC) διακοπή ρεύματος || (faint) σκοτοδίνη, λιποθυμία || ~**smith** n σιδεράς.

bladder [ˈblædə*] n κύστη || (of football etc) σαμπρέλλα.

blade [bleɪd] n (leaf etc) φύλλο || (of tool etc) λεπίδα, λάμα || (of oar etc) πτερύγιο, φτερό.

blame [bleɪm] n μομφή, ψόγος, φταίξιμο ♦ vt κατηγορώ, μέμφομαι || ~**less** a άψογος, ανεύθυνος.

bland [blænd] a ήπιος, μειλίχιος.

blank [blæŋk] a (empty) λευκός, άγραφος || (vacant) ανέκφραστος, χαμένα, συγχισμένος ♦ n κενό || (cartridge) άσφαιρο φυσίγγι.

blanket [ˈblæŋkɪt] n κλινοσκέπασμα nt, κουβέρτα.

blare [blɛə*] n δυνατός ήχος, ούρλιασμα nt ♦ vi αντηχώ, διασαλπίζω.

blasphemy [ˈblæsfɪmɪ] n βλαστήμια.

blast [blɑːst] n (gust) φύσημα nt, ριπή || (NAUT) σφύριγμα nt || (MINING) φουρνέλο || n βάζω φουρνέλο || ~**off** n (SPACE) εκτόξευση.

blatant [ˈbleɪtənt] a κραυγαλέος, ολοφάνερος.

blaze [bleɪz] n (fire) φλόγα, ανάφλεξη, φωτιά ♦ vi παίρνω φωτιά

|| (person) εξάπτομαι ♦ vt: to ~ a trail χαράσσω δρόμο.

blazer ['bleizə*] n σπορ σακάκι.

bleach [bli:tʃ] n άσπρισμα nt, μπουγάδα ♦ vt ασπρίζω, ξεβάφω || (hair) αποχρωματίζω.

bleak [bli:k] a ψυχρός, μελαγχολικός.

bleary-eyed ['bliəri'aid] a με θολωμένα μάτια.

bleat [bli:t] n βέλασμα nt ♦ vt βελάζω.

bled [bled] pt, pp of bleed.

bleed [bli:d] (irreg v) vi χύνω αίμα, χάνω αίμα ♦ vt φλεβοτομώ, παίρνω αίμα.

bleeding ['bli:diŋ] a ματωμένος.

blemish ['blemiʃ] n ελάττωμα nt, κηλίδα ♦ vt κηλιδώνω || (reputation) καταστρέφω.

blend [blend] n χαρμάνι, μίγμα nt ♦ vt ανακατεύω, συγχωνεύω ♦ vi (colours etc) ταιριάζω.

bless [bles] vt ευλογώ, δοξάζω || ~ing n ευλογία, ευτύχημα nt.

blew [blu:] pt of blow.

blight [blait] n (disease) ερυσίβη, συρίκι, συναπίδι || (fig) πληγή ♦ vt καταστρέφω.

blimey ['blaimi] excl (col) να με πάρει ο διάβολος.

blind [blaind] a τυφλός, στραβός || (alley etc) αδιέξοδος ♦ n τέντα || (excuse) πρόσχημα nt, υποκρισία ♦ vt τυφλώνω, στραβώνω || ~ fold a με δεμένα μάτια ♦ vt δένω τα μάτια || ~ly ad στα τυφλά, στα στραβά || ~ness n τυφλότητα, στραβωμάρα.

blink [bliŋk] vti ανοιγοκλείνω τα μάτια, μισοκλείνω τα μάτια || ~ers npl παρωπίδες fpl.

blinking ['bliŋkiŋ] a (col) = bloody.

bliss [blis] n μακαριότητα, ευδαιμονία.

blister ['blistə*] n (on skin)

φυσαλίδα, φουσκάλα || (on surfaces etc) φουσκάλα ♦ vti φουσκαλιάζω, φλυκταινούμαι.

blithe [blaið] a χαρούμενος, εύθυμος.

blitz [blits] n μπλίτς nt inv, βίαιη επίθεση.

blizzard ['blizəd] n χιονοθύελλα.

bloated ['bləutid] a φουσκωμένος, πρησμένος.

bloc [blɒk] n (POL) συνασπισμός, μπλόκ nt inv.

block [blɒk] n (piece) τεμάχιο, μεγάλο κομμάτι || (for chopping) επίκρανο, πικόνι || (traffic) συνωτισμός, διακοπή || (obstacle) εμπόδιο || (city) τετράγωνο ♦ vt φράσσω, εμποδίζω || ~ade n αποκλεισμός, μπλόκο ♦ vt αποκλείω, μπλοκάρω || ~age n εμπλοκή, μπλοκάρισμα nt.

bloke [bləuk] n (col) άνθρωπος.

blond(e) [blɒnd] a ξανθός, ξανθή ♦ n ξανθός, ξανθιά.

blood [blʌd] n αίμα nt || (kinship) συγγένεια || (descent) καταγωγή || ~ donor n αιμοδότης/τρια m/f || ~ group n ομάδα αίματος || ~ pressure n πίεση αίματος || ~ shed n αιματοχυσία || ~ shot a κόκκινος || ~ stained a αιματοστιγής, ματωμένος || ~ stream n κυκλοφοριακό σύστημα nt || ~ thirsty a αιμοβόρος || ~ transfusion n μετάγγιση αίματος || ~ y a (col) παλιο-, βρωμο- || (lit) αιματηρός || ~ y-minded a τζαναμπέτης.

bloom [blu:m] n (flower) λουλούδι || (perfection) άνθηση, ακμή ♦ vi ανθίζω || in ~ στην άνθησή του.

blossom ['blɒsəm] n άνθος nt ♦ vi ανθίζω.

blot [blɒt] n λεκές m || (disgrace) κηλίδα ♦ vt (stain) λεκιάζω || (dry ink)

στυπώνω, τραβώ || to ~ out *vt* εξαφανίζω, σβήνω.

blotchy ['blɒtʃɪ] *a* γεμάτος κοκκινίλες.

blotting paper ['blɒtɪŋpeɪpə*] *n* στυπόχαρτο.

blouse [blauz] *n* μπλούζα.

blow [bləʊ] *(irreg v)* *n* (with fist) κτύπημα *nt*, γροθιά || (with stick) ραβδισμός || (of air) φύσημα *nt* || (of fate) πλήγμα *nt* ♦ *vt* φυσάω || (a fuse) καίομαι || (col: squander) σπαταλάω || **at a single ~** μ'ένα κτύπημα || to ~ **one's top** ξεσπάω || to ~ **over** *vi* περνώ, ξεθυμαίνω || to ~ **up** *vi* σκάω, ανατινάζω ♦ *vt* (tyre) φουσκώνω || ~ **lamp** *n* καμινευτήρ || ~ **out** *n* (AUT) κλατάρισμα *nt* || ~ **y** *a* ανεμώδης.

blubber ['blʌbə*] *n* λίπος *nt* φάλαινας.

blue [bluː] *a* γαλάζιος, γαλανός || (paint) μπλέ || (with cold etc) μελανιασμένος ♦ *n*: to have the ~ **s** μελαγχολώ || ~ **bell** *n* ζημπούλι || ~ **bottle** *n* κρεατόμυγα || ~ **print** *n* κυανοτυπία, σχέδιο.

bluff [blʌf] *n* (deception) μπλόφα, απάτη ♦ *vt* μπλοφάρω, εξαπατώ ♦ *a* ντόμπρος.

blunder ['blʌndə*] *n* μεγάλο λάθος *nt*, χοντροκοπιά ♦ *vi* κάνω γκάφα.

blunt [blʌnt] *a* αμβλύς, στομωμένος || (person) μονόκομματος ♦ *vt* αμβλύνω, στομώνω || ~ **ly** *ad* απότομα, ντόμπρα.

blur [blɜː*] *n* θολούρα, θαμπάδα || (stain) μουτζούρα ♦ *vti* θολώνω, θαμπώνω.

blurt [blɜːt]: to ~ **out** *vt* λέω κάτι απερίσκεπτα, αποκαλύπτω.

blush [blʌʃ] *vi* κοκκινίζω ♦ *n* κοκκίνισμα *nt*.

bluster ['blʌstə*] *vi* (of wind) φυσώ δυνατά || (of person) κάνω φασαρία, κομπάζω.

boar [bɔː*] *n* γουρούνι αρσενικό, κάπρι.

board [bɔːd] *n* (of wood) σανίδα, τάβλα || (notice) πινακίδα, ταμπλό *nt inv* || (of paper) χαρτόνι || (meal) φαΐ || (of men) συμβούλιο, επιτροπή ♦ *vt* (feed) δίνω τροφή || (ship, train) επιβαίνω, μπαρκάρω || (with planks) σανιδώνω || ~ **and lodging** φαΐ και ύπνος || to ~ **up** *vt* (περι)φράσσω με σανίδες || ~ **er** *n* οικότροφος || (lodger) ένοικος || ~ **ing house** *n* πανσιόν *f inv* || ~ **ing school** *n* σχολή με οικοτροφείο || ~ **ing school pupil** *n* εσωτερικός.

boast [bəʊst] *vi* καυχώμαι, κομπορρημονώ ♦ *n* κομπασμός, καυχησιολογία || ~ **ful** *a* καυχησιάρης, φανφαρόνος.

boat [bəʊt] *n* βάρκα, καΐκι || (ship) καράβι || ~ **er** (hat) ναυτικό ψάθα || ~ **ing** *n* λεμβοδρομία με βάρκα || ~ **swain** ['bəʊsən] *n* λοστρόμος.

bob [bɒb] *vi* ανεβοκατεβαίνω.

bobbin ['bɒbɪn] *n* πηνίο, κουβαρίστρα || (ELEC) μπομπίνα.

bobsleigh ['bɒbsleɪ] *n* μποπσλέϊ *nt inv*, έλκηθρο.

bodice ['bɒdɪs] *n* στήθος *nt* φορέματος, μπούστος.

bodily ['bɒdɪlɪ] *ad* σωματικά || (together) συλλογικά, όλοι μαζί.

body ['bɒdɪ] *n* σώμα *nt*, κορμί || (legislative etc) σώμα, σωματείο || (collection) μεγάλο πλήθος *nt*, μάζα || (of car etc) σώμα, κύριο μέρος *nt* || ~ **guard** *n* σωματοφύλακας || ~ **work** *n* καρότσα.

bog [bɒg] *n* έλος *nt* ♦ *vi*: to get ~ **ged down** βουλιάζω.

boggle ['bɒgl] *vi* διστάζω.

bogus ['bəʊgəs] *a* ψεύτικος.

boil [bɔɪl] *vt* (potatoes etc) βράζω ♦ *vi* βράζω, κοχλάζω ♦ *n* (MED) καλόγερος || **to come to the ~** παίρνω βράση || ~ **er** *n* λέβης,

καζάν || ~ing point *n* σημείο βρασμού.

boisterous ['bɔɪstərəs] *a* θορυβώδης, ταραχώδης.

bold [bəʊld] *a* τολμηρός, θαρραλέος || ~ness *n* τολμηρότητα, θάρρος *nt*.

bollard ['bɒlɑd] *n* δέστρα.

bolster ['bəʊlstə*] *n* μαξιλάρα || to ~ up *vt* (υπο)στηρίζω.

bolt [bəʊlt] *n* (of door etc) σύρτης, μάνταλο || (rush away) εξόρμηση, φυγή ♦ *vt* (a door etc) μανταλώνω, κλειδώνω || (food) καταβροχθίζω ♦ *vi* (rush away) φεύγω, εξορμώ || (escape) δραπετεύω.

bomb [bɒm] *n* βόμβα ♦ *vt* βομβαρδίζω || ~ard [bɒmˈbɑːd] *vt* βομβαρδίζω, σφυροκοπώ || ~ardment *n* βομβαρδισμός || ~er *n* (person) βομβαρδιστής || (AVIAT) βομβαρδιστικό || ~ing *n* βομβαρδισμός || ~shell *n* (fig) κατάπληξη, σαν βόμβα.

bona fide ['bəʊnə'faɪdi] *a* καλής πίστεως.

bond [bɒnd] *n* (link) δεσμός, συνάφεια || (promise) υπόσχεση, σύμβαση || (ECON) ομολογία.

bone [bəʊn] *n* κόκκαλο ♦ *vt* ξεκοκκαλίζω || ~dry *a* εντελώς ξηρός, κατάξερος.

bonfire ['bɒnfaɪə*] *n* φωτιά.

bonnet ['bɒnit] *n* γυναικείο καπέλλο || (child's) σκουφίτσα || (cap) σκούφος, μπερές *m* || (Brit: of car) καπό.

bonus ['bəʊnəs] *n* επιμίσθιο, επίδομα *nt*.

bony ['bəʊni] *a* κοκκαλιάρης.

boo [buː] *vt* αποδοκιμάζω, γιουχαΐζω.

book [bʊk] *n* βιβλίο, κιτάπι ♦ *vt* (ticket etc) βγάζω εισιτήριο || (a room) κλείνω δωμάτιο || (person) πληρώνω, τιμωρούμαι || ~case *n* βιβλιοθήκη || ~ing office *n* πρακτορείο εισιτηρίων || ~-keeping *n* λογιστική

|| ~let *n* φυλλάδιο, βιβλιαράκι || ~maker *n* (RACING) μπουκμέικερ *m* *inv* || ~seller *n* βιβλιοπώλης || ~shop *n* βιβλιοπωλείο || ~stall *n* πάγκος βιβλιοπώλου || ~store *n* = ~shop.

boom [buːm] *n* (noise) κρότος, βόμβος || (NAUT) απώστης || (port) φράγμα *nt* || (busy period) μπούμ *nt* *inv*, κύμα *nt* ευημερίας, αιχμή ευημερίας ♦ *vi* ανέρχομαι, ανεβαίνω.

boon [buːn] *n* (blessing) όφελος *nt*.

boorish ['bʊəriʃ] *a* άξεστος, αγροίκος.

boost [buːst] *n* προώθηση ♦ *vt* προωθώ, ενισχύω.

boot [buːt] *n* μπότα || (Brit: of car) πορτμπαγκάζ *nt* *inv* ♦ *vt* (kick) λακτίζω, κλωτσάω || to ~ (in addition) επί πλέον.

booze [buːz] *n* ποτό || *vi* ξεφαντώνω, μεθοκοπώ.

border ['bɔːdə*] *n* (frontier) σύνορο, μεθόριος *f* || (edge) γύρος, σειρίτι, μπορντούρα || (page etc) πλαίσιο, βινιέτα || to ~ on *vt* συνορεύω με || ~line *n* (fig) εγγίζων τα όρια.

bore [bɔː*] *pt* of **bear** || *n* (person or thing) πληκτικός, ενοχλητικός, αφόρητος || (of gun etc) διαμέτρημα *nt* ♦ *vt* τρυπώ, ανοίγω τρύπα || (weary) πλήττω, λιμάρω || ~dom *n* πλήξη, ανία.

boring ['bɔːriŋ] *a* ανιαρός, βαρετός.

born [bɔːn] *pp*: **to be** ~ γεννιέμαι.

borough ['bʌrə] *n* (διοικητική) περιφέρεια.

borrow ['bɒrəʊ] *vt* δανείζομαι.

bosom ['bʊzəm] *n* στήθος *nt*, κόρφος.

boss [bɒs] *n* κύφωμα *nt*, καμπούρα || (master) το αφεντικό ♦ *vt* διευθύνω, κάνω το διευθυντή || ~y *a* αυταρχικός.

bosun ['bəʊsn] n = **boatswain** || see **boat**.

botanical [bə'tænɪkəl] a βοτανικός.

botanist ['bɒtənɪst] n βοτανολόγος m/f.

botany ['bɒtənɪ] n βοτανική.

botch [bɒtʃ] vt φτιάχνω τσαπατσούλικα, κουτσοφτιάχνω || (patch) κουτσομπαλώνω.

both [bəʊθ] a, pron αμφότεροι, και οι δύο ♦ ad και... και || οἱ όχι μόνο... αλλά και...

bother ['bɒðə*] n ενόχληση, μπελάς ♦ vt ενοχλώ, πειράζω, σκοτίζω ♦ vi στενοχωριέμαι, νοιάζομαι.

bottle ['bɒtl] n φιάλη, μπουκάλι, μποτίλια ♦ vt εμφιαλώνω, μπουκαλάρω, μποτιλιάρω || ~**neck** n (production) δυσκέρεια || (traffic) συνωστισμός || ~**opener** n ανοιχτήρι για μπουκάλες.

bottom ['bɒtəm] n κάτω μέρος nt, βάθος nt || (of sea etc) πυθμένας, βυθός || (seat) πισινός, ποπός || (ship) πλοίο || κάτω μέρος nt, κάτω-κάτω || (lowest) κατώτατος || ~**less** a απύθμενος.

bough [baʊ] n κλάδος, κλαδί.

bought [bɔːt] pt, pp of **buy**.

boulder ['bəʊldə*] n λίθος, λιθάρι, ογκόλιθος.

bounce [baʊns] n (rebound) αναπήδηση, γκελ at inv ♦ vi κάνω γκελ, αναπηδώ || (col: person) μπαίνω-βγαίνω ξαφνικά ♦ vt κάνω μπάλα να κάνει γκελ.

bound [baʊnd] pt, pp of **bind** || n όριο, σύνορο || (restriction) όρια ntpl || (leap) πήδημα nt ♦ vi (spring, leap) πηδώ, σκιρτώ || (limit) περιορίζω ♦ a προορίζόμενος για, κατευθυνόμενος προς.

boundary ['baʊndərɪ] n όριο, σύνορο.

bouquet ['bʊkeɪ] n μπουκέτο.

bout [baʊt] n (contest) γύρος,

αγώνας, συνάντηση || (of illness) προσβολή.

bow [bəʊ] n (curve) καμπή || (ribbon) φιόγκος || (weapon) τόξο, δοξάρι || (MUS) δοξάρι βιολιού.

bow [baʊ] vi υποκλίνομαι, σκύβω το κεφάλι ♦ vt κλίνω, κάμπτω || (submit) υποκύπτω, υποτάσσομαι ♦ n υπόκλιση, κλίση (της κεφαλής) || (of ship) πλώρη.

bowels [baʊəlz] npl έντερα ntpl, σπλάχνα ntpl || (fig) σπλάχνα ntpl.

bowl [bəʊl] n (basin) λεκάνη, γαβάθα || (of pipe) κούπα || (wooden ball) σφαίρα ♦ vti παίζω μπάλα, ρίχνω μπάλα || ~**s** npl παιχνίδι της μπάλας.

bow-legged ['bəʊlegɪd] a στραβοπόδης, στραβοκάνης.

bowler ['bəʊlə*] n παίκτης της μπάλας || (hat) μελόν nt.

bowling ['bəʊlɪŋ] n (game) παιχνίδι της μπάλας, μπόλιγκ nt inv.

bow tie ['bəʊ'taɪ] n παπιγιόν nt inv, πεταλούδα.

box [bɒks] n κιβώτιο || (small) κουτί || (THEAT) θεωρείο ♦ vt (s.o.'s ears) καρπαζώνω || (package) πακετάρω ♦ vi πυγμαχώ, παίζω μποξ || ~**er** n (person) πυγμάχος, μποξέρ m inv || (dog) μποξέρ m inv || ~**ing** n (SPORT) πυγμαχία, μποξ nt inv || ~ **office** n ταμείο (θεάτρου) || ~ **room** n αποθήκη οικίας.

boy [bɔɪ] n αγόρι, παιδί.

boycott ['bɔɪkɒt] n μπουκοτάρισμα ♦ vt αποκλείω, μπουκοτάρω.

boyfriend ['bɔɪfrend] n φίλος, αγαπημένος.

boyish ['bɔɪɪʃ] a παιδιάστικος, αγορίστικος.

bra [brɑː] n σουτιέν nt inv, στηθόδεσμος.

brace [breɪs] n (clamp) δεσμός || (pair) ζευγάρι || (support) στύλωμα nt || (tool) ματικάπι ♦ vt συνδέω,

στερεώνω || (o.s.) τονώνω, δυναμώνω
|| ~s npl τιράντες fpl.

bracelet ['breislit] n βραχιόλι.

bracing ['breisiŋ] a τονωτικός.

bracken ['brækən] n φτέρη.

bracket ['brækit] n (support)
υποστήριγμα nt, ωτίδα, κρεμάθρα ||
(round) παρένθεση || (square) αγκύλη
|| (group) ομάδα ♦ vt βάζω σε
παρένθεση || (associate) συνδέω.

brag [bræg] vi καυχώμαι.

braid [breid] n (of hair) πλεξίδα,
πλεξούδα || (officer's etc) σειρήτι,
κορδόνι.

Braille [breil] n Μπράιλ nt inv.

brain [brein] n εγκέφαλος, μυαλό ||
(person) διάνοια || ~s npl μυαλό ntpl
|| ~washing n πλύση εγκεφάλου ||
~wave n έμπνευση, επινόηση || ~y
a ευφυής.

braise [breiz] vt ψήνω στην
κατσαρόλα.

brake [breik] n (on vehicle)
τροχοπέδη, φρένο ♦ vti φρενάρω,
πατώ φρένο.

bramble ['bræmbl] n βάτος.

branch [brɑːntʃ] n (of tree) κλάδος,
κλαδί || (division) κλάδος || (office)
υποκατάστημα nt ♦ vi
διακλαδούμαι, χωρίζομαι.

brand [brænd] n (trademark) μάρκα ||
(on cattle) σφράγισμα με αναμμένο
σίρηρο.

brand-new ['brænd'njuː] a
κατακαίνουργιος, ολοκαίνουργιος,
του κουτιού.

brandy ['brændi] n κονιάκ nt inv.

brash [bræʃ] a αναιδής,
αδιάντροπος.

brass [brɑːs] n μπρούτζος || ~ **band**
n μπάντα, φανφάρα.

brat [bræt] n κουτσούβελο,
διαβολάκι.

bravado [brə'vɑːdəʊ] n
παλληκαρισμός.

brave [breiv] a γενναίος ♦ (show)

περίφημος ♦ n ερυθρόδερμος
πολεμιστής ♦ vt αψηφώ || ~ry n
θάρρος nt, ανδρεία.

brawl [brɔːl] n καυγάς ♦ vi
καυγαδίζω.

brawn [brɔːn] n μυϊκή δύναμη,
δύναμη || (COOKING) πηχτή.

brazen ['breizn] a (metal)
μπρούτζινος || (shameless) αναιδής,
ξετσίπωτος ♦ vt : to ~ **it out**
καυχώμαι ξετσίπωτα.

brazier ['breiziə*] n μαγκάλι,
φουφού f inv.

Brazil [brə'zil] n Βραζιλία || ~ian a
βραζιλιανός ♦ n Βραζιλιάνος/n m/f
|| ~ **nut** n Βραζιλιανό καρύδι.

breach [briːtʃ] n (in gap) ρήγμα nt,
τρύπα || (of trust, duty) παράβαση,
παράβαση || (quarrel) ρήξη, τσάκωμα
nt ♦ vt γκρεμίζω.

bread [brɛd] n ψωμί || (living)
καθημερινό ψωμί || ~ **and butter** n
μέσα συντηρήσεως || ~**crumbs** npl
ψίχουλα ntpl || ~**winner** n στήριγμα
nt της οικογενείας.

break [breik] (irreg v) vt (crush)
συντρίβω, τσακίζω || (apart) σπάω ||
(promise) αθετώ || (silence etc)
διακόπτω || (habit) κόβω || (the law)
παραβιάζω ♦ vi θραύομαι,
τσακίζομαι || (friendship etc) τα χαλώ ||
(dissolve) διαλύομαι ♦ n (gap) ρήξη,
άνοιγμα nt, χάσμα nt || (rest) διακοπή,
διάλειμμα nt || (chance) ευκαιρία,
τύχη || (fracture) ρωγμή || **to ~ free**
or **loose** vi δραπετεύω,
απελευθερώνομαι || **to ~ in** vt (a
horse etc) δαμάζω || (conversation)
διακόπτω ♦ vi (burglar) κάνω
διάρρηξη || **to ~ out** vi ξεσπώ || (of
prison) δραπετεύω || **to ~ up** vi
διαλύομαι ♦ vt χωρίζω, συντρίβω,
τεμαχίζω || ~**able** a εύθραυστος ||
~**age** n σπάσιμο, ράγισμα nt ||
~**down** n (in discussions) διακοπή ||
(of health) κατάρρευση || (mental)

breakfast

χάσιμο του μυαλού || **~er** *n (NAUT)* κύμα *nt.*

breakfast ['brɛkfəst] *n* πρωινό, κολατσιό.

breakthrough ['breɪkθruː] *n* δίοδος *f,* ρήγμα *nt.*

breakwater ['breɪkwɔːtə*] *n* κυματοθραύστης.

breast [brɛst] *n (of woman)* μαστός, βυζί || *(of man, animal)* στήθος *nt* || **~stroke** *n* απλωτή.

breath [brɛθ] *n* πνοή, αναπνοή || **out of ~** λαχανιασμένος.

breathe [briːð] *vti* αναπνέω || **~r** *n* ανάσα.

breathless ['brɛθlɪs] *a* λαχανιασμένος.

bred [brɛd] *pt, pp of* **breed.**

breed [briːd] *(irreg v) n* γενεά, ράτσα ♦ *vt* γεννώ, φέρνω || *(animals)* τρέφω ♦ *vi* αναπαράγομαι || **~er** *n (person)* αναπαραγωγός *m/f,* κτηνοτρόφος *m/f* || **~ing** *n* ανατροφή.

breeze [briːz] *n* αύρα, αεράκι.

breezy ['briːzɪ] *a* ευάερος || *(person)* γεμάτος ζωή.

brevity ['brɛvɪtɪ] *n* βραχύτητα, συντομία.

brew [bruː] *vt (drinks)* παρασκευάζω (μπύρα) αποστάζω || *(tea)* βράζω || *(plot)* μηχανορραφώ ♦ *vi* βράζομαι || *(storm etc)* έρχεται || **~ery** *n* ζυθοποιία, ποτοποιία.

bribe [braɪb] *n* δωροδοκία ♦ *vt* δωροδοκώ, λαδώνω || **~ry** *n* δωροδοκία, μπούκωμα *nt.*

brick [brɪk] *n* πλίνθος, τούβλο || **~layer** *n* τουβλάς || **~work** *n* πλινθοδομή.

bridal ['braɪdl] *a* νυφικός, γαμήλιος.

bride [braɪd] *n* νύφη || **~groom** *n* γαμπρός || **~smaid** *n* παράνυφη.

bridge [brɪdʒ] *n* γεφύρι, γιοφύρι || *(NAUT)* γέφυρα || *(CARDS)* μπριτζ *nt inv* || *(of nose)* ράχη της μύτης ♦ *vt* γεφυρώνω.

bridle ['braɪdl] *n* χαλινάρι, γκέμι ♦ *vt (a horse)* χαλινώνω || *(control)* χαλιναγωγώ.

brief [briːf] *a* σύντομος, βραχύς ♦ *n (LAW)* δικογραφία, φάκελος ♦ *vt* δίδω οδηγίες, ενημερώνω || **~s** *npl* κοντή κυλόττα || **~case** *n* χαρτοφύλακας || **~ing** *n* καταρτισμός, οδηγίες *fpl.*

brigade [brɪ'geɪd] *n (MIL)* ταξιαρχία || *see* **fire.**

brigadier [brɪgə'dɪə*] *n* ταξίαρχος.

bright [braɪt] *a (as light)* φωτεινός, λαμπερός, γυαλιστερός || *(weather)* φωτεινός, καθαρός || *(clever)* έξυπνος, ευφυής || *(colour)* ζωηρός, λαμπρός || **~en** *vti* ζωηρεύω, φωτίζομαι, αστράφτω.

brilliance ['brɪljəns] *n* λαμπρότητα, εξυπνάδα || *(of surface etc)* φωτεινότητα || *(of style)* ζωηρότητα.

brilliant ['brɪljənt] *a* φωτεινός, λαμπρός || *(person)* σπουδαίος, λαμπρός || *(splendid)* έξοχος.

brim [brɪm] *n (of cup)* χείλος *nt* || *(of hat)* γύρος, μπορ *nt inv* ♦ *vi* ξεχειλίζω || **~ful** *a* ξέχειλος.

brine [braɪn] *n* σαλαμούρα, άρμη.

bring [brɪŋ] *(irreg v) vt* φέρω, φέρνω || **to ~ about** *vt* επιτυγχάνω, καταφέρνω || **to ~ off** *vt* φέρω σε πέρας || **to ~ round** *or* **to** *vt* επαναφέρω, συνεφέρω || **to ~ up** *vt (raise)* ανατρέφω, μεγαλώνω || *(introduce)* προβάλλω, θέτω.

brisk [brɪsk] *a* ζωηρός.

bristle ['brɪsl] *n* γουρουνότριχα ♦ *vi* ανατριχιάζω.

Britain ['brɪtən] *n* Βρεττανία.

British ['brɪtɪʃ] *a* βρετανικός, αγγλικός || **the ~** *npl* οι 'Αγγλοι *mpl* || **~ Isles** *npl* Βρεττανικαί Νήσοι *fpl.*

Briton ['brɪtən] *n* Βρετανός/ίδα *m/f.*

brittle ['brɪtl] *a* εύθραυστος.

broach 34 buffalo

broach [brəʊtʃ] vt (subject) θίγω (ζήτημα).

broad [brɔːd] a ευρύς, φαρδύς, πλατύς || (daylight) το φως της ημέρας || (general) απλό, γενικό || (accent) χωριάτικη προφορά || **~ cast** n εκπομπή ♦ vti μεταδίδω ραδιοφωνικώς || **~ casting** n εκπομπή, μετάδοση || **~ en** vt ευρύνω, πλαταίνω ♦ vi ευρύνομαι, ανοίγω || **~ ly** ad ευρέως, πλατειά || **~ minded** a με ανοικτό μυαλό, ανεκτικός, ευρείας αντιλήψεως.

broccoli ['brɒkəli] n μπρόκολο.

brochure ['brəʊʃjʊə*] n φυλλάδιο, μπροσούρα.

broke [brəʊk] pt of **break** ♦ a απένταρος || **~ n** pp of **break** || **~ n-hearted** a με ραγισμένη καρδιά.

broker ['brəʊkə*] n μεσίτης, χρηματιστής.

bronchitis [brɒŋ'kaɪtɪs] n βρογχίτιδα.

bronze [brɒnz] n μπρούντζος || **~ d** a ηλιοψημένος, μαυρισμένος.

brooch [brəʊtʃ] n καρφίτσα.

brood [bruːd] n κλώσσισμα nt, γενιά ♦ vi κλωσσώ || (meditate) μελαγχολώ.

brook [brʊk] n (stream) ρυάκι, ρέμα nt.

broom [brʊm] n σκούπα || **~ stick** n σκουπόξυλο.

Bros. (abbr of Brothers) Αφοί (Αδελφοί mpl).

broth [brɒθ] n ζουμί κρέατος, σούπα.

brothel ['brɒθl] n μπορντέλο, οίκος ανοχής.

brother ['brʌðə*] n αδελφός || **~ in-law** n γαμπρός, κουνιάδος.

brought [brɔːt] pt, pp of **bring**.

brow [braʊ] n (forehead) κούτελο, μέτωπο || (eyebrow) φρύδι || (of hill etc) χείλος nt, φρύδι.

brown [braʊn] a καστανός, καφετής ♦ n καφετής ♦ vti σκουραίνω,

μαυρίζω || (cooking) καβουρδίζω || **~ ie** n (girl guide) προσκοπίνα.

browse [braʊz] vi (examine casually) ξεφυλλίζω, βόσκω, τριγυρίζω.

bruise [bruːz] n μελανιά, κτύπημα nt ♦ vti κτυπώ, κτυπιέμαι.

brunette [bruː'net] n μελαχροινή.

brunt [brʌnt] n ορμή, φόρα.

brush [brʌʃ] n βούρτσα || (paint) πινέλο || (fight) σύγκρουση ♦ vt βουρτσίζω || (lightly) ξεσκονίζω || to **~ aside** vt παραμερίζω || **~ wood** n θάμνοι mpl, χαμόκλαδα ntpl.

brusque [bruːsk] a απότομος, τραχύς.

Brussels sprout ['brʌslz'spraʊt] n (Βελγικό) λαχανάκι, πετί-σού.

brutal ['bruːtl] a κτηνώδης || **~ ity** n κτηνωδία.

brute [bruːt] n κτήνος nt, θηρίο.

B.Sc. abbr see **bachelor**.

bubble ['bʌbl] n μπουρμπουλήθρα, φουσκάλα ♦ vi κοχλάζω || (river, wine) αφρίζω || to **~ over** (fig) ξεχειλίζω.

buck [bʌk] n ελάφι αρσενικό || (rabbit) κούνελος ♦ vt ενθαρρύνω, δίνω κουράγιο || to **~ up** vi ενθαρρύνομαι, (ξανα) παίρνω κουράγιο.

bucket ['bʌkɪt] n κουβάς, κάδος.

buckle ['bʌkl] n πόρπη, φιούμπα ♦ vt κουμπώνω, θηλυκώνω || (bend) λυγίζω, στραβώνω.

bud [bʌd] n μπουμπούκι.

Buddhism ['budɪzəm] n Βουδδισμός.

budding ['bʌdɪŋ] a που μπουμπουκιάζει.

buddy ['bʌdɪ] n φιλαράκος.

budge [bʌdʒ] vti κινούμαι, υποχωρώ.

budgerigar ['bʌdʒərɪgɑː*] n παπαγαλάκι.

budget ['bʌdʒɪt] n προϋπολογισμός.

buff [bʌf] a (colour) σαμουά, κρεατί.

buffalo ['bʌfələʊ] n βουβάλι.

buffer ['bʌfə*] n αποσβεστήρας, αμορτισέρ nt inv.

buffet ['bʌfɪt] n πλήγμα nt, κτύπημα nt || ['bʊfeɪ] (bar) αναψυκτήριο || (food) μπουφές m inv ♦ vt πλήττω, κτυπώ.

buffoon [bə'fuːn] n παλιάτσος, καραγκιόζης.

bug [bʌg] n (insect) κοριός || (US) ζωύφιο || (spy device) κρυφό μικρόφωνο || (COMPUT) λάθος nt, σφάλμα nt.

bugle ['bjuːgl] n σάλπιγγα.

build [bɪld] (irreg v) vt οικοδομώ, χτίζω || ~ **er** n οικοδόμος, κατασκευαστής || ~**ing** n κτίριο, οικοδομή || ~**ing society** n οικοδομικός συνεταιρισμός || ~**-up** n διαφήμιση.

built [bɪlt] pt, pp of **build** || **well~** a (person) γεροδεμένος || ~**-in** a (cupboard) εντοιχισμένος.

bulb [bʌlb] n (BOT) βολβός || (ELEC) λάμπα, γλόμπος.

Bulgaria [bʌl'gɛərɪə] n Βουλγαρία.

bulge [bʌldʒ] n διόγκωση, φούσκωμα nt ♦ vti προεξέχω, εξογκούμαι, φουσκών ω.

bulk [bʌlk] n μέγεθος nt, όγκος || (greater part) μεγαλύτερο μέρος nt || ~ **head** n διάφραγμα nt || ~**y** a ογκώδης, χοντρός.

bull [bʊl] n ταύρος || ~ (rubbish) ψέματα ntpl, αρλούμπες fpl || ~**dog** n μπουλντόγκ m inv.

bulldozer ['bʊldəʊzə*] n μπουλντόζα.

bullet ['bʊlɪt] n σφαίρα, βόλι.

bulletin ['bʊlɪtɪn] n δελτίο, ανακοινωθέν nt.

bullfight ['bʊlfaɪt] n ταυρομαχία.

bullion ['bʊljən] n χρυσός (άργυρος) σε ράβδους.

bullock ['bʊlək] n βόδι, μοσχάρι.

bull's-eye ['bʊlzaɪ] n κέντρο (στόχου).

bully ['bʊlɪ] n τύραννος ♦ vt απειλώ, τρομοκρατώ.

bum [bʌm] n (col) πισινός || (tramp) αλήτες, ακαμάτης || **to** ~ **around** vi κοπροσκυλιάζω.

bump [bʌmp] n (blow) κτύπημα nt, τίναγμα nt || (bruise) πρήξιμο, καρούλα, καρούμπαλο ♦ vti κτυπώ, σκοντάφτω || ~**er** n (car) προφυλακτήρας ♦ a: ~**er harvest** πλούσια (σοδειά).

bumpy ['bʌmpɪ] a ανώμαλος (δρόμος).

bun [bʌn] n σταφιδόψωμο, κουλουράκι.

bunch [bʌntʃ] n μάτσο, φούχτα, χούφτα, δέμα nt.

bundle ['bʌndl] n δέμα nt, μπόγος nt πακέταρω, δένω || (also: ~ **off**) ξεφορτώνομαι.

bung [bʌŋ] n πώμα nt, τάπα ♦ vt (throw) ρίχνω, χώνω.

bungalow ['bʌŋgələʊ] n μπάγκαλο, εξοχικό σπίτι.

bungle ['bʌŋgl] vt τα κάνω θάλασσα, είμαι αδέξιος.

bunion ['bʌnjən] n κάλος.

bunk [bʌŋk] n κλίνη, κουκέτα.

bunker ['bʌŋkə*] n αποθήκη καυσίμων, καρβουνιέρα.

bunny ['bʌnɪ] n κουνελάκι.

bunting ['bʌntɪŋ] n σημαίες nt για σημαίες, σημαιοστολισμός.

buoy [bɔɪ] n (NAUT) σημαδούρα || (lifebuoy) σωσσίβιο || ~**ant** a (of person) εύθυμος, κεφάτος || **to** ~ **up** vt ενισχύω, αναθαρρύνω, ενθαρρύνω.

burden ['bɜːdn] n φόρτωμα nt, βάρος nt, δυσβάστακτο βάρος ♦ vt (επι)βαρύνω, φορτώνω.

bureau [bjʊə'rəʊ] n γραφείο που κλείνει || (for information etc) υπηρεσία πληροφοριών.

bureaucracy [bjʊə'rɒkrəsɪ] n γραφειοκρατία.

burglar ['bɜːglə*] n
διαρρήκτης/τρια m/f|| ~ **alarm** n
κουδούνι ασφαλείας|| ~ **ize** vt (US)
διαρρηγνύω|| ~ **y** n διάρρηξη.
burgle ['bɜːgl] vt διαρρηγνύω.
burial ['bɛrɪəl] n ταφή|| ~ **ground**
n νεκροταφείο.
burlesque [bɜːˈlɛsk] n επιθεώρηση,
μπυρλέσκ nt inv.
burly ['bɜːlɪ] a γεροδεμένος.
burn [bɜːn] (irreg v) n έγκαυμα nt
♦ vt καίω ♦ vi φλέγομαι|| **to ~ one's**
fingers (fig) βρίσκω το μπελά μου||
~ **ing question** n φλέγον ζήτημα nt.
burnt [bɜːnt] pt, pp of **burn** ♦ a
καμένος, ψημένος.
burrow ['bʌrəu] n φωλιά, τρύπα,
λαγούμι ♦ vti σκάβω λαγούμι,
ανοίγω τρύπα.
burst [bɜːst] (irreg v) n έκρηξη, ριπή
♦ vt (explode) προκαλώ έκρηξη||
(break) σπάζω|| (break out)
διαρρηγνύω, σπάω ♦ vi (tank etc)
διαρρηγνύομαι, σπάζω|| (flower)
σκάζω, ανοίγω|| (into pieces) γίνομαι
κομμάτια.
bury ['bɛrɪ] vt (inter) θάβω|| (hide)
κρύβομαι, χώνω, βυθίζομαι.
bus [bʌs] n λεωφορείο.
bush [buʃ] n θάμνος, χαμόκλαδο.
bushy ['buʃɪ] a δασύς, πυκνός.
busily ['bɪzɪlɪ] ad δραστήρια.
business ['bɪznɪs] n επιχείρηση,
δουλειά|| (concern) δουλειά|| ~ **man**
n επιχειρηματίας.
bus stop ['bʌsstɒp] n στάση
λεωφορείου.
bust [bʌst] n (statue) προτομή,
μπούστος|| (of woman) στήθος nt.
bustle ['bʌsl] n (θορυβώδης)
κίνηση, πάταγος ♦ vi
πηγαινοέρχομαι, βιάζομαι.
busy ['bɪzɪ] a απασχολημένος,
πολυάσχολος ♦ vt ασχολούμαι,
φροντίζω|| ~ **body** n
πολυπράγμονας, παπατρέχας.

but [bʌt] cj (still, yet, besides) αλλά, μα
♦ ad (only, except, as) μόνο, μόλις,
δεν... παρά ♦ prep (except) εκτός,
παρά.
butane ['bjuːteɪn] n βουτάνιο.
butcher ['butʃə*] n χασάπης||
(savage) σφαγέας ♦ vt σφάζω.
butler ['bʌtlə*] n μπάτλερ m inv,
αρχιυπηρέτης.
butt [bʌt] n (cask) βαρέλι, βουτσί||
(target) στόχος|| (of cigarette)
αποτσίγαρο, γόπα|| (thick end)
χοντρό άκρο ♦ vt κτυπώ με το
κεφάλι.
butter ['bʌtə*] n βούτυρο ♦ vt
βουτυρώνω|| **to ~ up** vt (fig)
κολακεύω, ξεσκονίζω.
butterfly ['bʌtəflaɪ] n πεταλούδα.
buttocks ['bʌtəks] npl γλουτοί mpl,
τα οπίσθια ntpl.
button ['bʌtn] n κουμπί ♦ vti
κουμπώνω|| ~ **hole** n κουμπότρυπα.
buttress ['bʌtrɪs] n αντέρεισμα nt.
buy [baɪ] (irreg v) vt αγοράζω|| **to ~**
up vt αγοράζω χονδρικώς|| ~ **er** n
αγοραστής.
buzz [bʌz] n βούισμα nt ♦ vi βουίζω.
buzzard ['bʌzəd] n ικτίνος.
buzzer ['bʌzə*] n βομβητής,
ψιθυριστής.
by [baɪ] prep (near, beside) παρά, πλάι,
δίπλα, κοντά|| (through) διά, από||
(with) από, με|| ~ **and large** κατά
κανόνα|| ~ **far** κατά πολύ|| ~
name κατ' όνομα.
by-election ['baɪɪlɛkʃn] n
αναπληρωματικές εκλογές fpl.
bygone ['baɪgɒn] a περασμένος,
παλιός ♦ n: **let ~s be ~s**
περασμένα, ξεχασμένα.
bypass ['baɪpɑːs] n (MECH)
βοηθητική δίοδος.
byproduct ['baɪprɒdʌkt] n
υποπροϊόν.
bystander ['baɪstændə*] n
παριστάμενος.

byte [baɪt] n (*COMPUT*) byte.

C

C. *abbr of* **centigrade.**

cab [kæb] n αμάξι, ταξί || (*of train, truck*) θέση οδηγού.

cabaret [ˈkæbəreɪ] n καμπαρέ nt inv.

cabbage [ˈkæbɪdʒ] n λάχανο.

cabin [ˈkæbɪn] n καλύβα || (*NAUT*) καμπίνα || ~ **cruiser** n θαλαμηγός f χωρίς κατάρτια.

cabinet [ˈkæbɪnɪt] n κομό || (*POL*) υπουργικό συμβούλιο || ~**maker** n επιπλοποιός.

cable [ˈkeɪbl] n καλώδιο || (*message*) τηλεγράφημα nt ♦ vti τηλεγραφώ || ~ **railway** n κρεμαστός σιδηρόδρομος.

cackle [ˈkækl] n κακάρισμα nt ♦ vi κακαρίζω.

cactus [ˈkæktəs] n κάκτος.

caddie, caddy [ˈkædɪ] n κάντι.

cadet [kəˈdet] n (*NAUT*) δόκιμος || (*MIL*) εύελπις || (*AVIAT*) ίκαρος.

cadge [kædʒ] vt ζητιανεύω, σελεμίζω.

Caesarean [siːˈzɛərɪən] a: ~ (**section**) καισαρική (τομή).

café [ˈkæfeɪ] n καφενείο || (*with food*) καφεστιατόριο || (*bar*) καφεμπάρ nt inv.

cafeteria n [kæfɪˈtɪərɪə] n καφετηρία.

cage [keɪdʒ] n κλουβί ♦ vt εγκλουβίζω.

cagey [ˈkeɪdʒɪ] a (*col*) πονηρός.

cajole [kəˈdʒəʊl] vt καλοπιάνω.

cake [keɪk] n κέικ nt inv, γλύκισμα nt || (*pie*) πίτα || (*of soap etc*) πλάκα.

calamity n [kəˈlæmɪtɪ] n συμφορά, καταστροφή.

calcium [ˈkælsɪəm] n ασβέστιο.

calculate [ˈkælkjʊleɪt] vti υπολογίζω, λογαριάζω.

calculating [ˈkælkjʊleɪtɪŋ] a υπολογιστικός, εσκεμμένος.

calculation [kælkjʊˈleɪʃən] n υπολογισμός.

calculus [ˈkælkjʊləs] n λογισμός.

calendar [ˈkæləndəˈ] n ημερολόγιο.

calf [kɑːf] n (*cow*) μοσχάρι || (*skin*) βιδέλο || (*ANAT*) κνήμη, γάμπα.

calibre, (*US*) **caliber** [ˈkælɪbəˈ] n διαμέτρημα nt || (*fig*) αξία ικανότητα.

call [kɔːl] vt καλώ, φωνάζω || (*meeting*) συγκαλώ || (*TEL*) κλήση, πρόσκληση ♦ vi (*visit*) επισκέπτομαι, έρχομαι ♦ n (*shout*) φωνή, κραυγή || (*visit*) επίσκεψη || ~**box** n τηλεφωνικός θάλαμος || ~**er** n (*visitor*) επισκέπτης/τρια m/f|| ~ **girl** n κοκότα || ~**ing** n (*profession*) επάγγελμα nt || to ~ **for** vt καλώ, έρχομαι || to ~ **off** vt ακυρώνω, σταματώ, διακόπτω || to ~ **on** vt (*visit*) επισκέπτομαι || to ~ **up** vt (*MIL*) επιστρατεύω || (*TEL*) (προς)καλώ, τηλεφωνώ.

callous [ˈkæləs] a σκληρός, άκαρδος.

calm [kɑːm] n αταραξία ♦ vti καθησυχάζω ♦ a ήρεμος, ατάραχος || ~**ness** n πουχία, κάλμα || to ~ **down** vi κατασταλάζω, καλμάρω ♦ vt ηρεμώ, καθησυχάζω.

calorie [ˈkælərɪ] n θερμίδα.

camber [ˈkæmbəˈ] n καμπυλότητα, κυρτότητα.

came [keɪm] pt of **come.**

camel [ˈkæməl] n καμήλα.

cameo [ˈkæmɪəʊ] n καμέα.

camera [ˈkæmərə] n φωτογραφική μηχανή || ~**man** n οπερατέρ m inv.

camouflage [ˈkæməflɑːʒ] n καμουφλάρισμα nt ♦ vt καμουφλάρω.

camp [kæmp] n κατασκήνωση || (*MIL*) στρατόπεδο ♦ vi κατασκηνώνω || (*MIL*) στρατοπεδεύω.

campaign [kæm'peɪn] n
εκστρατεία ♦ vi (also fig)
εκστρατεύω, κάνω καμπάνια.

campbed ['kæmp'bɛd] n κρεββάτι
εκστρατείας, ράντσο.

camper ['kæmpə*] n σκηνίτης,
εκδρομέας.

camping ['kæmpɪŋ] n: **to go ~**
πηγαίνω σε κατασκήνωση.

campsite ['kæmpsaɪt] n τόπος
κατασκηνώσεως.

can [kæn] auxiliary v (be able)
δύναμαι, μπορώ || (be allowed)
επιτρέπεται, μπορώ || (know how)
γνωρίζω, ξέρω ♦ n τενεκές m, κουτί
♦ vt κονσερβοποιώ.

Canada ['kænədə] n Καναδάς.

Canadian [kə'neɪdɪən] a καναδικός
♦ n Καναδός/n m/f.

canal [kə'næl] n (waterway) διώρυγα,
κανάλι || (ANAT) σωλήνας, πόρος.

canary [kə'nɛərɪ] n καναρίνι ♦ a
καναρινί (χρώμα).

cancel ['kænsəl] vt (check etc)
ακυρώνω || (strike out) διαγράφω ||
(MATH) εξαλείφω || **~lation** n
ακύρωση, ματαίωση.

cancer ['kænsə*] n καρκίνος.

candid ['kændɪd] a ειλικρινής.

candidate ['kændɪdeɪt] n
υποψήφιος/α m/f.

candle ['kændl] n κερί || **~stick** n
κηροπήγιο.

candour ['kændə*] n ευθύτητα,
ντομπροσύνη.

candy ['kændɪ] n καραμέλα.

cane [keɪn] n (bamboo etc) καλάμι ||
(stick) μπαστούνι ♦ vt (beat)
ραβδίζω.

canine ['kænaɪn] a σκυλίσιος.

canister ['kænɪstə*] n τενεκεδάκι,
κουτί.

cannabis ['kænəbɪs] n κάνναβη f.

canned ['kænd] a (food)
κονσερβοποιημένο.

cannibal ['kænɪbəl] n καννίβαλος

m/f, ανθρωποφάγος m/f|| **~ism** n
ανθρωποφαγία.

cannon ['kænən] n (gun) πυροβόλο,
κανόνι.

cannot ['kænɒt] = **can not** || see
can.

canoe [kə'nuː] n μονόξυλο, κανό ||
~ing n κανό.

canon ['kænən] n κανόνας ||
(criterion) κριτήριο || (clergyman)
εφημέριος.

can opener ['kænəʊpnə*] n
ανοιχτήρι.

canopy ['kænəpɪ] n σκιάδα,
προστέγασμα nt.

can't [kænt] = **can not** || see **can**.

cantankerous [kæn'tæŋkərəs] a
διεστραμμένος, καυγατζής.

canteen [kæn'tiːn] n (shop) καντίνα
|| (MIL) παγούρι.

canter ['kæntə*] n τριποδισμός ♦ vi
καλπάζω ελαφρά.

canvas ['kænvəs] n καννάβάτσο ||
(NAUT) πανιά ntpl || (ART) μουσαμάς ||
under ~ σε σκηνές.

canvass ['kænvəs] vt (election)
ψηφοθηρώ || (discuss) συζητώ,
ερευνώ.

canyon ['kænjən] n φαράγγι,
χαράδρα.

cap [kæp] n (hat) σκούφος,
τραγιάσκα || (top) κάλυμμα nt ♦ vt
στέφω, στεφανώνω || (bottle etc)
πωματίζω, σφραγίζω || (outdo)
υπερβάλλω.

capability [keɪpə'bɪlətɪ] n
ικανότητα.

capable ['keɪpəbl] a ικανός || **~ of**
ικανός να.

capacity [kə'pæsɪtɪ] n (space)
χωρητικότητα || (ability) ικανότητα ||
(position) ιδιότητα.

cape [keɪp] n (garment) κάπα,
μπελερίνα || (GEOG) ακρωτήρι.

capital ['kæpɪtl] n (city)
πρωτεύουσα || (ECON) κεφάλαιο ||

(letter) κεφαλαίο γράμμα || ~**ism** n
καπιταλισμός, κεφαλαιοκρατία ||
~**ist** a καπιταλιστής || ~
punishment n θανατική ποινή.
capitulate [kə'pɪtjuleɪt] vi
συνθηκολογώ.
capitulation [kəpɪtju'leɪʃən] n
συνθηκολόγηση.
capricious [kə'prɪʃəs] a
ιδιότροπος, ασταθής.
capsize [kæp'saɪz] vti ανατρέπω,
μπατάρω.
capstan ['kæpstən] n εργάτης.
capsule ['kæpsjuːl] n *(ANAT)* κάψα ||
(MED) καψούλα.
captain ['kæptɪn] n *(leader)*
αρχηγός || *(MIL)* λοχαγός || *(NAUT)*
πλοίαρχος ♦ vt οδηγώ, διευθύνω.
caption ['kæpʃən] n επικεφαλίδα ||
(of picture) λεζάντα.
captivate ['kæptɪveɪt] vt γοητεύω,
σαγηνεύω, δελεάζω.
captive ['kæptɪv] n, a αιχμάλωτος.
captivity [kæp'tɪvɪtɪ] n αιχμαλωσία.
capture ['kæptʃə*] vt συλλαμβάνω,
αιχμαλωτίζω || *(fort etc)* κυριεύω ♦ n
σύλληψη || *(objective)* κατάληψη.
car [kɑː*] n *(motor)* αυτοκίνητο,
αμάξι || *(railway)* βαγόνι.
carafe [kə'ræf] n καράφα.
caramel ['kærəməl] n καραμέλα.
carat ['kærət] n καράτι.
caravan ['kærəvæn] n καραβάνι ||
(house on wheels) τροχόσπιτο.
caraway ['kærəweɪ]: ~ **seed** n
κύμινο.
carbon ['kɑːbən] n *(CHEM)* άνθρακας ||
(paper) καρμπόν nt inv || ~ **copy** n
καρμπόν nt inv || ~ **ribbon** n ταινία
καρμπόν.
carburettor [kɑːbju'retə*] n
καρμπυρατέρ nt inv.
carcass ['kɑːkəs] n πτώμα nt,
κουφάρι, ψοφίμι.
card [kɑːd] n *(playing)*
τραπουλόχαρτο || *(visiting)*

επισκεπτήριο || *(general)* δελτάριο ||
~**board** n χαρτόνι || ~ **game** n
χαρτοπαιξία.
cardiac ['kɑːdɪæk] a καρδιακός.
cardigan ['kɑːdɪgən] n πλεκτή
ζακέτα.
cardinal ['kɑːdɪnl] a: ~ **number**
απόλυτος αριθμός.
care [kɛə*] n *(worry, attention)*
φροντίδα, μέριμνα, προσοχή ♦ vi
φροντίζω, με νοιάζει || ~ **of** *(abbr
c/o)* φροντίδι του || **to ~ about** vt με
ενδιαφέρει, με νοιάζει || **to take ~**
προσέχω || **to take ~ of** vt
ενδιαφέρομαι για, φροντίζω για || **to
~ for** vt ενδιαφέρομαι για || *(love)*
αγαπώ, αρέσω.
career [kə'rɪə*] n σταδιοδρομία,
καριέρα ♦ vi τρέχω, ορμώ.
carefree ['kɛəfriː] a αμέριμνος,
ξένοιαστος.
careful ['kɛəful] a προσεκτικός,
επιμελής || ~**ly** ad προσεκτικά.
careless ['kɛəlɪs] a απρόσεκτος,
απερίσκεπτος || ~**ness** n απροσεξία,
αμέλεια.
caress [kə'rɛs] n θωπεία, χάδι ♦ vt
θωπεύω, χαϊδεύω.
caretaker ['kɛəteɪkə*] n επιστάτης.
car-ferry ['kɑːferɪ] n πορθμείο
οχημάτων, φέρρυ-μποτ nt inv.
cargo ['kɑːgəu] n φορτίο.
caricature ['kærɪkətjuə*] n
γελοιογραφία, καρικατούρα.
carnation [kɑː'neɪʃən] n
γαρύφαλλο.
carnival ['kɑːnɪvəl] n *(public
celebration)* απόκρηες fpl, καρναβάλι.
carol ['kærəl] n *(Christmas)* κάλαντα
ntpl.
carp [kɑːp] n *(fish)* κυπρίνος, σαζάνι
|| **to ~ at** vt επικρίνω, κατσαδιάζω,
αντιλέγω.
car park ['kɑːpɑːk] n χώρος
παρκαρίσματος.

carpenter ['kɑ:pintə*] n
μαραγκός.

carpentry ['kɑ:pintri] n
ξυλουργική.

carpet ['kɑ:pit] n τάπης, χαλί ♦ vt
στρώνω με χαλί.

carriage ['kærıdʒ] n (vehicle)
άμαξα, όχημα nt || (carrying)
μεταφορά || (fees) μεταφορικά ntpl ||
(bearing) συμπεριφορά, ύφος nt || ~
return επαναφορά κυλίνδρου ||
~ **way** n (part of road) αμαξιτή οδός.

carrier ['kærıə*] n (μετα)φορέας,
κομιστής || ~**bag** n μεγάλη
χαρτοσακκούλα.

carrot ['kærət] n καρότο.

carry ['kæri] vt (transport, hold)
(μετα)φέρω, βαστάζω, κουβαλώ ||
(responsibility) έχω ευθύνες || **to be
carried away** (fig) παρασύρομαι ||
to ~ on vti συνεχίζω, επιμένω || **to
~ out** vt (orders) εκτελώ.

cart [kɑ:t] n κάρο ♦ vt μεταφέρω με
κάρο.

cartilage ['kɑ:tilidʒ] n χόνδρος,
τραγανό.

carton ['kɑ:tən] n κουτί από
χαρτόνι.

cartoon [kɑ:'tu:n] n (PRESS)
γελοιογραφία, σκίτσο || (CINE)
κινούμενες εικόνες fpl, μίκυ-μάους nt
inv.

cartridge ['kɑ:tridʒ] n (for gun)
φυσίγγι, φυσέκι.

carve [kɑ:v] vti σκαλίζω, χαράσσω,
κόβω.

carving ['kɑ:viŋ] n (in wood etc)
γλυπτική, σκάλισμα nt || ~ **knife** n
μαχαίρι για κόψιμο.

car wash ['kɑ:wɒʃ] n πλύσιμο
αυτοκινήτου.

cascade [kæs'keid] n καταρράκτης.

case [keis] n (box) θήκη, κιβώτιο,
κασόνι || (instance) περίπτωση ||
(state) κατάσταση, ζήτημα nt || (GRAM)
πτώση || (LAW) υπόθεση || **in ~** σε

περίπτωση που || **in any ~** εν πάσει
περιπτώσει.

cash [kæʃ] n μετρητά (χρήματα) ntpl
♦ vt εξαργυρώνω || ~**desk** n ταμείο.

cashier [kæ'ʃiə] n ταμίας, κασιέρης.

cashmere [kæʃ'miə*] n κασμήρι.

cash register ['kæʃ'redʒistə*] n
μηχανή ταμείου, ταμειακή μηχανή.

casing ['keisiŋ] n περίβλημα nt,
πλαίσιο, θήκη.

casino [kə'si:nəu] n καζίνο.

cask [kɑ:sk] n βαρέλι.

casket ['kɑ:skit] n (box) κουτί,
κασετίνα || (US) φέρετρο.

casserole ['kæsərəul] n (pot)
τσουκάλι, ντάβας || (meal) γιουβέτσι.

cassock ['kæsək] n ράσο.

cast [kɑ:st] (irreg v) vt (throw) ρίχνω,
πετώ || (shed) βγάζω, απορρίπτω ||
(THEAT) διανέμω ρόλους, αναθέτω
ρόλο || (metal) χύνω, καλουπώνω ♦ n
(THEAT) θίασος || **to ~ off** vti βγάζω
|| (NAUT) απολλύω.

caste [kɑ:st] n κοινωνική τάξη,
κάστα.

cast iron ['kɑ:st'aiən] n
χυτοσίδηρος.

castle ['kɑ:sl] n (fortress) φρούριο ||
(mansion) πύργος.

castor ['kɑ:stə*] n (wheel) καρούλι,
ρόδα || ~ **oil** n ρετσινόλαδο || ~
sugar n ψιλή ζάχαρη.

castrate [kæs'treit] vt μουνουχίζω.

casual ['kæʒjul] a (occasional) τυχαία
|| (work, attitude) τυχαίος,
απερίσκεπτος || (meeting) τυχαίος || ~
ly ad αδιάφορα.

casualty ['kæʒjulti] n τραυματίας.

cat [kæt] n γάτα.

catalogue, (US) **catalog**
['kætəlog] n κατάλογος ♦ vt
εγγράφω σε κατάλογο.

catalyst ['kætəlist] n καταλύτης.

catapult ['kætəpʌlt] n καταπέλτης.

cataract ['kætərækt] n (waterfall)
καταρράκτης || (MED) καταρράκτης.

catarrh [kə'tɑ:*] n κατάρρους m.

catastrophe [kə'tæstrəfı] n καταστροφή, συμφορά.

catch [kætʃ] (irreg v) n (for window etc) γάντζο, μπετούγια, ασφάλεια || (SPORT, breath) πιάσιμο || (fish) πιάνω (πολλά ψάρια) || (HUNT) θήραμα nt|| vt (seize) πιάνω, αρπάζω || (surprise) συλλαμβάνω || (in time) προφθάνω, πιάνω στα πρᾶσα || **to ~ a cold** αρπάζω κρύο.

catching ['kætʃıŋ] a (MED) μεταδοτικός, κολλητικός.

catch phrase ['kætʃfreız] n σύνθημα nt.

catchy ['kætʃı] a (tune) ελκυστικός.

categorical [kætı'gɒrıkəl] a κατηγορηματικός.

category ['kætıgərı] n κατηγορία, τάξη.

cater ['keıtə*] vi (food) τροφοδοτώ, σερβίρω || **~ing** n προμήθεια, τροφοδοσία || **to ~ for** (fig) φροντίζω, ικανοποιώ.

caterpillar ['kætəpılə*] n κάμπια.

cathedral [kə'θi:drəl] n καθεδρικός ναός, μητρόπολη.

catholic ['kæθəlık] a καθολικός, παγκόσμιος, ευρύς || **C~** n καθολικός/n m/f ♦ a (REL) καθολικός.

cattle ['kætl] npl κτήνη ntpl, ζώα ntpl.

catty ['kætı] a δηκτικός, πονηρός.

cauliflower ['kɒlıflauə*] n κουνουπίδι.

cause [kɒz] n (reason) αιτία, αφορμή, λόγος || (object) υπόθεση, χάρη ♦ vt προξενώ, κάνω να.

causeway ['kɒzweı] n υψωμένος δρόμος.

caustic ['kɒ:stık] a (burning) καυστικός || (sarcastic) σαρκαστικός.

caution ['kɒ:ʃən] n (care) προσοχή || (warning) προειδοποίηση ♦ vt προειδοποιώ.

cautious ['kɒ:ʃəs] a προσεκτικός.

cavalry ['kævəlrı] npl ιππικό.

cave [keıv] n σπηλιά || **~man** n τρωγλοδύτης ♦ **to ~ in** vi καταρρέω, σωριάζομαι.

cavern ['kævən] n σπηλιά.

caviar(e) ['kævıɑ:*] n χαβιάρι.

cavity ['kævıtı] n κοίλωμα nt, τρύπα.

C.B.I. abbr of Confederation of British Industry Συνομοσπονδία Βρεττανών Βιομηχάνων.

cc abbr of cubic centimetres; carbon copy.

cease [si:s] vti παύω, σταματώ, τελειώνω || **~fire** n ανακωχή || **~less** a ακατάπαυστος, αδιάκοπος.

cedar ['si:də*] n κέδρος.

ceiling ['si:lıŋ] n ταβάνι || (fig) ανώτατο ύψος.

celebrate ['sɛlıbreıt] vt γιορτάζω || (wedding etc) τελώ || **~d** a διάσημος.

celebration [sɛlı'breıʃən] n γιορτασμός, τελετή.

celebrity [sı'lɛbrıtı] n (person) διασημότητα.

celery ['sɛlərı] n σέλινο.

celestial [sı'lɛstıəl] a ουράνιος.

cell [sɛl] n (in monastery) κελλί || (in jail) φυλακή || (ELEC) στοιχείο || (BIOL) κύτταρο.

cellar ['sɛlə*] n υπόγειο, κελλάρι || (wine) κάβα.

'cello ['tʃɛləu] n βιολοντσέλο.

cellophane ['sɛləfeın] n (R) σελοφάν nt inv.

cellular ['sɛljulə*] a κυτταρικός, κυψελοειδής.

cellulose ['sɛljuləus] n κελλουλόζη, κυτταρίνη.

cement [sə'mɛnt] n τσιμέντο ♦ vt (lit) συγκολλώ με τσιμέντο || (fig) στερεώνω, κατοχυρώνω.

cemetery ['sɛmıtrı] n νεκροταφείο.

cenotaph ['sɛnətɑ:f] n κενοτάφιο.

censer ['sɛnsə*] n θυμιατήρι, λιβανιστήρι.

censor ['sɛnsə*] n λογοκριτής, ελεγκτής || **~ship** n λογοκρισία.

censure ['sɛnʃə*] vt επικρίνω, ψέγω.

census ['sɛnsəs] n απογραφή.

cent [sɛnt] n σέντ || (col) πεντάρα.

centenary [sɛn'tiːnərɪ] n εκατονταετηρίδα.

center ['sɛntə*] n (US) = **centre**.

centigrade ['sɛntɪɡreɪd] a εκατονταβάθμιος.

centilitre, (US) **centiliter** ['sɛntɪliːtə*] n εκατοστόλιτρο.

centimetre, (US) **centimeter** ['sɛntɪmiːtə*] n εκατοστόμετρο.

centipede ['sɛntɪpiːd] n σαρανταποδαρούσα.

central ['sɛntrəl] a κεντρικός || **~ heating** n κεντρική θέρμανση || **~ize** vt συγκεντρώνω || **~ processing unit (CPU)** (COMPUT) κεντρική μονάδα επεξεργασίας (ΚΜΕ).

centre ['sɛntə*] n κέντρο.

century ['sɛntjʊrɪ] n αιώνας.

ceramic [sɪ'ræmɪk] a κεραμικός.

cereal ['sɪərɪəl] n (any grain) δημητριακά ntpl, σιτηρά ntpl.

ceremony ['sɛrɪmənɪ] n εθιμοτυπία (religious) τελετή.

certain ['sɜːtən] a (sure) βέβαιος, σίγουρος, ασφαλής || (some, one) ωρισμένος, κάποιος || **for ~** σίγουρα || **~ly** ad ασφαλώς, σίγουρα || **~ty** n βεβαιότητα, σιγουριά.

certificate [sə'tɪfɪkɪt] n πιστοποιητικό, βεβαίωση.

certify ['sɜːtɪfaɪ] vti πιστοποιώ, βεβαιώ, κυρώνω.

cf. abbr = compare.

chafe [tʃeɪf] vti τρίβω, ερεθίζομαι, φθείρομαι.

chaffinch ['tʃæfɪntʃ] n σπίνος.

chain [tʃeɪn] n αλυσίδα, καδένα || (mountains) σειρά ♦ vt (also: **~ up**)

δένω με αλυσίδες, δεσμεύω || **~ reaction** n αλυσωτή αντίδραση || **~ store** n υποκατάστημα nt.

chair [tʃeə*] n καρέκλα || (UNIV etc) έδρα ♦ vt (preside) προεδρεύω || **~man** n πρόεδρος || (director) διευθυντής.

chalet ['ʃæleɪ] n σαλέ nt inv.

chalice ['tʃælɪs] n δισκοπότηρο.

chalk [tʃɔːk] n (GEOL) ασβεστόλιθος || (crayon) κιμωλία.

challenge ['tʃælɪndʒ] n πρόκληση ♦ vt προκαλώ || (dispute) αμφισβητώ || **~r** n διεκδικητής.

challenging ['tʃælɪndʒɪŋ] a προκλητικός.

chamber ['tʃeɪmbə*] n (compartment) δωμάτιο || (of gun etc) θαλάμη (όπλου) || **~ of commerce** n Εμπορικό Επιμελητήριο || **~maid** n καμαριέρα || **~ music** n μουσική δωματίου.

chamois ['ʃæmwɑː] n: **~ leather** n σαμουά nt inv.

champagne [ʃæm'peɪn] n σαμπάνια.

champion ['tʃæmpɪən] n (SPORT) πρωταθλητής/τρια m/f|| (of cause) πρόμαχος || **~ship** n πρωτάθλημα nt.

chance [tʃɑːns] n (opportunity) ευκαιρία || (possibility) ελπίδα, πιθανότητα ♦ a τυχαίος ♦ vt: **to ~ it** διακινδυνεύω, παίζω στην τύχη || **to take a ~** δοκιμάζω.

chancel ['tʃɑːnsəl] n ιερό (ναού).

chancellor ['tʃɑːnsələ*] n (UNIV) πρύτανης m || **C~ of the Exchequer** n Υπουργός Οικονομικών.

chandelier [ʃændə'lɪə*] n πολύφωτο, πολυέλαιος.

change [tʃeɪndʒ] vt αλλάζω, τροποποιώ (exchange) ανταλλάσσω || (trains) αλλάζω ♦ vi αλλάζω, μεταβάλλομαι ♦ n (alteration)

αλλαγή, μεταβολή || *(coins)* ψιλά *ntpl* || *(balance)* ρέστα *ntpl* || **~able** *a (weather)* άστατος || **~over** *n (to new system)* αλλαγή συστήματος.

changing ['tʃeɪndʒɪŋ] *a* ευμετάβλητος, αλλάξιμο || **~-room** *n (in shop)* βεστιάριο.

channel ['tʃænl] *n (of stream)* κοίτη || *(of bay etc)* δίαυλος, μπούκα || *(strait)* πορθμός, στενό || *(of communication)* οδός f, δρόμος || *(RAD etc)* ζώνη συχνοτήτων || *(TV)* κανάλι ♦ *vt* αυλακώνω || **the (English) C~** *n* Μάγχη || **C~ Islands** *npl* νησιά της Μάγχης.

chant [tʃɑ:nt] *n* τραγούδι || *(church)* ψαλμός ♦ *vt* τραγουδώ || *(church)* ψάλλω.

chaos ['keɪɒs] *n* χάος *nt*.

chap [tʃæp] *n* ρωγμή, σκάσιμο, τύπος ♦ *vt (skin)* σκάζω από το κρύο.

chapel ['tʃæpl] *n* παρεκκλήσι.

chaperon ['ʃæprəʊn] *n* συνοδός κοριτσιού ♦ *vt* συνοδεύω.

chaplain ['tʃæplɪn] *n* εφημέριος.

chapter ['tʃæptə*] *n (of book)* κεφάλαιο.

char [tʃɑ:*] *vt (burn)* μαυρίζω με κάψιμο ♦ *n (cleaner)* παραδουλεύτρα.

character ['kærɪktə*] *n (qualities)* χαρακτήρας || *(LITER, THEAT etc)* πρόσωπο, χαρακτήρας || *(peculiar person)* τύπος, χαρακτήρας || *(letter, sign, COMPUT)* χαρακτήρας, στοιχείο, γράμμα || **~s per second (c.p.s.)** *n* χαρακτήρες *mpl* ανά δευτερόλεπτο (χ.α.δ.) || **~istic** *a* χαρακτηριστικός ♦ *n* χαρακτηριστικό γνώρισμα *nt*.

charade [ʃə'rɑːd] *n* συλλαβόγριφος, φαρσα.

charcoal ['tʃɑːkəʊl] *n* ξυλοκάρβουνο.

charge [tʃɑːdʒ] *n (in price)* τίμημα *nt*, τιμή || *(accusation)* κατηγορία || *(load for gun)* γόμωση || *(attack)* έφοδος f,

προσβολή ♦ *vt (fill, load)* γεμίζω, φορτίζω || *(a price)* ζητώ (τιμή), χρεώνω || *(a battery)* επιφορτίζω || *(attack)* εφορμώ || *(accuse)* κατηγορώ ♦ *vi* επιπίπτω, προσβάλλω || **in ~ of** φροντίζω, που φροντίζει || **to take ~** αναλαμβάνω, είμαι υπεύθυνος.

charitable ['tʃærɪtəbl] *a* φιλάνθρωπος, ελεήμονας.

charity ['tʃærɪtɪ] *n (institution)* φιλανθρωπικό ίδρυμα || αγαθοεργία.

charlady ['tʃɑːleɪdɪ] *n* παραδουλεύτρα.

charm [tʃɑːm] *n (attractiveness)* γοητεία || *(for luck)* φυλαχτό ♦ *vt* μαγεύω, γοητεύω || **~ing** *a* γοητευτικός.

chart [tʃɑːt] *n (of information)* γραφική παράσταση, διάγραμμα *nt* || *(NAUT)* χάρτης.

charter ['tʃɑːtə*] *vt* ναυλώνω || καταστατικός χάρτης || **~ flight** *n* ναυλωμένη πτήση || **~ed accountant** *n* λογιστής.

charwoman ['tʃɑːwʊmən] *n* = **charlady**.

chase [tʃeɪs] *vt (run after)* κυνηγώ, (κατα-)διώκω ♦ *n (act of chasing)* κυνήγι, καταδίωξη.

chasm ['kæzəm] *n* χάσμα *nt*, κενό.

chassis ['ʃæsɪ] *n* σασσί *m inv*.

chastity ['tʃæstɪtɪ] *n* αγνότητα, παρθενία.

chat [tʃæt] *vi* κουβεντιάζω || *(friendly, casual talk)* φιλική κουβεντούλα.

chatter ['tʃætə*] *vi* φλυαρώ || *(of teeth)* τρέμω, κτυπώ ♦ *n* φλυαρία, τερετισμός || **~box** *n (esp child)* φλύαρος.

chatty ['tʃætɪ] *a (style)* ομιλητικός, πολυλογάς.

chauffeur ['ʃəʊfə*] *n* οδηγός, σωφέρ *m inv*.

cheap [tʃiːp] *a (joke)* άνοστο (αστείο) || *(poor quality)* φτηνός,

πρόστυχος, μικρής αξίας || ~en vt
(person) υποτιμώ, ξευτελίζω || ~ly ad
φτηνά.

cheat [tʃiːt] vti (εξ)απατώ,
κοροϊδεύω ♦ n αγύρτης,
κατεργάρης || ~ing n (at cards)
κλέψιμο || (general) παγαποντιά.

check [tʃɛk] vt (examine) ελέγχω ||
(halt) σταματώ, αναχαιτίζω ♦ n
(examination) έλεγχος, επαλήθευση ||
(restraint) περιορισμός || (restaurant
bill) λογαριασμός || (pattern) καρρώ
nt inv || (US) = cheque || ~ers npl
(US) ντάμα || ~mate n ματ nt inv ||
~point n σημείο ελέγχου || ~up n
(MED) γενική εξέταση.

cheek [tʃiːk] n παρειά, μάγουλο ||
(impudence) αναίδεια || ~bone n
μήλο (παρειάς) || ~y a αναιδής.

cheer [tʃiə*] n (joy) ευθυμία || (shout)
ζητωκραυγή ♦ vt (shout) επευφημώ,
ζητωκραυγάζω || (comfort) χαροποιώ
|| (encourage) ενθαρρύνω ♦ vi: to ~
up κάνω κέφι || **good** ~ n φαγητά
nt pl || ~**ful** a χαρωπός καλόκεφος ||
~**fulness** n ευθυμία || (of fireplace
etc) ζεστασιά || ~**ing** n ζητοκραυγές
fpl, χειροκροτήματα ntpl ♦ a
ενθαρρυντικός, προκαλών το κέφι ||
~**io** interj (in departure) γεια χαρά ||
(greeting) γεια σου || ~**less** a
μελαγχολικός, κακόκεφος.

cheese [tʃiːz] n τυρί.

chef [ʃef] n αρχιμάγειρας.

chemical [ˈkɛmɪkəl] a χημικός.

chemist [ˈkɛmɪst] n (MED)
φαρμακοποιός m/f || (scientist)
χημικός m/f || ~**ry** n χημεία || ~'s
(shop) n φαρμακείο.

cheque [tʃɛk] n επιταγή || ~ **book** n
βιβλιάριο επιταγών.

chequered [ˈtʃɛkəd] a (fig)
περιπετειώδης.

cherish [ˈtʃɛrɪʃ] vt (a hope) τρέφω ||
(love) λατρεύω || (look after)
περιποιούμαι.

cherry [ˈtʃɛrɪ] n (tree) κερασιά ||
(fruit) κεράσι.

chess [tʃɛs] n σκάκι || ~**board** n
σκακιέρα || ~**man** n πιόνι, πεσσός.

chest [tʃɛst] n (ANAT) στήθος nt ||
(box) κιβώτιο, μπαούλο || **to get sth
off one's** ~ ξελαφρώνω || ~ **of
drawers** n σιφονιέρα, κομό.

chestnut [ˈtʃɛsnʌt] n κάστανο || ~
(tree) n καστανιά.

chew [tʃuː] vti μασώ || ~**ing gum** n
τσίχλα.

chic [ʃiːk] a κομψός, σικ.

chick [tʃɪk] n πουλάκι.

chicken [ˈtʃɪkɪn] n (bird, food)
κοτόπουλο.

chickenpox [ˈtʃɪkɪnpɒks] n
ανεμοβλογιά.

chicory [ˈtʃɪkərɪ] n κιχώρι, αντίδι.

chief [tʃiːf] n αρχηγός m/f,
διευθυντής/διευθύντρια m/f ♦ a
κύριος, πρωτεύων, πρώτος || ~**ly** ad
κυρίως, προπάντων.

chilblain [ˈtʃɪlbleɪn] n χιονίστρα.

child [tʃaɪld] n παιδί || ~**birth** n
τοκετός, γέννα || ~**hood** n παιδικά
χρόνια ntpl || ~**ish** a παιδαριώδης,
παιδίατικος || ~**like** a αφελής,
παιδίατικος || ~**ren** [ˈtʃɪldrən] npl
of **child** παιδιά, παιδάκια ntpl.

chill [tʃɪl] n (coldness) ψυχρότητα,
κρυάδα || (cold) κρυολόγημα nt ♦ a
ψυχρός κρύος || ~**y** a ψυχρός,
κρύος.

chime [tʃaɪm] n κωδωνοκρουσία ♦
vi ηχώ αρμονικά.

chimney [ˈtʃɪmnɪ] n καπνοδόχος f,
καμινάδα.

chimpanzee [tʃɪmpænˈziː] n
χιμπαντζής.

chin [tʃɪn] n πηγούνι.

china [ˈtʃaɪnə] n πορσελάνη || (dishes,
cups) πιάτα ntpl.

China [ˈtʃaɪnə] n Κίνα.

Chinese [ˈtʃaɪˈniːz] a κινέζικος ♦ n

(person) Κινέζος/α m/f|| (language) κινεζική.

chink [tʃɪŋk] n (opening) ρωγμή, σκάσιμο || (noise) ήχος (μετάλλου κτλ).

chip [tʃɪp] n απόκομμα nt, θρύμμα nt ♦ vt θραύω, θρυμματίζω, αποκόπτω || to ~ in vi (CARDS) ποντάρω || (interrupt) παρεμβαίνω || συνεισφέρω.

chiropodist [kɪˈrɒpədɪst] n πεντικιουρίστας.

chirp [tʃɜːp] n τερετισμός, τιτίβισμα nt, κελάδημα nt ♦ vi τερετίζω, τιτιβίζω, κελαδώ.

chisel [ˈtʃɪzl] n σμίλη.

chit [tʃɪt] n σημείωμα nt, γραπτή άδεια.

chitchat [ˈtʃɪttʃæt] n κουβέντα.

chloride [ˈklɔːraɪd] n χλωρίδιο.

chlorine [ˈklɔːriːn] n χλώριο.

chloroform [ˈklɔrəfɔːm] n χλωροφόρμιο.

chock [tʃɒk] n μόρσος, τάκος.

chocolate [ˈtʃɒklɪt] n σοκολάτα.

choice [tʃɔɪs] n εκλογή, προτίμηση || (variety) ποικιλία ♦ a εκλεκτός.

choir [ˈkwaɪə*] n χορός || ~boy n παιδί χορωδίας.

choke [tʃəʊk] vi (be unable to breathe) πνίγομαι ♦ vt (stop breathing of) ασφυκτιώ, στραγγαλίζω || (block) εμφράσσω ♦ n (AUT) διακύπτης, εμφράκτης.

cholera [ˈkɒlərə] n χολέρα.

choose [tʃuːz] (irreg v) vt διαλέγω, προτιμώ || (decide) αρέσω, προτιμώ.

chop [tʃɒp] vt (cut with a blow) κόβω, αποκόβω || (into pieces) κατακόβω, διαμελίζω, λιανίζω ♦ vi: to ~ and change πωλώ και αγοράζω ♦ n (blow) κτύπημα nt || (meat) μπριζολάκι || ~py a ταραγμένος, κυματώδης || ~sticks npl ξυλαράκια ntpl (για το πιλάφι), κινέζικα ntpl/vi.

choral [ˈkɔːrəl] a χορικός.

chord [kɔːd] n χορδή.

chore [tʃɔː*] n βαρετή δουλειά.

choreographer [kɒrɪˈɒɡrəfə*] n χορογράφος m/f.

chortle [ˈtʃɔːtl] vi καγχάζω, κακαρίζω.

chorus [ˈkɔːrəs] n (choir etc) χορός, χορωδία || (many voices) τραγούδι εν χορώ || ~ of praise n (fig) συναυλία επαίνων.

chose [tʃəʊz] pt of **choose**.

chosen [ˈtʃəʊzn] pp of **choose**.

Christ [kraɪst] n Χριστός.

christen [ˈkrɪsn] vt βαφτίζω || ~ing n βάπτισμα nt.

Christian [ˈkrɪstɪən] n Χριστιανός/η m/f ♦ a χριστιανικά || ~ name n όνομα nt || ~ity n χριστιανισμός.

Christmas [ˈkrɪsməs] n Χριστούγεννα ntpl || ~ card n χριστουγεννιάτικη κάρτα.

chrome [krəʊm] n επιχρωμίωση.

chromium [ˈkrəʊmɪəm] n χρώμιο.

chronic [ˈkrɒnɪk] a (MED) χρόνιος.

chronicle [ˈkrɒnɪkl] n χρονικό, χρονογράφημα nt.

chronological [krɒnəˈlɒdʒɪkəl] a χρονολογικός.

chrysanthemum [krɪˈsænθəməm] n χρυσάνθεμο.

chubby [ˈtʃʌbɪ] a παχουλός, στρουμπουλός.

chuck [tʃʌk] vt πετώ, ρίχνω ♦ n σφιγκτήρας, τσόκ nt inv.

chuckle [ˈtʃʌkl] vi γελώ χαμηλόφωνα.

chum [tʃʌm] n στενός φίλος.

chunk [tʃʌŋk] n χοντρό κομμάτι.

church [tʃɜːtʃ] n (building) εκκλησία, ναός || ~yard n αυλόγυρος εκκλησίας, νεκροταφείο.

churlish [ˈtʃɜːlɪʃ] a άξεστος, δύστροπος.

churn [tʃɜːn] n (for butter) βουτινά, κάρδαρα, ντουρβάνι.

chute [ʃuːt] n τσουλήθρα.

chutney ['tʃʌtni] n τσάτνυ nt inv (αρωματικό).

CID n (abbr of Criminal Investigation Department) Ανακριτικό Τμήμα.

cider ['saɪdə*] n μηλίτης (οίνος).

cigar [sɪ'gɑː*] n πούρο.

cigarette [sɪgə'rɛt] n τσιγάρο, σιγαρέττο || ~ case n τσιγαροθήκη, ταμπακιέρα || ~ end n γόπα, αποτσίγαρο || ~ holder n πίπα.

cinder ['sɪndə*] n ανθρακιά, θράκα, στάκτη.

cine ['sɪnɪ]: ~-camera n κινηματογραφική μηχανή || ~-film n κινηματογραφική ταινία.

cinema ['sɪnəmə] n (THEAT) σινεμά nt inv|| (motion pictures) κινηματογράφος.

cinnamon ['sɪnəmən] n κανέλα.

cipher ['saɪfə*] n (zero) μηδενικό || (code) κρυπτογράφηση || (person) μηδενικός.

circle ['sɜːkl] n (ring, figure) κύκλος, γύρος || (of friends) κύκλος, συντροφιά ♦ vi περιστρέφομαι, στριφογυρίζω ♦ vt (surround) περικυκλώνω ♦ vi (move in a circle) κάνω τον κύκλο, κάνω κύκλους.

circuit ['sɜːkɪt] n (moving around) κυκλικός δρόμος, περιστροφή || (tour by judges) περιοδεία (δικαστού) || (ELEC) κύκλωμα nt|| ~ous a κυκλικός, έμμεσος.

circular ['sɜːkjulə*] a κυκλικός || (in a circle) κυκλοτερής ♦ n εγκύκλιος, διαφημιστικό γράμμα.

circulate ['sɜːkjuleɪt] vi κυκλοφορώ ♦ vt θέτω σε κυκλοφορία.

circulation [sɜːkju'leɪʃən] n κυκλοφορία.

circumcise ['sɜːkəmsaɪz] vt περιτέμνω.

circumference [sə'kʌmfərəns] n περιφέρεια.

circumspect ['sɜːkəmspɛkt] a προσεκτικός, μετρημένος.

circumstances ['sɜːkəmstənsɪz] npl (facts connected with sth) περιστάσεις fpl, συνθήκες fpl, συμβάντα ntpl|| (financial condition) οικονομική κατάσταση.

circus ['sɜːkəs] n τσίρκο.

cistern ['sɪstən] n δεξαμενή, ντεπόζιτο.

cite [saɪt] vt (mention, quote) αναφέρω, παραπέμπω.

citizen ['sɪtɪzn] n (city dweller) αστός/η m/f|| πολίτης/ισσα m/f|| ~ship n πολιτικά δικαιώματα ntpl.

citrus fruit ['sɪtrəs 'fruːt] n εσπεριδοειδή ntpl.

city ['sɪtɪ] n πόλη || the C~ το εμπορικόν κέντρο του Λονδίνου.

civic ['sɪvɪk] a αστικός, πολιτικός.

civil ['sɪvl] a πολιτικός || (polite) ευγενικός || ~ engineer n πολιτικός μηχανικός m/f|| ~ian n πολίτης/ισσα m/f, ιδιώτης m/f ♦ a πολιτικός || ~ law n αστικόν δίκαιο || ~ servant n δημόσιος m/f υπάλληλος || C~ Service n Δημόσιες Υπηρεσίες fpl|| ~ war n εμφύλιος πόλεμος.

civilization [sɪvɪlaɪ'zeɪʃən] n πολιτισμός.

civilized ['sɪvɪlaɪzd] a πολιτισμένος.

claim [kleɪm] vt απαιτώ, ζητώ, διεκδικώ ♦ n αίτηση, απαίτηση, αξίωση || ~ant n απαιτητής/τήτρια m/f|| (LAW) ενάγων/ουσα m/f, δικαιούχος a m/f.

clam [klæm] n αχιβάδα.

clamber ['klæmbə*] vi σκαρφαλώνω.

clammy ['klæmɪ] a ιδρωμένος, κολλώδης.

clamp [klæmp] n σφιγκτήρας, σύνδεσμος ♦ vt (συ)σφίγγω.

clang [klæŋ] n κλαγγή, κρότος ♦ vti αντηχώ, κροτώ.

clap [klæp] *vti* κτυπώ, χειροκροτώ || ~**ping** *n* χειροκρότημα *nt*.

claret ['klærət] *n* μαύρο κρασί, μπορντώ *nt inv.*

clarification [klærɪfɪ'keɪʃən] *n (fig)* διευκρίνιση.

clarify ['klærɪfaɪ] *vt* διευκρινίζω.

clarinet [klærɪ'net] *n* κλαρίνο.

clarity ['klærɪtɪ] *n* διαύγεια.

clash [klæʃ] *n* σύγκρουση, αντίθεση || *(sound)* δυνατό και πικρό κτύπημα ♦ *vi* συγκρούομαι.

clasp [klɑːsp] *n* πόρπη, κόπιτσα ♦ *vt* αγκαλιάζω, σφίγγω.

class [klɑːs] *n (rank)* τάξη || *(sort)* τάξη, είδος *nt*, κατηγορία || *(SCH)* τάξη ♦ *vt* ταξινομώ, βαθμολογώ.

classic ['klæsɪk] *n* κλασσικός ♦ *a (traditional)* κλασσικός || ~**al** *a* κλασσικός.

classification [klæsɪfɪ'keɪʃən] *n* ταξινόμηση, κατάταξη.

classify ['klæsɪfaɪ] *vt* ταξινομώ, κατατάσσω.

classroom ['klɑːsrum] *n* αίθουσα παραδόσεων, τάξη.

clatter ['klætə*] *n* θόρυβος, γδούπος ♦ *vi* κροτώ, θορυβώ.

clause [klɔːz] *n (of contract etc)* όρος, άρθρο, διάταξη || *(GRAM)* πρόταση.

claustrophobia [klɔːstrə'fəubɪə] *n* κλειστοφοβία.

claw [klɔː] *n* νύχι || *(of quadrupeds)* χηλή, οπλή ♦ *vt* νυχιάζω, γρατσουνίζω.

clay [kleɪ] *n* άργιλος, πηλός.

clean [kliːn] *a (free from dirt)* καθαρός, παστρικός || *(guiltless)* καθαρός, τίμιος || *(lines)* καθαρές (γραμμές), σαφείς περίγραμμα ♦ *vt* καθαρίζω, παστρεύω || ~**er** *n (person)* καθαριστής/ρια *m/f* || ~**ing** *n* κάθαρση, καθάρισμα *nt* || ~**liness** *n* καθαριότητα, πάστρα || ~**-up** *n* καθαρισμός || **to** ~ **out** *vt* καθαρίζω || *(col)* ξεπεντιαρίζω || **to** ~ **up** *vt*

κάνω καθαρισμό, σιάζω || *(col)* κερδίζω.

cleanse [klenz] *vt* αποκαθαίρω, καθαρίζω, πλένω.

clear [klɪə*] *a (water etc)* καθαρός, διαυγής || *(sound)* καθαρός (ήχος) || *(meaning)* σαφής, καθαρός || *(certain)* σαφής || *(road)* ανοικτός ♦ *vt* καθαρίζω, ξεκαθαρίζω ♦ *vi (become clear)* διευκρινίζεται || ~**ance** *n (sale)* εκπαίηση, ξεπούλημα *nt* || *(free space)* απελευθέρωση, εκκένωση || *(permission)* άδεια || ~**-cut** *a* σαφής, συγκεκριμένος || ~**ing** *n* καθάρισμα *nt* || ~**ly** *ad* σαφώς, προφανώς, ασφαλώς || ~**way** *n (Brit)* εθνική οδός χωρίς στάθμευση || **to** ~ **up** *vi* διαλύω, ξεκαθαρίζω ♦ *vt* τακτοποιώ, σιάζω || ξεκαθαρίζω.

clench [klentʃ] *vt (teeth etc)* σφίγγω.

clergy ['klɜːdʒɪ] *n* κλήρος, ιερατείο || ~**man** *n* κληρικός, ιερωμένος, παπάς.

clerical ['klerɪkəl] *a* κληρικός, ιερατικός || του γραφείου.

clerk [klɑːk, (US) klɜːrk] *n (US) (salesman, woman)* υπάλληλος *m/f* || *(in office)* γραφέας *m*.

clever ['klevə*] *a (with hands)* επιδέξιος, καπάτσος || *(in mind)* ευφυής, σπιρτόζος || ~**ly** *ad* ευφυώς, έξυπνα.

cliché ['kliːʃeɪ] *n* στερεότυπο, κλισέ *nt inv.*

click [klɪk] *vi* κτυπώ, κάνω τικ-τάκ ♦ *n* κλικ *nt inv*, ξηρός κρότος.

client ['klaɪənt] *n* πελάτης/ισσα *m/f* || ~**ele** [kliːãːn'tel] *n* πελατεία.

cliff [klɪf] *n* γκρεμός.

climate ['klaɪmɪt] *n* κλίμα *nt*.

climax ['klaɪmæks] *n* αποκορύφωμα *nt*.

climb [klaɪm] *vti* ανέρχομαι, ανεβαίνω, σκαρφαλώνω ♦ *n* ανέβασμα *nt*, ανηφοριά || ~**er** *n (of*

mountains) ορειβάτης m/f|| ~ing n:
to go ~ ing κάνω ορειβασία.

clinch [klɪntʃ] vt (fig: decide)
συνάπτω, κλείνω.

cling [klɪŋ] vi προσκολλιέμαι,
πιάνομαι.

clinic ['klɪnɪk] n κλινική|| ~al a
κλινικός.

clink [klɪŋk] n κτύπημα nt
(ποτηριών) ♦ vti κτυπώ, πχώ.

clip [klɪp] n συνδετήρας, τσιμπιδάκι
♦ vt (papers) συνδέω|| (hair)
κουρεύω, ψαλιδίζω|| (hedge) κόβω ||
~ pers npl (instrument) κουρευτική
μηχανή.

clique [kliːk] n κλίκα.

cloak [kləʊk] n πανωφόρι|| (fig)
κάλυμμα nt, πέπλο|| ~room n (for
coats etc) γκαρνταρόπα || (W.C.)
αποχωρητήριο, μέρος nt, καμπινέτο.

clock [klɒk] n ρολόι || ~wise ad
δεξιόστροφος|| ~work n
μηχανισμός ρολογιού.

clog [klɒg] n (shoe) τσόκαρο ♦ vti
εμποδίζω, κωλύω, φράσσω.

close [kləʊs] a (near) κοντινός,
εγγύς, διπλανός|| (atmosphere etc)
ασφυκτικός, πνιγηρός, στενός||
(mean) σφικτός || (weather)
βαρύς ♦ ad (near) κοντά, από κοντά,
σφικτά || ~ly ad φρθ προσεκτικά, στενά,
κατά πόδας.

close [kləʊz] vt (shut) κλείνω || (end)
τελειώνω, τερματίζω ♦ vi κλείνω ||
(end) τερματίζομαι ♦ n (end) τέλος nt
|| ~ down vti κλείνω, διακόπτω
|| ~ d a (road) απαγορεύεται η
διάβαση || ~d shop n βιομηχανία
κατάστημα nt.

closet ['klɒzɪt] n μικρό δωμάτιο ||
(store-room) αποθήκη.

close-up ['kləʊsʌp] n λεπτομέρεια.

closure ['kləʊzə*] n κλείσιμο,
τερματισμός.

clot [klɒt] n (esp blood) θρόμβος,
σβώλος ♦ vi θρομβούμαι, πήζω.

cloth [klɒθ] n (material) ύφασμα nt,
πανί|| (for cleaning) πατσαβούρα.

clothe [kləʊð] vt ντύνω, καλύπτω ||
~s npl ρούχα ntpl ~s brush n
βούρτσα || ~s line n σχοινί
απλώματος ρούχων || ~s peg n
μανταλάκι.

clothing ['kləʊðɪŋ] n = clothes ||
see clothe.

cloud [klaʊd] n σύννεφο || (of dust
etc) νέφος nt, σύννεφο || ~burst n
μπόρα || ~y a συνεφιασμένος ||
(wine etc) θολωμένο.

clout [klaʊt] n κτύπημα nt ♦ vt
κτυπώ, καρπαζώνω.

clove [kləʊv] n γαρύφαλο.

clover ['kləʊvə*] n τριφύλλι || ~
leaf n τριφύλλι.

clown [klaʊn] n παλιάτσος, κλόουν
nt inv ♦ vi κάνω τον παλιάτσο.

club [klʌb] n (stick) ρόπαλο,
ματσούκα || (society) λέσχη || (golf)
κλόμπ nt inv || (CARDS) σπαθί ♦ vt
κτυπώ με ρόπαλο, με κλόμπ ♦ vi: to
~ together συνεισφέρω, βάζω
ρεφενέ || ~house n λέσχη.

cluck [klʌk] vi κακαρίζω.

clue [kluː] n νύξη, ένδειξη || he
hasn't a ~ δεν έχει ιδέα.

clump [klʌmp] n συστάδα
(δεντρων), μεγάλο κομμάτι.

clumsy ['klʌmzɪ] a (person) αδέξιος,
ατζαμής || (object) άχαρος, άκομψος.

clung [klʌŋ] pt, pp of cling.

cluster ['klʌstə*] n συστάδα, ομάδα
|| (of grapes) τσαμπί || (of stars)
σύμπλεγμα nt ♦ vi συγκεντρώνομαι,
μαζεύομαι.

clutch [klʌtʃ] n (grip, grasp) άρπαγμα
nt, σφικτό πιάσιμο || (AUT) αμπραγιάζ
nt inv, συμπλέκτης ♦ vt αρπάζω,
πιάνω σφικτά.

clutter ['klʌtə*] nt παραγεμίζω,
κάνω ανωκάτω.

coach [kəʊtʃ] n (bus) λεωφορείο,
πούλμαν nt inv || (teacher)

coagulate 49 collaborate

φροντιστής || (RAIL) άμαξα, βαγόνι || (trainer) προγυμναστής/άστρια m/f|| ντ προγυμνάζω.

coagulate [kəʊˈægjʊleɪt] vti πήζω.

coal [kəʊl] n άνθρακας, κάρβουνο, γαιάνθρακας.

coalfield [ˈkəʊlfiːld] n ανθρακοφόρος περιοχή.

coalition [kəʊəˈlɪʃən] n συνασπισμός.

coalmine [ˈkəʊlmaɪn] n ανθρακωρυχείο.

coarse [kɔːs] a (lit) τραχύς, ακατέργαστος || (fig) άξεστος, χυδαίος.

coast [kəʊst] n παραλία, ακτή || ~al a παράκτιος, παραλιακός || ~er n ακτοπλοϊκό|| ~guard n ακτοφυλακή || ~line n ακτή, παραλία.

coat [kəʊt] n (garment) σακάκι || (of animal) προβιά || (layer etc) στρώμα nt, χέρι ♦ vt (with paint etc) επιχρίω || ~ of arms n οικόσημο || ~ hanger n κρεμαστάρι || ~ing n επίστρωμα nt, χέρι.

coax [kəʊks] vt καλοπιάνω, καταφέρνω.

cobbler [ˈkɒblə*] n μπαλωματής.

cobble(stone)s [ˈkɒbl(stəʊn)z] npl βότσαλα ntpl, καλντερίμι.

cobra [ˈkəʊbrə] n κόμπρα.

cobweb [ˈkɒbwɛb] n ιστός αράχνης, αραχνή.

cocaine [kəˈkeɪn] n (MED) κοκαΐνη.

cock [kɒk] n (poultry) κόκορας, πετεινός || (bird etc) αρσενικό πουλί || (tap, faucet etc) κρουνός, κάνουλα ♦ vt σηκώνω, βάζω στραβά (το καπέλο) || (a gun) σηκώνω το λύκο || ~erel n ο κοκαρλάκι.

cockle [ˈkɒkl] n κοχύλι.

cockney [ˈkɒknɪ] n Λονδρέζος κατωτέρας τάξης, κόκνυ inv.

cockpit [ˈkɒkpɪt] n (AVIAT) θέση χειριστού.

cockroach [ˈkɒkrəʊtʃ] n κατσαρίδα.

cocktail [ˈkɒkteɪl] n (drink) κοκτέιλ nt inv|| ~ cabinet n μπάρ nt inv|| ~ party n πάρτυ κοκτέιλ nt inv.

cocoa [ˈkəʊkəʊ] n κακάο.

coconut [ˈkəʊkənʌt] n καρύδα.

cocoon [kəˈkuːn] n κουκούλι.

cod [kɒd] n μουρούνα.

code [kəʊd] n (of laws) κώδικας || (signals) σύστημα nt κρυπτογραφίας.

codify [ˈkəʊdɪfaɪ] vt κωδικοποιώ.

coerce [kəʊˈɜːs] vt πιέζω, αναγκάζω.

coercion [kəʊˈɜːʃən] n καταπίεση.

coexistence [ˈkəʊɪgˈzɪstəns] n συνύπαρξη.

coffee [ˈkɒfɪ] n καφές m.

coffin [ˈkɒfɪn] n φέρετρο, κάσα.

cog [kɒg] n (of wheel etc) δόντι.

cognac [ˈkɒnjæk] n κονιάκ nt inv.

coherent [kəʊˈhɪərənt] a (consistent) συναφής, συνεπής.

coil [kɔɪl] n κουλούρα, σπείρωμα nt|| (ELEC) πηνίο ♦ vt συσπειρώνω, τυλίγω, κουλουριάζω.

coin [kɔɪn] n νόμισμα nt, κέρμα nt|| ~age n (system) νομισματικό σύστημα nt|| νόμισμα nt.

coincide [kəʊɪnˈsaɪd] vt συμπίπτω, συμφωνώ || ~nce [kəʊˈɪnsɪdəns] n σύμπτωση.

coke [kəʊk] n κώκ nt inv.

colander [ˈkʌləndə*] n τρυπητό, σουρωτήρι.

cold [kəʊld] a ψυχρός, κρύος ♦ n ψύχος nt, κρύο || (illness) κρυολόγημα nt|| to have ~ feet (γ)κιοτέβω || to give the ~ shoulder φέρομαι ψυχρά || ~ly ad ψυχρά, κρύα.

coleslaw [ˈkəʊlslɔː] n λαχανοσαλάτα.

colic [ˈkɒlɪk] n κωλικόπονος.

collaborate [kəˈlæbəreɪt] vi συνεργάζομαι.

collaboration [kəlæbəˈreɪʃən] n συνεργασία.

collapse [kəˈlæps] vi καταρρέω ♦ n κατάρρευση.

collapsible [kəˈlæpsəbl] a πτυσσόμενος, διπλωτός.

collar [ˈkɒlə*] n (of coat, shirt) κολλάρο, γιακάς || ~**bone** n κλειδί του ώμου.

collate [kɒˈleɪt] vt (αντι)παραβάλλω.

colleague [ˈkɒliːg] n συνάδελφος m/f, συνεργάτης m/f.

collect [kəˈlɛkt] vt συλλέγω, μαζεύω ♦ vi συναθροίζομαι || ~**ion** n συλλογή || (money) είσπραξη || ~**ive** a συλλογικός || (POL.) κολλεκτίβα.

collector [kəˈlɛktə*] n (of art etc) συλλέκτης/τρια m/f || (of money) εισπράκτορας.

college [ˈkɒlɪdʒ] n (non-specialized) κολλέγιο || (esp Oxford and Cambridge) πανεπιστήμιο.

collide [kəˈlaɪd] vi συγκρούομαι, τρακάρω.

collision [kəˈlɪʒən] n σύγκρουση.

colloquial [kəˈləʊkwɪəl] a της καθομιλουμένης.

colon [ˈkəʊlən] n (GRAM) διπλή στιγμή.

colonel [ˈkɜːnl] n συνταγματάρχης.

colonial [kəˈləʊnɪəl] a αποικιακός.

colonize [ˈkɒlənaɪz] vt αποικίζω.

colony [ˈkɒlənɪ] n αποικία || (of immigrants etc) παροικία.

color [ˈkʌlə*] n (US) = **colour.**

colossal [kəˈlɒsl] a κολοσσιαίος.

colour [ˈkʌlə*] n (of) n χρώμα nt || (paints etc) βαφή, μπογιά || (of skin) χρώμα nt ♦ vt χρωματίζω, βάφω || (news) χρωματίζω, γαρνίρω || ~**s** npl χρώματα ntpl || (NAUT) σημαία || ~-**blind** a δαλτωνικός || ~**ed** a χρωματιστός, έγχρωμος || (fig) εξογκωμένος || ~**film** n (for camera) έγχρωμο φιλμ || ~-**ful** a ζωντανός || ~**television** n έγχρωμη τηλεόραση.

colt [kəʊlt] n πώλος, πουλάρι.

column [ˈkɒləm] n (pillar) κίονας, στύλος, κολώνα || (of troops) φάλαγγα || (of page) στήλη || ~**ist** n αρθρογράφος m/f.

coma [ˈkəʊmə] n κώμα nt, λήθαργος.

comb [kəʊm] n (for hair) κτένι, χτένα || (of cock) λειρί || (honey) κηρήθρα ♦ vt (hair) κτενίζω || (search) ερευνώ, ψάχνω.

combat [ˈkɒmbæt] n πάλη, διαμάχη ♦ vt (κατα)πολεμώ.

combination [kɒmbɪˈneɪʃən] n συνδυασμός, ένωση.

combine [kəmˈbaɪn] vti συνδυάζω, συνεργάζομαι, ενούμαι ♦ [ˈkɒmbaɪn] n συνδυασμός, εταιρεία, συνδικάτο || ~ **harvester** n θεριστική και αλωνιστική μηχανή.

combustion [kəmˈbʌstʃən] n καύση, ανάφλεξη.

come [kʌm] (irreg v) vi (approach) έρχομαι, φθάνω || (reach) τελειώνω, φθάνω, βρίσκομαι || (become) γίνομαι, συμβαίνω || (result) καταλήγω || ~ **to about** vi συμβαίνει, γίνομαι || ~ **to across** vt συναντώ || ~ **to by** (visit) περνώ || (find) βρίσκω, αποκτώ || ~ **to in for** vt έχω μερίδιο, μετέχω || ~ **to into** vt (enter) μπαίνω μέσα, εμφανίζομαι || (inherit) κληρονομώ || (fashion) γίνομαι της μόδας || ~ **to out with** vt βγαίνω, βγάζω || ~ **to to** vt (bill) φθάνω || (grief) μού συμβαίνει δυστύχημα || (nothing) αποτυγχάνω || (notice) αντιλαμβάνομαι || ~ **to up** to vt ανεβαίνω || (amount) φθάνω || ~ **up with** vt προφταίνω || ~**back** n επάνοδος f.

comedian [kəˈmiːdɪən] n κωμικός.

comedown ['kʌmdaʊn] n ξεπεσμός.

comedy ['kɒmɪdɪ] n κωμωδία.

comet ['kɒmɪt] n κομήτης.

comfort ['kʌmfət] n (of body) άνεση || (of mind) παρηγοριά ♦ vt παρηγορώ || ~ **able** a αναπαυτικός, άνετος.

comic ['kɒmɪk] n (actor) κωμικός || (magazine) κόμικς ntpl inv ♦ a (also: ~ **al**) κωμικός, αστείος.

comma ['kɒmə] n (GRAM) κόμμα nt.

command [kə'mɑːnd] n (order) διαταγή || (control) εξουσία, κυριαρχία, διοίκηση || (COMPUT) εντολή ♦ vt (order) διατάζω || (be in charge) διοικώ, εξουσιάζω, ελέγχω || (be able to get) κατέχω, διαθέτω ♦ vi προστάζω || ~ **eer** [kɒmən'dɪə] vt επιτάσσω || ~ **er** n (MIL) διοικητής || (NAUT) πλωτάρχης.

commandment [kə'mɑːndmənt] n εντολή.

commando [kə'mɑːndəʊ] n κομμάντο m inv, καταδρομέας.

commemorate [kə'mɛməreɪt] vt γιορτάζω.

commemoration [kəmɛmə'reɪʃən] n: **in ~ of** εις μνήμην του.

commemorative [kə'mɛmərətɪv] a αναμνηστικός.

commence [kə'mɛns] vti αρχίζω.

commend [kə'mɛnd] vt συνιστώ, επαινώ || ~ **ation** [kɒmən'deɪʃən] n έπαινος.

commensurate [kə'mɛnʃərɪt] a ανάλογος.

comment ['kɒmɛnt] n σχόλιο, εξήγηση ♦ vi (+ on) σχολιάζω, επεξηγώ || ~ **ary** n (SPORT) ρεπορτάζ nt inv || σχόλιο || ~ **ator** n σχολιαστής/σχολιάστρια m/f.

commerce ['kɒmɜːs] n εμπόριο.

commercial [kə'mɜːʃəl] a

εμπορικός ♦ n (TV) διαφήμιση || ~ **ize** vt εμπορεύομαι.

commiserate [kə'mɪzəreɪt] vi: **to ~ with** συμπονώ, συλλυπούμαι.

commission [kə'mɪʃən] n (duty) εντολή, παραγγελία || (fee) προμήθεια || (MIL) βαθμός αξιωματικού || (reporting body) επιτροπή ♦ vt αναθέτω, επιφορτίζω || **out of ~** εκτός ενεργείας, χαλασμένο || ~ **aire** n θυρωρός || ~ **er** n μέλος nt επιτροπής, αρμοστής.

commit [kə'mɪt] vt (a crime) διαπράττω (έγκλημα) || (to paper) καταγράφω || (to memory) απομνημονεύω || (entrust) εμπιστεύομαι, αναθέτω || ~ **ment** n δέσμευση, υποχρέωση.

committee [kə'mɪtɪ] n επιτροπή.

commodity [kə'mɒdɪtɪ] n εμπόρευμα nt.

common ['kɒmən] a (shared) κοινός || (knowledge etc) κοινός, συνήθης || (ordinary, usual) συνήθης, συνηθισμένος || (mean, low) χυδαίος, πρόστυχος || (frequent) συνήθης ♦ n: **in ~** από κοινού || ~ **ly** ad συνήθως || **C ~ Market** n Κοινή Αγορά || ~ **place** a κοινοτοπία, πεζός || ~ **room** n αίθουσα καθηγητών || ~ **sense** n κοινός νούς || **the C ~ wealth** n Κοινοπολιτεία.

commotion [kə'məʊʃən] n ταραχή.

communal ['kɒmjuːnl] a κοινοτικός.

commune ['kɒmjuːn] n (group of people living communally) κοινότητα ♦ [kə'mjuːn] vi (+ with) συναναστρέφομαι.

communicate [kə'mjuːnɪkeɪt] vt (transmit) ανακοινώνω, μεταδίδω ♦ vi (connect) συγκοινωνώ || (be in touch) (+ with) επικοινωνώ.

communication [kəmjuːnɪ'keɪʃən] n ανακοίνωση, μετάδοση ||

συγκοινωνία, επικοινωνία || ~ s npl (transport etc) συγκοινωνία || ~ cord n κώδων m κινδύνου.

communion [kə'mjuːnɪən] n κοινότητα || (REL) θρησκευτική ομάδα || (Holy) C~ n (Αγία) Μετάληψη.

communiqué [kə'mjuːnɪkeɪ] n ανακοινωθέν nt.

communism ['kɒmjunɪzəm] n κομμουνισμός.

communist ['kɒmjunɪst] n κομμουνιστής/ίστρια m/f ♦ a κομμουνιστικός.

community [kə'mjuːnɪtɪ] n κοινότητα || (the public) κοινωνία, το κοινό || ~ **centre** n αίθουσα αναμύξης.

commutation ticket [kɒmjuː'teɪʃəntɪkɪt] n (US) εισιτήριο διαρκείας.

compact [kəm'pækt] a συμπαγής, σφικτός ♦ ['kɒmpækt] n (agreement) σύμβαση, συμφωνία || (powder) πουδριέρα.

companion [kəm'pænɪən] n σύντροφος m/f, συνάδελφος m/f, ταίρι || ~**ship** n συντροφία.

company ['kʌmpənɪ] n (business) εταιρεία || (of people) παρέα, συντροφιά || (MIL) λόχος || (guests) κόσμος || **to keep s.o.** ~ κάνω παρέα.

comparable ['kɒmpərəbl] a συγκρίσιμος, ανάλογος, παραβλητός.

comparative [kəm'pærətɪv] a συγκριτικός, σχετικός.

compare [kəm'pɛə*] vt συγκρίνω, παραβάλλω || (+ with) παρομοιάζω ♦ vi συγκρίνομαι.

comparison [kəm'pærɪsn] n σύγκριση || παρομοίωση || **in** ~ (**with**) συγκρινόμενος (με).

compartment [kəm'pɑːtmənt] n

(NAUT) διαμέρισμα nt || (RAIL) βαγκόν-λι nt inv.

compass ['kʌmpəs] n (instrument) πυξίδα || ~**es** npl διαβήτης.

compassion [kəm'pæʃən] n ευσπλαχνία, οίκτος || ~**ate** a φιλεύσπλαχνος.

compatible [kəm'pætɪbl] a συμβιβάσιμος, σύμφωνος.

compatibility [kəmpætɪ'bɪlɪtɪ] n (COMPUT) συμβατότητα.

compel [kəm'pɛl] vt αναγκάζω, υποχρεώνω.

compendium [kəm'pɛndɪəm] n σύνοψη, επιτομή.

compensate ['kɒmpenseɪt] vt αποζημιώνω ♦ vi: **to** ~ **for** αντισταθμίζω.

compensation [kɒmpen'seɪʃən] n (money) αποζημίωση || (satisfaction) ικανοποίηση.

compère ['kɒmpɛə*] n κομπέρ m/f inv.

compete [kəm'piːt] vi συναγωνίζομαι, ανταγωνίζομαι || (for prize) διαγωνίζομαι.

competence ['kɒmpɪtəns] n ικανότητα, επιδεξιότητα.

competent ['kɒmpɪtənt] a ικανός, επιδέξιος || (office etc) αρμόδιος.

competition [kɒmpɪ'tɪʃən] n άμιλλα || (rivalry) ανταγωνισμός, συναγωνισμός.

competitive [kəm'pɛtɪtɪv] a ανταγωνιστικός, συναγωνιστικός.

competitor [kəm'pɛtɪtə*] n ανταγωνιστής/ίστρια m/f, αντίπαλος m/f.

compile [kəm'paɪl] vt συλλέγω, συναθροίζω.

complacency [kəm'pleɪsnsɪ] n αυτάρκεια.

complacent [kəm'pleɪsənt] a αυτάρεσκος, ευχαριστημένος.

complain [kəm'pleɪn] vi παραπονιέμαι, γκρινιάζω || ~**t** n

πaράπονο, γκρίνια || *(illness)* αρρώστια.

complement [ˈkɒmplɪmənt] *n* πληρότητα || *(MATH)* συμπλήρωμα *nt* || *(esp ship's crew etc)* πλήρες πλήρωμα *nt*|| ~**ary** *a* συμπληρωματικός.

complete [kəmˈpliːt] *a* πλήρης, συμπληρωμένος, τέλειος ♦ *vt* συμπληρώνω, αποτελειώνω || ~**ly** πλήρως, εντελώς.

completion [kəmˈpliːʃən] *n* συμπλήρωση, αποπεράτωση.

complex [ˈkɒmplɛks] *a* πολύπλοκος, πολυσύνθετος ♦ *n (mental)* σύμπλεγμα *nt*, κόμπλεξ *nt inv*|| *(of buildings)* σύμπλεγμα *nt.*

complexion [kəmˈplɛkʃən] *n* χρώμα *nt*, χροιά.

complexity [kəmˈplɛksɪtɪ] *n* περιπλοκή.

complicate [ˈkɒmplɪkeɪt] *vt* περιπλέκω || ~**d** *a* μπλεγμένος.

complication [kɒmplɪˈkeɪʃən] *n* περιπλοκή.

compliment [ˈkɒmplɪmənt] *n* φιλοφρόνηση, κομπλιμέντο ♦ [ˈkɒmplɪment] *vt* κομπλιμεντάρω, συγχαίρω || ~**s** *npl* ευχές *fpl*, χαιρετισμοί *mpl*|| ~**ary** *a* φιλοφρονητικός, κομπλιμεντόζος.

comply [kəmˈplaɪ] *vi*: to ~ **with** συμμορφούμαι, ενδίδω, εκπληρώ.

component [kəmˈpəunənt] *a* συνθετικός, συστατικός ♦ *n* συστατικό || *(PHYS)* συνιστώσα δύναμη.

compose [kəmˈpəuz] *vt* συντάσσω, γράφω || *(MUS)* μελοποιώ, συνθέτω || *(calm)* ηρεμώ || ~ **a** στάραχος, ήρεμος || ~**r** *n (MUS)* μουσουργός, συνθέτης.

composite [ˈkɒmpəzɪt] *a* σύνθετος, μικτός.

composition [kɒmpəˈzɪʃən] *n* σύνθεση || *(structure)* σύσταση.

compost [ˈkɒmpɒst] *n (fertilizer)* φουσκί.

composure [kəmˈpəuʒə*] *n* ηρεμία αταραξία.

compound [ˈkɒmpaund] *n (GRAM)* σύνθετος λέξη || *(enclosure)* κλειστός χώρος || *(CHEM)* ένωση ♦ *a* σύνθετος.

comprehend [kɒmprɪˈhɛnd] *vt (understand)* καταλαβαίνω || *(include)* συμπεριλαμβάνω.

comprehension [kɒmprɪˈhɛnʃən] *n* κατανόηση, αντίληψη.

comprehensive [kɒmprɪˈhɛnsɪv] *a* περιεκτικός.

compress [kəmˈpres] *vt* συμπιέζω ♦ [ˈkɒmpres] *n (MED)* επίθεμα *nt*, κομπρέσσα || ~**ion** *n (συμ)* πίεση, σύμπτυξη.

comprise [kəmˈpraɪz] *vi* αποτελούμαι από.

compromise [ˈkɒmprəmaɪz] *n* συμβιβασμός ♦ *vt (expose)* εκθέτω ♦ *vi (agree)* συμβιβάζομαι.

compulsion [kəmˈpʌlʃən] *n* βία, καταναγκασμός.

compulsory [kəmˈpʌlsərɪ] *a (obligatory)* υποχρεωτικός.

computer [kəmˈpjuːtə*] *n* υπολογιστής.

comrade [ˈkɒmrɪd] *n* σύντροφος/φισσα *m/f*, συνάδελφος *m/f*|| ~**ship** *n* καμαραντερί.

concave [ˈkɒnˈkeɪv] *a* κοίλος, βαθουλός.

conceal [kənˈsiːl] *vt (απο)* κρύπτω.

concede [kənˈsiːd] *vt (admit)* παραδέχομαι ♦ *vi (yield)* παραχωρώ.

conceit [kənˈsiːt] *n* ματαιοδοξία, ξιππασιά || ~**ed** *a* φαντασμένος, ξιππασμένος.

conceivable [kənˈsiːvəbl] *a* διανοητός, δυνατός.

conceive [kənˈsiːv] *vt (imagine)* φαντάζομαι || *(child)* συλλαμβάνω.

concentrate [ˈkɒnsəntreɪt] *vi (+*

on) συγκεντρώνομαι ♦ *vt*
συγκεντρώνω.

concentration [kɔnsən'treiʃən] *n*
συγκέντρωση || ~ **camp** *n*
στρατόπεδο συγκεντρώσεως.

concept ['kɔnsɛpt] *n* ιδέα, έννοια.

conception [kən'sɛpʃən] *n*
σύλληψη, αντίληψη.

concern [kən'sɜːn] *n* (*affair*)
ενδιαφέρον, συμφέρον || (*business*)
επιχείρηση || (*anxiety*) ανησυχία ♦ *vt*
ενδιαφέρομαι, ενδιαφέρω || ~ **ed** *a*
(*anxious*) ανήσυχος || ~ **ing** *prep* όσο
αφορά.

concert ['kɔnsət] *n* συνεννόηση,
συμφωνία || (*MUS*) συναυλία || **in** ~
από συμφώνου, μαζί || ~ **hall** *n*
αίθουσα συναυλιών.

concertina [kɔnsə'tiːnə] *n*
ακορντεόν *nt inv.*

concerto [kən'tʃɛətəu] *n* κονσέρτο.

concession [kən'sɛʃən] *n*
παραχώρηση, εκχώρηση.

conciliation [kənsili'eiʃən] *n*
συμφιλίωση.

concise [kən'sais] *a* σύντομος,
συνοπτικός.

conclude [kən'kluːd] *vt* (*end*)
τελειώνω, περαίνω || (*settle*)
συνάπτω, κλείνω || (*decide*)
συμπεραίνω, καταλήγω ♦ *vi*
τερματίζω.

conclusion [kən'kluːʒən] *n*
συμπέρασμα *nt*, τέλος *nt* || **in** ~ εν
τέλει.

conclusive [kən'kluːsiv] *a*
αποφασιστικός, πειστικός.

concoct [kən'kɔkt] *vt* (*drink etc*)
κατασκευάζω || (*plan etc*) εφευρίσκω,
καταστρώνω.

concrete [kən'kriːt] *n*
σκυροκονίαμα *nt*, μπετό ♦ *a*
συγκεκριμένος.

concur [kən'kɜː*] *vi* συμπίπτω,
συμφωνώ.

concurrently [kən'kʌrəntli] *ad*
από κοινού.

concussion [kən'kʌʃən] *n*
τράνταγμα *nt* || (*MED*) διάσειση.

condemn [kən'dɛm] *vt* καταδικάζω
|| ~ **ation** *n* καταδίκη, μομφή.

condensation [kɔndɛn'seiʃən] *n*
συμπύκνωση.

condense [kən'dɛns] *vi*
συμπυκνούμαι ♦ *vt* συμπυκνώνω ||
~ **d milk** *n* συμπυκνωμένο γάλα.

condescend [kɔndi'sɛnd] *vi*
καταδέχομαι || ~ **ing** *a*
καταδεκτικός, ευπροσήγορος.

condition [kən'diʃən] *n* (*state*)
κατάσταση, συνθήκη || (*term*) όρος
♦ *vt* ρυθμίζω, καθορίζω || **on** ~ **that**
υπό τον όρο να || ~ **al** *a* υπό όρους,
προϋποθετικός.

condolences [kən'dəulənsiz] *npl*
συλλυπητήρια *ntpl.*

condone [kən'dəun] *vt* συγχωρώ,
παραβλέπω.

conducive [kən'djuːsiv] *a*
συντελεστικός.

conduct ['kɔndʌkt] *n* (*behaviour*)
διαγωγή || (*management*) διεξαγωγή
♦ [kən'dʌkt] *vt* (*people*) οδηγώ,
φέρω || (*affairs*) διευθύνω, εκτελώ ||
(*MUS*) διευθύνω || ~ **ed tour** *n*
ξενάγηση || ~ **or** *n* (*orchestra*)
μαέστρος || (*bus*) εισπράκτορας ||
~ **ress** *n* (*bus*) εισπράκτόρισσα.

cone [kəun] *n* (*MATH*) κώνος || (*ice
cream*) παγωτό χωνάκι || (*pine*)
κουκουνάρι.

confectioner [kən'fɛkʃənə*] *n*
ζαχαροπλάστης || ~ **'s** (**shop**) *n*
ζαχαροπλαστείο || ~ **y** *n*
ζαχαροπλαστείο.

confederation [kənfɛdə'reiʃən] *n*
συνομοσπονδία.

confer [kən'fɜː*] *vt* (*grant*)
απονέμω, παρέχω ♦ *vi* (*consult*)
συζητώ, διασκέπτομαι || ~ **ence**

confess 55 conk

['kɒnfərəns] n (συν)διάσκεψη, συμβούλιο.

confess [kən'fɛs] vti (admit) (εξ)ομολογώ || (REL) εξομολογούμαι || ~**ion** n ομολογία || (REL) εξομολόγηση.

confetti [kən'fɛtɪ] n χαρτοπόλεμος, κονφετί nt inv.

confide [kən'faɪd] vi: **to** ~ **in** εμπιστεύομαι.

confidence ['kɒnfɪdəns] n (trust) εμπιστοσύνη || (secret) μυστικό || ~ **trick** n κόλπο, απάτη.

confident ['kɒnfɪdənt] a βέβαιος, σίγουρος || ~**ial** a (secret) εμπιστευτικός || (trusted) της εμπιστοσύνης.

confine [kən'faɪn] vt περιορίζω || (shut up) εγκλείω || ~**d** a (space) περιορισμένος || ~**ment** n (limiting) περιορισμός || (birth) λοχεία, τοκετός.

confirm [kən'fɜːm] vt (report) επιβεβαιώνω || (appointment) επικυρώνω || (REL) χρίσμα nt, μύρωση || ~**ed** a έμμονος, αμετάπειστος.

confiscate ['kɒnfɪskeɪt] vt δημεύω.

confiscation [kɒnfɪs'keɪʃən] n δήμευση.

conflict ['kɒnflɪkt] n σύγκρουση, διαμάχη, αντίθεση ♦ [kən'flɪkt] vi συγκρούομαι, διαφέρω, αντιμάχομαι || ~**ing** a αντιφατικός, συγκρουόμενος.

conform [kən'fɔːm] vi (+ to) συμμορφώνομαι, προσαρμόζομαι.

confront [kən'frʌnt] vt αντιμετωπίζω || ~**ation** n αντιμετώπιση.

confuse [kən'fjuːz] vt συγχύζω, ταράσσω.

confusing [kən'fjuːzɪŋ] a συγκεχυμένος.

confusion [kən'fjuːʒən] n (disorder)

σύγχυση || (tumult) αναστάτωση, αναμουμπούλα || (embarrassment) σάστισμα nt.

congeal [kən'dʒiːl] vi πήζω.

congenial [kən'dʒiːnɪəl] a ταιριαστός, ευχάριστος.

congested [kən'dʒɛstɪd] a (overcrowded) συνωστισμένος.

congestion [kən'dʒɛstʃən] n (of traffic etc) συμφόρηση, συνωστισμός.

conglomeration [kənglɒmə'reɪʃən] n σύμφυρμα nt, σώμπηγμα nt.

congratulate [kən'grætjʊleɪt] vt (+ on) συγχαίρω.

congratulations [kəngrætjʊ'leɪʃənz] npl συγχαρητήρια ntpl.

congregate ['kɒŋgrɪgeɪt] vi συναθροίζομαι.

congregation [kɒŋgrɪ'geɪʃən] n συνάθροιση, εκκλησίασμα nt.

congress ['kɒŋgrɛs] n συνέλευση, συνέδριο || (US) Κογκρέσσο || ~**man** n (US) μέλος nt του Κογκρέσσου.

conical ['kɒnɪkəl] a κωνικός, κωνοειδής.

conifer ['kɒnɪfə*] n κωνοφόρο (δένδρο).

conjecture [kən'dʒɛktʃə*] n εικασία, συμπερασμός ♦ vti εικάζω, συμπεραίνω.

conjugal ['kɒndʒʊgəl] a συζυγικός.

conjunction [kən'dʒʌŋkʃən] n σύνδεσμος || **in** ~ **with** από κοινού με.

conjure ['kʌndʒə*] vti πλέκω, μηχανεύω || **to** ~ **up** vt επινοώ, επικαλούμαι || ~**r** n ταχυδακτυλουργός.

conjuring ['kʌndʒərɪŋ] n: ~ **trick** n ταχυδακτυλουργία.

conk [kɒŋk] **to** ~ **out** vi (col) σβήνω.

connect [kə'nɛkt] vti (train) συνδέω, συνδέομαι, συνδυάζω || ~ion n (joining) σύνδεση, συνάφεια || (relation) σχέση, συσχετισμός || in ~ ion with σχετικά με.

connexion [kə'nɛkʃən] n = connection | see **connect**.

connoisseur [kɔnə'sɜ:*] n ειδήμονας, τεχνοκρίτης.

conquer ['kɔŋkə*] vt (overcome) υπερνικώ, υποτάσσω || (by war) κατακτώ, κυριεύω || ~or n κατακτητής/ήτρια m/f, νικητής/ήτρια m/f.

conquest ['kɔŋkwɛst] n κατάκτηση.

conscience ['kɔnʃəns] n συνείδηση.

conscientious [kɔnʃi'ɛnʃəs] a ευσυνείδητος.

conscious ['kɔnʃəs] a συνειδητός, συναισθανόμενος || ~ness n συναίσθηση.

conscript ['kɔnskript] n στρατεύσιμος, κληρωτός || ~ion [kən'skripʃən] n στρατολογία.

consecrate ['kɔnsikreit] vt εγκαινιάζω, χειροτονώ || (devote) αφιερώνω.

consecutive [kən'sɛkjutiv] a διαδοχικός.

consensus [kən'sɛnsəs] n κοινή συναίνεση, επικρατούσα γνώμη.

consent [kən'sɛnt] n συγκατάθεση, συναίνεση ♦ vi (+ to) συγκατατίθεμαι.

consequence ['kɔnsikwəns] n (importance) σπουδαιότητα || (result, effect) συνέπεια, επακόλουθο.

consequently ['kɔnsikwəntli] ad επομένως, συνεπώς.

conservation [kɔnsə'veiʃən] n συντήρηση, διατήρηση.

conservative [kən'sɜ:vətiv] a συντηρητικός, μετριοπαθής || **C**~ a (party) συντηρητικός || n Συντηρητικός/ή m/f.

conservatory [kən'sɜ:vətri] n (greenhouse) θερμοκήπιο, σέρρα || (MUS) ωδείο.

conserve [kən'sɜ:v] vt συντηρώ, διατηρώ.

consider [kən'sidə*] vt (think over) μελετώ || (take into account) λαμβάνω υπόψη || (deem) θεωρώ.

considerable [kən'sidərəbl] a σημαντικός, αξιόλογος.

considerate [kən'sidərit] a διακριτικός, αβρός.

consideration [kənsidə'reiʃən] n (thoughtfulness) αβροφροσύνη, διακριτικότητα || (serious thought) μελέτη, σκέψη || (reason) λόγος || (reward) αμοιβή.

considering [kən'sidəriŋ] prep λαμβανομένου υπόψη.

consign [kən'sain] vt αποστέλλω, παραδίδω || ~ment n αποστολή.

consist [kən'sist] vi (+ of) συνίσταμαι, αποτελούμαι.

consistency [kən'sistənsi] n (firmness) συνοχή, συνέπεια, σταθερότητα || (density) πυκνότητα, στερεότητα.

consistent [kən'sistənt] a σταθερός, συνεπής, σύμφωνος.

consolation [kɔnsə'leiʃən] n παρηγορία.

console [kən'səul] vt παρηγορώ || (COMPUT) πληκτρολόγιο.

consolidate [kən'sɔlideit] vt συγκεντρώνω, παγιώνω.

consommé [kən'sɔmei] n ζωμός κρέατος, κονσομέ nt inv.

consonant ['kɔnsənənt] n (GRAM) σύμφωνο.

consortium [kən'sɔ:tiəm] n κοινοπραξία, κονσόρτσιουμ nt inv.

conspicuous [kən'spikjuəs] a καταφανής, περίβλεπτος || (prominent) αξιοσημείωτος, σημαντικός.

conspiracy ['kən'spɪrəsɪ] n
συνωμοσία.

conspire [kən'spaɪə*] vi συνωμοτώ,
συνεργώ.

constable ['kʌnstəbl] n
αστυφύλακας, χωροφύλακας.

constabulary [kən'stæbjulərɪ] n
αστυνομία.

constant ['kɒnstənt] a σταθερός,
συνεχής || ~**ly** ad σταθερά,
συνεχώς.

constellation [kɒnstə'leɪʃən] n
αστερισμός.

consternation [kɒnstə'neɪʃən] n
κατάπληξη.

constipated ['kɒnstɪpeɪtɪd] a
δυσκοίλιος.

constituency [kən'stɪtjuənsɪ] n
εκλογική περιφέρεια.

constituent [kən'stɪtjuənt] n
(elector) ψηφοφόρος m/f || (essential
part) συστατικό.

constitute ['kɒnstɪtjuːt] vt (amount
to) συνιστώ, αποτελώ.

constitution [kɒnstɪ'tjuːʃən] n
(laws) σύνταγμα nt || (health) κράση
|| ~**al** a συνταγματικός.

constrain [kən'streɪn] vt
εξαναγκάζω || ~**t** n εξαναγκασμός /
(feelings) ταραχή, τράκ nt inv.

constrict [kən'strɪkt] vt συσφίγγω ||
~**ion** n σύσφιγξη, σφίξιμο.

construct [kən'strʌkt] vt
κατασκευάζω, οικοδομώ || ~**ion** n
κατασκευή, οικοδόμηση || (GRAM)
σύνταξη, ερμηνεία || ~**ive** a
εποικοδομητικός, δημιουργικός.

construe [kən'struː] vt ερμηνεύω.

consul ['kɒnsəl] n πρόξενος || ~**ate**
['kɒnsjulɪt] n προξενείο.

consult [kən'sʌlt] vt
συμβουλεύομαι || ~**ant** n (MED)
ειδικός γιατρός || (other specialist)
σύμβουλος m/f || ~**ation** n
συμβούλιο, συνδιάσκεψη || ~**ing
room** n ιατρείο.

consume [kən'sjum] vt
καταναλίσκω || ~**r** n καταναλωτής.

consumption [kən'sʌmpʃən] n
κατανάλωση || (MED) φθίση,
φυματίωση.

contact ['kɒntækt] n επαφή ♦ vt
έρχομαι σε επαφή με || ~ **lenses** npl
φακοί mpl επαφής.

contagious [kən'teɪdʒəs] a
μεταδοτικός, κολλητικός.

contain [kən'teɪn] vt περιέχω || **to
~ o.s.** συγκρατούμαι || ~**er** n
(small) δοχείο || (TRANSPORT)
(εμπορευματικό) κιβώτιο.

contaminate [kən'tæmɪneɪt] vt
μολύνω, μιαίνω.

contamination [kəntæmɪ'neɪʃən] n
μόλυνση, μίανση.

contemplate ['kɒntempleɪt] vt
(look at) κυττάζω, παρατηρώ ||
(meditate) μελετώ, αναπολώ || (intend)
σχεδιάζω.

contemplation [kɒntem'pleɪʃən] n
σκέψη, συλλογή.

contemporary [kən'tempərərɪ] a
σύγχρονος ♦ n σύγχρονος/n m/f,
συνομήλικος/n m/f.

contempt [kən'tempt] n
περιφρόνηση || ~**ible** a
αξιοκαταφρόνητος || ~**uous** a
περιφρονητικός.

contend [kən'tend] vt (strive)
(συν)αγωνίζομαι || (argue)
ισχυρίζομαι || n (competitor)
ανταγωνιστής/ίστρια m/f.

content [kən'tent] a
ικανοποιημένος, ευχαριστημένος ♦
vt ικανοποιώ ♦ ['kɒntent] n (of article
etc) περιεχόμενο || ~**s** npl (of room)
περιεχόμενα ntpl || (of book) (πίνακας)
περιεχομένων || (of barrel)
περιεκτικότητα || ~**ed** a
ικανοποιημένος.

contention [kən'tenʃən] n (dispute)
αγώνας, διαμάχη || (opinion)
ισχυρισμός.

contentment [kən'tɛntmənt] *n*
ικανοποίηση.

contest ['kɒntɛst] *n* αγώνας, πάλη
♦ [kən'tɛst] *vt* διαμφισβητώ,
διεκδικώ, αγωνίζομαι || ~**ant** *n*
αγωνιζόμενος/η *m/f*,
διεκδικητής/ήτρια *m/f*.

context ['kɒntɛkst] *n*
συμφραζόμενα *ntpl*.

continent ['kɒntinənt] *n* ήπειρος *f* ||
the C~ Ευρώπη || ~**al** *a*
ηπειρωτικός.

contingency [kən'tɪndʒənsɪ] *n*
ενδεχόμενο, σύμπτωση.

contingent [kən'tɪndʒənt] *n*
ενδεχόμενος || *(MIL)* τμήμα στρατού
ή ναυτικού ♦ *a* (+ *(up)on)*
εξαρτώμενος από.

continual [kən'tɪnjuəl] *a (endless)*
συνεχής, αδιάκοπος || *(often repeated)*
συχνός || ~**ly** *ad* συνεχώς.

continuation [kəntɪnju'eɪʃən] *n*
συνέχεια, συνέχιση.

continue [kən'tɪnjuː] *vi* συνεχίζομαι
|| *(remain)* (παρα)μένω || συνεχίζω ||
(resume) εξακολουθώ.

continuity [kɒntɪ'njuːɪtɪ] *n*
συνέχεια.

continuous [kən'tɪnjuəs] *a*
συνεχής, αδιάκοπος.

contort [kən'tɔːt] *vt* συστρίβω,
παραμορφώνω || ~**ion** *n* στρίψιμο ||
(of face) μορφασμός || ~**ionist** *n*
ακροβάτης/ισσα *m/f*.

contour ['kɒntuə*] *n (shape)*
περίγραμμα *nt* || *(of map)* ισοϋψείς
καμπύλες *fpl*.

contraband ['kɒntrəbænd] *n*
λαθρεμπόριο, κοντραμπάντο.

contraception [kɒntrə'sɛpʃən] *n*
πρόληψη συλλήψεως.

contraceptive [kɒntrə'sɛptɪv] *n*
αντισυλληπτικό.

contract [kɒn'trækt] *n* συμβόλαιο,
συμφωνία ♦ [kən'trækt] *vi (to do sth)*
συμφωνώ, συμβάλλομαι || *(become*

smaller) συστέλλομαι, στενεύω ||
~**ion** *n* συστολή, μάζεμα *nt* || ~**or** *n*
εργολάβος, προμηθευτής.

contradict [kɒntrə'dɪkt] *vt (say the
opposite)* αντιλέγω || *(deny)* διαψεύδω
|| ~**ion** *n (in terms)* αντίφαση ||
(denial) διάψευση.

contralto [kən'træltəʊ] *n*
μεσόφωνος, κοντράλτο.

contraption [kən'træpʃən] *n*
μηχανή, μαραφέτι.

contrary ['kɒntrərɪ] *a (opposite)*
ενάντιος, αντίθετος || *(unfavourable)*
αντίθετος, δυσμενής || **on the** ~
τουναντίον.

contrast ['kɒntrɑːst] *n* σύγκριση,
αντίθεση ♦ [kən'trɑːst] *vt* συγκρίνω,
αντιπαραβάλλω.

contravene [kɒntrə'viːn] *vt (a rule
etc)* παραβαίνω, καταπατώ || *(conflict
with)* διαφεύδω, προσκρούω.

contribute [kən'trɪbjuːt] *vi (help)*
συμβάλλω, βοηθώ || *(subscribe)*
συνεισφέρω ♦ *vt* καταβάλλω.

contribution [kɒntrɪ'bjuːʃən] *n*
συνεισφορά, συνεργασία.

contributor [kən'trɪbjʊtə*] *n*
συνεισφέρων/ουσα *m/f*
συνεργάτης/ιδα *m/f*.

contrite ['kɒntraɪt] *a* συντριμμένος,
μετανοών.

contrive [kən'traɪv] *vt (bring about)*
καταφέρνω.

control [kən'trəʊl] *vt (check)*
συγκρατώ, χαλιναγωγώ || *(direct)*
διευθύνω, εξουσιάζω ♦ *n (in check)*
έλεγχος, επίβλεψη || *(restraint)*
χαλινός || ~**s** *npl* χειριστήριο,
έλεγχος || ~**key** *n (COMPUT)*
πλήκτρο ελέγχου.

controversial [kɒntrə'vɜːʃəl] *a*
συζητήσιμος.

controversy ['kɒntrəvɜːsɪ] *n*
συζήτηση, διαφωνία.

convalesce [kɒnvə'lɛs] *vi*

αναρρωνύω || ~**nce** n ανάρρωση ||
~**nt** a, a αναρρωνύων.
convene [kən'viːn] vti συγκαλώ,
συνέρχομαι.
convenience [kən'viːnɪəns] n
(being convenient) καταλληλότητα,
συμφωνία || (thing) ευκολία, άνεση.
convenient [kən'viːnɪənt] a
κατάλληλος, βολικός, χρήσιμος.
convent ['kɒnvənt] n μονή
γυναικών.
convention [kən'venʃən] n
(assembly) συνέδριο, συνέλευση ||
(custom) έθιμο, συνήθεια || ~**al** a
(traditional) εθιμοτυπικός,
συνθεσμένος.
converge [kən'vɜːdʒ] vi συγκλίνω.
conversant [kən'vɜːsənt] a (+
with) οικείος, γνωστός.
conversation [kɒnvə'seɪʃən] n
συνδιάλεξη, συνομιλία, κουβέντα ||
~**al** a ομιλητικός, καθομιλούμενος.
converse [kən'vɜːs] vi συνομιλώ,
συνδιαλέγομαι ♦ ['kɒnvɜːs] a
αντίθετος || ~**ly** ad αντίστροφα,
αντιθέτως.
conversion [kən'vɜːʃən] n
μετατροπή || (esp REL) προσηλύτιση ||
~ **table** n πίνακας μετατροπών.
convert [kən'vɜːt] vt (change)
μετατρέπω || (esp REL) προσηλυτίζω
♦ ['kɒnvɜːt] n προσήλυτος || ~**ible**
n (AUT) καμπριολέ κπ inv.
convex ['kɒn'veks] a κυρτός.
convey [kən'veɪ] vt (carry)
μεταφέρω || (communicate)
μεταβιβάζω, μεταδίδω || ~**or belt** n
μεταφορέας.
convict [kən'vɪkt] vt καταδικάζω ♦
['kɒnvɪkt] n κατάδικος/n m/f || ~**ion**
n (verdict) καταδίκη || (belief)
πεποίθηση.
convince [kən'vɪns] vt πείθω.
convincing [kən'vɪnsɪŋ] a
πειστικός.

convoy ['kɒnvɔɪ] n συνοδεία,
νηοπομπή.
convulse [kən'vʌls] vt (esp with
laughter) ξεραίνομαι στα γέλια.
convulsion [kən'vʌlʃən] n
σπασμός.
coo [kuː] vi (dove) τερετίζω σαν
περιστέρι.
cook [kuk] vt μαγειρεύω ♦ vi
ψήνομαι n μάγειρας || ~**book** n
βιβλίο μαγειρικής || ~**er** n συσκευή
μαγειρέματος || ~**ery** n μαγειρική ||
~**ery book** n = **cookbook** || ~**ie** n
(US) μπισκότο || ~**ing** n μαγειρική.
cool [kuːl] a (fairly cold) δροσερός ||
(calm) ψύχραιμος || (unfriendly)
ψυχρός, αδιάφορος || (impudent)
αναιδής, θρασύς ♦ vti δροσίζω,
κρυώνω || ~**ness** n ψύχρα,
ψυχρότητα.
coop [kuːp] n κοτέτσι, κλούβα ♦ vt:
to ~ **up** (fig) περιορίζω, κλείνω.
co-op ['kəʊ'ɒp] n =
cooperative.
cooperate [kəʊ'ɒpəreɪt] vi
συνεργάζομαι.
cooperation [kəʊɒpə'reɪʃən] n
συνεργασία.
cooperative [kəʊ'ɒpərətɪv] a
συνεργατικός ♦ n (farmers)
συνεταιρισμός || ~ **store** n (retail)
πρατήριο συνεταιρισμού.
coordinate [kəʊ'ɔːdɪneɪt] vt
συνδυάζω, συντονίζω.
coordination [kəʊɔːdɪ'neɪʃən] n
συντονισμός.
coot [kuːt] n φαλαρίδα, λούφα.
cope [kəʊp] vi (+ with) αντιμετωπίζω,
αντεπεξέρχομαι.
co-pilot ['kəʊ'paɪlət] n δεύτερος
χειριστής.
copper ['kɒpə*] n χαλκός, μπακίρι ||
(coin) δεκάρα || (sl: policeman)
αστυφύλακας.
coppice ['kɒpɪs] n, **copse** [kɒps] n
δασύλλιο, λόχμη.

copulate ['kɒpjuleɪt] vi
συνουσιάζομαι, γαμῶ.

copy ['kɒpɪ] n (imitation) αντίγραφο,
αντιγραφή || (of book) αντίτυπο ♦ vt
αντιγράφω, απομιμούμαι || (COMPUT)
αντιγράφω || ~ **book** n τετράδιο ||
~ **cat** n μιμητής/τρια m/f|| ~ **right**
n πνευματική ιδιοκτησία || ~ **right**
reserved απαγορεύεται η
αναδημοσίευση.

coral ['kɒrəl] n κοράλλιο || ~ **reef** n
κοραλλιογενές νησί.

cord [kɔːd] n σχοινί, χορδή || see
vocal.

cordial ['kɔːdɪəl] a εγκάρδιος || ~**ly**
ad (invite) εγκάρδια, θερμά.

cordon ['kɔːdn] n (ornamental)
κορδόνι || (of police etc) ζώνη.

corduroy ['kɔːdərɔɪ] n κοτλέ nt inv.

core [kɔː*] n πυρήνας, καρδιά ♦ vt
αφαιρώ το πυρήνα.

cork [kɔːk] n φελλός || (of bottle)
πώμα nt|| ~**screw** n τιρ-μπουσόν nt
inv.

cormorant ['kɔːmərənt] n
φαλακροκόρακας, καλικατζού f inv.

corn [kɔːn] n σιτηρά ntpl,
δημητριακά ntpl || (US: maize)
καλαμπόκι || (on foot) κάλος.

cornea ['kɔːnɪə] n κερατοειδής.

corned [kɔːnd]: ~ **beef** n βοδινό
κρέας σε κονσέρβα.

corner ['kɔːnə*] n (of street) γωνία ||
(of room) γωνία, κόχη || (fig) δύσκολη
θέση ♦ vt φέρνω σε δύσκολη θέση,
στριμώχνω || (ECON) μονοπωλώ ♦ vi
(turn) παίρνω στροφή || ~ **kick** n
κόρνερ nt inv|| ~**stone** n
ακρογωνιαίος λίθος, βάση.

cornet ['kɔːnɪt] n (MUS) κορνέτα ||
(ice cream) χωνάκι.

cornflour ['kɔːnflaʊə*] n
καλαμποκάλευρο, κορνφλάουερ nt
inv.

cornice ['kɔːnɪs] n κορνίζα.

cornstarch ['kɔːnstɑːtʃ] n (US) =
cornflour.

corny ['kɔːnɪ] a (joke) σαχλός.

coronary ['kɒrənərɪ] a στεφανιαίος
♦ n στεφανιαίά || ~ **thrombosis** n
θρόμβωση της στεφανιαίας.

coronation [kɒrə'neɪʃən] n στέψη.

coroner ['kɒrənə*] n
ιατροδικαστής m/f.

corporal ['kɔːpərəl] n (MIL)
δεκανέας || (AVIAT) υποσμηνίας ♦ a
σωματικός.

corporation [kɔːpə'reɪʃən] n
σωματείο || (esp business) εταιρεία.

corps [kɔː*] n (στρατιωτικό) σώμα
nt.

corpse [kɔːps] n πτώμα nt, κουφάρι.

corpulent ['kɔːpjulənt] a
παχύσαρκος.

corpuscle ['kɔːpʌsl] n σωματίδιο ||
(blood corpuscle) αιμοσφαίριο.

corral [kɔ'rɑːl] n μάντρα.

correct [kə'rekt] a (accurate)
ακριβής, ορθός, διορθωμένος ||
(proper) άμογος, όπως πρέπει ♦ vt
(papers etc) διορθώνω || (make right)
επανορθώνω || ~**ion** n διόρθωση ||
~**ly** ad ορθά, σωστά.

correlate ['kɒrɪleɪt] vi σχετίζομαι,
συσχετίζω.

correlation [kɒrɪ'leɪʃən] n
συσχετισμός, συσχέτιση.

correspond [kɒrɪs'pɒnd] vi (agree
with) ανταποκρίνομαι, ταιριάζω ||
(write) αλληλογραφώ || ~**ence** n
(letters) αλληλογραφία || (similarity)
αντιστοιχία, αντανάκριση || ~**ence**
course n μάθημα δι' αλληλογραφίας
|| ~**ent** n (reporter)
ανταποκριτής/τρια m/f|| ~**ing** a
αντίστοιχος.

corridor ['kɒrɪdɔː*] n διάδρομος.

corroborate [kə'rɒbəreɪt] vt
επιβεβαιώνω, ενισχύω.

corroboration [kərɒbə'reɪʃən] n
επιβεβαίωση, επίρρωση.

corrode [kə'rəʊd] *vti* διαβρώνω, σκουριάζω.

corrosion [kə'rəʊʒən] *n* διάβρωση, σκωρίαση.

corrugated ['kɒrəgeitid] *a* κυματοειδής || ~ **cardboard** *n* κυματοειδές χαρτόνι || ~ **iron** *n* αυλακωτό έλασμα *nt*.

corrupt [kə'rʌpt] *a* διεφθαρμένος ♦ *vt* διαφθείρω || ~**ion** *n* διαφθορά, δεκασμός.

corset ['kɔːsit] *n* κορσές *m*.

cortège [kɔː'teiʒ] *n* νεκρώσιμος πομπή.

cortisone ['kɔːtizəʊn] *n* κορτιζόνη.

cosh [kɒʃ] *n* μαγκούρα, βούρδουλας ♦ *vt* κτυπώ με βούρδουλα.

cosiness ['kəʊzinis] *n* άνεση.

cosmetic [kɒz'metik] *n* καλλυντικό.

cosmic ['kɒzmik] *a* κοσμικός.

cosmonaut ['kɒzmənɔːt] *n* αστροναύτης, κοσμοναύτης.

cosmopolitan [kɒzmə'pɒlitən] *a* κοσμοπολιτικός.

cosmos ['kɒzmɒs] *n* κόσμος, σύμπαν *nt*.

cost [kɒst] *(irreg v)* *n* κόστος *nt*, τιμή, δαπάνη ♦ *vt* κοστίζω, || **it ~s £5** στοιχίζει πέντε λίρες, || **it ~s too much** στοιχίζει πολλά || **it ~ him his life** τού κόστισε τη ζωή || **at all ~s** πάση θυσία.

costly ['kɒstli] *a (expensive)* δαπανηρός || *(jewellery etc)* πολύτιμος.

cost price ['kɒstprais] *n* τιμή κόστους.

costume ['kɒstjuːm] *n (style of dress)* ένδυμα *nt*, φορεσιά, μόδα || *(woman's outer clothes)* ενδυμασία, κοστούμι || *(for bathing)* μπανιερό, μαγιό *nt inv*.

cosy ['kəʊzi] *a* αναπαυτικός, ζεστός.

cot [kɒt] *n (child's bed)* κρεββάτακι.

cottage ['kɒtidʒ] *n* εξοχικό σπιτάκι || ~ **cheese** *n* άσπρο τυρί.

cotton ['kɒtn] *n* βαμβάκι, μπαμπάκι || ~ **wool** *n* ακατέργαστο βαμβάκι.

couch [kaʊtʃ] *n* καναπές *m* ♦ *vt* εκφράζω, συγκαλύπτω.

cough [kɒf] *vi* βήχω ♦ *n* βήχας || ~ **drop** *n* παστίλια για το βήχα.

could [kʊd] *pt of* **can** || ~**n't** = **could not** | *see* **can**.

council ['kaʊnsl] *n* συμβούλιο || ~**lor** *n* σύμβουλος *m/f*.

counsel ['kaʊnsl] *n (LAW)* δικηγόρος *m/f*| *(opinion)* συμβουλή || ~**lor** *n* σύμβουλος.

count [kaʊnt] *vt (add up)* μετρώ, αριθμώ || *(include)* υπολογίζω, συμπεριλαμβάνω ♦ *vi (be of importance)* υπολογίζομαι, στηρίζομαι ♦ *n (reckoning)* αρίθμηση, μέτρηση, λογαριασμός || *(nobleman)* κόμης || **to ~ on** *vt* υπολογίζω, στηρίζομαι σε || **to ~ up** *vt* προσθέτω.

counter ['kaʊntə*] *n* θυρίδα, γκισέ *nt inv* || *(machine that counts)* μετρητής ♦ *vt* αντιτίθεμαι, ανταπαντώ || *ad* εναντίον, αντιθέτως || ~**act** *vt* αντιδρώ, εξουδετερώνω || ~**-attack** *n* αντεπίθεση || ~**balance** *vt* αντισταθμίζω || ~**-espionage** *n* αντικατασκοπεία.

counterfeit ['kaʊntəfit] *a* πλαστός, κίβδηλος ♦ *n* παραποίηση, απάτη ♦ *vt* πλαστογραφώ.

counterfoil ['kaʊntəfɔil] *n* στέλεχος *nt*.

counterpart ['kaʊntəpaːt] *n* αντίστοιχο, ταίρι.

countess ['kaʊntis] *n* κόμισσα, κοντέσσα.

countless ['kaʊntlis] *a* αναρίθμητος, αμέτρητος.

country ['kʌntri] *n (land)* χώρα || *(of birth)* πατρίδα || *(rural district)* ύπαιθρος *f*, εξοχή, επαρχία || *(region)* περιοχή || ~ **dancing** *n* εθνικός χορός, λαϊκός χορός || ~ **house** *n*

εξοχικό σπίτι || ～**man** *n (national)*
(συμ)πατριώτης || *(rural)* επαρκιώτης,
χωριάτης || ～**side** *n* ύπαιθρος *f.*

county ['kauntɪ] *n* κομπτεία,
επαρχία || ～ **town** *n* πρωτεύουσα
κομπτείας.

coup [ku:] *n (also:* ～ **d'état**)
πραξικόπημα *nt.*

coupé ['ku:peɪ] *n* κουπέ *nt inv.*

couple ['kʌpl] *n* ζευγάρι, δύο ♦ *vt*
ενώνω, ζευγαρώνω.

couplet ['kʌplɪt] *n* δίστοιχο.

coupling ['kʌplɪŋ] *n* σύζευξη.

coupon ['ku:pɔn] *n* κουπόνι,
απόκομμα *nt.*

courage ['kʌrɪdʒ] *n* θάρρος *nt,*
γενναιότητα || ～**ous** *a* θαρραλέος.

courier ['kurɪə*] *n* αγγελιοφόρος.

course [kɔːs] *n (path, track)*
διαδρομή || *(line of action)* πορεία,
δρόμος || *(series, procedure)* μάθημα
nt, κουρ *nt inv* || *(career, journey)*
πορεία || *(part of meal)* φαγητό, πιάτο
|| **of** ～ φυσικά, και βέβαια || **in the**
～ **of** κατά τη διάρκεια του || **in due**
～ εν καιρώ δέοντι || *see* **golf.**

court [kɔːt] *n (attendants of sovereign)*
αυλή || *(residence of sovereign)*
(βασιλική) αυλή || *(of justice)*
δικαστήριο ♦ *vt* κορτάρω,
προσκαλώ, επιδιώκω || *see* **tennis.**

courteous ['kɔːtɪəs] *a* ευγενής.

courtesy ['kɔːtɪsɪ] *n* ευγένεια.

courthouse ['kɔːthaus] *n (US)*
δικαστικό μέγαρο.

courtier ['kɔːtɪə*] *n* αυλικός.

court-martial ['kɔːt'mɑːʃəl] *n*
στρατοδικείο.

court room *n* αίθουσα
δικαστηρίου.

courtyard ['kɔːtjɑːd] *n* αυλή.

cousin ['kʌzn] *n* ξάδελφος/η *m/f.*

cove [kəuv] *n* όρμος.

cover ['kʌvə*] *vt (place over)*
καλύπτω, σκεπάζω || *(shield, screen)*
καλύπτω, προστατεύω, κρύβω || *(deal*

with) καλύπτω, περιλαμβάνω ||
(protect) προστατεύω ♦ *n* κάλυμμα
nt, σκέπασμα *nt* || ～**age** *n (of news)*
ρεπορτάζ *nt inv* || ～ **charge** *n*
κουβέρ *nt inv* || ～**ing** *n* κάλυψη,
σκέπασμα *nt,* επένδυση || ～**ing
letter** *n* επιβεβαιωτική επιστολή.

covet ['kʌvɪt] *vt* εποφθαλμιώ.

cow [kau] *n* αγελάδα.

coward ['kauəd] *n* άνανδρος/η *m/f,*
δειλός/η *m/f* || ～**ice** *n* δειλία || ～**ly**
a άνανδρος, δειλός.

cowboy ['kaubɔɪ] *n* καουμπόι *nt inv.*

cower ['kauə*] *vi* μαζεύομαι, τρέμω.

cowshed ['kauʃed] *n* βουστάσιο.

coxswain ['kɔksn] *n (abbr:* **cox**)
πηδαλιούχος.

coy [kɔɪ] *a* ντροπαλός, σεμνός.

c.p.s. *abbr see* **character.**

CPU *abbr see* **central.**

crab [kræb] *n* κάβουρας || ～ **apple**
n αγριόμηλο.

crack [kræk] *n (sharp noise)* κρότος,
τριγμός || *(of whip)* στράκα || *(split)*
ρωγμή, σκάσιμο ♦ *vt (noise)* κροτώ ||
(split) θραύω, ραγίζω ♦ *a* λαμπρός,
εκλεκτός || ～**er** *n (firework)*
βαρελότο, στράκα || *(biscuit)*
ναξιμαδάκι, μπισκότο || **to** ～ **up** *vi*
κομματιάζω || *(fig)* καταρρέω.

crackling ['kræklɪŋ] *n*
κροταλισμός, τρίξιμο || *(of pig)* νέσα
ψημένου γουρουνιού.

cradle ['kreɪdl] *n* κοιτίδα, λίκνο,
κούνια.

craft [krɑːft] *n (skill)* τέχνη,
χειροτεχνία, επάγγελμα *nt* || *(cunning)*
πανουργία, δόλος || *(boat)* σκάφος
nt, βάρκα || ～**sman** *n* τεχνίτης ||
～**smanship** *n* τέχνη || ～**y** *a*
πανούργος, πονηρός,
πολυμήχανος.

crag [kræg] *n* κατόβραχο, γκρεμός
|| ～**gy** *a* απόκρημνος, βραχώδης.

cram [kræm] *vt* μπάζω, χώνω.

cramp [kræmp] n (MED) σπασμός, κράμπα ♦ vt εμποδίζω, περιορίζω.

crane [kreɪn] n γερανός, κρένι.

crank [kræŋk] n (lever) (χειρο)στρόφαλος, μανιβέλα || (person) ιδιότυπος, εκκεντρικός ♦ vt βάζω μπρος με μανιβέλλα || ~**shaft** n στροφαλοφόρος (άξωνας).

cranny ['krænɪ] n σχισμή, ρωγμή.

crash [kræʃ] n κρότος, βρόντος || (AVIAT) συντριβή, πτώση || (AUT) σύγκρουση || (ECON) κραχ nt inv ♦ vti πέφτω, συντρίβομαι || ~ **helmet** n προστατευτικό κράνος || ~ **landing** n αναγκαστική προσγείωση.

crate [kreɪt] n κασόνι, κοφίνι, καφάσι.

crater ['kreɪtə*] n κρατήρας.

cravat(e) [krə'væt] n γραβάτα.

crave [kreɪv] vi (+ for) εκλιπαρώ, ποθώ.

craving ['kreɪvɪŋ] n πόθος, λαχτάρα.

crawl [krɔːl] vi έρπω, σέρνομαι ♦ n σύρσιμο, βραδυπορία || (swimming) κρώουλ nt inv.

crayon ['kreɪən] n κραγιόνι, παστέλ nt inv.

craze [kreɪz] n μανία, λόξα.

crazy ['kreɪzɪ] a (foolish) ανόητος || (insane) παράφρονας, τρελλός, μουρλός.

creak [kriːk] n τριγμός ♦ vi τρίζω.

cream [kriːm] n καϊμάκι, κρέμα, σαντιγί f inv || (polish) αλοιφή || (cosmetic) κρέμα || (colour) ιβουάρ nt inv, κρεμ || ~ **cake** n πάστα, τούρτα || ~**y** α καϊμακλίδικος, βουτιρένιος.

crease [kriːs] n πτυχή, τσάκισμα nt, τσαλάκωμα nt ♦ vti ζαρώνω, τσαλακώνω.

create [kriː'eɪt] vt (bring into being) δημιουργώ || (cause) προξενώ || (COMPUT: file) δημιουργώ.

creation [kriː'eɪʃən] n δημιούργημα nt.

creative [kriː'eɪtɪv] a δημιουργικός.

creator [kriː'eɪtə*] n δημιουργός.

creature ['kriːtʃə*] n πλάσμα nt, ον nt.

credentials [krɪ'dɛnʃəlz] npl (papers) διαπιστευτήρια ntpl, πιστοποιητικά ntpl.

credibility [kredə'bɪlɪtɪ] n αξιοπιστία, (το) πιστευτό.

credible ['kredɪbl] a πιστευτός, αξιόπιστος.

credit ['kredɪt] n πίστη, πίστωση || (recognition) αναγνώριση ♦ vt πιστεύω || ~**able** a έντιμος, αξιέπαινος || ~ **card** n κάρτα πιστώσεως || ~**or** n πιστωτής.

creed [kriːd] n πίστη, θρήσκευμα nt.

creek [kriːk] n κολπίσκος || (US) ρέμα nt.

creep [kriːp] (irreg v) vi έρπω, σύρομαι || ~**er** n (animal) ερπετό || (plant) αναρριχητικό || ~**y** a (frightening) ανατριχιαστικός.

cremate [krɪ'meɪt] vt αποτεφρώνω, καίω.

cremation [krɪ'meɪʃən] n καύση (νεκρού).

crematorium [kremə'tɔːrɪəm] n κρεματόριο.

crêpe [kreɪp] n κρέπ(ι) nt inv.

crept [krept] pt, pp of **creep.**

crescent ['kresnt] n ημισέληνος f || (esp street) ημικυκλικός δρόμος.

cress [kres] n κάρδαμο.

crest [krest] n (tuft) λοφίο, λειρί || (of wave) κορυφή || (badge) κορωνίδα, οικόσημο || ~**fallen** a κατηφής, αποθαρρημένος.

Crete [kriːt] n Κρήτη.

crevasse [krɪ'væs] n σχισμή.

crevice ['krevɪs] n ρωγμή, χαραμάδα.

crew [kruː] n πλήρωμα nt || ~-**cut** n πολύ κοντό μαλλί.

crib [krɪb] *n* (child's bed) παιδικό κρεβάτι || (copy) αντιγραφή.

crick [krɪk] *n* πιάσιμο.

cricket ['krɪkɪt] *n* (insect) γρύλλος, τριζόνι || (game) κρίκετ *nt inv*.

crime [kraɪm] *n* (wicked act) κακούργημα *nt* || (lawbreaking) έγκλημα *nt*.

criminal ['krɪmɪnl] *n* εγκληματίας, κακούργος ♦ *a* εγκληματικός, ποινικός.

crimson ['krɪmzn] *n* πορφυρό, βυσσινί ♦ *a* κατακόκκινος.

cringe [krɪndʒ] *vi* φέρομαι δουλοπρεπώς, σκύβω.

crinkle ['krɪŋkl] *vt* ζαρώνω, τσαλακώνω || (rustle) τρίβω.

cripple ['krɪpl] *n* ανάπηρος, χωλός ♦ *vt* τραυματίζω, σακατεύω, παραλύω.

crisis ['kraɪsɪs] *n* (time of danger etc) κρίση.

crisp [krɪsp] *a* τραγανός, αφράτος, φρέσκος ♦ *n* ξεροτηγανισμένη πατάτα.

criss-cross ['krɪskrɒs] *a* σταυρωτός, καφασωτός.

criterion [kraɪ'tɪərɪən] *n* κριτήριο.

critic ['krɪtɪk] *n* (THEAT etc) τεχνοκρίτης, κριτικός || επικριτής || ~al *a* (like a critic) κριτικός || (danger) κρίσιμος || (severe) αυστηρός || ~ally *ad* με κριτική διάθεση, κρίσιμος || ~ism ['krɪtɪsɪzəm] *n* (judgment) κριτική || (finding fault) επίκριση || ~ize ['krɪtɪsaɪz] *vt* (επι)κρίνω, κατακρίνω.

croak [krəuk] *vi* (crow) κρώζω || (frog) κοάζω ♦ *n* (of crow) κρωγμός || (of frog) κοασμός.

crochet ['krəuʃeɪ] *n* κροσέ *nt*.

crockery ['krɒkərɪ] *n* πήλινα σκεύη *ntpl*.

crocodile ['krɒkədaɪl] *n* κροκόδειλος.

crocus ['krəukəs] *n* κρόκος.

crook [kruk] *n* (criminal) λωποδύτης, απατεώνας || (of shepherd) γκλίτσα || ~ed *a* αγκυλωτός.

crop [krɒp] *n* συγκομιδή, σοδιά || to ~ up *vi* (fig) παρουσιάζομαι, προκύπτω.

croquet ['krəukeɪ] *n* κροκέ *nt*.

croquette [krəu'kɛt] *n* κροκέτα, κεφτές *m*.

cross [krɒs] *n* (of Christ) σταυρός || (mark) σταυρός || (breed) διασταύρωση || (misfortune) εμπόδιο, δυσκολία ♦ *vt* (pass over) διασχίζω, περνώ || (make sign) σταυροκοπιέμαι || (place across) σταυρώνω || (mix breeds) διασταυρώνω || (cheque) διαγραμμίζω ♦ *a* θυμωμένος, κακόκεφος || ~-country (race) *n* ανώμαλος δρόμος || ~-examination *n* εξέταση κατ'αντιπαράσταση || ~-examine *vt* εξετάζω κατ'αντιπαράσταση || ~-eyed *a* αλλοίθωρος || ~-ing *n* (road etc) διάβαση, πέρασμα *nt* || (sea passage) διάπλους *m* || (place for crossing) διάβαση || at ~-purposes παρεξηγημένοι, σε αντίθεση || ~-reference *n* παραπομπή || ~-roads *n* σταυροδρόμι || ~-section *n* εγκάρσια τομή || ~-wind *n* πλάγιος άνεμος || ~-word (puzzle) *n* σταυρόλεξο.

crotch [krɒtʃ] *n* διακλάδωση δένδρου, καβάλος του πανταλονιού.

crotchet ['krɒtʃɪt] *n* ιδιοτροπία, βίδα.

crotchety ['krɒtʃɪtɪ] *a* (person) ιδιότροπος.

crouch [krautʃ] *vi* σκύβω, μαζεύομαι.

crow [krəu] *n* κορώνη, κουρούνα ♦ *vi* κράζω, λαλώ || (fig) κομπάζω.

crowbar ['krəubɑ:*] *n* λοστός.

crowd [kraud] *n* πλήθος *nt*, όχλος, συρροή ♦ *vt* (fill) γεμίζω ♦ *vi* (flock

together) συνθούμαι, συνωστίζομαι || ~**ed** a γεματός.

crown [kraυn] n *(royal headdress)* στέμμα nt, κορώνα || *(of tooth)* κορώνα || *(top of head etc)* κορυφή, κορφή || *(of flowers)* στεφάνι ♦ vt *(put crown on)* στεφανώνω || *(be at top of)* πάνω απ'όλα, αποκορυφώνω || ~ **jewels** npl κοσμήματα του Στέμματος ntpl || ~ **prince** n διάδοχος του θρόνου.

crucial [ˈkruːʃəl] a αποφασιστικός, κρίσιμος.

crucifix [ˈkruːsifiks] n εσταυρωμένος || ~**ion** n σταύρωση.

crucify [ˈkruːsifaɪ] vt σταυρώνω, βασανίζω.

crude [kruːd] a *(unfinished)* ακατέργαστος || *(petroleum)* αργό πετρέλαιο || *(harsh)* ωμός, άξεστος || *(humour)* χοντρό χιούμορ.

cruel [krʊəl] a *(vicious)* ωμοβόρος, αμείλικτος || *(severe, distressing)* σκληρός, ωμός || *(hard-hearted)* σκληρόκαρδος || ~**ty** n σκληρότητα, ασπλαχνία || *(to wife)* κακοποίηση.

cruise [kruːz] n περίπλους m, κρουαζιέρα ♦ vi κάνω κρουαζιέρα, περιπλέω || ~ **r** n καταδρομικό.

crumb [krʌm] n ψίχουλο || *(fig)* απομεινάρι.

crumble [ˈkrʌmbl] vti καταρρέω, θρυμματίζομαι.

crumbly [ˈkrʌmblɪ] a εύθρυπτος.

crumpet [ˈkrʌmpɪt] n είδος τηγανίτας.

crumple [ˈkrʌmpl] vt τσαλακώνω, ζαρώνω.

crunch [krʌntʃ] n τραγάνισμα nt || *(sound)* τρίξιμο ♦ vt μασώ, τραγανίζω || ~**y** a τραγανιστός.

crusade [kruːˈseɪd] n σταυροφορία.

crush [krʌʃ] n σύνθλιψη, συνωστισμός ♦ vt συνθλίβω || *(a rebellion)* συντρίβω, καταβάλλω ♦ vi

(material) τσαλακώνω || ~**ing** a συντριπτικός.

crust [krʌst] n *(of bread)* κόρα || *(of cake etc)* κρούστα || *(of earth etc)* φλοιός, κρούστα.

crutch [krʌtʃ] n δεκανίκι, πατερίτσα.

crux [krʌks] n ουσία, κεντρικό σημείο.

cry [kraɪ] vi *(sell etc)* διαλαλώ || *(shout)* φωνάζω, βάζω τις φωνές || *(weep)* κλαίω, θρηνώ ♦ n φωνή, κλάμα nt.

crypt [krɪpt] n κρύπτη.

cryptic [ˈkrɪptɪk] a μυστικός, δυσνόητος.

crystal [ˈkrɪstl] n *(natural form)* κρύσταλλος || *(clear glass)* κρύσταλλο || ~-**clear** a κρυστάλλινος || ~**lize** vti (fig) (απο)κρυσταλλώνω || *(fig)* (απο)κρυσταλλούμαι.

cu. abbr. ~ **ft.** = cubic feet; ~ **in.** = cubic inches.

cub [kʌb] n νεογνό ζώο.

cube [kjuːb] n *(figure)* κύβος.

cubic [ˈkjuːbɪk] a κυβικός.

cubicle [ˈkjuːbɪkl] n θαλαμίσκος.

cuckoo [ˈkʊkuː] n κούκος.

cucumber [ˈkjuːkʌmbə*] n αγγούρι.

cuddle [ˈkʌdl] vti αγκαλιάζω, κουκουλώνομαι ♦ n αγκάλιασμα nt.

cue [kjuː] n *(hint)* νύξη, υπαινιγμός || *(in billiards)* στέκα.

cuff [kʌf] n *(of shirt, coat etc)* μανικέτι || *(US)* = **turn-up** || ~**link** n μανικετόκουμπο ntpl.

cuisine [kwɪˈziːn] n μαγειρική.

cul-de-sac [ˈkʌldəˈsæk] n αδιέξοδο.

culinary [ˈkʌlɪnərɪ] a μαγειρικός.

culminate [ˈkʌlmɪneɪt] vi αποκορυφώνομαι, μεσουρανώ.

culmination [kʌlmɪˈneɪʃən] n μεσουράνημα nt, κολοφών m.

culprit [ˈkʌlprɪt] n ένοχος.

cult [kʌlt] n *(religious)* λατρεία || *(mode)* μόδα, λόξα.

cultivate ['kʌltɪveɪt] vt καλλιεργώ.

cultivation [kʌltɪ'veɪʃən] n καλλιέργεια.

cultural ['kʌltʃərəl] a πνευματικός, μορφωτικός.

culture ['kʌltʃə*] n (refinement) καλλιέργεια || (intellectual development) ανάπτυξη, κουλτούρα || ~d a μορφωμένος, καλλιεργημένος.

cumbersome ['kʌmbəsəm] a ενοχλητικός, βαρύς, δυσκίνητος.

cumulative ['kjuːmjulətɪv] a επισωρευτικός, αθροιστικός.

cunning ['kʌnɪŋ] n πανουργία, καπατσοσύνη ♦ a πονηρός, τετραπέρατος.

cup [kʌp] n κούπα, φλυτζάνι || (prize) κύπελλο.

cupboard ['kʌbəd] n ντουλάπι, αρμάρι.

cupful ['kʌpful] n φλυτζανιά.

cupola ['kjuːpələ] n θόλος, τρούλλος.

curable ['kjuərəbl] a ιάσιμος, που γιατρεύεται.

curator [kjuə'reɪtə*] n έφορος (μουσείου).

curb [kɜːb] vt χαλιναγωγώ, ελέγχω ♦ n χαλινός, φραγμός || see **kerb(stone)**.

curfew ['kɜːfjuː] n απαγόρευση της κυκλοφορίας.

curiosity [kjuərɪ'ɒsɪtɪ] n περιέργεια || (strange object) περίεργο αντικείμενο.

curious ['kjuərɪəs] a (philo)περίεργος || (strange) περίεργος, παράξενος.

curl [kɜːl] n βόστρυχος, μπούκλα || (of lips etc) στρίψιμο ♦ vti (hair etc) σγουραίνω || (lips) στρίβω, στραβώνω || (wrap) τυλίγω || ~er n ρολά ntpl, μπικουτί nt inv.

curly ['kɜːlɪ] a κατσαρός, σγουρός.

currant ['kʌrənt] n Κορινθιακή σταφίδα.

currency ['kʌrənsɪ] n νόμισμα nt || (of ideas) κυκλοφορία, πέραση.

current ['kʌrənt] n ρεύμα nt, ροή, ρέμα nt ♦ a κυκλοφορών, εν χρήσει || ~ account n τρεχούμενος λογαριασμός || ~ affairs npl επίκαιρα ntpl || ~ly ad γενικώς, σήμερα.

curriculum [kə'rɪkjuləm] n κύκλος μαθημάτων || ~ vitae n περίληψη προσόντων.

curry ['kʌrɪ] n κάρρι nt inv || ~ powder n σκόνη κάρρι.

curse [kɜːs] vi βλαστημώ, υβρίζω ♦ vt καταριέμαι, αναθεματίζω ♦ n κατάρα, ανάθεμα nt || (bad language) βλαστήμια.

cursor ['kɜːsə*] n (COMPUT) δείκτης θέσεως.

cursory ['kɜːsərɪ] a γρήγορος, βιαστικός.

curt [kɜːt] a απότομος, κοφτός.

curtail [kɜː'teɪl] vt περικόπτω, περιορίζω.

curtain ['kɜːtn] n (esp at window) κουρτίνα || (THEAT) αυλαία, παραπέτασμα nt.

curtsy ['kɜːtsɪ] n υπόκλιση ♦ vi κάνω υπόκλιση.

curve [kɜːv] n καμπή.

cushion ['kuʃən] n μαξιλαράκι.

custard ['kʌstəd] n ψημένη κρέμα.

custodian [kʌs'təudɪən] n φύλακας, επιστάτης.

custody ['kʌstədɪ] n επιτήρηση, κηδεμονία || (under arrest) κράτηση.

custom ['kʌstəm] n (fashion) έθιμο, συνήθεια || (business) πελατεία || ~ary a συνηθισμένος || ~-made a καμωμένο επί παραγγελία.

customer ['kʌstəmə*] n πελάτης/τισσα m/f.

customs ['kʌstəmz] n (taxes) δασμοί

mpl || **C~** (place) τελωνείο || **C~ officer** *n* τελωνειακός υπάλληλος.

cut [kʌt] *vt* (irreg *v*) (divide) κόβω, χαράζω || (wound) πληγώνω || (reduce) κατεβάζω (τιμές) ♦ *n* (sharp stroke) κόψη, κόψιμο || (wound) τομή, κόψιμο, πληγή || (reduction) περικοπή, μείωση || (share) μερίδιο.

cute [kjuːt] *a* χαριτωμένος.

cuticle ['kjuːtikl] *n* (on nail) επιδερμίδα.

cutlery ['kʌtləri] *n* μαχαιροπήρουνα *ntpl*.

cutlet ['kʌtlit] *n* κοτολέττα.

cutout ['kʌtaut] *n* (ELEC) διακόπτης.

cutprice ['kʌtprais] τιμή ελαττωμένη.

cutting ['kʌtiŋ] *n* αιχμή, κόψη.

cwt *abbr of* **hundredweight(s)**.

cyanide ['saiənaid] *n* κυανίδη.

cycle ['saikl] *n* (bicycle) ποδήλατο || (series) κύκλος, περίοδος *f* || (of poems etc) κύκλος ♦ *vi* πηγαίνω με ποδήλατο.

cycling ['saikliŋ] *n* ποδηλατοδρομία, ποδήλατο.

cyclist ['saiklist] *n* ποδηλατιστής.

cyclone ['saikləun] *n* κυκλώνας.

cygnet ['signit] *n* μικρός κύκνος.

cylinder ['silində*] *n* κύλινδρος || (of gas etc) φιάλη, μπουκάλα || ~ **block** *n* συγκρότημα *nt* κυλίνδρου || ~ **capacity** *n* όγκος κυλίνδρου || ~ **head** *n* κεφαλή κυλίνδρου.

cymbals ['simbəlz] *npl* κύμβαλα *ntpl*.

cynic ['sinik] *n* κυνικός || ~**al** *a* κυνικός, δύσπιστος || ~**ism** ['sinisizəm] *n* κυνισμός, χοτηροκουβέντα.

cypress ['saipris] *n* κυπαρίσσι.

Cyprus ['saiprəs] *n* Κύπρος *f*.

cyst [sist] *n* κύστις.

czar [zaː] *n* τσάρος || ~**ina** *n* τσαρίνα.

Czech [tʃɛk] *a* τσεχικός || *n* Τσέχος/α *m/f.*

Czechoslavakia ['tʃekəuslou'vækiə] *n* Τσεχοσλοβακία.

D

dab [dæb] *vt* επαλείφω ♦ *n* (tap) ελαφρό κτύπημα *nt* || (smear) μικρή ποσότητα, λίγο.

dad(dy) ['dæd(i)] *n* μπαμπάς, μπαμπάκας || **daddy-long-legs** *n* τιπούλη, αλογατάκι.

daffodil ['dæfədil] *n* ασφόδελος.

daft [dɑːft] *a* ανόητος, τρελλός.

dagger ['dægə*] *n* εγχειρίδιο, στιλέττο.

dahlia ['deiliə] *n* ντάλια.

daily ['deili] *a* ημερήσιος ♦ *n* καθημερινή (εφημερίδα).

dainty ['deinti] *a* κομψός, νόστιμος.

dairy ['dɛəri] *n* (shop) γαλακτοπωλείο, γαλατάδικο || (on farm) γαλακτοκομείο ♦ *a* γαλακτοκομικό.

daisy ['deizi] *n* μαργαρίτα || ~ **wheel** *n* (on printer) μαργαρίτα || ~ **wheel printer** *n* εκτυπωτής μαργαρίτας.

dam [dæm] *n* (for water) φράγμα *nt*, ανάχωμα *nt* ♦ *vt* φράσσω.

damage ['dæmidʒ] *n* βλάβη, ζημιά ♦ *vt* βλάπτω, ζημιώνω || ~**s** *npl* (LAW) αποζημίωση.

dame [deim] *n* κυρία, κυρά.

damn [dæm] *vt* καταδικάζω ♦ *a* (col) διάβολος || ~ **it** να πάρει ο διάβολος!, να πάρει η ευχή! || ~**ing** *a* καταδικαστικός, επιβαρυντικός.

damp [dæmp] *a* υγρός, νοτερός ♦ *n* υγρασία, υγρότητα ♦ *vt* (also: ~**en**) υγραίνω, μουσκεύω || (discourage) μειώνω, ελαττώνω, κόβω || ~**ness** *n* υγρασία, υγρότητα.

damson ['dæmzən] n δαμάσκηνο.

dance [da:ns] n χορός || (party) χορευτική συγκέντρωση, πάρτυ nt inv ♦ vi χορεύω || ~ **hall** n χορευτικό κέντρο || ~ **r** n χορευτής, χορεύτρια.

dancing ['da:nsiŋ] n χορός.

dandelion ['dændɪlaɪən] n αγριοράδικι.

dandruff ['dændrəf] n πιτυρίδα.

dandy ['dændɪ] n κομψευόμενος, δανδής.

Dane [deɪn] n Δανός/έζα m/f.

danger ['deɪndʒə*] n κίνδυνος || ~! (sign) προσοχή || **in** ~ διατρέχω κίνδυνο || ~**ous** a επικίνδυνος.

dangle ['dæŋgl] vti αιωρούμαι, ταλαντεύομαι, κρέμομαι.

Danish ['deɪnɪʃ] a δανικός ♦ n Δανική γλώσσα.

dare [dɛə*] vt τολμώ ♦ vi: **to** ~ (**to**) **do sth** τολμώ να κάνω κάτι || **I** ~ **say** ασφαλώς, πιθανώς.

daring ['dɛərɪŋ] a τολμηρός, άφοβος.

dark [da:k] a (dim) σκοτεινός, μαύρος || (gloomy) σκοτεινός, μελαγχολικός || (colour) μελαχροινός, μελαψός ♦ n σκοτάδι || (ignorance) σε άγνοια || **after** ~ αφού νυχτώσει || ~ **en** vti σκοτεινιάζω || ~**ness** n σκότος n σκοτάδι || ~ **room** n σκοτεινός θάλαμος.

darling ['da:lɪŋ] n πολυαγαπημένος.

darn [da:n] n μαντάρισμα nt ♦ vt μπαλώνω, καρικώνω.

dart [da:t] n (quick move) ορμή || (weapon) βέλος nt, σαΐτα ♦ vi εξακοντίζω, ορμώ || ~ **s** n σαΐτα || ~**board** n στόχος σαΐτας.

dash [dæʃ] n (rush) εξόρμηση || (waves) χτύπημα nt, σπάσιμο || (mark) παύλα ♦ vt (hit) ρίχνω, χτυπώ, καταστρέφω ♦ vi εφορμώ, πέφτω ||

~**board** n ταμπλό nt inv || ~**ing** a (person) ορμητικός, ζωηρός.

data ['deɪtə] npl δεδομένα ntpl, στοιχεία ntpl || ~**base** n βάση δεδομένων || ~ **processing** n κατεργασία στοιχείων.

date [deɪt] n (point in time) χρονολογία, ημερομηνία || (with person) ραντεβού nt inv || (fruit) χουρμάς ♦ vt (letter etc) βάζω ημερομηνία || (person) δίνω ραντεβού || ~ **d** a με χρονολογία.

daub [dɔ:b] vt (smear) πασαλείβω, αλείφω || (paint badly) μουντζουρώνω.

daughter ['dɔ:tə*] n θυγατέρα, κόρη || ~**in-law** n νύφη.

dawdle ['dɔ:dl] vi χασομερώ, τεμπελιάζω.

dawn [dɔ:n] n αυγή ♦ vi υποφώσκω, χαράζω || (become apparent) αποκαλύπτω.

day [deɪ] n ημέρα, μέρα || (24 hours) εικοσιτετράωρο || (date, time) ημερομηνία || (daylight) φως nt της ημέρας || ~ **by** ~ ημέρα με την ημέρα || ~**break** n αυγή, χάραμα nt || ~**dream** n ονειροπόλημα nt, ρεμβασμός ♦ vi ονειροπολώ, ρεμβάζω || ~**light** n φως nt της ημέρας || ~**time** n ημέρα.

daze [deɪz] vt θαμπώνω, ζαλίζω ♦ n θάμπωμα nt, ζάλη.

dazzle ['dæzl] vt θαμπώνω, τυφλώνω ♦ n θάμπωμα nt, τύφλωμα nt.

dead [dɛd] a νεκρός, πεθαμένος || (without feeling) αναίσθητος || (exact) πλήρης, ακριβής ♦ ad τελείως, ακριβώς, απολύτως || **the** ~ npl οι νεκροί mpl, οι πεθαμένοι mpl || ~**en** vt νεκρώνω, κατασιγάζω || ~ **end** n αδιέξοδο || ~ **heat** n ισοπαλία || ~**line** n (χρονικό) όριο || ~**lock** n αδιέξοδο || ~**ly** a θανατηφόρος, θανάσιμος || (fig) αδυσώπητος,

αφόρητος || ~ pan a (ηθοποιός) χωρίς έκφραση.

deaf [dεf] a κουφός || ~-**aid** n ακουστικό κωφών || ~-**en** vt (ξε)κουφαίνω || ~**ening** a εκκωφαντικός || ~-**mute** n κωφάλαλος /n m/f|| ~**ness** n κουφαμάρα.

deal [di:l] (irreg v) n συμφωνία, δουλειά ♦ vti (CARDS) μοιράζω, δίνω || **a great** ~ **of** ποσότητα, πολύ || to ~ **with** vt αντιμετωπίζω, λαμβάνω μέτρα || ~**er** n έμπορος, αντιπρόσωπος || (CARDS) μοιραστής.

dear [diɔ*] a (beloved) αγαπητός, προσφιλής || (expensive) ακριβός, δαπανηρός ♦ n προσφιλής, αγαπημένος || ~ **me** θεέ μου || **D**~ **Sir** αξιότιμε, αγαπητέ κύριε || **D**~ **John** αγαπητέ Γιάννη || ~**ly** ad (love) με αγάπη || (pay) ακριβά.

death [dεθ] n θάνατος || ~**bed** n νεκροκρέββατο || ~ **certificate** n πιστοποιητικό θανάτου || ~ **duties** npl (Brit) φόρος κληρονομίας || ~**ly** a νεκρικός, ωχρός || ~ **penalty** n ποινή θανάτου || ~ **rate** n θνησιμότητα.

debase [di'beis] vt ξεφτελίζω, υποβιβάζω.

debate [di'beit] n συζήτηση ♦ vt συζητώ || (consider) σκέφτομαι.

debauchery [di'bɔːtʃəri] n ακολασία.

debit ['dεbit] n δούναι, παθητικό || vt χρεώνω.

debris ['dεbriː] n συντρίμματα ntpl, μπάζα.

debt [dεt] n χρέος nt, οφειλή || **to be in** ~ χρωστώ || ~**or** n οφειλέτης, χρεώστης.

debug [diː'bʌg] vt (COMPUT) αφαιρώ λάθη or σφάλματα.

début ['deibuː] n πρώτη εμφάνιση, ντεμπούτο.

decade ['dεkeid] n δεκαετία.

decadence ['dεkədəns] n παρακμή.

decay [di'kei] n παρακμή, φθορά, κατάπτωση ♦ vi παρακμάζω, μαραίνομαι.

decease [di'siːs] n θάνατος || ~**d** n μακαρίτης/ισσα m/f.

deceit [di'siːt] n απάτη, δόλος || ~**ful** a δόλιος, απατηλός.

deceive [di'siːv] vt εξαπατώ, κοροϊδεύω.

decelerate [diː'sεləreit] vti επιβραδύνω, κόβω ταχύτητα.

December [di'sεmbə*] n Δεκέμβρης, Δεκέμβριος.

decency ['diːsənsi] n (fit behaviour) ευπρέπεια, σεμνότητα || (respectability) κοσμιότητα.

decent ['diːsnt] a (respectable) ευπρεπής, συμμαζεμένος || (pleasant) αρκετά καλός.

deception [di'sεpʃən] n εξαπάτηση, τέχνασμα nt.

deceptive [di'sεptiv] a απατηλός.

decibel ['dεsibεl] n ντεσιμπέλ nt inv.

decide [di'said] vt (settle) κρίνω, αποφασίζω ♦ vi (determine) αποφασίζω, καταλήγω || **to** ~ **to do** αποφασίζω να κάνω || ~**d** a αποφασισμένος, οριστικός || ~**dly** ad αποφασιστικά, βεβαίως.

deciduous [di'sidjuəs] a φυλλοβόλος.

decimal ['dεsiməl] a δεκαδικός ♦ n δεκαδικό || ~ **point** n υποδιαστολή.

decimate ['dεsimeit] vt αποδεκατίζω.

decipher [di'saifə*] vt ξεδιαλύνω, βγάζω.

decision [di'siʒən] n απόφαση.

decisive [di'saisiv] a αποφασιστικός.

deck [dεk] n (NAUT) κατάστρωμα nt, κουβέρτα || (of bus) όροφος || (of cards) τράπουλα || ~-**chair** n σαιζ-λογκ f inv.

declaration [dɛklə'reɪʃən] n
δήλωση, διακήρυξη.

declare [dɪ'klɛə*] vt (state) δηλώνω
|| (war) κηρύσσω || (in customs)
δηλώνω.

decline [dɪ'klaɪn] n (decay)
παρακμή, πτώση, πέσιμο || (lessening)
πέσιμο, κατάπτωση ♦ vt (refuse)
αρνούμαι || (GRAM) κλίνω ♦ vi φθίνω,
εξασθενίζω, αδυνατίζω.

declutch ['di:'klʌtʃ] vi
ντεμπραγιάρω.

decode ['di:'kəʊd] vt
αποκρυπτογραφώ.

decompose [di:kəm'pəʊz] vi (rot)
αποσυντίθεμαι, σαπίζω.

decontaminate [di:kən'tæmɪneɪt]
vt απολυμαίνω.

décor ['deɪkɔ:*] n διακόσμηση,
ντεκόρ nt inv.

decorate ['dɛkəreɪt] vt (renew paint
etc) χρωματίζω, βάφω || (adorn)
(δια)κοσμώ, στολίζω || (give medal
etc) παρασημοφορώ.

decoration [dɛkə'reɪʃən] n (of
house) διακόσμηση || (MIL)
παράσημο.

decorator ['dɛkəreɪtə*] n
διακοσμητής/ήτρια m/f.

decoy ['di:kɔɪ] n δέλεαρ nt inv,
δόλωμα nt.

decrease [di:'kri:s] n μείωση,
ελάττωση ♦ vti μειώνω,
ελαττώνομαι.

decree [dɪ'kri:] n διάταγμα nt,
βούλευμα nt.

decrepit [dɪ'krɛpɪt] a
παραγηρασμένος || (furniture etc)
ξεχαρβαλωμένος.

dedicate ['dɛdɪkeɪt] vt αφιερώνω.

dedication [dɛdɪ'keɪʃən] n
αφιέρωμση.

deduce [dɪ'dju:s] vt συμπεραίνω.

deduct [dɪ'dʌkt] vt αφαιρώ || ~ion n
αφαίρεση, συμπέρασμα nt || (in price
etc) έκπτωση.

deed [di:d] n πράξη, έργο || (LAW)
έγγραφο.

deep [di:p] a (water) βαθύς || (breath)
βαθειά || (voice) βαθειά, βαρειά || in
~ water σε μεγάλη δυσκολία ||
~en vt εμβαθύνω, βαθαίνω || ~-
freeze n κατάψυξη || ~-seated a
βαθειά ριζωμένος.

deer [dɪə*] n ελάφι.

deface [dɪ'feɪs] vt παραμορφώνω.

defamation [dɛfə'meɪʃən] n
δυσφήμιση.

default [dɪ'fɔ:lt] n παράλειψη,
αθέτηση || (LAW) απουσία || (COMPUT)
παράλειψη ♦ vi παραλείπω
καθήκον, φυγοδικώ || by ~ ερήμην
|| ~er n φυγόδικος.

defeat [dɪ'fi:t] n (overthrow)
ανατροπή, ματαίωση || ήττα,
συντριβή ♦ vt νικώ, ανατρέπω ||
~ist n ηττοπαθής.

defect ['di:fɛkt] n ατέλεια,
ελάττωμα nt ♦ [dɪ'fɛkt] vi λιποτακτώ
|| ~ive a ελλιπής, ελαττωματικός.

defence [dɪ'fɛns] n (MIL, SPORT)
άμυνα, υπεράσπιση || δικαιολογία ||
~less a ανυπεράσπιστος.

defend [dɪ'fɛnd] vt υπερασπίζω ||
~ant n εναγόμενος || ~er n
υπερασπιστής, υπέρμαχος.

defensive [dɪ'fɛnsɪv] a αμυντικός ♦
n άμυνα.

defer [dɪ'fɜ:*] vt αναβάλλω.

deference ['dɛfərəns] n σεβασμός.

defiance [dɪ'faɪəns] n αψηφισιά,
περιφρόνηση.

defiant [dɪ'faɪənt] a προκλητικός,
αψηφών.

deficiency [dɪ'fɪʃənsɪ] n έλλειψη,
ατέλεια.

deficient [dɪ'fɪʃənt] a ατελής,
ελλιπής.

deficit ['dɛfɪsɪt] n έλλειμμα nt.

define [dɪ'faɪn] vt (καθ)ορίζω ||
(explain) εξηγώ, καθορίζω.

definite ['dɛfɪnɪt] a (fixed)

(καθ)ορισμένος || *(clear)* σαφής ||
(GRAM) οριστικό || ~ **ly** *ad* σαφώς.
definition [dɛfɪˈnɪʃən] *n*
(καθ)ορισμός.
definitive [dɪˈfɪnɪtɪv] *a* οριστικός,
τελικός.
deflate [diːˈfleɪt] *vt* ξεφουσκώνω ||
(currency) υποτιμώ.
deflation [diːˈfleɪʃən] *n* *(FIN)*
υποτίμηση.
deflect [dɪˈflɛkt] *vt* εκτρέπω,
παρεκκλίνω.
deform [dɪˈfɔːm] *vt* παραμορφώνω,
ασχημίζω || ~**ed** *a* δύσμορφος
παραμορφωμένος || ~**ity** *n*
δυσμορφία, παραμόρφωση.
defraud [dɪˈfrɔːd] *vt* εξαπατώ,
κλέβω.
defrost [diːˈfrɒst] *vt* *(fridge)*
ξεπαγώνω.
deft [dɛft] *a* επιτήδειος, επιδέξιος.
defunct [dɪˈfʌŋkt] *a* μακαρίτης.
defy [dɪˈfaɪ] *vt* *(challenge)* προκαλώ ||
(ignore) αψηφώ.
degenerate [dɪˈdʒɛnəreɪt] *vi*
εκφυλίζομαι ♦ [dɪˈdʒɛnərɪt] *a*
εκφυλισμένος.
degradation [dɛgrəˈdeɪʃən] *n*
ξεφτελισμός, υποβιβασμός.
degrading [dɪˈɡreɪdɪŋ] *a*
ξεφτελιστικός, ταπεινωτικός.
degree [dɪˈɡriː] *n* *(step, stage)*
βαθμός || *(UNIV)* πτυχίο ||
(measurement) μοίρα || **by** ~**s**
βαθμηδόν.
dehydrated [diːhaɪˈdreɪtɪd] *a*
αφυδατωμένος.
de-ice [diːˈaɪs] *vt* *(windscreen)*
ξεπαγώνω.
deign [deɪn] *vi* καταδέχομαι,
ευαρεστούμαι.
deity [ˈdiːɪtɪ] *n* θεότητα.
dejected [dɪˈdʒɛktɪd] *a* κατηφής,
άκεφος.
dejection [dɪˈdʒɛkʃən] *n* κατήφεια,
ακεφιά.

delay [dɪˈleɪ] *vt* αναβάλλω,
καθυστερώ ♦ *vi* βραδύνω, αργώ ♦ *n*
αργοπορία, αναβολή, επιβράδυνση
|| **without** ~ χωρίς καθυστέρηση.
delegate [ˈdɛlɪɡɪt] *n* αντιπρόσωπος,
απεσταλμένος ♦ [ˈdɛlɪɡeɪt] *vt*
εντέλλομαι, εξουσιοδοτώ.
delegation [dɛlɪˈɡeɪʃən] *n*
αντιπροσωπεία.
delete [dɪˈliːt] *vt* αφαιρώ, σβήνω.
deliberate [dɪˈlɪbərɪt] *a* *(intentional)*
εσκεμμένος || *(slow)* αργός,
επιφυλακτικός ♦ [dɪˈlɪbəreɪt] *vi*
διαλογίζομαι, συνδιασκέπτομαι ||
~**ly** *ad* εσκεμμένα.
delicacy [ˈdɛlɪkəsɪ] *n* *(daintiness)*
ευαισθησία, λεπτότητα || *(refinement)*
λεπτότητα || *(choice food)* λιχουδιές
fpl.
delicate [ˈdɛlɪkɪt] *a* *(fine)* λεπτός,
απαλός || *(fragile)* λεπτός || *(situation)*
λεπτός, δύσκολος || *(MED)* λεπτή,
ευπαθής.
delicious [dɪˈlɪʃəs] *a* νόστιμος,
ευχάριστος.
delight [dɪˈlaɪt] *n* ευχαρίστηση,
τέρψη ♦ *vt* χαιροποιώ, τέρπω ||
~**ful** *a* γοητευτικός, πολύ
ευχάριστος.
delinquency [dɪˈlɪŋkwənsɪ] *n*
εγκληματικότητα, αδίκημα *nt.*
delinquent [dɪˈlɪŋkwənt] *n*
εγκληματίας, παραπτωματίας ♦ *a*
παραπτωματικός || *(ECON)*
εκπρόθεσμος.
delirium [dɪˈlɪrɪəm] *n* παραλήρημα
nt.
deliver [dɪˈlɪvə*] *vt* *(distribute)*
(παρα)δίδω, διανέμω || *(pronounce)*
εκφωνώ, μεταδίδω || *(free)*
απαλλάσσω, ελευθερώνω, σώζω ||
~**y** *n* παράδοση, διανομή || *(of
speech)* παράδοση, εκφώνηση.
delta [ˈdɛltə] *n* δέλτα *nt.*
delude [dɪˈluːd] *vt* εξαπατώ.
deluge [ˈdɛljuːdʒ] *n* κατακλυσμός.

delusion [dɪˈluː ʒən] n (αυτ)απάτη.
de luxe [dɪˈlʌks] a ντε λουξ.
demand [dɪˈmaːnd] vt απαιτώ,
αξιώνω ♦ n αξίωση, απαίτηση || (call
for a commodity) ζήτηση || **in** ~
ζητούμαι || **on** ~ επί τη εμφανίσει ||
~**ing** a απαιτητικός, διεκδικητικός.
demarcation [diːmaːˈkeɪʃən] n
οροθεσία.
demented [dɪˈmentɪd] a
παράφρονας, τρελλός.
demise [dɪˈmaɪz] n αποβίωση.
demobilization
[ˈdiːməubɪlaɪˈzeɪʃən] n
αποστράτευση.
democracy [dɪˈmɒkrəsɪ] n
δημοκρατία.
democrat [ˈdeməkræt] n
δημοκράτης || ~**ic** a δημοκρατικός.
demolish [dɪˈmɒlɪʃ] vt (lit)
κατεδαφίζω, κατακρημνίζω || (fig)
συντρίβω.
demolition [deməˈlɪʃən] n
κατεδάφιση.
demonstrate [ˈdemənstreɪt] vt
αποδεικνύω || (protest) διαδηλώνω.
demonstration [demənˈstreɪʃən] n
απόδειξη, επίδειξη || (POL)
διαδήλωση.
demonstrator [ˈdemənstreɪtə*] n
(POL) διαδηλωτής.
demoralize [dɪˈmɒrəlaɪz] vt
εξαχρειώνω, αποθαρρύνω.
demote [dɪˈməut] vt υποβιβάζω.
demure [dɪˈmjuə*] a σοβαρός,
μετριόφρονας.
den [den] n τρώγλη, φωλιά || (room)
καμαρούλα.
denial [dɪˈnaɪəl] n άρνηση.
Denmark [ˈdenmaːk] n Δανία.
denomination [dɪnɒmɪˈneɪʃən] n
(name) ονομασία || (REL) δόγμα nt,
θρήσκευμα nt.
denote [dɪˈnəut] vt δείχνω, εμφαίνω.
denounce [dɪˈnauns] vt καταγγέλω.

dense [dens] a πυκνός || (stupid)
βλάκας, αμαθής.
density [ˈdensɪtɪ] n πυκνότητα.
dent [dent] n κοίλωμα nt, βαθούλωμα
nt ♦ vt κοιλαίνω, βαθουλώνω.
dental [ˈdentl] a (GRAM)
οδοντόφωνος || ~ **surgeon** n =
dentist.
dentist [ˈdentɪst] n οδοντίατρος m/f
|| ~**ry** n οδοντιατρική.
denture [ˈdentʃə*] n οδοντοστοιχία,
μασέλα.
deny [dɪˈnaɪ] vt (declare untrue)
διαψεύδω, αρνούμαι || (disown)
απαρνιέμαι, ανακαλώ || (refuse)
αρνούμαι.
deodorant [diːˈəudərənt] n
αποσμητικό.
depart [dɪˈpaːt] vi αναχωρώ.
department [dɪˈpaːtmənt] n τμήμα
nt, υπηρεσία, κλάδος || (UNIV, SCH)
τμήμα nt || (POL) διεύθυνση, γραφείο
|| (US) υπουργείο || ~ **store** n
μεγάλο εμπορικό κατάστημα nt.
departure [dɪˈpaːtʃə*] n
αναχώρηση || **new** ~ n νέα τάση.
depend [dɪˈpend] vi: it ~s
εξαρτάται || **to** ~ **on** vti εξαρτώμαι
από || ~**able** a αξιόπιστος || (car,
machine etc) απολύτου ασφαλείας ||
~**ent** n (person) προστατευόμενος
♦ a (+ on) εξαρτώμενος από ||
~**ence** n εξάρτηση || (trust)
εμπιστοσύνη.
depict [dɪˈpɪkt] vt περιγράφω,
απεικονίζω.
depleted [dɪˈpliːtɪd] a
εξηντλημένος.
deplorable [dɪˈplɔːrəbl] a
θλιβερός, αξιοθρήνητος.
deplore [dɪˈplɔː*] vt αποδοκιμάζω,
λυπούμαι πολύ.
deploy [dɪˈplɔɪ] vt αναπτύσσω.
depopulation [ˈdiːpɒpjuˈleɪʃən] n
ελάττωση πληθυσμού.
deport [dɪˈpɔːt] vt εκτοπίζω,

απελαύνω || ~ation n απέλαση, εκτοπισμός || ~ment n συμπεριφορά.

depose [dɪ'pəʊz] vt εκθρονίζω.

deposit [dɪ'pɒzɪt] n κατάθεση || (down payment) προκαταβολή, καπάρο || (CHEM) ίζημα nt, κατακάθι ♦ vt (bank) (παρα)καταθέτω, αποταμιεύω || (place) τοποθετώ, βάζω || ~ **account** n λογαριασμός καταθέσεως || ~or n καταθέτης.

depot ['dɛpəʊ] n αποθήκη || (MIL) βάση ανεφοδιασμού || (US: for buses etc) σταθμός.

depravity [dɪ'prævɪtɪ] n αχρειότητα, διαφθορά.

depreciate [dɪ'priːʃɪeɪt] vt υποτιμώ ♦ vi υποτιμούμαι, πέφτω.

depreciation [dɪpriːʃɪ'eɪʃən] n υποτίμηση, πέσιμο.

depress [dɪ'prɛs] vt (make sad) συντρίβω, αποθαρρύνω || (press down) κατεβάζω || ~ed a (person) μελαγχολικός, αποκαρδιωμένος || (area) φτωχός, υποανάπτυκτος || ~ing a καταθλιπτικός, αποθαρρυντικός || ~ion n (ECON) ύφεση, κρίση || (hollow) κοιλότητα, λακούβα || (METEOROLOGY) βαρομετρική ύφεση.

deprivation [dɛprɪ'veɪʃən] n στέρηση.

deprive [dɪ'praɪv] vt (+ of) στερώ του || ~d a στερημένος.

depth [dɛpθ] n βάθος nt, βαθύτητα || **in the ~s of** στην καρδιά του.

deputation [dɛpjʊ'teɪʃən] n αποστολή, επιτροπή.

deputize ['dɛpjʊtaɪz] vi (+ for) αναπληρώ, αντιπροσωπεύω.

deputy ['dɛpjʊtɪ] a αναπληρωτικός, βοηθητικός ♦ n αναπληρωτής, αντικαταστάτης.

derail [dɪ'reɪl] vt εκτροχιάζω || ~ment n εκτροχίαση.

deranged [dɪ'reɪndʒd] a παράφρονας, στριμμένος.

derelict ['dɛrɪlɪkt] a εγκαταλελειμμένος.

deride [dɪ'raɪd] vt χλευάζω, εμπαίζω.

derision [dɪ'rɪʒən] n εμπαιγμός, χλευασμός.

derivative [dɪ'rɪvətɪv] a παράγωγος.

derive [dɪ'raɪv] vt παράγω, αποκομίζω ♦ vi κατάγομαι, παράγομαι.

dermatitis [dɜːmə'taɪtɪs] n δερματίτιδα.

derogatory [dɪ'rɒgətərɪ] a ξεφτελιστικός, δυσφημιστικός, μειωτικός.

derrick ['dɛrɪk] n γερανός || (of oil well) κρίωμα nt γεωτρήσεως.

descend [dɪ'sɛnd] vti κατεβαίνω || (rain etc) πέφτω ♦ vi: **to ~ from** κατάγομαι || ~ant n απόγονος.

descent [dɪ'sɛnt] n (coming down) κάθοδος f, κατέβασμα nt || (origin) καταγωγή.

describe [dɪs'kraɪb] vt περιγράφω.

description [dɪs'krɪpʃən] n περιγραφή || (kind, sort) είδος nt, τύπος.

descriptive [dɪs'krɪptɪv] a περιγραφικός.

desecrate ['dɛsɪkreɪt] vt βεβηλώνω.

desert ['dɛzət] n έρημος f ♦ [dɪ'zɜːt] vt εγκαταλείπω ♦ vi (MIL) λιποτακτώ || ~er n λιποτάκτης || ~ion n λιποταξία.

deserve [dɪ'zɜːv] vt αξίζω.

deserving [dɪ'zɜːvɪŋ] a άξιος, αξιόλογος.

design [dɪ'zaɪn] n (plan) σχέδιο, σκοπός, επιδίωξη || (drawing) σχέδιο, τύπος || (the art) σχέδιο ♦ vt (plan) σχεδιάζω || (purpose) προορίζω || **to have ~s on** έχω βλέψεις σε.

designate ['dɛzɪgneɪt] vt
(προ)ορίζω, διορίζω ♦ ['dɛzɪgnɪt] a
εκλεγείς.

designation [dɛzɪg'neɪʃən] n
ορισμός, τίτλος.

designer [dɪ'zaɪnə*] n (TECH)
μελετητής || (ART) σχεδιαστής.

desirable [dɪ'zaɪərəbl] a
επιθυμητός.

desire [dɪ'zaɪə*] n επιθυμία, πόθος
♦ vt επιθυμώ, ποθώ || (ask for) ζητώ.

desk [dɛsk] n γραφείο || (of student)
θρανίο.

desolate ['dɛsəlɪt] a (barren, dismal)
έρημος.

desolation [dɛsə'leɪʃən] n ερήμωση,
καταστροφή.

despair [dɪs'pɛə*] n απόγνωση,
απελπισία ♦ vi (+ of) απελπίζομαι
για.

despatch [dɪs'pætʃ] = **dispatch**.

desperate ['dɛspərɪt] a (hopeless)
απελπιστικός || (reckless)
απεγνωσμένος, σκληρός.

desperation [dɛspə'reɪʃən] n
απόγνωση.

despicable [dɪs'pɪkəbl] a απηδής,
σιχαμερός, αξιοκαταφρόνητος.

despise [dɪs'paɪz] vt περιφρονώ.

despite [dɪs'paɪt] prep παρά, σε
πείσμα.

despondent [dɪs'pɒndənt] a
απελπισμένος, συντριμμένος.

dessert [dɪ'zɜːt] n επιδόρπιο ||
~**spoon** n κουταλάκι του γλυκού.

destination [dɛstɪ'neɪʃən] n
προορισμός.

destiny ['dɛstɪnɪ] n προορισμός ||
(fate) μοίρα.

destitute ['dɛstɪtjuːt] a άπορος.

destroy [dɪs'trɔɪ] vt καταστρέφω ||
~**er** n (NAUT) αντιτορπιλλικό.

destruction [dɪs'trʌkʃən] n
καταστροφή.

destructive [dɪs'trʌktɪv] a
καταστρεπτικός.

detach [dɪ'tætʃ] vt αποσπώ, αφαιρώ
|| ~**able** a αφαιρούμενος, κινητός ||
~**ed** a (attitude) ανεπηρέαστος ||
~**ment** n (MIL) απόσπασμα nt || (fig)
απόσπαση, αμερολήψία.

detail ['diːteɪl] n λεπτομέρεια || (MIL)
απόσπασμα nt ♦ vt εκθέτω
λεπτομερώς || (MIL) ορίζω, αποσπώ ||
in ~ λεπτομερώς.

detain [dɪ'teɪn] vt κρατώ, εμποδίζω ||
(imprison) φυλακίζω, κρατώ.

detect [dɪ'tɛkt] vt ανακαλύπτω,
διακρίνω || ~**ion** [dɪ'tɛkʃən] n
ανακάλυψη || ~**ive** n μυστικός
αστυνομικός, ντετέκτιβ m inv || ~**ive
story** n αστυνομικό μυθιστόρημα nt
|| ~**or** n ανιχνευτής.

detention [dɪ'tɛnʃən] n κράτηση.

deter [dɪ'tɜː*] vt αποτρέπω.

detergent [dɪ'tɜːdʒənt] n
απορρυπαντικό, καθαρτικό.

deteriorate [dɪ'tɪərɪəreɪt] vi
επιδεινούμαι, χειροτερεύω.

deterioration [dɪtɪərɪə'reɪʃən] n
επιδείνωση.

determination [dɪtɜːmɪ'neɪʃən] n
απόφαση, αποφασιστικότητα.

determine [dɪ'tɜːmɪn] vt
(καθ)ορίζω, αποφασίζω || ~**d** a
αποφασιστικός, αποφασισμένος.

deterrent [dɪ'tɛrənt] n προληπτικό
♦ a αποτρεπτικός.

detest [dɪ'tɛst] vt απεχθάνομαι,
αποστρέφομαι, σιχαίνομαι || ~**able**
a απεχθής, σιχαμένος.

detonate ['dɛtəneɪt] vti εκρηγνύω,
εκπυροκροτώ.

detonator ['dɛtəneɪtə*] n
επικρουστήρας, πυροκροτητής.

detour ['diːtuə*] n απόκλιση,
στροφή, λοξοδρόμηση.

detract [dɪ'trækt] vi (+ from)
δυσφημώ, μειώνω.

detriment ['dɛtrɪmənt] n: **to the** ~
of προς βλάβη του || ~**al** a
βλαβερός, επιζήμιος.

devaluation [dɪvælju'eɪʃən] n υποτίμηση.

devalue [di:'vælju:] vt υποτιμώ.

devastate ['dɛvəsteɪt] vt ερημώνω, καταστρέφω.

devastating ['dɛvəsteɪtɪŋ] a εξολοθρευτικός.

develop [dɪ'vɛləp] vt (make grow) αναπτύσσω || (film) εμφανίζω ♦ vi (unfold) αναπτύσσομαι, εκδηλούμαι || (grow) αναπτύσσομαι || ~ing a (country) αναπτυσσόμενη || ~ment n ανάπτυξη.

deviate ['di:vɪeɪt] vi εκτρέπομαι, παρεκκλίνω.

deviation [di:vɪ'eɪʃən] n παρέκκλιση.

device [dɪ'vaɪs] n επινόημα nt, τέχνασμα nt.

devil ['dɛvl] n διά(β)ολος, δαίμονας || ~ish a διαβολικός.

devious ['di:vɪəs] a (means) έμμεσος, παρεκκλίνων || (person) ύπουλος.

devise [dɪ'vaɪz] vt επινοώ, μηχανεύομαι.

devoid [dɪ'vɔɪd] a: ~ of στερημένος, χωρίς...

devote [dɪ'vəut] vt αφιερώνω || ~d a αφοσιωμένος || ~e n λάτρης, οπαδός.

devotion [dɪ'vəuʃən] n αφοσίωση, λατρεία.

devour [dɪ'vauə*] vt καταβροχθίζω.

devout [dɪ'vaut] a ευσεβής, θρήσκος.

dew [dju:] n δρόσος, δροσιά.

dexterity [dɛks'tɛrɪtɪ] n επιδεξιότητα.

diabetes [daɪə'bi:ti:z] n διαβήτης.

diabetic [daɪə'bɛtɪk] a, n διαβητικός.

diagnose ['daɪəgnəuz] vt κάνω διάγνωση.

diagnosis [daɪəg'nəusɪs] n διάγνωση.

diagonal [daɪ'ægənl] a, n διαγώνιος.

diagram ['daɪəgræm] n διάγραμμα nt, σχέδιο.

dial ['daɪəl] n (esp TEL) δίσκος επιλογής, καντράν nt inv ♦ vt καλώ, παίρνω || ~ling tone n ένδειξη ελεύθερης γραμμής.

dialect ['daɪəlɛkt] n διάλεκτος f.

dialogue ['daɪəlɔg] n διάλογος.

diameter [daɪ'æmɪtə*] n διάμετρος f.

diamond ['daɪəmənd] n διαμάντι || (CARDS) καρρό.

diapers ['daɪəpəz] npl (US) πάνες fpl.

diaphragm ['daɪəfræm] n διάφραγμα nt.

diarrhoea [daɪə'rɪə] n διάρροια.

diary ['daɪərɪ] n ημερολόγιο.

dice [daɪs] npl ζάρια ntpl ♦ vt (vegetables) κόβω σε κύβους.

Dictaphone ['dɪktəfəun] n (R) Dictaphone nt.

dictate [dɪk'teɪt] vt υπαγορεύω || (impose) επιβάλλω ♦ ['dɪkteɪt] n πρόσταγμα nt, διαταγή.

dictation [dɪk'teɪʃən] n υπαγόρευση.

dictator [dɪk'teɪtə*] n δικτάτορας.

dictatorship [dɪk'teɪtəʃɪp] n δικτατορία.

diction ['dɪkʃən] n ύφος λόγου, λεκτικό.

dictionary ['dɪkʃənrɪ] n λεξικό.

did [dɪd] pt of **do** || ~n't = **did not** || see **do**.

die [daɪ] vi πεθαίνω, τα τινάζω || (end) σβήνω || **to** ~ **away** vi εξασθενίζω, σβήνω || **to** ~ **down** vi εξασθενίζω, πέφτω || **to** ~ **out** vi αποθνήσκω, σβήνω.

Diesel ['di:zəl]: ~ **engine** n ντήζελ nt inv.

diet ['daɪət] n (food) (δια)τροφή || (special course) δίαιτα ♦ vi κάνω δίαιτα.

differ ['dɪfə*] vi διαφέρω, ξεχωρίζω

|| (disagree) διαφωνώ || ~ence n διαφορά || (disagreement) διαφωνία, διαφορά || ~ent a διάφορος, διαφορετικός || ~ential [dɪfə'renʃəl] n (AUT) διαφορικό || (wages) διαφορική || ~entiate vti διαφοροποιώ, ξεχωρίζω.

difficult ['dɪfɪkəlt] a δύσκολος || ~y n δυσκολία, δυσχέρεια.

diffidence ['dɪfɪdəns] n επιφυλακτικότητα, ντροπαλότητα.

diffident ['dɪfɪdənt] a διστακτικός, άτολμος.

diffuse [dɪ'fjuːs] a διάχυτος ♦ [dɪ'fjuːz] vt διαχέω, σκορπίω.

dig [dɪg] (irreg v) vt (hole, garden) σκάβω || (nails) χώνω || (delve into) ψάχνω, τρυπώ ♦ n (prod) κάρφωμα nt, πείραγμα nt || (ARCH) εκσκαφή || to ~ up vt εκσκάπτω, ξερριζώνω, ξεθάβω.

digest [daɪ'dʒest] vt χωνεύω || (work over) επεξεργάζομαι ♦ ['daɪdʒest] n περίληψη, σύνοψη || ~ion n χώνευση.

digit ['dɪdʒɪt] n (number) ψηφίο, αριθμός || (toe, finger) δάκτυλος.

dignified ['dɪgnɪfaɪd] a αξιοπρεπής.

dignity ['dɪgnɪtɪ] n αξιοπρέπεια.

digress [daɪ'gres] vi εκτρέπομαι, ξεφεύγω || ~ion n εκτροπή, παρέκβαση.

digs [dɪgz] npl (Brit col) δωμάτιο.

dilapidated [dɪ'læpɪdeɪtɪd] a σαραβαλιασμένος.

dilate [daɪ'leɪt] vti διαστέλλω, πλαταίνω, διαστέλλομαι.

dilemma [daɪ'lemə] n δίλημμα nt.

diligent ['dɪlɪdʒənt] a επιμελής.

dilute [daɪ'luːt] vt αραιώνω, νερώνω ♦ a αραιός.

dim [dɪm] a αμυδρός, μουντός, σκοτεινός || (stupid) κουτός ♦ vt χαμηλώνω, θολώνω.

dime [daɪm] n (US) δέκατο του δολλαρίου.

dimension [dɪ'menʃən] n διάσταση, έκταση || ~s npl διαστάσεις fpl.

diminish [dɪ'mɪnɪʃ] vti ελαττώνω, ελαττώνομαι.

diminutive [dɪ'mɪnjutɪv] a υποκοριστικός ♦ n υποκοριστικό.

din [dɪn] n θόρυβος, πάταγος.

dine [daɪn] vi γευματίζω, τρώγω || ~r n τραπεζαρία τραίνου || (person) γευματίζων.

dinghy ['dɪŋgɪ] n μικρή βάρκα.

dingy ['dɪndʒɪ] a μαυρισμένος, βρώμικος.

dining car ['daɪnɪŋkɑː*] n βαγκόν-ρεστωράν nt inv.

dining room ['daɪnɪŋrum] n τραπεζαρία.

dinner ['dɪnə*] n γεύμα nt, φαΐ || (public) επίσημο γεύμα || ~ jacket n σμόκιν nt inv || ~ party n τραπέζι || ~ time n ώρα φαγητού.

diocese ['daɪəsɪs] n επισκοπή.

dip [dɪp] n (slope) κλίση, πλαγιά || (bath) βουτιά ♦ vt εμβαπτίζω, βουτώ || (AUT) χαμηλώνω || (flag) κατεβάζω ♦ vi (slope) γέρνω, κατηφορίζω, χαμηλώνω.

diphtheria [dɪf'θɪərɪə] n διφθερίτιδα.

diphthong ['dɪfθɒŋ] n δίφθογγος f.

diploma [dɪ'pləumə] n δίπλωμα nt.

diplomacy [dɪ'pləuməsɪ] n διπλωματία.

diplomat ['dɪpləmæt] n διπλωμάτης || ~ic a διπλωματικός.

dipstick ['dɪpstɪk] n βυθομετρικός ράβδος f.

dire [daɪə*] a καταστρεπτικός, τρομερός, έσχατος.

direct [daɪ'rekt] a (straight) ευθύς, ίσιος || (immediate) άμεσος ♦ vt (manage) διευθύνω, διοικώ || (aim) κατευθύνω, δείχνω.

direction [dɪ'rekʃən] n (control) διεύθυνση, διαχείριση || (of traffic) ρύθμιση || (of movement) κατεύθυνση,

φορά || ~ s npl (for use) οδηγίες fpl || ~ al a κατά διεύθυνση.

directly [dɪ'rektlɪ] ad (in straight line) κατευθείαν, ίσια || (at once) αμέσως.

director [dɪ'rektə*] n διευθυντής/ρια m/f, ο γενικός.

directory [dɪ'rektərɪ] n (esp TEL) (τηλεφωνικός) κατάλογος || (COMPUT) κατάλογος.

dirt [dɜːt] n ακαθαρσία, βρωμιά, ρύπος nt || ~ **road** n (US) χωματόδρομος || ~ **y** a ρυπαρός λερωμένος, ακάθαρτος || (mean) βρώμικος, πρόστυχος ♦ vt λερώνω, μουντζουρώνω.

disability [dɪsə'bɪlɪtɪ] n ανικανότητα || (physical) αναπηρία.

disabled [dɪs'eɪbld] a ανίκανος, σακατεμένος, ανάπηρος.

disadvantage [dɪsəd'vɑːntɪdʒ] n μειονέκτημα nt, ελάττωμα nt || (sell at) ζημιά || ~ **ous** [dɪsædvɑːn'teɪdʒəs] a ασύμφορος, δυσμενής.

disagree [dɪsə'griː] vi διαφωνώ || to ~ **with** vt δεν ταιριάζω, δεν πηγαίνω || (food) πειράζω || ~ **able** a δυσάρεστος, αντιπαθητικός || ~ **ment** n διαφωνία, διάσταση, ασυμφωνία.

disallow [dɪsə'laʊ] vt αρνούμαι, απορρίπτω, απαγορεύω.

disappear [dɪsə'pɪə*] vi εξαφανίζομαι || ~ **ance** n εξαφάνιση.

disappoint [dɪsə'pɔɪnt] vt απογοητεύω, χαλώ, στενοχωρούμαι || ~ **ing** a απογοητευτικός || ~ **ment** n απογοήτευση, λύπη.

disapproval [dɪsə'pruːvəl] n αποδοκιμασία.

disapprove [dɪsə'pruːv] vi (+ of) αποδοκιμάζω, επικρίνω.

disarm [dɪs'ɑːm] vt αφοπλίζω || ~ **ament** n αφοπλισμός.

disaster [dɪ'zɑːstə*] n συμφορά, δυστύχημα nt.

disastrous [dɪ'zɑːstrəs] a ολέθριος, καταστρεπτικός.

disband [dɪs'bænd] vt απολύω, διαλύω.

disbelief ['dɪsbə'liːf] n δυσπιστία.

disc [dɪsk] n δίσκος.

discard [dɪs'kɑːd] vt απορρίπτω, αφήνω.

discern [dɪ'sɜːn] vt διακρίνω, ξεχωρίζω || ~ **ing** a οξυδερκής, διακριτικός.

discharge [dɪs'tʃɑːdʒ] vt (unload ship etc) ξεφορτώνω || (fire a gun) πυροβολώ || (dismiss) απολύω || (MIL) αποστρατεύω || (perform duties) εκτελώ, εκπληρώ ♦ n (MED) απέκκριμα nt || (MIL) αποστράτευση || (flow) εκκένωση.

disciple [dɪ'saɪpl] n μαθητής/ήτρια m/f, οπαδός.

discipline ['dɪsɪplɪn] n πειθαρχία ♦ vt πειθαρχώ, τιμωρώ.

disclaim [dɪs'kleɪm] vt απαρνούμαι.

disclose [dɪs'kləʊz] vt αποκαλύπτω.

disclosure [dɪs'kləʊʒə*] n αποκάλυψη, εκδήλωση.

disco ['dɪskəʊ] n abbr of **discothèque**.

discoloured [dɪs'kʌləd] a ξεθωριασμένος, ξεθωριασμένη.

discomfort [dɪs'kʌmfət] n (uneasiness) δυσφορία, στενοχωρία || (lack of comfort) έλλειψη ανέσεως, κακουχία.

disconcert [dɪskən'sɜːt] vt ταράσσω, συγχύζω.

disconnect ['dɪskə'nekt] vt διασπώ, αποσυνδέω.

discontent [dɪskən'tent] n δυσαρέσκεια || ~ **ed** a δυσαρεστημένος.

discontinue ['dɪskən'tɪnjuː] vti διακόπτω, καταργώ.

discord [dɪs'kɔːd] n (quarrelling) διαφωνία, διχόνοια || (MUS)

παραφωνία || ~ant α ασύμφωνος, παράφωνος.

discothèque ['dɪskəutɛk] n δισκοθήκη.

discount ['dɪskaunt] n έκπτωση, σκόντο || (bank) προεξόφληση, υφαίρεση ♦ [dɪs'kaunt] vt (disbelieve) περιφρονώ, δεν πιστεύω.

discourage [dɪs'kʌrɪdʒ] vt (take away confidence) αποθαρρύνω || (disapprove) αποδοκιμάζω, αποτρέπω.

discouraging [dɪs'kʌrɪdʒɪŋ] a αποθαρρυντικός.

discourteous [dɪs'kɜːtɪəs] a αγενής.

discover [dɪs'kʌvə*] vt ανακαλύπτω || ~y n ανακάλυψη.

discredit [dɪs'krɛdɪt] vt δυσπιστώ, υποτιμώ.

discreet [dɪs'kriːt] a νουνεχής, διακριτικός.

discrepancy [dɪs'krɛpənsɪ] n διαφορά, ασυμφωνία.

discretion [dɪs'krɛʃən] n (prudence) φρόνηση, σύνεση || (right to decide) βούληση.

discriminate [dɪs'krɪmɪneɪt] vi κάνω διάκριση, ξεχωρίζω.

discriminating [dɪs'krɪmɪneɪtɪŋ] a διακριτικός, μεροληπτικός.

discrimination [dɪskrɪmɪ'neɪʃən] n διάκριση, ορθοφροσύνη.

discuss [dɪs'kʌs] vt συζητώ || ~ion n συζήτηση.

disdain [dɪs'deɪn] vt περιφρονώ || n περιφρόνηση || ~ful a υπεροπτικός, περιφρονητικός.

disease [dɪ'ziːz] n νόσημα nt, ασθένεια.

disembark [dɪsɪm'bɑːk] vti αποβιβάζω, αποβιβάζομαι.

disengage [dɪsɪn'geɪdʒ] vt (AUT) αποσυμπλέκω.

disentangle ['dɪsɪn'tæŋgl] vt διαχωρίζω, ξεμπλέκω.

disfigure [dɪs'fɪgə*] vt παραμορφώνω.

disgrace [dɪs'greɪs] n (general) δυσμένεια || (thing) αίσχος nt, ντροπή ♦ vt ντροπιάζω, ξεφτελίζω || ~ful a επονείδιστος.

disgruntled [dɪs'grʌntld] a δυσαρεστημένος, κατσουφιασμένος.

disguise [dɪs'gaɪz] vt (change appearance) μεταμφιέζω || (hide) αποκρύπτω ♦ n μεταμφίεση, απόκρυψη.

disgust [dɪs'gʌst] n αηδία ♦ vt αηδιάζω || ~ing a αηδιαστικός, σιχαμερός.

dish [dɪʃ] n πιάτο || (meal) φαγητό || to ~ up vt παρουσιάζω, σερβίρω || ~cloth n πιατόπανο.

dishearten [dɪs'hɑːtn] vt αποθαρρύνω, απελπίζω.

dishevelled [dɪ'ʃɛvəld] a ξεμαλλιασμένος, ανακατωμένος.

dishonest [dɪs'ɒnɪst] a ανέντιμος, κακοήθης || ~y n κακοήθεια, ατιμία.

dishonour [dɪs'ɒnə*] n αίσχος nt, ατιμία.

dishwasher ['dɪʃwɒʃə*] n πλυντήριο πιάτων.

disillusion [dɪsɪ'luːʒən] n απογοήτευση.

disinfect [dɪsɪn'fɛkt] vt απολυμαίνω || ~ant n απολυμαντικό.

disintegrate [dɪs'ɪntɪgreɪt] vi αποσυντίθεμαι, θρυμματίζομαι.

disinterested [dɪs'ɪntrɪstɪd] a αφιλοκερδής, αδιάφορος.

disjointed [dɪs'dʒɔɪntɪd] a ασυνάρτητος, εξαρθρωμένος.

disk [dɪsk] n = **disc**.

diskette [dɪs'kɛt] n (COMPUT) δισκέτα.

dislike [dɪs'laɪk] n αντιπάθεια, αποστροφή ♦ vt αντιπαθώ, απεχθάνομαι.

dislocate ['dɪsləukeɪt] vt (bone)

εξαρθρώνω, στραμπουλίζω ||
ξεχαρβαλώνω, χαλνώ.
dislodge [dɪs'lɔdʒ] vt εκτοπίζω,
εκδιώκω.
disloyal [dɪs'lɔɪəl] a άπιστος.
dismal ['dɪzməl] a ζοφερός,
μελαγχολικός.
dismantle [dɪs'mæntl] vt
παροπλίζω, λύω.
dismay [dɪs'meɪ] n κατάπληξη,
φόβος ♦ vt (dishearten) πτοώ,
φοβίζω, απογοητεύω.
dismiss [dɪs'mɪs] vt (discharge)
απολύω, παύω || (out of mind) διώχνω,
βγάζω || (send away) απομακρύνω,
διώχνω || (LAW) απορρίπτω,
απαλλάσσω || ~**al** n απόλυση,
παύση.
disobedience [dɪsə'biːdɪəns] n
ανυπακοή, παρακοή.
disobedient [dɪsə'biːdɪənt] a
ανυπάκουος, πεισματάρης.
disobey ['dɪsə'beɪ] vt παρακούω,
παραβαίνω.
disorder [dɪs'ɔːdə*] n (confusion)
ακαταστασία, αταξία || (commotion)
ταραχή, φασαρία || (MED) διαταραχή.
disorderly [dɪs'ɔːdəlɪ] a (untidy)
ακατάστατος || (unruly) άτακτος,
απείθαρχος.
disown [dɪs'əun] vt απαρνούμαι,
αποκηρύττω.
disparaging [dɪs'pærɪdʒɪŋ] a
δυσφημιστικός.
disparity [dɪs'pærɪtɪ] n ανισότητα,
διαφορά.
dispatch [dɪs'pætʃ] vt (goods)
στέλνω, διεκπεραιώνω ♦ n
αποστολή, διεκπεραίωση || (esp MIL)
αναφορά, μήνυμα nt.
dispel [dɪs'pel] vt διασκορπίζω.
dispensary [dɪs'pensərɪ] n
φαρμακείο.
dispense [dɪs'pens] vt διανέμω,
χορηγώ || **to** ~ **with** vt κάνω χωρίς.

disperse [dɪs'pɜːs] vt διασκορπίζω
♦ vi διασκορπίζομαι.
displace [dɪs'pleɪs] vt εκτοπίζω ||
~**d person** n πρόσφυγας.
display [dɪs'pleɪ] n (of goods) έκθεση,
επίδειξη || (of feeling) εκδήλωση ||
(MIL) επίδειξη ♦ vt επιδεικνύω,
εκθέτω.
displease [dɪs'pliːz] vt δυσαρεστώ.
displeasure [dɪs'pleʒə*] n
δυσαρέσκεια.
disposal [dɪs'pəuzəl] n (of property)
διάθεση || **at one's** ~ στη διάθεση.
dispose [dɪs'pəuz] vt: **to** ~ **of** vt
απαλλάσσομαι, ξεφορτώνομαι.
disposed [dɪs'pəuzd] a
διατεθειμένος.
disposition [dɪspə'zɪʃən] n
(character) προδιάθεση,
χαρακτήρας.
disproportionate [dɪsprə'pɔːʃnɪt]
a δυσανάλογος.
disprove [dɪs'pruːv] vt αναιρώ,
ανασκευάζω.
dispute [dɪs'pjuːt] n αμφισβήτηση,
φιλονεικία ♦ vt αμφισβητώ,
διεκδικώ.
disqualify [dɪs'kwɔlɪfaɪ] vt καθιστώ
ακατάλληλο || (SPORT) αποκλείω.
disregard [dɪsrɪ'gaːd] vt
παραβλέπω, αγνοώ, περιφρονώ.
disreputable [dɪs'repjutəbl] a
ανυπόληπτος, κακόφημος.
disrespectful [dɪsrɪ'spektful] a
ασεβής.
disrupt [dɪs'rʌpt] vt διασπώ, διαλύω
|| ~**ion** n διάσπαση.
dissatisfaction ['dɪssætɪs'fækʃən]
n δυσαρέσκεια.
dissatisfied ['dɪs'sætɪsfaɪd] a
δυσαρεστημένος.
dissect [dɪ'sekt] vt κατατέμνω,
διαμελίζω.
dissent [dɪ'sent] n διχογνωμία,
διαφωνία ♦ vi διαφωνώ.

dissident ['dɪsɪdənt] *a* διιστάμενος, διαφωνών.

dissipate ['dɪsɪpeɪt] *vt (waste)* σπαταλώ, ασωτεύω || *(disperse)* (δια)σκορπίζω.

dissociate [dɪ'səʊʃɪeɪt] *vt* αποσπώ, διαχωρίζω, αποχωρίζω.

dissolute ['dɪsəluːt] *a* άσωτος, έκλυτος.

dissolve [dɪ'zɒlv] *vt* διαλύω ♦ *vi* διαλύομαι, λυώνω.

dissuade [dɪ'sweɪd] *vt* αποτρέπω, μεταπείθω.

distance ['dɪstəns] *n* απόσταση, διάστημα *nt* || **in the ~** μακρυά.

distant ['dɪstənt] *a (far away)* μακρυά, μακρυνός || απομεμακρυσμένος, επιφυλακτικός.

distaste ['dɪs'teɪst] *n* αποστροφή, απέχθεια || **~ful** *a* δυσάρεστος, απεχθής.

distil [dɪs'tɪl] *vt* αποστάζω, διυλίζω || **~lery** *n* ποτοποιείο.

distinct [dɪs'tɪŋkt] *a (different)* διαφορετικός || *(clear)* ευδιάκριτος, σαφής || **~ion** *n (difference)* διαφορά || *(honour etc)* διάκριση, τιμή || *(medal etc)* παράσημο || **~ive** *a* διακριτικός, χαρακτηριστικός || **~ly** *ad* ευδιάκριτα, καθαρά.

distinguish [dɪs'tɪŋgwɪʃ] *vt* διακρίνω, ξεχωρίζω, διαφοροποιώ || **~ed** *a (eminent)* διακεκριμένος || **~ing** *a* χαρακτηριστικός, διακριτικός.

distort [dɪs'tɔːt] *vt (out of shape)* διαστρέφω, στραβώνω || *(fig)* διαστρεβλώνω, παραποιώ || **~ion** *n* παραμόρφωση, διαστρέβλωση.

distract [dɪs'trækt] *vt* αποσπώ, περισπώ || *(drive mad)* περιπλέκω, τρελλαίνω || **~ion** *n (inattention)* περίσπαση, αφηρημάδα || *(distress)* αναταραχή, αναστάτωση || *(diversion)* διασκέδαση.

distraught [dɪs'trɔːt] *a* ταραγμένος, συγχυσμένος.

distress [dɪs'trɛs] *n (grief)* απελπισία, αγωνία, πίκρα || *(suffering)* αθλιότητα, δυστυχία || *(difficulty)* κίνδυνος, σε δύσκολη θέση ♦ *vt* θλίβω, στενοχωρώ || **~ing** *a* δυσάρεστος, οδυνηρός || **~ signal** *n* σήμα *nt* κινδύνου.

distribute [dɪs'trɪbjuːt] *vt (give out)* διανέμω, μοιράζω || *(spread)* εξαπλώνω.

distribution [dɪstrɪ'bjuːʃən] *n* διανομή, κατανομή.

distributor [dɪs'trɪbjutə*] *n (COMM)* διανομέας, αντιπρόσωπος || *(AUT etc)* διανομέας.

district ['dɪstrɪkt] *n (of country)* περιοχή, περιφέρεια || *(of town)* συνοικία || **~ attorney** *n (US)* εισαγγελέας || **~ nurse** *n (Brit)* επισκέπτρια νοσοκόμος.

distrust [dɪs'trʌst] *n* δυσπιστία, υποψία ♦ *vt* δυσπιστώ προς, υποπτεύομαι.

disturb [dɪs'tɜːb] *vt (upset)* ταράσσω, ενοχλώ || *(agitate)* ταράσσω, κλονίζω || **~ance** *n* διατάραξη, φασαρία || **~ing** *a* ενοχλητικός, ανησυχητικός.

disused ['dɪs'juːzd] *a* αχρησιμοποίητος, απηρχαιωμένος.

ditch [dɪtʃ] *n* τάφρος *f*, χαντάκι.

ditto ['dɪtəʊ] *n* ομοίως.

divan [dɪ'væn] *n (bed)* ντιβάνι.

dive [daɪv] *n (into water)* βουτιά || *(AVIAT)* βύθιση ♦ *vi* βυθίζομαι, βουτώ || **~r** *n (professional)* δύτης.

diverge [daɪ'vɜːdʒ] *vi* διίσταμαι, αποκλίνω.

diverse [daɪ'vɜːs] *a* διάφορος, ποικίλος.

diversify [daɪ'vɜːsɪfaɪ] *vt* διαφοροποιώ, ποικίλλω.

diversion [daɪ'vɜːʃən] *n* απόκλιση,

λοξοδρομία || (of traffic) διοχέτευση || (pastime) διασκέδαση.

diversity [dai'vɔ:siti] n ανομοιότητα, ποικιλία.

divert [dai'vɔ:t] vt αποσπώ, εκτρέπω || (entertain) διασκεδάζω.

divide [di'vaid] vt διανέμω, (δια)μοιράζω, χωρίζω ♦ vi διαιρώ, χωρίζω.

dividend ['dividend] n μέρισμα nt, τοκομερίδιο || (MATH) διαιρετέος.

divine [di'vain] a θείος, θεϊκός.

diving board ['daiviŋbɔ:d] n εξέδρα για βουτιές.

divinity [di'viniti] n θεότητα || (study) θεολογία.

division [di'viʒən] a (dividing) διανομή, μοιρασιά || (MATH) διαίρεση || (MIL) μεραρχία || (part) τμήμα nt || (of opinion) διχόνοια, διαίρεση.

divorce [di'vɔ:s] n διαζύγιο, διάζευξη ♦ vt χωρίζω || ~d a χωρισμένος.

divulge [dai'vʌldʒ] vt αποκαλύπτω, φανερώνω.

dizziness ['dizinis] n ίλιγγος, ζάλη.

dizzy ['dizi] a ζαλισμένος.

do [du:] (irreg v) vt κάνω, εκτελώ, εκπληρώ, τελειώνω, ταιριάζω, αρκώ ♦ vi (act, proceed) κάνω || (be suitable) ταιριάζω, κάνω ♦ n (party) πάρτυ nt inv.

docile ['dousail] a πειθήνιος, υπάκουος.

dock [dɒk] n (NAUT) νεοδόχος, δεξαμενή || (court) εδώλιο ♦ vi (NAUT) δεξαμενίζομαι || ~er n φορτοεκφορτωτής, λιμενεργάτης.

docket ['dɒkit] n περιληπτική επιγραφή.

dockyard ['dɒkjɑ:d] n ναύσταθμος.

doctor ['dɒktə*] n (MED) γιατρός m/f || (UNIV) διδάκτωρ m/f.

doctrine ['dɒktrin] n δόγμα nt, θεωρία.

document ['dɒkjumənt] n έγγραφο

|| ~ary [dɒkju'mentəri] n (film) ντοκυμαντέρ nt inv.

dodge [dɒdʒ] n υπεκφυγή, τέχνασμα nt ♦ vt ξεφεύγω, αποφεύγω ♦ vi εκφεύγω, παραμερίζω, κάνω πλάι.

dog [dɒg] n σκυλί || (human) παλιάνθρωπος || ~ biscuit n μπισκότο για σκύλους || ~ collar n λαιμοδέτης (σκύλου) || (col) κολλάρο κληρικού.

dogged ['dɒgid] a ισχυρογνώμων, πεισματάρης.

dogma ['dɒgmə] n δόγμα nt || ~tic [dɒg'mætik] a (stubborn) κατηγορηματικός, δογματικός.

doings ['du:iŋz] npl (activities) πράξεις fpl, έργα ntpl.

doldrums ['dɒldrəmz] npl: in the ~ άκερφος.

dole [dəul] n (Brit: for unemployed) επίδομα ανεργίας || to be on the ~ παίρνω επίδομα ανεργίας || to ~ out vt διανέμω, μοιράζω.

doleful ['dəulful] a λυπητερός, πένθημος.

doll [dɒl] n κούκλα ♦ vt: to ~ o.s. up στολίζομαι.

dollar ['dɒlə*] n δολλάριο, τάληρο.

dolphin ['dɒlfin] n δελφίνι.

dome [dəum] n θόλος, τρούλλος.

domestic [də'mestik] a (of the house) οικιακός, του σπιτιού || (of the country) εσωτερικός, εγχώριος || (tame: of animal) οικιακός || ~ated a εξημερωμένος.

dominant ['dɒminənt] a επικρατών, υπερισχύων.

dominate ['dɒmineit] vt δεσπόζω, κυριαρχώ.

domination [dɒmi'neiʃən] n κυριαρχία.

domineering [dɒmi'niəriŋ] a δεσποτικός, αυταρχικός.

dominion [də'miniən] n (rule) κυριαρχία, εξουσία || (land) κτήση (αποικία).

dominoes ['dɒmɪnəʊz] *npl* ντόμινο.

donate [dəʊ'neɪt] *vt* δωρίζω.

donation [dəʊ'neɪʃən] *n* δωρεά.

done [dʌn] *pp* of **do**.

donkey ['dɒŋkɪ] *n* γάιδαρος, γαϊδούρι.

donor ['dəʊnə*] *n* δωρητής.

don't [dəʊnt] = **do not** || *see* do.

doom [duːm] *n* (*fate*) μοίρα || (*death*) θάνατος, καταστροφή ◆ *vt*: to be ~ed είμαι καταδικασμένος.

door [dɔː*] *n* πόρτα || ~**bell** *n* κουδούνι (της πόρτας) || ~**handle** *n* πόμολο, (χειρο)λαβή || ~**man** *n* θυρωρός, πορτιέρης || ~**mat** *n* ψάθα εξώπορτας || ~**step** *n* σκαλοπάτι.

dope [dəʊp] *n* (*drug*) ναρκωτικό.

dopey ['dəʊpɪ] *a* (*col*) βλάκας || (*doped*) χασικλωμένος.

dormant ['dɔːmənt] *a* λανθάνων, κοιμώμενος.

dormitory ['dɔːmɪtrɪ] *n* υπνοθάλαμος.

dosage ['dəʊsɪdʒ] *n* δόση.

dose [dəʊs] *n* δόση ◆ *vt* δίνω φάρμακο.

dot [dɒt] *n* στιγμή || **on the** ~ στη στιγμή, στην ώρα.

dote [dəʊt]: **to** ~ **on** *vt* αγαπώ τρελλά.

double ['dʌbl] *a* διπλός, διπλάσιος ◆ *ad* διπλά, διπλάσια, δύο-δύο ◆ *n* (*match*) σωσίας, ταίρι ◆ *vt* διπλασιάζω || (*fold in two*) διπλώνω ◆ *vi* διπλασιάζομαι, διπλώνομαι || **at the** ~ τροχάδην || ~**s** *npl* (TENNIS) διπλός (αγώνας) || ~ **bass** *n* κοντραμπάσο || ~ **bed** *n* διπλό κρεββάτι || ~**-breasted** *a* σταυρωτός || ~**-cross** *n* προδοσία ◆ *vt* προδίδω, εξαπατώ || ~**-decker** *n* διόροφο (λεωφορείο) || ~ **room** *n* δίκλινο.

doubly ['dʌblɪ] *ad* διπλάσια.

doubt [daʊt] *n* αμφιβολία ◆ *vt* αμφιβάλλω, αμφισβητώ || **without** ~ χωρίς καμμιά αμφιβολία || ~**ful** *a* αμφίβολος || ~**less** *ad* αναμφιβόλως.

dough [dəʊ] *n* ζυμάρι || ~**nut** *n* τηγανίτα, λουκουμάς.

dove [dʌv] *n* περιστέρι.

dovetail ['dʌvteɪl] *n* ψαλιδωτή ένωση ◆ *vi* ταιριάζω.

dowdy ['daʊdɪ] *a* άκομψος, κακοντυμένος.

down [daʊn] *n* (*fluff*) πούπουλο, χνούδι ◆ *ad* κάτω, χάμω ◆ *prep* πιο κάτω, προς το κάτω, χαμηλότερα ◆ *vt* κατεβάζω, ρίχνω κάτω, νικώ || ~ **with X!** κάτω ο X || ~**-and-out** *a* κατεστραμμένος, στην ψάθα || ~**-at-heel** *a* μπατίρης || ~**cast** *a* κατηφής || ~**fall** *n* πτώση, παρακμή || ~**hearted** *a* αποθαρρημένος, κακόκεφος || ~**hill** *ad* κατηφορικώς, προς τα κάτω || ~**pour** *n* μπόρα || ~**right** *a* ευθύς, ειλικρινής, απόλυτος || ~**stairs** *ad* κάτω || *a* κάτω, στα κάτω πάτωμα || ~**stream** *ad* με το ρεύμα || ~**town** *ad* στην πόλη || ~**ward** *a* κατηφορικός, κατερχόμενος || ~**wards** *ad* προς τα κάτω, και κάτω.

dowry ['daʊrɪ] *n* προίκα.

doz. *abbr of* **dozen**.

doze [dəʊz] *vi* λαγοκοιμάμαι ◆ *n* υπνάκος.

dozen ['dʌzn] *n* δωδεκάδα.

Dr. *abbr of* **doctor** || *abbr of* **drive** (*n*).

drab [dræb] *a* (*dull*) μονότονος, ανιαρός.

drachma ['drækmə] *n* δραχμή.

draft [drɑːft] *n* (*rough copy*) (προ)σχέδιο || (ECON) γραμμάτιο, συναλλαγματική || (US MIL) στρατολογία ◆ *vt* συντάσσω, ετοιμάζω προσχέδιο || *see* **draught**.

drag [dræg] *vt* (*pull*) σέρνω || (NAUT) βυθοκορώ ◆ *vi* βραδυπορώ,

drain

σέρνομαι ♦ n *(bore)* φορτικός
άνθρωπος || **to ~ on** vi συνεχίζω
ανιαρά.

drain [dreɪn] n *(lit)* οχετός, αγωγός,
αυλάκι || *(fig)* φυγή, διαρροή,
εξάντληση ♦ vt *(water)* αποχετεύω ||
(fig) αδειάζω, απομυζώ ♦ vi *(of
water)* στάζω, στραγγίζω || ~**age** n
αποχέτευση, αποστράγγιση ||
~**pipe** n σωλήνας αποχετεύσεως,
υδρορροή.

dram [dræm] n δράμι || *(col)*
σταγόνα.

drama ['drɑ:mə] n δράμα nt || ~**tic**
[drə'mætɪk] a δραματικός || ~**tist** n
δραματουργός, δραματοποιός.

drank [dræŋk] pt of **drink**.

drape [dreɪp] vt κοσμώ με ύφασμα,
ντύνω || ~**s** npl *(US)* κουρτίνες fpl ||
~**r** n υφασματέμπορος.

drastic ['dræstɪk] a δραστικός,
αποφασιστικός.

draught [drɑ:ft] n *(air)* ρεύμα nt
(αέρος) || *(NAUT)* βύθισμα nt || ~**s** n
(game) ντάμα, νταμιέρα || *(beer)* on
~ (μπύρα) του βαρελιού || ~**board**
n αβάκιο.

draughtsman ['drɑ:ftsmən] n
σχεδιαστής.

draughty ['drɑ:ftɪ] a με πολλά
ρεύματα.

draw [drɔ:] *(irreg v)* vt *(pull)* σέρνω,
τραβώ, σπικώνω || *(attract)* ελκύω,
τραβώ || *(a picture)* χαράσσω,
σχεδιάζω, ζωγραφίζω || *(take out)*
εξάγω, βγάζω, τραβάω ♦ vi *(SPORT)*
έρχομαι ισόπαλος ♦ n *(SPORT)*
ισοφάρισση || *(lottery)* κλήρωση || **to
~ to a close** πλησιάζω στο τέλος ||
to ~ out vi *(train)* ξεκινώ || *(lengthen)*
παρατείνω, τραβώ σε μάκρος ♦ vt
(take out) αποσύρω, τραβώ || **to ~
up** vi *(stop)* φθάνω ♦ vt *(document)*
συντάσσω, καταστρώνω || ~**back** n
μειονέκτημα nt, ελάττωμα nt ||
~**bridge** n κρεμαστή γέφυρα.

drawer [drɔ:*] n συρτάρι.

drawing ['drɔ:ɪŋ] n σχέδιο, σκίτσο ||
(art of drawing) σχέδιο || ~ **pin** n
πινέζα || ~ **room** n σαλόνι, σάλα.

drawl [drɔ:l] n συρτή φωνή ♦ vi
σέρνω τη φωνή.

dread [dred] n τρόμος, φόβος,
ανησυχία ♦ vt φοβούμαι, τρέμω ||
~**ful** a φοβερός, τρομερός.

dream [dri:m] *(irreg v)* n όνειρο ||
(fancy) ονειροπόληση ♦ vi
ονειρεύομαι ♦ a ονειρώδης || ~**er** n
ονειροπόλος || ~**y** a ονειροπόλος,
φαντασιόπληκτος, θολός.

dreary ['drɪərɪ] a μονότονος,
πληκτικός.

dredge [dredʒ] vt βυθοκορώ,
εκβαθύνω || ~**r** n βυθοκόρος.

dregs [dregz] npl κατακάθι, μούργα.

drench [drentʃ] vt καταβρέχω,
μουσκεύω.

dress [dres] n ενδυμασία, ρούχα ntpl,
ντύσιμο || *(esp woman's)* φόρεμα nt,
φουστάνι ♦ vt ντύνω, στολίζω || *(a
wound)* επενδύω || *(food)* ετοιμάζω για
μαγείρεμα || **to ~ up** vi ντύνομαι ||
~ **circle** n πρώτος εξώστης || ~**er** n
(person) που ντύνεται καλά || *(US)*
κομμός || ~**ing** n *(MED)* επίδεση ||
(for food) ετοιμασία, σάλτσα || ~**ing
gown** n ρόμπα || ~**ing room** n
(THEAT) καμαρίνι || ~**ing table** n
τουαλέτα *(έπιπλο)* || ~**maker** n
ράφτρα, μοδίστρα || ~**making** n
ραπτική || ~ **rehearsal** n τελευταία
πρόβα, γενική δοκιμή.

drew [dru:] pt of **draw**.

dribble ['drɪbl] vi *(trickle)* στάζω ♦
vt *(SPORT)* κάνω τρίπλες.

dried [draɪd] a ξηρός,
απεζηραμένος, στεγνός.

drift [drɪft] n *(driven by tide etc)*
κατεύθυνση, διεύθυνση, ταχύτητα ||
(mass of snow etc) σωρός,
συσσώρευση || *(meaning)* έννοια,
νόημα nt ♦ vi *(off course)*

παρασύρομαι, ξεπέφτω || *(aimlessly)* περιφέρομαι άσκοπα || ~ **wood** *n* ξύλο που επιπλέει.

drill [drɪl] *n (tool)* τρυπάνι, δράπανο || *(MIL.)* γυμνάσια *ntpl*, άσκηση ♦ *vt (bore)* τρυπώ, ανοίγω || *(exercise)* εκπαιδεύω, γυμνάζω ♦ *vi* (+ *for*) κάνω γεώτρηση.

drink [drɪŋk] *(irreg v) n (liquid)* ποτό, αναψυκτικό || *(alcoholic)* ποτό ♦ *vti (swallow liquid)* πίνω || ~ **er** *n* πότης || ~**ing water** *n* πόσιμο νερό.

drip [drɪp] *n* στάξιμο, σταλαγματιά ♦ *vi* στάζω, σταλάζω || ~**ping** *n* στάξιμο || *(fat)* λίπος ψητού || ~**ping wet** *a* μουσκεμένος.

drive [draɪv] *(irreg v) n (trip in car)* κούρσα, διαδρομή || *(road)* δρόμος πάρκου || *(campaign)* καμπανία, έρανος || *(energy)* ενεργητικότητα, δραστηριότητα || *(SPORT)* κτύπημα *nt || (COMPUT. also:* **disk** ~*)* μονάδα δίσκου ♦ *vt (car etc)* οδηγώ, σωφάρω || *(urge)* διώκνω, σπρώχνω || *(nail etc)* καρφώνω, μπάζω || *(operate)* κινώ, βάζω μπρος || *(force)* αναγκάζω, παρακινώ ♦ *vi (at controls)* οδηγώ, χειρίζομαι || *(travel)* πηγαίνω, τρέχω.

driver ['draɪvə*] *n* οδηγός || ~'**s license** *n (US)* άδεια οδηγού.

driving ['draɪvɪŋ] *a (rain)* νεροποντή|| ~ **instructor** *n* δάσκαλος οδηγήσεως || ~ **lesson** *n* μάθημα *nt* οδηγήσεως || ~ **licence** *n (Brit)* άδεια οδηγού || ~ **school** *n* σχολή οδηγών || ~ **test** *n* εξέταση για άδεια οδηγού.

drizzle ['drɪzl] *n* ψιχάλισμα *nt* ♦ *vi* ψιχαλίζω.

droll [drəʊl] *a* αστείος, κωμικός.

dromedary ['drɒmɪdəri] *n* κάμηλος *f n* δρομάς.

drone [drəʊn] *n (bee)* κηφήνας || *(sound)* βόμβος, βουητό ♦ *vi* σαλιαρίζω, μωρολογώ.

droop [druːp] *vi* πέφτω, γέρνω, σκύβω.

drop [drɒp] *n (of liquid)* σταγόνα, στάλα || *(fall)* πτώση, πέσιμο || *(MED)* σταγόνα ♦ *vt (let fall)* ρίχνω, αφήνω να πέσει || *(lower)* κατεβάζω, χαμηλώνω || *(cease)* εγκαταλείπω, παρατώ, αφήνω ♦ *vi (fall)* πέφτω || **to** ~ **off** *vi (sleep)* αποκοιμιέμαι || **to** ~ **out** *vi (withdraw)* αποσύρομαι.

dross [drɒs] *n* ακαθαρσίες *fpl*, απορρίμματα *ntpl*.

drought [draʊt] *n* ξηρασία.

drove [drəʊv] *pt* of **drive** ♦ *n (crowd)* πλήθος *nt* ανθρώπων, κοπάδι.

drown [draʊn] *vt* πνίγω || *(flood)* πλημμυρίζω ♦ *vi* πνίγομαι.

drowsy ['draʊzi] *a* νυσταλέος, νυσταγμένος.

drudgery ['drʌdʒəri] *n* μόχθος, αγγαρεία.

drug [drʌg] *n (MED)* φάρμακο || *(narcotic)* ναρκωτικό ♦ *vt* δίνω ναρκωτικό σε, υποπάρω || ~ **addict** *n* τοξικομανής, πρεζάκιας || ~ **store** *n (US)* φαρμακοποιός *m/f* || ~**store** *n (US)* φαρμακείο.

drum [drʌm] *n (MUS)* τύμπανο, τούμπανο || *(barrel)* βαρέλι || ~ **mer** *n* τυμπανιστής.

drunk [drʌŋk] *pp* of **drink** ♦ *n* μέθυσος, μπεκρής || ~**ard** *n* μεθύστακας || ~**en** *a* μεθυσμένος || ~**enness** *n* μέθη, μεθύσι.

dry [draɪ] *a (not wet)* ξηρός, ξερός || *(of well)* στερεμένος || *(rainless)* άνυδρος || *(uninteresting)* ξερός, κρύος || *(wine)* μπρούσκο ♦ *vt* ξηραίνω, στεγνώνω, στίβω ♦ *vi* ξεραίνομαι, στεγνώνω || **to** ~ **up** *vi* ξεραίνομαι || *(of well)* στερεύω || ~ **cleaner** *n* καθαριστήριο || ~**er** *n* στεγνωτής, στεγνωτήριο || ~ **rot** *n* σαράκι.

dual ['djʊəl] *a* διπλός, δυϊκός || ~

nationality n διπλή υπηκοότητα || ~**-purpose** a διπλής χρήσεως.

dubbed [dʌbd] a (CINE) ντουμπλαρισμένο.

dubious ['djuːbɪəs] a αμφίβολος, αμφιβάλλων, αβέβαιος.

duchess ['dʌtʃɪs] n δούκισσα.

duck [dʌk] n πάπια ♦ vt βουτώ, σκύβω ♦ vi βουτώ || ~**ling** n παπάκι.

duct [dʌkt] n αγωγός, σωλήνας.

dud [dʌd] n un εκραγείσα οβίδα ♦ a άχρηστος, τενεκές m, αποτυχημένος.

due [djuː] a (owing) οφειλόμενος, λήγων || (deserved) ανήκων, δίκαιος, σωστός || (expected) αναμενόμενος ♦ ad κατ'ευθείαν, ίσια προς || ~**s** npl (debt) τέλη ntpl, δασμός || (balance) οφειλόμενο, ανήκον || ~ **to** οφειλόμενο σε, λόγω.

duel ['djuəl] n μονομαχία.

duet [djuː'et] n δυωδία, ντουέτο.

dug [dʌg] pt, pp of **dig**.

duke [djuːk] n δούκας.

dull [dʌl] a (person) βραδύνους, κουτός || (boring) ανήκων, ανιαρός || (weather) βαρύς, σκοτεινός ♦ vt (soften, weaken) εξασθενίζω, ξεθωριάζω.

duly ['djuːli] ad δεόντως, εγκαίρως.

dumb [dʌm] a (lit) βουβός, μουγγός || (stupid) ανόητος, κουτός, ηλίθιος.

dummy ['dʌmi] n (model) κούκλα, ανδρείκελο || (substitute) ομοίωμα nt || (for baby) πιπιλίστρα ♦ a πλαστός, ψεύτικος, εικονικός.

dump [dʌmp] n σκουπιδότοπος || (storing place) αποθήκη ♦ vt ξεφορτώνω, απορρίπτω || ~**ing** n (COMM) πουλώ φτηνά || (rubbish) ανατροπή, εκφόρτιση.

dumpling ['dʌmpliŋ] n κομμάτι ζύμης βρασμένο με κρέας || (pie) πίτα.

dunce [dʌns] n αμαθής, ντουβάρι.

dune [djuːn] n αμμόλοφος.

dung [dʌŋ] n κοπριά.

dungarees [dʌŋgə'riːz] npl φόρμα εργάτη.

dungeon ['dʌndʒən] n μπουντρούμι, φυλακή.

dupe [djuːp] n θύμα nt, απάτη, κορόιδο ♦ vt εξαπατώ, κοροϊδεύω.

duplicate ['djuːplɪkɪt] a διπλός, διπλάσιος ♦ n διπλότυπο ♦ ['djuːplɪkeɪt] vt αντιγράφω || **in** ~ εις διπλούν.

durable ['djuərəbl] a ανθεκτικός, διαρκής.

duration [djuə'reɪʃən] n διάρκεια.

during ['djuəriŋ] prep κατά τη διάρκεια.

dusk [dʌsk] n σούρουπο.

dust [dʌst] n σκόνη, κονιορτός, στάκτη ♦ vt ξεσκονίζω, πασπαλίζω || ~**bin** n (Brit) τενεκές nt σκουπιδιών || ~**er** n ξεσκονόπανο || (feather) φτερό || ~**man** n (Brit) οδοκαθαριστής, σκουπιδιάρης || ~**y** a σκονισμένος.

Dutch [dʌtʃ] a ολλανδικός ♦ n (LING) Ολλανδικά || **the** ~ npl οι Ολλανδοί || ~**man** n Ολλανδέζος || ~**woman** n Ολλανδέζα.

duty ['djuːti] n καθήκον nt || (job) καθήκον(τα), υποχρέωση || (MIL) υπηρεσία || (tax) δασμός, φόρος || **on** ~ εν υπηρεσία || ~**-free** a αφορολόγητος ♦ n αφορολόγητα ntpl.

dwarf [dwɔːf] n νάνος.

dwell [dwel] (irreg v) vi διαμένω, κατοικώ || **to** ~ **on** vt εμμένω σε, επιμένω || ~**ing** n κατοικία.

dwindle ['dwindl] vi ελαττώνομαι, μικραίνω.

dye [dai] n βαφή, χρωματισμός ♦ vt βάφω.

dying ['daiiŋ] a (man) ετοιμοθάνατος.

dynamic [daɪˈnæmɪk] *a* δυναμικός || ~**s** *n* δυναμική.

dynamite [ˈdaɪnəmaɪt] *n* δυναμίτιδα.

dynamo [ˈdaɪnəməʊ] *n* γεννήτρια, δυναμό.

dynasty [ˈdɪnəstɪ] *n* δυναστεία.

dysentery [ˈdɪsɪntrɪ] *n* δυσεντερία.

E

each [iːtʃ] *a* καθένας, κάθε ♦ *pron* κάθε || ~ **other** ο ένας τον άλλο, αλλήλους.

eager [ˈiːgəʳ] *a* ένθερμος, ανυπόμονος, πρόθυμος.

eagle [ˈiːgl] *n* αετός.

ear [ɪəʳ] *n* αυτί || (for music) λεπτή ακοή || (of corn) στάχυ *nt* || ~**ache** *n* ωταλγία, αυτόπονος || ~**drum** *n* τύμπανο.

earl [ɜːl] *n* κόμης, κόντες *m*.

early [ˈɜːlɪ] *a* (before the season) πρώϊμος, πρόωρος || (in the morning) πρωϊνός ♦ *ad* (in the morning) πρωΐ || (in time) ενωρίς.

earn [ɜːn] *vt* κερδίζω, βγάζω || (acquire) αποκτώ, κατακτώ.

earnest [ˈɜːnɪst] *a* σοβαρός || (ardent) διάπυρος, ένθερμος || **in** ~ *ad* στα σοβαρά.

earnings [ˈɜːnɪŋz] *npl* απολαβές *fpl*, αποδοχές *fpl* || (of a firm) κέρδη *ntpl*.

earphones [ˈɪəfəʊnz] *npl* ακουστικά *ntpl*.

earring [ˈɪərɪŋ] *n* σκουλαρίκι.

earth [ɜːθ] *n* (planet) γη, κόσμος || (soil) γη, έδαφος, χώμα *nt* || (ELEC) γη, προσγείωση ♦ *vt* (ELEC) προσγειώνω || ~**enware** *n* πήλινα *ntpl* || ~**quake** *n* σεισμός.

earwig [ˈɪəwɪg] *n* (insect) φορφικούλη, ψαλίδα.

ease [iːz] *n* (facility) ευχέρεια,

ευκολία, άνεση || (comfort) ανάπαυση, άνεση, ξεκούραση ♦ *vt* (reduce pain etc) ανακουφίζω, καταπραΰνω || (remove pressure) καθησυχάζω, ξεφορτώνω || **at** ~! ανάπαυση! || **to** ~ **off** or **up** *vi* ελαττώνω, εργάζομαι αργότερα.

easily [ˈiːzɪlɪ] *ad* ήρεμα, εύκολα.

east [iːst] *n* (direction) ανατολή || (in direction) ανατολικά *ntpl* ♦ *a* ανατολικός ♦ *ad* προς ανατολάς, ανατολικά || **the E**~ Ανατολή.

Easter [ˈiːstəʳ] *n* Πάσχα *nt*, Λαμπρή.

eastern [ˈiːstən] *a* (from, of the east) ανατολικός.

eastward(s) [ˈiːstwəd(z)] *ad* προς ανατολάς.

easy [ˈiːzɪ] *a* (not difficult) ευχερής, εύκολος || (life) ξεκούραστος, άνετος || (manner) άνετος, αβίαστος || (yielding) καλόβολος ♦ *ad* εύκολα, ήρεμα, άνετα.

eat [iːt] (*irreg v*) *vt* (swallow) τρώγω || (one's words) καταπίνω || (consume) (κατα)τρώγω, υπονομεύω || **to** ~ **away** *vt* κατατρώγω, προσβάλλω || ~**able** *a* φαγώσιμος.

eavesdrop [ˈiːvzdrɒp] *vi* (+ on) κρυφακούω.

ebb [eb] *n* άμπωτη || (fig) παρακμή, πέσιμο ♦ *vi* κατεβαίνω, πέφτω.

ebony [ˈebənɪ] *n* έβενος, αμπανός.

ebullient [ɪˈbʌlɪənt] *a* (enthusiastic) εκδηλωτικός, ενθουσιώδης.

eccentric [ɪkˈsentrɪk] *a* (odd) εκκεντρικός, παράξενος ♦ *n* (person) ιδιότροπος.

ecclesiastical [ɪkliːzɪˈæstɪkl] *a* εκκλησιαστικός.

echo [ˈekəʊ] *n* ηχώ *f*, αντήχηση, αντίλαλος ♦ *vt* αντηχώ ♦ *vi* αντηχώ, απηχώ, αντιλαλώ.

eclipse [ɪˈklɪps] *n* έκλειψη ♦ *vt* προκαλώ έκλειψη || (fig) επισκιάζω.

economic [iːkəˈnɒmɪk] *a* οικονομικός || ~**al** *a* οικονομικός.

(of person) φειδωλός || ~**s** npl οικονομικά ntpl.

economist [ɪ'kɒnəmɪst] n οικονομολόγος m/f.

economize [ɪ'kɒnəmaɪz] vi (+ on) οικονομώ, κάνω οικονομία σε.

economy [ɪ'kɒnəmɪ] n οικονομία.

ecstasy ['ɛkstəsɪ] n έκσταση, μάγεμα nt.

ecstatic [ɛk'stætɪk] a εκστατικός.

ecumenical [i:kju:'mɛnɪkl] a οικουμενικός.

eczema ['ɛksɪmə] n έκζεμα nt.

edge [ɛdʒ] n *(boundary)* όχθη, παρυφή, άκρη || *(of garment)* ούγια || *(brink)* ακμή, κόλαση, άκρη || *(of knife)* κόψη, ακμή || **on** ~ = **edgy.**

edgy ['ɛdʒɪ] a εκνευρισμένος.

edible ['ɛdɪbl] a φαγώσιμος.

edict ['i:dɪkt] n διάταγμα nt.

edifice ['ɛdɪfɪs] n οικοδόμημα nt, κτίριο.

edit ['ɛdɪt] vt εκδίδω, διευθύνω || *(COMPUT)* συντάσσω σαω επιμελούμαι || ~**ion** [ɪ'dɪʃən] n έκδοση || ~**or** n *(of newspaper)* (αρχι)συντάκτης || *(of book)* εκδότης, επιμελητής εκδόσεως || ~**orial** a εκδοτικός, συντακτικός ♦ n *(κύριο)* άρθρο.

educate ['ɛdjukeɪt] vt εκπαιδεύω, σπουδάζω, μαθαίνω.

education [ɛdju'keɪʃən] n *(system)* εκπαίδευση || *(schooling)* σπουδές fpl, εκπαίδευση, μόρφωση || ~**al** a εκπαιδευτικός, μορφωτικός.

EEC N *(abbr of European Economic Community)* Ε.Ο.Κ. f *(ευρωπαϊκή οικονομική Κοινότητα).*

eel [i:l] n χέλι.

eerie ['ɪərɪ] a μυστηριώδης, παράξενος, τρομακτικός.

effect [ɪ'fɛkt] n *(result)* ενέργεια, επίδραση, επιρροή, αποτέλεσμα nt || *(impression)* εντύπωση, αίσθηση ♦ vt πραγματοποιώ, επιτυγχάνω || ~**s** npl *(sound, visual)* σκηνικά ntpl εφφέ || **in**

~ πράγματι, πραγματικά || ~**ive** a αποτελεσματικός, ουσιαστικός.

effeminate [ɪ'fɛmɪnɪt] a θηλυπρεπής, γυναικωτός.

effervescent [ɛfə'vɛsnt] a *(ανα)βράζων, σεριούχος* || *(person)* ζωηρός.

efficiency [ɪ'fɪʃənsɪ] n αποτελεσματικότητα, δραστικότητα || *(of machine)* απόδοση.

efficient [ɪ'fɪʃənt] a αποτελεσματικός || *(person)* ικανός, επιδέξιος.

effigy ['ɛfɪdʒɪ] n ομοίωμα nt, εικόνα.

effort ['ɛfət] n προσπάθεια || ~**less** n χωρίς προσπάθεια, εύκολος.

effrontery [ɪ'frʌntərɪ] n αυθάδεια, αδιαντροπιά.

e.g. ad *(abbr of exempli gratia)* παραδείγματος χάρη, π.χ.

egalitarian [ɪgælɪ'tɛərɪən] a ισοπεδωτικός.

egg [ɛg] n αυγό || ~ **to** ~ **on** vt εξωθώ, παρακινώ, σπρώχνω || ~**cup** n αυγοθήκη || ~**plant** n μελιτζανιά || ~**shell** n τσόφλι αυγού.

ego ['i:gəu] n το εγώ.

egotist ['ɛgəutɪst] n περιαυτολόγος.

Egypt ['i:dʒɪpt] n Αίγυπτος || ~**ian** [i:'dʒɪpʃən] n Αιγύπτιος ♦ a αιγυπτιακός.

eiderdown ['aɪdədaun] n *(quilt)* πουπουλένιο πάπλωμα nt.

eight [eɪt] num οκτώ, οχτώ || ~**een** num δέκα οκτώ || ~**eighth** a όγδοος || ~**y** num ογδόντα.

Eire ['ɛərə] n Ιρλανδία.

either ['aɪðə]* a εκάτερος, έκαστος, καθένας ♦ pron ή ο ένας ή ο άλλος, έκαστος || cj ή ... ή, είτε...είτε ♦ ad ούτε...ούτε.

eject [ɪ'dʒɛkt] vt εκβάλλω, βγάζω || *(throw out)* διώχνω, βγάζω έξω || ~**or seat** n εκτοξευόμενο κάθισμα nt.

elaborate [ɪ'læbərɪt] a επιμελημένος, εξονυχιστικός,

περίπλοκος ♦ [ɪ'læbəreɪt] vt επεξεργάζομαι, δουλεύω, επιμελούμαι.

elapse [ɪ'læps] vi παρέρχομαι, περνώ.

elastic [ɪ'læstɪk] n ελαστικό, λάστιχο ♦ a ελαστικός, εύκαμπτος || ~ **band** n λαστιχάκι.

elated [ɪ'leɪtɪd] a συνεπαρμένος, έξαλλος.

elation [ɪ'leɪʃən] n έπαρση, χαρά, κέφι.

elbow ['elbəʊ] n αγκώνας.

elder ['eldə*] a πρεσβύτερος, μεγαλύτερος ♦ n μεγαλύτερος || *(tree)* ακτή, σαμπούκος || ~ **ly** a ηλικιωμένος.

elect [ɪ'lekt] vt εκλέγω ♦ a εκλεκτός || ~ **ion** n εκλογή || ~ **ioneering** n ψηφοθηρία || ~ **or** n ψηφοφόρος m/f || ~ **oral** a εκλογικός || ~ **orate** n οι ψηφοφόροι mpl.

electric [ɪ'lektrɪk] a *(appliance)* ηλεκτρικός || ~ **al** a ηλεκτρικός || ~ **blanket** n θερμοφόρα κουβέρτα || ~ **chair** n *(US)* ηλεκτρική καρέκλα || ~ **cooker** n n. κουζίνα, μάτι || ~ **current** n n. ρεύμα nt || ~ **fire** n ηλεκτρικό σόμπα.

electrician [ɪlek'trɪʃən] n ηλεκτρολόγος.

electricity [ɪlek'trɪsɪtɪ] n ηλεκτρισμός.

electrify [ɪ'lektrɪfaɪ] vt (εξ)ηλεκτρίζω.

electrocute [ɪ'lektrəkjuːt] vt θανατώνω με ηλεκτρισμό, με ηλεκτροπληξία.

electron [ɪ'lektrɒn] n ηλεκτρόνιο.

electronic [elək'trɒnɪk] a ηλεκτρονικός || ~ **s** n ηλεκτρονική.

elegance ['elɪgəns] n κομψότητα.

elegant ['elɪgənt] a κομψός.

element ['elɪmənt] n *(all senses)* στοιχείο || ~ **ary** [elɪ'mentərɪ] a στοιχειώδης.

elephant ['elɪfənt] n ελέφαντας.

elevate ['elɪveɪt] vt (αν)υψώνω.

elevation [elɪ'veɪʃən] n *(height)* ύψος, ύψωμα nt.

elevator ['elɪveɪtə*] n ανελκυστήρας, ασανσέρ nt inv.

eleven [ɪ'levən] a έντεκα ♦ n *(team)* ομάδα έντεκα παικτών || ~ **ses** npl κολατσιό.

elf [elf] n έλφα, αγερικό, ξωτικό.

elicit [ɪ'lɪsɪt] vt εξάγω, αποσπώ, βγάζω.

eligible ['elɪdʒɪbl] a εκλέξιμος, κατάλληλος.

eliminate [ɪ'lɪmɪneɪt] vt αποβάλλω, διαγράφω || *(MATH)* εξαλείφω.

elimination [ɪlɪmɪ'neɪʃən] n αποκλεισμός, διαγραφή.

elite [ɪ'liːt] n εκλεκτή τάξη, αφρόκρεμα.

elm [elm] n φτελιά.

elocution [elə'kjuːʃən] n ευγλωττία, απαγγελία.

elongated ['iːlɒŋgeɪtɪd] a επιμήκης, μακρύς.

elope [ɪ'ləʊp] vi απάγομαι, φεύγω εκουσίως κλέβομαι || ~ **ment** n εκουσία απαγωγή.

eloquence ['eləkwəns] n ευφράδεια.

eloquent ['eləkwənt] a ευφραδής, εύγλωττος.

else [els] ad οπωσδήποτε άλλος, επί πλέον, αλλού || *(otherwise)* άλλως, αλλοιώς || ~ **where** ad αλλού.

elucidate [ɪ'luːsɪdeɪt] vt διευκρινίζω, δι ασαφηνίζω.

elude [ɪ'luːd] vt ξεφεύγω, διαφεύγω.

elusive [ɪ'luːsɪv] a άπιαστος, απατηλός.

emaciated [ɪ'meɪsɪeɪtɪd] a αδυνατισμένος, πετσί και κόκκαλο.

emanate ['eməneɪt] vi απορρέω, προέρχομαι, πηγάζω.

emancipate [ɪ'mænsɪpeɪt] vt απελευθερώνω.

emancipation [ɪmænsɪ'peɪʃən] n
χειραφέτηση, απελευθέρωση.

embalm [ɪm'baːm] vt ταριχεύω,
βαλσαμώνω.

embankment [ɪm'bæŋkmənt] n
ανάχωμα nt.

embargo [ɪm'baːgəʊ] n
απαγόρευση, περιορισμός.

embark [ɪm'baːk] vi επιβιβάζω ♦ vi
επιβιβάζομαι || **to ~ on** vt αρχίζω ||
~ation [ɛmbaːˈkeɪʃən] n
μπαρκάρισμα nt.

embarrass [ɪm'bærəs] vt φέρω σε
αμηχανία, στενοχωρώ || **~ing** a
(humiliating) ενοχλητικός,
ξεφτελιστικός || **~ment** n
στενοχώρια, αμηχανία, μπλέξιμο.

embassy ['ɛmbəsɪ] n πρεσβεία.

embed [ɪm'bɛd] vt χώνω, θάβω.

embellish [ɪm'bɛlɪʃ] vt καλλωπίζω,
στολίζω.

embers ['ɛmbəz] npl θράκα.

embezzle [ɪm'bɛzl] vt καταχρώμαι ||
~ment n κατάχρηση, σφετερισμός.

embitter [ɪm'bɪtə*] vt πικραίνω.

emblem ['ɛmbləm] n (symbol)
σύμβολο || (badge etc) έμβλημα nt.

embodiment [ɪm'bɒdɪmənt] n
ενσάρκωση, προσωποποίηση.

embody [ɪm'bɒdɪ] vt (ideas)
ενσαρκώνω, πραγματοποιώ || (new
features) ενσωματώνω, περιλαμβάνω.

emboss [ɪm'bɒs] vt αναγλύφω,
χαράσσω αναγλύφως.

embrace [ɪm'breɪs] vt (clasp)
εναγκαλίζομαι, αγκαλιάζω || (include)
περιλαμβάνω, περικλείω ♦ n
εναγκαλισμός, αγκαλιά.

embroider [ɪm'brɔɪdə*] vt κεντώ,
κάνω κέντημα || **~y** n κέντημα nt.

embryo ['ɛmbrɪəʊ] n (fig) έμβρυο.

emerald ['ɛmərld] n σμαράγδι.

emerge [ɪ'məːdʒ] vi αναδύομαι,
(ξε) βγαίνω, ξεπροβάλλω.

emergence [ɪ'məːdʒəns] n
εμφάνιση.

emergency [ɪ'məːdʒənsɪ] n
επείγουσα ανάγκη ♦ a (action)
έκτακτος || **~ exit** n έξοδος f
κινδύνου.

emery ['ɛmərɪ] n: **~ board** n
γυαλόχαρτο || **~ paper** n
σμυριδόχαρτο.

emetic [ɪ'mɛtɪk] n εμετικό.

emigrant ['ɛmɪgrənt] n
μετανάστης/ρια m/f ♦ a
μεταναστευτικός.

emigrate ['ɛmɪgreɪt] vi
μεταναστεύω.

emigration [ɛmɪ'greɪʃən] n
μετανάστευση.

eminence ['ɛmɪnəns] n (distinction)
ανωτερότητα, διασημότητα || (ECCL)
εξοχότητα.

eminent ['ɛmɪnənt] a
διακεκριμένος, έξοχος, διάσημος.

emission [ɪ'mɪʃən] n (of gases)
εκπομπή, αποβολή.

emit [ɪ'mɪt] vt εκπέμπω, αναδίνω.

emotion [ɪ'məʊʃən] n συγκίνηση,
(ψυχική) αναταραχή || **~al** a
(person) ευσυγκίνητος, ευαίσθητος ||
(scene) συγκινητικός || **~ally** ad με
συγκίνηση, συναισθηματικά.

emotive [ɪ'məʊtɪv] a συγκινητικός.

emperor ['ɛmpərə*] n
αυτοκράτορας.

emphasis ['ɛmfəsɪs] n έμφαση.

emphasize ['ɛmfəsaɪz] vt τονίζω,
υπογραμμίζω.

emphatic [ɪm'fætɪk] a εμφατικός.

empire ['ɛmpaɪə*] n αυτοκρατορία.

empirical [ɛm'pɪrɪkl] a εμπειρικός.

employ [ɛm'plɔɪ] vt (use)
χρησιμοποιώ, εφαρμόζω || (hire)
απασχολώ, έχω || **~ee** n υπάλληλος
m/f || **~er** n εργοδότης/ρια m/f ||
~ment n (job) απασχόληση,
δουλειά, εργασία || (jobs collectively)
χρήση, χρησιμοποίηση.

empress ['ɛmprɪs] n αυτοκράτειρα.

emptiness ['ɛmptɪnɪs] n κενό.

empty ['εmptɪ] *a* κενός, άδειος ♦ *vt (contents)* κενώνω, αδειάζω || *(container)* αδειάζω || ~-**handed** *a* με άδεια χέρια.

emulate ['εmjʊleɪt] *vt* αμιλλώμαι, μιμούμαι, ακολουθώ.

emulsion [ε'mʌlʃən] *n* γαλάκτωμα *nt.*

enable [ɪ'neɪbl] *vt* καθιστώ ικανό, διευκολύνω, επιτρέπω.

enamel [ɪ'næml] *n* βερνίκι, σμάλτο, λάκα || *(of teeth)* σμάλτο.

enamoured [ɪ'næməd] *a* (+ *of*) ερωτευμένος.

enchant [ɪn'tʃɑːnt] *vt (bewitch)* μαγεύω || *(delight)* γοητεύω || ~**ing** *a (delightful)* γοητευτικός.

encircle [ɪn'sɜːkl] *vt* (περι)κυκλώνω, (περι)σφίγγω.

enclose [ɪn'kləʊz] *vt (shut in)* περικλείω, (περι)μαντρώνω || *(in a letter etc)* εγκλείω, εσωκλείω.

enclosure [ɪn'kləʊʒə*] *n (space)* φράκτης, μαντρότοιχος || *(in a letter)* συνημμένο, εσώκλειστο.

encore ['ɒŋkɔː*] *n* πάλι, μπιζ.

encounter [ɪn'kaʊntə*] *n* συνάντηση || *(battle)* σύγκρουση ♦ *vt (meet)* συναντώ.

encourage [ɪn'kʌrɪdʒ] *vt* ενθαρρύνω, δίνω κουράγιο || ~**ment** *n* εμψύχωση, ενθάρρυνση.

encroach [ɪn'krəʊtʃ] *vi* (+ *(up)on)* καταπατώ.

encyclop(a)edia [ɛnsaɪkləʊ'piːdɪə] *n* εγκυκλοπαίδεια.

end [ɛnd] *n (finish)* τέρμα *nt*, τέλος *nt* || *(of book, day, rope, street, queue)* άκρη, τέλος *nt*, ουρά || *(purpose)* σκοπός, επιδίωξη ♦ *a* τελικός, ακραίος ♦ *vt* τερματίζω, τελειώνω ♦ *vi* τερματίζομαι, καταλήγω.

endanger [ɪn'deɪndʒə*] *vt* διακινδυνεύω, (εκ)θέτω σε κίνδυνο.

endeavour [ɪn'dɛvə*] *n*

προσπάθεια ♦ *vi* προσπαθώ, πασχίζω.

ending ['ɛndɪŋ] *n* τέλος *nt*, κατάληξη.

endless ['ɛndlɪs] *a* ατελείωτος, απέραντος.

endorse [ɪn'dɔːs] *vt (cheque etc)* οπισθογραφώ, θεωρώ || *(approve)* υποστηρίζω, εγκρίνω || ~**ment** *n* οπισθογράφηση || *(of action)* έγκριση.

endow [ɛn'daʊ] *vt* προικίζω || *(equip)* διωρίζω.

end product ['ɛndprɒdʌkt] *n* τελικό προϊόν.

endurance [ɪn'djʊərəns] *n* αντοχή.

endure [ɪn'djʊə*] *vt* υπομένω, ανέχομαι ♦ *vi* διαρκώ, αντέχω.

enemy ['ɛnəmɪ] *n* εχθρός ♦ *a* εχθρικός.

energetic [ɛnə'dʒɛtɪk] *a* ενεργητικός, δραστήριος.

energy ['ɛnədʒɪ] *n (of person)* ενέργεια, δύναμη || *(PHYS)* ενέργεια.

enforce [ɪn'fɔːs] *vt* επιβάλλω, εκτελώ, εφαρμόζω.

engage [ɪn'geɪdʒ] *vt (hire)* προσλαμβάνω, παίρνω || *(take part in)* απασχολώ, επισύρω, τραβώ || *(begin fight)* επιτίθεμαι || *(TECH)* συνδέω, βάζω || ~**d** *a (to marry)* αρραβωνιασμένος || *(TEL)* κατειλημμένη, μιλάει || *(in use)* αποσχολημένος, πιασμένος || *(person)* είμαι προσκεκλημένος, έχω κλείσει || ~**ment** *n (appointment)* δέσμευση, ραντεβού *nt inv* || *(to marry)* μνηστεία, αρραβώνιασμα *nt* || *(MIL)* συμπλοκή, σύγκρουση || ~**ment ring** *n* βέρα.

engaging [ɛn'geɪdʒɪŋ] *a* θελκτικός, που τραβάει.

engender [ɛn'dʒɛndə*] *vt* γεννώ, προκαλώ.

engine ['ɛndʒɪn] *n (AUT)* μηχανή, κινητήρας, μοτέρ *nt inv* || *(RAIL)* ατμομηχανή, ωτομοτρίς || ~

failure *or* **trouble** *n* βλάβη μηχανής ή κινητήρα.

engineer [endʒɪ'nɪə*] *n* μηχανικός || *(US RAIL)* μηχανοδηγός.

engineering [endʒɪ'nɪərɪŋ] *n* μηχανολογία.

England ['ɪŋglənd] *n* Αγγλία.

English ['ɪŋglɪʃ] *a* αγγλικός ♦ *n* *(LING)* (τα) Αγγλικά || **the ~** *npl* οι Άγγλοι *mpl* || **the ~ Channel** *n* Μάγχη || **~man** *n* Άγγλος, Εγγλέζος || **~woman** *n* Αγγλίδα.

engrave [en'greɪv] *vt* χαράσσω.

engraving [en'greɪvɪŋ] *n* χαρακτική.

engrossed [en'grəʊst] *a* απορροφημένος.

engulf [en'gʌlf] *vt* καταβροχθίζω, καταποντίζω.

enhance [en'hɑːns] *vt* εξαίρω, ανυψώ, ανεβάζω.

enigma [e'nɪgmə] *n* α ίνιγμα *nt* || **~tic** [enɪg'mætɪk] *a* αινιγματικός, μυστηριώδης.

enjoy [en'dʒɔɪ] *vt* μου αρέσει, χαίρομαι (κάτι) || *(privileges etc)* απολαμβάνω, κατέχω || **~able** *a* απολαυστικός, ευχάριστος || **~ment** *n* απόλαυση.

enlarge [en'lɑːdʒ] *vt* μεγεθύνω, επεκτείνω || *(PHOT)* μεγεθύνω, μεγαλώνω || **~ment** *n* μεγέθυνση.

enlighten [en'laɪtn] *vt* διαφωτίζω || **~ed** *a* φωτισμένος || **~ment** *n* διαφώτιση.

enlist [en'lɪst] *vt* στρατολογώ, προσλαμβάνω ♦ *vi* στρατολογούμαι, κατατάσσομαι.

enmity ['enmɪtɪ] *n* έχθρα, εχθρότητα.

enormity [ɪ'nɔːmɪtɪ] *n* μέγεθος *nt*, τερατωδία.

enormous [ɪ'nɔːməs] *a* τεράστιος, πελώριος, κολοσσιαίος || **~ly** *ad* πάρα πολύ, καταπληκτικά.

enough [ɛ'nʌf] *a* αρκετός, επαρκής, ικανός ♦ *a* αρκετός, ♦ *ad* αρκετά.

enquire [en'kwaɪə*] = **inquire.**

enrich [en'rɪtʃ] *vt* (εμ)πλουτίζω.

enrol [en'rəʊl] *vt* *(MIL)* στρατολογώ ♦ *vi* εγγράφομαι, προσλαμβάνω, παίρνω || **~ment** *n* στρατολογία || *(SCH)* αριθμός μαθητών.

ensign ['ensaɪn] *n* *(flag)* σημαία || *(NAUT)* σημαιοφόρος.

enslave [en'sleɪv] *vt* υποδουλώνω, σκλαβώνω.

ensue [en'sjuː] *vi* έπομαι, επακολουθώ.

ensure [ɪn'ʃʊə*] *vt* *(make certain)* (εξ)ασφαλίζω.

entail [en'teɪl] *vt* συνεπάγομαι, επιφέρω.

enter ['entə*] *vt* *(go into)* εισέρχομαι, μπαίνω || *(join)* εισέρχομαι, κατατάσσομαι, γίνομαι || *(write in)* εγγράφομαι, γράφω ♦ *vi* εισέρχομαι, μπαίνω || **to ~ for** *vt* εγγράφομαι || **to ~ into** *(agreement)* μπαίνω, συνάπτω, μετέχω || *(argument)* μπαίνω || **to ~ upon** *vt* αναλαμβάνω, αρχίζω.

enterprise ['entəpraɪz] *n* τόλμη, θάρρος *nt* || *(COMM)* επιχείρηση.

enterprising ['entəpraɪzɪŋ] *a* τολμηρός.

entertain [entə'teɪn] *vt* *(as guest)* φιλοξενώ, περιποιούμαι || *(amuse)* διασκεδάζω || **~ er** *n* ντιζέρ *m/f inv* || **~ing** *a* διασκεδαστικός || **~ment** *n* *(amusement)* διασκέδαση || *(show)* θέαμα *nt*.

enthralled [ɪn'θrɔːld] *a* γοητευμένος, κατακτημένος.

enthusiasm [ɪn'θuːzɪæzəm] *n* ενθουσιασμός.

enthusiast [ɪn'θuːzɪæst] *n* θαυμαστής/ρια *m/f*, λάτρης *m/f* || **~ic** [ɪnθuːzɪ'æstɪk] *a* ενθουσιώδης, μανιώδης.

entice [ɪn'taɪs] vt (tempt) δελεάζω, ξεμυαλίζω.

entire [ɪn'taɪə*] a ολόκληρος, ολάκαιρος, πλήρης || **~ly** ad ακέραια, πλήρως || **~ty** n: **in its ~ty** συνολικά.

entitle [ɛn'taɪtl] vt (allow) εξουσιοδοτώ, δίνω το δικαίωμα, επιτρέπω || (name) τιτλοφορώ.

entrance ['ɛntrəns] n είσοδος f, μπάσιμο ♦ [ɛn'traɪns] vt γοητεύω, μαγεύω || **~ examination** n εισαγωγικές εξετάσεις fpl || **~ fee** n τιμή εισιτηρίου, τιμή εγγραφής.

entrant ['ɛntrənt] n αρχάριος a m/f, υποψήφιος/a m/f.

entrenched [ɪn'trɛntʃt] a οχυρωμένος.

entrust [ɪn'trʌst] vt (confide) εμπιστεύομαι || (put in charge) επιφορτίζω, αναθέτω.

entry ['ɛntrɪ] n (place) είσοδος f|| (act) είσοδος f, εμφάνιση || (in dictionary) εγγραφή, καταχώριση || **'no ~'** 'απαγορεύεται η είσοδος' || **~ form** n αίτηση εγγραφής, δελτίο εγγραφής.

enunciate [ɪ'nʌnsɪeɪt] vt προφέρω.

envelop [ɪn'vɛləp] vt (περι)καλύπτω, τυλίγω, σκεπάζω.

envelope ['ɛnvələup] n φάκελλος.

envious ['ɛnvɪəs] a ζηλόφθονος, φθονερός, ζηλιάρης.

environment [ɪn'vaɪərənmənt] n περιβάλλον || **~al** a του περιβάλλοντος.

envoy ['ɛnvɔɪ] n απεσταλμένος.

envy ['ɛnvɪ] n φθόνος, ζήλεια || (object of envy) αντικείμενο ζήλειας ♦ vt φθονώ, ζηλεύω.

enzyme ['ɛnzaɪm] n ένζυμο.

ephemeral [ɪ'fɛmərəl] a εφήμερος.

epic ['ɛpɪk] n έπος, ηρωϊκό ποίημα ♦ a επικός.

epidemic [ɛpɪ'dɛmɪk] n επιδημία.

epilepsy ['ɛpɪlɛpsɪ] n επιληψία.

epileptic [ɛpɪ'lɛptɪk] a, n επιληπτικός.

epilogue ['ɛpɪlɒg] n επίλογος.

episode ['ɛpɪsəud] n επεισόδιο.

epistle [ɪ'pɪsl] n επιστολή, γράμμα nt.

epitome [ɪ'pɪtəmɪ] n επιτομή, περίληψη, σύνοψη.

epitomize [ɪ'pɪtəmaɪz] vt συνοψίζω, κάνω περίληψη.

epoch ['iːpɒk] n εποχή.

equable ['ɛkwəbl] a ομοιόμορφος, ίσος.

equal ['iːkwl] a (same) ίσος || (qualified) αντάξιος, ανταποκρίνομαι προς ♦ n ίσος, ομότιμος, όμοιος ♦ vt ισούμαι, είμαι ίσος || **~ to** αντάξιος, ανταποκρινόμενος || **without ~** ασυναγώνιστος || **~ity** n ισότητα || **~ize** vt εξισώνω, αντισταθμίζω || **~izer** n εξισωτής, αντισταθμιστής || **~ly** ad εξ ίσου, ομοίως || **~(s) sign** n σημείο ισότητας.

equanimity [ɛkwə'nɪmɪtɪ] n γαλήνη, πρεμία.

equate [ɪ'kweɪt] vt εξισώνω.

equation [ɪ'kweɪʒən] n εξίσωση.

equator [ɪ'kweɪtə*] n ισημερινός || **~ial** [ɛkwə'tɔːrɪəl] a ισημερινός.

equilibrium [iːkwɪ'lɪbrɪəm] n ισορροπία.

equinox ['iːkwɪnɒks] n ισημερία.

equip [ɪ'kwɪp] vt εφοδιάζω, εξοπλίζω || **~ment** n εφόδια ntpl, εφοδιασμός, υλικά ntpl.

equitable ['ɛkwɪtəbl] a δίκαιος.

equity ['ɛkwɪtɪ] n δίκαιο, τιμιότητα.

equivalent [ɪ'kwɪvələnt] a ισότιμος || (TECH) ισοδύναμη ♦ n αντίστοιχο.

equivocal [ɪ'kwɪvəkl] a (doubtful) διφορούμενος, αμφίβολος || (suspicious) ύποπτος.

era ['ɪərə] n εποχή.

eradicate [ɪ'rædɪkeɪt] vt ξεριζώνω.

erase [ɪ'reɪz] vt εξαλείφω, σβήνω.

(COMPUT) διαγράφω || ~r n γομολάστιχα, γόμα.

erect [ɪˈrɛkt] a ορθός, όρθιος, στητός, σηκωμένος ♦ vt υψώνω, ανεγείρω, κτίζω.

erection [ɪˈrɛkʃən] n όρθωση, σήκωμα nt, ανέργεση.

ermine [ˈɜːmɪn] n ερμίνα.

erode [ɪˈrəʊd] vt διαβρώνω, τρώγω.

erosion [ɪˈrəʊʒən] n διάβρωση.

erotic [ɪˈrɒtɪk] a ερωτικός || ~ism [ɪˈrɒtɪsɪzm] n ερωτισμός.

err [ɜː] vi (make mistakes) σφάλλω, σφάλλομαι || (sin) πλανώμαι, αμαρτάνω.

errand [ˈɛrənd] n παραγγελία, αποστολή || ~ boy n ο μικρός.

erratic [ɪˈrætɪk] a άτακτος, ακανόνιστος, εκκεντρικός.

erroneous [ɛˈrəʊnɪəs] a εσφαλμένος, λανθασμένος.

error [ˈɛrə*] n σφάλμα nt, λάθος nt.

erudite [ˈɛrjʊdaɪt] a πολυμαθής, διαβασμένος.

erupt [ɪˈrʌpt] vi κάνω έκρηξη || ~ion n έκρηξη, ξέσπασμα nt.

escalate [ˈɛskəleɪt] vt ανεβάζω ♦ vi ανεβαίνω.

escalator [ˈɛskəleɪtə*] n κυλιόμενη κλίμακα.

escapade [ɛskəˈpeɪd] n ξέσπασμα nt, περιπέτεια.

escape [ɪsˈkeɪp] n (getting away) (δια)φυγή, δραπέτευση, σκάσιμο || (leakage) εκφυγή, διαρροή ♦ vi (get free) δραπετεύω, (δια)σώζομαι || (unpunished) ξεφεύγω, γλυτώνω || (leak) διαφεύγω, διαρρέω, τρέχω ♦ vt (be forgotten) διαφεύγω, είμαι απαρατήρητος.

escort [ˈɛskɔːt] n (MIL) συνοδεία, φρουρά || (of lady) συνοδός, καβαλιέρος ♦ [ɪsˈkɔːt] vt συνοδεύω.

Eskimo [ˈɛskɪməʊ] n Εσκιμώος/α m/f.

especially [ɪsˈpɛʃəlɪ] ad ειδικώς, ιδιαιτέρως, κυρίως.

espionage [ˈɛspɪənɑːʒ] n κατασκοπεία.

esquire [ɛsˈkwaɪə*] n (abbr Esq.): **J. Brown E~** Κύριο J. Brown.

essay [ˈɛseɪ] n (SCH) άσκηση || (LITER) δοκίμιο.

essence [ˈɛsns] n (quality) ουσία || (perfume) άρωμα nt, μυρουδιά.

essential [ɪˈsɛnʃl] a (necessary) ουσιώδης, ουσιαστικός || (basic) βασικός, απαράιτητος ♦ n ουσία, το απαράιτητο || ~ly ad ουσιαστικά, κυρίως.

establish [ɪsˈtæblɪʃ] vt (set up) ιδρύω, θεμελιώνω, εγκαθιστώ || (prove) στηρίζω, στερεώνω, αποδεικνύω || ~ment n (setting up) ίδρυση, δημιουργία, επιβολή || (house of business) ίδρυμα nt, κατάστημα nt, οίκος || (MIL) σύνθεση (μονάδας) || **the E~ment** το Κατεστημένο.

estate [ɪsˈteɪt] n (landed property) κτήμα nt, ακίνητο || (property left) κληρονομία || ~ **agent** n κτηματομεσίτης|| ~ **car** n (Brit) στέισον-βάγκον nt inv.

esteem [ɪsˈtiːm] n εκτίμηση.

estimate [ˈɛstɪmɪt] n (opinion) εκτίμηση || (price quoted) (προ)υπολογισμός, τιμολόγιο ♦ [ˈɛstɪmeɪt] vt εκτιμώ, υπολογίζω, λογαριάζω.

estimation [ɛstɪˈmeɪʃən] n (judgment) κρίση, γνώμη || (esteem) εκτίμηση, υπόληψη.

estuary [ˈɛstjʊərɪ] n εκβολή.

etching [ˈɛtʃɪŋ] n χαλκογραφία.

eternal [ɪˈtɜːnl] a αιώνιος, ατελείωτος || ~ly ad αιωνίως.

eternity [ɪˈtɜːnɪtɪ] n αιωνιότητα.

ether [ˈiːθə*] n αιθέρας.

ethical [ˈɛθɪkl] a ηθικός.

ethics [ˈɛθɪks] npl ηθική.

ethnic [ˈɛθnɪk] a εθνικός.

etiquette ['ɛtɪkɛt] n εθιμοτυπία, ετικέτα.

eulogy ['juːlədʒɪ] n εγκώμιο.

euphemism ['juːfəmɪzəm] n ευφημισμός.

euphoria [juː'fɔːrɪə] n ευφορία.

Europe ['juərəp] n Ευρώπη || **~an a** η ευρωπαϊκός.

euthanasia [juːθə'neɪzɪə] n ευθανασία.

evacuate [ɪ'vækjueɪt] vt εκκενώνω, μεταφέρω.

evacuation [ɪvækju'eɪʃən] n εκκένωση, εκκένωμα.

evade [ɪ'veɪd] vt αποφεύγω, ξεφεύγω, διαφεύγω.

evaluate [ɪ'væljueɪt] vt εκτιμώ, υπολογίζω.

evangelist [ɪ'vændʒəlɪst] n Ευαγγελιστής.

evaporate [ɪ'væpəreɪt] vi εξατμίζομαι, ξεθυμαίνω ♦ vt εξατμίζω || **~d milk** n γάλα πυ εβαπορέ.

evaporation [ɪvæpə'reɪʃən] n εξάτμιση.

evasion [ɪ'veɪʒən] n (avoiding question) υπεκφυγή, πρόφαση.

evasive [ɪ'veɪsɪv] a ασαφής, ακαθόριστος.

even ['iːvən] a ομαλός, επίπεδος, ίσιος || (score etc) ισόπαλος, πάτσι || (number) άρτιος, ζυγός ♦ vt σιάζω, ισώνω, εξισώνω ♦ ad ακόμη, και αν, ή ακόμη || (emphasis) και αν ακόμα || **~ if** και αν || **to ~ out** ή **up** vi πατσίζω, ανταποδίδω τα ίσα.

evening ['iːvnɪŋ] n (time) βράδυ nt || (event) εσπερίδα, βραδινή συγκέντρωση || **in the ~** το βράδυ || **~ class** n βραδινό μάθημα || **~ dress** n (men's) φράκο || (woman's) βραδυνή τουαλέτα.

evenly ['iːvənlɪ] ad ομοιόμορφα, ομαλά, κανονικά.

event [ɪ'vɛnt] n (happening) γεγονός,

περίπτωση, έκβαση || (SPORT) άθλημα nt, αγώνας, ματς nt inv || **in the ~ of** σε περίπτωση || **~ful a** γεμάτος γεγονότα, αλησμόνητος.

eventual [ɪ'vɛntʃuəl] a (final) οριστικός, αναπόφευκτος, τελικός || **~ity** n πιθανότητα || **~ly** ad (at last) τελικά || (given time) πιθανώς.

ever ['ɛvə*] ad ποτέ, καμμιά φορά || (always) πάντα, πάντοτε || **~ so big** τόσος δα || **~ so many** τόσοι και τόσοι || **~green** a αειθαλής || **~lasting** a αιώνιος, διαρκής, άφθαρτος.

every ['ɛvrɪ] a καθένας, κάθε || **~ other day** κάθε παρά μέρα || **~body** pron όλοι, όλος ο κόσμος, καθένας || **~day** a (daily) κάθε μέρα, καθημερινός || (commonplace) συνηθισμένος, κοινός || **~one** = **~body** || **~thing** pron τα πάντα, όλα, κάθε τι || **~where** ad παντού.

evict [ɪ'vɪkt] vt εκδιώκω, εξώνω, διώχνω || **~ion** n έξωση, εκβολή.

evidence ['ɛvɪdəns] n (sign) σημάδι, σημείο, ένδειξη || (proof) απόδειξη, μαρτυρία || **in ~** (obvious) διακρίνομαι, ξεχωρίζω.

evident ['ɛvɪdənt] a προφανής, κατάδηλος, φανερός || **~ly** ad προφανώς, ολοφάνερα.

evil ['iːvɪl] a κακός ♦ n το κακό || (sin) κακία, αμαρτία.

evocative [ɪ'vɒkətɪv] a επικλητικός.

evoke [ɪ'vəuk] vt επικαλούμαι, ξαναφέρνω στο νου.

evolution [iːvə'luːʃən] n εξέλιξη, ανέλιξη.

evolve [ɪ'vɒlv] vt αναπτύσσω, συνάγω ♦ vi εξελίσσομαι, απορρέω.

ewe [juː] n προβατίνα.

ex- [ɛks] a (former) πρώην, τέως.

exact [ɪg'zækt] a ακριβής, σωστός ♦ vt (obedience etc) απαιτώ, ζητώ || (payment) αποσπώ, παίρνω || **~ing** a

απαιτητικός, κουραστικός || ~ ly ad ακριβώς, σωστά.

exaggerate [eg'zædʒəreɪt] vti υπερβάλλω, μεγαλοποιώ, (παρα)φουσκώνω.

exaggeration [egzædʒə'reɪʃən] n υπερβολή, μεγαλοποίηση.

exalt [eg'zɔːlt] vt εξυμνώ, εκθειάζω, επαινώ.

exam [eg'zæm] n abbr of **examination**.

examination [egzæmɪ'neɪʃən] n (SCH, UNIV) εξετάσεις fpl, διαγωνισμός || (MED) ιατρική εξέταση || (inquiry) ανάκριση, εξέταση || (CUSTOMS) έλεγχος, έρευνα.

examine [eg'zæmɪn] vt (MED, SCH) εξετάζω || (consider) εξετάζω, ερευνώ || (baggage) ερευνώ, ελέγχω || ~r n εξεταστής/ρια m/f, επιθεωρητής/ρια m/f.

example [ɪg'zɑːmpl] n δείγμα nt, παράδειγμα nt, υπόδειγμα nt || for ~ παραδείγματος χάριν, λόγου χάριν.

exasperate [ɪg'zɑːspəreɪt] vt εξάπτω, εξαγριώνω.

excavate ['ekskəveɪt] vt (hollow out) σκάπτω, ανοίγω, βαθαίνω || (unearth) ανασκάπτω, κάνω ανασκαφές.

excavation [ekskə'veɪʃən] n ανασκαφή.

excavator ['ekskəveɪtə*] n εκσκαφέας.

exceed [ek'siːd] vt (number) υπερβαίνω, (ξε)περνώ || (limit) υπερβαίνω (powers) υπερβαίνω, εξέρχομαι || (hopes) υπερβάλλω || ~ingly ad υπερβολικά, πολύ.

excel [ek'sel] vi διακρίνομαι, διαπρέπω, ξεπερνώ ♦ vt υπερέχω, υπερτερώ, ξεπερνώ.

excellence ['eksələns] n αξία, υπεροχή, αρετή.

Excellency ['eksələnsɪ] n: His ~ n Αυτού Εξοχότης.

excellent ['eksələnt] a εξαίρετος, θαυμάσιος, εξαίσιος.

except [ek'sept] prep (also: ~ for) εκτός, έξω από, εξαιρουμένου του ♦ vt εξαιρώ, αποκλείω || ~ing prep = except || ~ion n εξαίρεση || to take ~ion to προσβάλλομαι, αντιλέγω || ~ional a εξαιρετικός, έξοχος, ασύγκριτος.

excerpt ['eksɜːpt] n απόσπασμα nt.

excess [ek'ses] n υπερβολή, πληθώρα ♦ a (fare, baggage) υπερβάλλων || ~ive a υπερβολικός.

exchange [eks'tʃeɪndʒ] n ανταλλαγή || (foreign money) συνάλλαγμα nt || (TEL) κέντρο ♦ vt (goods) ανταλλάσσω, αλλάζω || (greetings, blows) ανταλλάσσω || see **rate**.

exchequer [eks'tʃekə*] n δημόσιο ταμείο, θησαυροφυλάκιο.

excise [ek'saɪz] n φόρος ♦ [ek'saɪz] vt φορολογώ.

excitable [ek'saɪtəbl] a ευερέθιστος, ευέξαπτος.

excite [ek'saɪt] vt (εξ)ερεθίζω, εξεγείρω, κεντρίζω || ~d a συγκινημένος, εκνευρισμένος || to get ~d εξάπτομαι || ~ment n έξαψη, αναστάτωση.

exciting [ek'saɪtɪŋ] a συναρπαστικός, συγκινητικός.

exclaim [eks'kleɪm] vi φωνάζω, αναφωνώ.

exclamation [eksklə'meɪʃən] n αναφώνηση, κραυγή || ~ mark n θαυμαστικό.

exclude [ɪks'kluːd] vt αποκλείω.

exclusion [ɪks'kluːʒən] n απόκλειση.

exclusive [ɪks'kluːsɪv] a (select) αποκλειστικός, περιορισμένος || (sole) αποκλειστικός, μοναδικός || (news etc) αποκλειστικός || ~ly ad αποκλειστικά, μόνο.

excommunicate

[ekskə'mju:nɪkeɪt] vt αφορίζω, αναθεματίζω.

excrement ['ekskrɪmənt] n απόπατμα nt, σκατά ntpl.

excruciating [eks'kru:ʃɪeɪtɪŋ] a φρικτός, ανυπόφορος.

excursion [eks'kɜːʃən] n εκδρομή.

excuse [eks'kju:s] n δικαιολογία, πρόφαση ♦ [eks'kju:z] vt (let off) απαλλάσσω, συγχωρώ|| (overlook) δικαιολογώ|| ~ me! συγγνώμη, με συγχωρείτε.

execute ['eksɪkju:t] vt (perform) εκτελώ, εκπληρώ, ενεργώ|| (put to death) εκτελώ, θανατώνω.

execution [eksɪ'kju:ʃən] n εκτέλεση || ~er n δήμιος, μπόγιας.

executive [eg'zekjutɪv] n (COMM) διευθυντής/ρια m/f|| (POL) εκτελεστική εξουσία ♦ a εκτελεστικός.

executor [eg'zekjutə*] n εκτελεστής.

exemplary [ɪg'zemplərɪ] a υποδειγματικός.

exemplify [ɪg'zemplɪfaɪ] vt παραδειγματίζω.

exempt [ɪg'zempt] a απαλλαγμένος, εξαιρεμένος ♦ vt εξαιρώ, απαλλάσσω|| ~ion n απαλλαγή.

exercise ['eksəsaɪz] n (of duties) άσκηση|| (physical) γυμναστική|| (SCH) σχολική άσκηση, γυμναστική|| (MIL) άσκηση, γυμνάσια ntpl ♦ vt (muscle) ασκώ, γυμνάζω|| (power) εξασκώ|| to ~ patience εξαντλώ υπομονή, κάνω υπομονή|| ~ book n τετράδιο (μαθητού).

exhaust [ɪg'zɔ:st] n (fumes) εξάτμιση, καυσαέρια ntpl|| (pipe) σωλήνας εξαγωγής ♦ vt (weary) εξαντλώ, κατακουράζω|| (use up) εξαντλώ, στειρεύω|| ~ed a εξαντλημένος|| ~ing a εξαντλητικός, κουραστικός|| ~ion

n εξάντληση, αποκάμωμα nt, τσάκισμα nt|| ~ive a εξαντλητικός, πλήρης.

exhibit [ɪg'zɪbɪt] n (ART) έκθεμα nt, έκθεση|| (LAW) τεκμήριο ♦ vt εκθέτω, παρουσιάζω, επιδεικνύω|| ~ion [eksɪ'bɪʃən] n (ART) έκθεση || (of temper etc) επίδειξη, γελοιοποίηση|| ~ionist n επιδείξιας || ~or n εκθέτης/ρια m/f.

exhilarating [ɪg'zɪləreɪtɪŋ] a φαιδρυντικός, ευχάριστος.

exhort [eg'zɔ:t] vt προτρέπω, ενθαρρύνω.

exile ['eksaɪl] n εξορία|| (person) εξόριστος.

exist [eg'zɪst] vi υπάρχω, υφίσταμαι, είμαι, ζω|| ~ence n (state of being) ύπαρξη|| (way of life) ζωή.

exit ['eksɪt] n έξοδος f.

exotic [ɪg'zɒtɪk] a εξωτικός.

expand [ɪks'pænd] vt (spread) διαστέλλω, ευρύνω, απλώνω|| (operations) επεκτείνω, αναπτύσσω ♦ vi διαστέλλομαι, φουσκώνω.

expanse [eks'pæns] n έκταση.

expansion [ɪks'pænʃən] n επέκταση, ανάπτυξη|| (PHYS) διαστολή, εκτόνωση.

expatriate [eks'pætrɪeɪt] vt εκπατρίζω, εκπατρίζομαι.

expect [ɪks'pekt] vt (anticipate) αναμένω, προσδοκώ, περιμένω|| (require) απαιτώ, αξιώνω|| (suppose) σκέπτομαι, φρονώ, πιστεύω|| (baby) περιμένω ♦ vi: to be ~ing περιμένω παιδί|| ~ant a (hopeful) περιμένων, αναμένων|| (mother) επίτοκος|| ~ation [ekspek'teɪʃən] n (hope) προσδοκία, ελπίδα|| ~ations npl ελπίδες fpl.

expedience [eks'pi:dɪəns] n, **expediency** [eks'pi:dɪənsɪ] n σκοπιμότητα, ωφελιμότητα.

expedient [eks'pi:dɪənt] a

σκόπιμος, πρόσφορος, κατάλληλος
♦ n μέσο, τρόπος, τέχνασμα nt.

expedite ['ɛkspɪdaɪt] vt επισπεύδω,
επιταχύνω.

expedition [ɛkspɪ'dɪʃn] n (journey)
αποστολή, εκστρατεία.

expel [ɛks'pɛl] vt διώκνω, βγάζω ||
(alien) απελαύνω.

expend [ɛks'pɛnd] vt (time)
αφιερώνω, διαθέτω || (money)
δαπανώ, ξοδεύω || (effort) δαπανώ,
εξαντλώ || ~**able** α αναλώσιμος ||
~**iture** n δαπάνη, κατανάλωση,
έξοδα ntpl.

expense [ɛks'pɛns] n (cost) δαπάνη,
έξοδα ntpl || (high cost) βάρος,
ακρίβεια || ~**s** npl αποζημίωση,
δαπάνες fpl || **at the** ~ **of** με τη
θυσία του, εις βάρος του || ~
account n έξοδα npl παραστάσεως.

expensive [ɛks'pɛnsɪv] α
πολυδάπανος, δαπανηρός, ακριβός.

experience [ɛks'pɪərɪəns] n
(happening) δοκιμασία, περιπέτεια ||
(knowledge) πείρα, εμπειρία ♦ vt
δοκιμάζω, υφίσταμαι, αισθάνομαι ||
~**d** α πεπειραμένος, έμπειρος.

expert ['ɛkspɜːt] n ειδικός,
εμπειρογνώμων, πραγματογνώμων
♦ α έμπειρος, ειδικός || ~**ise** n
πραγματογνωμοσύνη.

expiration [ɛkspɪ'reɪʃn] n εκπνοή.

expire [ɛks'paɪə*] vi (end) εκπνέω,
λήγω, τελειώνω || (die) αποθνήσκω,
πεθαίνω || (ticket) λήγω.

expiry [ɛks'paɪərɪ] n εκπνοή, λήξη.

explain [ɛks'pleɪn] vt (make clear)
· εξηγώ, λύω, ερμηνεύω || (account for)
εξηγούμαι, δικαιολογούμαι || **to** ~
away vt εξηγώ, δικαιολογώ.

explanation [ɛksplə'neɪʃn] n
εξήγηση.

explanatory [ɛks'plænətərɪ] α
ερμηνευτικός, εξηγητικός.

explicit [ɛks'plɪsɪt] α ρητός, σαφής,
καθαρός, κατηγορικός.

explode [ɛks'pləʊd] vi σκάω,
ανατινάζομαι.

exploit ['ɛksplɔɪt] n κατόρθωμα nt,
ανδραγάθημα nt ♦ [ɪks'plɔɪt] vt
εκμεταλλεύομαι || ~**ation** n
εκμετάλλευση.

exploration [ɛksplɔ'reɪʃn] n
εξερεύνηση, έρευνα.

exploratory [ɛks'plɔrətərɪ] α (fig)
δοκιμαστικός.

explore [ɛks'plɔː*] vt (for discovery)
εξερευνώ || (examine) εξετάζω,
(εξ)ερευνώ || ~ **r** n εξερευνητής.

explosion [ɛks'pləʊʒən] n (lit)
έκρηξη, εκτόνωση || (fig) ξεείλισμα
nt, ξέσπασμα nt.

explosive [ɛks'pləʊzɪv] α
εκρηκτικός ♦ n εκρηκτική ύλη.

exponent [ɛks'pəʊnənt] n
ερμηνευτής/ρια m/f, υπέρμαχος ||
(MATH) εκθέτης.

export [ɛks'pɔːt] vt εξάγω ♦
['ɛkspɔːt] n εξαγωγή ♦ α (trade)
εξαγωγικός || ~**ation** n εξαγωγή ||
~**er** n εξαγωγέας.

expose [ɛks'pəʊz] vt (uncover)
εκθέτω, αποκαλύπτω, ξεσκεπάζω ||
(leave unprotected) αφήνω
απροστάτευτο, εκθέτω || (plot)
αποκαλύπτω.

exposed [ɛks'pəʊzd] α (position)
εκτεθειμένος.

exposure [ɛks'pəʊʒə*] n τράβηγμα
nt, πόζα, φωτογραφία || (MED)
έκθεση || ~ **meter** n φωτόμετρο.

expound [ɛks'paʊnd] vt
αναπτύσσω, εκθέτω, εξηγώ.

express [ɛks'prɛs] α (clearly stated)
σαφής, ρητός || (speedy) ταχύς ♦ n
(fast train) ταχεία, εξπρές nt inv ♦ α
(speedily) γρήγορα, χωρίς σταθμό ♦
vt (idea) εκφράζω, διατυπώνω ||
(feeling) εκφράζω, εκδηλώνω || **to** ~
o.s. εκφράζομαι || ~**ion** n (phrase)
φράση, έκφραση, τρόπος
εκφράσεως || (look on face) έκφραση

|| (showing) εκδήλωση || ~ive a εκφραστικός || ~ly ad ρητώς, επίτηδες.

expulsion [eks'pʌlʃən] n απέλαση, αποβολή.

exquisite [eks'kwizit] a άριστος, ευχάριστος, λεπτός.

extend [eks'tend] vt (visit) παρατείνω || (building) επεκτείνω, μεγαλώνω || (hand) τείνω, δίνω || **to ~ a welcome** εύχομαι, καλωσορίζω.

extension [eks'tenʃən] n (general) έκταση, επέκταση, άπλωμα nt || (building) επέκταση, εύρυνση || (TEL) εσωτερική γραμμή.

extensive [eks'tensiv] a εκτεταμένος, εκτενής, μεγάλος || ~ly ad (travel) ευρέως || (use) εκτεταμένα.

extent [eks'tent] n έκταση, σημασία, μέγεθος nt.

exterior [eks'tiəriə*] a εξωτερικός ♦ n εξωτερικό, έξω.

exterminate [eks'tɜːmineit] vt εξοντώνω, εξολοθρεύω.

extermination [ekstɜːmi'neiʃən] n εξολόθρευση, εκρίζωση.

external [eks'tɜːnl] a εξωτερικός.

extinct [eks'tiŋkt] a (animal etc) εξαλειμμένος, εξαφανισμένος || ~ion n εξαφάνιση, σβήσιμο.

extinguish [eks'tiŋgwiʃ] vt σβήνω || ~er n πυροσβεστήρας.

extort [iks'tɔːt] vt (+ from) αποσπώ || ~ion [iks'tɔːʃən] n αναγκαστική είσπραξη, απόσπαση || ~ionate a υπερβολικός.

extra ['ekstrə] a πρόσθετος, έκτακτος, έξτρα ♦ ad πέρα από, εξαιρετικά, πολύ ♦ n συμπλήρωμα || (newspaper) έκτακτος έκδοση || (THEAT) κομπάρσος.

extract [eks'trækt] vt (distil) αποστάζω || (select) εξάγω, βγάζω, παίρνω ♦ ['ekstrækt] n (LITER)

απόσπασμα nt, εκλογή || (COOKING) εκχύλισμα nt || ~ion n εξαγωγή, βγάλσιμο || (origin) καταγωγή, προέλευση.

extradite ['ekstrədait] vt εκδίδω (εγκληματία).

extradition [ekstrə'diʃən] n έκδοση (εγκληματία).

extraneous [eks'treiniəs] a ξένος, άσχετος.

extraordinary [eks'trɔːdnri] a έκτακτος, εξαιρετικός || (strange) παράξενος, αλλόκοτος.

extravagant [eks'trævəgənt] a (lavish) υπερβολικός, παράλογος || (wasteful) σπάταλος, άσωτος.

extreme [eks'triːm] a (last) ακραίος, έσχατος, μακρυνός || (very great) υπερβολικός, μέγιστος || (not moderate) των άκρων, εξαιρετικός ♦ n άκρο, άκρη || ~s npl άκρα ntpl || ~ly ad υπερβολικά, εις το έπακρο.

extremist [eks'triːmist] a αδιάλλακτος, των άκρων ♦ n εξτρεμιστής/ρια m/f.

extremity [eks'tremiti] n (farthest end) άκρο, άκρη || (necessity) εσχάτη ανάγκη || **extremities** npl (ANAT) τα άκρα ntpl.

extricate ['ekstrikeit] vt εξάγω, βγάζω, ξεμπλέκω.

extrovert ['ekstrəuvɜːt] a, n εξωστρεφής.

exuberant [ig'zjuːbərənt] a διαχυτικός, ζωηρός.

exude [ig'zjuːd] vt εξιδρώ, εκχύνω.

exult [ig'zʌlt] vi χαίρομαι, αγάλλομαι, θριαμβεύω.

eye [ai] n (ANAT) οφθαλμός, μάτι || (of needle) μάτι, τρύπα || (for perception) καλό μάτι, μάτι ζωγράφου κτλ ♦ vt υποβλέπω, εποφθαλμιώ, κοιτάζω || **to keep an ~ on** προσέχω, επιβλέπω, παρακολουθώ || **in the ~s of** ενώπιο, στα μάτια || **(in the public ~)** διάσημος || **up to the**

~s in πνιγμένος στο, φορτωμένος
με || ~**ball** n βολβός οφθαλμού ||
~**brow** n φρύδι || ~**lash** n
βλεφαρίδα, ματοτσίνουρο || ~**lid** n
βλέφαρο || ~**-opener** n έκπληξη,
αποκάλυψη || ~**shadow** n σκιά
ματιών || ~**sight** n όραση || ~**sore** n
ασχήμια || ~**witness** n αυτόπτης
μάρτυρας.

F

F. abbr of **Fahrenheit**.
fable ['feibl] n μύθος, παραμύθι.
fabric ['fæbrik] n (cloth) ύφασμα nt,
πανί.
fabulous ['fæbjuləs] a (imaginary)
μυθικός, μυθώδης || (wonderful)
μυθικός || (unbelievable)
υπερβολικός.
facade [fə'sɑːd] n πρόσοψη.
face [feis] n (ANAT) πρόσωπο, φάτσα,
μούρη || (appearance) φυσιογνωμία ||
(grimace) μορφασμός || (front) όψη,
εμφάνιση || (of clock) καντράν nt inv
♦ vt (look towards) αντικρύζω, γυρίζω
|| (bravely) αντιμετωπίζω || **in the** ~
of ενώπιον, μπρος από, σε || **to** ~ **up**
to vt αντιμετωπίζω || ~ **cream** n
κρέμα (του προσώπου).

facet ['fæsit] n (single part) μέρος,
πλευρά || (of gem) έδρα διαμαντιού.
facetious [fə'siːʃəs] a ευτράπελος,
αστείος, περιπαικτικός || ~**ly** ad
ευτράπελα, πειραχτά.
face to face ['feistu'feis] ad
πρόσωπο με πρόσωπο, φάτσα με
φάτσα.
face value ['feis'væljuː] n
ονομαστική αξία.
facial ['feiʃəl] a του προσώπου,
καθάριση, μάσκα.
facile ['fæsail] a (US: easy) εύκολος.
facilitate [fə'siliteit] vt
(δι)ευκολύνω.

facility [fə'siliti] n (ease) ευχέρεια,
ευκολία || **facilities** npl ανέσεις fpl,
ευκολίες fpl.
facsimile [fæk'simili] n
πανομοιότυπο || (also: ~ **machine**)
τηλεαντιγραφικό.
fact [fækt] n γεγονός, nt,
πραγματικότητα || see **matter**.
faction ['fækʃən] n φατρία, κόμμα
nt.
factor ['fæktə*] n παράγων,
συντελεστής.
factory ['fæktəri] n εργοστάσιο.
factual ['fæktjuəl] a πραγματικός.
faculty ['fækəlti] n (ability)
ικανότητα, προσόν || (UNIV) σχολή ||
(US: teaching staff) διδακτικό
προσωπικό.
fade [feid] vt (cause to fade)
ξεθωριάζω, ξεβάφω ♦ vi (grow dim)
εξασθενίζω, αδυνατίζω, πέφτω ||
(lose colour) ξασπρίζω ξεθωριάζω,
ξεβάφω || (wither) μαραίνομαι.
fag [fæg] n αγγαρεία, μόχθος || (col:
cigarette) τσιγάρο || ~**ged** a
(exhausted) εξαντλημένος.
Fahrenheit ['færənhait] n
Φαρενάιτ inv.
fail [feil] vt (exam) απορρίπτω,
αποτυχχάνω ♦ vi (run short) λείπω ||
(lose power) εγκαταλείπω, χάνω,
εξα σθενίζω || (light) εξασθενίζω,
πέφτω, σβήνω || (remedy)
αποτυχχάνω || **to** ~ **to do sth**
(neglect) παραλείπω κάνω κάτι || (be
unable) αποτυχχάνω || **without** ~
χωρίς άλλο || ~**ing** n (shortcoming)
ελάττωμα nt, αδυναμία ♦ prep
ελλείψει || ~**ure** n (person)
αποτυχημένος || (MECH) διακοπή,
βλάβη.
faint [feint] a αδύνατος, ασθενής,
αμυδρός, δειλός ♦ n λιποθυμία,
αναισθησία ♦ vi λιποθυμώ ||
~**hearted** a δειλός, μικρόψυχος,
φοβιτσιάρης || ~**ly** ad ντροπαλά,

αδύνατα, άτονα, μόλις || ~**ness** n (of voice) αδυναμία || (of light) αμυδρότητα.

fair [fɛə*] a (beautiful) ωραίος, όμορφος || (light) ξανθός, άσπρος || (weather) καλός καιρός, καλοκαιριά || (just, honest) δίκαιος, έντιμος, τίμιος || (tolerable) υποφερτός || (conditions) έτσι και έτσι || (sizeable) αρκετός, μεγάλος ♦ ad (play) τίμια, δίκαια, έντιμα ♦ n (COMM) πανήγυρη, έκθεση || (fun fair) λούνα-παρκ nt inv, πανηγύρι || ~**ly** ad έντιμα, δίκαια || (rather) αρκετά καλά, σχεδόν, καλούτσικα || ~**ness** n τιμιότητα, εντιμότητα.

fairy [ˈfɛəri] n νεράιδα || ~ **tale** n παραμύθι.

faith [feiθ] n (trust) εμπιστοσύνη, πίστη || (REL) πίστη, θρήσκευμα nt, θρησκεία || **in good** ~ με καλή πίστη || ~**ful** a πιστός || ~**fully** ad πιστά, έντιμα || (in letter) υμέτερος.

fake [feik] n (thing) ψεύτικο είδος nt, απομίμηση || (person) απατεώνας ♦ a ψεύτικο, πλαστό ♦ vt παραποιώ, πλαστογραφώ.

falcon [ˈfɔːlkən] n γεράκι.

fall [fɔːl] (irreg v) n πτώση, κατέβασμα nt || (drop) πτώση, πέσιμο || (of snow) πτώση || (US: autumn) φθινόπωρο ♦ vi πέφτω || ~**s** npl (water fall) καταρράκτης || **to ~ down** vi (person) πέφτω κάμω || (building) καταρρέω, γκρεμίζομαι || (fail) αποτυγχάνω, πέφτω || **to ~ flat** vi πάω χαμένο, πέφτω στα κούφια, πέφτω || **to ~ for** vt (trick) πιάνομαι κορόιδο, πέφτω στην παγίδα || **to ~ off** vi (drop off) πέφτω || (diminish) πέφτω, φθίνω, μειώνομαι, ολιγοστεύω || **to ~ out** vi τσακώνομαι, τα χαλώ || **to ~ through** vi αποτυχάνω, γκρεμίζομαι || **to ~ under** vi υπάγομαι σε.

fallacy [ˈfæləsi] n σόφισμα nt, πλάνη.

fallen [ˈfɔːlən] pp of **fall**.

fallible [ˈfæləbl] a σφαλερός.

fallout [ˈfɔːlaut] n ραδιενεργός σκόνη.

fallow [ˈfæləu] a χέρσος, ακαλλιέργητος.

false [fɔːls] a (untrue) ψεύτικος, λαθεμένος || (sham) πλαστός, τεχνητός, κίβδηλος || **under ~ pretences** με απάτη || **~ alarm** n αδικαιολόγητος φόβος || ~**ly** ad ψεύτικα, απατηλά || ~ **teeth** npl μασέλες fpl.

falter [ˈfɔːltə*] vi διστάζω, κοντοστέκω, κομπιάζω || (in speech) τραυλίζω, ψευδίζω || ~**ing** a διστακτικός, ασταθής.

fame [feim] n φήμη.

familiar [fəˈmiliə*] a (well-known) γνωστός, γνώριμος || (intimate) οικείος, στενός, φιλικός || **to be ~ with** ξέρω, γνωρίζω || ~**ity** n οικειότητα, εξοικείωση || ~**ize** vt εξοικειούμαι με, συνηθίζω.

family [ˈfæmili] n οικογένεια, φαμίλια || ~ **allowance** n επίδομα nt οικογενείας || ~ **business** n οικογενειακή επιχείρηση || ~ **doctor** n οικογενειακός γιατρός || ~ **life** n οικογενειακή ζωή.

famine [ˈfæmin] n λιμός, πείνα.

famished [ˈfæmiʃt] a πεινασμένος.

famous [ˈfeiməs] a διάσημος, περίφημος, φημισμένος.

fan [fæn] n (folding) βεντάλια || (ELEC) ανεμιστήρας || (SPORT etc) φανατικός θαυμαστής/ρια m/f, λάτρης m/f ♦ vt αερίζω, ανεμίζω || **to ~ out** vi αναπτύσσω, απλώνω.

fanatic [fəˈnætik] n φανατικός || ~**al** a φανατικός.

fan belt [ˈfænbelt] n ιμάντας, ταινία, λουρί.

fancied ['fænsɪd] a φανταστικός, φαντασιώδης.

fanciful ['fænsɪful] a (odd) παράξενος, ιδιότροπος || (imaginative) φαντασιώδης.

fancy ['fænsɪ] n (liking) συμπάθεια, αγάπη, τσίμπημα sτ || (imagination) φαντασία ♦ a φαντασιώδης, φαντακτερός, φανταχτά ♦ vt (like) συμπαθώ, μου αρέσει || (imagine) φαντάζομαι, υποθέτω || **(just)** ~ **(that)!** για φαντάσου || ~ **dress** n μεταμφίεση || ~-**dress ball** n χορός μεταμφιεσμένων, μπάλ μασκέ nt inv.

fang [fæŋ] n δόντι || (of snake) φαρμακερό δόντι.

fantastic [fæn'tæstɪk] a παράξενος, φαντασιώδης, αλλόκοτος.

fantasy ['fæntəzɪ] n φαντασία, καπρίτσιο.

far [fɑː*] a μακρυνός, απώτερος ♦ ad μακρυά || (very much) κατά πολύ, τόσο πολύ || ~ **away**, ~ **off** πολύ μακρυά || **by** ~ ασυγκρίτως, κατά πολύ || **so** ~ ως εδώ, μέχρι εδώ || ~**away** a μακρυνός || **the F** ~ **East** 'Απω Ανατολή.

farce [fɑːs] n κωμωδία, φάρσα.

farcical ['fɑːsɪkəl] a γελοίος, κωμικός, σαν φάρσα.

fare [fɛə*] n εισητήριο, ναύλα nt(pl) || (food) φαΐ ♦ vi τα πάω, πηγαίνω || ~ **well** n αποχαιρετισμός ♦ excl αντίο!, χαίρετε!, γειά σου! ♦ a αποχαιρετιστήριος.

far-fetched ['fɑː'fɛtʃt] a εξεζητημένος, παρατραβηγμένος.

farm [fɑːm] n αγρόκτημα nt, φάρμα ♦ vt καλλιεργώ || ~**er** n γεωργός m/f, αγρότης/ισσα m/f, αγραμοδόρος || ~-**hand** n αγροτικός εργάτης || ~**house** n αγροικία || ~**ing** n γεωργία, καλλιέργεια || ~**land** n αγροτική έκταση || ~**yard** n περίβολος αγροικίας.

far-reaching ['fɑː'riːtʃɪŋ] a μεγάλης εκτάσεως, μεγάλης σημασίας.

far-sighted ['fɑː'saɪtɪd] a προνοητικός, διορατικός.

fart [fɑːt] (col) n πορδή ♦ vi πέρδομαι, κλάνω.

farther ['fɑːðə*] a μακρυνότερος, απώτερος ♦ ad μακρύτερα, περαιτέρω.

farthest ['fɑːðɪst] a απώτατος, μακρυνότερος ♦ ad μακρύτατα, πιο μακρυά.

fascinate ['fæsɪneɪt] vt γοητεύω, μαγεύω.

fascinating ['fæsɪneɪtɪŋ] a γοητευτικός, μαγευτικός.

fascination [fæsɪ'neɪʃən] n γοητεία, μάγεμα nt.

fascism ['fæʃɪzəm] n φασισμός.

fascist ['fæʃɪst] n φασίστας, φασίστας/ρια m/f ♦ a φασιστικός.

fashion ['fæʃən] n (custom) ράψιμο, μόδα || (manner) τρόπος, συνήθεια, μορφή ♦ vt σχηματίζω, διαμορφώνω, πλάθω || **in** ~ της μόδας || **out of** ~ ντεμοντέ || **after a** ~ όπως-όπως, έτσι κι έτσι || ~**able** a (clothes) της μόδας, μοντέρνος || (place) κοσμικός || ~**show** n επίδειξη μόδας.

fast [fɑːst] a (swift) ταχύς, γρήγορος || (ahead of time) που τρέχει, που πάει εμπρός || (steady, firm) σταθερός, στερεός, σφιχτός || (firmly fixed) στερεός, γερός ♦ ad (rapidly) γρήγορα || (firmly) στερεά, γερά ♦ n νηστεία ♦ vi νηστεύω.

fasten ['fɑːsn] vt (attach) στερεώνω, σφίγγω || (with rope) δένω || (coat) κουμπώνω ♦ vi δένομαι, κουμπώνομαι || ~**er** n, ~**ing** n (on box) συνδετήρας, ενδέτης || (on clothes) αγκράφα, φερμουάρ nt inv.

fastidious [fæs'tɪdɪəs] a δύσκολος, δύστροπος, στριφνός.

fat [fæt] a παχύς, χονδρός, εύσωμος

♦ n (of person) ξύγγι, πάχος nt || (on meat) λίπος nt, ξύγγι || (for cooking) λίπος nt.

fatal ['feɪtl] a (ending in death) θανάσιμος || (disastrous) μοιραίος, καταστρεπτικός, ολέθριος || **~ism** n μοιρολατρεία, φαταλισμός || **~ity** n (road death etc) θάνατος, θύμα nt || **~ly** ad μοιραία, αναπόφευκτα, θανάσιμα.

fate [feɪt] n (destiny) μοίρα, πεπρωμένο, το γραφτό || (death) μοίρα, θάνατος || **~ful** a (prophetic) προφητικός || (important) υψίστης σημασίας, αποφασιστικός.

father ['fɑːðə*] n (parent) πατέρας || (priest) πάτερ, πατήρ || (early leader) πατέρας, δημιουργός || **~-in-law** n πεθερός || **~ly** a πατρικός, σαν πατέρας.

fathom ['fæðəm] n οργυιά ♦ vt (sound) βυθομετρώ || (understand) βολιδοσκοπώ, καταλαβαίνω.

fatigue [fə'tiːg] n (weariness) κούραση, κόπωση, κάματος ♦ vt κουράζω, καταπονώ.

fatten ['fætn] vt παχαίνω, σιτεύω ♦ vi παχαίνω, χοντραίνω.

fatty ['fætɪ] a (food) παχύς, λιπαρός.

fatuous ['fætjuəs] a ανόητος, ηλίθιος, χαζός.

faucet ['fɔːsɪt] n (US) κάνουλε, βρύση.

fault [fɔːlt] n (offence) σφάλμα, λάθος nt || (defect) ελάττωμα nt || (blame) λάθος nt, φταίξιμο || (GEOL) ρήγμα nt, ρωγμή || **at ~** σφάλλω, λαθεύω, είμαι φταίστης || **~ess** a άμεμος, τέλειος || **~y** a ελαττωματικός, λανθασμένος.

fauna ['fɔːnə] n πανίδα.

favour, (US) **favor** ['feɪvə*] n (approval) εύνοια, συμπάθεια || (kindness) χάρη, χατήρι || (plan) προτιμώ, υποστηρίζω, μεροληπτώ || (in race) παίζω το φαβορί || **in ~ of**

unfavér || **~able** a ευνοϊκός || **~ably** ad ευνοϊκά, συμπαθητικά || **~ite** a ευνοούμενος, αγαπητός ♦ n ευνοούμενος || **~itism** n ευνοιοκρατία, ρουσφετολογία.

fawn [fɔːn] a, n (colour) πυρόξανθος.

fax [fæks] n (machine) τηλεαντιγραφικό έντυπο || (machine) τηλεαντιγραφικό ♦ vt στέλλω με το τηλεαντιγραφικό.

fear [fɪə*] n φόβος, τρόμος || vt φοβούμαι, τρέμω, ανησυχώ || **no ~!** μη φοβάσαι, δεν είναι πιθανό!! || **~ful** a (timid) δειλός, φοβιτσιάρης || (terrible) φοβερός, τρομερός || **~less** a ατρόμητος, άφοβος.

feasibility [fiːzə'bɪlɪtɪ] n (το) πραγματοποιήσιμο.

feasible ['fiːzəbl] a δυνατός, κατορθωτός.

feast [fiːst] n τραπέζι, φαγοπότι, γλέντι ♦ vi (+ on) απολαμβάνω, χορταίνω || **~ day** n (REL) γιορτή.

feat [fiːt] n κατόρθωμα nt.

feather ['feðə*] n φτερό.

feature ['fiːtʃə*] n χαρακτηριστικό || (article) κύριο άρθρο || (film) κυρία ταινία ♦ vti χαρακτηρίζω, τονίζω, εμφανίζω || **~less** a πλαδαρός, ασήμαντος.

February ['fɛbruərɪ] n Φεβρουάριος.

fed [fɛd] pt, pp of **feed** || **to be ~ up** vi βαριέμαι, μπουχτίζω, χάσκω.

federal ['fɛdərəl] a ομοσπονδικός, ομοσπονδιακός.

federation [fɛdə'reɪʃən] n ομοσπονδία, συνασπισμός.

fee [fiː] n (payment) αμοιβή || (for entrance) δίδακτρα ntpl, τέλος nt.

feeble ['fiːbl] a (person) φιλασθενής, αρρωστιάρης || (excuse) ασθενής, αμφίβολος || **~-minded** a διανοητικώς ανεπαρκής.

feed [fiːd] (irreg v) n τροφή, τάισμα nt, τροφοδότηση ♦ vt ταΐζω, θρέφω || (machine etc) τροφοδοτώ ||

to ~ on vt τρέφω με, τρέφομαι με || **~ back** n ανάδραση.

feel [fi:l] (irreg v) n (touch) αφή, πιάσιμο || (feeling) αίσθηση, αίσθημα nt ♦ vt (touch) αγγίζω || (examine) ψηλαφώ, ψαύω, πιάνω || (be mentally aware of) αισθάνομαι, νοιώθω || (think, believe) νοιώθω ♦ vi (give impression) αισθάνομαι, νοιώθω || **~er** n βολιδοσκόπηση || **~ing** n (sensation) αφή, αίσθημα nt || (emotion) ευαισθησία, συγκίνηση || (opinion) εντύπωση, γνώμη, αίσθημα nt.

feet [fi:t] npl of **foot**.

feign [fein] vt προσποιούμαι, υποκρίνομαι || **~ed** a προσποιητός, ψεύτικος.

feint [feint] n προσποίηση || (MIL) ψευδεπίθεση.

fell [fel] pt of **fall** ♦ vt (tree) κόβω, ρίχνω κάτω ♦ n (hill) βραχώδης λόφος.

fellow ['feləu] n (companion) σύντροφος, συνάδελφος || (member of society) εταίρος, μέλος || (man) άνθρωπος, φουκαράς, τύπος || **~ citizen** n συμπολίτης/ρια m/f|| **~ countryman** n συμπατριώτης || **~ feeling** n συναδελφοσύνη || **~ men** npl ανθρώπινοι || **~ship** n (group) (συν)αδελφότητα, εταιρεία || (friendliness) συντροφιά, συντροφικότητα.

felony ['feləni] n κακούργημα nt.

felt [felt] pt, pp of **feel** ♦ n πίλημα nt, τσόχα.

female ['fi:meil] n θηλυκό, γυναίκα ♦ a θηλυκός, γυναικείος.

feminine ['feminin] a (GRAM) θηλυκό || (qualities) θηλυκός, γυναικείος.

feminist ['feminist] n φεμινιστής, φεμινίστρια m/f.

fence [fens] n φράγμα nt, φράχτης ♦

vt (also ~ in, ~ off) περιφράσσω, (περι) μαντρώνω ♦ vi ξιφομαχώ.

fencing ['fensiŋ] n (swordplay) ξιφασκία, ξιφομαχία || (fences) περίφραξη, φράκτης.

fend [fend] vi: **to ~ for o.s.** φροντίζω, συντηρούμαι, καταφέρνω.

fender ['fendə*] n κιγκλίδωμα, πυρομάχος || (US: wing, mudguard) προφυλακτήρας.

fennel ['fenl] n μάραθο.

ferment [fə'ment] vi ζημούμαι, βράζω ♦ ['fз:ment] n ζύμωση, αναβρασμός || **~ation** n ζύμωση, βράσιμο.

fern [fз:n] n φτέρη.

ferocious [fə'rəuʃəs] a άγριος, θηριώδης.

ferry ['feri] n (small) πέραμα nt, πορθμείο || (large: also ~ boat) φέρρυ-μποτ nt inv ♦ vt διεκπεραιώ, διαπορθμεύω, περνώ.

fertile ['fз:tail] a (AGR) εύφορος, γόνιμος || (BIOL) γονιμοποιός.

fertility [fə'tiliti] n ευφορία, γονιμότητα.

fertilize ['fз:tilaiz] vt γονιμοποιώ || **~r** n λίπασμα nt.

fervent ['fз:vənt] a θερμός, φλογερός.

festival ['festivəl] n (REL etc) γιορτή, πανηγύρι || (ART, MUS) φεστιβάλ nt inv.

festive ['festiv] a γιορταστικός, γιορτάσιμος || (person) εύθυμος, κεφάτος || **the ~ season** (Christmas) εποχή γιορτών.

fetch [fetʃ] vt πηγαίνω να φέρω || (a price) αποφέρω, πιάνω.

fetching ['fetʃiŋ] a γοητευτικός, ελκυστικός.

fête [feit] n γιορτή, πανηγύρι.

fetters ['fetəz] npl δεσμά ntpl, αλυσίδες pl.

fetus ['fi:təs] n (US) = **foetus**.

feud [fju:d] n έχθρα, έριδα, βεντέτα

♦ vi είμαι στα χέρια με || ~ **al a**
φεουδαλικός, τιμαριωτικός ||
~ **alism** n φεουδαλισμός.

fever ['fi:və*] n πυρετός, θέρμη ||
~ **ish a** (MED) πυρετώδης || ~ **ishly**
ad (fig) πυρετωδώς, με τα μούτρα.

few [fju:] a λίγοι, μερικοί || **a** ~
μερικοί, λίγοι || ~ **er** λιγότεροι,
σπανιότεροι || ~ **est** ελάχιστοι,
λιγοστοί.

fiancé [fi'ɑ:ŋsei] n μνηστήρας,
αρραβωνιαστικός || ~ **e** n
αρραβωνιαστικιά.

fiasco [fi'æskəu] n φιάσκο,
αποτυχία.

fib [fib] n ψεμματάκι, μπούρδα ♦ vi
ψεύδομαι.

fibre, (US) **fiber** ['faibə*] n ίνα ||
~ **glass** n υαλοβάμβακας.

fickle ['fikl] a αλλοπρόσαλλος,
αλαφρομυαλός.

fiction ['fikʃən] n (invention)
φαντασία || (novels) μυθιστορήματα
ntpl || ~ **al** a των μυθιστορημάτων.

fictitious [fik'tiʃəs] a φανταστικός.

fiddle ['fidl] n (violin) βιολί || (swindle)
κομπίνα ♦ vt (cheat) ξεγελώ ♦ vi
παίζω, μαστορεύω, χάνω τον χρόνο
|| **to** ~ **with** vi παίζω, μαστορεύω ||
~ **r** n βιολιστής/ρια m/f.

fidelity [fi'deliti] n πίστη,
αφοσίωση, πιστότητα.

fidget ['fidʒit] n νι κάνω νευρικές
κινήσεις || ~ **y** a ασκίνητος,
νευρικός, ανήσυχος.

field [fi:ld] n (land) χωράφι, κάμπος,
περιοχή || (SPORT: ground) γήπεδο ||
(SPORT: in race) τα άλογα ntpl || (range)
έκταση, πεδίο || (battleground) πεδίο ||
(COMPUT) πεδίο || ~ **marshal** n
στρατάρχης || ~ **work** n (MIL) έργο
εκστρατείας.

fiend [fi:nd] n δαίμονας, τέρας ntpl ||
~ **ish** a διαβολικός.

fierce [fiəs] a θηριώδης,
μανιασμένος.

fiery ['faiəri] a (of fire) φλογερός,
καφτερός, φλεγόμενος || (person)
ζωηρός, ορμητικός, ζωντανός.

fifteen [fif'ti:n] num δέκα πέντε.

fifth [fifθ] a πέμπτος.

fiftieth ['fiftiiθ] a πεντηκοστός.

fifty ['fifti] num πενήντα.

fig [fig] n σύκο || (tree) συκιά.

fight [fait] (irreg v) n (between people)
καυγάς, πιάσιμο || (campaign) μάχη,
αγώνας, πάλη ♦ vt πολεμώ, μάχομαι
♦ vi (struggle against) μάχομαι,
αγωνίζομαι, παλεύω || ~ **er** n
πολεμιστής, μαχητής || (AVIAT)
καταδιωτικό || ~ **ing** n μάχη,
καυγάς || (SPORT) πυγμαχία.

figurative ['figərətiv] a
μεταφορικός, παραστατικός.

figure ['figə*] n (shape) μορφή,
σχήμα nt || (of person) παράστημα nt,
κορμοστασιά, σιλουέττα || (picture)
εικόνα, απεικόνιση || (person)
πρόσωπο, άνθρωπος ||
προσωπικότητα || (MATH) σχήμα nt
|| (cipher) αριθμός, ψηφίο, νούμερο ♦
vt (US: imagine) υπολογίζω,
λογαριάζω ♦ vi (appear)
εμφανίζομαι, φαντάζομαι || **to** ~
out vt υπολογίζω, λογαριάζω ||
~ **head** n (NAUT) ξόανο, γοργόνα ||
(fig) διακοσμητικό πρόσωπο.

filament ['filəmənt] n νήμα nt.

file [fail] n (tool) ρίνη, λίμα || (dossier)
φάκελος, αρχείο || (folder)
φάκελλος, ντοσιέ nt ιn || (row)
στοίχος, γραμμή, αράδα || (COMPUT)
αρχείο ♦ vt (wood) λιμάρω || (nails)
λιμάρω || (papers) ταξινομώ,
αρχειοθετώ || (claim) καταθέτω,
υποβάλλω ♦ vi: **to** ~ **in/out**
μπαίνω/βγαίνω ένας-ένας || **in**
single ~ σε μονή γραμμή.

filing ['failiŋ] n (of papers)
ταξινόμηση, αρχειοθέτηση || ~ **s** npl
ρινίσματα ntpl, λιμαδούρα ||
~ **cabinet** n δελτιοθήκη, αρχειοθήκη.

fill [fɪl] vt (make full) πληρώ, γεμίζω || (occupy completely) συμπληρώνω, γεμίζω || (satisfy) ικανοποιώ, χορταίνω || (position etc) κατέχω, γεμίζω ♦ n πλησμονή, κορεσμός, γέμισμα nt || **to ~ the bill** (fig) ανταποκρίνομαι || **to ~ in** vt (hole) γεμίζω, βουλώνω || (form) συμπληρώνω || **to ~ up** vt (container) γεμίζω τελείως || (form) συμπληρώνω.

fillet ['fɪlɪt] n (food) φιλέτο ♦ vt χωρίζω τα φιλέτα.

filling ['fɪlɪŋ] n (for cakes, pies etc) γέμιση || (for tooth) σφράγισμα nt, βούλωμα nt || **~ station** n πρατήριο βενζίνης, βενζινάδικο.

fillip ['fɪlɪp] n (reviver) αναζωογόνηση, τόνωση.

film [fɪlm] n (thin layer) ελαφρό στρώμα nt, μεμβράνη || (PHOT) (φωτο)ταινία, φιλμ nt inv, πλάκα || (moving picture) ταινία, φιλμ nt inv ♦ vt (scene) γυρίζω ταινία, φιλμάρω || **~ star** n αστέρας του κινηματογράφου.

filter ['fɪltə*] n φίλτρο || (PHOT) φίλτρο ♦ vt διυλίζω, φιλτράρω, λαμπικάρω ♦ vi (fig) διεισδύω, εισχωρώ || **~ tip** n επιστόμιο φίλτρο.

filth [fɪlθ] n (lit) ακαθαρσίες fpl, σκουπίδια ntpl, βρώμα || (fig) ηθική φθορά, βρωμιά, αισχρολογία || **~y** a ακάθαρτος, ρυπαρός, βρώμικος.

fin [fɪn] n (fish) πτερύγιο, φτερό.

final ['faɪnl] a τελικός, τελευταίος, οριστικός ♦ n (SPORT) τελικός (αγώνας) || **~s** npl (UNIV) απολυτήριοι εξετάσεις fpl || **~e** [fɪ'nɑːlɪ] n (THEAT) φινάλε nt inv || (MUS) φινάλε nt inv || **~ist** n (SPORT) φιναλίστής || **~ize** vt οριστικοποιώ || **~ly** ad (lastly) τελικά || (eventually) στο τέλος || (irrevocably) οριστικά, τελικά.

finance [faɪ'næns] n οικονομία ♦ vt χρηματοδοτώ || **~s** npl οικονομικά ntpl.

financial [faɪ'nænʃəl] a (policy) οικονομικ (πολιτική) || (year) οικονομικών (έτος).

financier [faɪ'nænsɪə*] n κεφαλαιούχος, χρηματοδότης.

find [faɪnd] (irreg v) vt (come across) βρίσκω || (discover, get) ανακαλύπτω, βρίσκω || (learn) ανακαλύπτω, διαπιστώνω || (declare) αποφαίνομαι, κηρύσσω ♦ n ανακάλυψη, εύρημα nt || **to ~ out (about)** vt ανακαλύπτω, αναζητώ, πληροφορούμαι || **~ings** npl (LAW) απόφαση, ετυμηγορία || (of report) διαπίστωση, συμπέρασμα nt.

fine [faɪn] a (thin, slender) λεπτός, ψιλός, ψιλόλιγνος || (delicate) λεπτός, φίνος || (handsome) ωραίος, όμορφος || (pure) καθαρός || (rainless) ωραίος, καλός ♦ ad (well) θαυμάσια, περίφημα || (small) λεπτά, λεπτομερώς, ψιλά ♦ n (LAW) ποινική ρήτρα, πρόστιμο ♦ vt (LAW) επιβάλλω πρόστιμο || **~ arts** n καλές τέχνες fpl.

finery ['faɪnərɪ] n στολίδια ntpl, στόλισμα nt.

finesse [fɪ'nes] n τέχνασμα nt, πανουργία, φινέτσα.

finger ['fɪŋgə*] n δάκτυλος, δάχτυλο ♦ vt ψαύω, ψηλαφώ, πιάνω || **~nail** n νύχι || **~print** n δακτυλικό αποτύπωμα || **~tip** n άκρη του δακτύλου.

finicky ['fɪnɪkɪ] a μικρολόγος, λεπτολόγος.

finish ['fɪnɪʃ] n (end) τέλος nt || (SPORT) τερματισμός, τέλος, τέρμα nt || (completion) τελείωμα nt, αποπεράτωση, συμπλήρωμα nt ♦ vt (also: **~ off, ~ up**) τερματίζω, τελειώνω, αποτελειώνω ♦ vi (general) τελειώνω, τερματίζομαι, λήγω || (SPORT) τερματίζω || **~ing**

line n τέρμα nt|| ~ing school n
σχολείο γενικής μορφώσεως.
finite ['faɪnaɪt] a πεπερασμένος,
περιωρισμένος.
Finland ['fɪnlənd] n Φινλανδία.
Finn [fɪn] n Φινλανδός/n m/f|| ~ish
a φινλανδικός ♦ n (LING) φιννική.
fiord [fjɔːd] n φιόρδ nt inv.
fir [fɜː*] n έλατο.
fire [faɪə*] n (element) πύρ nt|| (in
grate) φωτιά || (damaging) πυρκαγιά ||
(MIL) πύρ nt, βολή ♦ vt (cause to burn)
ανάβω, βάζω φωτιά || (gun etc)
πυροδοτώ, βάλλω, ρίχνω || (fig:
imagination) ενθουσιάζω, εξάπτω ||
(col: dismiss) απολύω, παύω, διώχνω
♦ vi (gun) πυροβολώ|| ~ on ~
καίομαι, παίρνω φωτιά|| ~ alarm n
σειρήνα πυρκαγιάς || ~arm n
(πυρόβολο) όπλο || ~ brigade n
πυροσβεστική (υπηρεσία) ||
~engine n πυροσβεστική αντλία || ~
escape n σκάλα πυρκαγιάς ||
~extinguisher n πυροσβεστήρας ||
~man n πυροσβέστης || (RAIL)
θερμαστής n τζάκι ||
~place n τζάκι ||
~side n κοντά στο τζάκι || ~
station n πυροσβεστικός σταθμός ||
~wood n καυσόξυλα ntpl ||
~works npl (lit) πυροτεχνήματα
ntpl.
firing ['faɪərɪŋ] n (MIL) βολή,
πυροβολισμός, πύρ nt|| ~ squad n
εκτελεστικό απόσπασμα nt.
firm [fɜːm] a (solid) στερεός,
σφιχτός || (determined) αμετάκινητος,
σταθερός n οίκος, εταιρεία, φίρμα
|| ~ly ad σταθερά, στερεά, γερά.
first [fɜːst] a (time) πρώτος n (place)
πρώτος ♦ ad (before others) πρώτος ||
(firstly = in the first place) πρωτίστως,
πρώτα-πρώτα || (sooner = before then)
στην αρχή, μάλλον, καλύτερα ♦ n
(person: in race) πρώτος || (UNIV) λίαν
καλώς, άριστα || (AUT) πρώτη
(ταχύτητα) || at ~ κατά πρώτο,

στην αρχή || ~ of all πριν απ'όλα,
κατ'αρχή || ~-aid kit n σακκίδιο
πρώτων βοηθειών || ~-class a
πρώτης τάξης || ~-hand a από
πρώτο χέρι || ~ lady n (US) πρώτη
κυρία || ~ly ad πρωτίστως,
πρώτα-πρώτα || ~ name n μικρό
όνομα || ~ night n πρώτη, πρεμιέρα
|| ~-rate a πρώτης τάξεως.
fiscal ['fɪskəl] a οικονομικός.
fish [fɪʃ] n ψάρι ♦ vi
ψαρεύω || to go ~ing πάω για
ψάρεμα || ~erman n ψαράς ||
~ery n αλιεία, ψαρική || ~ing boat
n ψαρόβαρκα || ~ing line n αρμίδι,
πετονιά || ~ing rod n καλάμι || ~
market n ιχθυαγορά || ~monger n
ιχθυοπώλης || ~y a (suspicious)
ύποπτος, βρώμικος.
fission ['fɪʃən] n διάσπαση.
fissure ['fɪʃə*] n σχισμή, ρωγμή.
fist [fɪst] n πυγμή, γροθιά.
fit [fɪt] a (MED, SPORT) σε φόρμα, υγιής
|| (suitable) κατάλληλος, αρμόζων,
καλός || (qualified, worthy) ικανός ♦ vt
(suit) συμφωνώ, ταιριάζω || (insert,
attach) πηγαίνω, μπαίνω ♦ vi
(correspond) εφαρμόζω, πιάνω || (of
clothes) πηγαίνω, έρχομαι ♦ n (of
clothes) εφαρμογή, ταίριασμα nt ||
(MED: mild, of coughing) παροξυσμός ||
(MED: serious, epilepsy) προσβολή || (of
anger) ξέσπασμα nt, έκρηξη || (of
laughter) ξέσπασμα || to ~ in vi
συμφωνώ, ταιριάζω ♦ vt ενώνω,
συνδέω || to ~ out vt εξαρτίζω,
εφοδιάζω, ντύνω || to ~ up vt
εφαρμόζω, ταιριάζω, μοντάρω ||
~fully, by ~s and starts
ακανόνιστα, άστατα || ~ness n
(suitability) ικανότητα,
καταλληλότητα || (MED) υγεία || ~ter
n εφαρμοστής || ~ting a κατάλληλος,
πρέπων, ταιριαστός ♦ n (of dress)
πρόβα, προβάρισμα nt|| (piece of

equipment) εφαρμογή, μοντάρισμα *nt*
|| ~ **tings** *npl* επιπλώσεις *fpl*,
εξαρτήματα *ntpl*, σύνεργα *ntpl*.

five [faiv] *num* πέντε || ~ **r** *n* (Brit)
πεντάρι (λίρες).

fix [fɪks] *vt (fasten)* τοποθετώ,
στερεώνω, καρφώνω || *(determine)*
καθορίζω, (προσδι)ορίζω, ρυθμίζω ||
(repair) επισκευάζω, επιδιορθώνω ||
(drink) ετοιμάζω, φτιάχνω ♦ *n*: **in a**
~ σε μπελάδες, σε μπλέξιμο, σε
σκοτούρες || ~ **ed** *a* σταθερός,
αμετάβλητος, στερεωμένος ||
~ **ture** *n* ακινητοποιημένο έπιπλο,
εξάρτημα *nt*.

fizz [fɪz] *n* σπίθισμα *nt*, άφρισμα ♦ *vi*
σπιθίζω.

fizzle [ˈfɪzl] *vi* αφρίζω, τσιρίζω || **to**
~ **out** *vi* σθήνω, αποτυχαίνω.

fizzy [ˈfɪzɪ] *a* αεριούχος, αφρώδης.

fjord [fjɔːd] *n* = **fiord**.

flabbergasted [ˈflæbəɡɑːstɪd] *a*
κατάπληκτος, εμβρόντητος.

flabby [ˈflæbɪ] *a* πλαδαρός, άτονος.

flag [flæɡ] *n (banner)* σημαία || *(also:*
~ **stone)** πλάκα, πλακόλιθος ♦ *vi*
(strength) εξασθενίζω, χαλαρούμαι ||
(spirit) κάμπτομαι, πέφτω, σβήνω || **to**
~ **down** *vt* σταματώ.

flagon [ˈflæɡən] *n* καράφα.

flagpole [ˈflæɡpəʊl] *n* κοντάρι.

flagrant [ˈfleɪɡrənt] *a* κατάφωρος,
καταφανής.

flair [flɛə*] *n* φυσική κλίση,
ικανότητα.

flake [fleɪk] *n (of rust)* λέπι, τρίμα *nt*,
φύλλο || *(of snow)* νιφάδα, στούπα ♦
vi (also: ~ **off)** ξελεπίζω,
ξεφλουδίζομαι.

flame [fleɪm] *n* φλόγα.

flamingo [fləˈmɪŋɡəʊ] *n* φλαμίγκος.

flange [flændʒ] *n* φλάντζα.

flank [flæŋk] *n (side)* λαγόνα, πλαγιά
|| *(MIL)* πλευρά ♦ *vt* ευρίσκομαι πλάι.

flannel [ˈflænl] *n* φανέλλα || ~ **s** *npl*
(trousers) φανελένιο παντελόνι.

flap [flæp] *n* καπάκι || *(of pocket)*
καπάκι (τσέπης) || *(of envelope)*
κλείσιμο (φακέλλου) ♦ *vt (of birds)*
φτερουγίζω ♦ *vi (sail, flag)*
ανεμίζομαι, κυματίζω.

flare [flɛə*] *n* φωτοβολίδα || *(in skirt
etc)* φάρδεμα *nt* || **to** ~ **up** *vi (into
flame)* ξεσπάω, ανάβω || *(in anger)*
ανάβω, εξάπτομαι.

flash [flæʃ] *n* αναλαμπή, λάμψη ||
(news flash) τελευταία είδηση || *(PHOT)*
φλας *nt inv* ♦ *vt (light)* κάνω να
λάμψει, ρίχνω || *(torch)* ρίχνω, ανάβω
|| *(message)* μεταδίδω ♦ *vi* αστράφτω,
γυαλίζω || **in a** ~ στη στιγμή || **to** ~
by *or* **past** *vi* περνώ σαν αστραπή ||
~ **back** *n* αναδρομή || ~ **bulb** *n*
λάμπα φλας || ~ **er** *n (AUT)* φανάρι του
στόπ.

flashy [ˈflæʃɪ] *a (pej)* φανταχτερός,
χτυπητός.

flask [flɑːsk] *n* τσότρα, φλασκί ||
(CHEM) φιάλη || *(vacuum flask)* θερμό.

flat [flæt] *a (level)* επίπεδος, ίσιος ||
(dull) χωρίς προοπτικής, θαμπό ||
(below pitch) σε ύφεση, υπεμβλή ||
(beer) ξεθυμασμένη || *(tyre)*
ξεφουσκωμένο, πεσμένο ♦ *n*
(rooms) διαμέρισμα *nt* || *(MUS)* ύφεση ||
(AUT) ξεφουσκωμένο λάστιχο || ~
broke *a* απένταρος, πατήρης ||
~ **footed** *a* με πλατειά πόδια || ~ **ly**
ad σαφώς, κατηγορηματικά || ~ **ten**
vt (also: ~ **ten out)** επιπεδώνω,
ισιώνω.

flatter [ˈflætə*] *vt* κολακεύω || ~ **er**
n κόλακας || ~ **ing** *a* κολακευτικός ||
~ **y** *n* κολακεία.

flaunt [flɔːnt] *vt* επιδεικνύω, δείχνω.

flavour, *(US)* **flavor** [ˈfleɪvə*] *n*
γεύση ♦ *vt* καρικεύω, αρωματίζω ||
~ **ing** *n* καρίκευμα *nt*, άρωμα *nt*.

flaw [flɔː] *n* ελάττωμα *nt* || ~ **less** *a*
άψογος, τέλειος.

flax [flæks] *n* λινάρι || ~ **en** *a*
κατάξανθος.

flea [fliː] n ψύλλος.

fled [flɛd] pt, pp of **flee**.

flee [fliː] (irreg v) vi (κατα)φεύγω ♦ vt φεύγω.

fleece [fliːs] n δορά, δέρμα, vt τομάρι ♦ vt (rob) ληστεύω, γδέρνω, γδύνω.

fleet [fliːt] n (NAUT) στόλος || (of cars) συνοδεία, πομπή.

fleeting [ˈfliːtɪŋ] a φευγαλέος, περαστικός.

Flemish [ˈflɛmɪʃ] a Φλαμανδικός ♦ n (LING) Φλαμανδική.

flesh [flɛʃ] n σάρκα || (meat) κρέας nt || (of fruit) σάρκα.

flew [fluː] pt of **fly**.

flex [flɛks] n εύκαμπτο καλώδιο ♦ vt κάμπτομαι || ~**ibility** η ευκαμψία || ~**ible** a εύκαμπτος || (plans) ελαστικός.

flick [flɪk] vt κτυπώ ελαφρά.

flicker [ˈflɪkə*] n (of light) τρεμούλιασμα nt, παίξιμο ♦ vi τρέμω, τρεμοσβήνω.

flier [ˈflaɪə*] n ιπτάμενος, αεροπόρος.

flight [flaɪt] n (flying) πτήση, πέταμα nt || (of squadron) σμήνος nt || (journey) διαδρομή || (also: ~ of steps) σκαλοπάτια ntpl, κλίμακα || **to take** ~ τρέπομαι σε φυγή || **to put to** ~ τρέπω σε φυγή || ~ **deck** n κατάστρωμα nt απογειώσεως.

flimsy [ˈflɪmzɪ] a σαθρός, λεπτός, μικρής αντοχής || (weak) αδύνατος, ασθενής, πρόχειρος.

flinch [flɪntʃ] vi υποχωρώ, δειλιάζω.

fling [flɪŋ] (irreg v) vt ρίχνω, πετώ.

flint [flɪnt] n (in lighter) τσακμακόπετρα.

flip [flɪp] vt δίνω ελαφρό κτύπημα.

flippant [ˈflɪpənt] a ελαφρός, αφελής.

flirt [flɜːt] vi φλερτάρω ♦ (woman) n φιλάρεσκη, κοκέτα || ~**ation** n φλερτ nt inv, φλερτάρισμα nt.

flit [flɪt] vi πηγαινοέρχομαι.

float [fləʊt] n πλωτήρας, φλοτέρ nt inv || (esp in procession) αποκριάτικο άρμα ♦ vi (επι)πλέω || (swimming) κολυμπώ ανάσκελα || (in air) πλέω ♦ vt (company) ιδρύω || (loan) εκδίδω δάνειο || (rumour) διαδίδω, κυκλοφορώ || ~**ing** a (lit) επιπλέων || (fig: population) κινητός πληθυσμός.

flock [flɒk] n ποίμνιο, κοπάδι || (of people) πλήθος nt, κοπάδι.

flog [flɒg] vt μαστιγώνω, ραβδίζω.

flood [flʌd] n πλημμύρα, κατακλυσμός ♦ vt πλημμυρίζω, κατακλύζω || ~**ing** n πλημμύρισμα nt, ξεχείλισμα || ~**light** n προβολέας ♦ vt φωτίζω με προβολέα.

floor [flɔː*] n (of room) δάπεδο, πάτωμα nt || (storey) όροφος, πάτωμα nt ♦ vt (person) ρίχνω κάτω || **ground** ~ (Brit), **first** ~ (US) ισόγειο || **first** ~ (Brit), **second** ~ (US) πρώτο πάτωμα || ~**board** n σανίδα || ~ **show** n νούμερα ntpl.

flop [flɒp] vi (fail) αποτυγχάνω, καταρρέω || (fall) κάνω πλάφ, σωριάζομαι.

floppy [ˈflɒpɪ] a πλαδαρός || (COMPUT: also: ~ **disk**) δισκέτα, εύκαμπτος (δίσκος).

flora [ˈflɔːrə] npl χλωρίδα || ~**l** a ανθικός, λουλουδένιος.

florid [ˈflɒrɪd] a ανθηρός, γεμάτος στολίδια.

florist [ˈflɒrɪst] n ανθοπώλης || ~'**s (shop)** n ανθοπωλείο.

flounce [flaʊns] n βολάν ♦ vi: **to** ~ **in/out** μπαίνω/βγαίνω απότομα.

flounder [ˈflaʊndə*] vi παραπατώ, σπαρταρώ, τσαλαβουτώ.

flour [ˈflaʊə*] n αλεύρι.

flourish [ˈflʌrɪʃ] vi (thrive, prosper) προοδεύω, ανθώ, προκόβω ♦ vt κραδαίνω, κουνώ ♦ n (ornament) στόλισμα nt, κόσμημα nt, τζίφρα||

επίδειξις, φανφάρα || ~ing a *(thriving)* ακμαίος.

flout [flaut] *vt* αψηφώ, περιφρονώ.

flow [fləu] *n (movement)* ροή, ρεύμα *nt* || *(stream: lit, fig)* ρους *m*, χύση, χείμαρρος || *(of dress)* χυτές γραμμές *fpl*, ντραπέ *nt inv* ♦ *vi* ρέω, χύνομαι || κυνώ || *(traffic, supply)* κυκλοφορώ, κινούμαι || *(robes, hair)* χύνομαι, πέφτω.

flower ['flauə*] *n* άνθος *nt*, λουλούδι ♦ *vi* ανθίζω || ~ **bed** *n* παρτέρι, βραγιά || ~**pot** *n* γλάστρα || ~**y** a πολυγαρνιρισμένος.

flowing ['fləuɪŋ] a *(movement)* ρέων || *(hair)* χυτός || *(style)* ρέων, άνετος.

flown [fləun] *pp* of **fly.**

flu [fluː] *n* γρίππη.

fluctuate ['flʌktjueɪt] *vi* κυμαίνομαι.

fluctuation [flʌktju'eɪʃən] *n* διακύμανση.

fluency ['fluːənsɪ] *n* ευγλωττία, ευφράδεια.

fluent ['fluːənt] a ευφράδης, στρωτός || ~**ly** ad ευχερώς, άνετα.

fluff [flʌf] *n* χνούδι || ~**y** a χνουδάτος.

fluid ['fluːɪd] *n* ρευστό, υγρό ♦ a *(of)* ρευστός, ρέων || *(fig: plans)* ρευστός, ευμετάβλητος.

fluke [fluːk] *n (col: lucky stroke)* κατά τύχη.

flung [flʌŋ] *pt, pp* of **fling.**

fluorescent [fluə'resnt] a φθορίζων.

fluoride ['fluːəraɪd] *n* φθοριούχο.

flurry ['flʌrɪ] *n (of activity)* αναστάτωση, ταραχή.

flush [flʌʃ] *n (blush)* κοκκίνισμα *nt*, ερύθημα *nt* || *(of excitement)* ξέσπασμα *nt* || *(CARDS)* χρώμα *nt*, φλας *nt inv* ♦ *vt* ποτίζω, καθαρίζω, τραβώ (το καζανάκι) ♦ *vi (blush)* κοκκινίζω ♦ a επίπεδος, λείος, στην ίδια επιφάνεια || ~**ed** a *(blushing)*

κόκκινος, ξαναμμένος || *(with anger)* κόκκινος.

fluster ['flʌstə*] *n* αναστάτωση || ~**ed** a ταραγμένος.

flute [fluːt] *n* φλογέρα, φλάουτο.

fluted ['fluːtɪd] a αυλακωτός.

flutter ['flʌtə*] *n (of wings)* φτερούγισμα *nt* || *(of excitement)* αναστάτωση, συγκίνηση ♦ *vi (of birds)* φτερουγίζω || τρέμω, ταράσσομαι.

flux [flʌks] *n*: **in a state of** ~ σε ρευστή κατάσταση.

fly [flaɪ] *n (insect)* μύγα || *(on trousers: also* **flies***)* μπροστινό άνοιγμα *nt* ♦ *vt (plane)* πετώ, πιλοτάρω || *(passengers)* μεταφέρω αεροπορικώς ♦ *vi (travel by air)* πετώ || *(flee)* φεύγω, τρέχω || *(of flag)* κυματίζω || ~**er** *n* = **flier** || ~**ing** *n (activity)* πτήση, αεροπορία ♦ a *(rapid)* γρήγορος, πεταχτός, σύντομος, βιαστικός || ~**ing saucer** *n* ιπτάμενος δίσκος || ~**ing start** *n* καλή αρχή, ταχύ ξεκίνημα *nt* || ~**over** *n (Brit)* εναέριος ή διάβαση || ~**past** *n* παρέλαση αεροπλάνων || ~**wheel** *n* σφόνδυλος, βολάν *nt inv.*

foal [fəul] *n* πουλάρι.

foam [fəum] *n* αφρός || *(plastic etc)* αφρολέξ *nt inv* ♦ *vi* αφρίζω.

fob [fɔb]: **to** ~ **off** *vt* πασσάρω, κοροϊδεύω.

focal ['fəukəl] a εστιακός.

focus ['fəukəs] *n* εστία ♦ *vt* συγκεντρώνω, ρυθμίζω || **in** ~ ρυθμισμένος, ευκρινής || **out of** ~ μη ρυθμισμένος, θαμπός.

fodder ['fɔdə*] *n* φορβή, χόρτο.

foe [fəu] *n* εχθρός, αντίπαλος.

foetus ['fiːtəs] *n* έμβρυο.

fog [fɔg] *n* ομίχλη ♦ *vt (issue)* θολώνω, περιπλέκω || ~**gy** a ομιχλώδης.

foible ['fɔɪbl] *n* αδυναμία.

foil [fɔɪl] *vt* ανατρέπω, προλαμβάνω

♦ n (of metal) έλασμα nt, φύλλο ||
(person) αντίθεση || (fencing) ξίφος nt.

fold [fəuld] n (bend, crease) πτυχή,
ζάρα, δίπλα ♦ vt διπλώνω, πτυχώνω
|| **to ~ up** vi (map etc) τυλίγω,
διπλώνω || (business) κλείνω το
μαγαζί, χρεωκοπώ || **~er** n
(pamphlet) διαφημιστικό φυλλάδιο ||
(portfolio) φάκελλος, ντοσιέ nt inv ||
~ing a (chair, bed etc) πτυσσόμενος,
τσακιστός.

foliage ['fəuliidʒ] n φυλλωσιά.

folio ['fəuliəu] n φύλλο.

folk [fəuk] n άνθρωποι mpl ♦ a
λαϊκός || **~s** npl άνθρωποι mpl,
συγγενείς mpl, δικοί μου mpl ||
~lore n λαογραφία || **~song** n
δημοτικό τραγούδι.

follow ['fɔləu] vt (come after)
(παρ)ακολουθώ || (obey) ακολουθώ ||
(go along path) ακολουθώ, παίρνω ||
(profession) ακολουθώ, ασκώ ||
(understand) καταλαβαίνω,
παρακολουθώ ♦ vi (after)
ακολουθώ, συνοδεύω || (result)
έπομαι, προκύπτω || **to ~ up** vt
συνεχίζω, εκμεταλλεύομαι || **~er** n
οπαδός || **~ing** a ακολουθών,
επόμενος ♦ n οπαδοί mpl,
ακολουθία.

folly ['fɔli] n ανοησία, τρέλλα.

fond [fɔnd] a: **to be ~ of** (person)
είμαι αφοσιωμένος, συμπαθώ,
αγαπώ || (thing) μου αρέσει,
τρελλαίνομαι για || **~ness** n (+ for)
αφοσίωση, συμπάθεια σε || αγάπη
για τάση στο.

font [fɔnt] n κολυμβήθρα.

food [fu:d] n τροφή, τρόφιμα ntpl,
φαΐ, φαγητό || **~ poisoning** n
δηλητηρίαση || **~stuffs** npl είδη
διατροφής.

fool [fu:l] n (silly person) πλίθιος,
βλάκας, κουτός, χαζός || (clown)
παλιάτσος ♦ vt (deceive) εξαπατώ, ♦
vi (act like a fool) κάνω το βλάκα ♦

~hardy a παράτολμος,
απερίσκεπτος || **~ish** a παράλογος,
γελοίος || **~proof** a (plan etc)
αλάνθαστος.

foot [fut] n (of person) πόδι, ποδάρι ||
(of animal) πόδι || (base) πέλμα nt,
πόδι, κάτω άκρο || (measure) αγγλικό
πόδι (0.3μ) ♦ vt (bill) πληρώνω, κάνω
τα έξοδα || **on ~** πεζή, με τα πόδια ||
~ball n (ball) μπάλα || (game)
ποδόσφαιρο || **~baller** n
ποδοσφαιριστής || **~brake** n
ποδόφρενο || **~bridge** n γέφυρα
πεζών || **~hills** npl χαμηλοί λόφοι
mpl || **~hold** n πάτημα nt, στήριγμα
nt || **~ing** n (lit) σίγουρη θέση,
πάτημα nt || (fig) θέση, κατάσταση ||
~lights npl ράμπα, προσκήνιο ||
~man n (servant) υπηρέτης, λακές
m || **~-and-mouth (disease)** n
αφθώδης πυρετός || **~note** n
υποσημείωση || **~path** n μονοπάτι ||
~sore a με πονεμένα πόδια ||
~step n βήμα nt, πάτημα nt || (trace)
ίχνος m, πατησιά || **~wear** n
παπούτσι.

for [fɔː*] prep για || (in spite of) μόλο ||
cj διότι, γιατί || **what ~?** γιατί;, για
ποιο λόγο;.

forage ['fɔridʒ] n βοσκή,
χορτονομή, χόρτο || vi (col) ψάχνω
για.

foray ['fɔrei] n επιδρομή, διαρπαγή.

forbearing [fɔː'bɛəriŋ] a
υπομονητικός, ανεκτικός.

forbid [fə'bid] (irreg v) vt
απαγορεύω || **~den** a
απαγορευμένος || **~ding** a
αποκρουστικός, δυσάρεστος.

force [fɔːs] n (strength) δύναμη,
ισχύς || (compulsion) εξαναγκασμός,
ζόρι || (body of men) δύναμη ♦ vt
(compel) εξαναγκάζω, εκβιάζω ||
(break open) παραβιάζω || **to ~ into**
vt πιέζω, σπρώχνω, μπάζω || **be in ~**
ισχύω || **the F~s** npl οι δυνάμεις fpl

|| ~**d** a *(smile)* προσποιητός, ψεύτικος || *(landing)* αναγκαστικός || ~**ful** a αποφασιστικός, δραστήριος.

forcibly ['fɔːsəbli] ad με το ζόρι, αποφασιστικά.

ford [fɔːd] n πέραμα ♦ vt περνώ.

fore [fɔː*] a πρόσθιος, μπροστινός ♦ n: **to the** ~ στο προσκήνιο, διαπρέπων.

forearm ['fɔːrɑːm] n αντιβράχιο.

foreboding [fɔː'bəudɪŋ] n κακό προαίσθημα nt, κακός οιωνός.

forecast ['fɔːkɑːst] n πρόβλεψη, πρόγνωση ♦ vt προβλέπω.

forecourt ['fɔːkɔːt] n προαύλιο.

forefathers ['fɔːfɑːðəz] npl πρόγονοι mpl.

forefinger ['fɔːfɪŋgə*] n δείκτης.

forefront ['fɔːfrʌnt] n πρόσοψη || *(fig)* πρώτη σειρά.

forego [fɔː'gəu] vt προηγούμαι, ~**ing** a προειρημένος || ~**ne** ['fɔːgɒn] a *(conclusion)* προκαθορισμένος.

foreground ['fɔːgraund] n πρώτο πλάνο.

forehead ['fɒrɪd] n μέτωπο, κούτελο.

foreign ['fɒrɪn] a *(country)* ξένος, ασχετος || *(trade)* εξωτερικός || *(accent)* ξενικός || *(body)* ξένος || ~**er** n ξένος, αλλοδαπός || ~**exchange** n συνάλλαγμα nt || **F**~ **Minister** n υπουργός εξωτερικών.

foreman ['fɔːmən] n προϊστάμενος, εργοδηγός.

foremost ['fɔːməust] a πρώτος, πρώτιστος, επί κεφαλής.

forensic [fə'rɛnsik] a: ~ **medicine** n ιατροδικαστική.

forerunner ['fɔːrʌnə*] n πρόδρομος.

foresee [fɔː'siː] vt προβλέπω || ~**able** a δυνάμενος να προβλεφθεί.

foresight ['fɔːsaɪt] n πρόβλεψη, πρόνοια.

forest ['fɒrɪst] n δάσος nt, ρουμάνι.

forestall [fɔː'stɔːl] vt προλαμβάνω.

forestry ['fɒrɪstrɪ] n δασοκομία.

foretaste ['fɔːteɪst] n προαίσθηση.

foretell [fɔː'tɛl] vt προλέγω, προμηνύω.

forever [fə'rɛvə*] ad παντοτεινά, για πάντα.

foreword ['fɔːwɜːd] n πρόλογος.

forfeit ['fɔːfɪt] n ποινική ρήτρα ♦ vt χάνω (δια κατασχέσεως), χάνω.

forge [fɔːdʒ] n καμίνι, σιδεράδικο ♦ vt *(falsely)* πλάθω, πλαστογραφώ || *(shape)* σφυρηλατώ || **to** ~ **ahead** vi προηγούμαι, προχωρώ || ~**r** n *(criminal)* πλαστογράφος, παραχαράκτης || ~**ry** n *(activity)* πλαστογράφηση || *(article)* πλαστός, κίβδηλο (αντικείμενο).

forget [fə'gɛt] vti λησμονώ, ξεχνώ, παραλείπω || ~**ful** a ξεχασιάρης, απρόσεκτος || ~**fulness** n απερισκεψία, έλλειψη μνήμης.

forgive [fə'gɪv] vt συγχωρώ || ~**ness** n συγχώρηση.

forgo [fɔː'gəu] vt παραιτούμαι, αποφεύγω, κάνω χωρίς.

fork [fɔːk] n *(for food)* πηρούνι || *(farm tool)* δικράνι, δικάλα || *(branch)* διακλάδωση ♦ vi *(road)* διακλαδίζομαι, χωρίζομαι || **to** ~ **out** vti *(col: pay)* πληρώνω || ~**ed** a δικαλωτός.

form [fɔːm] n *(structure)* μορφή, σχήμα nt, φόρμα || *(class)* τάξη || *(bench)* μπάγκος || *(document)* έντυπο, τύπος || *(also: mental, physical condition)* κατάσταση, φόρμα ♦ vt *(shape)* διαμορφώνω, σχηματίζω, φτιάνω || *(make part of)* συγκροτώ, σχηματίζω.

formal ['fɔːməl] a *(according to rule)* επίσημος, εθιμοτυπικός || *(stiff)* τυπικός || *(dress)* επίσημος || ~**ity** n *(of occasion)* τύπος, τυπικότητα ||

~ly ad *(ceremoniously)* τυπικά, με διατυπώσεις || *(officially)* επίσημα, τυπικά.

format ['fɔːmæt] n σχήμα nt ♦ vt *(COMPUT)* τρόπος παρουσιάσεως.

formation [fɔː'meɪʃən] n διαμόρφωση, σχηματισμός || *(forming)* σχηματισμός, διάπλαση || *(group)* σχηματισμός, διάταξη, τάξη.

formative ['fɔːmətɪv] a *(years)* διαπλαστικός, μορφωτικός.

former ['fɔːmə*] a παλαιότερος, προγενέστερος, πρώην, τέως || *(opposite of latter)* πρώτος || ~ly ad άλλοτε, παλαιότερα.

formidable ['fɔːmɪdəbl] a φοβερός, τρομερός.

formula ['fɔːmjulə] n τύπος || *(fig)* τύπος, στερεοτυπία, κλισέ nt inv || *(MATH)* τύπος || ~te ['fɔːmjuleɪt] vt διατυπώνω.

forsake [fə'seɪk] *(irreg v)* vt εγκαταλείπω, αφήνω, αρνούμαι.

fort [fɔːt] n φρούριο.

forte ['fɔːtɪ] n δύναμη, φόρτε nt inv.

forth [fɔːθ] ad προς τα εμπρός, προς τα έξω || *(in space)* εμπρός, μπροστά || *(in time)* από τώρα και εμπρός || ~coming a *(επ)*ερχόμενος, προσεχής.

fortieth ['fɔːtɪɪθ] a τεσσαρακοστός.

fortification [fɔːtɪfɪ'keɪʃən] n *(walls etc)* οχύρωμα nt, οχύρωση.

fortify ['fɔːtɪfaɪ] vt *(strengthen)* ενισχύω, δυναμώνω, τονώνω || *(protect)* οχυρώνω.

fortnight ['fɔːtnaɪt] n δεκαπενθήμερο || a δεκαπενθήμερος ♦ ad κάθε δεκαπέντε.

fortress ['fɔːtrɪs] n φρούριο, κάστρο.

fortunate ['fɔːtʃənɪt] a ευτυχής, τυχερός, ευμενής || ~ly ad ευτυχώς.

fortune ['fɔːtʃən] n *(chance)* τύχη, σύμπτωση, καλοτυχία || *(wealth)*

πλούτος, περιουσία || ~teller n μάντης, χαρτορίχτρα.

forty ['fɔːtɪ] num σαράντα.

forward ['fɔːwəd] a *(lying ahead)* πρόσθιος, μπροστινός || *(movement)* κίνηση προστά, προοδευτικός || *(advanced)* με πρώρον ♦ ad *(pros* τα) εμπρός, μπρος || *(SPORT)* κυνηγός ♦ vt *(mail etc)* αποστέλλω, διεκπεραιώνω || *(help)* προωθώ, ευνοώ, προάγω || ~s ad από τώρα και στο εξής.

fossil ['fɒsl] n απολίθωμα nt.

foster ['fɒstə*] vt καλλιεργώ, τρέφω || ~ child n θετό παιδί || ~ mother n θετή μητέρα, ψυχομάνα.

fought [fɔːt] pt, pp of **fight**.

foul [faul] a ακάθαρτος, ρυπαρός, βρωμερός, μολυσμένος || *(language)* βρωμολόχος, πρόστυχος, αισχρός || *(weather)* κακοκαιρίας || n *(SPORT)* φάουλ nt inv ♦ vt *(mechanism)* φράσσω, μπλέκω, πιάνω || *(SPORT)* κάνω φάουλ.

found [faund] pt, pp of **find** ♦ vt *(establish)* ιδρύω, θεμελιώνω, κτίζω || ~ation n *(act)* ίδρυση, θεμελίωση, θεμέλιο nt || *(fig)* ίδρυμα nt, κληροδότημα nt || ~ations npl *(building)* θεμέλια ntpl.

founder ['faundə*] n ιδρυτής ♦ vi *(NAUT)* βυθίζομαι, βουλιάζω.

foundry ['faundrɪ] n χυτήριο.

fount [faunt] n *(source)* πηγή || ~ain n πηγή || *(jet of water)* συντριβάνι || ~ain pen n στυλογράφος, στυλό.

four [fɔː*] num τέσσερα || **on all** ~s με τα τέσσερα || ~some n διπλή παρτίδα || ~teen num δέκα τέσσερα || ~teenth a δέκατος τέταρτος || ~th a τέταρτος.

fowl [faul] n πουλί, πουλερικό.

fox [fɒks] n αλεπού f.

foyer ['fɔɪeɪ] n φουαγιέ nt inv.

fraction ['frækʃən] n *(part)* κομμάτι || *(MATH)* κλάσμα nt.

fracture ['fræktʃə*] n (of bone)
κάταγμα nt ♦ vt θραύω, τσακίζω,
προκαλώ κάταγμα.

fragile ['frædʒaɪl] a εύθραυστος.

fragment ['frægmənt] n θραύσμα
nt, θρύμμα nt, σύντριμμα nt|| (part)
κομμάτι, απόκομμα nt, απόσπασμα
nt|| ~ary a αποσπασματικός,
τμηματικός.

fragrance ['freɪgrəns] n άρωμα nt,
μυρωδιά.

fragrant ['freɪgrənt] a εύοσμος,
μυρωδάτος.

frail [freɪl] a ευπαθής, ασθενικός.

frame [freɪm] n σκελετός, πλαίσιο||
(border) πλαίσιο, κορνίζα ♦ vt (put
into frame) πλαισιώνω, κορνιζάρω||
(put together) κατασηράψνω,
διαμορφώνω, κατασκευάζω|| (col:
incriminate) μηχανορραφώ,
σκηνοθετώ|| ~ of mind n
πνευματική κατάσταση, διάθεση||
~ work n σκελετός, πλαίσιο.

France [frɑːns] n Γαλλία.

franchise ['fræntʃaɪz] n προνόμιο.

frank [fræŋk] a ειλικρινής|| ~ly ad
ειλικρινά, ντόμπρα|| ~ness n
ειλικρίνεια.

frantic ['fræntɪk] a έξαλλος,
μανιώδης|| ~ally ad μανιασμένα,
έξαλλα.

fraternal [frə'tɜːnl] a αδελφικός.

fraternity [frə'tɜːnɪtɪ] n (club)
οργάνωση|| (spirit) αδελφότητα||
(US SCH) φοιτητική οργάνωση.

fraternize ['frætənaɪz] vi (with)
συναδελφώνομαι με.

fraud [frɔːd] n (trickery) δόλος,
απάτη|| (trick) κόλπο, απάτη, παγίδα||
(person) απατεώνας, κατεργάρης.

fraudulent ['frɔːdjʊlənt] a δόλιος,
απατηλός.

fray [freɪ] n σύρραξη, καυγάς,
σύγκρουση ♦ vt τρίβω, ταράζω,
ξεφτίζω ♦ vi ξεφτίζομαι, τρίβομαι||
~ed a τριμμένος, φαγωμένος.

freak [friːk] n ιδιοτροπία, καπρίτσιο
|| (col) τέρας nt ♦ a περίεργο
φαινόμενο.

freckle ['frekl] n φανάδα.

free [friː] a (at liberty) ανεξάρτητος,
ελεύθερος|| (loose) ελεύθερος|| (not
occupied) ελεύθερος|| (gratis)
δωρεάν, τζάμπα|| (liberal)
φιλελεύθερος, γενναιόφρων,
ανοικτός ♦ vt (set free)
(απ)ελευθερώνω|| (unblock)
αποφράσσω, καθαρίζω|| ~dom n
ελευθερία, ανεξαρτησία|| ~lance a
ανεξάρτητος|| ~ly ad ελεύθερα,
αβίαστα|| ~mason n μασώνος|| ~
trade n ελεύθερο εμπόριο|| ~way
n (US) αυτοκινητόδρομος|| ~wheel
vi πηγαίνω με ελεύθερο τροχό|| ~
will n ελευθέρα θέληση.

freeze [friːz] (irreg v) vi (become ice)
ψύχω, καταψύχω, παγώνω|| (feel
cold) κρυώνω ♦ vt (lit) (κατα)ψύχω,
παγώνω|| (fig) δεσμεύω,
ακινητοποιώ ♦ n (lit) (κατά)ψυξη,
παγωνιά|| (fig, ECON) δέσμευση|| ~r
n καταψύκτης, ψυγείο καταψύξεως.

freezing ['friːzɪŋ] a ~ cold a
παγερό κρύο|| ~ point n σημείο
ψύξεως, πήξεως.

freight [freɪt] n (goods) φορτίο,
εμπορεύματα ntpl|| (money charged)
ναύλος|| ~ car n (US) φορτηγό
βαγόνι|| ~er n (NAUT) φορτηγό.

French [frentʃ] a γαλλικός ♦ n
(LING) (τα) Γαλλικά|| the ~ npl οι
Γάλλοι|| ~ fried potatoes npl
πατάτες τηγανιτές fpl|| ~man n
Γάλλος|| ~ window n τζαμόπορτα
|| ~woman n Γαλλίδα.

frenzy ['frenzɪ] n φρενίτιδα, τρέλλα,
παραλήρημα nt.

frequency ['friːkwənsɪ] n
συχνότητα, πυκνότητα|| (PHYS)
συχνότητα.

frequent ['friːkwənt] a (happening
often) συχνός, διαδεδομένος,

συνηθισμένος || (numerous) άφθονος, πολυάριθμος ♦ [fri: 'kwɛnt] vt συχνάζω || ~ly ad συχνά.

fresco ['frɛskəʊ] n νωπογραφία, φρέσκο.

fresh [frɛʃ] a (new, additional) νέος, καινούριος, φρέσκος || (recent) νέος, πρωτότυπος || (not stale) νωπός, φρέσκος || (not tired) ρωμαλαίος, ξεκούραστος, φρέσκος || (cool) καθαρός, δροσερός || (cheeky) αναιδής, ζωηρός || ~en (also: ~en up) vi φρεσκάρω, συνέρχομαι ♦ vt αναζωογονώ, φρεσκάρω || ~ly ad πρόσφατα, νεο-, φρέσκος || ~ness n φρεσκάδα, δροσερότητα || ~water a του γλυκού νερού.

fret [frɛt] vi ταράσσομαι, ανησυχώ, στενοχωριέμαι.

friar ['fraɪə*] n μοναχός, καλόγηρος.

friction ['frɪkʃən] n (resistance) τριβή, τρίψιμο || (disagreement) προστριβή, τσάκωμα nt.

Friday ['fraɪdɪ] n Παρασκευή || see good.

fridge [frɪdʒ] n ψυγείο.

fried [fraɪd] a τηγανισμένο.

friend [frɛnd] n φίλος, γνωστός, γνώριμος || ~liness n φιλία || ~ly a (person) ευμενής, φιλικός || (attitude) φιλικός || ~ship n φιλία.

frieze [fri:z] n (ARCHIT) διάζωμα nt, ζωφόρος.

frigate ['frɪgɪt] n φρεγάτα.

fright [fraɪt] n τρόμος, φόβος || (ugly) άσχημος, σκίαχτρο || ~en vt (κατα)τρομάζω, φοβίζω || ~ening a τρομακτικός, τρομερός || ~ful a (col) τρομερός, φρικτός || ~fully ad τρομερά, τρομακτικά.

frigid ['frɪdʒɪd] a ψυχικός, παγερός, κρύος.

frill [frɪl] n βολάν nt inv.

fringe [frɪndʒ] n (border) κροσσός, κρόσι || (fig) περιθώριο, παρυφή.

frisky ['frɪskɪ] a παιχνιδιάρης, κεφάτος.

fritter ['frɪtə*] n τηγανίτα, αβήγγος || to ~ away vt σπαταλώ.

frivolity [frɪ'vɒlɪtɪ] n επιπολαιότητα.

frivolous ['frɪvələs] a επιπόλαιος.

frizzy ['frɪzɪ] a σγουρός.

fro [frəʊ] see to.

frock [frɒk] n (of monk) ράσο || (of woman) φουστάνι.

frog [frɒg] n βάτραχος || ~man n βατραχάνθρωπος.

frolic ['frɒlɪk] n παιχνίδι, γλέντι ♦ vt διασκεδάζω, παιχνιδίζω.

from [frɒm] prep από.

front [frʌnt] n (of house) πρόσοψη, μπροστινή, φάτσα || (MIL) μέτωπο || (POL) μέτωπο || (meteorology) μέτωπο || (fig: appearances) όψη, μούτρα ntpl, αναίδεια ♦ a (forward) πρόσθιος, μπροστινός || (first) μπροστινός, πρώτος || (door) κυρία είσοδος f, μπροστινή πόρτα || ~al a μετωπικός || ~ier n σύνορο, μεθόριος f || ~page a της πρώτης σελίδας || ~wheel drive n κίνηση στους προσινούς τροχούς.

frost [frɒst] n παγετός, παγωνιά || ~bite n κρυοπάγημα nt || ~ed a (glass) μάτ, αδιαφανές || ~y a παγερός, παγωμένος.

froth [frɒθ] n αφρός || (on beer) κολλάρο.

frown [fraʊn] n συνοφρύωση, κατσούφιασμα nt ♦ vi συνοφρυούμαι, σκυθρωπάζω || to ~upon vt κάνω μούτρα σε.

froze [frəʊz] pt of freeze || ~n pp of freeze || (COMM) παγωμένος || ~n food n κατεψυγμένο.

frugal ['fru:gəl] a λιτός, οικονομικός.

fruit [fru:t] n φρούτο, καρπός || ~s

npl καρποί *mpl*, κέρδη *ntpl*|| ~**ful** a καρποφόρος, γόνιμος || ~**ion** [frʌˈIʃən] *n* εκπλήρωση, απόλαυση.

frustrate [frʌsˈtreit] *vt* ματαιώνω, εξουδετερώνω, εμποδίζω|| ~**d** a απογοητευμένος.

frustration [frʌsˈtreiʃən] *n* ματαίωση, απογοήτευση.

fry [frai] *vt* τηγανίζω || **small** ~ *npl* οι ανθρωπάκοι *mpl*|| ~**ing pan** *n* τηγάνι.

ft. *abbr of* **foot, feet.**

fuchsia [ˈfjuːʃə] *n* φούξια.

fudge [fʌdʒ] *n* ζαχαρωτό.

fuel [fjuəl] *n* (*oil*) καύσιμη ύλη, πετρέλαιο || (*petrol*) καύσιμα *ntpl*, βενζίνη || (*wood*) καυσόξυλα *ntpl*|| (*coal*) κάρβουνο || (*gas*) καύσιμο αέριο || ~ **oil** a (*diesel fuel*) ακάθαρτο πετρέλαιο || ~ **tank** *n* ντεπόζιτο βενζίνης.

fugitive [ˈfjuːdʒitiv] *n* φυγάδας, δραπέτης.

fulfil [fulˈfil] *vt* (*accomplish*) εκπληρώνω || (*obey*) εκτελώ, εισακούω || ~**ment** *n* εκπλήρωση, εκτέλεση.

full [ful] a (*box, bottle*) πλήρης, γεμάτος || (*vehicle*) πλήρης, γεμάτος || (*person: satisfied*) χορτάτος, μπουκωμένος || (*session*) ολομέλεια || (*complete*) ολόκληρος || (*moon*) πανσέληνος || (*price*) ολόκληρος || (*speed*) ολοταχώς || (*skirt*) φαρδύς, μπουφάν || **in** ~ χωρίς έκπτωση, ολογράφως, στο ακέραιο || ~**back** *n* οπισθοφύλακας || ~ **stop** *n* τελεία || ~**-time** a (*work*) με πλήρες ωράριο ♦ *ad* ακριβώς, τελείως || ~**y** *ad* πλήρως, τελείως, απολύτως.

fumble [ˈfʌmbl] *vti* ψαχουλεύω, χειρίζομαι αδέξια.

fume [fjuːm] *vi* (*smoke*) βγάζω καπνό, κανίζω || (*be furious*) εξάπτομαι, λυσσάζω || ~**s** *npl* ατμοί *mpl*, αναθυμιάσεις *fpl*, καπνιές *fpl*.

fumigate [ˈfjuːmigeit] *vt* απολυμαίνω.

fun [fʌn] *n* διασκέδαση, κέφι, αστείο, χωρατό || **to make** ~ **of** κοροϊδεύω, περιπαίζω.

function [ˈfʌŋkʃən] ɪ (*use*) λειτουργία, έργο, δουλειά || (*public occasion*) τελετή, δεξίωση ♦ *vi* λειτουργώ || ~**al** a λειτουργικός || ~ **key** *n* (*COMPUT*) πλήκτρο λειτουργίας.

fund [fʌnd] *n* (*capital*) ταμείο, κεφάλαιο, παρακαταθήκη || (*store*) απόθεμα *nt*, πηγή.

fundamental [fʌndəˈmentl] a θεμελιώδης || ~**s** *npl* στοιχεία *ntpl*, βασικές αρχές *fpl*|| ~**ly** *ad* ουσιαστικά, βασικά.

funeral [ˈfjuːnərəl] *n* κηδεία ♦ a νεκρώσιμος, πένθιμος.

fun fair [ˈfʌnfɛə*] a λούνα-παρκ *pl inv.*

fungus [ˈfʌŋgəs] *n* μύκητας, μανιτάρι.

funnel [ˈfʌnl] *n* χωνί || (*of ship*) φουγάρο.

funny [ˈfʌni] a (*comical*) αστείος, κωμικός || (*strange*) παράξενος, περίεργος.

fur [fəː*] *n* γούνα, γουναρικό || ~ **coat** *n* γούνινο παλτό.

furious [ˈfjuəriəs] a μαινόμενος, λυσσαλέος, αγριεμένος || ~**ly** *ad* άγρια, με μανία.

furlong [ˈfəːlɒŋ] *n* = 220 υάρδες (201 μέτρα).

furlough [ˈfəːləu] *n* (*US*) άδεια.

furnace [ˈfəːnis] *n* κλίβανος, κάμινος, φούρνος.

furnish [ˈfəːniʃ] *vt* (*with furniture*) επιπλώνω || (*supply*) παρέχω, προμηθεύω, προσφέρω || ~**ings** *npl* έπιπλα *ntpl*, επίπλωση.

furniture [ˈfəːnitʃə*] *n* έπιπλα *ntpl*.

furrow [ˈfʌrəu] *n* αυλακώνω.

furry [ˈfəːri] a γούνινος.

further ['fɜːðə*] comp of **far** || a (additional) νέος, πρόσθετος, μεταγενέστερος || (more distant) μακρινότερος ♦ ad (more) περαιτέρω, περισσότερο || (moreover) άλλωστε, επί πλέον ♦ vt προάγω, υποστηρίζω || ~ **more** ad εκτός απ'αυτό, εξάλλου.

furthest ['fɜːðist] superl of **far**.

furtive ['fɜːtiv] a λαθραίος, κρυμμένος, ύπουλος.

fury ['fjʊəri] n οργή, θυμός, μανία.

fuse [fjuːz] n (ELEC) ασφάλεια || (cord) φυτίλι ♦ vt τήκω, λειώνω ♦ vi (ELEC) τήκομαι, λιώνω || ~ **box** n κιβώτιο ασφαλειών.

fuselage ['fjuːzəlɑː ʒ] n άτρακτος, σκελετός.

fusion ['fjuː ʒən] n (union) συγχώνευση, σύμπραξη.

fuss [fʌs] n (dispute) φασαρία, θόρυβος, ταραχή || (bustle) φασαρία, αναστάτωση, || ~ **y** a λεπτολόγος, ιδιότροπος.

futile ['fjuːtail] a (useless) φρούδος, μάταιος || (unimportant) ασήμαντος, κούφιος.

futility [fjuː'tiliti] n ματαιότητα.

future ['fjuːtʃə*] a μέλλων, μελλοντικός ♦ n μέλλον || **in (the)** ~ στο μέλλον.

futuristic [fjuːtʃə'ristik] a φουτουριστικός.

fuze [fjuːz] (US) = **fuse**.

fuzzy ['fʌzi] a (indistinct) θαμπός || (from drink) σουρωμένος.

G

g. abbr of **gram(s)**.

gabble ['ɡæbl] vi φλυαρώ.

gable ['ɡeibl] n αέτωμα nt.

gadget ['ɡædʒit] n μαραφέτι.

gag [ɡæɡ] n φίμωτρο || (funny phrase)

αστείο, κασκαρίκα ♦ nt φιμώνω, αποστομώνω.

gaiety ['ɡeiti] n ευθυμία.

gaily ['ɡeili] ad εύθυμα, χαρούμενα.

gain [ɡein] vt (obtain) αποκτώ, κερδίζω || (win over) κερδίζω, παίρνω || (make progress) προχωρώ, προηγούμαι ♦ vi (improve) κερδίζω, κατακτώ || (clock etc) τρέχω μπρος ♦ n κέρδος nt, αύξηση || ~ **ful** a επικερδής.

gal. abbr of **gallon**.

gala ['ɡɑːlə] n γιορτή.

galaxy ['ɡæləksi] n (stars) γαλαξίας.

gale [ɡeil] n θύελλα, φουρτούνα || ~ **warning** n αναγγελία θύελλας.

gallant ['ɡælənt] a (fine, brave) γενναίος, ηρωικός || (to women) γαλάντης, περιποιητικός || ~ **ry** n γενναιότητα, λεβεντιά || (to women) περιποιητικότητα.

gall-bladder ['ɡɔːlblædə*] n χοληδόχος κύστη.

gallery ['ɡæləri] n (ART) πινακοθήκη || (THEAT) γαλαρία, εξώστης.

galley ['ɡæli] n (of ship) μαγειρείο || (vessel) γαλέρα.

gallon ['ɡælən] n γαλόνι (04.54 χλγρ.).

gallop ['ɡæləp] n καλπασμός, γκάλοπ nt inv ♦ vi καλπάζω.

gallows ['ɡæləuz] npl αγχόνη, κρεμάλα.

gallstone ['ɡɔːlstəun] n χολόλιθος.

gamble ['ɡæmbl] vi παίζω ♦ vt (risk) ριψοκινδυνεύω || n (τυχερό) παιχνίδι || ~ **r** n (χαρτο)παίκτης.

gambling ['ɡæmbliŋ] n παιχνίδι, παίξιμο.

game [ɡeim] n (play) παιχνίδι, διασκέδαση || (animals) θήραμα nt, κυνήγι ♦ a θαρραλέος, τολμηρός || ~ **keeper** n φύλακας κυνηγιού.

gammon ['ɡæmən] n οπίσθια μπούτια ntpl, χοιρομέρι.

gang [ɡæŋ] n συμμορία, σπείρα.

gangrene ['gæŋgriːn] n γάγγραινα.

gangster ['gæŋstə*] n γκάνγκστερ m inv.

gangway ['gæŋwei] n (of ship) διαβάθρα, μαδέρι || (aisle) διάδρομος.

gaol [dʒeil] n = **jail**.

gap [gæp] n (opening) τρύπα, ρήγμα nt || (empty space) διάκενο.

gape [geip] vi χάσκω, χασμουριέμαι.

gaping ['geipiŋ] a χαίνων.

garage ['gærɑːʒ] n γκαράζ nt inv.

garbage ['gɑːbidʒ] n σκουπίδια ntpl || ~ **can** n (US) σκουπιδοτενεκές m.

garbled ['gɑːbld] a (story) παραμορφωμένος, αλλοιωμένος.

garden ['gɑːdn] n κήπος, μπαξές m ♦ vi ασχολούμαι με κηπουρική || ~**er** n κηπουρός, περιβολάρης || ~**ing** n κηπουρική.

gargle ['gɑːgl] vi γαργαρίζω ♦ n γαργάρα.

gargoyle ['gɑːgɔil] n υδρορρόη.

garish ['gɛəriʃ] a φανταχτερός, κακόγουστος.

garland ['gɑːlənd] n στέφανος, γιρλάντα.

garlic ['gɑːlik] n σκόρδο.

garment ['gɑːmənt] n φόρεμα nt.

garnish ['gɑːniʃ] vt (food) γαρνίρω ♦ n γαρνιτούρα.

garret ['gærit] n σοφίτα.

garrison ['gærisən] n φρουρά ♦ vt εγκαθιστώ φρουρά.

garrulous ['gæruləs] a φλύαρος, πολυλογάς.

garter ['gɑːtə*] n καλτσοδέτα.

gas [gæs] n αέριο || (coal gas) φωταέριο, γκάζ nt inv || (MED) αναισθητικό || (US: gasoline) βενζίνη ♦ vt δηλητηριάζω με αέριο || ~ **cooker** n κουζίνα || ~ **cylinder** n φιάλη αερίου || ~ **fire** n σόμπα του γκαζιού.

gash [gæʃ] n εγκοπή, μαχαιριά ♦ vt κόβω, πληγώνω.

gasket ['gæskit] n (TECH) παρένθεμα nt.

gasmask ['gæsmɑːsk] n αντιασφυξιογόνα μάσκα.

gas meter ['gæsmiːtə*] n μετρητής του γκαζιού.

gasoline ['gæsəliːn] n (US) βενζίνη.

gasp [gɑːsp] vi ασθμαίνω, λαχανιάζω ♦ n κομμένη αναπνοή, ρόγχος.

gas ring ['gæsriŋ] n μάτι του γκαζιού.

gas station ['gæssteiʃən] n (US) βενζινάδικο.

gas stove ['gæs'stəuv] n κουζίνα του γκαζιού.

gassy ['gæsi] a (drink) αεριούχος.

gastric ['gæstrik] a γαστρικός.

gastronomy [gæs'trɒnəmi] n γαστρονομία.

gate [geit] n πύλη, πόρτα || (of estate etc) καγκελόπορτα, αυλόπορτα || ~**crasher** n (party) απρόσκλητος επισκέπτης, τζαμπατζής || ~**way** n πύλη, είσοδος f.

gather ['gæðə*] vt συλλέγω, μαζεύω || (gain) συμπεραίνω, συνάγω ♦ vi (assemble) συγκεντρούμαι, μαζεύομαι || ~**ing** n συγκέντρωση, μάζεμα nt.

gauche [gəuʃ] a χωρίς τακτ.

gaudy ['gɔːdi] a επιδεικτικός, φανταχτερός.

gauge [geidʒ] n (of metal) διάμετρος, διαμέτρημα nt || (RAIL) πλάτος, μεταράτόχιο || (measure) μετρητής, (εν)δείκτης ♦ vt (δια)μετρώ, εκτιμώ.

gaunt [gɔːnt] a (lean) ισχνός, κοκκαλιάρης || (grim) άγριος, συντετραμμένος.

gauze [gɔːz] n γάζα.

gave [geiv] pt of **give**.

gay [gei] a (merry) εύθυμος || (brightly coloured) λαμπρός, ζωηρός || (homosexual) ομοφυλόφιλος.

gaze [geiz] n ατενές βλέμμα nt || ~ **at** vt ατενίζω, καρφώνω.

gazelle [gə'zɛl] n γαζέλα.

G.B. abbr see great.

G.C.E. n abbr of General Certificate of Education.

gear [gɪə*] n (equipment) είδη ntpl|| (MECH) μηχανισμός, οδοντωτός τροχός || (AUT) γρανάζι || in ~ κινούμενος, στην ταχύτητα || out of ~ νεκρό σημείο, εκτός λειτουργίας || ~box n κιβώτιο ταχυτήτων || ~-lever, (US) ~shift n μοχλός ταχυτήτων.

geese [giːs] npl of goose.

gelatin(e) ['dʒɛlətiːn] n ζελατίνη, πηκτή.

gelignite ['dʒɛlɪgnaɪt] n ζελινίτης.

gem [dʒɛm] n πολύτιμος λίθος, πέτρα.

gender ['dʒɛndə*] n γένος nt.

general ['dʒɛnərəl] n στρατηγός ♦ a γενικός || ~ election n γενικές εκλογές fpl || ~ization n γενίκευση || ~ize vi γενικεύω, κλαδικεύω || ~ly ad γενικά, κατά κανόνα || ~ practitioner (G.P.) n γιατρός m/f παθολόγος.

generate ['dʒɛnəreɪt] vt παράγω, (επι)φέρω προκαλώ || (ELEC) παράγω.

generation [dʒɛnə'reɪʃən] n (into being) γέννηση, γένεση || (descent in family) γενεά, γενιά || (of same period) (σημερινή) γενεά || (about 30 years) (μια) γενεά || third/fourth ~ a (COMPUT) τρίτης/τέταρτης γενεάς.

generator ['dʒɛnəreɪtə*] n γεννήτρια.

generosity [dʒɛnə'rɒsɪtɪ] n γενναιοδωρία, γενναιοψυχία.

generous ['dʒɛnərəs] a γενναιόδωρος, μεγαλόψυχος || (col) γενναίος, πλούσιος || ~ly ad γενναιόδωρα, μεγαλόψυχα.

genetics [dʒɪ'nɛtɪks] npl γενετική.

genial ['dʒiːnɪəl] a εύκρατος, ήπιος, προσηνής.

genitals ['dʒɛnɪtlz] npl γεννητικά όργανα ntpl.

genitive ['dʒɛnɪtɪv] n γενική (πτώση).

genius ['dʒiːnɪəs] n (person) ιδιοφυΐα, μεγαλοφυΐα || (ability) πνεύμα nt.

genteel [dʒɛn'tiːl] a ευγενής, κομψός.

gentile ['dʒɛntaɪl] n εθνικός, μη Ιουδαίος.

gentle ['dʒɛntl] a ήπιος, μαλακός, ευγενής.

gentleman ['dʒɛntlmən] n ευγενής, κύριος, τζέντλεμαν m inv.

gentleness ['dʒɛntlnɪs] n λεπτότητα.

gently ['dʒɛntlɪ] ad ήρεμα, μαλακά.

gentry ['dʒɛntrɪ] n αρχοντολόι.

gents [dʒɛnts] n άνδρες mpl, κύριοι mpl.

genuine ['dʒɛnjuːɪn] a γνήσιος, αυθεντικός, αληθινός || ~ly ad ειλικρινά, γνησίως.

geographical [dʒɪə'græfɪkəl] a γεωγραφικός.

geography [dʒɪ'ɒgrəfɪ] n γεωγραφία.

geological [dʒɪə'lɒdʒɪkəl] a γεωλογικός.

geologist [dʒɪ'ɒlədʒɪst] n γεωλόγος.

geology [dʒɪ'ɒlədʒɪ] n γεωλογία.

geometric(al) [dʒɪə'mɛtrɪk(əl)] a γεωμετρικός.

geometry [dʒɪ'ɒmɪtrɪ] n γεωμετρία.

geranium [dʒɪ'reɪnɪəm] n γεράνι.

germ [dʒɜːm] n (of disease) μικρόβιο || (bud or seed) σπέρμα nt || (beginning) σπέρμα nt.

German ['dʒɜːmən] a γερμανικός ♦ n (person) Γερμανός || (LING) Γερμανικά.

Germany ['dʒɜːmənɪ] n Γερμανία.

germination [dʒɜːmɪ'neɪʃən] n βλάστηση, κύηση.

gesticulate [dʒɛs'tɪkjʊleɪt] vi χειρονομώ.

gesture ['dʒɛstʃə*] n χειρονομία, νεύμα nt.

get [gɛt] (irreg v) vt (fetch) (πηγαίνω να) φέρω || (become) γίνομαι || (persuade) πείθω, καταφέρνω || (catch) (συλ)λαμβάνω, πιάνω ♦ vi (reach) πηγαίνω, φθάνω, γίνομαι || **to ~ along** vi (of people) πηγαίνω καλά || (depart) ποχωρώ, (ώρα) να φύγω || **to ~ at** vt (facts) φθάνω, βρίσκω, πλησιάζω || **to ~ away** vi (leave) αναχωρώ, ποχωρώ || (escape) φεύγω, το σκάω || **to ~ down** vt κατεβάζω, γράφω || **to ~ in** vi (train) μπαίνω, πιάνω φιλίες || **to ~ on** vi (well, badly etc) τα πάω καλά || **to ~ out** vi βγάζω, αφαιρώ, βγαίνω || **to ~ over** vt (illness) συνέρχομαι, τελειώνω || **to ~ up** vi (in morning) σηκώνομαι || **~away** n φυγή, δραπέτευση.

geyser ['giːzə*] n θερμοπίδακας, γκάιζερ nt inv || (heater) θερμοσίφωνας.

ghastly ['gaːstlɪ] a φρικτός, τρομερός || (pale) ωχρός.

gherkin ['gɜːkɪn] n αγγουράκι.

ghetto ['gɛtəʊ] n γκέτο.

ghost [gəʊst] n φάντασμα nt || **~ly** a σαν φάντασμα.

giant ['dʒaɪənt] n γίγαντας ♦ a γιγαντιαίος.

gibberish ['dʒɪbərɪʃ] n αλαμπουρνέζικα ntpl.

gibe [dʒaɪb] n σκώμμα nt, πείραγμα nt.

giblets ['dʒɪblɪts] npl εντόσθια ntpl (πουλερικών).

giddiness ['gɪdɪnɪs] n ίλιγγος, ζάλη.

giddy ['gɪdɪ] a (dizzy) ζαλισμένος || (frivolous) επιπόλαιος.

gift [gɪft] n δώρο || (talent) προσόν, ταλέντο || **~ed** a προικισμένος, με ταλέντο.

gigantic [dʒaɪˈgæntɪk] a γιγαντιαίος.

giggle ['gɪgl] vi χασκογελώ ♦ n νευρικό γέλιο.

gild [gɪld] (irreg v) vt (επι)χρυσώνω.

gill [dʒɪl] n (measure = ¼ pint) ⅛ του λίτρου ♦ [gɪl] n (fish) βράγχιο, σπάραχνο.

gilt [gɪlt] pp of gild || n επιχρύσωση, χρύσωμα nt ♦ a (επι)χρυσωμένος.

gin [dʒɪn] n (liquor) τζίν nt inv.

ginger ['dʒɪndʒə*] n πιπερόριζα || **~ beer** n τζιτζιμπύρα || **~bread** n μελόψωμο || **~-haired** a κοκκινοτρίχης.

gingerly ['dʒɪndʒəlɪ] ad προσεκτικά, μαλακά.

gipsy ['dʒɪpsɪ] n τσιγγάνος, γύφτος.

giraffe [dʒɪˈrɑːf] n καμηλοπάρδαλη.

girder ['gɜːdə*] n δοκός f.

girdle ['gɜːdl] n ζωνάρι ♦ vt (περι)ζώνω.

girl [gɜːl] n (child) κοριτσάκι, κορίτσι || (young woman) νέα, κοπέλα || **~friend** n (of girl) φιλενάδα || (of boy) φιλενάδα, φίλη || **~ish** a κοριτσίστικος.

girth [gɜːθ] n (measurement) περιφέρεια, περίμετρος || (strap) έποχο, ίγγλα.

gist [dʒɪst] n ουσία, έννοια.

give [gɪv] (irreg v) vt (hand over) δίνω, χαρίζω || (supply) παρέχω, απονέμω ♦ vi (break) υποχωρώ, λυγίζω || **to ~ away** vt (give free) χαρίζω || (betray) καταδίδω, προδίδω || **to ~ back** vt αποδίδω, ξαναδίδω, γυρίζω || **to ~ in** vi (yield, agree) υποχωρώ, υποκύπτω ♦ vt (hand in) παραδίδω || **to ~ up** vi (surrender) παραδίδομαι ♦ vt (post, office) παραιτούμαι, εγκαταλείπω || **to ~ way** vi θραύομαι, υποχωρώ, αντικαθίσταμαι || **~r** n δωρητής, δότης.

glacier ['glæsɪə*] n παγετώνας.

glad [glæd] a ευχαριστημένος, ευχάριστος || ~**den** vt χαροποιώ.

gladly ['glædli] ad ευχαρίστως, με χαρά.

glamorous ['glæmərəs] a γοητευτικός, μαγευτικός.

glamour ['glæmə*] n γοητεία, μαγεία.

glance [glɑːns] n βλέμμα nt, ματιά ♦ vi (+ at) (look) ρίχνω ματιά || γλιστρώ πλαγίως.

glancing ['glɑːnsɪŋ] a (blow) πλάγιος.

gland [glænd] n αδένας || ~**ular** a αδενικός.

glare [glεə*] n (light) εκτυφλωτική λάμψη || (fierce stare) άγριο βλέμμα nt ♦ vi απαστράπτω, λάμπω || (angrily) αγριοκοιτάζω.

glaring ['glεərɪŋ] a (mistake) έκδηλος, ολοφάνερος.

glass [glɑːs] n (substance) γυαλί || (vessel) ποτήρι || (mirror) καθρέφτης || ~**es** npl γυαλιά ntpl || ~**house** n (AGR) θερμοκήπιο, σέρρα || ~**ware** n γυαλικά ntpl || ~**y** a (eye) σαν γυαλί, ανέκφραστος.

glaze [gleiz] vt (furnish with glass) βάζω τζάμια || (finish) βερνικώνω, γυαλίζω ♦ n βερνίκι.

glazier ['gleiziə*] n τζαμιτζής.

gleam [gliːm] n ακτίδα, λάμψη ♦ vi ακτινοβολώ, λάμπω || ~**ing** a αστραφτερός.

glee [gliː] n ευθυμία, χαρά || ~**ful** a εύθυμος, χαρούμενος.

glen [glεn] n χαράδρα, δερβένι.

glib [glɪb] a εύγλωττος, επιπόλαιος || ~**ly** ad εύκολα, πονηρά.

glide [glaɪd] vi γλυστρώ, κυλώ ♦ n γλίστρημα || ~**r** n (AVIAT) ανεμόπτερο.

gliding ['glaɪdɪŋ] n ολίσθηση, ανεμοπορία.

glimmer ['glɪmə*] n αμυδρό φως nt.

glimpse [glɪmps] n γρήγορη ματιά ♦ vt βλέπω φευγαλέα.

glint [glɪnt] n λάμψη ♦ vi λάμπω, αστράφτω.

glisten ['glɪsn] vi απαστράπτω, σπιθίζω.

glitter ['glɪtə*] vi λάμπω, σπινθηροβολώ ♦ n λαμποκόπημα nt, γυάλισμα nt.

gloat [gləʊt]: **to ~ over** vt κοιτάζω με χαιρεκακία.

global ['gləʊbl] a παγκόσμιος.

globe [gləʊb] n (light) γλόμπος, λάμπα || (earth) σφαίρα, υδρόγειος σφαίρα.

gloom [gluːm] n (also: ~**iness**) (darkness) σκότος nt, σκοτάδι || (depression) μελαγχολία, ακεφιά μελαγχολικά, σκυθρωπά || ~**y** a σκοτεινός, βαρύς, μελαγχολικός.

glorify ['glɔːrɪfaɪ] vt εκθειάζω, εξυμνώ, δοξάζω.

glorious ['glɔːrɪəs] a ένδοξος, δοξασμένος, λαμπρός.

glory ['glɔːrɪ] n (splendour) δόξα, μεγαλείο || (fame) τιμή, φήμη, δόξα.

gloss [glɒs] n (shine) στιλπνότητα, λούστρο, γυαλάδα.

glossary ['glɒsərɪ] n λεξιλόγιο, γλωσσάριο.

glossy ['glɒsɪ] a (surface) στιλπνός, γυαλιστερός.

glove [glʌv] n γάντι.

glow [gləʊ] vi πυρακτούμαι, κοκκινίζω || (look hot) ζεσταίνομαι, ανάβω || (with emotion) αστράφτω, λάμπω ♦ n (heat) πυράκτωση || (colour) ρόδισμα || (feeling) σφρίγος nt, φλόγα.

glower ['glaʊə*] vi στραβοκοιτάζω.

glucose ['gluːkəʊs] n γλυκόζη.

glue [gluː] n κόλλα ♦ vt κολλώ.

glum [glʌm] a σκυθρωπός, κατσούφης.

glut [glʌt] n υπεραφθονία ♦ vt (ECON) πλημμυρίζω.

glutton

121

good

glutton ['glʌtn] n λαίμαργος, φαγάς || ~**ous** a αδηφάγος || ~**y** n λαιμαργία.

glycerin(e) ['glɪsəriːn] n γλυκερίνη.

gm, gms abbr of **gram(s)**.

gnarled [nɑːld] a ροζιάρικος.

gnat [næt] n σκνίπα.

gnaw [nɔː] vt ροκανίζω, τραγανίζω.

gnome [nəum] n νάνος.

go [gəu] (irreg v) vi (travel) πηγαίνω, πάω || (progress) κινούμαι, πάω || (function) πάω, τρέχω, λειτουργώ || (depart) αναχωρώ, φεύγω || (disappear) χάνομαι || (be sold) (+ for) πουλιέμαι για || (fit, suit) πηγαίνω, ταιριάζω || (become) γίνομαι || (break etc) σπάζω, κόβομαι, πωλούμαι ♦ n (energy) δραστηριότητα, διάθεση || (attempt) δοκιμή, προσπάθεια, απόπειρα || **to** ~ **ahead** vi (proceed) προχωρώ, προοδεύω || **to** ~ **along with** vi (agree to support) συμφωνώ, ταιριάζω || **to** ~ **away** vi (depart) φεύγω || **to** ~ **back** vi (return) επιστρέφω || **to** ~ **back on** vi (promise) παραβαίνω, αθετώ || **to** ~ **by** vi (years, time) περνώ || **to** ~ **down** vi (sun) κατεβαίνω, γέρνω, πέφτω || **to** ~ **for** vt (fetch) πάω για || (like) συμπαθώ || **to** ~ **in** vi (enter) εισέρχομαι, μπαίνω || (fit) μπαίνω || **to** ~ **into** vt (enter) μπαίνω || (study) εξετάζω, μελετώ || **to** ~ **off** vi (depart) εξέρχομαι, φεύγω || (milk) ξυνίζω || (explode) εκπυρσοκροτώ ♦ vt (dislike) ξεθυμαίνω, αντιπαθώ || **to** ~ **on** vi (continue) συνεχίζω, εξακολουθώ || **to** ~ **out** vi (fire, light) σβήνω || (of house) βγαίνω || **to** ~ **over** vi (examine, check) εξετάζω, επαναλαμβάνω || **to** ~ **up** vi (price) ανεβαίνω || (explode) ανατινάζομαι || **to** ~ **without** vt περνώ χωρίς.

goad [gəud] vt κεντρίζω, προκαλώ ♦ n βούκεντρο, κίνητρο.

go-ahead ['gəuəhɛd] a δραστήριος.

goal [gəul] n (purpose) σκοπός || (on sports field) τέρμα nt || (score) γκολ nt inv || ~**keeper** n τερματοφύλακας || ~**post** n δοκός f.

goat [gəut] n κατοίκα, γίδα.

gobble ['gɒbl] vt καταβροχθίζω.

go-between ['gəubitwiːn] n μεσάζων, μεσολαβητής.

god [gɒd] n θεός || **G**~ Θεός || ~**child** n βαφτιστικός || ~**dess** n θεά || ~**father** n νονός || ~**forsaken** a εγκαταλειμμένος, καταραμένος || ~**mother** n νουνά || ~**send** n θείο δώρο, κελεπούρι.

goggle ['gɒgl] vi γουρλώνω || ~**s** npl προστατευτικά γυαλιά ntpl.

going ['gəuiŋ] n (condition of ground) κατάσταση εδάφους ♦ a (rate) τρέχουσα (τιμή) || (concern) δραστήριος || ~**s-on** npl συμβάντα ntpl.

gold [gəuld] n χρυσός, χρυσάφι || ~**en** a χρυσός, χρυσαφένιος || ~**fish** n χρυσόψαρο || ~ **mine** n χρυσορυχείο.

golf [gɒlf] n γκόλφ nt inv || ~ **club** (society) λέσχη του γκόλφ || (stick) κλόμπ nt inv || ~ **course** n γήπεδο του γκόλφ || ~**er** n παίκτης του γκόλφ.

gondola ['gɒndələ] n γόνδολα.

gone [gɒn] pp of **go**.

gong [gɒŋ] n γκόγκ nt inv, κουδούνι.

good [gud] n (well-being) το καλό, όφελος || (goodness) αρετή, καλό ♦ a (well-behaved) καλός, έντιμος || (virtuous) τίμιος, αγαθός, καλός || (well-done) εξαιρετικός, καλός || (suitable) ταιριαστός, που πάει || (sound) σε καλή κατάσταση || ~**s** npl κινητά, αγαθά, είδη || **a** ~ **deal, a many** αρκετός, πολύς || ~ **bye!** αντίο! || γειά σου! || στο καλό! || **G**~ **Friday** n Μεγάλη Παρασκευή || ~**looking** a όμορφος || ~ **morning!**

goose

888

granite ['grænɪt] n γρανίτης.

granny ['grænɪ] n (col) γιαγιά, γρηούλα.

grant [grɑːnt] vt (bestow) απονέμω, δίνω || (allow) (απο)δέχομαι ♦ n δωρεά, επιχορήγηση.

granule ['grænjuːl] n κοκκίδιο, κοκκίο.

grape [greɪp] n σταφύλι, ρώγα.

grapefruit ['greɪpfruːt] n φράπα, γκρέιπ-φρουτ nt inv.

graph [grɑːf] n διάγραμμα nt, γραφική παράσταση || ~ic a (vivid) ζωηρός, εκφραστικός || (drawing, writing) γραφικός.

grapple ['græpl] vi (+ with) πιάνομαι, έρχομαι στα χέρια.

grasp [grɑːsp] vt πιάνω, αρπάζω, αρπάζω || (understand) συλλαμβάνω, κατανοώ ♦ n (handgrip) λαβή, πιάσιμο, σφίξιμο || (possession) έλεγχος, εξουσία || (understanding) αντίληψη, γνώση || ~ing a άπληστος, πλεονέκτης.

grass [grɑːs] n χορτάρι, γρασίδι || ~hopper n ακρίδα || ~land n λιβάδι || ~snake n νερόφιδο || ~y a χορταριασμένος, πράσινος.

grate [greɪt] n σχάρα, κάγκελο ♦ vi (scrape) ξύνω || (make harsh sound) τρίζω || (irritate) ενοχλώ ♦ vt (into small pieces) τρίβω.

grateful ['greɪtful] a ευγνώμονας, ευχάριστος || ~ly ad με ευγνωμοσύνη.

grater ['greɪtə*] n ξύστρα, τρίφτης.

gratify ['grætɪfaɪ] vt ευχαριστώ, ικανοποιώ.

gratifying ['grætɪfaɪɪŋ] a ευχάριστος.

grating ['greɪtɪŋ] n (iron bars) κιγκλίδωμα nt, κάγκελα ntpl ♦ a (noise) κακόηχος, στριγκός.

gratitude ['grætɪtjuːd] n ευγνωμοσύνη.

gratuity [grə'tjuːɪtɪ] n φιλοδώρημα nt.

grave [greɪv] n τάφος ♦ a βαρύς, σοβαρός, δυσάρεστος || ~digger n νεκροθάφτης.

gravel ['grævəl] n χαλίκι.

gravestone ['greɪvstəun] n επιτάφιος πλάκα.

graveyard ['greɪvjɑːd] n νεκροταφείο.

gravitate ['græviteɪt] vi έλκομαι, ρέπω προς.

gravity ['grævɪtɪ] n βαρύτητα, βάρος nt || (seriousness) σοβαρότητα.

gravy ['greɪvɪ] n είδος nt σάλτσας.

gray [greɪ] a = **grey**.

graze [greɪz] vi (feed) βόσκω ♦ vt (touch) ψαύω, εγγίζω || (scrape) ξύνω ♦ n (ΜΕD) ξεγδαρμα nt.

grease [griːs] n (fat) λίπος nt, ξύγγι || (lubricant) γράσο, λάδι ♦ vt λαδώνω, γρασάρω || ~proof a μη διαπερατός από λάδι.

greasy ['griːsɪ] a λιπαρός, λαδωμένος.

great [greɪt] a (large) μεγάλος || (important) σπουδαίος || (distinguished) μεγάλος || G~ Britain (G.B.) n Μεγάλη Βρετανία || ~-grandfather n πρόπαππος || ~-grandmother n προμάμη || ~ness n μεγαλείο, μέγεθος nt.

Greece [griːs] n Ελλάδα

greed [griːd] n (also: ~iness) απληστία, πλεονεξία || ~ily ad άπληστα || ~y a άπληστος, πλεονέκτης || (gluttonous) λαίμαργος, αδηφάγος.

Greek [griːk] n (person) Έλληνας/νίδα m/f || (LING) Ελληνικά ntpl ♦ a ελληνικός.

green [griːn] a πράσινος, άγουρος || (inexperienced) άπειρος || ~grocer n μανάβης || ~house n θερμοκήπιο.

greet [griːt] vt χαιρετίζω || ~ing n

χαιρετισμός || ~ings! χαιρετισμούς! *mpl.*

gregarious [grɪˈgɛərɪəs] *a* κοινωνικός.

grenade [grɪˈneɪd] *n* (χειρο)βομβίδα.

grew [gruː] *pt of* **grow**.

grey [greɪ] *a* σταχτής, γκρίζος, ψαρός || (*dismal*) σκοτεινός || ~-haired *a* γκρίζομάλλης, ψαρομάλλης || ~hound *n* λαγωνικό.

grid [grɪd] *n* (*of bars*) σχάρα, πλέγμα *nt* || (*network*) πλέγμα, δίκτυο || (*of map*) δικτυωτό, τετραγωνισμός || ~iron *n* σχάρα.

grief [griːf] *n* θλίψη, λύπη, ατύχημα *nt.*

grievance [ˈgriːvəns] *n* παράπονο.

grieve [griːv] *vi* λυπούμαι, θλίβομαι ♦ *vt* λυπώ, πικραίνω.

grill [grɪl] *n* (*on cooker*) σχάρα || (*of food*) της σχάρας ♦ *vt* ψήνω στη σχάρα || (*interrogate*) ανακρίνω.

grille [grɪl] *n* (*on car etc*) γρίλλιες *fpl.*

grim [grɪm] *a* φρικαλέος, απειλητικός, σκληρός.

grimace [grɪˈmeɪs] *n* γκριμάτσα ♦ *vi* μορφάζω.

grime [graɪm] *n* ακαθαρσία, λέρα, φούμο.

grimly [ˈgrɪmlɪ] *ad* απαίσια, σκληρά, αυστηρά.

grimy [ˈgraɪmɪ] *a* ακάθαρτος, βρώμικος.

grin [grɪn] *n* χαμόγελο, μειδίαμα *nt* ♦ *vi* χαμογελώ, μορφάζω.

grind [graɪnd] (*irreg v*) *vt* (*crush*) τρίβω, αλέθω, κοπανίζω || (*sharpen*) τροχίζω, τορνάρω, λειαίνω || (*teeth*) τρίζω ♦ *n* (*bore*) αγγαρεία, μαγγανοπήγαδο.

grip [grɪp] *n* (*firm hold*) σφίξιμο, πιάσιμο || (*handle*) λαβή || (*mastery*) πυγμή, εποχή, επιβολή || (*suitcase*) βαλιτσάκι ♦ *vt* πιάνω, σφίγγω.

gripes [graɪps] *npl* (*bowel pains*) κωλικόπονοι *mpl.*

gripping [ˈgrɪpɪŋ] *a* (*exciting*) συγκινητικός, συναρπαστικός.

grisly [ˈgrɪzlɪ] *a* φρικαστικός, τρομακτικός.

gristle [ˈgrɪsl] *n* χόνδρος, τραγανό.

grit [grɪt] *n* (*sand*) αμμόλιθος, ακαθαρσίες *fpl* || (*courage*) τόλμη, θάρρος *nt* ♦ *vt* (*teeth*) τρίζω.

groan [grəʊn] *n* αναστεναγμός ♦ *vi* (ανα)στενάζω.

grocer [ˈgrəʊsə*] *n* μπακάλης || ~ies *npl* είδη μπακαλικής.

groggy [ˈgrɒgɪ] *a* (*dazed, staggering*) κλονιζόμενος, σουρωμένος, ασταθής.

groin [grɔɪn] *n* βουβών *m.*

groom [gruːm] *n* ιπποκόμος || (*bridegroom*) γαμπρός ♦ *vt* (*o.s.*) ντύνομαι.

groove [gruːv] *n* αυλάκι, διάξυσμα *nt* || (*rut*) ρουτίνα.

grope [grəʊp] *vi* ψηλαφώ, ψάχνω.

gross [grəʊs] *a* (*coarse*) χονδροειδής, σωματώδης || (*very bad*) χοντρός, καταφανής || (*total*) ολικός, χονδρικός || *n* γρόσσα, δώδεκα δωδεκάδες || ~ly *ad* χονδροειδώς, υπερβολικά.

grotesque [grəʊˈtɛsk] *a* αλλόκοτος, παράλογος.

grotto [ˈgrɒtəʊ] *n* σπηλιά, κρύπτη.

ground [graʊnd] *pt, pp of* **grind** ♦ *n* (*surface*) έδαφος *nt*, γη, χώμα *nt* || (*piece of land*) οικόπεδο, γη || (*generally pl: reason*) λόγος, αιτία, βάση || ~s *npl* (*dregs*) κατακάθι, ίζημα *nt* || (*land*) περιοχή, κήποι *mpl*, πάρκο ♦ *vt* (*run ashore*) προσαράσσω, εξοκέλλω || (*compel to stay*) καθηλώνω || (*instruct*) διδάσκω εντατικά ♦ *vi* εξοκέλλω || ~ing *n* (*instruction*) οι βάσεις *fpl* || ~sheet *n* μουσαμάς εδάφους || ~work *n* θεμέλις *ntpl*, βάσις.

group [gruːp] n ομάδα, παρέα ♦ vt συνδυάζω, συνδέω, συγκεντρώνω.

grouse [graus] n (bird) χαμωτίδα, αγριόγαλος || (complaint) γκρίνια ♦ vi (complain) γκρινιάζω.

grove [grəuv] n άλσος nt, ασύλιο.

grovel ['grɒvl] vi (in fear) σέρνομαι, κυλίομαι || (abase o.s.) ταπεινώνομαι, πέφτω στα πόδια.

grow [grəu] (irreg v) vi (in size) μεγαλώνω, αναπτύσσομαι || (be produced) φύομαι || (become) καθίσταμαι, γίνομαι ♦ vt (raise crops etc) καλλιεργώ || **to ~ up** vi μεγαλώνω || **~er** n καλλιεργητής || **~ing** a αυξανόμενος, που μεγαλώνει.

growl [graul] vi μουγγρίζω ♦ n μουγγρισμα nt, βρυχηθμός.

grown-up ['grəun'ʌp] a ώριμος ♦ n ενήλικος.

growth [grəuθ] n (development) ανάπτυξη || (increase) αύξηση, μεγάλωμα nt || (what has grown) καλλιέργεια || (MED) σάρκωμα nt.

grub [grʌb] n (larva) σκουλήκι || (col: food) φαγητό || **~by** a ακάθαρτος, βρώμικος.

grudge [grʌdʒ] n (mutual) κακία, έχθρα ♦ vt ζηλεύω για, δείχνω απροθυμία || **to bear a ~** κρατώ κακία για.

grudging ['grʌdʒɪŋ] a απρόθυμος, φειδωλός.

gruelling ['gruəlɪŋ] a εξαντλητικός.

gruesome ['gruːsəm] a φρικτός, απαίσιος.

gruff [grʌf] a τραχύς, απότομος.

grumble ['grʌmbl] vi γκρινιάζω, μουγγρίζω ♦ n μουγγρητό, γκρίνια.

grumpy ['grʌmpɪ] a κατσούφης, γκρινιάρης.

grunt [grʌnt] n γρύλλισμα nt ♦ vi γρυλλίζω.

guarantee [gærən'tiː] n (of goods)

εγγύηση || (promise to pay) εγγύηση, ενέχυρο ♦ vt εγγυώμαι.

guard [gɑːd] n (defence) φρουρά, προφύλαξη || (sentry) σκοπός || (official) φύλακας ♦ vt φυλάσσω, προστατεύω, φρουρώ || **~ed** a υπό φρούρησιν || (words etc) επιφυλακτικός || **~ian** n (keeper) φύλακας, προστάτης || (of child) κηδεμόνας.

guerilla [gə'rɪlə] n αντάρτης || **~ warfare** n ανταρτοπόλεμος.

guess [ges] vti μαντεύω || (US) νομίζω ♦ n εικασία, γνώμη.

guest [gest] n καλεσμένος, ξένος || (of hotel) πελάτης || **~ house** n πανσιόν f inv || **~ room** n (in private house, for friends) δωμάτιο των ξένων.

guffaw [gʌ'fɔː] n καγχασμός ♦ vi ξεσπώ στα γέλια.

guidance ['gaɪdəns] n (control) καθοδήγηση || (advice) συμβουλές fpl, οδηγίες fpl.

guide [gaɪd] n (person) οδηγός m/f, συνοδός m/f, ξεναγός m/f || (book etc) οδηγός vt (καθοδηγώ || **girl ~** n προσκοπίνα || **~book** n οδηγός || **~d missile** n κατευθυνόμενο βλήμα nt || **~lines** npl οδηγός.

guild [gɪld] n (old: company) συντεχνία || (society) ένωση, σωματείο || **~hall** n (Brit: town hall) δημαρχείο.

guile [gaɪl] n τέχνασμα nt, δόλος || **~less** a άδολος.

guillotine ['gɪlətiːn] n λαιμητόμος f, γκιλοτίνα.

guilt [gɪlt] n ενοχή || **~y** a ένοχος.

guise [gaɪz] n (appearance) μορφή, εμφάνιση.

guitar [gɪ'tɑː*] n κιθάρα || **~ist** n κιθαριστής.

gulf [gʌlf] n κόλπος, κόρφος || (abyss) χάσμα nt.

gull [gʌl] n γλάρος.

gullet ['gʌlɪt] n οισοφάγος.

gullible ['gʌlɪbl] a εύπιστος, αφελής.

gully ['gʌlɪ] n ρεματιά, στενό, υπόνομος.

gulp [gʌlp] vi (hastily) καταπίνω, καταβροχθίζω || (choke) κομπιάζομαι, πνίγομαι ♦ n ρουφηξιά, γουλιά.

gum [gʌm] n (of teeth) ούλο || (for sticking) γόμα, γόμμι || (for chewing) τσίχλα, μαστίχα ♦ vt κολλώ, αλείφω με γόμα || ~**boots** npl μπότες από καουτσούκ.

gun [gʌn] n (cannon) πυροβόλο, κανόνι || (rifle) τουφέκι || (revolver) πιστόλι || ~ **fire** n βολή, πύρ nt, κανονιοβολισμός || ~**man** n ληστής, κακοποιός || ~**ner** n πυροβολητής || ~**powder** n πυρίτιδα, μπαρούτι || ~**shot** n τουφεκιά, κανονιά.

gurgle ['gɜ:gl] n παφλασμός, κελάρισμα nt.

gush [gʌ] n εκροή, διάχυση, ξέσπασμα nt ♦ vi (out) εκχύνομαι, αναπηδώ || (be moved) συγκινούμαι, αναλύομαι σε.

gusset ['gʌsɪt] n (MECH) επένθεμα nt.

gust [gʌst] n ανεμορριπή, μπουρίνι.

gut [gʌt] n (intestine) έντερο, σπλάχνο || (string) χορδή || ~**s** npl θάρρος nt.

gutter ['gʌtə*] n (channel) λούκι, σούγελο || (of street) ρείθρο, χαντάκι.

guttural ['gʌtərəl] a λαρυγγικό.

guy [gai] n (NAUT) πρόδρομος, γκάγια f || (effigy) ανδρείκελο, σκιάχτρο || (man, fellow) τύπος, παιδί.

guzzle ['gʌzl] vi καταβροχθίζω, ρουφώ.

gym(nasium) [dʒɪm('neɪzɪəm)] n γυμναστήριο.

gymnast ['dʒɪmnæst] n γυμναστής || ~**ics** n γυμναστική.

gyn(a)ecologist [gaɪnɪ'kɔlədʒɪst] n γυναικολόγος.

gypsy ['dʒɪpsɪ] n = **gipsy**.

gyrate [dʒaɪ'reɪt] vi περιστρέφομαι.

H

habit ['hæbɪt] n συνήθεια, έθιμο || (dress) φόρεμα nt.

habitation [hæbɪ'teɪʃən] n κατοικία, διαμονή.

habitual [hə'bɪtjuəl] a συνήθης, συνηθισμένος || ~**ly** ad συνήθως.

hack [hæk] vt κατακόβω, πετσοκόβω ♦ n άλογο που νοικιάζεται.

hackneyed ['hæknɪd] a ξεφτελισμένος, φθαρμένος.

had [hæd] pt, pp of **have**.

haddock ['hædək] n βακαλάος.

haemorrhage, hemorrhage (US) ['hemərɪdʒ] n αιμορραγία.

haemorrhoids, hemorrhoids (US) ['hemərɔɪdz] npl αιμορροΐδες fpl.

haggard ['hægəd] a κάτωχρος, χαμένος.

haggle ['hægl] vi κάνω παζάρι.

hail [heɪl] n (meteorology) χαλάζι ♦ vt (greet) χαιρετώ ♦ vi (meteorology) ρίχνει χαλάζι || **to** ~ **from** vt προέρχομαι από || ~**stone** n κόκκος χαλάζης.

hair [hɛə*] n (general) τρίχα, μαλλιά ntpl || (one hair) τρίχα || ~**'s breadth** n παρά τρίχα || ~**brush** n βούρτσα μαλλιών || ~**cut** n κούρεμα nt|| ~**do** n κτένισμα nt|| ~**dresser** n κομμωτής/ώτρια m/f, κουρέας || ~**drier** n στεγνωτήρας || ~**net** n δίχτυ nt για τα μαλλιά || ~**oil** n λάδι για τα μαλλιά || ~**pin** n (lit) φουρκέτα || (bend) απότομη στροφή || ~**-raising** a τρομακτικός || ~**-style** n κόμμωση, χτενισιά || ~**y** a τριχωτός, μαλλιαρός.

half [hɑ:f] n μισό ♦ a μισός ♦ ad κατά το ήμισυ, μισό || ~**-breed**, ~**-caste** n μιγάδας || ~**-hearted** a

χλιαρός, με μισή καρδιά || ~-**hour** n
ημίωρο, μισή (ώρα) || ~ **penny** n
μισή πένυα || ~-**price** μισή τιμή,
μισό εισιτήριο || ~ **way** ad στο ήμισυ
της αποστάσεως, μισοστρατής.

halibut ['hælɪbət] n ιππόγλωσσος,
είδος γλώσσας.

hall [hɔ:l] n μεγάλη αίθουσα ||
(building, house) δημόσιο κτίριο ||
(dining) τραπεζαρία || (entrance)
είσοδος f, χωλ nt inv.

hallo [hə'ləʊ] excl = **hello.**

hallucination [həlu:sɪ'neɪʃən] n
παραίσθηση, αυταπάτη.

halo ['heɪləʊ] n (of saint)
φωτοστέφανος || (of sun, moon) άλως
f, αλώνι.

halt [hɔ:lt] n στάση, σταμάτημα nt ♦
vt σταματώ ♦ vi σταθμεύω,
σταματώ.

halve [hɑ:v] vt χωρίζω στα δύο,
μοιράζω.

ham [hæm] n χοιρομέρι, ζαμπό nt
inv.

hamburger ['hæmbɜ:gə*] n
μπιφτέκι από κιμά.

hamlet ['hæmlɪt] n χωριουδάκι.

hammer ['hæmə*] n σφυρί ♦ vt
κτυπώ δυνατά, σφυρηλατώ.

hammock ['hæmək] n αιάκ nt inv,
κούνια || (NAUT) αιώρα, μπράντα.

hamper ['hæmpə*] n καλάθι ♦ vt
εμποδίζω, παρακωλύω.

hand [hænd] n χέρι || (of clock)
δείκτης || (worker) εργάτης || (help)
βοήθεια ♦ vt δίνω || βοηθώ || ~ **s** npl
(NAUT) πλήρωμα nt || **to ~ down** vt
μεταβιβάζω || **to ~ over** vt
παραδίδω || **at ~** κοντά || **in ~** στη
διάθεσή μου || υπό τον έλεγχό μου ||
~ **s up** ψηλά τα χέρια || ~ **bag** n
τσάντα || ~ **book** n εγχειρίδιο ||
(guide) οδηγός || ~ **brake** n
χειρόφρενο || ~ **cuffs** npl
χειροπέδες fpl || ~ **ful** n φούχτα,
φουχτιά.

handicap ['hændɪkæp] n εμπόδιο,
μειονέκτημα nt || (SPORT) χάντικαπ nt
inv ♦ vt παρεμποδίζω, δυσχεραίνω ||
(SPORT) βάζω χάντικαπ.

handicraft ['hændɪkrɑ:ft] n
χειροτεχνία, τέχνη.

handkerchief ['hæŋkətʃɪf] n
μαντήλι.

handle ['hændl] n (of door etc)
πόμολο, (χειρο)λαβή || (of cup etc)
χερούλι || (for winding) χειρολαβή,
χερούλι ♦ vt (use, treat)
μεταχειρίζομαι || (manipulate)
χειρίζομαι || (touch) πιάνω, αγγίζω ||
(COMM) διεκπεραιώνω, διαχειρίζομαι.

hand-luggage ['hændlʌgɪdʒ] n
αποσκευές fpl του χεριού.

handmade ['hændmeɪd] a
χειροποίητος.

handsome ['hænsəm] a ωραίος,
όμορφος || (generous) σημαντικός,
γενναιόδωρος.

handwriting ['hændraɪtɪŋ] n
γραφή, γράψιμο.

handy ['hændɪ] a επιδέξιος || (useful)
βολικός, χρήσιμος.

handyman ['hændɪmən] n
πολυτεχνίτης.

hang [hæŋ] (irreg v) vt αναρτώ,
κρεμώ || (one's head) σκύβω ||
(wallpaper) κολλώ ♦ vi κρέμομαι || **to**
~ **about** vi περιφέρομαι, τριγυρίζω,
τεμπελιάζω.

hangar ['hæŋə*] n υπόστεγο.

hanger ['hæŋə*] n κρεμάστρα.

hanger-on ['hæŋər'ɒn] n
κολλιτσίδα.

hangover ['hæŋəʊvə*] n (MED)
πονοκέφαλος (από μέθυσι).

hanker ['hæŋkə*] vi: **to ~ after**
ποθώ διακαώς, λαχταρώ.

haphazard [hæp'hæzəd] a στην
τύχη, τυχαία.

happen ['hæpən] vi συμβαίνω,
τυγχάνω || ~ **ing** n συμβάν, γεγονός
nt.

happily ['hæpɪlɪ] ad ευτυχώς,

happiness

happiness ['hæpɪnɪs] n ευτυχία.

happy ['hæpɪ] a ευτυχισμένος, τυχερός, επιτυχημένος || ~**go-lucky** a ξένοιαστος.

harass ['hærəs] vt παρενοχλώ, βασανίζω.

harbour, harbor (US)['hɑːbɔ*] n λιμάνι, καταφύγιο ♦ vt στεγάζω, παρέχω άσυλο.

hard [hɑːd] a σκληρός, στερεός || (task) δύσκολος, σκληρός || (person etc) αυστηρός, αλύπητος || (work) επίπονος, σκληρός ♦ ad δυνατά, σκληρά, δύσκολα || ~ **by** κοντά || ~-**boiled** a (egg) σφικτό || (person) σκληρός || ~ **en** vi σκληραίνω || ~-**hearted** a σκληρόκαρδος, αλύπητος.

hardly [hɑːdlɪ] ad μόλις.

hardship ['hɑːdʃɪp] n κακουχία, δοκιμασία, ταλαιπωρία.

hard-up [hɑːd'ʌp] a απένταρος.

hardware ['hɑːdwɛə*] n σιδηρικά ntpl, είδη ntpl, καγκελαρίας.

hardy ['hɑːdɪ] a σκληραγωγημένος || (brave) τολμηρός, θαρραλέος.

hare [hɛə*] n λαγός.

harem [hɑː'riːm] n χαρέμι.

harm [hɑːm] n κακό, βλάβη, ζημιά ♦ vt βλάπτω, θίγω || ~**ful** a επιβλαβής, βλαβερός || ~**less** a άκακος, αβλαβής, ακίνδυνος.

harmonica [hɑː'mɒnɪkə] n φυσαρμόνικα.

harmonious [hɑː'məʊnɪəs] a αρμονικός || (MUS) μελωδικός.

harmonize ['hɑːmənaɪz] vt εναρμονίζω || (agree) συμφωνώ ♦ vi εναρμονίζομαι, ταιριάζω.

harmony ['hɑːmənɪ] n (MUS) αρμονία || (agreement) συμφωνία.

harness ['hɑːnɪs] n σαγή, χάμουρα ntpl, χαμούρωμα || n (horse) χαμούρωμα.

harp [hɑːp] n άρπα || ~**ist** n αρπιστής.

harpoon [hɑː'puːn] n καμάκι.

harrow ['hærəʊ] n βωλοκόπος, σβάρνα ♦ vt βωλοκοπώ.

harrowing ['hærəʊɪŋ] a θλιβερός, σπαρακτικός.

harsh [hɑːʃ] a σκληρός, τραχύς || ~**ly** ad σκληρά, απότομα || ~**ness** n τραχύτητα, σκληρότητα || (of taste) ξυνίλα.

harvest ['hɑːvɪst] n συγκομιδή, εσοδεία || (season) θέρος nt, εποχή θερισμού ♦ vt θερίζω, μαζεύω.

harvester ['hɑːvɪstə*] n θεριστική μηχανή.

has [hæz] see **have**.

hash [hæʃ] n κιμάς ♦ vt κατακόπτω, κάνω κιμά.

hashish ['hæʃiːʃ] n χασίς nt inv.

haste [heɪst] n βία, βιασύνη, γρηγοράδα || ~ n vi σπεύδω, επιταχύνω ♦ vi βιάζομαι, κάνω γρήγορα.

hastily ['heɪstɪlɪ] ad βιαστικά.

hasty ['heɪstɪ] a βιαστικός, οξύθυμος.

hat [hæt] n καπέλο.

hatch [hætʃ] n καταπακτή, μπουκαπόρτα ♦ vi εκκολάπτομαι, βγαίνω, σκάω ♦ vt κλωσσώ.

hatchet ['hætʃɪt] n τσεκούρι.

hate [heɪt] vt μισώ ♦ n μίσος nt || ~**ful** a μισητός.

hatred ['heɪtrɪd] n έχθρα, μίσος nt.

haughty ['hɔːtɪ] a υπεροπτικός, αυθάδης.

haul [hɔːl] n τράβηγμα nt || (fish) δίχτυά ♦ vt έλκω, τραβώ, σύρω || ~**age** n μεταφορά εμπορευμάτων.

haunch [hɔːntʃ] n ισχίο, γοφός.

haunt [hɔːnt] n καταφύγιο, στέκι ♦ vt συνχάζω σε || (of ghosts) στοιχειώνω.

have [hæv] (irreg v) vt έχω, κατέχω || (be obliged) αναγκάζω, έχω να, πρέπει να || (meal) λαμβάνω, παίρνω || (obtain) παίρνω || (children etc) γεννώ, κάνω || ~ **to** ~ **on** vt φορώ.

haven ['heɪvən] n λιμάνι || (refuge) καταφύγιο, άσυλο.

haversack ['hævəsæk] n σακκίδιο || (MIL.) γυλιός.

havoc ['hævək] n πανωλεθρία, καταστροφή.

hawk [hɔːk] n γεράκι.

hay [heɪ] n σανός, άχυρο || ~ **fever** n αλλεργικό συνάχι || ~**stack** n θημωνιά.

haywire ['haɪwaɪə*] a (col) **it's gone ~** δεν πάει καλά.

hazard ['hæzəd] n (chance) τύχη || (danger) κίνδυνος ♦ vt διακινδυνεύω, ριψοκινδυνεύω || ~**ous** a ριψοκίνδυνος.

haze [heɪz] n καταχνιά.

hazelnut ['heɪzlnʌt] n φουντούκι.

hazy ['heɪzɪ] a (weather) καταχνιασμένος || (vague) αμυδρός, αόριστος.

he [hiː] pron αυτός, εκείνος ♦ αρσενικός.

head [hɛd] n (ANAT) κεφάλι || (leader) αρχηγός, προϊστάμενος, διευθυντής || (top) άκρο ♦ a πρωτεύων, αρχηγός ♦ vt ηγούμαι, διευθύνω, διοικώ || **to ~ for** vt κινούμαι προς, κατευθύνομαι || ~**ache** n κεφαλόπονος, πονοκέφαλος || ~**ing** n επικεφαλίδα, τίτλος || ~ **lamp** n προβολέας, φανάρι || ~ **land** n ακρωτήρι || ~ **light = ~ lamp** || ~**line** n επικεφαλίδα, τίτλος || ~ **long** ad με το κεφάλι, απερίσκεπτος || ~**master** n διευθυντής σχολείου || ~**mistress** n διευθύντρια (σχολείου) || ~**-on** a κατά μέτωπο || ~**quarters (H.Q.)** npl αρχηγείο, στρατηγείο || ~**rest** n προσκέφαλο || ~**strong** a ισχυρογνώμονας, ξεροκέφαλος || ~**waiter** n αρχισερβιτόρος, μαίτρ m inv|| ~**way** n πρόοδος f|| ~**wind** n αντίθετος άνεμος, αέρας κόντρα ||

~**y** a ορμητικός, φουριόζος || (drink etc) που ζαλίζει, βαράει στο κεφάλι.

heal [hiːl] vt θεραπεύω, γιατρεύω ♦ vi επουλώνομαι, γιατρεύομαι.

health [hɛlθ] n υγεία || (toast) πρόποση || ~**y** a υγιής, εύρωστος, γερός.

heap [hiːp] n σωρός|| πλήθος nt ♦ vt γεμίζω, συσσωρεύω.

hear [hɪə*] (irreg v) vt ακούω || (learn) ακούω, μαθαίνω || ~**ing** n (sense) ακοή || (LAW) (ακροαματική) εξέταση μαρτύρων || ~**ing aid** n ακουστικά npl βαρυκοΐας || ~**say** n φήμη, διάδοση.

hearse [hɜːs] n νεκροφόρα.

heart [hɑːt] n (ANAT) καρδιά || (centre) καρδιά || (courage) θάρρος || (emotion) ψυχή || (tenderness) καρδιά, ψυχή || (CARDS) κούπα || ~**attack** n καρδιακή προσβολή || ~**beat** n παλμός καρδιάς || ~**breaking** a θλιβερός, λυπητερός || ~**broken** a περίλυπος, θλιμμένος || ~**burn** n καρδιαλγία, καούρα (στομάχου) || ~**felt** a εγκάρδιος, υκαρδιακός.

hearth [hɑːθ] n τζάκι || εστία, πυροστιά.

heartily ['hɑːtɪlɪ] ad ειλικρινά, με όρεξη, τελείως.

heartless ['hɑːtlɪs] a άκαρδος.

hearty ['hɑːtɪ] a εγκάρδιος || (healthy) εύρωστος || (meal) πλούσιος, θρεπτικός.

heat [hiːt] n θερμότητα || (weather) ζέστη, κάψα || (anger) έξαψη, οργή || (SPORT) αγώνας δρόμου, κούρσα || vt θερμαίνω, ζεσταίνω || **to ~ up** vi ανάβω, (υπερ-) θερμαίνομαι || ~**ed** a ζεστός, θερμασμένος || ~**er** n θερμάστρα, σόμπα.

heath [hiːθ] n (Brit) χέρσα γη, ρεικιά || ρείκη.

heathen ['hiːðən] n ειδωλολάτρης, εθνικός ♦ a ειδωλολατρικός.

heather ['hɛðə*] n (ε)ρείκι.

heating ['hi:tɪŋ] n θέρμανση.

heatstroke ['hi:tstrəʊk] n θερμοπληξία.

heatwave ['hi:tweɪv] n κύμα nt ζέστης, καύσωνας.

heave [hi:v] (irreg v) vt σηκώνω, ανυψώνω || (throw) ρίχνω ♦ vi ανυψούμαι || (NAUT) βιράρω ♦ n ανύψωση, σήκωμα nt || φούσκωμα nt.

heaven ['hɛvn] n ουρανός || **for ~'s sake!** για όνομα του Θεού! || **good ~s!** Θεέ μου! || ~**ly** a ουράνιος || (col) περίφημος.

heavily ['hɛvɪlɪ] ad βαρειά, δυνατά.

heavy ['hɛvɪ] a βαρύς || (difficult) δύσκολος, δύσβατος || (abundant) άφθονος.

Hebrew ['hi:bru:] n (person) Εβραίος/α m/f|| (LING) Εβραϊκά nt pl ♦ a εβραϊκός.

heckle ['hɛkl] vt βομβαρδίζω με ενοχλητικές ερωτήσεις.

hectic ['hɛktɪk] a πυρετώδης || ταραχώδης.

hedge [hɛdʒ] n φράχτης, φραγμός ♦ vt (surround) περιφράσσω, φράσσω ♦ vi υπεκφεύγω, μασώ τα λόγια μου.

hedgehog ['hɛdʒhɒg] n σκαντζόχοιρος.

heed [hi:d] vt προσέχω ♦ n προσοχή || ~**less** a απρόσεκτος, αμέριμνος.

heel [hi:l] n (of foot) φτέρνα || (of shoe) τακούνι ♦ vt (shoe) βάζω τακούνι σε.

hefty ['hɛftɪ] a δυνατός, ρωμαλέος.

heifer ['hɛfə*] n δαμάλα.

height [haɪt] n (of person) ανάστημα nt, μπόι || (of object) ύψος nt, ύψωμα nt || (of mountain) κορυφή || ~**en** vt υψώνω, αυξάνω.

heir [ɛə*] n κληρονόμος || ~**ess** n η κληρονόμος || ~**loom** n οικογενειακό κειμήλιο.

held [hɛld] pt, pp of **hold**.

helicopter ['hɛlɪkɒptə*] n ελικόπτερο.

hell [hɛl] n κόλαση.

he'll [hi:l] = **he will, he shall** || see **will, shall.**

hellish ['hɛlɪʃ] a απαίσιος, καταχθόνιος.

hello [hə'ləʊ] excl (greeting) γεια σου! || (TEL) αλλό! || (surprise) μπα, μπα!

helm [hɛlm] n τιμόνι, δοιάκι.

helmet ['hɛlmɪt] n κράνος nt, κάσκα || περικεφαλαία.

helmsman ['hɛlmzmən] n πηδαλιούχος.

help [hɛlp] n βοήθεια ♦ vt βοηθώ, ενισχύω || (prevent) αποφεύγω, εμποδίζω || (serve food) σερβίρω || ~**er** n βοηθός m/f|| ~**ful** a χρήσιμος || ~**ing** n μερίδα || ~**less** a αβοήθητος, σε αμηχανία.

hem [hɛm] n στρίφωμα nt || **to ~ in** vt περικυκλώνω, στρυμώνω.

hemisphere ['hɛmɪsfɪə*] n ημισφαίριο.

hemp [hɛmp] n κάνναβη, καννάβι.

hen [hɛn] n κότα, θηλυκό πουλί || ~**coop** n κοτέτσι.

hence [hɛns] ad αn'εδώ, από τώρα || (therefore) αn'αυτό.

henchman ['hɛntʃmən] n πιστός οπαδός, μπράβος.

her [hɜ:*] pron αυτή ♦ a δικός της.

herald ['hɛrəld] n κήρυκας, πρόδρομος ♦ vt αναγγέλλω, προμηνύω, προαγγέλλω.

heraldry ['hɛrəldrɪ] n οικοσημολογία.

herb [hɜ:b] n βότανο, χόρτο.

herd [hɜ:d] n (of cattle) αγέλη || (of animals) κοπάδι.

here [hɪə*] ad εδώ ♦ n εδώ || ~! na! || **come ~!** έλα (δω)! || ~**after** ad στο εξής ♦ n μέλλουσα ζωή || ~ **by** ad αn'αυτό, διά του παρόντος.

hereditary [hɪ'rɛdɪtrɪ] a κληρονομικός.

heredity [hɪ'redɪtɪ] n
κληρονομικότητα.

heresy ['herɪsɪ] n αίρεση.

heretic ['herɪtɪk] n αιρετικός || ~**al**
[hɪ'retɪkəl] a αιρετικός.

herewith ['hɪə'wɪð] ad με το
παρόν, μ'αυτό.

heritage ['herɪtɪdʒ] n κληρονομία.

hermit ['hɜːmɪt] n ερημίτης.

hernia ['hɜːnɪə] n κήλη.

hero ['hɪərəu] n ήρωας, παλικάρι ||
(of a story) πρωταγωνιστής || ~**ic** a
ηρωικός.

heroin ['herəuɪn] n ηρωίνη.

heroine ['herəuɪn] n ηρωίδα,
πρωταγωνίστρια.

heroism ['herəuɪzm] n ηρωισμός.

heron ['herən] n ερωδιός, τσικνιάς.

herring ['herɪŋ] n ρέγγα.

hers [hɜːz] pron αυτής, δικός της.

herself [hɜː'self] pron η ίδια, τον
εαυτό της.

he's [hiːz] = he is, he has || see
be, have.

hesitant ['hezɪtənt] a διστακτικός.

hesitate ['hezɪteɪt] vi διστάζω.

hesitation [hezɪ'teɪʃən] n
δισταγμός, ενδοιασμός.

het up ['het'ʌp] a θυμωμένος,
στενοχωρημένος.

hew [hjuː] (irreg v) vt κατακόπτω,
πελεκώ.

hexagon ['heksəgən] n εξάγωνο.

heyday ['heɪdeɪ] n ακμή, άνθος nt,
καλές μέρες fpl.

hi [haɪ] excl εί, ου! || (US) καλημέρα!,
γεια σου!

hibernate ['haɪbəneɪt] vi
διαχειμάζω.

hiccough, hiccup ['hɪkʌp] vi έχω
λόξυγγα || ~**s** npl λόξυγγας.

hid [hɪd] pt of hide.

hidden ['hɪdn] pp of hide.

hide [haɪd] n δέρμα nt, πετσί,
τομάρι ♦ vt (από) κρύβω ♦ vi
κρύβομαι || ~**-and-seek** n κρυφτό.

hideous ['hɪdɪəs] a φρικτός,
αποκρουστικός, άσχημος.

hiding ['haɪdɪŋ] n (beating) σπάσιμο
στο ξύλο || **in** ~ (concealed)
κρυμμένος || ~ **place** n κρυψώνας.

hierarchy ['haɪərɑːkɪ] n ιεραρχία.

high [haɪ] a (far up) ψηλός || (tall)
ψηλός || (rank) ανώτερος,
σπουδαίος || (class) ανώτερος ||
(price) μεγάλος, ψηλός || (pressure
etc) ψηλός, μεγάλος || (opinion)
μεγάλη εκτίμηση σε ♦ ad ψηλά,
πλούσια || ~**chair** n ψηλό
καρεκλάκι για μωρά || ~**-handed** a
αυθαίρετα || ~**-heeled** a με ψηλά
τακούνια || ~**light** n (fig)
αποκορύφωμα nt, το μεγάλο
νούμερο || ~**ly** ad εξαιρετικά, πάρα
πολύ || ~**ly strung** a ευερέθιστος,
νευρικός || **H**~ **Mass** n μεγάλη
λειτουργία (των Καθολικών) ||
~**ness** n (title) υψηλότητα || ~**-
pitched** a (voice) διαπεραστικός,
οξύς.

high school ['haɪskuːl] n γυμνάσιο.

highway ['haɪweɪ] n εθνική οδός f.

hijack ['haɪdʒæk] vt κάνω
αεροπειρατία || ~**er** n (AVIAT)
αεροπειρατής.

hike [haɪk] vi πεζοπορώ ♦ n
πεζοπορία || ~**r** n πεζοπόρος.

hiking ['haɪkɪŋ] n πεζοπορία.

hilarious [hɪ'leərɪəs] a ιλαρός,
εύθυμος.

hilarity [hɪ'lærɪtɪ] n ιλαρότητα,
ευθυμία.

hill [hɪl] n λόφος || ~**y** a λοφώδης.

hilt [hɪlt] n λαβή (ξίφους) || **up to the**
~ τελείως.

him [hɪm] pron αυτόν, σ'αυτόν.

himself [hɪm'self] pron τον εαυτό
του, (αυτός) ο ίδιος.

hind [haɪnd] a οπίσθιος ♦ n έλαφος
f.

hinder ['hɪndə*] vt εμποδίζω,
κωλύω.

hindrance ['hɪndrəns] n εμπόδιο.
Hindu ['hɪn'duː] n Ινδός/ή m/f.
hinge [hɪndʒ] n άρθρωση, μεντεσές m ♦ vt κρεμώ σε μεντεσέδες ♦ vi (fig) εξαρτώμαι.
hint [hɪnt] n νύξη, υπαινιγμός ♦ vi υπαινίσσομαι.
hip [hɪp] n ισχίο, γοφός.
hippopotamus [hɪpə'pɒtəməs] n ιπποπόταμος.
hire ['haɪə*] n μίσθωση, ενοικίαση ♦ vt (worker) μισθώνω, πληρώνω, προσλαμβάνω || (rent) ενοικιάζω | (car) νοικιάζω || **'for ~'** 'ελεύθερον', 'ενοικιάζεται' || **~ purchase (H.P.)** n με δόσεις.
his [hɪz] pron δικός του ♦ a αυτού, (δικός) του.
hiss [hɪs] n σφύριγμα nt ♦ vi αποδοκιμάζω, σφυρίζω.
historian [hɪs'tɔːrɪən] n ιστορικός.
historic(al) [hɪs'tɒrɪk(əl)] a ιστορικός.
history ['hɪstərɪ] n ιστορία.
hit [hɪt] (irreg v) n κτύπημα nt || (success) επιτυχία ♦ vt κτυπώ, πλήττω || (target) ευστοχώ.
hitch [hɪtʃ] n τίναγμα nt, τράβηγμα nt || (bend) θηλειά || (fig) εμπόδιο ♦ vt δένω, προσδένω || (jerk) τραντάζω.
hitch-hike ['hɪtʃhaɪk] vi κάνω ωτοστόπ || **~r** n αυτός που κάνει ωτοστόπ.
hive [haɪv] n κυψέλη.
H.M.S. abbr of His (Her) Majesty's Ship.
hoard [hɔːd] n θησαυρός, σωρός ♦ vt συσσωρεύω, θησαυρίζω, αποκρύπτω.
hoarding ['hɔːdɪŋ] n αποθησαυρισμός, απόκρυψη.
hoarse [hɔːs] a βραχνιασμένος.
hoax [həʊks] n αστείο, τέχνασμα nt, φάρσα.
hobble ['hɒbl] vi χωλαίνω, κουτσαίνω.
hobby ['hɒbɪ] n μεράκι, χόμπι nt inv.

hobo ['həʊbəʊ] n (US) αλήτης.
hock [hɒk] n (wine) άσπρο κρασί του Ρήνου.
hockey ['hɒkɪ] n χόκεϋ nt inv.
hoe [həʊ] n σκαλιστήρι ♦ vt σκαλίζω.
hog [hɒg] n γουρούνι.
hoist [hɔɪst] n ανελκυστήρας || τράβηγμα nt, σηκώσιμο nt ♦ vt ανυψώνω.
hold [həʊld] (irreg v) n λαβή, πιάσιμο || (influence) έχω επιρροή πάνω σε || (NAUT) αμπάρι ♦ vt (grasp) κρατώ || (keep) κρατώ, φέρω || (contain) περιέχω || (keep back) συγκρατώ, σταματώ || (meeting etc) συγκαλώ, κάνω || (title) κατέχω, έχω || **to ~ back** vt συγκρατώ || (secret) αποκρύβω || (control) αναχαιτίζω || **to ~ down** vt κρατώ || **to ~ out** vt εκτείνω || (resist) αντέχω || **to ~ up** vt (support) υποστηρίζω || (display) επιδεικνύω || (stop) σταματώ, καθυστερώ || (rob) ληστεύω ♦ vi (withstand pressure) αντέχω || **~er** n κάτοχος m/f|| (handle) λαβή, σφιγκτήρας || **~ing** n (share) μετοχή || **~up** n καθυστέρηση || (robbery) ληστεία.
hole [həʊl] n τρύπα ♦ vt τρυπώ, ανοίγω.
holiday ['hɒlɪdeɪ] n γιορτή, αργία || (annual) διακοπές fpl || **~maker** n παραθεριστής/ρια m/f.
holiness ['həʊlɪnɪs] n αγιότητα.
Holland ['hɒlənd] n Ολλανδία.
hollow ['hɒləʊ] a βαθουλός, κοίλος || (empty) κούφιος || (false) ψεύτικος ♦ n κοίλωμα nt, βαθούλωμα nt, γούβα || **to ~ out** vt βαθουλώνω, σκάβω.
holly ['hɒlɪ] n (tree) πουρνάρι.
holster ['həʊlstə*] n πιστολιοθήκη.
holy ['həʊlɪ] a άγιος, ιερός || (divine) θείος.
homage ['hɒmɪdʒ] n υποταγή.
home [həʊm] n σπίτι, κατοικία ||

(native country) πατρίδα || *(institution)*
άσυλο ♦ a *(country)* πατρίδα || *(local)*
εγχώριος, ντόπιος ♦ *ad* στο σπίτι,
στην πατρίδα || **at ~** στο σπίτι || *(at
ease)* άνετα || **~ coming** n επάνοδος
f, επαναπατρισμός || **~ less** a
άστεγος || **~-made** a σπιτήσιος,
ντόπιος || **~ sick** a νοσταλγός ||
~ ward(s) *ad* προς το σπίτι ||
~ work n κατ'οίκον εργασία.
homicide ['hɒmisaid] n *(US)*
ανθρωποκτονία.
homogeneous [hɔmə'dʒiːnios] a
ομοιογενής.
homosexual ['hɔməu'seksjuəl] a
ομοφυλόφιλος ♦ n ομοφυλόφιλος,
ανώμαλος.
honest ['ɒnist] a τίμιος, έντιμος,
ευθύς || **~ly** *ad* τίμια || **~y** n
εντιμότητα.
honey ['hʌni] n μέλι || **~ comb** n
κερήθρα || **~ moon** n μήνας του
μέλιτος.
honk [hɒŋk] n *(AUT)* κορνάρισμα nt ♦
vi κορνάρω.
honor ['ɒnə*] *(US)* = **honour.**
honorary ['ɒnərəri] a τιμητικός ||
(degree etc) επίτιμος.
honour ['ɒnə*] n τιμή, υπόληψη ♦
vt τιμώ || *(bill)* εξοφλώ, πληρώνω ||
~ s npl *(UNIV)* τίτλος, τιμητική
διάκριση || **~ able** a έντιμος || *(title)*
εντιμότατος.
hood [hud] n κουκούλα, σκούφος ||
(cover) κάλυμμα nt || *(US AUT)* καπό ||
~ wink vt εξαπατώ, κοροϊδεύω.
hoof [huːf] n οπλή, πέλμα nt, νύχι.
hook [huk] n αγκίστρι, γάντζος ♦ vt
αγκιστρώνω, γαντζώνω.
hooligan ['huːligən] n ταραχοποιός.
hoop [huːp] n στεφάνι, τσέρκι.
hoot [huːt] n *(of owl)* σκούξιμο || *(AUT)*
κορνάρισμα nt ♦ vi γιουχαΐζω,
σφυρίζω || **~ er** n *(NAUT)* σειρήνα,
σφυρίχτρα || *(AUT)* κλάξον nt inv,
κόρνα.

hop [hɒp] n χοροπήδημα nt, πήδημα
nt || vi σκιρτώ, πηδώ, χοροπηδώ.
hope [həup] n ελπίδα ♦ vt ελπίζω ||
~ ful a γεμάτος ελπίδες,
ελπιδοφόρος || **~ less** a *(without
hope)* απελπισμένος || *(useless)*
μάταιος.
hops [hɒps] npl λυκίσκος.
horde [hɔːd] n ορδή, στίφος.
horizon [hə'raizn] n ορίζοντας ||
~ tal [hɒri'zɒntl] a οριζόντιος.
hormone ['hɔːməun] n ορμόνη.
horn [hɔːn] n κέρατο || *(insect)* κεραία
|| *(MUS)* κέρας nt, κόρνα || *(AUT)*
κλάξον nt inv|| **~ ed** a με κέρατα.
hornet ['hɔːnit] n σφήκα.
horny ['hɔːni] a κεράτινος,
σκληρός.
horoscope ['hɒrəskəup] n
ωροσκόπιο.
horrible ['hɒribl] a φρικτός,
φρικώδης, απαίσιος.
horrid ['hɒrid] a φρικτός,
αποτρόπαιος || *(col)* κακός.
horrify ['hɒrifai] vt τρομάζω ||
(shock) σκανδαλίζω.
horror ['hɒrə*] n φρίκη, τρόμος.
hors d'oeuvres [ɔ'dəːvr] npl
ορεκτικά ntpl, μεζεδάκια ntpl,
ορντέβρ nt inv.
horse [hɔːs] n άλογο || **on ~ back**
καβάλα || **~ chestnut** n
αγριοκάστανο || **~ drawn** a
ιπποκίνητο || **~ power** n *(h.p.)*
ιπποδύναμη || **~ racing** n
ιπποδρομίες fpl || **~ shoe** n πέταλο.
horticulture ['hɔːtikʌltʃə] n
κηπουρική.
hose [həuz] n *(water)* σωλήνας
ποτίσματος || **~ pipe** n μάνικα,
σωλήνας.
hosiery ['həuʒəri] n πλεκτά είδη και
κάλτσες pl.
hospitable [hɒs'pitəbl] a
φιλόξενος.
hospital ['hɒspitl] n νοσοκομείο.

hospitality [hɒspɪ'tælɪtɪ] *n*
φιλοξενία.

host [həʊst] *n* οικοδεσπότης || *(hotel)*
ξενοδόχος, χανιτζής || *(large number)*
πλήθος *nt*, στρατιά.

hostage [ˈhɒstɪdʒ] *n* όμηρος.

hostel [ˈhɒstəl] *n* οικοτροφείο, χάνι.

hostess [ˈhəʊstɛs] *n* οικοδέσποινα.

hostile [ˈhɒstaɪl] *a* εχθρικός.

hostility [hɒsˈtɪlɪtɪ] *n* εχθρότητα ||
hostilities *npl* εχθροπραξίες *fpl*.

hot [hɒt] *a* θερμός, ζεστός || *(fiery)*
οξύθυμος, αναμμένος || ~ **dog** *n*
λουκάνικο || ~**-water bottle** *n*
θερμοφόρα.

hotel [həʊˈtɛl] *n* ξενοδοχείο ||
(residential) πανσιόν *f inv*.

hound [haʊnd] *n* σκυλί, λαγωνικό ♦
vt καταδιώκω, παροτρύνω.

hour [ˈaʊə*] *n* ώρα || ~**ly** *a, ad* κάθε
ώρα.

house [haʊs] *n* σπίτι, κατοικία ||
(PARL) Βουλή || *(THEAT)* θέατρο αποτρίο
♦ [haʊz] *vt* στεγάζω || *(store)*
αποθηκεύω || ~**boat** *n* πλωτό σπίτι ||
~**breaking** *n* διάρρηξη σπιτιού ||
~**hold** *n* σπίτι || οικογένεια, σπιτικό ||
~**keeper** *n* οικονόμος *m/f*||
~**keeping** *n* νοικοκυριό || ~**wife** *n*
νοικοκυρά || ~**work** *n* δουλειές του
νοικοκυριού.

housing [ˈhaʊzɪŋ] *n* στέγαση.

hovel [ˈhɒvl] *n* καλύβα.

hover [ˈhɒvə*] *vi* μετεωρίζομαι,
πλανώμαι || *(between)* διστάζω,
ταλαντεύομαι || ~**craft** *n*
χόβερκραφτ *nt inv*.

how [haʊ] *ad* πώς, με ποιο τρόπο ||
(extent) πόσο || **and** ~! *(US)* και
βέβαια!, ασφαλώς! || ~**ever** *ad* όπως
κι αν || *(much)* οσοδήποτε, όσο κι αν
|| *(yet)* ωστόσο, κι όμως.

howl [haʊl] *n* ούρλιασμα *nt*,
ουρλιαχτό ♦ *vi* ουρλιάζω, σκούζω.

howler [ˈhaʊlə*] *n* ωρυόμενος ||
(mistake) γκάφα, χοντροκοπιά.

h.p., H.P. *see* **hire; horse**.

H.Q. *abbr of* **headquarters**.

hub [hʌb] *n* *(of wheel)* αφαλός || *(of
activity)* κέντρο.

hubbub [ˈhʌbʌb] *n* φασαρία,
θόρυβος, οχλοβοή.

huddle [ˈhʌdl] *n* σωρός, κουβάρι ♦
vi συσσωρεύω, μαζεύομαι,
κουλουριάζομαι.

hue [hjuː] *n* χροιά, χρώμα,
απόχρωση.

huff [hʌf] *n* παραφορά, θυμός.

hug [hʌg] *n* αγκάλιασμα *nt* ♦ *vt*
αγκαλιάζω, σφίγγω || *(NAUT)* **to** ~
the shore παραπλέω, πλέω
πλάι-πλάι στην ακτή.

huge [hjuːdʒ] *a* πελώριος, θεόρατος,
τεράτιος.

hulk [hʌlk] *n* *(NAUT)* ξαρματωμένο
πλοίο, σαπιοκάραβο || *(person)*
μπατάλης, χοντράνθρωπος || ~**ing**
a δυσκίνητος, χοντρός, βαρύς.

hull [hʌl] *n* σκάφος *nt*, κουφάρι
πλοίου.

hullo [həˈləʊ] *excl* = **hello**.

hum [hʌm] *n* βόμβος, βουητό,
ψίθυρος ♦ *vi* βουίζω, ψιθυρίζω ||
μουρμουρίζω.

human [ˈhjuːmən] *a* ανθρώπινος ♦
n άνθρωπος.

humane [hjuːˈmeɪn] *a*
ανθρωπιστικός, φιλάνθρωπος.

humanity [hjuːˈmænɪtɪ] *n*
ανθρωπότητα || *(kindness)*
φιλανθρωπία.

humble [ˈhʌmbl] *a* ταπεινός, απλός
|| *(unimportant)* ασήμαντος ♦ *vt*
ταπεινώνω, ξευτελίζω.

humbly [ˈhʌmblɪ] *ad* ταπεινά, απλά.

humdrum [ˈhʌmdrʌm] *a*
μονότονος, ανιαρός, πληκτικός.

humid [ˈhjuːmɪd] *a* υγρός, νοτερός
|| ~**ity** *n* υγρασία, νότισμα *nt*.

humiliate [hjuːˈmɪlɪeɪt] *vt*
ταπεινώνω, ξευτελίζω, κουρελιάζω.

humiliation [hjuːˈmɪlɪˈeɪʃən] n ταπείνωση, κουρέλιασμα nt.

humility [hjuːˈmɪlɪtɪ] n ταπεινότητα, μετριοφροσύνη.

humor [ˈhjuːmə*] (US) = **humour**.

humorist [ˈhjuːmərɪst] n χιουμορίστας.

humorous [ˈhjuːmərəs] a γεμάτος χιούμορ, εύθυμος.

humour [ˈhjuːmə*] n χιούμορ nt inv, κέφι, διάθεση ♦ vt κάνω τα χατήρια, κάνω τα κέφια.

hump [hʌmp] n καμπούρα.

hunch [hʌntʃ] n ύβος, καμπούρα || (suspicion) υποψία ♦ vt κυρτώνω, καμπουριάζω || ~**back** n καμπούρης/α m/f.

hundred [ˈhʌndrɪd] num, n εκατό || ~**weight** n (weight = 112 pounds) στατήρας.

hung [hʌŋ] pt, pp of **hang**.

Hungarian [hʌŋˈɡɛərɪən] a ουγγρικός ♦ n (person) Ούγγρος/Ουγγαρέζα m/f || (LING) (τα) Ουγγρικά.

Hungary [ˈhʌŋɡərɪ] n Ουγγαρία.

hunger [ˈhʌŋɡə*] n πείνα || (desire) σφοδρή επιθυμία ♦ vi: να πεινώ λαχταρώ.

hungrily [ˈhʌŋɡrɪlɪ] ad άπληστα, αχόρταγα, πεινασμένα.

hungry [ˈhʌŋɡrɪ] a πεινασμένος.

hunt [hʌnt] n hunting ♦ (seeking) αναζήτηση ♦ vt κυνηγώ || (search) διώκνω ♦ vi κυνηγώ || (seek) ψάχνω || ~**er** n κυνηγός || ~**ing** n κυνήγι.

hurdle [ˈhɜːdl] n (lit) φράκτης || (fig) εμπόδιο.

hurl [hɜːl] vt εκσφενδονίζω, ρίχνω.

hurrah [huˈrɑː] n, **hurray** [huˈreɪ] n ζητωκραυγή.

hurricane [ˈhʌrɪkən] n καταιγίδα, λαίλαπας.

hurried [ˈhʌrɪd] a βιαστικός || ~**ly** ad βιαστικά.

hurry [ˈhʌrɪ] n βία, βιασύνη ♦ vi

βιάζομαι, είμαι βιαστικός ♦ vt επισπεύδω, βιάζω.

hurt [hɜːt] (irreg v) n κακό || (wound) τραύμα nt, πληγή || (damage) βλάβη, ζημιά ♦ vt κτυπώ, τραυματίζω, πληγώνω || (insult) προσβάλλω, πειράζω ♦ vi πονώ, θίγομαι || ~**ful** a βλαβερός.

hurtle [ˈhɜːtl] vt εκσφενδονίζω ♦ vi (rush) εφορμώ, ρίχνομαι.

husband [ˈhʌzbənd] n άνδρας, σύζυγος.

hush [hʌʃ] n σιωπή, σιγή ♦ vt (καθ)ησυχάζω ♦ vi σωπαίνω || ~! σιωπή!, σούτ!

husk [hʌsk] n φλοιός, φλούδα, τσόφλι.

husky [ˈhʌskɪ] a (voice) βραχνός || γεροδεμένος ♦ n σκύλος ελκύθρου.

hustle [ˈhʌsl] n σπουδή, βιασύνη || (push) σπρωξίδι ♦ vt (push) σπρώχνω || σκουντώ, βιάζω.

hut [hʌt] n καλύβα || (MIL) παράπηγμα nt.

hutch [hʌtʃ] n κλουβ.

hyacinth [ˈhaɪəsɪnθ] n υάκινθος.

hybrid [ˈhaɪbrɪd] n μιγάδας, μικτογενής, νόθος ♦ a νόθος, μπασταρδεμένος.

hydrant [ˈhaɪdrənt] n σωλήνας πυρκαϊάς, στόμιο υδρολημψίας.

hydraulic [haɪˈdrɔːlɪk] a υδραυλικός.

hydroelectric [ˈhaɪdrəʊɪˈlɛktrɪk] a υδροηλεκτρικός.

hydrogen [ˈhaɪdrədʒən] n υδρογόνο.

hyena [haɪˈiːnə] n ύαινα.

hygiene [ˈhaɪdʒiːn] n υγιεινή.

hygienic [haɪˈdʒiːnɪk] a υγιεινός.

hymn [hɪm] n ύμνος, υμνωδία.

hyphen [ˈhaɪfən] n ενωτικό σημείο.

hypnosis [hɪpˈnəʊsɪs] n ύπνωση.

hypnotism [ˈhɪpnətɪzəm] n υπνωτισμός.

hypnotist [ˈhɪpnətɪst] n υπνωτιστής.

hypnotize ['hipnətaiz] *vt* υπνωτίζω.
hypocrisy [hi'pɒkrisi] *n* υποκρισία.
hypocrite ['hipɒkrit] *n* υποκριτής.
hypocritical [hipɒ'kritikl] *a* υποκριτικός.
hypothesis [hai'pɒθisis] *n* υπόθεση.
hypothetic(al) [haipɒ'θetik(əl)] *a* υποθετικός.
hysteria [his'tiəriə] *n* υστερία.
hysterical [his'tcrikl] *a* υστερικός.
hysterics [his'tcriks] *npl* υστερία.

I

I [ai] *pron* εγώ.
ice [ais] *n* πάγος || *(refreshment)* παγωτό ♦ *vt (cake)* γκλασάρω ▲ *vi (also ~ up)* παγώνω || ~ **axe** *n* πέλεκυς *m* πάγου || ~**berg** *n* παγόβουνο || ~**box** *n (US)* ψυγείο || ~ **cream** *n* παγωτό || ~-**cold** *a* παγερός, παγωμένος || ~ **hockey** *n* χόκεϊ στον πάγο.
icicle ['aisikl] *n* σταλακτίτης πάγου.
icing ['aisiŋ] *n* κρούστα για κέικ, γκλασάρισμα *nt*.
icon ['aikɒn] *n* εικόνα.
icy ['aisi] *a (slippery)* γλιστερός || *(frozen)* παγωμένος, παγωμένος.
I'd [aid] = **I would, I had** || *see* **would, have.**
idea [ai'diə] *n* ιδέα || *(plan)* σκοπός, ιδέα.
ideal [ai'diəl] *n* ιδανικό, ιδεώδες *nt* ♦ *a* ιδανικός, ιδεώδης || ~**ist** *n* ιδεαλιστής.
identical [ai'dentikəl] *a* όμοιος, ίδιος, απαράλλακτος.
identification [aidentifi'keiʃən] *n* εξακρίβωση ταυτότητας, συντάυτιση.
identify [ai'dentifai] *vt (person)* διαπιστώνω, εξακριβώνω || *(regard as same)* ταυτίζω.

identity [ai'dentiti] *n* ταυτότητα.
ideology [aidi'ɒlədʒi] *n* ιδεολογία.
idiocy ['idiəsi] *n* ηλιθιότητα.
idiom ['idiəm] *n* ιδίωμα *nt* || *(dialect)* διάλεκτος.
idiosyncrasy [idiə'siŋkrəsi] *n* ιδιοσυγκρασία.
idiot ['idiət] *n* ηλίθιος, ανόητος || ~**ic** [idi'ɒtik] *a* ηλίθιος.
idle ['aidl] *a* αργός || *(lazy)* οκνηρός, τεμπέλης || *(useless)* μάταιος, ανωφελής || ~**ness** *n* αργία, τεμπελιά || ~**r** *n* αργόσχολος.
idol ['aidl] *n* είδωλο || ~**ize** *vt* λατρεύω, θαυμάζω.
idyllic [i'dilik] *a* ειδυλλιακός.
i.e. *ad (abbr of id est)* δηλ. (δηλαδή).
if [if] *cj (condition)* εάν, αν, όταν || *(whether)* αν.
ignite [ig'nait] *vt* αναφλέγω, ανάβω.
ignition [ig'niʃən] *n* ανάφλεξη || ~ **key** *n (AUT)* κλειδί (ξεκινήσεως).
ignorance ['ignərəns] *n* άγνοια.
ignorant ['ignərənt] *a* αμαθής, αγνών.
ignore [ig'nɔː] *vt* αγνοώ, αψηφώ.
I'll [ail] = **I will, I shall** || *see* **will, shall.**
ill [il] *a* άρρωστος || *(evil)* κακός ♦ *n* κακό, ατυχία || ~-**advised** *a* ασύνετος, απερίσκεπτος || ~-**at-ease** *a* στενοχωρημένος, ανήσυχος.
illegal [i'liːgəl] *a* παράνομος || ~**ly** *ad* παράνομα.
illegible [i'lcdʒəbl] *a* δυσανάγνωστος.
illegitimate [ili'dʒitimit] *a* νόθος.
ill-fated ['il'feitid] *a* κακότυχος.
ill-feeling ['il'fiːliŋ] *n* κακία, έχθρα.
illicit [i'lisit] *a* παράνομος, αθέμιτος.
illiterate [i'litərit] *a* αγράμματος.
ill-mannered ['il'mænəd] *a* κακότροπος, κακομαθημένος.

illness ['ɪlnɪs] n ασθένεια, αρρώστεια.

illogical [ɪ'lɒdʒɪkəl] a παράλογος.

ill-treat ['ɪl'triːt] vt κακομεταχειρίζομαι.

illuminate [ɪ'luːmɪneɪt] vt φωτίζω, φωταγωγώ.

illumination [ɪluːmɪ'neɪʃən] n φωτισμός, φωταγώγηση.

illusion [ɪ'luːʒən] n αυταπάτη, πλάνη.

illusive [ɪ'luːsɪv] a, **illusory** [ɪ'luːsərɪ] a απατηλός.

illustrate ['ɪləstreɪt] vt εικονογραφώ.

illustration [ɪləs'treɪʃən] n εικονογράφηση, εικόνα.

illustrious [ɪ'lʌstrɪəs] a ένδοξος, επιφανής.

ill will ['ɪl'wɪl] n κακοβουλία, κακία.

I'm [aɪm] = **I am** || *see* be.

image ['ɪmɪdʒ] n *(statue)* εικόνα, είδωλο || *(likeness)* ομοίωμα nt, αναπαράσταση || *(reflection)* είδωλο || ~**ry** n ρητορικά σχήματα ntpl.

imaginable [ɪ'mædʒɪnəbl] a διανοητός.

imaginary [ɪ'mædʒɪnərɪ] a φανταστικός.

imagination [ɪmædʒɪ'neɪʃən] n φαντασία.

imaginative [ɪ'mædʒɪnətɪv] a ευφάνταστος, επινοητικός.

imagine [ɪ'mædʒɪn] vt φαντάζομαι, διανοούμαι.

imbalance [ɪm'bæləns] n ανισότητα, ανισορροπία.

imbecile ['ɪmbəsiːl] n βλάκας, ηλίθιος.

imbue [ɪm'bjuː] vt (εμ)ποτίζω, διαποτίζω.

imitate ['ɪmɪteɪt] vt μιμούμαι, αντιγράφω.

imitation [ɪmɪ'teɪʃən] n (απο)μίμηση.

imitator ['ɪmɪteɪtə*] n μιμητής.

immaculate [ɪ'mækjʊlɪt] a άσπιλος, άψογος.

immaterial [ɪmə'tɪərɪəl] a ασήμαντος, άυλος.

immature [ɪmə'tjʊə*] a ανώριμος, άγουρος.

immediate [ɪ'miːdɪət] a *(near)* άμεσος, προσεχής || *(present)* επείγων, άμεσος || *(not separated)* πλησιέστερος || *(instant)* άμεσος, στιγμιαίος || ~**ly** ad *(at once)* αμέσως, στη στιγμή.

immense [ɪ'mɛns] a απέραντος, άπειρος || ~**ly** ad απέραντα.

immerse [ɪ'mɜːs] vt εμβαπτίζω, βυθίζω, βουτώ.

immigrant ['ɪmɪgrənt] n μετανάστης.

immigration [ɪmɪ'greɪʃən] n μετανάστευση.

imminent ['ɪmɪnənt] a επικείμενος, άμεσος.

immobilize [ɪ'məʊbɪlaɪz] vt ακινητοποιώ.

immoral [ɪ'mɒrəl] a ανήθικος, κακοήθης || ~**ity** [ɪmə'rælɪt] n ανηθικότητα.

immortal [ɪ'mɔːtl] a αθάνατος, άφθαρτος ♦ n αθάνατος || ~**ize** vt αποθανατίζω.

immune [ɪ'mjuːn] a απρόσβλητος.

immunize ['ɪmjʊnaɪz] vt ανοσοποιώ.

impact [ɪm'pækt] n *(lit)* σύγκρουση, κτύπημα nt|| *(fig)* επίδραση.

impair [ɪm'pɛə*] vt βλάπτω, εξασθενίζω.

impale [ɪm'peɪl] vt ανασκολοπίζω, παλουκώνω.

impartial [ɪm'pɑːʃl] a αμερόληπτος || ~**ity** n αμεροληψία.

impassable [ɪm'pɑːsəbl] a αδιάβατος.

impatience [ɪm'peɪʃəns] n ανυπομονησία.

impatient [ɪm'peɪʃənt] a

ανυπόμονος || ~ ly ad ανυπόμονα,
βιαστικά.

impeccable [ɪmˈpɛkəbl] a άψογος,
τέλειος.

impede [ɪmˈpiːd] vt εμποδίζω,
παρακωλύω.

impediment [ɪmˈpɛdɪmənt] n
κώλυμα nt, εμπόδιο.

impending [ɪmˈpɛndɪŋ] a
επικείμενος.

imperative [ɪmˈpɛrətɪv] a
επιτακτικός ♦ n (GRAM) προστακτική.

imperceptible [ɪmpəˈsɛptəbl] a
ανεπαίσθητος, αδιόρατος.

imperfect [ɪmˈpɜːfɪkt] a
ελαττωματικός || (incomplete)
ελλειπής || ~ ion n ατέλεια,
ελάττωμα nt.

imperial [ɪmˈpɪərɪəl] a
αυτοκρατορικός || (majestic)
μεγαλοπρεπής.

impersonal [ɪmˈpɜːsnl] a
απρόσωπος.

impersonate [ɪmˈpɜːsəneɪt] vt
προσωποποιώ, υποδύομαι,
παριστάνω.

impersonation [ɪmpɜːsəˈneɪʃən] n
προσωποποίηση, ενσάρκωση,
μίμηση.

impertinent [ɪmˈpɜːtɪnənt] a
αυθάδης, άσχετος.

impervious [ɪmˈpɜːvɪəs] a
αδιαπέραστος, στεγανός,
ανεπηρέαστος.

impetuous [ɪmˈpɛtjuəs] a
ορμητικός, βίαιος.

impetus [ˈɪmpɪtəs] n ώθηση, ορμή.

impinge [ɪmˈpɪndʒ]: **to ~ on** vt
συγκρούομαι, καταπατώ.

implausible [ɪmˈplɔːzəbl] a
απίθανος.

implement [ˈɪmplɪmənt] n όργανο,
εργαλείο, σύνεργο ♦ [ˈɪmplɪmɛnt] vt
εφαρμόζω.

implicate [ˈɪmplɪkeɪt] vt εμπλέκω,
αναμιγνύω.

implication [ɪmplɪˈkeɪʃən] n
ενοχοποίηση, υπαινιγμός.

implicit [ɪmˈplɪsɪt] a
υπονοούμενος, σιωπηρός ||
(complete) απόλυτος, αμέριστος.

implore [ɪmˈplɔː*] vt ικετεύω,
εκλιπαρώ.

imply [ɪmˈplaɪ] vt υπονοώ,
υπαινίσσομαι, προϋποβέτω.

impolite [ɪmpəˈlaɪt] a αγενής.

imponderable [ɪmˈpɒndərəbl] a
αστάθμητος, ανεξιχνίαστος.

import [ɪmˈpɔːt] vt εισάγω ♦
[ˈɪmpɔːt] n εισαγωγή || (meaning)
σημασία.

importance [ɪmˈpɔːtəns] n
σπουδαιότητα, σοβαρότητα || (value)
σημασία, αξία.

important [ɪmˈpɔːtənt] a
σημαντικός, σπουδαίος.

importer [ɪmˈpɔːtə*] n εισαγωγέας.

impose [ɪmˈpəuz] vt επιβάλλω,
επιτάσσω || (on s.o.) εκμεταλλεύομαι.

imposing [ɪmˈpəuzɪŋ] a
επιβλητικός.

impossibility [ɪmpɒsəˈbɪlɪti] n (το)
αδύνατο.

impossible [ɪmˈpɒsəbl] a
αδύνατος, ακατόρθωτος,
ανυπόφορος.

impostor [ɪmˈpɒstə*] n αγύρτης,
απατεώνας.

impotence [ˈɪmpətəns] n (esp
sexual) ανικανότητα.

impotent [ˈɪmpətənt] a ανίκανος,
ανίσχυρος.

impound [ɪmˈpaund] vt κατάσχω.

impoverished [ɪmˈpɒvərɪʃt] a
πάμπτωχος, εξαντλημένος.

impracticable [ɪmˈpræktɪkəbl] a
ακατόρθωτος, απραγματοποίητος.

impractical [ɪmˈpræktɪkəl] a μη
πρακτικός.

impregnable [ɪmˈprɛgnəbl] a
απόρθητος.

impregnate ['ɪmprɛgneɪt] vt
γονιμοποιώ, εμποτίζω.

impress [ɪm'prɛs] vt (influence)
κάνω εντύπωση || (imprint)
εντυπώνω, εγχαράσσω.

impression [ɪm'prɛʃən] n (mark)
αποτύπωση, αποτύπωμα nt || (printed
copy) έκδοση || (effect) εντύπωση,
αίσθηση || (belief) ιδέα, εντύπωση,
γνώμη || ~**able** α ευαίσθητος,
ευσυγκίνητος || ~**ist** n
ιμπρεσσιονιστής.

impressive [ɪm'prɛsɪv] a
εντυπωσιακός, συγκινητικός.

imprison [ɪm'prɪzn] vt φυλακίζω ||
~**ment** n φυλάκιση.

improbable [ɪm'prɒbəbl] a
απίθανος.

impromptu [ɪm'prɒmptjuː] a
αυτοσχέδιος, εκ του προχείρου ♦ ad
εκ του προχείρου.

improper [ɪm'prɒpə*] a (wrong)
εσφαλμένος || (unsuitable)
ανάρμοστος || (indecent) απρεπής.

impropriety [ɪmprə'praɪətɪ] n
απρέπεια, ακαταλληλότητα.

improve [ɪm'pruːv] vt βελτιώνω,
κάνω καλύτερο ♦ vi (become better)
βελτιούμαι, καλυτερεύω || ~**ment** n
βελτίωση, πρόοδος f.

improvisation [ɪmprəvaɪ'zeɪʃən] n
αυτοσχεδιασμός.

improvise ['ɪmprəvaɪz] vi
αυτοσχεδιάζω || vt κάνω εκ του
προχείρου.

impudent ['ɪmpjudənt] a αναιδής,
αναίσχυντος.

impulse ['ɪmpʌls] n (sudden desire)
ορμή, ορμέμφυτο || ώθηση,
αυθόρμητη διάθεση.

impulsive [ɪm'pʌlsɪv] a
αυθόρμητος, ορμέμφυτος.

impunity [ɪm'pjuːnɪtɪ] n
ατιμωρησία.

impure [ɪm'pjuə*] a ακάθαρτος ||
(bad) μιαρός, αισχρός.

impurity [ɪm'pjuərɪtɪ] n ακαθαρσία,
ξένο σώμα nt.

in [ɪn] prep μέσα σε, εντός, σε || (made
of) σε || (expressed in) σε, με || (dressed
in) με ♦ ad εντός, μέσα || ~**s and
outs** npl τα μέσα και τα έξω.

in., ins abbr of **inch(es).**

inability [ɪnə'bɪlɪtɪ] n ανικανότητα,
αδυναμία.

inaccessible [ɪnæk'sɛsəbl] a
απρόσιτος, απλησίαστος.

inaccuracy [ɪn'ækjʊrəsɪ] n
ανακρίβεια.

inaccurate [ɪn'ækjʊrɪt] a
ανακριβής, εσφαλμένος.

inactivity [ɪnæk'tɪvɪtɪ] n αδράνεια,
αργία.

inadequacy [ɪn'ædɪkwəsɪ] n
ανεπάρκεια, ατέλεια.

inadequate [ɪn'ædɪkwɪt] a
ανεπαρκής, ατελής.

inadvertently [ɪnəd'vəːtəntlɪ] ad
απρόσεκτα, από αμέλεια.

inadvisable [ɪnəd'vaɪzəbl] a
ασύμφορος.

inane [ɪ'neɪn] a κενός, ανόητος.

inanimate [ɪn'ænɪmɪt] a άψυχος.

inappropriate [ɪnə'prəʊprɪɪt] a
ακατάλληλος, ανάρμοστος.

inapt [ɪn'æpt] a ανεπιτήδειος,
αδέξιος || ~**itude** n ανικανότητα,
αδεξιότητα.

inarticulate [ɪnɑː'tɪkjʊlɪt] a
άναρθρος, βουβός, ασύνδετος.

inasmuch [ɪnəz'mʌtʃ]: ~ **as** ad
επειδή, εφόσον.

inattention [ɪnə'tɛnʃən] n
απροσεξία, αφηρημάδα.

inattentive [ɪnə'tɛntɪv] a
απρόσεκτος, αμελής.

inaudible [ɪn'ɔːdəbl] a
ανεπαίσθητος, ασθενής.

inaugural [ɪ'nɔːgjʊrəl] a
εναρκτήριος.

inaugurate [ɪ'nɔːgjʊreɪt] vt
εγκαινιάζω.

inauguration [ɪnɔːgjuˈreɪʃən] n εγκαινιασμός, εγκαίνια ntpl.

inborn [ˈɪnˈbɔːn] a έμφυτος.

inbred [ˈɪnˈbrɛd] a έμφυτος, φυσικός.

Inc. abbr see **incorporated.**

incapability [ɪnkeɪpəˈbɪlɪtɪ] n ανικανότητα.

incapable [ɪnˈkeɪpəbl] a ανίκανος.

incapacitate [ɪnkəˈpæsɪteɪt] vt καθιστώ ανίκανο.

incarnate [ɪnˈkaːnɪt] a ενσαρκωμένος.

incarnation [ɪnkaːˈneɪʃən] n ενσάρκωση.

incendiary [ɪnˈsɛndɪərɪ] a εμπρηστικός ♦ n εμπρηστής.

incense [ˈɪnsɛns] n θυμίαμα nt, λιβάνι ♦ [ɪnˈsɛns] vt εξοργίζω, εξαγριώνω.

incentive [ɪnˈsɛntɪv] n κίνητρο, ελατήριο, τονωτικό.

incessant [ɪnˈsɛsnt] a αδιάκοπος || ~ly ad αδιάκοπα.

incest [ˈɪnsɛst] n αιμομιξία.

inch [ɪntʃ] n ίντσα (.0254 μ.).

incidence [ˈɪnsɪdəns] n πρόσπτωση, περίπτωση.

incident [ˈɪnsɪdənt] n επεισόδιο, περιπέτεια || ~al a τυχαίος, συμπτωματικός || ~ally ad παρεπιπτόντως.

incinerate [ɪnˈsɪnəreɪt*] n αποτεφρωτήρας.

incision [ɪnˈsɪʒən] n εντομή, χαραματιά.

incisive [ɪnˈsaɪsɪv] a κοφτερός || (cutting) δηκτικός.

incite [ɪnˈsaɪt] vt υποκινώ, παροτρύνω.

inclination [ɪnklɪˈneɪʃən] n κλίση, τάση, διάθεση.

incline [ˈɪnklaɪn] n κλίση ♦ [ɪnˈklaɪn] vi κλίνω, γέρνω || (be disposed) ρέπω, τείνω.

include [ɪnˈkluːd] vt (συμ)περιλαμβάνω, περιέχω.

inclusion [ɪnˈkluːʒən] n συμπερίληψη.

inclusive [ɪnˈkluːsɪv] a συμπεριλαμβάνων, περιέχων.

incognito [ɪnˈkɒgnɪtəu] ad ινκόγνιτο.

incoherent [ɪnkəuˈhɪərənt] a ασυνάρτητος.

income [ˈɪnkʌm] n εισόδημα nt || ~ tax n φόρος εισοδήματος.

incoming [ˈɪnkʌmɪŋ] a (tide) ανερχόμενος, εισερχόμενος.

incompatible [ɪnkəmˈpætəbl] a ασυμβίβαστος.

incompetence [ɪnˈkɒmpɪtəns] n αναρμοδιότητα, ανικανότητα

incompetent [ɪnˈkɒmpɪtənt] a ανίκανος, αναρμόδιος.

incomplete [ɪnkəmˈpliːt] a ατελής.

incomprehensible [ɪnkɒmprɪˈhɛnsəbl] a ακατανόητος, ακατάληπτος.

inconclusive [ɪnkənˈkluːsɪv] a μη πειστικός.

incongruous [ɪnˈkɒŋgruəs] a ασύμφωνος, ανάρμοστος.

inconsequential [ɪnkɒnsɪˈkwɛnʃəl] a ανακόλουθος, ασήμαντος.

inconsiderate [ɪnkənˈsɪdərɪt] a απερίσκεπτος, αδιάκριτος.

inconsistent [ɪnkənˈsɪstənt] a ασυνεπής, αντιφατικός.

inconspicuous [ɪnkənˈspɪkjuəs] a αφανής, απαρατήρητος.

inconstant [ɪnˈkɒnstənt] a ευμετάβολος, ασταθής.

incontinent [ɪnˈkɒntɪnənt] a ακρατής.

inconvenience [ɪnkənˈviːnɪəns] n δυσχέρεια, ενόχληση, μπελάς.

inconvenient [ɪnkənˈviːnɪənt] a στενόχωρος, ενοχλητικός, ακατάλληλος.

incorporate [ɪn'kɔːpəreɪt] vt
ενσωματώνω, συγχωνεύω.
incorporated [ɪn'kɔːpəreɪtɪd] a
ενσωματωμένος, συγχωνευμένος ||
~ **company** (US, abbr **Inc.**)
ανώνυμος (εταιρεία).
incorrect [ɪnkə'rekt] a
εσφαλμένος, ανακριβής.
incorruptible [ɪnkə'rʌptɪbl] a
αδιάφθορος, ακέραιος, αδέκαστος.
increase ['ɪnkriːs] n αύξηση ♦
[ɪn'kriːs] vt αυξάνω, μεγαλώνω ♦ vi
αυξάνομαι.
increasingly [ɪn'kriːsɪŋlɪ] ad
διαρκώς περισσότερο.
incredible [ɪn'kredəbl] a
απίστευτος.
incredulous [ɪn'kredjuləs] a
δύσπιστος.
increment ['ɪnkrɪmənt] n αύξηση.
incriminate [ɪn'krɪmɪneɪt] vt
ενοχοποιώ.
incubation [ɪnkju'beɪʃən] n
επώαση, κλώσημα nt.
incubator ['ɪnkjubeɪtə*] n
κλωσσομηχανή.
incur [ɪn'kɜː*] vt υφίσταμαι,
διατρέχω, προκαλώ.
incurable [ɪn'kjuərəbl] a ανίατος,
αγιάτρευτος.
incursion [ɪn'kɜːʃən] n επιδρομή.
indebted [ɪn'detɪd] a
υποχρεωμένος, υπόχρεος.
indecent [ɪn'diːsnt] a απρεπής,
άσεμνος.
indecision [ɪndɪ'sɪʒən] n
αναποφασιστικότητα, αοριστία.
indecisive [ɪndɪ'saɪsɪv] a μή
αποφασιστικός.
indeed [ɪn'diːd] ad πράγματι,
πραγματικά, αληθινά.
indefinable [ɪndɪ'faɪnəbl] a
απροσδιόριστος.
indefinite [ɪn'defɪnɪt] a αόριστος ||
~ **ly** ad επ'αόριστον.
indelible [ɪn'delɪbl] a ανεξίτηλος.

indemnify [ɪn'demnɪfaɪ] vt
αποζημιώνω, εξασφαλίζω.
indentation [ɪnden'teɪʃən] n
(typing) οδόντωση, χάραγμα nt.
independence [ɪndɪ'pendəns] n
ανεξαρτησία.
independent [ɪndɪ'pendənt] a
ανεξάρτητος.
indescribable [ɪndɪs'kraɪbəbl] a
απερίγραπτος.
index ['ɪndeks] n ευρετήριο || ~
finger n δείκτης.
India ['ɪndɪə] n Ινδία || ~ **n** a
Ινδός/Ινδή m/f || (of America)
ερυθρόδερμος ♦ a ινδικός,
ινδιάνικος.
indicate ['ɪndɪkeɪt] vt δεικνύω,
εμφαίνω, έδηλω.
indication [ɪndɪ'keɪʃən] n ένδειξη,
σημείο.
indicative [ɪn'dɪkətɪv] a (GRAM)
οριστική (έγκλιση).
indicator ['ɪndɪkeɪtə*] n (sign)
δείκτης.
indict [ɪn'daɪt] vt μηνύω, ενάγω,
κατηγγέλλω || ~**able** a ενακτέος ||
~**ment** n μήνυση, κατηγορία.
indifference [ɪn'dɪfrəns] n
αδιαφορία.
indifferent [ɪn'dɪfrənt] a (not
caring) αδιάφορος || (unimportant)
αδιάφορος || (neither good nor bad)
συνηθισμένος, έτσι κι έτσι ||
(moderate) μέτριος, ουδέτερος ||
(impartial) αμερόληπτος.
indigenous [ɪn'dɪdʒɪnəs] a γηγενής,
ιθαγενής, ντόπιος.
indigestible [ɪndɪ'dʒestɪbl] a
δυσκολοχώνευτος.
indigestion [ɪndɪ'dʒestʃən] n
δυσπεψία.
indignant [ɪn'dɪgnənt] a
αγανακτισμένος.
indignation [ɪndɪg'neɪʃən] n
αγανάκτηση.

indignity [ɪn'dɪgnɪtɪ] n προσβολή, ταπείνωση.

indirect [ɪndɪ'rɛkt] a πλάγιος, έμμεσος || ~**ly** ad έμμεσα.

indiscreet [ɪndɪs'kriːt] a αδιάκριτος, απρόσεκτος.

indiscretion [ɪndɪs'krɛʃən] n αδιακρισία, ακριτομύθια.

indiscriminate [ɪndɪs'krɪmɪnɪt] a χωρίς διακρίσεις, τυφλός.

indispensable [ɪndɪs'pɛnsəbl] a απαραίτητος.

indisposed [ɪndɪs'pəuzd] a αδιάθετος, απρόθυμος.

indisputable [ɪndɪs'pjuːtəbl] a αναμφισβήτητος, αναμφίβολος.

indistinct [ɪndɪs'tɪŋkt] a αδιόρατος, συγκεχυμένος, αμυδρός.

individual [ɪndɪ'vɪdjuəl] n άτομο, πρόσωπο ♦ a ιδιαίτερος, ατομικός || ~**ist** n ατομικιστής || ~**ity** n ατομικότητα, προσωπικότητα.

indoctrinate [ɪn'dɒktrɪneɪt] vt διδάσκω, κατηχώ, εμποτίζω.

indoctrination [ɪndɒktrɪ'neɪʃən] n εμποτισμός, διδασκαλία.

indolent ['ɪndələnt] a νωθρός, τεμπέλης.

Indonesia [ɪndəu'niːzɪə] n Ινδονησία || ~**n** a n Ινδονήσιος, ο ♦ a ινδουησιακός.

indoor ['ɪndɔː*] a του σπιτιού, εσωτερικός || ~**s** ad μέσα στο κτίριο.

indubitable [ɪn'djuːbɪtəbl] a αναμφίβολος, βέβαιος.

induce [ɪn'djuːs] vt πείθω, προτρέπω, προκαλώ || ~**ment** n προτροπή, κίνητρο.

indulge [ɪn'dʌldʒ] vt ικανοποιώ || *(allow pleasure)* εντρυφώ, παραδίδομαι || ~**nce** n επιείκια, διασκέδαση, εντρύφηση || ~**nt** a επιεικής, συγκαταβατικός.

industrial [ɪn'dʌstrɪəl] a

βιομηχανικός || ~**ist** n βιομήχανος || ~**ize** vt εκβιομηχανίζω.

industrious [ɪn'dʌstrɪəs] a φιλόπονος, επιμελής.

industry ['ɪndəstrɪ] n βιομηχανία || *(diligence)* φιλοπονία.

inebriated [ɪ'niːbrɪeɪtɪd] a μεθυσμένος.

inedible [ɪn'ɛdɪbl] a μη φαγώσιμος.

ineffective [ɪnɪ'fɛktɪv] a, **ineffectual** [ɪnɪ'fɛktjuəl] a ατελέσφορος, μάταιος.

inefficiency [ɪnɪ'fɪʃənsɪ] n ανικανότητα, ανεπάρκεια.

inefficient [ɪnɪ'fɪʃənt] a ανίκανος, ατελέσφορος.

inelegant [ɪn'ɛlɪgənt] a άκομψος, άγαρμπος.

ineligible [ɪn'ɛlɪdʒəbl] a μη εκλέξιμος, ακατάλληλος.

inept [ɪ'nɛpt] a άτοπος, ανόητος.

inequality [ɪnɪ'kwɒlɪtɪ] n ανισότητα.

ineradicable [ɪnɪ'rædɪkəbl] a αξερρίζωτος.

inert [ɪ'nɜːt] a αδρανής.

inertia [ɪ'nɜːʃə] n αδράνεια.

inescapable [ɪnɪs'keɪpəbl] a αναπόφευκτος.

inessential [ˈɪnɪˈsɛnʃəl] a μη απαραίτητος.

inestimable [ɪn'ɛstɪməbl] a ανεκτίμητος.

inevitable [ɪn'ɛvɪtəbl] a αναπόφευκτος.

inexact [ɪnɪg'zækt] a ανακριβής.

inexhaustible [ɪnɪg'zɔːstəbl] a ανεξάντλητος.

inexorable [ɪn'ɛksərəbl] a αδυσώπητος, αμείλικτος.

inexpensive [ɪnɪks'pɛnsɪv] a φθηνός, ανέξοδος.

inexperience [ɪnɪks'pɪərɪəns] n απειρία || ~**d** a άπειρος.

inexplicable [ɪnɪks'plɪkəbl] a ανεξήγητος.

inextricable [ɪnɪks'trɪkəbl] *a* αδιέξοδος, άλυτος.

infallibility [ɪnfælə'bɪlɪtɪ] *n* (το) αλάνθαστο.

infallible [ɪn'fæləbl] *a* αλάνθαστος, σίγουρος.

infamous ['ɪnfəməs] *a* κακόφημος.

infamy ['ɪnfəmɪ] *n* ατιμία, κακοήθεια.

infancy ['ɪnfənsɪ] *n* νηπιακή ηλικία || (*early stages*) απαρχές *fpl*, πρώτη περίοδος.

infant ['ɪnfənt] *n* νήπιο, βρέφος *nt* || ~ **ile** α παιδικός, παιδιάστικος || ~ **school** *n* κατώτερο δημοτικό σχολείο.

infantry ['ɪnfəntrɪ] *n* πεζικό || ~ **man** *n* στρατιώτης, φαντάρος.

infatuated [ɪn'fætjueɪtɪd] *a* ξεμυαλισμένος, συνεπαρμένος.

infatuation [ɪnfætju'eɪʃən] *n* ξεμυάλισμα *nt*, τρέλα.

infect [ɪn'fekt] *vt* μολύνω, μιαίνω, βρωμίζω || (*influence*) επηρεάζω || ~ **ion** *n* μόλυνση, επίδραση || ~ **ious** *a* μολυσματικός, μεταδοτικός.

infer [ɪn'fɜː*] *vt* συνάγω, συμπεραίνω, υπονοώ || ~ **ence** ['ɪnfərəns] *n* συμπέρασμα *nt*, πόρισμα *nt*.

inferior [ɪn'fɪərɪə*] *a* κατώτερος, υποδεέστερος, ♦ *n* κατώτερος, υφιστάμενος || ~ **ity** *n* κατωτερότητα, μειονεκτικότητα || ~ **ity complex** *n* (σύμ)πλεγμα *nt* κατωτερότητας.

infernal [ɪn'fɜːnl] *a* καταχθόνιος, διαβολικός, απαίσιος.

inferno [ɪn'fɜːnəʊ] *n* κόλαση.

infertile [ɪn'fɜːtaɪl] *a* άγονος, άκαρπος.

infertility [ɪnfɜː'tɪlɪtɪ] *n* (το) άγονο, στειρότητα.

infest [ɪn'fest] *vt* λυμαίνομαι, κατακλύζω.

infidelity [ɪnfɪ'delɪtɪ] *n* απιστία.

infiltrate ['ɪnfɪltreɪt] *vti* (δι)εισδύω, εισχωρώ.

infinite ['ɪnfɪnɪt] *a* άπειρος, απέραντος.

infinitive [ɪn'fɪnɪtɪv] *n* απαρέμφατο.

infinity [ɪn'fɪnɪtɪ] *n* άπειρο, απεραντοσύνη.

infirmary [ɪn'fɜːmərɪ] *n* νοσοκομείο, θεραπευτήριο.

infirmity [ɪn'fɜːmɪtɪ] *n* αδυναμία, αναπηρία.

inflame [ɪn'fleɪm] *vt* (*excite*) εξάπτω, ερεθίζω.

inflammable [ɪn'flæməbl] *a* εύφλεκτος.

inflammation [ɪnflə'meɪʃən] *n* φλόγωση, ερεθισμός.

inflate [ɪn'fleɪt] *vt* φουσκώνω || (*ECON*) προκαλώ πληθωρισμό.

inflation [ɪn'fleɪʃən] *n* πληθωρισμός.

inflexible [ɪn'fleksəbl] *a* άκαμπτος, αλύγιστος.

inflict [ɪn'flɪkt] *vt* καταφέρω, δίνω, επιβάλλω || ~ **ion** *n* επιβολή, βάρος *nt*, τιμωρία.

inflow ['ɪnfləʊ] *n* εισροή.

influence ['ɪnflʊəns] *n* επίδραση, επιρροή ♦ *vt* επηρεάζω, επιδρώ.

influential [ɪnflʊ'enʃəl] *a* σημαίνων, με επιρροή.

influenza [ɪnflʊ'enzə] *n* γρίπη.

influx ['ɪnflʌks] *n* εισροή, διείσδυση.

inform [ɪn'fɔːm] *vt* πληροφορώ, ειδοποιώ.

informal [ɪn'fɔːməl] *a* ανεπίσημος, παράτυπος || ~ **ity** *n* ανεπισημότητα.

information [ɪnfə'meɪʃən] *n* πληροφορίες *fpl*, είδηση.

informative [ɪn'fɔːmətɪv] *a* κατατοπιστικός, πληροφοριακός.

informer [ɪn'fɔːmə*] *n* καταδότης, χαφιές *m inv*.

infra-red [ɪnfrə'red] *a* υπέρυθρος.

infrequent [ɪn'friːkwənt] a σπάνιος.

infringe [ɪn'frɪndʒ] vt παραβαίνω, παραβιάζω ♦ vi καταπατώ || ~ment n παράβαση.

infuriating [ɪn'fjuərɪeɪtɪŋ] a εξοργιστικός.

ingenious [ɪn'dʒiːnɪəs] a οξύνους, πολυμήχανος.

ingenuity [ɪndʒɪ'njuːɪtɪ] n ευφυΐα, οξύνοια.

ingot ['ɪŋɡət] n ράβδος f, χελώνα.

ingratiate [ɪn'greɪʃɪeɪt] vt αποκτώ εύνοια.

ingratitude [ɪn'grætɪtjuːd] n αγνωμοσύνη.

ingredient [ɪn'griːdɪənt] n συστατικό.

inhabit [ɪn'hæbɪt] vt κατοικώ, μένω || ~ant n κάτοικος m/f.

inhale [ɪn'heɪl] vt εισπνέω, ρουφώ.

inherent [ɪn'hɪərənt] a (+ in) συμφυής, έμφυτος.

inherit [ɪn'herɪt] vt κληρονομώ || ~ance n κληρονομία.

inhibit [ɪn'hɪbɪt] vt εμποδίζω, αναχαιτίζω, απαγορεύω || ~ion n απαγόρευση, αναχαίτιση.

inhospitable [ɪnhɒs'pɪtəbl] a αφιλόξενος.

inhuman [ɪn'hjuːmən] a απάνθρωπος.

inimitable [ɪ'nɪmɪtəbl] a αμίμητος.

iniquity [ɪ'nɪkwɪtɪ] n αδικία, κακόθεια.

initial [ɪ'nɪʃəl] a αρχικός, πρώτος ♦ n αρχικό ♦ vt μονογράφω || ~ly ad αρχικά, κατ' αρχήν.

initiate [ɪ'nɪʃɪeɪt] vt αρχίζω, εισάγω || (in a society) μυώ.

initiation [ɪnɪʃɪ'eɪʃən] n μύηση.

initiative [ɪ'nɪʃɪətɪv] n πρωτοβουλία.

inject [ɪn'dʒekt] vt εγχέω, εισάγω, κάνω ένεση || ~ion n έγχυση, ένεση.

injure ['ɪndʒə*] vt βλάπτω, ζημιώνω, πληγώνω.

injury ['ɪndʒərɪ] n βλάβη, τραύμα nt, ζημιά.

injustice [ɪn'dʒʌstɪs] n αδικία.

ink [ɪŋk] n μελάνι.

inkling ['ɪŋklɪŋ] n υποψία, υπόνοια.

inlaid ['ɪn'leɪd] a εμπαιστός.

inland [ɪn'lænd] a εσωτερικός, μεσόγειος ♦ ad στο εσωτερικό, στα ενδότερα || ~ revenue n (Brit) Τμήμα Εσωτερικών Προσόδων.

in-laws ['ɪnlɔːz] npl πεθερικά ntpl.

inlet ['ɪnlet] n ορμίσκος, είσοδος f.

inmate ['ɪnmeɪt] n ένοικος/η m/f.

inn [ɪn] n πανδοχείο, ξενοδοχείο.

innate [ɪ'neɪt] a έμφυτος.

inner ['ɪnə*] a εσωτερικός.

innocence ['ɪnəsns] n αθωότητα, αφέλεια.

innocent ['ɪnəsnt] a αθώος, αγνός, αφελής.

innocuous [ɪ'nɒkjuəs] a αβλαβής.

innovation [ɪnəʊ'veɪʃən] n καινοτομία, νεωτερισμός.

innuendo [ɪnju'endəʊ] n υπαινιγμός.

innumerable [ɪ'njuːmərəbl] a αναρίθμητος.

inoculation [ɪnɒkjʊ'leɪʃən] n μπόλιασμα nt.

inopportune [ɪn'ɒpətjuːn] a άκαιρος, άτοπος.

inordinately [ɪ'nɔːdɪnɪtlɪ] ad υπερβολικά.

inorganic [ɪnɔː'gænɪk] a ανόργανος.

in-patient ['ɪnpeɪʃənt] n εσωτερικός (ασθενής).

input ['ɪnput] n εισαγωγή ♦ vt εισάγω, τροφοδοτώ.

inquest ['ɪnkwest] n ανάκριση, έρευνα.

inquire [ɪn'kwaɪə*] vi ρωτώ, ζητώ vt (price) ρωτώ την τιμή || **to ~ into** vt ερευνώ, εξετάζω.

inquiring [ɪnˈkwaɪərɪŋ] a *(mind)* ερευνητικός.

inquiry [ɪnˈkwaɪərɪ] n ερώτηση || *(search)* έρευνα, ανάκριση || **~ office** n υπηρεσία πληροφοριών.

inquisitive [ɪnˈkwɪzɪtɪv] a περίεργος, αδιάκριτος.

inroad [ˈɪnrəʊd] n εισβολή, επιδρομή.

insane [ɪnˈseɪn] a παράφρονας, τρελός.

insanitary [ɪnˈsænɪtərɪ] a ανθυγιεινός.

insanity [ɪnˈsænɪtɪ] n παραφροσύνη, τρέλα.

insatiable [ɪnˈseɪʃəbl] a ακόρεστος, άπληστος.

inscription [ɪnˈskrɪpʃən] n επιγραφή, αφιέρωση.

inscrutable [ɪnˈskruːtəbl] a ανεξιχνίαστος, μυστηριώδης.

insect [ˈɪnsɛkt] n έντομο, ζουζούνι || **~icide** n εντομοκτόνο.

insecure [ɪnsɪˈkjʊə*] a επισφαλής.

insecurity [ɪnsɪˈkjʊərɪtɪ] n ανασφάλεια, (το) επισφαλές nt.

insensible [ɪnˈsɛnsəbl] a αναισθητος, αναίσθητος.

insensitive [ɪnˈsɛnsɪtɪv] a αναίσθητος, χωρίς ντροπή.

inseparable [ɪnˈsɛpərəbl] a αχώριστος, αναπόσπαστος.

insert [ɪnˈsɜːt] vt παρεμβάλλω, καταχωρώ, εισάγω ♦ [ˈɪnsɜːt] n παρεμβολή, ένθεμα nt || **~ion** n παρεμβολή, καταχώρηση, βάλσιμο.

inshore [ˈɪnˈʃɔː*] a, ad κοντά στην ακτή.

inside [ˈɪnˈsaɪd] n (το) μέσα, εσωτερικό (μέρος) ♦ a εσωτερικός ♦ ad εσωτερικά, μέσα ♦ prep εντός, μέσα || **~forward** n (SPORT) μέσος κυνηγός || **~ out** ad ανάποδα, το μέσα έξω|| **~r** n μεμυημένος, γνώστης.

insidious [ɪnˈsɪdɪəs] a ύπουλος, δόλιος.

insight [ˈɪnsaɪt] n διορατικότητα, οξύνοια.

insignificant [ɪnsɪgˈnɪfɪkənt] a ασήμαντος, τιποτένιος.

insincere [ɪnsɪnˈsɪə*] a ανειλικρινής.

insinuate [ɪnˈsɪnjʊeɪt] vt αφήνω να εννοηθεί, υπαινίσσομαι.

insinuation [ɪnsɪnjʊˈeɪʃən] n υπαινιγμός.

insipid [ɪnˈsɪpɪd] a ανούσιος, σαχλός.

insist [ɪnˈsɪst] vi (+ on) επιμένω, εμμένω || **~ence** n επιμονή || **~ent** a επίμονος.

insolence [ˈɪnsələns] n αναίδεια, θρασύτητα.

insolent [ˈɪnsələnt] a αναιδής, θρασύς.

insoluble [ɪnˈsɒljʊbl] a άλυτος, αδιάλυτος.

insolvent [ɪnˈsɒlvənt] a αφερέγγυος, αναξιόχρεος.

insomnia [ɪnˈsɒmnɪə] n αϋπνία.

inspect [ɪnˈspɛkt] vt επιθεωρώ, επιτηρώ, επιβλέπω || **~ion** n επιθεώρηση, επιτήρηση || **~or** n επιθεωρητής/τρια m/f|| (RAIL) επιστάτης/άτρια m/f, επόπτης/όπτρια m/f.

inspiration [ɪnspəˈreɪʃən] n έμπνευση.

inspire [ɪnˈspaɪə*] vt εμπνέω.

inspiring [ɪnˈspaɪərɪŋ] a εμπνέων.

instability [ɪnstəˈbɪlɪtɪ] n αστάθεια.

install [ɪnˈstɔːl] vt εγκαθιστώ, μοντάρω || (in office) εγκαθιστώ || **~ation** n εγκατάσταση, τοποθέτηση.

instalment, installment (US) [ɪnˈstɔːlmənt] n δόση, παρτίδα.

instance [ˈɪnstəns] n περίπτωση, παράδειγμα nt || **for ~** παραδείγματος χάρη.

instant ['ɪnstənt] n στιγμή ♦ a
άμεσος, επείγων || ~ **coffee** n
στιγμιαίος καφές || ~**ly** ad αμέσως,
στη στιγμή.

instead [ɪn'stɛd] ad αντί γι' αυτό ||
~ **of** αντί.

instigation [ɪnstɪ'geɪʃən] n
παρακίνηση, υποκίνηση.

instil [ɪn'stɪl] vt εμποτίζω, βάζω.

instinct ['ɪnstɪŋkt] n ένστικτο,
ορμέμφυτο || ~**ive** a ενστικτώδης ||
~**ively** ad ενστικτωδώς.

institute ['ɪnstɪtjuːt] n ίδρυμα nt,
ινστιτούτο ♦ vt θεσπίζω, ιδρύω,
εγκαθιστώ.

institution [ɪnstɪ'tjuːʃən] n (custom)
θεσμός, θέσμιο || (organization)
ίδρυμα nt, οργάνωση || (beginning)
ίδρυση, σύσταση.

instruct [ɪn'strʌkt] vt (order)
παραγγέλλω, διατάσσω || (teach)
διδάσκω, μαθαίνω || ~**ion** n
διδασκαλία || (direction) οδηγία ||
~**ions** npl εντολές fpl, οδηγίες fpl ||
~**ive** a διδακτικός, ενημερωτικός ||
~**or** n δάσκαλος/άλα m/f,
εκπαιδευτής/εύτρια m/f || (US)
επιμελητής/ήτρια m/f.

instrument ['ɪnstrumənt] n
(implement) εργαλείο, όργανο || (MUS)
όργανο || ~**al** a ενόργανος ||
(helpful) συντελεστικός, συμβάλλων
|| ~**alist** n οργανοπαίκτης ||
panel n ταμπλό nt inv.

insubordinate [ɪnsə'bɔːdɪnɪt] a
ανυπότακτος, ανυπάκουος.

insubordination
['ɪnsəbɔːdɪ'neɪʃən] n ανυπακοή,
ανυποταξία.

insufferable [ɪn'sʌfərəbl] a
ανυπόφορος, αφόρητος.

insufficient [ɪnsə'fɪʃənt] a
ανεπαρκής, λειψός || ~**ly** ad
ανεπαρκώς.

insular ['ɪnsjʊlə] a (narrow-minded)
με στενές αντιλήψεις.

insulate ['ɪnsjʊleɪt] vt μονώνω || (set
apart) απομονώνω.

insulating ['ɪnsjʊleɪtɪŋ]: ~ **tape** n
μονωτική ταινία.

insulation [ɪnsjʊ'leɪʃən] n (ELEC)
μόνωση.

insulin ['ɪnsjʊlɪn] n (for diabetic)
ινσουλίνη.

insult ['ɪnsʌlt] n προσβολή, βρισιά
♦ [ɪn'sʌlt] vt βρίζω, προσβάλλω ||
~**ing** a προσβλητικός.

insuperable [ɪn'suːpərəbl] a
ανυπέρβλητος.

insurance [ɪn'ʃʊərəns] n ασφάλεια ||
~ **agent** n πράκτορας ασφαλειών ||
~ **policy** n ασφαλιστήριο.

insure [ɪn'ʃʊə*] vt (εξ)ασφαλίζω.

insurrection [ɪnsə'rɛkʃən] n
επανάσταση, εξέγερση.

intact [ɪn'tækt] a άθικτος,
απείραχτος.

intake ['ɪnteɪk] n (MECH) εισαγωγή.

intangible [ɪn'tændʒəbl] a
ακαθόριστος.

integral ['ɪntɪgrəl] a (essential)
αναπόσπαστος || (complete)
ολοκληρωτικός.

integrate ['ɪntɪgreɪt] vti
ολοκληρώνω.

integration [ɪntɪ'greɪʃən] n
ολοκλήρωση.

integrity [ɪn'tɛgrɪtɪ] n ακεραιότητα,
εντιμότητα.

intellect ['ɪntɪlɛkt] n διάνοια,
νόηση, μυαλό || ~**ual** a
διανοητικός, πνευματικός ♦ n
διανοούμενος.

intelligence [ɪn'tɛlɪdʒəns] n
νοημοσύνη || (information)
πληροφορία.

intelligent [ɪn'tɛlɪdʒənt] a ευφυής,
νοήμων, μυαλωμένος || ~**ly** ad
ευφυώς, έξυπνα.

intelligible [ɪn'tɛlɪdʒəbl] a
(κατα)νοητός, καταληπτός.

intemperate [in'tempərit] a ακρατής, μέθυσος.

intend [in'tend] vt (mean) προτίθεμαι || **to ~ to do sth** σκοπεύω να κάνω κάτι.

intense [in'tens] a έντονος, ισχυρός || **~ ly** ad υπερβολικά, έντονα.

intensify [in'tensifai] vt εντείνω, επιτείνω.

intensity [in'tensiti] n ένταση, σφοδρότητα, ορμή.

intensive [in'tensiv] a εντατικός.

intent [in'tent] n πρόθεση || **to all ~s and purposes** ουσιαστικά, πραγματικά.

intention [in'tenʃən] n πρόθεση || (plan) σκοπός || **~ al** a σκόπιμος, εσκεμμένος || **~ ally** ad εσκεμμένα, σκόπιμα.

intently [in'tentli] ad προσεκτικά, έντονα.

inter [in'tɜː] vt ενταφιάζω, θάβω.

inter- ['intə*] prefix διά-, μεσ(ο)-, μεταξύ.

interact [intər'ækt] vi αλληλεπιδρώ || **~ ion** n αλληλεπίδραση.

intercede [intə'siːd] vi επεμβαίνω, μεσολαβώ, μεσιτεύω.

intercept [intə'sept] vt ανακόπτω, συλλαμβάνω, πιάνω || **~ ion** n σύλληψη, υποκλοπή.

interchange ['intə'tʃeindʒ] n (exchange) ανταλλαγή || (roads) μεταλλαγή ♦ [intə'tʃeindʒ] vt ανταλλάσσω || **~ able** a ανταλλάξιμος, εναλλάξιμος.

intercom ['intəkom] n σύστη .α εσωτερικής επικοινωνίας.

interconnect [intəkə'nekt] vt αλληλοσυνδέω.

intercontinental [intəkonti'nentl] a διηπειρωτικός.

intercourse ['intəkɔːs] n συναλλαγή, σχέσεις 'pl || (sexual) συνουσία.

interest ['intrist] n (curiosity) ενδιαφέρον nt || (advantage) συμφέρον nt || (money paid) τόκος || (COMM: stake) συμφέροντα ntpl, συμμετοχή ♦ vt ενδιαφέρω, προσελκύω || **~ed** a ενδιαφερόμενος || (attentive) με ενδιαφέρον || **to be ~ed in** ενδιαφέρομαι για || **~ing** a ενδιαφέρων.

interface ['intəfeis] n (COMPUT) θύρα, υποδοχή.

interfere [intə'fiə*] vi επεμβαίνω || (+ with) συγκρούομαι με, ανακατεύομαι || **~nce** n (general) επέμβαση, ανάμιξη || (TV) παράσιτα ntpl.

interim ['intərim] a προσωρινός ♦ n: **in the ~** στο μεταξύ.

interior [in'tiəriə*] n εσωτερικό || (inland) ενδοχώρα ♦ a εσωτερικός.

interjection [intə'dʒekʃən] n (GRAM) επιφώνημα nt.

interlock [intə'lok] vi συνδέομαι ♦ vt συνδέω, συμπλέκω.

interloper ['intələupə*] n παρείσακτος.

interlude ['intəluːd] n διάλειμμα nt || (THEAT) ιντερμέτζο.

intermarry ['intə'mæri] vi επιμιγνύομαι.

intermediary [intə'miːdiəri] n μεσάζων/άζουσα m/f, μεσίτης/τρια m/f.

intermediate [intə'miːdiət] a μεσολαβών, ενδιάμεσος.

intermission [intə'miʃən] n διάλειμμα nt, διακοπή.

intermittent [intə'mitənt] a διαλείπων || **~ ly** ad διακεκομμέ α.

intern [in'tɜːn] vt περιορίζω ♦ ['intɜːn] n (US) εσωτερικός γιατρ ός m/f.

internal [in'tɜːnl] a εσωτερικός || **~ ly** ad (MED) εσωτερικά || **~**

revenue n (US) Τμήμα Εσωτερικών Προσόδων.

international [ɪntə'næʃnəl] a διεθνής ♦ n (SPORT) διεθνής (παίκτης).

internment [ɪn'tɜːnmənt] n εγκάθειρξη, περιορισμός.

interplay ['ɪntəpleɪ] n αλληλεπίδραση.

interpret [ɪn'tɜːprɪt] vt εξηγώ || (translate) μεταφράζω || (THEAT) ερμηνεύω || ~ation n ερμηνεία, εξήγηση || ~er n διερμηνέας m/f.

interrelated [ɪntərɪ'leɪtɪd] a αλληλένδετος.

interrogate [ɪn'terəgeɪt] vt ερωτώ, ανακρίνω.

interrogation [ɪntərə'geɪʃən] n ανάκριση, εξέταση.

interrogative [ɪntə'rɒgətɪv] a ερωτηματικός.

interrogator [ɪn'terəgeɪtə*] n ανακριτής.

interrupt [ɪntə'rʌpt] vt διακόπτω, εμποδίζω || ~ion n διακοπή.

intersect [ɪntə'sekt] vt τέμνω, διακόπτω, κόβω ♦ vi (roads) διασταυρώνομαι || ~ion n (roads) διασταύρωση, σταυροδρόμι.

intersperse [ɪntə'spɜːs] vt διασπείρω, αναμιγνύω.

interval ['ɪntəvəl] n διάλειμμα nt, διάστημα nt || (MUS) διάστημα nt || **at ~s** κατά διαστήματα.

intervene [ɪntə'viːn] vi μεσολαβώ, παρεμβαίνω, επεμβαίνω.

intervention [ɪntə'venʃən] n μεσολάβηση, παρέμβαση.

interview ['ɪntəvjuː] n (PRESS etc) συνέντευξη || (for job) συνάντηση, ραντεβού nt inv ♦ vt παίρνω συνέντευξη || ~er n εκείνος που παίρνει συνέντευξη.

intestate [ɪn'testɪt] a χωρίς διαθήκη.

intestine [ɪn'testɪn] n έντερο.

intimacy ['ɪntɪməsɪ] n οικειότητα || (sexual) συνουσία.

intimate ['ɪntɪmɪt] a ενδόμυχος, ιδιαίτερος || (familiar) οικείος, στενός ♦ ['ɪntɪmeɪt] vt υποδηλώ, εκδηλώνω, υπαινίσσομαι || ~ly ad στενά, κατά βάθος.

intimidate [ɪn'tɪmɪdeɪt] vt (εκ)φοβίζω, φοβερίζω.

intimidation [ɪntɪmɪ'deɪʃən] n εκφοβισμός.

into ['ɪntuː] prep (movement) σε, εντός, μέσα || (change) σε.

intolerable [ɪn'tɒlərəbl] a ανυπόφορος, αφόρητος.

intolerance [ɪn'tɒlərəns] n μισαλλοδοξία.

intolerant [ɪn'tɒlərənt] a μισαλλόδοξος, αδιάλλακτος.

intonation [ɪntəu'neɪʃən] n διακύμανση της φωνής.

intoxicate [ɪn'tɒksɪkeɪt] vt μεθώ, ζαλίζω || ~d a μεθυσμένος.

intoxication [ɪntɒksɪ'keɪʃən] n μεθύσι, παραζάλη.

intractable [ɪn'træktəbl] a ανυπάκουος, σπίθασος.

intransigent [ɪn'trænsɪdʒənt] a αδιάλλακτος.

intransitive [ɪn'trænsɪtɪv] a αμετάβατος.

intravenous [ɪntrə'viːnəs] a ενδοφλέβιος.

intrepid [ɪn'trepɪd] a ατρόμητος, άφοβος.

intricacy ['ɪntrɪkəsɪ] n περιπλοκή, (το) περίπλοκο.

intricate ['ɪntrɪkɪt] a περίπλοκος || (of thoughts) συγκεχυμένος.

intrigue [ɪn'triːg] n μηχανορραφία ♦ vt (make curious) διεγείρω την περιέργεια.

intriguing [ɪn'triːgɪŋ] a (fascinating) περίεργος, μυστηριώδης.

intrinsic [ɪn'trɪnsɪk] a ουσιαστικός, πραγματικός.

introduce [ɪntrəˈdjuːs] vt (person) συνιστώ, συστήνω || (sth new) παρουσιάζω, μπάζω || (subject) εισάγω.

introduction [ɪntrəˈdʌkʃən] n παρουσίαση, σύσταση || (book) εισαγωγή, πρόλογος.

introductory [ɪntrəˈdʌktərɪ] a εισαγωγικός.

introspective [ɪntrəʊˈspɛktɪv] a ενδοσκοπικός.

introvert [ˈɪntrəʊvɜːt] a, n ενδόστροφος.

intrude [ɪnˈtruːd] vi (+ on) επιβάλλω, επεμβαίνω || ~r n παρείσακτος.

intrusion [ɪnˈtruːʒən] n επέμβαση, διείσδυση.

intuition [ɪntjuːˈɪʃən] n διαίσθηση, ενόραση.

intuitive [ɪnˈtjuːɪtɪv] a διαισθητικός, ενστικτώδης.

inundate [ˈɪnʌndeɪt] vt (fig) κατακλύζω, πλημμυρίζω.

invade [ɪnˈveɪd] vt εισβάλλω, καταπατώ || ~r n επιδρομέας, εισβολέας.

invalid [ˈɪnvəlɪd] n ασθενής m/f, ανάπηρος/η m/f ♦ [ɪnˈvælɪd] a (not valid) άκυρος || ~ate vt ακυρώνω, αναιρώ.

invaluable [ɪnˈvæljuəbl] a ανεκτίμητος.

invariable [ɪnˈvɛərɪəbl] a αμετάβλητος.

invasion [ɪnˈveɪʒən] n εισβολή, επιδρομή.

invective [ɪnˈvɛktɪv] n βρισιά, λοιδωρία.

invent [ɪnˈvɛnt] vt εφευρίσκω || (make up) πλάθω || ~ion n εφεύρεση || ~ive a εφευρετικός, δημιουργικός || ~or n εφευρέτης.

inventory [ˈɪnvəntrɪ] n απογραφή, κατάλογος.

inverse [ˈɪnvɜːs] n αντίστροφος, ανάστροφος.

invert [ɪnˈvɜːt] vt αντιστρέφω || ~ed commas npl εισαγωγικά ntpl.

invertebrate [ɪnˈvɜːtɪbrɪt] n ασπόνδυλο.

invest [ɪnˈvɛst] vt (ECON) επενδύω || (control) παρέχω, αναθέτω.

investigate [ɪnˈvɛstɪgeɪt] vt ερευνώ, εξετάζω.

investigation [ɪnvɛstɪˈgeɪʃən] n έρευνα, εξέταση.

investigator [ɪnˈvɛstɪgeɪtə*] n ερευνητής/ήτρια m/f, αναζητητής/ήτρια m/f.

investiture [ɪnˈvɛstɪtʃə*] n τελετή απονομής αξιώματος.

investment [ɪnˈvɛstmənt] n επένδυση.

investor [ɪnˈvɛstə*] n κεφαλαιούχος m/f, επενδύτης m/f.

inveterate [ɪnˈvɛtərɪt] a (habitual) φανατικός, αδιόρθωτος.

invigorating [ɪnˈvɪgəreɪtɪŋ] a αναζωογονητικός, τονωτικός.

invincible [ɪnˈvɪnsɪbl] a αήττητος.

inviolate [ɪnˈvaɪəlɪt] a απαραβίαστος, απαράβατος.

invisible [ɪnˈvɪzɪbl] a (general) αόρατος, άδηλος || (ink) συμπαθητική μελάνη.

invitation [ɪnvɪˈteɪʃən] n πρόσκληση.

invite [ɪnˈvaɪt] vt (προς)καλώ || (attract) ελκύω, προκαλώ.

inviting [ɪnˈvaɪtɪŋ] a δελεαστικός, ελκυστικός.

invoice [ˈɪnvɔɪs] n τιμολόγιο ♦ vt τιμολογώ.

invoke [ɪnˈvəʊk] vt επικαλούμαι, απαιτώ.

involuntarily [ɪnˈvɒləntərɪlɪ] ad ακουσίως, αθέλητα.

involuntary [ɪnˈvɒləntərɪ] a ακούσιος, αθέλητος.

involve [ɪnˈvɒlv] vt (include)

συνεπάγομαι || (entangle)
(περι)πλέκω, ανακατώνω || ~d a
πλεγμένος || ~ment n ανάμιξη,
μπλέξιμο.
invulnerable [ɪn'vʌlnərəbl] a
άτρωτος.
inward ['ɪnwəd] a εσωτερικός, προς
τα μέσα || ~ (s) ad προς τα μέσα ||
~ly ad εσωτερικά, μέσα.
iodine ['aɪədi:n] n ιώδιο.
iota [aɪ'əʊtə] n (fig) γιώτα nt, τίποτε,
ελάχιστη ποσότητα.
I O U n (abbr of I owe you) γραμμάτιο.
I.Q. n (abbr of intelligence quotient)
δείκτης ευφυΐας.
Iran [ɪ'rɑːn] n Ιράν nt inv, Περσία.
Iraq [ɪ'rɑːk] n Ιράκ nt inv.
irascible [ɪ'ræsɪbl] a ευέξαπτος,
οξύθυμος.
irate [aɪ'reɪt] a θυμωμένος,
εξαγριωμένος.
Ireland ['aɪələnd] n Ιρλανδία.
iris ['aɪərɪs] n (ANAT) ίριδα || (BOT)
ίριδα, ρίδι.
Irish ['aɪərɪʃ] a ιρλανδικός || the ~
npl οι Ιρλανδοί || ~man n Ιρλανδός
|| ~woman n Ιρλανδή.
irk [ɜːk] vt ενοχλώ, στενοχωρώ.
iron ['aɪən] n σίδηρος || (flat iron)
σίδερο || (golf club) ρόπαλο του
γκόλφ ♦ a σιδερένιος ♦ vt
σιδερώνω || ~s npl (chains) αλυσίδες
fpl, δεσμά ntpl || to ~ out (crease)
σιδερώνω || (difficulties) εξομαλύνω ||
~ curtain n σιδηρούν
παραπέτασμα nt.
ironic(al) [aɪ'rɒnɪk(əl)] a ειρωνικός
|| ~ally ad ειρωνικά.
ironing ['aɪənɪŋ] n σιδέρωμα nt || ~
board n σανίδα σιδερώματος.
ironmonger ['aɪənmʌŋɡə*] n
σιδηροπώλης || ~'s (shop) n
σιδηροπωλείο.
iron ore ['aɪənɔː*] n
σιδηρομετάλλευμα nt.

ironworks ['aɪənwɜːks] n
σιδηρουργείο.
irony ['aɪərənɪ] n ειρωνεία.
irrational [ɪ'ræʃənl] a παράλογος.
irreconcilable [ɪrɛkən'saɪləbl] a
αδιάλλακτος, ασυμβίβαστος.
irredeemable [ɪrɪ'diːməbl] a
(COMM) ανεξαγόραστος.
irrefutable [ɪrɪ'fjuːtəbl] a
ακαταμάχητος, αδιάψευστος.
irregular [ɪ'rɛɡjʊlə*] a (not regular)
ακανόνιστος, άτακτος || (not smooth)
ανώμαλος || (against rule)
αντικανονικός, αντίθετος || ~ity n
ανωμαλία.
irrelevance [ɪ'rɛləvəns] n (το)
άσχετο.
irrelevant [ɪ'rɛləvənt] a άσχετος,
ξεκάρφωτος.
irreparable [ɪ'rɛpərəbl] a
ανεπανόρθωτος, αγιάτρευτος.
irreplaceable [ɪrɪ'pleɪsəbl] a
αναντικατάστατος.
irrepressible [ɪrɪ'prɛsəbl] a
ακατάσχετος, ακάθεκτος.
irreproachable [ɪrɪ'prəʊtʃəbl] a
άμεμπτος, άψογος.
irresistible [ɪrɪ'zɪstəbl] a
ασυγκράτητος, ακαταμάχητος.
irresolute [ɪ'rɛzəluːt] a
αναποφάσιστος, διστακτικός.
irrespective [ɪrɪ'spɛktɪv]: ~ of
prep ανεξάρτητα από.
irresponsible [ɪrɪs'pɒnsəbl] a
απερίσκεπτος, ελαφρόμυαλος.
irreverent [ɪ'rɛvərənt] a ασεβής,
ανευλαβής.
irrevocable [ɪ'rɛvəkəbl] a
αμετάκλητος, ανέκκλητος.
irrigate ['ɪrɪɡeɪt] vt αρδεύω,
ποτίζω.
irrigation [ɪrɪ'ɡeɪʃən] n άρδευση,
πότισμα nt.
irritable ['ɪrɪtəbl] a οξύθυμος,
ευέξαπτος.
irritate ['ɪrɪteɪt] vt (annoy)

(εξ)ερεθίζω, εκνευρίζω || (skin etc) ερεθίζω.

irritation [ɪrɪ'teɪʃən] n ερεθισμός, θυμός.

is [ɪz] see be.

Islam ['ɪzlɑːm] n Ισλάμ nt inv.

island ['aɪlənd] n νησί || ~er νησιώτης/ιώτισσα m/f.

isle [aɪl] n νήσος f, νησάκι.

isn't ['ɪznt] = **is not** || see be.

isolate ['aɪsəleɪt] vt (απο)μονώνω || ~d a απομονωμένος, απόμερος.

isolation [aɪsə'leɪʃən] n απομόνωση.

isotope ['aɪsətəup] n ισότοπο.

Israel ['ɪzreɪl] n Ισραήλ m inv || ~i n Ισραηλινός/ή m/f ♦ adj ισραηλινός.

issue ['ɪʃuː] n (question) υπόθεση, ζήτημα nt || (giving out) έκδοση, διανομή, χορήγηση || (copy) τεύχος, φύλλο || (offspring) απόγονοι mpl ♦ vt (rations) διανέμω || (orders) εκδίδω, δημοσιεύω || (equipment) διανέμω, εκδίδω || at ~ υπό συζήτηση.

isthmus ['ɪsməs] n ισθμός.

it [ɪt] pron τον, την, το, αυτό.

Italian [ɪ'tæliən] a ιταλικός ♦ n (person) Ιταλός/ίδα m/f || (LING) Ιταλικά ntpl.

italic [ɪ'tælɪk] a κυρτός, πλάγιος || ~s npl πλάγια γραφή.

Italy ['ɪtəlɪ] n Ιταλία.

itch [ɪtʃ] n (fig) πόθος, όρεξη || (MED) φαγούρα, ψώρα ♦ vi έχω φαγούρα || ~ing n φαγούρα.

it'd ['ɪtd] = **it would, it had** || see would, have.

item ['aɪtəm] n (on list) είδος nt, κονδύλι, εγγραφή || (in programme) νούμερο || (in agenda) θέμα nt || (in newspaper) είδηση || ~ize vt αναλύω.

itinerant [ɪ'tɪnərənt] a περιοδεύων n δρομολόγιο.

itinerary [aɪ'tɪnərərɪ] n δρομολόγιο.

it'll ['ɪtl] = **it will, it shall** || see will, shall.

its [ɪts] poss a του || poss pron δικό του.

it's [ɪts] = **it is, it has** || see be, have.

itself [ɪt'self] pron τον εαυτό του.

I.T.V. n (abbr of Independent Television) Ανεξάρτητο Τηλεοπτικό Κανάλι.

I've [aɪv] = **I have** || see have.

ivory ['aɪvərɪ] n ελεφαντοστούν nt || ~ **tower** n (fig) τόπος μονώσεως.

ivy ['aɪvɪ] n κισσός.

J

jab [dʒæb] vti κτυπώ, κεντώ, χώνω.

jabber ['dʒæbə*] vi φλυαρώ, τραυλίζω.

jack [dʒæk] n (MECH) γρύλλος || (CARDS) βαλές m, φάντης || to ~ **up** vt σηκώνω με γρύλλο.

jacket ['dʒækɪt] n ζακέτα, σακάκι || (MECH) χιτώνιο, πουκάμισο.

jack-knife ['dʒæknaɪf] n μεγάλος σουγιάς, κολοκοτρώνης.

jade [dʒeɪd] n (stone) νεφρίτης.

jaded ['dʒeɪdɪd] a κουρασμένος, τσακισμένος.

jagged ['dʒægɪd] a ανώμαλος, οδοντωτός, μυτερός.

jail [dʒeɪl] n φυλακή || ~**break** n δραπέτευση || ~**er** n δεσμοφύλακας.

jam [dʒæm] n (fruit) μαρμελάδα || (stoppage) εμπλοκή, φρακάρισμα nt, στρίμωγμα nt ♦ vi σφηνώνω, σφίγγω, στριμώχνω ♦ vi σφίγγομαι, φρακάρω, κολλώ.

jangle ['dʒæŋgl] vti ηχώ κακόηχα, κουδουνίζω.

janitor ['dʒænɪtə*] n (caretaker) θυρωρός m/f, επιστάτης/ρια m/f.

January ['dʒænjuərɪ] n Ιανουάριος.

Japan [dʒə'pæn] n ιαπωνία || ~**ese** a ιαπωνικός ♦ n (LING) Ιαπωνικά ntpl.

jar [dʒɑː*] n (glass) βάζο, λαγήνι,

στάμπα ♦ vi τραντάζω,
συγκρούομαι.

jargon ['dʒɑːgən] n επαγγελματική
φρασεολογία, αλαμπουρνέζικα ntpl.

jasmin(e) ['dʒæzmɪn] n γιασεμί.

jaundice ['dʒɔːndɪs] n ίκτερος,
χρυσή || ~**d** a (attitude) κακόβουλος,
φθονερός.

jaunt [dʒɔːnt] n βόλτα, περίπατος ||
~**y** a ζωηρός, ξένοιαστος.

javelin ['dʒævlɪn] n ακόντιο,
κοντάρι.

jaw [dʒɔː] n σαγόνι, μασέλα.

jazz [dʒæz] n τζαζ f inv || to ~ **up** vt
ζωηρεύω, επιταχύνω || ~ **band** n
τζαζ-μπαντ f inv.

jealous ['dʒeləs] a (envious)
ζηλιάρης || (watchful) ζηλότυπος,
προσεκτικός || ~**ly** ad ζηλότυπα, με
επιμέλεια || ~**y** n ζήλεια.

jeans [dʒiːnz] npl ντρίλινο
παντελόνι.

jeep [dʒiːp] n τζιπ nt inv.

jeer [dʒɪə*] vi (+ at) κοροϊδεύω,
χλευάζω, γιουχαΐζω ♦ n εμπαιγμός,
γιούχα.

jelly ['dʒelɪ] n ζελέ f || ~**fish** n
μέδουσα, τσούχτρα.

jeopardize ['dʒepədaɪz] vt
διακινδυνεύω.

jeopardy ['dʒepədɪ] n: **in** ~ σε
κίνδυνο.

jerk [dʒɜːk] n τίναγμα nt, τράνταγμα
nt || (US: idiot) χαζός ♦ vti τινάζω,
τραντάζω.

jerkin ['dʒɜːkɪn] n πέτσινο σακκάκι.

jerky ['dʒɜːkɪ] a απότομος, κοφτός.

jersey ['dʒɜːzɪ] n φανέλα.

jest [dʒest] n χωρατό, αστείο ♦ vi
κάνω αστεία, αστειεύομαι.

jet [dʒet] n (stream) πίδακας,
αναπήδηση || (spout) στόμιο, μπεκ nt
inv || (AVIAT) τζετ nt inv || ~**-black** a
κατάμαυρος || ~ **engine** n
κινητήριος τζέτ.

jettison ['dʒetɪsn] vt απορρίπτω.

jetty ['dʒetɪ] n μώλος, αποβάθρα.

Jew [dʒuː] n Εβραίος.

jewel ['dʒuːəl] n κόσμημα nt || (fig)
πολύτιμη, πέτρα || ~**ler**, (US) ~**er** n
κοσμηματοπώλης || ~(**l**)**er's** (**shop**)
n κοσμηματοπωλείο || ~(**le**)**ry** n
κοσμήματα ntpl, διαμαντικά ntpl.

Jewess ['dʒuːɪs] n Εβραία.

Jewish ['dʒuːɪʃ] a εβραϊκός.

jib [dʒɪb] n (NAUT) αρτέμων inv,
φλόκος ♦ vi αρνούμαι, κωλώνω,
κλωτσώ.

jibe [dʒaɪb] n πείραγμα nt, αστείο.

jiffy ['dʒɪfɪ] n (col): **in a** ~ στη
στιγμή, αμέσως.

jigsaw ['dʒɪgsɔː] n (also: ~ **puzzle**)
(παιχνίδι) σουναρμολόγησης.

jilt [dʒɪlt] vt διώχνω, στρίβω.

jingle ['dʒɪŋgl] n κουδούνισμα nt, ♦
vti κουδουνίζω.

jinx [dʒɪŋks] n (col) γρουσούζης.

jitters ['dʒɪtəz] npl (col): **to get the**
~ τρέμω, φοβάμαι.

job [dʒɔb] n έργο, εργασία || (position)
θέση, δουλειά || (difficult task)
αγγαρεία || ~**less** a άνεργος.

jockey ['dʒɔkɪ] n τζόκεϊ m inv ♦ vi
ελίσσομαι, μανουβράρω.

jocular ['dʒɔkjulə*] a αστείος,
εύθυμος.

jog [dʒɔg] vt σπρώχνω, σκουντώ ♦ vi
(move jerkily) κλυδωνίζω, τραντάζω.

join [dʒɔɪn] vt (fasten) ενώνω,
συνδέω, ματίζω || (club) εγγράφομαι,
γίνομαι μέλος ♦ vi (the army)
κατατάσσομαι ♦ n ένωση, ραφή.

joiner ['dʒɔɪnə*] n μαραγκός || ~**y** n
ξυλουργική.

joint [dʒɔɪnt] n (TECH) αρμός,
άρθρωση || (of meat) κομμάτι
κρέατος || (col: place) καταγώγιο,
τρώγλη || ~**ly** ad μαζί.

joist [dʒɔɪst] n δοκάρι, πατερό.

joke [dʒəuk] n αστείο, χωρατό,
καλαμπούρι ♦ vi αστειεύομαι || ~ **r** n

αστειολόγος || *(CARDS)* μπαλαντέρ *m inv.*

jolly [ˈdʒɒlɪ] *a* εύθυμος, χαρούμενος, κεφάτος ♦ *ad (col)* εξαιρετικά, πολύ.

jolt [dʒəʊlt] *n* τίναγμα *nt*, τράνταγμα *nt* || *(col)* ξάφνιασμα ♦ *vt* τινάζω, κουνώ.

jostle [ˈdʒɒsl] *vt* σπρώχνω.

jot [dʒɒt] *n*: **not one ~** ούτε ίχνος, ούτε κατά κεραία || **to ~ down** *vt* σημειώνω, γράφω || **~ter** *n* σημειωματάριο.

journal [ˈdʒɜːnl] *n* εφημερίδα, περιοδικό || **~ese** *n* δημοσιογραφικό ύφος || **~ism** *n* δημοσιογραφία || **~ist** *n* δημοσιογράφος *m/f.*

journey [ˈdʒɜːnɪ] *n* ταξίδι, διαδρομή.

joy [dʒɔɪ] *n* χαρά, ευθυμία || **~ful** *a* περιχαρής, χαρμόσυνος || **~ous** *a* εύθυμος || **~ride** *n* περίπατος με αυτοκίνητο.

Jr., Jun., Junr. *abbr of* **junior.**

jubilant [ˈdʒuːbɪlənt] *a* χαρούμενος, πανηγυρίζων.

jubilation [dʒuːbɪˈleɪʃən] *n* αγαλλίαση, χαρά.

jubilee [ˈdʒuːbɪliː] *n* γιορτή.

judge [dʒʌdʒ] *n (in court)* δικαστής *m* ♦ *vt* δικάζω, κρίνω ♦ *vi (estimate)* υπολογίζω, θεωρώ || **judg(e)ment** *n (sentence)* δικαστική απόφαση || *(opinion)* κρίση, γνώμη.

judicial [dʒuːˈdɪʃl] *a (LAW)* δικαστικός.

judicious [dʒuːˈdɪʃəs] *a* συνετός, γνωστικός, φρόνιμος.

judo [ˈdʒuːdəʊ] *n* τζούντο *nt inv.*

jug [dʒʌg] *n* κανάτι, στάμνα.

juggle [ˈdʒʌgl] *vi* ταχυδακτυλουργώ, εξαπατώ || **~r** *n* ταχυδακτυλουργός.

Jugoslav [ˈjuːgəʊˈslɑːv] = **Yugoslav.**

juice [dʒuːs] *n* χυμός, ζουμί.

juicy [ˈdʒuːsɪ] *a* χυμώδης, ζουμερός.

jukebox [ˈdʒuːkbɒks] *n* τζουκ μποξ *nt inv.*

July [dʒuːˈlaɪ] *n* Ιούλιος.

jumble [ˈdʒʌmbl] *n* ανακάτεμα *nt*, κυκεώνας, μπέρδεμα ♦ *vt (also:* **~ up)** ανακατεύω, μπερδεύω.

jumbo [ˈdʒʌmbəʊ] *attr.* ~ **jet** *n* τζάμπο τζετ *nt inv.*

jump [dʒʌmp] *vi* πηδώ ♦ *vi* πηδώ πάνω από, υπερπηδώ ♦ *n* πήδημα *nt*, άλμα *nt* || **~ed-up** *a (col)* νεόπλουτος.

jumper [ˈdʒʌmpə*] *n* μπλούζα, ριχτή ζακέτα.

jumpy [ˈdʒʌmpɪ] *a* νευρικός.

junction [ˈdʒʌŋkʃən] *n (road)* διασταύρωση || *(RAIL)* διακλάδωση.

juncture [ˈdʒʌŋktʃə*] *n*: **at this ~** στο σημείο αυτό.

June [dʒuːn] *n* Ιούνιος.

jungle [ˈdʒʌŋgl] *n (tropical)* ζούγκλα.

junior [ˈdʒuːnɪə*] *a (in age)* νεώτερος || *(in rank)* κατώτερος, υφιστάμενος ♦ *n (US: school)* πρωτελειόφοιτος/η *m/f.*

junk [dʒʌŋk] *n (rubbish)* σκουπίδια *ntpl*, παλιοπράγματα *ntpl* || *(ship)* τζόγκα || **~shop** *n* παλιατζίδικο.

jurisdiction [dʒʊərɪsˈdɪkʃən] *n* δικαιοδοσία.

jurisprudence [dʒʊərɪsˈpruːdəns] *n* νομολογία, νομομάθεια.

juror [ˈdʒʊərə*] *n* ένορκος *m/f.*

jury [ˈdʒʊərɪ] *n* ένορκοι *mpl* || *(of contest)* κριτική επιτροπή || **~man** *n* = **juror.**

just [dʒʌst] *a (fair, right)* δίκαιος, σωστός || *(exact)* ακριβής ♦ *ad (exactly)* ακριβώς || *(barely)* μόλις || **~ as I arrived** μόλις έφθασα || **I have ~ arrived** μόλις ήλθα || **~ a little ~** τόσο δα, λίγο || **~ now** πριν λίγο, μόλις τώρα || **~ you and me** εμείς μόνο συ κι εγώ.

justice ['dʒʌstɪs] n (fairness) δικαιοσύνη || (magistrate) δικαστικός, δικαστής.

justifiable [dʒʌstɪ'faɪəbl] a δικαιολογήσιμος, εύλογος.

justification [dʒʌstɪfɪ'keɪʃən] n δικαίωση, δικαιολογία.

justify ['dʒʌstɪfaɪ] vt (prove right) αιτιολογώ || (defend etc) δικαιώνω, δικαιολογώ.

justly ['dʒʌstlɪ] ad δίκαια, ορθά.

justness ['dʒʌstnɪs] n ορθότητα, το δίκαιο.

jut [dʒʌt] vi (also: ~ out) προεξέχω.

juvenile ['dʒuːvənaɪl] a νεανικός, παιδικός ♦ n νέος/α m/f.

juxtapose ['dʒʌkstəpəuz] vt (αντι)παραθέτω.

K

K (abbr of one thousand) K.

kaleidoscope [kə'laɪdəskəup] n καλειδοσκόπιο.

kangaroo [kæŋgə'ruː] n καγκουρό f inv.

keel [kiːl] n τρόπιδα, καρίνα.

keen [kiːn] a (eager) επιμελής, θερμός || ~ness n ζήλος, ενθουσιασμός.

keep [kiːp] (irreg v) vt (have) έχω, κρατώ, συντηρώ || (take care of) φυλάω, συντηρώ, τρέφω || (detain) (κατα)κρατώ, καθυστερώ || (be faithful) τηρώ, σέβομαι, μένω πιστός σε ♦ vi (continue) συνεχίζω, εξακολουθώ || (of food) διατηρούμαι, κρατώ || (remain: quiet etc) μένω, στέκομαι ♦ n τροφή, συντήρηση, έξοδα ntpl συντηρήσεως || (tower) (ακρο) πύργος || to ~ back vti κρατώ, πίσω, απομακρύνομαι, κρύβω || to ~ on vi συνεχίζω, εξακολουθώ να φορώ || '~ out' 'απαγορεύεται η είσοδος' || to ~ up

vi (+ with) διατηρώ, καλλιεργώ || ~ing n (care) φύλαξη, συντήρηση || in ~ing with σύμφωνα με, ανάλογα με.

keg [keg] n βαρελάκι.

kennel ['kɛnl] n σπιτάκι σκύλου.

kept [kɛpt] pt, pp of **keep**.

kerb(stone) ['kɜːb(stəun)] n κράσπεδο πεζοδρομίου.

kernel ['kɜːnl] n πυρήνας, κόκκος, ψύχα.

kerosene ['kɛrəsiːn] n φωτιστικό πετρέλαιο, παραφίνη.

ketchup ['kɛtʃəp] n κέτσαπ nt inv, σάλτσα τομάτας.

kettle ['kɛtl] n χύτρα.

key [kiː] n κλειδί || (to problem) κλείδα || (set of answers) κλείδα, λύση || (lever) μπλήκτρο || (MUS) τόνος ♦ a (position etc) βασικός, καίριος || to ~ in vt πληκτρολογώ || ~board n πλήκτρο, κλαβιέ nt inv || (of computer, typewriter) πληκτρολόγιο ♦ vt (COMPUT) πληκτρολογώ || ~hole n κλειδαρότρυπα || ~note n κύρια ιδέα || ~ ring n κρίκος κλειδιών.

khaki ['kɑːkɪ] n, a χακί.

kick [kɪk] vt λακτίζω, κλωτσώ || (col) παραπονιέμαι, αντιρρώ ♦ n λάκτισμα nt, κλωτσιά || (thrill) συγκίνηση || to ~ around vi (col) σέρνομαι, χαζεύω || to ~ off vi (SPORT) δίνω την πρώτη κλωτσιά || ~off n (SPORT) εναρκτήριο λάκτισμα.

kid [kɪd] n (child) πιτσιρίκος, παιδάκι || (goat) κατσικάκι, ρίφι || (leather) σεβρό.

kidnap ['kɪdnæp] vt απάγω, κλέβω || ~per n παρανομέγεας || ~ping n απαγωγή.

kidney ['kɪdnɪ] n νεφρό.

kill [kɪl] vt (murder) φονεύω, σκοτώνω || (destroy) ξεριζώνω, αφανίζω ♦ n κυνήγι || ~er n φονιάς/φόνισσα m/f.

kiln [kıln] n καμίνι, κλίβανος.

kilo ['kiːləu] n κιλό || ~**gramme**, ~**gram** (US) n χιλιόγραμμο || ~**metre**, ~**meter** (US) n χιλιόμετρο || ~**watt** n κιλοβάτ nt inv.

kilt [kılt] n φουστανέλα.

kimono [kı'məunəu] n κιμονό.

kin [kın] n συγγενείς mpl, συγγενολόι.

kind [kaınd] a καλός, καλοκάγαθος, καλόβολος ♦ n είδος nt || a ~ **of** ας το πούμε, κάποιος || **two of a** ~ του ιδίου φυράματος || **in** ~ (merchandise) σε είδος || (same way) με το ίδιο νόμισμα.

kindergarten ['kındəgɑːtn] n νηπιαγωγείο.

kindhearted ['kaınd'hɑːtıd] a καλόκαρδος.

kindle ['kındl] vt ανάβω || (rouse) εξάπτω, προκαλώ.

kindly ['kaındlı] a καλός, ευγενικός ♦ ad ευγενικά, μαλακά, φιλικά.

kindness ['kaındnıs] n αγαθότητα, καλωσύνη.

kindred ['kındrıd] n συγγενείς, συγγενικός.

king [kıŋ] n βασιλιάς || (CARDS) ρήγας || ~**dom** n βασίλειο || ~**fisher** n ψαροφάγος, μπιρμπίλι.

kink [kıŋk] n ζάρα, στράβωμα nt || ~**y** a (fig) ιδιότροπος || (hair) σγουρός.

kiosk ['kiːɒsk] n (TEL) θάλαμος || (shop) κιόσκι, περίπτερο.

kipper ['kıpə*] n καπνιστή ρέγγα.

kiss [kıs] n φιλί, φίλημα nt ♦ vt φιλώ nt ♦ vi: **they** ~**ed** φιλήθηκαν.

kit [kıt] n σύνεργα ntpl, ατομικά είδη ntpl || ~**bag** n σάκκος.

kitchen ['kıtʃın] n κουζίνα || ~**garden** n λαχανόκηπος || ~**sink** n νεροχύτης.

kite [kaıt] n (χαρτ) αετός || (bird) τσίφτης.

kitten ['kıtn] n γατάκι.

kitty ['kıtı] n (pool of money) κοινό ταμείο.

kleptomaniac [kleptəu'meınıæk] n κλεπτομανής m/f.

knack [næk] n επιδεξιότητα, κόλπο.

knapsack ['næpsæk] n δισάκκι, γυλιός.

knead [niːd] vt ζυμώνω.

knee [niː] n γόνατο || ~**cap** n επιγονατίδα.

kneel [niːl] (irreg v) vi γονατίζω.

knell [nel] n καμπάνισμα nt, κωδωνοκρουσία.

knelt [nelt] pt, pp of **kneel**.

knew [njuː] pt of **know**.

knickers ['nıkəz] npl κιλότα.

knife [naıf] n μαχαίρι ♦ vt μαχαιρώνω.

knight [naıt] n ιππότης || (CHESS) άλογο || ~**hood** n ιπποτισμός, ο τίτλος του ιππότη.

knit [nıt] vt πλέκω ♦ vi συγκολλώ || ~**ting** n πλέξιμο, πλεκτική || ~**ting machine** n πλεκτομηχανή || ~**ting needle** n βελόνα (του πλεξίματος) || ~**wear** n πλεκτό, τρικό.

knives [naıvz] npl of **knife**.

knob [nɒb] n (of door) πόμολο || (butter etc) κομμάτι.

knock [nɒk] vt (criticize) βρίζω, κακολογώ ♦ vi προσκρούω, χτυπώ ♦ n κτύπημα nt || **to** ~ **off** vi (finish) σταματώ || **to** ~ **out** vt βγάζω, τινάζω, || (SPORT) βγάζω νοκ-άουτ || ~ **er** n (on door) κτυπητήρι || ~ - **kneed** a στραβοπόδης, στραβοκάνης || ~ **out** n (lit) νοκ-άουτ nt inv.

knot [nɒt] n (of rope etc) κόμπος, δεσμός || (of ribbon) κόμπος || (measure) κόμβος ♦ vt δένω κόμπο.

know [nəu] (irreg v) vti (be aware of) ξέρω || (recognize) γνωρίζω, διακρίνω, ξέρω || **to** ~ **how to do** ξέρω πώς || ~**all** n παντογνώστης/τρια m/f || ~**how** n μέθοδος f, τέχνη || ~**ing** a

έξυπνος, πονηρός|| ~**ingly** ad
σκόπιμας, πονηρά.

knowledge ['nɒlɪdʒ] n (what one
knows) γνώση, μάθηση || (information)
είδηση, πληροφορίες fpl|| ~**able** a
καλά πληροφορημένος,
μορφωμένος.

known [nəʊn] pp of **know**.

knuckle ['nʌkl] n φάλαγγα,
κλείδωση.

K.O. n abbr of **knockout**.

koran [kɔ'rɑː] n κοράνιο.

L

l. abbr of **litre**.

lab [læb] n abbr of **laboratory**.

label ['leɪbl] n ετικέτα ♦ vt
επιγράφω, κολλώ ετικέτα.

labor ['leɪbə*] n (US) = **labour**.

laboratory [lə'bɒrətərɪ] n
εργαστήριο.

laborious [lə'bɔːrɪəs] a κοπιώδης,
επίπονος.

labour ['leɪbə*] n εργασία, μόχθος ||
(workmen) εργάτες mpl|| ~**er** n
εργάτης/τρια m/f|| **L ~ Party** n
εργατικό κόμμα.

lace [leɪs] n δαντέλα || (braid) σειρήτι
|| (cord) κορδόνι ♦ vt δένω, πλέκω,
βάζω δαντέλες.

lack [læk] vt στερούμαι n έλλειψη
|| **for ~** of λόγω ελλείψεως.

lackadaisical [lækə'deɪzɪkəl] a
άτονος, νωθρός.

laconic [lə'kɒnɪk] a λακωνικός.

lacquer ['lækə*] n βερνίκι, λάκα.

lad [læd] n (boy) αγόρι || (young man)
παλληκάρι.

ladder ['lædə*] n (lit) σκάλα,
ανεμόσκαλα || (fig) (κοινωνική)
κλίμακα.

laden ['leɪdn] a φορτωμένος.

ladle ['leɪdl] n κουτάλα.

lady ['leɪdɪ] n κυρία || (title) λαίδη ||

'Ladies' (lavatory) 'Κυριών',
'Γυναικών' || ~**bird**, ~**bug** (US) n
λαμπρίτσα, πασχαλίτσα|| ~**-in-
waiting** n Κυρία των Τιμών || ~**like**
a αρχοντικός, ευγενικός.

lag [læg] n (delay) καθυστέρηση,
επιβράδυνση ♦ vi (also: ~ **behind**)
βραδυπορώ ♦ vt (pipes) επενδύω,
φασκιώνω.

lager ['lɑːgə*] n ελαφρά μπύρα,
λάγκερ f inv.

lagging ['lægɪŋ] n μονωτική
επένδυση.

lagoon [lə'guːn] n λιμνοθάλασσα.

laid [leɪd] pt, pp of **lay** || **to be ~ up**
είμαι κρεβατωμένος.

lair [lɛə*] n φωλιά, άντρο.

lake [leɪk] n λίμνη.

lamb [læm] n αρνάκι || (meat) αρνί ||
~ **chop** n παϊδάκι.

lame [leɪm] a κουτσός || (excuse) μη
πειστικός.

lament [lə'ment] n θρήνος ♦ vt
θρηνώ, οδύρομαι || ~**able** a
αξιοθρήνητος.

laminated ['læmɪneɪtɪd] a
φυλλωτός.

lamp [læmp] n λύχνος, λυχνάρι ||
(globe) λάμπα || (in street) φανάρι ||
~**post** n φανοστάτης || ~**shade** n
αμπαζούρ nt inv.

lance [lɑːns] n λόγχη ♦ vt εγχειρίζω,
ανοίγω || ~ **corporal** n
υποδεκανέας.

lancet ['lɑːnsɪt] n νυστέρι.

land [lænd] n γη, στερεά || (ground)
γη, έδαφος nt || (country) γη, χώρα ||
(estate) κτήμα || vi (from ship)
αποβιβάζομαι || (AVIAT)
προσγειούμαι || (fig: arrive, fall)
πέφτω ♦ vt (obtain) πιάνω, λαμβάνω
|| (passengers, goods) αποβιβάζω,
ξεφορτώνω || ~**ing** n απόβαση ||
(AVIAT) προσγείωση || (platform)
πλατύσκαλο || ~**ing craft** n
αποβατικό σκάφος || ~**ing stage** n

αποβάθρα || ~ing strip n λωρίδα
προσγειώσεως || ~lady n
σπιτονοικοκυρά || ~locked a
μεσόγειος || ~lord n
σπιτονοικοκύρης || (innkeeper)
ξενοδόχος || ~lubber n στεριανός ||
~mark n ορόσημο || ~owner n
γαιοκτήμονας.
landscape ['lændskeip] n τοπίο ||
(painting) ζωγραφική τοπίων.
landslide ['lændslaid] n (GEOG)
(κατ)ολίσθηση || (POL) εντυπωσιακή
στροφή.
lane [lein] n δρομίσκος, μονοπάτι ||
(of road) λωρίδα, διάδρομος || (SPORT)
ατομική πίστα, λωρίδα.
language ['læŋgwidʒ] n γλώσσα ||
(national) γλώσσα, διάλεκτος ΄|
(style) γλώσσα, ομιλία.
languid ['læŋgwid] a νωθρός,
αδρανής.
languish ['læŋgwiʃ] vi λυώνω,
μαραίνομαι.
lank [læŋk] a μακρυά και ίσια || ~y
a μακρύς και λεπτός.
lanolin ['lænəulin] n λανολίνη.
lantern ['læntən] n φανάρι.
lap [læp] n ποδιά, γόνατα ntpl ||
(SPORT) γύρος, βόλτα ♦ vt γλείφω ♦
vi (of waves) παφλάζω || ~dog n
χαϊδεμένο σκυλάκι.
lapel [lə'pel] n πέτο.
lapse [læps] n σφάλμα nt || (moral)
παράβαση || (of time) παρέλευση,
εκπνοή.
larceny ['lɑːsəni] n κλοπή.
lard [lɑːd] n λαρδί.
larder ['lɑːdə*] n αποθήκη
τροφίμων, κελλάρι.
large [lɑːdʒ] a (broad) ευρύχωρος,
εκτενής || (big, numerous) μεγάλος ||
at ~ (free) ελεύθερος || (extensively)
γενικά || ~ly ad σε μεγάλο βαθμό ||
~scale a σε μεγάλη κλίμακα,
μεγάλος.
lark [lɑːk] n (bird) κορυδαλός || (joke)

αστείο, φάρσα || **to** ~ **about** vi (col)
αστιεύομαι, κάνω φάρσες.
larva ['lɑːvə] n νύμφη.
laryngitis [lærin'dʒaitis] n
λαρυγγίτιδα.
larynx ['læriŋks] n λάρυγγι.
lash [læʃ] n (stroke) καμτσικιά ♦ vt
(beat against) δέρνω, ξεσπώ, κτυπώ ||
(whip) μαστιγώνω || (bind)
(προσ)δένω || **to** ~ **out** vi (with fists)
επιτίθεμαι, εφορμώ || (spend money)
κάνω σπατάλες.
lass [læs] n κορίτσι, κοπέλα.
lasso [læ'suː] n λάσσο ♦ vt πιάνω με
λάσσο.
last [lɑːst] a τελευταίος, τελικός ♦ ad
τελευταία ♦ n (person or thing)
τελευταίος, ύστατος || (for shoe)
καλαπόδι ♦ vi (continue, hold out)
διαρκώ, παραμένω || (remain)
συντηρούμαι, διατηρούμαι || **at** ~
επί τέλους|| ~ **night** χθες το βράδυ
|| ~ **week** την περασμένη βδομάδα
|| ~**ing** a διαρκείας, που κρατά || ~-
minute a της τελευταίας στιγμής.
latch [lætʃ] n μάνταλο, σύρτης || (yale
lock) λουκέτο || ~**key** n απλό κλειδί,
αντικλείδι.
late [leit] a καθυστερημένος,
αργοπορημένος || (not early) αργά ||
(recent) παλιός, πρώην, τέως ||
(recently dead) μακαρίτης ♦ ad
καθυστερημένα, αργά || (late hour)
αργά || **of** ~ πρόσφατα || ~ **in the
day** αργά το βραδάκι || ~**comer** n
αργοπορημένος || ~**ly** ad
πρόσφατα, τελευταία || ~**ness** n (of
person) αργοπορία || (of hour)
προχωρημένη ώρα.
latent ['leitənt] a αφανής, κρυφός.
later ['leitə*] comp a, comp ad of
late.
lateral ['lætərəl] a πλάγιος,
πλευρικός.
latest ['leitist] sup a, sup ad of **late** ||

n (news) το νεώτερο || **at the ~** το αργότερο.

lathe [leɪð] *n* τόρνος.

lather ['lɑːðəˠ] *n* σαπουνάδα ♦ *vt* σαπουνίζω ♦ *vi* κάνω αφρό.

Latin ['lætɪn] *n* Λατινική (γλώσσα) ♦ *a* λατινικός || **~America** *n* Λατινική Αμερική || **~American** *a* λατινοαμερικανικός ♦ *n* Λατινοαμερικανός/ίδα *m/f.*

latitude ['lætɪtjuːd] *n* γεωγραφικό πλάτος *nt* || *(freedom)* ευρυχωρία, περιθώριο.

latrine [lə'triːn] *n* αποχωρητήριο, μέρος *nt.*

latter ['lætəˠ] *a (more recent)* ο δεύτερος, άλλος || *(later)* τελευταίος, πρόσφατος ♦ *n (opposite of former)* ο δεύτερος, άλλος || **~ly** *ad* τώρα τελευταία, πρόσφατα.

lattice work ['lætɪswɜːk] *n* δικτυωτό, καφάσι.

laudible ['lɔːdəbl] *a* αξιέπαινος.

laugh [lɑːf] *n* γέλιο ♦ *vi* γελώ || **to ~ at** *vt* διασκεδάζω, περιγελώ, γελώ για || **to ~ off** *vt* γελοιοποιώ || **~able** *a* γελοίος, αστείος, διασκεδαστικός || **~ing stock** *n* περίγελος, κορόιδο || **~ter** *n* γέλιο.

launch [lɔːntʃ] *n (of ship)* καθέλκυση || *(of rocket)* εκτόξευση || *(ship)* άκατος || *(motor)* βενζινάκατος *f* ♦ *vt (ship)* καθελκύω || *(ship)* προβάλλω, βάζω εμπρός || **~ing** *n* καθέλκυση, εκτόξευση || **~(ing) pad** *n* πλατφόρμα εκτόξευσης.

launder ['lɔːndəˠ] *vt* πλένω και σιδερώνω || **~ette** *n* πλυντήριο αυτοεξυπηρέτησης.

laundry ['lɔːndrɪ] *n (place)* πλυντήριο || *(clothes)* ρούχα *ntpl* για πλύσιμο.

laureate ['lɔːrɪɪt] *a see* poet.

laurel ['lɒrəl] *n* δάφνη.

lava ['lɑːvə] *n* λάβα.

lavatory ['lævətrɪ] *n* αποχωρητήριο, τουαλέτα.

lavender ['lævɪndəˠ] *n* λεβάντα.

lavish ['lævɪʃ] *a* γενναιόδωρος, σπάταλος || *(abundant)* άφθονος, πλούσιος ♦ *vt* κατασπαταλώ, διασπαβίζω || **~ly** *ad* άφθονα, σπάταλα.

law [lɔː] *n* νόμος, νομικά *ntpl* || *(system of laws)* δίκαιο || *(of game etc)* κανόνες *mpl* || **~-abiding** *a* νομοταγής || **~-breaker** *n* παραβάτης του νόμου || **~ court** *n* δικαστήριο || **~ful** *a* νόμιμος || **~less** *a* άνομος, παράνομος.

lawn [lɔːn] *n* πρασιά, γρασίδι || **~ mower** *n* χορτοκόπτης || **tennis** *n* τέννις *nt inv.*

law school ['lɔːskuːl] *n* σχολή νομικής.

law student ['lɔːstjuːdənt] *n* φοιτητής/ήτρια *m/f* νομικής.

lawsuit ['lɔːsuːt] *n* δίκη.

lawyer ['lɔːjəˠ] *n* νομικός *m/f,* δικηγόρος *m/f.*

lax [læks] *a* χαλαρός || *(morals etc)* έκλυτος, άτακτος.

laxative ['læksətɪv] *n* καθάρσιο.

laxity ['læksɪtɪ] *n* χαλαρότητα.

lay [leɪ] *(irreg v) pt of* lie || *a* λαϊκός, μη ειδικός ♦ *vt (put down)* τοποθετώ, θέτω, βάζω || *(lay low)* ξαπλώνω, σωριάζω || *(prepare)* βάζω, στρώνω || *(eggs)* γεννώ, κάνω || **to ~ aside** *vt* θέτω κατά μέρος, βάζω || **to ~ by** *vt* αποταμιεύω, οικονομώ || **to ~ down** *vt παραδίδω* || *(plan)* σχεδιάζω || **to ~ off** *vt (workers)* απολύω || **to ~ on** *vt* επιβάλλω, επιθέτω || **to ~ out** *vt* απλώνω || *(spend)* ξοδεύω || *(plan)* σχεδιάζω || **to ~ up** *vt (store)* αποθηκεύω || *(ship)* παροπλίζω || **~by** *n* βοηθητική λωρίδα στάθμευσης.

layer ['leɪəˠ] *n* στρώμα *nt.*

layette [lei'ɛt] n τα μωρουδιακά ntpl.

layman [lei'mən] n λαϊκός.

layout ['leiaut] n σχέδιο.

laze [leiz] vi τεμπελιάζω, χασομερώ || **laziness** ['leizinis] n τεμπελιά, χάζεμα nt || **lazy** ['leizi] a οκνηρός, τεμπέλης.

lb. abbr. of **pound** (weight).

lead [led] n μόλυβδος || (of pencil) μολύβι, γραφίτης.

lead [li:d] (irreg v) n (front position) πρώτη θέση, αρχηγία || (distance, time ahead) προπορεία || (example) καθοδήγηση, παράδειγμα nt || (clue) υπαινιγμός || (THEAT) πρωταγωνιστής/ίστρια m/f ♦ vt οδηγώ, καθοδηγώ || (group etc) ηγούμαι, διευθύνω ♦ vi άγω, καταλήγω, πηγαίνω || **to ~ astray** vt παραπλανώ || **to ~ away** vt (παρα)σύρω || **to ~ back** vt επαναφέρω || **to ~ on** vt προτρέπω κεντρίζω || **to ~ to** vt (street) οδηγώ σε, πηγαίνω σε || (result in) καταλήγω || **to ~ up to** vt οδηγώ σε || **~ er** n αρχηγός, ηγέτης || (newspaper) κύριο άρθρο || **~ ership** n ηγεσία, αρχηγία || **~ ing** a κύριος, ηγετικός, σημαίνων || **~ ing lady** n (THEAT) πρωταγωνίστρια || **~ ing light** n (person) ηγετική φυσιογνωμία.

leaf [li:f] n φύλλο || (thin sheet) φύλλο || (table) φύλλο (τραπεζιού).

leaflet ['li:flit] n φυλλάδιο.

league [li:g] n σύνδεσμος, ένωση, συμμαχία || (measure) λεύγα.

leak [li:k] n διαφυγή, διαρροή || (hole) τρύπα ♦ vt (liquid etc) διαρρέω (δια)φεύγω || (NAUT) κάνω νερά ♦ vi (of pipe etc) διαρρέω, τρέχω || **to ~ out** vi (liquid etc) διαρρέω || (information) διαδίδομαι.

lean [li:n] (irreg v) a (thin) λιγνός || (meat) άπαχος || (poor) ισχνός, φτωχός ♦ n άπαχο κρέας nt ♦ vi κλίνω, γέρνω ♦ vt ακουμπώ, στηρίζομαι || **to ~ back** vi γέρνω προς τα πίσω || **to ~ forward** vi γέρνω προς τα εμπρός || **to ~ on** vt στηρίζομαι, ακουμπώ || **to ~ over** vi κύπτω || **~ ing** n κλίση, τάση || **~ t** [lent] pt, pp of **lean** || **~ -to** n υπόστεγο.

leap [li:p] (irreg v) n πήδημα nt ♦ vi πηδώ || **by ~ s and bounds** αλματωδώς, καλπάζων || **~ frog** n καβάλες fpl, βαρελάκια ntpl || **~ t** [lept] pt, pp of **leap** || **~ year** n δίσεκτος χρόνος.

learn [lɜ:n] (irreg v) vti μαθαίνω || **~ ed** a μορφωμένος, πολυμαθής || **~ er** n (also AUT) μαθητευόμενος, αρχάριος || **~ ing** n (εκ)μάθηση, μόρφωση.

lease [li:s] n εκμίσθωση, ενοικίαση, συμβόλαιο ♦ vt εκμισθώνω, ενοικιάζω.

leash [li:ʃ] n λουρί, αλυσίδα.

least [li:st] a ελάχιστος, μικρότατος, λιγότερος ♦ n (το) λιγότερο, (το) μικρότερο || **at ~** τουλάχιστο || **not in the ~** καθόλου, ποτέ.

leather ['leðə*] n δέρμα nt, πετσί ♦ a δερμάτινος, πέτσινος.

leave [li:v] (irreg v) vt (go away from) φεύγω, εγκαταλείπω || (go without taking) αφήνω || (let stay) αφήνω || (give by will) αφήνω ♦ vi (depart) φεύγω ♦ n άδεια || (MIL) άδεια || **on ~** με άδεια || **to take one's ~ of** αποχαιρετώ, φεύγω || **to ~ out** vt παραλείπω.

leaves [li:vz] npl of **leaf.**

Lebanon ['lebənɒn]: **the ~ o** Λίβανος.

lecherous ['letʃərəs] a λάγνος, ασελγής.

lecture ['lektʃə*] n διάλεξη, μάθημα nt ♦ vi κάνω διάλεξη, κάνω μάθημα || **~ r** n ομιλητής/ήτρια m/f, υφηγητής/ήτρια m/f.

led [lɛd] *pt, pp of* **lead.**

ledge [lɛdʒ] *n* άκρο, χείλος *nt*, ράφι || *(of rock)* ύφαλος, ξέρα.

ledger ['lɛdʒəʳ] *n* καθολικό (κατάστιχο).

lee [liː] *n (from wind)* προκάλυμμα *nt*.

leek [liːk] *n* πράσο.

leer [lɪəʳ] *vi* στραβοκοιτάζω.

leeway ['liːweɪ] *n (fig)* χαμός χρόνου, περιθώριο.

left [lɛft] *pt, pp of* **leave** ♦ *a* αριστερός ♦ *n* (το) αριστερό, *n* αριστερά || the **L**~ *(POL)* η αριστερά || ~**-handed** *a* αριστερόχειρας || ~**-luggage (office)** *n* γραφείο καταθέσεως αποσκευών || ~**-overs** *npl* πλεονάσματα *ntpl*, υπολείμματα *ntpl* || ~**-wing** *n (POL)* αριστερός.

leg [lɛg] *n* πόδι, γάμπα || *(of table etc)* πόδι || *(on trouser etc)* γάμπα.

legacy ['lɛgəsɪ] *n* κληροδότημα *nt* || *(from ancestors)* κληρονομιά.

legal ['liːgəl] *a* νομικός || *(allowed)* νόμιμος || ~**ize** *vt* νομιμοποιώ || ~**ly** *ad* νόμιμα, νομικώς || ~ **tender** *n* νόμισμα *nt* (υποχρεωτικά δεκτό).

legend ['lɛdʒənd] *n* θρύλος, μύθος || ~**ary** *a* θρυλικός, μυθικός.

legible ['lɛdʒɪbl] *a* ευανάγνωστος.

legion ['liːdʒən] *n* λεγεώνα ♦ *a (countless)* αναρίθμητος.

legislate ['lɛdʒɪsleɪt] *vi* νομοθετώ.

legislation [lɛdʒɪs'leɪʃən] *n* νομοθεσία.

legislative ['lɛdʒɪslətɪv] *a* νομοθετικός.

legislature ['lɛdʒɪslətʃəʳ] *n* νομοθετικό σώμα *nt*.

legitimacy [lɪ'dʒɪtɪməsɪ] *n* νομιμότητα, γνησιότητα.

legitimate [lɪ'dʒɪtɪmɪt] *a* νόμιμος, λογικός.

leisure ['lɛʒəʳ] *n* σχόλη, άνεση, ελεύθερες ώρες *fpl* ♦ *a* της σχόλης, της αργίας || **at** ~ ελεύθερος, έχων

καιρό || ~**ly** *a* αβίαστος, αργός, άνετος.

lemon ['lɛmən] *n* λεμόνι || *(colour)* λεμονής || ~**ade** *n* λεμονάδα.

lend [lɛnd] *(irreg v) vt* δανείζω || *(dignity etc)* (προσ)δίδω || **it** ~**s itself to** προσφέρεται, κάνει για || ~**er** *n* δανειστής/ίσρια *m/f*|| ~**ing library** *n* δανειστική βιβλιοθήκη.

length [lɛŋθ] *n* μήκος *nt*, μάκρος *nt* || *(of road, pipe etc)* μήκος *nt* || *(of material)* κομμάτι || **at** ~ *(finally)* επί τέλους || *(time)* για πολλή ώρα || *(extent)* εν εκτάσει || ~**en** *vt* μακραίνω, επιμηκύνω ♦ *vi* επεκτείνομαι, παρατείνομαι || ~**ways** *ad* κατά μήκος, στο μάκρος || ~**y** *a* μακροσκελής, εκτενής.

leniency ['liːnɪənsɪ] *n* ηπιότητα, επιείκεια.

lenient ['liːnɪənt] *a* ήπιος, επιεικής.

lens [lɛnz] *n* φακός.

lent [lɛnt] *pt, pp of* **lend** || **L** ~ *n* Σαρακοστή.

lentil ['lɛntɪl] *n* φακή.

leopard ['lɛpəd] *n* λεοπάρδαλη.

leper ['lɛpəʳ] *n* λεπρός/*n m/f*.

leprosy ['lɛprəsɪ] *n* λέπρα.

lesbian ['lɛzbɪən] *n* λεσβιακός ♦ *n* λεσβία.

less [lɛs] *a comp of* **little** || λιγότερος ♦ *ad* λιγότερο ♦ *n* λιγότερο.

lessen ['lɛsn] *vi* μειούμαι, μικραίνω, λιγοστεύω ♦ *vt* μειώνω, ελαττώνω, μικραίνω.

lesson ['lɛsn] *n* μάθημα *nt*.

lest [lɛst] *cj* μήπως, μη τυχόν.

let [lɛt] *(irreg v) vt (allow)* αφήνω, επιτρέπω || *(lease)* ενοικιάζω, εκμισθώνω ♦ *n:* **without** ~ **or hindrance** χωρίς εμπόδιο, ελεύθερα || ~**'s go** ας πάμε || **'to** ~' 'ενοικιάζεται' || **to** ~ **down** *vt* κατεβάζω || *(disappoint)* απογοητεύω, εγκαταλείπω || **to** ~ **go** *vti* ελευθερώνω, χαλαρώνω || **to** ~ **off**

lethal [ˈliːθl] a θανατηφόρος.

lethargic [leˈθɑːdʒɪk] a ληθαργικός, νυσταλέος.

lethargy [ˈleθədʒɪ] n λήθαργος, ατονία.

letter [ˈletə*] n (sign) γράμμα nt, στοιχείο || επιστολή, γράμμα || ~box n γραμματοκιβώτιο || ~ing n γράμματα ntpl, μαρκάρισμα nt.

lettuce [ˈletɪs] n μαρούλι.

let-up [ˈletʌp] n (col) μείωση, χαλάρωση.

leukaemia, leukemia (US) [luːˈkiːmɪə] n λευκαιμία.

level [ˈlevl] a επίπεδο, οριζόντιος ♦ ad οριζοντίως ♦ n επίπεδο, επίπεδος επιφάνεια || (height) στάθμη ♦ vt ισοπεδώνω, οριζοντιώνω || **on the ~** (lit) επίπεδος, στο αλφάδι || (fig: honest) τίμια, εντάξει || **to ~ off** or **out** vi εξισώνω || ~ **crossing** n επίπεδο διάβαση || ~-**headed** a ισορροπημένος, ψύχραιμος.

lever [ˈliːvə*] n μοχλός ♦ vt κινώ μοχλό || ~**age** n ενέργεια μοχλού, μόχλευση.

levity [ˈlevɪtɪ] n ελαφρότητα, έλλειψη σοβαρότητας.

levy [ˈlevɪ] n (taxes) είσπραξη || (MIL) στρατολογία ♦ vt εισπράττω, επιβάλλω || (MIL) στρατολογώ.

lewd [luːd] a λάγνος, ασελγής.

liability [laɪəˈbɪlɪtɪ] n (being liable) ευθύνη, υποχρέωση || (debt) υποχρέωση, οφειλή || (disadvantage) προδιάθεση, τάση.

liable [ˈlaɪəbl] a (responsible) υπεύθυνος || (likely) ποκείμενος.

liaison [liːˈeɪzɒn] n (coordination) σύνδεσμος.

liar [ˈlaɪə*] n ψεύτης.

libel [ˈlaɪbəl] n λίβελλος, δυσφήμιση ♦ vt διασύρω, δυσφημώ.

liberal [ˈlɪbərəl] a (generous) γενναιόδωρος || (open-minded) φιλελεύθερος ♦ n φιλελεύθερος || **L~ Party** Φιλελεύθερο Κόμμα.

liberate [ˈlɪbəreɪt] vt απελευθερώνω.

liberation [lɪbəˈreɪʃən] n απελευθέρωση.

liberty [ˈlɪbətɪ] n ελευθερία || **at ~** ελεύθερος, εύκαιρος.

librarian [laɪˈbrɛərɪən] n βιβλιοθηκάριος m/f.

library [ˈlaɪbrərɪ] n βιβλιοθήκη.

libretto [lɪˈbretəʊ] n λιμπρέτο.

Libya [ˈlɪbɪə] n Λιβύη || ~**n** a λιβικός ♦ n (person) Λίβυος/α m/f.

lice [laɪs] npl of **louse**.

licence, license (US) [ˈlaɪsəns] n (permit) άδεια, έγκριση, προνόμιο || (lack of control) κατάχρηση || ~ **plate** n (US AUT) πινακίδα.

license [ˈlaɪsəns] vt δίνω άδεια, παρέχω άδεια || ~**d** a (for alcohol: premises) με άδεια πωλήσεως ποτού || ~**e** n προνομιούχος.

licentious [laɪˈsɛnʃəs] a ακόλαστος.

lichen [ˈlaɪkən] n λειχήνα.

lick [lɪk] vt γλείφω || (of flames etc) παίζω με, εγγίζω, καταβροχθίζω ♦ n γλείψιμο || (small amount) μικρή ποσότητα.

licorice [ˈlɪkərɪs] n γλυκόριζα.

lid [lɪd] n κάλυμμα nt, καπάκι.

lido [ˈliːdəʊ] n (for swimming) δημόσια πισίνα.

lie [laɪ] (irreg v) n ψέμα nt ♦ vi (speak) λέω ψέματα || (rest) είμαι ξαπλωμένος, μένω || (of object: be situated) κείμαι, ευρίσκομαι.

lieu [luː]: **n in ~ of** αντί του, στη θέση του.

lieutenant [lɛfˈtɛnənt] n (army)

υπολοχαγός || [luː ˈtɛnənt] (US) υποσμηναγός.

life [laɪf] n (being alive) ζωή || (way of living) τρόπος ζωής, ζωή || (time of life) ζωή, διάρκεια ζωής, βίος || (story) βίος, βιογραφία || (energy, vigour) ζωηρότητα, ζωή, κίνηση || ~ **assurance** n ασφάλεια ζωής || ~ **- belt** n σωσίβιο || ~ **boat** n ναυαγοσωστική λέμβος /|| ~ **-guard** n ναυαγοσώστης || ~ **jacket** n σωσίβιο || ~ **-less** a (dead) νεκρός, χωρίς ζωή, χωρίς κέφι || ~ **-like** a ρεαλιστικός, ζωντανός || ~ **-line** n (lit) σωσίβιο σχοινί || ~ **-long** a ισόβιος, ολόκληρης ζωής || ~ **-sized** a φυσικού μεγέθους || ~ **span** n διάρκεια ζωής, μέσος όρος ζωής || ~ **time** n ζωή.

lift [lɪft] vt (αν)υψώνω, σηκώνω || (col: steal) κλέβω ♦ vi υψώνομαι, σηκώνομαι ♦ n ανύψωση, σήκωμα nt || (AVIAT) άνωση || (machine, elevator) ανελκυστήρας, ασανσέρ nt inv || (free ride) παίρνω στο αυτοκίνητο.

ligament [ˈlɪɡəmənt] n σύνδεσμος.

light [laɪt] (irreg v) n φως nt || (giving light) φως nt, φωτισμός || (for cigarette) φωτιά || (lamp) φως nt, λάμπα || (brightness) λάμψη || (of dawn) λάμψη || (information) διαφώτιση || (aspect) φως nt, όψη, άποψη ♦ vt ανάβω || (set burning) ανάβω || (brighten) φωτίζω, φέγγω ♦ a (bright) φωτεινός || (colour) ανοιχτόχρωμος, ξανθός || (not heavy) ελαφρός || (easy to do) εύκολος || (delicate) ελαφρός, απαλός || (cheerful) εύθυμος || to ~ **up** vi (lamps) ανάβω, φωτίζω || (face) αστράφτω, λάμπω ♦ vt (illuminate) (δια)φωτίζω || ~ **bulb** n λάμπα, λαμπτήρας || ~ **en** vi (brighten) φωτίζομαι || (flash lightning) αστράφτω ♦ vt (give light to) φωτίζω

|| (make less heavy) ελαφρώνω || ~ **er** n (cigarette lighter) αναπτήρας || (boat) φορτηγίδα || ~ **-headed** a ζαλισμένος || (thoughtless) επιπόλαιος, απερίσκεπτος || ~ **-hearted** a εύθυμος, χαρούμενος || ~ **house** n φάρος || ~ **ing** n (on road) φωτισμός || (in theatre) φωτισμός || ~ **ly** ad ελαφρά, ελαφρά || ~ **meter** n (PHOT) μετρητής φωτός || ~ **ness** n ελαφρότητα.

lightning [ˈlaɪtnɪŋ] n αστραπή, κεραυνός || ~ **conductor** n αλεξικέραυνο.

light year [ˈlaɪtjɪə*] n έτος φωτός.

like [laɪk] vt μου αρέσει, συμπαθώ, προτιμώ ♦ prep σαν, όπως, ως ♦ a (similar) όμοιος, ίδιος || (equal) ίσος, παρόμοιος ♦ ad όπως, σαν ♦ n όμοιος || ~ **able** a ευχάριστος, συμπαθητικός.

likelihood [ˈlaɪklɪhud] n πιθανότητα.

likely [ˈlaɪklɪ] a πιθανός, που μπορεί να ♦ ad πιθανό, ίσως.

like-minded [laɪkˈmaɪndɪd] a με την αυτή γνώμη.

liken [ˈlaɪkən] vt συγκρίνω, παρομοιάζω.

likewise [ˈlaɪkwaɪz] ad ομοίως, επίσης, επί πλέον.

liking [ˈlaɪkɪŋ] n κλίση, τάση, συμπάθεια, γούστο.

lilac [ˈlaɪlək] n πασχαλιά.

lily [ˈlɪlɪ] n κρίνο.

limb [lɪm] n μέλος nt, άκρο || (of tree) κλάδος.

limber [ˈlɪmbə*] : to ~ **up** vi γίνομαι ευλύγιστος.

limbo [ˈlɪmbəʊ] n: to be in ~ (fig) είμαι σε κατάσταση αβεβαιότητας.

lime [laɪm] n (tree) γλυκολεμονιά, κίτριο || (fruit) γλυκολέμονο, κίτρο || (GEOL) ασβέστης.

limelight ['laɪmlaɪt] n (fig) το
προσκήνιο, δημοσιότητα.

limestone ['laɪmstəʊn] n
ασβεστόλιθος.

limit ['lɪmɪt] n όριο, σύνορο, πέρας
nt ♦ vt περιορίζω || ~**ation** n
περιορισμός, ανικανότητα || ~**ed** a
περιωρισμένος, στενός || ~**ed
company (Ltd.)** n εταιρεία
περιωρισμένης ευθύνης.

limousine ['lɪməziːn] n λιμουζίνα.

limp [lɪmp] n χωλότητα ♦ vi
χωλαίνω, κουτσαίνω ♦ a απαλός,
πλαδαρός, μαλακός || (without
energy) λυωμένος, τσακισμένος.

limpet ['lɪmpɪt] n πεταλίδα.

line [laɪn] n (cord, wire, string) σχοινί,
γραμμή, σπάγγος nt || (narrow mark)
γραμμή || (row, series) σειρά, γραμμή
|| (course, direction) κατεύθυνση,
τρόπος, πορεία || (class of goods)
σειρά, συλλογή, είδος nt || (poetry
etc) στίχος, γραμμή ♦ vt (coat etc)
φοδράρω || (border) χαράσσω || **in –
with** σύμφωνα με || **to ~ up** vi
μπαίνω στη γραμμή || σχηματίζω
ουρά ♦ vt παρατάσσω, βάζω στη
γραμμή.

linear ['lɪnɪə*] a (of length) του
μήκους, γραμμικ.

linen ['lɪnɪn] n λινό ύφασμα nt ||
(articles) ασπρόρουχα ntpl.

liner ['laɪnə*] n πλοίο γραμμής.

linesman ['laɪnzmən] n (SPORT)
λάινσμαν m inv.

line-up ['laɪnʌp] n παράταξη.

linger ['lɪŋgə*] vi (remain long)
χρονοτριβώ, παρατείνομαι || (delay)
αργοπορώ, βραδύνω.

lingerie ['lænʒəriː] n γυναικεία
εσώρουχα ntpl.

lingering ['lɪŋgərɪŋ] a
παρατετομένος, βραδύς, αναιρός.

lingo ['lɪŋgəʊ] n (col) γλώσσα,
διάλεκτος f.

linguist ['lɪŋgwɪst] n γλωσσολόγος
m/f, γλωσσομαθής m/f.

linguistic [lɪŋ'gwɪstɪk] a
γλωσσολογικός || ~**s** n
γλωσσολογία.

lining ['laɪnɪŋ] n φόδρα.

link [lɪŋk] n (of chain) κρίκος ||
δεσμός σύνδεσμος ♦ vt συνδέω,
ενώνω || ~**s** npl γήπεδο γκόλφ || ~-
up n (communication) σύνδεση.

linoleum [lɪ'nəʊlɪəm] n μουσαμάς,
δαπέδου.

lion ['laɪən] n λιοντάρι || ~**ess** n
λέαινα.

lip [lɪp] n χείλι, χείλος nt || **to pay ~
service** (+ to) κάνω ψεύτικες
υποσχέσεις || ~**stick** n κραγιόν nt
inv.

liqueur [lɪ'kjʊə*] n λικέρ nt inv.

liquid ['lɪkwɪd] n υγρό ♦ a
(substance) υγρός, ρευστός || (asset)
ρευστός, διαθέσιμος || ~**ate** vt
διαλύω, ξεκαθαρίζω, χρεωκοπώ ||
~**ation** n διάλυση, εξόφλnση,
χρεωκόπηση..

liquor ['lɪkə*] n (strong drink)
οινοπνευματώδες ποτό.

lisp [lɪsp] n τραυλισμός, ψεύδισμα nt.

list [lɪst] n (of names etc) κατάλογος ||
(on ship) κλίση, γέρσιμο ♦ vt (write
down) εγγράφω, καταγράφω ♦ vi (of
ship) κλίνω, γέρνω.

listen ['lɪsn] vi ακούω, προσέχω || **to
~ to** vt ακούω || ~**er** n
ακροατής/άτρια m/f.

listless ['lɪstlɪs] a άτονος, νωθρός,
αδιάφορος.

lit [lɪt] pt, pp of **light**.

litany ['lɪtənɪ] n Λιτανεία.

liter ['liːtə*] n (US) = **litre**.

literacy ['lɪtərəsɪ] n βαθμός
μόρφωσης.

literal ['lɪtərəl] a (word for word)
κατά λέξη || (usual meaning) κατά
κυριολεξία || ~**ly** ad κυριολεκτικά.

literary ['lɪtərərɪ] a λογοτεχνικός, φιλολογικός.

literate ['lɪtərɪt] a εγγράμματος.

literature ['lɪtərɪtʃə*] n φιλολογία, λογοτεχνία.

litre ['liːtə*] n λίτρο.

litter ['lɪtə*] n (untidy bits) σκουπίδια ntpl || (young animals) γέννα, νεογνά ntpl ♦ vt κάνω άνω-κάτω, βρωμίζω με σκουπίδια.

little ['lɪtl] a (small) μικρός, λίγος, κοντός || (unimportant) ασήμαντος ♦ ad ελάχιστα, λίγο ♦ n λίγο.

liturgy ['lɪtədʒɪ] n λειτουργία.

live [lɪv] vi ζω || (pass one's life) ζω || (last) ζω, διαρκώ || (dwell) κατοικώ, διαμένω, ζω || to ~ down vt κάνω να ξεχαστεί, υπερνικώ || to ~ on vi τρέφομαι με, συντηρούμαι με || to ~ up to vt εφαρμόζω, τιμώ, εκπληρώνω.

live [laɪv] a (living) ζωντανός || (burning) αναμμένος || (wire) ηλεκτρισμένος με ρεύμα || (broadcast) ζωντανό πρόγραμμα.

livelihood ['laɪvlɪhʊd] n τα προς το ζην.

lively ['laɪvlɪ] a ζωηρός.

liver ['lɪvə*] n (ANAT) συκώτι.

livery ['lɪvərɪ] n στολή υπηρέτη.

lives [laɪvz] npl of **life**.

livestock ['laɪvstɒk] n ζώα ntpl, κτήνη ntpl.

livid ['lɪvɪd] a (lit) πελιδνός, ωχρός || (furious) φουριόζος.

living ['lɪvɪŋ] n τα προς το ζην, βίος ♦ a ζωντανός || (wage) βασικός μισθός || ~ room n σαλόνι.

lizard ['lɪzəd] n σαύρα.

load [ləʊd] n φορτίο, φόρτωμα nt ♦ vt φορτώνω, γεμίζω.

loaf [ləʊf] n καρβέλι || vi χαζεύω, τεμπελιάζω.

loan [ləʊn] n δάνειο, δανεισμός ♦ vt δανείζω || on ~ επασπασμένος.

loathe [ləʊð] vt σιχαίνομαι.

loathing ['ləʊðɪŋ] n σιχαμός, απδία.

loaves [ləʊvz] npl of **loaf**.

lobby ['lɒbɪ] n προθάλαμος, είσοδος f ♦ vt επηρεάζω βουλευτές.

lobe [ləʊb] n λοβός.

lobster ['lɒbstə*] n αστακός.

local ['ləʊkəl] a τοπικός, επιτόπιος ♦ n (pub) ταβέρνα || the ~s npl ντόπιοι mpl || ~ity n θέση, μέρος, τοποθεσία || ~ly ad τοπικά, επιτόπια.

locate [ləʊ'keɪt] vt εντοπίζω || (establish) τοποθετώ.

location [ləʊ'keɪʃən] n τοποθεσία.

loch [lɒx] n λίμνη.

lock [lɒk] n (of door) κλειδαριά || (of canal etc) υδροφράκτης, φράγμα nt || (of hair) βόστρυχος, μπούκλα ♦ vt κλειδώνω || σφίγγω, στερεώνω ♦ vi (door etc) ασφαλίζομαι || (wheels) σφηνώνω, μπλοκάρομαι.

locker ['lɒkə*] n αρμάρι, ντουλάπι, αποθήκη.

locket ['lɒkɪt] n μενταγιόν nt inv.

locomotive [ləʊkə'məʊtɪv] n ατμάμαξα, ατμομηχανή.

locust ['ləʊkəst] n ακρίδα.

lodge [lɒdʒ] n εξοχικό σπίτι || (at gate) σπιτάκι του φύλακα || (meeting place) στοά ♦ vi αποξενούμαι, διαμένω || (rent a room) είμαι νοικάρης || (stick) αφηνώνομαι, πιάνομαι ♦ vt καταθέτω, υποβάλλω || ~n n ένοικος m/f.

lodgings ['lɒdʒɪŋz] npl δωμάτια ntpl.

loft [lɒft] n υπερώο, σοφίτα.

lofty ['lɒftɪ] a ψηλός || (proud) υπεροπτικός, αγέρωχος.

log [lɒg] n (of wood) κούτσουρο || (of ship etc) ημερολόγιο.

logarithm ['lɒgərɪθəm] n λογάριθμος.

logbook ['lɒgbʊk] n ημερολόγιο (πλοίου).

loggerheads ['lɒgəhɛdz] n: at ~ τσακωμένος, στα μαχαίρια.

logic ['lɔdʒɪk] n λογική || **~al** a λογικός.

loin [lɔɪn] n πλευρό ntpl, λαγόνες mpl.

loiter ['lɔɪtə*] vi χρονοτριβώ, χαζεύω.

loll [lɔl] vi ξαπλώνω, χουζουρεύω.

lollipop ['lɔlɪpɔp] n γλειφιτζούρι.

London ['lʌndən] n Λονδίνο n || **~er** n (person) Λονδρέζος a m/f.

lone [ləun] a (solitary) μόνος, μοναχικός || **~liness** n μοναξιά, ερημιά || **~ly** a (sad) μελαγχολικός, έρημος, ακατοίκητος.

long [lɔŋ] a μακρύς, εκτενής || (length) μάκρος ♦ ad (time) για πολλή ώρα || (during) όλη, σ όλη ♦ vi (+ for) ποθώ, λαχταρώ || **before** ~ σύντομα || **as ~ as** εφ' όσο || **in the ~ run** στο τέλος, τελικά || **~-distance** a (TEL) υπεραστικός || (SPORT) μεγάλων αποστάσεων || **~-haired** a μακρυμάλλης || **~hand** n κανονική γραφή || **~ing** n πόθος, λαχτάρα ♦ a γεμάτος λαχτάρα.

longitude ['lɔŋgɪtjuːd] n μήκος.

long: ~ jump n άλμα εις μήκος || **~-lost** a χαμένος προ πολλού || **~-playing record (L.P.)** n δίσκος μακράς διαρκείας || **~-range** a μεγάλης διαρκείας, μεγάλης ακτίνος || **~-sighted** a πρεσβύωπας, οξυδερκής || **~-standing** a παλιός, μακροχρόνιος || **~-suffering** a υπομονητικός, μακρόθυμος || **~-term** a μακροπρόθεσμος, μακροχρόνιος || **~-wave** n μακρύ κύμα || **~-winded** a ατελείωτος, φλύαρος.

loo [luː] n μέρος nt.

loofah ['luːfə] n (ελ)λύφι.

look [luk] vi (see) κοιτάζω, βλέπω || (seem) φαίνομαι || (face) βλέπω, αντικρύζω ♦ n βλέμμα nt, ματιά || **~s** npl όψη, εμφάνιση || **to ~ after** vt φροντίζω για || **to ~ down on** vt (fig) περιφρονώ || **to ~ for** vt

ψάχνω, ζητώ || (expect) προσδοκώ || **to ~ forward to** vt προσδοκώ || **to ~ out for** vt αναζητώ, ψάχνω, προσέχω || **to ~ to** vt φροντίζω για, βασίζομαι σε || **to ~ up** vt καλυτερεύω ♦ vi επισκέπτομαι, ψάχνω (σε βιβλίο) || **to ~ up to** vt σέβομαι || **~out** n (watch) προσοχή || (view) θέα || (MIL.) φρούρηση, φρουρός.

loom [luːm] n αργαλειός ♦ vi διαφαίνομαι, διακρίνομαι.

loop [luːp] n βρόχος, θηλιά ♦ vt κάνω θηλιά, δένω με θηλιά || **~hole** n (for escape) υπεκφυγή, διέξοδος f.

loose [luːs] a χαλαρός || (free) ελεύθερος, λυμένος || (slack) απρόσεκτος, απαλός ♦ vt λύνω, λασκάρω, χαλαρώνω || **at a ~ end** χωρίς απασχόληση || **~ly** ad χαλαρά, ασαφώς || **~n** vt λύνω, λασκάρω.

loot [luːt] n λάφυρο, λεία, πλιάτσικο ♦ vt λαφυραγωγώ, λεηλατώ || **~ing** n λεηλασία.

lop [lɔp] **to ~ off** vt (απο)κόβω, κλαδεύω.

lop-sided ['lɔp'saɪdɪd] a ετερόβαρής, που γέρνει.

lord [lɔːd] n άρχοντας, αφέντης || (Brit) λόρδος || **the L~** ο Κύριος || **~ly** a μεγαλοπρεπής, αγέρωχος || **~ship** n (title) εξοχότητα.

lore [lɔː*] n ειδική γνώση, παραδόσεις fpl.

lorry ['lɔrɪ] n φορτηγό (αυτοκίνητο), καμιόνι || **~ driver** n οδηγός φορτηγού.

lose [luːz] (irreg v) vt (most senses) χάνω || (waste) σπαταλώ, χάνω || vi χάνω || **~r** n νικημένος χαμένος.

loss [lɔs] n απώλεια, χάσιμο || (what is lost) απώλεια || (harm) ζημιά || **to be at a ~** τα έχω χαμένα, βρίσκομαι σε αμηχανία.

lost [lɔst] pt, pp of **lose** ♦ a χαμένος

|| ~ **property** n (γραφείο) απολεσθέντων αντικειμένων.

lot [lɒt] n (large quantity) πολύ || (for prize) κλήρος || (group of objects) σύνολο, σε παρτίδες || **a** ~ of ένα σωρό, πολύ || ~**s of** πλήθος, ένα σωρό.

lotion ['ləuʃən] n λοσιόν f inv.

lottery ['lɒtəri] n λαχείο.

loud [laud] a βροντερός, θορυβώδης, μεγαλόφωνος || (showy) κτυπητός ♦ ad δυνατά, μεγαλόφωνα || ~**ly** ad δυνατά, μεγαλόφωνα || ~**speaker** n μεγάφωνο.

lounge [laundʒ] n μικρό σαλόνι, χωλ nt inv ξενοδοχείου || vi περιφέρομαι άσκοπα, χαζεύω || ~ **suit** n καθημερινό κοστούμι.

louse [laus] n ψείρα.

lousy ['lauzi] a (lit) ψειριάρης || (fig) βρωμερός, άθλιος.

lout [laut] n άξεστος, ντουβάρι.

lovable ['lʌvəbl] a αξιαγάπητος.

love [lʌv] n αγάπη, έρωτας, στοργή || (person loved) αγαπημένος, ερωμένος || (SPORT) μηδέν ♦ vt (person) αγαπώ || (activity) λατρεύω, αγαπώ || **to** ~ **to do** θα μου άρεσαι να κάνω || **to make** ~ κάνω έρωτα, φλερτάρω || ~ **affair** n ερωτική υπόθεση || ~ **letter** n ερωτικό γράμμα nt || ~ **life** n ερωτική ζωή.

lovely ['lʌvli] a ωραίος, χαριτωμένος, ευχάριστος.

lovemaking ['lʌvmeikiŋ] n ερωτοτροπία, κόρτε nt inv.

lover ['lʌvə*] n (in general) φιλο- || (man) εραστής, φίλος.

lovesong ['lʌvsɒŋ] n ερωτικό τραγούδι.

loving ['lʌviŋ] a τρυφερός, στοργικός.

low [ləu] a (not tall) χαμηλός || (rank) ταπεινός, κατώτερος || (common) χυδαίος, άξεστος || (not loud)

αδύνατος, χαμηλός || (weak) κακόκεφος || (tide) άμπωτη ♦ ad χαμηλά || (not loudly) χαμηλόφωνα, χαμηλά ♦ n (low point) ναδίρ nt inv || (meteorology) βαρομετρικό χαμηλό || ~-**cut** a (dress) ντεκολτέ.

lower ['ləuə*] vt κατεβάζω, χαμηλώνω || (make less) ελαττώνω.

lowly ['ləuli] a ταπεινός, μετριόφρονας.

loyal ['lɔiəl] a πιστός, αφοσιωμένος || ~**ty** n πίστη, αφοσίωση.

lozenge ['lɒzindʒ] n παστίλια.

L.P. n abbr see **long-playing record**.

Ltd. abbr see **limited**.

lubricant ['luːbrikənt] n λιπαντικό, γράσο.

lubricate ['luːbrikeit] vt λιπαίνω, λαδώνω, γρασάρω.

lucid ['luːsid] a σαφής, διαυγής || ~**ity** n σαφήνεια, διαύγεια.

luck [lʌk] n τύχη || ~**ily** ad ευτυχώς || ~**y** a τυχερός.

lucrative ['luːkrətiv] a επικερδής.

ludicrous ['luːdikrəs] a αλλόκοτος, γελοίος, αστείος.

lug [lʌg] vt σέρνω με δυσκολία.

luggage ['lʌgidʒ] n αποσκευές fpl || ~ **rack** n (in train etc) δίχτυ nt για βαλίτσες.

lukewarm ['luːkwɔːm] a χλιαρός || (indifferent) αδιάφορος.

lull [lʌl] n ανάπαυλα, κόπαση ♦ vt νανουρίζω || (calm) καθησυχάζω, καταπραΰνω.

lullaby ['lʌləbai] n νανούρισμα nt.

lumbago [lʌm'beigəu] n οσφυαλγία.

lumber ['lʌmbə*] n (old articles) παλιατσούρες fpl || (wood) ξυλεία || ~**jack** n ξυλοκόπος.

luminous ['luːminəs] a φωτεινός, φωτισμένος.

lump [lʌmp] n (σ)βώλος, μεγάλο κομμάτι || (swelling) εξόγκωμα nt, καρούμπαλο || (of sugar) κομμάτι ♦ vt

σβωλιάζω, συσσωρεύω||a ~ sum στρογγυλό ποσό, ολική τιμή|| ~y a σβωλιασμένος.

lunacy ['luːnəsi] n παραφροσύνη.

lunar ['luːnə*] a σεληνιακός.

lunatic ['luːnətik] n παράφρονας ♦ a παράφρονας, τρελός.

lunch [lʌntʃ] n (also: ~eon) γεύμα|| ~ time n μεσημβρινή διακοπή.

lung [lʌŋ] n πνεύμονας|| ~ cancer n καρκίνος των πνευμόνων.

lunge [lʌndʒ] vi μπήγω, κτυπώ ξαφνικά, εφορμώ.

lurch [lɜːtʃ] vi τρικλίζω, ταλαντεύομαι ♦ n τρίκλισμα nt, μπότζι.

lure [ljuə*] n δελέασμα nt, δόλωμα nt, έλξη ♦ vt δελεάζω, θέλγω.

lurid ['ljuərid] a (shocking) τρομερός.

lurk [lɜːk] vi παραμονεύω, κρύβομαι.

luscious ['lʌʃəs] a γευστικός, χυμώδης, γλυκύτατος.

lush [lʌʃ] a (of) χυμούς|| (countryside) πλούσιος σε βλάστηση.

lust [lʌst] n σαρκική επιθυμία ♦ vi (+ after) εποφθαλμιώ, ορέγομαι|| ~ful a λάγνος.

lustre, luster (US) ['lʌstə*] n λάμψη, στιλπνότητα.

lusty ['lʌsti] a εύρωστος, σφριγηλός.

lute [luːt] n λαούτο.

Luxembourg ['lʌksəmbɜːg] n Λουξεμβούργο.

luxuriant [lʌg'zjuəriənt] a άφθονος, πλούσιος.

luxurious [lʌg'zjuəriəs] a πολυτελής, πλούσιος.

luxury ['lʌkʃəri] n πολυτέλεια, λούσο.

lying ['laiiŋ] n κείμενος || (not truthful) ψευδόμενος ♦ a ψεύτικος.

lynch [lintʃ] vt λυντσάρω.

lyre ['laiə*] n λύρα.

lyric ['lirik] n λόγια ntpl τραγουδιού ♦ a λυρικός|| ~al a (fig) ενθουσιώδης, λυρικός.

M

M. abbr of **metre, mile, million.**

M. A. abbr see **master.**

mac [mæk] n (raincoat) αδιάβροχο.

macaroni [mækə'rəuni] n μακαρόνια ntpl.

mace [meis] n (spice) μοσχοκάρυδο.

machine [mə'ʃiːn] n (general) μηχανή, μηχάνημα nt ♦ vt (dress etc) επεξεργάζομαι, κατεργάζομαι|| ~ gun n πολυβόλο|| ~ry n μηχανές fpl|| (parts) μηχανικά μέρη ntpl|| (of government) μηχανισμός.

machinist [mə'ʃiːnist] n μηχανουργός.

mackerel ['mækrəl] n σκουμπρί.

mackintosh ['mækintɔʃ] n αδιάβροχο.

mad [mæd] a παράφρονας, τρελός || (foolish) παράλογος.

madam ['mædəm] n κυρία.

madden ['mædn] vt τρελαίνω.

made [meid] pt, pp of **make** || ~-to-measure a κατά παραγγελία.

madly ['mædli] ad τρελά, άγρια.

madman ['mædmən] n (maniac) φρενοβλαβής, τρελός.

madness ['mædnis] n παραφροσύνη, τρέλα.

Madonna [mə'dɔnə] n Παναγία.

magazine [mægə'ziːn] n περιοδικό.

maggot ['mægət] n σκουλίκι.

magic ['mædʒik] n μαγεία ♦ a μαγικός, μαγεμένος|| ~al a μαγικός|| ~ian n μάγος.

magistrate ['mædʒistreit] n ειρηνοδίκης.

magnanimous [mæg'næniməs] a μεγαλόψυχος.

magnate ['mægneit] n μεγιστάνας.

magnet ['mægnɪt] n μαγνήτης ||
~**ic** a μαγνητικός || ~**ism** n
μαγνητισμός.

magnification [mægnɪfɪ'keɪʃən] n
μεγέθυνση.

magnificence [mæg'nɪfɪsəns] n
μεγαλοπρέπεια.

magnificent [mæg'nɪfɪsənt] a
μεγαλοπρεπής.

magnify ['mægnɪfaɪ] vt μεγεθύνω,
υπερβάλλω || ~**ing glass** n
μεγεθυντικός φακός.

magnitude ['mægnɪtjuːd] n
μέγεθος nt, σπουδαιότητα.

magnolia [mæg'nəʊlɪə] n μανόλια.

magpie ['mægpaɪ] n καρακάξα.

mahogany [mə'hɒgənɪ] n μαόνι.

maid [meɪd] n (servant) υπηρέτρια.

maiden ['meɪdən] n κορίτσι,
παρθένος f ♦ a (lady) άγαμος || ~
name n οικογενειακό όνομα || ~
speech n παρθενικός λόγος || ~
voyage n παρθενικό ταξίδι.

mail [meɪl] n επιστολές fpl,
ταχυδρομείο || (system) ταχυδρομείο
♦ vt (US) ταχυδρομώ || ~**box** n
γραμματοκιβώτιο || ~**order** n
ταχυδρομική εντολή.

maim [meɪm] vt ακρωτηριάζω,
σακατεύω.

main [meɪn] a κύριος, πρωτεύων ♦ n
(pipe) κεντρικός αγωγός || **in the** ~
γενικά, ως επί το πλείστο || ~**frame
(computer)** n Η/Υ μεγάλου
μεγέθους || ~**land** n στερεά,
ηπειρωτική χώρα || ~ **road** n
κεντρική οδός f || ~**stay** n (fig)
κύριο έρεισμα nt, στήριγμα nt.

maintain [meɪn'teɪn] vt (machine)
διατηρώ, συντηρώ || (support)
συντηρώ, τρέφω || (traditions)
συντηρώ, συνεχίζω || (an opinion)
υποστηρίζω.

maintenance ['meɪntɪnəns] n
(TECH) συντήρηση.

maisonette [meɪzə'nɛt] n
διαμέρισμα nt, μονοκατοικία.

maize [meɪz] n αραποσίτι,
καλαμπόκι.

majestic [mə'dʒɛstɪk] a
μεγαλοπρεπής.

majesty ['mædʒɪstɪ] n μεγαλείο ||
His/Her M ~ n Αυτού/Αυτή
Μεγαλειότης.

major ['meɪdʒə*] n (MIL)
ταγματάρχης ♦ a (MUS) μείζων.

majority [mə'dʒɒrɪtɪ] n πλειοψηφία
|| (number) πλειονότητα.

make [meɪk] (irreg v) vt (build, shape,
produce) κάνω, φτιάχνω, δημιουργώ
|| (appoint) κάνω, ορίζω || (cause to do)
αναγκάζω, κάνω, υποχρεώνω ||
(reach) φθάνω || (earn) κάνω,
αποκτώ, κερδίζω, βγάζω || (do,
perform) κάνω || (amount to) κάνω ||
(prepare) φτιάχνω ♦ n (style)
κατασκευή, τύπος || (kind) μάρκα || **to**
~ **for** vt (place) κατευθύνομαι,
πηγαίνω || **to** ~ **out** vi επιτυγχάνω,
καταφέρνω ♦ vt (write out)
συντάσσω, βγάζω, ετοιμάζω ||
(understand) καταλήγω, καταλαβαίνω
|| (pretend) προσποιούμαι, παριστάνω
|| **to** ~ **up** vt (make) συντάσσω,
φτιάχνω, πλάθω || (face) βάφομαι,
μακιγιάρομαι, φτιάχνομαι || (settle)
ρυθμίζω, συμφιλιώνω, διευθετώ || **to**
~ **up for** vi ανακτώ, αναπληρώνω ||
~**believe** n προσποίηση, υπόκριση
♦ a προσποιητός, ψεύτικος || ~**r** n
κατασκευαστής/άστρια m/f,
δημιουργός m/f || ~**shift** a
προσωρινή λύση || ~**up** n
(cosmetics) μακιγιάζ nt inv || σύσταση
|| (THEAT) μακιγιάζ nt inv, βάψιμο.

making ['meɪkɪŋ] n: **in the** ~ εν
εξελίξει.

malaise [mæ'leɪz] n αδιαθεσία.

malaria [mə'lɛərɪə] n ελονοσία.

Malaysia [mə'leɪzɪə] n Μαλαισία.

male [meɪl] n άνδρας ♦ a αρσενικός.

malevolent [mɔ'levələnt] a κακόβουλος.

malfunction [mæl'fʌŋkʃən] vi λειτουργώ ελαττωματικά.

malice ['mælɪs] n κακεντρέχεια, έχθρα.

malicious [mɔ'lɪʃəs] a κακόβουλος, μοχθηρός.

malign [mɔ'laɪn] vt δυσφημίζω, κακολογώ.

malignant [mɔ'lɪgnənt] a (tumour) κακοήθης.

malleable ['mælɪəbl] a ελάσιμος, μαλακός.

mallet ['mælɪt] n ξύλινο σφυρί, κόπανος.

malnutrition [mælnju'trɪʃən] n υποσιτισμός.

malpractice [mæl'præktɪs] n αδίκημα nt, κατάχρηση.

malt [mɔːlt] n βύνη.

Malta ['mɔːltə] n Μάλτα.

maltreat [mæl'triːt] vt κακομεταχειρίζομαι.

mammal ['mæməl] n θηλαστικό, μαστοφόρο.

mammoth ['mæməθ] a γιγαντιαίος, πελώριος.

man [mæn] n άνθρωπος || (male) άνδρας || (race) ανθρωπότητα ♦ vt επανδρώνω.

manage ['mænɪdʒ] vi (succeed) καταφέρνω ♦ vt χειρίζομαι, διευθύνω, διοικώ || ~**able** a ευχείριστος || (person) εύκολος || ~**ment** n χειρισμός, διαχείριση || (directors) διεύθυνση, διοίκηση || ~**r** n διευθυντής || ~**ress** n διευθύντρια || ~**rial** a διευθυντικός, τεχνοκρατικός.

managing ['mænɪdʒɪŋ] a: ~ **director** n γενικός διευθυντής.

mandarin ['mændərɪn] n (orange) μανταρίνι || (man) μανδαρίνος.

mandate ['mændeɪt] n (instruction) εντολή || (commission) εντολή.

mandatory ['mændətərɪ] a υποχρεωτικός.

mandolin(e) ['mændəlɪn] n μαντολίνο.

mane [meɪn] n χαίτη.

maneuver [mɔ'nuːvə*] (US)= **manoeuvre**.

manfully ['mænfəlɪ] ad παλληκαρίσια.

mangle ['mæŋgl] vt κατακεσκίζω, κατακόβω.

mango ['mæŋgəʊ] n μάγγο.

manhandle ['mænhændl] vt ξυλοφορτώνω, κακομεταχειρίζομαι.

manhole ['mænhəʊl] n ανθρωποθυρίδα, είσοδος f υπονόμου.

manhood ['mænhʊd] n ανδρικότητα, ανδρική ηλικία.

man-hour ['mæn'aʊə*] n ώρα εργασίας.

manhunt ['mænhʌnt] n ανθρωποκυνήγι.

mania ['meɪnɪə] n (craze) μανία, πάθος nt || (madness) τρέλα || ~**c** n μανιακός.

manicure ['mænɪkjʊə*] n μανικιούρ nt inv ♦ vt φτιάχνω τα νύχια || ~ **set** n κασετίνα του μανικιούρ.

manifest ['mænɪfest] vt επιδεικνύω, εκδηλώνω ♦ a έκδηλος, προφανής || ~**ation** n εκδήλωση.

manifesto [mænɪ'festəʊ] n διακήρυξη, μανιφέστο.

manipulate [mɔ'nɪpjʊleɪt] vt χειρίζομαι, μανουβράρω.

mankind [mæn'kaɪnd] n ανθρωπότητα.

manly ['mænlɪ] a ανδρικός, ανδροπρεπής, αντρίκιος.

manner ['mænə*] n τρόπος || (custom) συμπεριφορά, είδος nt || ~**s** npl συμπεριφορά, τρόποι mpl ||

~ism n (of person) ιδιορρυθμία, ιδιοτροπία.

manoeuvre [mə'nuːvə*] vti ελίσσομαι, μανουβράρω ♦ n (MIL) ελιγμός, άσκηση.

manor ['mænə*] n τιμάριο, κτήμα nt || **~ house** n αρχοντικό σπίτι.

manpower ['mænpauə*] n το εργατικό δυναμικό.

manservant ['mænsːvənt] n υπηρέτης, καμαριέρης.

mansion ['mænʃən] n μέγαρο.

manslaughter ['mænslɔːtə*] n ανθρωποκτονία.

mantelpiece ['mæntlpiːs] n γείσωμα nt τζακιού.

mantle ['mæntl] n μανδύας.

manual ['mænjuəl] a χειρωνακτικός ♦ n εγχειρίδιο.

manufacture [mænju'fæktʃə*] vt κατασκευάζω, βιομηχανοποιώ ♦ n κατασκευή, βιομηχανία || **~r** n βιομήχανος.

manure [mə'njuə*] n κοπριά, λίπασμα nt.

manuscript ['mænjuskript] n χειρόγραφο.

many ['mɛni] a πολλοί, αρκετοί ♦ n αρκετοί, πολλοί, όσοι.

map [mæp] n χάρτης ♦ vt χαρτογραφώ || to **~ out** vt χαράσσω, καθορίζω, κανονίζω.

maple ['meipl] n σφεντάμι.

mar [maː*] vt βλάφτω, χαλώ, παραμορφώνω.

marathon ['mærəθən] n μαραθώνιος.

marauder [mə'rɔːdə*] n λεηλάτης, ληστής.

marble ['maːbl] n μάρμαρο || **~s** n (game) βώλος, μπίλια.

March [maːtʃ] n Μάρτιος, Μάρτης.

march [maːtʃ] vi βαδίζω, βηματίζω, οδηγώ ♦ n (tune) εμβατήριο || (walk) πορεία, βάδισμα nt || **~-past** n παρέλαση.

mare [mɛə*] n φοράδα.

margarine [maːdʒə'riːn] n μαργαρίνη.

margin ['maːdʒin] n (page) περιθώριο || (extra amount) περιθώριο || **~al** a περιθωριακός.

marigold ['mærigəuld] n κατιφές m.

marijuana [mæri'waːnə] n μαριχουάνα.

marina [mə'riːnə] n (for boats) μαρίνα.

marine [mə'riːn] a θαλάσσιος, ναυτικός || (MIL) πεζοναυτικός ♦ n (MIL) πεζοναύτης.

marital ['mæritl] a συζυγικός.

maritime ['mæritaim] a θαλασσινός, ναυτικός.

marjoram ['maːdʒərəm] n μαντζουράνα.

mark [maːk] n (coin) μάρκα || (scar etc) σημάδι, ίχνος, στίγμα nt || (sign) σημείο, ένδειξη || (target) στόχος, σημάδι || (grade) βαθμός ♦ vt (make a mark) μαρκάρω, σημαδεύω || (indicate) δεικνύω, εκδηλώνω, δείχνω || (watch etc) προσέχω, κοιτάζω || (exam) διορθώνω, βαθμολογώ || to **~ time** κάνω βήμα σημειωτό || (make no progress) δεν προχωρώ || to **~ out** vt σημαδεύω || **~ed** a έντονος, σαφής, φανερός, εμφανής || **~er** n (sign) δείκτης.

market ['maːkit] n αγορά || (overseas) αγορά || (demand) ζήτηση ♦ vt (COMM: new product) πουλώ || (project) προβάλλω || **~ day** n ημέρα αγοράς || **~ garden** n (Brit) περιβόλι κηπουρικών || **~ing** n αγορά, πώληση || **~ place** n αγορά, παζάρι.

marksman ['maːksmən] n σκοπευτής || **~ship** n σκοπευτική ικανότητα.

marmalade ['maːməleid] n μαρμελάδα.

maroon [mə'ruːn] vt (usually passive) εγκαταλείπω σε έρημη ακτή ♦ a (colour) ερυθρόφαιος.

marquee [maː'kiː] n μεγάλη τέντα.

marquess, marquis ['maːkwɪs] n μαρκήσιος.

marriage ['mærɪdʒ] n (institution) παντρειά || (wedding) γάμος.

married ['mærɪd] a (person, life) έγγαμος.

marrow ['mærəʊ] n μυελός, μεδούλι || (vegetable) κολοκύθι.

marry ['mærɪ] vt νυμφεύω, παντρεύω ♦ vi (also: **get married**) νυμφεύομαι, παντρεύομαι.

Mars [maːz] n 'Αρης.

marsh [maːʃ] n έλος nt, βάλτος.

marshal ['maːʃəl] n (US) σερίφης ♦ vt παρατάσσω, συγκεντρώνω || see **field**.

marshy ['maːʃɪ] a ελώδης.

martial ['maːʃəl] a πολεμικός, στρατιωτικός || ~ **law** n στρατιωτικός νόμος.

martyr ['maːtə*] n μάρτυρας || (fig) βασανιζόμενος || ~**dom** n μαρτύριο.

marvel ['maːvəl] n θαύμα nt ♦ vi (+ at) εκπλήσσομαι, θαυμάζω || ~**lous**, (US) ~**ous** a θαυμάσιος, καταπληκτικός.

Marxism ['maːksɪzm] n μαρξισμός.

Marxist ['maːksɪst] n μαρξιστής.

mascara [mæs'kaːrə] n μάσκαρα.

mascot ['mæskət] n μασκότ nt inv.

masculine ['mæskjulɪn] a αρσενικός || (manly) ανδροπρεπής, ρωμαλέος || (GRAM) αρσενικός ♦ n το αρσενικό.

masculinity [mæskju'lɪnɪtɪ] n αρρενότητα, ανδρικό ύφος.

mashed [mæʃt] a: ~ **potatoes** npl πατάτες fpl πουρέ.

mask [maːsk] n προσωπίδα, μάσκα ||

(pretence) προσωπείο ♦ vt καλύπτω, αποκρύπτω.

masochist ['mæsəʊkɪst] n μαζοχιστής.

mason ['meɪsn] n (stonemason) κτίστης || (freemason) τέκτονας || ~**ic** [mə'sɒnɪk] a τεκτονικός, μασονικός || ~**ry** ['meɪsnrɪ] n λιθοδομή, χτίσιμο.

masquerade [mæskə'reɪd] n μεταμφίεση ♦ vi μεταμφιέζομαι.

mass [mæs] n (PHYS) μάζα || (information, people) όγκος, μάζα, πλήθος nt || (majority) το μεγαλύτερο μέρος, η πλειοψηφία || (REL) λειτουργία ♦ vt συγκεντρώνω, αθροίζω, μαζεύω ♦ vi συγκεντρώνομαι, μαζεύομαι.

massacre ['mæsəkə*] n σφαγή, μακελειό ♦ vt σφάζω.

massage ['mæsaːʒ] n μάλαξη, μασάζ nt inv ♦ vt μαλάσσω, κάνω μασάζ.

masseur [mæ'sɜː*] n μασέρ m inv.

masseuse [mæ'sɜːz] n μασέζ f inv.

massive ['mæsɪv] a ογκώδης, δυνατός.

mass media ['mæs'miːdɪə] npl μέσα ntpl μαζικής επικοινωνίας.

mass production ['mæsprə'dʌkʃən] n μαζική παραγωγή.

mast [maːst] n ιστός, κατάρτι || (pole) στήλη, στύλος.

master ['maːstə*] n κύριος, αφεντικό || (teacher) δάσκαλος, καθηγητής || (head) αρχηγός || (of ship) καπετάνιος || (artist) μεγάλος καλλιτέχνης ♦ vt εξουσιάζω, ελέγχω || (learn) μαθαίνω τέλεια || ~**ly** a έντεχνος, αριστοτεχνικός || ~**mind** n εγκέφαλος ♦ vt συλλαμβάνω, πραγματοποιώ || **M** ~ **of Arts (M.A.)** n ανώτερος πτυχιούχος θετικών επιστημών || ~**piece** n αριστούργημα nt || ~ **stroke** n

αριστοτεχνικό κτύπημα *nt* || ~ **y** *n* εξουσία, υπεροχή, μαεστρία.

masturbate ['mæstəbeɪt] *vi* μαλακίζομαι.

masturbation [mæstə'beɪʃən] *n* μαλακία.

mat [mæt] *n* ψάθα, χαλάκι || (*material for table*) στρωσίδι τραπεζιού || (*tangled mass*) μπλεγμένα νήματα *ntpl* κτλ ♦ *vti* μπλέκω, μπερδεύω.

match [mætʃ] *n* (*matchstick*) σπίρτο || (*game*) αγώνας || (*equal*) ταίρι || (*marriage*) συνοικέσιο ♦ *vt* (*be like*) εναρμονίζω, ταιριάζω || (*equal strength etc*) εξισούμαι με, φθάνω ♦ *vi* συμβιβάζομαι, συμφωνώ, ταιριάζω || ~ **box** *n* κουτί σπίρτα || ~ **ing** *a* προσαρμογή || ~ **less** *a* απαράμιλλος.

mate [meɪt] *n* σύντροφος, συνάδελφος || (*husband, wife*) σύζυγος, ταίρι || (*NAUT*) υποπλοίαρχος ♦ *n* (*chess*) κάνω ματ || (*of animal*) ζευγαρώνομαι.

material [mə'tɪərɪəl] *n* ύλη, υλικό ♦ *a* σημαντικός, ουσιώδης || (*of matter*) υλικός || (*opposite of spirit*) υλικός || ~ **s** *npl* υλικά *ntpl*, εφόδια *ntpl* || ~ **istic** *a* υλιστικός || ~ **ize** *vi* πραγματοποιούμαι, γίνομαι.

maternal [mə'tɜ:nl] *a* μητρικός || (*relatives*) από τη μητέρα.

maternity [mə'tɜ:nɪtɪ] *n* μητρότητα || ~ **dress** φόρεμα *nt* εγγύου || ~ **hospital** *n* μαιευτήριο.

mathematical [mæθə'mætɪkəl] *a* μαθηματικός.

mathematician [mæθəmə'tɪʃən] *n* μαθηματικός *m/f*.

mathematics [mæθə'mætɪks] *n*, **maths** [mæθs] *n* μαθηματικά *ntpl*.

matinée ['mætɪneɪ] *n* παράσταση (απογευματινή).

mating ['meɪtɪŋ] *n* ζευγάρωμα *nt*, βάτεμα *nt*.

matriarchal [meɪtrɪ'ɑːkl] *a* μητριαρχικός.

matrimonial [mætrɪ'məʊnɪəl] *a* γαμήλιος, συζυγικός.

matrimony ['mætrɪmənɪ] *n* γάμος, έγγαμη ζωή.

matron ['meɪtrən] *n* (*MED*) προϊσταμένη || (*SCH*) επιμελήτρια, οικονόμος *f* || ~ **ly** *a* σεβάσμιος, ατάραχος.

matt [mæt] *a* (*paint*) μουντός, ματ.

matter ['mætə*] *n* ουσία, ύλη || (*affair*) υπόθεση, θέμα *nt*, πράγμα *nt* || (*question, issue etc*) ζήτημα *nt* || (*discharge*) πύο, έμπυο ♦ *vi* έχω σημασία, ενδιαφέρω || **what is the ~?** τι συμβαίνει; || **as a ~ of fact** στην πραγματικότητα || ~ - **of-fact** *a* πεζός, πρακτικός.

mattress ['mætrɪs] *n* στρώμα *nt*.

mature [mə'tjʊə*] *a* ώριμος ♦ *vi* ωριμάζω.

maturity [mə'tjʊərɪtɪ] *n* ωριμότητα.

maul [mɔːl] *vt* κακοποιώ, κοπανίζω.

mauve [məʊv] *a* (*colour*) μώβ.

max. *abbr of* **maximum.**

maxim ['mæksɪm] *n* απόφθεγμα *nt*, γνωμικό.

maximum ['mæksɪməm] *a* ανώτατος, μεγαλύτερος ♦ *n* ανώτατο όριο, μάξιμουμ *nt inv*.

May [meɪ] *n* Μάιος.

may [meɪ] (*irreg v*) *vi* (*be possible*) ίσως να || (*have permission*) έχω την άδεια να, μπορώ να.

maybe ['meɪbiː] *ad* ίσως, πιθανό.

May Day ['meɪdeɪ] *n* Πρωτομαγιά.

mayonnaise [meɪə'neɪz] *n* μαγιονέζα.

mayor [mɛə*] *n* δήμαρχος || ~ **ess** *n* (*wife*) κυρία δημάρχου || (*lady mayor*) n δήμαρχος.

maze [meɪz] *n* (*network*) λαβύρινθος, κυκελώνας.

me [miː] *pron* (*after prep*) με, εμένα.

meadow ['mɛdəʊ] *n* λειβάδι.

meagre, meager (US) ['mi:gə*] a ισχνός, πενιχρός.

meal [mi:l] n φαγητό || (grain) χοντράλευρο || ~**time** n ώρα φαγητού.

mean [mi:n] (irreg v) a άθλιος, φτωχός, ταπεινός || (stingy) φιλάργυρος, τσιγκούνης || (average) μέσος, μεσαίος ♦ vt (signify) εννοώ, σημαίνω, θέλω να πω || (intend) προτίθεμαι, σκοπεύω || (be resolved) προορίζω ♦ n (average) μέσος όρος, μέσο || ~**s** npl μέσα ntpl, τρόποι mpl || (wealth) πόροι mpl, μέσα ntpl, περιουσία || **by** ~**s of** με τη βοήθεια του/της || **by all** ~**s** οπωσδήποτε.

meander [mi'ændə*] vi ελίσσομαι, σχηματίζω μαιάνδρους.

meaning ['mi:niŋ] n (intention) λόγος, σκοπός || (sense of word) έννοια, σημασία, νόημα nt || ~**ful** a με σημασία, που λέει πολλά || ~**less** a χωρίς νόημα.

meanness ['mi:nnis] n μικρότητα, μικροπρέπεια.

meant [mɛnt] pt, pp of **mean**.

meantime ['mi:ntaim] ad, **meanwhile** ['mi:nwail] ad εν τω μεταξύ, στο μεταξύ.

measles ['mi:zlz] n ιλαρά || **German** ~ n ερυθρά.

measly ['mi:zli] a (col) ασήμαντος, ανάξιος, τιποτένιος.

measure ['mɛʒə*] vt (find size) μετρώ || (test) δοκιμάζω, αναμετρώμαι ♦ vi (be certain size) είναι, έχει διαστάσεις ♦ n (unit) μέτρο || (tape measure) μεζούρα, μέτρο || (plan) μέτρο, ενέργεια, πράξη || (a law) μέτρο || ~**d** a μετρημένος || ~**ment** n (way of measuring) μέτρηση, μέτρημα nt || (amount measured) μέτρα ntpl, διαστάσεις fpl.

meat [mi:t] n (flesh) κρέας nt || ~ **pie** n κρεατόπιτα || ~**y** a (lit) σαρκώδης.

mechanic [mi'kænik] n τεχνίτης, μηχανικός || ~**s** n μηχανική || ~**al** a μηχανικός || (automatically) μηχανικός, αυτόματος.

mechanism ['mɛkənizəm] n μηχανισμός.

mechanization [mɛkənai'zeiʃən] n μηχανοποίηση.

medal ['mɛdl] n μετάλλιο || ~**lion** [mi'dæliən] n μενταγιό || ~**list**, ~**ist** (US) n κάτοχος μεταλλίου.

meddle ['mɛdl] vi (+ with) ανακατεύομαι, επεμβαίνω.

media ['mi:diə] npl (of communication) μέσα ntpl.

mediate ['mi:dieit] vi μεσολαβώ.

mediation [mi:di'eiʃən] n μεσολάβηση.

mediator ['mi:dieitə*] n μεσολαβητής.

medical ['mɛdikəl] a (science) ιατρικός || (student) (φοιτητής) ιατρικής.

medicated ['mɛdikeitid] a εμποτισμένος με φάρμακο.

medicinal [mɛ'disinl] a φαρμακευτικός, ιατρικός, θεραπευτικός.

medicine ['mɛdsin] n ιατρική || (drugs) φάρμακο, γιατρικό || ~**chest** n φαρμακείο.

medieval [mɛdi'i:vəl] a μεσαιωνικός.

mediocre [mi:di'əukə*] a μέτριος, της αράδας.

mediocrity [mi:di'ɒkriti] n μετριότητα.

meditate ['mɛditeit] vi (+ on) μελετώ, σκέπτομαι, συλλογίζομαι.

meditation [mɛdi'teiʃən] n συλλογισμός, διαλογισμός.

Mediterranean (Sea) [mɛditə'reiniən(si:)] n Μεσόγειος (θάλασσα).

medium ['miːdɪəm] a μεσαίος, μέτριος ♦ n μέσο, μέσος όρος || *(means)* μέσο, όργανο.

medley ['medlɪ] n σύμφυρμα nt, κυκεώνας, μίγμα nt.

meek [miːk] a πράος, ήρεμος, πειθήνιος.

meet [miːt] vt συναντώ, απαντώ, ανταμώνω || *(come across)* βρίσκω, απαντώ, διασταυρώνομαι || *(go towards)* προχωρώ, πηγαίνω || *(pay, satisfy)* εκπληρώνω, ανταποκρίνομαι, τιμώ ♦ vi *(by arrangement)* συναντώμαι, βλέπομαι || *(fight)* αντιμετωπίζω || *(join)* συναντώμαι, συναθροίζομαι, συνέρχομαι || **to ~ with** vt *(problems)* συναντώ, αντιμετωπίζω || *(US: people)* συναντώ, γνωρίζω || **~ing** n συνάντηση, συνάθροιση, συνέλευση || **~ing place** n τόπος συναντήσεως.

megaphone ['megəfəʊn] n μεγάφωνο.

melancholy ['melənkəlɪ] n μελαγχολία, κατήφεια ♦ a μελαγχολικός.

mellow ['meləʊ] a ώριμος || *(delicate)* απαλός, γλυκός || *(aged)* απαλός ♦ vi ωριμάζω, απαλύνομαι.

melodious [mɪˈləʊdɪəs] a μελωδικός.

melodrama ['meləʊdrɑːmə] n μελόδραμα n.

melody ['melədɪ] n μελωδία.

melon ['melən] n πεπόνι.

melt [melt] vi τήκομαι, λυώνω || *(disappear)* χάνομαι, διαλύομαι ♦ vt τήκω, λυώνω || **to ~ away** vi λυώνω, διαλύομαι || **to ~ down** vt λυώνω, τήκω || **~ing point** n σημείο τήξεως || **~ing pot** n *(fig)* χωνευτήριο, ρευστή κατάσταση.

member ['membə*] n μέλος nt || **M~ of Parliament (M.P.)** n βουλευτής/ίνα m/f || **~ship** n μέλη ntpl, αριθμός μελών.

membrane ['membreɪn] n μεμβράνη.

memento [məˈmentəʊ] n ενθύμιο, ενθύμηση.

memo ['meməʊ] n *(COMM)* υπόμνημα nt, σημείωση.

memoirs ['memwɑːz] npl απομνημονεύματα ntpl.

memorable ['memərəbl] a αξιομνημόνευτος, αξέχαστος.

memorandum [meməˈrændəm] n *(COMM)* υπόμνημα nt, σημείωση.

memorial [mɪˈmɔːrɪəl] n μνημείο ♦ a αναμνηστικός, επιμνημόσυνος.

memorize ['meməraɪz] vt αποστηθίζω, μαθαίνω απ' έξω.

memory ['memərɪ] n μνήμη, μνημονικό, θυμητικό || *(thing recalled)* ανάμνηση, θύμηση || *(COMPUT)* μνήμη || **in ~ of** εις μνήμην του, εις ανάμνηση του.

men [men] npl of **man.**

menace ['menɪs] n απειλή, φοβέρα ♦ vt απειλώ, φοβερίζω.

menacing ['menɪsɪŋ] a απειλητικός.

menagerie [mɪˈnædʒərɪ] n θηριοτροφείο.

mend [mend] vt (επι)διορθώνω, βελτιώνω ♦ vi αναρρώνω ♦ n επιδιόρθωση, επισκευή || **to be on the ~** συνέρχομαι, πάω καλύτερα.

menial ['miːnɪəl] a ταπεινός, δουλοπρεπής.

meningitis [menɪnˈdʒaɪtɪs] n μηνιγγίτιδα.

menopause ['menəʊpɔːz] n εμμηνόπαυση.

menstruation [menstrʊˈeɪʃən] n εμμηνόρροια, περίοδος f.

mental ['mentl] a διανοητικός, νοερός, πνευματικός || *(col: abnormal)* τρελός || **~ity** n νοοτροπία.

mention ['menʃən] n μνεία ♦ vt αναφέρω || **don't ~ it!** παρακαλώ!

menu ['mɛnjuː] n (also COMPUT)
μενού nt inv.

mercantile ['mɜːkəntaɪl] a
εμπορικός.

mercenary ['mɜːsɪnərɪ] a
φιλοχρήματος, πλεονέκτης ♦ n
μισθοφόρος.

merchandise ['mɜːtʃəndaɪz] n
εμπορεύματα ntpl.

merchant ['mɜːtʃənt] n έμπορος ♦
a εμπορικός || ~ **navy** n εμπορικό
ναυτικό.

merciful ['mɜːsɪful] a εύσπλαχνος.

merciless ['mɜːsɪlɪs] a ανελέητος,
άσπλαχνος.

mercury ['mɜːkjʊrɪ] n
υδράργυρος.

mercy ['mɜːsɪ] n ευσπλαχνία, έλεος
nt || (blessing) ευλογία || **at the ~ of**
στο έλεος τού.

mere [mɪə*] a απλός, τίποτε άλλο
από || ~**ly** ad απλώς, μόνο.

merge [mɜːdʒ] vt απορροφώ,
συγχωνεύω || (COMPUT) αναμιγνύω ♦
vi (become absorbed) απορροφούμαι,
συγχωνεύομαι || ~**r** n (COMM)
συγχώνευση.

meridian [mə'rɪdɪən] n
μεσημβρινός.

meringue [mə'ræŋ] n μαρέγγα.

merit ['mɛrɪt] n αξία, προσόν ♦ vt
αξίζω.

mermaid ['mɜːmeɪd] n γοργόνα.

merriment ['mɛrɪmənt] n ευθυμία,
διασκέδαση.

merry ['mɛrɪ] a εύθυμος, φαιδρός,
χαρωπός || (col: after drink) στο κέφι,
πιωμένος.

mesh [mɛʃ] n θηλειά (δικτύου) ♦ vti
(gears) εμπλέκω, εμπλέκομαι.

mesmerize ['mɛzmᵊraɪz] vt
μαγνητίζω, υπνωτίζω.

mess [mɛs] n σαλάτα, θάλασσα ||
(untidy state) ακαθαρσία, άνω-κάτω ||
(MIL) συσσίτιο, τραπέζι || (officers'
mess) λέσχη αξιωματικών || **to ~**

about vi χασομερώ || **to ~ about
with** vt πασπατεύω, σαχλαμαρίζω ||
to ~ up vt χαλώ, μπλέκω,
περιπλέκω.

message ['mɛsɪdʒ] n μήνυμα nt,
διάγγελμα nt, είδηση.

messenger ['mɛsɪndʒə*] n
αγγελιαφόρος.

messy ['mɛsɪ] a ακάθαρτος,
ακατάστατος.

met [mɛt] pt, pp of **meet**.

metabolism [mɛ'tæbᵊlɪzəm] n
μεταβολισμός.

metal ['mɛtl] n μέταλλο || ~**lic** a
μεταλλικός || ~**lurgy** n
μεταλλουργία.

metaphor ['mɛtᵊfɔː*] n μεταφορά.

metaphysics [mɛtᵊ'fɪzɪks] n
μεταφυσική.

meteor ['miːtɪə*] n μετέωρο || ~**ic**
a μετεωρικός, λαμπρός || ~**ological**
a μετεωρολογικός || ~**ology** n
μετεωρολογία.

meter ['miːtə*] n (instrument)
μετρητής || (US) = **metre**.

method ['mɛθəd] n μέθοδος f ||
~**ical** a μεθοδικός.

Methodist ['mɛθədɪst] a, n
Μεθοδιστής.

methylated spirits
['mɛθɪleɪtɪd'spɪrɪts] n (also: **meths**)
μεθυλικό οινόπνευμα nt.

meticulous [mɪ'tɪkjʊləs] a
λεπτολόγος, σχολαστικός.

metre ['miːtə*] n μέτρο.

metric ['mɛtrɪk] a μετρικός.

metronome ['mɛtrᵊnəʊm] n
μετρονόμος.

metropolis [mɪ'trɒpəlɪs] n
μητρόπολη.

mews [mjuːz] n αδιέξοδο.

Mexican ['mɛksɪkən] a μεξικανικός
♦ n Μεξικανός/ίδα m/f.

Mexico ['mɛksɪkəʊ] n Μεξικό.

mezzanine ['mɛzᵊniːn] n
ημιόροφος, μέτζο.

miaow [mi:'au] vi νιαουρίζω.

mice [maɪs] npl of **mouse**.

microbe ['maɪkrəʊb] n μικρόβιο.

microcomputer
['maɪkrəʊkəm'pjuːtə*] n
μικροϋπολογιστής.

microfilm ['maɪkrəʊfɪlm] n
μικροφίλμ nt inv.

microphone ['maɪkrəfəʊn] n
μικρόφωνο.

microscope ['maɪkrəskəʊp] n
μικροσκόπιο.

microscopic [maɪkrə'skɒpɪk] a
μικροσκοπικός.

mid [mɪd] a μέσος, μεσαίος || **in ~
course** στο μέσο, στην ακμή.

midday ['mɪd'deɪ] n μεσημέρι.

middle ['mɪdl] n μέσο ♦ a μέσος,
μεσαίος || **~-aged** a μεσήλικας || **the
M ~ Ages** npl ο Μεσαίωνας || **~
class** n μεσαία τάξη, αστική τάξη ||
~-class a αστικός || **M ~ East** n
Μέση Ανατολή || **~man** n
μεταπωλητής, μεσίτης || **~ name** n
όνομα nt πατρός.

midge [mɪdʒ] n σκνίπα.

midget ['mɪdʒɪt] n νάνος,
ανθρωπάκι ♦ a μικρός,
μικροσκοπικός.

midnight ['mɪdnaɪt] n μεσάνυχτα
ntpl.

midst [mɪdst] n: **in the ~ of** στο
μέσο.

midsummer ['mɪd'sʌmə*] n
μεσοκαλόκαιρο.

midway ['mɪd'weɪ] ad (+ between)
στο μέσο ♦ a μέσος.

midweek ['mɪd'wiːk] ad στα μέσα
της εβδομάδας.

midwife ['mɪdwaɪf] n μαία, μαμμή ||
~ry ['mɪdwɪfərɪ] n μαιευτική.

midwinter ['mɪd'wɪntə*] n στο
μέσο του χειμώνα, μεσοχείμωνο.

might [maɪt] pt of **may** || n ισχύς,
δύναμη || **~y** a ισχυρός, δυνατός ♦
ad (col) πολύ, τρομερά.

migraine ['miːgreɪn] n ημικρανία.

migrant ['maɪgrənt] n
μεταναστευτικός, περαστικός ♦ a
αποδημητικός, μεταναστευτικός.

migrate [maɪ'greɪt] vi (birds)
αποδημώ.

migration [maɪ'greɪʃən] n
μετανάστευση.

mike [maɪk] n (microphone)
μικρόφωνο.

mild [maɪld] a (rebuke) επιεικής,
μαλακός || (warm) ήπιος, εύκρατος ||
(taste) ελαφρός || (slight) ελαφρός ♦
n (beer) ελαφριά μπύρα.

mildew ['mɪldjuː] n μούχλα,
σείρηκας.

mildness ['maɪldnɪs] n ηπιότητα,
γλύκα, επιείκεια.

mile [maɪl] n μίλι (1609 μ) || **~age** n
απόσταση σε μίλια || **~stone** n
μιλιοδείκτης || (fig) ιστορικός
σταθμός.

militant ['mɪlɪtənt] n οπαδός της
αμέσου δράσεως ♦ a μαχητικός.

military ['mɪlɪtərɪ] a στρατιωτικός
♦ n οι στρατιωτικοί mpl, στρατός.

militate ['mɪlɪteɪt] vi (+ against)
αντιστρατεύομαι, αντιμάχομαι.

militia [mɪ'lɪʃə] n εθνοφυλακή.

milk [mɪlk] n γάλα nt ♦ vt (cow)
αρμέγω || (fig) εκμεταλλεύομαι,
μαδώ || **~man** n γαλατάς || **M ~ y**
Way n Γαλαξίας.

mill [mɪl] n μύλος || (building) μύλος ||
(factory) εργοστάσιο ♦ vt (grind)
αλέθω ♦ vi (move around)
στριφογυρίζω.

millenium [mɪ'lɛnɪəm] n
χιλιετηρίδα.

miller ['mɪlə*] n μυλωνάς.

millet ['mɪlɪt] n κεχρί, σόργο.

milligram(me) ['mɪlɪgræm] n
χιλιοστόγραμμο.

millilitre, milliliter (US)
['mɪlɪliːtə*] n χιλιοστόλιτρο.

millimetre, millimeter (US)
[ˈmilimiːtə*] n χιλιοστόμετρο.

milliner [ˈmilinə*] n καπελλού f|| **~y** n γυναικεία καπέλλα ntpl.

million [ˈmiljən] n εκατομμύριο || **~aire** n εκατομμυριούχος.

mime [maim] n μίμος, μιμόδραμα nt ♦ vti μιμούμαι, παίζω με μιμική.

mimic [ˈmimik] a μιμικός, μιμητής/ήτρια m/f ♦ vti μιμούμαι, κοροϊδεύω, αντιγράφω || **~ry** n μίμηση, μιμική.

min. abbr of **minute(s)**, **minimum.**

mince [mins] vt ψιλοκόβω, κάνω κιμά || (words) μασώ ♦ vi βαδίζω με προσποιητή χάρη ♦ n (meat) κιμάς || **~meat** n μείγμα απ με φρούτα και σταφίδες || **~ pie** n πίτα με φρούτα και σταφίδες, κρεατόπιτα || **~r** n κρεατομηχανή.

mind [maind] n νούς m, μυαλό || (intelligence) σκέψη, γνώμη, ιδέα || (memory) μνήμη, ανάμνηση, θύμηση ♦ vti φροντίζω, προσέχω || (be careful) προσέχω || (object to) έχω αντίρρηση, ενοχλούμαι, πειράζομαι || **on my ~** στη σκέψη μου, ανησυχώ || **to my ~** κατά τη γνώμη μου || **out of one's ~** τρελός || **never ~!** δεν πειράζει, άστο, μην ανησυχείς || **to bear** or **keep in ~** δεν ξεχνώ, λαμβάνω υπόψη || **to make up one's ~** αποφασίζω || **~the step'** 'πρόσεχε το σκαλοπάτι' || **~ful** a προσεκτικός, || **~less** a απερίσκεπτος, αδιάφορος, απρόσεκτος.

mine [main] poss pron δικός μου, δική μου, δικό μου ♦ n (explosive, metal) ορυχείο || (NAUT) νάρκη || (source) πηγή ♦ vt εξορύσσω || (NAUT) ναρκοθετώ ♦ vi εκμεταλλεύομαι || **~field** n ναρκοπέδιο || **~r** n μεταλλωρύχος, ανθρακωρύχος.

mineral [ˈminərəl] a ορυκτός,

μεταλλευτικός ♦ n ορυκτό, μετάλλευμα nt|| **~ water** n επιτραπέζιο νερό, μεταλλικό νερό.

minesweeper [ˈmainswiːpə*] n ναρκαλιευτικό.

mingle [ˈmiŋgl] vt αναμιγνύω ♦ vi (+ with) αναμιγνύομαι.

mingy [ˈmindʒi] a (col) στριμμένος, γύφτος, μίζερος.

miniature [ˈminitʃə*] a μικρογραφικός ♦ n μικρογραφία, μινιατούρα || (model) μακέτα || **in ~** μικρού σχήματος.

minibus [ˈminibʌs] n μικρό λεωφορείο.

minicab [ˈminikæb] n μικρό ταξί.

minicomputer
[ˈminikəmˈpjuːtə*] n μικρο-υπολογιστής.

minimal [ˈminiml] a ελάχιστος.

minimize [ˈminimaiz] vt ελαττώνω, μικραίνω, περιορίζω.

minimum [ˈminiməm] n ελάχιστο, κατώτατο όριο, μίνιμουμ nt inv ♦ a κατώτατος, ελάχιστος.

mining [ˈmainiŋ] n εξόρυξη || (NAUT) ναρκοθέτηση ♦ a μεταλλευτική, ορυκτικόν.

miniskirt [ˈminiskɜːt] n κοντή φούστα, μίνι.

minister [ˈministə*] n υπουργός m/f|| (ECCL) ιερέας || **~ial** [minisˈtiəriəl] a υπουργικός, κυβερνητικός.

ministry [ˈministri] n (government) υπουργείο, κυβέρνηση || (ECCL) το ιερατείο, κλήρος.

mink [miŋk] n είδος νιφίτσας ♦ a: **~ coat** n παλτό από μινκ.

minor [ˈmainə*] a μικρότερος, μικρός || (MUS) ελάσσων ♦ n (under 18: Brit) ανήλικος.

minority [maiˈnoriti] n μειοψηφία, μειονότητα.

minstrel [ˈminstrəl] n ραψωδός, τραγουδιστής.

mint [mɪnt] n (plant) δυόσμος || (sweet) μέντα || (for coins) νομισματοκοπείο ♦ a (condition) καινούργιος, κατακαίνουργιος || ~ **sauce** n σάλτσα με δυόσμο.

minuet [mɪnjuˈɛt] n μενουέτο.

minus [ˈmaɪnəs] n σημείο του πλην ♦ prep πλην, μείον.

minute [maɪˈnjuːt] a μικροσκοπικός, ελάχιστος || (detailed) λεπτομερής ♦ [ˈmɪnɪt] n λεπτό (της ώρας) || (moment) στιγμή || ~s npl πρακτικά ntpl.

miracle [ˈmɪrəkl] n (esp REL) θαύμα nt.

miraculous [mɪˈrækjuləs] a θαυματουργός, υπερφυσικός, θαυμαστός.

mirage [ˈmɪrɑːʒ] n αντικατοπτρισμός, οπτική απάτη.

mirror [ˈmɪrə*] n καθρέφτης, κάτοπτρο ♦ vt αντικατοπτρίζω, αντανακλώ.

mirth [mɜːθ] n ευθυμία, χαρά, κέφι.

misadventure [mɪsədˈventʃə*] n κακοτυχία, ατύχημα nt.

misapprehension [ˈmɪsæprɪˈhenʃən] n (misunderstanding) παρεξήγηση.

misbehave [ˈmɪsbɪˈheɪv] vi φέρομαι άσχημα.

miscalculate [ˈmɪsˈkælkjuleɪt] vt υπολογίζω λανθασμένα.

miscalculation [ˈmɪskælkjuˈleɪʃən] n λανθασμένος υπολογισμός.

miscarriage [ˈmɪskærɪdʒ] n αποτυχία || (of justice) δικαστικό λάθος || (MED) αποβολή.

miscellaneous [mɪsɪˈleɪnɪəs] a ποικίλος, ανάμικτος.

mischance [mɪsˈtʃɑːns] n αποτυχία, ατύχημα nt.

mischievous [ˈmɪstʃɪvəs] a κατεργάρης, σκανταλιάρης.

misconception [ˈmɪskənˈsepʃən] n εσφαλμένη αντίληψη.

misconduct [mɪsˈkɒndʌkt] n παράπτωμα nt, κακή διαγωγή.

miscount [ˈmɪsˈkaunt] vt μετρώ λανθασμένα.

misdemeanour, misdemeanor (US) [ˈmɪsdɪˈmiːnə*] n (less important offence) παράπτωμα, πλημμέλημα nt.

misdirect [ˈmɪsdɪˈrekt] vt (person, letter) δίνω λανθασμένες οδηγίες, διευθύνω άσχημα.

miser [ˈmaɪzə*] n φιλάργυρος, τσιγκούνης.

miserable [ˈmɪzərəbl] a δυστυχισμένος, θλιβερός || (poor) άθλιος, ελεεινός, φτωχός.

miserly [ˈmaɪzəlɪ] a τσιγκούνικος.

misery [ˈmɪzərɪ] n δυστυχία, βάσανο || (poverty) αθλιότητα, φτώχια.

misfire [ˈmɪsˈfaɪə*] vi ρετάρω, παθαίνω αφλογιστία || (plan) πέφτω στο κενό.

misfit [ˈmɪsfɪt] n (person) απροσάρμοστος.

misfortune [mɪsˈfɔːtʃən] n ατυχία, ατύχημα nt.

misgiving [mɪsˈgɪvɪŋ] n (often pl) ανησυχία, αμφιβολία, φόβος.

misguided [ˈmɪsˈgaɪdɪd] a πλανώμενος, παρασυρόμενος.

mishandle [ˈmɪsˈhændl] vt (manage badly) κακομεταχειρίζομαι.

mishap [ˈmɪshæp] n ατυχία, αναποδιά.

mishear [ˈmɪsˈhɪə*] vt (hear wrongly) παρακούω.

misinform [ˈmɪsɪnˈfɔːm] vt πληροφορώ κακώς.

misinterpret [ˈmɪsɪnˈtɜːprɪt] vt παρερμηνεύω.

misjudge [ˈmɪsˈdʒʌdʒ] vt κρίνω λανθασμένα.

mislay — 179 — moat

mislay ['mɪs'leɪ] vt (misplace, lose) παραπετώ, χάνω.

mislead ['mɪs'liːd] vt (deceive) παραπλανώ, εξαπατώ || ~ing a παραπλανητικός.

misnomer ['mɪs'nəʊmə*] n λανθασμένη ονομασία.

misogynist [mɪ'sɔdʒɪnɪst] n μισογύνης.

misplace ['mɪs'pleɪs] vt (mislay) τοποθετώ κατά λάθος, χάνω.

misprint ['mɪsprɪnt] n τυπογραφικό λάθος.

misread ['mɪs'riːd] vt κακοδιαβάζω, παρερμηνεύω.

misrepresent ['mɪsrɛprɪ'zɛnt] vt διαστρέφω, παραμορφώνω.

miss [mɪs] vt αστοχώ, αποτυγχάνω || (not notice) δε βλέπω, χάνω || (train etc) χάνω || (omit) παραλείπω || (regret absence) μού λείπει, αποζητώ ♦ vi αντιλαμβάνομαι ♦ n (fall short) αστοχία || (failure) αποτυχία.

Miss [mɪs] n: ~ X Δεσποινίδα Χ, Δεσποινίς Χ, Δις Χ || ~ Smith Δεσποινίδα Σμιθ, Δις Σμιθ.

misshapen ['mɪs'ʃeɪpən] a παραμορφωμένος.

missile ['mɪsaɪl] n (esp nuclear) βλήμα nt.

missing ['mɪsɪŋ] a (person) απών, αγνοούμενος || (thing) χαμένος.

mission ['mɪʃən] n αποστολή || (church) ιεραποστολή || ~ary n ιεραπόστολος.

misspent ['mɪs'spɛnt] a (youth) χαμένα (νειάτα).

mist [mɪst] n ομίχλη, καταχνιά ♦ vi (also: ~ over, ~ up) σκεπάζω με ομίχλη, θαμπώνω.

mistake [mɪs'teɪk] n σφάλμα nt, λάθος nt ♦ vt παρανοώ, παρερμηνεύω || (for another) παίρνω για άλλο, παραγνωρίζω || ~n a (person) σφάλλω, κάνω λάθος || (identity) παραγνωρίζω.

mister ['mɪstə*] n (abbr Mr) κύριος (Κος) || see Mr.

mistletoe ['mɪsltəʊ] n ιξός, γκι.

mistreat ['mɪs'triːt] vt κακομεταχειρίζομαι.

mistress ['mɪstrɪs] n (teacher) δασκάλα || (of house) κυρία, οικοδέσποινα || (lover) ερωμένη, μαιτρέσσα || see Mrs.

mistrust ['mɪs'trʌst] vt δυσπιστώ, υποπτεύομαι.

misty ['mɪstɪ] a ομιχλώδης, θαμπός, σκοτεινιασμένος.

misunderstand ['mɪsʌndə'stænd] vti παρανοώ, παρεξηγώ || ~ing n παρανόηση, παρεξήγηση.

misunderstood ['mɪsʌndə'stʊd] a (person) παρεξηγημένος.

misuse ['mɪs'juːs] n κακή χρήση || ['mɪs'juːz] vt κάνω κατάχρηση, χρησιμοποιώ λανθασμένα.

miter ['maɪtə*] n (US) = **mitre**.

mitigate ['mɪtɪgeɪt] vt μετριάζω, καταπραΰνω.

mitre ['maɪtə*] n λοξή ένωση, ονυχωτή ένωση || (ECCL) μίτρα.

mitt(en) ['mɪt(n)] n είδος nt γαντιού.

mix [mɪks] vt αναμιγνύω, ανακατώνω ♦ vi αναμιγνύομαι, ταιριάζω ♦ n (mixture) μίξη, μίγμα nt || **to ~ up** vt ανακατεύω || (confuse) μπερδεύω || ~ed a (assorted) ανάμικτος || (school etc) μικτός || ~ed-up a (confused) συγχυσμένος, μπερδεμένος || ~r n (for food) μίξερ || (person) κοινωνικός || ~ture n (assortment) αμάλγαμα nt, ανακάτεμα nt || (MED) μίγμα nt || ~up n (confusion) σύγχυση, ανακατωσούρα.

moan [məʊn] n (groan) γογγυσμός, βογγητό || (complaint) γκρίνια, μουρμουρητό ♦ vi στενάζω, βογγώ, γογγύζω.

moat [məʊt] n τάφρος f.

mob [mɔb] n όχλος, το πλήθος nt ♦
vt (star etc) πολιορκώ, κυκλώνω.

mobile [ˈməubail] a ευκίνητος,
κινητός, ευμετάβολος.

mobility [məuˈbiliti] n ευκινησία,
κινητικότητα.

mock [mɔk] vt εμπαίζω, κοροϊδεύω,
περιπαίζω ♦ a ψεύτικος, φτιαστός ||
~**ery** n (derision) εμπαιγμός,
κοροϊδία || (object) περίγελος,
κορόιδο || ~**ing** a (tone) ειρωνικός,
σαρκαστικός || ~**up** n υπόδειγμα nt
|| (model) μακέτα.

model [ˈmɔdl] n ομοίωμα nt,
μοντέλο || (example) πρότυπο,
υπόδειγμα nt || (person) μοντέλο || (of
clothes) μανεκέν nt inv ♦ vt
(δια)πλάθω, διαμορφώνω, σχεδιάζω
|| (display clothes) κάνω επίδειξη
(ρούχων) ♦ a (railway: toy) τραινάκι ||
(child) πρότυπο, ιδεώδης || ~**ing**,
~**ing** (US) n σχεδίασμα nt, πλάσιμο ||
(of styles) επίδειξη μόδας.

modem [ˈməudem] n (COMPUT)
modem.

moderate [ˈmɔdərit] a μέτριος,
μέσος || (fairly good) μέτριος, της
σειράς ♦ n (POL) μετριοπαθής ♦
[ˈmɔdəreit] vi προΐσταμαι,
προεδρεύω ♦ vt μετριάζω,
περιορίζω || ~**ly** ad μετρημένα,
συγκρατημένα, μέτρια.

moderation [mɔdəˈreiʃən] n
μετριασμός, μετριοπάθεια.

modern [ˈmɔdən] a σύγχρονος,
μοντέρνος || ~**ization** n
(εκ)συγχρονισμός || ~**ize** vt
συγχρονίζω, ανανεώνω.

modest [ˈmɔdist] a (attitude)
μετριόφρων, σεμνός || (meal, home)
ταπεινός, μέτριος || ~**y** n
μετριοφροσύνη, σεμνότητα,
ταπεινότητα.

modicum [ˈmɔdikəm] n: with a ~
of με ελάχιστο, με λίγο.

modification [mɔdifiˈkeiʃən] n
τροποποίηση, μετριασμός.

modify [ˈmɔdifai] vt τροποποιώ,
μετριάζω.

module [ˈmɔdjuːl] n (space)
θαλαμίσκος.

mohair [ˈməuheə*] n μαλλί μοχαίρ
nt inv.

moist [mɔist] a υγρός, νοτισμένος ||
~**en** vt υγραίνω, μουσκεύω || ~**ure**
n υγρασία.

molar [ˈməulə*] n γομφίος, μυλίτης,
τραπεζίτης.

mold [məuld] (US) = **mould.**

mole [məul] n (spot) κρεατοελιά ||
(animal) τυφλοπόντικας || (pier)
κυματοθραύστης, μώλος.

molecule [ˈmɔlikjuːl] n μόριο.

molest [məuˈlest] vt (παρ)ενοχλώ,
πειράζω.

molt [məult] (US) = **moult.**

molten [ˈməultən] a χυτός,
λιωμένος.

moment [ˈməumənt] n στιγμή ||
(importance) βαρύτητα,
σπουδαιότητα || ~**ary** a στιγμιαίος,
προσωρινός || ~**ous** a
βαρυσήμαντος, σημαντικός.

momentum [məuˈmentəm] n
ορμή, φόρα.

monarch [ˈmɔnək] n μονάρχης ||
~**y** n μοναρχία.

monastery [ˈmɔnəstri] n
μοναστήρι.

monastic [məˈnæstik] a μοναχικός,
μοναστικός.

Monday [ˈmʌndi] n Δευτέρα.

monetary [ˈmʌnitəri] a
νομισματικός, χρηματικός.

money [ˈmʌni] n χρήμα nt, νόμισμα
nt, παράς || (wealth) χρήματα ntpl,
πλούτη ntpl || ~**lender** n τοκιστής,
τοκογλύφος || ~**order** n
ταχυδρομική επιταγή.

mongol [ˈmɔŋgəl] n (child) πάσχων
εκ μογγολισμού ♦ a μογγολικός.

mongrel ['mʌŋgrəl] n μιγάδας ♦ a μιγαδικός, μιξιγενής.

monitor ['mɒnitə*] n παρεναίτης, επιμελητής || (television monitor) ελεγκτής || (COMPUT) οθόνη ♦ vt (broadcasts) ελέγχω.

monk [mʌŋk] n καλόγηρος, μοναχός.

monkey ['mʌŋki] n πίθηκος, μαϊμού f|| ~ **nut** n αραποφύστικο || ~ **wrench** n γαλλικό κλειδί.

mono- ['mɒnəu] prefix μον(ο).

monochrome ['mɒnəkrəum] a (TV) μονόχρωμος.

monocle ['mɒnəkl] n μονύελο, μονόκλ n inv.

monogram ['mɒnəgræm] n μονόγραμμα nt, μονογραφή.

monolithic [mɒnəu'liθik] a μονολιθικός.

monologue ['mɒnəlɒg] n μονόλογος.

monopoly [mə'nɒpəli] n μονοπώλιο.

monorail ['mɒnəureil] n μονόραβδος f.

monosyllabic ['mɒnəusi'læbik] a (person) μονοσυλλαβικός.

monotone ['mɒnətəun] n μονοτονία ήχου, μονότονη ομιλία.

monotonous [mə'nɒtənəs] a μονότονος.

monotony [mə'nɒtəni] n μονοτονία.

monsoon [mɒn'su:n] n θερινός μουσσώνας.

monster ['mɒnstə*] n (huge animal) τέρας nt, τερατούργημα nt || (wicked person) τέρας.

monstrosity [mɒns'trɒsiti] n τερατωδία, κτηνωδία.

monstrous ['mɒnstrəs] a τερατώδης, εκτρωματικός.

montage [mɒn'tɑ:ʒ] n (picture) μοντάζ n inv, μοντάρισμα nt.

month [mʌnθ] n μήνας || ~**ly** a

μηνιαίος, μηνιάτικος ♦ ad μηνιαίως, κάθε μήνα ♦ n (magazine) μηνιαίο περιοδικό.

monument ['mɒnjumənt] n μνημείο || ~**al** a μνημειακός || (work etc) μνημειώδης.

moo [mu:] vi (cow) μυκώμαι, μουγκρίζω.

mood [mu:d] n διάθεση, κέφι || (GRAM) έγκλιση || ~**y** a κακόκεφος, κατσούφης, σκυθρωπός, ιδιότροπος.

moon [mu:n] n σελήνη, φεγγάρι || ~**light** n σεληνόφως nt, φεγγάρι || ~**lit** a φεγγαρόλουστος.

moor [muə*] n (Brit: heath) έλος nt, βάλτος, ρεικότοπος ♦ vt (ship) πρυμνοδετώ, δένω (πλοίο) ♦ vi πλευρίζω, πέφτω δίπλα.

moorings ['muəriŋz] npl πρυμνήσια ntpl, πρυμάτσες fpl, ναύδετα ntpl.

moorland ['muələnd] n έλος nt, βάλτος, ρεικότοπος.

moose [mu:s] n άλκη n Αμερικανική.

mop [mɒp] n πατσαβούρα || (duster) ξεσκονιστήρι ♦ vt σφουγγαρίζω || ~ **of hair** n ξεντένιστα μαλλιά ntpl.

mope [məup] vi μελαγχολώ, αθυμώ.

moral ['mɒrəl] a ηθικός, ψυχικός || ~s npl ήθη ntpl|| ~**e** n ηθικό || ~**ity** n ηθικότητα, ηθικό αίσθημα nt.

morass [mə'ræs] n έλος nt|| (fig) βόρβορος.

morbid ['mɔ:bid] a νοσηρός, αρρωστιάρικος.

more [mɔ:*] a περισσότερος ♦ ad περισσότερο, πιο πολύ || ~ **or less** σχεδόν, πάνω κάτω || ~ **than ever** περισσότερο παρά ποτέ.

moreover [mɔ:'rəuvə*] ad επί πλέον, εκτός τούτου.

morgue [mɔ:g] n νεκροτομείο.

moribund ['mɒribʌnd] a ετοιμοθάνατος.

morning ['mɔːnɪŋ] *n* πρωΐ ♦ *a* πρωϊνός || **in the ~** το πρωΐ.

Moroccan [məˈrɒkən] *a, n* Μαροκινός.

Morocco [məˈrɒkəʊ] *n* Μαρόκο.

moron ['mɔːrɒn] *n* καθυστερημένος || (*col*) ηλίθιος, βλάκας || **~ic** [məˈrɒnɪk] *a* ηλίθιος, βλακώδης.

morose [məˈrəʊs] *a* κακότροπος, σκυθρωπός.

morphine ['mɔːfiːn] *n* μορφίνη.

Morse [mɔːs]: **~ code** *n* μοραϊκός κώδικας.

morsel ['mɔːsl] *n* (*of food*) μπουκιά, κομματάκι.

mortal ['mɔːtl] *a* θνητός || (*deadly*) θανάσιμος, θανατηφόρος || (*very great*) τρομερός ♦ *n* (*human being*) θνητός (άνθρωπος) || **~ity** *n* θνητότητα || (*death rate*) θνησιμότητα.

mortar ['mɔːtə*] *n* ασβεστοκονίαμα *nt*, πηλός, λάσπη || (*bowl*) λάσπη || (*weapon*) όλμος.

mortgage ['mɔːgɪdʒ] *n* υποθήκη.

mortuary ['mɔːtjʊərɪ] *n* νεκροθάλαμος.

mosaic [məʊˈzeɪɪk] *n* μωσαϊκό, ψηφιδωτό.

Moscow ['mɒskəʊ] *n* Μόσχα.

Moslem ['mɒzləm] *n* Μουσουλμάνος/α *m/f* ♦ *a* μουσουλμανικός.

mosque [mɒsk] *n* τέμενος *nt*, τζαμί.

mosquito [mɒsˈkiːtəʊ] *n* κουνούπι.

moss [mɒs] *n* βρύο || **~y** *a* βρυώδης, βρυόφυτος.

most [məʊst] *a* περισσότερος, πιο πολύς ♦ *ad* πιο, πιο πολύ ♦ *n* οι περισσότεροι || **at the (very) ~** το πιο πολύ || **to make the ~ of** επωφελούμαι || **~ly** *ad* ως επί το πλείστο, κυρίως, συνήθως.

M.O.T. *n* (*abbr of Ministry of Transport*): **the ~ (test)**

αναγκαστικός, ετήσιος τεχνικός έλεγχος οχημάτων.

motel [məʊˈtɛl] *n* μοτέλ *nt inv*.

moth [mɒθ] *n* βότριδα, σκώρος || **~ ball** *n* ναφθαλίνη (σε μπάλλες) || **~-eaten** *a* σκωροφαγωμένος.

mother ['mʌðə*] *n* μητέρα, μάνα *vt* (*spoil*) χαϊδεύω, κανακεύω ♦ *a* (*tongue, country*) μητρική (γλώσσα) || **~hood** *n* μητρότητα || **~-in-law** *n* πεθερά || **~ly** *a* μητρικά, σαν μάνα || **~-to-be** *n* σε ενδιαφέρουσα.

motif [məʊˈtiːf] *n* μοτίφ *nt inv*, θέμα *nt*, μοτίβο.

motion ['məʊʃən] *n* κίνηση || (*proposal*) πρόταση ♦ *vi* κάνω νόημα, νεύω || **~less** *a* ακίνητος || **~ picture** *n* ταινία, φιλμ *nt inv*.

motivated ['məʊtɪveɪtɪd] *a* αιτιολογούμενος, κινητήριος.

motivation [məʊtɪˈveɪʃən] *n* κίνητρο, ελατήριο.

motive ['məʊtɪv] *n* κίνητρο, αίτιο, ελατήριο ♦ *a* κινητήριος.

motley ['mɒtlɪ] *a* (*heterogeneous*) πολύχρωμος, ετερογενής.

motor ['məʊtə*] *n* κινητήρας, μηχανή || (*automobile*) αυτοκίνητο ♦ *vi* ταξιδεύω με αυτοκίνητο || **~ bike** *n* μοτοσυκλέτα || **~ boat** *n* βενζινάκατος *f* || **~ car** *n* αυτοκίνητο || **~cycle** *n* = **~ bike** || **~ cyclist** *n* μοτοσυκλετιστής || **~ ing** *n* χρήση του αυτοκινήτου, οδήγηση ♦ *a* του αυτοκινήτου, της οδηγήσεως || **~ ist** *n* αυτοκινητιστής || **~ oil** *n* λάδι κινητήρων || **~ racing** *n* αυτοκινητοδρομία || **~ scooter** *n* σκούτερ *nt inv*, βέσπα || **~ vehicle** *n* όχημα *nt* || **~ way** *n* (*Brit*) αυτοκινητόδρομος.

mottled ['mɒtld] *a* διάστικτος, ποικιλόχρωμος.

motto ['mɒtəʊ] *n* ρητό, μόττο, αρχή.

mould [məʊld] *n* τύπος, μήτρα, καλούπι || (*shape*) τύπωμα *nt*,

πρότυπο || (mildew) μούχλα ♦ vt χύνω σε τύπους || (fig) διαπλάθω, διαμορφώνω || ~**er** vi (decay) σαπίζω, φθείρομαι || ~**ing** n (in plaster) τυποποιία, χυτό αντικείμενο || (in wood) κορνίζα || ~**y** a (food etc) μουχλιασμένος.

moult [məult] vi μαδώ.

mound [maund] n ανάχωμα nt, λοφίσκος, πρόχωμα nt.

mount [maunt] n (high hill) όρος nt, βουνό || (horse) άλογο || (for jewel etc) κορνίζα, υποστήριγμα nt, σκελετός ♦ vt (get on horse) ανεβάζω, ανεβαίνω στο || (put in setting) μοντάρω, δένω, κορνιζάρω || (exhibition) ανεβάζω ♦ (attack) οργανώνω επίθεση ♦ vi (also: ~ up) ανέρχομαι, ανεβαίνω.

mountain ['mauntin] n όρος nt, βουνό || (pile) σωρός, πλήθος nt || ~**eer** n (climber) ορειβάτης || ~**eering** n ορειβασία || **to go** ~**eering** κάνω ορειβασία || ~**ous** a ορεινός || ~ **side** n πλευρά βουνού.

mourn [mɔːn] vt πενθώ, θρηνώ ♦ vi (+ for) θρηνώ, κλαίω || ~**er** n πενθών, πενθοφορών || ~**ful** a πένθιμος || ~**ing** n πένθος nt || in ~**ing** (period etc) έχω πένθος || (dress) πένθιμα ρούχα ntpl, μαύρα ntpl.

mouse [maus] n ποντικός || ~**trap** n ποντικοπαγίδα, φάκα.

moustache [məs'taːʃ] n μουστάκι.

mouth [mauθ] n (ANAT) στόμα nt || (opening) στόμιο || (entrance) εκβολή, στόμιο ♦ [mauð] vt (words) ομιλώ με στόμφο || ~**ful** n μπουκιά || ~**organ** n φυσαρμόνικα || ~**piece** n επιστόμιο || (speaker) όργανο, φερέφωνο, εκπρόσωπος || ~**wash** n γαργάρα || ~**watering** a γαργαλιστικός.

movable ['muːvəbl] a κινητός.

move [muːv] n (movement) κίνηση || (in game) κίνηση || (step) ενέργεια, βήμα nt || (from house) μετακόμιση ♦ vt (μετα)κινώ, μετατοπίζω || (stir, rouse) συγκινώ, γίνομαι (εξωφρενών κλ) ♦ vi (general) κινούμαι, κουνιέμαι || (travel) μετακινούμαι, φεύγω || (take action) ενεργώ || (go elsewhere) μετακομίζω || **to get a** ~ **on** σπεύδω, κάνω γρήγορα || **to** ~ **house** μετοικώ, μετακομίζω || **to** ~ **about** vi περιφέρομαι, τριγυρίζω || ~ **away** vi απομακρύνομαι, φεύγω || **to** ~ **back** vi υποχωρώ, ξαναγυρίζω πίσω || **to** ~ **forward** vi προχωρώ ♦ vt κινώ προς τα εμπρός || **to** ~ **in** (house) μετακομίζω (στο νέο σπίτι), εγκαθίσταμαι || **to** ~ **on** vi προχωρώ, τραβώ το δρόμο μου ♦ vt κάνω να κυκλοφορεί || **to** ~ **out** vi (house) μετακομίζω (αλλού), αδειάζω || ~**ment** n κίνηση, μετακίνηση || (social etc) κίνημα nt, κίνηση || (MUS) μέρος nt.

movie ['muːvɪ] n (film) φιλμ nt inv || **the** ~**s** (cinema) σινεμά nt inv || ~ **camera** n (amateur) κινηματογραφική μηχανή.

moving ['muːvɪŋ] a (lit) κινούμενος, κινητός || (stirring) συνταρακτικός, συγκινητικός || (touching) συγκινητικός.

mow [məu] (irreg v) vt θερίζω || **to** ~ **down** vt θερίζω || ~**er** n (machine) θεριστική μηχανή.

M.P. abbr see **member**.

m.p.g. (abbr of miles per gallon) x.α.λ. (χιλιόμετρα ανά λίτρο).

m.p.h. (abbr of miles per hour) x.α.ω. (χιλιόμετρα ανά ώρα).

Mr ['mɪstə*] n: ~ **Smith** Εύριος Σμιθ, Κος Σμιθ.

Mrs ['mɪsɪz] n: ~ **Smith** Κυρία Σμιθ, Κα Σμιθ.

much [mʌtʃ] a πολύς ♦ ad πολύ, συχνά, σχεδόν ♦ n πολλά, πολύ ||

how ~ is it? πόσο κάνει; || **too ~** πάρα πολύ.

muck [mʌk] n (lit) κοπριά, βρωμιά || (fig) σύγχυση, καταστροφή || **to ~ about** vi (col) περιφέρομαι άσκοπα, χαζεύω ♦ vt (col) λασπώνω, βρωμίζω || **to ~ up** vt (col: ruin) χαλάω μια δουλειά || **~y** a (dirty) βρώμικος, βρωμερός.

mud [mʌd] n λάσπη.

muddle [ˈmʌdl] n ακαταστασία, σαλάτα, μπέρδεμα nt ♦ vt (also: ~ up) μπερδεύω, κάνω άνω-κάτω || **to ~ through** vi καταφέρνω κουτσά-στραβά.

muddy [ˈmʌdi] a λασπώδης, λασπωμένος.

mudguard [ˈmʌdɡɑːd] n φτερό (αυτοκινήτου).

mudpack [ˈmʌdpæk] n μάσκα (από πηλό).

mud-slinging [ˈmʌdsliŋiŋ] n συκοφαντία, κακογλωσσιά.

muffle [ˈmʌfl] vt πνίγω (ήχο) || (wrap up) κουκουλώνω, σκεπάζω || **~d** a υπόκουρος, πνιγμένος.

mug [mʌg] n (cup) μεγάλο φλυτζάνι, φλυτζάνα || (col: face) μούτρο, φάτσα || (col: dupe) χαζός, κορόιδο ♦ vt (assault) κτυπώ από πίσω || **~ging** n (assault) επίθεση με ληστεία.

muggy [ˈmʌgi] a (weather) βαρύς (καιρός), υγρός.

mule [mjuːl] n ημίονος, μουλάρι.

mull [mʌl]: **to ~ over** vt γυροφέρνω στο μυαλό.

mulled [mʌld] a (wine) ζεστό κρασί με κανέλλα.

multi [ˈmʌlti] prefix πολυ-.

multicoloured, multicolored (US) [ˈmʌltiˈkʌləd] a πολύχρωμος.

multiple [ˈmʌltipl] n πολλαπλάσιο ♦ a πολλαπλός || **~ store** n κατάστημα nt με πολλά υποκαταστήματα.

multiplication [mʌltiplɪˈkeiʃən] n πολλαπλασιασμός.

multiply [ˈmʌltiplai] vt πολλαπλασιάζω ♦ vi πολλαπλασιάζομαι.

multitude [ˈmʌltitjuːd] n πλήθος nt.

mum [mʌm] n (col) μαμά.

mumble [ˈmʌmbl] vti μουρμουρίζω, μασώ ♦ n μπερδεμένα λόγια ntpl, μουρμούρα.

mummy [ˈmʌmi] n μούμια || (col) μαμά.

mumps [mʌmps] n παρωτίτιδα μαγουλάδες fpl.

munch [mʌntʃ] vti μασουλίζω, τραγανίζω.

mundane [ˈmʌnˈdein] a εγκόσμιος, γήινος.

municipal [mjuːˈnisipəl] a δημοτικός.

munitions [mjuːˈniʃənz] npl πολεμοφόδια ntpl.

mural [ˈmjuərəl] n τοιχογραφία.

murder [ˈmɜːdə*] n φόνος, δολοφονία || (fig: col) φονικό ♦ vt φονεύω, σκοτώνω, δολοφονώ || **~er** n φονιάς, δολοφόνος || **~erous** a (δολο)φονικός || **~ess** n φόνισσα.

murky [ˈmɜːki] a σκοτεινός, ζοφερός.

murmur [ˈmɜːmə*] n ψίθυρος, μουρμουρητό ♦ vi ψιθυρίζω, μουρμουρίζω, παραπονούμαι.

muscle [ˈmʌsl] n μυς m.

muscular [ˈmʌskjulə*] a μυϊκός, γεροδεμένος.

Muse [mjuːz] n Μούσα.

muse [mjuːz] vi ρεμβάζω, ονειροπολώ.

museum [mjuːˈziəm] n μουσείο.

mush [mʌʃ] n πολτός.

mushroom [ˈmʌʃrum] n μανιτάρι ♦ vi ξεφυτρώνω.

mushy [ˈmʌʃi] a πολτώδης, μαλακός.

music ['mjuːzɪk] n μουσική || **to face the ~** ακούω εξάψαλμο || **~al** n μουσική παράσταση ♦ a μουσικός, φιλόμουσος || **~ian** n μουσικός m/f || **~ stand** n αναλόγιο μουσικού.

muslin ['mʌzlɪn] n μουσελίνα.

mussel ['mʌl] n μύδι.

must [mʌst] auxiliary v (obligation) **I ~ do it** πρέπει να το κάνω || **I ~ not do it** δεν πρέπει να το κάνω || (probability) **he ~ be there by now** πρέπει να είναι εκεί τώρα ♦ n γλύκος, μούστος || **it is a ~** είναι αναγκαίο.

mustache ['mʌstæʃ] n (US) = moustache.

mustard ['mʌstəd] n (condiment) μουστάρδα.

mustn't ['mʌsnt] = must not.

musty ['mʌstɪ] a μουχλιασμένος || (col) παλιατσούρα, μπαγιάτικος.

mute [mjuːt] n βουβός/ή m/f, μουγγός/ή m/f.

mutilate ['mjuːtɪleɪt] vt ακρωτηριάζω, σακατεύω.

mutilation [mjuːtɪ'leɪʃən] n ακρωτηριασμός, σακάτεμα nt.

mutinous ['mjuːtɪnəs] a στασιαστικός, ανταρτικός.

mutiny ['mjuːtɪnɪ] n στάση, ανταρσία ♦ vi στασιάζω.

mutter ['mʌtə*] vti μουρμουρίζω.

mutton ['mʌtn] n αρνίσιο κρέας nt.

mutual ['mjuːtjuəl] a αμοιβαίος, κοινός || **~ly** ad αμοιβαίως.

muzzle ['mʌzl] n (mouth and nose) ρύγχος nt, μουσούδα || (straps) φίμωτρο || (of gun) στόμιο, στόμα nt ♦ vt φιμώνω.

my [maɪ] poss a δικός μου, μου.

myopic [maɪ'ɒpɪk] a μυωπικός.

myself [maɪ'self] pron εγώ ο ίδιος, τον εαυτό μου.

mysterious [mɪs'tɪərɪəs] a μυστηριώδης.

mystery ['mɪstərɪ] n μυστήριο.

mystic ['mɪstɪk] n μυστικός, μυστικιστής || **~al** a μυστικιστικός, μυστηριώδης.

mystification [mɪstɪfɪ'keɪʃən] n αμηχανία, απάτη.

mystify ['mɪstɪfaɪ] vt προκαλώ έκπληξη.

myth [mɪθ] n μύθος || **~ical** a μυθικός || **~ological** a μυθολογικός || **~ology** n μυθολογία.

N

nab [næb] vt αρπάζω, συλλαμβάνω.

nag [næg] n (horse) μικρό άλογο (ιπποασίας) || (person) γκρινιάρης, καυγατζής ♦ vti γκρινιάζω, καυγαδίζω || **~ging** n καυγάς, φασαρία.

nail [neɪl] n νύχι || (spike) καρφί, πρόκα ♦ vt καρφώνω || **to ~ down** vt (fig) δεσμεύω || **~ brush** n βούρτσα των νυχιών || **~ file** n λίμα (για νύχια) || **~ polish** n βερνίκι των νυχιών, μανό || **~ scissors** npl ψαλιδάκι (για νύχια) || **~ varnish** n βερνίκι για τα νύχια.

naïve [naɪ'iːv] a αφελής.

naked ['neɪkɪd] a γυμνός || (uncovered) εκτεθειμένος, καθαρός || **~ness** n γυμνότητα.

name [neɪm] n όνομα nt || (reputation) φήμη, υπόληψη ♦ vt ονομάζω || (call by name) αναφέρω, κατονομάζω || (appoint) ορίζω, διορίζω || **in the ~ of** εξ ονόματός του || (authority of) εν ονόματι || **~less** a άγνωστος, ανώνυμος || **~ly** ad δηλαδή || **~sake** n ομώνυμος, συνονόματος.

nanny ['nænɪ] n (for child) νταντά.

nap [næp] n (sleep) υπνάκος || **to have a ~** τον παίρνω λιγάκι.

nape [neɪp] n αυχένας, σβέρκος.

napkin ['næpkɪn] n πετσέτα

φαγητού || (Brit) χαρτοπετσέτα, πάνα (βρέφους).

nappy ['næpi] n (for baby) πάνα.

narcissus [naː'sisəs] n νάρκισσος.

narcotic [naː'kɒtik] n ναρκωτικόν nt.

nark [naːk] vt (col: annoy) εξερεθίζω, εξαγριώνω.

narration [nə'reiʃən] n διήγηση.

narrative ['nærətiv] n διήγημα nt, αφήγηση ♦ a αφηγηματικός.

narrator [nə'reitə*] n αφηγητής.

narrow ['nærəu] a στενός, στενόχωρος ♦ vi στενεύω || **to ~ down** vt περιορίζω || **~ly** ad (miss) μόλις, παρά λίγο || **~-minded** a στενοκέφαλος.

nasal ['neizəl] a ένρινος, ρινικός, της μύτης.

nastiness ['naːstinis] n κακία, αχρειότητα, προστυχιά.

nasty ['naːsti] a (mess) δυσάρεστος, βρώμικος || (business) δύσκολος, επικίνδυνος, φοβερός || (person) πρόστυχος, ρεμάλι, κακός.

nation ['neiʃən] n έθνος nt || ['næʃənl] a εθνικός ♦ n υπήκοος m/f, πολίτης/τισσα m/f || **~al anthem** n εθνικός ύμνος || **~alism** n εθνικισμός || **~alist** a, n εθνικιστής/ίστρια m/f, εθνικόφρων || **~ality** n εθνικότητα || **~alization** n εθνικοποίηση || **~alize** vt εθνικοποιώ || **~ally** ad από εθνική άποψη || **~-wide** a πανεθνικό ♦ ad σ' ολόκληρη τη χώρα.

native ['neitiv] n ντόπιος/ια m/f || (non-European) ιθαγενής m/f ♦ a εγχώριος || (country etc) γενέθλιος, μητρικός || (inborn) έμφυτος, φυσικός.

NATO [neitəu] n ΝΑΤΟ (Οργανισμός Βορειοατλαντικού Συμφώνου).

natter ['nætə*] vi (col: chat) κουβεντιάζω.

natural ['nætʃrəl] a φυσικός ||

(inborn) έμφυτος, φυσικός || **~ist** n φυσιοδίφης || **~ize** vt πολιτογραφώ || (plant etc) εγκλιματίζω || **~ly** ad φυσικά, βέβαια || **~ness** n φυσικότητα.

nature ['neitʃə*] n φύση || (sort, kind) είδος nt, χαρακτήρας || **by ~** εκ φύσεως.

naughty ['nɔːti] a (child) άτακτος, κακός.

nausea ['nɔːsiə] n ναυτία, αναγούλα || (disgust) αηδία, αποστροφή || **~te** vt αηδιάζω (κάτι), προ ξενώ ναυτία.

nauseating ['nɔːsieitiŋ] a αηδιαστικός, σιχαμερός.

nautical ['nɔːtikəl] a ναυτικός.

naval ['neivəl] a ναυτικός.

nave [neiv] n κλίτος, νάρθηκας.

navel ['neivəl] n ομφαλός, αφαλός.

navigable ['nævigəbl] a πλωτός.

navigate ['nævigeit] vt (ship etc) κυβερνώ, διευθύνω ♦ vi ναυσιπλοώ, πλέω, ταξιδεύω.

navigation [nævi'geiʃən] n ναυτιλία, πλους m, διάπλους m.

navigator ['nævigeitə*] n ναυτίλος, πλοηγός || (explorer) θαλασσοπόρος || (AVIAT) αεροναυτίλος.

navy ['neivi] n ναυτικό || **~ blue** n (colour) σκούρος μπλε, μπλε μαρίν.

nay [nei] ad (no) όχι || (also) τι λέω, ή καλύτερα.

Nazi ['naːtsi] n Ναζιστής.

neap tide ['niːptaid] n άμπωτη.

near [niə*] a (close) εγγύς, κοντινός || (related) πλησίον, στενός ♦ ad (space) κοντά, πλησίον || (time) περί, εγγύς, κοντά || **~ to** κοντά σε, παρά || (time) περί, κοντά, κοντά || (time) περί, κοντά ♦ vt πλησιάζω || **~by** a κοντινός, πλησίον ♦ ad πολύ κοντά, εγγύτατα || **N ~ East** n Εγγύς Ανατολή || **~ly** ad σχεδόν, περίπου || **~ miss** n λίγο έλειψε (να), παρά λίγο (να) ||

~ness *n* εγγύτητα, στενότητα ||
~side *n* (AUT) αριστερή πλευρά.

neat [niːt] *a* (tidy) καθαρός,
καλοβαμένος, κομψός || (clever)
καλοβαλμένος, επιτυχής, κομψός ||
(pure) καθαρός, αγνός, χωρίς νερό.

nebulous [ˈnɛbjuləs] *a* νεφελώδης.

necessarily [ˈnɛsɪsrɪlɪ] *ad*
απαραιτήτως, κατ' ανάγκη.

necessary [ˈnɛsɪsərɪ] *a* αναγκαίος,
απαραίτητος.

necessitate [nɪˈsɛsɪteɪt] *vt* κάνω
αναγκαίο, υποχρεώνω.

necessity [nɪˈsɛsɪtɪ] *n* ανάγκη.

neck [nɛk] *n* λαιμός, αυχένας,
τράχηλος, σβέρκος || (narrow part)
λαιμός, στένωμα *nt* || ~ and ~ στα
ίσια, ισόπαλος πλάι-πλάι.

necklace [ˈnɛklɪs] *n* περιδέραιο,
κολιέ *nt inv*.

neckline *n* [ˈnɛklaɪn] λαιμός,
ντεκολτέ *nt inv*.

necktie *n* [ˈnɛktaɪ] γραβάτα.

née [neɪ] *a* το γένος.

need [niːd] *n* ανάγκη, χρεία ||
(poverty) ένδεια, φτώχια ♦ *vt* (of
person) χρειάζομαι || (of thing) απαιτώ,
ζητώ (κάτι) || to ~ to do έχω
ανάγκη να κάνω.

needle [ˈniːdl] *n* βελόνι *n* || (knitting)
βελόνα *f* || (compass etc) βελόνη *f*.

needless [ˈniːdlɪs] *a* άχρηστος,
περιττός.

needlework [ˈniːdlwɜːk] *n*
εργόχειρο.

needy [ˈniːdɪ] *a* ενδεής, άπορος.

negation [nɪˈgeɪʃən] *n* άρνηση.

negative [ˈnɛgətɪv] *n* (PHOT)
αρνητικό ♦ *a* αρνητικός.

neglect [nɪˈglɛkt] *vt* παραμελώ ♦ *n*
αμέλεια, παραμέληση.

negligée [ˈnɛglɪʒeɪ] *n* νυχτικό.

negligence [ˈnɛglɪdʒəns] *n*
αμέλεια.

negligent [ˈnɛglɪdʒənt] *a* αμελής,

απρόσεκτος || ~ly *ad* απρόσεκτα,
αμελώς.

negligible [ˈnɛglɪdʒəbl] *a*
αμελητέος.

negotiable [nɪˈgəʊʃɪəbl] *a* (cheque)
εμπορεύσιμος, μετατρεπτός,
μεταβιβάσιμος.

negotiate [nɪˈgəʊʃɪeɪt] *vi*
διαπραγματεύομαι ♦ *vt* (treaty)
διαπραγματεύομαι || (difficulty)
διαβαίνω, ξεπερνώ.

negotiation [nɪgəʊʃɪˈeɪʃən] *n*
διαπραγμάτευση.

negotiator [nɪˈgəʊʃɪeɪtəʳ] *n*
διαπραγματευτής.

Negress [ˈniːgrɛs] *n* νέγρα, μαύρη.

Negro [ˈniːgrəʊ] *n* νέγρος, μαύρος.

neighbour, neighbor (US)
[ˈneɪbəʳ] *n* γείτονας/γείτονισσα *m/f*
|| ~hood *n* γειτονιά, περιοχή || ~ing
a γειτονικός || ~ly *a* καλός
γείτονας, γειτονικός.

neither [ˈnaɪðəʳ] *a* ούτε ο ένας
ούτε ο άλλος, κανένας || *cj* ούτε ...
ούτε, ούτε (και) ♦ *pron* κανένας.

neo- [ˈniːəʊ] prefix νεο-.

neon [ˈniːɒn] *n* νέο || ~ light *n* φως
με νέο.

nephew [ˈnɛvjuː] *n* ανεψιός.

nerve [nɜːv] *n* νεύρο || (courage)
σθένος *nt*, θάρρος *nt* || (impudence)
θράσος *nt* || ~-racking *a*
εκνευριστικός.

nervous [ˈnɜːvəs] *a* νευρικός ||
(timid) ντροπαλός, νευρικός, δειλός
|| ~ breakdown *n* νευρικός
κλονισμός || ~ly *ad* δειλά,
φοβισμένα || ~ness *n* νευρικότητα,
δειλία.

nest [nɛst] *n* φωλιά.

nestle [ˈnɛsl] *vi* φωλιάζω,
κουλουριάζομαι.

net [nɛt] *n* δίκτυο, δίχτυ *nt* || (hair)
φιλές *m*, δίχτυ *nt* ♦ *a* καθαρός.

Netherlands [ˈnɛðələndz] *npl*
Ολλανδία.

netting ['netɪŋ] n δικτύωμα nt, πλέγμα nt.

network ['netwɜːk] n δίκτυο.

neurotic [njuː'rɒtɪk] a νευρωτικός ♦ n νευροπαθής.

neuter ['njuːtə*] a ουδέτερος ♦ n ουδέτερο.

neutral ['njuːtrəl] a ουδέτερος || ~**ity** n ουδετερότητα.

never ['nevə*] ad ποτέ || ~**-ending** a ατελείωτος || ~**theless** ad εντούτοις, παρ' όλα αυτά.

new [njuː] a νέος, καινούργιος || (clothes etc) καινούργής, καινούργιος || (modern) σύγχρονος, μοντέρνος || (at work etc) αρχάριος, άπειρος || ~**born** a νεογέννητος || ~**comer** n φρεσκοφερμένος/vn m/f, νεοφερμένος/vn m/f || ~**ly** ad τελευταία, πρόσφατα || ~**moon** n καινούργιο φεγγάρι || ~**ness** n νεότητα, φρεσκάδα.

news [njuːz] n τα νέα ntpl, ειδήσεις fpl || ~**agent** n πράκτορας εφημερίδων || ~**flash** n έκτακτη είδηση || ~**letter** n δελτίο ειδήσεων || ~**paper** n εφημερίδα || ~**reel** n ταινία επικαίρων.

New Year [njuː'jɪə*] n Νέο Έτος || ~**'s Day** n Πρωτοχρονιά || ~**'s Eve** n παραμονή της Πρωτοχρονιάς.

New Zealand [njuː'ziːlənd] n Νέα Ζηλανδία.

next [nekst] a πλησιέστερος, γειτονικός, πλαϊνός || (in time) προσεχής, επόμενος ♦ ad έπειτα, κατόπιν, μετά ♦ prep: ~ **to** κοντά σε, σχεδόν || **the** ~ **day** την άλλη μέρα, την επομένη || ~ **year** επόμενο έτος nt, άλλος χρόνος, του χρόνου || ~ **of kin** n πλησιέστερο συγγενής.

N.H.S. abbr of National Health Service.

nibble ['nɪbl] vt δαγκώνω, μασουλίζω, τρώγω σιγά-σιγά.

nice [naɪs] a ευχάριστος, καλός,

ωραίος || (exact) λεπτός, ευαίσθητος || ~**-looking** a ωραίος, όμορφος || ~**ly** ad ωραία, ευχάριστα.

nick [nɪk] n (cut) χαραγή, εγκοπή || **in the** ~ **of time** στην κατάλληλη στιγμή.

nickel ['nɪkl] n νικέλιο || (US) πεντάρα (5 σέντς).

nickname ['nɪkneɪm] n παρατσούκλι.

nicotine ['nɪkətiːn] n νικοτίνη.

niece [niːs] n ανεψιά.

niggling ['nɪglɪŋ] a ασημαντολόγος.

night [naɪt] n νύχτα, βράδυ || **good** ~ καλή νύχτα || at or **by** ~ τη νύχτα || ~ **cap** n (drink) νυκτερινό ρόφημα nt || ~ **club** n νυκτερινό κέντρο || ~ **dress** n νυχτικό || ~ **fall** n σούρουπο || ~ **life** n νυχτερινή ζωή || ~**ly** a νυχτερινός, βραδυνός ♦ ad κάθε νύχτα, κάθε βράδυ || ~**mare** n εφιάλτης || ~ **school** n βραδινή σχολή || ~**time** n νύχτα || ~ **watchman** n νυκτοφύλακας.

nightingale ['naɪtɪŋgeɪl] n αηδόνι.

nil [nɪl] n μηδέν, τίποτε.

nimble ['nɪmbl] a εύστροφος, ευκίνητος.

nine [naɪn] num εννέα, εννιά || ~**teen** num δεκαεννιά || ~**ty** num ενενήντα.

ninth [naɪnθ] a ένατος.

nip [nɪp] vt (pinch etc) τσιμπώ, δαγκώνω ♦ n τσίμπημα nt, δάγκωμα nt.

nipple ['nɪpl] n (ANAT) θηλή, ρώγα.

nitrogen ['naɪtrədʒən] n άζωτο.

no [nəu] a κανείς, καθόλου ♦ ad όχι, καθόλου, μη ♦ n άρνηση, αρνητική ψήφος f.

nobility [nəu'bɪlɪtɪ] n (social class) ευγενείς mpl.

noble ['nəubl] a ευγενής, μεγαλοπρεπής ♦ n ευγενής, ευπατρίδης.

nobody ['nəubədɪ] pron κανείς, κανένας, ♦ n (unimportant person) μηδαμινότητα, τιποτένιος.

nod [nɒd] vi νεύω, νέφω, κάνω νόημα || (droop with sleep) νυστάζω, κουτουλώ ♦ n νεύμα nt, νόημα nt, κουτούλισμα nt.

noise [nɔɪz] n κρότος, βοή || (unpleasant) θόρυβος.

noisily ['nɔɪzɪlɪ] ad θορυβωδώς, με φασαρία.

noisy ['nɔɪzɪ] a θορυβώδης.

nomad ['nəumæd] n νομάδας || -ic a νομαδικός.

nominal ['nɒmɪnl] a ονομαστικός, εικονικός.

nominate ['nɒmɪneɪt] vt προτείνω, ονομάζω || (appoint) διορίζω.

nomination [nɒmɪ'neɪʃn] n πρόταση, υποψηφιότητα, διορισμός.

nominee [nɒmɪ'niː] n υποψήφιος/ήφρια m/f.

non- [nɒn] prefix αν-, αντι-, αν, α-|| ~alcoholic a χωρίς οινόπνευμα.

nonchalant ['nɒnʃələnt] a ψύχραιμος, αδιάφορος.

nondescript ['nɒndɪskrɪpt] a ακαθόριστος, χαρακτηριστικός.

none [nʌn] a κανένας ♦ pron κανένας, καμμιά, κανένα ♦ ad καθόλου.

nonentity [nɒ'nentɪtɪ] n μηδαμινότητα, ασήμαντος άνθρωπος.

nonplussed ['nɒn'plʌst] a (τα έχω) χαμένα, βρίσκομαι σε αμηχανία.

nonsense ['nɒnsəns] n ανοησία, παραλογισμός.

non-stop ['nɒn'stɒp] a χωρίς σταθμό.

noodles ['nuːdlz] npl φιδές m.

noon [nuːn] n μεσημέρι.

no one ['nəuwʌn] pron = **nobody.**

noose [nuːs] n βρόχος, θηλειά.

nor [nɔː*] cj ούτε, μήτε.

norm [nɔːm] n κανόνας, τύπος, μέτρο.

normal ['nɔːməl] a κανονικός, συνηθισμένος, ομαλός || ~ly ad κανονικά.

north [nɔːθ] n βορράς, βοριάς || (of country etc) τα βόρεια ♦ a βόρειος ♦ ad βορείως, προς βορρά|| ~-east a βορειοανατολικός|| ~ern a βόρειος, βορεινός || N~ Pole n Βόρειος Πόλος|| N~ Sea n Βόρειος Θάλασσα || ~ward(s) ad προς βορρά|| ~-west a βορειοδυτικός.

Norway ['nɔːweɪ] n Νορβηγία.

Norwegian [nɔː'wiːdʒən] a νορβηγικός ♦ n Νορβηγός/Νορβηγίδα m/f.

nose [nəuz] n μύτη || (smell) όσφρηση, μύτη || ~bleed n ρινορραγία, μάτωμα nt της μύτης || ~-dive n κάθετη εφόρμηση || ~y a περίεργος, αδιάκριτος.

nostalgia [nɒs'tældʒɪə] n νοσταλγία.

nostalgic [nɒs'tældʒɪk] a νοσταλγικός.

nostril ['nɒstrɪl] n ρουθούνι.

not [nɒt] ad δεν, μη, όχι.

notable ['nəutəbl] a αξιοσημείωτος, σημαντικός.

notch [nɒtʃ] n εγκοπή, χαραγή, οδόντωση.

note [nəut] n νότα, τόνος, πλήκτρο || (short letter) γραμματάκι, σημείωμα nt || (remark) σημείωση, υπόμνημα nt || (reputation) φήμη διάκριση ♦ vt σημειώνω, παρατηρώ || (write down) σημειώνω, (κατα)γράφω ~book n σημειωματάριο, καρνέ nt inv || ~-case n πορτοφόλι || ~d a σημαίνων, διακεκριμένος, διάσημος || ~paper n χαρτί αλληλογραφίας.

nothing ['nʌθɪŋ] n μηδέν, τίποτε || for ~ (free) δωρεάν, τζάμπα.

notice ['nəutɪs] n (announcement) αγγελία, αναγγελία || (attention)

proσοχή, παρατήρηση || (warning) ειδοποίηση, προειδοποίηση ♦ vt (observe) παρατηρώ, αντιλαμβάνομαι, προσέχω || ~able a αξιοσημείωτος, αξιοπρόσεκτος || ~ board n (Brit) ενοικιαστήριο, πίνακας ανακοινώσεων.

notification [nɔʊtɪfɪˈkeɪʃən] n (αν)αγγελία, ανακοίνωση, δήλωση, γνωστοποίηση.

notify [ˈnəʊtɪfaɪ] vt πληροφορώ, ειδοποιώ, γνωστοποιώ.

notion [ˈnəʊʃən] n αντίληψη, ιδέα || (fancy) γνώμη, ιδέα, σκέψη.

notorious [nəʊˈtɔːrɪəs] a περιβόητος, πασίγνωστος.

notwithstanding [nɒtwɪθˈstændɪŋ] ad παρ', όλα αυτά, εντούτοις, όμως.

nougat [ˈnuːgɑː] n μαντολάτο.

nought [nɔːt] n (zero) μηδέν || τίποτε, μηδέν.

noun [naʊn] n όνομα, ουσιαστικό.

nourish [ˈnʌrɪʃ] vt (δια)τρέφω || ~ing a θρεπτικός.

novel [ˈnɒvəl] n μυθιστόρημα nt ♦ a νέος, πρωτότυπος || ~ist n μυθιστοριογράφος m/f || ~ty n νεωτερισμός.

November [nəʊˈvɛmbə*] n Νοέμβριος.

novice [ˈnɒvɪs] n αρχάριος, μαθητευόμενος.

now [naʊ] ad τώρα, λοιπόν || right ~ αμέσως, στη στιγμή || ~ and then κάπου-κάπου, καμμιά φορά, || ~ and again κάθε τόσο, μερικές φορές, που και που || ~adays ad σήμερα.

nowhere [ˈnəʊwɛə*] ad πουθενά.

nozzle [ˈnɒzl] n στόμιο (σωλήνα), προφύσιο, ακροφύσιον.

nuclear [ˈnjuːklɪə*] a (energy etc) πυρηνικός.

nucleus [ˈnjuːklɪəs] n πυρήνας.

nude [njuːd] a γυμνός, γδυτός ♦ n (ART) γυμνό.

nudge [nʌdʒ] vt αγκωνίζω, σκουντώ.

nudist [ˈnjuːdɪst] n γυμνιστής/ γυμνίστρια m/f.

nudity [ˈnjuːdɪtɪ] n γυμνότητα.

nuisance [ˈnjuːsns] n ενόχληση, μπελάς.

null [nʌl] a άκυρος.

numb [nʌm] a ναρκωμένος, μουδιασμένος ♦ vt ναρκώνω, μουδιάζω.

number [ˈnʌmbə*] n αριθμός, ψηφίο, νούμερο || (sum) αριθμός, σύνολο, άθροισμα nt || (quantity) πολλοί mpl, πλήθος nt || (GRAM) αριθμός || (issue) αριθμός (τεύχους) ♦ vt (an)αριθμώ, μετρώ || (amount to) ανέρχομαι, φθάνω, αριθμώ || ~ plate n (Brit AUT) πινακίδα κυκλοφορίας αυτοκινήτου.

numeral [ˈnjuːmərəl] n αριθμός.

numerical [njuːˈmɛrɪkəl] a (order) αριθμητικός.

numerous [ˈnjuːmərəs] a πολυάριθμος.

nun [nʌn] n μοναχή, καλόγρια.

nurse [nɜːs] n νοσοκόμος/ νοσοκόμα m/f || (for children) παραμάνα, τροφός f ♦ vt (patient, invalid) περιποιούμαι, νοσηλεύω || (fig) φροντίζω, επιμελούμαι, συγκρατώ.

nursery [ˈnɜːsərɪ] n παιδικός σταθμός, βρεφοκομείο || (plants) φυτώριο || ~ rhyme n παιδικό τραγουδάκι || ~ school n νηπιαγωγείο.

nursing [ˈnɜːsɪŋ] n (profession) επάγγελμα nt νοσοκόμου || ~ home n (ιδιωτική) κλινική.

nut [nʌt] n περικόχλιο, παξιμάδι || (fruit) καρύδι, ξηρός καρπός || ~s a (col: crazy) τρελός.

nutcracker [ˈnʌtkrækə*] n καρυοθραύστης.

nutmeg ['nʌtmeg] n μοσχοκάρυδο.

nutrient ['nju:trɪənt] n θρεπτικό, τρόφιμο.

nutritious [nju:'trɪʃəs] a θρεπτικός.

nutshell ['nʌtʃel] n: **in a ~** σύντομος, με λίγα λόγια.

nylon ['naɪlɒn] a, n νάυλον nt inv.

O

oaf [əuf] n αδέξιος, άξεστος.

oak [əuk] n δρύς, βαλανιδιά ♦ a δρύινος.

O.A.P. abbr see **old.**

oar [ɔ:*] n κώπη, κουπί.

oasis [əu'eɪsɪs] n όαση.

oath [əuθ] n όρκος || (swearword) βλαστήμια.

oats [əuts] npl βρώμη.

obedience [ə'bi:dɪəns] n υπακοή, ευπείθεια.

obedient [ə'bi:dɪənt] a υπάκουος.

obesity [əu'bi:sɪtɪ] n παχυσαρκία.

obey [ə'beɪ] vti υπακούω.

obituary [ə'bɪtjuərɪ] n νεκρολογία.

object ['ɒbdʒɪkt] n αντικείμενο || (target) στόχος, σκοπός, αντικείμενη || (GRAM) αντικείμενο ♦ [əb'dʒekt] vi (+ to) (proposal) αντιτίθεμαι, αποδοκιμάζω || (a noise etc) αποκρούω, επικρίνω || **~ion** n αντίρρηση, αντιλογία || (obstacle) εμπόδιο, δυσκολία || **~ionable** a απαράδεκτος, ανεπιθύμητος || **~ive** n αντικειμενικός σκοπός ♦ a (impartial) αντικειμενικός || **~or** n αντιρρησίας, αντιλέγων.

obligation [ɒblɪ'geɪʃən] n υποχρέωση.

obligatory [ɒ'blɪgətərɪ] a υποχρεωτικός.

oblige [ə'blaɪdʒ] vt υποχρεώνω, επιβάλλω || (do a favour) εξυπηρετώ, υποχρεώνω.

obliging [ə'blaɪdʒɪŋ] a υποχρεωτικός, εξυπηρετικός.

oblique [ə'bli:k] a λοξός, πλάγιος.

obliterate [ə'blɪtəreɪt] vt εξαλείφω, σβήνω, καταστρέφω.

oblivious [ə'blɪvɪəs] a (+ of) επιλήσμων, ξεχασιάρης.

oblong ['ɒblɒŋ] n επιμήκες σχήμα nt, ορθογώνιο ♦ a επιμήκης, μακρουλός.

obnoxious [əb'nɒkʃəs] a απεχθής, δυσάρεστος.

oboe ['əubəu] n όμποε nt.

obscene [əb'si:n] a αισχρός, πρόστυχος.

obscenity [əb'senɪtɪ] n αισχρότητα, αχρειότητα.

obscure [əb'skjuə*] a σκοτεινός, σκούρος || (unnoticed) άσημος, ταπεινός ♦ vt συσκοτίζω, σκεπάζω.

obscurity [əb'skjuərɪtɪ] n σκοτάδι, αφάνεια.

obsequious [əb'si:kwɪəs] a δουλοπρεπής.

observance [əb'zɜ:vəns] n τήρηση, τύπος.

observant [əb'zɜ:vənt] a παρατηρητικός, προσεκτικός.

observation [ɒbzə'veɪʃən] n παρατήρηση, παρακολούθηση.

observatory [əb'zɜ:vətrɪ] n αστεροσκοπείο.

observe [əb'zɜ:v] vt (the law etc) τηρώ, κρατώ || (study) παρατηρώ, κοιτάζω || (understand) διακρίνω, αντιλαμβάνομαι || **~r** n παρατηρητής, τηρητής.

obsess [əb'ses] vt κατέχω, βασανίζω || **~ion** n εμμονή ιδέα || **~ive** a καταθλιπτικός, βασανιστικός.

obsolescence [ɒbsə'lesns] n τάση προς αχρηστία, παλαίωση nt.

obsolete ['ɒbsəli:t] a απαρχαιωμένος.

obstacle ['ɒbstəkl] n εμπόδιο,

πρόσκομμα || ~ **race** n δρόμος μετ' εμποδίων.

obstetrics [ɒb'stɛtrɪks] n μαιευτική.

obstinate ['ɒbstɪnɪt] a επίμονος, πεισματάρης || ~**ly** ad επίμονα.

obstruct [ɒb'strʌkt] vt φράσσω, εμποδίζω || ~**ion** n κωλυσιεργία, εμπόδιο.

obtain [ɒb'teɪn] vt παίρνω, αποκτώ, επιτυγχάνω || ~**able** a επιτευκτός, εφικτός.

obtrusive [ɒb'truːsɪv] a ενοχλητικός, φορτικός.

obvious ['ɒbvɪəs] a προφανής, ευνόητος || ~**ly** ad προφανώς, φανερά.

occasion [ə'keɪʒən] n (time) ευκαιρία, φορά || (event) αφορμή, περίσταση || (reason) λόγος, αιτία ♦ vt προξενώ || ~**al** a σποραδικός, τυχαίος || (drink) που και που || ~**ally** ad κάπου-κάπου.

occult [ɒ'kʌlt] n: the ~ οι απόκρυφες επιστήμες.

occupant ['ɒkjupənt] n κάτοχος m/f || (of house) ένοικος m/f.

occupation [ɒkju'peɪʃən] n απασχόληση, ασχολία, επάγγελμα nt || (of country) κατάληψη, κτήση || ~**al** a (hazard) επαγγελματικός.

occupier ['ɒkjupaɪə*] n (of house) ένοικος m/f.

occupy ['ɒkjupaɪ] vt (take possession) κατέχω, κατακτώ || (live in) κατοικώ || (hold) κατέχω || (employ) απασχολώ.

occur [ə'kɜː*] vi συμβαίνω, γίνομαι, λαμβάνω χώρα || (be found) συναντώμαι, εμφανίζομαι || (+ to) παρουσιάζεται στη σκέψη || **it** ~**s to me** μου έρχεται || ~**rence** n γεγονός nt, συμβάν nt.

ocean ['əuʃən] n ωκεανός || ~-**going** a υπερωκεάνειος.

ochre ['əukə*] n ώχρα.

o'clock [ə'klɒk] ad: **it is 5** ~ είναι πέντε n (ώρα).

octagonal [ɒk'tægənl] a οκταγώνιος.

octane ['ɒkteɪn] n οκτάνιο.

octave ['ɒktɪv] n οχτάβα.

October [ɒk'təubə*] n Οκτώβριος.

octopus ['ɒktəpəs] n χταπόδι.

odd [ɒd] a (number) περιττός, μονός || (not part of set) μονός, παράταιρος || (with some left over) αυτός που περισσεύει || (strange) περίεργος, παράξενος || (casual) τυχαίος || ~**ity** n παραδοξότητα || (person) παράξενος άνθρωπος || ~**ly** ad περίεργως, περίεργα || ~**ments** npl υπολείμματα ntpl || ~**s** npl ανισότητα, διαφορά || (advantage) πλεονέκτημα nt, πιθανότητες fpl || (chances) πιθανότητες fpl || (at racetrack) στοίχημα nt, ποντάρισμα nt || **at** ~ **s** διαφωνώ, είμαι τσακωμένος || ~**s and ends** npl απομεινάρια ntpl, μικροπράγματα ntpl.

ode [əud] n ωδή.

odious ['əudɪəs] a απεχθής, μισητός.

odour, odor (US) ['əudə*] n οσμή, μυρουδιά || ~**less** a άοσμος.

of [ɒf] ad (absent) μακριά || (of switch) κλειστό || (milk) όχι φρέσκος, χαλασμένος ♦ prep από, μακριά από, λιγότερο από.

offal ['ɒfəl] n εντόσθια ntpl.

off-colour, off-color (US) ['ɒf'kʌlə*] a (ill) χλωρός.

offence [ə'fɛns] n (crime) παράπτωμα nt, αδίκημα nt || (insult) προσβολή.

offend [ə'fɛnd] vt προσβάλλω || ~**er** n παραβάτης m/f || ~**ing** a προσβλητικός, πειρακτικός.

offense [ə'fɛns] n (US) = **offence.**

offensive [ə'fɛnsɪv] a προσβλητικός, δυσάρεστος || (weapon) επιθετικός.

offer ['ɒfə*] n προσφορά ♦ vt

προσφέρω, προτείνω || ~ing n (esp REL) θυσία, προσφορά.

offhand ['υf'hænd] a αυθόρμητος, απότομος ♦ ad στη στιγμή, απότομα.

office ['υfιs] n (position) γραφείο || ~ r n (MIL) αξιωματικός, αξιωματούχος || ~ **work** n εργασία γραφείου.

official [ə'fιʃəl] a (authorized) επίσημος, υπηρεσιακός ♦ n υπάλληλος m/f (δημόσιος) || ~**ly** ad επίσημα.

officious [ə'fιʃəs] a αυταρχικός, ενοχλητικός.

offing ['υfιŋ] n: **in the** ~ εν όψει, στα ανοιχτά.

off line [υf'laιn] a (COMPUT) έμμεση σύνδεση και προπέλαση || (switched off) αποσυνδεόμενος.

off-season ['υfsizzn] a μη εποχιακός, εκτός εποχής, νεκρή εποχή.

offset ['υfset] vt αντισταθμίζω, αποζημιώνω.

offshore ['υf'ʃɔ:*] ad στα ανοιχτά ♦ a χερσαίου, στεριανός.

offside ['υf'saιd] a (AUT) έξω πλευρά, δεξιά πλευρά ♦ n (SPORT) οφσάιντ.

offspring ['υfsprιŋ] n απόγονος, βλαστός.

often ['υfən] ad συχνά, πολλές φορές.

oh [υ] excl ω!, αχ!

oil [ɔιl] n πετρέλαιο, λάδι ♦ vt λαδώνω || ~ **can** n λαδωτήρι || ~**field** n πετρελαιοφόρος περιοχή || ~**-fired** a καίων πετρέλαιο || ~ **painting** n ελαιογραφία || ~ **refinery** n διυλιστήριο || ~**skins** npl μουσαμάς || ~ **tanker** n δεξαμενόπλοιο || ~ **well** n πετρελαιοπηγή || ~**y** a ελαιώδης, λαδερός.

ointment ['ɔιntmənt] n αλοιφή.

O.K., okay ['υ'keι] excl πολύ καλά, εντάξει ♦ n έγκριση ♦ vt εγκρίνω.

old [əυld] a γέροντας, γέρος, ηλικιωμένος || (of age) της ηλικίας, χρονών || (worn) παλιός || (former) παλιός, πρώην, τέως || (friend) παλιός (σύντροφος) || ~ **age** n (βαθειά) γεράματα ntpl || ~ **age pensioner (O.A.P.)** n συνταξιούχος m/f || ~**en** a (old) παλιό, του παλιού || ~**-fashioned** a οπαδός του παλιού καιρού || (out of date) απαρχαιωμένος, παλιάς μόδας || ~ **maid** n γεροντοκόρη.

olive ['υlιv] n (fruit) ελιά, ελαία ♦ a (colour) λαδής, ελαιόχρους || ~ **oil** n ελαιόλαδο, λάδι.

Olympic [υ'lιmpιk] a Ολυμπιακός || ~ **Games** npl (also: ~**s**) Ολυμπιακοί αγώνες mpl.

omelet(te) ['υmlιt] n ομελέτα.

omen ['υmen] n οιωνός, σημάδι.

ominous ['υmιnəs] a δυσοίωνος, δυσμενής.

omission [υ'mιʃən] n παράλειψη, παραδρομή.

omit [υ'mιt] vt παραλείπω.

on [υn] prep πάνω σε, σε, κατά, περί ♦ ad εμπρός, προς τα εμπρός, σε λειτουργία || ~ **and off** κάπου-κάπου || ~ **the left** αριστερά, στ, αριστερά || ~ **Friday** την Παρασκευή.

once [wʌns] ad μια φορά, άλλοτε, κάποτε || cj μόλις, από τη στιγμή που, μια και || at ~ αμέσως, στη στιγμή || (same time) ταυτόχρονα, σύγχρονα || all at ~ (suddenly) εντελώς ξαφνικά || (speaking etc) όλοι μαζί || ~ **more** ακόμη μια φορά, **more than** ~ πολλές φορές || ~ **and for all** μια και καλή || ~ **upon a time** μια φορά και (σε κάποιο καιρό).

oncoming ['υnkʌmιŋ] a (traffic) επερχόμενος, προσεγγίζων.

one [wʌn] a ένας, μία, ένα || *(only)* μόνος, μοναδικός ♦ n ένα, ένας, μια ♦ *pron* ένας, αυτός, κανείς, τέτοιος || **this** ~ αυτός εδώ|| **that** ~ αυτός εκεί || ~ **by** ~ ένας-ένας || ~ **another** αλλήλους || ~**-man** a *(business)* (δουλειά) για έναν άνθρωπο || ~**self** *pron* εαυτού || ~**-way** a *(street, traffic)* μονής κατευθύνσεως.

onion [ˈʌnjən] n κρεμμύδι.

on line [ɒnˈlaɪn] a *(COMPUT)* άμεση σύνδεση και προσπέλαση || *(switched on)* συνδεδεμένος.

onlooker [ˈɒnlʊkə*] n θεατής.

only [ˈəʊnlɪ] ad μόνο ♦ a μόνος.

onset [ˈɒnsɛt] n *(beginning)* απαρχή.

onshore [ˈɒnʃɔː*] a, ad προς την ακτή.

onslaught [ˈɒnslɔːt] n εφόρμηση, επίθεση.

onto [ˈɒntu] *prep* = **on to**.

onus [ˈəʊnəs] n βάρος nt, ευθύνη, καθήκον nt.

onwards [ˈɒnwədz] ad *(place)* προς τα εμπρός, και πέρα || *(time)* και στο εξής.

ooze [uːz] vi *(liquid)* στάζω, εκρέω, διειδύω.

opaque [əʊˈpeɪk] a αδιαφανής, θαμπός.

open [ˈəʊpən] a ανοικτός || *(unlimited)* ανοικτός, απεριόριστος || *(without cover)* ακάλυπτος, ξέσκεπος || *(clear)* φανερός, έκδηλος || *(question)* φανερός, έκδηλος || *(free)* ελεύθερος, ανοικτός || *(sincere)* ειλικρινής, απροκάλυπτος ♦ vt ανοίγω || *(letter)* αποσφραγίζω, ανοίγω || *(box)* Μίνω, ανοίγω ♦ vi αρχίζω, ανοίγω || *(shop)* ανοίγω || *(play)* αρχίζω || **to** ~ **out** vt ανοίγω, ξεδιπλώνω || **to** ~ **up** vt *(route)* ανοίγω, χαράσσω, διανοίγω || ~**-air** a υπαίθριος || ~**er** n *(for cans)* ανοικτήρι || ~**ing** n άνοιγμα nt,

ρωγμή || *(beginning)* έναρξη || *(good chance)* ευκαιρία || ~**ly** ad φανερά, ειλικρινά, δημόσια || ~**-minded** a απροκάλυπτος με ανοικτό μυαλό || ~**-necked** a ανοικτό || *(φόρεμα)* ντεκολτέ.

opera [ˈɒprə] n μελόδραμα nt, όπερα || ~ **house** n λυρική σκηνή, όπερα.

operate [ˈɒpəreɪt] vt *(machine)* ενεργώ, κινώ, δικινδύνω ♦ vi λειτουργώ, δρώ, ενεργώ || *(MED)* *(+ on)* χειρουργώ, εγχειρίζω.

operation [ɒpəˈreɪʃən] n λειτουργία, δράση || *(MED)* εγχείρηση || *(MIL)* επιχείρηση.

operative [ˈɒprətɪv] a ενεργός, ισχύων, χειρουργικός.

operator [ˈɒprəreɪtə*] n *(of machine)* χειριστής, οπερατέρ m inv || *(TEL)* τηλεφωνήτρια.

operetta [ɒprəˈrɛtə] n οπερέττα.

opinion [əˈpɪnjən] n γνώμη, ιδέα, δοξασία.

opium [ˈəʊpɪəm] n όπιο.

opponent [əˈpəʊnənt] n αντίπαλος.

opportune [ˈɒpətjuːn] a επίκαιρος, εύθετος, κατάλληλος.

opportunist [ɒpəˈtjuːnɪst] n καιροσκόπος.

opportunity [ɒpəˈtjuːnɪtɪ] n ευκαιρία.

oppose [əˈpəʊz] vt αντιτάσσω, αντικρούω, καταπολεμώ || ~**d** a *(+ to)* αντίθετος (προς), αντιτιθέμενος.

opposing [əˈpəʊzɪŋ] a *(side)* αντίθετος, αντίπαλος.

opposite [ˈɒpəzɪt] a αντίθετος, αντικρυνός || *(direction)* αντίθετος ♦ ad απέναντι, αντίκρυ ♦ *prep* απέναντι || n αντίστοιχο, αντίθετο || ~ **number** n *(person)* αντίστοιχος.

opposition [ɒpəˈzɪʃən] n αντίσταση, αντίθεση || *(party)* αντιπολίτευση.

oppress [əˈprɛs] vt καταπιέζω, καταδυναστεύω || *(heat etc)*

καταθλίβω, βασανίζω || ~ion n
καταπίεση, στενοχώρια || ~ive a
καταθλιπτικός, πνιγηρός.

opt [ɒpt] vi: to ~ for διαλέγω,
επιλέγω.

optical ['ɒptikəl] n οπτικός.

optician [ɒp'tiʃən] n οπτικός.

optimism ['ɒptimizəm] n
αισιοδοξία.

optimist ['ɒptimist] n αισιόδοξος ||
~ ic a αισιόδοξος.

optimum ['ɒptiməm] a ευνοϊκός,
άριστος.

option ['ɒpʃən] n εκλογή || (right to
choose) δικαίωμα nt εκλογής || ~al a
προαιρετικός.

opulent ['ɒpjulənt] a πλούσιος,
άφθονος.

or [ɔː*] cj ή.

oracle ['ɒrəkl] n χρησμός, μαντείο.

oral ['ɔːrəl] a προφορικός ♦ n
(exam) προφορικές (εξετάσεις) fpl.

orange ['ɒrindʒ] n πορτοκάλι ||
(colour) πορτοκαλλί.

oration [ɔː'reiʃən] n λόγος.

orbit ['ɔːbit] n τροχιά ♦ vt (earth)
περιστρέφομαι.

orchard ['ɔːtʃəd] n οπωρόκηπος,
περιβόλι.

orchestra ['ɔːkistrə] n ορχήστρα ||
~l [ɔː'kestrəl] a ορχηστρικός.

orchid ['ɔːkid] n ορχεοειδές φυτό.

ordain [ɔː'dein] vt (pro)ορίζω,
θεσπίζω διορίζω || (ECCL) χειροτονώ.

ordeal [ɔː'diːl] n βασανιστήριο.

order ['ɔːdə*] n (arrangement) τάξη,
σειρά, διαδοχή || (instruction)
διαταγή, εντολή, διάταγμα nt || (rank,
class) τάξη || (ECCL) βαθμός
ιερωσύνης || (MIL) τάγμα nt ||
(decoration) παράσημο || (COMM)
επιταγή, παραγγελία ♦ vt διατάσσω
|| διευθετώ, ταξινομώ || (COMM)
παραγγέλλω || ~ form n έντυπο
εντολής || ~ly n ευελιφόρμος,
ορτινάντσα ♦ a φρόνιμος, τακτικός,

ήσυχος || (tidy) συγυρισμένος,
τακτικός.

ordinary ['ɔːdnri] a συνήθης,
συνηθισμένος || (commonplace) της
αράδας, κοινός.

ore [ɔː*] n ορυκτό, μετάλλευμα nt.

organ ['ɔːgən] n (all senses) όργανο ||
~ic [ɔː'gænik] a οργανικός,
ενόργανος.

organism ['ɔːgənizəm] n
οργανισμός.

organist ['ɔːgənist] n
οργανοπαίκτης.

organization [ɔːgənai'zeiʃən] n
οργάνωση, οργανισμός.

organize ['ɔːgənaiz] vt οργανώνω ||
~r n (δι)οργανωτής.

orgasm ['ɔːgæzəm] n οργασμός,
παροξυσμός.

orgy ['ɔːdʒi] n όργιο.

Orient ['ɔːriənt] n: the ~ Ανατολή,
Άπω Ανατολή.

oriental [ɔːri'entəl] a ανατολικός,
ασιατικός ♦ n Ασιάτης.

orientate ['ɔːrienteit] vt
προσανατολίζω.

origin ['ɒridʒin] n αρχή, γένεση,
καταγωγή.

original [ə'ridʒinl] a (first) αρχικός ||
(new) πρωτότυπος || (individual)
ιδιότυπος, πρωτότυπος ♦ n
πρωτότυπο || ~ ity [ɒridʒi'næliti] n
πρωτοτυπία || ~ly ad αρχικά, εξ
αρχής.

originate [ə'ridʒineit] vi κατάγομαι,
προέρχομαι ♦ vt γεννώ, δημιουργώ.

originator [ə'ridʒineitə*] n
δημιουργός, εγκαινιαστής.

ornament ['ɔːnəmənt] n κόσμημα
nt, στολίδι || ~al a (δια)κοσμητικός.

ornate [ɔː'neit] a διακοσμημένος,
φανταχτερός.

ornithology [ɔːni'θɒlədʒi] n
ορνιθολογία.

orphan ['ɔːfən] n ορφανός/ή m/f ♦

νt ορφανεύω || ~age n
ορφανοτροφείο.
orthodox [ˈɔːθədɒks] a ορθόδοξος ||
(conventional) καθιερωμένος.
orthopaedic, orthopedic *(US)*
[ɔːθəuˈpiːdɪk] a ορθοπεδικός.
ostensibly [ɒsˈtɛnsəblɪ] ad κατά τα
φαινόμενα, δήθεν.
ostentatious [ɒstɛnˈteɪʃəs] a
επιδεικτικός, φιγουρατζής,
φανταχτερός.
ostracize [ˈɒstrəsaɪz] νt
εξοστρακίζω.
ostrich [ˈɒstrɪtʃ] n
στρουθοκάμηλος f.
other [ˈʌðə*] a άλλος || *(additional)*
άλλος, επιπρόσθετος || *(opposite)*
άλλος, απέναντι ♦ pron άλλος ♦ ad:
~ **than** διαφορετικός από, εκτός
από || ~**wise** ad αλλιώς, αλλιώτικα ||
(in other ways) κατά τα άλλα || *(or else)*
διαφορετικά, αλλιώς, ειδεμή.
otter [ˈɒtə*] n ενυδρίδα.
ought [ɔːt] auxiliary ν πρέπει, θα
έπρεπε || I ~ **to do it** πρέπει να το
κάνω || **you** ~ **to go** πρέπει να
φύγεις || **he** ~ **to win** πρέπει να
κερδίσει.
ounce [auns] n ουγγιά.
our [auə*] poss a δικός μας || ~**s** poss
pron δικός μας || ~**selves** pron εμείς
οι ίδιοι.
oust [aust] νt διώχνω, εκτοπίζω.
out [aut] ad έξω || *(not indoors)* εκτός ||
(not alight) σβησμένος || *(open)* που
βγήκε, βγαλμένος || *(made known)*
γνωστός, που απεκαλύφθη || *(in
reckoning)* σε λάθος, έξω || ~ **of** prep
έξω από || *(from among)* από ||
(without) χωρίς || ~ **made** ~ **of wood**
καμωμένος από ξύλο || ~**of-
bounds** a απαγορευμένος || ~**of-
date** a ξεπερασμένος || ~ **of doors**
ad έξω, στο ύπαιθρο || ~ **of order** a
χαλασμένος || ~**of-the-way** a

παράμερος, απόμερος || *(unusual)*
ασυνήθης, ασυνήθιστος.
outboard (motor)
[ˈautbɔːd(ˈməutə*)] n εξωλέμβιος
(κινητήρας).
outbreak [ˈautbreɪk] n έκρηξη,
ξέσπασμα nt, έναρξη.
outburst [ˈautbɜːst] n έκρηξη,
ξέσπασμα nt.
outcast [ˈautkɑːst] n απόβλητος.
outcome [ˈautkʌm] n έκβαση,
πέρας nt.
outcry [ˈautkraɪ] n (κατα)κραυγή.
outdated [autˈdeɪtɪd] a
παλιωμένος, ξεπερασμένος.
outdo [autˈduː] νt υπερβαίνω,
υπερέχω.
outdoor [ˈautdɔː*] a υπαίθριος,
εξωτερικός.
outdoors [autˈdɔːz] ad στο
ύπαιθρο.
outer [ˈautə*] a εξωτερικός || ~
space n διάστημα nt.
outfit [ˈautfɪt] n εξοπλισμός,
εργαλεία ntpl, απαιτούμενα ntpl.
outgoings [ˈautgɔuɪŋz] npl
(expenses) έξοδα ntpl, πληρωμές fpl.
outgrow [autˈgrəu] νt γίνομαι
ψηλότερος από, ξεπερνώ.
outing [ˈautɪŋ] n εκδρομή.
outlaw [ˈautlɔː] n ληστής,
παράνομος ♦ νt βάζω εκτός νόμου.
outlay [ˈautleɪ] n δαπάνη, έξοδα
ntpl.
outlet [ˈautlɛt] n διέξοδος f,
άνοιγμα nt.
outline [ˈautlaɪn] n περίμετρος f,
περίγραμμα nt || *(summary)*
περίληψη.
outlive [autˈlɪv] νt επιζώ.
outlook [ˈautluk] n (prospect)
πρόβλεψη.
outlying [ˈautlaɪɪŋ] a απόκεντρος,
απόμερος.
outmoded [autˈməudɪd] a ντεμοντέ.

outnumber [aut'nʌmbə*] vt
υπερτερώ αριθμητικά.

outpatient ['autpeiʃənt] n
εξωτερικός ασθενής m/f.

outpost ['autpəust] n (people, also
place) προφυλακή, φυλάκιο.

output ['autput] n παραγωγή,
απόδοση, προϊόν nt ♦ vt (COMPUT)
εκτυπώνω.

outrage ['autreidʒ] n προσβολή,
κατάφωρο αδίκημα nt ♦ vt
προσβάλλω, πληγώνω, ταράζω ||
~ous a σκανδαλώδης, τερατώδης,
αχρείος.

outright ['autrait] ad απερίφραστα,
ωμά, ξάστερα || (once and for all)
τελείως, εντελώς ♦ a τέλειος,
οριστικός.

outset ['autset] n αρχή, ξεκίνημα nt.

outside ['aut'said] n εξωτερικό ♦ a
εξωτερικός, πιθανός ♦ ad απ' έξω,
έξω ♦ prep έξω από, εκτός, από,
πέραν του || ~r n (in race etc) χωρίς
πιθανότητες fpl|| (independent)
ξένος/η m/f, θεατής.

outsize ['autsaiz] a μεγάλων
διαστάσεων.

outskirts ['autskə:ts] npl προάστια
ntpl, περίχωρα ntpl.

outspoken [aut'spəukən] a
ειλικρινής, ντόμπρος.

outstanding [aut'stændiŋ] a
προέχων, κύριος, σημαντικός ||
(person) διακεκριμένος, σπουδαίος,
διαπρεπής || (unsettled) εκκρεμής,
απλήρωτος.

outstay [aut'stei] vt (welcome) μένω
περισσότερο από.

outstretched ['autstretʃt] a (hand)
απλωμένος, με ανοιχτές αγκάλες.

outward ['autwəd] a (sign)
εξωτερικός || (journey) προς τα έξω,
έξω || ~ly ad εξωτερικά,
φαινομενικά.

outwit [aut'wit] vt ξεγελώ.

oval ['əuvəl] a ωοειδής,
ελλειψοειδής ♦ n ωοειδές σχήμα nt.

ovary ['əuvəri] n ωοθήκη.

ovation [əu'veiʃən] n επευφημία.

oven ['ʌvn] n κλίβανος, φούρνος.

over ['əuvə*] ad (above) από πάνω,
πάνω από || (across) απέναντι, πέρα ||
(finished) περασμένος, τελειωμένος ||
(too much) πέραν του δέοντος, επί
πλέον || (again) φορές (συνέχεια),
πάλι ♦ prep (above) από πάνω, πάνω
|| (across) απέναντι || (in rank)
υπεράνω, ανώτερος || (about) περί,
για || all ~ (everywhere) παντού, σ'
όλο || (finished) τελειωμένος,
περασμένος || ~ and ~ πολλές
φορές, επανειλημμένα || ~ and
above πέρα από.

over- ['əuvə*] prefix υπέρ-, παρά-.

overall ['əuvərɔːl] n (Brit: for woman
etc) ποδιά || ~s npl (industrial etc)
φόρμα.

overbalance [əuvə'bæləns] vi
ανατρέπω, υπερέχω.

overbearing [əuvə'bɛəriŋ] a
αυταρχικός, δεσποτικός,
υπεροπτικός.

overboard ['əuvəbɔːd] ad στη
θάλασσα (από πλοίο).

overcast ['əuvəkɑːst] a
συννεφιασμένος, σκοτεινιασμένος.

overcharge [əuvə'tʃɑːdʒ] vt (price)
παίρνω πολλά, πουλώ σε,
υπερβολική τιμή.

overcoat ['əuvəkəut] n επανωφόρι,
παλτό.

overcome [əuvə'kʌm] vt νικώ,
καταβάλλω.

overcrowded [əuvə'kraudid] a
υπερπλήρης, παραγεμισμένος.

overdo [əuvə'duː] vt (cook)
παραψήνω || (exaggerate)
υπερβάλλω, μεγαλοποιώ,
παρακάνω.

overdose ['əuvədəus] n υπερβολική
δόση.

overdraft 198 overwhelm

overdraft ['əυvədrɑːft] *n* ανάληψη χωρίς αντίκρισμα.

overdrawn [əυvə'drɔːn] *a (account) see* **overdraft.**

overdrive ['əυvədraiv] *n (AUT)* οβερντράιβ.

overdue ['əυvə'djuː] *a* καθυστερημένος, εκπρόθεσμος.

overestimate ['əυvər'estimeit] *vt* υπερεκτιμώ, υπερτιμώ.

overexcited ['əυvərik'saitid] *a* υπερδιεγειρόμενος.

overexpose ['əυvəriks'pəυz] *vt (PHOT)* υπερεκθέτω, υπερφωτίζω.

overflow [əυvə'fləυ] *vi* ξεχειλίζω ♦ ['əυvəfləυ] *n* υπερχείλιση, ξεχείλισμα *nt.*

overgrown ['əυvə'grəυn] *a (garden)* κατάφυτος, γεμάτος από, σκεπασμένος με.

overhaul [əυvə'hɔːl] *vt (repair)* εξετάζω, επιθεωρώ, ελέγχω ♦ ['əυvəhɔːl] *n* προσεκτική εξέταση, επιθεώρηση, επισκευή.

overhead [əυvə'hed] *a* εναέριος, γενικός ♦ ['əυvə'hed] *ad* επάνω, υπεράνω, ψηλά || ~ **s** *npl* γενικά έξοδα *ntpl.*

overhear [əυvə'hiə*] *vt* ακούω τυχαία, κρυφακούω.

overjoyed [əυvə'dʒɔid] *a* περίχαρης, γεμάτος χαρά.

overland ['əυvəlænd] *a* χερσαίος, στεριανός ♦ [əυvə'lænd] *ad (journey)* διά ξηράς.

overlap [əυvə'læp] *vi* καβαλικεύω, σκεπάζω μερικώς ♦ ['əυvəlæp] *n* επικάλυψη, καβαλίκεμα *nt.*

overleaf [əυvə'liːf] *ad* στο πίσω μέρος (της σελίδας).

overload [əυvə'ləυd] *vt* παραφορτώνω, υπερφορτίζω.

overlook [əυvə'luk] *vt* κοιτάζω πάνω από, δεσπόζω || *(not notice)* παραβλέπω, παραμελώ || *(pardon)* παραβλέπω, συγχωρώ.

overnight ['əυvə'nait] *a* ολονύκτιος, ξενυχτισμένος ♦ *ad* όλη τη νύκτα, ξενύχτι.

overpass ['əυvəpɑːs] *n (road)* ανυψωμένη διάβαση.

overpower [əυvə'pauə*] *vt* καταβάλλω, συντρίβω, καταπνίγω || ~**ing** *a* συντριπτικός, αποπνικτικός.

overrate ['əυvə'reit] *vt* υπερτιμώ.

override [əυvə'raid] *vt (invalidate)* υπερβαίνω, ανατρέπω.

overriding [əυvə'raidiŋ] *a* πρωταρχικός, δεσπόζων.

overrule [əυvə'ruːl] *vt* ανατρέπω, αγνοώ, αναιρώ.

overseas ['əυvə'siːz] *ad* στο εξωτερικό ♦ *a (trade)* εξωτερικός.

overshadow [əυvə'ʃædəυ] *vt* επισκιάζω.

overshoot [əυvə'ʃuːt] *vt (runway)* προσγειώνομαι μακριά.

oversight ['əυvəsait] *n* παράβλεψη, παραδρομή.

oversleep ['əυvə'sliːp] *vi* παρακοιμάμαι.

overstate [əυvə'steit] *vt (case)* μεγαλοποιώ, υπερβάλλω || ~**ment** *n* υπερβολή, μεγαλοποίηση.

overt [əυ'vɜːt] *a* έκδηλος, καταφανής, φανερός.

overtake [əυvə'teik] *vt* προσπερνώ, ξεπερνώ ♦ *vi* συμβαίνω σε, τυχαίνω σε.

overtaking [əυvə'teikiŋ] *n* ξεπέρασμα *nt.*

overthrow [əυvə'θrəυ] *vt* ανατρέπω || *(vanquish)* συντρίβω.

overtime ['əυvətaim] *n* υπερωρία.

overture ['əυvətjuə*] *n (MUS)* εισαγωγή, ουβερτούρα.

overturn [əυvə'tɜːn] *vt* ανατρέπω, αναποδογυρίζω ♦ *vi* ανατρέπομαι.

overweight ['əυvə'weit] *a* με βάρος ανώτερο του κανονικού.

overwhelm [əυvə'welm] *vt* συντρίβω, κατακλύζω, καταβάλλω ||

~ing n συντριπτικός, ακαταμάχητος.

overwork ['əuvə'wɜːk] n κατάπονηση, υπερκόπωση ♦ vt παραφορτώνω, παρακουράζω ♦ vi εργάζομαι υπερβολικά, παρακουράζομαι.

overwrought ['əuvə'rɔːt] a σε υπερένταση, παρακουρασμένος.

owe [əu] vt οφείλω, χρωστώ.

owing to ['əuɪŋtu:] prep λόγω, ένεκα, συνεπεία, εξ αιτίας.

owl [aul] n κουκουβάγια.

own [əun] vt (κατ)έχω, είμαι κύριος ♦ a δικός (μου) ♦ n δικός (μου), ιδιαίτερος || **all my ~** μου ανήκει, όλο δικό μου || **on one's ~** ανεξάρτητα, μόνος (μου) || **to ~ up** vi (confess) ομολογώ || **~er** n ιδιοκτήτης/ήτρια m/f, κύριος/ία m/f || **~ership** n κυριότητα, ιδιοκτησία.

ox [ɒks] n βόδι.

oxide ['ɒksaɪd] n οξείδιο.

oxygen ['ɒksɪdʒən] n οξυγόνο || **~ mask** n μάσκα οξυγόνου || **~ tent** n ασκός οξυγόνου.

oyster ['ɔɪstə*] n στρείδι.

oz. abbr of **ounce(s).**

ozone ['əuzəun] n όζον nt.

P

p [pi:] abbr of **penny, pence.**

p.a. abbr of **per annum.**

pace [peɪs] n βήμα nt, βάδισμα nt|| (speed) ταχύτητα ♦ vi βαδίζω, βηματίζω, περπατώ || **to keep with** συμβαδίζω || **~maker** n προπονητής || (MED) βηματοδότης.

Pacific (Ocean) [pə'sɪfɪk('əuʃən)] n Ειρηνικός (Ωκεανός).

pacifist ['pæsɪfɪst] n ειρηνόφιλος/η m/f.

pacify ['pæsɪfaɪ] vt ειρηνεύω, καθησυχάζω.

pack [pæk] n (bundle) δέμα nt, πακέτο || (wolves) αγέλη, κοπάδι || (cards) δεσμίδα, τράπουλα || (gang) συμμορία ♦ vt (case) συσκευάζω, πακετάρω, κάνω βαλίτσα || (bags) μαζεύω (τα ρούχα μου).

package ['pækɪdʒ] n δέμα nt.

packet ['pækɪt] n δεματάκι, πακέτο.

pack ice ['pækaɪs] n σωρός πάγων, ογκόπαγοι mpl.

packing ['pækɪŋ] n (action) πακετάρισμα nt|| (material) συσκευασία || **~ case** n κιβώτιο συσκευασίας, κασόνι.

pact [pækt] n συμφωνία, συνθήκη.

pad [pæd] n (pillow) μαξιλαράκι || (notebook) μπλόκ nt inv|| (for inking) ταμπόν nt inv ♦ vt (παρα)γεμίζω.

paddle ['pædl] n (oar) κουπί, αναδευτήρας ♦ vt (boat) κωπηλατώ, τραβώ κουπί ♦ vi (in sea) κωπηλατώ ήρεμα, τσαλαβουτώ.

paddling pool ['pædlɪŋpu:l] n λιμνούλα (για παιδιά).

paddock ['pædək] n περίβολος, μάντρα (για άλογα).

paddy ['pædɪ] n: **~ field** n ορυζοφυτεία.

padlock ['pædlɒk] n λουκέτο.

padre ['pɑːdrɪ] n παπάς.

paediatrics [pi:dɪ'ætrɪks] n παιδιατρική.

pagan ['peɪgən] a ειδωλολατρικός.

page [peɪdʒ] n (of book) σελίδα || (boy servant) νεαρός υπηρέτης, γκρούμ m inv|| (wedding) παράνυμφος ♦ vt (in hotel etc) στέλνω μικρό να φωνάξει (κάποιον).

pageant ['pædʒənt] n φαντασμαγορικό θέαμα nt, επιβλητική πομπή.

paid [peɪd] pt, pp of **pay.**

pail [peɪl] n κάδος, κουβάς.

pain [peɪn] n πόνος || **~s** npl (efforts) κόπος || **~ed** a (expression)

θλιμένος, πικραμένος, πονεμένος || ~ **ful** a οδυνηρός || (physically) που πονεί || (difficult) επίπονος ||
~ **killing drug** n παυσίπονο ||
~ **less** a ανώδυνος || **painstaking** a φιλόπονος, προσεκτικός.

paint [peint] n μπογιά ♦ vt ζωγραφίζω, απεικονίζω || (house etc) μπογιατίζω, χρωματίζω || ~ **brush** n χρωστήρας, πινέλο || ~ **er** n (ART) ζωγράφος m/f || (decorator) χρωματιστής, μπογιατζής || ~ **ing** n (action) ζωγραφική || (picture) πίνακας, ζωγραφιά.

pair [peə*] n ζευγάρι || (of shoes) ζεύγος nt || ~ **of scissors** n ψαλίδι || ~ **of trousers** n παντελόνι.

pajamas [pə'dʒɑ:məz] npl (US) πιτζάμες fpl.

pal [pæl] n (col) σύντροφος, φίλος.

palace ['pælis] n ανάκτορο, παλάτι.

palatable ['pælətəbl] a εύγευστος, νόστιμος.

palate ['pælit] n υπερώα, ουρανίσκος || (taste) γεύση.

pale [peil] a (face) ωχρός, χλωμός || (colour) ανοιχτός.

palette ['pælit] n παλέτα.

palisade [pæli'seid] n φράκτης από πασσάλους.

pall [pɔ:l] n (of smoke) σύννεφο ♦ vi κουράζω, βαρίεμαι.

pally ['pæli] a (col) που πιάνει εύκολα φιλίες.

palm [pɑ:m] n (tree) φοίνικας || (of hand) παλάμη || ~ **ist** n χειρομάντης/ισσα m/f || P~ **Sunday** n Κυριακή των Βαΐων || ~ **tree** n φοινικιά, χουρμαδιά.

palpable ['pælpəbl] a (obvious) φανερός, καταφανής.

palpitation [pælpi'teiʃən] n παλμός, σπαρτάρισμα nt.

paltry ['pɔ:ltri] a μηδαμινός, τιποτένιος, άθλιος.

pamper ['pæmpə*] vt (παρα)χαϊδεύω.

pamphlet ['pæmflit] n φυλλάδιο.

pan [pæn] n τηγάνι, κατσαρόλα ♦ vi (+ out) επιτυγχάνω, αποδίδω.

panacea [pænə'siə] n (fig) πανάκεια.

pancake ['pænkeik] n τηγανίτα.

panda ['pændə] n πάντα.

pandemonium [pændi'məuniəm] n πανδαιμόνιο.

pander ['pændə*] vi (+ to) κάνω το ρουφιάνο, κολακεύω πρόστυχα.

pane [pein] n τζάμι.

panel ['pænl] n (of wood) φάτνωμα nt, φύλλο || (of people) επιτροπή || ~ **ling**, ~ **ing** (US) n ξυλεπένδυση.

pang [pæŋ] n δυνατός πόνος || (pain) αγωνία.

panic ['pænik] n πανικός ♦ a (reaction) πανικόβλητος ♦ vi πανικοβάλλομαι || ~ **ky** a (person) πανικόβλητος, έντρομος, φοβισμένος.

pannier ['pæniə*] n κοφίνι, πανέρι.

panorama [pænə'rɑ:mə] n πανόραμα nt.

pansy ['pænzi] n (flower) πανσές m.

pant [pænt] vi λαχανιάζω.

panther ['pænθə*] n πάνθηρας.

panties ['pæntiz] npl (woman's) κυλότα.

pantomime ['pæntəmaim] n παντομίμα.

pantry ['pæntri] n κελάρι || (butler's) κάβα.

pants [pænts] npl (woman's) κυλότα || (man's) σώβρακο || (US: trousers) παντελόνι.

papal ['peipəl] a παπικός.

paper ['peipə*] n (material) χαρτί || (newspaper) εφημερίδα || (essay) μελέτη, διατριβή, υπόμνημα nt ♦ a χάρτινος ♦ vt σκεπάζω με χαρτί, στολίζω με χαρτί || ~ **s** npl (identity) πιστοποιητικά ntpl || (documents) έγγραφα ntpl || ~ **back** n χαρτόδετο

(βιβλίου) || ~ **bag** n χαρτοσακούλα || ~ **clip** n συνδετήρας || ~**weight** n πρες παπιέ nt inv || ~ **work** n γραφική εργασία.

papier-mâché ['pæpɪeɪ'mæʃeɪ] n πεπιεσμένο χαρτί.

par [pɑː*] n (COMM) ισοτιμία, άρτιο, ισότητα || **on a** ~ **with** ίσος με, ίση αξία με.

parable ['pærəbl] n παραβολή.

parachute ['pærəʃuːt] n αλεξίπτωτο ♦ vi πέφτω με αλεξίπτωτο.

parade [pə'reɪd] n (procession) παρέλαση || (review) παράταξη, παρέλαση ♦ vt επιδεικνύω, κάνω παρέλαση ♦ vi παρελαύνω.

paradise ['pærədaɪs] n παράδεισος.

paradox ['pærədɒks] n παράδοξο, παραδοξολογία || ~**ical** a παράδοξα.

paraffin ['pærəfɪn] n παραφίνη.

paragraph ['pærəɡrɑːf] n παράγραφος f.

parallel ['pærəlel] a παράλληλος || (similar) όμοιος, παράλληλος, ανάλογος ♦ n παράλληλος.

paralysis [pə'rælɪsɪs] n παράλυση.

paralyze ['pærəlaɪz] vt παραλύω.

paramount ['pærəmaʊnt] a ύψιστος, υπέρτατος, εξαίρετος.

paranoia [pærə'nɔɪə] n παράνοια.

paraphernalia [pærəfə'neɪlɪə] n διάφορα ntpl, καλαμπαλίκια ntpl.

paraphrase ['pærəfreɪz] vt παραφράζω.

paraplegic [pærə'pliːdʒɪk] a παραπληγικός.

parasite ['pærəsaɪt] n παράσιτο.

parasol [pærə'sɒl] n ομπρέλα του ήλιου.

paratrooper ['pærətruːpə*] n αλεξιπτωτιστής.

parcel ['pɑːsl] n δέμα nt, πακέτο ♦ vt (also: ~ **up**) πακετάρω.

parch [pɑːtʃ] vt ξηραίνω, καψαλίζω,

ψήνω || ~**ed** a ξηρός, στεγνός, άνυδρος.

parchment ['pɑːtʃmənt] n περγαμηνή.

pardon ['pɑːdn] n συγγνώμη, συγχώρηση ♦ vt (free from punishment) δίνω χάρη σε || ~! συγγνώμη!! || ~ **me!** με συγχωρείτε! || I **beg your** ~! συγγνώμη!! || I **beg your** ~? παρακαλώ;

parent ['pɛərənt] n γονέας || ~**al** a πατρικός, μητρικός.

parenthesis [pə'renθɪsɪs] n παρένθεση.

parish ['pærɪʃ] n ενορία, κοινότητα || ~**ioner** n ενορίτης/ισσα m/f.

park [pɑːk] n πάρκο || (cars) χώρος σταθμεύσεως ♦ vti στάθμευση, παρκάρω || ~**ing** n στάθμευση, παρκάρισμα nt, πάρκινγκ nt inv || '**no** ~**ing**' 'απαγορεύεται η στάθμευση' || ~**ing lot** n (US) χώρος σταθμεύσεως || ~**ing meter** n παρκόμετρο || ~**ing place** n θέση σταθμεύσεως.

parliament ['pɑːləmənt] n κοινοβούλιο || (in Britain) κοινοβούλιο, βουλή || ~**ary** a κοινοβουλευτικός.

parody ['pærədɪ] n παρωδία.

parole [pə'rəʊl] n: **on** ~ ελεύθερος (προσωρινά) επί λόγου.

parquet ['pɑːkeɪ] n παρκέτο.

parrot ['pærət] n παπαγάλος || ~**fashion** ad (learn) παπαγαλίστικα.

parry ['pærɪ] vt αποκρούω, αποφεύγω, ξεφεύγω.

parsimonious [pɑːsɪ'məʊnɪəs] a φειδωλός, σφιχτός, τσιγγούνης || ~**ly** ad με φειδωλότητα, μετρημένα.

parsley ['pɑːslɪ] n μαϊντανός.

parsnip ['pɑːsnɪp] n δαυκί.

parson ['pɑːsn] n εφημέριος, παπάς.

part [pɑːt] n μέρος nt, κομμάτι || (in play) ρόλος || (of machine) τμήμα nt,

μέρος nt, εξάρτημα nt, κομμάτι ♦ a
μερικός, ημι-, μισο- ♦ ad = **partly** ♦
vt χωρίζω, διαιρώ, κόβω || vi (people)
χωρίζομαι || (roads) παρεκκλίνω,
χωρίζομαι || **for my** ~ όσο για μένα
|| **for the most** ~ ως επί το
πλείστον || **to** ~ **with** vt
εγκαταλείπω, παραδίδω || ~**ial**
['pɑ:ʃəl] a μερικός || (favouring)
μεροληπτικός || (+ to) έχω
συμπάθεια σε, έχω προτίμηση σε ||
~**ially** ad μερικά, εν μέρει.

participate [pɑ:'tɪsɪpeɪt] vi (+ in)
συμμετέχω, παίρνω μέρος.

participation [pɑ:tɪsɪ'peɪʃən] n
συμμετοχή.

participle ['pɑ:tɪsɪpl] n μετοχή.

particular [pə'tɪkjʊlə*] a
συγκεκριμένος || (single) ιδιαίτερος ||
(hard to please) ιδιότροπος,
ακριβόλογος || n λεπτομέρεια,
ιδιομορφία || ~**s** npl (details)
χαρακτηριστικά ntpl, περιγραφή ||
~**ly** ad ιδιαίτερα, ειδικά,
συγκεκριμένα.

parting ['pɑ:tɪŋ] n (separation)
αναχώρηση, χωρισμός || (of hair)
χωρίστρα ♦ a διαχωριστικός.

partisan [pɑ:tɪ'zæn] n οπαδός,
παρτιζάνος ♦ a μερολπτικός.

partition [pɑ:'tɪʃən] n (wall) χώρισμα
nt, μεσότοιχος.

partly ['pɑ:tlɪ] ad εν μέρει.

partner ['pɑ:tnə*] n εταίρος,
συνέταιρος || (in dance etc)
καβαλιέρος, ντάμα ♦ vt
συνεταιρίζομαι, συμπράττω ||
~**ship** n συνεταιρισμός,
συνεργασία.

partridge ['pɑ:trɪdʒ] n πέρδικα.

part-time ['pɑ:t'taɪm] ad για λίγες
ώρες, μερικώς απασχολούμενος.

party ['pɑ:tɪ] n (POL) κόμμα nt||
(group) ομάδα, συντροφιά || (lawsuit)
διάδικος || μέτοχος || (agreement)
πρόσωπο || (celebration) πάρτυ nt inv

♦ a (dress) του πάρτυ, της
διασκεδάσεως|| (POL) του κόμματος,
κομματικός.

pass [pɑ:s] vt περνώ, διαβαίνω ||
(surpass) υπερβαίνω, ξεπερνώ,
προσπερνώ || (move one to another)
μεταβιβάζω, διαβιβάζω, δίνω ||
(spend time) περνώ || (be successful)
επιτυχχάνω, περνώ || (approve)
εγκρίνω ♦ vi μεταβαίνω, διαβαίνω,
διέρχομαι ♦ n (passage) στενό,
πέρασμα nt || (permission) άδεια ||
(success) περνώ || (SPORT) πάσα || **to**
~ **away** (to die) πεθαίνω ||
(disappear) εξαφανίζομαι || **to** ~ **by**
vi περνώ || παραμελώ || **to** ~ **for** vt
περνώ για || **to** ~ **out** vi (faint)
λιποθυμώ || ~**able** a διαβατός
(fairly good) υποφερτός,
καλούτσικος.

passage ['pæsɪdʒ] n (corridor)
διάδρομος || (part of book etc)
απόσπασμα nt, κομμάτι || (crossing)
διάβαση, πέρασμα f, διάβα nt|| ~**way**
n δίοδος f, πέρασμα nt || (sidestreet)
πάροδος f.

passenger ['pæsɪndʒə*] n
επιβάτης/ρια m/f.

passer-by ['pɑ:sə'baɪ] n διαβάτης,
περαστικός.

passing ['pɑ:sɪŋ] n (death) θάνατος
♦ a (car) διερχόμενος, διαβατικός ||
in ~ παρεμπιπτόντως.

passion ['pæʃən] n πάθος nt, θέρμη,
μανία || (love) έρωτας, πάθος nt||
~**ate** a σφοδρός, φλογερός, βίαιος
|| ~**ately** ad παράφορα, βίαια.

passive ['pæsɪv] a (GRAM)
παθητικός.

Passover ['pɑ:səʊvə*] n Λαμπρή,
Πάσχα nt.

passport ['pɑ:spɔ:t] n διαβατήριο.

password ['pɑ:swɜ:d] n σύνθημα
nt, παραούνθημα nt.

past [pɑ:st] ad, prep (beyond) πέρα,
πέρα από || (with numbers)

περασμένος || (with time) μετά, περασμένα ♦ a (years) περασμένος, τον παλιό καιρό || (president etc) τέως, πρώην.

paste [peist] n (for paper) κόλλα || (for cooking) πάστα, ζυμάρι.

pastel ['pæstəl] a (colour) παστέλ.

pasteurized ['pæstəraizd] a παστεριωμένος.

pastille ['pæstil] n παστίλια.

pastime ['pɑːstaim] n διασκέδαση, παιχνίδι.

pastor ['pɑːstə*] n πάστορας, παπάς.

pastry ['peistri] n ζύμη, πάστα || (pies, tarts etc) γλυκό.

pasture ['pɑːstʃə*] n (ground) βοσκότόπι.

pasty ['pæsti] n κρεατόπιτα ♦ ['peisti] a ζυμαρένιος, ωχρός.

pat [pæt] n ελαφρό κτύπημα nt, χάδι ♦ vt κτυπώ ελαφρά, χαϊδεύω.

patch [pætʃ] n μπάλωμα nt || (stain) λεκές m ♦ vt μπαλώνω || **~ work** n σύρραμα nt, συνονθύλευμα nt || **~y** a (irregular) ανομοιόμορφος.

patent ['peitənt] n προνόμιο, πατέντα ♦ vt πατεντάρω ♦ a προφανής, απλός, προνομιακός, πρωτότυπος || **~ leather** n λουστρίνι.

paternal [pə'tɜːnl] a πατρικός.

path [pɑːθ] n δρομάκος, μονοπάτι || (of sun etc) διαδρομή, πορεία γραμμη.

pathetic [pə'θεtik] a συγκινητικός, αξιολύπητος || **~ally** ad παθητικά, συγκινητικά.

pathologist [pə'θɒlədʒist] n παθολόγος.

pathology [pə'θɒlədʒi] n παθολογία.

pathos ['peiθɒs] n πάθος nt, συγκίνηση.

pathway ['pɑːθwei] n μονοπάτι, πέρασμα nt.

patience ['peiʃəns] n υπομονή.

patient ['peiʃənt] n νοσηλευόμενος/η m/f, άρρωστος/n m/f ♦ a υπομονητικός.

patio ['pætiəu] n πλακόστρωτη αυλή.

patriotic [pætri'ɒtik] a πατριωτικός.

patrol [pə'trəul] n περίπολος f, περιπολία || vti περιπολώ || **on** ~ σε περιπολία || ~ **car** n περιπολικό || ~ **man** n (US) αστυφύλακας.

patron ['peitrən] n πάτρωνας, προστάτης/ρια m/f, υποστηρικτής/ίκτρια m/f || (COMM) τακτικός πελάτης || **~age** ['pætrənidʒ] n προστασία, υποστήριξη || ~**ize** ['pætrənaiz] vt υποστηρίζω || (manner) μεταχειρίζομαι συγκαταβατικά || ~**izing** a (attitude) συγκαταβατικός || ~ **saint** n προστάτης/ρια m/f, άγιος/α m/f.

patter ['pætə*] n (sound) ελαφρά συνεχή κτυπήματα ntpl || (sales talk) φλυαρία, κορακίστικα ntpl ♦ vi κτυπώ ελαφρά και συνεχώς.

pattern ['pætən] n υπόδειγμα nt, πρότυπο, μοντέλο || (design) σχέδιο, τύπος, μοντέλο.

paunch [pɔːntʃ] n κοιλιά.

pauper ['pɔːpə*] n άπορος/n m/f, πτωχός/n m/f.

pause [pɔːz] n παύση, διακοπή, ανάπαυλα, διάλειμμα nt ♦ vi σταματώ, διστάζω, κοντοστέκομαι.

pave [peiv] vt επιστρώνω || **to** ~ **the way for** ανοίγω το δρόμο, προετοιμάζω το έδαφος.

pavement ['peivmənt] n (Brit) πεζοδρόμιο.

pavilion [pə'viliən] n (building) περίπτερο, υπόστεγο.

paving ['peiviŋ] n στρώσιμο.

paw [pɔː] n πέλμα nt ζώου, πόδι ♦ vt

χτυπώ με το πόδι || (person) πασπατεύω.

pawn [pɔːn] n ενέχυρο ♦ vt ενεχυριάζω, βάζω ενέχυρο || ~**broker** n ενεχυροδανειστής || ~**shop** n ενεχυροδανειστήριο.

pay [pei] (irreg v) n πληρωμή, μισθός ♦ vt πληρώνω, καταβάλλω, ξοδεύω || (be profitable to) συμφέρω, αποδίδω ♦ vi πληρώνομαι, είναι συμφέρον || **to ~ attention (to)** προσέχω || **to ~ for** vt πληρώνω, κερνώ || **to ~ up** vi εξοφλώ || ~**able** a πληρωτέος || ~ **day** n μέρα πληρωμής || ~**ee** n δικαιούχος || ~**ing** a επικερδής, αποδοτικός || ~**ment** n πληρωμή || (compensation) αποζημίωση, ανταπόδοση || ~**roll** n μισθοδοτική κατάσταση.

p.c. abbr of **per cent**.

pea [piː] n (seed) μπιζέλι.

peace [piːs] n ειρήνη, ησυχία || ~**ful** a γαλήνιος, ήσυχος || ~ **offering** n δώρο συμφιλιώσεως.

peach [piːtʃ] n ροδάκινο.

peacock ['piːkɔk] n παγόνι.

peak [piːk] n κορυφή || (of cap) γείσο.

peal [piːl] n κωδωνοκρουσία, κτύπημα nt.

peanut ['piːnʌt] n αράπικο φυστίκι.

pear [pɛə*] n απίδι, αχλάδι.

pearl [pɜːl] n μαργαριτάρι.

peasant ['pɛznt] n χωρικός/ή m/f, χωριάτης/ισσα m/f, αγρότης/ισσα m/f.

peat [piːt] n τύρφη, ποάνθρακας.

pebble ['pɛbl] n χαλίκι.

peck [pɛk] vti ραμφίζω, τσιμπώ ♦ n (with beak) ραμφισμός, τσίμπημα nt || (kiss) φιλάκι.

peckish ['pɛkiʃ] a (col): **to feel ~** νοιώθω το στομάχι άδειο.

peculiar [pi'kjuːlɪə*] a (interest) ειδικός, ιδιαίτερος || (+to) ιδιαίτερο χαρακτηριστικό, ιδιάζων || ~**ity** n

ιδιομορφία, ιδιορρυθμία || (oddness) παραξενιά.

pedal ['pɛdl] n ποδωστήριο, πεντάλ nt inv ♦ vti χρησιμοποιώ πεντάλ, ποδηλατώ.

pedantic [pi'dæntik] a σχολαστικός.

peddle ['pɛdl] vt κάνω το μικροπωλητή, πουλώ στους δρόμους.

pedestal ['pɛdistl] n βάθρο, βάση αγάλματος.

pedestrian [pi'dɛstrɪən] n πεζός, διαβάτης ♦ a με τα πόδια, πεζός || (humdrum) μονότονος, πεζός || ~ **crossing** n διάβαση πεζών.

pediatrics [piːdi'ætriks] n (US) = **paediatrics**.

pedigree ['pɛdigriː] n γενεαλογικό δέντρο, καταγωγή ♦ a (animal) καθαρόαιμος.

pee [piː] (col) n ούρα ntpl ♦ vi κατουρώ, κάνω πιπί.

peek [piːk] n ματιά ♦ vi κρυφοκοιτάζω, ξεπροβάλλω.

peel [piːl] n φλούδα ♦ vi (paint etc) ξεφλουδίζομαι, φεύγω.

peep [piːp] n (look) φευγαλέο βλέμμα nt, ματιά || (sound) τιτίβισμα nt, σκούξιμο, τσίριγμα nt ♦ vi (look) κρυφοκοιτάζω.

peer [pɪə*] vi κοιτάζω με προσοχή || (+ at) κοιτάζω προσεκτικά || (peer) κρυφοκοιτάζω ♦ n (nobleman) λόρδος, ευγενής || (equal) ισάξιος, ίσος, ταίρι || ~**age** n τάξη ευγενών || ~**less** a απαράμιλλος, ασύγκριτος.

peeve [piːv] vt (col) εκνευρίζω || ~**d** a εκνευρισμένος.

peevish ['piːvɪʃ] a ευερέθιστος, δύστροπος.

peg [pɛg] n γόμφος, πάσσαλος, κρεμάστρα || **to buy clothes off the ~** αγοράζω έτοιμα ρούχα.

pekinese [piːki'niːz] n πεκινουά nt inv.

pelican ['pelikən] n πελεκάνος.
pellet ['pelit] n (of paper, bread etc) σφαιρίδιο, σβώλος || (pill) δισκίο.
pelt [pelt] vt πετροβολώ, πετώ, κτυπώ ♦ vi (fall heavily) πέφτω με δύναμη ♦ n δορά, δέρμα nt, προβειά.
pelvis ['pelvis] n λεκάνη.
pen [pen] n (for writing) γραφίδα, πένα, στυλό || (for sheep) μάντρα.
penal ['piːnl] a ποινικός || ~ize vt επιβάλλω ποινή σε, τιμωρώ || ~ty ['penəlti] n ποινή, τιμωρία || ~ty kick n πέναλτυ nt inv.
penance ['penəns] n αυτοτιμωρία, μετάνοια.
pence [pens] npl πένες fpl.
pencil ['pensl] n μολύβι || (of light) δέσμη || ~ sharpener n ξύστρα.
pendant ['pendənt] n κρεμαστό κόσμημα nt.
pending ['pendiŋ] prep κατά τη διάρκεια του, μέχρι ♦ a εκκρεμής.
pendulum ['pendjuləm] n εκκρεμές nt.
penetrate ['penitreit] vt εισχωρώ σε, διεισδύω || (pierce) διαπερνώ, τρυπώ|| **penetrating** a διαπεραστικός, οξύς.
penetration [peni'treiʃən] n (lit) διείσδυση.
penfriend ['penfrend] n φίλος από αλληλογραφία.
penguin ['peŋgwin] n πιγκουίνος.
penicillin [peni'silin] n πενικιλίνη.
peninsula [pi'ninsjulə] n χερσόνησος f.
penis ['piːnis] n πέος nt.
penitence ['penitəns] n μετάνοια.
penitent ['penitənt] a μετανοημένος.
penitentiary [peni'tenʃəri] n (US) σωφρονιστήριο.
penknife ['pennaif] n σουγιάς.
pen name n ['penneim] n ψευδώνυμο (φιλολογικό).

pennant ['penənt] n τριγωνικό σημαία.
penniless ['penilis] a απένταρος.
penny ['peni] n πένα.
pension ['penʃən] n (from job) σύνταξη || ~er n συνταξιούχος.
pensive ['pensiv] a σκεπτικός, συλλογισμένος.
pentagon ['pentəgən] n πεντάγωνο.
Pentecost ['pentikɒst] n Πεντηκοστή.
penthouse ['penthaus] n ρετιρέ nt inv, υπόστεγο.
pent-up ['pentʌp] a (feelings) συγκρατημένη συγκίνηση.
penultimate [pi'nʌltimit] a προτελευταίος.
people ['piːpl] n άνθρωποι mpl, κόσμος || (nation) λαός, έθνος nt ♦ vt κατοικώ, οικίζω.
pep [pep] n (col) κέφι, ζωή || to ~ up vt ενθαρρύνω, δίνω κέφι σε.
pepper ['pepə*] n πιπέρι || (green) πιπεριά ♦ vt (pelt) κοπανίζω, βομβαρδίζω || ~mint n (plant) δυόσμος, μέντα || (sweet) μέντα (καραμέλα).
per [pɜː*] prep κατά, ανά, διά || ~ cent τοις εκατό || ~ annum το χρόνο.
perceive [pə'siːv] vt διακρίνω, βλέπω || (understand) αντιλαμβάνομαι, καταλαβαίνω.
percentage [pə'sentidʒ] n ποσοστό, τοις εκατό.
perception [pə'sepʃən] n αντίληψη, αίσθηση.
perceptive [pə'septiv] a αντιληπτικός.
perch [pɜːtʃ] n κούρνια, ξύλο || (fish) πέρκα ♦ vi κουρνιάζω, τοποθετώ ψηλά.
percolator ['pɜːkəleitə*] n καφετιέρα με φίλτρο.
percussion [pə'kʌʃən] n (MUS) κρουστά όργανα ntpl.

peremptory [pə'remptəri] a τελικός, αμετάκλητος, αποφασιστικός.

perennial [pə'reniəl] a αιώνιος, μόνιμος, πολυετής ♦ n πολυετές φυτό.

perfect [pə'fikt] a τέλειος, πλήρης, τελειωμένος || (GRAM) τετελεσμένος ♦ n (GRAM) παρακείμενος ♦ [pə'fekt] vt τελειοποιώ, συμπληρώνω || ~ion [pə'fekʃən] n τελειότητα, εντέλεια, τελειοποίηση || ~ly ad εντελώς, τέλεια.

perforate [pə'fəreit] vt διατρυπώ, διαπερνώ || ~d a διάτρητος.

perforation [pəfə'reiʃən] n διάτρηση, τρύπα.

perform [pə'fɔːm] vt εκτελώ, εκπληρώ, επιτελώ || (THEAT) παριστάνω, παίζω ♦ vi (THEAT) παίζω || ~ance n εκτέλεση, κατόρθωμα nt || (THEAT) παράσταση || ~er n εκτελεστής, ηθοποιός m/f || ~ing a (animal) γυμνασμένο (ζώο).

perfume [pə'fjuːm] n οσμή, μυρωδιά || (scent) άρωμα nt, μυρωδικό.

perhaps [pə'hæps] ad ίσως.

peril [peril] n κίνδυνος || ~ous a επικίνδυνος || ~ously ad επικίνδυνα.

perimeter [pə'rimitə*] n περίμετρος f.

period [piəriəd] n εποχή, περίοδος f || (stop) τελεία || (MED) στάδιο, φάση, περίοδος f ♦ a (costume) της εποχής || ~ic a περιοδικός || ~ical a περιοδικός ♦ n περιοδικό || ~ically ad κατά περιόδους.

peripheral [pə'rifərəl] a περιφερειακός, περιμετρικός ♦ n (COMPUT) περιφερειακή μονάδα.

periphery [pə'rifəri] n περιφέρεια, περίμετρος f.

periscope [periskəup] n περισκόπιο.

perish [periʃ] vi χάνομαι, αφανίζομαι, πεθαίνω || ~able a φθαρτός || ~ing a (col: cold) τρομερό κρύο.

perjury [pə'dʒəri] n επιορκία, ψευδομαρτυρία.

perk [pɜːk] to ~ up vi ξανακάνω κέφι, ξαναζωντανεύω || ~y a (cheerful) ζωηρός, εύθυμος.

perm [pɜːm] n περμανάντ f inv.

permanent ['pɜːmənənt] a μόνιμος, διαρκής || ~ly ad μόνιμα.

permissible [pə'misəbl] a επιτρεπόμενος, ανεκτός.

permission [pə'miʃən] n άδεια, έγκριση.

permissive [pə'misiv] a επιτρεπτικός.

permit ['pɜːmit] n άδεια ♦ [pə'mit] vt επιτρέπω.

permutation [pɜːmjuː'teiʃən] n (αντι)μετάθεση, αντιμετάταξη.

pernicious [pɜː'niʃəs] a ολέθριος, καταστρεπτικός.

perpendicular [pɜːpən'dikjulə*] a κάθετος, κατακόρυφος.

perpetrate ['pɜːpitreit] vt διαπράττω.

perpetual [pə'petjuəl] a αδιάκοπος, συνεχής, παντοτινός.

perpetuate [pə'petjueit] vt διαιωνίζω, αποθανατίζω.

perplex [pə'pleks] vt περιπλέκω, φέρνω σε αμηχανία, μπερδεύω || ~ed a σε αμηχανία || ~ing a μπερδεμένος || ~ity n αμηχανία, παραζάλη, δίλημμα nt.

persecute ['pɜːsikjuːt] vt (oppress) καταδιώκω, διώκω.

persecution [pɜːsi'kjuːʃən] n διωγμός, καταδίωξη.

perseverance [pɜːsi'viərəns] n καρτερία, εμμονή, επιμονή.

persevere [pɜːsi'viə*] vi εμμένω, επιμένω.

Persia ['pɜːʃə] n Περσία || ~n a

περσικός ♦ n (person) Πέρσης/ίδα m/f|| (LING) Περσικά ntpl|| ~n Gulf n Περσικός Κόλπος.

persist [pə'sɪst] vi επιμένω, μένω, σταθερός|| (keep saying) επιμένω, εμμένω|| ~ence n επιμονή, εμμονή || ~ent a επιμονος, διαρκής.

person ['pɜːsn] n πρόσωπο, άνθρωπος, άτομο|| ~able n ευπαρουσίαστος, ωραίος|| ~al a προσωπικός, ατομικός|| (of body) σωματικός|| ~ality n προσωπικότητα || ~ally ad προσωπικά|| ~ify vt προσωποποιώ.

personnel [pɜːsə'nel] n προσωπικό || ~ manager n διευθυντής προσωπικού.

perspective [pə'spektɪv] n προοπτική|| (view) άποψη, θέα.

perspex ['pɜːspeks] n (R) άθραυστο γυαλί, περσπέξ nt inv.

perspiration [pɜːspə'reɪʃən] n εφίδρωση, ιδρώτας.

perspire [pəs'paɪə*] vi ιδρώνω.

persuade [pə'sweɪd] vt πείθω, καταπείθω.

persuasion [pə'sweɪʒən] n πειθώ f, πειστικότητα|| (belief) πεποίθηση, θρήσκευμα nt.

persuasive [pə'sweɪsɪv] a πειστικός.

pert [pɜːt] a αναιδής, αυθάδης, τσαχπίνης.

pertaining [pɜː'teɪnɪŋ]: ~ to prep σχετικά με.

pertinent ['pɜːtɪnənt] a σχετικός, κατάλληλος, σωστός.

perturb [pə'tɜːb] vt διαταράσσω, προκαλώ αντησυχία.

perusal [pə'ruːzəl] n ανάγνωση, διάβασμα nt.

pervade [pɜː'veɪd] vt εμποτίζω, διαπερνώ, επικρατώ.

perverse [pɜː'vɜːs] a διεστραμμένος, κακότροπος.

perversion [pə'vɜːʃən] n διαστροφή, ανωμαλία.

pervert ['pɜːvɜːt] n διεστραμμένος, ανώμαλος τύπος, εκφυλισμένος ♦ [pə'vɜːt] vt διαστρέφω, στρεβλώνω, διαφθείρω.

pessimism ['pesimizəm] n απαισιοδοξία.

pessimist ['pesimist] n απαισιόδοξος/n nt|| ~ic a απαισιόδοξος.

pest [pest] n επιβλαβές φυτό (ή έντομο)|| (fig: person, thing) ενοχλητικός/ή m/f, πληγή.

pester ['pestə*] vt ενοχλώ, πειράζω.

pestle ['pesl] n κόπανος, γουδοχέρι.

pet [pet] n χαϊδεμένος n m/f|| (animal) ζώο του σπιτιού ♦ vt χαϊδεύω.

petal ['petl] n πέταλο.

peter ['piːtə*]: to ~ out vi εξαφανίζομαι, σβήνω.

petition [pə'tɪʃən] n αίτηση, αναφορά.

petrified ['petrifaɪd] a απολιθωμένος.

petrol ['petrəl] n (Brit) βενζίνη|| ~ engine n βενζινομηχανή.

petroleum [pɪ'trəʊliəm] n πετρέλαιο.

petrol: ~ pump n (in car) αντλία βενζίνης|| ~ station n πρατήριο βενζίνης|| ~ tank n δεξαμενή|| (car) ρεζερβουάρ nt inv βενζίνης.

petticoat ['petikəut] n μεσοφόρι.

petty ['peti] a μικρός, ασήμαντος, κατώτερος|| (mean) μικρόνους, στενοκέφαλος|| ~ cash n μικροέξοδα ntpl, πρόχειρο ταμείο || ~ officer n υπαξιωματικός, υποκελευστής.

petulant ['petjulənt] a οξύθυμος, ευερέθιστος.

pew [pjuː] n στασίδι.

pewter ['pjuːtə*] n κράμα nt κασσιτέρου και μολύβδου.

phantom ['fæntəm] *n* φάντασμα *nt*.

Pharaoh ['fɛərəʊ] *n* Φαραώ *m*.

pharmacist ['fɑ:məsɪst] *n* φαρμακοποιός *m/f.*

pharmacy ['fɑ:məsɪ] *n* (*shop*) φαρμακείο || (*science*) φαρμακευτική.

phase [feɪz] *n* φάση.

Ph.D. (*abbr = Doctor of Philosophy*) = διδακτορικό δίπλωμα *nt.*

pheasant ['fɛznt] *n* φασιανός.

phenomenon [fɪ'nɒmɪnən] *n* φαινόμενο.

philanthropist [fɪ'lænθrəpɪst] *n* φιλάνθρωπος.

philately [fɪ'lætəlɪ] *n* φιλοτελισμός.

philosopher [fɪ'lɒsəfə*] *n* φιλόσοφος.

philosophical [fɪlə'sɒfɪkəl] *a* φιλοσοφικός.

philosophy [fɪ'lɒsəfɪ] *n* φιλοσοφία.

phlegm [flɛm] *n* φλέγμα *nt.*

phobia ['fəʊbɪə] *n* φοβία, φοβοπάθεια.

phone [fəʊn] (*abbr of* **telephone**) *n* τηλέφωνο ♦ *vt* τηλεφωνώ.

phonetics [fəʊ'nɛtɪks] *n* φωνολογία, φωνητική.

phon(e)y ['fəʊnɪ] (*col*) *a* ψεύτικος ♦ *n* απατεώνας.

phosphate ['fɒsfeɪt] *n* φωσφορικό αλάτι.

phosphorus ['fɒsfərəs] *n* φωσφόρος.

photo ['fəʊtəʊ] *n* φωτογραφία.

photocopier ['fəʊtəʊ'kɒpɪə*] *n* φωτοτυπική μηχανή.

photocopy ['fəʊtəʊkɒpɪ] *n* φωτοαντίτυπο, φωτοτυπία ♦ *vt* κάνω φωτοτυπία.

photogenic [fəʊtəʊ'dʒɛnɪk] *a* φωτογενής.

photograph ['fəʊtəʊɡræf] *n* φωτογραφία ♦ *vt* φωτογραφίζω, βγάζω φωτογραφίες || ~**er** [fə'tɒɡrəfə*] *n* φωτογράφος || ~**ic** *a*

φωτογραφικός || ~**y** *n* φωτογραφική τέχνη, φωτογράφιση.

photostat ['fəʊtəʊstæt] *n* φωτοστατικό αντίτυπο.

phrase [freɪz] *n* φράση ♦ *vt* διατυπώνω || ~ **book** *n* συλλογή εκφράσεων.

physical ['fɪzɪkəl] *a* φυσικός || (*of the body*) σωματικός || ~**ly** *ad* φυσικά, σωματικά.

physician [fɪ'zɪʃən] *n* ιατρός *m/f.*

physicist ['fɪzɪsɪst] *n* φυσικός *m/f.*

physics ['fɪzɪks] *n* φυσική.

physiology [fɪzɪ'ɒlədʒɪ] *n* φυσιολογία.

physiotherapy [fɪzɪə'θɛrəpɪ] *n* φυσιοθεραπεία.

physique [fɪ'zi:k] *n* σωματική διάπλαση.

pianist ['pɪənɪst] *n* πιανίστας/ρια *m/f.*

piano ['pjɑ:nəʊ] *n* πιάνο.

pick [pɪk] *n* (*a tool*) αξίνα, κασμάς, σκαπάνη || (*choice*) εκλογή || (*best*) ότι εκλεκτό, αφρόκρεμα ♦ *vti* μαζεύω, κόβω, συλλέγω || (*choose*) εκλέγω, διαλέγω || **I** ~ **a pocket** βουτώ από την τσέπη, κλέβω το πορτοφόλι || **to** ~ **out** *vt* διαλέγω || **to** ~ **up** *vi* (*improve*) βελτιώνομαι ♦ *vt* (*arrest*) συλλαμβάνω, πιάνω || (*from ground*) σηκώνω, μαζεύω || (*in car etc*) παίρνω || ~**axe** *n* σκαπάνη, κασμάς.

picket ['pɪkɪt] *n* (*stake*) πάσσαλος, παλούκι || (*strikers*) σκοπός απεργών ♦ *vt* βάζω σκοπούς.

pickle ['pɪkl] *n* (*also:* ~**s**: *as condiment*) τουρσί, άλμη ♦ *vt* διατηρώ σε άλμη, παστώνω.

pickpocket ['pɪkpɒkɪt] *n* πορτοφολάς.

pickup ['pɪkʌp] *n* (*on record player*) φωνολήπτης, πικάπ *nt inv* || (*small truck*) μικρό φορτηγό || (*casual acquaintance*) ψάρεμα *nt*, τσίμπημα *nt* πελάτου.

picnic ['pɪknɪk] n εκδρομή, πικνίκ nt inv ♦ vi τρώγω στην εξοχή || ~**ker** n εκδρομέας.

pictorial [pɪk'tɔːrɪəl] a εικονογραφικός || (graphic) γραφικός || (illustrated) εικονογραφημένος.

picture ['pɪktʃə*] n εικόνα, ζωγραφιά, προσωποποίηση ♦ vt ζωγραφίζω, απεικονίζω, φαντάζομαι || the ~s npl κινηματογράφος || ~ **book** n βιβλίο με εικόνες.

picturesque [pɪktʃə'rɛsk] a γραφικός.

pie [paɪ] n πίτα.

piece [piːs] n κομμάτι || in ~s (broken) (σε) κομματάκια || (taken apart) σε κομμάτια || ~ **meal** ad λίγο-λίγο, κομματιαστά || ~**work** n εργασία με το κομμάτι.

pier [pɪə*] n (landing place) προκυμαία, αποβάθρα.

pierce [pɪəs] vt τρυπώ, διεισδύω, εισχωρώ.

piercing ['pɪəsɪŋ] a (cry) διαπεραστικός.

piety ['paɪətɪ] n ευσέβεια, θρησκολιψία.

pig [pɪg] n γουρούνι, παλιάνθρωπος, γουρούνι.

pigeon ['pɪdʒən] n περιστέρι || ~**hole** n (compartment) θυρίδα, γραμματοθήκη ♦ vt βάζω στο αρχείο.

piggy bank ['pɪgɪbæŋk] n κουμπαράς.

pigheaded ['pɪg'hɛdɪd] a πεισματάρης, ξεροκέφαλος.

piglet ['pɪglɪt] n γουρουνόπουλο.

pigment ['pɪgmənt] n χρώμα nt, βαφή.

pigmy ['pɪgmɪ] n = **pygmy**.

pigskin ['pɪgskɪn] n γουρουνόδερμα nt.

pigsty ['pɪgstaɪ] n χοιροστάσιο.

pigtail ['pɪgteɪl] n κοτσίδα.

pilchard ['pɪltʃəd] n μεγάλη σαρδέλα.

pile [paɪl] n (of books) σωρός, στοίβα || (in ground) πάσσαλος, παλούκι, κολώνα || (on carpet) τρίχα, χνούδι ♦ vti (also: ~ **up**) συσσωρεύω, στοιβάζω.

piles [paɪlz] npl αιμορροΐδες fpl, ζοχάδες fpl.

pilfer ['pɪlfə*] vt κλέβω, βουτώ, σουφρώνω.

pilgrim ['pɪlgrɪm] n προσκυνητής/ήτρια m/f|| ~**age** n προσκύνημα nt.

pill [pɪl] n χάπι || the P~ n χάπι αντισυλληπτικό.

pillage ['pɪlɪdʒ] vt λεηλατώ.

pillar ['pɪlə*] n κίονας, κολώνα, στύλος || (fig) στύλος || ~ **box** n (Brit) ταχυδρομικό κουτί.

pillion ['pɪljən] n πισινό κάθισμα nt.

pillory ['pɪlərɪ] vt διαπομπεύω, στηλιτεύω.

pillow ['pɪləʊ] n προσκέφαλο, μαξιλάρι || ~**case** n μαξιλαροθήκη.

pilot ['paɪlət] n πλοηγός, πιλότος || (AVIAT) χειριστής, πιλότος ♦ vt (AVIAT) οδηγώ, πιλοτάρω || ~ **light** n καυστήρας (θερμάστρας φωταερίου).

pimp [pɪmp] n μαστροπός, ρουφιάνος.

pimple ['pɪmpl] n εξάνθημα nt, σπυρί.

pin [pɪn] n καρφίτσα || (peg) περόνη ♦ vt καρφιτσώνω || (hold fast) καρφώνω, πλακώνομαι || (on) ~s **and needles** στα κάρβουνα || to ~ **down** vt (fig: person) καθηλώνω.

pinafore ['pɪnəfɔː*] n ποδιά.

pincers ['pɪnsəz] npl τανάλια.

pinch [pɪntʃ] n μικρή ποσότητα, πρέζα || (nip) τσίμπημα nt, τσιμπιά ♦ vt (with fingers) τσιμπώ || (col: steal) αποσπώ, σουφρώνω, βουτώ ♦ vi

(shoe) στενεύω, σφίγγω || **at a ~** στην ανάγκη, σε ώρα ανάγκης.

pincushion ['pinkuʃən] *n* μαξιλαράκι για καρφίτσες.

pine [pain] *n (also:* **~ tree)** πεύκο ♦ *vi:* **to ~ for** ποθώ, μαραζώνω.

pineapple ['painæpl] *n* ανανάς.

ping [piŋ] *n (noise)* σφύριγμα *nt*, κουδούνισμα *nt* || **~-pong** *n* πινγκ-πονγκ *nt inv.*

pink [piŋk] *n (plant)* γαρουφαλιά || *(pale red)* ροζ *nt*, ρόδινος.

pin money ['pinmʌni] *n* χαρτζιλίκι.

pinnacle ['pinəkl] *n (highest point)* κορυφή, κολοφώνας.

pinpoint ['pinpɔint] *vi* υποδεικνύω ακριβώς.

pint [paint] *n* πίντα (.567 λ.).

pioneer [paiə'niə*] *n* πρωτοπόρος/α *m/f.*

pious ['paiəs] *a* ευσεβής, θρήσκος.

pip [pip] *n (seed)* κουκούτσι || *(on uniform)* άστρο *(επωμίδας)*.

pipe [paip] *n* σωλήνας, οχετός || *(smoking)* πίπα, τσιμπούκι || *(instrument)* αυλός || *(of bird)* κελάδημα *nt* || **to ~ down** *vi (be quiet)* το βουλώνω || **~ dream** *n* μάταιη ελπίδα || **~ line** *n* αγωγός || **~ r** *n* αυλητής, παίκτης γκάιντας || **~ tobacco** *n* καπνός πίπας.

piping ['paipiŋ] *ad:* **~ hot** καυτερός, ζεματιστός, αχνιστός.

piquant ['pi:kənt] *a* πικάντικος.

pique [pi:k] *n* μνησικακία, φούρκα.

piracy ['paiərəsi] *n* πειρατεία.

pirate ['paiərit] *n* πειρατής || **~ radio** *n* πειρατικός σταθμός.

pirouette [piru'et] *n* πιρουέτα ♦ *vi* κάνω πιρουέτες, στριφογυρίζω.

pissed [pist] *a (col)* μεθυσμένος.

pistol ['pistl] *n* πιστόλι.

piston ['pistən] *n* έμβολο, πιστόνι.

pit [pit] *n* λάκκος, ανθρακωρυχείο ♦ *vt* σημαδεύω, κόβω || *(put to test)* έχω κάποιον σαν αντίπαλο.

pitch [pitʃ] *n (way of throwing)* βολή, ριξιά || *(ground)* γήπεδο || *(degree)* βαθμός, κλίση || *(of note)* ύψος τόνου, διαπασών *nt* || *(tar)* πίσσα, κατράμι ♦ *vt (throw)* πετώ || *(tent)* στήνω *(σκηνή)* ♦ *vi (fall headlong)* πέφτω || *(of ship)* σκαμπανεβάζω || **~-black** *a* μαύρος σαν κατράμι || **~ed battle** *n* μάχη εκ του συστάδην.

pitcher ['pitʃə*] *n* στάμνα, κανάτα.

pitchfork ['pitʃfɔːk] *n* δίκρανο, τσουγκράνα, φούρκα ♦ *vt* φορτώνω με δικράνι.

pitfall ['pitfɔːl] *n (trap)* παγίδα.

pith [piθ] *n (essence)* ουσία, σθένος *nt.*

pithy ['piθi] *a (concise)* με ουσία, ουσιαστικός.

pitiable ['pitiəbl] *a* αξιολύπητος, αξιοθρήνητος, οικτρός.

pitiful ['pitiful] *a* αξιολύπητος || *(mean)* ελεεινός || **~ly** *ad* θλιβερά, ελεεινά.

pitiless ['pitilis] *a* ανελέητος, άσπλαχνος, άκαρδος || **~ly** *ad* σκληρά, ανελέητα.

pittance ['pitəns] *n* εξευτελιστικός μισθός.

pity ['piti] *n* έλεος, οίκτος, λύπηση || *(of regret)* κρίμα *nt* || **what a ~** τι κρίμα!

pivot ['pivət] *n* άξονας, κέντρο περιστροφής, κεντρικό σημείο ♦ *vi (turn)* περιστρέφομαι.

pixie ['piksi] *n* ξωτικό, νεράιδα.

placard ['plækɑːd] *n* τοιχοκόλληση, ταμπέλα, πινακίδα.

placate [plə'keit] *vt* κατευνάζω.

place [pleis] *n* τόπος, μέρος *nt*, τοποθεσία || *(position)* σημείο, μέρος *nt* || *(location)* τοποθεσία || *(town etc)* τόπος || *(employment, rank)* θέση, υπηρεσία, βαθμός || *(seat)* θέση, κάθισμα *nt* ♦ *vt (object)* τοποθετώ, βάζω || *(order)* τοποθετώ, πουλώ || *(in*

race| έρχομαι πλασέ|| **in** ~ στη σωστή θέση|| **out of** ~ άτοπος|| **in the first** ~ εν πρώτοις.

placid ['plæsɪd] *a* γαλήνιος, ήρεμος, ατάραχος.

plagiarism ['pleɪdʒərɪzəm] *n* λογοκλοπή, λογοκλοπία.

plague [pleɪg] *n* πληγή, μάστιγα, λοιμός, πανούκλα.

plaice [pleɪs] *n* γλώσσα (ψάρι).

plaid [plæd] *n* καρό ύφασμα *nt*.

plain [pleɪn] *a* (clear) σαφής, φανερός|| (simple) απλός, λιτός|| (not beautiful) κοινός, όχι ωραίος ♦ *ad* καθαρά, ευδιακρίτως, ειλικρινά|| *n* πεδιάδα, κάμπος|| **in** ~ **clothes** (police) με πολιτικά|| ~**ly** *ad* προφανώς, ολοφάνερα|| (simply) απλά.

plaintiff ['pleɪntɪf] *n* ενάγων/ουσα *m/f*, μηνυτής/ύτρια *m/f*.

plait [plæt] *n* πλόκαμος, πλεξούδα ♦ *vt* πλέκω.

plan [plæn] *n* σχέδιο, προσχέδιο, πρόγραμμα *nt*|| (of house etc) σχέδιο, πλάνο, σχεδιάγραμμα *nt*|| (POL, ECON) σχέδιο ♦ *a* (holiday etc) σχεδιάζω ♦ *vi* (make a plan) καταστρώνω, σχεδιαγραφώ.

plane [pleɪn] *n* (tree) πλάτανος|| (tool) ροκάνι, ροκάνι, πλάνια|| (level) επίπεδο, επίπεδος (επιφάνειας)|| (AVIAT) αεροπλάνο ♦ *a* επίπεδος ♦ *vt* (with tool) ροκανίζω, πλανίζω.

planet ['plænɪt] *n* πλανήτης.

plank [plæŋk] *n* σανίδα, μαδέρι.

planner ['plænə*] *n* προγραμματιστής *m/f*, σχεδιαστής/άστρια *m/f*.

planning ['plænɪŋ] *n* χάραξη (σχεδίου), κατάστρωση, προγραμματισμός.

plant [plɑːnt] *n* φυτό|| (factory) εγκατάσταση, εργοστάσιο, μηχανήματα *ntpl* || *n* φυτεύω|| (set firmly) καρφώνω, εγκαθιστώ.

plantation [plæn'teɪʃən] *n* φυτεία.

plaque [plæk] *n* (on wall) πλάκα (αναμνηστική)|| (on teeth) πέτρα.

plasma ['plæzmə] *n* πλάσμα *nt*, πρωτόπλασμα *nt*.

plaster ['plɑːstə*] *n* σουβάς, κονίαμα *nt*, γύψος|| (for wounds) έμπλαστρο, τσιρότο ♦ *vt* σοβατίζω|| φορτώνω, σκεπάζω|| **in** ~ (leg etc) σε γύψο|| ~**ed** *a* (col) μεθυσμένος|| ~**er** *n* σουβατζής.

plastic ['plæstɪk] *n* πλαστική ύλη ♦ *a* πλαστικός|| (easily shaped) εύπλαστος|| **P**~**ine** ® (R) πλαστιλίνη|| ~ **surgery** *n* πλαστική εγχείρηση.

plate [pleɪt] *n* πιάτο, δίσκος|| (table utensils) χρυσά ή αργυρά επιτραπέζια σκεύη *ntpl*, ασημικά *ntpl* || (flat sheet) πλάκα, λάμα, φύλλο.

plateau ['plætəu] *n* υψίπεδο, οροπέδιο.

plateful ['pleɪtful] *n* πιάτο γεμάτο.

plate glass ['pleɪt'glɑːs] *n* κρύσταλλο, υαλοπίνακας.

platform ['plætfɔːm] *n* (at meeting) εξέδρα, βήμα *nt*|| (RAIL) αποβάθρα, εξέδρα.

platinum ['plætɪnəm] *n* λευκόχρυσος, πλατίνη.

platitude ['plætɪtjuːd] *n* κοινοτοπία.

platoon [plə'tuːn] *n* διμοιρία, ουλαμός.

platter ['plætə*] *n* πιατέλα.

plausible ['plɔːzəbl] *a* εύλογος, πιθανός.

play [pleɪ] *n* παιχνίδι, διασκέδαση|| (stage) έργο|| (of shadows etc) παίξιμο || (MECH) ανοχή, παίξιμο ♦ *vt* παίζω, διασκεδάζω|| (trick) παιχνιδιάζω, κάνω αστείο|| (part) παίζω, υποδύομαι ρόλο, ερμηνεύω|| (instrument) παίζω ♦ *vi* (amuse o.s.) διασκεδάζω, παίζω, παιχνιδίζω|| (of light etc) σπιθοβολώ, παίζω, χοροπηδώ|| ~**boy** *n* γλεντζές *m*, έκλυτος νέος ||

~**ed-out** a εξαντλημένος, αποκαμωμένος || ~**er** n παίκτης/ρια m/f, ηθοποιός m/f|| ~**ful** a παιχνιδιάρικος, παιχνιδιάρης ||
~**ground** n προαύλιο, τόπος διασκεδάσεως || ~**ing card** n τραπουλόχαρτο || ~**ing field** n γήπεδο || ~**mate** n συμπαίκτης, σύντροφος στο παιχνίδι || ~**thing** n παιχνίδι, παιχνιδάκι || ~**wright** n θεατρικός συγγραφέας m/f.

plea [pliː] n (LAW) έκκληση, αγωγή.

plead [pliːd] vt επικαλούμαι, προβάλλω ♦ vi παρακαλώ, ικετεύω || (LAW) υποστηρίζω, υπερασπίζω, απολογούμαι.

pleasant ['pleznt] a ευχάριστος || ~**ry** n ευθυμία, κέφι, χιούμορ.

please [pliːz] vt αρέσω, ευχαριστώ || ~! παρακαλώ! || **my bill,** ~ το λογαριασμό, παρακαλώ || ~ **yourself!** κάνε το κέφι σου! || ~**d** a (happy, glad) ευχαριστημένος, ικανοποιημένος.

pleasing ['pliːziŋ] a ευχάριστος.

pleasurable ['pleʒərəbl] a ευχάριστος, τερπνός.

pleasure ['pleʒə*] n τέρψη, ευχαρίστηση, χαρά || (amusement) απολαύσεις fpl, ηδονές fpl, χαρές || **it's a** ~! χαίρομαι!, παρακαλώ!

pleat [pliːt] n πτυχή, πιέτα.

plebs [plebz] npl λαουτζίκος.

plectrum ['plektrəm] n πλήκτρο.

pledge [pledʒ] n ενέχυρο, δεσμευτική υπόσχεση, τεκμήριο ♦ vi δίνω το λόγο μου, υπόσχομαι.

plentiful ['plentiful] a άφθονος πλουσιοπάροχος.

plenty ['plenti] n αφθονία, πλήθος nt|| (enough) αρκετό ♦ ad (col) πάρα πολύ || ~ **of** άφθονα, με το τσουβάλι.

plethora ['pleθərə] n πληθώρα.

pleurisy ['pluərisi] n πλευρίτιδα.

pliable ['plaiəbl] a εύκαμπτος, ευλύγιστος.

pliers ['plaiəz] npl τανάλια, λαβίδα.

plight [plait] n κατάσταση, θέση.

plinth [plinθ] n πλίνθος, πλινθίο.

plod [plɒd] vi περπατώ βαρειά, σέρνομαι || ~**der** n φιλόπονος, ευσυνείδητος.

plot [plɒt] n (conspiracy) συνωμοσία || (of story) πλοκή, υπόθεση || (land) οικόπεδο, χωράφι ♦ vt χαράσσω, σχεδιάζω ♦ vt (plan secretly) συνωμοτώ, μηχανορραφώ.

plough, plow (US) [plau] n άροτρο, αλέτρι ♦ vt (earth) αροτριώ, αλετρίζω || (col: exam candidate) απορρίπτω (μαθητή) || **to** ~ **back** vt (COMM) επενδύω (τα κέρδη) στην ίδια επιχείρηση || **to** ~ **through** vt (book) διαβάζω με κόπο || ~**ing** n άροση, αλέτρισμα nt.

pluck [plʌk] vt (fruit) κόβω || (feathers) μαδώ ♦ n (col) κουράγιο, θάρρος nt|| **to** ~ **up courage** παίρνω κουράγιο|| ~**y** a θαρραλέος, παλικάρι.

plug [plʌg] n (for hole) πώμα nt, βούλωμα nt, τάπα || (wall socket) πρίζα || (col: publicity) διαφήμιση, προβολή || (AUT) μπουζί ♦ vt (hole) βουλώνω, ταπώνω || (col: advertise) διαφημίζω, προβάλλω.

plum [plʌm] n (fruit) δαμάσκηνο ♦ a (choice) εκλεκτό πράμα, καλύτερη θέση.

plumage ['pluːmidʒ] n φτέρωμα nt, φτερά ntpl.

plumb [plʌm] n κατακόρυφος ♦ a πλήρης, αληθής ♦ ad (exactly) ακριβώς || (wholly) τελείως ♦ vt βυθομετρώ, σταθμίζω.

plumber ['plʌmə*] n υδραυλικός.

plumbing ['plʌmiŋ] n (craft) υδραυλική τέχνη || (piping) σωληνώσεις fpl, υδραυλικά ntpl.

plume [pluːm] n λοφίο, φτερό.

plump [plʌmp] a στρογγυλός, παχουλός, αφράτος ♦ vi σωριάζομαι, πέφτω βαριά ♦ vt πετώ απότομα || **to ~ for** vt (col: choose) υποστηρίζω, ψηφίζω υπέρ.

plunder ['plʌndə*] n λεία, λεηλασία, πλιάτσικο ♦ vt λεηλατώ, λαφυραγωγώ.

plunge [plʌndʒ] n κατάδυση, βουτιά ♦ vt (κατα)βυθίζω, βουτώ, χώνω ♦ vi καταδύομαι, βουτώ.

plunging ['plʌndʒiŋ] a (neckline) μεγάλο (ντεκολτέ).

pluperfect ['pluː'pɜːfikt] n υπερσυντέλικος.

plural ['pluərəl] a πληθυντικός, πολλαπλός ♦ n πληθυντικός.

plus [plʌs] prep πλέον, συν, μαζί με ♦ a θετικός.

plush [plʌʃ] a (col: luxurious) πολυτελής, πλούσιος.

ply [plai] n (layer) φύλλο, φλοίωμα nt || **three-~ wool** τρίκλωνο μαλλί ♦ vt (with questions) ταλαιπωρώ (με ερωτήσεις) || **to ~ a trade** ασκώ επάγγελμα ♦ vi ταξιδεύω, εκτελώ γραμμή || **~wood** n κοντραπλακέ nt inv.

P.M. abbr see **prime**.

p.m. ad (abbr of post meridiem) μ.μ. (μετά το μεσημέρι).

pneumatic [njuː'mætik] a πνευματικός, του πεπιεσμένου αέρα.

pneumonia [njuː'məuniə] n πνευμονία.

P.O. abbr see **post office**.

poach [pəutʃ] vt (cook) βράζω ξεφλουδισμένο αυγό, ποσάρω || (steal) κλέβω ♦ vi λαθροθηρώ || **~ed** a (egg) (αυγό) ποσέ || **~er** n λαθροθήρας || **~ing** n λαθροθηρία, κλοπή.

pocket ['pɒkit] n τσέπη || (hollow) θύλακας, λάκκος || (of resistance) νησίδα αντιστάσεως ♦ vt τσεπώνω,

βάζω στην τσέπη || **out of ~** ζημιωμένος, βγαίνω χαμένος || **~book** n (US: wallet) πορτοφόλι || (notebook) σημειωμάτάριο (της τσέπης) || (small book) βιβλίο τσέπης || **~ful** n όσο χωρεί μια τσέπη || **~knife** n σουγιάς (της τσέπης) || **~money** n χαρτζιλίκι.

pod [pɒd] n περικάρπιο.

podgy ['pɒdʒi] a κοντόχονδρος, χοντρός.

poem ['pəuim] n ποίημα nt.

poet ['pəuit] n ποιητής/ήτρια m/f || **~ic** [pəu'etik] a ποιητικός || **~laureate** n επίσημος ποιητής || **~ry** n ποίηση.

poignant ['pɔinjənt] a οξύς, δριμύς, τσουχτερός, δυνατός.

point [pɔint] n (sharp end) ακίδα, άκρα, αιχμή, μύτη || (dot) στίξη, σημείο || (moment) στιγμή, σημείο || (detail) λεπτομέρεια, στοιχείο, σημείο || (headland) ακρωτήριο || (RAIL) κλειδί, διασταύρωση || (of compass) ρόμβος πυξίδας, κάρτα || (degree) βαθμός, σημείο || (decimal point) κόμμα nt ♦ vt στρέφω, κατευθύνω, δείχνω || (gun etc) σκοπεύω με, σημαδεύω ♦ vi δείχνω, δακτυλοδεικτώ || **~s** npl κλειδί || **~ of view** n άποψη || **what's the ~?** τι το όφελος; || **to ~ out** vt δείχνω, επισύρω την προσοχή, υπογραμμίζω || **to ~ to** vt δείχνω, δακτυλοδεικτώ || **~-blank** ad κατ' ευθείαν, απερίσταφτος || **~ duty** n υπηρεσία τροχαίας || **~ed** a (shape) αιχμηρός, μυτερός || (remark) δηκτικός, καυστικός, τσουχτερός || **~er** n δείκτης || **~less** a άσκοπος, μάταιος.

poise [pɔiz] n παρουσιαστικό, κορμοστασιά ♦ vti ισορροπώ, σταθμίζω.

poison ['pɔizn] n δηλητήριο ♦ vt

δηλητηριάζω, μολύνω || ~ous a
δηλητηριώδης, φαρμακερός.

poke [pǝʊk] vt (stick into) κτυπώ,
χώνω || (fire) συδαυλίζω, σκαλίζω ♦
n (jab) κτύπημα nt, σπρωξιά || **to ~
one's nose into** ανακατεύομαι σε ||
to ~ about vi ψηλαφώ, ψάχνω ||
~r n σκαλιστήρι || (CARDS) πόκερ nt
inv.

poky ['pǝʊkɪ] a μικρός, στενόχωρος.

Poland ['pǝʊlǝnd] n Πολωνία.

polar ['pǝʊlǝ*] a πολικός || **~ bear**
n πολική άρκτος || **~ize** vt πολώνω
♦ vi πολούμαι.

pole [pǝʊl] n (of wood) στύλος, ιστός,
κοντάρι || (ELEC) στύλος || (GEOG)
πόλος || **~cat** a (US) είδος νυφίτσας
|| **~ star** n πολικό αστέρι || **~vault**
n άλμα nt επί κοντώ.

police [pǝ'liːs] n αστυνομία ♦ vt
αστυνομεύω, ελέγχω, τηρώ (την
τάξη) || **~ car** n αστυνομικό
(αυτοκίνητο) || **~man** n
αστυφύλακας, αστυνομικός,
πολισμάνος || **~ state** n αστυνομικό
κράτος nt|| **~ station** n αστυνομικό
τμήμα nt || **~woman** n n
αστυνομικός, αστυνομικίνα.

policy ['pɒlɪsɪ] n πολιτική ||
(prudence) φρόνηση || (insurance)
ασφαλιστήριο.

polio ['pǝʊlɪǝʊ] n πολυομυελίτιδα.

Polish ['pǝʊlɪʃ] a πολωνικός ♦ n
(LING) Πολωνικά ntpl.

polish ['pɒlɪʃ] n βερνίκι || (surface)
γυαλάδα, στιλπνότητα, λούστρο ||
(fig: refinement) ευγένεια, καλοί
τρόποι mpl ♦ vt στιλβώνω, γυαλίζω,
λουστράρω || (refine) εξευγενίζω || **to
~ off** vt (work) τελειώνω βιαστικά ||
(food) αδειάζω, καταβάζω, καθαρίζω
|| **~ed** a (fig) ευγενικός, λεπτός ||
εκλεπτισμένος.

polite [pǝ'laɪt] a ευγενής,
φιλόφρονος || **~ness** n ευγένεια,
λεπτότητα.

politic ['pɒlɪtɪk] a (wise) συνετός,
προνοητικός || **~al** [pǝ'lɪtɪkǝl] a
πολιτικός || **~ian** [pɒlɪ'tɪʃǝn] n
πολιτικός, πολιτικάντης || **~s** npl (n)
πολιτική || (US) πολιτικολογία.

polka [pɒlkǝ] n πόλκα || **~ dot**
(φόρεμα) με πίκες fpl, με βούλες fpl.

poll [pǝʊl] n ψηφοφορία, αριθμός
ψήφων ♦ vt συγκεντρώνω ψήφους,
ψηφίζω.

pollen ['pɒlǝn] n γύρη
(λουλουδιού).

pollination [pɒlɪ'neɪʃǝn] n
επικονίαση, γονιμοποίηση.

polling booth ['pǝʊlɪŋbuːθ] n
απομονωτήριο εκλογικού τμήματος.

polling day ['pǝʊlɪŋdeɪ] n μέρα
εκλογών.

polling station ['pǝʊlɪŋsteɪʃǝn] n
εκλογικό τμήμα nt.

pollute [pǝ'luːt] vt μολύνω,
βρωμίζω.

pollution [pǝ'luːʃǝn] n μίανση,
μόλυνση.

polo ['pǝʊlǝʊ] n πόλο nt inv.

poly- ['pɒlɪ] prefix πολυ-.

polygamy [pǝ'lɪgǝmɪ] n πολυγαμία.

polytechnic [pɒlɪ'tɛknɪk] n
πολυτεχνείο.

polythene ['pɒlɪθiːn] n πολυθένιο.

pomegranate ['pɒmǝgrænɪt] n
ρόδι.

pommel ['pʌml] vt γρονθοκοπώ,
κοπανίζω.

pomp [pɒmp] n λαμπρότητα,
επίδειξη.

pompous ['pɒmpǝs] a πομπώδης,
φανφαρόνος || **~ly** ad με
επιδεικτικότητα, με στόμφο.

ponce [pɒns] n (col) σωματέμπορος.

pond [pɒnd] n δεξαμενή, λιμνούλα.

ponder ['pɒndǝ*] vti
ξανασκέπτομαι, μελετώ, ζυγίζω ||
~ous a βαρύς, βραδύς, ανιαρός.

pontificate [pɒn'tɪfɪkeɪt] vi (fig)
μιλώ με ύφος ποντιφικό.

pontoon [pɒn'tuːn] n πλωτό στήριγμα nt γέφυρας || *(CARDS)* είκοσι ένα.

pony ['pəʊnɪ] n αλογάκι || ~**tail** n αλογοουρά.

poodle ['puːdl] n σγουρόμαλλο σκυλάκι.

pool [puːl] n *(of liquid)* λιμνούλα, νερόλακκος || *(at cards)* πόστα, πότ || *(billiards)* μπάτοκια || ~**s** *(football)* προ-πο at inv ♦ vt *(money etc)* ενώνω, συγκεντρώνω.

poor [pʊə*] a φτωχός, δυστυχισμένος || *(feeble)* αδύνατος, άθλιος || *(pitied)* κακόμοιρος, αξιολύπητος ♦ n: **the** ~ οι φτωχοί mpl|| ~**ly** ad φτωχικά, άθλια ♦ a αδιάθετος.

pop [pɒp] n *(noise)* ξηρός κρότος || *(MUS)* μουσική ποπ || *(col US: father)* μπαμπάς ♦ vt *(put suddenly)* θέτω απότομα ♦ vi *(explode)* κάνω ποπ, κροτώ|| *(come suddenly)* μπαίνω ξαφνικά, βγαίνω|| ~ **concert** n λαϊκή συναυλία *(non)*|| ~**corn** n ψημένο καλαμπόκι, ποπ-κορν nt inv.

Pope [pəʊp] n Πάπας.

poplar ['pɒplə*] n λεύκη.

poppy ['pɒpɪ] n παπαρούνα.

populace ['pɒpjʊlɪs] n λαός, το πλήθος.

popular ['pɒpjʊlə*] a δημοφιλής, κοσμοαγάπητος || *(of the people)* λαϊκός|| ~**ity** n δημοτικότητα, δημοφιλία|| ~**ize** vt εκλαϊκεύω.

populate ['pɒpjʊleɪt] vt (συν)οικίζω, κατοικώ.

population [pɒpjʊ'leɪʃən] n πληθυσμός.

porcelain ['pɔːslɪn] n πορσελάνη.

porch [pɔːtʃ] n προστέγασμα nt|| *(US)* βεράντα.

porcupine ['pɔːkjʊpaɪn] n σκαντζόχοιρος.

pore [pɔː*] n πόρος || **to** ~ **over** vt προσηλώνομαι.

pork [pɔːk] n χοιρινό.

pornographic [pɔːnə'græfɪk] a πορνογραφικός.

pornography [pɔː'nɒɡrəfɪ] n πορνογραφία.

porous ['pɔːrəs] a πορώδης.

porpoise ['pɔːpəs] n φώκαινα.

porridge ['pɒrɪdʒ] n χυλός (βρώμης).

port [pɔːt] n λιμένας, λιμάνι || *(town)* πόρτο || *(COMPUT)* σύνδεση εισόδου/εξόδου || *(NAUT: left side)* αριστερή πλευρά || *(wine)* πορτό, οίνος Πορτογαλίας.

portable ['pɔːtəbl] a φορητός.

portal ['pɔːtl] n είσοδος, πύλη.

portcullis [pɔːt'kʌlɪs] n καταρχτή θύρα, καταρχτή.

portent ['pɔːtɛnt] n κακός οιωνός || *(good)* θαυμάσιο πράγμα nt, οιωνός.

porter ['pɔːtə*] n αχθοφόρος, χαμάλης || *(doorkeeper)* θυρωρός.

porthole ['pɔːthəʊl] n *(NAUT)* φινιστρίνι.

portion ['pɔːʃən] n μερίδα, μερίδιο.

portly ['pɔːtlɪ] a παχύς, επιβλητικός.

portrait ['pɔːtrɪt] n προσωπογραφία, πορτραίτο.

portray [pɔː'treɪ] vt *(describe)* περιγράφω|| ~**al** a απεικόνιση, περιγραφή.

Portugal ['pɔːtjʊɡəl] n Πορτογαλία.

Portuguese ['pɔːtjʊ'ɡiːz] a πορτογαλικός ♦ n *(person)* Πορτογάλος/ίδα m/f|| *(LING)* Πορτογαλικά ntpl.

pose [pəʊz] n *(position)* στάση || *(affectation)* προσποίηση, πόζα ♦ vi *(take up attitude)* ποζάρω|| *(assume false pose)* εμφανίζομαι, παριστάνω ♦ vt *(put question)* θέτω|| ~**r** n *(problem)* δύσκολο πρόβλημα nt.

posh [pɒʃ] a *(col)* πλούσιος.

position [pə'zɪʃən] n θέση, στάση || *(place)* θέση, σειρά || *(location)* τοποθεσία || *(attitude)* θέση, πρόταση

|| (rank) θέση, βαθμός || (job) θέση, εργασία.

positive ['pɒzitiv] a θετικός, καταφατικός || (confident) βέβαιος, σίγουρος || (real) πραγματικός, αληθινός || (character) θετικός.

posse ['pɒsi] n (US) απόσπασμα nt (αστυνομικών).

possess [pə'zɛs] vt (κατ)έχω, διατηρώ || ~ion n κατοχή, κτήμα nt || (owning) κατοχή || ~ive a κτητικός, παθολογικά στοργικός || (GRAM) κτητικό.

possibility [pɒsi'biliti] n (chance) πιθανότητα || (event) δυνατότητα.

possible ['pɒsəbl] a δυνατός, ενδεχόμενος, λογικός || **if** ~ αν μπορώ, αν είναι δυνατό.

possibly ['pɒsəbli] ad κατά το δυνατό, πιθανό, ίσως.

post [pəʊst] n (pole) στύλος, πάσσαλος, κολώνα || (mail) ταχυδρομείο || (man) ταχυδρόμος || (station) θέση, φυλακή, πόστο || (job) θέση, πόστο ♦ vt (notice) τοιχοκολλώ || (letters) ταχυδρομώ || (station) εγκαθιστώ, τοποθετώ || ~age n ταχυδρομικά ntpl, γραμματόσημα ntpl || ~al a ταχυδρομικός || ~al order n ταχυδρομική επιταγή || ~box n ταχυδρομικό κουτί || ~card n καρτποστάλ f inv, κάρτα.

postdate ['pəʊst'deit] vt (cheque) μεταχρονολογώ, επιχρονολογώ.

poster ['pəʊstə*] n διαφήμιση, αφίσα.

poste restante [pəʊst'rɛstɑ̃:nt] n ποστ-ρεστάντ.

posterior [pɒs'tiəriə*] n (col) ο πισινός, κώλος.

posterity [pɒs'tɛriti] n (οι) μεταγενέστεροι.

postgraduate ['pəʊst'grædjuit] n μεταπτυχιακός σπουδαστής.

posthumous ['pɒstjʊməs] a (works) κατάλοιπα ntpl.

postman ['pəʊstmən] n ταχυδρόμος.

postmark ['pəʊstmɑ:k] n ταχυδρομική σφραγίδα.

postmaster ['pəʊstmɑ:stə*] n διευθυντής ταχυδρομείου.

post-mortem ['pəʊst'mɔ:təm] n (examination) νεκροψία.

post office ['pəʊstɒfis] n ταχυδρομείο || ~ **box (P.O. Box)** n ταχυδρομική θυρίδα (Τ.Θ.), ταχυδρομικό κιβώτιο.

postpone [pəʊst'pəʊn] vt αναβάλλω.

postscript ['pəʊsskript] n υστερόγραφο.

postulate ['pɒstjuleit] vt απαιτώ, αξιώνω.

posture ['pɒstʃə*] n στάση, θέση, κατάσταση ♦ vi τοποθετώ, στήνω, ποζάρω.

postwar ['pəʊst'wɔ:*] a μεταπολεμικός.

posy ['pəʊzi] n μπουκέτο (από λουλούδια), ανθοδέσμη.

pot [pɒt] n (for cooking) χύτρα, δοχείο, γλάστρα || (sl: marijuana) ναρκωτικά ntpl ♦ vt (plant) βάζω σε γλάστρα, φυτεύω σε γλάστρα.

potash ['pɒtæʃ] n ποτάσα.

potato [pə'teitəʊ] n πατάτα.

potent ['pəʊtənt] a ισχυρός, πειστικός.

potential [pəʊ'tɛnʃəl] a δυνητικός, λανθάνων, πιθανός, δυνατός ♦ n δυναμικό || ~**ly** ad ενδεχομένως, πιθανώς.

pothole ['pɒthəʊl] n πηγάδι, σπήλαιο || (in road) λακκούβα, λάκκος.

potholing ['pɒthəʊliŋ] n σπηλαιολογία.

potion ['pəʊʃən] n δόση (φαρμάκου).

potted ['pɔtɪd] a (food)
διατηρημένος || (plant) στη γλάστρα,
της γλάστρας.

potter ['pɔtə*] n κεραμοποιός,
τσουκαλάς ♦ vi χασομερώ,
ψευδοδουλεύω || ~ y n
αγγειοπλαστική, κεραμική || (place)
κεραμοποιείο.

potty ['pɔtɪ] a (mad) λοξός, τρελός
♦ n (child's) δοχείο (μωρού).

pouch [paʊtʃ] n (ZOOL) θύλακας ||
(tobacco) ταμπακιέρα.

poultice ['pəʊltɪs] n κατάπλασμα nt.

poultry ['pəʊltrɪ] n πουλερικά ntpl ||
~ **farm** n ορνιθοτροφείο.

pounce [paʊns] vi (+ on) εφορμώ,
πηδώ πάνω σε, χυμώ ♦ n πήδημα nt,
εφόρμηση.

pound [paʊnd] n (weight) λίμπρα (435
γρ), λίβρα, λίτρα || (sterling) λίρα
(Αγγλίας) || (area) περίβολος,
μάντρα ♦ vt κτυπώ, κοπανίζω ||
(crush to powder) λειοτριβώ,
κονιοποιώ, κοπανίζω || ~ **ing** n
σφυροκόπημα nt.

pour [pɔ:*] vt (cause) χύνω ♦ vi
μπαίνω σαν ποτάμι, τρέχω, χύνομαι
|| **to ~ away** or **off** vt χύνω (έξω),
ξεχύνομαι || **to ~ in** vi (people)
μπαίνω κατά κύματα || ~ **ing rain** n
βροχή με το τουλούμι,
καταρρακτώδης βροχή.

pout [paʊt] n κατσούφιασμα nt ♦ vi
κατσουφιάζω, στραβομουριάζω.

poverty ['pɔvətɪ] n φτώχεια || ~-
stricken a φτωχός, άπορος.

powder ['paʊdə*] n σκόνη ||
(medicine) σκόνη || (cosmetic) πούδρα
♦ vt (make into powder) κονιοποιώ,
τρίβω || (put on powder) πουδράρω ||
to ~ one's nose πουδράρομαι ||
(fig) πάω στη τουαλέτα || ~ **room** n
τουαλέτα || ~ **y** a κονιώδης, σαν
σκόνη.

power [paʊə*] n (ability to act)
εξουσία, δύναμη, ικανότητα ||

(strength) δύναμη || (mighty nation)
(μεγάλη) δύναμη || (mental)
ικανότητα, ιδιοφυΐα, ταλέντο ||
(ELEC) ενέργεια, δύναμη || (POL: of
party or leader) εξουσία, επιρροή,
ισχύς ♦ vt παρέχω ενέργεια σε, κινώ
|| ~ **cut** n διακοπή ρεύματος || ~-**ful**
a (person) ρωμαλέος, μεγάλος,
δυνατός || (government) ισχυρός ||
(engine) ισχυρός, αποδοτικός ||
~-**less** a ανίσχυρος, αδύναμος || ~-
line n γραμμή μεταφοράς || ~-
station n εργοστάσιο παραγωγής
ρεύματος.

p.p. abbr: ~ **P. Smith** Δια τον κον Π.
Σμιθ.

P.R. abbr of **public relations**.

practicable ['præktɪkəbl] a
δυνατός, κατορθωτός,
εφαρμόσιμος.

practical ['præktɪkəl] a πρακτικός,
θετικός, εφαρμόσιμος || ~ **joke** n
βαρύ αστείο, φάρσα || ~**ly** ad
(almost) σχεδόν, ουσιαστικά.

practice ['præktɪs] n άσκηση,
εξάσκηση || (habit) συνήθεια, έθιμο ||
(business) άσκηση, εξάσκηση ||
(clients) πελατεία || **in ~** (in reality)
στην πραγματικότητα || **to be out of
~** (SPORT) ξεσυνηθίζω, δεν είμαι σε
φόρμα.

practicing ['præktɪsɪŋ] a (US) =
practising.

practise, practice (US) ['præktɪs]
vt ασκώ, εφαρμόζω, ακολουθώ,
συνηθίζω || (SPORT) εκγυμνάζω ||
(piano) μελετώ, κάνω ασκήσεις ||
(profession) επαγγέλλομαι, (εξ)ασκώ.

practising ['præktɪsɪŋ] a (Christian
etc) που ασκεί τα θρησκευτικά του
καθήκοντα.

practitioner [præk'tɪʃənə*] n
επαγγελματίας.

pragmatic [præg'mætɪk] a
πρακτικός, πραγματικός.

prairie ['prɛərɪ] n λιβάδι, κάμπος.

praise [preiz] n έπαινος, εγκώμιο ♦ νt επαινώ, εξυμνώ || (worship) δοξάζω || ~**worthy** a αξιέπαινος.

pram [præm] n καροτσάκι μωρού.

prance [prɑːns] vi ανασκιρτώ, αναπηδώ || (strut) κορδώνομαι, καμαρώνω.

prank [præŋk] n ζαβολιά, κατεργαριά, κόλπο.

prattle ['prætl] vi φλυαρώ.

prawn [prɔːn] n είδος nt γαρίδας.

pray [prei] vi προσεύχομαι, παρακαλώ || ~**er** n προσευχή || (praying) παράκληση || ~**er book** n ευχολόγιο, προσευχητήριο.

pre- [priː] prefix προ-.

preach [priːtʃ] vi κηρύσσω || ~**er** n ιεροκήρυκας.

preamble [priːˈæmbl] n προοίμιο, εισαγωγή.

prearranged ['priːəˈreindʒd] a προκαθορισμένος, συμφωνημένος από πριν.

precarious [priˈkɛəriəs] a επισφαλής, επικίνδυνος, αβέβαιος.

precaution [priˈkɔːʃən] n προφύλαξη.

precede [priːˈsiːd] vti προηγούμαι, προπορεύομαι || ~**nt** ['presidənt] n προηγούμενο.

preceding [priːˈsiːdiŋ] a προηγούμενος.

precept ['priːsept] n κανόνας, δίδαγμα nt, διαταγή.

precinct ['priːsiŋkt] n περίβολος, περιοχή.

precious ['preʃəs] a πολύτιμος || (affected) επιτηδευμένος, προσποιητός.

precipice ['presipis] n γκρεμός.

precipitate [priˈsipitit] a (hasty) βιαστικός, εσπευσμένος || ~**ly** ad βιαστικά.

precipitous [priˈsipitəs] a (steep) κρημνώδης || ~**ly** ad απότομα.

precise [priˈsais] a ακριβής,

ορισμένος, συγκεκριμένος || (careful) ακριβολόγος, τυπικός.

preclude [priˈkluːd] vt αποκλείω, προλαμβάνω.

precocious [priˈkouʃəs] a πρόωρος.

preconceived ['priːkənˈsiːvd] a (idea) προκαταληπτικός.

precondition [priːkənˈdiʃən] n προϋπόθεση.

precursor [priːˈkɜːsə*] n πρόδρομος.

predator ['predətə*] n ληστής, αρπακτικό || (animal) ζώο.

predecessor ['priːdisesə*] n προκάτοχος.

predestination [priːdestiˈneiʃən] n προκαθορισμός.

predetermine ['priːdiˈtɜːmin] vt προκαθορίζω, προαποφασίζω.

predicament [priˈdikəmənt] n δύσκολη θέση, δυσχέρεια.

predicate ['predikit] n βεβαίωση, υποδηλώ.

predict [priˈdikt] vt προλέγω, προφητεύω || ~**ion** n πρόβλεψη, προφητεία.

predominance [priˈdominəns] n επικράτηση, υπεροχή.

predominant [priˈdominənt] a υπερισχύων, επικρατών.

predominate [priˈdomineit] vi επικρατώ, υπερισχύω.

pre-eminent [priːˈeminənt] a διαπρεπής, υπερέχων.

pre-empt [priːˈempt] vt αποκτώ πρώτος.

preen [priːn] vt: to ~ **o.s.** στολίζομαι, καμαρώνω.

prefabricated ['priːˈfæbrikeitid] a προκατασκευασμένος.

preface ['prefis] n πρόλογος, εισαγωγή, προοίμιο.

prefect ['priːfekt] n (of school) επιμελητής/ήτρια m/f.

prefer [priˈfɜː*] vt προτιμώ,

υποβάλλω, προάγω || ~**able**
['prεfərəbl] a (+ to) προτιμότερος,
καλύτερος (από) || ~**ence** n
προτίμηση || ~**ential** a
προνομιακός, προνομιούχος.

prefix ['pri:fiks] n πρόθεμα nt.

pregnancy ['prεgnənsı] n
εγκυμοσύνη.

pregnant ['prεgnənt] a έγκυος || (of
ideas) γόνιμος (σε), γεμάτος
συνέπειες.

prehistoric ['pri:hɪs'tɒrɪk] a
προϊστορικός.

prehistory ['pri:'hɪstərı] n
προϊστορία.

prejudice ['prεdʒudɪs] n
προκατάληψη, πρόληψη || (harm)
ζημιά, βλάβη ♦ vt ζημιώνω,
επηρεάζω || ~**d** a
προκατειλημμένος,
προδιατεθειμένος.

prelate ['prεlɪt] n ιεράρχης.

preliminary [prɪ'lɪmɪnərı] a
προκαταρκτικός.

prelude ['prεljuːd] n πρόλογος,
προοίμιο || (MUS) προανάκρουσμα nt,
πρελούντιο.

premarital ['pri:'mærɪtl] a
προγαμιαίος.

premature ['prεmətʃʊə*] a
πρόωρος || ~**ly** ad πρόωρα.

premeditated [pri:'mεdɪteɪtɪd] a
προεσκεμμένος, εκ προμελέτης.

premier ['prεmɪə*] a πρώτος,
κύριος ♦ n (head of country)
πρωθυπουργός m/f|| ~**e**
[prεmɪ'εə*] n πρεμιέρα.

premise ['prεmɪs] n πρόταση || ~**s**
npl οίκημα nt, κτίριο.

premium ['pri:mɪəm] n (insurance)
ασφάλιστρο.

premonition [pri:mə'nɪʃən] n
προαίσθημα nt.

preoccupied [pri:'ɒkjupaɪd] a
απορροφημένος, αφηρημένος.

prep [prεp] n (SCH: study) βραδυνή,
μελέτη.

preparation [prεpə'reɪʃən] n
προπαρασκευή, προετοιμασία.

preparatory [prɪ'pærətərı] a (SCH)
προπαρασκευαστικός,
προεισαγωγικός.

prepare [prɪ'pεə*] vt προετοιμάζω,
προπαρασκευάζω ♦ vi
προετοιμάζομαι,
προπαρασκευάζομαι || ~**d for** είμαι
έτοιμος για || ~**d to** είμαι
διατεθειμένος να.

preponderance [prɪ'pɒndərəns] n
υπεροχή, επικράτηση.

preposition [prεpə'zɪʃən] n
πρόθεση.

preposterous [prɪ'pɒstərəs] a
παράλογος, γελοίος.

prerequisite [pri:'rεkwɪzɪt] n
προϋπόθεση, αναγκαίος όρος.

prerogative [prɪ'rɒgətɪv] n
προνόμιο.

Presbyterian [prεzbɪ'tɪərɪən] a, n
Πρεσβυτεριανός.

preschool ['pri:'sku:l] a
προσχολικός.

prescribe [prɪs'kraɪb] vt ορίζω,
παραγγέλλω || (medicine) δίνω
συνταγή.

prescription [prɪs'krɪpʃən] n (for
medicine) συνταγή.

presence ['prεzns] n παρουσία
(bearing) ύφος nt, παρουσιαστικό,
εμφάνιση || ~ **of mind** ψυχραιμία,
ετοιμότητα πνεύματος.

present ['prεznt] a παρών || (time)
σημερινός ♦ n (time) το παρόν, το
σήμερα || (gift) δώρο (GRAM)
ενεστώτας ♦ ['prɪ'zεnt] vt
παρουσιάζω, παρουσιάζομαι ||
(introduce) συστήνω, παρουσιάζω ||
(offer, give) καταθέτω, προσφέρω,
δίνω || **at** ~ τώρα, προς το παρόν ||
~**able** a παρουσιάσιμος || ~**ation** n
παρουσίαση, παράσταση || ~-**day** a

σημερινός || ~**ly** ad (soon) σε λίγο,
αμέσως, σύντομα || (at present) τώρα.

preservation [prezə'veɪʃən] n
διατήρηση, διαφύλαξη.

preservative [prɪ'zɜːvətɪv] n
συντηρητικό ♦ a διατηρητικός.

preserve [prɪ'zɜːv] vt διαφυλάσσω
|| (keep up) συντηρώ ♦ n μέρος nt
διατηρήσεως ζώων || (jam) γλυκό
κουταλιού, μαρμελάδα.

preside [prɪ'zaɪd] vi προεδρεύω.

presidency ['prezɪdənsɪ] n
προεδρία.

president ['prezɪdənt] n πρόεδρος
|| (of university) πρύτανης || (of a
country) πρόεδρος || ~**ial** a
προεδρικός.

press [pres] n (machine) πιεστήριο,
πρέσσο || (printing house)
(τυπογραφικό) πιεστήριο,
τυπογραφείο || (newspapers) τύπος,
εφημερίδες fpl || (journalists) τύπος,
δημοσιογράφοι mpl ♦ vt πιέζω,
συνθλίβω || (urge) πιέζω, επιμένω ||
(clothes) σιδερώνω ♦ vi πιέζομαι,
σφίγγομαι || **to be** ~**ed for** δεν έχω
αρκετό, πιέζομαι για || **to** ~ **for**
αξιώνω, επιμένω σε, ασκώ πίεση για
|| **to** ~ **on** vi σπεύδω, επισπεύδω,
συνεχίζω || ~ **agency** n πρακτορείο
ειδήσεων || ~ **conference** n
δημοσιογραφική συνέντευξη || ~
cutting n απόκομμα nt εφημερίδας ||
~**ing** a (urgent) επείγων || (persistent)
επίμονος, πιεστικός || ~ **stud** n
κουμπί με πίεση.

pressure ['preʃə*] n πίεση || ~
cooker n χύτρα ταχύτητας,
καταρρόλα ταχύτητας || ~ **gauge** a
θλιβόμετρο, πιεζόμετρο, μανόμετρο
|| ~ **group** n ομάδα με ισχυρή
επιρροή.

pressurized ['preʃəraɪzd] a
πιεζόμενος, υπό πίεση.

prestige [pres'tiːʒ] n γόητρο.

presumably [prɪ'zjuːməblɪ] ad
κατά το φαινόμενο, πιθανώς.

presume [prɪ'zjuːm] vti υποθέτω,
προϋποθέτω || (venture) τολμώ,
παίρνω το θάρρος.

presumption [prɪ'zʌmpʃən] n
υπόθεση, παραδοχή || (impudence)
αναίδεια.

presuppose [priːsə'pəʊz] vt
προϋποθέτω.

pretence [prɪ'tens] n προσποίηση ||
(false excuse) πρόσχημα nt, πρόφαση.

pretend [prɪ'tend] vt (feign)
προσποιούμαι, υποκρίνομαι ♦ vi
προσποιούμαι.

pretense [prɪ'tens] n (US) =
pretence.

pretension [prɪ'tenʃən] n (claim to
merit) αξίωση, απαίτηση.

pretentious [prɪ'tenʃəs] a
απαιτητικός, επιδεικτικός.

pretext ['priːtekst] n πρόφαση,
πρόσχημα nt.

pretty ['prɪtɪ] a χαριτωμένος,
ωραίος.

prevail [prɪ'veɪl] vi επικρατώ,
υπερισχύω || (succeed) επιβάλλω,
πείθω || ~**ing** a (current) επικρατών,
ισχύων.

prevalent ['prevələnt] a
διαδεδομένος, επικρατών.

prevent [prɪ'vent] vt αποτρέπω,
προλαμβάνω || (hinder) εμποδίζω,
(παρα)κωλύω || ~**able** a
αποφεύξιμος || ~**ative** a
προληπτικά (φάρμακο) || ~**ion** n
πρόληψη, εμπόδιση || ~**ive** a
προληπτικός, προφυλακτικός.

preview ['priːvjuː] n
προκαταρκτική προβολή,
δοκιμαστική προβολή.

previous ['priːvɪəs] a
προηγούμενος || ~**ly** ad
προηγούμενος, πρώτερα.

prewar ['priːwɔː*] a
προπολεμικός.

prey [preɪ] n λεία, βορά, θύμα nt|| to
~ **on** vt (chase) κυνηγώ || (eat)
τρώγω || (mind) βασανίζω.

price [praɪs] n τιμή, τίμημα nt||
(value) αξία ♦ vt διατιμώ, καθορίζω
τιμή || ~**less** a ανεκτίμητος.

prick [prɪk] n τσίμπημα nt ♦ vt
τσιμπώ, κεντρώ, τρυπώ.

prickle ['prɪkl] n αγκάθι.

prickly ['prɪklɪ] a (lit) αγκαθωτός,
τσουχτερός || (fig: person) δύσκολος.

pride [praɪd] n (self-respect) φιλότιμο
|| (something to be proud of)
υπερηφάνεια, καμάρι || (conceit)
αλαζονεία, υπεροψία || to ~ o.s. on
sth υπερηφανεύομαι, καμαρώνω για
κάτι.

priest [priːst] n ιερέας, παπάς ||
~**ess** n ιέρεια || ~**hood** n ιερωσύνη,
ιερείς mpl.

prig [prɪg] n φαντασμένος,
ξιππασμένος.

prim [prɪm] a ακριβής, τυπικός,
μαζεμένος.

primarily ['praɪmərɪlɪ] ad
πρωτίστως, κυρίως || (at first) αρχικά,
πρώτα-πρώτα.

primary ['praɪmərɪ] a πρώτος,
αρχικός || (basic) βασικός || (first in
importance) πρωταρχικός, κύριος,
ουσιώδης || (education) στοιχειώδης ||
(election) προκριματική εκλογή || ~
colours npl πρωτεύοντα χρώματα
ntpl || ~ **school** n δημοτικό σχολείο.

primate ['praɪmɪt] n
αρχιεπίσκοπος, πριμάτος ||
['praɪmeɪt] (ZOOL) πρωτεύον
θηλαστικό.

prime [praɪm] a πρώτος, πρώτιστος,
κύριος || (excellent) εξαίρετος,
πρώτης ποιότητας || vt κατηχώ,
δασκαλεύω || (gun, pump) γεμίζω || ~
minister n πρωθυπουργός m/f ||
~ **r** n αλφαβητάριο, πρώτον βιβλίο.

primeval [praɪˈmiːvəl] a
πρωτόγονος, αρχέγονος.

primitive ['prɪmɪtɪv] a
πρωτόγονος.

primrose ['prɪmrəʊz] n πράνθεμο,
δακράκι, πασχαλούδα.

primula ['prɪmjʊlə] n πριμούλη.

primus (stove) ['praɪməs(stəʊv)]
n (R) γκαζιέρα.

prince [prɪns] n (of royal family)
πρίγκιπας, βασιλόπουλο || ~**ss** n
πριγκήπισσα.

principal ['prɪnsɪpəl] a κύριος,
κυριότερος ♦ n (capital) κεφάλαιο ||
(of school) προϊστάμενος/n m/f,
διευθυντής/ύντρια m/f || ~**ly** ad
κυρίως, προπαντός, κατά το
πλείστον.

principle ['prɪnsɪpl] n αρχή.

print [prɪnt] n φόρμα, τύπος ||
(fingerprint) αποτύπωμα nt || (PHOT)
αντίτυπο, κόπια || (picture) εικόνα ||
(pattern) εμπριμέ nt inv ♦ vt τυπώνω,
εκτυπώνω || to ~ **out** (text) τυπώνω
|| ~**ed matter** n έντυπα ntpl || ~**er**
n τυπογράφος || ~**ing** n (εκ)τύπωση,
τυπογραφία || ~**ing press** n
πιεστήριο (τυπογραφείου).

prior ['praɪə*] a προγενέστερος,
προηγούμενος ♦ n (ECCL)
ηγούμενος.

priority [praɪˈɒrɪtɪ] n
προτεραιότητα.

priory ['praɪərɪ] n μοναστήρι,
κοινόβιο.

prise [praɪz] vt: to ~ **open** ανοίγω
με μοχλό.

prism ['prɪzəm] n πρίσμα nt.

prison ['prɪzn] n φυλακή || ~**er** n
φυλακισμένος/n m/f, υπόδικος/n
m/f, κατάδικος m/f || (of war)
αιχμάλωτος/n m/f.

pristine ['prɪstaɪn] a πρωτόγονος,
αρχικός.

privacy ['prɪvəsɪ] n μοναξιά ||
(secrecy) μυστικότητα.

private ['praɪvɪt] a ιδιωτικός,
ιδιαίτερος || (secret) μυστικός ♦ n

(MIL) φαντάρος || '~' (sign) 'ιδιωτικό', 'ιδιαίτερον' || **in ~** ιδιαιτέρως, μυστικά || **~ eye** *n* ιδιωτικός αστυνομικός || **~ly** *ad* ιδιωτικά || (in confidence) εμπιστευτικά.

privet ['prɪvɪt] *n* λιγούστρο, αγριομυρτιά.

privilege ['prɪvɪlɪdʒ] *n* προνόμιο || **~d** *a* προνομιούχος.

privy ['prɪvɪ] *a:* **~ council** ανακτοβούλιο.

prize [praɪz] *n* βραβείο, έπαθλο ♦ *a* (example) λαμπρό υπόδειγμα || (idiot) υπόδειγμα ηλιθίου ♦ *vt* εκτιμώ, τιμώ || **~ fight** *n* πυγμαχικός αγώνας || **~ giving** *n* βράβευση || **~winner** *n* βραβευμένος/η *m/f.*

pro- [prəʊ] prefix (in favour) υπέρ, αντί-|| **the pros and cons** τα υπέρ και το κατά.

pro [prəʊ] *n* (professional) επαγγελματίας.

probability [prɒbə'bɪlɪtɪ] *n* πιθανότητα.

probable ['prɒbəbl] *a* ενδεχόμενος, πιθανός.

probably ['prɒbəblɪ] *ad* πιθανώς, πιθανόν.

probation [prə'beɪʃən] *n* δοκιμασία || (in court etc) αστυνομική επιτήρηση || **on ~** υπό δοκιμασία || **~er** *n* δόκιμος.

probe [prəʊb] *n* (MED) καθετήρας, μήλη || (enquiry) εξερεύνηση, διερεύνηση ♦ *vti* (εξ)ερευνώ, διερευνώ.

probity ['prəʊbɪtɪ] *n* τιμιότητα, ακεραιότητα.

problem ['prɒbləm] *n* πρόβλημα *nt* || **~atic** *a* προβληματικός.

procedure [prə'siːdʒə*] *n* διαδικασία, μέθοδος *f.*

proceed [prə'siːd] *vi* προχωρώ, συνεχίζω || (begin) προβαίνω || **~ings** *npl* συζητήσεις *fpl,* πρακτικά

ntpl || (LAW) δικαστική ενέργεια, δίκη || **~s** ['prəʊsiːdz] *npl* εισπράξεις *fpl.*

process ['prəʊses] *n* πορεία, εξέλιξη || (method) μέθοδος *f,* τρόπος ♦ *vt* επεξεργάζομαι, κατεργάζω.

procession [prə'seʃən] *n* πομπή, παρέλαση || (orderly progress) παράταξη, σειρά, συνοδεία.

proclaim [prə'kleɪm] *vt* κηρύσσω, ανακηρύσσω, αναγορεύω || (show) φανερώνω, δείχνω.

procure [prə'kjʊə*] *vt* προμηθεύω, προμηθεύομαι.

prod [prɒd] *vt* σκαλίζω, κεντρίζω, εξάπτω ♦ *n* (push, jab) μήξιμο, κέντρισμα *nt.*

prodigal ['prɒdɪgəl] *a* άσωτος.

prodigious [prə'dɪdʒəs] *a* τεράστιος, καταπληκτικός.

prodigy ['prɒdɪdʒɪ] *n* φαινόμενο, θαύμα *nt.*

produce [n 'prɒdjuːs; vt 'prədjuːs] *n* (AGR) προϊόν, καρπός ♦ *vt* (show) παρουσιάζω, δείχνω || (make) παράγω, γεννώ, προξενώ || (play) ανεβάζω, παρουσιάζω || **~r** *n* παραγωγός || (THEAT) σκηνοθέτης, παραγωγός.

product ['prɒdʌkt] *n* προϊόν || (result) αποτέλεσμα *nt.*

production [prə'dʌkʃən] *n* παραγωγή, κατασκευή || (THEAT) σκηνοθέτηση, παράσταση, ανέβασμα *nt* || **~ line** *n* γραμμή παραγωγής.

productive [prə'dʌktɪv] *a* παραγωγικός || (fertile) γόνιμος.

productivity [prɒdʌk'tɪvɪtɪ] *n* παραγωγικότητα || (fertility) γονιμότητα.

profane [prə'feɪn] *a* βέβηλος || (language) βλάσφημος.

profess [prə'fes] *vt* διακηρύττω || (confess) ομολογώ || (claim) προσποιούμαι.

profession [prə'feʃən] *n* επάγγελμα

nt || *(declaration)* ομολογία, διακήρυξη || ~ **al** *n* επαγγελματίας ♦ *a* επαγγελματικός || ~ **alism** *n* επαγγελματισμός.

professor [prəˈfesə*] *n* καθηγητής/ήτρια *m/f*.

proficient [prəˈfiʃənt] *a* ικανός, ειδικός.

profile [ˈprəufail] *n* (of face) κατατομή, προφίλ *nt inv* || (fig report) σύντομη βιογραφία.

profit [ˈprɔfit] *n* κέρδος *nt*, όφελος *nt*, ωφέλεια ♦ *vi* (+ by, from) ωφελούμαι (από) επωφελούμαι || ~ **able** *a* επικερδής, επωφελής || ~ **ably** *ad* επωφελώς, επικερδώς, ωφέλιμα.

profiteering [prɔfiˈtiəriŋ] *n* κερδοσκοπία.

profound [prəˈfaund] *a* βαθύς || (mysterious) μυστηριώδης.

profuse [prəˈfjuːs] *a* άφθονος, γενναιόδωρος.

programing [ˈprəugræmiŋ] *n* = **programming**.

programme, program (US, COMPUT) [ˈprəugræm] *n* πρόγραμμα *nt*.

programmer [ˈprəugræmə*] *n* προγραμματιστής *m/f*.

programming [ˈprəugræmiŋ] *n* προγραμματισμός || ~ **language** *n* γλώσσα προγραμματισμού.

progress [ˈprəugres] *n* πρόοδος *f*, εξέλιξη ♦ [prəˈgres] *vi* προοδεύω, προχωρώ, εξελίσσομαι || **to make** ~ σημειώνω πρόοδο, προοδεύω || ~ **ion** *n* πρόοδος *f* || ~ **ive** *a* προοδευτικός.

prohibit [prəˈhibit] *vt* απαγορεύω || ~ **ion** *n* απαγόρευση || (US: of alcohol) ποτοαπαγόρευση || ~ **ive** *a* (price etc) απαγορευτικός, απλησίαστος.

project [ˈprɔdʒekt] *n* (plan) σχέδιο || (study) μελέτη ♦ [prəˈdʒekt] *vt* (throw) εκτοξεύω, εξακοντίζω ||

(extend) προεκτείνω || (film etc) προβάλλω ♦ *vi* (προ)εξέχω, προβάλλω.

projectile [prəˈdʒektail] *n* βλήμα *nt*.

projection [prəˈdʒekʃən] *n* προεξοχή, προβολή.

projector [prəˈdʒektə*] *n* (film) προβολέας, μηχάνημα *nt* προβολής.

proletariat [prəuləˈtɛəriət] *n* προλεταριάτο.

proliferate [prəˈlifəreit] *vi* πολλαπλασιάζομαι.

prolific [prəˈlifik] *a* γόνιμος || (plentiful) άφθονος.

prologue [ˈprəulɔg] *n* πρόλογος.

prolong [prəˈlɔŋ] *vt* παρατείνω || (extend) προεκτείνω.

prom [prɔm] *n* abbr of **promenade** abbr of **promenade concert** || (US: college ball) συναυλία με λαϊκές τιμές.

promenade [prɔmiˈnɑːd] *n* περίπατος || (place) τόπος περιπάτου || ~ **concert** *n* συναυλία || ~ **deck** *n* (NAUT) κατάστρωμα *nt* περιπάτου.

prominent [ˈprɔminənt] *a* περίφημος, διακεκριμένος.

promiscuity [prɔmisˈkjuːiti] *n* σμίξιμο, ανακάτεμα *nt*, ελεύθερες ερωτικές σχέσεις.

promise [ˈprɔmis] *n* υπόσχεση, τάξιμο || (hope) υπόσχεση ♦ *vti* υπόσχομαι, δίνω υποσχέσεις, προμηνύω.

promising [ˈprɔmisiŋ] *a* γεμάτος υποσχέσεις, ενθαρρυντικός.

promote [prəˈməut] *vt* προάγω, προβιβάζω || (support) υποστηρίζω || ~ **r** *n* υποστηρικτής, υποκινητής || (organiser) διοργανωτής.

promotion [prəˈməuʃən] *n* (of sales etc) διαφήμιση, προαγωγή || (in rank) προαγωγή, προβιβασμός.

prompt [prɔmpt] *a* άμεσος, πρόθυμος, ταχύς ♦ *ad* (punctually) στην ώρα ♦ *vt* παρακινώ

|| *(remind)* υποβάλλω|| ~**er** n *(THEAT)*
υποβολέας|| ~**ness** n ταχύτητα,
ετοιμότητα, προθυμία.
prone [prɔʊn] a πεσμένος
μπρούμυτα|| *(inclined)* (+ *to*)
επιρρεπής (τιρος), αυτός που έχει
τάση (τιρος).
prong [prɒŋ] n δόντι πηρουνιού,
πηρούνα, διχάλα.
pronoun [ˈprɔʊnaʊn] n αντωνυμία.
pronounce [prəˈnaʊns] vt *(GRAM)*
προφέρω|| *(LAW)* εκδίδω, επιβάλλω,
γνωματεύω|| ~**d** a *(marked)*
έντονος, ζωηρός.
pronto [ˈprɒntəʊ] ad *(col)* αμέσως,
γρήγορα.
pronunciation [prənʌnsɪˈeɪʃən] n
προφορά.
proof [pruːf] n απόδειξη, τεκμήριο ||
(test) δοκιμή, δοκιμασία || *(copy)*
δοκίμιο ♦ a αδιαπέραστος,
στεγανός|| *(resistant)* ανθεκτικός.
prop [prɒp] n στήριγμα nt, έρεισμα
nt, υποστήριγμα nt|| *(THEAT)*
βοηθητικά ntpl, αξεσουάρ nt inv ♦ vt
(also: ~ **up**) (υπο)στηρίζω,
στηλώνω.
propaganda [prɒpəˈɡændə] n
προπαγάνδα.
propagation [prɒpəˈɡeɪʃən] n *(of
plants)* αναπαραγωγή,
πολλαπλασιασμός || *(of knowledge)*
διάδοση.
propel [prəˈpel] vt προωθώ|| ~**ler**
n έλικας, προπέλα.
proper [ˈprɒpə*] a πρέπων,
αρμόζων || ~**ly** ad καλά,
καταλλήλως, σωστά || ~ **noun** n
κύριο όνομα nt.
property [ˈprɒpətɪ] n ιδιοκτησία,
περιουσία || *(quality)* ιδιότητα,
χαρακτηριστικό || *(THEAT)* βοηθητικό,
αξεσουάρ nt inv|| *(land)* κτήμα nt,
ακίνητο || ~ **owner** n
ιδιοκτήτης/ρια m/f.

prophecy [ˈprɒfɪsɪ] n *(prediction)*
προφητεία.
prophesy [ˈprɒfɪsaɪ] vt προφητεύω,
προλέγω.
prophet [ˈprɒfɪt] n προφήτης || ~**ic**
a προφητικός.
proportion [prəˈpɔːʃən] n σχέση,
αναλογία || *(share)* μέρος, τμήμα nt ♦
vt ρυθμίζω, μοιράζω κατ' αναλογία ||
~**al** a ανάλογος, συμμετρικός,
αναλογικός || ~**ate** a ανάλογος.
proposal [prəˈpəʊzl] n πρόταση,
εισήγηση || *(of marriage)* πρόταση
γάμου.
propose [prəˈpəʊz] vt προτείνω,
σκοπεύω ♦ vi *(marriage)* κάνω
πρόταση γάμου.
proposition [prɒpəˈzɪʃən] n
πρόταση, σχέδιο, υπόθεση.
proprietary [prəˈpraɪətərɪ] a της
ιδιοκτησίας, της κυριότητας.
proprietor [prəˈpraɪətə*] n
ιδιοκτήτης/τρια m/f.
propulsion [prəˈpʌlʃən] n
(προ)ώθηση.
pro rata [prəʊˈrɑːtə] ad κατ'
αναλογία.
prosaic [prəʊˈzeɪɪk] a *(ordinary)*
πεζός.
prose [prəʊz] n πεζός λόγος,
πεζογραφία, πρόζα.
prosecute [ˈprɒsɪkjuːt] vt
υποβάλλω μήνυση.
prosecution [prɒsɪˈkjuːʃən] n
(noινική) δίωξη || *(people bringing
action)* κατηγορία, μηνυτής.
prosecutor [ˈprɒsɪkjuːtə*] n
εισαγγελέας.
prospect [ˈprɒspekt] n *(expectation)*
προσδοκία || *(hope)* ελπίδα || ~**ing**
n *(for minerals)* αναζήτηση
(μεταλλευμάτων) || ~**ive** a πιθανός,
μελλοντικός || ~**or** n μεταλλοδίφης
|| *(for gold)* χρυσοθήρας.
prospectus [prəˈspektəs] n
αγγελία, πρόγραμμα nt.

prosper ['prɒspə*] vi ευδοκιμώ, ακμάζω, ευημερώ || ~ity n ευημερία, ευδαιμονία || ~ous a ευημερών, ακμάζων || (successful) επιτυχής.

prostitute ['prɒstitjuːt] n πόρνη, πουτάνα.

prostrate ['prɒstreit] a (lying flat) πρηνής, μπρούμυτος.

protagonist [prəʊ'tægənist] n πρωταγωνιστής/ίστρια m/f.

protect [prə'tɛkt] vt προστατεύω, προφυλάσσω, υπερασπίζω, καλύπτω || ~ion n προστασία, υπεράσπιση, άμυνα || (shelter) σκέπαστρο, προστατευτικό μέσο || ~ive a προστατευτικός || ~or n προστάτης, προφυλακτήρας.

protégé ['prɒteʒei] n προστατευόμενος || ~e προστατευόμενη

protein ['prəʊtiːn] n πρωτεΐνη.

protest ['prəʊtest] n διαμαρτυρία ♦ [prə'test] vi (+ against) διαμαρτύρομαι.

Protestant ['prɒtistənt] a, n Διαμαρτυρόμενος, Προτεστάντης.

protocol ['prəʊtəkɒl] n πρωτόκολλο.

prototype ['prəʊtəutaip] n πρωτότυπο.

protractor [prə'træktə*] n μοιρογνωμόνιο.

protrude [prə'truːd] vi προεξέχω, βγαίνω έξω.

proud [praud] a περήφανος || (snobbish) φαντασμένος || (condescending) ακατάδεκτος.

prove [pruːv] vt (show) αποδεικνύω, επαληθεύω || (turn out) δείχνομαι.

proverb ['prɒvɜːb] n παροιμία.

provide [prə'vaid] vt προμηθεύω, χορηγώ || ~d cj εφόσον, αρκεί να.

province ['prɒvins] n επαρχία || (fig) αρμοδιότητα.

provincial [prə'vinʃəl] a επαρχιακός.

provision [prə'viʒən] n (supply) προμήθεια || (condition) όρος || ~s npl (food) τρόφιμα ntpl || (equipment) εφόδια ntpl || ~al προσωρινός.

provocation [prɒvə'keiʃən] n πρόκληση.

provocative [prə'vɒkətiv] a προκλητικός, ερεθιστικός.

provoke [prə'vəʊk] vt προκαλώ, διεγείρω, εξερεθίζω.

prow [prau] n πρώρα, πλώρη.

prowess ['praus] n γενναιότητα || (bravery) ανδρεία, παλικαριά.

prowl [praul] vt (streets) περιφέρομαι, τριγυρίζω ♦ n: on the ~ ψάχνω διαρκώς || ~er n νυχτοπάτης, τριγυρριστής.

proximity [prɒk'simiti] n εγγύτητα, αμεσότητα.

proxy ['prɒksi] n πληρεξούσιος, αντιπρόσωπος || by ~ δι' αντιπροσώπου.

prudent ['pruːdənt] a συνετός, φρόνιμος.

prudish ['pruːdiʃ] a σεμνότυφος || ~ness n σεμνοτυφία.

prune [pruːn] n ξερό δαμάσκηνο ♦ vt κλαδεύω.

pry [prai] vi (+ into) ψάχνω, χώνω τη μύτη (σε).

psalm [sɑːm] n ψαλμός.

pseudo- ['sjuːdəu] prefix ψεύτικος, κίβδηλος || (in compds) ψευδο-.

pseudonym ['sjuːdəunim] n ψευδώνυμο.

psyche ['saiki] n (soul, mind, intelligence) ψυχή.

psychiatric [saiki'ætrik] a ψυχιατρικός.

psychiatrist [sai'kaiətrist] n ψυχιατρος m/f.

psychiatry [sai'kaiətri] n ψυχιατρική.

psychic(al) ['saikik(əl)] a ψυχικός.

psychoanalyst [saɪkəʊˈænəlɪst] n ψυχαναλυτής/ύτρια m/f.

psychological [saɪkəˈlɒdʒɪkəl] a ψυχολογικός || ~**ly** ad ψυχολογικά.

psychologist [saɪˈkɒlədʒɪst] n ψυχολόγος m/f.

psychology [saɪˈkɒlədʒɪ] n ψυχολογία.

psychopath [ˈsaɪkəʊpæθ] n ψυχοπαθής m/f.

psychosomatic [ˈsaɪkəʊsəʊˈmætɪk] a ψυχοσωματικός.

psychotherapy [ˈsaɪkəʊˈθɛrəpɪ] n ψυχοθεραπεία.

psychotic [saɪˈkɒtɪk] a, n ψυχωτικός.

p.t.o. abbr of please turn over.

pub [pʌb] n (Brit) = **public house** || see **public**.

puberty [ˈpjuːbətɪ] n ήβη, εφηβεία.

public [ˈpʌblɪk] a δημόσιος || (generally known) πασίγνωστος ♦ n (also: **the general** ~) το κοινό || ~ **house** n ταβέρνα.

publican [ˈpʌblɪkən] n (innkeeper) ταβερνιάρης, κάπελας.

publication [pʌblɪˈkeɪʃən] n (something published) δημοσίευση, έκδοση || (making known) κοινοποίηση, δημοσίευση.

publicity [pʌbˈlɪsɪtɪ] n δημοσιότητα || (advertising) διαφήμιση.

publicly [ˈpʌblɪklɪ] ad δημόσια, ολοφάνερα.

public: ~ **opinion** n κοινή γνώμη || ~ **relations** n δημόσιες σχέσεις fpl || ~ **school** n (Brit) ιδιωτικό σχολείο (Αγγλίας) || ~**-spirited** a ενδιαφερόμενος για το κοινό καλό.

publish [ˈpʌblɪʃ] vt εκδίδω, δημοσιεύω || (figures etc) αναγγέλω, δημοσιεύω || ~**er** n εκδότης/ρια m/f || ~**ing** n έκδοση, δημοσίευση.

pucker [ˈpʌkə*] vt ζαρώνω.

pudding [ˈpʊdɪŋ] n πουτίγκα.

puddle [ˈpʌdl] n (pool) λακκούβα, λιμνούλα.

puff [pʌf] n ξεφύσημα nt, φύσημα nt ♦ vt ξεφυσώ, βγάζω καπνό ♦ vi φυσώ, λαχανιάζω || ~**ed** a (col: out of breath) λαχανισμένος.

puff pastry [ˈpʌfˈpeɪstrɪ] n, **puff paste** (US) [ˈpʌfˈpeɪst] n γλύκισμα με φύλλα.

puffy [ˈpʌfɪ] a φουσκωμένος, φουσκωτός.

pull [pʊl] n (tug) έλξη, τράβηγμα nt || (fig) επιρροή, μέσο ♦ vt (trolley) σύρω, έλκω, τραβώ, σέρνω || (hair) τραβώ || (trigger) πατώ, τραβώ ♦ vi (on rope etc) τραβώ, σύρω || '~' (sign) 'σύρατε' || **to** ~ **a face** κάνω μούτρα, μορφάζω || **to** ~ **to pieces** τραβώ και κομματιάζω, κάνω κομμάτια || **to** ~ **o.s. together** συνέρχομαι || **to** ~ **apart** (break) σχίζω στα δυο, αποχωρίζω || (dismantle) λύω || **to** ~ **down** vt (house) κατεδαφίζω, γκρεμίζω || **to** ~ **in** vi (RAIL) μπαίνω (στο σταθμό) || **to** ~ **off** vt (deal etc) επιτυγχάνω (κάτι) || **to** ~ **out** vi φεύγω, ξεκινώ, αναχωρώ || (vehicle) βγαίνω από τη λωρίδα ♦ vt αφαιρώ, βγάζω, τραβώ || **to** ~ **round or through** vi συνέρχομαι, γλιτώνω || (from illness) αναρρώνω || **to** ~ **up** vi σταματώ.

pulley [ˈpʊlɪ] n τροχαλία.

pullover [ˈpʊləʊvə*] n πουλόβερ nt inv.

pulp [pʌlp] n πολτός, σάρκωμα nt.

pulpit [ˈpʊlpɪt] n άμβωνας.

pulsate [pʌlˈseɪt] vi πάλλομαι, πάλλω, σφύζω.

pulse [pʌls] n σφυγμός, παλμός || (vegetable) όσπρια ntpl.

pulverize [ˈpʌlvəraɪz] vt κάνω σκόνη, κονιοποιώ.

pummel [ˈpʌml] vt γρονθοκοπώ.

pump [pʌmp] n αντλία || (bicycle)

τρόμπα ♦ vt αντλώ || **to ~ up** vt (tyre) φουσκώνω (λάστιχο).

pumpkin ['pʌmpkɪn] n κολοκύθα.

pun [pʌn] n λογοπαίγνιο.

punch [pʌntʃ] n τρυπητήρι, ζουμπάς || (blow) γροθιά || (drink) πόντς nt inv, πόντσι ♦ vt γρονθοκοπώ, δίνω μια γροθιά || (a hole) τρυπώ, ανοίγω.

punctual ['pʌŋktjʊəl] a ακριβής.

punctuate ['pʌŋktjʊeɪt] vt στίζω || (fig) τονίζω, υπογραμμίζω.

punctuation [pʌŋktjʊ'eɪʃən] n στίξη.

puncture ['pʌŋktʃə*] n (παρα)κέντηση || (tyre) σκάσιμο, τρύπημα σε λάστιχο ♦ vt παρακεντώ, τρυπώ, σπάζω.

pungent ['pʌndʒənt] a δριμύς, σουβλερός, οξύς.

punish ['pʌnɪʃ] vt τιμωρώ, δέρνω || (in boxing etc) δίνω άγριο ξύλο, μαστιγώνω || **~able** a αξιόποινος, τιμωρητέος || **~ment** n τιμωρία.

punitive ['pjuːnɪtɪv] a τιμωρητικός || (MIL) **~ expedition** n εκστρατεία αντιποίνων.

punt [pʌnt] n πλοιάρι, ρηχή βάρκα.

punter ['pʌntə*] n (gambler) παίκτης.

puny ['pjuːnɪ] a μικροκαμωμένος, αδύνατος, ασήμαντος.

pup [pʌp] n σκυλάκι, κουτάβι.

pupil ['pjuːpɪl] n μαθητής/ήτρια m/f || (of eye) κόρη (οφθαλμού).

puppet ['pʌpɪt] n μαριονέτα || (person) ανδρείκελο.

puppy ['pʌpɪ] n σκυλάκι.

purchase ['pɜːtʃɪs] n ψώνισμα, ψώνιο || (buying) αγορά, ψώνισμα nt ♦ vt αγοράζω, ψωνίζω || **~r** n αγοραστής.

pure [pjuə*] a καθαρός || (innocent) άδολος, αγνός || (unmixed) αμιγής, ανόθευτος.

purée ['pjuəreɪ] n πουρές m inv.

purge [pɜːdʒ] n καθάρσιο || (POL) εκκαθάριση ♦ vt (εκ)καθαρίζω.

purify ['pjuərɪfaɪ] vt καθαρίζω, εξαγνίζω.

purist ['pjuərɪst] n: **Greek language ~** καθαρευουσιάνος, καθαρολόγος.

puritan ['pjuərɪtən] n πουριτανός || **~ical** a πουριτανικός.

purity ['pjuərɪtɪ] n καθαρότητα || (authenticity) γνησιότητα.

purl [pɜːl] n ανάποδη βελονιά ♦ vt πλέκω ανάποδα.

purple ['pɜːpl] (colour) a πορφυρός ♦ n πορφύρα, πορφυρό (χρώμα).

purpose ['pɜːpəs] n σκοπός, πρόθεση || **on ~** σκόπιμα || **~ful** a (προ)εσκεμμένος, σκόπιμος || **~ly** ad επίτηδες, σκόπιμα.

purr [pɜː*] vi (of cat) ρουθουνίζω, κάνω ρονρό ♦ n γουργούρισμα.

purse [pɜːs] n πορτοφόλι ♦ vt ζαρώνω.

purser ['pɜːsə*] n λογιστής (πλοίου).

pursue [pə'sjuː] vt (κατα)διώκω, κυνηγώ || (carry on) συνεχίζω, ακολουθώ || **~r** n διώκτης.

pursuit [pə'sjuːt] n (κατα)δίωξη, κυνήγημα nt || (occupation) επιδίωξη, επάγγελμα nt.

purveyor [pɜː'veɪə*] n προμηθευτής (τροφίμων).

pus [pʌs] n πύο.

push [puʃ] n ώθηση, σκούντημα nt, σπρωξιά || (MIL) προώθηση ♦ vt σπρώχνω, σκουντώ || (forward) προχωρώ, προοδεύω ♦ vi σπρώχνω, ωθώ, ασκώ πίεση || (make one's way) προχωρώ (με δυσκολία) || **~! (sign)** 'ωθήσετε' || **at a ~** (if necessary) στην ανάγκη || **to ~ aside** vt απωθώ, παραμερίζω || **to ~ off** vi (col) φεύγω, ξεκινώ || **to ~ on** vi (continue) προχωρώ, συνεχίζω, επισπεύδω || **to ~ through** vt

(measure) περνώ (νομοσχέδιο κτλ) ||
~ **chair** *n* καροτσάκι, παιδικό
αμαξάκι || ~**ing** *a* δραστήριος,
επίμονος || ~**over** *n* (col) εύκολο
πράμα *nt*, εύκολη κατάκτηση.

puss [pus] *n* (also: **pussy cat**) γατάκι,
ψιμίνα.

put [put] *(irreg v)* vt θέτω, τοποθετώ,
βάζω || *(express)* εκφράζω, εξηγώ,
υποβάλλω || **to ~ about** *vi*
στρέφομαι, αναστρέφομαι ♦ *vt*
διαδίδω, θέτω σε κυκλοφορία || **to
~ across** *vt (succeed)* επιτυγχάνω,
βγάζω πέρα || *(meaning)* δίνω να
καταλάβει || **to ~ away** *vt (store)*
βάζω κατά μέρος, φυλάω || **to ~
back** *vt (replace)* βάζω πίσω ||
(postpone) αναβάλλω || **to ~ by** *vt
(money)* αποταμιεύω || **to ~ down** *vt
(lit)* κατεβάζω || *(in writing)* γράφω,
σημειώνω || **to ~ forward** *vt (idea)*
αναπτύσσω, εισηγούμαι, προτείνω ||
(date) αναβάλλω || **to ~ off** *vt
(postpone)* αναβάλλω || *(discourage)*
μεταπείθω, εμποδίζω, αποθαρρύνω
|| **to ~ on** *(clothes etc)* φορώ ||
(light etc) ανάβω || *(play etc)* ανεβάζω
|| *(brake)* φρενάρω || *(false air)*
προσποιούμαι || **to ~ out** *vt (hand
etc)* εκτείνω, απλώνω || *(news, rumour)*
διαδίδω || *(light etc)* σβήνω || *(person:
inconvenience)* στενοχωρώ, ενοχλώ ||
to ~ up *vt (raise)* σηκώνω, υψώνω ||
(guest) φιλοξενώ || **to ~ up with** *vt*
ανέχομαι.

putrid ['pjuːtrɪd] *a* σαπρός, σάπιος.
putt [pʌt] *vt* σέρνω (τη μπάλα) ♦ *n*
συρτό χτύπημα *nt*, πάτιγκ *nt inv*.

putty ['pʌtɪ] *n* στόκος.

put-up ['putʌp] *a*: ~ **job** δουλειά
σκαρωμένη, στημένη μηχανή.

puzzle ['pʌzl] *n* αίνιγμα *nt*, δύσκολο
πρόβλημα *nt*, μπέρδεμα *nt* || *(toy)*
παιχνίδι συναρμολογήσεως, γρίφος
♦ *vt (perplex)* περιπλέκω, συγχίζω ♦
vi σπάζω το κεφάλι μου.

puzzling ['pʌzlɪŋ] *a* πολύπλοκος,
δύσκολος, μπλεγμένος.

pygmy ['pɪgmɪ] *n* πυγμαίος.

pyjamas [pɪ'dʒɑːməz] *npl* πυζάμες
fpl.

pylon ['paɪlən] *n* στύλος.

pyramid ['pɪrəmɪd] *n* πυραμίδα.

python ['paɪθən] *n* πύθωνας.

Q

quack [kwæk] *n* κραυγή πάπιας ||
(dishonest person) κομπογιαννίτης.

quad [kwɒd] *n abbr of* **quadrangle,
quadruple, quadruplet.**

quadrangle ['kwɒdræŋgl] *n (court)*
τετράγωνη αυλή.

quadruped ['kwɒdruped] *n*
τετράποδο.

quadruple ['kwɒdrupl] *a*
τετραπλός, τετραπλάσιος,
τετράδιπλος ♦ [kwɒ'druːpl] *vti*
τετραπλασιάζω, τετραπλασιάζομαι.

quadruplet [kwɒ'druːplɪt] *n*
τετράδυμα.

quaint [kweɪnt] *a* παράξενος,
αλλόκοτος.

quake [kweɪk] *vi* τρέμω, σείομαι ||
Q~**r** *n* Κουάκερος.

qualification [kwɒlɪfɪ'keɪʃən] *n*
ικανότητα, προσόν *nt* || *(reservation)*
επιφύλαξη, όρος, περιορισμός.

qualified ['kwɒlɪfaɪd] *a* έχων τα
προσόντα, κατάλληλος || *(reserved)*
επιφυλακτικός, περιωρισμένος,
μετριασμένος.

qualify ['kwɒlɪfaɪ] *vt* καθιστώ
κατάλληλο, αποκτώ τα προσόντα ||
(limit) τροποποιώ, προσδιορίζω ♦ *vi
(acquire degree)* λαμβάνω δίπλωμα.

quality ['kwɒlɪtɪ] *n (kind)* ποιότητα ||
(of person) ιδιότητα, χαρακτηριστικό,
ικανότητα ♦ *a* καλής ποιότητας.

qualm [kwɑːm] *n (misgiving)* τύψη,
ενδοιασμός.

quandary ['kwɒndərɪ] n αμηχανία, δίλημμα nt.

quantity ['kwɒntɪtɪ] n ποσότητα || (large amount) μεγάλη ποσότητα || πολύ, κε το σωρό.

quarantine ['kwɒrəntiːn] n καραντίνα.

quarrel ['kwɒrəl] n (argument) φιλονεικία, διένεξη, καυγάς, τσακωμός ♦ vi (argue) φιλονεικώ, τσακώνομαι || ~some α ευέξαπτος, καυγατζής.

quarry ['kwɒrɪ] n (of stone) λατομείο || (animal) θήραμα nt, κυνήγι.

quart [kwɔːt] n τέταρτο του γαλονιού.

quarter ['kwɔːtə*] n τέταρτο || (of year) τριμηνία ♦ vt κόβω στα τέσσερα || (MIL) στρατωνίζω || ~s npl (esp MIL) κατάλυμα nt, στρατώνας || (accommodation) στέγαση || ~ of an hour ένα τέταρτο (της ώρας) || ~ past three τρεις και τέταρτο || ~ to three τρεις παρά τέταρτο || ~-deck n πρυμναίο κατάστρωμα nt, κάσαρο || ~ly α τριμηνιαίος || ~master n (NAUT) υποναύκληρος || (MIL) επιμελητής.

quartet(te) [kwɔː'tɛt] n τετραφωνία, κουαρτέτο.

quartz [kwɔːts] n χαλαζίας.

quash [kwɒʃ] vt (verdict) αναιρώ, ακυρώνω.

quasi ['kwɑːzɪ] a σαν, σχεδόν, τρόπον τινά.

quaver ['kweɪvə*] n (MUS) όγδοο ♦ vi τρέμω, κάνω τρίλιες.

quay [kiː] n αποβάθρα, προκυμαία.

queasy ['kwiːzɪ] a ευαίσθητος, αηδιαστικός.

queen [kwiːn] n βασίλισσα || (CARDS) ντάμα || ~ mother n βασιλομήτωρ f.

queer [kwɪə*] a αλλόκοτος, παράξενος ♦ n (col: homosexual) 'τοιούτος'.

quell [kwɛl] vt καταινύγω, καταβάλλω, κατευνάζω.

quench [kwɛntʃ] vt κόβω (τη δίψα μου), κατευνάζω || (fire etc) σβήνω.

query ['kwɪərɪ] n ερώτηση, απορία nt ♦ vt ερωτώ, ερευνώ.

quest [kwɛst] n αναζήτηση, έρευνα.

question ['kwɛstʃən] n ερώτηση, ερώτημα nt || (problem) ζήτημα nt, θέμα nt|| (doubt) αμφιβολία, αμφισβήτηση ♦ vt ρωτώ, εξετάζω || (doubt) αμφισβητώ || beyond ~ αναμφισβήτητα || out of the ~ εκτός συζητήσεως, απαράδεκτος || ~able α αμφίβολος, αμφισβητήσιμος || ~er n εξεταστής, ανακριτής || ~ing α ερώτηση, ανάκριση || ~ mark n ερωτηματικό.

questionnaire [kwɛstʃə'nɛə*] n ερωτηματολόγιο.

queue [kjuː] n (in line) ουρά ♦ vi μπαίνω στην ουρά, σχηματίζω ουρά.

quibble ['kwɪbl] n (petty objection) υπεκφυγή.

quick [kwɪk] a (fast) ταχύς, γρήγορος, γοργός || (impatient) βιαστικός, ευέξαπτος || (keen) ζωηρός, ζωντανός, έξυπνος ♦ ad γρήγορα ♦ n (ANAT) ευαίσθητο σημείο, σάρκα, κρέας nt || (old: the living) οι ζωντανοί || ~en vt (hasten) επιταχύνω || (rouse) (ανα)ζωογονώ, ζωντανεύω || vi (ανα)ζωντανεύω, αναζωπυρούμαι || ~ly ad γρήγορα || ~sand n κινητή άμμος f|| ~step n (MUSIC) ταχύς ρυθμός || ~witted a ξύπνιος, ατσίδα.

quid [kwɪd] n (Brit col: £1) λίρα (Αγγλίας).

quiet ['kwaɪət] a (without noise) σιωπηλός, ήσυχος, αθόρυβος || (still) ήρεμος, γαλήνιος, ήσυχος || (peaceful) ήρεμος, ατάραχος ♦ n ησυχία, ηρεμία || ~en vt (also: ~en down) (καθ)ησυχάζω, καλμάρω || ~ly ad ήρεμα, απαλά, σιγαλά,

σιωπηλά || ~ness n πρεμιά, γαλήνη, κάλμα.

quill [kwɪl] n (pen) πένα από φτερό.

quilt [kwɪlt] n πάπλωμα nt, εφάπλωμα nt.

quin [kwɪn] n abbr of **quintuplet**.

quince [kwɪns] n κυδώνι.

quinine [kwɪˈniːn] n κινίνη.

quintet(te) [kwɪnˈtet] n κουιντέτο.

quintuplet [kwɪnˈtjuːplɪt] n πεντάδυμο.

quip [kwɪp] n ευφυολόγημα nt, πείραγμα nt, σαρκασμός ♦ vi ευφυολογώ.

quit [kwɪt] (irreg) vt εγκαταλείπω, φεύγω ♦ vi (give up) παραιτούμαι, εγκαταλείπω.

quite [kwaɪt] ad τελείως, εντελώς || (fairly) μάλλον, πολύ || ~ (so)! σωστά!, σύμφωνοι!

quits [kwɪts] ad στα ίσια, πάτσι.

quiver [ˈkwɪvə*] vi τρέμω, τρεμουλιάζω ♦ n (for arrows) φαρέτρα, σαϊτοθήκη.

quiz [kwɪz] n στραβόκατσαγμα nt || (test) προφορική εξέταση ♦ vt (question) εξετάζω || (puzzle) n αινιγματώδης, ερωτηματικός.

quorum [ˈkwɔːrəm] n απαρτία.

quota [ˈkwəʊtə] n ανάλογο μερίδιο, μερίδα.

quotation [kwəʊˈteɪʃən] n (from book) απόσπασμα nt || (price) προσφορά || ~ marks npl εισαγωγικά ntpl.

quote [kwəʊt] n (quotation) απόσπασμα nt ♦ vti (price) καθορίζω, δίνω τιμή || (cite) παραθέτω, αναφέρω.

quotient [ˈkwəʊʃənt] n πηλίκο nt.

R

rabbi [ˈræbaɪ] n ραββίνος.

rabbit [ˈræbɪt] n κουνέλι || ~ hutch n κλουβί κουνελιού.

rabble [ˈræbl] n όχλος.

rabid [ˈræbɪd] a (fig) μανιασμένος, αδιάλλακτος.

rabies [ˈreɪbiːz] n λύσσα.

R.A.C. abbr of Royal Automobile Club.

race [reɪs] n (people) ράτσα, φυλή || (generation) γενιά || (animals) ράτσα || (competition) αγώνας δρόμου || (rush) βία, γρηγοράδα ♦ vt κάνω αγώνα δρόμου ♦ vi τρέχω || (compete) συναγωνίζομαι || ~course n (for horses) ιππόδρομος || ~horse n άλογο ιπποδρομιών || ~ meeting n (for horses) ιπποδρομία || ~ relations npl φυλετικές σχέσεις fpl || ~track n (for cars etc) πίστα (αγώνων).

racial [ˈreɪʃəl] a φυλετικός || ~ism n φυλετισμός, ρα(τ)σισμός || ~ist a ρα(τ)σιστικός.

racing [ˈreɪsɪŋ] n αγώνες mpl, συμμετοχή σε αγώνες || ~ car n αυτοκίνητο αγώνων || ~ driver n οδηγός αυτοκινήτου αγώνων.

racist [ˈreɪsɪst] a ρατσιστής.

rack [ræk] n (clothes etc) κρεμάστρα ♦ vt βασανίζω || ~ and ruin n καταστροφή, κατά διαβόλου.

racket [ˈrækɪt] n θόρυβος, φασαρία || (dishonest scheme) κομπίνα || (for tennis) ρακέτα.

racquet [ˈrækɪt] n ρακέτα.

racy [ˈreɪsɪ] a (spirited) ζωηρός, κεφάτος.

radar [ˈreɪdɑː*] n ραντάρ nt inv.

radiant [ˈreɪdɪənt] a λαμπερός || (giving out rays) ακτινοβόλος.

radiate [ˈreɪdɪeɪt] vt (of heat) ακτινοβολώ, εκπέμνω ♦ vi (lines) εκτείνω ακτινοειδώς.

radiation [reɪdɪˈeɪʃən] n ακτινοβολία.

radiator [ˈreɪdɪeɪtə*] n σώμα nt καλοριφέρ || (AUT) ψυγείο.

radical [ˈrædɪkəl] a ριζικός || (POL)
ριζοσπαστικός.
radio [ˈreɪdɪəʊ] n ραδιόφωνο.
radio... [ˈreɪdɪəʊ] prefix: ~**active** a
ραδιενεργός || ~**activity** n
ραδιενέργεια || ~**grapher** n
ακτινογράφος || ~**telephone** n
ασύρματο τηλέφωνο || ~ **telescope**
n ραδιοτηλεσκόπιο || ~**therapist** n
ακτινολόγος ιατρός.
radish [ˈrædɪʃ] n ρεπανάκι.
radium [ˈreɪdɪəm] n ράδιο.
radius [ˈreɪdɪəs] n ακτίνα.
raffia [ˈræfɪə] n ραφία.
raffle [ˈræfl] n λαχείο, λοταρία.
raft [rɑːft] n σχεδία.
rafter [ˈrɑːftəʳ] n δοκάρι, καδρόνι.
rag [ræg] n (of cloth) ράκος nt,
κουρέλι || (col: newspaper) εφημερίδα
♦ vt κάνω φάρσα, κάνω καζούρα ||
~ **bag** n (fig) κακοντυμένη γυναίκα.
rage [reɪdʒ] n (fury) λύσσα, μανία ||
(fashion) μανία της μόδας ♦ vi
(person) μαίνομαι, είμαι έξω φρενών
|| (storm) μαίνομαι, είμαι αγριεμένος.
ragged [ˈrægɪd] a (edge) τραχύς,
απότομος.
raging [ˈreɪdʒɪŋ] a μαινόμενος,
αγριεμένος.
raid [reɪd] n (MIL) επιδρομή ||
(invasion) εισβολή || (criminal)
επιδρομή, γιουρούσι || (by police)
επιδρομή, μπλόκος ♦ vt εισβάλλω
σε, κάνω μπλόκο || ~**er** n
επιδρομέας.
rail [reɪl] n (on stair) κάγκελο,
κιγκλίδωμα nt || (of ship) κουπαστή, ||
(RAIL) σιδηροτροχιά, γραμμή || ~s
npl (RAIL) τροχιά, γραμμές fpl || **by** ~
σιδηροδρομικώς, με τραίνο ||
~**ings** npl κάγκελα ntpl, φράχτης ||
~**road** n (US), ~**way** n (Brit)
σιδηρόδρομος, σιδηροδρομική
γραμμή || ~**road** or ~**way station**
n σιδηροδρομικός σταθμός.
rain [reɪn] n βροχή || vti βρέχω ||

~**bow** n ουράνιο τόξο || ~**coat** n
αδιάβροχο || ~**drop** n σταγόνα
βροχής || ~**storm** n καταιγίδα,
(flood) κατακλυσμός || ~**y** a (region)
βροχερός || (day) βροχερή (μέρα) ||
(fig) ώρα ανάγκης || (season) εποχή
των βροχών.
raise [reɪz] n (esp US: increase)
αύξηση (μισθού) ♦ vt (build) κτίζω,
στήνω || (lift) σηκώνω, υψώνω,
ανεβάζω || (a question) προβάλλω,
θέτω || (doubts) προκαλώ, γεννώ ||
(collect) μαζεύω, συλλέγω || (bring up)
ανατρέφω, τρέφω.
raisin [ˈreɪzən] n σταφίδα.
rake [reɪk] n τσουγκράνα || (dissolute
person) έκλυτος, ακόλαστος ♦ vt
(AGR) μαζεύω με τσουγκράνα,
σκαλίζω || (with shots) γαζώνω ||
(search keenly) εξετάζω, ερευνώ || to
~ **in** or **together** etc vt μαζεύω.
rally [ˈrælɪ] n (POL etc)
συγκέντρωση, συναγερμός || (AUT)
ράλλυ nt inv || (improvement)
ανάκτηση, βελτίωση ♦ vt
συναθροίζω, συγκεντρώνω ♦ vi
(health) συνέρχομαι, αναρρώνω || to
~ **round** vti συσπειρώνομαι.
ram [ræm] n κριάρι || (beam) έμβολο,
κριός ♦ vt εμβολίζω, πηγνύω || (strike)
κτυπώ || (stuff) παραγεμίζω, χώνω.
ramble [ˈræmbl] n περίπατος,
περιπλάνηση ♦ vi κάνω βόλτες,
περιφέρομαι || (be delirious) μιλώ
ασυνάρτητα.
rambling [ˈræmblɪŋ] a (plant)
αναρριχητικός || (speech) ασύνδετος,
ασυνάρτητος.
ramification [ræmɪfɪˈkeɪʃən] n
διακλάδωση.
ramp [ræmp] n (incline) κεκλιμένο
επίπεδο, ανωφέρεια.
rampage [ræmˈpeɪdʒ] n: to be on
the ~ vi (also: ~) συμπεριφέρομαι
βίαια.
rampant [ˈræmpənt] a (unchecked)

αχαλίνωτος, ξαπλωμένος || (on hind legs) όρθιος.

rampart ['ræmpɑːt] n έπαλξη, προμαχώνας, ντάπια.

ramshackle ['ræmʃækl] a ετοιμόρροπος, ερειπιωμένος, ρημάδι.

ran [ræn] pt of **run**.

ranch [rɑːntʃ] n αγρόκτημα nt, ράντσο.

rancid ['rænsɪd] a ταγγός, τσαγγός.

rancour, rancor (US)['ræŋkə*] n μνησικακία, έχθρα.

random ['rændəm] a τυχαίος ♦ n: **at** ~ στην τύχη, στα κουτουρού.

randy ['rændɪ] a (col) ασελγής, λάγνος.

rang [ræŋ] pt of **ring**.

range [reɪndʒ] n (row, line) σειρά, οροσειρά || (extent, series) έκταση, σειρά, περιοχή || (of gun) βεληνεκές nt, εμβέλεια || (for shooting) πεδίο βολής, σκοπευτήριο || (cooking stove) κουζίνα, μαγειρική συσκευή ♦ vt παρατάσσω, βάζω στη σειρά || (roam) περιπλανώμαι, περιφέρομαι ♦ vi (extend) εκτείνομαι, απλώνομαι || ~ **r** n (of forest) δασόφρος, δασονόμος.

rank [ræŋk] n (row, line) στοίχος, γραμμή || (social position) (κοινωνική) τάξη || (high position) ανώτερη θέση, βαθμός ♦ vi (of place) κατατάσσομαι, έρχομαι ♦ a (bad smelling) δύσοσμος, ταγγός || (extreme) πλήρης, τέλειος, απόλυτος || **the** ~ **s** npl (MIL) οι στρατιώτες, φαντάροι mpl || **the** ~ **and file** (fig) ο απλός λαός.

ransack ['rænsæk] vt λεηλατώ, κάνω άνω-κάτω, ψάχνω καλά.

ransom ['rænsəm] n λύτρα ntpl || to hold to ~ ζητώ λύτρα.

rant [rænt] vi κομπάζω || ~ **ing** n στόμφος.

rap [ræp] n κτύπημα nt, κτύπος, κρότος ♦ vt κρούω, κτυπώ.

rape [reɪp] n βιασμός ♦ vt βιάζω.

rapid ['ræpɪd] a ταχύς, γρήγορος || ~ **s** npl μικρός καταρράκτης || ~ **ly** ad γρήγορα, γοργά.

rapist ['reɪpɪst] n βιαστής.

rapture ['ræptʃə*] n έκσταση, μεγάλη χαρά.

rapturous ['ræptʃərəs] a εκστατικός, ενθουσιασμένος.

rare [rɛə*] a σπάνιος, συνηθιστός || αραιός || (air) αραιός || (especially good) θαυμάσιος, σπουδαίος || (in cooking) μισοψημένος.

rarity ['rɛərɪtɪ] n σπάνιο πράγμα nt || (scarcity) σπανιότητα.

rascal ['rɑːskəl] n παλιάνθρωπος, μασκαράς.

rash [ræʃ] a παράτολμος, απερίσκεπτος ♦ n εξάνθημα nt.

rasher ['ræʃə*] n ψιλή φέτα μπέικον.

raspberry ['rɑːzbəri] n σμέουρο, φραμπουάζ nt inv, βατόμουρο.

rasping ['rɑːspɪŋ] a (noise) οξύς, στριγγλός.

rat [ræt] n (animal) αρουραίος, μεγάλος ποντικός.

ratable ['reɪtəbl] a: ~ **value** φορολογήσιμο τεκμαρτό ενοίκιο (ακινήτου).

ratchet ['rætʃɪt] n οδοντωτός τροχός, καστάνια ntpl.

rate [reɪt] n (proportion) αναλογία, ανάλογο ποσό, ανάλογος αριθμός || (price) ποσοστό, τόκος || (speed) ρυθμός, ταχύτητα ♦ vt εκτιμώ, ταξινομώ || ~ **s** npl (Brit) τοπικός φόρος || **at any** ~ οπωσδήποτε, εν πάσει περιπτώσει || **at this** ~ έτσι || ~ **of exchange** n τιμή συναλλάγματος || ~ **payer** n φορολογούμενος || **see first**.

rather ['rɑːðə*] ad μάλλον,

καλύτερα, παρά || (somewhat) λίγο, κάπως, μάλλον, σχετικά.

ratify ['rætɪfaɪ] vt επικυρώνω, εγκρίνω.

rating ['reɪtɪŋ] n (classification) εκτίμηση, τάξη || (NAUT) μέλος πληρώματος, ειδικότητα.

ratio ['reɪʃɪəʊ] n λόγος, αναλογία.

ration ['ræʃən] n μερίδα || (usually pl, food) σιτηρέσιο, τροψη ♦ vt περιορίζω, επιβάλλω μερίδες.

rational ['ræʃənl] a λογικός || **rationale** [ræʃə'nɑːl] n λογική εξήγηση, λογική βάση || ~**ize** vt ορθολογίζομαι, οργανώνω ορθολογικά.

rationing ['ræʃnɪŋ] n καθορισμός μερίδων, διανομή με δελτίο.

rattle ['rætl] n κρότος, κροταλισμός || (toy) ροκάνα, κρόταλο ♦ vi κροταλίζω, κροτώ || ~**snake** n κροταλίας.

raucous ['rɔːkəs] n βραχνός.

ravage ['rævɪdʒ] vt ερημώνω, αφανίζω, ρημάζω || ~ s npl (of time etc) φθορά του χρόνου.

rave [reɪv] vi παραληρώ, παραμιλώ || (rage) μαίνομαι, ουρλιάζω.

raven ['reɪvn] n κοράκι, κόρακας.

ravenous ['rævənəs] a (hungry) πεινασμένος, λιμασμένος.

ravine [rə'viːn] n φαράγγι.

raving ['reɪvɪŋ] a: ~ **lunatic** μανιακός, παράφρονας.

ravioli [rævɪ'əʊlɪ] n ραβιόλια ntpl.

ravish ['rævɪʃ] vt απάγω, κλέβω || (rape) βιάζω || ~**ing** a γοητευτικός, μαγευτικός.

raw [rɔː] a (uncooked) ωμός, άψητος || (not manufactured) ακατέργαστος || (tender) ευαίσθητος, ματωμένος || (inexperienced) άξεστος, ατζαμής || ~ **material** n πρώτες ύλες fpl.

ray [reɪ] n ακτίδα.

raze [reɪz] vt ισοπεδώνω, κατεδαφίζω, γκρεμίζω.

razor ['reɪzə*] n ξυράφι || ~ **blade** n ξυριστική λεπίδα.

Rd abbr of **road**.

re- [riː] prefix αντι-, ανά-, ξανά-.

reach [riːtʃ] n έκταση, άπλωμα nt, τέντωμα nt (χεριού) || (distance) εντός βολής, κοντά ♦ vt απλώνω, τεντώνω || (arrive at) φθάνω ♦ vi (επ)εκτείνομαι || **to** ~ **out** vi απλώνω (το χέρι).

react [riː'ækt] vi αντιδρώ || ~**ion** n αντίδραση || ~**ionary** a αντιδραστικός.

reactor [riː'æktə*] n αντιδραστήρας.

read [riːd] (irreg v) n ανάγνωση, διάβασμα nt ♦ vti διαβάζω || (aloud) διαβάζω δυνατά || (understand) ερμηνεύω, δείχνω || (find in book) διαβάζομαι || (COMPUT) διαβάζω || ~ **able** a αναγνώσιμος, που διαβάζεται || ~**er** n αναγνώστης/ρια m/f|| (book) αναγνωστικό || ~**ership** n (of newspaper etc) αναγνωστικό κοινό.

readily ['redɪlɪ] ad πρόθυμα, αδίστακτα, εύκολα.

readiness ['redɪnɪs] n προθυμία || (being ready) ετοιμότητα.

reading ['riːdɪŋ] n ανάγνωση, διάβασμα nt || ~ **lamp** n λάμπα του τραπεζιού || ~ **room** n αναγνωστήριο.

readjust ['riːə'dʒʌst] vt αναπροσαρμόζω, διορθώνω, σιάζω.

ready ['redɪ] a έτοιμος || (willing) πρόθυμος, διατεθειμένος || (condition) έτοιμος || (quick, facile) γρήγορος, εύκολος || (available) πρόχειρος ♦ ad τελείως n: **at the** ~ έτοιμος || ~-**made** a έτοιμος.

real [rɪəl] a πραγματικός, αληθινός || ~ **estate** n ακίνητη περιουσία, οικιόλα ntpl || ~**ism** n πραγματισμός, ρεαλισμός || ~**ist** n

πραγματιστής, ρεαλιστής/ίστρια m/f || ~istic a ρεαλιστικός.

reality [riː'ælɪtɪ] n πραγματικότητα, αλήθεια || in ~ πράγματι, πραγματικά.

realization [rɪəlaɪ'zeɪʃən] n συνειδητοποίηση || (fulfilment) πραγματοποίηση.

realize ['rɪəlaɪz] vt (understand) κατανοώ, αντιλαμβάνομαι, καταλαβαίνω || (bring about) πραγματοποιώ.

really ['rɪəlɪ] ad πραγματικά, αλήθεια, όχι δα.

realm [relm] n σφαίρα, δικαιοδοσία || (kingdom) βασίλειο.

reap [riːp] vt θερίζω || (harvest) συγκομίζω, μαζεύω || ~er n (machine) θεριστική μηχανή.

reappear ['riːə'pɪə*] vi επανεμφανίζομαι, ξαναφαίνομαι || ~ance n επανεμφάνιση, επάνοδος f.

reapply ['riːə'plaɪ] vi (+ to, for) ξαναϋποβάλλω (αίτηση).

reappoint ['riːə'pɔɪnt] vt επαναδιορίζω.

rear [rɪə*] a οπίσθιος, πισινός ♦ n νώτα ntpl, οπίσθια ntpl, οπισθοφυλακή ♦ vt (bring up) (ανα)τρέφω ♦ vi ανορθούμαι, σηκώνομαι σούζα || ~guard n οπισθοφυλακή.

rearm ['riː'ɑːm] vti επανεξοπλίζω, επανεξοπλίζομαι || ~ament n επανεξοπλισμός.

rearrange ['riːə'reɪndʒ] vt τακτοποιώ πάλι, αναδιαρρυθμίζω.

rear-view ['rɪəvjuː] a: ~ mirror καθρέπτης οδήγησης.

reason ['riːzn] n (cause) λόγος, αιτία || (ability to think) λογικό, λογική || (judgment) κρίση ♦ vi σκέπτομαι, συλλογίζομαι, συμπεραίνω || ~able a λογικός || (fair) μετριοπαθής, μέτριος || ~ably ad λογικά || ~ed a

(argument) αιτιολογημένος, δικαιολογημένος|| ~ing n συλλογισμός, επιχείρημα nt.

reassert ['riːə'səːt] vt επαναβεβαιώνω.

reassure [riːə'ʃuə*] vt ενθαρρύνω καθησυχάζω.

reassuring [riːə'ʃuərɪŋ] a καθησυχαστικός|| (encouraging) ενθαρρυντικός.

rebate ['riːbeɪt] n έκπτωση.

rebel ['rebl] n αντάρτης/ισσα m/f, επαναστάτης/ρια m/f ♦ a επαναστατημένος, ανταρτικός || ~lion [rɪ'beliən] n ανταρσία|| ~lious a ανταρτικός, ανυπότακτος.

rebirth ['riː'bəːθ] n αναγέννηση.

rebound [rɪ'baund] vi αναπηδώ ♦ ['riːbaund] n αναπήδηση.

rebuff [rɪ'bʌf] n απόκρουση, άρνηση ♦ vt αποκρούω, αρνούμαι.

rebuild [riː'bɪld] vt ανοικοδομώ || ~ing n ανοικοδόμηση.

rebuke [rɪ'bjuːk] n επίπληξη, μομφή ♦ vt επιπλήττω, επιτιμώ.

recalcitrant [rɪ'kælsɪtrənt] a ανυπάκουος, δύστροπος.

recall [rɪ'kɔːl] vt (call back) ανακαλώ || (remember) ξαναθυμίζω, ξαναθυμάμαι || (withdraw) ανακαλώ.

recant [rɪ'kænt] vi ανακαλώ, αναιρώ, αναθεωρώ.

recap ['riːkæp] vti ξαναβουλώνω.

recede [rɪ'siːd] vi αποσύρομαι, υποχωρώ, τραβιέμαι.

receipt [rɪ'siːt] n απόδειξη παραλαβής || (receiving) λήψη, παραλαβή || ~s npl εισπράξεις fpl, έσοδα ntpl.

receive [rɪ'siːv] vt λαμβάνω || (welcome) (υπο)δέχομαι || ~r n (TEL) ακουστικό.

recent ['riːsnt] a πρόσφατος, νέος || ~ly ad τελευταία, πρόσφατα.

receptacle [rɪ'septəkl] n δοχείο.

reception [rɪ'sepʃən] n (welcome)

υποδοχή || (party) δεξίωση || (at hotel etc) γραφείο υποδοχής || ~**ist** n υπάλληλος m/f επί της υποδοχής.

receptive [rɪˈsɛptɪv] a δεκτικός.

recess [rɪˈsɛs] n (interval) διακοπή, διάλειμμα nt || (in wall) εσοχή, βαθούλωμα nt || (inner place) μυστικό μέρος nt.

recharge [ˈriːˈtʃɑːdʒ] vt (battery) αναφορτίζω, ξαναγεμίζω.

recipe [ˈrɛsɪpɪ] n συνταγή.

recipient [rɪˈsɪpɪənt] n δέκτης, λήπτης, παραλήπτης.

reciprocal [rɪˈsɪprəkəl] a αμοιβαίος, αντίστροφος.

recital [rɪˈsaɪtl] n (MUS) ρεσιτάλ nt inv.

recite [rɪˈsaɪt] vt απαγγέλλω, αποστηθίζω || (tell one by one) εξιστορώ, απαριθμώ.

reckless [ˈrɛklɪs] a αδιάφορος, απρόσεκτος, απερίσκεπτος || ~**ly** ad απερίσκεπτα, παράτολμα.

reckon [ˈrɛkən] vt (count) υπολογίζω, λογαριάζω, μετρώ || (consider) εκτιμώ, λογαριάζω ♦ vi υπολογίζω || **to** ~ **on** vt στηρίζομαι σε, υπολογίζω σε || ~**ing** n υπολογισμός.

reclaim [rɪˈkleɪm] vi (land) εκγεώσιμων, αποκτώ || (demand back) ξαναζητώ.

recline [rɪˈklaɪn] vi ξαπλώνω, πλαγιάζω, ακουμπώ.

reclining [rɪˈklaɪnɪŋ] a πλαγιαστός, ξαπλωμένος.

recluse [rɪˈkluːs] n ερημίτης.

recognition [rɛkəɡˈnɪʃən] n αναγνώριση.

recognize [ˈrɛkəɡnaɪz] vt αναγνωρίζω || (admit) ομολογώ, παραδέχομαι.

recoil [rɪˈkɔɪl] vi οπισθοδρομώ, μαζεύομαι || (spring) αναπηδώ.

recollect [rɛkəˈlɛkt] vt θυμούμαι, ανασπολώ || ~**ion** n ανάμνηση (memory) μνημονικός.

recommend [rɛkəˈmɛnd] vt συνιστώ || ~**ation** n σύσταση || (qualification) προσόν nt.

recompense [ˈrɛkəmpɛns] n ανταμοιβή, αποζημίωση ♦ vt ανταμείβω, αποζημιώνω.

reconcile [ˈrɛkənsaɪl] vt (make agree) συμβιβάζω || (make friendly) συμφιλιώνω.

reconciliation [rɛkənsɪlɪˈeɪʃən] n συμφιλίωση, συμβιβασμός.

reconditioned [ˈriːkənˈdɪʃnd] a επισκευασμένος, ανακαινισθείς.

reconnoitre, reconnoiter (US) [rɛkəˈnɔɪtə*] vti κάνω αναγνώριση, εξερευνώ.

reconsider [ˈriːkənˈsɪdə*] vti αναθεωρώ, επανεξετάζω.

reconstitute [riːˈkɒnstɪtjuːt] vt επαναφέρω στη φυσική κατάσταση.

reconstruct [ˈriːkənˈstrʌkt] vt ανοικοδομώ, ανασυγκροτώ || ~**ion** n ανοικοδόμηση, ανασυγκρότηση.

record [ˈrɛkɔːd] n αναγραφή, καταγραφή, σημείωση || (disc) δίσκος, πλάκα || (best performance) πρωτάθλημα nt, ρεκόρ nt inv, επίδοση || (COMPUT) εγγραφή ♦ (a time) με μεγάλη ταχύτητα, σε διάστημα του σημειώνει ρεκόρ ♦ [rɪˈkɔːd] vt (set down) καταγράφω, αναγράφω || (music etc) ηχογραφώ, εγγράφω || ~**ed** a (music) ηχογραφημένος || ~**er** n μηχάνημα nt εγγραφής || (tape recorder) μαγνητόφωνο || ~**holder** n (SPORT) πρωταθλητής/ήτρια m/f || ~**ing** n (music) ηχογράφηση || ~**player** n πικάπ nt inv.

recount [rɪˈkaʊnt] vt (tell in detail) αφηγούμαι, εξιστορώ.

re-count [rɪˈkaʊnt] n νέα καταμέτρηση ♦ [riːˈkaʊnt] vt ξαναμετρώ.

recoup [rɪˈkuːp] vt αποζημιώνω, ξαναπέρνω.

recourse [rɪ'kɔːs] n καταφυγή, προσφυγή.

recover [rɪ'kʌvə*] vt ανακτώ, ξαναβρίσκω ♦ vi ανακτώ (την υγεία μου), θεραπεύομαι || ~y n ανάκτηση, ανεύρεση || (from illness) ανάρρωση.

recreation [rɛkrɪ'eɪʃən] n αναψυχή, διασκέδαση || ~al a διασκεδαστικός.

recrimination [rɪkrɪmɪ'neɪʃən] n αντέγκληση, αντικατηγορία.

recruit [rɪ'kruːt] n νεοσύλλεκτος ♦ vt στρατολογώ || ~ment n στρατολογία.

rectangle ['rɛktæŋgl] n ορθογώνιο.

rectangular [rɛk'tæŋgjʊlə*] a ορθογώνιος.

rectify ['rɛktɪfaɪ] vt επανορθώνω, διορθώνω.

rectory ['rɛktərɪ] n (ECCL) πρεσβυτέριο, εφημερείο.

recuperate [rɪ'kuːpəreɪt] vi αναλαμβάνω, αναρρώνω.

recur [rɪ'kɜː*] vi επανέρχομαι, ξαναομιλβαίνω || ~rence n επανάληψη.

red [rɛd] n (colour) κόκκινο n (Communist) κομμουνιστής/ίστρια m/f, αριστερός/ή m/f ♦ a κόκκινος, ερυθρός || **to be in the** ~ έχω έλλειμα nt || R ~ **Cross** n Ερυθρός Σταυρός || ~**den** vti κοκκινίζω || ~**dish** a κοκκινωπός.

redeem [rɪ'diːm] vt αντισταθμίζω, εξοφλώ, εξαγοράζω.

red-haired ['rɛd'hɛəd] a κοκκινομάλλης.

red-handed ['rɛd'hændɪd] a επ' αυτοφώρω, στα πράσα.

redhead ['rɛdhɛd] n κοκκινομάλλα.

red herring ['rɛd'hɛrɪŋ] n (fig) ξεγέλασμα nt, άσχετο θέμα nt.

red-hot ['rɛd'hɒt] a

ερυθροπυρωμένος || (fig) φανατικός, ένθερμος.

redirect [riːdaɪ'rɛkt] vt (mail) απευθύνω σε νέα διεύθυνση.

rediscovery ['riːdɪs'kʌvərɪ] n εκ νέου ανακάλυψη.

red-letter ['rɛd'lɛtə*] a: ~ **day** μέρα ευτυχισμένων γεγονότων, αξιομνημόνευτη μέρα.

redness ['rɛdnɪs] n κοκκινίλα, κοκκινάδα.

redo ['riː'duː] vt ξανακάνω.

redouble [riː'dʌbl] vt αναδιπλασιάζω.

red tape ['rɛd'teɪp] n γραφειοκρατία.

reduce [rɪ'djuːs] vt (decrease) ελαττώνω, μικραίνω, περιορίζω || (in strength) αδυνατίζω || (lower) υποβιβάζω, κατεβάζω || (change state) μεταβάλλω || ~d a (price) μειωμένη (τιμή).

reduction [rɪ'dʌkʃən] n ελάττωση || (in size) σμίκρυνση || (in price) έκπτωση.

redundancy [rɪ'dʌndənsɪ] n περίσσευμα nt, πλεόνασμα nt.

redundant [rɪ'dʌndənt] a πλεονάζων, περιττός.

reed [riːd] n καλάμι || (of clarinet etc) γλωσσίδι.

reef [riːf] n (at sea) ύφαλος, ξέρα.

reek [riːk] vi αναδίδω κακή μυρωδιά, βρομάω.

reel [riːl] n (for rope) ανέμη || (for cotton, film etc) πηνίο, καρούλι, μασούρι || (dance) ζωηρός (σκωτικός) χορός ♦ vt τυλίγω || (stagger) τρικλίζω, ζαλίζομαι.

re-election [riːɪ'lɛkʃən] n επανεκλογή.

re-entry [riː'ɛntrɪ] n επάνοδος f, ξαναμπάσιμο.

re-examine ['riːɪg'zæmɪn] vt επανεξετάζω.

ref [rɛf] n (col: abbr of referee) διαιτητής.

refectory [rɪ'fɛktərɪ] n τραπεζαρία μοναστηριού ή κολλεγίου.

refer [rɪ'fɜː*] vt παραπέμπω || **to ~ to** vt αναφέρομαι σε || (consult) συμβουλεύομαι.

referee [rɛfə'riː] n διαιτητής || (for job application) υπέγγυος, εγγυητής ♦ vt (SPORT) διαιτητεύω.

reference ['rɛfrəns] n αναφορά || (in book etc) παραπομπή || (of character) πιστοποιητικό, σύσταση || (person referred to) αυτός που δίνει τη σύσταση, ο εγγυητής || (allusion) μνεία, υπαινιγμός || ~ **book** n βιβλίο οδηγός, σύμβουλος.

referendum [rɛfə'rɛndəm] n δημοψήφισμα nt.

refill [riː'fɪl] n (for pen etc) ανταλλακτικό.

refine [rɪ'faɪn] vt καθαρίζω, διυλίζω, ραφινάρω || (make finer) εκλεπτύνω, εξευγενίζω || ~**d** a (person) λεπτός, καλλιεργημένος || ~**ment** n εξευγενισμός, λεπτή διάκριση || ~**ry** n διϋλιστήριο.

reflect [rɪ'flɛkt] vt αντανακλώ ♦ vi (meditate) σκέπτομαι, συλλογίζομαι, μελετώ || ~**ion** n αντανάκλαση || (thought) σκέψη || ~**or** n ανακλαστήρας, καθρέπτης.

reflex ['riːflɛks] a (involuntary) αντανακλαστικός || ~**ive** a (GRAM) αυτοπαθής.

reform [rɪ'fɔːm] n μεταρρύθμιση, αποκατάσταση, ανασχηματισμός ♦ vt μεταρρυθμίζω, αποκαθιστώ, αναμορφώνω.

reformat [riː'fɔːmæt] vt (COMPUT) ανασχηματίζω.

refrain [rɪ'freɪn] vi (+ from) απέχω, συγκρατούμαι.

refresh [rɪ'frɛʃ] vt αναζωογονώ, δροσίζω, φρεσκάρω || ~**er course** n επανάληψη, μετεκπαίδευση ||

~**ing** a ευχάριστος, ζωογόνος, δροσιστικός || ~**ments** npl (food, drink) αναψυκτικά ntpl.

refrigerator [rɪ'frɪdʒəreɪtə*] n ψυγείο.

refuel ['riːfjuəl] vti ανεφοδιάζομαι (με καύσιμα).

refuge ['rɛfjuːdʒ] n καταφύγιο, καταφυγή, προστασία || **refugee** [rɛfju'dʒiː] n πρόσφυγας.

refund ['riːfʌnd] n επιστροφή χρημάτων, απόδοση ♦ [rɪ'fʌnd] vt επιστρέφω (χρήματα).

refurbish [riː'fɜːbɪʃ] vt (decorate) ανακαινίζω, φρεσκάρω.

refusal [rɪ'fjuːzəl] n άρνηση.

refuse ['rɛfjuːs] n απορρίμματα ntpl, σκουπίδια ntpl ♦ [rɪ'fjuːz] vti αρνούμαι, απορρίπτω.

refute [rɪ'fjuːt] vt ανασκευάζω, ανατρέπω.

regain [rɪ'geɪn] vt επανακτώ.

regal ['riːɡəl] a βασιλικός.

regard [rɪ'ɡɑːd] n (respect) εκτίμηση, σεβασμός ♦ vt (consider) θεωρώ || ~**s** npl (greetings) χαιρετισμοί mpl, χαιρετίσματα ntpl || ~**ing**, **as ~s** όσον αφορά, σχετικά με || **as ~s, with ~ to** ως προς, όσο για || ~**less** a (+ of) αδιάφορος, άσχετος ♦ ad αδιάφορα, αδιαφορώντας.

regatta [rɪ'ɡætə] n λεμβοδρομία.

régime [reɪ'ʒiːm] n καθεστώς nt.

regiment ['rɛdʒɪmənt] n σύνταγμα nt || ~**al** a του συντάγματος.

region ['riːdʒən] n περιοχή || ~**al** a τοπικός, περιφερειακός.

register ['rɛdʒɪstə*] n κατάλογος, ληξιαρχικό βιβλίο, μητρώο ♦ vt καταγράφω, εγγράφω || (write down) σημειώνω ♦ vi (at hotel) εγγράφομαι || (make impression) δείχνω || ~**ed** a (letter) συστημένο γράμμα.

registrar [redʒıs'trɑː*] n
ληξίαρχος, γραμματέας m/f.

registration [redʒıs'treıʃən] n (act)
καταγραφή, εγγραφή || (number)
αριθμός εγγραφής.

registry ['redʒıstrı] n ληξιαρχείο ||
~ **office** n (for civil marriage)
ληξιαρχείο.

regret [rı'gret] n λύπη, μετάνοια ♦
vt λυπούμαι, μετανοώ || ~**fully** ad
με λύπη, με πόνο || ~**table** a
δυσάρεστος, λυπηρός.

regular ['regjulə*] a τακτικός,
κανονικός, συνηθισμένος || (not
varying) ομαλός ♦ n (client etc)
τακτικός (πελάτης) || ~**ity** n
κανονικότητα, ομαλότητα.

regulate ['regjuleıt] vt κανονίζω,
τακτοποιώ, ρυθμίζω.

regulation [regju'leıʃən] n
κανονισμός || (control) ρύθμιση.

rehabilitation [ˈriːəbılıˈteıʃən] n
αποκατάσταση, παλινόρθωση.

rehash ['riː'hæʃ] vt (col)
ξαναδουλεύω, ανασκευάζω.

rehearsal [rı'hɜːsəl] n δοκιμή,
πρόβα.

rehearse [rı'hɜːs] vt (practise) κάνω
δοκιμές, κάνω πρόβα.

reign [reın] n (period) βασιλεία ♦ vi
βασιλεύω.

reimburse [riːım'bɜːs] vt
επιστρέφω (χρήματα), αποζημιώνω.

rein [reın] n ηνία ntpl, χαλινάρι.

reindeer ['reındıə*] n τάρανδος.

reinforce [riːın'fɔːs] vt ενισχύω,
δυναμώνω || ~**d concrete** n μπετό
αρμέ nt inv|| ~**ment** n ενίσχυση ||
~**ments** npl (MIL.) ενισχύσεις fpl.

reinstate [riːın'steıt] vt
επαναφέρω στη θέση του,
αποκαθιστώ, επανεγκαθιστώ.

reiterate [riː'ıtəreıt] vt
επαναλαμβάνω.

reject [rı'dʒekt] vt απορρίπτω,
αποκρούω ♦ ['riːdʒekt] n

απόρριμμα nt, σκάρτο || ~**ion** n
απόρριψη.

rejoice [rı'dʒɔıs] vi χαίρομαι, χαίρω.

relapse [rı'læps] n υποτροπή.

relate [rı'leıt] vt διηγούμαι,
εξιστορώ || (connect) συσχετίζω || ~**d**
a (subjects) σχετιζόμενος, σχετικά με
|| (people) (+ to) συγγενής.

relating [rı'leıtıŋ] prep: ~ **to**
σχετικός με, ότι αφορά.

relation [rı'leıʃən] n (of family)
συγγενής m/f|| (connection) σχέση,
συγγένεια || ~**ship** n συγγένεια,
σχέση.

relative ['relətıv] n συγγενής m/f ♦
a αναφορικός, σχετικός || ~**ly** ad
σχετικά || ~ **pronoun** n αναφορική
αντωνυμία.

relax [rı'læks] vi χαλαρώνω,
λασκάρω || (rest) ανακουφίζω ♦ vt
χαλαρούμαι, αναπαύομαι,
ξεκουράζομαι || ~**ation** n αναψυχή,
διασκέδαση || ~**ed** a χαλαρός,
λάσκος || ~**ing** a ξεκουραστικός.

relay ['riːleı] n (SPORT)
σκυταλοδρομία ♦ vt (message)
αναμεταδίδω.

release [rı'liːs] n (relief) απαλλαγή,
απόλυση || (from prison)
αποφυλάκιση || (device) διακόπτης ♦
vt απελευθερώνω || (prisoner)
απολύω, αποφυλακίζω || (grip)
χαλαρώνω, λασκάρω, απομπλέκω ||
(report, news) θέτω σε κυκλοφορία,
επιτρέπω δημοσίευση.

relegate ['relıgeıt] vt (put down)
υποβιβάζω.

relent [rı'lent] vi κάμπτομαι,
μαλακώνω || ~**less** a αδιάλλακτος,
αμείλικτος, ανελέητος.

relevant ['reləvənt] a σχετικός.

reliable [rı'laıəbl] a αξιόπιστος.

reliably [rı'laıəblı] ad
μ'εμπιστοσύνη, σίγουρα.

reliance [rı'laıəns] n εμπιστοσύνη,
πεποίθηση.

relic ['rɛlɪk] n απομεινάρι, ενθύμιο || (of saint) λείψανο.

relief [rɪ'liːf] n (from pain etc) ανακούφιση, ξελάφρωμα nt || (help) βοήθεια || (from duty) αντικατάσταση, αλλαγή || (design) ανάγλυφο || (distinctness) προβολή, ευδιακρισία.

relieve [rɪ'liːv] vt (pain etc) ανακουφίζω, ξαλαφρώνω || (bring help) βοηθώ, περιβάλλω || (take place of) αντικαθιστώ, απαλλάσσω || **to ~ of** παίρνω, απαλλάσσω.

religion [rɪ'lɪdʒən] n θρησκεία, θρήσκευμα nt.

religious [rɪ'lɪdʒəs] a θρησκευτικός || (pious) ευσεβής.

relinquish [rɪ'lɪŋkwɪʃ] vt παραιτούμαι, εγκαταλείπω.

relish ['rɛlɪʃ] n (sauce) καρύκευμα nt, σάλτσα ♦ vt απολαμβάνω, τρώγω ευχάριστα.

relive ['riː'lɪv] vt ξαναζώ.

reluctant [rɪ'lʌktənt] a απρόθυμος || **~ly** ad με το ζόρι, με το στανιό.

rely [rɪ'laɪ]: **to ~ on** vt βασίζομαι, στηρίζομαι, εμπιστεύομαι.

remain [rɪ'meɪn] vi (be left) απομένω || (stay) παραμένω, μένω || **~der** n υπόλοιπο || **~ing** a υπόλοιπος || **~s** npl υπολείμματα ntpl || (corpse) λείψανα ntpl.

remand [rɪ'mɑːnd] n: **on ~** παραπομπή (κατηγορουμένου) ♦ vt: **to ~ in custody** προφυλακίζω.

remark [rɪ'mɑːk] n παρατήρηση, σημείωση ♦ vt (say) λέγω || (notice) παρατηρώ || **~able** a αξιοσημείωτος || (unusual) ασυνήθιστος || **~ably** ad αξιόλογα, εξαιρετικά.

remarry ['riː'mærɪ] vi ξαναπαντρεύομαι.

remedial [rɪ'miːdɪəl] a θεραπευτικός.

remedy ['rɛmədɪ] n θεραπεία || (MED) φάρμακο, γιατρικό ♦ vt θεραπεύω, διορθώνω.

remember [rɪ'mɛmbə*] vt θυμούμαι || (give regards) δίνω χαιρετισμούς σε.

remembrance [rɪ'mɛmbrəns] n ανάμνηση, μνήμη.

remind [rɪ'maɪnd] vt υπενθυμίζω, θυμίζω || **~er** n κάτι που θυμίζει, ενθύμημα nt.

reminisce [rɛmɪ'nɪs] vi αναπολώ, ξαναθυμάμαι.

reminiscences [rɛmɪ'nɪsnsɪz] npl αναμνήσεις fpl, απομνημονεύματα ntpl.

reminiscent [rɛmɪ'nɪsnt] a (+ of) που θυμίζει κάτι.

remission [rɪ'mɪʃən] n (from sins) άφεση, ελάττωση || (release) χάρη, μείωση (ποινής).

remit [rɪ'mɪt] vt (send money) εμβάζω, μεταβιβάζω || **~tance** n έμβασμα nt (χρηματικό).

remnant ['rɛmnənt] n υπόλειμμα nt.

remorse [rɪ'mɔːs] n τύψη, μεταμέλεια || **~ful** a γεμάτος τύψεις, μετανοιωμένος || **~less** a άσπλαχνος, αμετανόητος.

remote [rɪ'məʊt] a μακρινός, απομονωμένος, απόμερος || (slight) αμυδρός, ελαφρός || (vague) αόριστος || **~ control** n τηλερρυθμιστής || **~ly** ad αόριστα, μακριά.

remould ['riː'məʊld] vt (tyre) ξαναφορμάρω.

removable [rɪ'muːvəbl] a μεταθέσιμος, κινητός, φορητός.

removal [rɪ'muːvəl] n αφαίρεση, βγάλσιμο || (from house) μετακόμιση, μετακίνηση || (from office) απόλυση, ανάκληση || **~ van** n φορτηγό μετακομίσεων.

remove [rɪ'muːv] vt αφαιρώ, βγάζω, μεταφέρω || (dismiss) απολύω, απομακρύνω || **~r** (for paint etc) εξαλειπτικό μέσο || **~rs** npl

(company) εταιρεία μεταφορών οικοσκευών.

remuneration [rɪmjuːnəˈreɪʃən] n αμοιβή, πληρωμή.

rend [rend] *(irreg v)* vt σχίζω, αποσπώ.

render [ˈrendə*] vt *(make)* καθιστώ, κάνω || *(translate)* μεταφράζω || ~ing n *(MUS)* ερμηνεία, απόδοση.

rendezvous [ˈrɒndɪvuː] n συνάντηση, ραντεβού nt inv.

renew [rɪˈnjuː] vt *(make new)* ανανεώνω || *(begin again)* ανασυνδέω, ξαναπιάνω || *(negotiations)* επαναλαμβάνω || ~al n ανανέωση, ανασύνδεση.

renounce [rɪˈnauns] vt *(give up)* εγκαταλείπω, αποκηρύσσω || *(disown)* αρνούμαι, αποποιούμαι.

renovate [ˈrenəuveɪt] vt ανακαινίζω || *(repair)* επισκευάζω.

renovation [rɛnəuˈveɪʃən] n ανακαίνιση || *(repair)* επισκευή.

renown [rɪˈnaun] n φήμη || ~ed a φημισμένος, ονομαστός.

rent [rent] n *(of dwelling)* ενοίκιο || *(hiring)* μίσθωμα, νοίκι ♦ vt ενοικιάζω || *(hire)* μισθώνω || *(AUT etc)* ενοικιάζω *(αυτοκίνητο)* || ~al n μίσθωμα, νοίκι.

renunciation [rɪnʌnsɪˈeɪʃən] n απάρνηση.

reorganize [riːˈɔːɡənaɪz] vt αναδιοργανώνω.

rep [rep] n *(COMM: abbr of representative)* αντιπρόσωπος || *(THEAT: abbr of repertory)* ρεπερτόριο.

repair [rɪˈpɛə*] n επισκευή, επιδιόρθωση || *(in good condition)* σε καλή κατάσταση ♦ vt επισκευάζω, επιδιορθώνω || ~ kit n σύνεργα ntpl επισκευή || ~man n επισκευαστής, κτλ.

repartee [rɛpɑːˈtiː] n ετοιμολογία, εύστοχη απάντηση.

repay [riːˈpeɪ] vt *(pay back)* ανταποδίδω || *(money)* ξεπληρώνω || ~ment n ανταπόδοση.

repeal [rɪˈpiːl] n ανάκληση, ακύρωση ♦ vt ανακαλώ, ακυρώνω.

repeat [rɪˈpiːt] n *(RAD, TV)* επανάληψη ♦ vt επαναλαμβάνω || ~edly ad επανειλημμένα, πολλές φορές.

repel [rɪˈpel] vt αποκρούω, απωθώ || ~lent a αποκρουστικός, απωθητικός ♦ n: insect ~lent n εντομοαπωθητικ ή λοσιόν f inv.

repent [rɪˈpent] vi μετανοιώνω, μεταμελούμαι || ~ance n μετάνοια, μεταμέλεια.

repercussion [riːpəˈkʌʃən] n *(effect)* αντίκτυπος, αντίκτυπος.

repertoire [ˈrepətwɑː*] n δραματολόγιο, ρεπερτόριο.

repertory [ˈrepətərɪ] n *(THEAT)* ρεπερτόριο.

repetition [repɪˈtɪʃən] n επανάληψη.

repetitive [rɪˈpetɪtɪv] a επαναληπτικός.

replace [rɪˈpleɪs] vt αντικαθιστώ || *(put back)* ξαναβάζω || ~ment n αντικατάσταση || *(person)* αντικαταστάτης.

replenish [rɪˈplenɪʃ] vt ξαναγεμίζω, συμπληρώνω.

replica [ˈreplɪkə] n πανομοιότυπο, αντίγραφο έργου τέχνης.

reply [rɪˈplaɪ] n απάντηση ♦ vi απαντώ, αποκρίνομαι.

report [rɪˈpɔːt] n *(account)* έκθεση, εξιστόρηση, αναφορά || *(bang)* κρότος, πυροβολισμός || vt αναφέρω || *(give account of)* εξιστορώ || *(news)* κάνω ρεπορτάζ ♦ vi *(make a report)* εκθέτω, αναφέρω, κάνω αναφορά || *(present o.s.)* παρουσιάζομαι || ~er n δημοσιογράφος.

reprehensible [reprɪˈhensɪbl] a αξιόμεμπτος.

represent [reprɪˈzent] vt (describe) παριστάνω, παρουσιάζω || (act) αντιπροσωπεύω || **~ation** n παράσταση, αναπαράσταση || (in parliament) αντιπροσώπευση, αντιπροσωπεία || **~ative** n αντιπρόσωπος ♦ a αντιπροσωπευτικός, παραστατικός.

repress [rɪˈpres] vt καταβάλλω, καταστέλλω, καταπνίγω || **~ion** n καταστολή, κατάπνιξη || **~ive** a κατασταλτικός, καταπιεστικός.

reprieve [rɪˈpriːv] n αναστολή (θανατικής ποινής), αναβολή ♦ vt αναστέλλω, ανακουφίζω.

reprimand [ˈreprɪmɑːnd] n επιτίμηση, επίπληξη ♦ vt επιτιμώ, επιπλήττω.

reprint [ˈriːprɪnt] n ανατύπωση ♦ [riːˈprɪnt] vt ανατυπώνω.

reprisal [rɪˈpraɪzl] n αντεκδίκηση, αντίποινο.

reproach [rɪˈprəʊtʃ] n επίπληξη, μομφή ♦ vt επιπλήττω, μέμφομαι, ψέγω.

reproduce [riːprəˈdjuːs] vt αναπαράγω || (make copy) ανατυπώνω ♦ vi αναπαράγομαι, πολλαπλασιάζομαι.

reproduction [riːprəˈdʌkʃən] n (copy) αναπαράσταση, αντίγραφο || (breeding) αναπαραγωγή.

reproductive [riːprəˈdʌktɪv] a αναπαραγωγικός.

reproving [rɪˈpruːvɪŋ] a επικριτικός, αποδοκιμαστικός.

reptile [ˈreptaɪl] n ερπετό.

republic [rɪˈpʌblɪk] n δημοκρατία || **~an** a δημοκρατικός || (party: US) ρεπουμπλικανικός ♦ n δημοκράτης || (US) ρεπουμπλικανός.

repudiate [rɪˈpjuːdɪeɪt] vt απαρνούμαι, αποκρούω, αποκηρύσσω.

repugnant [rɪˈpʌgnənt] a απεχθής, αηδιαστικός, σιχαμερός.

repulse [rɪˈpʌls] vt απωθώ, αποκρούω || (reject) αποκρούω, απορρίπτω.

repulsive [rɪˈpʌlsɪv] a αποκρουστικός, σιχαμερός.

reputable [ˈrepjʊtəbl] a έντιμος, αξιοπρεπής.

reputation [repjʊˈteɪʃən] n φήμη, υπόληψη || (good name) όνομα nt.

repute [rɪˈpjuːt] n εκτίμηση, υπόληψη || **~d** a φημισμένος, υποτιθέμενος || **~dly** ad κατά την κοινή γνώμη.

request [rɪˈkwest] n αίτηση, παράκληση || (demand) ζήτηση ♦ vt ζητώ, παρακαλώ.

requiem [ˈrekwɪem] n μνημόσυνο.

require [rɪˈkwaɪə*] vt ζητώ, απαιτώ || (oblige) χρειάζομαι || **~ment** n απαίτηση, ανάγκη.

requisite [ˈrekwɪzɪt] n απαιτούμενο πράγμα nt, προϋπόθεση ♦ a απαιτούμενος.

requisition [rekwɪˈzɪʃən] n επίταξη, απαίτηση ♦ vt απαιτώ, επιτάσσω.

reroute [ˈriːˈruːt] vt χαράσσω νέα πορεία, κάνω άλλο δρόμο.

resale [ˈriːˈseɪl] n μεταπώληση, ξαναπούλημα nt.

rescue [ˈreskjuː] n διάσωση, απολύτρωση ♦ vt (save) σώζω, λυτρώνω || **~r** n σωτήρας, λυτρωτής.

research [rɪˈsɜːtʃ] n έρευνα ♦ vi (+ into) κάνω έρευνα || vt ερευνώ || **~er** n ερευνητής.

resemblance [rɪˈzembləns] n ομοιότητα.

resemble [rɪˈzembl] vt μοιάζω.

resent [rɪˈzent] vt φέρω βαρέως, θίγομαι από || **~ful** a μνησίκακος, πειραγμένος || **~ment** n μνησικακία, έχθρα, πίκρα.

reservation [rezəˈveɪʃən] n

επιφύλαξη || (place) εξασφάλιση, κλείσιμο || (doubt) επιφύλαξη.
reserve [rɪ'zɜːv] n απόθεμα nt, αποθεματικό || (self-restraint) επιφύλαξη, συντηρητικότητα || (area of land) επιφυλασσόμενη περιοχή || (SPORT) εφεδρικός παίκτης ♦ vt (seats etc) κρατώ, αγκαζάρω, κλείνω || ~s npl (MIL) εφεδρείες fpl|| in ~ κατά μέρος, για ρεζέρβα || ~d a επιφυλακτικός, συγκρατημένος || '~d' (notice) 'κλεισμένος', 'κρατημένος'.
reservoir ['rezəvwɑː*] n δεξαμενή, ντεπόζιτο, ρεζερβουάρ nt inv|| (store) απόθεμα nt.
reshape ['riː'ʃeɪp] vt μεταπλάθω, τροποποιώ, ανασχηματίζω.
reshuffle ['riː'ʃʌfl] n (POL) ανασχηματισμός.
reside [rɪ'zaɪd] vi διαμένω, ανήκω || **residence** ['rezɪdəns] n κατοικία, σπίτι || (living) διαμονή, παραμονή || **resident** n κάτοικος ♦ a εγκατεστημένος || **residential** a της μόνιμου διαμονής, με ιδιωτικές κατοικίες.
residue ['rezɪdjuː] n υπόλοιπο, υπόλειμμα nt, κατάλοιπο.
resign [rɪ'zaɪn] vt παραιτούμαι || (submit) υποτάσσομαι, εγκαταλείπομαι || **resignation** [rezɪg'neɪʃən] n παραίτηση || (submission) υποταγή, υπομονή || ~**ed** a ανεκόμενος, υποτακτικός.
resilient [rɪ'zɪlɪənt] a ελαστικός.
resin ['rezɪn] n ρητίνη, ρετσίνη.
resist [rɪ'zɪst] vt αντιστέκομαι σε, αντιδρώ κατά || ~**ance** n αντίσταση.
resolute ['rezəluːt] a αποφασιστικός, σταθερός.
resolution [rezə'luːʃən] n αποφασιστικότητα || (decision) απόφαση.
resolve [rɪ'zɔlv] n απόφαση ♦ vt αναλύω, διαλύω, λύω ♦ vi

διαλύομαι, αναλύομαι || (decide) αποφασίζω || ~**d** a αποφασισμένος.
resonant ['rezənənt] a αντηχών, αντηχητικός.
resort [rɪ'zɔːt] n τόπος διαμονής, θέρετρο || (help) καταφυγή, μέσο, βοήθεια ♦ vi (+ to) προσφεύγω, καταφεύγω (σε) || **in the last ~** σαν τελευταία λύση.
resound [rɪ'zaund] vi αντηχώ, απηχώ || ~**ing** a απηχών, πηχηρός.
resource [rɪ'sɔːs] n καταφύγιο, μέσο, βοήθημα nt || ~**s** npl (of fuel) πλούτος (σε καύσιμα) || (of a country etc) οι πόροι mpl, πλούτος || ~**ful** a εφευρετικός.
respect [rɪs'pekt] n σεβασμός || (way) αναφορά ♦ vt σέβομαι || (treat with consideration) προσέχω || ~**s** npl (greetings) σέβη ntpl, χαιρετίσματα ntpl|| **with ~ to** όσον αφορά || **in ~ of** σχετικά με || **in this ~** ως προς αυτό το σημείο || ~**able** a έντιμος, ευυπόληπτος || (fairly good) υποφερτός, αρκετά καλός || ~**ed** a σεβαστός || ~**ful** a γεμάτος σεβασμό || ~**ive** a σχετικός, αμοιβαίος, αντίστοιχος || ~**ively** ad αντιστοίχως.
respiration [respɪ'reɪʃən] n αναπνοή.
respite ['respaɪt] n ανάπαυλα, διακοπή.
resplendent [rɪs'plendənt] a (bright) λαμπρός || (magnificent) μεγαλοπρεπής.
respond [rɪs'pɔnd] vi απαντώ, αποκρίνομαι || (act in answer) ανταποκρίνομαι, ανταποδίδω.
response [rɪs'pɔns] n απάντηση, ανταπόκριση.
responsibility [rɪspɔnsə'bɪlɪtɪ] n ευθύνη.
responsible [rɪs'pɔnsəbl] a υπεύθυνος, υπόλογος || (reliable) αξιόπιστος.

responsive [rɪs'pɒnsɪv] a ευαίσθητος, που ανταποκρίνεται.

rest [rest] n ανάπαυση, ξεκούραση || *(pause)* πτώση, ανάπαυλα || *(remainder)* υπόλοιπο ♦ vi αναπαύομαι, ξεκουράζομαι || *(be supported)* στηρίζομαι, ακουμπώ || *(remain)* στηρίζομαι, βασίζομαι || **the ~ of them** οι υπόλοιποι.

restaurant ['restarɔ:ŋ] n εστιατόριο || **~ car** n βαγκόν-ρεστωράν nt inv.

rest cure ['restkjʊə*] n θεραπεία αναπαύσεως.

restful ['restful] a ξεκούραστος, ήσυχος, αναπαυτικός.

rest home ['resthəʊm] n πρεβαντόριο, αναρρωτήριο.

restive ['restɪv] a ατίθασος, ανήσυχος.

restless ['restlɪs] a ανήσυχος, ασείκινητος, άυπνος || **~ly** ad ανήσυχα, νευρικά, ταραγμένα.

restore [rɪs'tɔ:*] vt επιστρέφω, αποκαθιστώ || *(repair)* επισκευάζω, αναστηλώνω.

restrain [rɪs'treɪn] vt ανακαιτίζω, συγκρατώ || **~ed** *(style etc)* ήρεμος, συγκρατημένος, μετρημένος || **~t** n περιορισμός, περιστολή || *(self-control)* συγκράτηση.

restrict [rɪs'trɪkt] vt περιορίζω || **~ed** a περιορισμένος || **~ion** n περιορισμός || **~ive** a περιοριστικός.

rest room ['restrʊm] n *(US)* αποχωρητήριο, τουαλέτα.

result [rɪ'zʌlt] n αποτέλεσμα nt, συνέπεια || *(of test)* αποτέλεσμα ntpl ♦ vi (+ in) καταλήγω, απολήγω.

resume [rɪ'zju:m] vt επαναρχίζω, ξαναρχίζω.

résumé ['reɪzju:meɪ] n περίληψη.

resumption [rɪ'zʌmpʃən] n (επ)ανάληψη, συνέχιση.

resurgence [rɪ'sɜ:dʒəns] n αναζωογόνηση, ανανέωση || *(uprising)* ξεσήκωμα nt.

resurrection [rezə'rekʃən] n ανάσταση, αναναβίωση.

resuscitate [rɪ'sʌsɪteɪt] vt αναστaίνω, επαναφέρω στη ζωή.

resuscitation [rɪsʌsɪ'teɪʃən] n αναζωογόνηση, ανάσταση.

retail ['ri:teɪl] n λιανική πώληση ♦ a λιανικός ♦ [ri:'teɪl] vt πουλάω λιανικά || **~er** n μεταπωλητής, λιανέμπορος || **~ price** n τιμή λιανικής πωλήσεως.

retain [rɪ'teɪn] vt διατηρώ, συγκρατώ, κρατώ || **~er** n υπηρέτης || *(fee)* προκαταβολή δικηγόρου.

retaliate [rɪ'tælɪeɪt] vi αντεκδικούμαι, ανταποδίδω.

retarded [rɪ'tɑ:dɪd] a καθυστερημένος.

retention [rɪ'tenʃən] n διατήρηση, συγκράτηση.

retentive [rɪ'tentɪv] a συνεκτικός, ισχυρός.

rethink [ri:'θɪŋk] vt ξανασκέπτομαι.

reticent ['retɪsənt] a λιγομίλητος, επιφυλακτικός.

retina ['retɪnə] n αμφιβληστροειδής (χιτών).

retinue ['retɪnju:] n ακολουθία, συνοδεία.

retire [rɪ'taɪə*] vi αποχωρώ, γίνομαι συνταξιούχος || *(withdraw, retreat)* υποχωρώ, αποσύρομαι || *(go to bed)* πάω για ύπνο || **~d** a *(person)* συνταξιούχος || **~ment** n αποχώρηση, συνταξιοδότηση.

retiring [rɪ'taɪərɪŋ] a επιφυλακτικός, ακοινώνητος || *(shy)* ντροπαλός.

retort [rɪ'tɔ:t] n *(reply)* οξεία απάντηση, έξυπνη απάντηση ♦ vi ανταναντώ, αποκρίνομαι.

retrace [ri:'treɪs] vt ανατρέχω, ξαναγυρίζω.

retract [rɪˈtrækt] vti ανακαλώ, παίρνω πίσω || ~**able** a (aerial) εισελκόμενος.

retread [ˈriːˈtred] vt (AUT: tyre) ανεπιστρώνω, ξαναφορράρω.

retreat [rɪˈtriːt] n υποχώρηση, οπισθοχώρηση || (escape) καταφύγιο ♦ vi υποχωρώ, οπισθοχωρώ.

retribution [retrɪˈbjuːʃən] n τιμωρία, ανταπόδοση, εκδίκηση.

retrieve [rɪˈtriːv] vt επανακτώ, αποδίδω || (rescue) επανορθώνω, σώζω || ~**r** n κυνηγετικός σκύλος, ριτρίβερ.

retrograde [ˈretrəʊɡreɪd] a (step, action) οπισθοδρομικός, παλινδρομικός.

retrospect [ˈretrəʊspekt] n: **in** ~ σε αναδρόμηση, όταν το σκέφτομαι || ~**ive** a (LAW) αναδρομικός.

return [rɪˈtɜːn] n επιστροφή, επάνοδος f, γύρισμα || (arrival) ερχομός || (profits) κέρδος, εισπράξεις fpl || (rail ticket etc) εισιτήριο μετ' επιστροφής || (journey) ταξίδι επιστροφής || (match) αγώνας ανταποδόσεως || ~**s** npl (report) έκθεση, δήλωση || (statistics) στατιστική ♦ vi επιστρέφω, γυρίζω, επανέρχομαι ♦ vt (give back) επιστρέφω, δίνω πίσω, γυρίζω || (pay back) επιστρέφω, πληρώνω || (elect) εκλέγω || ~**able** a (bottle etc) επιστρεφόμενος, επιστρεπτός || ~ **key** n (COMPUT) πλήκτρο επαναφοράς.

reunion [riːˈjuːnjən] n συνάντηση, συγκέντρωση.

reunite [ˈriːjuːˈnaɪt] vt ξανασμίγω, συναντώμαι.

rev [rev] n (AUT) στροφές fpl ♦ vti (also: ~ **up**) φουλάρω.

reveal [rɪˈviːl] vt αποκαλύπτω, φανερώνω || ~**ing** a αποκαλυπτικός.

reveille [rɪˈvælɪ] n εγερτήριο σάλπισμα nt.

revel [ˈrevl] vi (+ in) διασκεδάζω, γλεντώ.

revelation [revəˈleɪʃən] n αποκάλυψη.

reveller [ˈrevlə*] n γλεντζές m.

revelry [ˈrevlrɪ] n διασκέδαση, γλέντι.

revenge [rɪˈvendʒ] n εκδίκηση ♦ vt εκδικούμαι.

revenue [ˈrevənjuː] n πρόσοδος f, έσοδα ntpl, εισόδημα nt.

reverberate [rɪˈvɜːbəreɪt] vi αντηχώ, αντανακλώμαι.

revere [rɪˈvɪə*] vt σέβομαι, τιμώ || ~**nce** [ˈrevərəns] n σέβας nt, σεβασμός || **the R** ~ **nd Smith** ο αιδεσιμώτατος Σμιθ || ~**nt** a ευσεβής.

reversal [rɪˈvɜːsəl] n αντιστροφή, αναστροφή.

reverse [rɪˈvɜːs] n αντίστροφο || (defeat) ήττα || (misfortune) ατυχία || (AUT: gear) όπισθεν f inv ♦ a (order, direction) αντίθετος, αντίστροφος ♦ vt (put upside down) αναστρέφω || (change) αντιστρέφω ♦ vi βάζω την όπισθεν.

revert [rɪˈvɜːt] vi επανέρχομαι, επιστρέφω.

review [rɪˈvjuː] n επιθεώρηση || (of critic) κριτική (βιβλίου) || (magazine) επιθεώρηση, περιοδικό ♦ vt (look back on) ανασκοπώ, εξετάζω || (troops) επιθεωρώ || (a book) γράφω κριτική || ~**er** n (critic) κριτικογράφος, κριτικός.

revise [rɪˈvaɪz] vt αναθεωρώ, ξανακοιτάζω || (correct) διορθώνω.

revision [rɪˈvɪʒən] n αναθεώρηση || (correct) επανεξέταση.

revitalize [riːˈvaɪtəlaɪz] vt αναζωογονώ.

revival [rɪˈvaɪvəl] n αναγέννηση || (of play) επανάληψη.

revive [rɪ'vaɪv] vt αναζωογονώ, ανασταίνω, ξαναζωντανεύω ♦ vi αναζωογονούμαι, ξαναζωντανεύω, αναζωπυρούμαι.

revoke [rɪ'vəʊk] vt ανακαλώ, ακυρώνω.

revolt [rɪ'vəʊlt] n στάση, επανάσταση ♦ vi επαναστατώ || ~**ing** a αηδιαστικός, σκανδαλώδης.

revolution [revə'luːʃən] n (of wheel) περιστροφή || (change, POL) επανάσταση || ~**ary** a επαναστατικός, ανατρεπτικός ♦ n επανάσταση || ~**ize** vt αλλάζω οριστικά.

revolve [rɪ'vɒlv] vi περιστρέφομαι.

revolver [rɪ'vɒlvə*] n περίστροφο.

revue [rɪ'vjuː] n επιθεώρηση (θεατρική).

revulsion [rɪ'vʌlʃən] n μεταστροφή.

reward [rɪ'wɔːd] n (αντ)αμοιβή ♦ vt ανταμείβω || ~**ing** a ανταμειπτικός || (fig) που αξίζει τον κόπο.

rewind [riː'waɪnd] vt ξανατυλίγω, ξανακουρδίζω.

rewire [riː'waɪə*] vt (house) αλλάζω τα σύρματα (σπιτιού).

reword [riː'wɜːd] vt ανασυντάσσω, ξαναγράφω με άλλες λέξεις.

rewrite [riː'raɪt] vt ξαναγράφω.

rhapsody ['ræpsədɪ] n ραψωδία.

rhetoric ['retərɪk] n ρητορική, ρητορία || ~**al** a ρητορικός.

rheumatic [ruː'mætɪk] a ρευματικός.

rheumatism ['ruːmətɪzəm] n ρευματισμός.

rhinoceros [raɪ'nɒsərəs] n ρινόκερως m.

rhododendron [rəʊdə'dendrən] n ροδόδεντρο.

rhubarb ['ruːbɑːb] n ραβέντι, ρουμπάρμπαρο.

rhyme [raɪm] n ομοιοκαταληξία, ρίμα.

rhythm ['rɪðəm] n ρυθμός, μέτρο || ~**ic(al)** a ρυθμικός || ~**ically** ad ρυθμικά, με ρυθμό.

rib [rɪb] n πλευρά, πλευρό ♦ vt (mock) εμπαίζω, κοροϊδεύω.

ribald ['rɪbəld] a αισχρός, πρόστυχος, σόκιν.

ribbed [rɪbd] a ραβδωτός, με νευρώσεις.

ribbon ['rɪbən] n ταινία, κορδέλα.

rice [raɪs] n ρύζι || ~ **pudding** n ρυζόγαλο.

rich [rɪtʃ] a πλούσιος || (fertile) εύφορος, πλούσιος, γόνιμος || (splendid) πολυτελής, λαμπρός, υπέροχος || (of food) πλούσιο, από εκλεκτά συστατικά || **the** ~ οι πλούσιοι || ~**es** npl πλούτη ntpl, αφθονία || ~**ly** a πλούσια || ~**ness** n πλούτος || (abundance) αφθονία.

rickety ['rɪkɪtɪ] a (unsteady) που τρέμει, σαθρός, σαραβαλιασμένος.

rickshaw ['rɪkʃɔː] n δίτροχη άμαξα συρόμενη από άνθρωπο.

ricochet ['rɪkəʃeɪ] n εποστρακισμός ♦ vi εποστρακίζω, αναπηδώ.

rid [rɪd] (irreg v) vt απαλλάσσω, ελευθερώνω || **to get** ~ **of** απαλλάσσομαι από || **good riddance!** καλά ξεκουμπίστε!· ας πάει στο καλό!

riddle ['rɪdl] n (puzzle) αίνιγμα nt ♦ vt (esp passive) κάνω κόσκινο.

ride [raɪd] (irreg v) n διαδρομή, περίπατος, ταξίδι ♦ vt τρέχω, διασκίζω || (horse, bicycle) καβαλικεύω ♦ vi πάω καβάλα, καβαλικεύω, πηγαίνω με αμάξι || (NAUT) είμαι αγκυροβολημένος || ~**r** ιππέας, καβαλάρης || (in contract etc) προσθήκη, παράρτημα nt, συμπληρωματική διάταξη.

ridge [rɪdʒ] n (hill) κορυφογραμμή, ράχη || (of roof) κολοφώνας,

καβελαριά, κορφιάς || (narrow raised strip) πτυχή, ζάρα, προεξοχή.

ridicule ['ridikju:l] n περίγελος, εμπαιγμός, κοροϊδία ♦ vt κοροϊδεύω, γελοποιώ.

ridiculous [ri'dikjuləs] a γελοίος.

riding ['raidiŋ] n: to go ~ πηγαίνω ιππασία || ~ **school** n σχολή ιππασίας.

rife [raif] a: ~ **with** μεστός, γεμάτος από.

riffraff ['rifræf] n αλητεία, σκυλολόι.

rifle ['raifl] n όπλο, τουφέκι ♦ vt (rob) αδειάζω, διαρπάζω || ~ **range** n πεδίο βολής, σκοπευτήριο.

rift [rift] n σχισμή, ρωγμή.

rig [rig] n (outfit) φορεσιά, στόλισμα nt || (oil rig) γεωτρύπανο ♦ vt (election etc) νοθεύω τις εκλογές || ~**ging** n ξάρτια ntpl || to ~ **out** vt ντύνω, στολίζω || to ~ **up** vt στήνω, μαντάρω.

right [rait] a (correct, proper) ορθός, σωστός, κανονικός || (just, good) ευθύς, δίκαιος, έντιμος || (on right side) στα δεξιά ♦ n (what is just or true) το δίκαιο, η δικαιοσύνη || (title, claim) δικαίωμα nt, προνόμιο || (not left) δεξιά (πλευρά), το δεξιό || (POL) n Δεξιά ♦ ad (straight) κατευθείαν, ίσια || (completely, thoroughly) ακριβώς, κατευθείαν, τελείως ♦ vt ανορθώνω, ισορροπώ, ξαναφέρνω στα ίσια ♦ excl σωστά!, σύμφωνοι!, έχεις δίκιο! || to be ~ έχω δίκαιο || all ~! εντάξει! || ~ **now** αμέσως || by ~s στα νομικά, νομίμως || on the ~ στα δεξιά || ~ **angle** n ορθή γωνία || ~**eous** a ευθύς, ηθικός || ~**eousness** n ορθότητα, τιμιότητα || ~**ful** a νόμιμος, δίκαιος || ~-**hand drive** n με δεξιό τιμόνι || ~-**handed** a δεξιόχειρας, δεξιόστροφος || ~-**hand man** n το δεξί χέρι || ~-**hand side** n τα δεξιά || ~**ly** ad δίκαια,

ορθά || ~-**minded** a λογικός, ορθοφρονών || ~ **of way** n n προτεραιότητα || ~-**winger** n δεξιός.

rigid ['ridʒid] a άκαμπτος, αλύγιστος || (strict) αυστηρός || ~**ity** n ακαμψία, αλυγισία || ~**ly** ad άκαμπτα, αλύγιστα, αυστηρά.

rigmarole ['rigmərəul] n ασυναρτησίες fpl, κουραφέξαλα ntpl.

rigor ['rigə*] n (US) = **rigour.**

rigorous ['rigərəs] a αυστηρός, τραχύς.

rigour ['rigə*] n αυστηρότητα, δριμύτητα.

rim [rim] n στεφάνη, χείλος nt || (of wheel) στεφάνη, ζάντα || ~**less** a χωρίς σκελετό, χωρίς γείσο || ~**med** a με στεφάνη, με σκελετό.

rind [raind] n φλοιός, φλούδα.

ring [riŋ] n (irreg v) n δακτύλιος, δακτυλίδι || (of people) συντροφιά, φατρία, συμμορία || (arena) παλαίστρα, στίβος, πίστα, αρένα || (of bell) ρίγκ nt inv || (TEL) τηλεφώνημα nt, κτύπημα nt τηλεφώνου ♦ vi κτυπώ το κουδούνι ♦ vi (TEL) (also: ~ up) τηλεφωνώ || (resound) αντηχώ, κτυπώ || (bell) κουδουνίζω || to ~ **off** vi διακόπτω τη συνομιλία, κλείνω το τηλέφωνο || ~**leader** n (of gang) αρχηγός συμμορίας.

ringlets ['riŋlits] npl (hair) μπούκλες fpl.

ring road n (Brit) η περιφερειακή οδός ƒ.

rink [riŋk] n πίστα πατινάζ.

rinse [rins] n ξέπλυμα nt ♦ vt ξεπλένω, ξεβγάζω.

riot ['raiət] n στάση, οχλαγωγία ♦ vi οχλαγωγώ, θορυβώ || ~**ous** a ταραχώδης, οχλαγωγικός, οργιαστικός.

rip [rip] n σχισμή, σχίσιμο ♦ vti σχίζω, ξεσχίζω.

ripcord ['rɪpkɔːd] n σχοινί ανοίγματος.

ripe [raɪp] a ώριμος, γινομένος || **~n** vti ωριμάζω, γίνομαι || **~ness** n ωριμότητα.

ripple ['rɪpl] n κυματισμός, ρυτίδα ♦ vti κυματίζω, ρυτιδώνω.

rise [raɪz] (irreg v) n ύψωμα nt, ανήφορος, κλίση || (esp in wages) αύξηση, άνοδος f ♦ vi (from chair) σηκώνομαι όρθιος || (from bed) ξυπνώ, σηκώνομαι || (sun) ανατέλλω, βγαίνω || (smoke, prices) υψώνομαι, ανεβαίνω || (mountain) υψώνομαι || (ground) ανηφορίζω, υψώνομαι || (revolt) εξεγείρομαι, ξεσηκώνομαι, επαναστατώ || **to give ~ to** προκαλώ || **to ~ to the occasion** φαίνομαι αντάξιος των περιστάσεων.

risk [rɪsk] n κίνδυνος, ριψοκινδύνευση ♦ vt ριψοκινδυνεύω || **~y** a επικίνδυνος, ριψοκίνδυνος.

risqué ['riːskeɪ] a τολμηρό.

rissole ['rɪsəʊl] n κεφτές m, κροκέτα.

rite [raɪt] n ιεροτελεστία, εκκλησιαστική τελετή.

ritual ['rɪtjʊəl] n τυπικό, λειτουργικό ♦ a τυπικός, καθιερωμένος.

rival ['raɪvəl] n a αντίπαλος, αντίζηλος, ανταγωνιστής ♦ vt ανταγωνίζομαι, συναγωνίζομαι || **~ry** n ανταγωνισμός, συναγωνισμός.

river ['rɪvə*] n ποταμός, ποτάμι || **~bank** n όχθη (ποταμού) || **~bed** n κοίτη ποταμού || **~side** n όχθη ♦ a της όχθης.

rivet ['rɪvɪt] n καζανόκαρφο, καρφί ♦ vt καθηλώνω, καρφώνω || (fix) προσηλώνω, καρφώνω.

Riviera [rɪvɪ'eərə] n: **the ~** n Ριβιέρα.

R.N. abbr of Royal Navy.

road [rəʊd] n οδός f, δρόμος || **~block** n οδόφραγμα nt || **~hog** n κακός οδηγός || **~map** n οδικός χάρτης || **~side** a dκρη του δρόμου, δίπλα στο δρόμο ♦ a στο δρόμο, του δρόμου || **~sign** n πινακίδα δρόμου || **~way** n αμαξητή οδός || **~worthy** a κατάλληλος για κυκλοφορία.

roam [rəʊm] vi περιπλανώμαι, περιφέρομαι ♦ vt διασχίζω, διατρέχω, τριγυρίζω.

roar [rɔː*] n βρυχηθμός, μουγγρητό ♦ vi βρυχώμαι, ωρύομαι || **~ing** a (fire) γερή (φωτιά), δυνατή (φωτιά) || (trade) ακμάζον (εμπόριο), καλές (δουλειές).

roast [rəʊst] n ψητό κρέας nt, ψητό ♦ vt ψήνω || (coffee beans) καβουρντίζω.

rob [rɒb] vt κλέβω, ληστεύω, αποστερώ || **~ber** n ληστής, κλέφτης || **~bery** n ληστεία.

robe [rəʊb] n ρόμπα, φόρεμα nt || (of office) στολή, τήβεννος ♦ vt περιβάλλω, ντύνω.

robin ['rɒbɪn] n κοκκινολαίμης, κομπογιάννης.

robot ['rəʊbɒt] n αυτόματο, ρομπότ nt inv.

robust [rəʊ'bʌst] a εύρωστος, ρωμαλέος.

rock [rɒk] n βράχος || (GEOL) πέτρωμα nt || (candy) είδος καραμέλας ♦ vti λικνίζω, κουνώ, κουνιέμαι || **on the ~s** (drink) με πάγο, χωρίς νερό || (ship) πέφτω στα βράχια || (marriage etc) υπό διάλυση, σε δύσκολη θέση || **~bottom** n (fig) κατώτερο σημείο || **~ climber** n ορειβάτης βράχων || **~ery** n τεχνητοί βράχοι mpl.

rocket ['rɒkɪt] n ρουκέτα, πύραυλος, βολίδα.

rock fall ['rɒkfɔːl] n πτώση βράχων.

rocking chair ['rɒkɪŋtʃeə*] n κουνιστή πολυθρόνα.

rocking horse ['rɒkɪŋhɔːs] n αλογάκι (παιδικό).

rocky ['rɒkɪ] a βραχώδης.

rod [rɒd] n (bar) ράβδος f, βέργα.

rode [rəud] pt of **ride**.

rodent ['rəudənt] n τρωκτικό.

rodeo ['rəudɪəu] n διαγωνισμός (καουμπόιδων).

roe [rəu] n (deer) δορκάδα, ζαρκάδι || (of fish) αυγά ntpl ψαριών.

rogue [rəug] n παλιάνθρωπος || (mischievous) κατεργάρης, πειρακτήριο, πονηρός.

roguish ['rəugɪʃ] a (playful) κατεργάρικος, τσαχπίνικος || (cheating) δόλιος, πανούργος.

role [rəul] n ρόλος.

roll [rəul] n (paper, meat etc) κύλινδρος, ρολό, τόπι || (bread) φρατζολάκι, κουλουράκι || (list) κατάλογος, λίστα || (of drum) συνεχής τυμπανοκρουσία ♦ vt (over) περιστρέφω, κυλώ || (wind round) τυλίγω, κάνω ρολό || (smooth out) ισοπεδώνω, πατώ, στρώνω ♦ vi (swing) στριφογυρίζω, κουνώ || (make deep sound) ηχώ, βροντώ || **to ~ by** vi (time) περνώ γρήγορα || **to ~ in** vi (mail) φθάνω σε μεγάλες ποσότητες || **to ~ over** vi ανατρέπομαι, κυλιέμαι || **to ~ up** vi (arrive) φθάνω, κουβαλιέμαι ♦ vt (carpet) τυλίγω || **~ call** n ονομαστική κλήση, προσκλητήριο || **~ed** a (umbrella) τυλιγμένος || **~er** n κύλινδρος, τροχός|| **~er skates** npl πατίνια ntpl με ρόδες.

rolling ['rəulɪŋ] a (landscape) ανώμαλο έδαφος || **~ pin** n πλάστης (για άνοιγμα φύλλου) || **~ stock** n τροχαίο υλικό.

roly-poly ['rəulɪ'pəulɪ] n (pudding) πουτίγγα ρολό με φρούτα.

ROM abbr of read only memory μνήμη ROM, μνήμη που μόνο διαβάζεται.

Roman ['rəumən] n ρωμαϊκός ♦ n Ρωμαίος || **~ Catholic** a, n ρωμαιοκαθολικός.

romance [rəu'mæns] n ρομάντζο || (story) ρομαντική ιστορία ♦ vi υπερβάλλω, φαντασιολογώ.

Romanesque [rəumə'nesk] a ρωμανικός (ρυθμός).

romantic [rəu'mæntɪk] a ρομαντικός.

romp [rɒmp] n εύθυμο παιχνίδι, φασαρία ♦ vi (also: **~ about**) θορυβώ, κάνω φασαρία, στακτό || **~ers** npl μπλούζα, ποδιά παιδιών, φόρμα.

rondo ['rɒndəu] n (MUS) ροντό nt inv, ρόντο nt inv.

roof [ruːf] n στέγη, σκεπή || (of car etc) σκεπή || (of mouth) ουρανίσκος ♦ vt στεγάζω, σκεπάζω || **~ garden** n κήπος σε ταράτσα || **~ing** n στέγαση, ταβάνωμα.

rook [ruk] n (bird) κορώνη, κουρούνα, χαβαρόνι || (thief) κλέφτης, λωποδύτης ♦ vt (cheat) κλέβω.

room [rum] n (in house) δωμάτιο, κάμαρα || (space) χώρος, τόπος || (opportunity) περιθώριο || **~s** npl (flat) δωμάτια ntpl, διαμέρισμα nt || (lodgings) δωμάτια ntpl με φαγητό || **~iness** n ευρυχωρία || **~ing house** n οικία ενοικιαζόμενα επιπλωμένα δωμάτια || **~mate** n συγκάτοικος || **~ service** n υπηρεσία || **~y** a ευρύχωρος.

roost [ruːst] n κούρνια, κοτέτσι ♦ vi κουρνιάζω.

root [ruːt] n ρίζα || (source) πηγή, αιτία, ρίζα ♦ vt ριζώνω || **to ~ about** vi (fig) ψάχνω || **to ~ for** vt

rope [rəup] n σχοινί ♦ vt δένω με σχοινί || to ~ in vt περικλείω, προσπλυτίζω, παρασύρω || **to know the ~s** ξέρω τη δουλειά μου, είμαι μπασμένος || ~ **ladder** n ανεμόσκαλα.

rosary ['rəuzəri] n κομβολόι.

rose [rəuz] pt of **rise** || (flower) n τριανταφυλλιά, ρόδο ♦ a ροδόχρους, ρόζ.

rosé ['rəuzei] n (wine) κοκκινέλι.

rosebed ['rəuzbed] n ρωδωνιά, βραγιά με τριανταφυλλιές.

rosebud ['rəuzbʌd] n μπουμπούκι τριανταφύλλου.

rosebush ['rəuzbuʃ] n τριανταφυλλιά.

rosemary ['rəuzməri] n δενδρολίβανο.

rosette [rəu'zet] n ροζέττα.

roster ['rɒstə*] n κατάλογος, κατάσταση.

rostrum ['rɒstrəm] n άμβωνας, βήμα nt.

rosy ['rəuzi] a (colour) ροδόχρους, ρόδινος, ρόζ || (hopeful) ρόδινα.

rot [rɒt] n σήψη, σαπίλα, σάπισμα nt || (nonsense) ανονσία, μπούρδα ♦ vti αποσυντίθεμαι, σαπίζω.

rota ['rəutə] n κατάλογος, πίνακας.

rotary ['rəutəri] a περιστροφικός.

rotate [rəu'teit] vt (two or more things in order) εναλλάσσω, εκτελώ εκ περιτροπής ♦ vi περιστρέφομαι, γυρίζω (γύρω από).

rotating [rəu'teitiŋ] a περιστρεφόμενος, περιστροφικός.

rotation [rəu'teiʃən] n περιστροφή.

rotor ['rəutə*] n στροφείο, ρώτωρ m. inv, ρότορ m inv.

rotten ['rɒtn] a (smell) σάπιος, σάπιος, σαπισμένος || (dishonest) πρόστυχος, κακής ποιότητας.

rotund [rəu'tʌnd] a στρογγυλός, παχουλός.

rouble ['ru:bl] n ρούβλι.

rouge [ru:ʒ] n κοκκινάδι, βαφή.

rough [rʌf] a (uneven) ανώμαλος, τραχύς || (violent, coarse) χονδροειδής, πρόστυχος, τραχύς, απότομος || (stormy, wild) άγριος, σφοδρός, τρικυμιώδης || (without comforts) πρόχειρος, στοιχειώδης || (unfinished drawing) πρόχειρο, του προσχέδιο || (stones) ακατέργαστος || (makeshift) βιαστικός, πρόχειρος || (approximate) κατά προσέγγιση || n (uncut grass) ψηλό χορτάρι || (violent person) μάγκας, κουτσαβάκης ♦ vt: to ~ **it** στερούμαι τις ανέσεις, αντιμετωπίζω δυσκολίες || **to play ~** παίζω σκληρό παιχνίδι || **to ~ out** vt (draft) προσχεδιάζω, κάνω πρόχειρα || ~**en** vt τραχύνω || ~**ly** ad δυνατά || (draft) πρόχειρα || ~**ness** n τραχύτητα, σκληρότητα.

roulette [ru:'let] n ρουλέτα.

Roumania [ru:'meiniə] n Ρουμανία || ~**n** n (person) Ρουμάνος/α m/f ♦ a ρουμανικός.

round [raund] a στρογγυλός, σφαιρικός, κυκλικός || (rough) στρογγυλός ♦ ad γύρω, τριγύρω ♦ prep γύρω από, περί ♦ n κύκλος, γύρος || (duty) γύρος, βόλτα, περιοδεία, καθημερινή δουλειά || (SPORT) γύρος ♦ vt (corner) κάμπτω, στρίβω, κάνω στροφή, παίρνω τη στροφή || **to ~ off** vt στρογγυλεύω, τελειώνω || **to ~ up** vt συγκεντρώνω, μαζεύω, πιάνω, περικυκλώνω || ~ **of ammunition** n φυσίγγι || ~ **of applause** n ομοβροντία χειροκροτημάτων || ~ **of drinks** n ένας γύρος ποτών || ~**about** n ένας κυκλικός διασταύρωση δρόμων || (merry-go-round) περιστρεφόμενα ξύλινα αλογάκια

ntpl ♦ η κυκλικός, περιφερειακός ||
~**ed** a στρογγυλεμένος || ~**ly** *ad*
(*fig*) τέλεια, ολοσχερώς, πλήρως ||
~-**shouldered** a με κυρτούς ώμους,
σκυφτός || ~**up** η περιμάζεμα *nt.*

rouse [rauz] *vt* σηκώνω || (*stir up*)
προκαλώ, διεγείρω, ξεσηκώνω.

rousing ['rauziŋ] a (*welcome*)
θορυβώδης, ζωηρός.

rout [raut] *n* φυγή, άτακτη φυγή ♦ *vt*
κατατροπώνω, τρέπω σε φυγή.

route [ruːt] *n* δρομολόγιο, δρόμος,
πορεία || ~ **map** *n* οδικός χάρτης.

routine [ruː'tiːn] *n* ρουτίνα,
στερεότυπη πορεία ♦ a κανονικός,
τακτικός.

roving ['rəʊviŋ] a περιφερόμενος,
περιπλανώμενος.

row [rəʊ] *n* (*line*) σειρά, στοίχος,
γραμμή, αράδα ♦ *vi* (*boat*) κινώ με
κουπί, μεταφέρω με τα κουπιά ♦ *vi*
(*in boat*) κωπηλατώ, τραβώ κουπί ♦
[rəʊ] *n* (*noise*) θόρυβος, φασαρία,
σαματάς || (*dispute*) φιλονεικία,
καυγάς, σκηνή || (*scolding*) επίπληξη,
κατσάδα, λούσιμο ♦ *vi* φιλονεικώ,
καυγαδίζω, αρπάζομαι.

rowdy ['raudɪ] a θορυβώδης, που
κάνει σαματά ♦ *n* (*person*)
θορυβοποιός, καυγατζής.

rowing ['rəʊiŋ] *n* κωπηλασία, κουπί
|| ~ **boat** *n* βάρκα με κουπιά.

rowlock ['rɒlək] *n* σκαλμός.

royal ['rɔɪəl] a βασιλικός || ~**ist** *n*
βασιλόφρων *m*, βασιλικός ♦ a
βασιλικός.

royalty ['rɔɪəltɪ] *n* (*royal family*)
βασιλική οικογένεια || (*payment: to
inventor*) δικαιώματα *ntpl* εφευρέτου
|| (*: to author*) συγγραφικά
δικαιώματα *ntpl*.

r.p.m. *abbr* (= *revs per minute*)
στρ./λεπ., σ.α.λ. (στροφές ανά
λεπτό).

R.S.V.P. *abbr* (= *répondez s'il vous
plaît*) R.S.V.P.

Rt. Hon. *abbr* (= *Right Honourable*)
Εντιμότατος.

rub [rʌb] *n* (*polish, with cloth*) τρίψιμο,
σφουγγάρισμα *nt* ♦ *vt* τρίβω,
επαλείφω, προστρίβω || (*clean*)
στεγνώνω, σκουπίζω || **to** ~ **off** *vi*
τρίβω, σβήνω.

rubber ['rʌbə*] *n* (*substance*)
καουτσούκ *nt inv*|| (*Brit*)
γομμολάστιχα || ~ **band** *n* λάστιχο ||
~ **plant** *n* φυτό δέντρο καουτσούκ
|| ~ **stamp** *n* (*lit*) σφραγίδα || (*fig*) ο
εγκρίνων τυφλά.

rubbish ['rʌbɪʃ] *n* σκουπίδια *ntpl*,
απορρίμματα *ntpl*|| (*nonsense*)
ανοησίες *fpl*, κολοκύθια *ntpl*|| ~
dump *n* τόπος απορρίψεως
σκουπιδιών || ~**y** a άχρηστος, της
πεντάρας.

rubble ['rʌbl] *n* χαλίκι, σκύρο.

ruble ['ruːbl] *n* (*US*) = **rouble**.

ruby ['ruːbɪ] *n* ρουμπίνι ♦ a κόκκινο,
ρουμπινί.

rucksack ['rʌksæk] *n* σακκίδιο.

rudder ['rʌdə*] *n* πηδάλιο, τιμόνι.

ruddy ['rʌdɪ] a (*colour*)
ροδοκόκκινος, ερυθρωπός || (*col:
bloody*) τρομερός.

rude [ruːd] a (*vulgar*) πρόστυχος ||
(*impolite*) βάναυσος, απολίτιστος,
αγενής || (*rough*) τραχύς,
πρωτόγονος || ~**ly** *ad* πρωτόγονα,
απότομα || ~**ness** *n* χοντροκοπιά,
αγένεια.

rudiment ['ruːdɪmənt] *n* στοιχείο,
υποτυπώδης αρχή || ~**ary** a
στοιχειώδης.

ruff [rʌf] *n* τραχηλιά.

ruffian ['rʌfiən] *n* παλιάνθρωπος,
κακούργος.

ruffle ['rʌfl] *vt* ρυτιδώνω,
τσαλακώνω, ανακατεύω.

rug [rʌg] *n* τάπης, χαλί|| (*for knees*)
κουβέρτα, χράμι.

rugby ['rʌgbɪ] *n* ράγκμπυ *nt inv*.

rugged ['rʌgɪd] a τραχύς || (surface) ανώμαλος.

rugger ['rʌgə*] n ράγκμπι nt inv.

ruin ['ruːɪn] n καταστροφή, συμφορά, αφανισμός ♦ vt καταστρέφω, αφανίζω || ~s npl ερείπια ntpl || ~ation n καταστροφή, όλεθρος, ρήμαγμα nt.

rule [ruːl] n (guide) κανόνας || (what is usual) συνήθεια, το κανονικό || (government) εξουσία, αρχή, κυριαρχία || (stick) κανόνας ♦ vt κυβερνώ, διοικώ || (pervade) διέπω || (lines) χαρακώνω || **as a ~** κατά κανόνα, συνήθως || ~**d** a (paper) ριγωτός, χαρακωμένος || ~**r** n κυβερνήτης, άρχοντας || (straight edge) χάρακας, ρίγα, μέτρο.

ruling ['ruːlɪŋ] a (party) άρχοντας, διευθύνων, κυβερνών || (class) άρχουσα (τάξη).

rum [rʌm] n ρούμι ♦ a (col) παράξενος, αλλόκοτος.

rumble ['rʌmbl] n υπόκωφος βοή, βροντή ♦ vi βροντώ, βουίζω, γουργουρίζω.

rummage ['rʌmɪdʒ] n έρευνα, ψάξιμο ♦ vt ερευνώ, ψάχνω.

rumour, rumor (US) ['ruːmə*] n φήμη, διάδοση ♦ vt: **it is ~ed that** λέγεται ότι, διαδίδεται ότι, φημολογείται ότι.

rump [rʌmp] n γλουτός, οπίσθια μέρη || ~**steak** n κόντρα φιλέτο.

rumpus ['rʌmpəs] n θόρυβος, ταραχή || (col) καυγάς, σαματάς.

run [rʌn] (irreg v) n (running) δρόμος, τρέξιμο || (AUT) διαδρομή, βόλτα || (series) σειρά, συνέχεια || (sudden demand) ζήτηση || (enclosed space) χώρος κλειστός || (ski run) πίστα του σκί, κατάβαση για σκι ♦ vt (cause to run) κατευθύνω, λειτουργώ || (train, bus) κυκλοφορώ, κάνω διαδρομή || (manage) διευθύνω || (compete in race) τρέχω σε αγώνα || (stand for election)

βάζω υποψηφιότητα || (force) περνώ || (pass: hand, eye) περνώ || (COMPUT: program) τρέχω ♦ vi (move quickly) τρέχω, το βάζω στα πόδια || (in election) θέτω υποψηφιότητα || (in race) τρέχω σε αγώνες || (machine) λειτουργώ || (flow) ρέω, κυλώ, τρέχω || (colours) ξεβάφω, βγαίνω, τρέχω || **on the ~** σε φυγή || **to ~ riot** οργιάζω || **to ~ a risk** ριψοκινδυνεύω || **to ~ about** vi (children) τρέχω εδώ και κει || **to ~ across** vt (find) συναντώ τυχαία || **to ~ away** vi δραπετεύω || **to ~ down** vi (clock) ξεκουρδίζω ♦ vt (run over) κτυπώ, πατώ (κάποιον), πλακώνω || (talk against) δυσφημώ, κατηγορώ || **to be ~-down** είμαι εξαντλημένος, είμαι τσακισμένος || **to ~ off** vi φεύγω, τρέπομαι σε φυγή || **to σκάω** || **to ~ out** vi (person) βγαίνω τρέχοντας || (liquid) χύνομαι, τρέχω, στάζω || (lease) λήγω || (money) τελειώνω, εξαντλούμαι || **to ~ out of** vt εξαντλώ, τελειώνω, μένω από || **to ~ over** vt κτυπώ, πλακώνω, πατώ || (read) ρίχνω μια ματιά || **to ~ through** vt (instructions) διαβάζω γρήγορα, εκτελώ βιαστικά || **to ~ up** vt (debt) αφήνω να ανεβεί, χρεώνομαι περισσότερα || (dress) ράβω γρήγορα-γρήγορα || **to ~ up against** vt (difficulties) συναντώ, αντιμετωπίζω || ~**about** n (small car) αυτοκίνητο δύο θέσεων || ~**away** a (horse) αφηνιασμένο (άλογο) || (person) ο δραπέτης.

rung [rʌŋ] pp of **ring** ♦ n βαθμίδα || (of rope ladder) σκαλί ανεμόσκαλας.

runner ['rʌnə*] n (messenger) αγγελιαφόρος || (of sleigh) πατίνι || ~-**up** n ο επιλαχών, ο δεύτερος (νικητής).

running ['rʌnɪŋ] n (of business) διεύθυνση || (of machine) λειτουργία, κίνηση ♦ a (water) τρεχούμενος || ~

commentary n σύγχρονη περιγραφή, (ραδιο) ρεπορτάζ nt inv.

run-of-the-mill ['rʌnəvðə'mɪl] a κοινός, συνηθισμένος.

runt [rʌnt] n κοντοστούμπης.

run-through ['rʌnθruː] n γρήγορο διάβασμα nt, γρήγορη επανάληψη.

runway ['rʌnweɪ] n διάδρομος απογειώσεως.

rupture ['rʌptʃə*] n (MED) ρήξη, διάρρηξη ♦ vt: to ~ o.s. πάσχω από κήλη.

rural ['ruərəl] a αγροτικός, υπαίθριος.

ruse [ruːz] n τέχνασμα nt, πανουργία, κόλπο.

rush [rʌʃ] n (dash) βιασύνη || (sudden demand) μεγάλη ζήτηση || (current) εκτόξευση, εισροή ♦ vt ορμώ, τρέχω επειγόντως || (attack) κάνω έφοδο || (col: overcharge) γδέρνω ♦ vi (dash) (εξ)ορμώ, εφορμώ, σπεύδω, τρέχω || **~es** npl (BOT) βούρλο, σπάρτο || ~ **hour** n ώρα συνωστισμού, ώρα πολλής δουλειάς.

rusk [rʌsk] n παξιμάδι.

Russia ['rʌʃə] n Ρωσία || **~n** n Ρώσος/ίδα m/f ♦ a ρωσικός, ρούσικος.

rust [rʌst] n σκουριά, σκουριά ♦ vi σκουριάζω.

rustic ['rʌstɪk] a (of the country) αγροτικός, χωριάτικος || (roughly made) χοντροκαμωμένος.

rustle ['rʌsl] n ψίθυρος, τρίξιμο, μουρμούρισμα nt ♦ vi τρίζω, μουρμουρίζω ♦ vt (US: animals) κλέβω, είμαι ζωοκλέπτης.

rustproof ['rʌstpruːf] a ανοξείδωτος.

rusty ['rʌstɪ] a σκουριασμένος.

rut [rʌt] n (track) αυλάκι, τροχιά, ροδιά || (routine) ρουτίνα, μονοτονία.

ruthless ['ruːθlɪs] a ανελέητος, άσπλαχνος, ωμός || ~**ly** ad χωρίς

οίκτο, αλύπητα || ~**ness** n ασπλαχνία, σκληρότητα.

rye [raɪ] n σίκαλη || ~ **bread** n ψωμί από σίκαλη.

S

sabbath ['sæbəθ] n (Jewish) Σάββατο || (Christian) Κυριακή.

sabbatical [sə'bætɪkəl] a: ~ **year** άδεια ενός χρόνου (καθηγητού).

saber ['seɪbə*] n (US) = **sabre**.

sabotage ['sæbətɑːʒ] n σαμποτάζ nt inv.

sabre ['seɪbə*] n σπαθί.

saccharin(e) ['sækərɪn] n σακχαρίνη.

sack [sæk] n σάκος, τσουβάλι || (dismissal) απόλυση ♦ vt απολύω || (town) λεηλατώ || ~**ful** n σακιά, τσουβάλι || ~**ing** n (material) σακόπανο || (dismissal) απόλυση, παύση.

sacrament ['sækrəmənt] n μυστήριο, μετάληψη.

sacred ['seɪkrɪd] a ιερός, άγιος || (duty etc) απαραβίαστος.

sacrifice ['sækrɪfaɪs] n θυσία ♦ vt θυσιάζω.

sacrilege ['sækrɪlɪdʒ] n ιεροσυλία || βεβήλωση.

sacrosanct ['sækrəʊsæŋkt] a ιερός και απαραβίαστος.

sad [sæd] a λυπημένος, θλιμένος, (dull) θλιβερός || ~**den** vt λυπώ, θλίβω.

saddle ['sædl] n σέλα ♦ vt (burden) φορτώνω || ~**bag** n δισάκι.

sadism ['seɪdɪzm] n σαδισμός.

sadist ['seɪdɪst] n σαδιστής/ίστρια m/f || ~**ic** [sə'dɪstɪk] a σαδιστικός.

sadness ['sædnɪs] n θλίψη, μελαγχολία.

safari [sə'fɑːrɪ] n σαφάρι.

safe [seɪf] a ασφαλής, σώος ||

(cautious) προσεκτικός, σίγουρος ||
(sure) ασφαλής, ακίνδυνος ♦ *n*
χρηματοκιβώτιο || ~**guard** *n*
εξασφάλιση, προστασία ♦ *vt*
προστατεύω || ~**keeping** *n*
ασφάλεια || ~**ly** *ad* ασφαλώς,
σίγουρα.

safety ['seifti] *n* ασφάλεια, σιγουριά
|| ~ **belt** *n* ζώνη ασφαλείας || ~
curtain *n* αυλαία ασφαλείας || ~
pin *n* παραμάνα.

sag [sæg] *vi* κάμπτομαι, βουλιάζω.

sage [seidʒ] *n (herb)* φασκομηλιά,
αλιφασκιά || *(man)* σοφός.

sago ['seigəu] *n (food)* σάγος.

said [sɛd] *pt, pp of* **say** || *a* λεγόμενος,
λεχθείς.

sail [seil] *n* ιστίο, πανί || *(trip)* ταξίδι,
απόπλους ♦ *vt* κυβερνώ *(πλοίο)* ♦
vi πλέω, πάω με το πανί || *(depart)*
αποπλέω || *(fig: cloud etc)* τρέχω,
περνώ || ~**boat** *n (US)* βάρκα με πανί
|| ~**ing** *n (SPORT)* ιστιοπλοΐα || **to go**
~**ing** κάνω ιστιοπλοΐες || ~**ing**
ship *n* ιστιοφόρο πλοίο || ~**or** *n*
ναύτης, ναυτικός.

saint [seint] *n* άγιος/α *m/f.*

sake [seik] *n:* **for the** ~ **of** για χάρη
του || **for your** ~ για το καλό σου.

salad ['sæləd] *n* σαλάτα || ~
dressing *n* λάδι *nt* μαγιονέζας || ~
oil *n* λάδι για σαλάτα.

salary ['sæləri] *n* μισθός.

sale [seil] *n* πώληση, πούλημα *nt* ||
(for short periods) ξεπούλημα *nt* ||
εκπτώσεις *fpl* || ~**room** *n*
δημοπρατήριο || **salesman** *n*
πωλητής || **saleswoman** *n* πωλήτρια.

salient ['seiliənt] *a* προεξέχων,
εντυπωσιακός.

saliva [sə'laivə] *n* σάλιο.

sallow ['sæləu] *a* ωχρός, χλωμός.

salmon ['sæmən] *n* σολομός.

salon ['sælɔn] *n* κομμωτήριο.

saloon [sə'luːn] *n (AUT)* κλειστό
(αυτοκίνητο) || *(ship's lounge)* σαλόνι.

salt [sɔːlt] *n* άλας *nt*, αλάτι || *(CHEM)*
άλας *nt* ♦ *vt (cure)* αλατίζω,
παστώνω || *(flavour)* αλατίζω ||
~**cellar** *n* αλατιέρα || ~**y** *a*
αλμυρός.

salutary ['sæljutəri] *a* ωφέλιμος,
σωτήριος.

salute [sə'luːt] *n (MIL)* χαιρετισμός
♦ *vt (MIL)* χαιρετίζω, αποδίδω
χαιρετισμό.

salvage ['sælvidʒ] *n* διάσωση ||
(property saved) διασωθέν, υλικό ♦ *vt*
διασώζω.

salvation [sæl'veiʃən] *n* σωτηρία ||
S ~ **Army** *n* ο Στρατός της
Σωτηρίας.

salver ['sælvə*] *n* δίσκος.

salvo ['sælvəu] *n* κανονιοβολισμός,
ομοβροντία.

same [seim] *a* ίδιος || **all the** ~ παρ'
όλα αυτά.

sample ['saːmpl] *n* δείγμα *nt* ♦ *vt*
(test) δοκιμάζω.

sanatorium [sænə'tɔːriəm] *n*
σανατόριο.

sanctimonious [sæŋkti'məuniəs]
a ψευτοθεοφοβούμενος, υποκριτής.

sanction ['sæŋkʃən] *n (POL, ECON)*
*(επι)κύρωση.

sanctity ['sæŋktiti] *n* αγιότητα,
αγιοσύνη || *(sacredness)* ιερότητα, το
απαράβιαστο.

sanctuary ['sæŋktjuəri] *n* ιερό,
άδυτο || *(for fugitive)* άσυλο || *(refuge)*
καταφύγιο.

sand [sænd] *n* άμμος *f* ♦ *vt* στρώνω
με άμμο || ~**s** *npl* αμμουδιά.

sandal ['sændl] *n* σανδάλι, πέδιλο.

sandbag ['sændbæg] *n* σάκος
άμμου.

sand dune ['sænddjuːn] *n*
αμμόλοφος.

sandpaper ['sændpeipə*] *n*
γυαλόχαρτο.

sandpit ['sændpit] *n (for children)*
αμμόκουτο.

sandstone ['sændstəʊn] n ψαμμίτης, ψαμμόλιθος.

sandwich ['sænwɪdʒ] n σάντουιτς ♦ vt παρεμβάλλω, στριμώχνω.

sandy ['sændɪ] a (with sand) αμμώδης, αμμουδερός || (colour) πυρόξανθος.

sane [seɪn] a συνετός || (sensible) λογικός.

sang [sæŋ] pt of **sing**.

sanitarium [sænɪ'tɛərɪəm] n (US) = **sanatorium**.

sanitary ['sænɪtərɪ] a υγιεινός || (protective) υγιεινονομικός || ~ **napkin** (US), ~ **towel** n πετσέτα υγείας.

sanitation [sænɪ'teɪʃən] n υγιεινή.

sanity ['sænɪtɪ] n πνευματική υγεία, υγιής νούς || (good sense) λογική.

sank [sæŋk] pt of **sink**.

Santa Claus [sæntə'klɔːz] n 'Αη Βασίλη.

sap [sæp] n (of plants) χυμός, οπός ♦ vt (wear away) υπονομεύω, υποσκάπτω.

sapling ['sæplɪŋ] n δενδρύλιο.

sapphire ['sæfaɪə*] n σάπφειρος.

sarcasm ['sɑːkæzəm] n σαρκασμός.

sarcastic [sɑː'kæstɪk] a σαρκαστικός.

sardine [sɑː'diːn] n σαρδέλα.

sash [sæʃ] n ζώνη αξιωματικών.

sat [sæt] pt, pp of **sit**.

Satan ['seɪtn] n Σατανάς || ~**ic** [sə'tænɪk] a σατανικός.

satchel ['sætʃəl] n (SCH) τσάντα, σάκα.

satellite ['sætəlaɪt] n δορυφόρος ♦ a δορυφορικός.

satin ['sætɪn] n σατέν nt inv ♦ a σατινέ, από σατέν.

satire ['sætaɪə*] n σάτυρα.

satirical [sə'tɪrɪkl] a σατυρικός.

satisfaction [sætɪs'fækʃən] n ικανοποίηση || ευχαρίστηση.

satisfactory [sætɪs'fæktərɪ] a ικανοποιητικός.

satisfy ['sætɪsfaɪ] vt ικανοποιώ || (convince) πείθω, διαβεβαιώ || ~**ing** a ικανοποιητικός.

saturate ['sætʃəreɪt] vt διαβρέχω, διαποτίζω, μουσκεύω.

Saturday ['sætədɪ] n Σάββατο.

sauce [sɔːs] n σάλτσα || ~ **pan** n κατσαρόλα.

saucer ['sɔːsə*] n πιατάκι.

saucy ['sɔːsɪ] a αναιδής, αυθάδης.

saunter ['sɔːntə*] vi σουλατσάρω, περπατώ άσκοπα ♦ n βόλτα.

sausage ['sɒsɪdʒ] n λουκάνικο || ~ **roll** n λουκάνικο με ζύμη.

savage ['sævɪdʒ] a άγριος, θηριώδης || (uncivilized) απολίτιστος, βάρβαρος ♦ n άγριος ♦ vt (fig) επιτίθεμαι άγρια || ~**ry** n αγριότητα, βαρβαρότητα.

save [seɪv] vt σώζω, γλυτώνω || (store up) (εξ)οικονομώ, αποταμιεύω, μαζεύω || (avoid using up) αποφεύγω || (COMPUT) φυλάω ♦ prep, cj εκτός από εκτός, εξαιρουμένου.

saving ['seɪvɪŋ] a (redeeming) σωτήριος ♦ n οικονομία || ~s npl αποταμιεύσεις fpl, καταθέσεις fpl, οικονομίες fpl || ~s **bank** n ταμιευτήριο.

saviour, savior (US) ['seɪvjə*] n σωτήρας.

savour, savor (US) ['seɪvə*] n ουσία, γεύση, γούστο ♦ vt γεύομαι || (enjoy) απολαμβάνω || ~**y** a γευστικός, νόστιμος, ορεκτικός.

saw [sɔː] (irreg v) n (tool) πριόνι ♦ vt πριονίζω || pt of **see** || ~**dust** n πριονίδια ntpl || ~**mill** n πριονιστήριο.

saxophone ['sæksəfəʊn] n σαξόφωνο.

say [seɪ] (irreg v) n λόγος ♦ vt (tell) λέγω || (suppose) υποθέτω || ~**ing** n ρητό.

scab [skæb] n κάρκαδο || (pej: industry) απεργοσπάστης.

scabby ['skæbɪ] a ψωριάρης.

scaffold ['skæfəld] n ικρίωμα nt|| ~**ing** n σκαλωσιά.

scald [skɔːld] n ζεμάτισμα nt ♦ vt ζεματίζω.

scale [skeɪl] n (of fish) λέπι || (MUS) κλίμακα, σκάλα || (for measuring) κλίμακα, διαβάθμιση || (on map) κλίμακα || (size) κλίμακος ♦ vt (climb) αναρριχώμαι, σκαρφαλώνω || ~**s** npl (balance) ζυγός, ζυγαριά || **on a large** ~ σε μεγάλη κλίμακα || ~ **drawing** n σχέδιο υπό κλίμακα.

scallop ['skɔləp] n (shellfish) χτένι.

scalp [skælp] n τριχωτό δέρμα nt κεφαλής ♦ vt γδέρνω το κρανίο.

scalpel ['skælpəl] n νυστέρι.

scamper ['skæmpə*] vi τρέχω τρελά, το στρίβω.

scan [skæn] vt εξονυχίζω, διερευνώ || (POET) διαβάζω μετρικά.

scandal ['skændl] n σκάνδαλο || (gossip) κακολογία, κουτσομπολιό || ~**ize** vt σκανδαλίζω || ~**ous** a σκανδαλώδης.

Scandinavia [skændɪ'neɪvɪə] n Σκανδιναβία || ~**n** a σκανδιναβικός ♦ n Σκανδιναβός/ή m/f.

scant [skænt] a πενιχρός, ανεπαρκής, λιγοστός || ~**y** a ανεπαρκής, λιγοστός.

scapegoat ['skeɪpgəut] n αποδιοπομπαίος τράγος.

scar [skɑː*] n ουλή, σημάδι ♦ vt αφήνω σημάδι.

scarce [skɛəs] a σπάνιος || ~**ly** ad μόλις, σχεδόν καθόλου || ~**ness** n σπανιότητα έλλειψη.

scarcity ['skɛəsɪtɪ] n σπανιότητα, έλλειψη.

scare [skɛə*] n εκφόβιση, τρομάρα ♦ vt φοβίζω, τρομάζω || ~**crow** n σκιάχτρο.

scarf [skɑːf] n σάρπα, κασκόλ nt inv.

scarlet ['skɑːlɪt] a (colour) κατακόκκινος ♦ n κτυπητό κόκκινο || ~ **fever** n οστρακιά, σκαρλατίνα.

scarves [skɑːvz] npl of **scarf**.

scathing ['skeɪðɪŋ] a καυστικός, δηκτικός.

scatter ['skætə*] n διασπορά, σκόρπισμα nt ♦ vt (sprinkle) σκορπίζω || (an enemy) διασκορπίζω ♦ vi διαλύομαι, σκορπίζω || ~**brained** a αμυαλός, ξεμυαλισμένος || ~**ing** n μικρή ποσότητα, σκόρπισμα nt.

scavenger ['skævɪndʒə*] n (animal) ζώο που τρώει ψοφίμια.

scene [siːn] n (of accident etc) τόπος, θέατρο || (of play) σκηνή || (division of play) σκηνή || (view) τοπείο, άποψη, θέα || (fuss) σκηνή, φασαρία, επεισόδιο || (incident) σκηνή || **on the** ~ στον τόπο, επί σκηνής || ~**ry** n σκηνικό, σκηνογραφία, σκηνή || (view) τοπίο, θέα.

scenic ['siːnɪk] a σκηνικός, θεαματικός.

scent [sɛnt] n οσμή, άρωμα nt, μυρουδιά || (sense of smell) όσφρηση ♦ vt (make fragrant) αρωματίζω, μοσχοβολώ.

scepter ['sɛptə*] n (US) = **sceptre**.

sceptic ['skɛptɪk] n σκεπτικιστής || ~**al** a σκεπτικός, δύσπιστος || ~**ism** n σκεπτικισμός.

sceptre ['sɛptə*] n σκήπτρο.

schedule ['ʃɛdjuːl, (US) 'skɛdjuːl] n πρόγραμμα, nt|| (of trains) δρομολόγιο || (of prices) κατάλογος ♦ vt καταγράφω, προγραμματίζω || **on** ~ στην ώρα || σύμφωνα με το πρόγραμμα || **behind** ~ καθυστερημένος.

scheme [skiːm] n διάταξη || (plan) σχέδιο || (plot) μηχανορραφία, δολοπλοκία ♦ vti (plot) μηχανορραφώ || (plan) σχεδιάζω.

scheming ['ski:miŋ] a δολοπλόκος, κομπιναδόρος.

schism ['sizəm] n σχίσμα nt.

schizophrenic [skitsəʊ'frɛnik] a σχιζοφρενικός.

scholar ['skɒlə*] n μελετητής, μορφωμένος || (with scholarship) υπότροφος || ~**ly** a μορφωμένος || ~**ship** n υποτροφία || (learning) μόρφωση.

school [sku:l] n σχολείο || (group) σχολή || (department) σχολή ♦ attr a σχολικός, του σχολείου ♦ vt διδάσκω, γυμνάζω, μορφώνω || ~**book** n σχολικό βιβλίο || ~**boy** n μαθητής || ~**days** npl σχολικά χρόνια ntpl || ~**girl** n μαθήτρια || ~**ing** n εκπαίδευση, μόρφωση δάσκαλος, καθηγητής || ~**mistress** n δασκάλα, καθηγήτρια || ~**teacher** n δημοδιδάσκαλος/ισσα m/f.

schooner ['sku:nə*] n (ship) σκούνα || (glass for sherry etc) ποτηράκι.

sciatica [sai'ætikə] n ισχιαλγία.

science ['saiəns] n επιστήμη.

scientific [saiən'tifik] a επιστημονικός.

scientist ['saiəntist] n επιστήμονας m/f.

scintillating ['sintileitiŋ] a σπινθοβολικός, σπινθηροβόλος.

scissors ['sizəz] npl (also: a pair of ~) ψαλίδι.

scoff [skɒf] n vt (eat) τρώγω, καταβροχθίζω ♦ vi (mock) (+at) σκόπτω, κοροϊδεύω.

scold [skəʊld] vt επιπλήττω, μαλώνω.

scone [skɒn] n είδος pt κέικ.

scoop [sku:p] n φτυάρι, σέσουλα ♦ vt: to ~ **out** αδειάζω || to ~ **up** vt βγάζω.

scooter ['sku:tə*] n (motorcycle) βέσπα || (child's toy) πατίνι.

scope [skəʊp] n αντίληψη, ικανότης || (opportunity) ευκαιρία || (margin) περιθώριο.

scorch [skɔ:tʃ] n καφάλωμα nt, κάψιμο ♦ vt καψαλίζω, τσουρουφλίζω || (wither) ψήνω, ξεραίνω || ~**ing** a καφτερός.

score [skɔ:*] n (points) σκορ nt inv || (MUS) παρτιτούρα || (reason) σημείο || (twenty) εικοσάρα, εικοσαριά ♦ vt (win points) σημειώνω, κάνω πόντους || (mark) χαράσσω, χαρακώνω ♦ vi (keep record) κρατώ σκόρ || ~**board** n πίνακας των σκορ || ~**r** n (player) ο επιτυχών τέρμα || (recorder) μαρκαδόρος.

scorn ['skɔ:n] n περιφρόνηση ♦ vt περιφρονώ.

scorpion ['skɔ:piən] n σκορπιός.

Scot [skɒt] n Σκωτσέζος/α m/f.

Scotch n (whisky) (σκωτσέζικο) ουίσκυ.

scotch [skɒtʃ] vt (terminate) αποτρέπω, καταπνίγω.

Scotland ['skɒtlənd] n Σκωτία.

Scots [skɒts] npl Σκωτσέζοι mpl ♦ a σκωτσέζος || ~**man** n Σκωτσέζος || ~**woman** n Σκωτίδα, Σκωτσέζα.

Scottish ['skɒtiʃ] a σκωτικός, σκωτσέζικος.

scoundrel ['skaʊndrəl] n παλιάνθρωπος.

scour ['skaʊə*] vt (search) διατρέχω, ερευνώ || (clean) καθαρίζω || ~**er** n (for pans) σύρμα nt.

scourge [skə:dʒ] n (plague) πληγή.

scout [skaʊt] n ανιχνευτής || (boy scout) πρόσκοπος ♦ vi (reconnoitre) ανιχνεύω, κάνω αναγνώριση.

scowl [skaʊl] n συνοφρύωση, σκυθρωπότητα ♦ vi συνοφρυούμαι, κατσουφιάζω.

scraggy ['skrægi] a ισχνός, κοκκαλιάρης.

scram [skræm] vi (col) στρίβω, το βάζω στα πόδια || ~**!** στρίβε!, δίνε του!

scramble ['skræmbl] n σκαρφάλωμα nt || (struggle) αγώνας,

πάλη ♦ vi: to ~ for αγωνίζομαι || ~d eggs npl αυγά χτυπητά ntpl.

scrap [skræp] n κομματάκι, απόρριμμα nt, ψίχουλο || (fight) συμπλοκή, καυγάς || (scrap iron) παλιοσίδερα ntpl ♦ a για πέταμα, άχρηστος ♦ vt πετώ σαν άχρηστο, απορρίπτω ♦ vi (fight) πιάνομαι στα χέρια || ~s npl (waste) απομεινάρια ntpl, απορρίμματα ntpl || ~book n λεύκωμα nt αποκομμάτων.

scrape [skreip] n απόξεση, ξύσιμο || (awkward position) αμηχανία, μπελάς ♦ vt ξύνω, ξεγδέρνω || (clean) καθαρίζω, τρίβω ♦ vi ξύνω || ~r n ξύστρα, ξυστήρι.

scrap heap ['skræphiːp] n σωρός παλιοσίδερων.

scrap merchant ['skræpmɜːtʃənt] n έμπορος παλιοσίδερων.

scrappy ['skræpi] a ασύνδετος, ασυνάρτητος, ανακατεμένος.

scratch ['skrætʃ] n νυχιά, αμυχή, γρατσουνιά || (itch) ξύσιμο ♦ a πρόχειρος ♦ vt ξύνω, τρίβω || (wound) γρατσουνίζω, ξεγδέρνω ♦ vi (rub) ξύνομαι.

scrawl [skrɔːl] n ορνιθοσκαλίσματα ntpl ♦ vti κακογράφω, ορνιθοσκαλίζω.

scream [skriːm] n κραυγή, ξεφωνητό, στριγγλιά ♦ vi ξεφωνίζω || (speak loudly) στριγγλίζω.

screech [skriːtʃ] n κραυγή, στριγγλιά ♦ vi σκούζω, στριγγλίζω, ουρλιάζω.

screen [skriːn] n παραπέτασμα nt, προπέτασμα nt, παραβάν nt inv || (for films) οθόνη, πανί || (church) κιγκλίδωμα nt ♦ vt προφυλάσσω, προστατεύω || (film) κινηματογραφώ, γυρίζω.

screw [skruː] n κοχλίας, βίδα || (NAUT) έλικας, προπέλα ♦ vt βιδώνω, σφίγγω || (col) καταπιέζω || ~driver

n κατσαβίδι || ~y a (col) μουρλός, ξεβιδωμένος.

scribble ['skribl] n κακογραφία ♦ vt γράφω βιαστικά, ορνιθοσκαλίζω.

script [skript] n χειρόγραφο || (of play) κείμενο, σενάριο.

Scripture ['skriptʃə*] n n Αγία Γραφή.

scriptwriter ['skriptraitə*] n σεναριογράφος.

scroll [skrəul] n κύλινδρος, ρόλος (περγαμηνής) ♦ vt (COMPUT) μετακινώ τα περιεχόμενα της οθόνης πάνω/κάτω.

scrounge [skraundʒ] vt (col) διακονεύω ♦ n: on the ~ πάω τσάρκα.

scrub [skrʌb] n (clean) τριβή, τρίψιμο, βούρτσισμα nt || (countryside) χαμόκλαδα ntpl, αγριμιά ♦ vt πλένω, βουρτσίζω, τρίβω || (erase) σκυρώνω, σβήνω.

scruff [skrʌf] n σβέρκο.

scrum(mage) ['skrʌm(idʒ)] n συμπλοκή.

scruple ['skruːpl] n ενδοιασμός, δισταγμός της συνείδησης.

scrupulous ['skruːpjuləs] a ευσυνείδητος || ~ly ad ευσυνείδητα.

scrutinize ['skruːtinaiz] vt εξετάζω προσεκτικά, διερευνώ.

scrutiny ['skruːtini] n αυστηρός έλεγχος, διερεύνηση.

scuff [skʌf] vt (shoes) σέρνω.

scuffle ['skʌfl] n συμπλοκή, καυγάς.

scullery ['skʌləri] n πλυντήριο μαγειρίου, λάντσα.

sculptor ['skʌlptə*] n γλύπτης/τρια n/f.

sculpture ['skʌlptʃə*] n γλυπτική || (statue) γλυπτό.

scum [skʌm] n βρώμικος αφρός, βρωμιά || (people) κατακάθια ntpl, αποβράσματα ntpl.

scurrilous ['skʌrɪləs] a υβριστικός, αχρείος, βρώμικος.

scurry ['skʌrɪ] vi τρέχω, σπεύδω.

scurvy ['skɜːvɪ] n σκορβούτο.

scuttle ['skʌtl] vt (plans) εγκαταλείπω, υποχωρώ ♦ vi (scamper) τρέχω βιαστικά, το στρίβω.

scythe [saɪð] n δρεπάνι.

sea [siː] n θάλασσα || (broad stretch) ωκεανός, θάλασσα ♦ a θαλασσινός, της θάλασσας || ~ **bird** n θαλασσοπούλι || ~ **board** n ακτή, παραλία || ~ **breeze** n θαλασσινή αύρα, μπάτης || ~ **farer** n θαλασσινός, θαλασσοπόρος || ~ **food** n θαλασσινά ntpl || ~ **front** n παραλία, προκυμαία || ~ **going** a ποντοπόρος || ~ **gull** n γλάρος.

seal [siːl] n (animal) φώκια || (stamp) σφραγίδα, βούλα || (impression) σφραγίδα ♦ vt σφραγίζω || (close) κλείνω, σφραγίζω, βουλώνω.

sea level ['siːlɛvl] n επιφάνεια της θάλασσας.

sealing wax ['siːlɪŋwæks] n βουλοκέρι.

sea lion ['siːlaɪən] n είδος φώκιας.

seam [siːm] n ραφή || (joining) ένωση, ραφή || (of coal etc) φλέβα.

seaman ['siːmən] n ναυτικός, ναύτης.

seamy ['siːmɪ] a ανάποδος, άσχημος.

seaport ['siːpɔːt] n λιμάνι.

search [sɜːtʃ] n έρευνα, αναζήτηση ♦ vt ερευνώ, αναζητώ || (COMPUT) διερευνώ || ~ **ing** a ερευνητικός, προσεκτικός || ~ **light** n προβολέας || ~ **party** n απόσπασμα ή έρευνας.

seashore ['siːʃɔː*] n ακτή, παραλία.

seasick ['siːsɪk] a αυτός που έχει ναυτία || ~ **ness** n ναυτία.

seaside ['siːsaɪd] n παραλία, γιαλός.

season ['siːzn] n εποχή ♦ vt αρτύω, καρυκεύω || ~ **al** a εποχιακός || ~ **ing** n καρύκευμα, άρτυμα ntpl,

μπαχαρικό || ~ **ticket** n διαρκές εισιτήριο.

seat [siːt] n κάθισμα nt, καρέκλα || (PARL etc) έδρα || (manner of sitting) κάθισμα nt, στάση || (bottom) πισινός, οπίσθια ntpl ♦ vt καθίζω || **lt** ~ **s 20 people** είναι 20 θέσεων || ~ **belt** n ζώνη ασφαλείας.

sea water ['siːwɔːtə*] n θαλασσινό νερό.

seaweed ['siːwiːd] n φύκι, φύκια ntpl.

seaworthy ['siːwɜːðɪ] a πλόιμος, ικανός να πλεύσει.

sec. abbr of **second(s).**

secluded [sɪˈkluːdɪd] a παράμερος, απομονωμένος.

seclusion [sɪˈkluːʒən] n απομόνωση.

second ['sɛkənd] num δεύτερος ♦ ad (in second position) δεύτερος || (RAIL) δεύτερη (θέση) ♦ n (of time) δευτερόλεπτο || (COMM: imperfect) δεύτερο χέρι ♦ vt υποστηρίζω, βοηθώ || ~ **ary** a δευτερεύων, ασήμαντος || ~ **ary education** μέση εκπαίδευση || ~ **ary school** n σχολείο μέσης εκπαιδεύσεως || ~ **er** n υποστηρικτής/ίκτρια m/f || ~ **hand** a μεταχειρισμένος, δεύτερο χέρι || (not original) μη πρωτότυπος || ~ **ly** ad κατά δεύτερο λόγο || ~ **rate** a μέτριος, δεύτερας ποιότητας || ~ **thoughts** npl δεύτερες σκέψεις fpl.

secrecy ['siːkrəsɪ] n μυστικότητα, εχεμύθεια.

secret ['siːkrɪt] n μυστικό ♦ a μυστικός, κρυφός, απόρρητος.

secretariat [sɛkrəˈtɛərɪət] n γραμματεία.

secretary ['sɛkrətrɪ] n γραμματέας m/f || (minister etc) υπουργός m/f.

secretive ['siːkrətɪv] a κρυψίνους.

sect [sɛkt] n αίρεση || ~ **arian** a αιρετικός, στενοκέφαλος, κομματικός.

section ['sɛkʃən] n χωρισμός, κόψιμο || (piece) τμήμα nt, μέρος nt, τομή || ~**al** a τμηματικός, τοπικός.

sector ['sɛktə*] n (private or public sector) τομέας.

secular ['sɛkjulə*] a λαϊκός, κοσμικός.

secure [sɪ'kjuə*] a βέβαιος, ακίνδυνος || (fixed) ασφαλής ♦ vt (fix) στερεώνω, σφίγγω || (obtain) εξασφαλίζω.

security [sɪ'kjuərɪtɪ] n ασφάλεια, σιγουριά || (bond) εγγύηση, χρεώγραφο || (national security) ασφάλεια || see **social**.

sedate [sɪ'deɪt] a στάρκος, ήρεμος.

sedation [sɪ'deɪʃən] n (MED) καταπράϋνση.

sedative ['sɛdətɪv] n καταπραϋντικό ♦ a καταπραϋντικός.

sedentary ['sɛdntrɪ] a αδρανής, καθιστικός.

sediment ['sɛdɪmənt] n κατακάθι, ίζημα.

seduce [sɪ'djuːs] vt (general) δελεάζω, παρασύρω || (sexually) διαφθείρω, αποπλανώ.

seduction [sɪ'dʌkʃən] n αποπλάνηση, δελεασμός.

seductive [sɪ'dʌktɪv] a γοητευτικός, αποπλανητικός.

see [siː] (irreg v) vt βλέπω || (find out) κοιτάζω || (understand) αντιλαμβάνομαι || (make sure) φροντίζω || (accompany) συνοδεύω || (visit) πηγαίνω, βλέπω, επισκέπτομαι ♦ vi (understand) αντιλαμβάνομαι ♦ n (bishop's) επισκοπή || **to ~ through** vt φροντίζω μέχρι τέλους, παρακολουθώ || **to ~ to** vt φροντίζω για || **to ~ off** vt συνοδεύω, ξεπροβοδίζω.

seed [siːd] n ο σπόρος || (grain) κόκκος, σπειρί || ~**ling** n σπορό φυτό || ~**y** a (ill) αδιάθετος, τσακισμένος || (shabby) κουρελιασμένος.

seeing ['siːɪŋ] cj: ~ **(that)** εφόσον, αφού, δεδομένου ότι.

seek [siːk] (irreg v) vt αναζητώ, ψάχνω, ζητώ.

seem [siːm] vi φαίνομαι, μοιάζω || ~**ingly** ad φαινομενικά, κατά τα φαινόμενα.

seen [siːn] pp of **see**.

seep [siːp] vi διαρρέω, περνώ από.

seesaw ['siːsɔː] n (plank) τραμπάλα.

seethe [siːð] vi (be agitated) αναταράσσομαι, βράζω.

segment ['sɛgmənt] n τμήμα nt.

segregate ['sɛgrɪgeɪt] vt απομονώνω, χωρίζω.

segregation [sɛgrɪ'geɪʃən] n απομόνωση, χωρισμός.

seismic ['saɪzmɪk] a σεισμικός.

seize [siːz] vt αρπάζω, πιάνω || (take possession) κατάσχω || (understand) αντιλαμβάνομαι, συλλαμβάνω || **to ~ up** vi (MECH) σφηνώνομαι, μαγκώνω, κολλώ.

seizure ['siːʒə*] n (illness) απότομη προσβολή.

seldom ['sɛldəm] ad σπανίως, σπάνια.

select [sɪ'lɛkt] a εκλεκτός, διαλεκτός ♦ vt εκλέγω, διαλέγω || ~**ion** n εκλογή, διαλογή, επιλογή || ~**ive** a εκλεκτικός || ~**or** n (person) επιλογέας, εκλέκτωρ m || (TECH) επιλογέας.

self [sɛlf] n εαυτός, το πρόσωπο, το άτομο || ~**-appointed** a αυτοδιοριζόμενος || ~**-assured** a επηρρεένος, γεμάτος αυτοπεποίθηση || ~**-confidence** n αυτοπεποίθηση || ~**-conscious** a δειλός, ενουνείδητος || ~**-contained** a αυτοτελής, ανεξάρτητος || (reserved) επιφυλακτικός || ~**-defence** n αυτοάμυνα || ~**-evident** a αυταπόδεικτος || ~**-indulgent** a αυτεντρύφηλος, τρυφηλός || ~-

interest n ιδιοτέλεια || ~**ish** a εγωιστικός, ιδιοτελής || ~**ishness** n εγωισμός, ιδιοτέλεια || ~**lessly** ad αλτρουιστικά || ~**portrait** n αυτοπροσωπογραφία || ~**reliant** a ανεξάρτητος || ~**respect** n αυτοσεβασμός || ~**righteous** a υποκριτικός || ~**satisfied** a αυτάρεσκος, ικανοποιημένος από τον εαυτό του || ~**service** n αυτοσερβίρισμα || ~**sufficient** a αυτάρκης || ~**supporting** a (FIN) αυτοσυντήρητος, αυτάρκης.

sell [sel] (irreg v) vt πουλώ ♦ vi (COMM) πωλούμαι || ~**er** n πωλητής/τρια m/f || ~**ing price** n τιμή πωλήσεως.

selves [selvz] pl of self.

semaphore ['seməfɔː*] n (system) σηματοφόρος.

semi ['semi] prefix ημι- || ~**circle** n ημικύκλιο || ~**colon** n άνω τελεία || ~**conscious** a ημιαναίσθητος || ~**detached house** n ριζόντιος διπλοκατοικία || ~**final** n ημιτελικός.

seminar ['seminaː*] n σεμινάριο.

semitone ['semitəun] n (MUS) ημιτόνιο.

semolina [semə'liːnə] n σιμιγδάλι.

senate ['senit] n σύγκλητος f || (US) γερουσία.

senator ['senitə*] n γερουσιαστής.

send [send] (irreg v) vt πέμπω, στέλνω, αποστέλλω || (col: inspire) ενθουσιάζω, τρελαίνω || **to ~ away** vt απολύω, διώχνω || **to ~ back** vt στέλνω πίσω, επιστρέφω || **to ~ for** vt στέλνω να φωνάξω, καλώ || **to ~ off** vt (goods) αποστέλλω, στέλνω || (player) αποβάλλω || **to ~ out** vi (invitation) στέλνω || **to ~ up** vt (general) ανεβάζω, στέλνω, ανυψώνω || ~**er** n αποστολέας || ~**off** n αποχαιρετισμός.

senile ['siːnail] a γεροντικός.

senility [si'niliti] n γεράματα ntpl, ξεμωράματα ntpl.

senior ['siːniə*] a μεγαλύτερος, πρεσβύτερος || (rank) αρχαιότερος, ανώτερος ♦ n πρεσβύτερος, γηραιότερος, μεγαλύτερος || (US) τελειόφοιτος/η m/f || ~**ity** n αρχαιότητα (βαθμού).

sensation [sen'seiʃən] n αίσθηση, αίσθημα nt || (state of excitement) αίσθηση, εντύνωση || ~**al** a εντυπωσιακός.

sense [sens] n αίσθηση || (understanding) λογική, λογικό || (meaning) έννοια, νόημα nt || (feeling) (συν)αίσθημα nt ♦ vt (δι)αισθάνομαι || ~**less** a ανόητος, παράλογος || (unconscious) αναίσθητος.

sensibility [sensi'biliti] n ευαισθησία, αίσθημα.

sensible ['sensəbl] a λογικός.

sensitive ['sensitiv] a (+ to) ευαίσθητος, ευπαθής || (easily hurt) ευσυγκίνητος, εύθικτος.

sensitivity [sensi'tiviti] n ευαισθησία, ευπάθεια.

sensual ['sensjuəl] a αισθησιακός, σαρκικός, φιλήδονος.

sensuous ['sensjuəs] a ηδυπαθής, αισθησιακός.

sent [sent] pt, pp of send.

sentence ['sentəns] n (GRAM) πρόταση || (LAW) απόφαση, ποινή.

sentiment ['sentimənt] n αίσθημα nt, αισθηματικότητα || (thought) γνώμη, άποψη || ~**al** a αισθηματικός || ~**ality** n αισθηματισμός.

sentry ['sentri] n σκοπός, φρουρός.

separate ['seprit] a χωριστός ♦ ['sepəreit] vt χωρίζω, ξεχωρίζω || ~**ly** ad ξεχωριστά.

separation [sepə'reiʃən] n χωρισμός, διαχώριση.

September [sep'tembə*] n Σεπτέμβριος.

septic ['sɛptɪk] *a* σηπτικός.

sequel ['siːkwəl] *n* συνέπεια, αποτέλεσμα *nt*|| *(continuation)* συνέχεια.

sequence ['siːkwəns] *n* διαδοχή, συνέχεια, ακολουθία.

sequin ['siːkwɪn] *n* πούλι *nt*.

serenade [sɛrə'neɪd] *n* σερενάτα ♦ *vt* κάνω σερενάτα.

serene [sə'riːn] *a* γαλήνιος, ατάραχος|| ~**ly** *ad* ήρεμα, γαλήνια.

serenity [sɪ'rɛnɪtɪ] *n* γαλήνη, ηρεμία.

sergeant ['sɑːdʒənt] *n* λοχίας *(police)* ενωμοτάρχης.

serial ['sɪərɪəl] *n* ιστορία σε συνέχειες|| ~ **number** *n* αύξοντας αριθμός|| ~**ize** *vt* δημοσιεύω σε συνέχειες.

series ['sɪərɪz] *n* σειρά.

serious ['sɪərɪəs] *a* σοβαρός|| ~**ly** *ad* σοβαρά|| ~**ness** *n* σοβαρότητα.

sermon ['sɜːmən] *n* κήρυγμα *nt*, ομιλία.

serrated [sɛ'reɪtɪd] *a* οδοντωτός, πριονωτός.

serum ['sɪərəm] *n* ορός.

servant ['sɜːvənt] *n* υπηρέτης/έτρια *m/f*|| *see* civil.

serve [sɜːv] *vt* υπηρετώ|| *(do work of)* εξυπηρετώ, εκπληρώνω|| *(supply)* προμηθεύω ♦ *vi (be useful)* χρησιμεύω για|| *(in army)* υπηρετώ|| *(wait at table, tennis)* σερβίρω ♦ *n (tennis)* σερβίρισμα *nt*|| **it ~s him right** καλά να πάθει|| **to ~ out** or **up** *vt (food)* σερβίρω.

service ['sɜːvɪs] *n* υπηρεσία *n (work done)* εξυπηρέτηση|| *(government department)* υπηρεσία *(civil etc)* υπηρεσία, εργασία|| *(help)* διάθεση, χρησιμότητα|| *(REL)* λειτουργία *(set of dishes)* σερβίτσιο|| *(tennis)* σερβίς *nt inv*|| *(AUT: maintenance)* συντήρηση, επισκευή ♦ *vt (AUT, MECH)* συντηρώ, επισκευάζω|| **the**

S~s *npl (armed forces)* τα όπλα *ntpl*, οι ένοπλες δυνάμεις *fpl*|| ~**able** *a* εύχρηστος, ανθεκτικός, χρήσιμος|| ~**men** *npl (soldier etc)* άντρες των ενόπλων δυνάμεων|| ~ **station** *n* γκαράζ *nt inv*.

serviette [sɜːvɪ'ɛt] *n* πετσέτα (φαγητού).

servile ['sɜːvaɪl] *a* δουλικός, δουλοπρεπής.

session ['sɛʃən] *n* συνεδρίαση, συνεδρία.

set [sɛt] *(irreg v)* *n (of things)* σειρά, συλλογή|| *(RAD, TV)* συσκευή|| *(tennis)* γύρος, σέτ *nt inv*|| *(group of people)* ομάδα, κατηγορία, συντροφιά, κόσμος|| *(CINE)* συσκευή|| *(THEAT)* διάκοσμος, σκηνικό ♦ *a (specified)* καθωρισμένος|| *(determined)* αποφασισμένος ♦ *vt* θέτω, τοποθετώ, βάζω|| *(arrange)* κανονίζω|| *(adjust)* ρυθμίζω, βάζω, κανονίζω|| *(exam)* δίδω τα θέματα ♦ *vi (of sun)* δύω, βασιλεύω|| *(fix)* σκληραίνομαι, σφίγγω, πιάνω|| **to ~ on fire** καίω, πυρπολώ, βάζω φωτιά|| **to ~ free** ελευθερώνω|| **to ~ going** ξεκινώ|| **to ~ sail** απολύω|| **to ~ about** *vt (task)* αρχίζω|| **to ~ aside** *vt* ξεχωρίζω, βάζω κατά μέρος, απορρίπτω|| **to ~ back** *vt (in time)* επιβραδύνω, καθυστερώ|| *(cost)* κοστίζω|| **to ~ off** *vi* ξεκινώ, φεύγω ♦ *vt (explode)* εκτοξεύω, ρίχνω, εκπυρούω|| *(show up well)* εξαίρω, αναδεικνύω, τονίζω, υπογραμμίζω|| **to ~ out** *vi* ξεκινώ, φεύγω ♦ *vt (arrange)* ρυθμίζω, κανονίζω, σιάζω|| *(state)* καθορίζω|| **to ~ up** *vt (organization)* ιδρύω, οργανώνω|| ~**back** *n (reverse)* αποτυχία, ατυχία, αναποδιά.

settee [sɛ'tiː] *n* καναπές *m*.

setting ['sɛtɪŋ] *n (scenery)* τοποθεσία, πλαίσιο *(MUS)* μελοποίηση, μουσική τραγουδιού.

settle ['sɛtl] vt (MED: calm) καθησυχάζω, καταπραϋνω || (pay) εξοφλώ, πληρώνω || (agree) ρυθμίζω κανονίζω ♦ vi (also: ~ **down**) εγκαθίσταμαι || (person) σοβαρεύω || ~**ment** n (payment) εξόφληση || (colony) εποικισμός || ~**r** n άποικος.

setup ['sɛtʌp] n (arrangement) τοποθέτηση, οργάνωση || (situation) κατάσταση.

seven ['sɛvn] num επτά || ~**teen** num δεκαεπτά || ~**th** a έβδομος || ~**ty** num εβδομήντα.

sever ['sɛvə*] vt κόβω || (fig) διακόπτω.

several ['sɛvrəl] a διάφορος, ξεχωριστός ♦ pron μερικοί.

severance ['sɛvərəns] n διαχωρισμός || (fig) διακοπή.

severe [si'viə*] a αυστηρός, σκληρός || (serious) σοβαρός || (hard, rigorous) δριμύς, σκληρός, άγριος || (unadorned) αυστηρός, απέριττος, λιτός || ~**ly** ad αυστηρά, σκληρά.

severity [si'vɛriti] n αυστηρότητα, σκληρότητα, δριμύτητα.

sew [səu] (irreg v) vti ράβω || **to** ~ **up** vt ράβω.

sewage ['sju:idʒ] n ακαθαρσίες ftpl υπονόμων, βρωμόνερα ntpl.

sewer ['sjuə*] n οχετός, υπόνομος.

sewing ['səuiŋ] n ράψιμο || ~ **machine** n ραπτομηχανή.

sewn [səun] pp of **sew**.

sex [sɛks] n φύλο, σέξ nt inv || (activity) γενετήσια ορμή || ~ **act** n συνουσία.

sexual ['sɛksjuəl] a γενετήσιος, σεξουαλικός || ~**ly** ad σεξουαλικά.

sexy ['sɛksi] a ελκυστικός, σεξουαλικός.

shabby ['ʃæbi] a κουρελιασμένος, σαραβαλιασμένος || (mean) μικροπρεπής, αχρείος.

shack [ʃæk] n καλύβα.

shackles ['ʃæklz] npl δεσμά, χειροπέδες fpl.

shade [ʃeid] n σκιά, ίσκιος || (for lamp) αμπαζούρ nt inv || (of colour) απόχρωση || (small quantity) ίχνος m, μικρή ποσότητα ♦ vt σκιάζω.

shadow ['ʃædəu] n σκιά, σκοτάδι ♦ vt (follow) παρακολουθώ || ~**y** a σκιερός, σκιασμένος || (dim) ασαφής, θαμπός.

shady ['ʃeidi] a σκιερός || (dubious) ύποπτος.

shaft [ʃɑ:ft] n κοντάρι, στέλεχος, λαβή || (of mine) φρέαρ nt || (of machine) άξονας, άτρακτος f || (of light) ακτίδα.

shaggy ['ʃægi] a τραχύς, τριχωτός.

shake [ʃeik] (irreg v) vt σείω, κουνώ, τινάζω || (fist etc) απειλώ με τη γροθιά μου || (rock) (συγ)κλονίζω, κουνώ, τραντάζω || (weaken) κλονίζω || (alarm) συγκλονίζω, αναστατώνω ♦ vi τρέμω, κλονίζομαι, τραντάζομαι ♦ n τίναγμα nt, κούνημα nt, δόνηση || **to** ~ **off** vt τινάζω || (fig) απαλλάσσομαι από || **to** ~ **up** vt (lit) ταράζω, κουνώ || (fig) ξυπνώ || ~**-up** n πρόχειρο πράμα.

shaky ['ʃeiki] a ασταθής, τρεμουλιαστός || (weak) κλονισμένος, αδύνατος.

shall [ʃæl] auxiliary v: **I** ~ **go** θα φύγω, θα πάω || **you** ~ **do it!** θα το κάμεις.

shallot [ʃə'lɔt] n μικρό κρεμμύδι.

shallow ['ʃæləu] a (lit) ρηχός || (fig) επιπόλαιος.

sham [ʃæm] n προσποίηση, απομίμηση, ψευτιά ♦ a προσποιητός, ψεύτικος.

shambles ['ʃæmblz] n sing χάος nt.

shame [ʃeim] n ντροπή || (pity) ντροπή, αμαρτία, κρίμα nt ♦ vt (humiliate) ντροπιάζω || **what a** ~! τι κρίμα! || ~**-faced** a ντροπιασμένος || ~**ful** a

ντροπιασμένος || ~less a αναίσχυντος, αδιάντροπος.

shampoo [ʃæm'pu:] n σαμπουάν nt inv ♦ vt λούζω (τα μαλλιά μου).

shamrock ['ʃæmrɔk] n τριφύλλι.

shandy ['ʃændɪ] n (beer and lemonade) μπύρα με λεμονάδα.

shan't [ʃɑ:nt] = shall not || see shall.

shanty ['ʃæntɪ] n καλύβα, παράγγα || ~ **town** n παραγγούπολη.

shape [ʃeɪp] n σχήμα nt, μορφή, φόρμα, καλούπι ♦ vt σχηματίζω, διαμορφώνω, διαπλάθω || **to take** ~ διαμορφούμαι, παίρνω μορφή || ~less a άμορφος, ακανόνιστος || ~ly a καλοσχηματισμένος, όμορφος.

share [ʃɛə*] n (thing received) μερίδιο || (contribution) μετοχή, μερίδιο || (FIN) μετοχή, τίτλος, αξία ♦ vt μοιράζω, διανέμω || (in common) (συμ)μετέχω || ~holder n μέτοχος.

shark [ʃɑ:k] n (fish) σκυλόψαρο, καρχαρίας.

sharp [ʃɑ:p] a (razor, knife) κοφτερός || (distinct) ξεκαθαριστός, έντονος, καθαρός || (biting) δριμύς, διαπεραστικός || (quick-witted) οξύνους, έξυπνος || (unscrupulous) πονηρός, κατεργάρης ♦ n (MUS) δίεση ♦ ad ακριβώς, έντονα, καθαρά || **look** ~! κάνε γρήγορα!, κουνήσου!|| ~en vt ακονίζω, τροχίζω, ξεμυτίζω || ~ener n ξύστρα || ~-eyed a που κόβει το μάτι του || ~ness n κόψη || ~-witted a οξύνους, έξυπνος.

shatter ['ʃætə*] vt θρυμματίζω, σπάζω, κάνω κομμάτια || (fig) συντρίβω, κλονίζω || vi συντρίβομαι, σπάω.

shave [ʃeɪv] (irreg v) n ξύρισμα nt ♦ vt ξυρίζω || (fig) περνώ ξυστά ♦ vi ξυρίζομαι || ~r n (ELEC) ξυριστική μηχανή.

shaving ['ʃeɪvɪŋ] n (action) ξύρισμα nt|| ~s npl (of wood etc) ροκανίδια ntpl, ρινίσματα ntpl|| ~ **brush** n πινέλο του ξυρίσματος || ~ **cream** n κρέμα ξυρίσματος.

shawl [ʃɔ:l] n σάλι.

she [ʃi:] pron αυτή ♦ a θηλυκός.

sheaf [ʃi:f] n δέσμη, δεμάτι.

shear [ʃɪə*] (irreg v) vt (sheep etc) κουρεύω || **to** ~ **off** vt κόβω || ~s npl (for hedge) ψαλίδα.

sheath [ʃi:θ] n θήκη, κολεός, θηκάρι.

shed [ʃed] (irreg v) n υπόστεγο ♦ vt αποβάλλω, βγάζω || (pour out) χύνω.

she'd [ʃi:d] = she had, she would || see have, would.

sheep [ʃi:p] n πρόβατο || ~-**dog** n τσοπανόσκυλο || ~**ish** a δειλός, ντροπαλός || ~-**skin** n προβιά.

sheer [ʃɪə*] a καθαρός πραγματικός, γνήσιος || (steep) κατακόρυφος, απότομος || (almost transparent) διαφανής, λεπτός ♦ ad τελείως, πλήρως, απολύτως.

sheet [ʃi:t] n σεντόνι || (thin piece) έλασμα nt, φύλλο, λαμαρίνα || (paper) φύλλο, κόλλα.

sheik(h) [ʃeɪk] n σεϊχης.

shelf [ʃelf] n ράφι.

she'll [ʃi:l] = she will, she shall || see will, shall.

shell [ʃel] n κέλυφος nt, τσόφλι, φλοιός || (explosive) οβίδα, βλήμα nt|| (of building) σκελετός ♦ vt ξεφλουδίζω || (MIL) βομβαρδίζω.

shellfish ['ʃelfɪʃ] n (ZOOL) οστρακοειδές nt|| (as food) θαλασσινά ntpl.

shelter ['ʃeltə*] n καταφύγιο || (protection) προστασία ♦ vt προφυλάσσω, προστατεύω, στεγάζω ♦ vi προφυλάσσομαι, φυλάγομαι || ~ed a (life) αποτραβηγμένος, περιορισμένος || (spot) προφυλαγμένος, προστατευμένος.

shelve [ʃεlv] vt (put aside) βάζω στο ράφι || ~s npl of **shelf**.

shepherd ['ʃεpəd] n ποιμένας, βοσκός ♦ vt (guide) οδηγώ, συνοδεύω || ~ess n βοσκοπούλα || ~'s pie n κιμάς σκεπασμένος με πουρέ και ψημένος στο φούρνο.

sheriff ['ʃεrif] n σερίφης.

sherry ['ʃεri] n σέρυ nt inv.

she's [ʃiːz] = **she is, she has** || see **be, have**.

shield [ʃiːld] n ασπίδα, σκουτάρι || (protection) προστατευτικό κάλυμμα nt ♦ vt προασπίζω, προστατεύω || καλύπτω.

shift [ʃift] n (change) αλλαγή || (group of workers, period) βάρδια ♦ vt μετατοπίζω, μεταθέτω, μετακινώ || (remove) αλλάζω, μεταβάλλω ♦ vi μετακινούμαι, μετατοπίζομαι || ~y a πονηρός, ύπουλος.

shilling ['ʃiliŋ] n (old) σελίνι.

shimmer ['ʃimə*] n ανταύγεια, μαρμαρυγή ♦ vi σπιθοβολώ, λαμπυρίζω, γυαλίζω.

shin [ʃin] n αντικνήμιο, καλάμι (ποδιού).

shine [ʃain] (irreg v) n (gleam) γυάλισμα nt, στιλπνότητα, γυαλάδα ♦ vt (polish) στίλβω, λουστράρω, γυαλίζω || (torch) ακτινοβολώ, λάμπω ♦ vi λάμπω, αστράφτω, γυαλίζω || (excel) διακρίνομαι, ξεπροβάλλω.

shingle ['ʃiŋgl] n ξυλοκέραμος, ταβανοσάνιδο || (on beach) βότσαλα ntpl, κροκάλες fpl || ~s npl (MED) έρπης, ζωστήρ n.

shiny ['ʃaini] a λαμπερός, γυαλιστερός.

ship [ʃip] n πλοίο, σκάφος nt ♦ vt επιβιβάζω, μπαρκάρω || (transport as cargo) φορτώνω, αποστέλλω || ~building n ναυπηγική || ~ment n φόρτωση || (goods) φορτίο, εμπόρευμα nt || ~per n (sender) αποστολέας || ~ping n (act)

φόρτωση || (ships) πλοία ntpl, ναυτιλία || (ships of country) εμπορική ναυτιλία || ~shape a περίφημος, εξαιρετικός || ~wreck n ναυάγιο || ~yard n ναυπηγείο.

shire ['ʃaiə*] n κομητεία.

shirk [ʃəːk] vt αποφεύγω, ξεφεύγω, φυγοπονώ.

shirt [ʃəːt] n (man's shirt) πουκάμισο.

shiver ['ʃivə*] n ρίγος nt, τρεμούλα ♦ vi (with cold) τρέμω, τουρτουρίζω.

shoal [ʃəul] n (of fish) κοπάδι (ψαριών).

shock [ʃɔk] n δόνηση, σύγκρουση, τίναγμα nt || (ELEC) ηλεκτρικό σόκ nt inv, ηλεκτροπληξία || (emotional) συγκλονισμός, ταραχή || (MED) καταπληξία, σόκ ♦ vt σκανδαλίζω, σοκάρω || ~ absorber n αποσβεστήρας κρούσεων, αμορτισέρ nt inv || ~ing a σκανδαλώδης || συγκλονιστικός || ~proof a (watch) προφυλαγμένος από δονήσεις.

shod [ʃɔd] pt, pp of **shoe**.

shoddiness ['ʃɔdinis] n κακή ποιότητα.

shoddy ['ʃɔdi] a κακής ποιότητας, της πεντάρας.

shoe [ʃuː] (irreg v) n υπόδημα nt, παπούτσι || (of horse) πέταλο ♦ vt πεταλώνω (άλογο) || ~brush n βούρτσα των παπουτσιών || ~horn n κόκκαλο των παπουτσιών || ~lace n κορδόνι || ~shop n παπουτσάδικο υποδηματοπωλείο.

shone [ʃɔn] pt, pp of **shine**.

shook [ʃuk] pt of **shake**.

shoot [ʃuːt] (irreg v) n (branch) βλαστός, βλαστάρι ♦ vt (gun) πυροβολώ, εκκενώνω || (kill) σκοτώνω || (film) τραβώ, γυρίζω (ταινία) ♦ vi (move swiftly) (εξ)ορμώ, τρέχω, πετώ || (let off gun) πυροβολώ, κτυπώ || to ~ down vt (plane) καταρρίπτω || ~ing n (shots)

πυροβολισμός, πόλεμος || (hunting) κυνήγι || ~ing star n διάττων αστέρας.

shop [ʃɔp] n κατάστημα nt, μαγαζί || (workshop) εργαστήριο, μαγαζί nt ♦ vi (also: go ~ping) ψωνίζω || ~ assistant n υπάλληλος m/f καταστήματος || ~keeper n καταστηματάρχης, μικρέμπορος || ~lifter n κλέφτης καταστημάτων || ~lifting n κλοπή καταστημάτων || ~per n πελάτης/τρια m/f, αγοραστής/άστρια m/f|| ~ping n αγορές fpl, ψώνια ntpl || ~ping bag n τσάντα για τα ψώνια || ~ping centre, ~ping center (US) n αγορά, εμπορικό κέντρο || ~-soiled a στραπατσαρισμένος || ~ steward n (industry) αντιπρόσωπος του συνδικάτου || ~ window n προθήκη, βιτρίνα || see talk.

shore [ʃɔː*] n (of sea, lake) ακτή, παραλία ♦ vt: to ~ up υποστηρίζω, στηλώνω.

shorn [ʃɔːn] pp of shear.

short [ʃɔːt] a βραχύς, κοντός || (not tall) κοντός || (too finished) βραχύς, σύντομος || (curt) απότομος, κοφτός || (in measure) λιποβαρής, ελλειπής, λειψός || (ELEC: short-circuit) (βραχυκύκλωμα nt) ♦ ad απότομα || ~ of εκτός || vti (ELEC) βραχυκυκλώνω, βραχυκυκλούμαι || to cut ~ τερματίζω απότομα, συντομεύω, διακόπτω || to fall ~ πέφτω κοντά, δεν πετυχαίνω || to stop ~ σταματώ ξαφνικά || ~age n ανεπάρκεια, έλλειψη || ~bread n είδος nt κέικ || ~circuit n βραχυκύκλωμα nt ♦ vi βραχυκυκλούμαι || ~coming n ελάττωμα nt, ατέλεια, μειονέκτημα nt|| ~ cut n συντομώτερος δρόμος || ~ en vti μικραίνω, κονταίνω || ~hand n στενογραφία || ~hand typist n στενοδακτυλογράφος m/f ||

~-lived a βραχύβιος, εφήμερος || ~ly ad (soon) προσεχώς, σύντομα, σε λίγο || ~ness n βραχύτητα, συντομία || ~-sighted a (lit) μυωπικός || (fig) μη προνοητικός, κοντόθαμνος || ~story n διήγημα nt || ~-tempered a απότομος, ευέξαπτος || ~-term a (FIN) βραχυπρόθεσμος || ~-wave n (RAD) βραχύ κύμα nt.

shot [ʃɔt] pt, pp of **shoot** ♦ n (firing etc) πυροβολισμός, τουφεκιά || (person) σκοπευτής || (attempt) δοκιμή, προσπάθεια, απόπειρα || (injection) ένεση || (PHOT) λήψη φωτογραφίας || like a ~ (very readily) αμέσως, πρόθυμα || ~gun n κυνηγετικό όπλο.

should [ʃud] auxiliary v: I ~ go now πρέπει να φύγω τώρα || he ~ be there now πρέπει να έχει φθάσει τώρα || I ~ like θα ήθελα.

shoulder ['ʃəuldə*] n ώμος ♦ vt επωμίζομαι || ~ blade n ωμοπλάτη.

shouldn't ['ʃudnt] = **should not** || see **should**.

shout [ʃaut] n κραυγή, φωνή ♦ vi κραυγάζω || vi κραυγάζω, φωνάζω || ~ing n φωνές fpl, κραυγές fpl.

shove [ʃʌv] n ώθηση, σπρωξιά, σπρώξιμο ♦ vt σπρώχνω || to ~ off vi (NAUT) απωθώ || (fig, col) φεύγω, ξεκινώ.

shovel ['ʃʌvl] n φτυάρι ♦ vt φτυαρίζω.

show [ʃəu] (irreg) n (indication) n επίδειξη, προβολή || (appearance) εμφάνιση, όψη || (exhibition) έκθεση, θέαμα nt || (THEAT, CINE) θέατρο, σινεμά nt inv, παράσταση ♦ vt δείκνυω, οδηγώ || (demonstrate) παρουσιάζω, αποδεικνύω || (explain) δείχνω, εξηγώ || (give) δείχνω ♦ vi (be visible) εμφανίζομαι, φαίνομαι, ξεπροβάλλω || to ~ in vi πες να μπει || to ~ out vi συνοδεύω στην έξοδο || to ~ off

vi (pej) επιδεικνύομαι, καμαρώνω ♦ *vt (display)* επιδεικνύω, δείχνω, διαφημίζω || **to ~ up** *vi (appear)* εμφανίζομαι, παρουσιάζομαι ♦ *vt* δείχνω || **~down** *n* αναμέτρηση, διακήρυξη προθέσεων.

shower ['ʃauə] *n* μπόρα || (stones etc) βροχή από πέτρες κτλ || (shower bath) ντους, *nt inv* ♦ *vt (fig only)* δίνω άφθονα || **~ y** *a (weather)* βροχερός.

showing ['ʃəuɪŋ] *n (of film)* εμφάνιση, προβολή.

shown [ʃəun] *pp of* **show.**

show-off ['ʃəuf] *n (col: person)* κορδωμένος.

showroom ['ʃəurum] *n* αίθουσα εκθέσεων.

shrank [ʃræŋk] *pt of* **shrink.**

shrapnel ['ʃræpnl] *n* βολιδοφόρο βλήμα *nt.*

shred [ʃred] *n (generally pl)* κομμάτι, λουρίδα, κουρέλι || *vt* κατατμίζω, σχίζω σε λουρίδες || **in ~s** ξεσχισμένος, κουρελιασμένος.

shrewd [ʃruːd] *a* διορατικός, επιδέξιος || **~ness** *n* ευφυΐα, εξυπνάδα.

shriek [ʃriːk] *n* ξεφωνητό, στριγγλιά ♦ *vti* ξεφωνίζω, στριγγλίζω.

shrill [ʃrɪl] *a* οξύς, διαπεραστικός.

shrimp [ʃrɪmp] *n* γαρίδα.

shrine [ʃraɪn] *n* λειψανοθήκη, βωμός, ιερός τόπος.

shrink [ʃrɪŋk] *(irreg v) vi* συστέλλομαι, μαζεύομαι ♦ *vt (make smaller)* ζαρώνω, συστέλλω, κάνω να μαζέψει || **~age** *n* συστολή, μπάσιμο, μάζεμα *nt.*

shrivel ['ʃrɪvl] *vti (also: ~ up)* μαραίνομαι, ζαρώνω, ξεραίνομαι.

shroud [ʃraud] *n* σάβανο ♦ *vt* σκεπάζω, καλύπτω.

Shrove Tuesday ['ʃrəuv'tjuːzdɪ] *n* Καθαρή Τρίτη.

shrub [ʃrʌb] *n* θάμνος, χαμόδεντρο || **~bery** *n* θαμνώνας, λόγγος.

shrug [ʃrʌg] *n* σήκωμα *nt* των ώμων || **to ~ off** *vt* αφηγώ, απορρίπτω.

shrunk [ʃrʌŋk] *pp of* **shrink.**

shudder ['ʃʌdə*] *n* ρίγος *nt*, φρικίαση, τρεμούλα ♦ *vi* τρέμω.

shuffle ['ʃʌfl] *n (CARDS)* ανακάτεμα *nt (*τράπουλας) ♦ *vti* ανακατεύω ♦ *vi* σέρνω τα πόδια.

shun [ʃʌn] *vt* αποφεύγω.

shush [ʃuʃ] *excl (col)* σουτ!

shut [ʃʌt] *(irreg v) vi* κλείνω ♦ *vi* κλείσιμαι, κλείνω || **to ~ down** *vti* κλείνω, σταματώ εργασίες || **to ~ off** *(supply)* διακόπτω, αποκόπτω, αποκλείω || **to ~ up** *vi (keep quiet)* σωπαίνω, βουλώνω ♦ *vt (close)* κλείνω καλά, κλειδώνω || *(silence)* αποστομώνω, κλείνω το στόμα || **~ up!** σκασμός! || **~ter** *n* παραθυρόφυλλο, παντζούρι || *(of camera)* φωτοφράκτης.

shuttlecock ['ʃʌtlkɒk] *n* φτερωτή σφαίρα, βολάν *nt inv.*

shy [ʃaɪ] *a* ντροπαλός, δειλός || **~ly** *ad* ντροπαλά, δειλά || **~ness** *n* δειλία, ντροπαλότητα.

Siamese [saɪə'miːz] *a:* **~ cat** Σιαμαία γάτα.

sick [sɪk] *a* ασθενής, άρρωστος || (inclined to vomit) έχω τάση προς εμετό || *(disgusting)* αηδιαστικός, σιχαμερός || **~ bay** *n* νοσοκομείο πλοίου || **~en** *vt* αρρωσταίνω, αηδιάζω ♦ *vi* αηδιάζω || **~ening** *a (fig)* αηδιαστικός.

sickle ['sɪkl] *n* δρεπάνι.

sick leave ['sɪkliːv] *n* αναρρωτική άδεια.

sickly ['sɪklɪ] *a* αρρωστιάρης, ωχρός, ασθενικός || *(nauseating)* που προκαλεί αναγούλα.

sickness ['sɪknɪs] *n* ασθένεια, αρρώστια, νόσος *f* || *(vomiting)* ναυτία, αναγούλα, εμετός.

sick pay ['sɪkpeɪ] *n* επίδομα *nt* ασθενείας.

side [saɪd] n πλευρά, πλευρό, μέρος nt, μεριά || (of body) πλευρά, μεριά || (of lake) όχθη || (aspect) πλευρά, όψη, άποψη ♦ a (door, entrance) πλαγία (είσοδος), πλαϊνή (είσοδος f) ♦ vi: **to ~ with** πάω με, παίρνω το μέρος του || **by the ~** of στο πλευρό του, σε σύγκριση με || **on all ~s** από παντού || **to take ~s (with)** υποστηρίζω, μεροληπτώ || **~board** n μπουφές m inv || **~boards, ~burns** npl (whiskers) φαβορίτες fpl || **~ effect** n (MED) παρενέργεια || **~light** n (AUT) πλευρικός φανός || **~line** n (RAIL) δευτερεύουσα γραμμή || (fig: hobby) πάρεργο || **~road** n πάροδος f || **~ show** n δευτερεύον θέαμα nt || **~track** n (fig) παραμερίζω || **~walk** n (US) πεζοδρόμιο || **~ways** ad πλάγια, λοξά.

siding ['saɪdɪŋ] n πλευρική διακλάδωση.

sidle ['saɪdl] vi: **to ~ up** πλησιάζω δειλά και πλάγια.

siege [siːdʒ] n πολιορκία.

sieve [sɪv] n κόσκινο ♦ vt κοσκινίζω.

sift [sɪft] vt κοσκινίζω || (examine) ξεχωρίζω, εξονυχίζω.

sigh [saɪ] n αναστεναγμός ♦ vi (ανα)στενάζω.

sight [saɪt] n όραση || (scene) θέα, θέαμα nt || (of rifle) κλισίοσκόπιο, στόχαστρο ♦ vt αντικρύζω, βλέπω, παρατηρώ || **in ~** φαίνομαι, γίνομαι ορατός || **out of ~** δε φαίνομαι || **~seeing** n επίσκεψη αξιοθέατων || **to go ~seeing** επισκέπτομαι τα αξιοθέατα.

sign [saɪn] n (with hand) νεύμα n, νόημα nt || (indication) ένδειξη, σημάδι || (notice, road etc) σήμα nt, ταμπέλα, πινακίδα || (written symbol) σημείο, σημάδι ♦ vt υπογράφω || **to ~ off** vi ξεμπαρκάρω || **to ~ up** vti (MIL) κατατάσσομαι.

signal ['sɪgnl] n σύνθημα nt, σημείο, σήμα nt ♦ vt σηματοδοτώ, στέλνω με σήματα.

signature ['sɪgnətʃə*] n υπογραφή.

significance [sɪg'nɪfɪkəns] n σημασία, έννοια, νόημα nt || (importance) σπουδαιότητα, σημαντικότητα.

significant [sɪg'nɪfɪkənt] a με σημασία, σημαντικός || (important) σημαντικός, σπουδαίος, σημαίνων || **~ly** ad με έννοια, με σημασία.

signify ['sɪgnɪfaɪ] vt σημαίνω, εννοώ || (express) είμαι ένδειξη, (εκ)δηλώνω.

sign language ['saɪnlæŋgwɪdʒ] n γλώσσα του νεύματα.

signpost ['saɪnpəʊst] n σήμα nt κυκλοφορίας, πινακίδα της τροχαίας.

silence ['saɪləns] n σιγή, σιωπή, ησυχία ♦ vt σιωπαίνω, πνιγάζω || n σιγαστήρας, σιλανσιέ nt inv.

silent ['saɪlənt] a σιωπηλός, αθόρυβος, σιγαλός || (saying nothing) άφωνος, αμίλητος.

silhouette [sɪluː'et] n (outline) σιλουέτα ♦ vt διαγράφομαι σα σιλουέτα.

silk [sɪlk] n μετάξι ♦ a μεταξωτός || **~y** a μεταξένιος, απαλός, στιλπνός.

silliness ['sɪlɪnɪs] n μωρία, ανοησία, χαζομάρα.

silly ['sɪlɪ] a ανόητος, μωρός.

silt [sɪlt] n βόρβορος, λάσπη.

silver ['sɪlvə*] n άργυρος, ασήμι ntpl || (coins) αργυρά νομίσματα ntpl || (objects) ασημικά ntpl ♦ a αργυρός, ασημένιος || **~ paper** n ασημόχαρτο || **~-plated** a επάργυρος || **~smith** n αργυροχόος || **~y** a ασημένιος.

similar ['sɪmɪlə*] a (+ to) όμοιος (με) || **~ity** n ομοιότητα, ομοιία || **~ly** ad παρόμοια, ομοίως.

simile ['sɪmɪlɪ] n παρομοίωση.

simmer ['sɪmə*] vi σιγοβράζω.

simple ['sɪmpl] a (easy) απλός, εύκολος || (natural) απλός, απλοϊκός || (plain) απλός, απλοϊκός || (of one kind) απλός || (weak-minded) αφελής, μωρόπιστος || ~-minded a αφελής, απλοϊκός.

simplicity [sɪm'plɪsɪtɪ] n απλότητα.

simplify ['sɪmplɪfaɪ] vt απλουστεύω, απλοποιώ.

simulation [sɪmju'leɪʃən] n (imitation) απομίμηση, προσποίηση.

simultaneous [sɪməl'teɪnɪəs] a ταυτόχρονος || ~ly ad ταυτόχρονα, σύγχρονα με.

sin [sɪn] n αμαρτία ♦ vi αμαρτάνω.

since [sɪns] ad έκτοτε, από τότε ♦ prep από || cj (time) αφότου, από τότε που || (because) αφού, εφόσον.

sincere [sɪn'sɪə*] a ειλικρινής || ~ly ad ειλικρινά.

sincerity [sɪn'serɪtɪ] n ειλικρίνεια.

sinful ['sɪnful] a αμαρτωλός.

sing [sɪŋ] (irreg v) vt (song) τραγουδώ ♦ vi (gen) τραγουδώ || (bird) κελαηδώ || (ears) βουίζω.

singe [sɪndʒ] vt τσουρουφλίζω, καψαλίζω.

singer ['sɪŋə*] n αοιδός m/f, τραγουδιστής/ίστρια m/f.

singing ['sɪŋɪŋ] n τραγούδι.

single ['sɪŋgl] a μόνος, μοναδικός || (bed, room) μονό (κρεββάτι, δωμάτιο) || (unmarried) άγαμος || (ticket) απλό (εισιτήριο) || (one part) απλός, ένας ♦ n (ticket) απλό εισιτήριο || ~s npl (tennis) απλό παιχνίδι, σιγκλ at inv || **to ~ out** vt διαλέγω, επιλέγω, ξεχωρίζω || **in ~ file** κατ' άνδρα, στη γραμμή, ένας-ένας || **~-handed** a ολομόναχος, αβοήθητος, μόνος || **~-minded** a για ένα μόνο σκοπό || **~-sided disk** n (COMPUT) δίσκος μιας όψεως.

singlet ['sɪŋglɪt] n φανελίτσα.

singular ['sɪŋgjulə*] a ενικός || (odd) παράξενος, σπάνιος, μοναδικός ♦ n (GRAM) ενικός αριθμός.

sinister ['sɪnɪstə*] a απαίσιος, δυσοίωνος, μοχθηρός.

sink [sɪŋk] (irreg v) n νεροχύτης ♦ vt (put under) καταποντίζω, βουλιάζω || (dig) σκάβω, ανοίγω ♦ vi (fall slowly) καταβυθίζομαι, βουλιάζω, καθίζω || **to ~ in** vi (news etc) χαράσσομαι στο μυαλό || **~ing** a (feeling) απογοητευτικός || **with ~ing heart** με σφιγμένη καρδιά.

sinner ['sɪnə*] n αμαρτωλός.

sinus ['saɪnəs] n (ANAT) κόλπος.

sip [sɪp] n ρουφηξιά, γουλιά ♦ vt πίνω γουλιά-γουλιά, ρουφώ.

siphon ['saɪfən] n σιφόνι || **to ~ off** vt αναρροφώ, σιφωνίζω.

sir [sɜ:*] n κύριε || (title) κύριος || **yes S~** μάλιστα, κύριε.

siren ['saɪərən] n σειρήνα.

sirloin ['sɜːlɔɪn] n κόντρα φιλέτο.

sister ['sɪstə*] n αδελφή || (MED) αρχινοσοκόμος || (nun) αδελφή, καλογριά, αδελφή || **~-in-law** n κουνιάδα, νύφη.

sit [sɪt] (irreg v) vi κάθομαι || (at session) συνεδριάζω ♦ vt (exam) δίνω εξετάσεις, εξετάζομαι || **to ~ tight** δεν το κουνώ, βάζω τα δυνατά μου || **to ~ down** vi κάθομαι || **to ~ up** vi (after lying) ανασηκώνομαι || (at night) αγρυπνώ, ξενυχτώ.

site [saɪt] n τοποθεσία, θέση ♦ vt τοποθετώ, εγκαθιστώ.

sit-in ['sɪtɪn] n (demonstration) καταλαμβάνω σαν ένδειξη διαμαρτυρίας.

sitting ['sɪtɪŋ] n συνεδρίαση || **~ room** n σαλόνι.

situated ['sɪtjueɪtɪd] a κείμενος, ευρισκόμενος.

situation [sɪtju'eɪʃən] n (state of affairs) κατάσταση || (place)

τοποθεσία, θέση || *(post)* θέση, εργασία, δουλειά.

six [sɪks] *num* έξι || ~**teen** *num* δεκαέξι || ~**th** a έκτος || ~**ty** *num* εξήντα.

size [saɪz] *n* μέγεθος, διάσταση, έκταση, όγκος || *(glue)* κόλλα || *(of clothing)* νούμερο || **to** ~ **up** *vt (assess)* εκτιμώ (το μέγεθος), σχηματίζω γνώμη για || ~**able** a αρκετά μεγάλος, μεγαλούτσικος.

sizzle [ˈsɪzl] *n* σφύριγμα *nt*, τσιτσίρισμα *nt* ♦ *vi* τσιτσιρίζω, σφυρίζω.

skate [skeɪt] *n* πέδιλο, πατίνι ♦ *vi* πατινάρω, παγοδρομώ || ~**r** *n* πατινέρ *m/f inv*, παγοδρόμος.

skating [ˈskeɪtɪŋ] *n*: **to go** ~ πηγαίνω για πατινάζ || ~ **rink** *n* παγοδρόμιο, αίθουσα πατινάζ.

skeleton [ˈskelɪtn] *n* σκελετός.

skeptic [ˈskeptɪk] *n (US)* = **sceptic**.

sketch [sketʃ] *n* σκαρίφημα *nt*, σκιαγραφία || *(play)* σκίτσο, σκετς *nt inv* ♦ *vt* σκιαγραφώ, σκιτσάρω || ~**book** *n* σημειωματάριο || ~ **pad** *n* καρνέ *nt inv* για σκίτσα || ~**y** a ατελής, ασαφής, ακαθόριστος.

skewer [ˈskjuːə*] *n* σούβλα.

ski [skiː] *n* σκι ♦ *vi* κάνω σκι || ~ **boot** *n* παπούτσι του σκι.

skid [skɪd] *n (skid-pan)* τροχοπέδη ♦ *vi* γλυστρώ πλαγίως, ντεραπάρω.

skidmark [ˈskɪdmaːk] *n* ίχνη *ntpl* ντεραπαρίσματος.

skier [ˈskiːə*] *n* σκιέρ *m/f inv*.

skiing [ˈskiːɪŋ] *n*: **to go** ~ πάω για σκι.

skijump [ˈskiːdʒʌmp] *n* πήδημα *nt* με σκι.

skilful [ˈskɪlful] a ικανός, επιδέξιος, επιτήδειος.

skill [skɪl] *n* ικανότητα, επιδεξιότητα || ~**ed** a επιδέξιος || *(trained)* ειδικευμένος.

skim [skɪm] *vt* ξαφρίζω, βγάζω || *(read)* ξεφυλλίζω || *(glide over)* περνώ ξυστά.

skimp [skɪmp] *vt* τσιγγουνεύομαι || *(do carelessly)* εκτελώ γρήγορα και επιπόλαια || ~**y** a *(work, dress)* ανεπαρκής || *(meal)* φτωχός.

skin [skɪn] *n* δέρμα *nt*, πετσί, τομάρι || *(peel, rind)* φλοιός, φλούδα || *(on milk)* πέτσα ♦ *vt* γδέρνω, ξεφλουδίζω || ~**deep** a επιπόλαιος, επιφανειακός || ~ **diving** *n* υποβρύχιο κολύμπι || ~**ny** a αδύνατος, κοκκαλιάρης, τσίρος || ~**tight** a *(dress etc)* (φόρεμα) εφαρμοστό.

skip [skɪp] *n (ανα)*πήδημα *nt*, σκίρτημα *nt* ♦ *vi* σκιρτώ, πηδώ, πετάγομαι ♦ *vt* παραλείπω, πηδώ.

ski pants [ˈskiː pænts] *npl* παντελόνι του σκι.

skipper [ˈskɪpə*] *n (NAUT, SPORT)* καπετάνιος.

skipping rope [ˈskɪpɪŋrəup] *n* σχοινάκι.

skirmish [ˈskɜːmɪʃ] *n* αψιμαχία.

skirt [skɜːt] *n* φούστα ♦ *vt* περιτρέχω, φέρνω βόλτα.

skit [skɪt] *n* ευθυμογράφημα *nt*, παρωδία, νούμερο.

skittle [ˈskɪtl] *n (one pin)* τσούκι || ~**s** *n (game)* τσούνια.

skull [skʌl] *n* κρανίο.

skunk [skʌŋk] *n* μεφίτη, είδος ασβού.

sky [skaɪ] *n* ουρανός || ~**-blue** a ανοιχτό μπλε || ~ **blue** *n* ουρανί (χρώμα) || ~**light** *n* φεγγίτης || ~**scraper** *n* ουρανοξύστης.

slab [slæb] *n* πλάκα.

slack [slæk] a χαλαρός, λάσκος || *(slow, dull)* νεκρός, νεκρή (εποχή) || *(careless)* αμελής, αδρανής ♦ *vi* ατονώ, τεμπελιάζω ♦ *n (in rope etc)* χαλαρότητα || ~**s** *npl* σπορ παντελόνι || ~**en** *(also:* ~ **en off)** *vi*

χαλαρώμαι, μειώμαι, πέφτω ♦ *vt* χαλαρώνω, μετριάζω, επιβραδύνω, λασκάρω.

slag [slæg] *n* σκουριά || ~ **heap** *n* σωρός σκουριάς.

slam [slæm] *n* κρότος, κτύπημα πόρτας ♦ *vt (door)* κλείνω απότομα, κτυπώ || *(throw down)* πετάω με δύναμη ♦ *vi* κλείνω με κρότο.

slander ['slɑ:ndə*] *n* κακολογία, διαβολή, συκοφαντία ♦ *vt* συκοφαντώ, κακολογώ, διαβάλλω || ~ **ous** *a* συκοφαντικός.

slang [slæŋ] *n* μάγκικη γλώσσα, λαϊκό, ιδίωμα *nt*.

slant [slɑ:nt] *n (lit)* κλίση, γέρσιμο || *(fig)* άποψη, αντίληψη ♦ *vti* κλίνω, γέρνω || ~**ing** *a* λοξός, πλάγιος.

slap [slæp] *n* κτύπημα *nt*, χαστούκι, μπάτσος, καρπαζιά ♦ *vt* ραπίζω, μπατσίζω, καρπαζώνω ♦ *ad (directly)* κατευθείαν || ~**dash** *ad* ξένοιαστα, απρόσεκτα || ~**stick** *n (comedy)* φάρσα.

slash [slæʃ] *n* δυνατό κτύπημα *nt*, σχίσιμο ♦ *vt* κόβω, σχίζω, πετσοκόβω.

slate [sleit] *n* σχιστόλιθος || *(piece of slate)* αβάκιο, πλάκα ♦ *vt (criticize)* επικρίνω, κουρελιάζω.

slaughter ['slɔ:tə*] *n* σφαγή, σφάξιμο ♦ *vt* σφάζω.

Slav [slɑ:v] *n (person)* Σλάβος/α *m/f* ♦ *a* σλαβικός.

slave [sleiv] *n* σκλάβος, δούλος ♦ *vi* δουλεύω σκληρά, μοχθώ || ~**ry** *n* δουλεία, σκλαβιά.

slavish ['sleiviʃ] *a* δουλικός || ~**ly** *ad* δουλικά.

sledge [sledʒ] *n* έλκηθρο || ~**hammer** *n* βαριά, μεγάλο σφυρί.

sleek [sli:k] *a* λείος, απαλός, προσποιητός.

sleep [sli:p] *(irreg v)* *n* ύπνος ♦ *vi* κοιμούμαι, πλαγιάζω || **to go to** ~ αποκοιμούμαι || **to** ~ **in** *vi (late)*

ξυπνώ αργά || ~**er** *n* υπναράς || *(RAIL)* κλινάμαξα || ~**ily** *ad* κοιμισμένα || ~**iness** *n* υπνηλία, νυσταγμός, νύστα ||~**ing bag** *n* σάκκος ύπνου || ~**ing car** *n* κλινάμαξα, βαγκόν-λι *nt inv*|| ~**ing pill** *n* υπνωτικό χάπι || ~**lessness** *n* αϋπνία, αγρυπνία || ~**walker** *n* υπνοβάτης/άτρια *m/f*|| ~**y** *a* νυσταλέος, νυσταγμένος.

sleet [sli:t] *n* χιονόνερο.

sleeve [sli:v] *n* μανίκι || ~**less** *a (garment)* χωρίς μανίκια.

sleigh [slei] *n* έλκηθρο.

sleight [slait] *n*: ~ **of hand** ταχυδακτυλουργία.

slender ['slendə*] *a* λεπτός, λιγνός || *(small)* ισχνός, ασθενής.

slept [slept] *pt, pp of* **sleep.**

slice [slais] *n (of bread)* φέτα || *(of cake, cheese etc)* κομμάτι ♦ *vt* τεμαχίζω, κόβω σε φέτες.

slick [slik] *a (smart)* γλυστερός, δόλιος, επιτήδειος.

slid [slid] *pt, pp of* **slide.**

slide [slaid] *(irreg v)* *n* τσουλήθρα, ολισθητήριο, στίβος || *(PHOT: transparency)* διαφάνεια, σλάϊντ *nt inv* || *(brooch)* τσιμπιδάκι || *(fall in prices)* πτώση τιμών ♦ *vt* παρακάμπτω, ξεφεύγω ♦ *vi* γλυστρώ.

sliding ['slaidiŋ] *a (door)* συρτή (πόρτα).

slight [slait] *a* λεπτός || *(trivial)* ελαφρός, ασήμαντος || *(small)* μικροκαμωμένος, μικρούλης ♦ *n* υποτίμηση, περιφρόνηση ♦ *vt (offend)* προσβάλλω, θίγω || ~**ly** *ad* ελαφρά, κάπως, λιγάκι.

slim [slim] *a* λεπτός, μικρός ♦ *vi* κάνω δίαιτα.

slime [slaim] *n* λάσπη, βούρκος.

slimming ['slimiŋ] *n* αδυνάτισμα *nt.*

slimy ['slaimi] *a* βορβορώδης, γλοιώδης.

sling [slɪŋ] *(irreg v)* n *(bandage)* ανωμπής, κρεμαστάρι ♦ *vt* εκσφενδονίζω, ρίχνω.

slip [slɪp] n *(slipping)* ολίσθημα nt, γλύστρημα nt || *(petticoat)* μισοφόρι || *(of paper)* φύλλο, χαρτί ♦ *vt* γλυστρώ αθόρυβα, χώνω || *(escape from)* ξεφεύγω από ♦ *vi* *(lose balance)* γλυστρώ || *(move smoothly)* κινούμαι αθόρυβα || *(make mistake)* κάνω γκάφα, σφάλλω || *(decline)* παρεκτρέπομαι, παραστρατώ || **to ~ away** *vi* γλιστρώ, φεύγω απαρατήρητα || **to ~ in** *vt* βάζω, χώνω || **to ~ out** *vi* βγαίνω (κρυφά).

slipper ['slɪpə*] n παντούφλα.

slippery ['slɪpərɪ] a ολισθηρός, γλυστερός || *(tricky)* πανούργος, πονηρός.

slipshod ['slɪpʃɒd] a ακατάστατος, απρόσεκτος.

slip-up ['slɪpʌp] n *(mistake)* σφάλμα nt, γκάφα.

slipway ['slɪpweɪ] n ναυπηγική κλίνη.

slit [slɪt] *(irreg v)* n σχίσιμο, σχισμή ♦ *vt* κόβω, σχίζω, σχίζομαι.

slither ['slɪðə*] *vi* σέρνομαι, γλιστρώ.

slob [slɒb] n *(col: unpleasant person)* ατζαμής.

slog [slɒg] n *(great effort)* αγγαρεία, βαρειά δουλειά ♦ *vi* *(work hard)* δουλεύω σκληρά.

slogan ['sləʊgən] n *(catchword)* σύνθημα nt.

slop [slɒp] *vi* ξεχειλίζω, χύνομαι ♦ *vt* χύνω.

slope [sləʊp] n κατηφοριά, πλαγιά || *(slant)* κλίση ♦ *vi:* **to ~ down** κατηφορίζω || **to ~ up** *vi* ανηφορίζω.

sloping ['sləʊpɪŋ] a λοξός, πλάγιος.

sloppy ['slɒpɪ] a λασπωμένος, λασπώδης || *(untidy)* πρόχειρος,

ακατάστατος || *(weak, silly)* άτονος, σαχλός.

slot [slɒt] n σχισμή, χαραμάδα ♦ *vt:* **to ~ in** βάζω, τοποθετώ || **~ machine** n αυτόματος πωλητής || μηχάνημα τυχερών παιχνιδιών.

slouch [slaʊtʃ] *vi* κινούμαι αδέξια.

slovenly ['slʌvnlɪ] a ακατάστατος, απρόσεκτος.

slow [sləʊ] a βραδύς, αργός || *(of clock)* πάω, πίσω || *(stupid)* βραδύνους, χοντροκέφαλος ♦ *ad* σιγά, αργά || '**~**' *(roadsign)* 'αργά' || **to ~ down** *vi* επιβραδύνω, μειώνω, κόβω (ταχύτητα) ♦ *vt* επιβραδύνω || **to ~ up** *vi* σταματώ, φρενάρω ♦ *vt* επιβραδύνω || **~ly** ad σιγά, αργά || **in ~ motion** σε αργό ρυθμό, ρελαντί.

sludge [slʌdʒ] n λάσπη, βούρκος.

slug [slʌg] n γυμνοσάλιαγκας || *(bullet)* μικρή σφαίρα || **~gish** a αδρανής, τεμπέλικος, νωθρός || **~gishly** ad νωθρά, τεμπέλικα || **~gishness** n νωθρότητα, βραδύτητα.

sluice [sluːs] n υδροφράκτης, φράγμα nt.

slum [slʌm] n φτωχογειτονιά.

slumber ['slʌmbə*] n γαλήνιος ύπνος.

slump [slʌmp] n πτώση, ελάττωση ζητήσεως ♦ *vi* πέφτω απότομα.

slung [slʌŋ] pt, pp of **sling**.

slur [slɜː*] n βιαστική προφορά, τραύλισμα nt || *(insult)* στίγμα nt προσβολή ♦ *vt* *(also:* **~ over**) κακοποορφέρω, τραυλίζω.

slush [slʌʃ] n λασπωμένο χιόνι || **~y** a *(lit)* λασπωμένος || *(fig: sentimental)* σαχλός, γλυκανάλατος.

slut [slʌt] n τσούλια, παλιοθήλυκο.

sly [slaɪ] a πονηρός, πανούργος, ύπουλος.

smack [smæk] n *(slap)* κτύπημα nt, χαστούκι, μπάτσος ♦ *vt* *(slap)*

ραπίζω, καρπαζώνω ‖ **to ~ one's lips** κτυπώ τα χείλη.

small [smɔːl] a μικρός, λίγος ‖ **~ holding** n μικρό κτήμα nt ‖ **~ hours** npl πολύ πρωινές ώρες fpl ‖ **~ish** a μάλλον μικρός, μικρούτσικος ‖ **~ pox** n ευλογιά, βλογιά ‖ **~ talk** n φλυαρία.

smart [smɑːt] a (well-dressed) κομψός, μοντέρνος ‖ (clever) έξυπνος, επιδέξιος ‖ (sharp, quick) οξβέλτος, γρήγορος, ζωηρός ♦ vi πονώ, τσούζω, υποφέρω ‖ **to ~en up** vi ζωηρεύω, κάνω κέφι ‖ κομμεύομαι ♦ vt επισπεύδω.

smash [smæʃ] n (collision) σύγκρουση ♦ vt τσακίζω, θρυμματίζω, κομματιάζω ‖ (destroy) καταστρέφω, συντρίβω ♦ vi θραύομαι, κομματιάζομαι ‖ **~ing** a (col) σπουδαίος, περίφημος.

smattering ['smætəriŋ] n επιπόλαια γνώση, πασάλειμμα.

smear [smɪə*] n κηλίδα, λεκές m ‖ επίχρισμα nt ♦ vt λερώνω, μουντζουρώνω.

smell [smɛl] (irreg v) n όσφρηση ‖ (odour) οσμή, μυρωδιά ♦ vt (breathe in) μυρίζω ♦ vi μυρίζω, παίρνω μυρωδιά ‖ (give out smell) μυρίζω, βρωμώ ‖ **~ y** a (unpleasant) δύσοσμος, βρωμερός.

smile [smaɪl] n χαμόγελο ♦ vi χαμογελώ.

smiling ['smaɪliŋ] a χαμογελαστός, γελαστός.

smirk [smɜːk] n ψεύτικο χαμόγελο ♦ vi χαμογελώ ψεύτικα.

smith [smɪθ] n σιδηρουργός, σιδεράς ‖ **~ y** ['smɪðɪ] n σιδηρουργείο, σιδεράδικο.

smock [smɒk] n μπλούζα, φόρμα.

smoke [sməuk] n καπνός, καπνίλα ‖ (tobacco) κάπνισμα nt, τσιγάρο ♦ vt (puff) καπνίζω ‖ (dry food) καπνίζω ♦ vi αναδίδω καπνούς, καπνίζω ‖ (of

cigarette) καπνίζω ‖ **~d** a (bacon etc) καπνιστός ‖ **~ r** n (person) καπνιστής ‖ (RAIL) όχημα nt καπνιστών.

smoking ['sməukiŋ] n κάπνισμα nt ‖ **'no ~'** (sign) 'απαγορεύεται το κάπνισμα'.

smoky ['sməuki] a γεμάτος καπνό, καπνισμένος.

smolder ['sməuldə*] vi (US) = **smoulder.**

smooth [smuːð] a (in consistency) απαλός ‖ (wine) γλυκόπιοτος ‖ (movement) ομαλός, μαλακός, αθόρυβος ‖ (person) γλυκομίλητος, γαλίφης ♦ vt (also: ~ out) λειαίνω, εξομαλύνω, ισιώνω.

smother ['smʌðə*] vt πνίγω, καταπνίγω.

smoulder ['sməuldə*] vi σιγοκαίω, υποβόσκω.

smudge [smʌdʒ] n κηλίδα, λεκές m, βρωμιά ♦ vt λεκιάζω, λερώνω, βρωμίζω.

smug [smʌg] a αυτάρεσκος, καμαρωτός.

smuggle ['smʌgl] vt κάνω λαθρεμπόριο, περνώ λαθραία ‖ **~r** n λαθρέμπορος, κοντραμπαντζής.

smuggling ['smʌgliŋ] n λαθρεμπόριο, κοντραμπάντο.

smutty ['smʌti] a (fig: obscene) αισχρός, βρώμικος, πρόστυχος.

snack [snæk] n ελαφρό φαγητό, κολατσό ‖ **~ bar** n σνακ-μπαρ nt inv.

snag [snæg] n (obstacle) εμπόδιο, κώλυμα nt ‖ (in stocking) τράβηγμα nt κλωστής.

snail [sneil] n σαλιγκάρι.

snake [sneik] n φίδι.

snap [snæp] n (sound) ψαλίδια, κράκ nt inv, ξηρός κρότος ‖ (photograph) στιγμιότυπο, ενσταντανέ nt inv, φωτογραφία ♦ a βιαστικός, (unexpected) απροσδόκητος ♦ vt (make sound) κροταλίζω ‖ (break)

θραύω, σπάζω, τσακίζω ||
(photograph) φωτογραφίζω, τραβώ,
πέρνω ♦ vi (break) σπάω || to ~ off
vt (break) σπάω || to ~ up vt
αρπάζω, βουτώ || ~py α δηκτικός,
απότομος, ζωηρός || ~shot n
φωτογραφία εναστιγμιαία τανέ.

snare [snɛə*] n παγίδα ♦ vt
παγιδεύω, πιάνω.

snarl [snɑːl] n γρυλισμός,
μούγγρισμα nt ♦ vi (also person)
γρυλίζω.

snatch [snætʃ] n άρπαγμα nt || (small
amount) κομμάτι ♦ vt αρπάζω,
βουτώ.

sneak [sniːk] vi κινούμαι κρυφά.

sneer [snɪə*] n καγχασμός,
σαρκασμός ♦ vi κοροϊδεύω,
σαρκάζω, χλευάζω.

sneeze [sniːz] n φτέρνισμα nt ♦ vi
φτερνίζομαι.

sniff [snɪf] n εισπνοή, ρούφηγμα nt
♦ vi ξεφυσώ, είμαι συναχωμένος ♦
vt (smell) μυρίζω, ρουφώ.

snigger [ˈsnɪgə*] n πνιχτό γέλιο,
πονηρό γέλιο ♦ vi κρυφογελώ,
ξερογελώ.

snip [snɪp] n ψαλίδισμα nt,
κομματάκι || (bargain) ευκαιρία, καλή
δουλειά ♦ vt ψαλίδίζω, κόβω.

sniper [ˈsnaɪpə*] n (marksman)
ελεύθερος σκοπευτής.

snippet [ˈsnɪpɪt] n κομματάκι,
απόσπασμα nt.

snivelling [ˈsnɪvlɪŋ] a (whimpering)
κλαψιάρικος.

snob [snɒb] n ο νόμμ m inv,
ψωροπερήφανος/n m/f|| ~bery n
σνομπισμός || ~bish α σνόμπι,
φαντασμένος, πόζάτος.

snooker [ˈsnuːkə*] n είδος nt
μπιλιάρδου.

snoop [snuːp] vi: to ~ about χώνω
τη μύτη, παραφυλάω.

snooty [ˈsnuːtɪ] a (col: snobbish)
υπερόπτης, ψηλομύτης.

snooze [snuːz] n υπνάκος ♦ vi
παίρνω έναν υπνάκο, μισοκοιμάμαι.

snore [snɔː*] vi ροχαλίζω.

snorkel [ˈsnɔːkl] n αναπνευστικός
σωλήνας.

snort [snɔːt] n φρίμασμα nt,
ξεφύσημα nt, ρουθούνισμα nt ♦ vi
ρουθουνίζω, φριμάζω, ξεφυσώ.

snout [snaut] n ρύγχος nt,
μουσούδα, μύτη.

snow [snəu] n χιόνι ♦ vi χιονίζω,
ρίχνω χιόνι || ~ball n μπάλα χιόνι,
χιονόσφαιρα || ~bound a
(απο)κλεισμένος από τα χιόνια ||
~drift n χιονοστιβάδα || ~drop n
γάλανθος ο χιονώδης || ~fall n
χιονόπτωση || ~flake n νιφάδα ||
~man n χιονάνθρωπος ||
~plough, ~plow (US) n
εκχιονιστήρας || ~storm n
χιονοθύελλα.

snub [snʌb] vt αποκρούω,
προσβάλλω, κόβω ♦ n επίπληξη,
προσβολή, κατάδα.

snuff [snʌf] n ταμπάκο, πρέζα.

snug [snʌg] a άνετος, βολικός,
ζεστός, αναπαυτικός.

so [səu] ad (extent) τόσο(ν) || (in such
manner) έτσι || (thus) μ' αυτόν τον
τρόπο || (to such an extent) τόσο ♦ cj
επομένως, γι αυτό, έτσι λοιπόν || or
~ περίπου, πάνω κάτω || ~ long!
(goodbye) γεια σου!, αντίο! || ~
many, ~ much τόσος || ~ that
ούτως ώστε.

soak [səuk] vt διαποτίζω, μουσκεύω ||
(leave in liquid) διαποτίζω, μουσκεύω
|| to ~ in vi διεισδύω, διαποτίζω,
ποτίζω.

soap [səup] n σαπούνι || ~flakes npl
τριμμένο σαπούνι || ~ powder n
σαπούνι σε σκόνη || ~y α γεμάτος
σαπούνι.

soar [sɔː*] vi πετώ ψηλά,
ανυψώνομαι.

sob [sɒb] n λυγμός, αναφυλλητό ♦ vi κλαίω με αναφιλητά.

sober ['səubə*] a νηφάλιος, ξεμέθυστος || (calm) σοβαρός, εγκρατής, ήρεμος || **to ~ up** vi συνέρχομαι, ξεμεθάω.

Soc. abbr of **society**.

so-called ['səu'kɔːld] a δήθεν, λεγόμενος.

soccer ['sɒkə*] n ποδόσφαιρο.

sociable ['səuʃəbl] a κοινωνικός, φιλικός, ομιλητικός.

social ['səuʃəl] a κοινωνικός || **~ism** n σοσιαλισμός || **~ist** a σοσιαλιστής/ίστρια m/f ♦ a σοσιαλιστικός || **~ly** ad κοινωνικώς || **~ science** n κοινωνική επιστήμη || **~ security** n κοινωνική ασφάλεια || **~ work** n κοινωνική εργασία || **~worker** n κοινωνικός λειτουργός m/f.

society [sə'saiəti] n (people and customs) κοινωνία || (club) εταιρεία || (fashionable life) κοσμική ζωή, καλός κόσμος.

sociologist [səusi'ɒlədʒist] n κοινωνιολόγος.

sociology [səusi'ɒlədʒi] n κοινωνιολογία.

sock [sɒk] n (κοντή) κάλτσα ♦ vt (hit) δίνω γροθιά.

socket ['sɒkit] n ντουί, πρίζα.

sod [sɒd] n (of earth) χορταρισμένο χώμα || (col: term of abuse) παλιάνθρωπος.

soda ['səudə] n (CHEM) νάτριο, σόδα || (drink) σόδα || **~ water** n αεριούχο νερό, σόδα.

sodden ['sɒdn] a βρεγμένος, μουσκεμένος || (moist and heavy) λασπιωμένος.

sofa ['səufə] n σοφάς, καναπές m.

soft [sɒft] a μαλακός, απαλός || (not loud) απαλός, γλυκός, ελαφρός || (kind) τρυφερός, καλός || (weak, silly) ανόητος, χαζός || **~ drink** n

αναψυκτικό || **~en** vt μαλακώνω ♦ vi μαλακώνω, γίνομαι μαλακός || **~hearted** a ευαίσθητος, με τρυφερή καρδιά || **~ly** ad απαλά, μαλακά, αθόρυβα || **~ness** n μαλακότητα, απαλότητα.

soggy ['sɒgi] a υγρός, μουσκεμένος.

soil [sɔil] n (earth) έδαφος nt, χώμα nt ♦ vt λερώνω || **~ed** a λερωμένος, ακάθαρτος.

solar ['səulə*] a ηλιακός.

sold [səuld] pt, pp of **sell**.

solder ['səuldə*] vt (συγ)κολλώ ♦ n συγκόλληση || (material) καλάι.

soldier ['səuldʒə*] n στρατιώτης.

sole [səul] n πέλμα nt, πατούσα || (of shoe) σόλα || (fish) γλώσσα ♦ a μόνος, μοναδικός || **~ly** ad (only) μόνο, μοναδικά.

solemn ['sɒləm] a σοβαρός || (formal) επίσημος, σεμνός.

solicitor [sə'lisitə*] n δικηγόρος m/f, σύμβουλος, συνήγορος.

solid ['sɒlid] a στερεός, συμπαγής || (hard) στερεός, γερός, σκληρός || (reliable) σοβαρός, βάσιμος || (meal) γερός, ολόκληρος ♦ n στερεό || **~arity** n ενότητα, αλληλεγγύη || **~ify** [sə'lidifai] vi στερεοποιούμαι, πήζω ♦ vt στερεοποιώ, πήζω, παγώνω || **~ity** n στερεότητα.

solitaire [sɒli'tɛə*] n (game) πασιέντσα || (gem) μονό διαμάντι, μονόπετρο.

solitary ['sɒlitəri] a μόνος || (lonely) ολομόναχος, μοναχικός.

solitude ['sɒlitjuːd] n μοναξιά, ερημιά.

solo ['səuləu] n σόλο || **~ist** n σολίστας m, σολίστ m/f.

soluble ['sɒljubl] a διαλυτός, ευδιάλυτος || (able to be solved) επιδεικτικός λύσεως.

solution [sə'luːʃən] n λύση, λύσιμο || (explanation) λύση, εξήγηση || (in liquid) διάλυση, διάλυμα nt.

solve [sɒlv] vt λύω, εξηγώ.
solvent ['sɒlvənt] a αξιόχρεος.
sombre, somber (US) ['sɒmbə*] a σκοτεινός, μελαγχολικός || ~**ly** ad μελαγχολικά.
some [sʌm] a (uncertain number) λίγοι, λίγοι, μερικοί || (indefinite) κάποιος || (remarkable) σπουδαίος, περίφημος || (partitive) μερικός ♦ pron μερικοί, κάτι ♦ ad περίπου || ~**body** pron κάποιος || ~ **κάποιος** || ~**day** ad (μιά) κάποια μέρα || ~**how** ad κάπως, κατά κάποιο τρόπο || ~**one** pron = **somebody** || ~**place** ad (US) = **somewhere.**
somersault ['sʌməsɔ:lt] n τούμπα, κουτρουβάλα ♦ vi κάνω τούμπα.
something ['sʌmθɪŋ] pron κάτι, οτιδήποτε.
sometime ['sʌmtaɪm] ad κάποτε || ~**s** ad μερικές φορές, κάπου-κάπου.
somewhat ['sʌmwɒt] ad κάπως.
somewhere ['sʌmwɛə*] ad κάπου.
son [sʌn] n υιός.
song [sɒŋ] n τραγούδι || ~**writer** n (μουσικο)συνθέτης.
sonic ['sɒnɪk] a ηχητικός.
son-in-law ['sʌnɪnlɔ:] n γαμπρός.
sonnet ['sɒnɪt] n σονέτο.
soon [su:n] ad γρήγορα || (early) σύντομα, νωρίς || **as ~ as** = **as possible** το συντομότερο δυνατό || ~**er** ad (time) γρηγορότερα || (of preference) καλύτερα, κάλιο.
soot [sut] n αιθάλη, φούμο, καπνιά.
soothe [su:ð] vt καταπραΰνω, παρηγορώ.
sophisticated [sə'fɪstɪkeɪtɪd] a (person) κοσμικός, μοντέρνος || (machinery) πιο σύγχρονος.
soporific [sɒpə'rɪfɪk] a υπνωτικός, ναρκωτικός.
sopping ['sɒpɪŋ] a (very wet) καταβρεγμένος, μουσκεμένος.
soppy ['sɒpɪ] a (col: sentimental) δακρύβρεκτος, σαχλός.

soprano [sə'prɑ:nəʊ] n υψίφωνος f, σοπράνο f.
sordid ['sɔ:dɪd] a ακάθαρτος, ρυπαρός || (mean) άθλιος, χυδαίος.
sore [sɔ:*] a πονεμένος, ερεθισμένος, nt || (offended) πειραγμένος, θυμωμένος ♦ n πληγή, τραύμα || ~**ly** ad (tempted) βαθειά, σοβαρά.
sorrow ['sɒrəʊ] n λύπη, θλίψη, μετάνοια || ~**ful** a θλιμμένος, λυπημένος.
sorry ['sɒrɪ] a λυπημένος, πονεμένος || (pitiable) άθλιος, αξιολύπητος.
sort [sɔ:t] n είδος, τάξη ♦ vt (COMPUT) ταξινομώ || (also: ~ **out**) (papers) ταξινομώ, ξεκαθαρίζω || (problems) τακτοποιώ, (ξε)χωρίζω.
so-so ['səʊsəʊ] ad έτσι κι έτσι.
soufflé ['su:fleɪ] n σουφλέ nt inv.
sought [sɔ:t] pt, pp of **seek.**
soul [səʊl] n ψυχή || ~**-destroying** a ψυχοφθόρος, αποκτηνωτικός || ~**ful** a αισθηματικός, συγκινητικός || ~**less** a άψυχος, άκαρδος.
sound [saʊnd] a (healthy) υγιής, γερός || (safe) στερεός, ασφαλής, σίγουρος || (reasonable) λογικός, (deep, hearty) γερός ♦ n (noise) ήχος, θόρυβος || (GEOG) στενό, πορθμός ♦ vt (alarm) κτυπώ ♦ vi (find depth) βυθομετρώ || (seem) φαίνομαι, μοιάζω || **to ~ out** (opinions) βολιδοσκοπώ || ~ **barrier** n φράγμα του ήχου || ~**ing** n (NAUT etc) βυθομέτρηση, βολιδοσκόπηση || ~**ly** ad (sleep) βαθειά, καλά, ήσυχα || (beat) γερά, τελείως || ~**proof** a (room) ηχομονωτικός ♦ vt κάνω αδιαπέρατο από ήχο || ~**track** n (of film) ηχητική ζώνη (ταινίας).
soup [su:p] n σούπα, ζωμός || **in the** ~ σε δύσκολη θέση || ~**spoon** n κουτάλι της σούπας.

sour ['sauə*] *a* ξινός || *(milk)* ξινός || *(bad-tempered)* στριφνός, γκρινιάρης.

source [sɔːs] *n* πηγή, προέλευση.

south [sauθ] *n* νότος ♦ *a* νότιος ♦ *ad* προς νότο, νοτίως || **~-east** *n* το νοτιοανατολικό || **~-easterly** *a* νοτιοανατολικός || **~ern** *a* νότιος, μεσημβρινός || S~ **Pole** *n* Νότιος Πόλος || **~ward(s)** *ad* προς νότο || **~-west** *n* το νοτιοδυτικό.

souvenir [suːvə'nıə*] *n* ενθύμιο, σουβενίρ *nt inv*.

sovereign ['sɒvrın] *n* μονάρχης βασιλέας ♦ *a (independent)* κυρίαρχος || **~ty** *n* ηγεμονία, κυριαρχία.

soviet ['sɔuviət] *a* σοβιετικός.

sow [sau] *n* γουρούνα || [sɔu] *(irreg v) vt* σπέρνω || *(spread abroad)* ενσπείρω.

soya bean ['sɔıə'biːn] *n* σόγια.

spa [spɑː] *n* ιαματική πηγή || *(place)* λουτρόπολη.

space [speıs] *n* χώρος, τόπος || *(distance)* απόσταση || *(length of time)* διάστημα *nt* || *(universe)* διάστημα *nt* || **to ~ out** *vt* αραιώνω, τοποθετώ κατ' αποστάσεις || **~craft** *n* διαστημόπλοιο || **~man** *n* κοσμοναύτης.

spacing ['speısıŋ] *n* αραίωση.

spacious ['speıʃəs] *a* ευρύς, ευρύχωρος, απλόχωρος.

spade [speıd] *n (tool)* φτυάρι, τσάπα, τσαπί || **~s** *npl (CARDS)* μπαστούνι, πίκα.

spaghetti [spə'getı] *n* σπαγέτο, μακαρονάδα.

Spain [speın] *n* Ισπανία.

span [spæn] *n (of arch)* άνοιγμα *nt*, απόσταση || *(of time)* διάρκεια *(ζωής)* ♦ *vt* συνδέω, καλύπτω.

Spaniard ['spænjəd] *n* Ισπανός.

spaniel ['spænjəl] *n* σπάνιελ *nt inv*.

Spanish ['spænıʃ] *n (LING)* Ισπανικά *ntpl* ♦ *a* ισπανικός.

spank [spæŋk] *vt* δέρνω (στον πισινό).

spanner ['spænə*] *n* κλειδί (υδραυλικού).

spare [spεə*] *a* περίσσιος, λιτός, ισχνός || *n* = ~ **part** || *vt (do without)* οικονομώ, φυλάγω || *(save from hurt)* λυπούμαι, χαρίζω, φειδομαι || *(lend, give)* περισσεύω, δίνω, παραχωρώ, διαθέτω || **to ~** περισσεύω || **~ part** *n* ανταλλακτικό, εξάρτημα *nt* || **~ wheel** *n* ρεζέρβα || **~ time** *n* ελεύθερες ώρες.

spark [spɑːk] *n* σπινθήρας, σπίθα || *(fig)* ίχνος, σπίθα || **~ plug** *n* σπινθηριστής, μπουζί *nt inv*.

sparkle ['spɑːkl] *n* σπινθήρας, σπίθα, λάμψη || *(gaiety)* σπιρτάδα ♦ *vi* σπινθηρίζω, σπιθοβολώ, αστράφτω.

sparkling ['spɑːklıŋ] *a (lit)* αστραφτερός, σπινθηροβόλος || *(wine)* αφρώδης || *(conversation)* πνευματικός (ομιλία).

sparrow ['spærəu] *n* σπουργίτης.

sparse [spɑːs] *a* αραιός, σποραδικός.

spasm ['spæzəm] *n* σπασμός, σπαρτάρισμα *nt* || *(short spell)* κρίση, έξαψη || **~odic** [-'mɔdık] *a* σπασμωδικός, σπαστικός.

spastic ['spæstık] *n* σπαστικός.

spat [spæt] *pt, pp of* **spit**.

spate [speıt] *n (fig)* πλημμύρα, πλημμύρισμα *nt* || **in ~** *(river)* φουσκωμένος, πλημμυρισμένος.

spatter ['spætə*] *n* πιτσίλισμα *nt*, ράντισμα *nt* || *vi* πιτσιλίζω, ραντίζω ♦ *vi* αναπηδώ, (ξε)πετιέμαι, στάζω.

spatula ['spætjulə] *n* σπάτουλα.

spawn [spɔːn] *vt* αφήνω αυγά *(fig)* γεννώ.

speak [spiːk] *(irreg v) vt* λέγω, προφέρω, εκφράζω || *(truth)* λέγω, λέω || *(language)* μιλώ ♦ *vi (+ to)* μιλώ (σε) || μιλώ, συζητώ || *(make speech)*

αγορεύω, μιλώ|| to ~ for vt συνηγορώ, μιλώ για|| **to ~ up** vi υψώνω τη φωνή μιλώ σε κάποιο|| **~er** n ομιλητής/ήτρια m/f, συνομιλητής/ήτρια m/f|| (chairman) πρόεδρος|| (loudspeaker: on record player) μεγάφωνο.

spear [spɪə*] n ακόντιο, δόρυ nt, κοντάρι ♦ vt τρυπώ με κοντάρι, πιάνω με κοντάρι.

special ['spɛʃəl] a ειδικός, ίδιος|| (particular kind) εξαιρετικός, ασυνήθιστος|| (particular purpose) ιδιαίτερος, ξεχωριστός ♦ n (RAIL) ειδική αμαξοστοιχία|| (cooking) ειδικός, ιδιαίτερος|| **~ist** n ειδικός|| **~ity** n ιδιότητα|| (food) σπεσιαλιτέ nt inv (+ in) ειδικεύομαι σε|| **~ly** ad ειδικά, ιδιαίτερα, προ παντός, πάνω απ' όλα.

species ['spiːʃiːz] n είδος nt.

specific [spə'sɪfɪk] a ειδικός, ορισμένος, ακριβής, σαφής|| **~ally** ad ειδικά, συγκεκριμένα|| **~ation** [spɛsɪfɪ'keɪʃən] n περιγραφή, καθορισμός, προδιαγραφή.

specify ['spɛsɪfaɪ] vt καθορίζω, προσδιορίζω.

specimen ['spɛsɪmɪn] n δείγμα nt.

speck [spɛk] n κηλίδα, σταγόνα|| (particle) κόκκος, μόριο.

speckled ['spɛkld] a διάστικτος, πιτσιλισμένος.

specs [spɛks] npl (col) γυαλιά ntpl.

spectacle ['spɛktəkl] n θέαμα nt|| **~s** npl ματογυάλια ntpl, γυαλιά ntpl.

spectacular [spɛk'tækjulə*] a θεαματικός.

spectator [spɛk'teɪtə*] n θεατής.

spectre, (US) **specter** ['spɛktə*] n φάντασμα nt, σκίαχτρο.

spectrum ['spɛktrəm] n φάσμα nt.

speculate ['spɛkjuleɪt] vi κάνω υποθέσεις|| (FIN) κερδοσκοπώ.

speculation [spɛkju'leɪʃən] n (FIN) κερδοσκοπία.

sped [spɛd] pt, pp of **speed.**

speech [spiːtʃ] n λόγος, λαλιά|| (talk) λόγος, αγόρευση, ομιλία|| **~ day** n (SCH) απονομή των πτυχίων|| **~less** a άλαλος, βουβός, άφωνος|| **~ therapy** n θεραπευτική αγωγή λόγου.

speed [spiːd] (irreg v) n ταχύτητα, σπουδή|| (gear) ταχύτητα ♦ vi σπεύδω, κάνω γρήγορα, τρέχω|| **to ~ up** vi επιταχύνω ♦ vt επισπεύδω, επιταχύνω|| **~boat** n εξωλέμβιος|| **~ily** ad γρήγορα, εσπευσμένα, βιαστικά|| **~ing** n υπερβολική ταχύτητα|| **~ limit** n όριο ταχύτητας|| **~ometer** n ταχύμετρο, κοντέρ nt inv|| **~way** n αυτοκινητόδρομος|| **~y** a ταχύς, γρήγορος.

spell [spɛl] (irreg v) n (magic) γοητεία, μαγεία, μάγια ntpl|| (period of time) διάστημα nt, χρονική περίοδος ♦ vt ορθογραφώ|| (word) συλλαβίζω|| (mean) σημαίνω|| **~bound** a γοητευμένος, μαγεμένος|| **~ing** n συλλαβισμός, ορθογραφία.

spelt [spɛlt] pt, pp of **spell.**

spend [spɛnd] (irreg v) vt ξοδεύω, δαπανώ|| (use up) εξαντλώ, χρησιμοποιώ.

spent [spɛnt] pt, pp of **spend** ♦ a (patience) εξαντλημένος.

sperm [spɜːm] n (BIOL) σπέρμα nt.

spew [spjuː] vt ξερνώ, κάνω εμετό.

sphere [sfɪə*] n σφαίρα, υδρόγειος.

spherical ['sfɛrɪkəl] a σφαιρικός.

sphinx [sfɪŋks] n σφίγγα.

spice [spaɪs] n καρύκευμα nt, μπαχαρικό ♦ vt καρυκεύω.

spicy ['spaɪsɪ] a αρωματισμένος, πικάντικος.

spider ['spaɪdə*] n αράχνη|| **~y** a αράχνινος.

spike [spaɪk] n αιχμή, καρφί, στάχυ nt, πάσσαλος.

spill [spɪl] (irreg v) vt (upset) ανατρέπω, αναποδογυρίζω || (pour out) χύνω ♦ vi (flow over) χύνομαι.

spin [spɪn] (irreg v) n (revolution of wheel) περιστροφή, στριφογύρισμα || (trip in car) περίπατος, βόλτα || (AVIAT) σπινάρισμα nt ♦ vt (wool etc) κλώθω, γνέθω || (turn) γυρίζω ♦ vi περιστρέφομαι, (στριφο)γυρίζω | to ~ out vi (of money etc) οικονομώ (τα λεφτά μου) ♦ vt παρατείνω, παρατραβώ.

spinach ['spɪnɪdʒ] n σπανάκι.

spinal ['spaɪnl] a νωτιαίος, ραχιαίος, σπονδυλικός || ~ **cord** n νωτιαίος μυελός.

spindly ['spɪndlɪ] a λιγνός.

spin-drier ['spɪn'draɪə*] n στεγνωτήρας.

spine [spaɪn] n σπονδυλική στήλη, ραχοκοκκαλιά || (thorn) αγκάθι || ~**less** a (fig) δειλός, άβολος.

spinning ['spɪnɪŋ] n (of thread) κλώσιμο, στρίψιμο || ~ **wheel** n ροδάνι, ανέμη.

spinster ['spɪnstə*] n γεροντοκόρη.

spiral ['spaɪərəl] n σπείρα, έλικα ♦ a ελικοειδής, σπειροειδής ♦ vi κινούμαι σπειροειδώς || ~ **staircase** n γυριστή σκάλα, στριφτή σκάλα.

spire ['spaɪə*] n κορυφή κωδωνοστασίου.

spirit ['spɪrɪt] n πνεύμα nt, ψυχή || (ghost) φάντασμα nt || (humour, mood) διάθεση, κέφι || (courage) κουράγιο, θάρρος nt || (alcoholic) οινοπνευματώδες ποτό, σπίρτο || **in good** ~ s κεφάτος, καλόκεφος || ~ **ed** a ζωηρός, έντονος, θαρραλέος || ~ **level** n αλφάδι.

spiritual ['spɪrɪtjʊəl] a πνευματικός, ψυχικός ♦ n θρησκευτικό τραγούδι || ~**ism** n πνευματισμός.

spit [spɪt] (irreg v) n (for roasting) σούβλα || (saliva) φτύσιμο, σάλιο ♦ vi φτύνω || (of motor) ρετάρω.

spite [spaɪt] n μίσος, έχθρα, κακία ♦ vt ενοχλώ, πεισμώνω, φουρκίζω || **in** ~ **of** παρά το, παρ' όλα || ~**ful** a μοχθηρός, εκδικητικός.

splash [splæʃ] n πιτσίλισμα nt, πλαταούλισμα nt, λεκές || (of colour) πολυχρωμία ♦ vti πλατσουλίζω, πιτσιλίζω.

spleen [spliːn] n σπλήνα.

splendid ['splendɪd] a λαμπρός, μεγαλοπρεπής || (fine) εξαίσιος, περίφημος.

splendour, (US) **splendor** ['splendə*] n λαμπρότητα, λάμψη || (glory) μεγαλοπρέπεια.

splint [splɪnt] n νάρθηκας.

splinter ['splɪntə*] n θραύσμα nt ♦ vi θραύομαι, σπάζω..

split [splɪt] (irreg v) n σχισμή, σχίσιμο, ρωγμή, διαίρεση ♦ vt σχίζω, θραύω, σπάζω ♦ vi (divide) διασπώ || (col: depart) αναχωρώ || to ~ **up** vi διαιρούμαι ♦ vt διαιρώ, χωρίζω, διασπώ.

splutter ['splʌtə*] vti τραυλίζω || (of motor) ρετάρω.

spoil [spɔɪl] (irreg v) vt χαλώ || ~**s** npl λεία, λάφυρα ntpl || ~**sport** n αυτός που χαλάει το κέφι.

spoke [spəʊk] n ακτίνα (τροχού) || pt of speak || ~**n** pp of speak || ~**sman** n εκπρόσωπος.

sponge [spʌndʒ] n σφουγγάρι ♦ vt πλένω, σφουγγίζω ♦ vi (+ on) ζω σε βάρος κάποιου || ~ **bag** n σάκκος για σφουγγάρι || ~ **cake** n παντεσπάνι.

spongy ['spʌndʒɪ] a σπογγώδης.

sponsor ['spɒnsə*] n ανάδοχος, εγγυητής/ήτρια m/f, εισηγητής/ήτρια m/f ♦ vt

υποστηρίζω, εισηγούμαι || ~**ship** n
υποστήριξη.

spontaneous [spɔn'teiniəs] a
αυτόματος || *(natural)* αυθόρμητος.

spool [spuːl] n καρούλια, μασούρι.

spoon [spuːn] n κουτάλι || ~**-feed** vt
(lit) ταΐζω με το κουτάλι || *(fig)*
επιχορηγώ || ~**ful** n κουταλιά.

sporadic [spə'rædik] a σποραδικός.

sport [spɔːt] n *(games)* αθλητισμός,
σπόρ nt inv || *(fun)* διασκέδαση,
παιχνίδι || *(good-humoured person)*
καλός άνθρωπος || ~**ing** a *(fair)*
τίμιος || ~**s car** n αυτοκίνητο σπόρ
|| ~**(s) coat** n, ~**(s) jacket** n
σακκάκι σπόρ || ~**sman** n
φίλαθλος, τίμιος παίκτης ||
~**smanship** n τιμιότητα στο σπορ ||
~**swear** n είδη ntpl αθλητισμού ||
~**swoman** n αθλήτρια.

spot [spɔt] n στίγμα nt, κηλίδα, λεκές
m || *(place)* τόπος, μέρος nt,
τοποθεσία || *(small amount)* στάλα,
λίγο ♦ vt *(notice)* διακρίνω,
σημειώνω || *(make spots on)* λεκιάζω
|| ~**check** n αιφνιδιαστικός έλεγχος
|| ~**less** a δασπιλος, ακηλίδωτος,
καθαρός || ~**light** n προβολέας
θεάτρου || *(position)* το προσκήνιο,
κέντρο, ~**ted** a διάστικτος,
πιτσιλωτός || ~**ty** a *(face)* με
πανάδες, με σπειριά.

spouse [spauz] n σύζυγος m/f.

spout [spaut] n στόμιο, σωλήνας ||
(jet) εκροή, πίδακας ♦ vi ξεπιτώ,
αναπηδώ, ξεχύνομαι.

sprain [sprein] n διάστρεμμα nt,
στραμπούλιγμα nt ♦ vt
στραμπουλίζω.

sprang [spræŋ] pt of **spring**.

sprawl [sprɔːl] vi εκτείνομαι,
ξαπλώνομαι.

spray [sprei] n *(sprinkle)*
πιτσιλίσματα ntpl || *(of sea)* αφρός ||
(instrument) ψεκαστήρας,

βαποριζατέρ nt inv || *(branch)*
κλωνάρι ♦ vt ψεκάζω, καταβρέχω.

spread [spred] *(irreg v)* n *(extent)*
επέκταση, διάδοση || *(col)* τραπέζι,
πλούσιο γεύμα nt ♦ vt απλώνω,
στρώνω || *(scatter)* σκορπίζω,
στρώνω, δια διαδίδω || *(smear)* αλείφω,
χύνω.

spree [spriː] n διασκέδαση,
ξεφάντωμα nt, γλέντι.

sprightly [ˈspraitli] a ζωηρός,
κεφάτος.

spring [spriŋ] *(irreg v)* n *(leap)*
πήδημα nt || *(of water)* πηγή || *(coil)*
ελατήριο || *(season)* άνοιξη ♦ vi
*(ανα)πηδώ, ξεπετάγομαι || *to ~ up*
vi *(problem)* δημιουργούμαι,
εμφανίζομαι || ~**board** n βατήρας,
τραμπλίν nt inv || ~**-clean** n γενικός
καθαρισμός ♦ vt κάνω γενικό
καθαρισμό || ~**-cleaning** n γενικός
καθαρισμός *(ανοιξιάτικος)* ||
~**iness** n ελαστικότητα || ~**time** n
άνοιξη || ~**y** a ελαστικός,
εύκαμπτος.

sprinkle [ˈspriŋkl] n ράντισμα nt ♦
vt ραντίζω, ραίνω.

sprint [sprint] n δρόμος ταχύτητας
♦ vi τρέχω σε δρόμο ταχύτητας ||
~**er** n δρομέας ταχύτητας.

sprite [sprait] n ξωτικό, στοιχειό.

sprout [spraut] vi βλασταίνω,
φυτρώνω || *see* **Brussels sprout**.

spruce [spruːs] n έλατο ♦ a
κομψός, περιποιημένος.

sprung [sprʌŋ] pp of **spring**.

spry [sprai] a ζωηρός, ενεργητικός.

spun [spʌn] pt, pp of **spin**.

spur [spɜː*] n σπηρούνι || *(fig)*
κίνητρο, ελατήριο ♦ vt *(also: ~ on)*
κεντρίζω, παρακινώ || *on the ~ of
the moment* χωρίς σκέψη,
αυθόρμητα.

spurn [spɜːn] vt περιφρονώ,
αποκρούω.

spurt [spɜːt] n *(effort)* σφίξιμο,

φουλάρισμα nt, ξέσπασμα nt|| (jet)
ανάβλυση, πίδακας ♦ vti ξεχύνομαι,
φουλάρω.

spy [spaɪ] n κατάσκοπος m/f ♦ vi
κατασκοπεύω ♦ vt διακρίνω, βλέπω,
παρατηρώ|| ~**ing** n (espionage)
κατασκοπεία.

sq. (MATH), **Sq,** (in address) abbr of
square.

squabble ['skwɔbl] n φιλονεικία,
καυγάς ♦ vi φιλονεικώ, καυγαδίζω,
πιάνομαι (με).

squad [skwɔd] n (MIL) απόσπασμα nt,
ουλαμός|| (police) υπηρεσία
διώξεως.

squadron ['skwɔdrən] n μοίρα.

squalid ['skwɔlɪd] a βρώμικος,
βρωμερός, άθλιος.

squall [skwɔːl] n (scream) κραυγή,
στριγγλιά.

squalor ['skwɔlə*] n ακαθαρσία,
βρώμα, αθλιότητα.

squander ['skwɔndə*] vt σπαταλώ.

square [skwɛə*] n (figure)
τετράγωνο|| (of town) πλατεία||
(instrument) γωνία, γνώμονας||
(product) τετράγωνο|| (col: person)
ανίαρος, ατάίριαστος ♦ a
τετραγωνικός|| (honest) τίμιος,
καθαρός, δίκαιος|| (ample)
ικανοποιητικός, άφθονος ♦ ad
(exactly) ακριβώς, κάθετα ♦ vt
(arrange) ρυθμίζω, κανονίζω,
τακτοποιώ|| (MATH) τετραγωνίζω ♦
vi (agree) (+ with) συμφωνώ,
συμβιβάζομαι|| **all** ~ στα ίσια,
πάτσι|| **2 metres** ~ **4** τετραγωνικά
μέτρα|| **1** ~ **metre** 1 τετραγωνικό
μέτρο|| ~**ly** ad τίμια, ντόμπρα.

squash [skwɔʃ] n (drink) χυμός
(φρούτων) ♦ vt συνθλίβω, ζουλώ,
στύβω.

squat [skwɔt] a κοντόχοντρος ♦ vi
κάθομαι σταυροπόδι|| ~**ter** n
σφετεριστής γης.

squawk [skwɔːk] n κράξιμο, βραχνή

squeak [skwiːk] n τσιριχτή φωνή,
σκούξιμο ♦ vi σκούζω, τσιρίζω,
τρίζω.

squeal [skwiːl] n διαπεραστικός
ήχος, κραυγή, στριγγλιά ♦ vi
στριγγλίζω, σκούζω.

squeamish ['skwiːmɪʃ] a
ευαίσθητος, με τάση στον εμετό||
(easily shocked) σιχασιάρης,
δύστροπος.

squeeze [skwiːz] n (lit) σύνθλιψη,
σφίξιμο, στρίμωγμα nt|| (ECON) πίεση
♦ vt συνθλίβω, σφίγγω, στύβω|| **to**
~ **out** vt στύβω.

squid [skwɪd] n σουπιά.

squint [skwɪnt] n αλλοιθωρισμός,
στραβισμός ♦ vi αλλοιθωρίζω,
στραβοκοιτάζω.

squirm [skwɜːm] vi συστρέφω το
σώμα, στενοχωριέμαι, ντρέπομαι.

squirrel ['skwɪrəl] n σκίουρος.

squirt [skwɜːt] n εκτόξευση,
πιτσίλισμα nt, ριπή ♦ vi αναβλύζω,
πετάγομαι, εκτοξεύω.

Sr abbr of **senior.**

St abbr of **saint, street.**

stab [stæb] n (blow) κτύπημα nt,
μπαμπεσιά nt|| (col: try) **to have a** ~
δοκιμάζω.

stability [stə'bɪlɪtɪ] n σταθερότητα.

stabilize ['steɪbəlaɪz] vt
σταθεροποιώ|| ~**r** n
ζυγοσταθμιστής, σταθεροποιητής.

stable ['steɪbl] n στάβλος ♦ vt
σταβλίζω ♦ a σταθερός, μόνιμος.

stack [stæk] n θημωνιά, σωρός ♦ vt
συσσωρεύω, στοιβάζω.

stadium ['steɪdɪəm] n στάδιο.

staff [stɑːf] n (stick) ράβδος f,
μπαστούνι, κοντάκι|| (people)
προσωπικό, επιτελείο ♦ vt (with
people) επανδρώνω με προσωπικό.

stag [stæg] n ελάφι.

stage [steɪdʒ] n (theatre) σκηνή||

(actors) θέατρο || (degree) στάδιο ♦ vt
(play) ανεβάζω, σκηνοθετώ ||
(demonstration) οργανώνω,
σκηνοθετώ || **in ~s** βαθμηδόν, κατά
στάδια || ~ **coach** n ταχυδρομική
άμαξα || ~ **door** n είσοδος f
ηθοποιών || ~ **manager** n
σκηνοθέτης.

stagger ['stægə*] vi κλονίζομαι,
τρικλίζω, παραπατώ || vt (person)
ζαλίζω, συγκλονίζω, κάνω να τα
χάσει || (hours) κλιμακώνω (τις ώρες)
|| ~**ing** a (amazing) καταπληκτικός,
συγκλονιστικός.

stagnant ['stægnənt] a στάσιμος,
λιμνασμένος || (dull) αδρανής,
άγονος.

stagnate [stæg'neɪt] vi είμαι
στάσιμος, αδρανώ.

staid [steɪd] a θετικός, σοβαρός.

stain [steɪn] n λεκές m, κηλίδα ||
(colouring) χρώμα nt, βαφή, μπογιά ♦
vt λεκιάζω, λερώνω || ~**ed glass** n
χρωματιστό γυαλί || ~**less** a (steel)
ανοξείδωτος.

stair [stɛə*] n (one step) σκαλοπάτι,
σκαλί || ~**case** n κλίμακα, σκάλα ||
~**s** npl σκάλα || ~**way** n σκάλα.

stake [steɪk] n πάσσαλος, παλούκι ||
(gambling) στοίχημα nt, μίζα,
ποντάρισμα nt ♦ vt ποντάρω || (fig)
παίζω.

stalactite ['stæləktaɪt] n
σταλακτίτης.

stalagmite ['stæləgmaɪt] n
σταλαγμίτης.

stale [steɪl] a μπαγιάτικος || ~**mate**
n αδιέξοδο.

stalk [stɔːk] n κοτσάνι, στέλεχος nt
μίσχος ♦ vt παρακολουθώ αθλέιος
♦ vi (walk stiffly) βαδίζω με μεγάλα
βήματα.

stall [stɔːl] n παράπηγμα nt στάβλου,
παχνί || (stand) μπάγκος, περίπτερο
♦ vt (AUT) κολλώ, μπλοκάρω ♦ vi
(AUT) κολλώ || (delay) αναβάλλω,

χρονοτριβώ || ~**s** npl (THEAT)
καθίσματα ntpl (ορχήστρας).

stallion ['stælɪən] n επιβήτορας,
βαρβάτο αλογο.

stalwart ['stɔːlwət] a ρωμαλέος,
σταθερός ♦ n παλληκάρι.

stamina ['stæmɪnə] n σφρίγος nt,
ζωτική δύναμ.

stammer ['stæmə*] n τραύλισμα nt,
τσέβδισμα nt ♦ vi τραυλίζω,
ψευδίζω, ψελλίζω.

stamp [stæmp] n (postage)
γραμματόσημο || (official) ένσημο ||
(of foot) κτήπημα nt του ποδιού,
ποδοβολητό || (on document)
σφραγίδα, βούλα, στάμπα ♦ vi
χτυπώ το πόδι, περπατώ βαρειά ♦ vt
(make mark) σφραγίζω, μαρκάρω,
σταμπάρω || (fix postage) κολλώ
γραμματόσημο || ~ **album** n
συλλογή γραμματοσήμων || ~
collecting n φιλοτελισμός.

stampede [stæm'piːd] n
εσπευσμένη φυγή, πανικός.

stance [stæns] n (posture) στάση.

stand [stænd] (irreg v) n (position)
στάση || (MIL) αντίσταση || (rest)
υποστήριγμα nt, πόδι, στήριγμα nt ||
(seats) εξέδρα ♦ vi (erect) στέκομαι ||
(rise) σηκώνομαι || (place, set) κείμαι,
βρίσκομαι, είμαι || (halt, stop)
σταματώ, στέκομαι ♦ vt (place)
τοποθετώ, βάζω, κουμπώ (όρθιο) ||
(endure) υποφέρω, αντέχω, υπομένω
|| **to make a ~** αντιστέκομαι,
αντιτίθεμαι || **it ~s to reason**
είναι λογικό || **to ~ by** vi (be ready)
είμαι έτοιμος, είμαι σε επιφυλακή ♦
vt (opinion) μένω πιστός σε || **to ~
for** vt (defend) υπερασπίζομαι,
υποστηρίζω || (signify)
αντιπροσωπεύω || (permit, tolerate)
υπομένω, ανέχομαι || **to ~ in for**
vt αντικαθιστώ || **to ~ out** vi (be
prominent) (προ)εξέχω, ξεχωρίζω || **to**

~ **up** vi (rise) σηκώνομαι || **to** ~ **up for** vt υποστηρίζω.

standard ['stændəd] n (measure) υπόδειγμα nt, κανόνας, μέτρο || (flag) σημαία, λάβαρο ♦ a (size etc) πρότυπος, κανονικός, συνηθισμένος || ~ize vt τυποποιώ || ~ **of living** n βιωτικό επίπεδο.

standby ['stændbaɪ] n (person) αντικαταστάτης/τρια m/f.

stand-in ['stændɪn] n αντικαταστάτης/τρια m/f, αναπληρωτής/ώτρια m/f.

standing ['stændɪŋ] a όρθιος || (lasting) μόνιμος, διαρκής ♦ n διάρκεια || (reputation) κοινωνική θέση, υπόληψη || ~ **orders** npl (MIL) μόνιμες διατάξεις fpl, κανονισμοί mpl || ~ **room only** μόνο όρθιοι.

stand-offish ['stænd'ɔfɪʃ] a υπεροπτικός.

standpoint ['stændpɔɪnt] n άποψη, σκοπιά.

standstill ['stændstɪl] n: **at a** ~ στασιμότητα, νεκρό σημείο || **to come to a** ~ καταλήγω σε αδιέξοδο, σταματώ.

stank [stæŋk] pt of **stink**.

stanza ['stænzə] n στροφή, στάντσα.

staple ['steɪpl] n άγκιστρο, συνδετήρας || (product) κύριο προϊόν ♦ a κύριος, πρωτεύων ♦ vt στερεώνω, συνδέω || ~**r** n συνδετήρας.

star [stɑ:*] n άστρο, αστέρι || (actor) αστέρας, πρωταγωνιστής/ίστρια m/f, στάρ m/f inv || (shape) αστέρι ♦ vi (in film) πρωταγωνιστώ, παίζω σε ταινία ♦ vt (**to star an actor**) παρουσιάζω σαν πρωταγωνιστή.

starboard ['stɑ:bəd] n δεξιά πλευρά, n δεξιά.

starch [stɑ:tʃ] n άμυλο nt || ~**ed** a (collar) κολλαριστός || ~**y** a

αμυλώδης, αμυλούχος || (formal) υπεροπτικός, ποζάτος.

stardom ['stɑ:dəm] n θέση αστέρα.

stare [stɛə*] n ατενές βλέμμα nt, καρφωτή ματιά ♦ vi (+ **at**) ατενίζω, καρφώνω με το μάτι.

starfish ['stɑ:fɪʃ] n αστερίας.

stark [stɑ:k] a ψυχρός, σκληρός ♦ ad: ~ **naked** ολόγυμνος, θεόγυμνος, τσίτσιδος.

starlight ['stɑ:laɪt] n αστροφεγγιά.

starling ['stɑ:lɪŋ] n ψαρώνι, καραβέλι.

starry ['stɑ:rɪ] a έναστρος, αστερόφεγγος, λαμπερός || ~-**eyed** a (innocent) ονειροπαρμένος αφελής.

start [stɑ:t] n αρχή, σημείο εκκίνησης, εκκίνηση || (beginning) αρχή, αρχίνισμα nt || (sudden movement) ξάφνιασμα nt, ανατίναγμα nt ♦ vt (set going) αρχίζω, ανοίγω, βγάζω ♦ vi (begin journey) αρχίζω, ξεκινώ || (make sudden movement) αναπηδώ, ξαφνίζομαι || **to** ~ **doing** αρχίζω με, πιάνομαι με || **to** ~ **off** vi (begin) αρχίζω, ξεκινώ || **to** ~ **up** vi βάζω μπρος || ~ **er** n (AUT) εκκινητήρας, μίζα || (for race) αφέτης || ~**ing point** n αφετηρία, σημείο εκκινήσεως.

startle ['stɑ:tl] vt ξαφνιάζω, φοβίζω, εκπλήσσω.

startling ['stɑ:tlɪŋ] a καταπληκτικός, εντυπωσιακός, χτυπητός.

starvation [stɑ:'veɪʃən] n λιμός, λιμοκτονία, ασιτία, πείνα.

starve [stɑ:v] vi (die of hunger) πεθαίνω από πείνα || (suffer from hunger) ψοφώ της πείνας, πεινώ ♦ vt (keep without food) στερώ τροφής.

starving ['stɑ:vɪŋ] a πεινασμένος, λιμασμένος, ψόφιος της πείνας.

state [steɪt] n κατάσταση, θέση || (government) κράτος nt, πολιτεία || (anxiety) αναστάτωση ♦ vt δηλώνω,

λέγω, ανακοινώνω || ~ly a
μεγαλοπρεπής, αξιοπρεπής ||
~ment n δήλωση, έκθεση ||
~sman n πολιτικός.

static ['stætɪk] n στατική ♦ a
ακίνητος, αδρανής || (PHYS) στατικός
|| ~ electricity n στατικός
ηλεκτρισμός.

station ['steɪʃən] n (RAIL) σταθμός ||
(post) σταθμός, θέση || (position in life)
κοινωνική θέση, βαθμός ♦ vt
τοποθετώ, βάζω.

stationary ['steɪʃənərɪ] a στάσιμος,
ακίνητος.

stationer ['steɪʃənə*] n
χαρτοπώλης || ~'s (shop) n
χαρτοπωλείο || ~y n χαρτικά είδη
ntpl.

station master ['steɪʃənmɑːstə*] n
σταθμάρχης.

station wagon ['steɪʃənwægən] n
(US AUT) στέισον-βάγκον nt inv.

statistic [stə'tɪstɪk] n στατιστική
(στοιχείο) || ~al a στατιστικός || ~s
npl στατιστική.

statue ['stætjuː] n άγαλμα nt.

stature ['stætʃə] n ανάστημα nt.

status ['steɪtəs] n θέση, κατάσταση ||
the ~ quo n καθεστώς nt, στάτους
κβο nt inv.

statute ['stætjuːt] n νόμος,
θέσπισμα nt.

statutory ['stætjutərɪ] a
νομοθετημένος, θεσπισμένος.

staunch [stɔːntʃ] a αξιόπιστος,
πιστός, δυνατός.

stave [steɪv] vt: to ~ off (attack)
αποκρούω, απωθώ || (threat)
αποτρέπω, αποφεύγω.

stay [steɪ] n διαμονή, παραμονή ♦ vi
(παραμένω) || (at place) διαμένω || to
~ put μένω στην ίδια θέση || to ~
with friends μένω με φίλους || to
~ the night μένω το βράδυ || to ~
behind vi παρακολουθώ από πίσω ||
μένω πίσω || to ~ in vi (at home)

μένω (στο σπίτι) || to ~ on vi
(continue) παραμένω || to ~ out vi (of
house) μένω έξω, δεν επιστρέφω || to
~ up vi (at night) αγρυπνώ, ξενυχτώ.

STD n (abbr of Subscriber Trunk
Dialling) τηλεφωνικός κώδικας (Τηλ.
Κωδ.).

steadfast ['stɛdfəst] a σταθερός.

steadily ['stɛdɪlɪ] ad σταθερά.

steady ['stɛdɪ] a σταθερός, στερεός
|| (regular) κανονικός, συνεχής,
σταθερός || (reliable) σταθερός,
συνεπής, τακτικός ♦ vt
σταθεροποιώ, στερεώνω || to ~ o.s.
σταθεροποιούμαι, καθησυχάζω.

steak [steɪk] n (meat) μπριζόλα,
μπιφτέκι || (fish) φέτα.

steal [stiːl] (irreg v) vt κλέβω, βουτώ,
σουφρώνω ♦ vi φεύγω κλεφτά ||
~th ['stɛlθ] n: by ~th κρυφά,
κλεφτά, μυστικά || ~thy a κρυφός,
φευγαλέος, προσεκτικός.

steam [stiːm] n ατμός ♦ vt βράζω
στον ατμό ♦ vi αναδίνω ατμό,
αχνίζω || (ship) κινούμαι, πλέω (με
ατμό) || ~ engine n ατμομηχανή ||
~er n ατμόπλοιο, βαπόρι ||
~roller n οδοστρωτήρας || ~y a
θολός, γεμάτος ατμούς.

steel [stiːl] n χάλυβας, ατσάλι ♦ a
χαλύβδινος, ατσάλινος || ~works n
χαλυβδουργείο.

steep [stiːp] a απότομος,
απόκρημνος || (price) εξωφρενική ♦
vt διαποτίζω, μουσκεύω, βουτώ.

steeple ['stiːpl] n κωδωνοστάσιο ||
~chase n ιπποδρομία με εμπόδια ||
~jack n επιδιορθωτής
καπνοδόχων.

steeply ['stiːplɪ] ad απότομα,
κατηφορικά.

steepness ['stiːpnɪs] n το απότομο,
το απόκρημνο.

steer [stɪə*] n μικρός ταύρος ♦ vt
(car) οδηγώ || (boat) πηδαλιουχώ ♦ vi
κατευθύνομαι, βάζω πλώρη για

~ing n (AUT) σύστημα nt
διεύθυνσης || ~ing wheel n βολάν
nt inv, τιμόνι.

stem [stem] n στέλεχος nt, κορμός
♦ vt σταματώ, ανακόπτω || to ~
from vt προέρχομαι από.

stench [stentʃ] n δυσοσμία,
δυσωδία.

stencil ['stensl] n μεμβράνη ♦ vt
γράφω μεμβράνες, πολυγραφώ.

stenographer [ste'nɒgrəfə*] n
στενογράφος m/f.

step [step] n βήμα nt, πάτημα nt ||
(stair) βαθμίδα, σκαλοπάτι, σκαλί ||
(action) διάβημα nt, ενέργεια || (sound)
βήμα nt, βάδισμα nt ♦ vi βηματίζω,
βαδίζω || ~s npl = stepladder || to
~ down vi (fig) παραιτούμαι || to ~
up vi αυξάνω, ανεβάζω || ~brother
n ετεροθαλής αδελφός || ~child n
προγονός, προγονή m/f|| ~father
n πατριός || ~ladder n σκάλα
(φορητή) || ~mother n μητριά.

stepping stone ['stepɪŋstəʊn] n
σκαλοπάτι, ενδιάμεσος σταθμός.

stereo ['stɪərɪəʊ] n (RAD)
στερεοφωνικό ραδιόφωνο ||
~phonic a στερεοφωνικό || ~type
n στερεοτυπία ♦ vt τυπώνω διά
στερεοτυπίας.

sterile ['steraɪl] a στείρος, άγονος,
άκαρπος || (free from germs)
αποστειρωμένος.

sterility [ste'rɪlɪtɪ] n στειρότητα,
αγονία.

sterilization [sterɪlaɪ'zeɪʃən] n
αποστείρωση.

sterilize ['sterɪlaɪz] vt στειρώνω ||
(from germs) αποστειρώνω.

sterling ['stɜːlɪŋ] a στερλίνα || (top
quality) αμιγής, καλής ποιότητας.

stern [stɜːn] a αυστηρός, βλοσυρός
♦ n πρύμνη, πρύμη.

stethoscope ['steθəskəʊp] n
στηθοσκόπιο.

stevedore ['stiːvɪdɔː*] n
φορτοεκφορτωτής.

stew [stjuː] n κρέας nt με χορταρικά
♦ vt κάνω κρέας στην κατσαρόλα ♦
vi σιγοβράζω.

steward ['stjuːəd] n (AVIAT, NAUT,
RAIL, in club etc) φροντιστής,
οικονόμος, καμαρότος || ~ess n
(AVIAT) αεροσυνοδός.

stick [stɪk] (irreg v) n βέργα, ράβδος
f || (cane) μπαστούνι ♦ vt μπήγω,
χώνω, καρφώνω || (gum) κολλώ || (col:
tolerate) ανέχομαι, υποφέρω ♦ vi
(stop) πιάνομαι, κολλώ, φρακάρω ||
(hold fast) κολλιέμαι, κολλώ || to ~
out (project) κρατώ μέχρι τέλους,
επιμένω || to ~ up vi (project)
υψώνομαι, στήνω || to ~ up for vt
(defend) υπερασπίζομαι, παίρνω το
μέρος || ~er n ετικέτα.

stickler ['stɪklə*] n (+ for)
άκαμπτος, στενοκέφαλος (σε).

stick-up ['stɪkʌp] n (col: robbery)
ληστεία.

sticky ['stɪkɪ] a κολλώδης,
γλοιώδης.

stiff [stɪf] a δύσκαμπτος, σκληρός,
άκαμπτος || (examination etc)
δύσκολος || (paste) σκληρός,
σφιχτός || (formal) επιτηδευμένος,
τυπικός, ψυχρός || (strong) ισχυρός,
δυνατός || ~en vt σκληραίνω,
δυναμώνω ♦ vi σκληραίνομαι,
γίνομαι άκαμπτος || ~ness n
σκληρότητα, πιάσιμο.

stifle ['staɪfl] vt (keep back)
καταπνίγω, συγκρατώ.

stifling ['staɪflɪŋ] a (atmosphere)
αποπνικτικός, ασφυκτικός.

stigma ['stɪgmə] n στίγμα nt,
κηλίδα.

stile [staɪl] n στύλος.

still [stɪl] a ακίνητος, αθόρυβος,
σιωπηλός ♦ ad (yet) ακόμη || (even)
ακόμη (περισσότερο) || ~born a
θνησιγενής || ~ life n νεκρή φύση.

stilt [stɪlt] n ξυλοπόδαρο.

stilted ['stɪltɪd] a άκαμπτος, τυπικός, τεχνητός.

stimulant ['stɪmjulənt] n διεγερτικό, τονωτικό.

stimulate ['stɪmjuleɪt] vt διεγείρω, εξάπτω.

stimulating ['stɪmjuleɪtɪŋ] a διεγερτικός, τονωτικός.

stimulation [stɪmju'leɪʃən] n διέγερση, τόνωση.

stimulus ['stɪmjuləs] n κίνητρο.

sting [stɪŋ] (irreg v) n δήγμα nt, κέντρισμα nt ♦ vt κεντρίζω, τσιμπώ.

stingy ['stɪndʒɪ] a φιλάργυρος, τσιγγούνης, σφιχτοχέρης.

stink [stɪŋk] (irreg v) n δυσοσμία, βρώμα ♦ vi βρωμώ, βρωμάω || ~ ing a (fig) τρομερός.

stint [stɪnt] n όριο, καθήκον ♦ vt στερώ, περιορίζω.

stipend ['staɪpend] n (to vicar etc) μισθός, επίδομα nt.

stipulate ['stɪpjuleɪt] vt αποφαίνομαι, συμφωνώ, συνομολογώ.

stipulation [stɪpju'leɪʃən] n όρος, διάταξη, συμφωνία.

stir [stɜ:*] n ταραχή, σάλεμα nt, κούνημα nt, κίνηση ♦ vt (mix) ανακατώνω, αναδεύω ♦ vi (move) κουνιέμαι, σαλεύω || to ~ up vt υποκινώ, υποδαυλίζω || ~ring a συγκλονιστικός, συγκινητικός.

stirrup ['stɪrəp] n αναβολέας, σκάλα.

stitch [stɪtʃ] n βελονιά, ραφή || (sudden pain) σουβλιά πόνου, σουβλιά ♦ vt ράβω, κάνω βελονιές.

stock [stɒk] n (supply) απόθεμα nt, στοκ nt inv, προμήθεια || (trader's goods) ρουφόρευματα ntpl, στοκ nt inv || (farm animals) κτήνη ntpl, ζώα ntpl || (liquid) ζωμός, κονσομέ nt inv || (ECON) χρεώγραφο, τίτλος, αξία ♦ a της σειράς, κανονικός,

συνηθισμένος ♦ vt εφοδιάζω, έχω παρακαταθήκη από || to take ~ κάνω απογραφή || (+ of) κρίνω, εκτιμώ || to ~ up with vt αποθηκεύω.

stockade [stɒ'keɪd] n πασσαλόπηγμα nt, φράκτης.

stockbroker ['stɒkbrəʊkə*] n χρηματομεσίτης, χρηματιστής.

stock exchange ['stɒkɪkstʃeɪndʒ] n χρηματιστήριο.

stocking ['stɒkɪŋ] n κάλτσα.

stock market ['stɒkmɑ:kɪt] n αγορά κρεωγράφων.

stockpile ['stɒkpaɪl] n αποθέματα ntpl ♦ vt δημιουργώ αποθέματα.

stocktaking ['stɒkteɪkɪŋ] n (COMM) απογραφή.

stocky ['stɒkɪ] a κοντόχοντρος.

stodgy ['stɒdʒɪ] a βαρύς, ανιαρός.

stoical ['stəʊɪkəl] a στωικός.

stoke [stəʊk] vt τροφοδοτώ φωτιά, διατηρώ φωτιά.

stole [stəʊl] pt of **steal** ♦ n (fur) γούνα, σάρπα || ~n pp of **steal** ♦ a κλεμμένος.

stomach ['stʌmək] n στομάχι || (inclination) όρεξη, διάθεση ♦ vt ανέχομαι, χωνεύω || ~ ache n στομαχόπονος.

stone [stəʊn] n λίθος, πέτρα || (gem) πολύτιμος λίθος, πετράδι, κόσμημα nt || (of fruit) πυρήνας, κουκούτσι || (weight) βάρος 14 λιβρών ♦ a από λίθους, πέτρινος ♦ vt βγάζω κουκούτσια από || ~-**cold** a κρύος σαν μάρμαρο || ~-**deaf** a θεόκουφος || ~-**work** n λιθοδομή.

stony ['stəʊnɪ] a πετρώδης, γεμάτος πέτρες.

stood [stʊd] pt, pp of **stand.**

stool [stu:l] n σκαμνί.

stoop [stu:p] vi σκύβω.

stop [stɒp] n στάση || (punctuation) σημείο στίξεως ♦ vt (prevent) σταματώ || (bring to end) διακόπτω,

stoppage ['stɔpɪdʒ] n σταμάτημα nt, παύση, διακοπή.

stopper ['stɔpə*] n πώμα nt, βούλωμα nt.

stopwatch ['stɔpwɔtʃ] n χρονόμετρο.

storage ['stɔːrɪdʒ] n (εν)αποθήκευση, αποθήκη.

store [stɔː*] n παρακαταθήκη, εφόδιο || (place) αποθήκη || (large shop) κατάστημα nt, μαγαζί ♦ vt εφοδιάζω, αποθηκεύω || (COMPUT) αποθηκεύω || **to ~ up** vt συσσωρεύω, συγκεντρώνω, μαζεύω || **~room** n αποθήκη, κελάρι.

storey ['stɔːrɪ] n (Brit) όροφος, πάτωμα nt.

stork [stɔːk] n πελαργός, λελέκι.

storm [stɔːm] n θύελλα, καταιγίδα, φουρτούνα || (disturbance) θύελλα, καταιγισμός ♦ vi μαίνομαι ♦ vt (attack) εξαπολύω έφοδο || **to take by ~** (lit) καταλαμβάνω με έφοδο || (fig) κατακτώ, παρασύρω || **~ cloud** n μαύρο σύννεφο || **~y** a (weather) θυελλώδης.

story ['stɔːrɪ] n (account) ιστορία, αφήγηση, διήγημα nt || (lie) παραμύθι, ψέμα nt || (US: storey) όροφος, πάτωμα nt || **~book** n βιβλίο διηγημάτων || **~teller** n αφηγητής, παραμύθας.

stout [staut] a (bold) δυνατός, γερός,

θαρραλέος || (too fat) χονδρός, σωματώδης, παχύς ♦ n είδος μπύρας.

stove [stəuv] n (for cooking) κουζίνα, συσκευή μαγειρεύματος || (for heating) θερμάστρα, σόμπα.

stow [stəu] vt στοιβάζω, αποθηκεύω || **~away** n λαθρεπιβάτης.

straddle ['strædl] vt κάθομαι καβαλικευτά, καβαλικεύω.

straggle ['strægl] vi σκορπίζω, βραδυπορώ || **~ r** n παραπλανημένος, ο βραδυπορών.

straight [streɪt] a ευθύς, ευθύγραμμος, ίσιος || (honest) δίκαιος, ευθύς, τίμιος, ντόμπρος || (in order) τακτικός, τακτοποιημένος, σιαγμένος ♦ ad ίσια, κατευθείαν, αμέσως || (drink) σκέτο ♦ n ευθεία || **~ away** ad (at once) αμέσως || **~ off** ad (without stopping) στη στιγμή, αυτοστιγμεί || **~en** vt (also: **~ out**) ισιώνω || (fig) τακτοποιώ || **~ forward** a (simple) χωρίς περιστροφές, ντόμπρος, ειλικρινής.

strain [streɪn] n (mental) ένταση, κούραση || (streak, trace) φυσική διάθεση, κλίση, τάση ♦ vt (stretch) εντείνω, τεντώνω || (filter) διυλίζω, φιλτράρω ♦ vi (make effort) μοχθώ, κοπιάζω, εντείνω || **~ s** npl (MUS) τόνος, ύφος nt || **~ed** a (laugh) βιασμένος, ψεύτικος || (relations) τεταμένος || **~er** n σουρωτήρι, φίλτρο, τρυπητό.

strait [streɪt] n (GEOG) στενό, πορθμός || **~ jacket** n ζουρλομανδύας || **~-laced** a ηθικολόγος, σεμνότυφος.

strand [strænd] n (thread) κλώνος, κλωνί, κλωστή ♦ vt εξοκέλλω || **~ed** a εγκαταλειμμένος, αφισμένος πίσω.

strange [streɪndʒ] a ξένος || (unusual) ασυνήθιστος, παράξενος || **~ness** n το περίεργο, παράξενο || **~r** n ξένος/n m/f, άγνωστος/n m/f ||

|| *(new to a place)* νεοαφιχθείς/είσα m/f, καινούργιος/α m/f.

strangle ['stræŋgl] *vt* στραγγαλίζω, πνίγω, καταπνίγω.

strangulation [stræŋgju'leɪʃən] *n* στραγγαλισμός.

strap [stræp] *n* λωρίδα, λουρί ♦ *vt* δένω με λουρί || *(beat)* δέρνω με λουρί || ~**ping** *a* γεροδεμένος.

strata ['strɑːtə] *npl of* **stratum**.

stratagem ['strætɪdʒəm] *n* στρατήγημα *nt*, κόλπο.

strategic [strə'tiːdʒɪk] *a* στρατηγικός || ~**ally** *ad* στρατηγικά.

strategy ['strætɪdʒɪ] *n* στρατηγική, τέχνασμα *nt*.

stratum ['strɑːtəm] *n* στρώμα *nt*.

straw [strɔː] *n (AGR)* άχυρο, χόρτο || *(drinking straw)* καλάμι, καλαμάκι ♦ *a (hat, basket)* ψάθινος, αχυρένιος.

strawberry ['strɔːbərɪ] *n* φράουλα.

stray [streɪ] *n* χαμένος, ζώο που έχει ξεκόψει από το κοπάδι ♦ *vi* περιπλανιέμαι, απομακρύνομαι ♦ *a (animal)* περιπλανώμενος, αδέσποτος || *(thought)* ξεκάρφωτος, σκόρπιος, ξεκλάριστος.

streak [striːk] *n* γραμμή, λωρίδα, ρίγα || *(strain)* δόση *vt* χαράσσω, ριγώνω, σχηματίζω ραβδώσεις || ~**y** *a* ραβδωτός, γραμμωτός, ριγωτός.

stream [striːm] *n* ποτάμι, ρυάκι, ρέμα *nt* || *(flow)* ροή, ρυμός, χείμαρρος || *(crowd)* κύματα *ntpl*, αδιάκοπη σειρά ♦ *vi* ρέω, τρέχω, κυλώ.

streamer ['striːmə*] *n* σερπαντίνα, ταινία, σημαία.

streamlined ['striːmlaɪnd] *a* αεροδυναμικός.

street [striːt] *n* οδός f, δρόμος || ~ **car** *n (US: tram)* τράμ *nt inv* || ~ **lamp** *n* φανοστάτης.

strength [streŋθ] *n (lit)* δύναμη, ισχύς f|| *(fig)* **on the ~of**

βασιζόμενος σε, στηριζόμενος σε || ~**en** *vt* ενισχύω, δυναμώνω.

strenuous ['strenjuəs] *a* κουραστικός, δραστήριος || *(requiring effort)* επίπονος, σκληρός.

stress [stres] *n (force, pressure)* πίεση, καταναγκασμός || *(mental strain)* ένταση || *(accent)* τόνος ♦ *vt* τονίζω.

stretch [stretʃ] *n (area)* έκταση || *vt* τεντώνω, απλώνω || *vi* εκτείνομαι, πλαταίνω || **at a ~** *(continuously)* χωρίς διακοπή || **to ~ out** *vi* επεκτείνομαι, αραιώνω ♦ *vt* τείνω, απλώνω || ~**er** *n* φορείο.

stricken ['strɪkən] *a (person)* χτυπημένος, λιμμένος || *(city, country)* χτυπημένος.

strict [strɪkt] *a* ακριβής, αυστηρός || δριμύς || ~**ly** *ad* αυστηρά, ακριβώς || ~**ly speaking** κυριολεκτικώς, για να πούμε την αλήθεια || ~**ness** *n* αυστηρότητα.

stride [straɪd] *(irreg v)* *n* μεγάλο βήμα *nt*, δρασκελιά ♦ *vi* δρασκελίζω, βηματίζω.

strident ['straɪdənt] *a* οξύς, στριγγός, στρίγγλικος.

strife [straɪf] *n* αγώνας, πάλη, σύγκρουση.

strike [straɪk] *(irreg v)* *n* απεργία || *(discovery)* ανακάλυψη, συνάντηση || *(attack)* επιχείρηση, πλήγμα *nt* ♦ *vt* κτυπώ, προσκρούω, σκουντώ || *(come into mind)* έρχομαι (στο μυαλό), μου φαίνεται || *(find gold)* ανακαλύπτω, βρίσκω ♦ *vi (stop work)* κηρύσσω απεργία, απεργώ || *(clock)* ηχώ, χτυπώ, σημαίνω || **to ~ down** *vt (lay low)* χάμω χτυπώ || **to ~ out** *vt (cross out)* εξαλείφω, διαγράφω, σβήνω || **to ~ up** *vt (music)* αρχίζω (να παίζω) || *(friendship)* πιάνω φιλία || ~**r** *n* απεργός.

striking ['straɪkɪŋ] *a* κτυπητός,

ελκυστικός, ενδιαφέρων || ~ **ly** ad
εντυπωσιακά, χτυπητά.

string [strɪŋ] n σπάγγος, κορδόνι ||
(series) σειρά || *(MUS)* χορδή ||
(COMPUT) διεταγμένη σειρά
χαρακτήρων || ~ **bean** n φρέσκο
φασολάκι.

stringent ['strɪndʒənt] a αυστηρός,
στενός.

strip [strɪp] n λουρίδα, ταινία ♦ vt
γυμνώνω, γδύνω, βγάζω || *(machine
etc)* αποσυνθέ ♦ vi γδύνομαι,
γυμνώνομαι || ~ **cartoon** n σειρά
εύθυμων σκίτσων.

stripe [straɪp] n γραμμή, λουρίδα,
ράβδωση || ~**d** a ραβδωτός,
ριγωτός.

stripper ['strɪpə*] n στριπτηζέζ f inv.

striptease ['strɪptiːz] n στριπτήζ nt
inv.

strive [straɪv] *(irreg v)* vi (+ for)
αγωνίζομαι (για), προσπαθώ || ~**n**
['strɪvn] pp of **strive**.

strode [strəud] pt, pp of **stride**.

stroke [strəuk] n κτύπημα nt,
πλήγμα nt || *(TECH)* κίνηση, διαδρομή,
ρυθμός || *(sudden attack)* προσβολή ||
(caress) θωπεία, χάδι, χλίδεμα nt ||
χαιδεύω, τρίβω, ρίγλιω || **at a ~ μ'**
ένα κτύπημα, με μιας || **on the ~ of
5** στις 5 ακριβώς.

stroll [strəul] n περίπατος, βόλτα ♦
vi κάνω περίπατο, κάνω βόλτες.

strong [strɒŋ] a δυνατός, ισχυρός,
γερός || *(firm)* στερεός, γερός ||
(flavour) δυνατός, έντονος || *(protest)*
έντονος || *(wind)* ισχυρός, δυνατός ||
they are 50 ~ δυνάμεως 50
ανδρών || ~**hold** n φρούριο, οχυρό,
προπύργιο || ~**ly** ad δυνατά, γερά ||
~**room** n αίθουσα
χρηματοκιβωτίων.

strove [strəuv] pt of **strive**.

struck [strʌk] pt, pp of **strike**.

structural ['strʌktʃərəl] a δομικός.

structure ['strʌktʃə*] n κατασκευή,

δομή || *(building)* οικοδόμημα nt,
κτίριο, κτίσμα nt.

struggle ['strʌgl] n αγώνας, πάλη,
σκληρή προσπάθεια ♦ vi (+ to)
αγωνίζομαι, παλεύω.

strum [strʌm] vt *(guitar)* παίζω
αδέξια, παίζω άτεχνα.

strut [strʌt] n *(support)* στήριγμα nt,
υποστήριγμα nt ♦ vi περιφέρομαι
καμαρωτός, κορδώνομαι.

stub [stʌb] n *(cigarette etc)* υπόλειμμα
nt, γόπα.

stubble ['stʌbl] n καλαμιά, ρίζες fpl ||
(on face) γένια πολ ημερών.

stubborn ['stʌbən] a επίμονος,
πεισματάρης, ξεροκέφαλος || ~**ly**
ad πεισματικά, επίμονα.

stubby ['stʌbɪ] a κοντόχοντρος.

stuck [stʌk] pt, pp of **stick** || ~-**up** a
υπεροπτικός, φαντασμένος.

stud [stʌd] n πλατυκέφαλο καρφί ||
(of shirt) κουμπί, ξενόκουμπο || *(of
horses)* στάθλος αλόγων, ιπποστάσιο
♦ vt διαστίζω, κοσμώ με καρφιά.

student ['stjuːdənt] n
φοιτητής/ήτρια m/f,
σπουδαστής/άστρια m/f, μελετητής.

studio ['stjuːdɪəu] n εργαστήριο,
ατελιέ nt inv || *(also TV)* στούντιο.

studious ['stjuːdɪəs] a μελετηρός,
φιλομαθής || *(careful)* προσεκτικός ||
~**ly** ad *(carefully)* επιμελώς.

study ['stʌdɪ] n σπουδή, μελέτη ||
(something studied) μελέτη, έρευνα ||
(room) σπουδαστήριο,
αναγνωστήριο ♦ vt σπουδάζω,
μελετώ || *(examine)* μελετώ,
παρατηρώ ♦ vi επιμελούμαι, μελετώ.

stuff [stʌf] n ύλη, υλικό, ουσία ♦ vt
(παρα)γεμίζω || ~**ing** n
παραγέμισμα nt, γέμιση || *(of fowl etc)*
γέμισμα nt || ~ **y** a *(room)* πνιγηρός,
χωρίς αέρα || *(ideas: old-fashioned)*
σεμνότυφος.

stumble ['stʌmbl] vi σκοντάφτω,

προσκρούω || **to** ~ **on** vt ανακαλύπτω αναπάντεχα.

stumbling block ['stʌmblɪŋblɒk] n εμπόδιο.

stump [stʌmp] n κούτσουρο, στέλεχος nt ♦ vt (puzzle) μπερδεύω, τα χάνω.

stun [stʌn] vt ζαλίζω, ταράζω.

stung [stʌŋ] pt, pp of **sting**.

stunk [stʌŋk] pp of **stink**.

stunning ['stʌnɪŋ] a εξαίσιος, καταπληκτικός.

stunt [stʌnt] n εκπληκτική παράσταση, άθλος ♦ vt περιστέλλω, εμποδίζω την ανάπτυξη || **~ed** a κατισχναμένος.

stupefy ['stju:pɪfaɪ] vt καταπλήσσω.

stupendous [stju:'pɛndəs] a τεράστιος, πελώριος, καταπληκτικός || **~ly** ad καταπληκτικά.

stupid ['stju:pɪd] a ηλίθιος, βλάκας, κουτός || **~ity** n βλακεία, κουταμάρα || **~ly** ad ηλίθια, βλακωδώς.

stupor ['stju:pə*] n νάρκη, λήθαργος, χαύνωση.

sturdy ['stɜːdɪ] a δυνατός, σθεναρός, γεροδεμένος.

stutter ['stʌtə*] n ψέλλισμα nt, τραύλισμα nt ♦ vi τραυλίζω, τσεβδίζω.

sty [staɪ] n χοιροστάσιο, γουρνοστάσι.

stye [staɪ] n χαλάζιο, κριθαράκι.

style [staɪl] n στύλ nt inv, τεχνοτροπία, ύφος nt || (fashion) ρυθμός, στύλ nt inv, μόδα || (distinction) επιδεξιότητα, μεγαλοπρέπεια.

stylish ['staɪlɪʃ] a μοντέρνος, κομψός || **~ly** ad κομψά, με σικ.

stylus ['staɪləs] n στύλος, γραφίδα.

suave [swɑːv] a ευγενικός, απαλός, ευχάριστος.

sub- [sʌb] prefix υπο-.

subconscious ['sʌb'kɒnʃəs] a

υποσυνείδητος ♦ n: **the** ~ το υποσυνείδητο.

subdivide ['sʌbdɪ'vaɪd] vt υποδιαιρώ.

subdivision ['sʌbdɪvɪʒən] n υποδιαίρεση.

subdue [səb'dju:] vt κατακτώ, υποτάσσω, μαλακώνω || **~d** a συντριμμένος, μαλακωμένος.

subject ['sʌbdʒɪkt] n υποκείμενο m/f || (theme) θέμα nt, αντικείμενο || (GRAM) υποκείμενο ♦ [səb'dʒɛkt] vt: **to** ~ **s.o. to sth** υποβάλλω κάποιον σε κάτι || **to be** ~ **to** υπόκειμαι σε, εξαρτώμαι από || **~ion** n καθυπόταξη, υποταγή || **~ive** a υποκειμενικός || **~ matter** n θέμα nt, περιεχόμενο.

sublet ['sʌb'lɛt] vt υπενοικιάζω.

sublime [sə'blaɪm] a θείος, ανώτερος, έξοχος.

submarine [sʌbmə'ri:n] n υποβρύχιο.

submerge [səb'mɜːdʒ] vt βυθίζω, χώνω στο νερό ♦ vi καταδύομαι, βυθίζομαι, βουλιάζω.

submission [səb'mɪʃən] n υποταγή, υπακοή || (presentation) υποβολή.

submit [səb'mɪt] vt υποβάλλω ♦ vi υποτάσσομαι, υποβάλλομαι.

subnormal ['sʌb'nɔ:məl] a κάτω του κανονικού.

subordinate [sə'bɔ:dɪnɪt] a κατώτερος, εξαρτημένος ♦ n υφιστάμενος.

subpoena [səb'pi:nə] n κλήση (μορτύρων) ♦ vt καλώ, αποστέλλω κλήση.

subscribe [səb'skraɪb] vi (pay contribution) εγγράφομαι, συνεισφέρω || (+ to) επιδοκιμάζω, αποδέχομαι, παραδέχομαι || **~r** n (to periodical, TEL) συνδρομητής/ήτρια m/f.

subscription [səb'skrɪpʃən] n συνεισφορά, συνδρομή.

subsequent ['sʌbsɪkwənt] a επακόλουθος, μεταγενέστερος || **~ly** ad έπειτα, αργότερα.

subside [səb'saɪd] vi κατακαθίζω, υποχωρώ, κοπάζω || **~nce** n καθίζηση, κόπαση.

subsidiary [səb'sɪdɪərɪ] a βοηθητικός, δευτερεύων ♦ n θυγατρική εταιρεία.

subsidize ['sʌbsɪdaɪz] vt επιχορηγώ, επιδοτώ.

subsidy ['sʌbsɪdɪ] n επιχορήγηση, βοήθημα nt, επίδομα nt.

subsistence [səb'sɪstəns] n ύπαρξη, συντήρηση, επιβίωση.

substance ['sʌbstəns] n ουσία || (wealth) περιουσία, αξία.

substandard ['sʌb'stændəd] a κάτω του μέσου όρου, κακής ποιότητας.

substantial [səb'stænʃəl] a (strong) στερεός, γερός || (important) σημαντικός, ουσιώδης || **~ly** ad ουσιαστικά, πραγματικά.

substantiate [səb'stænʃɪeɪt] vt επαληθεύω, αποδεικνύω, αιτιολογώ.

substitute ['sʌbstɪtjuːt] n αντικαταστάτης, υποκατάστατο ♦ vt υποκαθιστώ, αντικαθιστώ.

substitution [sʌbstɪ'tjuːʃən] n αντικατάσταση, υποκατάσταση.

subterfuge ['sʌbtəfjuːdʒ] n υπεκφυγή, τέχνασμα nt, πρόφαση.

subterranean [sʌbtə'reɪnɪən] a υπόγειος.

subtitle ['sʌbtaɪtl] n (CINE) υπότιτλος.

subtle ['sʌtl] a (faint) λεπτός, διακριτικός || (clever, sly) έξυπνος, πανούργος || **~ty** n λεπτότητα.

subtly ['sʌtlɪ] ad διακριτικά, με λεπτότητα.

subtract [səb'trækt] vt αφαιρώ || **~ion** n αφαίρεση.

subtropical ['sʌb'trɒpɪkəl] a υποτροπικός.

suburb ['sʌbɜːb] n προάστειο || **~an** a των προαστείων.

subversive [səb'vɜːsɪv] a ανατρεπτικός.

subway ['sʌbweɪ] n (US) υπόγειος σιδηρόδρομος.

succeed [sək'siːd] vi επιτυγχάνω, πετυχαίνω ♦ vt διαδέχομαι || **~ing** a (following) επόμενος, μελλοντικός.

success [sək'ses] n επιτυχία, ευτυχής έκβαση || (person) επιτυχημένος άνθρωπος || **~ful** a επιτυχής, επιτυχημένος || **~fully** ad επιτυχώς, με επιτυχία.

succession [sək'seʃən] n διαδοχή.

successive [sək'sesɪv] a διαδοχικός, συνεχής, αλλεπάλληλος.

successor [sək'sesə*] n διάδοχος.

succinct [sək'sɪŋkt] a σύντομος και σαφής.

succulent ['sʌkjulənt] a εύχυμος, ζουμερός, νόστιμος.

succumb [sə'kʌm] vi (+ to) υποκύπτω, υποτάσσομαι, ενδίδω.

such [sʌtʃ] a (of that kind) τέτοιος, τέτοιου είδους || (so great etc) τόσος ♦ pron αυτός, αυτοί, τέτοια.

suck [sʌk] vt (toffee) πιπιλίζω || **~er** n (col) κορόιδο.

suction ['sʌkʃən] n αναρρόφηση, άντληση.

sudden ['sʌdn] a ξαφνικός, αιφνίδιος || **all of a ~** αιφνιδίως, ξαφνικά || **~ly** ad ξαφνικά.

sue [suː] vt ενάγω, κάνω αγωγή.

suede [sweɪd] n καστόρι, σουέντ nt inv.

suet [suɪt] n λίπος nt, ξύγγι.

suffer ['sʌfə*] vt (of death) θανατούμαι, εκτελούμαι || (permit) υποφέρω, ανέχομαι, δέχομαι ♦ vi υποφέρω, πάσχω || **~er** n υποφέρων, πάσχων || **~ing** n πόνος, βάσανα ntpl, πάθη ntpl.

suffice [sə'fais] vi (εn)αρκώ, φθάνω.

sufficient [sə'fɪʃənt] a επαρκής, αρκετός || **~ly** ad αρκετά.

suffix ['sʌfɪks] n κατάληξη, πρόσφυμα nt.

suffocate ['sʌfəkeit] vi πνίγομαι, ασφυκτιώ.

suffocation [sʌfə'keiʃən] n ασφυξία, πνίξιμο.

sugar ['ʃugə*] n ζάχαρη ♦ vt ζαχαρώνω, βάζω ζάχαρη || **~ beet** n ζαχαρότευτλο || **~ cane** n ζαχαροκάλαμο || **~ y** a ζαχαρένιος, ζαχαρωμένος, γλυκύτατος.

suggest [sə'dʒest] vt εισηγούμαι, προτείνω || (show indirectly) υπαινίσσομαι, υπονοώ || (propose) προτείνω, υποβάλλω, υποδεικνύω || **~ion** n πρόταση, υποβολή || **~ive** a υπαινισσόμενος, υποβλητικός, με υπονοούμενα.

suicidal [sui'saidl] a της αυτοκτονίας.

suicide ['suisaid] n αυτοκτονία || (person) αυτόχειρας.

suit [su:t] n (of clothes) κοστούμι || (in cards) τα τέσσερα χρώματα ♦ vt ταιριάζω, πηγαίνω || (satisfy) ικανοποιώ, βολεύω || (adapt) προσαρμόζω || **~able** a κατάλληλος, αρμόζων, ταιριαστός || **~ably** ad καταλλήλως, όπως πρέπει.

suitcase ['su:tkeis] n βαλίτσα.

suite [swi:t] n (of rooms) διαμέρισμα nt, σουίτα || (MUS) σουίτα.

sulfur ['sʌlfə*] n (US) = sulphur.

sulk [sʌlk] vi κάνω μούτρα, κατσουφιάζω || **~ y** a κακόκεφος, κατσούφης.

sullen ['sʌlən] a (gloomy) κατηφής, μελαγχολικός || (bad-tempered) κακόκεφος, αγέλαστος.

sulphur ['sʌlfə*] n θείο, θειάφι.

sultan ['sʌltən] n σουλτάνος || **~ a** n σουλτάνα || (raisin) σουλτανίνα.

sultry ['sʌltri] a αποπνικτικός, πνιγηρός.

sum [sʌm] n (total) σύνολο || (calculation) άθροισμα nt || (of money) ποσό (χρημάτων) || **to ~ up** vt συνοψίζω, ανακεφαλαιώνω ♦ vi κρίνω, εκτιμώ.

summarize ['sʌməraiz] vt συνοψίζω, συγκεφαλαιώνω.

summary ['sʌməri] n (συνοπτική) περίληψη, σύνοψη.

summer ['sʌmə*] n καλοκαίρι ♦ attr a (clothing) καλοκαιρινός || **~house** n (in garden) περίπτερο κήπου || **~time** n καλοκαίρι, θερινή ώρα.

summit ['sʌmit] n κορυφή || **~ conference** n συνεδρίαση κορυφής.

summon ['sʌmən] vt (συγ)καλώ, προσκαλώ || (gather up) συγκεντρώνω, μαζεύω || **~s** n κλήση ♦ vt κλητεύω, καλώ.

sump [sʌmp] n λεκάνη αποστραγγίσεως, κάρτερ nt inv.

sumptuous ['sʌmptjuəs] a πολυτελής, πολυδάπανος.

sun [sʌn] n ήλιος || (sunshine) λιακάδα || **~bathe** vi κάνω ηλιοθεραπεία || **~burn** n έγκαυμα nt από τον ήλιο || **~burnt** a ηλιοκαμμένος, μαυρισμένος.

Sunday ['sʌndi] n Κυριακή.

sundial ['sʌndaiəl] n ηλιακό ρολόι.

sundry ['sʌndri] a διάφορος || **sundries** npl διάφορα είδη ntpl.

sunflower ['sʌnflauə*] n ήλιος, ηλίανθος.

sung [sʌŋ] pp of sing.

sunglasses ['sʌnglɑ:siz] npl γυαλιά ntpl του ηλίου.

sunk [sʌŋk] pp of sink.

sunlight ['sʌnlait] n ηλιακό φώς, λιακάδα.

sunlit ['sʌnlit] a ηλιόλουστος.

sunny ['sʌnɪ] a ευήλιος, ηλιόλουστος || (cheerful) χαρωπός, γελαστός.

sunrise ['sʌnraɪz] n ανατολή του ηλίου.

sunset ['sʌnset] n ηλιοβασίλεμα nt.

sunshade ['sʌnʃeɪd] n (over table) αλεξήλιο, ομπρέλα του ηλίου.

sunshine ['sʌnʃaɪn] n λιακάδα.

sunspot ['sʌnspɒt] n ηλιακή κηλίδα.

sunstroke ['sʌnstrəʊk] n ηλίαση.

suntan ['sʌntæn] n μαύρισμα nt από τον ήλιο.

super ['suːpə*] a (col) υπέροχος, περίφημος, σπουδαίος || prefix υπερ-.

superannuation [suːpərænjʊ'eɪʃən] n συνταξιοδότηση.

superb [suː'pɜːb] a υπέροχος, έξοχος, εξαίσιος || ~ly ad υπέροχα, έξοχα, λαμπρά.

supercilious [suːpə'sɪlɪəs] a αγέρωχος, υπεροπτικός.

superficial [suːpə'fɪʃəl] a επιφανειακός || (shallow) επιπόλαιος, επιφανειακός.

superfluous [sʊ'pɜːflʊəs] a περιττός.

superhuman [suːpə'hjuːmən] a (effort) υπεράνθρωπος.

superimpose ['suːpərɪm'pəʊz] vt βάζω από πάνω, υπερθέτω.

superintendent [suːpərɪn'tendənt] n (police) αξιωματικός της αστυνομίας.

superior [sʊ'pɪərɪə*] a ανώτερος, υπέρτερος, εξαιρετικός || (proud) υπεροπτικός, ακατάδεκτος ♦ n προϊστάμενος, ανώτερος || ~ity n υπεροχή, ανωτερότητα.

superlative [sʊ'pɜːlətɪv] a ανώτατος, υπερθετικός ♦ n (το) υπερθετικό.

superman ['suːpəmæn] n υπεράνθρωπος.

supermarket ['suːpəmɑːkɪt] n σουπερμάρκετ f inv, υπεραγορά.

supernatural [suːpə'nætʃərəl] a υπερφυσικός.

superpower ['suːpəpaʊə*] n (POL) υπερδύναμη.

supersede [suːpə'siːd] vt αντικαθιστώ, παραμερίζω.

supersonic ['suːpə'sɒnɪk] a υπερηχητικός.

superstition [suːpə'stɪʃən] n δεισιδαιμονία, πρόληψη.

superstitious [suːpə'stɪʃəs] a δεισιδαίμονας, προληπτικός.

supertanker ['suːpətæŋkə*] n υπερδεξαμενόπλοιο.

supervise ['suːpəvaɪz] vt επιβλέπω, εποπτεύω, διευθύνω.

supervision [suːpə'vɪʒən] n εποπτεία, επιθεώρηση, διεύθυνση.

supervisor ['suːpəvaɪzə*] n επιθεωρητής/ήτρια m/f, επόπτης/όπτρια m/f, επιστάτης/άτρια m/f.

supper ['sʌpə*] n δείπνο.

supple ['sʌpl] a εύκαμπτος, ευλύγιστος, λυγερός.

supplement ['sʌplɪmənt] n συμπλήρωμα nt || (newspaper) παράρτημα nt ♦ [sʌplɪ'ment] vt συμπληρώνω || ~ary a συμπληρωματικός, πρόσθετος.

supplier [sə'plaɪə*] n προμηθευτής.

supply [sə'plaɪ] vt παρέχω, εφοδιάζω, προμηθεύω ♦ n εφόδιο, απόθεμα nt, προμήθεια || (supplying) εφοδιασμός, τροφοδότηση || **supplies** npl (food) τρόφιμα ntpl || (MIL) εφόδια ntpl || ~ **and demand** προσφορά και ζήτηση.

support [sə'pɔːt] n (moral, financial etc) υποστήριξη, ενίσχυση || (TECH) στήριγμα nt, υποστήριγμα nt, έρεισμα nt ♦ vt (υπο)στηρίζω, ενισχύω || (provide for) συντηρώ, κρατώ || (speak for) υποστηρίζω,

ενισχύω || (endure) υπομένω, υποφέρω || ~ **er** n (POL etc) οπαδός, υπερασπιστής/ίστρια m/f || (SPORT) οπαδός, υποστηρικτής/ίκτρια m/f || ~ **ing** a (programme, role) βοηθητικός, δευτερεύων.

suppose [sə'pəʊz] vti υποθέτω, προϋποθέτω || (think, imagine) φαντάζομαι, νομίζω || ~ **he comes** ... αν έρθει ... || ~ **dly** ad υποθετικά, δήθεν.

supposing [sə'pəʊzɪŋ] cj εάν, ας υποθέσουμε ότι.

supposition [sʌpə'zɪʃən] n υπόθεση, γνώμη.

suppress [sə'pres] vt καταπνίγω, καταστέλλω || (hold back) συγκρατώ, σκεπάζω || ~ **ion** n κατάπνιξη, συγκράτηση, απόκρυψη.

supremacy [su'preməsɪ] n υπεροχή, ανώτατη εξουσία.

supreme [su'priːm] a υπέρτατος, ανώτατος, ύψιστος.

surcharge ['sɜːtʃɑːdʒ] n πρόσθετη επιβάρυνση.

sure [ʃʊə*] a βέβαιος, ασφαλής, σίγουρος ♦ ad βεβαίως, ασφαλώς || ~**!** (of course) βέβαια!, ασφαλώς! || **to make ~ of** βεβαιώνω || ~**-footed** a με σίγουρο πόδι || ~**ly** ad ασφαλώς, βεβαίως || (firmly) αναμφιβόλα || (gladly) βεβαίως, μετά χαράς.

surf [sɜːf] n κύμα nt, αφρός.

surface ['sɜːfɪs] n (top side) επιφάνεια || (outward appearance) εξωτερικό, εμφάνιση ♦ vt (roadway) επιστρώνω, στρώνω ♦ vi βγαίνω στην επιφάνεια || ~ **mail** n τακτικό ταχυδρομείο.

surfboard ['sɜːfbɔːd] n σανίδα κυματοδρομίας, σέρφμπορντ nt inv.

surfeit ['sɜːfɪt] n υπεραφθονία, πλήθώρα, κόρος.

surge [sɜːdʒ] n μεγάλο κύμα nt || (fig) μεγάλη αύξηση ♦ vi ορμώ, ξεχύνομαι.

surgeon ['sɜːdʒən] n χειρούργος.

surgery ['sɜːdʒərɪ] n χειρουργική || (room) ιατρείο, χειρουργείο.

surgical ['sɜːdʒɪkəl] a χειρουργικός.

surly ['sɜːlɪ] a αγροίκος, κατσούφης, αγενής.

surmise [sɜː'maɪz] vt εικάζω, υποθέτω, μαντεύω.

surmount [sɜː'maʊnt] vt (difficulty) υπερνικώ, ξεπερνώ.

surname ['sɜːneɪm] n επώνυμο.

surpass [sɜː'pɑːs] vt υπερτερώ, υπερβαίνω, ξεπερνώ.

surplus ['sɜːpləs] n περίσσευμα nt, πλεόνασμα nt ♦ a πλεονάζων, υπεράριθμος.

surprise [sə'praɪz] n έκπληξη, κατάπληξη, ξάφνισμα nt ♦ vt αιφνιδιάζω || (astonish) εκπλήσσω, καταπλήσσω, ξαφνίζω.

surprising [sə'praɪzɪŋ] a εκπληκτικός, καταπληκτικός.

surrender [sə'rendə*] n παράδοση, εγκατάλειψη ♦ vi παραδίδομαι, παραδίδω, παραχωρώ.

surreptitious [sʌrəp'tɪʃəs] a λαθραίος, κρυφός.

surround [sə'raʊnd] vt περιβάλλω, περικυκλώνω || ~ **ing** a (countryside) περιβάλλων, εξοχικός || ~ **ings** npl περιβάλλον, περίχωρο ntpl.

surveillance [sɜː'veɪləns] n (observation) επιτήρηση, εποπτεία.

survey [sɜː'veɪ] n (inquiry) επισκόπηση || (of land) χωρογράφηση, τοπογράφηση ['sɜː'veɪ] vt επισκοπώ, εξετάζω || (measure land) χωρογραφώ, τοπογραφώ || ~ **ing** n (of land) χωρογράφηση, τοπογραφία || ~ **or** n (of land) τοπογράφος.

survival [sə'vaɪvəl] n επιβίωση || (from past) υπόλειμμα, επιβίωμα nt.

survive [sə'vaɪv] vi επιζώ ♦ vt

επιζώ || *(a shipwreck etc)* σώζομαι, γλυτώνω.

survivor [sə'vaivə*] *n* επιζών, διασωθείς.

susceptible [sə'sɛptəbl] *a* (+ *to*) επιδεκτικός, τρωτός.

suspect ['sʌspɛkt] *n* ύποπτος ♦ *a* ύποπτος ♦ [səs'pɛkt] *vt* υποπτεύομαι, υποψιάζομαι || *(think likely)* υποψιάζομαι, φαντάζομαι.

suspend [səs'pɛnd] *vt* αναστέλλω, διακόπτω || *(hang up)* αναρτώ, κρεμώ || ~**ers** *npl* καλτσοδέτες *fpl* || *(US)* τιράντες *fpl*.

suspense [səs'pɛns] *n* εκκρεμότητα, ανησυχία, αβεβαιότητα.

suspension [səs'pɛnʃən] *n* αναστολή, ανακοπή || *(being suspended)* απόλυση || *(AUT)* ανάρτηση || ~ **bridge** *n* κρεμαστή γέφυρα.

suspicion [səs'piʃən] *n* υποψία, υπόνοια || *(small amount)* μικρή δόση.

suspicious [səs'piʃəs] *a* ύποπτος, καχύποπτος || ~**ly** *ad* ύποπτα, δύσπιστα.

sustain [səs'tein] *vt* υποστηρίζω, στηρίζω, βαστάζω || *(confirm)* αποδέχομαι || *(injury)* αναδέχομαι, παθαίνω, δέχομαι || ~**ed** *a (effort)* επίμονος, συνεχής.

sustenance ['sʌstinəns] *n* συντήρηση, τροφή.

swab [swɒb] *n (pad)* ξέστρο.

swagger ['swægə*] *vi* περπατώ καμαρωτός, επιδεικνύομαι.

swallow ['swɒləu] *n (bird)* χελιδόνι || *(of food etc)* μπουκιά ♦ *vt* καταπίνω, χάφτω || **to** ~ **up** *vt* καταπίνω, καταβροφίζω.

swam [swæm] *pt of* **swim**.

swamp [swɒmp] *n* έλος *nt*, βάλτος ♦ *vt (overwhelm)* συντρίβω, σαρώνω.

swan [swɒn] *n* κύκνος.

swap [swɒp] *n (exchange)* ανταλλαγή ♦ *vt (+ for)* ανταλλάσσω, αλλάζω.

swarm [swɔːm] *n (of bees)* σμήνος *nt*, πλήφος *nt* || *(of insects)* σύννεφο || *(of people)* μπουλούκι, τσούρμο ♦ *vt (crowd)* συρρέω, συγκεντρώνομαι.

swarthy ['swɔːði] *a* μελαψός, μελαχροινός.

swastika ['swɒstikə] *n* αγκυλωτός σταυρός.

swat [swɒt] *vt* κτυπώ, βαρώ.

sway [swei] *vi* ταλαντεύομαι, κουνιέμαι, τρικλίζω ♦ *vt* ταλαντεύω, κουνώ || *(influence)* διευθύνω, επηρεάζω, παρασύρω.

swear [swɛə*] *(irreg v) vi* ορκίζομαι || *(curse)* βλαστημώ, βρίζω || **to** ~ **to** ορκίζομαι σε, βεβαιώ || ~**word** *n* βλαστήμια, βρισιά.

sweat [swɛt] *n* ιδρώτας || *(MED)* ίδρωμα *nt* ♦ *vi* ιδρώνω || *(toil)* μοχθώ, σπάω στη δουλειά.

sweater ['swɛtə*] *n* πουλόβερ *nt inv*.

sweaty ['swɛti] *a* ιδρωμένος.

Swede [swiːd] *n* Σουηδός/ή *m/f*.

swede [swiːd] *n (turnip)* ραπίτσα.

Sweden ['swiːdn] *n* Σουηδία.

Swedish ['swiːdiʃ] *a* σουηδικός ♦ *n (LING)* Σουηδικά *ntpl*.

sweep [swiːp] *(irreg v) n* σκούπισμα *nt*, σάρωμα *nt* || *(wide curve)* κυκλική κίνηση, καμπή || *(range)* άνοιγμα *nt*, ευρύτητα || *(of chimney)* καπνοδοχοκαθαριστής ♦ *vt* σκουπίζω, καθαρίζω, σαρώνω ♦ *vi (move in curve)* εκτείνομαι, απλώνομαι || *(move majestically)* προχωρώ μεγαλόπρεπα || **to** ~ **away** *vt* σκουπίζω, σαρώνω || **to** ~ **past** *vi* περνώ γρήγορα || **to** ~ **up** *vi* φθάνω, ανεβαίνω ♦ *vt* σκουπίζω, μαζεύω || ~**ing** *a (gesture)* πλατειά (χειρονομία) || *(statement)* γενικός, ριζικός.

sweet [swiːt] *n* γλυκό || *(candy)*

ζαχαρωτό, καραμέλα ♦ *a* γλυκός ||
(fresh) δροσερός, φρέσκος || *(gentle,
pretty)* χαριτωμένος, γλυκός,
συμπαθητικός || ~**breads** *npl*
γλυκάδια *ntpl* || ~**en** *vt* γλυκαίνω ||
~**heart** *n* αγαπητικός, αγαπημένος
|| ~**ly** *ad* γλυκά, μελωδικά,
ευχάριστα || ~**ness** *n* γλυκύτητα,
γλύκα || ~ **pea** *n* λάθυρος,
μοσχομπίζελο || ~**tooth** *n*
αδυναμία για γλυκά.

swell [swɛl] *(irreg v) n* (*in wave*) μεγάλο
κύμα *nt* ♦ *a* (*col: excellent*)
εξαιρετικός, πρώτης τάξης ♦ *vt*
(*numbers*) εξογκώνω, αυξάνω ♦ *vi*
(*also:* ~ **up**) εξογκούμαι, φουσκώνω
|| (*become louder*) δυναμώνω || (*MED*)
πρήζομαι || ~**ing** *n* εξόγκωση,
πρήξιμο.

sweltering ['swɛltərɪŋ] *a*
ιδρωμένος, αποπνικτικός.

swept [swɛpt] *pt, pp of* **sweep.**

swerve [swɜːv] *n* παρέκκλιση,
παρατιμονιά || *vti* παρεκκλίνω,
παρστρατίζω, στρίβω.

swift [swɪft] *n* (*bird*) κλαδευτήρα,
πετροχελίδονο ♦ *a* ταχύς,
γρήγορος, άμεσος.

swig [swɪg] *n* (*col: of drink*) μεγάλη
ρουφηξιά.

swill [swɪl] *n* (*for pigs*) τροφή χοίρων
♦ *vt* (*also:* ~ **out,** ~ **down**)
ξεπλένω.

swim [swɪm] *(irreg v) n* κολύμπι ♦ *vi*
(*person*) κολυμπώ || (*be flooded*)
πλημμυρίζω, είμαι πλημμυρισμένος
|| (*feel dizzy*) ιλιγγιώ, ζαλίζομαι ♦ *vt*
(*cross by swimming*) περνώ
κολυμπώντας || ~**mer** *n*
κολυμβητής/ήτρια *m/f*|| ~**ming** *n*
κολύμπι || **to go** ~**ming** πάω
κολύμπι || ~**ming baths** *npl*
κολυμβητικές δεξαμενές *fpl* || ~
ming cap *n* σκουφί || ~**ming
costume** *n* μαγιό || ~**ming pool** *n*
πισίνα|| ~**suit** *n* μαγιό.

swindle ['swɪndl] *n* απάτη ♦ *vt*
(εξ)απατώ|| ~**r** *n* απατεώνας,
κατεργάρης.

swine [swaɪn] *n* χοίρος, γουρούνι ||
(*person*) γουρούνι, παλιάνθρωπος.

swing [swɪŋ] *(irreg v) n* κούνια ||
(*swinging*) αιώρηση, ταλάντευση ||
(*music*) ρυθμός ♦ *vt* ταλαντεύω,
κουνώ || (*move round*) περιστρέφω,
στρέφω ♦ *vi* αιωρούμαι, κουνιέμαι ||
(*move round*) στρέφομαι, κάνω
μεταβολή || **in full** ~ σε πλήρη
δράση || ~ **bridge** *n*
περιστρεφόμενη γέφυρα || ~ **door**
n περιστρεφόμενη πόρτα.

swipe [swaɪp] *n* δυνατό κτύπημα *nt*
♦ *vt* (*hit*) κτυπώ δυνατά || (*col: steal*)
κλέβω, βουτώ.

swish [swɪʃ] *a* (*col: smart*) κομψός,
μοντέρνος ♦ *vt* θροΐζω.

Swiss [swɪs] *a* ελβετικός ♦ *n* (*person*)
Ελβετός/ίδα *m/f.*

switch [swɪtʃ] *n* (*for light, radio etc*)
διακόπτης || (*change*) αλλαγή ♦ *vti*
διακόπτω || (*turn*) γυρίζω απότομα ||
to ~ **off** *vt* πραίνω του
ανεβοκατεβαίνει διακόπτω, σβήνω ||
to ~ **on** *vt* ανάβω, ανοίγω || ~**back**
n (*at fair*) σε λούνα παρκ || ~**board** *n*
πίνακας διανομής, τηλεφωνικό
κέντρο.

Switzerland ['swɪtsələnd] *n*
Ελβετία.

swivel ['swɪvl] *vti* (*also:* ~ **round**)
(περι)στρέφομαι, στρέφω.

swollen ['swəʊlən] *pp of* **swell** ♦ *a*
(*ankle etc*) πρησμένος, διογκωμένος.

swoon [swuːn] *vi* λιποθυμώ.

swoop [swuːp] *n* (*esp by police*)
ξαφνική επίθεση, εφόρμηση ♦ *vi*
(*also:* ~ **down**) εφορμώ, πέφτω.

swop [swɒp] = **swap.**

sword [sɔːd] *n* ξίφος *nt*, σπαθί || ~
fish *n* ξιφίας.

swore [swɔː] *pt of* **swear.**

sworn [swɔːn] *pp of* **swear.**

swum [swʌm] pp of **swim.**

swung [swʌŋ] pt, pp of **swing.**

sycamore ['sɪkəmɔː*] n συκομουριά.

syllable ['sɪləbl] n συλλαβή.

syllabus ['sɪləbəs] n διδακτέα ύλη.

symbol ['sɪmbəl] n σύμβολο, σημείο || ~**ic(al)** [sɪm'bɒlɪk(əl)] a συμβολικός || ~**ism** n συμβολισμός || ~**ize** vt συμβολίζω, παριστάνω.

symmetrical [sɪ'metrɪkəl] a συμμετρικός.

symmetry ['sɪmɪtrɪ] n συμμετρία.

sympathetic [sɪmpə'θetɪk] a συμπαθητικός || (agreeing) ευνοϊκός με.

sympathize ['sɪmpəθaɪz] vi (+ with) συμπάσχω με, συμπονώ, συμπαθώ || ~**r** n οπαδός.

sympathy ['sɪmpəθɪ] n συμπάθεια, συμπόνια.

symphony ['sɪmfənɪ] n (composition) συμφωνία || ~ **orchestra** n συμφωνική ορχήστρα.

symposium [sɪm'pəʊzɪəm] n (meeting for discussion) συγκέντρωση, συμπόσιο.

symptom ['sɪmptəm] n σύμπτωμα nt || ~**atic** a συμπτωματικός.

synagogue ['sɪnəgɒg] n συναγωγή.

synchronize ['sɪŋkrənaɪz] vt συγχρονίζω ♦ vi (+ with) γίνομαι ταυτόχρονως.

syndicate ['sɪndɪkɪt] n συνδικάτο.

syndrome ['sɪndrəʊm] n (MED) σύνδρομο.

synonym ['sɪnənɪm] n συνώνυμο || ~**ous** [sɪ'nɒnɪməs] a συνώνυμος.

synopsis [sɪ'nɒpsɪs] n σύνοψη, περίληψη.

syntax ['sɪntæks] n σύνταξη, συντακτικό || ~ **error** n (COMPUT) συντακτικό λάθος nt.

synthesis ['sɪnθəsɪs] n σύνθεση.

synthetic [sɪn'θetɪk] a (artificial) συνθετικός.

syphilis ['sɪfɪlɪs] n σύφιλη.

syphon ['saɪfən] = **siphon.**

syringe [sɪ'rɪndʒ] n σύριγγα.

syrup ['sɪrəp] n σιρόπι || ~**y** a σιροπιασμένος.

system ['sɪstəm] n σύστημα nt || (railway etc) δίκτυο || (method) σύστημα nt, μέθοδος f || ~**atic** a συστηματικός, μεθοδικός.

T

tab [tæb] n θηλειά.

tabby ['tæbɪ] n (cat) γάτα.

table ['teɪbl] n τραπέζι || (list) πίνακας.

tablecloth ['teɪblklɒθ] n τραπεζομάντηλο.

table d'hôte ['taːbl'dəʊt] a ταμπλ ν' τοτ.

table lamp ['teɪbllæmp] n πορτατίφ nt inv.

tablemat ['teɪblmæt] n ψάθα για ζεστά πιάτα.

tablespoon ['teɪblspuːn] n κουτάλι του σερβιρίσματος || ~**ful** n κουταλιά του σερβιρίσματος.

tablet ['tæblɪt] n πλάκα || (notebook) σημειωματάριο || (pellet) δισκίο, χάπι.

table tennis ['teɪbltenɪs] n πινγκ πονγκ nt inv.

table wine ['teɪblwaɪn] n επιτραπέζιο κρασί.

taboo [tə'buː] n ταμπού nt inv ♦ a απαγορευμένος, ταμπού.

tacit ['tæsɪt] a σιωπηρός, υπονοούμενος.

taciturn ['tæsɪtɜːn] a σιωπηλός, λιγόλογος.

tack [tæk] n πινέζα || (stitch) μεγάλη βελονιά, τρύπωμα nt || (NAUT) αναστροφή, διαδρομή || (course) πορεία.

tackle ['tækl] n (for lifting) πτροχαλία, παλάγκο || fishing ~

σύνεργα *ntpl* ψαρικής ♦ *vt*
αντιμετωπίζω, καταπίνομαι με || *(a player)* κάνω τάκελ.

tacky ['tækι] *a* κολλώδης.

tact [tækt] *n* τάκτ *nt inv*, λεπτότητα ||
~**ful** *a* με τάκτ, διακριτικός.

tactical ['tæktιkəl] *a* τακτικός.

tactics ['tæktιks] *npl* τακτική.

tactless ['tæktlιs] *a* στερούμενος
τάκτ, αδέξιος.

tadpole ['tædpəʊl] *n* γυρίνος.

taffeta ['tæfιtə] *n* ταφτάς.

tag [tæg] *n* (*label*) ετικέτα.

tail [teιl] *n* ουρά || **to ~ off** *vi* (*in size, quality etc*) ελαττώνομαι, αραιώνω ||
~ **end** *n* τελευταίο τμήμα *nt*, ουρά,
τέλος *nt*.

tailor ['teιlə*] *n* ράπτης || ~**ing** *n*
ραπτική || ~**-made** *a* καμωμένο
ειδικά.

tailwind ['teιlwιnd] *n* ούριος
άνεμος.

tainted ['teιntιd] *a* μολυσμένος,
χαλασμένος.

take [teιk] (*irreg v*) *vt* παίρνω, βγάζω
|| (*seize*) πιάνω, παίρνω,
καταλαμβάνω || (*require*) απαιτώ,
χρειάζομαι || (*hire*) νοικιάζω
|| (*understand*) δέχομαι, παραδέχομαι,
συμπεραίνω || (*choose*) διαλέγω
(*PHOT*) φωτογραφίζω,
φωτογραφίζομαι || **to ~ part in**
συμμετέχω || **to ~ place** συμβαίνω ||
to ~ after νι μοιάζω || **to ~ back** *vt*
(*return*) φέρνω πίσω, παίρνω πίσω ||
to ~ down *vt* κατεβάζω, ξεκρεμώ ||
(*demolish*) κατεδαφίζω || (*write*)
σημειώνω καταγράφω || **to ~ in** *vt*
(*deceive*) εξαπατώ, ξεγελώ ||
(*understand*) καταλαβαίνω,
αντιλαμβάνομαι || (*include*)
περιλαμβάνω || **to ~ off** *vi*
(*aeroplane*) απογειούμαι, ξεκινώ ♦ *vt*
(*remove*) αφαιρώ, βγάζω, παίρνω ||
(*imitate*) μιμούμαι, παρωδώ || **to ~
on** *vt* (*undertake*) αναλαμβάνω ||

(*engage*) μισθώνω, προσλαμβάνω ||
(*accept as opponent*) δέχομαι την
πρόσκληση || **to ~ out** *vt* (*licence etc*) βγάζω, κάνω || (*stain*) βγάζω || **to
~ over** *vt* αναλαμβάνω || (*succeed*)
διαδέχομαι || **to ~ to** *vt* (*person*)
συμπαθώ || (*sport, hobby*) επιδίδομαι
σε, μ' αρέσει να || **to ~ up** *vt* (*raise*)
σηκώνω, μαζεύω || (*occupy*)
καταλαμβάνω, πιάνω || (*absorb*)
απορροφώ, τραβώ || (*engage in*)
απασχολούμαι σε || ~**off** *n* (*AVIAT*)
απογείωση || (*imitation*) μίμηση ||
~**over** *n* (*COMM*) ανάληψη
επιχειρήσεως, κτήση.

takings ['teιkιnz] *npl* (*COMM*)
εισπράξεις *fpl*.

talc [tælk] *n* (*also:* ~**um powder**)
τάλκ *nt inv*.

tale [teιl] *n* αφήγηση, παραμύθι,
ιστορία.

talent ['tælənt] *n* ταλέντο || ~**ed** *a*
με ταλέντο.

talk [tɔ:k] *n* συζήτηση, συνομιλία,
κουβέντα || (*rumour*) φλυαρία,
διάδοση || (*speech*) λόγος, ομιλία || **to
~ shop** συζητώ για την εργασία
μου || **to ~ over** *vt* συζητώ ||
~**ative** *a* φλύαρος.

tall [tɔ:l] *a* ψηλός || ~**boy** *n*
(*furniture*) ψηλό κομμό, ψηλός
καθρέφτης || ~**story** *n* μπούρδα,
αρλούμπα.

tally ['tælι] *n* (*account*)
λογαριασμός ♦ *vi* συμφωνώ,
αντιστοιχώ.

tambourine [tæmbə'ri:n] *n* ντέφι.

tame [teιm] *a* ήμερος, δαμασμένος ||
(*dull*) άτονος || ~**ness** *n* ημερότητα.

tamper ['tæmpə*]: **to ~ with** *vt*
ανακατεύομαι με || (*falsify*)
παραποιώ.

tan [tæn] *n* (*colour*) (*also:* **sun ~**)
μελαχροινό χρώμα, μαύρισμα *nt* ♦ *a*
(*colour*) φαιοκίτρινος, καφέ.

tandem ['tændəm] n διπλό ποδήλατο.

tang [tæŋ] n οξεία γεύση, δυνατή οσμή.

tangent ['tændʒənt] n εφαπτομένη.

tangerine [tændʒə'riːn] n μανταρίνι.

tangible ['tændʒəbl] a απτός, ψηλαφητός || (real) πραγματικός, αισθητός.

tangle ['tæŋgl] n μπέρδεμα nt, ανακάτωμα nt || (complication) περιπλοκή ♦ vti μπερδεύομαι || (complicate) περιπλέκω.

tango ['tæŋgəu] n ταγκό nt inv.

tank [tæŋk] n δεξαμενή, ντεπόζιτο || (MIL.) τάνκ nt inv, άρμα μάχης.

tankard ['tæŋkəd] n κύπελλο, μαστραπάς.

tanker ['tæŋkə*] n (ship) δεξαμενόπλοιο, τάνκερ nt inv || (truck) βυτιοφόρο.

tankful ['tæŋkful] n γεμάτο δοχείο.

tantalizing ['tæntəlaɪzɪŋ] a προκλητικός, δελεαστικός.

tantrum ['tæntrəm] n έκρηξη οργής, ξέσπασμα nt, παραφορά.

tap [tæp] n βρύση || (on barrel) κάνουλα || (gentle blow) ελαφρό κτύπημα nt ♦ vt (strike) κτυπώ ελαφρά || (supply) παίρνω, τροφοδοτώ, ανοίγω.

tap-dance ['tæpdɑːns] vi χορεύω με κλακέτες.

tape [teɪp] n ταινία || magnetic ~ μαγνητοταινία ♦ vt (to record) μαγνητογραφώ, ηχογραφώ || ~ measure n μετρική ταινία, μέτρο.

taper ['teɪpə*] n λαμπάδα, κερί ♦ vi λεπτύνομαι, λιγοστεύω.

tape recorder n ['teɪprɪkɔːdə*] n μαγνητόφωνο.

tapestry ['tæpɪstrɪ] n ταπετσαρία τοίχου, ταπεταρία.

tar [tɑː*] n πίσσα.

tardy ['tɑːdɪ] a βραδύς, αργός.

target ['tɑːgɪt] n στόχος.

tariff ['tærɪf] n (list of charges) τιμολόγιο || (duty) δασμός, δασμολόγιο.

tarmac ['tɑːmæk] n (AVIAT) διάδρομος απογειώσεως.

tarnish ['tɑːnɪʃ] vt (lit) θαμπώνω, σκοτεινιάζω || (fig) μαυρίζω, κηλιδώνω.

tarpaulin [tɑː'pɔːlɪn] n κηρόπανο, μουσαμάς.

tart [tɑːt] n (pie) τούρτα, τάρτα || (col: low woman) τσούλα ♦ a ξινός, οξύς, δριμύς.

tartan ['tɑːtən] n σκωτσέζικο ύφασμα nt.

tartar ['tɑːtə*] n τρυγία, πουρί.

task [tɑːsk] n καθήκον, έργο, δουλειά, αποστολή.

tassel ['tæsəl] n θύσανος, φούντα.

taste [teɪst] n γεύση, γούστο || (preference) προτίμηση ♦ vt γεύομαι, δοκιμάζω || ~ful a κομψός, με γούστο, καλαίσθητος || ~less a άγευστος, άνοστος || (bad taste) χωρίς γούστο, κακόγουστος.

tasty ['teɪstɪ] a γευστικός, νόστιμος.

tatters ['tætəz] npl: in ~ (also: **tattered**) κουρελιασμένος.

tattoo [tə'tuː] n (nighttime) στρατιωτική επίδειξη || (on skin) δερματοστιξία, τατουάζ nt inv ♦ vt διαστίζω, τατουάρω.

tatty ['tætɪ] a (col: cheap, of poor quality) ψιτινός, πρόστυχος.

taught [tɔːt] pt, pp of **teach**.

taunt [tɔːnt] n χλευασμός, λοιδορία, κοροϊδία ♦ vt χλευάζω, κοροϊδεύω.

taut [tɔːt] a τεντωμένος, τεταμένος.

tavern ['tævən] n ταβέρνα.

tawdry ['tɔːdrɪ] a φανταχτερός, φτηνός, τιποτένιος.

tawny ['tɔːnɪ] a φαιοκίτρινος.

tax [tæks] n φόρος ♦ vt φορολογώ || (burden) εξαντλώ, βάζω σε δοκιμασία || ~ation n φορολογία ||

~ **collector** n εισπράκτορας φόρων || ~**-free** a αφορολόγητος.

taxi ['tæksi] n ταξί ♦ vi (AVIAT) τροχοδρομώ || ~ **driver** n οδηγός ταξί, ταξιτζής || ~ **rank** n, ~ **stand** n στάση ταξί, πιάτσα.

taxpayer ['tækspeɪə*] n φορολογούμενος.

T.B. abbr of **tuberculosis**.

tea [tiː] n τέιο, τσάι || (drink) τσάι || (meal) απογευματινό τσάι, γεύμα nt με τσάι || ~ **bag** n σακκουλάκι τσαγιού || ~ **break** n διάλειμμα nt για τσάι.

teach [tiːtʃ] (irreg v) vti διδάσκω, μαθαίνω || ~ **er** n δάσκαλος/δασκάλα m/f|| ~**ing** n διδασκαλία.

tea cosy ['tiːkəʊzi] n σκέπασμα nt τσαγιέρας.

teacup ['tiːkʌp] n φλυτζάνι τσαγιού.

teak [tiːk] n τικ, τεκ ♦ a από τικ.

tea leaves ['tiːliːvz] npl φύλλα ntpl τσαγιού.

team [tiːm] n ομάδα, συνεργείο || (of animals) ζευγάρι || ~ **work** n ομαδικό παίξιμο, συνεργασία.

tea party ['tiːpɑːti] n δεξίωση με τσάι.

teapot ['tiːpɒt] n τσαγιέρα.

tear [tɛə*] n (rip) σχίσιμο, σκισμή δάκρυ nt ♦ (irreg v) vt ανοίγω τρύπα || (pull apart) σχίζω, σπαράσσω ♦ vi (become torn) σχίζομαι || (rush) τρέχω, ορμώ ♦ ['tiə*] n (cry) δάκρυ || **in** ~ **s** δακρυσμένος, βουτηγμένος στα δάκρυα || ~**ful** a δακρυσμένος, κλαμένος || ~ **gas** n δακρυγόνο αέριο.

tearoom ['tiːrum] n αίθουσα τσίου.

tease [tiːz] n πειραχτήριο, πείραγμα nt ♦ vt πειράζω, κοροϊδεύω.

tea set ['tiːset] n σερβίτσιο τσαγιού.

teaspoon ['tiːspuːn] n κουταλάκι

του τσαγιού || ~**ful** n κουταλιά του τσαγιού.

tea strainer ['tiːstreɪnə*] n σουρωτήρι του τσαγιού.

teat [tiːt] n θηλή, ρώγα.

teatime ['tiːtaɪm] n ώρα του τσαγιού.

technical ['teknɪkəl] a τεχνικός || ~**ity** n τεχνική λεπτομέρεια.

technician [tek'nɪʃən] n (craftsman) τεχνίτης, τεχνικός || (specialist) ειδικός.

technique [tek'niːk] n τεχνική, ειδική μέθοδος f.

technological [teknə'lɒdʒɪkəl] a τεχνολογικός.

technology [tek'nɒlədʒi] n τεχνολογία.

teddy (bear) ['tedɪ(bɛə*)] n αρκουδάκι (παιχνίδι).

tedious ['tiːdɪəs] a ανιαρός, βαρετός.

tedium ['tiːdɪəm] n ανιαρότητα, μονοτονία, ανία.

tee [tiː] n υψωματάκι, σωρός (άμμου).

teem [tiːm] vi βρίθω, αφθονώ || (pour) πέφτω καταρρακτωδώς.

teenage ['tiːneɪdʒ] a εφηβικός, μεταξύ 13 και 20 || ~ **r** n έφηβος.

teens [tiːnz] npl ηλικία μεταξύ 13 και 20 χρονών.

teeth [tiːθ] npl of **tooth**.

teethe [tiːð] vi βγάζω δόντια.

teething ring ['tiːðɪŋrɪŋ] n ροδέλα μωρού (στο οδοντοφυΐα).

teetotal ['tiː'təʊtl] a αντιαλκοολικός || ~**ler**, ~**er** (US) n απέχων από οινοπνευματώδη ποτά.

telecommunication ['telɪkəmjuːnɪ'keɪʃən] n τηλεπικοινωνία.

telegram ['telɪgræm] n τηλεγράφημα nt.

telegraph ['telɪgrɑːf] n τηλέγραφος || ~**ic** a (address)

τηλεγραφικός || ~ **pole** n
τηλεγραφικός στύλος.
telepathic [teli'pæθik] a
τηλεπαθητικός.
telepathy [ti'lepəθi] n τηλεπάθεια.
telephone ['telifəun] n τηλέφωνο
♦ vti τηλεφωνώ || ~ **booth**, ~ **box** n
τηλεφωνικός θάλαμος || ~ **call** n
τηλεφώνημα nt, κλήση || ~
directory n τηλεφωνικός
κατάλογος || ~ **exchange** n κέντρο
|| ~ **number** n αριθμός τηλεφώνου.
telephonist [ti'lefənist] n
τηλεφωνήτρια.
telephoto ['teli'fəutəu] a: ~ **lens**
τηλεφακός.
teleprinter ['teliprintə*] n
τηλέτυπο.
telescope ['teliskəup] n τηλεσκόπιο
♦ vti (compress) συμπτύσσω.
telescopic [telis'kɒpik] a
τηλεσκοπικός.
televise ['telivaiz] vt μεταδίδω
τηλεοπτικά.
television ['telivi3ən] n τηλεόραση
|| ~ **set** n δέκτης τηλεοράσεως.
telex ['teleks] n τέλεξ nt inv,
τηλέτυπο ♦ vti στέλλω με τον
τηλέτυπο.
tell [tel] (irreg v) vt λέγω, λέω || (make
known) αφηγούμαι, γνωστοποιώ ||
(order) διατάσσω, παραγγέλλω, λέω
σε || (person of sth) λέω κάτι,
ανακοινώνω ♦ vi (have effect)
αποφέρω, συνεπάγομαι, έχω || **to** ~
on vt (inform against) καταδίδω,
προδίδω || **to** ~ **off** vt μαλώνω,
κατσαδιάζω || ~**er** n (in bank) ταμίας
|| ~**ing** a αποτελεσματικός || ~**tale**
a μαρτυριάρης, κουτσομπόλης.
telly ['teli] n (col) abbr of
television.
temerity [ti'meriti] n θάρρος nt,
τόλμη.
temper ['tempə*] n (disposition)
διάθεση, τεμπεραμέντο || (burst of

anger) οργή, θυμός ♦ vt (moderate)
απαλύνω, μαλακώνω, συγκρατώ.
temperament ['tempramənt] n
διάθεση, ιδιοσυγκρασία,
τεμπεραμέντο || ~**al** a (moody)
ιδιότροπος || (fig) γεμάτος βίδες.
temperance ['temprəns] n (in
drinking) αποφυγή
οινοπνευματωδών ποτών ||
(moderation) εγκράτεια,
μετριοπάθεια.
temperate ['temprit] a
μετριοπαθής, εύκρατος.
temperature ['temprətʃə*] n
θερμοκρασία.
tempered ['tempəd] a (steel)
εσκληρυμένος, βαμμένος.
tempest ['tempist] n θύελλα,
τρικυμία, φουρτούνα.
temple ['templ] n (building) ναός ||
(ANAT) κρόταφος, μηλίγγι.
tempo ['tempəu] n ρυθμός, τέμπο ||
(of movement) ρυθμός, μέτρο.
temporal ['tempərəl] a (of time)
χρονικός, του χρόνου || (worldly)
εγκόσμιος, κοσμικός.
temporarily ['tempərərili] ad
προσωρινά, για λίγο.
temporary ['tempərəri] a
προσωρινός, πρόσκαιρος.
tempt [tempt] vt (persuade)
παροτρύνω, προτρέπω || (attract)
δελεάζω || ~**ation** n πειρασμός,
δελεασμός || ~**ing** a δελεαστικός.
ten [ten] num δέκα.
tenable ['tenəbl] a υπερασπίσιμος,
υποστηρίξιμος, λογικός.
tenacious [tə'neiʃəs] a εμμένων,
επίμονος.
tenacity [tə'næsiti] n εμμονή,
επιμονή.
tenancy ['tenənsi] n ενοικίαση,
μίσθωση.
tenant ['tenənt] n ενοικιαστής/
ενοικιάστρια m/f, μισθωτής/
μισθώτρια m/f.

tend [tɛnd] vt (look after) περιποιούμαι ♦ vi τείνω, ρέπω, κλίνω.

tendency ['tɛndənsɪ] n τάση, κλίση, ροπή.

tender ['tɛndə*] a τρυφερός, μαλακός || (delicate) λεπτός, ευπαθής, τρυφερός || (loving) στοργικός, ευαίσθητος, πονετικός ♦ n (COMM: offer) προσφορά || ~ness n τρυφερότητα, λεπτότητα, στοργικότητα.

tendon ['tɛndən] n τένων m.

tenement ['tɛnɪmənt] n λαϊκή πολυκατοικία.

tenet ['tɛnət] n αρχή, αξίωμα nt, δόγμα nt.

tennis ['tɛnɪs] n τένις nt inv, αντισφαίριση || ~ ball n μπάλα του τένις || ~ court n γήπεδο του τένις || ~ racket n ρακέτα του τένις.

tenor ['tɛnə*] n (male voice) οξύφωνος, τενόρος || (singer) τενόρος.

tense [tɛns] a (fig) σε υπερένταση, τεταμένος || (taut) τεντωμένος ♦ n χρόνος || ~ness n ένταση, τεταμένη κατάσταση.

tension ['tɛnʃən] n η ένταση || (stretching) τάση, τέντωμα nt.

tent [tɛnt] n σκηνή, τέντα.

tentacle ['tɛntəkl] n κεραία, πλόκαμος.

tentative ['tɛntətɪv] a δοκιμαστικός, προσωρινός.

tenterhooks ['tɛntəhʊks] npl: on ~ ανήσυχος, ανυπόμονος.

tenth [tɛnθ] a δέκατος, δέκατο.

tent peg ['tɛntpɛg] n πάσσαλος σκηνής.

tent pole ['tɛntpəʊl] n ορθοστάτης σκηνής.

tenuous ['tɛnjʊəs] a λεπτός, αραιός, ελαφρός.

tenure ['tɛnjʊə*] n κατοχή, κτήση.

tepid ['tɛpɪd] a χλιαρός.

term ['tɜːm] n όριο || (fixed time) περίοδος f, διάρκεια, χρόνος || (word) όρος, έκφραση, λέξη ♦ vt ονομάζω, καλώ || ~s npl όροι mpl, διατάξεις fpl || (relationship) σχέσεις fpl.

terminal ['tɜːmɪnl] a τελικός, άκρος ♦ n (ELEC) ακροδέκτης, πόλος || (for oil, ore etc) ακραίος σταθμός || (COMPUT) τερματικό.

terminate ['tɜːmɪneɪt] vi (+ in) τερματίζω, τελειώνω.

termination [tɜːmɪ'neɪʃən] n τερματισμός, περάτωση, κατάληξη.

terminology [tɜːmɪ'nɒlədʒɪ] n ορολογία.

terminus ['tɜːmɪnəs] n ακραίος, σταθμός, τέρμα nt.

termite ['tɜːmaɪt] n τερμίτης.

terrace ['tɛrəs] n σειρά σπιτιών || (in garden etc) επιπέδωμα nt, ταράτσα || ~d a (garden) σε βαθμίδες, κλιμακωτός || (house) ιδίου ρυθμού.

terrain [tɛ'reɪn] n έδαφος nt, πεδίο, έκταση.

terrible ['tɛrəbl] a (causing fear) τρομερός, τρομακτικός, φοβερός || (inferior) φοβερός, κατώτερος || (very great) απερίγραπτος, υπερβολικός.

terribly ['tɛrəblɪ] ad τρομερά, φρικτά, τρομακτικά.

terrier ['tɛrɪə*] n σκυλί τεριέ.

terrific [tə'rɪfɪk] a τρομερός, καταπληκτικός.

terrify ['tɛrɪfaɪ] vt τρομάζω, τρομοκρατώ.

territorial [tɛrɪ'tɔːrɪəl] a εδαφικός, τοπικός, κτηματικός.

territory ['tɛrɪtərɪ] n γη, περιοχή, έδαφος nt.

terror ['tɛrə*] n τρόμος, φρίκη, φόβος, τρομάρα || ~ism n τρομοκρατία || ~ist n τρομοκράτης || ~ize vt τρομοκρατώ.

terse [tɜːs] a σύντομος, βραχύς || (concise) περιληπτικός.

test [tɛst] n δοκιμή, δοκιμασία ||
(examination) εξέταση, ανάλυση ♦ vt
δοκιμάζω || (examine) εξετάζω.
testament ['tɛstəmənt] n διαθήκη.
testicle ['tɛstɪkl] n όρχις m, αρχίδι.
testify ['tɛstɪfaɪ] vi καταθέτω
(ενόρκως).
testimonial [tɛstɪ'məunɪəl] n
πιστοποιητικό, βεβαίωση || (gift)
δώρο ευγνωμοσύνης.
testimony ['tɛstɪmənɪ] n μαρτυρία,
κατάθεση || (proof) απόδειξη.
test match ['tɛstmætʃ] n (cricket,
rugby) μεγάλη διεθνής συνάντηση.
test pilot ['tɛstpaɪlət] n πιλότος
δοκιμών.
test tube ['tɛsttjuːb] n
δοκιμαστικός σωλήνας.
testy ['tɛstɪ] a (short-tempered)
ευέξαπτος, δύστροπος.
tetanus ['tɛtənəs] n τέτανος.
tether ['tɛðə*] vt δένω.
text [tɛkst] n κείμενο τ, θέμα ||
εγχειρίδιο, διδακτικό βιβλίο.
textiles ['tɛkstaɪlz] npl υφαντά είδη,
υφάσματα ntpl.
texture ['tɛkstʃə*] n (of surface) υφή.
than [ðæn] prep, cj ή, παρά, από.
thank [θæŋk] vt ευχαριστώ || ~ful a
ευγνώμων || ~fully ad με
ευγνωμοσύνη || ~less a αχάριστος
|| ~s excl ευχαριστώ || (gratitude)
ευγνωμοσύνη, ευχαριστίες fpl ||
T~sgiving n (US: festival) Ημέρα
των Ευχαριστιών.
that [ðæt] a αυτός, εκείνος ♦ pron
εκείνος, ο οποίος, που ♦ cj ότι,
ώστε, διότι, να ♦ ad πόσο, έτσι.
thatched [θætʃt] a (cottage)
αχυροστρωμένος.
thaw [θɔː] n τήξη, λυώσιμο ♦ vi
τήκομαι, λυώνω.
the [ðiː, ðə] definite article o, η, το ||
(pl) οι, τα.
theatre, theater (US) ['θɪətə*] n
θέατρο || (drama) θεατρική τέχνη,

δραματική τέχνη || (MED)
αμφιθέατρο || ~goer n
θεατρόφιλος.
theatrical [θɪ'ætrɪkəl] a θεατρικός,
θεαματικός || (showy) θεατρίνιστικος,
προσποιητός.
theft [θɛft] n κλοπή, κλεψιά.
their [ðɛə*] poss a δικός τους, δική
τους || ~s poss pron δικός τους,
δικοί τους.
them [ðɛm, ðəm] pron αυτούς, αυτές,
αυτά.
theme [θiːm] n θέμα nt, υπόθεση ||
(melody) θέμα, μοτίβο || ~ song n (of
film etc) κύρια μελωδία.
themselves [ðəm'sɛlvz] pl pron
τους εαυτούς τους || (they
themselves) αυτοί οι ίδιοι.
then [ðɛn] ad τότε || (next) κατόπιν,
έπειτα || cj λοιπόν, τότε, επί πλέον ♦
n τότε.
theological [θɪə'lɒdʒɪkəl] a
θεολογικός.
theology [θɪ'ɒlədʒɪ] n θεολογία.
theorem ['θɪərəm] n θεώρημα nt.
theoretical [θɪə'rɛtɪkəl] a
θεωρητικός.
theorize ['θɪəraɪz] vi κάνω θεωρίες.
theory ['θɪərɪ] n θεωρία || (idea) ιδέα.
therapeutic(al) [θɛrə'pjuːtɪk(l)] a
θεραπευτικός.
therapist ['θɛrəpɪst] n
θεραπευτής/ύτρια m/f.
therapy ['θɛrəpɪ] n θεραπεία.
there [ðɛə*] ad εκεί, να, έλα ♦ n
εκείνος εκεί || (interj) να || (never
mind) έλα, έλα || ~ is υπάρχει ||
are υπάρχουν || ~abouts ad εκεί
κοντά, περίπου || ~after ad έπειτα,
κατόπιν || ~fore ad γι'αυτό το λόγο,
επομένως || ~'s = there is, there
has.
Thermos ['θɜːməs] n (R) (flask)
θέρμο(ς).
thermostat ['θɜːməstæt] n
θερμοστάτης.

thesaurus [θɪˈsɔːrəs] n θησαυρός, συλλογή λέξεως.

these [diːz] pl pron αυτοί, αυτές, αυτά.

thesis [ˈθiːsɪs] n θέμα, θέση || (UNIV) διατριβή.

they [ðeɪ] pl pron αυτοί, αυτές, αυτά.

thick [θɪk] a χοντρός, παχύς, πυκνός, πηχτός || (person: slow, stupid) κουτός, χοντροκέφαλος ♦ n: **in the ~ of** στη φούρια, στο οξύτερο σημείο || **~ en** vi (fog) πυκνώνω, γίνομαι πυκνότερο ♦ vt (sauce etc) πήζω, πυκνώνω, δένω || **~ness** n (of object) πάχος, πυκνότητα || (of voice) βραχνάδα || **~set** a κοντόχοντρος || **~skinned** a παχύδερμος, χοντρόπετσος.

thief [θiːf] n κλέφτης, λωποδύτης.

thieves [θiːvz] npl of **thief.**

thieving [ˈθiːvɪŋ] n κλοπή, κλεψιά.

thigh [θaɪ] n μηρός, μπούτι.

thimble [ˈθɪmbl] n δακτυλήθρα.

thin [θɪn] a λεπτός, ψιλός, αδύνατος || (not abundant) αραιός, διεσπαρμένος || (person) ισχνός, λιγνός, αδύνατος || (crowd) αραιός, λιγοστός.

thing [θɪŋ] n πράγμα nt, αντικείμενο.

think [θɪŋk] (irreg v) vi σκέπτομαι || (believe) νομίζω || (have in mind) σκοπεύω || **to ~ over** vt σκέπτομαι, συλλογίζομαι || **to ~ up** vt σκέπτομαι, καταστρώνω.

thinly [ˈθɪnlɪ] ad (disguised) μόλις.

thinness [ˈθɪnɪs] n λεπτότητα, αδυναμία || (of liquids, crowds) αραιότητα.

third [θɜːd] a τρίτος ♦ n τρίτος, τρίτο || **~ly** ad κατά τρίτο λόγο, τρίτο || **~-party insurance** n ασφάλιση τρίτων || **~-rate** a τρίτης τάξεως, κακής ποιότητας.

thirst [θɜːst] n δίψα || (strong desire) δυνατή επιθυμία, πόθος || **~y** a διψασμένος.

thirteen [ˈθɜːˈtiːn] num δεκατρία.

thirty [ˈθɜːtɪ] num τριάντα.

this [ðɪs] pron, a αυτός, αυτή, αυτό || (this much) τόσος.

thistle [ˈθɪsl] n γαϊδουράγκαθο.

thorn [θɔːn] n αγκάθι || (plant) ακανθώδης θάμνος, αγκάθι || **~y** a ακανθώδης || (problem) ακανθώδης.

thorough [ˈθʌrə] a πλήρης, τέλειος || (accurate) λεπτομερής, εξονυχιστικός || **~bred** n καθαρόαιμος, από ράτσα ♦ a καθαρόαιμος || **~fare** n οδός f, διάβαση, αρτηρία || (main street) κεντρική λεωφόρος || **~ly** ad τέλεια, πλήρως, κατά βάθος.

those [ðəʊz] pl pron αυτές, αυτοί, αυτά ♦ a τούτοι, εκείνοι.

though [ðəʊ] cj άνκαι, μολονότι ♦ ad παρ' όλα αυτά, ωστόσο.

thought [θɔːt] n ιδέα, σκέψη || (thinking) σκέψη, συλλογισμός || pt, pp of **think** || **~ful** a σοβαρός, σκεπτικός || (also kind) διακριτικός, ευγενικός || **~less** a απερίσκεπτος, απρόσεκτος, αδιάκριτος.

thousand [ˈθaʊzənd] num χίλιοι, χίλιες, χίλια || **~th** a χιλιοστός.

thrash [θræʃ] vt (hit) κτυπώ, δέρνω, ξυλοφορτώνω || (fig) νικώ.

thread [θrɛd] n (of cotton, silk etc) νήμα nt, κλωστή || (of screw) σπείρωμα nt, βήμα nt || (of story) συνέχεια, ειρμός ♦ vt (needle) βάζω κλωστή σε, περνώ ♦ vi (pick one's way) περνώ με δυσκολία || **~bare** a ξεφτισμένος, παλιός.

threat [θrɛt] n το φοβέρα, φοβέρισμα nt || (sign of danger) απειλή || **~en** vti (person) απειλώ, φοβερίζω || (storm) απειλώ.

three [θriː] num τρεις, τρία || **~-dimensional** a τρισδιάστατος || **~-fold** a τριπλός, τρίδιπλος || **~-piece suit** n (clothes) τρουαπιές nt inv || **~-ply** a (wool) τρίκλωσο.

thresh [θrεʃ] *vt* αλωνίζω.

threshold ['θrεʃhəʊld] *n* (beginning) κατώφλι, αρχή || (doorway) κατώφλι.

threw [θru:] *pt of* throw.

thrift [θrɪft] *n* (economy) οικονομία, αποταμίευση || ~ **y** a οικονόμος, μετρημένος.

thrill [θrɪl] *n* ρίγος *nt*, ανατριχίλα, σύγκρυο, τρεμούλα ♦ *vt* προκαλώ ρίγος σε, συγκινώ, πλεκτρίζω ♦ *vi* φρικιώ, ριγώ, τρέμω. αγωνιώ || ~**er** *n* μυθιστόρημα *nt* αγωνίας.

thrive [θraɪv] *vi* (+ on) (plants) ευδοκιμώ || (business) ευημερώ || (children) αναπτύσσομαι.

thriving ['θraɪvɪŋ] a ακμαίος, ρωμαλέος, ακμάζων || (successful) επιτυχής.

throat [θrəʊt] *n* λαιμός || (internal passages) φάρυγγας, λάρυγγας, λαρύγγι.

throb [θrɒb] *n* κτύπημα *nt*, παλμός, δόνηση ♦ *vi* κτυπώ, πάλλομαι.

throes [θrəʊz] *npl* οδύνες *fpl*, πόνοι *ntpl* || **in the ~ of** αγωνιζόμενος με.

thrombosis [θrɒm'bəʊsɪs] *n* θρόμβωση.

throne [θrəʊn] *n* θρόνος.

throttle ['θrɒtl] *n* ρυθμιστική βαλβίδα μηχανής, δικλείδα ♦ *vt* (choke) στραγγαλίζω.

through [θru:] *prep* διαμέσου, καθ'όλη τη διάρκεια του || (because of) λόγω του, εξαιτίας του ♦ *ad* εξ ολοκλήρου, κατευθείαν, από την αρχή μέχρι το τέλος ♦ a (without a stop) κατευθείαν || (end to end) πέρα για πέρα || (ticket) ολοκλήρου διαδρομής (εισιτήριο) || (finished) τελειωμένος || ~**out** *prep* σε ολόκληρο, σ' όλο, παντού ♦ *ad* παντού, ολόκληρα.

throw [θrəʊ] (irreg *v*) *n* ρίξη, ρίξιμο, πέταγμα *nt*, βολή ♦ *vt* ρίχνω, πετώ || **to ~ out** *vt* (lit) πετώ έξω || (reject) απορρίπτω, αποκρούω || **to ~ up** *vi*

(vomit) ξερνώ, κάνω εμετό || ~**-in** *n* (SPORT) δίνω επιπλέον.

thru [θru:] (US) = **through**.

thrush [θrʌʃ] *n* κίχλη, τσίχλα.

thrust [θrʌst] (irreg *v*) *n* (TECH) ώθηση, σπρωξιά ♦ *vti* σπρώχνω, μηγνύω || (push one's way) διαπερνώ, διασχίζω, περνώ.

thud [θʌd] *n* γδούπος.

thug [θʌg] *n* γκάγκστερ *m inv*, μπράβος.

thumb [θʌm] *n* αντίχειρας ♦ *vt* (book) φυλλομετρώ || **to ~ a lift** κάνω ωτοστόπ || ~**tack** *n* (US) πινέζα.

thump [θʌmp] *n* βαρύ κτύπημα *nt*, γροθιά ♦ *vti* κτυπώ δυνατά, γρονθοκοπώ.

thunder ['θʌndə*] *n* βροντή ♦ *vi* βροντώ, βροντοφωνώ || ~**storm** *n* καταιγίδα, θύελλα || ~**struck** a εμβρόντητος, κατάπληκτος || ~**y** a (weather, sky) θυελλώδης.

Thursday ['θɜːzdɪ] *n* Πέμπτη.

thus [ðʌs] *ad* έτσι || (therefore) έτσι, λοιπόν.

thwart [θwɔːt] *vt* ματαιώνω, ανατρέπω, εμποδίζω.

thyme [taɪm] *n* θυμάρι.

thyroid ['θaɪrɔɪd] *n* θυρεοειδής (αδένας).

tiara [tɪ'ɑːrə] *n* διάδημα *nt*, τιάρα.

tic [tɪk] *n* (nervous) τικ, σπάσμα *nt*, σπασμός.

tick [tɪk] *n* τικ (ρολογιού), λεπτό || (small mark) σημείο ελέγχου, τσεκάρισμα ♦ *vi* κτυπώ, κάνω τικ ♦ *vt* σημειώνω, τσεκάρω.

ticket ['tɪkɪt] *n* (for travel etc) εισιτήριο, δελτίο || (label) σημείωση, ετικέτα || ~ **collector** *n* ελεγκτής εισιτηρίων || ~ **holder** *n* κάτοχος εισιτηρίου || ~ **office** *n* γραφείο εκδόσεως εισιτηρίων.

tickle ['tɪkl] *n* γαργάλισμα *nt* ♦ *vt*

γαργαλίζω, γαργαλώ || *(amuse)* διασκεδάζω.

ticklish ['tıklıʃ] a που γαργαλιέται εύκολα || *(difficult)* λεπτός, δύσκολος.

tidal ['taıdl] a παλιρροιακός.

tide [taıd] n παλίρροια, ρεύμα nt || *(season)* εποχή.

tidiness ['taıdınıs] n τάξη, συγύρισμα.

tidy ['taıdı] a συγυρισμένος, τακτοποιημένος, σιαγμένος ♦ vt τακτοποιώ, σιάζω, συγυρίζω.

tie [taı] n *(necktie)* γραβάτα, λαιμοδέτης || *(connection)* δεσμός || *(SPORT)* ισοπαλία ♦ vt προσδένω, δένω || *(into knot)* δένω, κάνω κόμπο ♦ vi έρχομαι ισόπαλος, ισοψηφώ || **to ~ down** vt *(lit)* στερεώνω, δένω καλά || *(fig)* δεσμεύω || **to ~ up** vt *(dog)* προσδένω, δένω || *(boat)* δένω.

tier [tıə*] n σειρά.

tiff [tıf] n μικροσακκμός, καυγαδάκι.

tiger ['taıgə*] n τίγρη.

tight [taıt] a σφιχτός, στερεός || *(stretched)* τεντωμένος || *(close)* στεγανός, ερμητικός || *(col)* πιωμένος, σκνίπα || *(miserly)* τσιγγούνης || **~s** npl καλτσόν nt inv|| **~ en** vti σφίγγω, σφίγγομαι || **~ - fisted** a σφιχτοχέρης, σπαγγοραμμένος || **~ ly** ad σφιχτοκλεισμένα, σφιχτά, γερά || **~ rope** n τεντωμένο σχοινί.

tile [taıl] n *(in roof)* κεραμίδι || *(on wall or floor)* πλακάκι || **~ d** a *(roof)* με κεραμίδια.

till [tıl] n συρτάρι ταμείου ♦ vt καλλιεργώ ♦ prep ώς, μέχρι ♦ cj έως ότου, ώς που.

tilt [tıll] vti γέρνω, κλίνω.

timber ['tımbə*] n ξυλεία || *(trees)* δάσος nt, ψηλά δέντρα npl.

time [taım] n χρόνος || *(period)* καιρός || *(hour)* ώρα || *(point in time)*

στιγμή, φορά || *(occasion)* καιρός, εποχή || *(rhythm, speed)* χρόνος, ρυθμός ♦ vt ρυθμίζω, χρονομετρώ || **in ~** έγκαιρα || *(MUS)* μέτρο, χρόνο || **on ~** στην ώρα || **five ~s** πέντε φορές || **local ~** τοπική ώρα || **what ~ is it?** τι ώρα είναι; || **~ keeper** n *(SPORT)* χρονομετρητής || **~ less** a *(beauty)* αιώνιος, άφθαρτος || **~ limit** n χρονικό όριο, προθεσμία || **~ ly** a έγκαιρος, επίκαιρος || **~ switch** n χρονοδιακόπτης || **~ table** n *(travel)* δρομολόγιο || *(schools)* ωρολόγιο πρόγραμμα nt|| **~ zone** n άτρακτος χρόνου, ωριαία ζώνη.

timid ['tımıd] a δειλός, φοβιτσιάρης.

timing ['taımıŋ] n ρύθμιση, χρονισμός, χρονομέτρηση.

timpani ['tımpənı] npl τύμπανα ntpl.

tin [tın] n κασσίτερος, καλάι || *(container)* τενεκές m, κουτί κονσέρβας || **~ foil** n ασημόχαρτο, αλουμινόχαρτο, χρυσόχαρτο.

tinge [tındʒ] n χροιά, απόχρωση, δόση ♦ vt χρωματίζω, βάφω.

tingle ['tıŋgl] n τσούξιμο, έξαψη ♦ vi τσούζω, τσιμπώ.

tinker ['tıŋkə*] n γανωματής || **to ~ with** vt σκαλίζω, φτιάχνω αδέξια.

tinkle ['tıŋkl] vi κουδουνίζω, πκω.

tinned [tınd] a *(food)* κονσέρβα, του κουτιού.

tin opener ['tınəʊpnə*] n ανοιχτήρι.

tinsel ['tınsl] n γυαλιστερές κορδέλες fpl μετάλλου, ασημένια βροχή.

tint [tınt] n χροιά, απόχρωση.

tiny ['taını] a μικροσκοπικός, μικρούτσικος.

tip [tıp] n άκρη, άκρο, μύτη || *(for protection)* σιδηρά άκρα ntpl, σίδερο, πετσάκι || *(of money)* φιλοδώρημα nt, πουρμπουάρ nt inv|| *(useful hint)* υπαινιγμός, μυστική πληροφορία ♦

vt (put end on) προσθέτω άκρη σε || *(tip over)* γέρνω αναποδογυρίζω || *(waiter)* φιλοδωρώ, δίνω πουρμπουάρ || **~-off** *n (hint)* πληροφορία, υπαινιγμός || **~ped** *a (cigarette)* με φίλτρο.

tipsy ['tipsi] *a* μεθυσμένος, πιωμένος.

tiptoe ['tiptəu] *n: on* ~ ακροποδητί, στα νύχια.

tiptop ['tip'top] *a:* **in** ~ **condition** σε καλή φόρμα, πρώτης τάξεως.

tire ['taiə*] *n (US)* = **tyre** ♦ *vti* κουράζω, εξαντλώ, κουράζομαι, βαριέμαι || **~d** *a* κουρασμένος, εξαντλημένος || **~d of** βαριέμαι || **~dness** *n* κόπωση, κούραση || **~less** *a* ακούραστος, ακαταπόνητος.

tiring ['taiəriŋ] *a* κουραστικός || *(boring)* πληκτικός, ανιαρός.

tissue ['tiʃu:] *n (BIOL)* ιστός, υφή || *(paper handkerchief)* χαρτομάντηλο || ~ **paper** *n* τσιγαρόχαρτο.

tit [tit] *n (bird)* αιγίθαλος, || *n (col: breast)* βυζί, μαστός || ~ **for tat** οφθαλμόν αντί οφθαλμού.

titbit ['titbit] *n* μεζές *m*.

title ['taitl] *n* τίτλος, επικεφαλίδα || *(rank etc)* τίτλος || *(legal)* τίτλος, δικαίωμα *nt* || *(SPORT)* (παγκόσμιος) τίτλος || ~ **deed** *n* τίτλος κυριότητας, τίτλος ιδιοκτησίας || ~ **role** *n* πρώτος ρόλος, ρόλος που δίνει το τίτλο του έργου.

titter ['titə*] *vi* γελώ ανόητα, κρυφογελώ.

titular ['titjulə*] *a* επίτιμος.

to [tu:, tə] *prep (towards)* προς, στο || *(as far as)* μέχρι || *(comparison)* προς το, έναντι || *(for infin)* για να || ~ **and fro** κάτω πάνω, πηγαινέλα, ανεβοκατέβασμα.

toad [təud] *n* φρύνος, βάτραχος || *(fig)* μπούφος || ~**stool** *n* βωλίτης *ο* δηλητηριώδης (μανιτάρι).

toast [təust] *n* φρυγανιά || *(drink)* πρόποση ♦ *vt (drink)* κάνω πρόποση || *(brown)* ψήνω, φρυγανίζω || *(warm)* ζεσταίνω || ~**er** *n* φρυγανιέρα.

tobacco [tə'bækəu] *n* καπνός || ~**nist** *n* καπνοπώλης || ~**nist's (shop)** *n* καπνοπωλείο.

toboggan [tə'bɒgən] *n* έλκηθρο, τόμπογκαν *nt inv.*

today [tə'dei] *n* το σήμερα ♦ *ad* σήμερα || *(present time)* σήμερα, τώρα.

toddy ['tɒdi] *n (warm, alcoholic drink)* ζεστό γκρόγκ *nt inv.*

toe [təu] *n* δάκτυλο του ποδιού ♦ *vt:* **to** ~ **the line** *(fig)* υπακούω, υποτάσσομαι || ~**nail** *n* νύχι του ποδιού.

toffee ['tɒfi] *n* καραμέλα με βούτυρο || ~ **apple** *n* ζαχαρωμένο μήλο.

together [tə'gɛðə*] *ad* μαζί, μόνοι, ο ένας με τον άλλο || *(at the same time)* μαζί, συγχρόνως || ~**ness** *n* πνεύμα συνεργασίας.

toggle switch ['tɒglswitʃ] *n (COMPUT)* διακόπτης με σκαλάκιος.

toil [tɔil] *n* μόχθος, κόπος, σκληρή δουλειά ♦ *vi* μοχθώ, εργάζομαι σκληρά.

toilet ['tɔilit] *n (lavatory)* αποχωρητήριο, μέρος *nt* ♦ *a* τουαλέτα || ~ **paper** *n* χαρτί τουαλέτας, χάρτης υγείας || ~**ries** *npl* είδη *npl* τουαλέτας || ~ **roll** *n* ρολό χαρτιού τουαλέτας || ~ **water** *n* κολώνια.

token ['təukən] *n* ένδειξη, τεκμήριο, σημείο.

told [təuld] *pt, pp of* **tell.**

tolerable ['tɒlərəbl] *a* ανεκτός, υποφερτός || *(moderate)* καλούτσικος.

tolerance ['tɒlərəns] *n* ανοχή, ανεκτικότητα || *(engineering)* ανοχή.

tolerant ['tɒlərənt] *a* ανεκτικός.

tolerate ['tɔləreɪt] vt ανέχομαι, υποφέρω.

toleration [tɔlə'reɪʃən] n ανοχή, ανεκτικότητα.

toll [təʊl] n (tax, charge) διόδια, φόρος ♦ vi (bell) κτυπώ (καμπάνα), καμπανίζω || ~ **bridge** n γέφυρα με διόδια ntpl.

tomato [tə'mɑːtəʊ] n ντομάτα.

tomb [tuːm] n τύμβος, τάφος.

tomboy ['tɔmbɔɪ] n αγοροκόριτσο.

tombstone ['tuːmstəʊn] n επιτύμβιος λίθος.

tomcat ['tɔmkæt] n γάτος.

tomorrow [tə'mɔrəʊ] n αύριο, αυριανή μέρα ♦ ad αύριο.

ton [tʌn] n τόνος (2240 λίμπρες) || (US) τόνος (2000 λίμπρες) || ~**s of** (col) μεγάλη ποσότητα, πολλές φορές.

tone [təʊn] n τόνος, ήχος || (character) τόνος, πνεύμα nt, τάση || (colour) τόνος, απόχρωση ♦ vi συντονίζομαι, ταιριάζω ♦ vt τονίζω, τονώνω, ρυθμίζω || **to ~ down** vt απαλύνω, μαλακώνω, μετριάζω.

tongs [tɔŋz] npl λαβίδα, τσιμπίδα, μασιά.

tongue [tʌŋ] n γλώσσα || (ox tongue: food) βοδινή γλώσσα || **with ~ in cheek** ειρωνικά || ~**-tied** a άφωνος, βουβός (από κατάπληξη) || ~**-twister** n γλωσσοδέτης.

tonic ['tɔnɪk] n τονωτικό, δυναμωτικό || (MUS) τονική, βασική νότα || ~ **water** n τόνικ.

tonight [tə'naɪt] n σήμερα το βράδυ ♦ ad απόψε.

tonnage ['tʌnɪdʒ] n χωρητικότητα, τοννάζ nt inv.

tonsil ['tɔnsl] n αμυγδαλή || ~**litis** n αμυγδαλίτιδα.

too [tuː] ad πολύ, πάρα πολύ, υπερβολικά || (also) επίσης.

took [tʊk] pt of take.

tool [tuːl] n εργαλείο || ~**-box** n κιβώτιο εργαλείων.

toot [tuːt] n κορνάρισμα nt ♦ vi κορνάρω.

tooth [tuːθ] n δόντι || (on gearwheel) δόντι || ~**-ache** n πονόδοντος, οδοντόπονος || ~**-brush** n οδοντόβουρτσα || ~**-paste** n οδοντόπαστα || ~**-pick** n οδοντογλυφίδα.

top [tɔp] n κορυφή, κορφή, απάνω (μέρος) || (at school) πρώτος, καλύτερος || (spinning toy) σβούρα ♦ a ανώτερος, ψηλότερος || (list) είμαι επικεφαλής, είμαι πρώτος || **from ~ to toe** από την κορυφή ως τα νύχια || ~ **coat** n παλτό || ~ **hat** n ψηλό καπέλο || ~**-heavy** a ασταθής, βαρύς στην κορυφή.

topic ['tɔpɪk] n θέμα nt, ζήτημα nt || ~**al** a επίκαιρος.

top-level ['tɔp'levl] a υψηλού επιπέδου.

topmost ['tɔpməʊst] a υψηλότερος, κορυφαίος, ύψιστος.

topple ['tɔpl] vti κλονίζομαι, πέφτω || (overturn) ανατρέπω.

topsy-turvy ['tɔpsɪ'tɜːvɪ] a, ad άνω κάτω.

torch [tɔːtʃ] n (electric) φακός, φανάρι || (Olympic) πυρσός, λαμπάδα, δαυλί.

tore [tɔː] pt of tear.

torment ['tɔːment] n βασανιστήριο, μαρτύριο || ['tɔːment] vt ενοχλώ, πειράζω || (distress) βασανίζω, τυραννώ.

torn [tɔːn] pp of tear || a (undecided: between) ταλαντευόμενος, αναποφάσιστος.

tornado [tɔː'neɪdəʊ] n ανεμοστρόβιλος, λαίλαπα.

torpedo [tɔː'piːdəʊ] n τορπίλη.

torrent ['tɔrənt] n χείμαρρος || ~**ial** a χειμαρρώδης.

torso ['tɔːsəʊ] n κορμός, τόρσο.

tortoise ['tɔ:təs] *n* χελώνα.

tortuous ['tɔ:tjuəs] *a* ελικοειδής, στρεβλός || *(deceitful)* ανέντιμος, δόλιος.

torture ['tɔ:tʃə*] *n* βασανιστήριο, βασανισμός, μαρτύριο ♦ *vt* βασανίζω.

Tory ['tɔ:rɪ] *n* συντηρητικός ♦ *a* συντηρητικός.

toss [tɒs] *vt* πετώ, τραντάζω || *(in the air)* ρίχνω, πετώ ♦ *n (of coin to decide)* στρίψιμο || **to ~ a coin,** *to* **~ up for** ρίχνω κορώνα-γράμματα.

tot [tɒt] *n* ποτηράκι, γουλιά || *(child)* παιδάκι, μωρό, μπέμπης.

total ['təʊtl] *n* σύνολο, όλα, άθροισμα *nt*, σούμα ♦ *a* (συν)ολικός, ολόκληρος, πλήρης ♦ *vt* προσθέτω, αθροίζω || *(amount to)* ανέρχομαι σε, φθάνω.

totem pole ['təʊtəmpəʊl] *n* στήλη του τότεμ.

totter ['tɒtə*] *vi* παραπατώ, τρικλίζω.

touch [tʌtʃ] *n* αφή, επαφή, άγγιγμα *nt* || *(sense)* επαφή, αφή || *(small amount)* μικρή δόση, ίχνος *nt*, υποψία || *(style)* νιελιά, μολυβιά, ύφος *nt* ♦ *vt* αγγίζω || *(come against)* εφάπτομαι, ακουμπώ || *(move)* θίγω, συγκινώ || **in ~ with** σ' επαφή με, διατηρώ επαφή || **to ~ on** *vt (topic)* θίγω (θέμα) || **to ~ up** *vt (paint)* ρετουσάρω, επισκευάζω || **~ -and-go** *a* επικίνδυνος, αβέβαιος, επισφαλής || **~ -down** *n* προσγείωση || **~ -ing** *a* συγκινητικός || **~ -line** *n* γραμμή του τέρματος || **~ -y** *a* ευαίσθητος, εύθικτος.

tough [tʌf] *a* σκληρός, στερεός || *(difficult)* δυσχερής, σκληρός, δύσκολος || *(meat)* σκληρός ♦ *n (gangster etc)* κακοποιός, μπράβος || **~ en** *vti* σκληραίνω, σκληρύνομαι || **~ ness** *n* σκληρότητα || *(resilience)* αντοχή.

toupee ['tu:peɪ] *n (wig)* περούκα.

tour ['tʊə*] *n* περιοδεία, περιήγηση ♦ *vi* περιηγούμαι, περιοδεύω || **~ ing** *n* περιοδεία.

tourism ['tʊərɪzəm] *n* τουρισμός.

tourist ['tʊərɪst] *n* τουρίστας/τουρίστρια *m/f*, περιηγητής/περιηγήτρια *m/f* || **~ office** *n* τουριστικό γραφείο.

tournament ['tʊənəmənt] *n* πρωτάθλημα *nt*, τουρνουά *nt inv*.

tousled ['tauzld] *a (hair)* αναστατωμένος, ξεντένιστος.

tow [təʊ] *n (pull)* ρυμούλκηση ♦ *vt (pull)* ρυμουλκώ.

toward(s) [tə'wɔ:d(z)] *prep* προς, κατά, για.

towel ['tauəl] *n* πετσέτα.

tower ['tauə*] *n* πύργος || **~ ing** *a* πανύψηλος || *(rage)* βίαιος, άγριος.

town [taun] *n* πόλη, πολιτεία, χώρα || **~ clerk** *n* γραμματέας δημαρχίας || **~ hall** *n* δημαρχείο || **~ planning** *n* πολεοδομία.

towrope ['təʊrəʊp] *n* σχοινί ρυμούλκησης.

toxic ['tɒksɪk] *a* τοξικός.

toy [tɔɪ] *n* παιχνίδι, παιχνιδάκι || **to ~ with** *vt* παίζω με, σκέπτομαι *n*.

trace [treɪs] *n* ίχνος *nt* || *(small amount)* ίχνος *nt*, υπόλειμμα *nt*, τεκμήριο ♦ *vt* παρακολουθώ || *(find out)* ανιχνεύω, διακρίνω || *(copy)* χαράσσω, αντιγράφω, ξεσηκώνω.

track [træk] *n* ίχνη *ntpl*, πέρασμα *nt*, πατημασιές *fpl* || *(path)* μονοπάτι || *(road)* δρομάκος || *(racing)* διάδρομος αγώνων, στίβος, πίστα || *(RAIL)* (σιδηροδρομική) γραμμή ♦ *vt* παρακολουθώ || *(persecute)* καταδιώκω || **to keep ~ of** παρακολουθώ, βρίσκομαι σε επαφή με || **to ~ down** *vt* ανακαλύπτω, βρίσκω || **~ er dog** *n* κυνηγόσκυλο.

tract [trækt] *n* περιοχή, έκταση || *(book)* φυλλάδιο.

tractor ['træktə*] n ελκυστήρας, τρακτέρ nt inv.

trade [treid] n εμπόριο || (business) επάγγελμα nt, δουλειά || (people) συντεχνία, κλάδος ♦ vi (+ in) εμπορεύομαι, συναλλάσσομαι, κάνω δουλειές || ~**mark** n σήμα nt (κατατεθέν) || ~ **name** n εμπορική επωνυμία, φίρμα || ~ **in** εμπορεύομαι || ~**sman** n καταστηματάρχης, λιανέμπορος || (skilled workman) τεχνίτης || ~ **union** n εργατική ένωση, συνδικάτο.

trading ['treidiŋ] n εμπόριο.

tradition [trə'diʃən] n παράδοση || ~**al** a παραδοσιακός, πατροπαράδοτος.

traffic ['træfik] n κίνηση, κυκλοφορία || (esp in drugs) εμπόριο, συναλλαγή ♦ vt (esp drugs) εμπορεύομαι (κάτι) || ~ **circle** n (US: roundabout) κυκλοφοριακός δρόμος || ~ **jam** n μποτιλιάρισμα || ~ **lights** npl φανάρια ntpl, φώτα ntpl κυκλοφορίας.

tragedy ['trædʒidi] n τραγωδία, δράμα nt.

tragic ['trædʒik] a τραγικός.

trail [treil] n ίχνος nt || (footsteps) πατήματα ntpl || (something trailing) γραμμή (καπνού), ουρά || (rough road) μονοπάτι ♦ vi (follow) σέρνομαι πίσω || (hang loosely) σέρνομαι, σέρνω || **to ~ behind** vi σέρνομαι πίσω || ~**er** n (truck) ρυμουλκούμενο όχημα nt || (film) απόσπασμα nt ταινίας || (US: caravan) τροχόσπιτο.

train [trein] n συρμός αμαξοστοιχίας, τραίνο || (of gown) ουρά || (series) σειρά, αλληλουχία, ειρμός ♦ vt εκπαιδεύω, διδάσκω, μαθαίνω || (plant) κατευθύνω, οδηγώ || (point gun) σκοπεύω ♦ vi (exercise) προπονώ, προγυμνάζω || ~**ed** a εκγυμνασμένος, εξασκημένος ||

~**ee** n ασκούμενος μαθητής || ~**er** n εκπαιδευτής || (sport) προπονητής, γυμναστής/ γυμνάστρια m/f|| ~**ing** n εκπαίδευση, εξάσκηση || (sport) προπόνηση || **in** ~ **ing** σε φόρμα || ~**ing college** n παιδαγωγική ακαδημία.

traipse [treips] vi (wander) σέρνομαι εδώ και κει, τριγυρίζω κουρασμένα.

trait [treit] n χαρακτηριστικό.

traitor ['treitə*] n προδότης/τρια m/f.

tram(car) ['træm(ka:*)] n τράμ nt inv.

tramp [træmp] n (vagabond) αλήτης/αλήτισσα m/f ♦ vi περπατώ βαρειά, βηματίζω βαρειά || (by foot) πεζοπορώ, πηγαίνω πεζή.

trample ['træmpl] vt ποδοπατώ, καταπατώ.

trampoline ['træmpəliːn] n τραμπολίνο.

trance [trɑːns] n έκσταση, ύπνωση, όραμα nt.

tranquil ['træŋkwil] a ήρεμος, ήσυχος || ~**lity** n πρεμία || ~**lizer** n (drug) καταπραϋντικό.

transact [træn'zækt] vt εκτελώ, διεξάγω, διεκπεραιώνω || ~**ion** n διεκπεραίωση, διεξαγωγή, συναλλαγή.

transatlantic ['trænzət'læntik] a υπερατλαντικός.

transcend [træn'send] vt υπερέχω, υπερβαίνω.

transcript ['trænskript] n αντίγραφο, αντιγραφή || ~**ion** n αντιγραφή, αντίγραφο.

transept ['trænsept] n πτέρυγα ναού, εγκάρσιο κλίτος nt.

transfer ['trænsfə*] n μεταφορά, (job) μετάθεση || (legal) μεταβίβαση, εκχώρηση, μεταγραφή || (design) χαλκομανία, στάμπα, αντιγραφή || (sport) μετάθεση, μεταφορά ♦ [træns'fɜː*] vt μεταφέρω, μεταθέτω,

transform 310 treachery

αλλάζω || ~able a μεταβιβάσιμος, μεταφερτός || 'not ~able' (on ticket) 'προσωπικό'.

transform [træns'fɔːm] vt μετασχηματίζω, μεταβάλλω, μεταμορφώνω || ~ation n μετασχηματισμός, μεταβολή, μεταμόρφωση || ~er n (ELEC) μετασχηματιστής.

transfusion [træns'fjuːʒən] n μετάγγιση.

transient ['trænziənt] a παροδικός.

transistor [træn'zistə*] n κρυσταλλικός πολλαπλασιαστής || (radio) τρανσίστορ nt inv, φορητό ραδιόφωνο.

transit ['trænzit] n: in ~ κατά την μεταφορά, υπό μεταφορά.

transition [træn'ziʃən] n μετάβαση, μεταβολή, αλλαγή || ~al a μεταβατικός.

transitive ['trænzitiv] a μεταβατικό (ρήμα).

transitory ['trænzitəri] a παροδικός, βραχύς, εφήμερος.

translate [trænz'leit] vt μεταφράζω.

translation [trænz'leiʃən] n μετάφραση.

translator [trænz'leitə*] n μεταφραστής/άστρια m/f.

transmission [trænz'miʃən] n (of information) μετάβδαση, διάδοση || (AUT) μετάδοση || (RAD) εκπομπή, μετάδοση.

transmit [trænz'mit] vt μεταδίδω, μεταβιβάζω, διαβιβάζω || ~ter n πομπός.

transparency [træns'peərənsi] n (PHOT: slide) διαφάνεια, ολάιντ nt inv.

transparent [træns'peərənt] a διαφανής, διουγής || (clear) καθαρός.

transplant [træns'plɑːnt] vt μεταφυτεύω, μεταφέρω ♦

[ˈtrænsplɑːnt] n (also MED) μεταφύτευση, μεταμόσχευση.

transport ['trænspɔːt] n μεταφορά ♦ [træns'pɔːt] vt μεταφέρω || ~able a μετακομιστός, φορητός || ~ation n μεταφορά.

transverse ['trænzvɜːs] a εγκάρσιος.

trap [træp] n (trick) παγίδα, απάτη || (snare) παγίδα, φάκα || (carriage) δίτροχη άμαξα || (col: mouth) στόμα nt ♦ vt παγιδεύω, πιάνω στην παγίδα || ~door n καταπακτή.

trapeze [trə'piːz] n τραπέζιο.

trappings ['træpiŋz] npl διακόσμηση, στολίδια ntpl.

trash [træʃ] n η σκουπίδια ntpl, χωρίς αξία || (nonsense) μπούρδες fpl, τρίχες fpl || ~ can n (US) σκουπιδοτενεκές m.

trauma ['trɔːmə] n τραύμα nt || ~tic a τραυματικός.

travel ['trævl] n ταξίδι, περίηγηση vi ταξιδεύω, κάνω ταξίδια ♦ vt (distance) πηγαίνω, βαδίζω, προχωρώ, μετακινούμαι || ~ler, ~er (US) n ταξιδιώτης/τισσα m/f || (salesman) πλασιέ m inv, αντιπρόσωπος || ~ler's cheque, ~er's check (US) n ταξιδιωτική επιταγή, τράβελερς τσεκ nt inv || ~ling, ~ing (US) n το ταξίδι ♦ attr a ταξιδιωτικός, του ταξιδιού || ~sickness n ναυτία.

traverse ['trævəs] vt διασχίζω, διαβαίνω, περνώ.

travesty ['trævisti] n διακωμώδηση, παρωδία.

trawler ['trɔːlə*] n αλιευτικό, τράτα.

tray [trei] n δίσκος.

treacherous ['tretʃərəs] a (person) δόλιος, ύπουλος || (road: dangerous, icy etc) επικίνδυνος, άστατος.

treachery ['tretʃəri] n δολιότητα, προδοσία, απιστία.

treacle ['triːkl] n μελάσσα, πετιμέζι.
tread [trɛd] *(irreg v)* n περπάτημα nt || *(way of walking)* βήμα nt, βηματισμός || *(stair, tyre)* βαθμίδα, πάτημα nt, πέλμα nt ελαστικού ♦ vi βαδίζω, περπατώ || **to ~ on** vt (ποδο)πατώ.
treason ['triːzn] n προδοσία.
treasure ['trɛʒə*] n θησαυρός ♦ vt αποθησαυρίζω || *(value highly)* εκτιμώ, θεωρώ πολύτιμο || **~ hunt** n θησαυροθηρία || **~r** n ταμίας.
treasury ['trɛʒərɪ] n θησαυροφυλάκειο, ταμείο.
treat [triːt] n ευχαρίστηση, απόλαυση ♦ vt μεταχειρίζομαι, φέρομαι || *(entertain)* κερνώ, προσφέρω.
treatise ['triːtɪz] n πραγματεία, διατριβή.
treatment ['triːtmənt] n μεταχείρηση, περιποίηση || *(MED)* κούρα, θεραπεία.
treaty ['triːtɪ] n συνθήκη.
treble ['trɛbl] a τριπλός, τριπλάσιος ♦ vt τριπλασιάζω ♦ n πρίμο || *(voice)* υψίφωνος, σοπράνο f inv.
tree [triː] n δέντρο || **~ trunk** n κορμός δέντρου.
trek [trɛk] n ταξίδι, μετανάστευση ♦ vi *(migrate)* μετοικώ, μεταναστεύω.
trellis ['trɛlɪs] n δικτυωτό πλέγμα nt, καφασωτό πλαίσιο.
tremble ['trɛmbl] vi τρέμω, δονούμαι.
trembling ['trɛmblɪŋ] n τρόμος, τρεμούλα ♦ a τρεμάμενος, τρεμουλιάρης.
tremendous [trə'mɛndəs] a *(vast)* πελώριος, τρομερός.
tremor ['trɛmə*] n τρεμούλιασμα nt.
trench [trɛntʃ] n τάφρος f, αυλάκι, χαντάκι || *(of war)* χαράκωμα nt.
trend [trɛnd] n τάση, πορεία ♦ vi τείνω.

trepidation [trɛpɪ'deɪʃən] n φόβος, ανυσυχία, τρεμούλα.
trespass ['trɛspəs] vi καταπατώ.
tress [trɛs] n βόστρυχος, πλεξούδα, κοτσίδα, μπούκλα.
trestle ['trɛsl] n υπόβαθρο, υποστήριγμα nt, καβαλέτο || **~ table** n τραπέζι σε καβαλέτο.
trial ['traɪəl] n *(in court)* δίκη, κρίση || *(test)* δοκιμή || *(hardship)* δοκιμασία, βάσανο || **by ~ and error** με τη μέθοδο της δοκιμής και πλάνης, εμπειρικά.
triangle ['traɪæŋgl] n τρίγωνο.
triangular [traɪ'æŋgjulə*] a τριγωνικός.
tribal ['traɪbl] a φυλετικός.
tribe [traɪb] n φυλή || **~sman** n μέλος m φυλής.
tribulation [trɪbju'leɪʃən] n δοκιμασία, συμφορά, πάθημα nt.
tribunal [traɪ'bjuːnl] n δικαστήριο.
tributary ['trɪbjutərɪ] n παραπόταμος.
tribute ['trɪbjuːt] n *(respect)* φόρος τιμής.
trice [traɪs] n: **in a ~** στη στιγμή.
trick [trɪk] n τέχνασμα nt, κόλπο, κατεργαριά || *(clever act)* δεξιοτεχνία, ταχυδακτυλουργία || *(habit)* συνήθεια || *(CARDS)* κόλπο, πιάσιμο, λεβέ nt inv ♦ vt εξαπατώ || **~ery** n απάτη, κοροϊδία.
trickle ['trɪkl] n λεπτή ροή, στάξιμο, στάλα (νερού) ♦ vi σταλάζω, στάζω.
tricky ['trɪkɪ] a *(problem, situation)* περίπλοκος, δύσκολος.
tricycle ['traɪsɪkl] n τρίκυκλο.
trifle ['traɪfl] n είδος nt τούρτας || *(of little importance)* μικροπράγματα ntpl, ασήμαντο γεγονός, μηδαμινό ποσό.
trifling ['traɪflɪŋ] a ασήμαντος, τιποτένιος.
trigger ['trɪgə*] n σκανδάλη.

trigonometry [trigə'nɒmitri] *n* τριγωνομετρία.

trim [trim] *a* κομψός, ευπρεπής ♦ *n* τάξη, φόρμα, ευπρεπής κατάσταση || *(haircut etc)* κόψιμο, φρεσκάρισμα *nt* (μαλλιών) ♦ *vt* κόβω, κουρεύω, κλαδεύω || *(decorate)* ευπρεπίζω || ~**mings** *npl* γαρνιτούρες *fpl*.

Trinity ['triniti] *n*: **the** ~ *(REL)* Αγία Τριάδα.

trinket ['trinkit] *n* μικρό κόσμημα *nt*, μπιμπελό *nt inv*.

trio ['tri:ǝʊ] *n* τριάδα || *(MUS)* τρίο.

trip [trip] *n* εκδρομή, ταξίδι || *(stumble)* παραπάτημα *nt*, τρικλοποδιά ♦ *vi* περπατώ ελαφρά, αλαφροπατώ || *(stumble)* σκοντάφτω, παραπατώ || **to** ~ **up** *vi* ανεβαίνω ελαφροπατώντας ♦ *vt* βάζω τρικλοποδιά *σε*.

tripe [traip] *n (food)* πατσάς || *(rubbish)* ανοησίες *fpl*, μπούρδες *fpl*.

triple ['tripl] *a* τριπλός, τρίδιπλος.

triplets ['triplits] *npl* τρίδυμα *ntpl*.

triplicate ['triplikit] *n*: **in** ~ *σε* τριπλούν.

tripod ['traipɒd] *n* τρίποδο.

trite [trait] *a* τριμμένος, κοινός, συνηθισμένος.

triumph ['traiʌmf] *n* θρίαμβος ♦ *vi* θριαμβεύω || ~**ant** *a* θριαμβευτικός.

trivial ['triviəl] *a* ασήμαντος, τιποτένιος || ~**ity** *n* ασημαντότητα, κοινοτοπία.

trod [trɒd] *pt of* **tread** || ~**den** *pp of* **tread**.

trolley ['trɒli] *n (small truck)* καροτσάκι || ~ **bus** *n* τρόλλεϊ *nt inv*.

trombone [trɒm'bəʊn] *n* τρομπόνι.

troop [tru:p] *n* ομάδα, όμιλος || ~**s** *npl* στρατεύματα *ntpl* || **to** ~ **in/out** *vi* μπαίνω/βγαίνω ομαδικά || ~**er** *n* ιππέας, έφιππος αστυνομικός.

trophy ['trǝʊfi] *n* τρόπαιο, έπαθλο.

tropic ['trɒpik] *n* τροπικός || ~**al** *a* τροπικός.

trot [trɒt] *n* τριποδισμός, ελαφρό τρέξιμο ♦ *vi* τρέχω σιγά.

trouble ['trʌbl] *n* στενοχώρια, ανησυχία, σκοτούρα || *(effort, care)* κόπος ♦ *vt* ενοχλώ, ανησυχώ || ~**d** *a* ανήσυχος, ταραγμένος || ~**-free** *a* χωρίς σκοτούρες || ~**maker** *n* ταραχοποιός, ταραξίας || ~**some** *a* ενοχλητικός, δύσκολος.

trough [trɒf] *n* σκάφη, ποτίστρα || *(channel)* τάφρος *f* || *(meteorology)* σφαίνα υφέσεως.

troupe [tru:p] *n* θίασος.

trousers ['traʊzǝz] *npl* πανταλόνι.

trousseau ['tru:sǝʊ] *n* προίκα (ασπρόρουχα και φορέματα).

trout [traʊt] *n* πέστροφα.

trowel ['traʊǝl] *n* μυστρί.

truant ['truǝnt] *n*: **to play** ~ *vi* το σκάω, απουσιάζω αδικαιολόγητα.

truce [tru:s] *n* ανακωχή.

truck [trʌk] *n* φορτηγό αμάξι, καμιόνι || *(RAIL)* φορείο || *(barrow)* χειράμαξα αχθοφόρου || ~ **driver** *n* οδηγός φορτηγού || ~ **farm** *n (US)* αγρόκτημα *nt* λαχανικών, περιβόλι.

truculent ['trʌkjʊlǝnt] *a* βίαιος, άγριος, επιθετικός.

trudge [trʌdʒ] *vi* βαδίζω με δυσκολία, σέρνομαι.

true [tru:] *a* αληθινός || *(precise)* ακριβής || *(genuine)* πραγματικός, αυθεντικός, γνήσιος || *(friend)* πιστός, τίμιος, αληθής.

truffle ['trʌfl] *n* τρούφα.

truly ['tru:li] *ad* ειλικρινά, πιστά, αληθινά || *(exactly)* με ακρίβεια, ακριβώς, ορθά || ~**s yours** ~ όλως υμέτερος.

trump [trʌmp] *n (CARDS)* ατού *nt inv* || ~**ed-up** *a* ψεύτικος, σκαρωμένος.

trumpet ['trʌmpit] *n* σάλπιγγα, τρουμπέτα.

truncheon ['trʌntʃǝn] *n* ρόπαλο, αστυνομικό γκλόμπ *nt inv*.

trundle ['trʌndl] vti: **to ~ along** κυλώ, τρέχω, τσουλώ.

trunk [trʌŋk] n κορμός, κούτσουρο || (body) κορμός, τόρσο nt inv|| (box) κιβώτιο, μπαούλο || (of elephant) προβοσκίδα || **~s** npl μαγιό || **call** n υπεραστική κλήση.

truss [trʌs] n (MED) κοιλεπίδεσμος, ζώνη.

trust [trʌst] n πίστη, εμπιστοσύνη || (property) καταπίστευμα nt ♦ vt εμπιστεύομαι σε || **~ed** a έμπιστος, της εμπιστοσύνης || **~ee** n επίτροπος, κηδεμόνας, έφορος || **~ful** a γεμάτος εμπιστοσύνη, ευκολόπιστος || **~ing** a πλήρης εμπιστοσύνης || **~worthy** a αξιόπιστος || **~y** a πιστός, αξιόπιστος.

truth [truːθ] n αλήθεια || **~ful** a φιλαλήθης, αληθινός || **~fully** ad αληθινά, ειλικρινά, πιστά || **~fulness** n φιλαλήθεια, ειλικρίνεια.

try [traɪ] (irreg v) n προσπάθεια || (test) δοκιμή, απόπειρα ♦ vt δοκιμάζω, κάνω δοκιμή || (in court) δικάζω || (strain) κουράζω ♦ vi (attempt) προσπαθώ, ζητώ να || **to ~ on** vt δοκιμάζω, προβάρω || **to ~ out** vt δοκιμάζω || **~ing** a δύσκολος, κουραστικός, σκληρός.

tsar [zɑː*] n τσάρος.

T-shirt ['tiː∫əːt] n φανέλα (αθλητική).

tub [tʌb] n μεγάλη λεκάνη, σκάφη, κάδος.

tuba ['tjuːbə] n μεγάλη κορνέτα, κοντραμπάσσο.

tubby ['tʌbɪ] a (fat) στρογγυλός σαν βαρέλι, κοντοπίθαρος.

tube [tjuːb] n σωλήνας, αγωγός, αυλός || (also for toothpaste etc) σωληνάριο || (in London) υπόγειος σιδηρόδρομος || (AUT: for tyre) σαμπρέλα || **~less** a (AUT) χωρίς σαμπρέλα.

tuber ['tjuːbə*] n βολβός, γογγύλι.

tuberculosis [tjubɜːkjuˈləʊsɪs] n φυματίωση.

tube station ['tjuːbsteɪ∫ən] n σταθμός του υπόγειου τραίνου.

tubing ['tjuːbɪŋ] n σωλήν(ωση).

tubular ['tjuːbjuːə*] a (steel, furniture) σωληνοειδής, σωληνωτός.

TUC n (abbr of Trades Union Congress) Συμβούλιο Αγγλικών Εργατικών Συνδικάτων.

tuck [tʌk] n (pleat) πιέτα, πτυχή ♦ vt (gather) διπλώνω, μαζεύω || **to ~ away** vt κώνω || **to ~ in** vt μαζεύω, κώνω ♦ vi (food) πέφτω με τα μούτρα στο φαΐ || **to ~ up** vt (child) σκεπάζω, τακτοποιώ.

Tuesday ['tjuːzdɪ] n Τρίτη.

tuft [tʌft] n θύσανος, φούντα.

tug [tʌg] n απότομο τράβηγμα nt|| (steamship) ρυμουλκό (πλοίο) ♦ vti σύρω, τραβώ δυνατά || **~-of-war** n διελκυστίνδα.

tuition [tjuːˈɪ∫ən] n διδασκαλία || (fees) δίδακτρα ntpl.

tulip ['tjuːlɪp] n τουλίπα.

tumble ['tʌmbl] n πέσιμο, τούμπα, κουτρουβάλα ♦ vi πέφτω, τουμπάρω || (somersault) κάνω τούμπες, αναποδογυρίζω ♦ vt (toss about) κατρακυλώ, σωριάζομαι || **to ~ to** vt συλλαμβάνω, αντιλαμβάνομαι || **~down** a ετοιμόρροπος, σαραβαλιασμένος || **~r** n (acrobat) ακροβάτης/τρια m/f|| (glass) ποτήρι.

tummy ['tʌmɪ] n (col: stomach, belly) στομάκι, κοιλιά.

tumour ['tjuːmə*] n όγκος.

tumult ['tjuːmʌlt] n θόρυβος, σαματάς, φασαρία || **~uous** a θορυβώδης, ταραχώδης, θυελλώδης.

tuna ['tjuːnə] n τόνος.

tune [tjuːn] n μελωδία, σκοπός || (pitch) τόνος, συντονισμός ♦ vti

κουρδίζω, συντονίζω || *(motorcar)* ρυθμίζω, εναρμονίζω, || in ~ μελωδικός, συντονισμένος || ~ out of ~ παραφωνία, έξω από το τόνο || to ~ up *vi (MUS)* συντονίζομαι, βρίσκω τον τόνο || ~ful a μελωδικός, αρμονικός.

tunic ['tjuːnɪk] n χιτώνιο, αμπέχονο.

tuning ['tjuːnɪŋ] n *(RAD)* συντονισμός || *(AUT)* ρύθμιση.

Tunisia [tjuːˈnɪzɪə] Τυνησία || ~n a τυπησιακός ♦ n Τυνήσιος.

tunnel ['tʌnl] n σήραγγα, τούνέλι ♦ vi ανοίγω σήραγγα.

tunny ['tʌnɪ] n τόνος.

turban ['tɜːbən] n σαρίκι, τουρμάνι.

turbine ['tɜːbaɪn] n στρόβιλος, τουρμπίνα.

turbulence ['tɜːbjʊləns] n *(AVIAT)* στροβιλισμός, αναταραχή.

turbulent ['tɜːbjʊlənt] a ταραγμένος, βίαιος, άτακτος.

turf [tɜːf] n χλόη, γρασίδι || *(sod)* χορταρισαμένος βώλος.

turgid ['tɜːdʒɪd] a *(pompous)* στομφώδης, πομπώδης.

Turk [tɜːk] n Τούρκος.

turkey ['tɜːkɪ] n γαλοπούλα, ινδιάνος || T~ n Τουρκία.

Turkish ['tɜːkɪʃ] a τουρκικός || *(LING)* Τουρκική || ~ bath n χαμάμ nt inv.

turmoil ['tɜːmɔɪl] n αναταραχή, αναστάτωση, πατιρντί.

turn [tɜːn] n περιστροφή, γύρισμα nt || *(turning)* στροφή || *(performance)* σειρά || *(shape, manner)* νοοτροπία, διάθεση || *(chance)* σειρά || *(MED)* κρίση ♦ vt περιστρέφω, γυρίζω, στρίβω || *(change position)* αλλάζω, γυρίζω || *(of colour)* αλλάζω χρώμα nt ♦ vi περιστρέφομαι, γυρίζω || *(change direction)* στρέφομαι, στρίβω || *(become sour)* ξυνίζω || to ~ back vti γυρίζω πίσω || to ~ down vt *(refuse)*

απορρίπτω || *(fold down)* διπλώνω, τσακίζω || to ~ in vi *(go to bed)* πάω για ύπνο ♦ vt *(fold)* γυρίζω (μέσα), στριφώνω || to ~ off vi *(from road)* αλλάζω δρόμο, στρίβω ♦ vt *(light)* κλείνω, σβήνω || *(RAD)* κλείνω, σβήνω || to ~ on vt *(light)* ανοίγω, ανάβω || *(RAD)* ανοίγω || to ~ out vt εξελίσσομαι, πάω || *(extinguish)* κλείνω, σβήνω || to ~ up vi *(person)* εμφανίζομαι, φθάνω ξαφνικά || *(lost object)* ξαναβρίσκω ♦ vt *(collar)* σηκώνω, ανασηκώνω || *(RAD: increase volume)* ανεβάζω, δυναμώνω || ~ing n *(in road)* καμπή, στροφή || ~ing point n κρίσιμο σημείο, αποφασιστικό σημείο.

turnip ['tɜːnɪp] n γογγύλι.

turnout ['tɜːnaʊt] n συνάθροιση, ακροατήριο.

turnover ['tɜːnəʊvə*] n τζίρος.

turnpike ['tɜːnpaɪk] n *(US: toll highway)* οδός f με διόδια.

turnstile ['tɜːnstaɪl] n περιστροφική είσοδος f.

turntable ['tɜːnteɪbl] n περιστροφική εξέδρα, περιστροφική βάση.

turn-up ['tɜːnʌp] n *(on trousers)* ρεβέρ nt inv.

turpentine ['tɜːpəntaɪn] n νέφτι.

turquoise ['tɜːkwɔɪz] n τουρκουάζ nt inv ♦ a *(colour)* κυανοπράσινος.

turret ['tʌrɪt] n πυργίσκος.

turtle ['tɜːtl] n χελώνα.

tusk [tʌsk] n χαυλιόδοντο.

tussle ['tʌsl] n τσακωμός, καυγάς.

tutor ['tjuːtə*] n ιδιαίτερος καθηγητής, οικοδιδάσκαλος || *(at college)* υφηγητής || ~ial n *(UNIV)* ιδιαίτερο μάθημα από καθηγητή.

TV [tiː'viː] n *(abbr of television)* TV f, τηλεόραση.

twaddle ['twɒdl] n *(col)* μωρολογία, φλυαρία, μπούρδες fpl.

twang [twæŋ] n οξύς ήχος χορδής,

évρινος τόνος, σβούρισμα nt ♦ vti
αφήνω τεντωμένη χορδή, αντηχώ,
κρούω.

tweed [twi:d] n τουήντ nt inv.

tweezers ['twi:zəz] npl τσιμπίδα.

twelfth [twelfθ] a δωδέκατος || **T ~
Night** n παραμονή των Φώτων.

twelve [twelv] num δώδεκα.

twentieth ['twentiiθ] a εικοστός.

twenty ['twenti] num είκοσι.

twerp [twə:p] n (col: fool) βλάκας.

twice [twais] ad δύο φορές,
διπλάσιος.

twig [twig] n κλαδί, κλωνάρι ♦ vt
(understand, realize) αντιλαμβάνομαι,
μπαίνω, πιάνω.

twilight ['twailait] n λυκόφως nt,
λυκαυγές nt.

twin [twin] n δίδυμος ♦ a δίδυμος.

twine [twain] n σπάγγος, χοντρή
κλωστή ♦ vi συστρέφομαι, στρίβομαι || (curve)
στρίβω.

twinge [twindʒ] n δυνατός πόνος,
σουβλιά.

twinkle ['twiŋkl] n σπινθηρισμός,
σπίθισμα nt ♦ vi σπινθηροβολώ,
σπιθίζω || (star) τρεμοσβήνω.

twirl [twə:l] n περιστροφή, στρίψιμο
♦ vti περιστρέφω, στρίβω.

twist [twist] n συστροφή, στρίψιμο,
στραμπούλημα nt ♦ vi συστρέφω,
πλέκω, στρίβω || (distort) στρεβλώνω,
στραβώνω || (cheat) εξαπατώ ♦ vi
συστρέφομαι, στρίβομαι || (curve)
στρίβω.

twit [twit] n (col: fool) κορόιδο,
βλάκας.

twitch [twitʃ] n σύσπαση, τίναγμα nt
♦ vi συσπώμαι νευρικά.

two [tu:] num δύο, δυο || ~-**door** a
(AUT) με δύο πόρτες || ~-**faced** a
(pej: person) διπρόσωπος || ~-**fold** ad
δύο φορές, διπλά ♦ a διπλός || ~-
piece (suit) ντεπιές || (swimsuit)
κοστούμι μπάνιου ντεπιές || ~-
seater n (plane) διθέσιο || (car)

διθέσιο || ~**some** n ζευγάρι || ~-
way a (traffic) διπλής κυκλοφορίας.

tycoon [tai'ku:n] n μεγιστάνας των
επιχειρήσεων.

type [taip] n τύπος || (example) είδος
nt, τάξη || (printing) χαρακτήρες mpl,
στοιχεία ntpl ♦ vt δακτυλογραφώ ||
~-**face** n τύπος γραφής || ~-**script** n
δακτυλογραφημένο κείμενο || ~-
writer n γραφομηχανή || ~-
written a δακτυλογραφημένο.

typhoid ['taifɔid] n τυφοειδής.

typhoon [tai'fu:n] n ο τυφώνας.

typhus ['taifəs] n τύφος.

typical ['tipikəl] a τυπικός,
χαρακτηριστικός.

typify ['tipifai] vt αντιπροσωπεύω,
συμβολίζω.

typing ['taipiŋ] n δακτυλογράφηση.

typist ['taipist] n δακτυλογράφος
m/f.

tyranny ['tirəni] n τυραννία.

tyrant ['taiərənt] n τύραννος.

tyre ['taiə*] n (AUT) ρόδα, λάστιχο.

U

udder ['ʌdə*] n μαστός, μαστάρι.

UFO ['ju:fəu] n (abbr of unidentified
flying object) αντικείμενο αγνώστου
ταυτότητας.

ugliness ['ʌglinis] n ασχήμια.

ugly ['ʌgli] a άσχημος, άσκημος ||
(bad) άσχημος, κακός || (dangerous)
δυσάρεστος, επικίνδυνος, άσχημος.

UHF abbr of ultra-high frequency
υπερυψηλή συχνότητα, UHF.

UK n abbr see **united**.

ulcer ['ʌlsə*] n (in mouth, stomach)
έλκος nt.

ulterior [ʌl'tiəriə*] a (hidden)
υστερόβουλος, κρυφός.

ultimate ['ʌltimit] a τελευταίος,
τελικός, ύστατος, βασικός || ~-**ly** ad
τελικά, βασικά.

ultimatum [ʌltɪˈmeɪtəm] n τελεσίγραφο.

ultraviolet [ˈʌltrəˈvaɪəlɪt] a: ~ **light** υπεριώδες φώς nt.

umbilical [ʌmbɪˈlaɪkəl] a: ~ **cord** ομφάλιος λώρος, ομφάλιος.

umbrella [ʌmˈbrɛlə] n ομπρέλα.

umpire [ˈʌmpaɪə*] n διαιτητής ♦ vti διαιτητεύω.

umpteen [ˈʌmptiːn] num (col) ένα σωρό, δεν ξέρω πόσοι.

UN abbr see **united.**

unable [ʌnˈeɪbl] a ανίκανος, μη δυνάμενος.

unaccompanied [ʌnəˈkʌmpənɪd] a (child, lady) ασυνόδευτος, μόνος.

unaccountably [ʌnəˈkaʊntəblɪ] ad ανεξήγητα.

unaccustomed [ʌnəˈkʌstəmd] a ασυνήθιστος || (+ to) ασυνήθιστος (σε, να).

unaided [ʌnˈeɪdɪd] a χωρίς βοήθεια, αβοήθητος.

unanimous [juːˈnænɪməs] a ομόθυμος, ομόφωνος || ~ly ad ομόφωνα, παμψηφεί.

unattached [ʌnəˈtætʃt] a (single) ελεύθερος, εργένης.

unattended [ʌnəˈtɛndɪd] a χωρίς συνοδεία, παραμελυμένος.

unattractive [ʌnəˈtræktɪv] a μη συμπαθητικός.

unauthorized [ʌnˈɔːθəraɪzd] a χωρίς άδεια, μη εξουσιοδοτημένος.

unavoidable [ʌnəˈvɔɪdəbl] a αναπόφευκτος.

unaware [ʌnəˈwɛə*] a ανίδεος, άγνωστ~ || ~s ad ξαφνικά, χωρίς προειδοποίηση.

unbalanced [ʌnˈbælənst] a μη ισορροπημένος, ανισόρροπος.

unbearable [ʌnˈbɛərəbl] a ανυπόφορος, αφόρητος.

unbeatable [ʌnˈbiːtəbl] a (team) αήττητος, ακαταγώνιστος.

unbeaten [ʌnˈbiːtn] a (team, record) αήττητος, αχτύπητο ρεκόρ.

unbeknown [ʌnbɪˈnəʊn] ad (+ to) εν αγνοία του.

unbelievable [ʌnbɪˈliːvəbl] a απίστευτος.

unbend [ʌnˈbɛnd] vi ευθυγραμμίζομαι, σιάζω ♦ vt χαλαρώνω, ξετεντώνω.

unbounded [ʌnˈbaʊndɪd] a απεριόριστος, απέραντος.

unbreakable [ʌnˈbreɪkəbl] a άθραυστος.

unbridled [ʌnˈbraɪdld] a αχαλίνωτος, ασυγκράτητος.

unbroken [ʌnˈbrəʊkən] a (inviolate) άθραυστος, άσπαστος || (undisturbed) απαράβατος, αδιατάρακτος.

unburden [ʌnˈbɜːdn] vt: to ~ o.s. ανακουφίζω, ξαλαφρώνω.

unbutton [ʌnˈbʌtn] vt ξεκουμπώνω.

uncalled-for [ʌnˈkɔːldfɔː*] a άκαιρος, αδικαιολόγητος.

uncanny [ʌnˈkænɪ] a παράξενος, αφύσικος, μυστηριώδης.

unceasing [ʌnˈsiːsɪŋ] a ακατάπαυστος.

uncertain [ʌnˈsɜːtn] a αβέβαιος, αμφίβολος || (weather etc) ασταθής || (vague) ακαθόριστος || ~ty n αβεβαιότητα, αμφιβολία, αστάθεια.

unchanged [ʌnˈtʃeɪndʒd] a αμετάβλητος.

uncharitable [ʌnˈtʃærɪtəbl] a άσπλαχνος, αφιλάνθρωπος.

uncharted [ʌnˈtʃɑːtɪd] a ανεξερεύνητος.

unchecked [ʌnˈtʃɛkt] a (unhindered) ανεμπόδιστος, ασταμάτητος || (not confirmed) ανεξέλεγκτος.

uncivil [ʌnˈsɪvɪl] a αγενής, άξεστος, κακότροπος.

uncle [ˈʌŋkl] n θείος, μπάρμπας.

uncomfortable [ʌnˈkʌmfətəbl] a (uneasy) ανήσυχος, δυσάρεστος.

unconscious

unconscious [ʌnˈkɒnʃəs] a
ασυνείδητος || (not aware)
αναίσθητος ♦ n: the ~ το
ασυνείδητο || ~ly ad ασυνείδητα,
χωρίς να το καταλάβω.

uncontrollable [ʌnkənˈtrəuləbl] a
αχαλίνωτος, ακατάσχετος,
ασυγκράτητος.

uncouth [ʌnˈkuːθ] a αδέξιος,
άξεστος.

uncover [ʌnˈkʌvə*] vt ξεσκεπάζω ||
(expose) αποκαλύπτω, εκθέτω.

undecided [ʌndɪˈsaɪdɪd] a
αναποφάσιστος || (pending)
εκκρεμής.

undeniable [ʌndɪˈnaɪəbl] a
αναμφισβήτητος.

under [ˈʌndə*] prep υπό, κάτω από ||
(in time of) επί, στην εποχή του ♦ ad
κάτω, από κάτω || ~ age a ανήλικος
|| ~ repair υπό επισκευή.

undercarriage [ˈʌndəkærɪdʒ] n,
undercart [ˈʌndəkɑːt] n σύστημα
nt, προσγειώσεως.

underclothes [ˈʌndəkləuðz] npl
εσώρουχα ntpl.

undercoat [ˈʌndəkəut] n (paint)
βασικό χρώμα nt.

undercover [ˈʌndəkʌvə] a
μυστικός, κρυφός.

undercurrent [ˈʌndəkʌrənt] n
ρεύμα nt, κάτω από την επιφάνεια.

undercut [ˈʌndəkʌt] n (cooking)
φιλέτο κρέατος ♦ vt πουλώ
φθηνότερα από.

underdeveloped [ˈʌndədɪˈveləpt]
a (country) υποανάπτυκτος.

underdog [ˈʌndədɒg] n ο πιο
αδύνατος.

underdone [ʌndəˈdʌn] a (cooking)
μισοψημένος.

underestimate [ʌndərˈestɪmeɪt] vt
υποτιμώ.

underfed [ʌndəˈfed] a
υποσιτιζόμενος.

underfoot [ʌndəˈfut] ad κάτω από
τα πόδια.

undergo [ʌndəˈgəu] vt υφίσταμαι,
παθαίνω.

undergraduate [ʌndəˈgrædjuɪt] n
φοιτητής/τήτρια m/f.

underground [ˈʌndəgraund] n
υπόγειος σιδηρόδρομος ♦ a (press
etc) μυστικός, κρυφός || (movement)
της αντιστάσεως.

undergrowth [ˈʌndəgrəuθ] n
θάμνοι mpl, χαμόκλαδα.

underhand [ˈʌndəhænd] a
πανούργος, ύπουλος.

underlie [ʌndəˈlaɪ] vt υπόκειμαι,
είμαι η βάση.

underline [ʌndəˈlaɪn] vt
υπογραμμίζω || (draw attention to)
υπογραμμίζω, τονίζω.

underling [ˈʌndəlɪŋ] n
υφιστάμενος, παραγιός,
υποτακτικός.

undermine [ʌndəˈmaɪn] vt
υπονομεύω, υποσκάβω.

underneath [ʌndəˈniːθ] ad κάτω
από, από κάτω ♦ prep κάτω από,
υπό.

underpaid [ʌndəˈpeɪd] a
κακοπληρωμένος.

underpass [ˈʌndəpɑːs] n υπόγεια
διάβαση.

underprivileged [ʌndəˈprɪvɪlɪdʒd]
a με μειωμένα προνόμια,
αδικημένος.

underrate [ʌndəˈreɪt] vt υποτιμώ.

underside [ˈʌndəsaɪd] n κάτω
πλευρά, το αποκάτω.

underskirt [ˈʌndəskɜːt] n
κομπινεζόν nt inv, μεσοφόρι.

understand [ʌndəˈstænd] vt
αντιλαμβάνομαι || (know) γνωρίζω,
καταλαβαίνω || (hear, believe)
μαθαίνω, πιστεύω, νομίζω || (GRAM)
υπονοώ || ~able a (κατα)νοητός,
καταληπτός, ευνόητος || ~ing

συνεννόηση, κατανόηση ||
(agreement) συμφωνία.

understatement ['ʌndəsteɪtmənt]
n δήλωση κάτω από την
πραγματικότητα.

understudy ['ʌndəstʌdɪ] n
αντικαταστάτης/τρια m/f.

undertake [ʌndə'teɪk] vt
αναλαμβάνω || ~ r n εργολάβος
κηδειών.

undertaking [ʌndə'teɪkɪŋ] n
επιχείρηση || *(promise)* δέσμευση,
υπόσχεση.

underwater [ʌndə'wɔːtə*] ad
υποβρυχίως ♦ a υποβρύχιος.

underwear ['ʌndəweə*] n
εσώρουχα ntpl.

underweight [ʌndə'weɪt] a
λιποβαρής, αδύνατος.

underworld ['ʌndəwɜːld] n *(of
crime)* υπόκοσμος.

underwriter ['ʌndəraɪtə*] n
(insurance) ασφαλιστής.

undesirable [ʌndɪ'zaɪərəbl] a
ανεπιθύμητος.

undies ['ʌndɪz] npl *(col)* εσώρουχα
(γυναικεία).

undisputed [ʌndɪs'pjuːtɪd] a
αδιαφιλονίκητος, αδιαμφισβήτητος.

undo [ʌn'duː] vt λύνω, ξεκουμπώνω,
ανοίγω || *(work)* καταστρέφω, χαλώ ||
~ing n καταστροφή, αφανισμός.

undoubted [ʌn'daʊtɪd] a
αναμφισβήτητος, αναμφίβολος ||
~ly ad αναμφιβόλως.

undress [ʌn'dres] vti γδύνομαι,
γδύνω.

undue [ʌn'djuː] a υπερβολικός,
αδικαιολόγητος.

undulating ['ʌndjʊleɪtɪŋ] a
κυμαινόμενος, ταλαντευόμενος.

unduly [ʌn'djuːlɪ] ad υπερβολικά,
άπρεπα.

unearth [ʌn'ɜːθ] vt ξεθάβω,
ανακαλύπτω || ~ly a υπερφυσικός,
απόκοσμος.

uneasy [ʌn'iːzɪ] a ανήσυχος,
στενοχωρημένος.

uneconomic(al)
['ʌniːkə'nɒmɪk(əl)] a ανοικονομικός,
σπάταλος, ασύμφορος.

uneducated [ʌn'edjʊkeɪtɪd] a
ασπούδαστος, αμόρφωτος.

unemployed [ʌnɪm'plɔɪd] a
άνεργος, αχρησιμοποίητος || npl: the
~ οι άνεργοι.

unemployment [ʌnɪm'plɔɪmənt] n
ανεργία.

unending [ʌn'endɪŋ] a ατελείωτος.

unerring [ʌn'ɜːrɪŋ] a αλάνθαστος,
ακριβής.

uneven [ʌn'iːvən] a *(surface)*
ανώμαλος || *(quality)* άνισος,
ακανόνιστος.

unfair [ʌn'feə*] a *(unkind,
unreasonable)* άδικος || ~ly ad άδικα,
άτιμα.

unfaithful [ʌn'feɪθfʊl] a *(to spouse)*
άπιστος.

unfasten [ʌn'fɑːsn] vt λύνω ||
(clothes) ξεκουμπώνω || *(open)*
ξεκλειδώνω.

unfavourable, *(US)*
unfavorable [ʌn'feɪvərəbl] a
δυσμενής, δυσοίωνος.

unfeeling [ʌn'fiːlɪŋ] a
σκληρόκαρδος, αναίσθητος.

unfinished [ʌn'fɪnɪʃt] a ατέλειωτος,
ασυμπλήρωτος.

unfit [ʌn'fɪt] a *(in health)* ανίκανος,
αδιάθετος || *(+ for)* ακατάλληλος
(για).

unflagging [ʌn'flægɪŋ] a
ακλόνητος, ακαταπόνητος,
αλύγιστος.

unfold [ʌn'fəʊld] vt ξεδιπλώνω,
ξετυλίγω, απλώνω || *(reveal)*
αποκαλύπτω || *(develop)* αναπτύσσω ||
(explain) εξηγώ ♦ vi *(develop)*
αναπτύσσομαι, εκτυλίσσομαι.

unforeseen [ʌnfɔː'siːn] a
απρόβλεπτος, απροσδόκητος.

unforgivable [ʌnfəˈgɪvəbl] a
ασυγχώρητος.

unfortunate [ʌnˈfɔːtʃnɪt] a άτυχος,
κακότυχος || **~ly** ad δυστυχώς.

unfounded [ʌnˈfaʊndɪd] a (rumour)
αβάσιμος.

unfriendly [ʌnˈfrɛndlɪ] a
δυσμενής, εχθρικός.

unfurnished [ʌnˈfɜːnɪʃt] a (flat)
χωρίς έπιπλα.

ungainly [ʌnˈgeɪnlɪ] a αδέξιος.

unhappiness [ʌnˈhæpɪnɪs] n
δυστυχία, στενοχώρια.

unhappy [ʌnˈhæpɪ] a
δυστυχισμένος, στενοχωρημένος.

unharmed [ʌnˈhɑːmd] a σώος,
αβλαβής, απείραχτος.

unhealthy [ʌnˈhɛlθɪ] a (lit)
ανθυγιεινός, αρρωστιάρης || (fig)
νοσηρός.

unheard-off [ʌnˈhɜːdɒv] a
πρωτάκουστος, ανήκουστος.

unhurt [ʌnˈhɜːt] a χωρίς τραύμα,
σώος και αβλαβής.

unidentified [ʌnaɪˈdɛntɪfaɪd] a μη
αναγνωρισθείς, άγνωστος.

uniform [ˈjuːnɪfɔːm] n στολή ♦ a
ομοιόμορφος, ίδιος || **~ity** n
ομοιομορφία.

unify [ˈjuːnɪfaɪ] vt ενοποιώ.

unilateral [juːnɪˈlætərəl] a
μονόπλευρος.

unintentional [ʌnɪnˈtɛnʃənl] a
ακούσιος, αθέλητος.

union [ˈjuːnjən] n ένωση || (alliance)
ένωση || (agreement) συμφωνία || (of
workers) εργατικό σωματείο,
συνδικάτο || **U ~ Jack** n Αγγλική
σημαία.

unique [juːˈniːk] a μοναδικός,
ιδιόρρυθμος, ασυνήθιστος.

unison [ˈjuːnɪsn] n: **in ~** ομόφωνα,
από κοινού || (MUS) αρμονία,
μονοφωνία, ομοιχία.

unit [ˈjuːnɪt] n μονάδα || (team, squad)
ομάδα, συγκρότημα nt.

unite [juːˈnaɪt] vt ενώνω ♦ vi
ενώνομαι (με) || **~d** a ενωμένος,
συνδυασμένος || **U ~ d Kingdom
(UK)** n Ηνωμένο Βασίλειο (Η.Β) ||
U ~ d Nations (UN) npl Ηνωμένα
Έθνη (O.H.E.) m || **U ~ d States (of
America) (US, USA)** npl Ηνωμένες
Πολιτείες (Αμερικής) (Η.Π.Α.) fpl.

unity [ˈjuːnɪtɪ] n ενότητα, αρμονία,
σύμπνοια, μονάδα.

universal [juːnɪˈvɜːsəl] a
οικουμενικός, καθολικός || (general)
γενικός || (of the world) παγκόσμιος.

universe [ˈjuːnɪvɜːs] n σύμπαν nt,
οικουμένη.

university [juːnɪˈvɜːsɪtɪ] n
πανεπιστήμιο.

unjust [ʌnˈdʒʌst] a άδικος.

unkempt [ʌnˈkɛmpt] a ατημέλητος,
ακτένιστος.

unkind [ʌnˈkaɪnd] a αγενής,
άστοργος, σκληρός.

unknown [ʌnˈnəʊn] a (+ to)
άγνωστος (σε), αγνοούμενος από.

unladen [ʌnˈleɪdn] a (col: weight)
χωρίς φορτίο, κενός.

unleash [ʌnˈliːʃ] vt λύνω,
ελευθερώνω.

unless [ənˈlɛs] cj εκτός εάν, εκτός
αν.

unlike [ʌnˈlaɪk] a ανόμοιος,
διαφορετικός από.

unlimited [ʌnˈlɪmɪtɪd] a
απεριόριστος.

unload [ʌnˈləʊd] vt εκφορτώνω,
ξεφορτώνω.

unlock [ʌnˈlɒk] vt ξεκλειδώνω.

unmarried [ʌnˈmærɪd] a άγαμος.

unmask [ʌnˈmɑːsk] vt (expose)
αποκαλύπτω || αφαιρώ προσωπείο
από.

unmistakable [ʌnmɪsˈteɪkəbl] a
αλάθητος, ολοφάνερος, σαφής.

unmitigated [ʌnˈmɪtɪgeɪtɪd] a
αμετρίαστος, απόλυτος.

unnecessary [ʌnˈnɛsɪsərɪ] a περιττός, άσκοπος, μάταιος.

unobtainable [ʌnəbˈteɪnəbl] a ανεπίτευκτος.

unoccupied [ʌnˈɒkjupaɪd] a (seat etc) ελεύθερος, διαθέσιμος.

unorthodox [ʌnˈɔːθədɒks] a ανορθόδοξος.

unpack [ʌnˈpæk] vti ξεπακετάρω, βγάζω από βαλίτσας.

unparalleled [ʌnˈpærəleld] a απαράμιλλος.

unpleasant [ʌnˈplɛznt] a δυσάρεστος.

unplug [ʌnˈplʌg] vt ξεβουλώνω || (ELEC) βγάζω την πρίζα.

unpopular [ʌnˈpɒpjulə*] a αντιδημοτικός.

unprecedented [ʌnˈprɛsɪdəntɪd] a χωρίς προηγούμενο.

unqualified [ʌnˈkwɒlɪfaɪd] a αναρμόδιος, ακατάλληλος || (success) αμετρίαστος, απόλυτος.

unravel [ʌnˈrævəl] vt ξεφτώ, ξηλώνω, ξετυλίγω || (clarify) διευκρινίζω || (solve) λύνω, διαλύω.

unreal [ʌnˈrɪəl] a απατηλός, φανταστικός.

unreasonable [ʌnˈriːznəbl] a (unfair) παράλογος.

unrelenting [ʌnrɪˈlɛntɪŋ] a αδυσώπητος, ανελέητος.

unrelieved [ʌnrɪˈliːvd] a (monotony) χωρίς ποικιλία, μονότονος.

unrepeatable [ʌnrɪˈpiːtəbl] a (offer) που δεν επαναλαμβάνεται.

unrest [ʌnˈrɛst] n (discontent, trouble) ανησυχία, ταραχή.

unroll [ʌnˈrəʊl] vt ξετυλίγω.

unruly [ʌnˈruːlɪ] a ανυπότακτος, ατίθασος, άτακτος.

unsafe [ʌnˈseɪf] a επικίνδυνος, ανασφαλής.

unsaid [ʌnˈsɛd] a: to leave sth ~ αποσιωπώ κάτι.

unsatisfactory [ˈʌnsætɪsˈfæktərɪ] a μη ικανοποιητικός, ανεπαρκής.

unsavoury, (US) unsavory [ʌnˈseɪvərɪ] a (of bad character) ύποπτος, σκοτεινός.

unscrew [ʌnˈskruː] vt ξεβιδώνω.

unscrupulous [ʌnˈskruːpjuləs] a ασυνείδητος, ανενδοίαστος.

unsettled [ʌnˈsɛtld] a ανήσυχος, αβέβαιος || (weather) ευμετάβλητος, αβέβαιος.

unshaven [ʌnˈʃeɪvn] a αξύριστος.

unsightly [ʌnˈsaɪtlɪ] a άσχημος, δύσμορφος.

unskilled [ʌnˈskɪld] a (workman) ανειδίκευτος.

unspeakable [ʌnˈspiːkəbl] a απερίγραπτος, ανείπωτος, ανέκφραστος || (very bad) αποκρουστικός, απδιάστατος, σιχαμερός.

unstuck [ʌnˈstʌk] a: to come ~ ξεκολλώ || (lit) ξεκολλώ, ξεκολλιέμαι || (fig) καταρρέω, γκρεμίζομαι.

unsuitable [ʌnˈsuːtəbl] a ακατάλληλος.

unsuspecting [ʌnsəsˈpɛktɪŋ] a ανυποψίαστος.

unswerving [ʌnˈswɜːvɪŋ] a (loyalty) σταθερός, πιστός.

untangle [ʌnˈtæŋgl] vt ξεχωρίζω, ξεμπλέκω.

untapped [ʌnˈtæpt] a (resources) ανεκμετάλλευτος.

unthinkable [ʌnˈθɪŋkəbl] a ασύλληπτος, πολύ απίθανος.

untidy [ʌnˈtaɪdɪ] a ακατάστατος.

untie [ʌnˈtaɪ] vt λύνω.

until [ənˈtɪl] prep μέχρι, έως || cj μέχρι ότου, έως ότου.

untimely [ʌnˈtaɪmlɪ] a (death) πρόωρος.

untold [ʌnˈtəʊld] a (countless) αμέτρητος, ανυπολόγιστος.

untoward [ʌntəˈwɔːd] a δυσάρεστος, δυσμενής.

unused [ʌn'juːzd] a αμεταχείριστος.

unusual [ʌn'juːʒʊəl] a ασυνήθιστος, σπάνιος || **~ly** ad εξαιρετικά, αφάνταστα, ασυνήθιστα.

unveil [ʌn'veɪl] vt αποκαλύπτω, ξεσκεπάζω.

unwell [ʌn'wel] a αδιάθετος, άρρωστος.

unwieldy [ʌn'wiːldɪ] a δυσκίνητος, βαρύς, αδέξιος.

unwilling [ʌn'wɪlɪŋ] a απρόθυμος, ακούσιος.

unwind [ʌn'waɪnd] vt (lit) ξετυλίγω, ξεκουρδίζω ♦ vi (relax) χαλαρώνομαι.

unwitting [ʌn'wɪtɪŋ] a χωρίς πρόθεση, ακούσιος.

unwrap [ʌn'ræp] vt ξετυλίγω.

unwritten [ʌn'rɪtn] a (law) άγραφος, προφορικός.

up [ʌp] prep προς τα πάνω, αντίθετα με το ρεύμα ♦ ad επάνω, άνω, τελείως || **it is ~ to you** εξαρτάται από σένα || **what is he ~ to?** τι επιδιώκει; τι θέλει; || **he is not ~ to it** δεν έχει την ικανότητα (να) || **~-and-coming** a εξαιρετικά δραστήριος, ανερχόμενος ♦ n: **~s and downs** διακυμάνσεις fpl, μεταβολές fpl της τύχης.

upbringing ['ʌpbrɪŋɪŋ] n ανατροφή.

update [ʌp'deɪt] vt ενημερώνω, εκσυγχρονίζω.

upheaval [ʌp'hiːvəl] n (violent disturbance) αναστάτωση, αναταραχή.

uphill [ʌp'hɪl] a ανηφορικός ♦ ad προς τα άνω.

uphold [ʌp'həʊld] vt (maintain) υποστηρίζω.

upholstery [ʌp'həʊlstərɪ] n ταπετσαρία.

upkeep ['ʌpkiːp] n συντήρηση, έξοδα ntpl συντηρήσεως.

upon [ə'pɒn] prep πάνω, σε.

upper ['ʌpə*] a ανώτερος, άνω, από πάνω || **the ~ class** n n ανωτέρα τάξη, η καλή κοινωνία || **~-class** a της ανωτέρας τάξεως || **~most** a υπέρτατος, ανώτατος.

upright ['ʌpraɪt] a όρθιος, κατακόρυφος, κάθετος || (honest) ευθύς, δίκαιος, τίμιος ♦ n ορθοστάτης.

uprising [ʌp'raɪzɪŋ] n εξέγερση, ξεσήκωμα nt.

uproar ['ʌprɔː*] n θόρυβος, φασαρία, αναστάτωση.

uproot [ʌp'ruːt] vt ξεριζώνω.

upset ['ʌpset] n αναστάτωση, ανατροπή, αναποδογύρισμα nt ♦ [ʌp'set] vt (overturn) ανατρέπω, αναποδογυρίζω || (distress) ταράσσω, αναστατώνω.

upshot ['ʌpʃɒt] n αποτέλεσμα nt, έκβαση, κατάληξη.

upside ['ʌpsaɪd]: **~ down** ad άνω-κάτω, ανάποδα, φύρδην-μίγδην.

upstairs ['ʌp'stɛəz] ad στο επάνω πάτωμα nt ♦ a (room) επάνω, του άνω ορόφου ♦ n επάνω.

upstart ['ʌpstɑːt] n νεόπλουτος, αναιδής άνθρωπος.

upstream [ʌp'striːm] ad αντίθετα με το ρεύμα.

uptake ['ʌpteɪk] n αντίληψη || **to be quick, (slow) on the ~** (δεν) παίρνω, (δεν) αρπάζω.

up-to-date ['ʌptə'deɪt] a σύγχρονος, μοντέρνος || (fashionable) της μόδας.

upturn ['ʌptɜːn] n (in luck) βελτίωση, άνοδος f.

upward ['ʌpwəd] a προς τα άνω || **~(s)** ad προς τα άνω.

uranium [juə'reɪnɪəm] n ουράνιο.

urban ['ɜːbən] a αστικός.

urbane [ɜː'beɪn] a ευγενικός, αβρός, ραφιναρισμένος.

urchin ['ɜːtʃɪn] n (boy) αλητάκι || **sea ~** αχινός.

urge [ɜːdʒ] n (desire) επίμονη επιθυμία, ώθηση ♦ vt (entreat) παροτρύνω.

urgency ['ɜːdʒənsɪ] n επείγουσα ανάγκη, επιμονή, πίεση.

urgent ['ɜːdʒənt] a επείγων, πιεστικός, άμεσος || **~ly** ad επειγόντως.

urinal ['juərɪnl] n ουρητήριο.

urine ['juərɪn] n ούρα ntpl.

urn [ɜːn] n υδρία, δοχείο, αγγείο || (teapot) σαμοβάρι.

us [ʌs] pron εμάς, μας.

US, USA n abbr see united.

usage ['juːzɪdʒ] n μεταχείριση, έθιμο, συνήθεια || (esp LING) χρήση.

use [juːs] n χρήση || (custom) συνήθεια, έθιμο || (employment) χρήση, χρησιμοποίηση || (value) χρησιμότητα ♦ [juːz] vt χρησιμοποιώ, μεταχειρίζομαι || (make most of) χρησιμεύω || **in ~** εν χρήσει || **out of ~** εν αχρηστία || **to** συνηθίζω να || **she ~d to do it** συνήθιζε να το κάνει || **to ~ up** vt καταναλίσκω, εξαντλώ || **~d a** (car) μεταχειρισμένος, δεύτερο χέρι || **~ful** a χρήσιμος || **~less a** άχρηστος || **~r** n χρήστης.

usher ['ʌʃə*] n (at wedding) παράνυμφος || **~ette** n (at cinema) ταξιθέτρια.

USSR n: **the ~** Ε.Σ.Σ.Δ ('Ενωση Σοσιαλιστικών Σοβιετικών Δημοκρατιών).

usual ['juːʒuəl] a συνηθισμένος || **~ly** ad συνήθως.

usurp [juː'zɜːp] vt σφετερίζομαι, αρπάζω.

utensil [juː'tɛnsl] n σκεύος nt, εργαλείο.

uterus ['juːtərəs] n μήτρα.

utilitarian [juːtɪlɪ'tɛərɪən] a κοινωφελής, ωφελιμιστικός.

utility [juː'tɪlɪtɪ] n χρησιμότητα, ευχρηστία || (useful thing) χρήσιμο πράγμα nt || (also public utility: electricity supply industry) δημοσία υπηρεσία, κοινωφελής επιχείρηση.

utilize ['juːtɪlaɪz] vt χρησιμοποιώ, εκμεταλλεύομαι.

utmost ['ʌtməust] a ακρότατος, απότατος, έσχατος || n: **to do one's ~** κάνω ότι μπορώ.

utter ['ʌtə*] a πλήρης, ολοσχερής ♦ vt αρθρώνω, εκστομίζω, προφέρω, λέω || **~ly** ad τελείως, εξ ολοκλήρου.

U-turn ['juː'tɜːn] n (AUT) στροφή 180 μοιρών.

V

v. (abbr of verse) ποιητ. (ποιητικός) || abbr of **versus** || (abbr of vide) βλ (βλέπετε) || abbr of **volt.**

vacancy ['veɪkənsɪ] n κενό, κενή θέση || (room) δωμάτιο.

vacant ['veɪkənt] a κενός || (not occupied) άδειος, ελεύθερος || (stupid) αφηρημένος, ανέκφραστος || **'~'** (on door) δωμάτιο.

vacate [və'keɪt] vt εκκενώνω, αδειάζω, εγκαταλείπω.

vacation [və'keɪʃən] n διακοπή, αργία.

vaccinate ['væksɪneɪt] vt εμβολιάζω, μπολιάζω.

vaccination [væksɪ'neɪʃən] n εμβολιασμός, μπόλιασμα nt.

vaccine ['væksiːn] n εμβόλιο, βατσίνα.

vacuum ['vækjum] n κενό || **~ bottle** n (US) φιάλη κενού, θερμός nt || **~ cleaner** n ηλεκτρική σκούπα || **~ flask** n (Brit) φιάλη κενού, θερμός nt.

vagina [və'dʒaɪnə] n κόλπος (γυναίκας).

vagrant ['veɪɡrənt] n περιπλανώμενος, αλήτης.

vague [veɪɡ] a ασαφής, αμυδρός, ακαθόριστος || ~ly ad αόριστα, ασαφώς.

vain [veɪn] a μάταιος, άκαρπος || (conceited) ματαιόδοξος || in ~ μάταια.

vale [veɪl] n κοιλάδα, λαγκάδι.

valid ['vælɪd] a έγκυρος, βάσιμος, νόμιμος, λογικός || ~ity n εγκυρότητα, ισχύς f.

valise [və'liːz] n (suitcase) βαλίτσα.

valley ['vælɪ] n κοιλάδα, λαγκάδι.

valuable ['væljʊəbl] a πολύτιμος || ~s npl αντικείμενα αξίας ntpl.

valuation [vælju'eɪʃən] n εκτίμηση, αξία.

value ['væljuː] n αξία, τιμή, σημασία, έννοια ♦ vt εκτιμώ || ~ added tax (VAT) n Φόρος Προστιθέμενης Αξίας (Φ.Π.Α.) m|| ~d a (appreciated) εκτιμώμενος.

valve [vælv] n βαλβίδα, δικλείδα, λυχνία.

vampire ['væmpaɪə*] n βρυκόλακας.

van [væn] n φορτηγό, σκευοφόρος.

vandal ['vændəl] n βάνδαλος || ~ism n βανδαλισμός.

vanilla [və'nɪlə] n βανίλια ♦ attr a (ice cream) παγωτό.

vanish ['vænɪʃ] vi εξαφανίζομαι, χάνομαι.

vanity ['vænɪtɪ] n ματαιοδοξία, εγωισμός || ~ case n γυναικείο τσαντάκι.

vantage ['vɑːntɪdʒ] n: ~ point (good viewpoint) πλεονεκτική θέση.

vapour, (US) **vapor** ['veɪpə*] n ατμός, πάχνη || (gas) ατμός, υδρατμός.

variable ['veərɪəbl] a μεταβλητός, ευμετάβλητος.

variance ['veərɪəns] n: at ~ σε διάσταση, σε διαφωνία.

variation [veərɪ'eɪʃən] n παραλλαγή, παρέκκλιση, μεταβολή.

varicose ['værɪkəʊs] a: ~ veins κιρσώδες φλέβες fpl.

varied ['veərɪd] a διάφορος, ποικίλος, μεταβαλλόμενος.

variety [və'raɪətɪ] n ποικιλία, διαφορά || (varied collection) ποικιλία, πολλά και διάφορα || (kind) ποικιλία || ~ show n (THEAT) επιθεώρηση.

various ['veərɪəs] a ποικίλος, διάφορος.

varnish ['vɑːnɪʃ] n βερνίκι, στιλβωμένη επιφάνεια ♦ vt βερνικώνω, στιλβώνω.

vary ['veərɪ] vt διαφοροποιώ, ποικίλω ♦ vi αλλάζω, μεταβάλλομαι, διαφέρω || ~ing a μεταβαλλόμενος, μεταβλητός, ποικίλος.

vase [vɑːz] n βάζο, αγγείο.

vast [vɑːst] a πελώριος, εκτεταμένος, απέραντος.

vat [væt] n κάδος, βούτα, δεξαμενή.

VAT [væt] n abbr see **value**.

Vatican ['vætɪkən] n: the ~ το Βατικανό.

vault [vɔːlt] n θόλος, καμάρα || (cellar) υπόγειο || (tomb) θολωτός τάφος || (leap) πήδημα nt, άλμα nt ♦ vt πηδώ, κάνω άλμα επί κοντώ.

VD n abbr see **venereal**.

VDU n abbr see **visual**.

veal [viːl] n μοσχάρι.

veer [vɪə*] vi στρέφω, αλλάζω κατεύθυνση, γυρίζω.

vegetable ['vedʒɪtəbl] n φυτό, λαχανικό, χορταρικό.

vegetarian [vedʒɪ'teərɪən] a, n (people) χορτοφάγος || (animal) φυτοφάγος.

vegetate ['vedʒɪteɪt] vi φυτοζωώ.

vegetation [vedʒɪ'teɪʃən] n βλάστηση.

vehement ['viːɪmənt] a βίαιος, ορμητικός.

vehicle ['viːɪkl] n όχημα nt, αμάξι.

veil [veɪl] n πέπλος, βέλο || (fig) κάλυμμα nt ♦ vt καλύπτω, κρύβω.

vein [veɪn] n φλέβα || (of ore) φλέβα, στρώμα nt || (streak) διάθεση, ταλέντο || (mood) πνεύμα nt, διάθεση, κέφι.

velocity [vɪ'lɒsɪtɪ] n ταχύτητα.

velvet ['vɛlvɪt] n βελούδο.

vendetta [vɛn'dɛtə] n βεντέτα, εκδίκηση.

vending machine ['vɛndɪŋməʃiːn] n μηχάνημα nt πωλήσεως.

vendor ['vɛndɔː*] n πωλητής.

veneer [və'nɪə*] n (lit) καπλαμάς, επίστρωση, επένδυση || (fig) επίχρισμα nt, επίστρωμα nt || (lustre) λούστρο.

venerable ['vɛnərəbl] a αξιοσέβαστος, σεβάσμιος.

venereal [vɪ'nɪərɪəl] a (disease) αφροδίσιος || ~ disease (VD) n αφροδίσιο νόσημα.

venetian [vɪ'niːʃən] a: ~ blind παντζούρι.

vengeance ['vɛndʒəns] n εκδίκηση.

venison ['vɛnɪsn] n κρέας nt ελαφιού.

venom ['vɛnəm] n δηλητήριο, φαρμάκι || ~ous a φαρμακερός.

vent [vɛnt] n τρύπα εξαερισμού, διέξοδος ♦ vt ξεσπώ, ξεθυμαίνω.

ventilate ['vɛntɪleɪt] vt αερίζω.

ventilation [vɛntɪ'leɪʃən] n (εξ)αερισμός.

ventilator ['vɛntɪleɪtə*] n εξαεριστήρας, ανεμιστήρας.

ventriloquist [vɛn'trɪləkwɪst] n εγγαστρίμυθος.

venture ['vɛntʃə*] n τόλμημα nt, εγχείρημα nt || (COMM) επιχείρηση ♦ vt ριψοκινδυνεύω, ρισκάρω ♦ vi αποτολμώ, τολμώ.

venue ['vɛnjuː] n τόπος συναντήσεως, τόπος δίκης.

veranda(h) [və'rændə] n βεράντα.

verb [vɜːb] n ρήμα nt || ~al a λεκτικός, προφορικός.

verbose [vɜː'bəʊs] a πολύλογος, μακροσκελής.

verdict ['vɜːdɪkt] n κρίση, γνώμη || (of jury) ετυμηγορία, απόφαση.

verge [vɜːdʒ] n (of road) άκρη (του δρόμου) || on the ~ of doing έτοιμος να ♦ vi: to ~ on πλησιάζω, τείνω προς.

verger ['vɜːdʒə*] n νεωκόρος.

verify ['vɛrɪfaɪ] vt επιβεβαιώνω, αποδεικνύω.

vermin ['vɜːmɪn] npl βλαβερά ζωύφια ntpl.

vermouth ['vɜːməθ] n βερμούτ nt inv.

vernacular [və'nækjʊlə*] n τοπική διάλεκτος f, κοινή γλώσσα.

versatile ['vɜːsətaɪl] a πολύπλευρος, εύστροφος.

verse [vɜːs] n ποίηση, ποιήματα ntpl || (line) στίχος || (of poem, song) στροφή || (of Bible) εδάφιο || ~d a (+ in) μυημένος, πεπειραμένος, μορφωμένος.

version ['vɜːʃən] n (account) έκδοση, ερμηνεία.

versus ['vɜːsəs] prep κατά, εναντίον.

vertebra ['vɜːtɪbrə] n σπόνδυλος, ραχοκόκκαλο.

vertebrate ['vɜːtɪbrɪt] a σπονδυλωτός.

vertical ['vɜːtɪkəl] a κάθετος, κατακόρυφος.

vertigo ['vɜːtɪgəʊ] n ίλιγγος, ζάλη.

very ['vɛrɪ] ad πολύ || (precisely) ακριβώς ♦ a (identical) ίδιος || (mere) και μόνο.

vespers ['vɛspəz] npl εσπερινός.

vessel ['vɛsl] n πλοίο, σκάφος nt || (container) αγγείο, σκεύος nt.

vest [vɛst] n φανελάκι || (US: waistcoat) γιλέκο ♦ vt περιβάλλω,

παραχωρώ, παρέχω || ~ed a
(interest) κεκτημένος.

vestibule ['vɛstibjuːl] n (of house)
προθάλαμος, χωλ nt inv.

vestige ['vɛstidʒ] n υπόλειμμα nt,
ίχνος nt.

vestry ['vɛstri] n ιεροφυλάκειο,
σκευοφυλάκιο, βεστιάριο.

vet [vɛt] n (abbr of veterinary surgeon)
κτηνίατρος ♦ vt εξετάζω.

veteran ['vɛtərən] n παλαίμαχος,
βετεράνος ♦ a του παλαιμάχου,
πεπειραμένος.

veterinary ['vɛtərinəri] a
κτηνιατρικός || ~ **surgeon** n
κτηνίατρος.

veto ['viːtəu] n δικαίωμα nt
αρνησικυρίας, βέτο || (prohibition)
απαγόρευση ♦ vt προβάλλω βέτο
(σε).

vex [vɛks] vt ενοχλώ, ερεθίζω,
ταράσσω || ~ed a θυμωμένος,
πειραγμένος.

VHF n (abbr of very high frequency)
πολύ υψηλή συχνότητα (Λ.Υ.Σ.).

via ['vaiə] prep μέσω, διά μέσου.

viable ['vaiəbl] a βιώσιμος.

viaduct ['vaiədʌkt] n οδογέφυρα,
αψιδωτή γέφυρα.

vibrate [vai'breit] vi πάλλομαι,
δονούμαι, ταλαντεύομαι || (resound)
ηχώ.

vibration [vai'breiʃən] n
ταλάντευση, δόνηση, κούνημα nt.

vicar ['vikə*] n εφημέριος || ~**age** n
πρεσβυτέριο, οικία εφημερίου.

vice [vais] n (evil) εκφυλισμός,
ακολασία, αμάρτημα nt || (TECH)
μέγγενη.

vice- [vais] prefix αντί-, υπό ||
~**chairman** n αντιπρόεδρος.

vice versa ['vaisi'vəːsə] ad
αντίστροφα.

vicinity [vi'siniti] n γειτονιά,
εγγύτητα, περιοχή.

vicious ['viʃəs] a (also cruel) κακός,
κακόηθης.

victim ['viktim] n θύμα nt ||
~**ization** n καταπίεση, αντίποινα
ntpl || ~**ize** vt καταπιέζω,
μεταχειρίζομαι σαν θύμα.

victor ['viktə*] n νικητής/ήτρια m/f.

Victorian [vik'tɔːriən] a
βικτωριανός.

victorious [vik'tɔːriəs] a
νικηφόρος, θριαμβευτής.

victory ['viktəri] n νίκη.

video ['vidiəu] n βίντεο.

vie [vai] vi (compete) (+ with)
αμιλλώμαι, ανταγωνίζομαι.

view [vjuː] n όψη, ματιά, βλέμμα nt ||
(scene) θέα, προοπτική, όψη ||
(opinion) άποψη, έκθεση || (intention)
πρόθεση, βλέψη, σκοπός ♦ vt
(situation) κυττάζω, επιθεωρώ,
εξετάζω || ~**er** n (viewfinder)
σκόπευτρο || (PHOT: small projector)
μικρό μηχάνημα nt προβολής || (TV)
θεατής || ~**finder** n σκόπευτρο,
εικονοσκόπιο || ~**point** n σημείο με
καλή θέα || (attitude) άποψη.

vigil ['vidʒil] n αγρυπνία, ξενύχτι,
ολονυχτία || ~**ant** a άγρυπνος,
προσεκτικός.

vigor ['vigə*] n (US) = **vigour.**

vigorous ['vigərəs] a ρωμαλέος,
σθεναρός, ζωηρός || ~**ly** ad γερά,
δυνατά.

vigour ['vigə*] n σθένος nt, σφρίγος
nt, ζωτικότητα, ζωηρότητα.

vile [vail] a ανήθικος, αχρείος,
αισχρός || (foul) ακάθαρτος,
βρωμερός, σιχαμερός.

villa ['vilə] n έπαυλη, βίλα.

village ['vilidʒ] n χωριό || ~**r** n
χωριάτης/άτισσα m/f.

villain ['vilən] n ο κακός,
παλιάνθρωπος.

vindicate ['vindikeit] vt δικαιώνω,
υπερασπίζω.

vindictive [vɪn'dɪktɪv] a εκδικητικός.

vine [vaɪn] n αμπέλι, κλήμα nt.

vinegar ['vɪnɪgə*] n ξύδι.

vineyard ['vɪnjəd] n αμπελώνας, αμπέλι.

vintage ['vɪntɪdʒ] n (wine) κρασί ωρισμένου έτους || (gathering) τρυγητός, τρύγος.

vinyl ['vaɪnl] n βινύλιο.

viola [vɪ'əʊlə] n (MUS) βιόλα.

violate ['vaɪəleɪt] vt (break promise) αθετώ, καταπατώ || (disturb) παραβιάζω || (desecrate) βεβηλώνω.

violation [vaɪə'leɪʃən] n παράβαση, παράβαση, αθέτηση.

violence ['vaɪələns] n σφοδρότητα, ένταση || (rough treatment) βία, βιαιότητα.

violent ['vaɪələnt] a βίαιος, ορμητικός || (extreme) ζωηρός, έντονος, οξύς, ισχυρός || ~ly ad βίαια, απότομα, εξαιρετικά, πολύ.

violet ['vaɪəlɪt] n βιολέτα, μενεξές m ♦ a μενεξεδένιος, μώβ.

violin [vaɪə'lɪn] n βιολί.

VIP n (abbr of very important person) Επίσημος/n m/f.

viper ['vaɪpə*] n έχιδνα, οχιά.

virgin ['vɜːdʒɪn] n παρθένα ♦ a παρθένος, παρθενικός, καθαρός || ~ity n παρθενία.

virile ['vɪraɪl] a ανδρικός, δυνατός, σθεναρός.

virility [vɪ'rɪlɪtɪ] n ανδρισμός, ανδροπρέπεια, αρρενωπότητα.

virtually ['vɜːtjʊəlɪ] ad (in fact) ουσιαστικά || (almost) σχεδόν.

virtue ['vɜːtjuː] n αρετή || (good quality) ικανότητα, δραστικότητα || **by** ~ **of** δυνάμει, συνεπεία, λόγω, εξαιτίας.

virtuoso [vɜːtjʊ'əʊzəʊ] n δεξιοτέχνης μουσικός, βιρτουόζος.

virtuous ['vɜːtjʊəs] a ενάρετος.

virulent ['vɪrʊlənt] a τοξικός,

θανατηφόρος || (bitter) εχθρικός, κακεντρεχής, φαρμακερός.

virus ['vaɪərəs] n ιός, μικρόβιο.

visa ['viːzə] n θεώρηση, βίζα.

vis-à-vis ['viːzæviː] prep απέναντι, αντίκρυ.

viscount ['vaɪkaʊnt] n υποκόμης.

visibility [vɪzɪ'bɪlɪtɪ] n ορατότητα.

visible ['vɪzəbl] a ορατός, εμφανής, φαλερός || **visibly** ad καταφανώς, προφανώς, ολοφάνερα.

vision ['vɪʒən] n όραση || (imagination) διορατικότητα || (dream) όραμα nt, οπτασία || ~**ary** n οραματιστής, ονειροπόλος.

visit ['vɪzɪt] n επίσκεψη ♦ vt επισκέπτομαι || (stay with) κάνω βίζιτα, φιλοξενούμαι || ~**or** n επισκέπτης/ρια m/f || ~**ors' book** n βιβλίο επισκεπτών.

visor ['vaɪzə*] n προσωπίδα.

vista ['vɪstə] n θέα, άνοιγμα nt, προοπτική, άποψη.

visual ['vɪzjʊəl] a οπτικός, ορατός, πραγματικός || ~ **display unit (VDU)** n μονάδα οφόνης βίντεο || ~**ize** vt φαντάζομαι, οραματίζομαι.

vital ['vaɪtl] a ουσιώδης, κεφαλαιώδης, ζωτικός || (necessary to life) ζωτικός, ουσιώδης || ~**ity** n ζωτικότητα, ανθεκτικότητα, ζωή.

vitamin ['vɪtəmɪn] n βιταμίνη.

vivacious [vɪ'veɪʃəs] a ζωηρός, εύθυμος, κεφάτος.

vivid ['vɪvɪd] a ζωντανός, ζωηρός || (bright, clear) ζωηρός, λαμπρός.

vivisection [vɪvɪ'sekʃən] n ζωοτομία.

vocabulary [vəʊ'kæbjʊlərɪ] n λεξιλόγιο.

vocal ['vəʊkəl] a φωνητικός, πηκτικός || ~ **cord** n φωνητική χορδή || ~**ist** n αοιδός m/f, τραγουδιστής/ίστρια n/f.

vocation [vəʊ'keɪʃən] n (calling)

προορισμός, κλήση || (profession) επάγγελμα nt, τέχνη.

vociferous [vəʊ'sifərəs] a κραυγαλέος, φωνακλάς.

vodka ['vɒdkə] n βότκα.

vogue [vəʊg] n μόδα || (popularity) δημοτικότητα.

voice [vɔɪs] n φωνή || (right of opinion) ψήφος, γνώμη || (GRAM) φωνή (του ρήματος) ♦ vt εκφράζω || **with one** ~ ομόφωνα.

void [vɔɪd] n κενό ♦ a (of meaning) κενός, άδειος.

volatile ['vɒlətaɪl] a άστατος, ευμετάβολος, ασταθής || (evaporating quickly) πτητικός.

volcanic [vɒl'kænɪk] a ηφαιστειώδης, εκρυκτικός.

volcano [vɒl'keɪnəʊ] n ηφαίστειο.

volition [və'lɪʃən] n: **of one's own** ~ με τη θέλησή μου.

volley ['vɒlɪ] n ομοβροντία || (shower) καταιγισμός, θύελλα || (TENNIS) βολλέ nt inv, κατευθείαν κτύπημα nt || ~**ball** n χειροσφαίριση, βόλλεϋ-μπωλ nt inv.

volt [vəʊlt] n βόλτ || ~**age** n τάση, βολτάζ nt inv.

volume ['vɒljuːm] n τόμος βιβλίου || (amount) μεγάλη ποσότητα || (space) όγκος || (loudness of sound) ένταση, όγκος.

voluntarily ['vɒləntərɪlɪ] ad εκουσίως, αυθόρμητα, εθελοντικά.

voluntary ['vɒləntərɪ] a εθελοντικός, εκούσιος.

volunteer [vɒlən'tɪə*] n εθελοντής/όντρια m/f ♦ vt προσφέρομαι.

voluptuous [və'lʌptjʊəs] a φιλήδονος, ηδυπαθής.

vomit ['vɒmɪt] n εμετός, ξέρασμα nt ♦ vti κάνω εμετό, ξερνώ.

vote [vəʊt] n ψηφοφορία, ψήφος || (right) δικαίωμα nt ψήφου || (result) αποτέλεσμα nt ψηφοφορίας ♦ vt

ψηφίζω, ♦ vi ψηφίζω || ~**r** n ψηφοφόρος m/f, εκλογέας.

voting ['vəʊtɪŋ] n ψηφοφορία.

vouch [vaʊtʃ]: **to** ~ **for** vt υποστηρίζω, εγγυώμαι για.

voucher ['vaʊtʃə*] n απόδειξη πληρωμής, δικαιολογητικό.

vow [vaʊ] n όρκος, τάξιμο, τάμα nt ♦ vt ορκίζομαι, διακηρύττω.

vowel ['vaʊəl] n φωνήεν nt.

voyage ['vɔɪɪdʒ] n ταξίδι.

vulgar ['vʌlgə*] a χυδαίος, πρόστυχος, άξεστος || (of common people) κοινός, λαϊκός || ~**ity** n χυδαιότητα, προστυχιά.

vulnerable ['vʌlnərəbl] a τρωτός, εύτρωτος, ευπρόσβλητος.

vulture ['vʌltʃə*] n γύπας, όρνιο.

W

wad [wɒd] n (bundle) δέσμη, μάτσο.

wade [weɪd] vi βαδίζω στο νερό.

wafer ['weɪfə*] n λεπτό μπισκότο.

waffle ['wɒfl] n (food) είδος nt τηγανίτα || (col: empty talk) φλυαρία ♦ vi (col) φλυαρώ.

waft [wɑːft] vti μεταφέρω, σκορπίζω.

wag [wæg] vti κινώ, κουνώ, κινούμαι.

wage [weɪdʒ] n ημερομίσθιο, μισθός, αμοιβή, μεροκάματο ♦ vt διεξάγω, διενεργώ || ~**s** npl μισθός || ~ **earner** n μισθωτός || ~ **freeze** n παγίωση μισθών.

wager ['weɪdʒə*] n στοίχημα nt.

waggle ['wægl] vti (tail) κουνώ, ταλαντεύομαι.

wag(g)on ['wægən] n (road, rail) άμαξα, βαγόνι.

wail [weɪl] n θρήνος, ολοφυρμός ♦ vi θρηνώ, κλαίω, ολοφύρομαι.

waist [weɪst] n μέση, ζώνη || ~**coat** n γιλέκο || ~**line** n μέση.

wait [weɪt] n αναμονή, στάση ♦ vi περιμένω, αναμένω, σερβίρω || **to** ~

for vt περιμένω, αναμένω, καρτερώ || ~**er** n σερβιτόρος, γκαρσόνι || ~**ing room** n αίθουσα αναμονής, προθάλαμος || ~**ress** n σερβιτόρα.

wake [weɪk] (irreg v) vt ξυπνώ ♦ vi αγρυπνώ, είμαι άυπνος ♦ n ξενύχτι νεκρού || ~**n** vt αφυπνίζω, ξυπνώ.

Wales [weɪlz] n Ουαλία.

walk [wɔ:k] n περπάτημα nt, βόλτα, περίπατος || (way of walking) βάδισμα nt, περπατησιά || (path, route) περίπατος, δρόμος, πεζοδρόμιο || (walk of life) επάγγελμα nt ♦ vi περπατώ, βαδίζω || ~**er** n πεζοπόρος/α m/f, περπατητής m/f || ~**ie-talkie** n φορητός ασύρματος || ~**ing** n πεζοπορία, περπάτημα nt ♦ attr a (holiday) με τα πόδια || ~**ing shoes** παπούτσια ntpl πεζοπορίας || ~**ing stick** n μπαστούνι || ~**out** n (of workers) απεργία || ~**over** n (col) εύκολη νίκη, εύκολη δουλειά.

wall [wɔ:l] n (of house) τοίχος || (of city) τείχος nt.

wallet [ˈwɒlit] n πορτοφόλι.

wallop [ˈwɒləp] n δυνατό χτύπημα.

wallow [ˈwɒləʊ] vi (+ in) κυλιέμαι (σε), πλέω (πε) || (in money) κολυμπώ στο χρήμα.

wallpaper [ˈwɔ:lpeɪpə*] n τοιχόχαρτο, χαρτί ταπετσαρίας.

walnut [ˈwɔ:lnʌt] n καρύδι || (tree) καρυδιά.

walrus [ˈwɔ:lrəs] n θαλάσσιος ίππος.

waltz [wɔ:lts] n βάλς nt inv ♦ vi χορεύω βάλς.

wand [wɒnd] n ράβδος f, ραβδί.

wander [ˈwɒndə*] vi περιπλανώμαι, περιφέρομαι, τριγυρίζω || ~**ing** a πλανόδιος, περιπλανώμενος.

want [wɒnt] vt θέλω, επιθυμώ || (need) χρειάζομαι, έχω ανάγκη ♦ n: **for** ~ of ελλείψει || ~**s** npl (needs) ανάγκες fpl.

wanton [ˈwɒntən] a ακόλαστος, λάγνος.

war [wɔ:*] n πόλεμος.

ward [wɔ:d] n (division) περιφέρεια, συνοικία || (hospital) θάλαμος ♦ vt: **to** ~ **off** αποκρούω, αποφεύγω.

warden [ˈwɔ:dn] n διευθυντής, φύλακας.

warder [ˈwɔ:də*] n φύλακας, δεσμοφύλακας.

wardrobe [ˈwɔ:drəʊb] n ντουλάπα || (clothing) γκαρνταρόμια, τα ρούχα ntpl.

warehouse [ˈwɛəhaʊs] n αποθήκη.

wares [wɛəz] npl εμπορεύματα ntpl.

warfare [ˈwɔ:fɛə*] n πόλεμος.

warhead [ˈwɔ:hɛd] n κώνος βλήματος.

warily [ˈwɛərɪlɪ] ad προσεκτικά, επιφυλακτικά.

warlike [ˈwɔ:laɪk] a πολεμικός, πολεμοχαρής, φιλοπόλεμος.

warm [wɔ:m] a θερμός || (fire) ζεστός || (welcome) θερμός, ζωηρός || **to** ~ **up** vti ζεσταίνω, ζωηρεύω, ενθουσιάζομαι || ~**-hearted** a με ζεστή καρδιά, συμπονετικός || ~**ly** ad θερμά, ενθουσιωδώς || ~**th** n θερμότητα, ζεστασιά, ενθουσιασμός.

warn [wɔ:n] vt προειδοποιώ || ~**ing** n προειδοποίηση || (caution) ειδοποίηση.

warp [wɔ:p] vt σκεβρώνω ♦ n παραμόρφωση || (in meaning) στημόνι.

warrant [ˈwɒrənt] n (police) ένταλμα nt.

warranty [ˈwɒrəntɪ] n εξουσιοδότηση, εγγύηση.

warrior [ˈwɒrɪə*] n πολεμιστής.

warship [ˈwɔ:ʃɪp] n πολεμικό πλοίο.

wart [wɔ:t] n κρεατοελιά.

wartime [ˈwɔ:taɪm] n πολεμική εποχή, πολεμική περίοδος f.

wary ['wεərɪ] a προσεκτικός, πονηρός, επιφυλακτικός.

was [wɒz, wəz] pt of **be**.

wash [wɒʃ] n πλύση, πλύσιμο || (face, hands) νίψιμο || (clothes) μπουγάδα ♦ vt πλένω ♦ vi πλένομαι || **to ~ away** vt παρασύρω, παίρνω || **~able** a που πλένεται || **~basin** n λεκάνη (νιπτήρα) || **~er** n ροδέλα || (person) πλύστρα || **~ing** n (linen etc) ρούχα ntpl για πλύσιμο, πλύση, πλύσιμο || **~ing machine** n πλυντήριο || **~ing powder** n σκόνη πλυσίματος || **~ing-up** n πλύσιμο των πιάτων || **~-out** n (col) αποτυχία, φιάσκο || **~room** n τουαλέτα.

wasn't ['wɒznt] = **was not** || see **be**.

wasp [wɒsp] n σφήκα.

wastage ['weɪstɪdʒ] n σπατάλη.

waste [weɪst] n σπατάλη || (what is wasted) άχρηστα υλικά ntpl, σκουπίδια ntpl, απορρίμματα ntpl || (wilderness) έρημος f ♦ a άχρηστος || (land) χέρσος, ερημωμένος ♦ vt (object) σπαταλώ, καταστρέφω || (time) σπαταλώ, χάνω ♦ vi: **to ~ away** φθίνω, αδυνατίζω || **~ful** a σπάταλος || **~paper basket** n κάλαθος αχρήστων.

watch [wɒtʃ] n επίβλεψη, επιτήρηση || (vigilance) επαγρύπνηση || (guard) φυλακή, φρουρός || (NAUT) φυλακή, βάρδια || (timepiece) ρολόι ♦ vt παρατηρώ, παρακολουθώ ♦ vi αγρυπνώ, προσέχω, φρουρώ || **~dog** n (fig) επιστάτης/ρια m/f, φύλακας || **~ful** a άγρυπνος, προσεκτικός || **~maker** n ωρολογοποιός, ρολογάς || **~man** n (νυκτο)φύλακας || **~strap** n λουρίδα ρολογιού.

water ['wɔːtə*] n νερό ♦ vt ποτίζω || (wet) βρέχω, καταβρέχω || (soak) διαβρέχω || **to ~ down** vt απαλύνω (έκφραση), εξασθενίζω || **~ closet**

n αποχωρητήριο, απόπατος, μέρος nt || **~colour**, (US) **~color** n πίνακας με νερομπογιά, ακουαρέλα || (paint) υδρόχρωμα nt, νερομπογιά || **~cress** n νεροκάρδαμο || **~fall** n καταρράκτης || **~hole** n νερόλακκος || **~ing can** n ποτιστήρι || **~ lily** n νούφαρο || **~line** n ίσαλος (γραμμή) || **~logged** a πλημμυρισμένος, διάβροχος, μουσκεμένος || **~melon** n καρπούζι || **~proof** a αδιάβροχος, υδατοστεγής || **~shed** n γραμμή διαχωρισμού υδάτων || **~skiing** n θαλάσσιο σκί || **~tight** a υδατοστεγής, στεγανός, αδιάβροχος || **~works** npl μηχανοστάσιο υδρεύσεως || **~y** a (colour) ξεπλυμένος, άτονος.

watt [wɒt] n βάτ(τ) nt inv.

wave [weɪv] n κύμα nt || (of hand) κούνημα nt του χεριού || (RAD) κύμα nt || (in hair) κυμάτωση, κατσάρωμα nt ♦ vt (hand) χαιρετώ με το χέρι, κουνώ το χέρι || (shape in curves) κατσαρώνω ♦ vi (flag) κυματίζω, ανεμίζω || **~length** n μήκος nt, κύματος.

waver ['weɪvə*] vi ταλαντεύομαι, κυμαίνομαι || (weaken) κλονίζομαι.

wavy ['weɪvɪ] a κυματώδης, κυματιστός.

wax [wæks] n κερί ♦ vt (floors) κερώνω, παρκετάρω || vi (moon) μεγαλώνω, γίνομαι.

way [weɪ] n οδός f, δρόμος || (manner) τρόπος || (direction) κατεύθυνση, δρόμος || (habit) τρόπος, συνήθεια, έθιμο || **in the ~** φράζω, εμποδίζω, είμαι στο δρόμο || **by the ~** με την ευκαιρία || **'~ in'** 'είσοδος' || **'~ out'** 'έξοδος'.

waylay [weɪ'leɪ] vt ενεδρεύω, καιροφυλακτώ.

wayward ['weɪwəd] a δύστροπος, πεισματάρης.

W.C. ['dʌblju:'si:] n τουαλέτα.

we [wi:] pl pron εμείς.

weak [wi:k] a αδύνατος, ασθενικός || (not powerful) ανίσχυρος || (diluted) αδύνατος, ελαφρός || ~**en** vti εξασθενίζω, αδυνατίζω, εξασθενώ || ~**ling** n αδύνατος άνθρωπος, ασθενικό πλάσμα nt|| ~**ness** n αδυναμία || (fault) ελάττωμα nt|| (fondness) προτίμηση, αδυναμία.

wealth [welθ] n πλούτος || (abundance) αφθονία || (things having value) περιουσία || ~**y** a πλούσιος.

wean [wi:n] vt απογαλακτίζω, αποκόβω.

weapon ['wepən] n όπλο.

wear [wɛə*] (irreg v) n ρούχα ntpl, ρουχισμός, φόρεμα nt|| (use) χρήση || (decay) φθορά ♦ vt φέρω, φορώ || (show) δείχνω, κρατιέμαι || (use) φθείρω, λυώνω ♦ vi (last long) αντέχω, διατηρούμαι || ~ **and tear** φθορά, χρήσεις || **to ~ away** vti φθείρω, φθείρομαι, τρώγω, τρίβω || **to ~ down** vt φθείρω, τρώγω || **to ~ off** vi εξασθενίζω, περνώ || **to ~ out** vt φθείρω, τρίβω, λυώνω || ~**er** n φορών.

weariness ['wɪərɪnɪs] n κόπωση, κούραση.

weary ['wɪərɪ] a κουρασμένος, αποκαμωμένος || (tiring) κουραστικός, πληκτικός, ανιαρός ♦ vti κουράζω, κουράζομαι.

weasel ['wi:zl] n νυφίτσα, κουνάβι.

weather ['wɛðə*] n καιρός ♦ vt αντιμετωπίζω || (season) εκθέτω στον καιρό || ~**-beaten** a ανεμοδαρμένος, ηλιοκαμένος, μαυρισμένος || ~**cock** n ανεμοδείκτης || ~ **forecast** n πρόβλεψη καιρού.

weave [wi:v] (irreg v) vt υφαίνω, πλέκω, συνθέτω || ~**r** n υφαντής/άντρια m/f.

weaving ['wi:vɪŋ] n ύφανση, πλέξιμο.

web [web] n ύφασμα nt, μεμβράνη || (of spider) ιστός αράχνης || ~**-bed** a μεμβρανώδης || ~**bing** n ύφασμα nt λωρίδων || (for reinforcement) ενισχυτική ταινία.

wed [wed] vt νυμφεύω, νυμφεύομαι, παντρεύομαι.

we'd [wi:d] = **we had**, **we would** || see **have**, **would**.

wedding ['wedɪŋ] n γάμος, παντρειά || ~ **day** n μέρα των γάμων, επέτειος f των γάμων || ~**present** n γαμήλιο δώρο || ~ **ring** n αρραβώνας, βέρα.

wedge [wedʒ] n σφήνα || vt ενσφηνώνω, χώνω, μπήγω || (pack tightly) σφηνώνω, στριμώχνω.

Wednesday ['wenzdɪ] n Τετάρτη.

wee [wi:] a (Scottish col) μικρούλης, λιγάκι, τόσος δα.

weed [wi:d] n ζιζάνιο, αγριόχορτο ♦ vt ξεχορταριάζω, σκαλίζω, βγάζω, καθαρίζω || ~**-killer** n ζιζανιοκτόνο.

week [wi:k] n βδομάδα || ~**-day** n καθημερινή || ~**-end** n Σαββατοκύριακο || ~**-ly** ad εβδομαδιαίως ♦ a εβδομαδιαίος.

weep [wi:p] (irreg v) vi κλαίω, χύνω δάκρυα, δακρύζω.

weigh [wei] vt σταθμίζω, ζυγίζω || (have weight) ζυγίζω ♦ vi (be important) ζυγίζω || **to ~ down** vt (υπερ)φορτώνω, βαραίνω, πιέζω || **to ~ up** vt εκτιμώ, ζυγίζω || ~**-bridge** n γεφυροπλάστιγγα.

weight [weit] n βαρύτητα || (something used on scales) σταθμό, μέτρο, ζύγι || (load) βάρος nt, φορτίο || (importance) κύρος nt, επιρροή, αξία || ~ **lifting** n άρση βαρών || ~**y** a βαρύς.

weir [wɪə*] n φράγμα nt ποταμού.

weird [wɪəd] a υπερφυσικός, παράξενος.

welcome ['wɛlkəm] n υποδοχή || (reception) δεξίωση ♦ vt καλωσορίζω, (υπο) δέχομαι.

welcoming ['wɛlkəmɪŋ] a καλής υποδοχής.

weld [wɛld] n συγκόλληση, κόλληση ♦ vt (συγ)κολλώ, ενώνω || ~ er n συγκολλητής.

welfare ['wɛlfɛə*] n ευημερία, κοινωνική πρόνοια || ~ state n κράτος nt κοινωνικής πρόνοιας.

well [wɛl] n πηγάδι, πηγή, πετρελαιοπηγή ♦ ad καλά || (to considerable extent) αρκετά, σχεδόν || (thoroughly) καλά, τελείως ♦ a υγιής, καλά || (satisfactory) καλός, καλά || interj (beginning conversation) λοιπόν, ίσως, καλά || (surprise) αδύνατον, μπά || as ~ (also) επίσης, ομοίως.

we'll [wiːl] = **we will, we shall** || see **will, shall.**

well-behaved ['wɛlbɪ'heɪvd] a φρόνιμος, πειθαρχημένος.

well-being ['wɛl'biːɪŋ] n ευημερία.

well-earned ['wɛl'ɜːnd] a (rest) δίκαιος, καλοκερδισμένος.

wellingtons ['wɛlɪŋtənz] npl ψηλές μπότες fpl.

well-known ['wɛl'nəun] a (person) πασίγνωστος, φημισμένος.

well-meaning ['wɛl'miːnɪŋ] a καλοπροαίρετος.

well-off ['wɛl'ɒf] a εύπορος, πλούσιος.

well-read ['wɛl'rɛd] a μορφωμένος, πολυδιαβασμένος.

well-to-do ['wɛltə'duː] a εύπορος.

well-wisher ['wɛlwɪʃə*] n καλοθελητής/ήτρα m/f.

Welsh [wɛlʃ] a ουαλικός ♦ n (LING) Ουαλικά || ~ man n Ουαλαός.

went [wɛnt] pt of **go.**

wept [wɛpt] pt, pp of **weep.**

were [wɜː*] pt, pl of **be.**

we're [wɪə*] = **we are** || see **be.**

weren't ['wɜːnt] = **were not** || see **be.**

west [wɛst] n δύση || (country) δύση, δυτικά ♦ a δυτικός ♦ ad δυτικά, προς δυσμάς || the **W** ~ n n Δύση || ~**erly** a δυτικός (άνεμος) || ~**ern** a δυτικός ♦ n (CINE) ταινία με καουμπόης || **W** ~ **Indies** npl Οι Αντίλλες || ~**ward**(s) ad προς τα δυτικά.

wet [wɛt] a υγρός, βρε(γ)μένος, μουσκεμένος || (rainy) βροχερός || '~ **paint**' προσοχή χρώμα' || ~ **blanket** n (fig) άνθρωπος που χαλάει το κέφι, κρύος.

we've [wiːv] = **we have** || see **have.**

whack [wæk] vt κτυπώ, δέρνω στα ψαχνά.

whale [weɪl] n φάλαινα.

wharf [wɔːf] n αποβάθρα, προκυμαία.

what [wɒt] a (relative) ότι, όσος || (quantity) όσος, πόσος || (interrogative) τι, πώς; ποιος || interj τι, πώς; || ~**ever** a όποιος...και, ό τι... και, οποιοσδήποτε.

wheat [wiːt] n σιτάρι, στάρι.

wheel [wiːl] n τροχός, ρόδα ♦ vt (περι)στρέφω, σπρώχνω ♦ vi περιστρέφομαι, γυρίζω γύρω-γύρω || ~**barrow** n χειράμαξα || ~**chair** n αναπηρική καρέκλα.

wheeze [wiːz] vi αναπνέω δύσκολα, ασθμαίνω, ρογχάζω.

when [wɛn] ad πότε || (relative) όταν || cj όταν, που || ~**ever** ad οποτεδήποτε.

where [wɛə*] ad πού || (relative) (εκεί) που, όπου || ~**abouts** ad πού; || (λοιπόν) || πού περίπου; ♦ n θέση, διαμονή, κατατόπια ntpl || ~**as** cj εφόσον, ενώ.

wherever [wɛə'rɛvə*] ad οπουδήποτε.

whet [wɛt] vt (appetite) διεγείρω, ανοίγω (την όρεξη).

whether ['wɛðə*] cj εάν, αν, είτε.

which [wɪtʃ] a ποιος ♦ pron (interrogative) ποιο || (relative) ο' οποίος, στο οποίο, του οποίου || ~ever a όποιος, απ' όπου ♦ pron οποσδήποτε.

whiff [wɪf] n πνοή, φύσημα nt, ρουφηξιά.

while [waɪl] n χρονική περίοδος f, καιρός, χρόνος || cj ενώ.

whim [wɪm] n παραξενιά, ιδιοτροπία, καπρίτσιο.

whimper ['wɪmpə*] vi κλαυθμυρίζω, βογγώ.

whimsical ['wɪmzɪkəl] a ιδιότροπος, παράξενος.

whine [waɪn] vi κλαυθμυρίζω, μεμψιμοιρώ.

whip [wɪp] n μαστίγιο, καμτσίκι || (PARL) κοινοβουλευτικός πγέτης ♦ vt μαστιγώνω, δέρνω, κτυπώ || (snatch) κινώ απότομα, αρπάζω || ~round n έρανος, συνεισφορά.

whirl [wɜːl] n στροβιλισμός, στριφογύρισμα nt, γύρισμα nt ♦ vti στροβιλίζω, στριφογυρίζω, περιστρέφομαι || ~pool n δίνη, ρουφήχτρα || ~wind n ανεμοστρόβιλος.

whirr [wɜː*] vi βουίζω, σβουρίζω.

whisk [wɪsk] n (for eggs) χτυπητήρι ♦ vt (cream etc) κτυπώ, ανακατεύω.

whisker ['wɪskə*] n φαβορίτα || (of cat) μουστάκι.

whisk(e)y ['wɪskɪ] n ουίσκυ.

whisper ['wɪspə*] n ψίθυρος, θρόισμα nt, ψιθύρισμα nt ♦ vi ψιθυρίζω, μουρμουρίζω ♦ vt (secretly) ψιθυρίζω, σφυρίζω.

whist [wɪst] n ουίστ nt inv.

whistle ['wɪsl] n σφύριγμα nt || (instrument) σφυρίχτρα ♦ vi σφυρίζω.

white [waɪt] n λευκό, άσπρο || (of egg,

eye) λεύκωμα nt, ασπράδι ♦ a λευκός, άσπρος || (with fear) άσπρος, χλωμός || ~-collar worker n υπάλληλος m/f σε γραφείο || ~ lie n αθώο ψέμα nt || ~wash n (paint) ασβεστόνερο, ασβεστόχρωμα nt ♦ vt ασβεστώνω, ασπρίζω || (fig) αποκαθιστώ, δικαιολογώ.

Whitsun ['wɪtsn] n (also Whit Sunday) Πεντηκοστή.

whittle ['wɪtl] vt: to ~ away or down ελαττώνω, περιορίζω.

whizz [wɪz] vi σφυρίζω, περνώ γρήγορα || ~ kid n (col) σπουδαίο παιδί.

who [huː] pron ποιος || (relative) όποιος, που || ~ever pron οποιοσδήποτε, οιοσδήποτε.

WHO n (abbr of World Health Organization) Παγκόσμιος Οργανισμός Υγείας (WHO).

whole [həʊl] a (complete) ολόκληρος, όλος, πλήρης || (uninjured) αβλαβής, σώος ♦ n σύνολο || (not broken) σύνολο, ακέραιο || ~hearted a ολόψυχος || ~sale n χοντρική πώληση, χοντρεμπόριο || attr a (trade) χοντρικός || (destruction) ολοκληρωτικός || ~saler n χοντρέμπορος, κατάστημα nt χοντρικής πωλήσεως || ~some a υγιεινός, υγιής.

wholly ['həʊlɪ] ad πλήρως, τελείως.

whom [huːm] pron (object) ποιον.

whooping cough ['huːpɪŋkɒf] n κοκκύτης.

whore [hɔː*] n πόρνη, πουτάνα.

whose [huːz] pron ποιου, τίνος ποιανού || (of whom) του οποίου.

why [waɪ] ad για τί || (relative) που, γιατί || interj μπα || ε.

wick [wɪk] n φυτίλι.

wicked ['wɪkɪd] a κακός, διεστραμμένος, κακοήθης.

wicker ['wɪkə*] n λυγαριά.

wicket ['wɪkɪt] n (cricket) φράκτης, στυλίσκοι mpl του κρίκετ.

wide [waɪd] a ευρύς, πλατύς, φαρδύς, εκτενής || (mouth) ορθάνοικτος || (in firing) έξω (από το στόχο) άστοχος ♦ ad (opening) διάπλατα || ~-**angle lens** n ευρυγώνιος φακός || ~-**awake** a εντελώς ξύπνιος || ~**ly** ad ευρύτατα, πλατειά || ~**n** vt (road) ευρύνω, πλαταίνω, διευρύνω || ~ **open** a (lit) ορθάνοικτος, ακάλυπτος || ~**spread** a εκτεταμένος || (rumour etc) διαδεδομένος, γενικός.

widow ['wɪdəʊ] n χήρα || ~**ed** a χηρευάμενος, χηρεύσασα || ~**er** n χήρος.

width [wɪdθ] n εύρος nt, πλάτος nt, φάρδος nt.

wield [wiːld] vt χειρίζομαι, ελέγχω, εξασκώ.

wife [waɪf] n η σύζυγος, γυναίκα.

wig [wɪg] n περούκα.

wiggle ['wɪgl] vti κινώ νευρικά, κουνώ, κουνιέμαι.

wild [waɪld] a άγριος || (not cultivated) σε άγρια κατάσταση || (excited) αχαλίνωτος, ξετρελαμένος, τρελός || ~**erness** ['wɪldənɪs] n έρημος, αγριότοπος || ~-**goose chase** n μάταιη αναζήτηση, άσκοπη επιχείρηση || ~**life** n άγρια ζώα ntpl || ~**ly** ad άγρια, σαν τρελός.

wilful ['wɪlful] a εσκεμμένος, εκ προμελέτης || (obstinate) ξεροκέφαλος, πεισματάρης.

will [wɪl] auxiliary v: he ~ **come** θα έρθει || **I** ~ **do it** θα το κάνω! ♦ n βούληση, θέληση || (purpose) απόφαση, βούληση, θέλημα nt || (inheritance) διαθήκη ♦ vt θέλω, αποφασίζω || ~**ing** a πρόθυμος.

willow ['wɪləʊ] n ιτιά.

will power ['wɪlpaʊə*] n θέληση, αυτοέλεγχος.

wilt [wɪlt] vi μαραίνομαι.

wily ['waɪlɪ] a πανούργος.

win [wɪn] (irreg v) n νίκη, επιτυχία ♦ vt νικώ, κερδίζω ♦ vi επιτυγχάνω || **to** ~ **over** vt κατακτώ, αποκτώ.

wince [wɪns] n σύσπαση, τρεμούλιασμα nt ♦ vi μορφάζω, σφίγγομαι.

winch [wɪntʃ] n βαρούλκο, βίντσι.

wind [waɪnd] (irreg v) vt (wrap) τυλίγω || (tighten) σφίγγω, κουρδίζω ♦ vi στρέφω, στρέφομαι, ελίσσομαι, τυλίγομαι || **to** ~ **up** vt (clock) κουρδίζω || (debate) κλείνω, τερματίζω.

wind [wɪnd] n άνεμος, αέρας || (MED) αέρια ntpl, τυμπανισμός || ~**fall** n (good luck) κελεπούρι.

winding ['waɪndɪŋ] a (road) ελισσόμενος, φιδίσιος, με κορδέλες, στριφτός.

wind instrument ['wɪndɪnstrʊmənt] n (MUS) πνευστό (όργανο).

windmill ['wɪndmɪl] n ανεμόμυλος.

window ['wɪndəʊ] n παράθυρο, βιτρίνα || (COMPUT) παράθυρο || ~-**box** n κιβώτιο λουλουδιών || ~-**cleaner** n (man) καθαριστής παραθύρων || ~ **frame** n πλαίσιο παραθύρου, κούφωμα ntl || ~ **ledge** n περβάζι παραθύρου || ~ **pane** n τζάμι || ~-**sill** n περβάζι παραθύρου.

windpipe ['wɪndpaɪp] n τραχεία, λαρύγγι.

windscreen ['wɪndskriːn], (US) **windshield** ['wɪndʃiːld] n παρμπρίζ nt inv || ~ **wiper** n υαλοκαθαριστήρας.

windswept ['wɪndswept] a ανεμοδαρμένος.

windy ['wɪndɪ] a ανεμώδης, εκτεθειμένος στους ανέμους.

wine [waɪn] n οίνος, κρασί || ~ **cellar** n κάβα || ~ **glass** n ποτήρι του κρασιού || ~ **list** n κατάλογος κρασιών || ~ **merchant** n

κρασέμπορος || ~ **tasting** n δοκιμή κρασιών || ~ **waiter** n σερβιτόρος για τα κρασιά.

wing [wiŋ] n (of bird, plane) φτερούγα, φτερό || (of building) πτέρυγα (κτιρίου) || (MIL πτέρυγα || ~s npl (THEAT) παρασκήνια ntpl.

wink [wiŋk] n ανοιγοκλείσιμο του ματιού, νεύμα ♦ vi κλείνω το μάτι, νεύω.

winner ['winə*] n νικητής/ήτρια m/f.

winning ['winiŋ] a (team) κερδίζων, νικήτρια (ομάδα) || (goal) κερδίζων γκόλ || ~s npl κέρδη ntpl || ~ **post** n τέρμα nt.

winter ['wintə*] n χειμώνας ♦ attr a (clothes) χειμωνιάτικα ♦ vi περνώ το χειμώνα (σε) || ~ **sports** npl χειμωνιάτικα σπόρ nt inv.

wintry ['wintri] a χειμωνιάτικος, ψυχρός.

wipe [waip] n σκούπισμα nt, στέγνωμα nt, σφούγγισμα nt ♦ vt σκουπίζω, στεγνώνω, σφουγγίζω || **to** ~ **out** vt (debt) σβήνω, εξοφλώ || (destroy) εξολοθρεύω, σαρώνω.

wire ['waiə*] n σύρμα nt || (cable) τηλεγράφημα nt ♦ vt ενώνω με σύρμα, τοποθετώ τα καλώδια.

wireless ['waiəlis] n ασύρματος || (radio) ραδιόφωνο.

wiry ['waiəri] a σαν σύρμα, νευρώδης, δυνατός.

wisdom ['wizdəm] n σοφία, φρόνηση || (good judgment) σωφροσύνη || (prudence) φρονιμάδα, γνώση || ~ **tooth** n φρονιμίτης.

wise [waiz] a σοφός, φρόνιμος, συνετός || -**wise** suffix κατά κάποιο τρόπο, σαν || ~ **crack** n ευφυολόγημα nt, καλαμπούρι.

wish [wiʃ] n (desire) επιθυμία, ευχή ♦ vt (desire) εύχομαι, επιθυμώ || **with best** ~ **es** με τις καλύτερες ευχές || **to** ~ **good-bye** εύχομαι καλό ταξίδι

|| **to** ~ **to do** επιθυμώ, θέλω να || ~ **ful thinking** n ευσεβείς πόθοι mpl.

wisp [wisp] n (of hair) τσουλούφι, τολύπη.

wistful ['wistful] a συλλογισμένος, πικραμένος.

wit [wit] n (sense) αντίληψη, κατανόηση, νους m, μυαλό || (cleverness) πνεύμα nt, ευφυΐα || (person) πνευματώδης άνθρωπος, ευφυής, σπίρτο || ~ s npl μυαλό, εξυπνάδα.

witch [witʃ] n μάγισσα || ~ **craft** n μαγεία.

with [wið, wiθ] prep μετά, μαζί, με || (by means of) με, από || (concerning) μαζί με, μετά || (notwithstanding) παρά, παρ όλο.

withdraw [wið'drɔː] vt αποσύρω, σύρω, τραβώ, φέρνω ♦ vi αποσύρομαι, αποτραβιέμαι, τραβιέμαι || ~ **al** n αποχώρηση, ανάκληση.

wither ['wiðə*] vi μαραίνομαι, ξεραίνομαι || ~ **ed** a μαραμένος, ξερός.

withhold [wið'həuld] vt αναστέλλω, κατακρατώ.

within [wið'in] prep εντός, μέσα σε.

without [wið'aut] prep εκτός, χωρίς, δίχως.

withstand [wið'stænd] vt αντιστέκομαι σε, αντέχω σε.

witness ['witnis] n μαρτυρία || (LAW) μάρτυρας ♦ vt (see) παρίσταμαι μάρτυς, βλέπω || (sign documents) επικυρώνω, βεβαιώνω, υπογράφω || ~ **box**, (US) ~ **stand** n θέση του εξεταζόμενου μάρτυρα.

witticism ['witisizəm] n ευφυολογία, ευφυολόγημα nt, εξυπνάδα, αστείο.

wittily ['witili] ad πνευματωδώς, έξυπνα, σπιρτόζικα.

witty ['witi] a πνευματώδης, σπιρτόζικος, έξυπνος.

wives [waivz] *npl* of **wife**.

wizard ['wizəd] *n* μάγος.

wk *abbr* of **week**.

wobble ['wɒbl] *vi* παραπατώ, ταλαντεύομαι, τρέμω.

woe [wəu] *n* συμφορά, δυστυχία, λύπη, θλίψη.

woke [wəuk] *pt, pp* of **wake**.

wolf [wulf] *n* λύκος.

wolves [wulvz] *npl* of **wolf**.

woman ['wumən] *n* γυναίκα ♦ *attr a* *(doctor)* ο γιατρός.

womb [wuːm] *n* μήτρα.

women ['wimin] *npl* of **woman**.

won [wʌn] *pt, pp* of **win**.

wonder ['wʌndə*] *n* θαύμα *nt* || *(feeling)* θαυμασμός, κατάπληξη ♦ *vi* *(want to know)* απορώ, διερωτώμαι || **~ful** *a* θαυμάσιος, εκπληκτικός.

won't [wəunt] = **will not** || *see* **will**.

wood [wud] *n* ξύλο, ξυλεία || *(forest)* δάσος *nt*, δρυμός, άλσος *nt* || **~ carving** *n* ξυλογλυπτική || **~en a** *a* ξύλινος || *(stiff)* αδέξιος, άκαμπτος || **~ pecker** *n* δρυοκολάπτης || **~wind** *n* ξύλινα πνευστά *ntpl* || **~work** *n* ξυλουργική || **~worm** *n* σκουλήκι του ξύλου.

wool [wul] *n* μαλλί || *(material)* μάλλινο ύφασμα *nt* || **~len**, *(US)* **~en a** μάλλινος || *(industry)* υφαντουργική || **~ly**, *(US)* **~y** *a* σαν μαλλί, σκεπασμένος με μαλλί.

word [wɜːd] *n* λέξη || *(talk, speech)* λόγος, παρατήρηση || *(news)* είδηση, ειδοποίηση, μήνυμα *nt*, νέα || *(promise)* λόγος ♦ *vt* διατυπώνω, εκφράζω με λέξεις || **~ing** *n* διατύπωση, φρασεολογία || **~ processing** *n* επεξεργασία κειμένου || **~ processor** *n* επεξεργαστής κειμένου.

wore [wɔː*] *pt* of **wear**.

work [wɜːk] *n* έργο || *(task)* εργασία, δουλειά, απασχόληση || *(ART, LITER)*

έργο, προϊόν εργασίας ♦ *vi* εργάζομαι, δουλεύω || *(have occupation)* εργάζομαι, ασχολούμαι με, δουλεύω ♦ *vt* *(cause to act)* λειτουργώ, επιτυγχάνω || **~s n** *(factory)* εργοστάσιο || **to ~ on** *vt* συνεχίζω || *(influence)* επηρεάζω || **to ~ out** *vi* *(sum)* υπολογίζομαι, ανέρχομαι σε ♦ *vt (problem)* λύνω, αναπτύσσω || *(plan)* επεξεργάζομαι || **to ~ up to** *vi* ανέρχομαι || **to get ~ed up** εξάπτομαι, θυμώνω || **~able** *a* επεξεργάσιμος, εκμεταλλεύσιμος, εφαρμόσιμος || **~er** *n* εργάτης/ρια *m/f*, **~ing class** *n* εργατική τάξη, εργαζόμενοι *mpl* || **~ing-class** *a* της εργατικής τάξης || **~ing man** *n* εργάτης, δουλευτής || **~man** *n* εργάτης, τεχνίτης || **~manship** *n* εκτέλεση, δούλεμα *nt*, επεξεργασία || **~shop** *n* εργαστήριο.

world [wɜːld] *n* σύμπαν *nt*, υφήλιος *f*, κόσμος *m* || *(the earth)* γη, κόσμος || *(mankind)* κόσμος, ανθρωπότητα || *(society)* κοινωνία, κόσμος || *(sphere)* κόσμος || *attr a (champion)* παγκόσμιος, διεθνής || **out of this ~** ανίσχυρος, περίφημος || **~-famous** *a* παγκοσμίου φήμης || **~ly** *a* εγκόσμιος, του κόσμου || **~-wide** *a* παγκόσμιος, διεθνής.

worm [wɜːm] *n* σκουλήκι.

worn [wɔːn] *pp* of **wear** || *a* εθθαρμένος, φορεμένος || **~-out a** *(object)* φθαρμένος, φαγωμένος || *(person)* εξαντλημένος, τσακισμένος.

worried ['wʌrid] *a* στενοχωρημένος, ανήσυχος.

worry ['wʌri] *n* στενοχώρια, σκοτούρα || *vt* βασανίζω, στενοχωρώ ♦ *vi* ανησυχώ, στενοχωρούμαι || **~ing** *a* ενοχλητικός, βασανιστικός.

worse [wɜːs] *a comp of* **bad** ♦ *ad comp of* **badly** ♦ *n* κάτι χειρότερο,

πιο κακό || ~**n** vt επιδεινώνω, χειροτερεύω ♦ vi επιδεινούμαι.

worship ['wɜːʃɪp] n λατρεία, προσκύνηση || (religious service) λατρεία, εκκλησίασμα nt || (title) n αυτού εντιμότης ♦ vt λατρεύω || (adore) αγαπώ, λατρεύω.

worst [wɜːst] a sup of **bad** ♦ ad sup of **badly** ♦ n ο χειρότερος, ο πιό κακός.

worsted ['wustɪd] n υφάσματα πενιέ, μαλλί πενιέ.

worth [wɜːθ] n αξία || a ~ άξιος || ~**less** a χωρίς αξία || (useless) άχρηστος || ~**while** a αξιόλογος.

worthy ['wɜːðɪ] a άξιος || (+ of) αντάξιος.

would ['wud] auxiliary v: **she** ~ **come** ερχόταν || **if you asked he** ~ **come** αν παρακαλούσες θα 'ρχόταν || **you like a drink?** θέλεις κανένα ποτό; || ~**be** α δήθεν || ~**n't** = **not**.

wound [waund] pt, pp of **wind** ♦ [wuːnd] n τραύμα nt, πληγή ♦ vt τραυματίζω, πληγώνω.

wove [wəuv] pt of **weave** || ~**n** pp of **weave**.

wpm n (abbr of words per minute) λεξ/λεπ., λ.α.λ. (λέξεις ανά λεπτό).

wrangle ['ræŋgl] n καυγάς, τσακωμός, λογομαχία ♦ vi καυγαδίζω, λογομαχώ, τσακώνομαι.

wrap [ræp] n εκνέασμα nt, σάλι ♦ vt (also: ~ **up**) τυλίγω, περιβάλλω, καλύπτω || ~ n περιτύλιγμα nt, κάλυμμα nt || (gown) ρόμπα || ~**ping paper** n χαρτί περιτυλίγματος.

wreath [riːθ] n στεφάνι.

wreck [rɛk] n ερείπιο, καταστροφή || (NAUT) ναυάγιο || (ruin) καταστροφή ♦ vt καταστρέφω || (NAUT) προκαλώ ναυάγιο || ~**age** n ναυάγιο, συντρίμματα ntpl.

wren [rɛn] n τρόχιλος, τρυποκαρύδα.

wrench [rɛntʃ] n (γαλλικό) κλειδί || (violent twist) βίαιη κίνηση στρέψεως, στρέβλωση ♦ vt στρεβλώνω, στραμπουλίζω.

wrestle ['rɛsl] vi (+ **with**) αγωνίζομαι || (SPORT) παλεύω.

wrestling ['rɛslɪŋ] n πάλη, πάλεμα nt || ~ **match** n αγώνισμα nt πάλης.

wretched ['rɛtʃɪd] a πολύ δυστυχισμένος άθλιος || (bad, poor) άθλιος, θλιβερός, αξιοθρήνητος.

wriggle ['rɪgl] n συστροφή στριφογύρισμα ♦ vi συστρέφομαι, σπαρταρώ στριφογυρίζω, γλιστρώ.

wring [rɪŋ] (irreg v) vt συστρέφω, στρίβω.

wrinkle ['rɪŋkl] n (on face) ρυτίδα || (in cloth) πτυχή ♦ vt ρυτιδώνω, ζαρώνω ♦ vi ρυτιδούμαι, ζαρώνω.

wrist [rɪst] n καρπός (του χεριού) || ~ **watch** n ρολόι του χεριού.

writ [rɪt] n (LAW) δικαστική πράξη, έντολμα nt.

write [raɪt] (irreg v) vt γράφω || (book) συντάσσω, γράφω ♦ vi (send letter) γράφω, στέλνω γράμμα || to ~ **down** vt διατυπώνω, (κατα) γράφω, σημειώνω, περιγράφω || to ~ **off** vt (dismiss) ακυρώνω, διαγράφω, ξεγράφω || to ~ **out** vt καθαρογράφω, αντιγράφω, συντάσσω || to ~ **up** vt (report) συντάσσω, γράφω || ~-**off** n (smashed car) τελείως κατεστραμμένο || ~**r** n συγγραφέας, συντάκτης.

writing ['raɪtɪŋ] n γράψιμο, γραφή || (books etc) λογοτεχνικό έργο || ~ **paper** n κόλλα, χαρτί γραμματειος.

written ['rɪtn] pp of **write**.

wrong [rɒŋ] a κακός, άδικος || (incorrect) ανακριβής, λανθασμένος || (to be mistaken) κάνω λάθος.

wrote [rəut] pt of **write**.

wrought [rɔːt] a: ~ **iron** κατεργασμένος σίδηρος.

wrung [rʌŋ] pt, pp of **wring**.
wry [raɪ] a στρεβλός, στριμμένος, στραβός.
wt. abbr of **weight**.

X

Xmas ['eksməs] n (col: Christmas) Χριστούγεννα ntpl.
X-ray ['eks'reɪ] n ακτινογραφία, ακτινοσκόπηση.
xylophone ['zaɪləfəʊn] n ξυλόφωνο.

Y

yacht [jɒt] n θαλαμηγός f, γιωτ nt inv, κότερο || ~**ing** n ενασχόληση με γιωτ, γιώτιχκ nt inv|| ~**sman** n άνθρωπος ασχολούμενος με γιώτ.
Yank [jæŋk] n (col: American) Αμερικάνος, Γιάνκης.
yap [jæp] vi (+ for) πόθω, λαχταρώ || ~**ing** n πόθος, λαχτάρα.
yard [jɑːd] n (of house etc) αυλή, προαύλιο, μάντρα || (measure) υάρδα (0.914 μ).
yarn [jɑːn] n νήμα nt, κλωστή || (tale) ιστορία φανταστική.
yawn [jɔːn] n χασμούρημα nt, χασμουρητό ♦ vi χασμουριέμαι.
yd. abbr of **yard(s)**.
year [jɪə*] n έτος nt, χρόνος || ~**ly** a ετήσιος ♦ ad ετησίως, κάθε χρόνο.
yearn [jɜːn] vi (+ for) ποθώ, λαχταρώ || ~**ing** n πόθος, λαχτάρα.
yeast [jiːst] n προζύμι, μαγιά.
yell [jɛl] n κραυγή, σκούξιμο ♦ vi ωρύομαι, φωνάζω δυνατά, σκούζω.
yellow ['jɛləʊ] a κίτρινος ♦ n κίτρινο.
yelp [jɛlp] vi γαυγίζω.
yes [jɛs] ad ναι, μάλιστα.
yesterday ['jɛstədeɪ] ad χθες, χτες.
yet [jɛt] ad (by now) ακόμη, τώρα ||

(still) ακόμη || (by that time) κι όμως, παρ' όλα αυτά || cj κι όμως, εντούτοις.
yew [juː] n τάξος.
Yiddish ['jɪdɪʃ] n (LING) γερμανοεβραϊκά.
yield [jiːld] n παραγωγή, απόδοση ♦ vt αποδίδω, αποφέρω ♦ vi (surrender) υποτάσσομαι, παραδίδομαι.
yodel ['jəʊdl] vi τραγουδώ (τυρολέξικα).
yoga ['jəʊgə] n γιόγκα nt inv.
yogurt ['jəʊgət] n γιαούρτι nt.
yoke [jəʊk] n ζυγός, ζευγάρι || (servitude) ζυγός.
yolk [jəʊk] n κρόκος, κροκάδι.
you [juː] pron (εσείς, (ε)σύ.
you'd [juːd] = **you had, you would** || see **have, would**.
you'll [juːl] = **you will, you shall** || see **will, shall**.
young [jʌŋ] a νέος, νεαρός, μικρός || **the** ~ οι νέοι mpl, n νεολαία || ~**ish** a μάλλον νέος, νεούτσικος || ~**ster** n νεαρός, νέος, αγόρι.
your ['jʊə*] poss a σου, σας.
you're ['jʊə*] = **you are** || see **be**.
yours [jʊəz] poss pron (δικός) σου, (δικός) σας || ~ **faithfully** υμέτερος || ~ **sincerely** όλως υμέτερος.
yourself [jə'sɛlf] pron συ (ο ίδιος), τον εαυτόν σας, χωρίς βοήθεια.
yourselves [jə'sɛlvz] pron pl σεις (οι ίδιοι), μόνοι σας.
youth [juːθ] n νεότητα, νιάτα, νιότη || (young man) νέος, νεαρός, έφηβος || (young people) νέοι mpl, νεολαία || ~**ful** a νεανικός, νεαρός || ~ **hostel** n ξενώνας νεότητας.
you've [juːv] = **you have** || see **have**.
Yugoslav ['juːgəʊ'slɑːv] a γιουγκοσλαβικός ♦ n (person) Γιουγκοσλάβος/α m/f || (LING)

zany ['zeɪnɪ] a πλίθιος, βλάκας.

zeal [zi:l] n ζήλος || ~**ous** a γεμάτος ζήλο.

zebra ['zi:brə] n ζέβρα || ~ **crossing** n διάβαση (πεζών).

zero ['zɪərəʊ] n μηδέν nt, μηδενικό || ~ **hour** n ώρα μηδέν, ώρα (επιθέσεως).

zest [zɛst] n ζέση, ενθουσιασμός, όρεξη.

z

Γιουγκοσλαβικά ntpl || ~ **ia** n Γιουγκοσλαβία.

zigzag ['zɪgzæg] n ζιγκ-ζαγκ nt inv ♦ vi κάνω ζιγκ-ζαγκ.

zinc [zɪŋk] n ψευδάργυρος, τσίγκος.

Zionism ['zaɪənɪzəm] n σιωνισμός.

zip [zɪp] n (also: ~ **fastener**, ~**per**) φερμουάρ nt inv ♦ vt (also: ~ **up**) κλείνω (με φερμουάρ).

zodiac ['zəʊdɪæk] n ζωδιακός κύκλος.

zone [zəʊn] n ζώνη.

zoo [zu:] n ζωολογικός κήπος || ~**logical** a ζωολογικός || ~**logist** n ζωολόγος || ~**logy** n ζωολογία.

zoom [zu:m] vi βομβώ, βουΐζω || ~ **lens** n φακός μεταβλητής εστιακής αποστάσεως, ζούμ nt inv.

ΑΓΓΛΙΚΑ ΑΝΩΜΑΛΑ ΡΗΜΑΤΑ

present	pt	pp	present	pt	pp
arise	arose	arisen	deal	dealt	dealt
awake	awoke	awaked	dig	dug	dug
be (am, is, are; being)	was, were	been	do (3rd person; he/she/it/does)	did	done
bear	bore	born(e)	draw	drew	drawn
beat	beat	beaten	dream	dreamed, dreamt	dreamed, dreamt
become	became	become			
befall	befell	befallen	drink	drank	drunk
begin	began	begun	drive	drove	driven
behold	beheld	beheld	dwell	dwelt	dwelt
bend	bent	bent	eat	ate	eaten
beseech	besought	besought	fall	fell	fallen
beset	beset	beset	feed	fed	fed
bet	bet, betted	bet, betted	feel	felt	felt
			fight	fought	fought
bid	bid	bid	find	found	found
bind	bound	bound	flee	fled	fled
bite	bit	bitten	fling	flung	flung
bleed	bled	bled	fly	flew	flown
blow	blew	blown	forbid	forbade	forbidden
break	broke	broken	forego	forewent	foregone
breed	bred	bred	foresee	foresaw	foreseen
bring	brought	brought	foretell	foretold	foretold
build	built	built	forget	forgot	forgotten
burn	burnt, burned	burnt, burned	forgive	forgave	forgiven
burst	burst	burst	forsake	forsook	forsaken
buy	bought	bought	freeze	froze	frozen
can	could	(been able)	get	got	got, (US) gotten
cast	cast	cast			
catch	caught	caught	give	gave	given
choose	chose	chosen	go	went	gone
cling	clung	clung	(goes)		
come	came	come	grind	ground	ground
cost	cost	cost	grow	grew	grown
creep	crept	crept	hang	hung, hanged	hung, hanged
cut	cut	cut			

339

present	pt	pp	present	pt	pp
have	had	had	ride	rode	ridden
hear	heard	heard	ring	rang	rung
hide	hid	hidden	rise	rose	risen
hit	hit	hit	run	ran	run
hold	held	held	saw	sawed	sawn
hurt	hurt	hurt	say	said	said
keep	kept	kept	see	saw	seen
kneel	knelt,	knelt,	seek	sought	sought
	kneeled	kneeled	sell	sold	sold
know	knew	known	send	sent	sent
lay	laid	laid	set	set	set
lead	led	led	shake	shook	shaken
lean	leant,	leant,	shall	should	—
	leaned	leaned	shear	sheared	shorn,
leap	leapt,	leapt,			sheared
	leaped	leaped	shed	shed	shed
learn	learnt,	learnt,	shine	shone	shone
	learned	learned	shoot	shot	shot
leave	left	left	show	showed	shown
lend	lent	lent	shrink	shrank	shrunk
let	let	let	shut	shut	shut
lie	lay	lain	sing	sang	sung
(lying)			sink	sank	sunk
light	lit,	lit,	sit	sat	sat
	lighted	lighted	slay	slew	slain
lose	lost	lost	sleep	slept	slept
make	made	made	slide	slid	slid
may	might	—	sling	slung	slung
mean	meant	meant	slit	slit	slit
meet	met	met	smell	smelt,	smelt,
mistake	mistook	mistaken		smelled	smelled
mow	mowed	mown,	sow	sowed	sown,
		mowed			sowed
must	(had to)	(had to)	speak	spoke	spoken
pay	paid	paid	speed	sped,	sped,
put	put	put		speeded	speeded
quit	quit,	quit,	spell	spelt,	spelt,
	quitted	quitted		spelled	spelled
read	read	read	spend	spent	spent
rend	rent	rent	spill	spilt,	spilt,
rid	rid	rid		spilled	spilled

present	pt	pp	present	pt	pp
spin	spun	spun	take	took	taken
spit	spat	spat	teach	taught	taught
split	split	split	tear	tore	torn
spoil	spoiled, spoilt	spoiled, spoilt	tell	told	told
			think	thought	thought
spread	spread	spread	throw	threw	thrown
spring	sprang	sprung	thrust	thrust	thrust
stand	stood	stood	tread	trod	trodden
steal	stole	stolen	wake	woke, waked	woken, waked
stick	stuck	stuck			
sting	stung	stung	waylay	waylaid	waylaid
stink	stank	stunk	wear	wore	worn
stride	strode	stridden	weave	wove, weaved	woven, weaved
strike	struck	struck, stricken	wed	wedded, wed	wedded, wed
strive	strove	striven			
swear	swore	sworn	weep	wept	wept
sweep	swept	swept	will	would	—
swell	swelled	swollen, swelled	win	won	won
			wind	wound	wound
swim	swam	swum	wring	wrung	wrung
swing	swung	swung	write	wrote	written

ΑΠΟΛΥΤΑ CARDINAL NUMBERS

μηδέν	0	zero
ένας, μία (μια), ένα	1	one
δύο	2	two
τρεις, τρία	3	three
τέσσερις, τέσσερα	4	four
πέντε	5	five
έξι	6	six
επτά (εφτά)	7	seven
οκτώ (οχτώ)	8	eight
εννέα (εννιά)	9	nine
δέκα	10	ten
έντεκα	11	eleven
δώδεκα	12	twelve
δεκατρείς, δεκατρία	13	thirteen
δεκατέσσερις,		
δεκατέσσερα	14	fourteen
δεκαπέντε	15	fifteen
δεκαέξι	16	sixteen
δεκαεπτά (δεκαεφτά)	17	seventeen
δεκαοκτώ (δεκαοχτώ)	18	eighteen
δεκαεννέα (δεκαεννιά)	19	nineteen
είκοσι	20	twenty
είκοσι ένας, μία, ένα	21	twenty-one
είκοσι δύο	22	twenty-two
είκοσι τρεις, τρία	23	twenty-three
τριάντα	30	thirty
σαράντα	40	forty
πενήντα	50	fifty
εξήντα	60	sixty
εβδομήντα	70	seventy
ογδόντα	80	eighty
ενενήντα	90	ninety
εκατό	100	one hundred
εκατόν ένας, εκατόν μία,		
εκατόν ένα	101	one hundred and one
εκατόν πενήντα έξι	156	one hundred and fifty-six
διακόσιοι,ες,α	200	two hundred
τριακόσιοι,ες,α	300	three hundred
τετρακόσιοι,ες,α	400	four hundred
πεντακόσιοι,ες,α	500	five hundred
εξακόσιοι,ες,α	600	six hundred
επτακόσιοι,ες,α		
(εφτακόσιοι,ες,α)	700	seven hundred
οκτακόσιοι,ες,α		
(οχτακόσιοι,ες,α)	800	eight hundred
εννιακόσιοι,ες,α	900	nine hundred
χίλιοι, χίλιες, χίλια	1,000	one thousand
δύο χιλιάδες	2,000	two thousand
τρεις χιλιάδες	3,000	three thousand
ένα εκατομμύριο	1,000,000	one million
ένα δισεκατομμύριο	1,000,000,000	one billion

342

TAKTIKA ORDINAL NUMBERS

πρώτος, πρώτη, πρώτο	1st	first
δεύτερος	2nd	second
τρίτος	3rd	third
τέταρτος	4th	fourth
πέμπτος	5th	fifth
έκτος	6th	sixth
έβδομος	7th	seventh
όγδοος	8th	eighth
ένατος	9th	ninth
δέκατος	10th	tenth
ενδέκατος (εντέκατος)	11th	eleventh
δωδέκατος	12th	twelfth
δέκατος τρίτος	13th	thirteenth
δέκατος τέταρτος	14th	fourteenth
δέκατος πέμπτος	15th	fifteenth
δέκατος έκτος	16th	sixteenth
δέκατος έβδομος	17th	seventeenth
δέκατος όγδοος	18th	eighteenth
δέκατος ένατος	19th	nineteenth
εικοστός	20th	twentieth
εικοστός πρώτος	21st	twenty-first
εικοστός δεύτερος	22nd	twenty-second
εικοστός τρίτος	23rd	twenty-third
τριακοστός	30th	thirtieth
τεσσαρακοστός	40th	fortieth
πεντηκοστός	50th	fiftieth
εξηκοστός	60th	sixtieth
εβδομηκοστός	70th	seventieth
ογδοηκοστός	80th	eightieth
ενενηκοστός	90th	ninetieth
εκατοστός	100th	(one) hundredth
διακοσιοστός	200th	two hundredth
τριακοσιοστός	300th	three hundredth
τετρακοσιοστός	400th	four hundredth
πεντακοσιοστός	500th	five hundredth
εξακοσιοστός	600th	six hundredth
επτακοσιοστός (εφτακοσιοστός)	700th	seven hundredth
οκτακοσιοστός (οχτακοσιοστός)	800th	eight hundredth
εννιακοσιοστός	900th	nine hundredth
χιλιοστός	1,000th	(one) thousandth
εκατομμυριοστός	1,000,000th	millionth
δισεκατομμυριοστός	1,000,000,000th	billionth

THE TIME

what time is it?		τι ώρα είναι;
it is ...		είναι ...
at what time?		τι ώρα;
at 8		στις οκτώ
at midnight		τα μεσάνυχτα
at one p.m.		στη μία μετά το μεσημέρι
00.00	midnight	μεσάνυχτα, δώδεκα τα μεσάνυχτα
00.10	ten past midnight, ten past twelve a.m.	δώδεκα και δέκα μετά τα μεσάνυχτα
00.15	a quarter past midnight, twelve fifteen a.m.	δώδεκα και τέταρτο μετά τα μεσάνυχτα, δώδεκα και δεκαπέντε π.μ.
00.30	half past twelve, twelve thirty a.m.	δώδεκα και μισή, δώδεκα και τριάντα π.μ.
01.10	ten past one, one ten	μία (μια) και δέκα
01.15	a quarter past one, one fifteen	μία (μια) και τέταρτο, μία και δεκαπέντε
01.30	half past one, one thirty	μία (μια) και μισή, μία και τριάντα
01.45	a quarter to two, one forty-five	δύο παρά τέταρτο, μία και σαράντα πέντε
01.50	ten to two, one fifty	δύο παρά δέκα, μία και πενήντα
12.00	midday	μεσημέρι, δώδεκα το μεσημέρι
12.30	half past twelve, twelve thirty p.m.	δώδεκα και μισή, δώδεκα και τριάντα μ.μ.
13.00	one (o'clock) (in the afternoon), one p.m.	μία (μια) η ώρα (το απόγευμα ή μ.μ.)
19.00	seven (o'clock) (in the evening), seven p.m.	επτά η ώρα (το βράδυ ή μ.μ.)
21.30	nine thirty (p.m. or at night)	εννέα και μισή (μ.μ. ή το βράδυ)
23.45	a quarter to twelve, eleven forty-five p.m.	δώδεκα παρά τέταρτο, έντεκα και σαράντα πέντε μ.μ.
in 20 minutes		σε είκοσι λεπτά
20 minutes ago		πριν από είκοσι λεπτά
wake me up at 7		ξυπνήστε με στις επτά
20 km.p.h.		είκοσι χιλιόμετρα την ώρα

DATES AND NUMBERS

1. The date

what's the date today?	τι ημερομηνία είναι σήμερα;
it's the ...	είναι η ...
1st of February	πρώτη Φεβρουαρίου
2nd of February	δευτέρα Φεβρουαρίου
28th of February	εικοστή ογδόη Φεβρουαρίου
he's coming on the 7th of May	θα φθάσει στις επτά Μαΐου
I was born in 1945	γεννήθηκα το χίλια εννιακόσια σαράντα πέντε
I was born on the 15th of July 19 ...	γεννήθηκα στις δεκαπέντε Ιουλίου χίλια εννιακόσια...
during the sixties	στη δεκαετία του εξήντα
in the twentieth century	στον εικοστό αιώνα
in May	το Μάιο
on Monday (the 15th)	τη Δευτέρα (στις δεκαπέντε)
on Mondays	κάθε Δευτέρα
next/last Monday	την επόμενη/την περασμένη Δευτέρα
in 10 days' time	σε δέκα μέρες

2. Telephone numbers

I would like Athens 24 35 56
θα ήθελα Αθήνα είκοσι τέσσερα/ τριάντα πέντε/ πενήντα έξι

could you get me Athens 22 00 79, extension 2233
μπορείτε να μου πάρετε Αθήνα είκοσι δύο/ μηδέν μηδέν/ εβδομήντα εννέα, εσωτερική γραμμή είκοσι δύο/ τριάντα τρία

the Athens prefix is 01
ο κωδικός της Αθήνας είναι μηδέν ένα

3. Using numbers

he lives at number 10	μένει στον αριθμό δέκα
it's in chapter 7, on page 7	είναι στο έβδομο κεφάλαιο, στη σελίδα επτά
he lives on the 3rd floor	μένει στο τρίτο πάτωμα
he came in 4th	ήρθε τέταρτος
a share of one seventh	μερίδιο ένα έβδομο
scale 1:25,000	κλίμακα ένα στις είκοσι πέντε χιλιάδες

345

BUILD UP YOUR GEM COLLECTION!

HarperCollins*Publishers*

This dictionary is just *one* of many in the best-selling series of **Gem** Dictionaries and Guides.

Gem Dictionaries can help you with writing and spelling – in English and many other languages. There are also Gem Basic Facts, Reference Gems and Gem Nature Guides, to interest and inform you in every subject.

Every Gem is the same handy size as this dictionary and the titles listed below are only a selection of the many titles available in the Gem series.

Collins Gems include:

English Dictionary	Spelling Guide
Thesaurus	English Grammar
Dictionary and Thesaurus	English Usage
Scots Dictionary	French Grammar
French Dictionary	French Verb Tables
German Dictionary	French 5000 Words
Spanish Dictionary	German Grammar
Italian Dictionary	German Verb Tables
Portuguese Dictionary	German 5000 Words
Greek Dictionary	Spanish Verb Tables
Latin Dictionary	and Grammar
Russian Dictionary	Dictionary of Quotations
Welsh Dictionary	